Fodor's Road Guide USA

Delaware
District of Columbia
Maryland
Pennsylvania
Virginia

First Edition

Fodor's Travel Publications
New York Toronto London Sydney Auckland
www.fodors.com

Fodor's Road Guide USA: Delaware, District of Columbia, Maryland, Pennsylvania, Virginia

Fodor's Travel Publications
President: Bonnie Ammer
Publisher: Kris Kliemann
Executive Managing Editor: Denise DeGennaro
Editorial Director: Karen Cure
Director of Marketing Development: Jeanne Kramer
Associate Managing Editor: Linda Schmidt
Senior Editor: Constance Jones
Director of Production and Manufacturing: Chuck Bloodgood
Creative Director: Fabrizio La Rocca

Contributors
Editing: Holly Hammond (Delaware), Anthony Laudato (Virginia), Laureen Miles (Maryland), Brigid Wilson (Pennsylvania), with Jinny Alpaugh, Donna Cornachio, Yvonne Daley, Nicole Davis, Linda Downs, Karen Fein, Gail Harrington, Shannon Kelly, Marni Keough, Fran Levine, Christa Malone, Doris Maxfield, Liz McGeehee, Pat Hadley-Miller, Elizabeth Minyard, Denise Mortensen, Candy Moulton, Anne O'Connor, Brian Rohan, Paula Szuchman, Justine Valenti, Susan Walton, and Ethan Young
Production Editorial: Ira-Neil Dittersdorf
Writing: John Briley (District of Columbia), Lynn Cothern (Virginia restaurants), Rob DeGiacomo (Pennsylvania introductions, lodgings, and events), Valerie Helmbreck (Delaware), Kim Korienek (Pennsylvania introductions, attractions, and dinings), Marcus Popiolek (Pennsylvania town introductions, attractions, and dinings), Maura Singleton (Virginia) and Greg Tasker (Maryland), with Kelly Demaret, Hannah Fons, William Fox, Sarah Gil, Keisha Hutchins, Gail Johnson, Alia Levine, Laurice Nemetz, Eric Reymond, Brendan Walsh, Rob DiGiacomo, Alia Levine, Laurice Nemetz, Sara Pepitone, Carrie Ann Sabato, Frances Schamberg, Ami Trivedi, and Brendan Walsh
Editorial Assistance: Shannon Kelly, Jennifer LiButti, Emmanuelle Morgen
Research: Kim Bacon, Lonette Fisher, Karene Grad, Josh Greenwald, Doug Hirlinger, Helen Kasimis, Hasan Khondker, Kristina Klurman, Mary Ann O'Grady, and Rupa Shah
Black-and-White Maps: Rebecca Baer, Robert Blake, David Lindroth, Todd Pasini
Production/Manufacturing: Robert B. Shields
Cover: John Skowronski (background photo), Bart Nagel (photo, illustration)
Interior Photos: Pete Morelewicz (Delaware and District of Columbia), Corbis (Maryland), Siobhan O'Hare (Pennsylvania), Photodisc (Virginia)

Special Sales
Fodor's Travel Publications are available at special discounts for bulk purchases for sales promotions or premiums. Special editions can be created in large quantities for special needs. Write to Special Markets, Fodor's Travel Publications, 280 Park Avenue, New York, NY 10017. Inquiries from Canada should be sent to Random House of Canada, Ltd., Marketing Department, 2775 Matheson Boulevard East, Mississauga, Ontario L4W 4P7. Inquiries from the United Kingdom should be sent to Fodor's Travel Publications, 20 Vauxhall Bridge Road, London SW1V 2SA, England.
PRINTED IN THE UNITED STATES OF AMERICA
10 9 8 7 6 5 4 3 2 1

CONTENTS

Great Road Trips

Of all the things that went wrong with Clark Griswold's vacation, one stands out: The theme park he had driven across the country to visit was closed when he got there. Clark, the suburban bumbler played by Chevy Chase in 1983's hilarious *National Lampoon's Vacation*, is fictional, of course. But his story is poignantly true. Although most Americans get only two precious weeks of vacation a year, many set off on their journeys with surprisingly little guidance. Many travelers find out about their destination from friends and family or wait to get travel information until they arrive in their hotel, where racks of brochures dispense the "facts," along with free city magazines. But it's hard to distinguish the truth from hype in these sources. And it makes no sense to spend priceless vacation time in a hotel room reading about a place when you could be out seeing it up close and personal.

Congratulate yourself on picking up this guide. Studying it—before you leave home—is the best possible first step toward making sure your vacation fulfills your every dream.

Inside you'll find all the tools you need to plan a perfect road trip. In the hundreds of towns we describe, you'll find thousands of places to explore. So you'll always know what's around the next bend. And with the practical information we provide, you can easily call to confirm the details that matter and study up on what you'll want to see and do, before you leave home.

By all means, when you plan your trip, allow yourself time to make a few detours. Because as wonderful as it is to visit sights you've read about, it's the serendipitous experiences that often prove the most memorable: the hole-in-the-wall diner that serves a transcendent tomato soup, the historical society gallery stuffed with dusty local curiosities of days gone by. As you whiz down the highway, use the book to find out more about the towns announced by roadside signs. Consider turning off at the next exit. And always remember: In this great country of ours, there's an adventure around every corner.

HOW TO USE THIS BOOK

Alphabetical organization should make it a snap to navigate through this book. Still, in putting it together, we've made certain decisions and used certain terms you need to know about.

LOCATIONS AND CATEGORIZATIONS

Color map coordinates are given for every town in the guide.

Attractions, restaurants, and lodging places are listed under the nearest town covered in the guide.

Parks and forests are sometimes listed under the main access point.

Exact street addresses are provided whenever possible; when they were not available or applicable, directions and/or cross-streets are indicated.

CITIES

For state capitals and larger cities, attractions are alphabetized by category. Shopping sections focus on good shopping areas where you'll find a concentration of interesting shops. We include malls only if they're unusual in some way and individual stores only when they're community institutions. Restaurants and hotels are grouped by price category then arranged alphabetically.

RESTAURANTS

All are air-conditioned unless otherwise noted, and all permit smoking unless they're identified as "no-smoking."

Dress: Assume that no jackets or ties are required for men unless otherwise noted.

Family-style service: Restaurants characterized this way serve food communally, out of serving dishes as you might at home.

Meals and hours: Assume that restaurants are open for lunch and dinner unless otherwise noted. We always specify days closed and meals not available.

Prices: The price ranges listed are for dinner entrées (or lunch entrées if no dinner is served).

Reservations: They are always a good idea. We don't mention them unless they're essential or are not accepted.

Fodor's Choice: Stars denote restaurants that are Fodor's Choices—our editors' picks of the state's very best in a given price category.

LODGINGS

All are air-conditioned unless otherwise noted, and all permit smoking unless they're identified as "no-smoking."

AP: This designation means that a hostelry operates on the American Plan (AP)—-that is, rates include all meals. AP may be an option or it may be the only meal plan available; be sure to find out.

Baths: You'll find private bathrooms with bathtubs unless noted otherwise.

Business services: If we tell you they're there, you can expect a variety on the premises.

Exercising: We note if there's "exercise equipment" even when there's no designated area; if you want a dedicated facility, look for "gym."

Facilities: We list what's available but don't note charges to use them. When pricing accommodations, always ask what's included.

Hot tub: This term denotes hot tubs, Jacuzzis, and whirlpools.

MAP: Rates at these properties include two meals.

No smoking: Properties with this designation prohibit smoking.

Opening and closing: Assume that hostelries are open year-round unless otherwise noted.

Pets: We note whether or not they're welcome and whether there's a charge.

Pools: Assume they're outdoors with fresh water; indoor pools are noted.

Prices: The price ranges listed are for a high-season double room for two, excluding tax and service charge.

Telephone and TV: Assume that you'll find them unless otherwise noted.

Fodor's Choice: Stars denote hostelries that are Fodor's Choices—our editors' picks of the state's very best in a given price category.

NATIONAL PARKS

National parks protect and preserve the treasures of America's heritage, and they're always worth visiting whenever you're in the area. Many are worth a long detour. If you will travel to many national parks, consider purchasing the National Parks Pass ($50), which gets you and your companions free admission to all parks for one year. (Camping and parking are extra.) A percentage of the proceeds from sales of the pass helps to fund important projects in the parks. Both the Golden Age Passport ($10), for those 62 and older, and the Golden Access Passport (free), for travelers with disabilities, entitle holders to free entry to all national parks, plus 50% off fees for the use of many park facilities and services. You must show proof of age and of U.S. citizenship or permanent residency (such as a U.S. passport, driver's license, or birth certificate) and, if requesting Golden Access, proof of your disability. You must get your Golden Access or Golden Age passport in person; the former is available at all federal recreation areas, the latter at federal recreation areas that charge fees. You may purchase the National Parks Pass by mail or through the Internet. For information, contact the National Park Service (Department of the Interior, 1849 C St. NW, Washington, DC 20240-0001, 202/208—4747, www.nps.gov). To buy the National Parks Pass, write to 27540 Ave. Mentry, Valencia, CA 91355, call 888/GO—PARKS, or visit www.national-parks.org.

IMPORTANT TIP

Although all prices, opening times, and other details in this book are based on information supplied to us at press time, changes occur all the time in the travel world, and Fodor's cannot accept responsibility for facts that become outdated or for inadvertent errors or omissions. So always confirm information when it matters, especially if you're making a detour to visit a specific place.

Let Us Hear from You

Keeping a travel guide fresh and up-to-date is a big job, and we welcome any and all comments. We'd love to have your thoughts on places we've listed, and we're interested in hearing about your own special finds, even the ones in your own back yard. Our guides are thoroughly updated for each new edition, and we're always adding new information, so your feedback is vital. Contact us via e-mail in care of roadnotes@fodors.com (specifying the name of the book on the subject line) or via snail mail in care of Road Guides at Fodor's, 280 Park Avenue, New York, NY 10017. We look forward to hearing from you. And in the meantime, have a wonderful road trip.

THE EDITORS

Important Numbers and On-Line Info

LODGINGS

Adam's Mark	800/444—2326	www.adamsmark.com
Baymont Inns	800/428—3438	www.baymontinns.com
Best Western	800/528—1234	www.bestwestern.com
	TDD 800/528—2222	
Budget Host	800/283—4678	www.budgethost.com
Clarion	800/252—7466	www.clarioninn.com
Comfort	800/228—5150	www.comfortinn.com
Courtyard by Marriott	800/321—2211	www.courtyard.com
Days Inn	800/325—2525	www.daysinn.com
Doubletree	800/222—8733	www.doubletreehotels.com
Drury Inns	800/325—8300	www.druryinn.com
Econo Lodge	800/555—2666	www.hotelchoice.com
Embassy Suites	800/362—2779	www.embassysuites.com
Exel Inns of America	800/356—8013	www.exelinns.com
Fairfield Inn by Marriott	800/228—2800	www.fairfieldinn.com
Fairmont Hotels	800/527—4727	www.fairmont.com
Forte	800/225—5843	www.forte-hotels.com
Four Seasons	800/332—3442	www.fourseasons.com
Friendship Inns	800/453—4511	www.hotelchoice.com
Hampton Inn	800/426—7866	www.hampton-inn.com
Hilton	800/445—8667	www.hilton.com
	TDD 800/368—1133	
Holiday Inn	800/465—4329	www.holiday-inn.com
	TDD 800/238—5544	
Howard Johnson	800/446—4656	www.hojo.com
	TDD 800/654—8442	
Hyatt & Resorts	800/233—1234	www.hyatt.com
Inns of America	800/826—0778	www.innsofamerica.com
Inter-Continental	800/327—0200	www.interconti.com
La Quinta	800/531—5900	www.laquinta.com
	TDD 800/426—3101	
Loews	800/235—6397	www.loewshotels.com
Marriott	800/228—9290	www.marriott.com
Master Hosts Inns	800/251—1962	www.reservahost.com
Le Meridien	800/225—5843	www.lemeridien.com
Motel 6	800/466—8356	www.motel6.com
Omni	800/843—6664	www.omnihotels.com
Quality Inn	800/228—5151	www.qualityinn.com
Radisson	800/333—3333	www.radisson.com
Ramada	800/228—2828	www.ramada.com
	TDD 800/533—6634	
Red Carpet/Scottish Inns	800/251—1962	www.reservahost.com
Red Lion	800/547—8010	www.redlion.com
Red Roof Inn	800/843—7663	www.redroof.com
Renaissance	800/468—3571	www.renaissancehotels.com
Residence Inn by Marriott	800/331—3131	www.residenceinn.com
Ritz-Carlton	800/241—3333	www.ritzcarlton.com
Rodeway	800/228—2000	www.rodeway.com

Sheraton	800/325—3535	www.sheraton.com
Shilo Inn	800/222—2244	www.shiloinns.com
Signature Inns	800/822—5252	www.signature-inns.com
Sleep Inn	800/221—2222	www.sleepinn.com
Super 8	800/848—8888	www.super8.com
Susse Chalet	800/258—1980	www.sussechalet.com
Travelodge/Viscount	800/255—3050	www.travelodge.com
Vagabond	800/522—1555	www.vagabondinns.com
Westin Hotels & Resorts	800/937—8461	www.westin.com
Wyndham Hotels & Resorts	800/996—3426	www.wyndham.com

AIRLINES

Air Canada	888/247—2262	www.aircanada.ca
Alaska	800/426—0333	www.alaska-air.com
American	800/433—7300	www.aa.com
America West	800/235—9292	www.americawest.com
British Airways	800/247—9297	www.british-airways.com
Canadian	800/426—7000	www.cdnair.ca
Continental Airlines	800/525—0280	www.continental.com
Delta	800/221—1212	www.delta.com
Midway Airlines	800/446—4392	www.midwayair.com
Northwest	800/225—2525	www.nwa.com
SkyWest	800/453—9417	www.delta.com
Southwest	800/435—9792	www.southwest.com
TWA	800/221—2000	www.twa.com
United	800/241—6522	www.ual.com
USAir	800/428—4322	www.usair.com

BUSES AND TRAINS

Amtrak	800/872—7245	www.amtrak.com
Greyhound	800/231—2222	www.greyhound.com
Trailways	800/343—9999	www.trailways.com

CAR RENTALS

Advantage	800/777—5500	www.arac.com
Alamo	800/327—9633	www.goalamo.com
Allstate	800/634—6186	www.bnm.com/as.htm
Avis	800/331—1212	www.avis.com
Budget	800/527—0700	www.budget.com
Dollar	800/800—4000	www.dollar.com
Enterprise	800/325—8007	www.pickenterprise.com
Hertz	800/654—3131	www.hertz.com
National	800/328—4567	www.nationalcar.com
Payless	800/237—2804	www.paylesscarrental.com
Rent-A-Wreck	800/535—1391	www.rent-a-wreck.com
Thrifty	800/367—2277	www.thrifty.com

Note: Area codes are changing all over the United States as this book goes to press. For the latest updates, check www.areacode-info.com.

Fodor's Road Guide USA

Delaware
District of Columbia
Maryland
Pennsylvania
Virginia

Delaware

Delaware's founding fathers were in something of a rush to ratify the U.S. Constitution, forever earning Delware the nickname "the First State." The Colonial capital, Philadelphia, is just 25 mi north of Wilmington, Delaware's largest city. Like its neighbor to the north, Delaware is rich in Colonial history, but nowadays it takes the lead in business, not politics. Half of the Fortune 500 companies are among the 200,000 businesses incorporated in Delaware for tax purposes, though you won't see much evidence on Wilmington's modest skyline—most firms maintain only an office here.

In its key physical features Delaware is known for being second: only Rhode Island is smaller and only Florida is flatter. Its blink-and-you-missed-it size is underscored for motorists who encounter it on I–95, which cuts for 14 mi across the northern tip of the state.

But for such a tiny place, Delaware offers travelers a surprisingly broad variety of experiences. From the Piedmont's rolling hills and hardwood forest in the north, through the tidal marshes along the Delaware Bay coast, to the Atlantic dunes and placid inland waterways in the south is a journey of barely 100 mi. It encompasses the corporate center of Wilmington (the midway point between New York and Washington for rail travelers), the Colonial charm of New Castle, the beach-season bustle of Rehoboth Beach, the Bombay Hook bird sanctuary, and the Cypress Swamp, the northernmost stand of bald cypress in America.

For generations Delaware was dominated by the DuPonts, both the family and the industrial giant. Virtually every public institution bears the stamp of one or the other. Family estates such as Winterthur and Nemours have become showplace museums and gardens (as has Longwood, a few miles over the Pennsylvania border). The company's early headquarters and gunpowder works along Brandywine Creek are preserved as Hagley Museum and Library, devoted to early American industrial history.

CAPITAL: DOVER	POPULATION: 706,000	AREA: 2,044 SQUARE MI
BORDERS: PA, MD, NJ, ATLANTIC OCEAN	TIME ZONE: EASTERN	POSTAL ABBREVIATION: DE
WEB SITE: WWW.STATE.DE.US/TOURISM		

Wilmington's Hotel DuPont, still owned by the company, houses the state's finest restaurant and its premier playhouse. Northern Delaware's major parks and nature preserves were carved from family holdings. Even Delaware's major north-south highway, U.S. 13—now supplanted in places by a new limited-access highway, Route 1—was built by a DuPont, with an eye to improving commerce in the early days of the automobile.

The DuPont influence wanes once you leave Delaware's industrialized north. Most of the state lies on the flat, fertile Delmarva Peninsula, a long finger of land between the Chesapeake Bay to the west and the Delaware Bay and Atlantic Ocean to the east, which it shares with Maryland and Virginia. Until the mid-20th century this region was devoted mostly to agriculture, while small towns devoted to shipping, fishing, and shipbuilding sprang up along the region's many meandering creeks. Most of the towns declined in importance with the advent of the railroad in the 1850s, leaving behind a rich architectural legacy.

Even the resorts along Delaware's short stretch of Atlantic coastline offer a glimpse at the past. Lewes, settled by the Dutch in 1637, was the first town in what is now Delaware. Rehoboth Beach, the state's largest seaside town, was developed toward the close of the Victorian period, and gingerbread-style cottages remain common in the central shopping district. Shopping, in fact, is helping to turn the area from a summer-only destination to a year-round draw. Route 1, the coast road that links all the state's beaches, is home to an ever-growing collection of outlet stores that never lack for bargain-hunters, especially since Delaware is one of the few states in the nation—and the only one in the generally tax-heavy Mid-Atlantic region—that imposes no sales tax on purchases.

History

Even in prehistoric times, Delaware apparently was a summer destination for people seeking sun, sand, and shellfish—a recent archaeological dig not far from the ocean uncovered the charred remains of an oyster feast from about 10,000 years ago. But its isolated peninsula kept the area a backwater even for ancient Americans. When Europeans arrived, they found the northern part occupied by tribes of what they called the Delawares, though the natives called themselves the Lenni Lenape, meaning "original people." The southern part of the peninsula was inhabited by the Nanticokes, a few hundred of whom remain in the state today.

Henry Hudson was the first European explorer to record an encounter with Delaware Bay, but he left quickly after realizing it was a river. The waterway got its name the next year, when an expedition from Virginia sailed in and named it for that colony's governor, Lord De La Warr. Because the Delaware lies about halfway between the two common sailing routes to North America, it was one of the last areas on the East Coast settled by Europeans, but few places have flown the flags of so many different countries. The Dutch arrived in 1631, followed by the Swedes (plus some Finns) by the end of the decade. The Dutch expelled the Scandinavians in 1655, but soon the British swept in, relieving the Dutch of Delaware in 1664, when they changed

DE Timeline

1610	1631	1632	1638
Captain Samuel Argall of the Virginia colony names De La Warr Bay for the governor of Virginia.	The Dutch build a settlement at Zwaanendael (now Lewes).	The colony is wiped out by Indians.	The Swedes found a colony where the Christina River meets the Delaware, near present-day Wilmington.

INTRODUCTION
HISTORY
REGIONS
WHEN TO VISIT
STATE'S GREATS
RULES OF THE ROAD
DRIVING TOURS

New Amsterdam's name to New York. But it was more than a century before Delaware became an independent colony.

The land was granted in 1682 to William Penn, who first set foot on American soil at New Castle before sailing up the river to found Philadelphia. Large tracts in northern Delaware originally belonged to Penn's children, and the Quaker presence is still felt today. Penn originally gave his "Three Lower Counties" an equal voice in Pennsylvania's legislature. As the rest of Pennsylvania grew in size, these counties received permission for their own legislature to meet, though they were still ruled by Pennsylvania's governor. Delaware's boundaries were long a source of friction between Pennsylvania and Maryland—a situation that wasn't settled until surveyors Charles Mason and Jeremiah Dixon traced their celebrated line, which forms Delaware's western boundary. In July 1776 Delaware's representatives declared independence from England; later that year they declared themselves free of Pennsylvania as well.

The DuPont family arrived in 1800, drawn by the easy access to creeks that could power mill wheels. They weren't alone—the area was an early center for production of everything from flour and paper to snuff and, in the DuPonts' case, gunpowder, which they began manufacturing in 1802. The remains of these early mills still dot the countryside, and a few have been restored. Many were owned by the industrious Quakers, who later distinguished themselves by operating way stations on the Underground Railroad to help slaves fleeing to freedom. Delaware, like Maryland, was a border state in the Civil War, officially siding with the Union but failing to abolish slavery until after the war. It was during the country's Gilded Age that the DuPonts amassed much of their vast wealth and built the sprawling estates that are among Delaware's premier tourist attractions today.

Regions

1. CHATEAU COUNTRY

The northern rim of Delaware lies in the Piedmont, an area of low hills and lush valleys where the state's early industry developed. Hundreds of the area's small farms were bought up in the 1800s by various members of the DuPont clan, many of whom built large country estates. Some, like Winterthur and Nemours, are now open to the public as museums. You will see others across the rolling hills as you drive along the region's scenic back roads.

Towns listed: Greenville

2. WILMINGTON METRO AREA

Delaware's only city of more than 50,000 residents is also its business and cultural capital. Since the 1950s, as its suburbs have spread to cover most of the northern half of New Castle County, Wilming-

1655	1664	1682	1704	1776
The Dutch attack and capture New Sweden.	The English seize Dutch holdings on the Delaware.	Delaware's three counties are granted to William Penn.	The first meeting of separate Delaware legislature is held.	Delaware declares independence from England and Pennsylvania.

ton's population and influence have declined, but city leaders have begun a revitalization plan by concentrating on the Christina River waterfront, a former industrial area that's now home to a minor-league baseball park and an arts center.

Towns listed: Arden, Claymont, Delaware City, Hockessin, Newark, New Castle, Odessa, Wilmington

3. TIDAL WETLANDS

The state's long Delaware Bay shoreline is strung like beads on a necklace with wetlands where wildlife abounds. The jewels among the marshes are national wildlife refuges at Bombay Hook, between Smyrna and the state capital, Dover, and Prime Hook, between Milford and Lewes. Both are important feeding grounds for a large variety of resident and migratory birds, making them popular stops for bird-watchers, especially in the spring and fall.

Towns listed: Dover, Milford, Smyrna

4. ATLANTIC COAST

Delaware's ocean shoreline extends just 28 mi from Cape Henlopen in the north to Fenwick Island in the south, but that short stretch includes a variety of vacation experiences. Rehoboth Beach draws a cosmopolitan crowd from Washington, Baltimore, and New York with sophisticated restaurants and eclectic boutiques. Families are attracted to its boardwalk and amusements. Lewes is steeped in history, Dewey Beach in nightlife. Bethany Beach and Fenwick Island, intent on staying small, are known as "the quiet resorts." There are also state parks with separate areas devoted to bathing, surf fishing, and wildlife.

Towns listed: Bethany Beach, Dewey Beach, Fenwick Island, Lewes, Rehoboth Beach

5. LOWER DELAWARE

The Chesapeake and Delaware Canal cuts through New Castle County, giving ships a shortcut between the bays. To the south lies what residents proudly call "Slower Lower Delaware," an area where city bustle gives way to country and small-town life. Most of the towns are indeed tiny, but few are so small that they don't have antique shops and historic sites. At the extreme southern end of the state lies the Pocomoke Swamp, where red cedars and the continent's northernmost stand of bald cypress poke through the shallow water.

Town listed: Georgetown

When to Visit

Delaware enjoys four distinct seasons, with a fair amount of rain year round. The state's coastline tends to keep it relatively mild in winter and prevents the summers from getting overly hot.

1777	1787	1802	1865	1880
British troops en route to Philadelphia win a skirmish at Cooch's Bridge, the only Revolutionary battle on Delaware soil. The state capital moves from New Castle to Dover.	On December 7 Delaware becomes the first state to ratify the U.S. Constitution.	French immigrant Eleuthere Irenee DuPont builds a gunpowder mill along the Brandywine Creek.	Fort Delaware, on Pea Patch Island off Delaware City, is used as a Civil War prison.	The first beauty contest in the U.S., called the "Miss United States Contest," is held in Rehoboth Beach, Delaware.

INTRODUCTION
HISTORY
REGIONS
WHEN TO VISIT
STATE'S GREATS
RULES OF THE ROAD
DRIVING TOURS

Winters are a little colder in the north around Wilmington and inland, but in general temperatures remain at around 40°F. Snow, however, is not uncommon.

Summers are warm and sometimes humid, but the sea breeze helps cool down the coastal regions. Temperatures seldom reach into the nineties. Spring and fall are mild, with a slight chill in the evenings. Late spring brings out the flowers in the lowland fields. Autumn is the best time to enjoy the foliage in the state parks and forests. These two seasons may be the most relaxing time to visit, with fewer tourists on the roads and beaches.

CLIMATE CHART
Average High/Low Temperatures (°F) and Monthly Precipitation (in inches)

	JAN.	FEB.	MAR.	APR.	MAY	JUNE
GEORGETOWN	42/23	44/25	54/33	63/40	73/51	82/60
	3.67	3.15	3.99	3.44	3.65	3.41
	JULY	AUG.	SEPT.	OCT.	NOV.	DEC.
	86/65	84/63	78/56	68/45	57/36	47/28
	3.70	3.6	3.41	3.27	3.18	3.46
	JAN.	FEB.	MAR.	APR.	MAY	JUNE
WILMINGTON	38/22	41/24	52/33	62/42	72/52	81/61
	3.03	2.91	3.43	3.39	3.84	3.55
	JULY	AUG.	SEPT.	OCT.	NOV.	DEC.
	85/67	84/65	77/58	67/45	55/37	43/27
	4.23	3.4	3.43	2.88	3.27	3.48

FESTIVALS AND SEASONAL EVENTS
WINTER

Feb.–Mar. **Merchants' Attic and Public Garage Sale.** Rehoboth holds the state's largest indoor garage sale; local businesses and citizens sell excess inventory and household items. | 800/441–1329, ext. 15.

SPRING

May **Old Dover Days.** Dover heritage street fair with crafts and events celebrating the town's history. | 302/734–1736.

SUMMER

July **Delaware State Fair.** The town of Harrington, 17 mi south of Dover, is taken over by livestock, midway rides, and concerts in a traditional state fair format. | 302/398–3269.

1901	1938	1971	1973	2000
Delaware native Eldridge Reeves Johnson founded the Victor Talking Machine Company producing the popular Victrola.	Wilmington-born novelist John Phillips Marquand wins the Pulitzer Prize for "The Late George Apley."	Delaware passes the nation's first Coastal Zone Act, which bars industries that pollute in order to protect beaches and wetlands.	Delaware native Henry Heimlich creates his famous life-saving maneuver.	Ruth Ann Minner becomes the first woman to be elected Governor of Delaware.

Oct.   **Delaware Nature Society Harvest Moon Festival.** Hockessin
holds a two-day celebration of the people and the land;
booths and events explain the history of the Lenape Indians,
and there are hayrides, butterflies on display, pumpkin deco-
rating, and much more. | 302/239–2334.

State's Greats

Both natural wonders and the monuments of human history draw visitors to the tiny
state of Delaware. The "First State" played a central part in the Colonial politics that
led to the emergence of a new nation. The large Native American population and pre-
English settlers from northern Europe left their mark on the Delaware landscape. Old
churches, mills, and museums stand as reminders of a time when few on the continent spoke the English tongue. When the British arrived, they proceeded to build
houses in the Colonial style that once dominated the whole Northeast. You'll find some
of the finest surviving examples of these elegant dwellings in northern Delaware.

Water dominates the environment of this river-filled coastal state. Beaches, fishing, watersports, boating, sailing—Delaware has them all in abundance. The 28-mi
Atlantic coast is a natural playground of wave and sand. The hardwood forests of Piedmont's rolling hills—perfect for a scenic drive—are only a short trip from the shore,
yet their serene, cool atmosphere could be a continent away. Delaware's marshlands
and national parks are popular with birdwatchers.

Beaches, Forests, and Parks

The Atlantic coast has many small and medium-sized seaside towns that cater to the
needs of visitors, especially families. **Rehoboth Beach** is the largest of them, with a busy
boardwalk for strolling and shopping. Nearby **Dewey Beach** attracts college kids and
a singles crowd. For a more serene coastal experience, **Fenwick Island,** south of the
Indian River, is famed for its fishing.

Delaware was settled early by farmers who set about clearing much of its forest
land. The best of the remaining woodlands stand in the Piedmont region to the north.
Bombay Hook National Wildlife Refuge consists of more than 15,000 acres of ponds
and fields, filled between April and November with both resident and migrating
waterfowl.

Culture, History, and the Arts

Wilmington, the only city in Delaware with a population over 50,000, is the state's
center of arts and culture. Its opera house, museums, and galleries draw visitors from
around the state and beyond. The city is also rich in Colonial history, with churches
and houses dating from the 1690s. **New Castle**—Delaware's capital until 1777—is a
barely commercialized gem of a town with restored Colonial houses, cobblestone
streets, and historic sites along the Delaware River. William Penn's first landing in North
America is noted in Battery Park. The culture and history of Delaware has for two centuries
been linked to the DuPont family. A number of the old family estates were given to
the state and are maintained as historic and cultural landmarks. **Winterthur Museum,
Garden, and Library** is the prize among them, with collections of Colonial furniture,
decorative arts, and fine art.

Sports

Wilmington has a minor-league baseball team, but otherwise professional sports are
thin on the ground. In Delaware sports means participation. Miles of hiking trails, lakes
and streams, and the seashore offer countless opportunities for the adventurous

INTRODUCTION
HISTORY
REGIONS
WHEN TO VISIT
STATE'S GREATS
RULES OF THE ROAD
DRIVING TOURS

spirit. Fishing (river or deep-sea), boating, and sailing are three of the major sports in Delaware. The flat terrain also makes the state popular with cyclists, and bike trails wind through many state parks. Tennis courts and golf courses can be found, especially near the popular seaside resort towns.

Rules of the Road

Right turn on red: Drivers are permitted to make a right turn on red after coming to a full stop, unless otherwise posted.

Speed limits may vary based on road conditions and/or specific areas, so always refer to posted signs.

Seatbelt and helmet laws: Seatbelts are mandatory for all front-seat passengers in any vehicle. Children under 40 pounds or 4 years of age must travel in an approved safety seat. Motorcycle operators and passengers under 18 are required to wear helmets.

Speed limits: Speed limits in Delaware are 55 mph on four-lane and major highways; 50 mph on two-lane roads; 25 mph in specially zoned areas such as business or residential districts; and 20 mph in school zones.

For more information: Delaware State Police | 302/739–5931.

Between the Old Capital and the New: Colonial Delaware

FROM WILMINGTON TO DOVER

Distance: 35 mi   Time: Minimum 1–2 days
Breaks: Overnight stops in Wilmington, Dover.

Between the old state capital of Wilmington and the new one at Dover lies the bulk of Delaware's Colonial history. Most of the trip is on Rte. 9, which follows the Delaware River down to the great bay. It was this waterway that allowed the early adventurers—including William Penn—to navigate the region and found their settlements.

❶ Begin in the medium-sized city of **Wilmington,** which is almost exactly halfway between New York and Washington. This advantageous location has attracted many of America's major corporations to set up offices here. But commerce has not robbed the town of its soul, and many attractions draw Colonial buffs. The **Delaware History Museum** is an ever-changing venue for exhibits on Delaware history, crafts, and culture in the First State. **Fort Christina Monument,** according to local legend, stands on the site of America's first log cabin, originally called New Sweden by its Finnish and Swedish founders. **Holy Trinity (Old Swedes) Church and Hendrickson House Museum** is said to be the oldest Anglican church in America, with its rectory near the Delaware River. **Willingtown Square** is a handsome cluster of four 18th-century houses now used as offices. **Winterthur Museum, Garden, and Library** has one of the world's foremost collections of American furniture and antiques.

❷ Five miles south of Wilmington on Route 9 lies **New Castle,** the town at the heart of Colonial Delaware, with restored Colonial houses, cobblestone streets, and historic sites along the Delaware River. William Penn first landed here, and the occasion is noted in **Battery Park.** Two blocks west, on the waterfront, the **Old New Castle Courthouse,** once

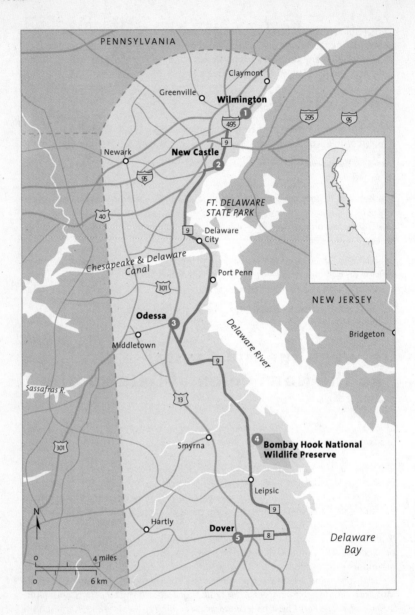

the seat of government, is now a pristine museum of state history. The **George Read II House** and formal gardens were built in 1801 in grand Federal style by a signer of the Declaration of Independence. The **Amstel House Museum** is housed in the restored brick mansion of a former governor, with Colonial furnishings and arts.

❸ Even Delawareans can't resist the rural road from New Castle to Dover, which winds through the flatlands and across the Chesapeake and Delaware Canal. About 10 mi south of New Castle sits the town of **Odessa**. The architecture of this old grain-shipping town is more Federal than Colonial and is well worth a few hours of exploration. The **Historic Houses of Odessa** are fine examples of 18th-century architecture, built for four of the town's major families.

INTRODUCTION
HISTORY
REGIONS
WHEN TO VISIT
STATE'S GREATS
RULES OF THE ROAD
DRIVING TOURS

➍ Another 12 mi south on Rte. 9 you'll spot the towering marsh grasses of **Bombay Hook National Wildlife Preserve,** some 15,000 acres of marshlands favored by hundreds of species of waterfowl.

➎ End your trip in **Dover** (from Bombay Hook, south on Rte. 9 to Rte. 8 west for 6 mi), the capital of Delaware since 1777, laid out by William Penn himself. The **John Dickinson Plantation** is the former home of one of Delaware's most distinguished sons of the Colonial era. **The Old State House,** built in 1802, is the second oldest seat of government in continuous use in the nation.

Rural Delmarva life circa 1890 is recreated at **Delaware Agricultural Museum and Village.** You can't pass through Dover without stopping off at the **Delaware State Museum.** The focus here is on Delaware's role as the first state to ratify the U.S. Constitution.

Delaware's Own Route 1:
The Towns of The Atlantic Coast
FROM LEWES TO FENWICK ISLAND

Distance: 28 mi   Time: Minimum 1–3 days
Breaks: Overnight stop in Bethany Beach

Delaware's ocean shoreline is just 28 mi from Cape Henlopen in the north to Fenwick Island in the south, but it includes hip Rehoboth Beach, historic coastal villages, and three state parks. Scenic Rte. 1 hugs the coast for the entire journey.

❶ Begin in **Lewes,** Delaware's oldest settlement and the site of an enclave of historic buildings and homes. The historical society maintains a number of these houses, including the **Fisher-Martin House,** built around 1728. **Zwaanendael Museum** features displays that trace the town's roots to the present day. Park the car and treat yourself to a ride on the **Queen Anne's Railroad,** an authentic steam engine.

❷ East of town, (approx. 3 mi on Rte. 404) on the shore, you'll find **Cape Henlopen State Park,** a large seaside park with beaches, well-protected dunes, and wildlife.

❸ From Cape Henlopen State Park proceed west on Rte. 404 and then south on Rte. 1 for 4 mi until you hit the seaside resort of **Rehoboth Beach.** "The nation's summer capital" got its nickname because it used to be so popular with Washington politicos. Besides the fancy shops and good restaurants, the real attraction is the **Delaware Seashore State Park,** a top-notch state park with beaches set within a wildlife preserve. The **Anna Hazzard Museum** has an impressive Native American exhibit.

❹ Two miles south of Rehoboth is the slightly shabbier but less busy **Dewey Beach.**

❺ **Bethany Beach,** another 7 mi south, is a delightfully serene coast town: a famous spot for fishing and bathing. **Holts Landing State Park** is 200 acres of boating, fishing, crabbing, and fun.

❻ **Fenwick Island,** at the southeastern tip of Delaware, is a fashionable summer resort popular across the mid-Atlantic states. **Fenwick Island Lighthouse,** now open to the public, was in continuous operation from 1859 to 1978. **Fenwick Island State Park**—another one of Delaware's wonderful coastal state parks—is good for surfing as well as swimming and fishing.

ARDEN

MAP 4, H1

(Nearby town also listed: Wilmington)

Delaware's only single-tax community was founded by artists and craftspeople in 1900, on the theory that no persons own the land on which they live. Instead they have 99-year leases, and their "rent" is their only local tax, covering property, school, sewer, and roads. The entire village of Arden is on the National Register of Historic Places.

Information: Greater Wilmington Convention and Visitors Bureau. | 100 W. 10th St., Wilmington, DE 19801 | 302/652–4088 or 800/422–1181 | info@wilmcvb.org | www.wilmcvb.org.

Attractions

Arden Gild Hall. The center of community life in Arden, the Gild Hall hosts town events, concerts, dances, theater performances, and just about any other cultural activity you can think of. | 2126 The Highway | 302/475–3126 | Varies | Call for event schedule.

ON THE CALENDAR

SEPT.: *Arden Fair.* Held at the beginning of September on the grounds of the Arden Gild Hall off Harvey Avenue, this festival showcases the work of local artisans. | 302/571–9590.

Dining

Anthony's on Shipley Street. American. It looks like a 1950s diner, but the dishes at this downtown eatery tend toward the Italian. Grills, seafood dishes, pasta, and salads make up the formal dinner menu. The seafood pescatore—shrimp, scallops, mussels, clams, and calamari sauteed in a marinara sauce and served with crustini—is a specialty. | 913 Shipley St. Wilmington | 302/652–7797 | fax 302/654–5064 | $18–$30 | AE, DC, D, MC, V.

Lodging

Comfort Suites. This all-suite hotel is a mile from Christiana Mall. Complimentary Continental breakfast. In-room data ports, some in-room safes, microwaves, some in-room hot tubs, cable TV. Indoor pool. Business services. | 56 Old Baltimore Pike Newark, | 302/266–6600 or 888/322–5999 | fax 302/226–6500 | comfsuide@aol.com | 65 rooms | $80–$124 | AE, DC, D, MC, V.

BETHANY BEACH

MAP 4, I4

(Nearby towns also listed: Fenwick Island, Lewes, Rehoboth Beach)

Bethany Beach and nearby Fenwick Island are billed as the "quiet resorts," because both towns are primarily residential. Bethany was founded as a site for revival camp meetings; hence the biblical name. It's just south of the Delaware Seashore State Park. The town entrance is marked by a modern interpretation of an Indian totem pole. Bethany's boardwalk is home to one of the best summertime arts and crafts shows in the region. Fenwick Island, the southernmost of Delaware's beach communities, is marked by the historic Fenwick Island Lighthouse and one of the original Transpeninsular Line Markers. Between the towns lies the Indian River Lifesaving Station, one of the oldest remaining on the Atlantic Coast; it was recently renovated as a museum. Local sites: Fenwick Island Lighthouse, Indian River Lifesaving Station.

Information: Bethany Beach and Fenwick Area Chamber of Commerce | Rte. 1, Box 1450, Bethany Beach, DE 19930 | 302/539–2100 or 800/962–SURF | fax 302/539–9434 | www.bethany-fenwick.org.

Attractions

Holts Landing State Park. One of Delaware's series of small, inland state parks. Its 200-plus acres are perfect for swimming, fishing, clamming, and sailing. | Millville | 302/539–9060 or 302/539–1055 | www.destateparks.com/holts | $2.50 (DE residents), $5 (out of state) | Daily 8–dusk.

South Bethany Seafood Market. If you're staying in lodgings with kitchen facilities, this is the spot to get fresh seafood, including clams, scallops, swordfish, tuna, salmon, crab, and local fish. If you like, the market will steam or grill your fish for you. | Rte. 1 | 302/537–1332 | Free | Daily.

ON THE CALENDAR

SEPT.: *Boardwalk Arts Festival.* Displays of arts and crafts from all over are sponsored by the local chamber of commerce. | Labor Day weekend | 302/539–2100.
SEPT.: *Coastal Music and Arts Festival.* Held at Lord Baltimore Elementary School in nearby Ocean View, this fest includes a juried arts and crafts competition, music from area performers, kids' art activities, food vendors, and an auction of everything from the work of local artisans to tee times at nearby golf courses. | 302/537–2700.

Dining

Magnolia's Restaurant and Pub. Continental. The pub serves sandwiches, burgers, salads, and finger foods for lunch and dinner. The formal dining room serves veal, seafood, and steak entrees. Try the flounder maguelia—flounder in an egg batter sauteed with mushrooms, capers, lemon, wine, and garlic, and topped with jumbo shrimp. | Cedar Neck Rd. Ocean View | 302/539–5671 or 888/415–3474 | fax 302/539–2506 | Lunch available only at the pub | $17–$35 | AE, D, MC, V.

Mango's. Caribbean. Mango's serves up large portions of Caribbean specialties, pasta, and American classics on the ocean front. Try a mai tai and a mambo combo: Jamaican jerk chicken with coconut shrimp, Cuban black beans, rice, and fresh vegetables. A steel band plays at Sunday brunch. | Garfield Pkwy. and Boardwalk | 302/537–6621 | fax 302/537–5490 | Limited fall, winter, and spring hours | $12–$23 | MC, V.

The Parkway Restauraunt. American. The Parkway is a cozy pub that recalls the TV show "Cheers." Like many restaurants in the area, the kitchen takes jumbo lump crab cakes seriously; they also have rack of lamb and white chocolate and vanilla crème brûlée. Kids' menu, early-bird dinner. | 114 Garfield Pkwy. | 302/537–7500 | $21–$29 | AE, DC, MC, V.

Sedona. Southwestern. An upscale restaurant with a feeling of the desert, Sedona avoids the usual coastal trappings. Game meats like elk, ostrich, antelope, boar, and buffalo are often available. | 26 Pennsylvania Ave. | 302/539–1200 | No lunch | $8–$15 | AE, D, MC, V.

Lodging

Adam's Ocean Front Motel. The rates at this motel on the beach vary widely by season, but rooms always have daily maid service. You can sunbathe in the protected area behind the motel. | 23 rooms. Complimentary Continental breakfast. Cable TV. Pool. | 4 Read St. | 302/227–3030 or 800/448–8080 | www.adamsoceanfront.com/hotel | $45–$185 | Nov.–Mar. | MC, V.

The Addy Sea Bed and Breakfast. This Victorian beachfront house was Bethany Beach's first inn. Rooms are furnished with period antiques. A large downstairs bedroom, the Captain's Quarters, was originally builder John Addy's office. | 14 rooms (7 share bath). Complimentary breakfast. | 99 N. Atlantic Ave. | 302/539–3707 | $120–$170 | MC, V | Closed Nov.–Mar.

The Atlantic Surf. These one-, two-, and three-bedroom units have fully stocked kitchens and individually controlled air conditioning. They do not have daily maid service. You can walk two blocks to the beach or enjoy the sunning and barbecue areas in the backyard. | 7 rooms. Picnic area. Kitchenettes, cable TV, no room phones. | 217 4th St. | 302/539–6552 | www.atbeach.com/lodging/de/apt/atlanticsurf/ | $65–$180 | MC, V.

Bethany Arms. At this boardwalk motel most of the rooms have ocean views; furnishings are simple. Room 36 has the best view of the sea. | 52 units. Many kitchenettes, cable TV. | 99 Hollywood St. | 302/539–9603 | $90–$145 | Closed mid-Oct.–Feb. | MC, V.

Blue Surf. This two-story motel right on the boardwalk has wraparound balconies. It is next to the bandstand in the center of town. | 35 units. Many kitchenettes, cable TV. Business services. | 302/539–7531 | $43–$63 | Closed mid Oct.–Apr. | MC, V.

Captain Ebe T. Chandler House. Eleven miles inland in Frankford, this B&B offers beach lovers a quiet and remote alternative to staying in the resort towns. You can relax in the garden or pool in the backyard, watch a video in the den, or borrow the inn's bikes, beach chairs, or picnic supplies for an outing. Complimentary Continental breakfast, TV in common area. Pool. | 13 Main St. Frankford | 302/732–3481 or 888/732–1300 | chandlerhouse@atbeach.com | 5 rooms | $75–$115 | No credit cards.

Harbor View. Every room at this motel has a balcony. The bay is nearby. | 81 rooms. Restaurant, picnic area, complimentary Continental breakfast. Some kitchenettes, cable TV. Pool. Laundry facilities. | RD 1, Box 302 | 302/539–0500 | fax 302/539–5170 | $119–$179 | AE, D, DC, MC, V.

Journey's End. This traditional guest house opened in 1927 and hasn't changed much since, with shared baths and no TVs. It harks back to a time when Bethany Beach was a modest religious retreat. | 8 rooms (with shared bath) | 101 Parkwood St. | 302/539–9502 | $55–$77 | No credit cards | Closed mid-Oct.–May.

Westward Pines Motel. Family-run and inland a bit, this motel is a quiet spot away from the hustle of the beach in high season. It looks like a log cabin. One room has a whirlpool tub. | 10 rooms | 10 Kent Ave. | 302/539–7426 | fax 302/539–3670 | $75–$90 | MC, V.

CLAYMONT

(Nearby town also listed: Greenville)

At New Castle County's northernmost edge, Claymont was once a dignified and elegant resort community on the Delaware River. It has lost its wealthy residents, but some of their stately homes remain, scattered among working-class housing developments of the post–World War II era. The mansion that F. Scott Fitzgerald and his wife, Zelda, rented in summers past is no more, but the Darley Manor Inn is now a bed-and-breakfast, where visitors can wander through rooms where Charles Dickens stayed.

Information: **New Castle County Chamber of Commerce.** | Box 11247, Claymont, DE 19850 | 302/737–4343 | fax 302/737–8450 | ncccc@dca.net | www.ncccc.com.

ON THE CALENDAR

DEC.: *Robinson House Christmas Tours.* On the first and second weekends in December, you can tour this historic 1723 house decorated for the holidays. It was once inhabited by George Washington, Anthony Wayne, Robert Morris, and General "Lighthorse" Harry Lee during Revolutionary War days. At Naamans Road and Philadelphia Pike. | 302/792–0285.

Dining

Fuel House. American. You can eat and get going fast at Fuel House, where they serve hamburgers, fries, onion rings, and the like for dine-in or carry-out. | 2616 Philadelphia Pike | 302/793–0920 | $4–$6 | No credit cards.

Lodging

Darley Manor. This 1790s Colonial manor house was the former residence of Felix O. C. Darley, mid-19th-century book illustrator of titles including *The Scarlet Letter*. Rooms have some period antiques. | 6 rooms (3 with shower only). Complimentary breakfast. Cable TV. Exercise equipment. Business services. No kids under 9. No smoking. | 3701 Philadelphia Pike (U.S. 13 Bus.), Claymont | 302/792–2127 or 800/824–4703 | fax 302/798–6143 | darley@dca.net | www.dca.net/darley | $99–$129 | AE, D, DC, MC, V.

Milan Motel. This one-story, drive-up motel retains its 1950s charms. The Coffield House is 3 mi away; Wilmington is 4 mi. | 20 rooms. Cable TV. No pets. | 3306 Philadelphia Pike | 302/798–6601 | $40–$45 | MC, V.

DELAWARE CITY

(Nearby town also listed: Newark)

This tiny "city" on the Delaware River hosts two main attractions: a mammoth oil refinery and Fort Delaware. Battery Park at the waterfront gives the town a modest charm, but the effect is muted by the aroma of refined petrol and the industrial nature of the river it fronts.

Information: **City of Delaware City** | 407 Clinton St., Box 4159, Delaware City 19706 | 302/834–4573 | ncccc@dca.net.

Attractions

Fort Delaware State Park. You can visit the state's somewhat decrepit, 19th-century army camp (which housed some 12,000 Confederate prisoners during the Civil War) in late spring to early fall, when Civil War buffs reenact military events. The fort sits on Pea Patch Island in the Delaware River, but it doesn't boast much of a view. However, this tiny spot of land is believed to be the largest heronry in the northeastern United States. More than 7,000 pairs of wading birds—including herons, egrets, and ibis—have been observed nesting on the highest elevation here. Two heronry overlooks and a nature trail have been established on the island. You can get there by taking a 10-minute boat ride from Delaware City. | Park Superintendent, 45 Clinton St., Box 170, Delaware City | 302/834–7941 | www.destateparks.com | $2.50 (DE residents), $5 (out of state) | Late Apr.–Sept., weekends 10–6; mid– Jun.–Labor day, Wed.–Fri. 10–6.

ON THE CALENDAR

APRIL: *Season Opens at Fort Delaware.* Locals celebrate with a grand send-off on the last weekend in April, when the ferry begins running from Fort Delaware to Pea Patch Island and on to Fort Mott State Park in New Jersey. | 302/834–7941.

Dining

The Reybold Room at the Olde Canal Inn. Contemporary. In a dining room with white table cloths and Colonial furnishings, you can enjoy fresh seafood, veal, and pasta. The veal Olde Canal is tenderized and served with crabmeat and mushrooms and topped with brie cheese. | Clinton and Harbor Sts. | 302/832–5100 | fax 302/834–7442 | Reservations essential | Closed Mon. No lunch weekends | $11–$20.

Lodging

Olde Canal Inn. Built in 1826 as a rest stop for government officials and gentry traveling between Baltimore, Philadelphia, and New York, the inn is within walking distance of all of Delaware City's historic attractions. Almost all rooms have ocean views. | 10 rooms. Restaurant, bar. | Clinton and Harbor Sts. | 302/832–5100 | fax 302/834–7442 | www.oldecanalinn.com | $49–$199 | AE, D, MC, V.

DEWEY BEACH

MAP 4, I4

(Nearby town also listed: Rehoboth Beach)

South of the more staid and artsy Rehoboth Beach, Dewey has been attempting in recent years to shed its "party hearty" reputation. New complexes such as Ruddertowne include dining, shopping, and entertainment. But vestiges of the old Dewey Beach party scene remain in the inexpensive motels and basic rental accommodations that abound. But with no boardwalk or town center, just a strip of Route 1 running through its center, Dewey Beach is still, as local bumper stickers proclaim, "A Way of Life."

Information: **Rehoboth/Dewey Chamber of Commerce** | 501 Rehoboth Ave., Box 216, Dewey Beach 19971 | 302/227–2233 or 800/441–1329, ext. 13 | fax 302/227–8351 | rehoboth@dmv.com | www.dmv.com/business/rehoboth.

Attractions

Delaware Seashore State Park. Set within the wildlife refuge that extends from Dewey Beach to Bethany Beach, this 2,000-acre state park has a campground, two ocean swimming areas, bathhouses, and sandy white beaches that are among Delaware's best. | Inlet 850, Rte. 1, south of Dewey Beach | 302/227–2800 | $2.50 (DE residents), $5 (out of state) | Daily 8–dusk.

Indian River Lifesaving Station. Three miles south of Dewey Beach is this historic museum, the only standing lifesaving station on the East Coast. Built in 1876, the station was the base of operations for "surfmen," who were experts in sea rescues. | 130 Coastal Hwy. | 302/227–0478 | www.irlss.org | Free | Summer daily 10–5, winter weekends 11–4.

ON THE CALENDAR

SEPT.: *Dewey Beach Triathalon.* If you're not up for participating in this half-mile swim, 16-mile bike ride, and three-mile run at Delaware Seashore State Park, you can certainly cheer on those who are. | 302/227–8018.

Dining

Juice Joint Cafe. Vegetarian. One of the few healthy food options right on the beach, the Juice Joint serves smoothies, juice, fruit, as well as creative sandwiches, salads, and burritos. The seared yellowfin tuna with pesto on a wholegrain bun is a popular choice. | 2000 Hwy. 1 | 302/226–2112 | No dinner | $4–$10 | No credit cards.

Lodging

Atlantic Oceanside Motel. Especially popular with singles vacationing from Maryland, Virginia, and Washington, D.C., this three-story motel is minutes from the beach and right across the street from the Bottle & Cork bar. | 61 rooms. In-room data ports, cable TV. Pool. | 1700 Hwy. 1 | 302/227–8811 or 800/422–0481 | www.atlanticoceanside.com/motel | $89–$109 | AE, D, MC, V.

Atlantic View Motel. This simply furnished notel is directly on the beach, steps from fishing, jet skiing, and clamming. | 35 rooms. Cable TV. Pool. Laundry facilities. | 2 Clayton St., North Dewey Beach | 302/227–3878 or 800/777–4162 | fax 302/226–2640 | $120–$180 | Closed Nov.–Mar. | AE, D, MC, V.

Best Western Gold Leaf. A half block from the beach and boardwalk, this hotel has parking available on every floor. Each room has a balcony. It's across the street from the Rusty Rudder, a dining and entertainment complex. | 75 rooms. Cable TV. Pool. Laundry facilities. Business services. | 1400 Rte. 1 | 302/226–1100 | fax 302/226–9785 or 800/422–8566 | www.bestwesterngoldleaf.com | $149–$199 | AE, D, DC, MC, V.

DOVER

MAP 4, H3

(Nearby towns also listed: Odessa, Smyrna)

Dover's downtown area, the Green, was laid out in 1722 on the orders of William Penn. Although today its surrounding buildings serve as the county seat and state capital, in Colonial times the Green hosted fairs and markets for the region. It was at an inn on the Green—the Golden Fleece Tavern—that Delaware became the first state to ratify the U.S. Constitution on December 7, 1787. Mercantile activities of the city shifted several blocks north to Loockerman Street as Dover grew after the Civil War. Many buildings on this street retain their turn-of-the-century facades. At the edge of town sits the Dover Air Force Base, jumping-off spot for most military airborne missions and the receiving facility for war and disaster casualties from abroad. Today, because of Delaware's liberal corporation laws, over 50,000 firms name Dover as their home for tax purposes.

Information: **Central Delaware Chamber of Commerce** | Treadway Towers, Suite 2-A, Box 576, Dover 19903 | 302/734–7513 | fax 302/678–0189 | jsteele@cdcc.net | www.cdcc.net.

WALKING TOUR

Start your Dover walking tour at the Delaware State Visitors Center at the corner of Federal and North streets, where you can pick up local maps and learn about current events and attractions. (If the Visitor Center parking lot is full, head 1½ blocks east and try the Archives building. From here, walk one block down Federal Street to the Green and the Delaware State House, built in 1792. It served as courtroom, governor's office, and legislative chambers until 1934, when official business was moved to Legislative Hall. After strolling across the Green, head one block west on Bank Lane to Governors Avenue, where you'll find the Delaware State Museum Complex, which includes the Johnson Victrola Museum, and the Delaware Agricultural Museum.

You'll need a car to visit some outlying attractions. Head west to Route 113 and take it south to the main entrance of the Dover Air Force Base Museum, a WWII hangar and outdoor display filled with vintage aircraft and memorabilia. Double back on Route 113 N to get to Harrington Raceway, where you can enjoy harness racing from May into fall. Continue north on Route 113 to the Delaware Agricultural Museum and Village, south of Delaware State University; this recreated 1890s village displays thousands of artifacts related to farming and agriculture in Delaware. From here you can head back to town on State Street and unwind at Silver Lake Park.

NEIGHBORHOODS

Around State Street: Victorian homes fill the area surrounding State Street and stretching from Dover Green to Silver Lake; all are well-preserved and some reflect the ministrations of TV personality Bob Vila. A good place to start exploring is the Old Statehouse on the Green. Walking north you will spot some of the original redbrick roadway and you'll pass Wesley College and signs toward the Governor's Mansion on Kings Highway. Many of the handsome State Street structures now house modern shops, restaurants, and bookstores. Silver Lake Park is not far away.

TRANSPORTATION

Airport: To get to Dover, you can either fly into Philadelphia International Airport or Baltimore–Washington International. | 215/937–6937 for Philadelphia, 410/859–7111 for BWI.

Airport Transportation: You can combine Amtrak via Wilmington and DART to get to Dover.

Car services are the fastest option from both airports. The cost is $60–$90 from Philadelphia, $85–$140 from BWI. Call Delaware Express (302/454–7800) or Mooney Transportation (302/674–3200).

Bus: There is no **Greyhound** service in Dover itself, but the line serves Wilmington at | 101 N. French Street | 800/872–7245 and 302/655–6111.

The **DART** bus system serves all of Delaware. The major commuter link between Dover and Wilmington, it provides local bus service in both cities. | 800/652–DART or 302/652–DART | www.dartfirststate.com.

Rail: The nearest town served by Amtrak is Wilmington, where you'll find the station at the juncture of | Martin Luther King, Jr., Boulevard and French St. | 800/872–8745 and 302/429–6529.

Driving around Town: Dover is in the busy eastern corridor, so expect congestion. Only two main roads lead into and out of town, Routes 113 and 13, both running north–south. Parking is a not a problem, as there are six municipal parking lots and parking on the street is free. Some lots reserved primarily for state employees have limited parking for visitors, and when the legislature is in session (January–June, Tues.–Thurs.), you'll do better to look for a space some distance away from government buildings. Outside town, remember that local roads are often used by Amish residents, who travel in picturesque but slow-moving horse-drawn buggies. Yield to them and exercise caution. And twice a year, when the NASCAR races are held at Dover Downs, 200,000 extra people—and their cars—fill the town to bursting.

Attractions

CULTURE, EDUCATION, AND HISTORY

Delaware Agricultural Museum and Village. Rural Delmarva life circa 1890 is recreated at this museum, with a village and farmstead. | 866 N. DuPont Hwy. (U.S. 13) | 302/734–1618 | $3; special rates for seniors and children | Apr.–Dec., Tues.–Sat. 10–4, Sun. 1–4.

Delaware State Museums. The focus here is on Delaware's role as the first state to ratify the U.S. Constitution. The 1880 Gallery reconstructs a period high street, complete with general store. | 316 S. Governors Ave. | 302/739–4266 | Free | Mon.–Sat. 8:30–4:30, Sun. 1:30–4:30.

John Dickinson Plantation. This restored farm complex is the former home of one of Delaware's most distinguished sons of the Colonial era. | Kitts Hummock Rd., at Rte. 9 | 302/739–3277 | www.destatemuseums.org/jdp | Free | Mar.–Dec., Tues.–Sat. 10–3:30, Sun. 1:30–4:30; Jan.–Feb. Tues.–Sat. 10–3:30.

Hall of Records. This museum includes Delaware's Colonial charter as well as the document ratifying the U.S. Constitution in 1787. | 121 Duke of York St. | 302/739–5318 | Free | Weekdays 8:30–4:15.

Johnson Victrola Museum. Designed as a 1920s Victrola store, this museum is a tribute to the inventor of the Victor Talking Machine. | Bank and New Sts. | 302/739–4266 | Free | Tues.–Sat. 10–3:30.

The Old State House. Built in 1792, the heart of Delaware's central county and state capital sits on the historic Green, surrounded by the halls of government. | Federal St. between Loockerman and Water Sts. | 302/739–4266 | Free | Tue.–Sat. 10:00–4:30, Sun. 1:30–4:30.

MUSEUMS

Delaware Air Force Base Museum. A World War II hangar, listed in the National Historic Register, is the new home of this museum. Special exhibitions, demonstrations, military weapons display, and low-cost airplane rides are featured throughout the year. Community Appreciation Day is held the third Saturday of each month from April to November. | 1301 Heritage Rd. | 302/677–5938 | Free | Daily 9–4.

PARKS, NATURAL AREAS, AND OUTDOOR RECREATION

Killens Pond State Park. This rural park has facilities for boating and camping. | U.S. 13, south of Felton | 302/284–4526 | Weekdays free, weekends $2.50 (DE residents), $5 (out of state) | Daily 8–dusk.
Silver Lake Park. This park has play areas, lake swimming, fishing, a small boat-launching ramp, and a fitness trail. | Kings Hwy. and Washington St. | 302/736–7050 | Free | Daily.

OTHER POINTS OF INTEREST

Delaware State Visitor Center. The center is a good starting point for touring the state capitol and State House complex. | 406 Federal St. | 302/739–4266 | Free | Daily.

Dover Downs International Speedway. Also known as "The Monster Mile," Dover Downs is one of the most popular race destinations in the Northeast. It claims to draw the biggest crowds to a sporting event between New York and North Carolina. Seating capacity is about 107,000. Dover, which was built and started hosting NASCAR Winston Cup Series races in 1969, expanded to two races a year in 1971. Drivers such as Richard Petty, David Pearson, Cale Yarborough and Bobby Allison drove to victory in races at the track that picked up its nickname because of the tremendous physical demands it placed upon a driver. The first NASCAR Busch Series Grand National Division race at Dover Downs was held there in the series' inaugural season of 1982. | 131 N. Dupont Hwy., one mile north of downtown, across from Delaware State University Campus | 302/674–4600, schedule; 800/441–RACE or 302/734–RACE for tickets.

ON THE CALENDAR

MAY: *Old Dover Days.* This Dover heritage street fair celebrates the town's history with a parade, house tours, and crafts. | 302/734–1736.

MAY: *Harrington Raceway.* Harness racing begins in May and continues throughout the summer and fall at Delaware State Fairgrounds. | Harrington | 5:30 PM | 302/398–3269.

JULY: *Delaware State Fair.* This traditional state fair includes livestock, midway rides, and concerts. | Harrington | 302/398–3269.

OCT.: *Ghost Walk at Delaware Agricultural Museum.* Local storyteller Ed Okonowicz and Jennifer Griffin, curator of the Agricultural Museum, take kids though a haunted village. Ghosts and goblins have been known to show up for the stories. Recommended for kids 8 and older. | 302/734–1618.

Dining

Barking Frog. Cafe. The Barking Frog is named after the native tree frog that sounds like, yes, a dog barking. The cafe serves up creative coffee drinks, sandwiches, wraps, salads, soups, and homemade baked goods. The marinated chicken salad is especially popular. | 33 W. Loockerman St. | 302/736–8300 | Sunday | $3–$6 | No credit cards.

The Hub Rock Cafe. American. This restaurant in the Sheraton Inn serves sandwiches and appetizers in fun, laid-back surroundings. | 1570 N. DuPont Hwy. (U.S. 13) | 302/678–8500 | $5–$13 | AE, D, DC, MC, V.

Paradiso. Italian. This stripmall restaurant serves Italian classics and American standbys. Lobster tail is a specialty. | 1151 E. Lebanon Rd. | 302/697–3055 | $12–$20 | AE, D, MC, V.

Where Pigs Fly. American. Pigs fly off the spit in the form of hickory-smoked baby back ribs and "pulled pig" sandwiches at this family restaurant. Chicken and trimmings are also served. | 617 Loockerman St. | 302/678–0586 | $10–$14 | AE, D, DC, MC, V.

Lodging

INEXPENSIVE

Days Inn. This drive-up chain motel in downtown Dover has simply appointed rooms. | 81 rooms. Complimentary Continental breakfast. In-room data ports, cable TV, some microwaves. | 272 N. DuPont Hwy. (U.S. 13) | 302/674–8002 | fax 302/674–2195 | $45–$60 | AE, MC, V.

Howard Johnson's. Plain but up-to-date accommodations on Dover's main road are convenient to Colonial sites. | 133 rooms. Restaurant. Pool. | 651 N. DuPont Hwy. (U.S. 13) | 302/678–8900 | fax 302/678–2245 | $45–$75 | AE, MC, V.

MODERATE

Best Western Galaxy Inn. This two-story motel is next to Dover Air Force Base, 2 mi from John Dickinson Plantation, and 3 mi from Dover Downs. | 64 rooms. Complimentary Continental breakfast. In-room data ports, cable TV. Pool. Laundry facilities. Business services. | 91700 East Lebanon Rd. | 302/735–4700 | fax 302/735–1604 | $54–$75 | AE, MC, V.

Budget Inn. Basic accommodations in a two-story drive-up motel on Dover's main road, half a mile from Dover Downs. | 68 rooms. Cable TV. Pool. Laundry facilities. No pets. | 1426 N. DuPont Hwy. (U.S. 13) | 302/734–4433 | fax 302/734–4433 | $50–$65 | AE, D, DC, MC, V.

Comfort Inn. This two-story motel is 5 blocks from historic Dover, just south of town. | 94 rooms. Complimentary Continental breakfast. Some refrigerators, cable TV. Pool. Exercise equipment. Some pets allowed. | 222 S. DuPont Hwy. (U.S. 13) | 302/674–3300 | fax 302/674–3300, ext. 190 | $55–$69 | AE, D, DC, MC, V.

Comfort Suites Dover. This three-story standard motel is a mile from Delaware State University and a half mile from Dover Downs. | 64 rooms. Restaurant. In-room data ports, some in-room hot tubs, cable TV. Pool. | 1654 N. Dupont Hwy. (U.S. 13). | 302/736–1204 | $59–$184 | AE, DC, D, MC, V.

Dover Inn. This one-story basic motel is less than a mile from Dover Downs. Restaurants are across the street. | 54 rooms. Some microwaves, some refrigerators, cable TV. Laundry facilities. | 428 N. DuPont Hwy. (U.S. 13) | 302/674–4011 | $55–$75 | AE, D, MC, V.

Ramada Inn. Bright, simple rooms with basic amenities, a mile from downtown Dover. | 122 rooms | 348 N. DuPont Hwy. (U.S. 13) | 302/734–5701 | fax 302/678–4788 | $59–$93 | AE, MC, V.

Hampton Inn. You can relax in the outdoor pool, use the free gym nearby, or lounge in your room with free HBO. The Hampton is three miles from downtown Dover and a mile from Dover Downs. | 88 rooms. Complimentary Continental breakfast. In-room data ports, cable TV. Pool. Business services. | 1568 N. DuPont Hwy. (U.S. 13) | 302/736–3500 | $92–$100 | AE, D, MC, V.

VERY EXPENSIVE

Sheraton Inn. Near Delaware State College and Dover Downs, this full-service conference center hotel is suited to the business traveler who wants convenience and comfort. Generously sized rooms are bright and well-appointed. | 152 rooms. Restaurant (see The Hub Rock Cafe), bars (with entertainment). In-room data ports, room service, cable TV. Indoor pool. Hot tub. Exercise equipment. Business services. | 1570 N. DuPont Hwy. (U.S. 13) | 302/678–8500 | fax 302/678–9073 | $106–$139 | AE, D, DC, MC, V.

FENWICK ISLAND

MAP 4, I4

(Nearby towns also listed: Bethany Beach, Rehoboth Beach)

Fenwick is technically an island—it sits on a tiny scrap of land between Delaware and Maryland—but it doesn't really feel like one. No great bridges or causeways connect it to terra firma. It was named for a Virginia landowner, Thomas Fenwick, who bought it in 1686. Salt-making was the big business here in the 19th century. One of the "quiet resorts" of the Delaware shore, the town's resident population of 230 swells in summer with an influx of vacationers. Fenwick was founded and incorporated in 1953 and boasts a historic lighthouse, on the Maryland-Delaware border.

Information: Bethany Beach and Fenwick Area Chamber of Commerce | Rte. 1, Box 1450, Fenwick Island 19930 | 302/539–2100 or 800/962–SURF | fax 302/539–9434 | info@wilm-cvb.org | www.wilmcvb.org.

Attractions

Fenwick Island Lighthouse. The lighthouse was in continuous operation from 1859 to 1978. Public outcry led to the reinstallation of the original 1,500-pound light in 1981. | Rte. 1, Fenwick Island | 410/250–1098 | Free | June–Aug., two Wed. afternoons per month, or by appointment.

Fenwick Island State Park. Delaware's southernmost state park lies on a 3-mi stretch of barrier island, between the Atlantic and Little Assawoman Bay. Its 344 acres are renowned for fishing, sailing, clamming, birdwatching, as well as bathing. | Rte. 1, Millville | 302/539–9060 or 302/539–1055 | $2.50 (DE residents), $5 (out of state) | Daily 8–dusk.

Transpeninsular Marker. A marker from the 1751 survey of the region now sits on the south side of the Fenwick Island Lighthouse. | 302/539–8129 | Free | Weekdays 9–5, weekends 10–4; Nov.–Mar., Mon.–Fri. 9–5, closed Sun.

JAN.: *Exercise Like the Eskimos.* Begin the New Year with low-impact aerobics at Bethany Beach. The truly bold will cool off with a dip in the frigid ocean afterward. | 302/539–2100.

MAY AND OCT.: *Surf-Fishing Tournaments.* Regularly scheduled weekend tournaments are sponsored by area chamber of commerce. | 302/539–2100.

Dining

Mancini's. Italian. The seven-foot brick pizza oven is the first thing you see when you enter this upscale, casual restaurant. It serves only pizza, pasta, and appetizers. You can get 17 pizza toppings and a wide variety of pasta dishes, some with fresh seafood. | 907 Coastal Hwy. | 302/537–4224 | Reservations not accepted | No lunch. Closed Mon., Tue | $10–$20 | AE, D, MC, V.

Tom and Terry's Seafood Restaurant. Seafood. Fresh seafood is prepared in the restaurant overlooking Assawoman Bay and is also sold in the market next door. Stuffed lobster tail is a favorite. Smoking is allowed at the bar. Early-bird supper. | Rte. 54 | 302/436–4161 | $30–$50 | MC, V.

Lodging

Atlantic Coast Inn. This inn is 500 feet from the beach. You can choose rooms in the back building, which are slightly larger or in the less expensive front building. | 48 rooms. Some kitchenettes, cable TV. Pool. Laundry facilities. | Rte. 54 and Ocean Hwy. | 302/539–7673 or 800/432–8038 | www.atlanticcoastinn.com | $42–$105 | Oct.–mid-Apr.

GEORGETOWN

MAP 4, H4

(Nearby towns also listed: Lewes, Milford)

In 1791 the Delaware General Assembly moved the Sussex County government seat from Lewes on the coast to a more central location at "James Pettyjohn's old field." Georgetown was eventually laid out in a circle, a half mile in all directions from its center. The town is unique in maintaining a post-election tradition called Return Day. Politicians, the media, and voters gather to hear official poll results and celebrate the end of the season's campaigns with speeches, parades, music, arts, and an ox roast.

Information: **Georgetown Chamber of Commerce** | Box 1, Georgetown 19947 | 302/856–1544 | fax 302/856–1577 | www.georgetownde.com.

Attractions

Nutter D. Marvel Museum. A collection of historic buildings and horse-drawn carriages along with thousands of photos and documents on the town's history are the highlights of this eclectic collection. Buildings include two barrel-roof barns, a century-old church, a blacksmith shop, a one-room schoolhouse, and two railroad freight buildings. | 508 S. Bedford St. | 302/855–9660.

JUNE: *Sussex County Fair.* Usually held the third weekend in June, this festival celebrates Americana. You can munch foot-long hot dogs and other treats, thrill to midway rides and games, and view arts and crafts creations. | 302/856–1793.

Dining

JW Pickles and Friends. American. Blues, rock, and country bands play on Saturday nights. Fried appetizers, steaks, pasta, and a variety of chicken sandwiches make up the menu. | 21 Georgetown Plaza | 302/855–1300 | $8–$15 | AE, MC, V.

Lodging

Hickman's Motel. Budget accommodations in a one-story drive-up motel on Rte. 13 in nearby Millsboro. | 27 rooms. Cable TV. | 520 W. DuPont Hwy., Millsboro | 302/934–7968 | $45–$50 | AE, D, MC, V.

GREENVILLE

MAP 4, H1

(Nearby towns also listed: Claymont, Newark, Wilmington)

Like many Delaware suburbs, Greenville has no real entertainment or gathering spots, but there is upscale shopping and dining.

Information: New Castle County Chamber of Commerce | 630 Churchman's Rd., Box 11247, Newark 19850 | 302/737–4343 | fax 302/737–8450 | ncccc@dca.net | www.ncccc.com.

Attractions

Delaware Museum of Natural History. The emphasis here is on life under the sea and in the wild. The prize exhibit is a 500-pound clam. | 4840 Kennett Pike, Wilmington | 302/658–9111 | www.delmnh.org | $5; special rates for seniors and children | Daily.

ON THE CALENDAR

MAY: *St. Hedwig Polish Festival.* This annual event held at St. Hedwig Church (at Linden and Harrison streets in Wilmington) features Polish food, arts and crafts, music, dancing, and history. | 302/594–1402.

Dining

Amalfi. Italian. Northern and southern Italian cuisines like cioppino and calamari are served along with salmon and veal in an intimate, elegant room. No smoking. | 3801 Greenville Center | 302/655–7719 | $12–$20 | AE, D, DC, MC, V.

Brandywine Brewing Company Restaurant and Brewery. American. This brew-pub is casual and upscale. The crab-and-corn chowder is popular, but the beer is the big draw. Kids' menu. | 3801 Kennett Pike | 302/655–8000 | $10–$15 | AE, D, DC, MC, V.

Cromwell's Tavern. American. Barnboard walls and Colonial-style lighting lend this neighborhood tavern an old-world charm. The grub is hearty and the portions large. Entertainment Saturday. Sunday brunch. | 3858 Kennett Pike | 302/571–0561 | $12–$16 | AE, D, DC, MC, V.

Lodging

Residence Inn by Marriott. This all-suite hotel off I-95 near the University Plaza Shopping Center in Newark includes the use of sports courts. | 120 rooms. Complimentary breakfast. In-room data ports, some kitchenettes, some refrigerators, cable TV. Pool., Outdoor hot tub. Gym. | 240 Chapman Rd. | 302/453–9200 | fax 302/453–8122 | scene.delawareonline.com/profiles/residenceinn/ | $99–$164 | AE, D, MC, V.

HOCKESSIN

MAP 4, H1

(Nearby town also listed: Greenville)

Once nothing more than a general store for local farmers, Hockessin still retains some of its country air. But most of its pastures are quickly being turned into housing developments and its barns razed to make way for shops. Still, the rolling hills and back roads that run into nearby Pennsylvania are a welcome respite from the congestion in most of New Castle County's suburbs. A library, public parks, firehouse, shops, and a tiny county police station make up the core of the village.

Information: New Castle County Chamber of Commerce | 630 Churchman's Rd., Box 11247, Newark 19850 | 302/737–4343 | fax 302/737–8450 | ncccc@dca.net | www.ncccc.com.

Attractions

Ashland Nature Center. Four self-guided nature trails meander through 200 acres of meadow, marsh, pond, and forest. There's also a native plant garden and a nature center with environmental displays and information. | Brackenville and Barley Mill Rds. | 302/239–2334 | www.delawarenaturesociety.org/ashland | Free | Nature center Mon.–Fri. 8:30–4:30, Sat. 9–3, Sun. 1–4, trails open daily.

ON THE CALENDAR

OCT.: *Delaware Nature Society Harvest Moon Festival.* In this two-day celebration of the people and the land, booths and events recount the history of the Lenape Indians, and there are hayrides, butterflies on display, pumpkin decorating, and more. | Ashland Nature Center | 302/239–2334.

Dining

Back Burner. American. This barn-like country restaurant serves a six-ounce filet en croute prepared in a puff pastry with brie. Other favorites are strip steak and rack of lamb. No smoking. | 425 Hockessin Corner | 302/239–2314 | $20–$23 | AE, D, DC, MC, V.

Back Burner to Go. American. You can take home a selection of foods prepared by the restaurant next door, including salads and crab cakes. | 425 Hockessin Corner | 302/239–2732 | $7–$15 | AE, D, DC, MC, V.

The Crownery. Chinese. This spacious family restaurant in Lantana Shopping Center serves Cantonese food at a reasonable price. | 228 Lantana Dr. | 302/239–3825 | $11–$15 | AE, D, DC, MC, V.

Lodging

Fairfield Inn by Marriott. This three-story hotel is just a mile from the Delaware Park Race Track and Casino. | 135 rooms. Complimentary Continental breakfast. In-room data ports, cable TV. Business services. | 65 Geoffrey Dr. | 302/292–1500 | www.fairfieldinn.com | $75–$95 | AE, DC, D, MC, V.

LEWES

MAP 4, I4

(Nearby towns also listed: Bethany Beach, Fenwick Island, Rehoboth Beach)

Settled by the Dutch in 1631, Lewes (pronounced LOO-is) is Delaware's oldest settlement. It's also the northernmost of the coastal towns, on Delaware Bay rather than the Atlantic. Known for its fishing marinas, Lewes is also the southern terminal of the

KODAK'S TIPS FOR TAKING GREAT PICTURES

Get Closer
- Fill the frame tightly for maximum impact
- Move closer physically or use a long lens
- Continually check the viewfinder for wasted space

Choosing a Format
- Add variety by mixing horizontal and vertical shots
- Choose the format that gives the subject greatest drama

The Rule of Thirds
- Mentally divide the frame into vertical and horizontal thirds
- Place important subjects at thirds' intersections
- Use thirds' divisions to place the horizon

Lines
- Take time to notice lines
- Let lines lead the eye to a main subject
- Use the shape of lines to establish mood

Taking Pictures Through Frames
- Use foreground frames to draw attention to a subject
- Look for frames that complement the subject
- Expose for the subject, and let the frame go dark

Patterns
- Find patterns in repeated shapes, colors, and lines
- Try close-ups or overviews
- Isolate patterns for maximum impact (use a telephoto lens)

Textures that Touch the Eyes
- Exploit the tangible qualities of subjects
- Use oblique lighting to heighten surface textures
- Compare a variety of textures within a shot

Dramatic Angles
- Try dramatic angles to make ordinary subjects exciting
- Use high angles to help organize chaos and uncover patterns, and low angles to exaggerate height

Silhouettes
- Silhouette bold shapes against bright backgrounds
- Meter and expose for the background illumination
- Don't let conflicting shapes converge

Abstract Composition
- Don't restrict yourself to realistic renderings
- Look for ideas in reflections, shapes, and colors
- Keep designs simple

Establishing Size
- Include objects of known size
- Use people for scale, where possible
- Experiment with false or misleading scale

Color
- Accentuate mood through color
- Highlight subjects or create designs through color contrasts
- Study the effects of weather and lighting

From *Kodak Guide to Shooting Great Travel Pictures* © 2000 by Fodor's Travel Publications

Cape May–Lewes Ferry, which crosses the mouth of the bay between Delaware and New Jersey. The town retains an enclave of historic buildings and homes, many of them painstakingly restored. Some still show cannonball marks from a British bombardment in the war of 1812. In 1984 the remains of the *De Braak,* a 17th-century Dutch vessel, were discovered by divers off the coast. Retrieval of the ship and its treasures made headlines nationwide. Lewes is also the site of the University of Delaware's College of Marine Studies. Coast Day is a popular annual event every fall.

Information: **Lewes Chamber of Commerce** | 120 Kings Hwy., Box 1, Lewes 19958 | 302/645–8073 | fax 302/645–8412 | www.leweschamber.com.

Attractions

Cape Henlopen State Park. This 4,000-acre seaside park includes beaches, well-protected dunes, wildlife, and bath houses. You can play golf, fish, and camp. | 42 Cape Henlopen Dr. | 302/645–8983 | www.destateparks.com | $2.50 (DE residents), $5 (out of state) | Daily 8–dusk.

Fisher-Martin House. Built around 1728, the house now serves as the information center of the Lewes Chamber of Commerce and Visitors Bureau. | 120 Kings Hwy. | 302/645–8073 | Free | Sept.–Memorial Day, weekdays 10–4; June–Aug., Sat. 9–3, Sun. 10–2.

Lewes–Cape May Ferry. This efficient (70-minute) ferry service connects Lewes with the Victorian beach village of Cape May, New Jersey. The ferry carries up to 100 cars and 800 passengers on the 17-mi journey. There are 22 daily crossings in summer, 7 in winter, between 7 and 13 in spring and fall. | 43 Henlopen Dr. | 302/645–6313 or 800/643–3779 | Call for rates and hours.

Prime Hook Wildlife Refuge. This 8,817- acre expanse of freshwater or tidal marsh, timber and brush, and grasslands and croplands, 10 mi northwest of Lewes, is home to many species of birds, mammals, fishes, reptiles, and amphibians. There are 15 miles of streams for canoeing and fishing. Refuge access is off Route 16. | Turtle Pond Rd., RD #13 Box 195, Milton, | 302/684–8419 | fax 302/684–8504 | Free | Refuge: daily dawn–dusk; visitor center April–Nov. weekdays 7:30–4, weekends 9–4.

Queen Anne's Railroad. You can take a 50-minute round-trip dinner excursion on an authentic steam train. | 730 Kings Hwy. | 888/456–8668 | $59 (dinner included) | Apr.–Dec., Sat. 5:30; Jun.–Sept., Wed. 5:30.

Zwaanendael Museum. This town museum gets its name from the Dutch whaling fishery founded near Lewes in 1631. Museum displays trace the town's roots to the present day. | Kings Hwy. and Savannah Rd. | 302/645–1148 | Free | Mon. 10–4, Tues.–Sat. 1:30–4:30.

ON THE CALENDAR

MAR. OR APR.: *Great Delaware Kite Festival.* Every Easter high-flying kites fill the skies above the state park's beaches. | Friday before Easter | 302/645–8073.
MAY: British Motorcar Show. Shine up your Triumph, Rolls, or Jaguar or admire other peoples' cars at this annual show held at Blackhouse Pond Park. A winners circle parade follows the judging. | 302/645–7777.
JUNE: *Zwaanendael Heritage Garden Tour.* You can visit Lewes's finest gardens in their spring finery. | 302/645–8073.
OCT: *Coast Day.* Marine studies come ashore with exhibits, cooking demonstrations, and conservation ideas, sponsored by the University of Delaware Sea Grant Program and the Graduate College of Marine Studies. | 302/831–8083.

Dining

La Rosa Negra. Italian. Try the rock fish in sundried tomato and butter sauce or more standard Italian fare in casual surroundings with a black-and-white color scheme. Kids' menu, early-bird supper. No smoking. | 128 2nd St. | 302/645–1980 | $15–$20 | AE, D, DC, MC, V.

Second Street Grille. American. Enjoy the popular crab cakes in an unpretentious restaurant with family-style service. Kids' menu, early-bird supper. Sunday brunch. | 115 W. 2nd St. | 302/644–4122 | $8–$20 | MC, V.

Lodging

Anglers. Two buildings in a fenced garden and picnic area are across the street from the fishing wharf. Rooms have two double beds or one queen. | 25 rooms, 2 with kitchenettes. Cable TV. Pool. | 110 Anglers Rd. | 302/645–2831 | $75–$110 | AE, MC, V.

Bay Moon Bed and Breakfast. This 1887 Victorian inn in the heart of old Lewes is furnished with antiques. You can relax in wicker chairs on the front porch, then curl up in a four-poster bed under a down comforter. Outdoor shower and free use of swimwear. | 4 rooms. Bar, complimentary breakfast. Outdoor hot tub. | 128 Kings Hwy. | 302/644–1802 | www.bay-moonbnb.com | $135–$150 | AE, D, MC, V.

Blue Water House Bed and Breakfast. A casual inn with guest rooms on the first floor, the Blue Water offers free use of grill, picnic tables, bikes, beach chairs, and boogie boards. The complimentary breakfast includes a different home-baked bread every day. | 6 rooms. Picnic area, complimentary breakfast. | 407 E. Market St. | 302/645–7832 or 800/493–2080 | $85–$150 | MC, V.

Inn at Canal Square. Downtown on the Lewes–Rehoboth canal, near restaurants and the fishing dock, this inn is something of a local landmark. Rooms are spacious and smartly furnished with reproduction antiques. They even have a houseboat for rent. | 22 rooms. Complimentary Continental breakfast. Cable TV. | 122 Market St. | 302/644–3377 or 800/222–7902 | fax 302/645–7083 | $155–$185 | AE, D, DC, MC, V.

New Devon Inn. A historically registered brick hotel built in 1926 is a mile from Henlopen State Park. Many antique stores are nearby. | 26 rooms. Restaurant. Business services. | 142 2nd St. | 302/645–6466 or 800/824–8754 | fax 302/645–7196 | $110–$140 | AE, MC, V.

MILFORD

MAP 4, H3

(Nearby towns also listed: Lewes, Georgetown)

Milford sits on the Mispillion River at the intersection of U.S. 13 and Route 1, half in Kent County and half in Sussex County. Settlers populated the area as early as 1660, and it was the center of a vibrant timber trade. Three historic areas in the town are listed on the National Register. Milford today has a saltwater-access marina and is within a few miles of several freshwater boat ramps.

Information: **Milford Chamber of Commerce** | 11 S. DuPont Blvd., Box 805, Milford 19963 | 302/422–3344 | fax 302/422–7503 | ccgm@milford-de.com | www.milford-de.com.

Attractions

Abbott's Mill Nature Center. About 4 mi south of Milford, you can learn about the environment of the area and take an easy hike along a six-acre bog, through meadows, and along a creek. | Abbotts Pond Rd., off Rte. 36 | 302/422–0847 | www.delawarenaturesociety.org/abbotts | Nature Center Mon.–Fri. 8:30–4:30, trails open daily.

ON THE CALENDAR

OCT.: *Autumn at Abbott's Mill Festival.* Held on the third Saturday in October, this festival includes guided canoe excursions, gristmill tours, a Colonial skills demonstration, Native American and environmental exhibits, a craft sale, and music. | 302/422–0847.

Dining

Sonny's Garden City Cafe. Eclectic. Seafood, salads, and Southwestern, Brazilian, and American cuisine will draw you to Sonny's. The gravies, salsas, guacamole, and mashed potatoes are all made from scratch, and the chef's wife performs Brazilian songs in English and Portuguese on Thursday and Friday nights. | 36 N. Walnut St. | 302/422–5760 | Closed Sun. Breakfast Sat. only | $6–$12 | No credit cards.

Lodging

The Towers. Once the residence of Delaware Governor William Burton, this 1783 Colonial was renovated by Burton's daughter in 1891 into a Steamboat Gothic Victorian mansion. Stained glass and carved woodwork adorn the interior, the Music Room has a massive fireplace and grand piano, and there is a walled garden with gazebo. Sherry is always available, compliments of the house. | 4 rooms. Complimentary breakfast. Pool. | 101 N.W. Front St. | 302/422–3814 or 800/366–3814 | fax 302/422–4703 | $95–$135 | AE, MC, V.

NEWARK

MAP 4, H2

(Nearby towns also listed: New Castle, Wilmington)

Fourteen miles southwest of Wilmington and home of the University of Delaware and its scenic Old College, Newark today is a thriving small city. The university dates from 1743; the Newark campus was established about 1765. The city is part of the Wilmington greater metropolitan area.

Information: Greater Wilmington Convention and Visitors Bureau | 100 W. 10th St., Wilmington 19801 | 302/652–4088 or 800/422–1181 | info@wilmcvb.org | www.wilmcvb.org.

Attractions

Cooch's Bridge. Local historians insist that the Stars and Stripes was first unfurled at this site during a Revolutionary War battle on September 3, 1777. | Old Baltimore Pike, Newark | No phone | Free | Daily.

Iron Hill Museum of Natural History. This former one-room schoolhouse contains collections of Delaware birds, mammals, insects, and fossils. Three nature trails fan out from the site. | 1355 Old Baltimore Pike | 302/368–5703 | $1 | Wed.–Fri. noon–4, Sat. 1–4.

University of Delaware. The beautiful and historic campus spreads through the town of Newark, but the main focus is its pastoral mall. | S. College Ave. (Rte. 896) | 302/831–8123 | Free | Daily.

University of Delaware Mineral Collection. This collection of more than 6,000 specimens is considered to be among the finest in the country. | Penny Hall, Academy St. | 302/831–2569 | Free | Weekends 1–4, Tues.–Thurs. noon–4.

White Clay Creek State Park. The creek runs through 2,500 acres of woodland and rock outcrops. You can fish, hike, and birdwatch. | 425 Wedgewood Rd. | 302/368–6900 | $2.50 (DE residents), $5 (out of state) | Daily 8–dusk.

ON THE CALENDAR

APR.: *Ag Day.* The University of Delaware shows off its renowned Agricultural College in Townsend Hall every spring. | 302/831–2508.
JUNE: *Newark Nite.* Games, food, and family fun extend into the wee hours in the streets and shops of downtown Newark. | 302/366–7036.

Dining

Iron Hill Brewery and Restaurant. American. The brew-pub fare here is a cut above most, especially the wood-fired pizzas. Don't miss the Louisiana barbecued shrimp. The Great American Beer Festival awarded a gold medal to Iron Hill's maibock—homemade sweet beer, higher in alcohol content than traditional beer, and brewed each May. Its American Pale Ale and Lodestone Lager have taken home awards, too. | 147 E. Main St. | 302/266–9000 | $10–$15 | AE, D, DC, MC, V.

Klondike Kate's. American. Kate's attracts the college crowd with its outdoor deck and laid-back atmosphere. Try the super nachos. Entertainment Thursday and Saturday. Kids' menu. Sunday brunch. | 158 E. Main St. | 302/737–6100 | $7–$15 | AE, D, DC, MC, V.

Sala Salu. American. The restaurant, whose name is taken from a Dr. Seuss story, is known for its vegetarian entrées. They make all soups and desserts on the premises, which are always lively. Entertainment Thursday and Friday. Kids' menu. Sunday brunch. | 16 Marrows Rd. | 302/368–4545 | $11–$13 | AE, D, DC, MC, V.

Lodging

Best Western. You can sing karaoke at Caesar's, the hotel lounge. It's a short drive to restaurants, nightclubs, Longwood Gardens, Winterthur, and Delaware Park. | 94 rooms. Restaurant, bar, complimentary Continental breakfast, room service. Cable TV. Pool. Business services. | 260 Chapman Rd. (Rte. 273). | 302/738–3400 | fax 302/738–3414 | $70–$75 | AE, D, DC, MC, V.

Comfort Inn. This reasonably priced motel is 2 mi from the University of Delaware and close to the New Castle County airport. Wilmington's waterfront area is 7 mi away. | 102 rooms. Restaurant, bar, complimentary Continental breakfast. In-room data ports, some refrigerators, cable TV. Pool. Business services. Some pets allowed. | 1120 S. College Ave. (Rte. 896) | 302/368–8715 | fax 302/368–6454 | $63–$90 | AE, D, DC, MC, V.

Hilton Inn Christiana. Ten acres of landscaped grounds and murals of the Brandywine Valley separate this Hilton from the pack. It's just south of Wilmington off I–95. | 266 rooms. Restaurant, bar. In-room data ports, cable TV. Pool. Hot tub. Exercise equipment. Business services. | 100 Continental Dr. | 302/454–1500 | fax 302/454–0233 | $130–$155 | AE, D, DC, MC, V.

Holiday Inn. This full-service hotel is 7 mi from downtown, 2 mi from Christiana Mall, and near all the Brandywine Valley attractions. | 144 rooms. Restaurant, bar. In-room data ports, room service, cable TV. Pool. Laundry facilities. Business services. Free parking. | 1203 Christiana Rd. | 302/737–2700 | fax 302/737–3214 | $99–$105 | AE, D, DC, MC, V.

Howard Johnson. These standard motel accommodations are 3 mi from the racetrack and 2 mi south of the University of Delaware. | 142 rooms. Complimentary Continental breakfast. In-room data ports, cable TV. Pool. Business services. Free parking. Some pets allowed. | 1119 S. College Ave. (Rte. 896) | 302/368–8521 | fax 302/368–9868 | $65–$125 | AE, D, DC, MC, V.

McIntosh Inn. A member of a small East Coast chain, this hotel is within walking distance of several restaurants. | 108 rooms. Complimentary Continental breakfast. In-room data ports, some microwaves, cable TV. | 100 McIntosh Plaza | 302/453–9100 or 800/444–2775 | fax 302/453–9114 | $55–$65 | AE, DC, MC, V.

Sleep Inn Newark. This two-story standard motel is just across the street from the University of Delaware stadium. | 97 rooms. Complimentary Continental breakfast. In-room data ports, cable TV. Laundry facilities, laundry service. | 630 S. College Ave. | 302/453–1700 | $55–$169 | AE, DC, D, MC, V.

NEW CASTLE

MAP 4, H2

(Nearby towns also listed: Newark, Wilmington)

New Castle, on the Delaware River just south of Wilmington, is an undiscovered jewel of the eastern seaboard. It was founded in 1651 by the Dutch on their way up the Delaware River and later was conquered by the Swedes and then the British. In 1682 it was the first landing site in North America of William Penn, an occasion commemorated in Battery Park. The Colonial assembly met here, and New Castle became the first capital. Cobblestone streets date from the Colonial era, as do the proud homes that line them. "A Day in Old New Castle" is held annually in May, and there are also Christmastime candlelight tours.

Information: New Castle County Chamber of Commerce | 630 Churchman's Rd., Box 11247, Newark 19850 | 302/737–4343 | fax 302/737–8450 | ncccc@dca.net | www.ncccc.com.

Attractions

Amstel House Museum. A bit of 18th-century life is preserved in this Colonial house where George Washington is said to have attended a wedding. | 2 E. 4th St. | 302/322–2794 | $2.25; special rates for children | Mar.–Dec., Tues.–Sat. 11–3:30, Sun. 1–3:30; Jan.–Feb. weekends 11–3:30.

George Read II House. Built in 1801 in the Federal style by the son of George Read I, signer of the Declaration of Independence and the U.S. Constitution, the house is surrounded by formal gardens designed in 1847. Twelve rooms are open to the public. | 42 The Strand | 302/322–8411 | $4; special rates for students, seniors, and children | Mar.–Dec., Tues.–Sat. 10–4, Sun. noon–4; Jan.–Feb. weekends 10–4.

The Green. Old New Castle's historic center is bordered by cobblestone pathways and Colonial buildings. | 3rd St. | Free | Daily.

Immanuel Episcopal Church. Built in 1703, the original church burned in a dramatic fire in the 1980s. It was carefully and lovingly restored by local experts, who were able to use the original walls and foundation. Tombstones in the adjoining graveyard date from 1707. | 100 Harmony St. | 302/328–2413 | Free | Daily 8–dusk.

New Castle–Frenchtown Railroad Ticket Office. Trains pulled by the Delaware steam locomotive operated in the pre-Civil War period. The ticket office was built in 1832 and occupied a number of locations before finding its current site in the 1950s. | Battery Park, Delaware St. | No phone | Free | Daily.

New Castle Presbyterian Church. The first congregation of Dutch settlers built this now-restored church in 1707. | 25 E. 2nd St. | 302/328–3279 | Free | Weekdays 9–6, Sun. 11 AM service.

Old Dutch House. Delaware's oldest dwelling, this tiny house reflects the 1651 founding of New Castle by the Dutch, who called the area Fort Casimir. Period furnishings and art are the main attractions. | 32 E. 3rd St. | 302/322–2794 | $2.25; special rates for children | Mar.–Dec., Tues.–Sat. 11–3:30, Sun. 1–3:30; Jan.–Feb. weekends 11–3:30.

Old Library Museum. This hexagonal Victorian building houses special exhibits related to the area. | 40 E. 3rd St. | 302/322–2794 | Free. Sat. 11–3:30, Sun. 1–3:30

Old New Castle Court House. The history and government of the Colonial capital are the focus of this museum, with exhibits on William Penn and the Delaware abolitionists. | 211 Delaware St. | 302/323–4453 | Free | Tues.–Sat. 10–3:30, Sun. 1:30–4:30.

MAY: *A Day in Old New Castle.* On the third Saturday in May some of New Castle's most spectacular and historic homes and gardens are open for public tours. | 302/328–2413.

JUNE: *Separation Day.* A historic anniversary celebrates Delaware's declaration of independence from the British. Events include a parade, craft show, and fireworks. | 302/322–9802.

JUNE–AUG: *Band Concerts.* Open-air music is played most Wednesday evenings in Battery Park. | 302/322–6334.

Dining

Salty Sam's Pier 13. Seafood. This casual place takes particular pride in its flounder Helina and seafood-stuffed Atlantic salmon. Kids' menu. | 130 S. DuPont Hwy. | 302/323–1408 | $12–$15 | AE, D, DC, MC, V.

Lodging

Fox Lodge at Lesley Manor. No televisions or phones disturb the peace in this 1855 Gothic Revival mansion, known as The Castle, just a few blocks from downtown. It has nine fireplaces, a hand-carved oak staircase, pressed tin ceilings, and rose, herb, and vegetable gardens. | 4 rooms. Complimentary breakfast. | 123 W. 7th St. | 302/328–0768 | www.foxlodge.com | $105–$185 | MC, V.

Ramada Inn. The location might not sound appealing—near the graveyard and state hospital—but this full-service hotel is a good value. | 131 rooms. Restaurant, bar, room service. In-room data ports, cable TV. Pool. Business services. Some pets allowed. | I–295 and Rte. 13, Manor Branch | 302/658–8511 | fax 302/658–3071 | $72–$90 | AE, D, DC, MC, V.

Rodeway Inn. The DuPont family built this Dutch-theme bungalow-style motel with Colonial furnishings. Historic New Castle is 2 mi away, and the Christiana Mall, with 260 stores, is a five-minute drive. | 40 rooms. Cable TV. Business services. Some pets allowed. | 111 S. DuPont Hwy. | 302/328–6246 | fax 302/328–9493 | $59–$74 | AE, D, DC, MC, V.

ODESSA

MAP 4, H2

(Nearby towns also listed: Delaware City, New Castle)

In 1855 the people of Cantwell's Bridge, a major grain-shipping port, decided to change their town name to Odessa, in memory of the great Black Sea port. Long gone are those hectic days, and now, near a sleepy intersection on U.S. 13, Odessa is easily missed. Many people are drawn to the tiny town because of its collection of 18th- and 19th-century houses that are part of the Winterthur Museum complex.

Information: **New Castle County Chamber of Commerce** | 630 Churchman's Rd., Box 11247, Newark 19850 | 302/737–4343 | fax 302/737–8450. | ncccc@dca.net | www.ncccc.com.

Attractions

Brick Hotel Gallery. This Federal-style building houses the country's largest collection of Victorian furniture made in the style of J. H. Belter, between 1840 and 1860. | 2nd and Main Sts. | 302/378–4069 | $7 | Mar.–Dec., Tues.–Sat. 10–4, Sun. 1–4.

Historic Houses of Odessa. A collection of historic 18th-century homes built for the town's elite have been renovated and are open for viewing. | 2nd and Main Sts. | 302/378–4069 | $9 | Mar.–Dec., Tues.–Sat. 10–4, Sun. 1–4.

Corbit-Sharp House. This handsome Georgian house was built in 1774 by William Corbit, who operated a tannery on the banks of the Appoquinimink Creek. | 2nd and Main Sts. | 302/378–4069 | $9 | Mar.–Dec., Tues.–Sat. 10–4, Sun. 1–4.

Wilson-Warner House. Odessa merchant David Wilson built this lovely home in 1769. It's been restored and furnished as it was in 1829, when the family went bankrupt. | 2nd and Main Sts. | 302/378–4069 | $9 | Mar.–Dec., Tues.–Sat. 10–4, Sun. 1–4.

Lums Pond State Park. This park provides a tranquil spot not far from busy Newark. Its 1,800 acres includes a 200-acre pond and numerous hiking trails. | 1068 Howell School Rd., Bear | 302/368–6989 | $2.50 (DE residents), $5 (out of state) | Daily 8–dusk.

Old Drawyer's Church. Construction began in 1773, but the church took nearly 60 years to complete. | U.S. 13 | 302/378–4069 | Free | First Sun. in June, or by appointment.

ON THE CALENDAR
JUNE: *Old Drawyer's Church Annual Service.* On the first Sunday in June a Presbyterian service is held at the church. | 302/378–4069.

Dining
Hearth Restaurant. American. The Hearth is a particularly popular spot after church on Sundays. It serves up gigantic plates of steaming turkey with mashed potatoes and gravy, open-faced roast beef sandwiches, and fried chicken. | U.S. 13 | 302/378–9901 | $5–$10 | MC, V.

Lodging
Pleasant Hill Motel. This 1950s drive-up motel one half mile south of town prides itself on friendly customer service. The innkeepers will be happy to tell you about local attractions and recommend restaurants. Cable TV. | 3155 S. Hwy. 13 | 302/378–2468 | 15 rooms | $45–$55 | MC, V.

REHOBOTH BEACH

MAP 4, I4

(Nearby towns also listed: Bethany Beach, Fenwick Island, Lewes)

Possibly one of the best restaurant towns on the mid-Atlantic coast, Rehoboth has undergone a dramatic facelift in recent years. Artsy shops, comfortable hotels, and a bustling boardwalk draw visitors and retirees from Delaware and Washington, D.C. The mood here is more staid and refined than in Ocean City, Maryland, to the south, due mostly to the local prohibition on high-rise apartments and condos. The area's biggest problem is summer parking and the town's vigilant meter police. Deep-sea fishing, boating, swimming, and biking are among the favored local pursuits.

Information: **Rehoboth/Dewey Chamber of Commerce** | 501 Rehoboth Ave., Box 216, Rehoboth Beach 19971 | 302/227–2233 or 800/441–1329, ext. 13 | fax 302/227–8351 | rehoboth@dmv.com | www.dmv.com/business/rehoboth.

Attractions
Anna Hazzard Museum. Once a camp meeting building, this small museum with its Native American exhibit is named for the former owner and civic leader. | 17 Christian St. | 302/226–1119 | Free | June–Aug., Wed. and Sat. 10–2.

ON THE CALENDAR
THROUGHOUT YEAR: *Merchants' Attic and Public Garage Sale.* At the state's largest indoor garage sale at the Convention Center, local businesses and citizens sell excess inventory and household items. | 800/441–1329, ext. 15.
MAY–SEPT.: *Bandstand concerts.* The local bandstand hosts open-air concerts weekends and some weeknights. | 800/441–1239.

OCT.: *Sea Witch Halloween Festival and Fiddler's Convention.* This Halloween weekend celebration throughout Rehoboth includes a gathering of some mighty fine fiddle players. | Halloween weekend | 800/441–1329, ext. 11.

Dining

Brew Ha Ha! Café. This coffeehouse is known for its creative sandwiches as well as its coffee drinks. Entertainment. No smoking. | 70 Rehoboth Ave. | 302/227–8160 | $9–$17 | No credit cards.

Celsius. Contemporary. The owners serve sophisticated food in a simple style: Spanish tapas appetizers and French and Mediterranean dishes like lobster croquettes and paella. If you enjoy dessert, order the award-winning chocolate cake. Early-bird supper. No smoking. | 50 Wilmington Ave. | 302/227–5767 | $20–$36 | MC, V.

Chez La Mer. French. This spot has a reputation in fine dining circles, and visiting celebs occasionally stop by. The bouillabaisse, roast duck, and filet with dijonnaise sauce are favorites. The *Wine Spectator* has repeatedly given La Mer awards for excellence. No smoking. | 210 2nd St. | 302/227–6494 | Closed Nov.–Mar. | $36–$45 | AE, D, DC, MC, V.

Cloud 9. American. The fish of the day is usually a good indication of the innovation and variety on the menu at this bistro. You can dance to live music most nights. Kids' menu. Sunday brunch. | 234 Rehoboth Ave. | 302/226–1999 | $20–$34 | D, DC, MC, V.

The Corner Cupboard Inn. American. The owners claim to serve "Eastern shore cooking with a southern flair." Fish and seafood are specialties. Sunday brunch; no lunch. BYOB. | 50 Park Ave. | 302/227–8553 | $20–$30 | AE, MC, V.

Jake's Seafood House. Seafood. Seafood bisque and 1½-pound lobsters are among the specialties of this family-style, Baltimore-based restaurant. Kids' menu. No smoking. | 29 Baltimore Ave. | 302/227–6237 | $15–$23 | AE, D, DC, MC, V.

La La Land. Contemporary. You can enjoy grilled rack of lamb or pan-seared halibut on the patio of this remodeled Victorian house. The interior is flamboyant, with bright colors and collages on the walls. There are three dining areas, including a lively bar. | 22 Wilmington Ave. | 302/227–3887 | Reservations essential | $35–$47 | AE, D, DC, MC, V.

1776 Restaurant. American. An upscale steak house serving New York strip, ribeye, prime rib chop, and more. Live jazz on weekends. | Rte. 1 | 302/644–4776 | Reservations essential weekends | $19–$23 | AE, D, DC, MC, V.

Victoria's Restaurant. American. Victoria's is in the Boardwalk Plaza Hotel and overlooks the ocean. There is outdoor dining during the summer. Live piano Sat. Kids' menu, early-bird supper. Sun. brunch with jazz trio, off-season. | 2 Olive Ave. | 302/227–0615 | $21–$27 | AE, D, DC, MC, V.

Lodging

Admiral Motel. Only 50 ft from the beach, this five-story hotel has balcony rooms with views of the ocean. | 73 rooms. In-room data ports, cable TV. Indoor pool. Hot tub. | 2 Baltimore Ave. | 302/227–2103 | fax 302/227–3620 | www.admiralrehoboth.com | $132–$225 | AE, D, MC, V.

Atlantic Budget Inn. Centrally located in downtown Rehoboth, this hotel is close to shopping and is a few blocks from the beach. The rooms are a little cramped. | 107 rooms. Some kitchenettes, cable TV. Pool. | 154 Rehoboth Ave. | 302/227–9446 or 800/245–2112 (MD, OH, PA, and VA only) | fax 302/227–9446 | $59–$159 | AE, D, DC, MC, V.

Beach View. The rooms are refurbished every two years and have views of the pool or the Atlantic Ocean, just 50 yds away. | 38 rooms. Complimentary Continental breakfast. Cable TV. Pool. Laundry facilities. | 6 Wilmington Ave. | 302/227–2999 or 800/288–5962 | fax 302/226–2640 | $115–$150 | Closed weekdays in Nov. | AE, D, MC, V.

Boardwalk Plaza Hotel. This Victorian-style, four-story hotel on the boardwalk has interior hallways, a rooftop sundeck, and off-street parking. | 84 rooms, 45 suites. Restaurant (see Victoria's Restaurant), room service. In-room data ports, some kitchenettes. Indoor-outdoor pool. Exercise equipment. Business services. | 2 Olive Ave. | 302/227–7169 or 800/332–3224 | fax 302/227–0561 | www.boardwalkplaza.com | $209–$399 | AE, D, DC, MC, V.

Brighton Suites. This pink hotel is just a block from the beach. Its suites have two double beds or one king, separate living room, wet bar, and room safe. | 66 suites. Cable TV. Pool. Exercise equipment. Childrens' programs. Business services. | 34 Wilmington Ave. | 302/227–5780 or 800/227–5788 | fax 302/227–6815 | $89–$152 | AE, D, DC, MC, V.

Chesapeake Landing Bed and Breakfast. This secluded property is in a pine and bamboo forest on the shore of Lake Comegys. | 4 rooms. Complimentary breakfast. TV in common area. Pool, lake. | 101 Chesapeake St. | 302/227–2973 | fax 302/227–0301 | www.chesapeake-landing.com | $95–$225 | MC, V.

Dinner Bell Inn. Surrounded by an English garden and two blocks from the ocean, the inn's rooms have pine-paneled rooms and Colonial-style furnishings. The gardener's cottage sleeps six; the house sleeps eight. | 28 rooms, house, cottage. Restaurant, bar, complimentary Continental breakfast. Some kitchenettes, cable TV. Business services. No kids under 12. | 2 Christian St. | 302/227–2561 or 800/425–2355 | fax 302/227–0323 | www.dinnerbellinn.com | $95–$145 | Closed Oct.–mid-Apr. | AE, MC, V.

Econo Lodge Resort. A motor inn close to three factory outlet stores and 2 mi from the beach and boardwalk. | 79 rooms. Complimentary breakfast. Cable TV. Pool. Laundry facilities. Business services. | 4361 Rte. 1 | 302/227–0500 or 800/553–2666 | fax 302/227–2170 | $100–$124 | AE, D, DC, MC, V.

Henlopen Hotel. This white oceanfront high-rise at the north end of the Boardwalk has covered parking. All rooms have balconies; most have water views. | 93 rooms. Complimentary Continental breakfast. Restaurant. Cable TV. Business services. | 511 N. Boardwalk | 302/227–2551 or 800/441–8450 | fax 302/227–8147 | $59–$179, $79–$249 suites | Closed Dec.–Mar. | AE, D, DC, MC, V.

Lord and Hamilton Seaside Inn. In this 1871 Victorian all guest rooms have private baths and some have ocean views. Wicker chairs on the wraparound porch and Victorian and English country antiques invite a return to times past. The inn is 50 ft from the boardwalk. | 7 rooms. Complimentary Continental breakfast. | 20 Brooklyn Ave. | 302/227–6960 or 877/227–6960 | www.lordhamilton.com | $130–$175 in season, $64–$125 off season | MC, V.

Sandcastle. This gray building designed to resemble a sand castle is two blocks from the beach. | 60 rooms. Indoor pool. Sauna. | 123 2nd St. | 302/227–0400 or 800/372–2112 | fax 302/226–9288 | $99–$149 | Closed end of Nov.–Mar. | AE, D, MC, V.

Sea'esta Motel Inn. All rooms in this three-story motel have balconies looking onto the bay; the ocean is a block away. There is covered parking; the Rusty Rudder restaurant is across the street. | 33 units. Kitchenettes, cable TV. Beach. | 1409 Rte. 1, Dewey Beach | 302/227–4343 or 302/227–7299 | $33–$129 | Closed Nov.–Mar. | AE, D, DC, MC, V.

The Sussex House. Two blocks from the beach and five blocks from downtown's nightlife and restaurants, this modern B&B has a front porch and back garden. | 6 roooms. Complimentary breakfast. Cable TV. | 601 Bayard Ave. | 302/227–7860 or 877/787–7392 | fax 302/227–0282 | www.thesussexhouse.com | $125–$209 | AE, DC, D, MC, V.

Tally-Ho Inn. A bit south and west in Selbyville, the Tally-Ho Inn is in a wooded area. It is furnished with antiques and includes a library with a fireplace, a formal dining room, and a Chinese parlor. You can stay in the Oriental Suite or opt for the Polo Room and sleep on Ralph Lauren linens. | 2 rooms. Dining room, complimentary breakfast. | Rte. 1 Selbyville | 302/436–2828 | tallyhoinn@hotmail.com | $125–$140 | MC, V.

SMYRNA

(Nearby towns also listed: Dover, Odessa)

Eight miles west of Delaware Bay and Bombay Hook Wildlife Refuge, Smyrna began about 1700 as an English Quaker settlement called Duck Creek Village, 1 mi north of the current town. The town was named after a Turkish port. The Smyrna Landing wharves were important centers of commerce in the 1800s. Many fine examples of Federal and Victorian architecture can still be found in the town. Locally the town is notorious for being home to the state penitentiary.

Information: **Smyrna Rest and Information Center** | 5500 DuPont Hwy., Smyrna 19977 | 302/653–8910 | www.townofsmyrna.com.

Attractions
Allee House. This 1753 brick plantation house in the Bombay Hook Wildlife Refuge is amazingly well preserved both inside and out. Tours give a glimpse of the life of early settlers. | Dutch Neck Rd., off Rte. 9 | 302/653–6872 | $4 | Weekends in spring and fall 2–5.

Bombay Hook National Wildlife Refuge. Marsh grasses and wildlife are preserved in 12,000 acres of tidal marshes and briny swamps south of Odessa. On a single day you might spot deer, snow geese, whistling swans, egrets, herons, and even a bald eagle or two. | 2591 Whitehall Neck Rd. | 302/653–6872 | $4 | Daily dawn–dusk.

Smyrna Museum. A Colonial home built in the 1790s houses a permanent display of artifacts from the region's Leni Lenape Indians, plus Colonial and Federal furnishings. | 11 S. Main St. | 302/653–8844, 302/653–9502 | Free | Sat. 10–1.

ON THE CALENDAR
OCT.: *Smyrna High School Homecoming.* Call to find out which Friday in October will be Smyrna High School's homecoming, then go cheer on the fighting Eagles varsity football team, as they tackle an area opponent. | 302/653–8491.

Dining
Boondock's. Seafood. Deep-fried seafood is popular here, but you can also get American classics like hamburgers and steaks. | 825 Lighthouse Rd. | 302/653–6962 | $8–$12 | AE, MC, V.

Lodging
Economy Inn. This one-story, independent motel is on the shores of Garrison Lake, a popular fishing spot. | 15 rooms. Cable TV. | 1896 S. DuPont Blvd. | 302/653–9154 | $32 | MC, V.

WILMINGTON

(Nearby towns also listed: Claymont, Greenville, New Castle)

First settled by Swedes in 1655, Wilmington was taken over by Peter Stuyvesant and the Dutch and later by the British. It was William Penn and the Quakers who brought prosperity, making Wilmington a major shipping and commerce hub.

In modern times the city's claim to fame has been its location, halfway between New York City and Washington, D.C. Many corporations like the equal access to both commerce and government so much that they have set up shop in the city, which is sometimes called the world's corporate capital. While the DuPont Co. has long called Wilmington home, the area's biggest businesses now are credit card banks, attracted by the state's laissez faire attitude to interest rate charges. Banks have gobbled up downtown real estate, but little has been done to improve the inner city blight of rundown neighborhoods and empty stores in the city center. After 5 PM it's quiet downtown, as all movie theaters and most restaurants and housing developments are in the suburbs. Current efforts to establish a commercial waterfront center, much like Baltimore's to the south, have been slowed by city government squabbling and power plays. Wilmington's minor league baseball park is one of the waterfront project's keystones, and the club complex Kahunaville draws visitors into town after dark.

Information: **Greater Wilmington Convention and Visitors Bureau** | 100 W 10th St., Wilmington 19801 | 302/652–4088 or 800/489–6664 | info@wilmcvb.org | www.wilmcvb.org.

WALKING TOUR

A tour of Wilmington is best done in two parts. The first half, which covers historical points downtown, is partly walkable. The second requires a car and will take you to museums and parks on the outskirts of town.

Start by visiting the Greater Wilmington Convention and Visitors Bureau on 10th Street between Orange and Shipley streets to pick up maps and information on current events. Walk northwest on Orange Street to 11th Street, and after turning right walk to the 12-story Italian Renaissance Hotel du Pont, built in 1913, and walk through its ornate lobby. Turn right on Market Street, heading south along the Market Street Mall, to the Grand Opera House, home of the Delaware Symphony. Continue south on Market Street until you come to the Delaware History Center and Old Town Hall. The former occupies a 1941 building, formerly a Woolworth's store, and features local art and a Discovery Room where children can try on costumes and learn the story of Delaware. The Old Town Hall, a Georgian home that was once a center of Delaware commerce, displays rotating exhibits covering Delaware history.

Although you can walk, you're better off driving from here east along 7th Street to its end to visit the Fort Christina Monument and Fort Christina Park. Near the park, at 1124 E. 7th, is the shipyard where a full-size recreation of the Swedish Tall Ship Kalmar Nyckel is berthed when not at sea. Go back out to Church Street and turn left (south) to the Holy Trinity (Old Swedes) Church, one of the nation's oldest Anglican churches still regularly used for worship. Nearby Hendrickson House Museum is a Swedish stone farmhouse dating from 1690. Continue down Church Street to East 4th Street and turn right (west). At Orange Street, a left turn takes you to 2 Sout Orange Street, where you'll find the Riverfront Market, opened as part of a local restoration in November 2000.

To see the Brandywine Zoo and Park, pick up your car and head north on Market Street, crossing the Brandywine River. To get to the Delaware Art Museum, head past the park and take the first left on the bridge over the river. Take Lovering Street west to Kentmere Parkway. You'll find the museum on your right near the entrance to Rockford Park.

The host of great attractions north of the city includes the Delaware Toy and Miniature Museum, the Hagley Museum, Nemours Mansion and Gardens, and the Winterthur Museum, Garden and Library. Most of these can be reached by heading north on Rt. 52 (Pennsylvania Ave.). To find out whether the tall ship Kalmar Nyckel is in port, call | 302/429–7447.

NEIGHBORHOODS

Market Street. To walk down Wilmington's Market Street is to experience everything that Delaware is today: a link to history and a bridge to the future. Market Street stretches between the Christina and Brandywine rivers, and along its length you'll find everything from well-preserved federal homes to the headquarters of the DuPont Corporation. Market Street has been the center of Delaware's commerce since the days when it was occupied by dime stores, old banks, and America's first shipping companies. Today it is a center for business, culture, and the arts. Many of the city's top museums are here, and the Grand Opera House and the Playhouse are in the area, in the Hotel du Pont . Shops, cafés, and restaurants fill the Market Street Mall, a pedestrian shopping center.

The Waterfront. Wilmington's waterfront area is undergoing a renaissance. It was the site of much of the nation's shipbuilding from the mid to the late 1800s. As the 1900s came around, Wilmington began to transform itself from a working-class town to a white-collar city, and the shipyards began to fall into disrepair. It wasn't until the late 20th century that an effort was made to halt the decline. Leading the way in the attempt to attract visitors is the First USA Riverfront Arts Center, which mounts world-class art exhibitions. Nearby are outlet shops and Frawley Stadium, home to the Blue Rocks, the Kansas City Royals' minor league A-team. Today the area known as the Riverfront runs parallel to the Christina River, south of West 1st Street. There's a mile-long brick path for joggers and bikers and three locations where you can pick up a water taxi—the Riverfront area, the Tubman-Garrett Park across from the Amtrak station, and a local restaurant called Up the Creek, at the end of East 7th Street on the Brandywine River.

TRANSPORTATION

Airport: There is no commercial airport in Delaware. To fly here, book yourself into Philadelphia International Airport or Baltimore-Washington International. | 215/937–6937 for Philadelphia, 410/859–7111 for BWI.

Airport Transportation: Ride services to Wilmington are available; the cost is about $30 between Wilmington and Philadelphia, $65–$140 from BWI. Delaware Express Shuttle (800/648–5466 or 302/454–7800). Limo Exchange (302/322–1200). Eagle Limousine Service (800/669–5460).

From Philadelphia, a less expensive but more time-consuming option is the SEPTA train. You'll take the R1 to the 30th St. station and catch the R2 to Wilmington. The trip takes between 1½ and 3 hours depending on the frequency of the R2. Check out | 215/580–7800 | www.septa.org | $6 one way. From BWI, buses travel to the BWI Amtrak station. From there, you can take an hour-long Amtrak ride to Wilmington. | www.amtrak.com | $38 one way. **Rail:** Northeast corridor **Amtrak** trains stop in the Wilmington station. | Luther King Blvd. and French St. | 302/429–6529. **Bus:** Bus service throughout Delaware is via **Greyhound.** | 101 N. French St. | 302/655–6111 for depot, 800/872–7245 for Greyhound lines.

The **DART** public bus serves all of Delaware and is a major commuter link between Dover and Wilmington; it also has local routes. | 800/652–DART or 302/652–DART. **Driving around Town:** Within downtown Wilmington, it's unlikely that you'll see heavy traffic. I–95, Delaware Avenue, and Route 13 can be briefly congested during evening rush hours. Downtown has ample on-street parking and many municipal garages. Meters cost between 50 cents and $2 per hour. RVs may have a hard time negotiating the narrow streets, so park when you can and see the sights on foot.

Attractions

ART AND ARCHITECTURE

Amtrak Station. Restored to its original glory, the Frank Furness–designed station has lovely tile work and well-polished brass that give a great first impression of the city. | M.L. King and French Sts. | 302/429–6527 | Free | Daily.

....

Candlelight Dinner Theatre. Open year-round, the dinner theatre presents musicals, revues, and comedies along with dinner and wine. | 2208 Millers Rd. | 302/475–2313 | Varies | Call for performance schedule.

....

Delaware Art Museum. This museum houses a well-organized and highly respected collection of late-19th-century English Pre-Raphaelite art. The American section includes works by Homer and Hopper. Take the children to the participatory gallery. | 2301 Kentmere Pkwy. | 302/571–9590 | Free | Tues.–Sat. 9–4., Sun. 10–4.

Grand Opera House. Restored and stately, this tall white building was constructed in 1871 and is home to the Delaware Symphony. It was originally built by masons in splendid Second Empire style. | 818 Market St. Mall | 302/658–7898 or 302/652–5577 (box office) | Prices vary with shows | Daily; times vary with shows.

CULTURE, EDUCATION, AND HISTORY

Delaware History Museum. This museum is home to an ever-changing schedule of exhibits on Delaware history, crafts, and culture. | 504 Market St. | 302/656–0637 | $4; special rates for students, seniors, and children | Weekdays noon–4, Sat. 10–4.

Fort Christina Monument. Local legend places America's first log cabin on this site, called New Sweden by its Finnish and Swedish founders. | Foot of 7th St. | No phone | Free | Daily.

Hagley Museum. The original site of the giant DuPont company, the museum displays industrial advances of the past two centuries. The site includes a working water mill and steam engine and a 19th-century schoolhouse. | Rte. 141, 3 mi north of Wilmington | 302/658–2400 | www.hagley.lib.de.us | $9.75; special rates students, seniors, and children | Daily 9:30–4:30.

Nemours Mansion and Gardens. The former home of philanthrophist Alfred I. DuPont, the mansion sits next to the world-renowned children's hospital that bears his name. The large formal gardens are perfect for a stroll. | Rockland Rd. | 302/651–6912 | $10 | May–Nov., Tues.–Sun., by appointment.

Rockwood Museum. This elegant Victorian house with English garden houses a museum of mainly decorative arts. | 610 Shipley Rd. | 302/761–4340 | $5; special rates for seniors and children | Tues.–Sat. 11–4.

Willingtown Square. This cluster of four 18th-century houses is now used as offices. | 500 block Market St. Mall | 302/655–7161 | Free | Daily.

Wilmington and Western Railroad. A turn-of-the-century railway offers rides through the Red Clay Valley, ending at a picnic spot. | 1601 Railroad Ave. | 302/998–1930 | $8; special rates for seniors and children | Mar.–Dec., call for hours.

Winterthur Museum, Garden, and Library. Probably the world's foremost collection of American furniture and antiques, the museum and its splendid gardens were once the home of Henry Francis DuPont. Each year the museum's Point-to-Point Race is the city's premier social and sporting event, attacting more than 10,000 visitors. | Rte. 52, 6 mi NW of Wilmington | 302/888–4600 or 800/448–3883 | $8–$21 | Daily.

MUSEUMS

Delaware Toy and Miniature Museum. The exhibits include antique and contemporary dollhouses, miniatures, and sample furniture as well as dolls, toys, trains, boats, and planes from Europe and America, dating from the 18th century to the present. | 6 Old Barley Mill Rd. | 302/427–8697 | $5; special rates for students and seniors | Tues.–Sat. 10–4, Sun. noon–4.

PARKS, NATURAL AREAS, AND OUTDOOR RECREATION

Bellevue State Park. The former estate of William DuPont, this sprawling complex includes stables, tennis courts, and a popular lawn and band shell for midsummer concerts. | 800 Carr Rd. | 302/577–3390 | $2.50 (DE residents), $5 (out of state) | Daily dawn–dusk.

Brandywine Creek State Park. Bordered by Greenville's Chateau Country and the tightly packed suburbia of North Wilmington, this state park is a wildlife and recreational refuge. | Adams Dam Rd. | 302/577–3534 | $2.50 (DE residents), $5 (out of state) | Daily dawn–dusk.

Brandywine Zoo and Park. This tiny (12-acre) zoo is nestled on the lush banks of the Brandywine River. Its highlights are a pair of Siberian tigers and Josephine Garden and fountain. | 1021 West 18th St. | 302/571–7747 | $3 | Daily 10–4.

RELIGION AND SPIRITUALITY

Holy Trinity (Old Swedes) Church and Hendrickson House Museum. Dating from 1698, it is said to be the oldest Anglican church in America. Its rectory, near the Delaware River, also dates from the 17th century and contains furniture and art from later periods. | 606 Church St. | 302/652–5629 | $2 | Mon.–Sat. 10–4.

OTHER POINTS OF INTEREST

Delaware Park Racetrack and Video Slots Casino. This pleasant rural racetrack has added a slots component to its operation. | Delaware Park Blvd. | 302/994–2521 | Free | Call for racing schedule; slots, Mon.–Sat. 8 AM–2 AM, Sun. 1 PM–2 AM.

ON THE CALENDAR

MAR.–NOV.: *Horse Racing.* Experience the thrill of live horse racing at an intimate track, or try your luck on brand-new slot machines. | Delaware Park Blvd. | 302/994–2521.
APR.: *Storybook Garden Party.* This festival of hands-on craft activities, music, and storytelling is very popular with kids. | 302/658–2400.
MAY: *Wilmington Garden Day.* The famous gardens and houses of Wilmington are open for public tours every spring. | 302/571–4180.
JULY: *Victorian Ice Cream Festival.* Every summer as many as 20,000 people listen to music, browse crafts booths, and eat gallons of ice cream in Rockwood Park. | 302/761–4340.

Dining

INEXPENSIVE

Big Sky Bread. Vegetarian. It's not open for dinner, but Big Sky serves lunch (soups, sandwiches, salads) and 100 different kinds of bread! No smoking. | 1812 Marsh Rd. | 302/475–9494 | $7–$15 | No credit cards.

Brew Ha Ha! Café. Brew Ha Ha! is a coffeehouse that serves salads and sandwiches during lunch and is usually closed by 8. | 1420 DuPont St., Trolley Sq. | 302/778–2656 | $9–$15 | No credit cards.

The Flavour of Britain. English. Scones and pastries are served with a wide assortment of teas in a cozy tearoom. | 1601 Concord Pike | 302/658–9975 | $7–$16 | AE, D, MC, V.

The Greenery Food Court and Caterers. American. Made-to-order buffet-style food can be taken outside to a patio or eaten indoors in a skylit dining room. | Chase Manhattan Center, 1201 Market St. | 302/652–3663 | Breakfast and lunch only | $6–$8 | MC, V.

Kid Shelleen's. American. Diners look on while their orders are prepared on a show grill in the center of the dining room. Kids' menu. Sun. brunch. | 1801 W. 14th St. | 302/658–4600 | $9–$22 | AE, D, DC, MC, V.

Rosauri's Pizza and Pasta. Italian. Pizza-making is regarded as an art form at this busy, casual restaurant with a super-friendly staff. Kids' menu. | 1323 McKennans Church Rd. | 302/996–0301 | $7–$17 | AE, D, DC MC, V.

MODERATE

Annie's Restaurant. American. Annie's is a New York deli-style restaurant where the "biggest sandwiches in the world" are served by a friendly waitstaff. Smoking is allowed in the lounge. | 500 Greenmill Ave. | 302/888–1229 | Closed Sun. | $8–$19 | AE, D, MC, V.

Dead Presidents Pub and Restaurant. American. Photos of former leaders of the free world adorn the walls of this pub-grub joint, where you can hear live music the last Thursday of every month. | 618 N. Union St. | 302/652–7737 | $13–$19 | AE, D, DC, MC, V.

El Tapatio. Southwestern. Sizzling fajitas and salsas ranging from mild to you-must-be-kidding are the mainstays at El Tapatio. Live music on Friday. Kids' menu. | 1700 Philadelphia Pike | 302/791–9566 | $11–$20 | AE, D, DC, MC, V.

Grotto Pizza. Italian. This is one of a chain of establishments found throughout Delaware. The Grotto gets especially busy on "Lotsa Pizza" and "Lotsa Pasta" nights (Tuesdays and Thursdays respectively), when prices drop for their already moderately priced food. | Fairfax Shopping Center | 302/575–0330 | Reservations not accepted | $12–$17 | AE, D, V.

Jessop's Tavern and Colonial Restaurant. American. Pub fare (fish 'n' chips, shepherd's pie) has been served at this establishment ever since Abraham Jessop hung out his shingle in 1724. The menu includes rich oyster chowder and double-crusted chicken potpie. Live music during the week. | 114 Delaware St., Old New Castle | 302/322–6111 | Closed Sun. | $16–$23 | AE, D, MC, V.

Kokopelli Bar and Grille. Tex-Mex. There are no fewer than 50 types of tequila to sample at Kokopelli; try a shot or one of their famous margaritas along with your taco or tostada. Kids' menu. | 729 N. Union St. | 302/652–0444 | $12–$15 | AE, MC, V.

Lamberti's Cucina. Italian. There are several Lamberti's in the state, but Centerville's boasts an especially fine capellini positano (made with tomato sauce and fresh crabmeat). Kids' menu. | 1300 Centerville Rd., Centerville | 302/995–6955 | $8–$15 | AE, D, DC, MC, V.

EXPENSIVE

The Black Trumpet Bistro. French. The eponymous mushroom is among the exotic fungi used in many of the entrées in this sunny, brick-walled eatery. Full bar. No smoking. | 1828 W. 11th St. | 302/777–0454 | Closed Sun. | $20–$25 | AE, MC, V.

Christina River Club. American. This upscale waterfront eatery has a heated tent on the deck. Steaks and chicken are popular dishes. Live music on Tuesday. Sunday brunch. | 201 A St. | 302/652–4787 | Closed Sun. | $16–$23 | AE, D, DC, MC, V.

Harry's Savory Grill. American. Harry's is known for live magic every Tuesday, on Harry Houdini night. The portobello mushroom pizza is a top seller. There are two patios for outdoor dining. Live music on weekends. Kids' menu, early-bird dinners. | 2020 Naamans Rd., N. Wilmington | 302/475–3000 | Reservations required | $20–$30 | AE, D, DC, MC, V.

Luigi Vitrone's Pastabilities. Italian. Luigi himself makes the pastas and tends to the milk-fed veal, fresh fish, and seafood. No smoking. | 415 N. Lincoln St. | 302/656–9822 | Closed Mon. | $20–$25 | AE, MC, V.

Sienna. Mediterranean. This upscale restaurant is known for its seafood paella and eclectic interior—heavy on the French mirrors and Mediterranean tiles. Live piano music Wed.–Sat. | 1616 Delaware Ave. | 302/652–0653 | Closed Mon. No lunch weekends | $19–$23 | AE, V.

VERY EXPENSIVE

Brandywine Room. Contemporary. Red leather chairs and banquettes and walnut-paneled walls with original Wyeth paintings add up to a classic club look in this Hotel Dupont restaurant. Try the rack of lamb with an herb crust, veal medallions with lump crabmeat in a tarragon sauce, or sea scallops with shrimp and shitake mushrooms on pasta. Kids' menu available. No smoking. Free parking. | 11th and Market Sts. | 302/594–3156 | $23–$50 | AE, D, DC, MC, V.

Deep Blue Bar and Grill. Seafood. The management of Deep Blue refers to the place as a "contemporary American fish house." The eclectic menu, with smooth tuna carpaccio and grilled octopus in olive oil and garlic, deserves all the kudos it's received. Live music in the lounge Thursday, Saturday. | 111 W. 11th St. | 302/777–2040 | Sun. | $35–$60 | AE, D, DC, MC, V.

Eclipse. American. Eclipse is known for its rare-game dishes and farm-raised fish like New Zealand warehou. The bustling dining room and exposed kitchen has a New York bistro flair. No smoking. | 1020 N. Union St. | 302/658–1588 | Closed Sun. | $30–$50 | AE, D, DC, MC, V.

Positano. Seafood. Eastern shore cuisine like filet of rockfish in a sesame crust, dover sole in sauce persillade, as well as steaks and chops are served in a quiet room with paneled walls and Mediterranean murals. | 2401 Pennsylvania Ave. | 302/656–6788 | Jacket and tie | Closed Sun. | $29–$42 | AE, D, DC, MC, V.

Raffaele's. Italian. Everything is homemade at this upscale family-run restaurant, from the osso buco melanize (braised veal roasted for six hours) to the salad croutons. Kids' menu available. | 1934 W. 6th St. | 302/658–3988 | Reservations essential weekends | Closed Mon. lunch | $27–$34 | AE, D, DC, MC, V.

Tavol Toscana. Italian. Northern Italian cuisine is presented in a relaxed, elegant restaurant. Try the tortellini. Smoking allowed at the bar. | 1412 N. DuPont St. | 302/654–8001 | $25–$30 | AE, D, DC, MC, V.

Walter's Steak House and Saloon. American. Prime rib and 8-oz filets are the most requested specialties at this intimate, softly lit eatery. Complimentary seafood bar. | 802 N. Union St. | 302/652–6780 | $32–$45 | AE, D, DC, MC, V.

Lodging

MODERATE

WILMINGTON

INTRO
ATTRACTIONS
DINING
LODGING

Best Western Brandywine Valley Inn. This hotel, a few miles from historic downtown, is just off I–95. A restaurant with cocktail lounge and kid's menu is next door. | 98 rooms, 12 suites. In-room data ports, some kitchenettes, cable TV. Hot tub. Pool, wading pool. Exercise equipment. Business services. Free parking. Some pets allowed. | 1807 Concord Pike (U.S. 202) | 302/656–9436 | fax 302/656–8564 | www.brandywineinn.com | $63–$95 | AE, D, DC, MC, V.

The Boulevard Bed and Breakfast. This three-story, 1913 red brick Colonial Revival mansion is just north of historic downtown on a tree-lined street. It boasts leaded glass windows and a grand central staircase. | 6 rooms, 2 with shared bath. Complimentary breakfast. In-room data ports, cable TV, VCRs and movies. | 1909 Baynard Blvd. | 302/656–9700 | fax 302/656–9701 | blvdbb@wserv.com | $55–$75 | AE, MC, V.

Days Inn. The Brandywine battlefield, Longwood Gardens, Hagley Museum, and Winterthur Museum are all a short drive from this Brandywine Valley hotel. The building is two stories. | 100 rooms. Complimentary Continental breakfast. In-room data ports, cable TV. Business services. | 5209 Concord Pike | 302/478–0300 | fax 302/478–2401 | $55–$75 | AE, D, MC, V.

Fairview Inn. South of downtown near the Christiana River and I-495, this hotel offers easy access to historic Wilmington and downtown nightlife. Suites and rooms are available. | 142 rooms. In-room data ports, some microwaves, some refrigerators, cable TV. Pool. | 1051 S. Market St. | 302/656–9431 | $60–$105 | AE, D, MC, V.

EXPENSIVE

Courtyard by Marriott. This large motor inn is in downtown Wilmington near restaurants, shopping outlets, historic sites. It's a short drive from the riverfront. | 125 rooms. In-room data ports, some in-room hot tubs, cable TV. Exercise equipment. Airport shuttle. | 1102 West St. | 302/429–7600 | fax 302/429–9167 | $69–$149 | AE, D, DC, MC, V.

Doubletree Hotel. Close to the Wintherthur and Hagley museums and Longwood Gardens, the full-service Doubletree is popular with business travelers. | 154 rooms. Restaurant, bar. In-room data ports, cable TV. Exercise equipment. Business services. | 4727 Concord Pike | 302/478–6000 | fax 302/477–1492 | www.radisson.com | $89–$139 | AE, D, DC, MC, V.

Holiday Inn–North. In north Wilmington, near Longwood Gardens, museums, and shopping, this two-story motel is 5 mi from downtown. | 138 rooms. Restaurant, bar, room service. In-room data ports, cable TV. Pool. Laundry facilities. Business services. Some pets allowed.

| 4000 Concord Pike (U.S. 202) | 302/478–2222 | fax 302/479–0850 | www.holiday-inn.com | $94–$135 | AE, D, DC, MC, V.

Sheraton Suites. These luxury accommodations are close to antique shops and fine dining in historic New Castle. | 230 suites. Restaurant, bar. In-room data ports, cable TV. Indoor pool. Exercise equipment. Laundry facilities. Business services. Airport shuttle. | 422 Delaware Ave. | 302/654–8300 | fax 302/654–6036 | www.ittsheraton.com | $89–$159 | AE, D, DC, MC, V.

VERY EXPENSIVE

Brandywine Suites. This four-story former store, tucked into a nondescript downtown block, has dramatic contemporary architecture. | 49 suites. Restaurant (see Mediterranean Grill), bar, complimentary breakfast. In-room data ports, cable TV. Exercise equipment. Business services. Airport shuttle. | 707 King St. | 302/656–9300 | fax 302/656–2459 | $129 | AE, DC, MC, V.

Courtyard Wilmington Brandywine. Four 18-hole golf courses are within 15 mi of this hotel, and almost every Wilmington attraction is within 10 mi. | 78 rooms, 3 suites. Restaurant, bar, room service. In-room data ports, cable TV. Indoor pool. Hot tub. Exercise equipment. Business services. | 320 Rocky Run Pkwy., Talleyville | 302/477–9500 | fax 302/477–0929 | www.courtyard.com/ilgbw/ | $144–$164 | AE, DC, D, MC, V.

Hotel DuPont. This hotel in the heart of downtown has been operating since 1913. French and Italian craftsmen carved and gilded the ornate lobby, where afternoon tea is still served. Each room has a separate sitting area. | 216 rooms. Restaurants, bar with entertainment, room service. In-room data ports, cable TV. Beauty salon, massage. Driving range, putting green. Gym. Business services. Airport shuttle. | 11th and Market Sts. | 302/594–3100 or 800/441–9019 | fax 302/656–2145 | www.dupont.com/hotel | $149–$309 | AE, D, DC, MC, V.

Homewood Suites by Hilton. This all-suite hotel is just off I–95 in the suburbs, about 8 mi from downtown. Shuttles to the Philadelphia, Baltimore, and Washington, D.C., airports are available for a modest fee. | 113 rooms. Complimentary Continental breakfast. In-room data ports, kitchenettes, cable TV. Pool. Exercise equipment. Laundry facilities, laundry service. Business services. | 350 Rocky Run Blvd. | 302/479–2000 or 800/225–5466 | fax 302/479–0770 | $135–$150 | AE, DC, D, MC, V.

Inn at Montchanin Village. This 19th-century, 11-building mill complex in rural Brandywine Valley is surrounded by gardens. Rooms are furnished with antiques, high-quality linens; some have fireplaces. | 22 rooms, 5 with shower only, 16 suites. Restaurant, picnic area, complimentary breakfast, room service. In-room data ports, some in-room hot tubs, cable TV. Business services. No smoking. | Rte. 100 and Kirk Rd., Montchanin | 302/888–2133 or 800/COWBIRD | fax 302/888–0389 | montchan@gte.com | www.montchanin.com | $160–$170, $450–$500 suites | AE, DC, MC, V.

Wyndham Garden Hotel. About 25 minutes south of Philadelphia, this nine-story hotel in the center of downtown is near museums, the Grand Opera, and the baseball stadium. The University of Delaware is 15 minutes away. | 217 rooms. Restaurant, bar. In-room data ports, cable TV. Indoor pool. Beauty salon. Hot tub. Exercise equipment. Business services. Some pets allowed. | 700 King St. | 302/655–0400 | fax 302/655–5488 | $99–$142 | AE, D, DC, MC, V.

TOP TIPS FOR TRAVELERS

Smart Sightseeings

Don't plan your visit in your hotel room. Don't wait until you pull into town to decide how to spend your days. It's inevitable that there will be much more to see and do than you'll have time for: choose sights in advance.

Organize your touring. Note the places that most interest you on a map, and visit places that are near each other during the same morning or afternoon.

Start the day well equipped. Leave your hotel in the morning with everything you need for the day—maps, medicines, extra film, your guidebook, rain gear, and another layer of clothing in case the weather turns cooler.

Tour museums early. If you're there when the doors open you'll have an intimate experience of the collection.

Easy does it. See museums in the mornings, when you're fresh, and visit sit-down attractions later on. Take breaks before you need them.

Strike up a conversation. Only curmudgeons don't respond to a smile and a polite request for information. Most people appreciate your interest in their home town. And your conversations may end up being your most vivid memories.

Get lost. When you do, you never know what you'll find—but you can count on it being memorable. Use your guidebook to help you get back on track. Build wandering-around time into every day.

Quit before you're tired. There's no point in seeing that one extra sight if you're too exhausted to enjoy it.

Take your mother's advice. Go to the bathroom when you have the chance. You never know what lies ahead.

Hotel How-Tos

How to get a deal. After you've chosen a likely candidate or two, phone them directly and price a room for your travel dates. Then call the hotel's toll-free number and ask the same questions. Also try consolidators and hotel-room discounters. You won't hear the same rates twice. On the spot, make a reservation as soon as you are quoted a price you want to pay.

Promises, promises. If you have special requests, make them when you reserve. Get written confirmation of any promises.

Settle in. Upon arriving, make sure everything works—lights and lamps, TV and radio, sink, tub, shower, and anything else that matters. Report any problems immediately. And don't wait until you need extra pillows or blankets or an ironing board to call housekeeping. Also check out the fire emergency instructions. Know where to find the fire exits, and make sure your companions do, too.

If you need to complain. Be polite but firm. Explain the problem to the person in charge. Suggest a course of action. If you aren't satisfied, repeat your requests to the manager. Document everything: Take pictures and keep a written record of who you've spoken with, when, and what was said. Contact your travel agent, if he made the reservations.

Know the score. When you go out, take your hotel's business cards (one for everyone in your party). If you have extras, you can give them out to new acquaintances who want to call you.

Tip up front. For special services, a tip or partial tip in advance can work wonders.

Use all the hotel resources A concierge can make difficult things easy. But a desk clerk, bellhop, or other hotel employee who's friendly, smart, and ambitious can often steer you straight as well. A gratuity is in order if the advice is helpful.

© Artville

District of Columbia

Washington, D.C. is the seat of our government, the home of our president, and the stomping grounds of countless members of Congress. The main business here is politics, so there's no shortage of politicians, lobbyists, lawyers, and public relations firms in town. The city isn't known for its fashionably dressed inhabitants, its hip arts scene, or its innovative dining establishments. But it's much more than an uptight political town. If you know where to look, D.C. has plenty to interest you—from nightlife and the arts to museums and fine dining.

There is entertainment practically every night of the year. If you like your performing arts classy, check the listings for the Kennedy Center, National Theater, and Warner Theater. If you want a little more kick, see who is on tap at Blues Alley and the 9:30 Club. Or if you're searching for a rendition of your favorite playwright's work, investigate Arena Stage, Ford's Theatre, and the Shakespeare Theatre. None of these venues are cheap, but they all tend to draw the cream of the crop, so you really get what you pay for.

As the nation's capital, Washington hosts an international array of visitors and new residents. This infusion of cultures means that the D.C. restaurant scene is getting better and more diverse. (And sometimes cheaper: More of the top dining rooms now offer reasonably priced fare and fixed-price specials.) You can find almost any type of food here, from Burmese to Ethiopian, health-conscious new American to appetizer-size Spanish tapas.

The city offers so much in the way of history, culture, and scenery that your visit almost certainly will be exhilarating and educational. The city's primary tourist area— the meticulously maintained National Mall, monuments, museums, Tidal Basin, and the grounds and gardens that surround these attractions—is lush and green in spring and summer and exudes a more subtle beauty in the colder months. Another plus: Admission to the national monuments, and many of the museums and parks, is free.

POPULATION: 606,900	AREA: 68 SQUARE MI	BORDERS: MD, VA
TIME ZONE: EASTERN STANDARD TIME	POSTAL ABBREVIATION: DC	
WEB SITE: WWW.CI.WASHINGTON.DC.US		

Washington today is more vibrant than it has been in years, thanks to a soaring national economy, resulting in more locals spending money and more tourists pouring in. Neighborhood revitalization programs have improved living conditions in some of the decaying areas of the District, and the bulk of downtown and federal tourist areas appear more polished than they did 10 years ago. With all the publicity D.C. received in the late 1980s and early 1990s as the murder capital of the U.S., it is important to note that Washington is a fairly safe city. Essentially, the same rules apply in D.C. as in any major city: Watch your personal belongings, be careful after dark, and be sure of what you're doing when you decide to wander from beaten paths.

History

D.C. was selected as the permanent site for the U.S. capital by Congress in 1790, and George Washington was given the authority to choose a precise spot for the original capital city—a 10-square-mile area on the Potomac on land that was donated by Maryland and Virginia. In 1791 French engineer Pierre Charles L'Enfant was hired to survey the land and design the city, and although his plans were ultimately implemented, he was fired in 1792 as a result of conflicts with politicians and investors. In 1793 the cornerstone for the Capitol was laid on the hill that L'Enfant had chosen.

In 1800, the Capitol was "inhabitable" (although far from completed) and President John Adams and the seat of federal government was moved to an "unfinished" city of Washington. There were no proper sidewalks, street lights, or sanitation systems, and large areas of the city were still occupied by swamp and farmland. Constitution Avenue was a canal, and early presidents took oar boats when traveling from the White House to the Capitol.

Development was slow and interrupted by the War of 1812. In 1814 the British arrived in Chesapeake Bay, made their way to the Capitol, and burned it, along with the Library of Congress and many ships and stores. President James Madison and First Lady Dolley were forced to move to Octagon House and then "The Seven Buildings" until the Capitol was rebuilt in 1817. By 1822 the city had been largely reconstructed and boasted a population of close to 15,000, but it was far from cosmopolitan, and progress was again interrupted by war—this time the Civil War.

It wasn't until after the Civil War, in 1870, and the term of city administrator Alexander ("Boss") Shepherd that sidewalks and sewer systems were laid and street lights installed. During Shepherd's term, L'Enfant's plans were finally realized—300 miles of half-laid streets were improved, oft-used thoroughfares were paved, Old Tiber Creek was filled in, and some 6,000 trees were planted. In 1901 a committee was appointed—including landscape architect Frederick Law Olmstead, sculptor Augustus Saint-Gaudens, and architects Daniel Burnham and Charles McKim—to continue laying out the city. Their main focus was development of the Mall, but they also laid the plans for a complete parks system, selected sites for government buildings, and designed the Lincoln Memorial and the Arlington Memorial Bridge. In 1912 the famous cherry trees were planted in the Tidal Basin.

DC Timeline

1608	1751	1775–83	1788
Captain John Smith explores the Potomac.	Georgetown is founded above the mouth of Rock Creek.	American Revolutionary War.	The 1788 U.S. Constitution is ratified. It gives Congress legislative control of D.C.

The late 19th and early 20th centuries brought an influx of wealthy immigrants and the benefits of their talents and economic resources. The Library of Congress and Union Station were built, and the Mall was laid out; its present-day form closely resembles the original. The latter half of the the 20th century brought still more politicians and bureaucrats to town as government got "bigger" and world politics more complex. During his short time in office in the early 1960s, John F. Kennedy passed bills to preserve historic houses, approved a plan for the Metro, and championed better housing conditions in deteriorating D.C. neighborhoods.

In the last 30 years, D.C. has weathered destructive riots, the resignation of a president, and the arrest and conviction of a mayor on drug charges. And there are still neighborhoods that need attention. But the city has rebounded from these and other challenges, and, although there's still work to be done, it is today a city that Americans can be proud of.

Convention and Visitors Bureau | 1212 New York Ave. NW | 202/789–7007 | fax 202/789–7037 | www.washington.org.
Visitors' Center | 1300 Pennsylvania Ave. NW | 202/347–2873 | fax 202/724–2445.

Neighborhoods

Washington is unique among major U.S. cities in that no private building may be higher than 160 feet (Pierre Charles L'Enfant's idea, supported by Congress). As a result, the 555-foot Washington Monument and clean, off-white Capitol dome rule the skyline below downtown and the gothic-looking towers of the National Cathedral loom above upper Northwest.

Pennsylvania Avenue runs from the east end of Georgetown all the way across town to Anacostia, in far southeast D.C., but you cannot drive the entire length continuously due to two notable structures placed squarely in the avenue's path: the White House and the Capitol. In fact, as a result of a flurry of security near-misses during Bill Clinton's presidency, the section of Pennsylvania Avenue directly in front of the White House and Treasury Department building is permanently closed to motorized traffic, making car travel in that area extremely slow during rush hours.

L'Enfant gave Washington a couple of other idiosyncrasies. First, there's the series of traffic circles—Dupont, Thomas, Scott, Washington, Sheridan, Chevy Chase, Logan, and more—spread throughout the city. These were intended to slow up any invading armies attempting to conquer D.C. by rushing up the town's broad avenues; their modern-day effect is to confound drivers who are not familiar with traffic circle etiquette. In the absence of other signs or traffic lights, the rule is to yield to traffic already in the circle. Inch out, look for your break, and go for it when you have the chance.

Second, L'Enfant divided D.C. into quadrants, placing the Capitol in the center. North Capitol Street, East Capitol Street, and South Capitol Street run from the Capitol into very distinct areas and neighborhoods, few of which hold any interest for you, although each boulevard serves up stirring views of the dome. To the Capitol's west lies the Mall, thus the absence of a West Capitol Street.

INTRODUCTION
HISTORY
NEIGHBORHOODS
WHEN TO VISIT
THE DISTRICT'S GREATS
TRANSPORTATION

1789	1790	1791–92	1800	1814
Georgetown University is founded.	President George Washington chooses a site on the Potomac for the new federal capital.	Pierre Charles L'Enfant begins planning the city, and work on the White House get under way.	The federal capital is moved from Philadelphia to D.C.	British forces raid Washington and burn the White House. President James Madison relocates to the Octagon while the original Capitol is restored.

Third, L'Enfant named one avenue after every state in the Union, and most avenues criss-cross town without adherence to D.C.'s otherwise well-organized grid system. Each state avenue has a distinct character. The planners of the stretch of Connecticut Avenue from Maryland to Woodley Park (which also includes the National Zoo) intentionally alternated business and residential zones so that the boulevard would not get buried by commerce. Massachusetts Avenue wends a stately path from upper Northwest D.C. past the naval observatory (where the U.S. vice president resides), ceding to an embassy-lined corridor around Dupont Circle and eventually skirting the run-down district just south of Shaw, one of the city's more crime-ridden neighborhoods. Independence and Constitution avenues frame the Mall and split duty between hosting federal agencies and Smithsonian museums. And many more, such as Utah and Colorado Avenues, are stashed in residential neighborhoods.

THE MALL

For you as a visitor, The Mall is likely to be the heart of Washington, with nearly a dozen museums ringing the expanse of green. Of course, the Mall is more than just a front yard for these museums. Bounded on the north and south by Constitution and Independence Avenues and on the east and west by 3rd and 14th Streets, it's a picnicking park and a jogging path, an outdoor stage for festivals and fireworks, and America's town green. Nine of the Smithsonian Institution's 14 museums in the capital lie within these boundaries.

CAPITOL HILL

Deriving its name from the Capitol building here, this neighborhood is more than just the center of government. "The Hill" also includes charming residential blocks lined with Victorian row houses and a fine assortment of restaurants, bars, and shops. Capitol Hill's boundaries are disputed: It's bordered to the west, north, and south by the Capitol, Union Station, and I Street, respectively. Some argue that Capitol Hill extends east to the Anacostia River, others that it ends at 11th Street near Lincoln Park. The neighborhood does in fact seem to grow as members of Capitol Hill's active historic-preservation movement restore an increasing number of 19th-century houses.

The neighborhood also serves as the point from which the city is divided into quadrants: northwest, southwest, northeast, and southeast. North Capitol Street, which runs north from the Capitol, separates northeast from northwest; East Capitol Street separates northeast and southeast; South Capitol Street separates southwest and southeast; and the Mall (Independence Avenue on the south and Constitution Avenue on the north) separates northwest from southwest.

GEORGETOWN

Perhaps the best known among D.C. neighborhoods is Georgetown, home to Georgetown University, tree-lined streets, and tastefully preserved architecture. The neighborhood's two must-walk streets—Wisconsin Avenue and M Street NW—hold most

1820	1846	1848	1861–65	1862
Under the Act of 1820, Washington residents are given the right to elect their own mayor.	Congress passes a law returning the land southwest of the Potomac, including Alexandria and Alexandria County, to the state of Virginia.	Work begins on the Washington Monument and the Mall.	American Civil War.	Slavery is abolished in the federal district (the City of Washington, Washington County, and Georgetown), predating both the Emancipation Proclamation and the adoption of the

INTRODUCTION
HISTORY
NEIGHBORHOODS
WHEN TO VISIT
THE DISTRICT'S GREATS
TRANSPORTATION

of Georgetown's shops, restaurants, and bars and seem to be lively and kicking seven days a week, from before noon to after midnight. Much of the area is presented in redbrick-fronted buildings and sidewalks, with small boutique storefronts perched aside major chain stores.

You can spend a fortune in the stores (Dean & Deluca, Patagonia, the boutique galleries), hotels (Four Seasons) and restaurants (Morton's of Chicago), but you can also find deals at some of the ethnic stores and chains like Urban Outfitters, and cheap meals at time-worn establishments Mr. Smith's and Garrett's.

Georgetown sits on a hill, which ends at the Georgetown Waterfront and the Potomac River (at the bottom of Wisconsin Avenue, on K Street). The waterfront is itself a lively scene on nice-weather days, especially weekends, when people pack the riverfront restaurants and bars and the wooden promenade to mingle, stroll, and people watch. The Foggy Bottom neighborhood and downtown are to the east of Georgetown, Georgetown University is to the west and on the side streets off Wisconsin Avenue, and to the north, rows of quaint town houses are home to a mix of university students and some of the city's wealthier residents.

FOGGY BOTTOM

The Foggy Bottom area of Washington—bordered roughly by the Potomac and Rock Creek to the west, 20th Street to the east, Pennsylvania Avenue to the north, and Constitution Avenue to the south—has three main claims to fame: the State Department, the Kennedy Center, and George Washington University. The neighborhood began as one filled with wharves, breweries, glassworks, and other factories. The opening of the State Department in 1947 sparked new interest—and building—in the area, and today the neighborhood is a mixed bag of tiny, one-room-wide row houses sitting next to large, mixed-use developments.

ADAMS-MORGAN

If you're seeking an edgy and colorful slice of nightlife, head for Adams-Morgan, where no fewer than three dozen eateries and bars pack a four-block stretch of 18th Street NW, and a few blocks of Columbia Road, which intersects 18th Street at the top of a hill. On almost any night, but especially during nice weather and on weekends, this neighborhood is teeming with young revelers and middle-aged diners.

At many of the establishments you can eat outdoors, either on rooftops or in sidewalk settings, and the best of these are superb for taking in the spectacle and feeling the pulse of the area's party scene.

MOUNT PLEASANT

Above Adams-Morgan, between Columbia Road and Rock Creek Park, is the mostly residential Mount Pleasant. (There are some restaurants and bars along Mount Pleasant Street NW, but they are primarily the haunts of locals and hold little allure otherwise.)

| 13th Amendment to the Constitution. | **1867** African-American males vote for the first time. | **1878** D.C. government is once again removed from the hands of residents, this time to a municipal corporation governed by 3 presidentially appointed commissioners. | **1884** Work on the Washington Monument is completed. | **1910** The city imposes height restrictions on buildings. |

The area is worth mentioning because it is home to the bulk of the city's Latino population, the largest urban El Salvadoran community outside El Salvador.

DUPONT CIRCLE

A neighborhood with a character of its own and the convenience of Metro service is Dupont Circle, a few blocks south of Adams-Morgan. The area's diverse businesses and building spaces create an eclectic choice of venues for shopping, dining, gallery hopping, and celebrating. Leisure activities are enjoyed in the shadow of stone-columned edifices, modern office buildings, and even a couple of embassies. The neighborhood's centerpiece is Dupont Circle itself, a wide, bench-rimmed gyre that draws all varieties of residents and workers during dry weather.

FARRAGUT SQUARE

From Dupont, it's only a three-block walk to the nucleus of Washington's business district, Farragut Square, at Connecticut Avenue and K Streets NW. Like nearby Lafayette Park and Franklin and McPherson Squares, Farragut is a one-block grassy area with benches and walkways surrounding a centerpiece monument. These parks are not destinations in themselves but are nice for a break during walking tours of the city; they can become quite vibrant during warm-season lunch hours. Mill about for 20 minutes and you'll get a good sense of the city's workaday dress code and office gossip topics.

DOWNTOWN

Nowhere else have the city's imperfections been more visible than on Pennsylvania Avenue. By the early 1960s it had become a national disgrace: The dilapidated buildings that lined it housed pawn shops and cheap souvenir stores. Washington's downtown—once within the diamond formed by Massachusetts, Louisiana, Pennsylvania, and New York avenues—had its problems, too, many the result of riots that rocked the capital in 1968 after the assassination of Dr. Martin Luther King Jr. In their wake, many businesses left the area and moved north of the White House.

In recent years developers have rediscovered "old downtown," and buildings are now being torn down or remodeled at an amazing pace. After several false starts, Pennsylvania Avenue is shining once again.

Most of downtown is within walking distance of some part of the Mall. However, if you prefer not to hoof it, taxis abound in this area and subway stations are positioned at least every half-dozen blocks.

When to Visit

The weather in D.C. can range from unbelievably perfect spring and fall days to miserably humid summer heat and wicked winter cold. When the city is at the height of its spring bloom, with azaleas, dogwoods, tulips, and hundreds of other colorful plants in full glory, Washington is one of the most beautiful cities on earth. It is almost

1931	1939	1943	1954	1961
Hunger March on Washington.	African-American opera singer Marion Anderson sings to a crowd of 75,000 on the steps of the Lincoln Memorial after being barred from Constitution Hall.	The Pentagon is completed.	Racial integration is introduced to Washington schools—the first of such integration in the country.	With the passing of the 23rd Amendment, District residents get the right to vote for president.

INTRODUCTION
HISTORY
NEIGHBORHOODS
WHEN TO VISIT
THE DISTRICT'S GREATS
TRANSPORTATION

impossible to overstate the effect that a crystal clear spring day, with temperatures in the low 70s and a light breeze, can have on your mood.

Likewise in the fall, when the area's army of deciduous trees turns colors, you may be treated to a beaming cloudless day beneath a deep blue sky that makes touring the nation's capital an unforgettable experience.

Although D.C. can experience utterly distressing summer heat and humidity, these conditions are not guaranteed. Heat waves tend to be sandwiched between respites of tolerable, sometimes glorious, weather (even in July and August) and often provide their own entertainment, in the form of violent thunderstorms that turn the sky dark green and the Potomac River into a roiling frenzy of whitecaps.

Just as summer offers breaks from the heat, D.C. winters also straddle a climatological fence. January daytime highs may be below 10 or above 60, though they generally settle between 35 and 50. Because tourist crowds tend to be lighter in winter months, you may want to take a chance on the weather and plan your visit for January, when the rest of the traveling public is still recovering from holiday spending. You'll find better deals on hotels and easier access to museums and other sites.

CLIMATE CHART
Average High/Low Temperatures (°F) and Monthly Precipitation (in inches)

JAN.	FEB.	MAR.	APR.	MAY	JUNE
42/28	46/30	58/38	66/48	77/57	87/67
3	3	3.3	3	3.8	3.5

JULY	AUG.	SEPT.	OCT.	NOV.	DEC.
89/70	88/69	80/62	70/53	60/45	50/30
3.8	4	3.3	3	3.1	3.1

ON THE CALENDAR
WINTER

Dec. **National Christmas Tree Lighting/Pageant of Peace.** This mid-December festival (usually the second Thursday) is accompanied by music and caroling and is kicked off with the lighting of the tree at dusk on the Ellipse grounds, south of the White House. For the following few weeks the Ellipse hosts choral performances, a Nativity scene, a Yule log, and a display of lighted Christmas trees representing each U.S. state and territory. | 202/619–7222 | www.nps.gov/whho/pageant.

Old Town Christmas Candlelight Tours. Music and refreshments are included in this tour of Alexandria's Ramsay House, Gadsby's Tavern Museum, Lee-Fendall House, and Carlyle House. | Old Town/Alexandria | 703/838–4200 | www.gadsby-tavern.org.

1963
Dr. Martin Luther King, Jr. delivers his "I Have a Dream" speech at National Hall after the March on Washington.

1973
Self-government, including the right to vote for their own mayor, is returned to D.C. residents.

1974
General elections are held for mayor and council on November 5, 1974.

1975
Newly elected Mayor Walter Washington and the first elected council take office.

1978
Parts of the Metrorail Red Line, the city's new subway system, open.

SPRING

Mar.–Apr.
Easter Egg Roll. This annual children's event, held on Easter Monday on the lawn of the White House, is open to the public, but get there early if you expect to gain admittance. | 1600 Pennsylvania Ave. NW | 202/456–2200.

Smithsonian Kite Festival. Kite makers and fliers of all shapes and sizes attend this festival on the Washington Monument grounds. | 202/456–3030.

Cherry Blossom Festival. A two-week-long springtime festival celebrates D.C.'s stunning Japanese cherry blossom trees that ring the Tidal Basin and crowd Hains Point—whether they bloom on schedule or not. Events take place at various locations throughout the city, mostly on or near the Mall. Features include an opening ceremony, Japanese lantern-lighting, a 10-kilometer foot race, rugby and kids' soccer tournaments, Japanese cultural activities, concerts, and a culminating parade on Constitution Avenue from 7th to 17th streets. | 202/619–7275.

Apr.
Georgetown House Tour. A walking tour takes you to Georgetown's lovely private homes. High tea, served at the old St. John's Georgetown Parish Church, is included in the admission. | 3240 O St. NW | 202/338–1796.

Apr.–May
Georgetown Garden Tour. Rain or shine, a walking tour goes to some of the more spectacular gardens in this quaint neighborhood. | 202/333–4953 or 202/244–0381.

May
Goodwill Industries Embassy Tour. Eight to 10 embassies are visited, via shuttle bus (unless you prefer to walk). The tour takes place on a Saturday, usually in May, from 10 to 5. | 202/636–4225 | www.dcgoodwill.org.

National Cathedral Flower Mart. Each year a different country is celebrated at this colorful event with flower booths, crafts, and demonstrations. | Massachusetts and Wisconsin Aves. NW | 202/537–6200 | www.cathedral.org.

Memorial Day Ceremony. A military commemoration of all the soldiers who served for the U.S. in armed conflicts is held annually on the grounds of Arlington National Cemetery in Arlington, Virginia. | Arlington, VA, 22211 | 703/607–8052.

May–Aug.
Evening Parade. This series of Friday evening parades features music and precision marching by the Marine Band and Bugle

1979
Marion Barry takes office as the mayor of D.C.

1987
Authority over and operation of two of the three D.C. area airports—Reagan National and Washington-Dulles International— transfers from the federal government to the newly created Metropolitan Washington Airports Authority.

1991
Mayor Sharon Pratt Dixon is the first woman to become mayor of D.C.

1993
Vietnam Women's Memorial is dedicated.

INTRODUCTION
HISTORY
NEIGHBORHOODS
WHEN TO VISIT
THE DISTRICT'S GREATS
TRANSPORTATION

Corps. The show starts at 8:45 and lasts an hour or so. Request reservations (generally required) in writing only to: US Marine Barracks, I Street between 8th and 9th Streets SE, Washington, DC, 20390. Include your name, phone number, return address, and preferred date plus alternate date. | 8th St. and I St., SE | 202/433–6060.

SUMMER

June–July   **Festival of American Folklife.** Begun in 1970, this annual celebration of the diversity of culture within the U.S.—as well as an introduction to peoples and customs from faraway lands—brings a lively collection of food, entertainment, and education to the Mall. There are some nighttime activities. | National Mall between 10th and 14th Sts. | Daily 11–5:30 | 202/357–4574 or 202/619–7222.

June–Aug.   **Fort Dupont Summer Theatre.** Free jazz concerts Friday and Saturday at 8:30 are given in Fort Dupont Park. | Minnesota and Randle Circle SE | 202/426–7723.

June–Sept.   **Carter Barron Amphitheater.** Surrounded by the woods of Rock Creek Park, the outdoor amphitheater shows plays, including a yearly Shakespeare series, and presents jazz, blues, and other concert fare, mostly Friday to Sunday. Tickets are available through Ticketmaster (202/432–7328) or at the box office. | 16th St. and Colorado Ave. NW | 202/426–0486.

July   **July 4th Celebration.** The mother of all American celebrations attracts hundreds of thousands of revelers who pack the Mall to listen to music, picnic, and celebrate all things American with family and friends as they await the evening's fireworks display, which begins just after dusk. The weather can be scorching, so plan accordingly. | 703/838–4200.

Hispanic Festival. A celebration of Latin American culture, food, music, dance, and theater takes place on the Mall. | 703/838–4200.

FALL

Sept.   **Washington National Cathedral Open House.** Open house allows you to tour the majestic shrine, though you won't see any more than you would during a normal tour. It's held on a Saturday in September from 10 until 5. | Massachusetts and Wisconsin Aves. NW | 202/537–6200 | www.cathedral.org.

1995
Marion Barry is elected Mayor of the District of Columbia for an unprecedented fourth term. The Korean War Veterans memorial is dedicated.

1999
Mayor Anthony Williams takes office.

Oct. **Taste of D.C.** One of the capital's newest annual festivals—held on the second weekend—presents a variety of dishes from its restaurants as well as an ample tasting of local culture. Also featured are arts and crafts displays, a "We are the World" children's parade, and musical entertainment. | Pennsylvania Ave. NW | 202/724–4093.

The District's Greats

D.C. can be an impressive spectacle any day of the year, but two events guarantee sizable crowds and planned activities: the annual spring **Cherry Blossom Festival** and the **July 4th Celebration.** The two weeks of the Cherry Blossom Festival are among the busiest of tourist seasons, so plan early for hotel space and expect to stand in lines at museums and other attractions.

The most popular monuments, such as the **Lincoln Memorial, Jefferson Memorial, Washington Monument,** and **Capitol** are impressive and pretty by day but are truly moving sites at night when they bask in the glow of spotlights and you are undistracted by daylight activities. On a nice evening, it's pleasant to take a stroll from the Lincoln Memorial to the Capitol (or at least to the Washington Monument, from which you have a magnificent view of the dome). Also rewarding is a lap around the Tidal Basin, including a tour of the Jefferson Memorial.

Dominating the D.C. museum circuit is the **Smithsonian Institution**'s family of 12 archival buildings, from the Museum of American History to the Museum of Natural History, the awe-inspiring exhibits at the National Gallery of Art and the Air and Space Museum. The aesthetic appeal of Washington is not confined to the Mall. **Rock Creek Park,** one of the largest urban parks in the world, is a dense, forested National Park bisected by Rock Creek. An interlude here will make you feel far from a major city. It is possible to hike in certain sections of the park—for instance, between Bingham and Wise roads—for an hour without crossing a street.

Transportation

Airports: The Washington area is served by three airports, none of which is in the city and only one of which, **Reagan National Airport,** is served directly by the Metro. Reagan National, on the Potomac River north of Alexandria, Virginia, is the closest to the city (about a 10-minute drive). **Dulles International Airport** is a solid 40-minute drive from D.C. in Loudon County, Virginia. A variety of buses, shuttles, and taxis run between D.C. and Dulles and you can pay vastly different rates to ride the same distance, so check at the airport's information desk—near baggage claim—for the option that best suits your needs. **Baltimore Washington International Airport (BWI)** lies just south of Baltimore, about a 45-minute drive from downtown D.C. The airport is accessible by shuttles and taxis, but the cheapest way to get there is via the MARC trains that run regularly from Union Station in Washington (though you have to hop on a shuttle bus after leaving the train in Baltimore to reach the terminal).

Driving around Town: Encircling the city and its suburbs is the famous Washington Beltway, a combination of I–95 and I–495. Access to the city itself is provided by five major highways: I–66 from the west; I–395 (a branch of I–95) and I–295 from the south; U.S. 50 from the east; and Route 295, also known as the Baltimore-Washington Parkway, from the north. Rush hour traffic begins clogging all roads at 6 in the morning, peaking around 8. In the afternoon congestion is thickest between 4:15 and 6:30. Backups are particularly problematic at the few bridges that cross the Potomac.

The layout of D.C., designed by French-born Pierre L'Enfant to resemble that of Paris, features broad avenues radiating from the center of the city, the U.S. Capitol. Streets are identified as east or west and north or south, based on their orientation to this landmark. Although many thoroughfares run perpendicular to one another, forming a grid, many cut diagonally across town. The numerous traffic circles where these diagonals intersect with other streets can be difficult and dangerous for a newcomer to navigate, especially at rush hour. Further complications are the city's many parks, rivers, and natural features. The city is notorious for its inadequate signage, although it has improved slightly.

Parking downtown is a challenge that requires much driving in circles as you wait for someone to leave a legitimate spot. Be attentive to signs; at most spots the meter limit is two hours. If you're lucky, you can sometimes find a place with a broken or missing meter. The police can tow your car away if it's parked illegally. (To reclaim your towed car, call 202/727–5000.) On weekends and holidays most street parking is free. Along the Mall, the long open stretch between the Capitol and the Lincoln Memorial, parking is always free, though you must pay attention to signs indicating how long you are allowed to park. Cars in violation may be booted or towed. Towing is especially common in the early evening, beginning around 4.

Bus: Greyhound Bus Lines runs service in and out of Washington, D.C. The company also has stations in nearby Silver Spring, Maryland, and in Arlington and Springfield, Virginia (1005 1st St. NE | 202/289–5160 or 800/231–2222). | www.greyhound.com.

Intra-City Transportation: D.C.'s subway system, the **Metro,** consists of five lines, each denoted by a color (red, orange, blue, green, or yellow), that spoke outward from the center of downtown. The system, however, misses some exciting neighborhoods and stops short of some integral suburban areas. Be sure to check a map before heading out to your destination. Admission to the system is via fare cards, which may be purchased at any station from automated machines. Fares start at $1.10 and you're charged more the farther you travel. **Washington Metropolitan Area Transit Authority (WMATA)** red, white, and blue Metrobuses crisscross the city and nearby suburbs. Free transfers, good for 1½ hours to 2 hours, are available on buses and in Metro stations. Rail-to-bus transfers, 25 cents each, must be picked up before boarding the train. There are no bus-to-rail transfers.

Trains: More than 80 trains a day arrive at Washington, D.C.'s **Union Station** on Capitol Hill (50 Massachusetts Ave. NE). **Amtrak** (800/872–7245); **MARC** (800/325–7245). **Washington Metropolitan Area Transit Authority (WMATA)** (202/637–7000 or 202/638–3780).

DISTRICT OF
COLUMBIA

INTRO
ATTRACTIONS
DINING
LODGING

Attractions

CULTURE, EDUCATION, AND HISTORY

American Red Cross. The three-building headquarters houses historical and educational displays about the organization, including a biography of founder Clara Barton. Governors Hall, in the 17th Street building, has beautiful Tiffany windows, while most full displays are in the E Street site, across the street. | 430 17th St. NW and 1730 E St. NW | 202/737–8300 | www.redcross.org | Free | Weekdays 9–5.

Bureau of Engraving and Printing. Here is where paper money has been made since 1914. Guided tours take you to see currency and stamps rolling off the presses. | 14th and C Sts. SW | 202/874–3019 or 202/874–3186 | www.moneyfactory.com | Free | Sept.–May, weekdays 9–1:40; June–Aug., weekdays 9–1:40 and 5–6:40.

★ **Capitol.** Worth seeing just for the architecture, this beautifully domed centerpiece of the U.S. Congress is steeped in American history. Here you can witness congressional sessions. Guided tours. | Between Constitution & Independence Aves., at Pennsylvania Ave. | 202/225–6827 | Free | Daily 9–6, tours Mon.–Sat.

The Catholic University of America. This old religious university, with its traditional campus (gray stone buildings, nice lawns), is in one of D.C.'s more culturally consistent neighborhoods. It's not really a visitor's destination, unless you are considering attending school or are visiting a student. | 620 Michigan Ave. NE | 202/319–5000 | www.cua.edu | Free | Daily.

Coolidge Auditorium. This Library of Congress hall, which was built in 1925 through a generous donation by Elizabeth Sprague Coolidge, presents classical and new music, as well as avant-garde jazz, in an elegant and intimate setting. It is said to be one of the finest acoustic environments in the world. | 1st St. and Independence Ave. SE | 202/707–5502 | www.loc.gov/rr/perform/concert/ | Ticket prices vary | Call for schedule.

District of Columbia Jewish Community Center. Performances of high educational value are presented in dance and theater, and include lectures and workshops. Some activities are dependent on membership. | 1529 16th St. NW | 202/518–9400 | fax 202/ 518–9420 | www.dcjcc.org | Prices vary | Call for schedule.

Department of the Interior. On the first floor of this government building, the museum blends 1930s era charm and dioramas with contemporary exhibits of natural history specimens, photos, art, and exceptional artifacts. Topics addressed are wildlife, land use, and American Indians. You'll need a photo ID for admission. A guided tour of the building's New Deal art murals is available by appointment only, made at least two weeks ahead. | 1849 C St. NW | 202/208–4743 | www.museums.doi.gov/museum/ | Free | Weekdays 8:30–4:30, 3rd Sat. of every month 1–4.

Department of State Building. You can tour the luxurious diplomatic reception rooms, designed to resemble the great European halls as well as colonial American plantations. Not recommended for children under 12. | 2201 C St. NW | 202/647–3241 | Free | Weekdays, tours 9:30, 10:30, 2:45; reservations required 3–4 wks in advance.

Department of the Treasury. You won't see money made here, but you will learn the history of the department and see the wonderfully constructed and appointed Greek Revival building, dating from 1869, which is right next door to the White House. Guided tours are 90 minutes. | Pennsylvania Ave. at 15th St. NW | 202/622–0896 | Free | Sat.; reservations required.

Dumbarton Oaks. A historic house, site of the famous meeting of the Allies in 1944, shares lush land with three museums. The Dumbarton Oaks Research Library and Collection is in a 19th-century Federal-style house built on the crest of a wooded valley in Georgetown. The name combines a reference to the original great oaks on the site—several still standing—with the 18th-century name "Dumbarton," taken from the Rock of Dumbarton in Scotland. The institution has important research resources relating to the history of landscape architecture and to Byzantine and pre-Columbian studies. On public display are collections of Byzantine and pre-Columbian art and rare books and prints relating to the gardens. | 1703 32nd St. NW; garden, 31st and R Sts. | 202/339–6400; 202/339–6409 for tour reservations | www.doaks.org | Museum free; garden Apr.–Oct. $5, free Nov.–Mar. | Museum, Tues.–Sun. 2–5; garden, Apr.–Oct., daily 2–6; Nov.–Mar., daily 2–5; closed in inclement weather; reservations required for tours.

Explorers Hall. The National Geographic Society's colorfully interactive display of scientific and natural wonders is housed here, including educational displays about animals, ancient and modern cultures, geographic regions, and climate phenomena. Great for kids and adults. | 17th and M Sts. NW | 202/857–7588 | www.ngs.org | Free | Mon.–Sat. 9–5, Sun. 10–5.

Federal Reserve Building. Since the main attraction here is the Fed's board room, where the Federal Open Market Committee meets, the building is open to the public for just 30 minutes per week on a guided tour. | C St. between 20th and 21st Sts NW | 202/452–3149 | www.federalreserve.gov | Free | Thurs. 2:30–3.

Federal Trade Commission Building. This building is not a big tourist attraction, but if trade is your thing you're welcome to step in and peruse the library and public information room.

VACATION COUNTDOWN Your checklist for a perfect journey

Way Ahead

- ❑ Devise a trip budget.
- ❑ Write down the five things you want most from this trip. Keep this list handy before and during your trip.
- ❑ Book lodging and transportation.
- ❑ Arrange for pet care.
- ❑ Photocopy any important documentation (passport, driver's license, vehicle registration, and so on) you'll carry with you on your trip. Store the copies in a safe place at home.
- ❑ Review health and home-owners insurance policies to find out what they cover when you're away from home.

A Month Before

- ❑ Make restaurant reservations and buy theater and concert tickets. Visit fodors.com for links to local events and news.
- ❑ Familiarize yourself with the local language or lingo.
- ❑ Schedule a tune-up for your car.

Two Weeks Before

- ❑ Create your itinerary.
- ❑ Enjoy a book or movie set in your destination to get you in the mood.
- ❑ Prepare a packing list.
- ❑ Shop for missing essentials.
- ❑ Repair, launder, or dry-clean the clothes you will take with you.
- ❑ Replenish your supply of prescription drugs and contact lenses if necessary.

A Week Before

- ❑ Stop newspaper and mail deliveries.
- ❑ Pay bills.
- ❑ Stock up on film and batteries.
- ❑ Label your luggage.
- ❑ Finalize your packing list—always take less than you think you need.
- ❑ Pack a toiletries kit filled with travel-size essentials.
- ❑ Check tire treads.
- ❑ Write down your insurance agent's number and any other emergency numbers and take them with you.
- ❑ Get lots of sleep. You want to be well-rested and healthy for your impending trip.

A Day Before

- ❑ Collect passport, driver's license, insurance card, vehicle registration, and other documents.
- ❑ Check travel documents.
- ❑ Give a copy of your itinerary to a family member or friend.
- ❑ Check your car's fluids, lights, tire inflation, and wiper blades.
- ❑ Get packing!

During Your Trip

- ❑ Keep a journal/scrapbook as a personal souvenir.
- ❑ Spend time with locals.
- ❑ Take time to explore. Don't plan too much. Let yourself get lost and use your Fodor's guide to get back on track.

© Corbis

| Pennsylvania Ave. NW between 6th and 7th Sts. | 202/326–2222 | www.ftc.gov | Free | Weekdays 9–5.

Folger Shakespeare Library. See the Elizabethan-style Great Hall, housing rotating exhibits, and check out the two interactive computer video screens that convey information on Shakespeare and his time. You can also visit the founder's room, once the office of Henry Clay Folger's wife and still containing her furniture and a fantastic picture of Queen Elizabeth. There's also an Elizabethan garden, theater, and museum shop. A guided tour daily at 11 provides the only access to the founder's room and theater. | 201 E. Capitol St. SE | 202/544–4600 | www.folger.edu | Mon.–Sat. 10–4.

Ford's Theatre. In this theater President Lincoln was shot on April 14, 1865, and he died at Petersen House across the street. Together, the buildings are preserved by the National Park Service as Ford's Theatre National Historic Site, on a redbrick street. You can visit the theatre—restored in the 1960s and holding a never-used presidential box in the spot Lincoln was shot—the Lincoln Museum, and the bookstore (in the museum), as well as Petersen House. Also, 15-minute narratives are presented during much of the day. | 511 10th St. NW | 202/426–6924 or 202/347–4833 | Free; ticket price charged for shows | Daily 9–5. In the basement of Ford's Theatre, the **Lincoln Museum** holds numerous assassination artifacts, such as John Wilkes Booth's derringer and the coat Lincoln wore that night. There are also informative displays about the the events prior to and after the murder. | 511 10th St. NW | 202/426–6924 | Free | Daily.

Frederick Douglass National Historic Site. Cedar Hill, a 21-room mansion built in 1855, was the home of Frederick Douglass for the last 17 years of his life. A slave who become a highly respected pillar of the community and adviser to numerous presidents, Douglass lived here despite proclamations from the former owner that no Africans be allowed into the neighborhood (the man went bankrupt). Thirteen rooms are open to the public. | 1411 W. St. SE | 202/426–5961 or 800/365–2267 | www.nps.gov/frdo | $3 | Daily 9–5.

★ **Georgetown University.** In addition to academic guided tours, geared heavily toward prospective students, you can take a self-guided walking tour of the campus for history and architectural information about the oldest Jesuit school in the country. A quick visit to the campus may be best as part of a longer tour of the Georgetown neighborhoods. | 37th and O Sts. NW | 202/687–3600 | www.georgetown.edu | Free | Weekdays, Sat., by reservation.

George Washington University. It has a somewhat diffuse urban campus, between downtown and Georgetown. University trolley and double-decker bus tours of the city are available, as well as walking tours of the campus, mostly for students but open to the public. | 801 22nd St. NW | 202/994–6602 | Free | Year-round, weekdays; Aug.–Nov., Apr. Sat.Campus tours: Mon.–Fri. 10 and, 2; Sat. 10 and 1. No Sat. tours Dec.– March.

Government Printing Office Bookstore. You'll find reams of federal publications in the bookstore of a large government building that does not offer public tours. | N. Capitol St. NW, between G and H Sts. | Bookstore, 202/512–0132 | www.mainbookstoregpo.gov | Weekdays 8–4.

House Office Buildings. You can walk the halls where the laws are made, in the Cannon, Longworth, and Rayburn buildings. Drop in on your congressperson, if you like, because it's your right. All three buildings are within a block of each other. | Cannon: Independence and New Jersey Aves.; Longworth: Independence Ave. and S. Capitol St.; Rayburn: Independence Ave. and 1st St. | 202/225–2456 | www.house.gov | Free | Weekdays 9–6.

Howard University. One of the premier African-American universities in the U.S., it rests on an urban campus in a quintessentially D.C. neighborhood. Campus tours, by appointment only, are geared primarily toward prospective students and their families, but others may join as well. | 2400 6th St. NW | 202/806–0970 | www.howard.edu | Free | Sept.–July, weekdays. Campus tours are by appointment only. To make arrangements call 202/806–2755. Tours last two hours and are given weekdays between 10 to 2.

J. Edgar Hoover Federal Bureau of Investigation Building A one-hour tour here is one of the most exciting things in the city. A brief film outlines the bureau's work, an exhibit describes the famous past cases, and there's a firearms demonstration by an agent. | 935 Pennsylvania Ave. NW (tour entrance on E St. NW) | 202/324–3447 | Free | Tours weekdays every 20 mins, 8:45–4:15.

John F. Kennedy Center for the Performing Arts. Home to the finest of D.C.'s performing arts. Inside it is grand, with high ceilings, lavishly decorated corridors, and comfortable, posh performance halls, while outdoors there's a terrace overlooking the river where you can chill out during intermission. There's always something playing at the Kennedy Center, and you can self-tour the center for free. | 2700 F Street NW | 202/467–4600 or 202/416–8340 | www.kennedy-center.org | Free | Daily, 10 AM–midnight.

Labor Department. See the building that keeps track of working America. Self-guided tours, which include cafeteria access, allow you to see the Labor Department's Great Hall, Hall of Fame, and library. Gardens and several pieces of sculpture surround the building. Group tours can be arranged in advance. | Francis H. Perkins Building, 200 Constitution Ave. NW | 202/219–5000 or 202/219–6992 | www.dol.gov | Free | Weekdays 8:15–4:45; photo ID required.

Library of Congress. Of the three library buildings, the Thomas Jefferson building is the oldest. Here you can learn about the library's art, architecture, and history as well as see the Main Reading Room, a Gutenberg Bible, and the Giant Bible of Mainz. There are also rotating exhibits. | 10 1st St. SE | 202/707–8000. 202/707–6400 | www.loc.gov | Free | Mon.–Sat. 10–5:30; tours 11:30, 1, 2:30, 4.

Lincoln Theatre. At this 1,250-seat theater major jazz artists play matinees for young audiences (ages five and up) before a show. At one time the theater hosted the same performers that appeared at New York's Cotton Club and Apollo Theatre. | 1215 U St. NW | 202/328–6000 | www.thelincolntheatre.org | Ticket prices vary | Call for schedule.

Martin Luther King Memorial Library. The largest public library in D.C., it has a mural on the first floor depicting events in the life of Dr. King. Summer hours vary. | 901 G St. NW | 202/727–1111 | Free | Mon.–Thurs. 10–9, Fri.–Sat. 10–5:30, Sun. 1–5.

Meridian International Center. Housed in two period-style mansions, this private, non-profit educational institution is devoted to international affairs. Adults only. | 1630 Crescent Pl. NW | 202/939–5544 | Free | Weekdays 2–5; hours vary weekends.

National Academy of Sciences. Lying on pleasantly landscaped grounds, this bastion of higher knowledge presents for public viewing an art exhibit, frequently on scientific themes, and a chamber music concert series. There is a massive memorial to Albert Einstein by Robert Berks on the academy's front lawn. Call for information on chamber music. | 2101 Constitution Ave., between 21st and 22nd Sts. NW | 202/334–2436 | www.nas.edu/about/ | Free | Weekdays 9–5.

The National Archives. Visit the document center of the world and check out the the Research Room, where you can discover the archives' nationwide holdings, learn about family history/genealogy research and veterans' service records, order reproductions, search the NARA Archival Information Locator (NAIL) database, locate government documents and library materials, and more. The Declaration of Independence, the Constitution, and the Bill of Rights are displayed behind bulletproof glass. | Pennsylvania Ave. between 7th and 9th Sts NW | 202/501–5000 or 202/501–5205 | www.nara.gov | Free | Research, Mon. and Wed. 8:45–5, Tues., Thurs., and Fri. 8:45–9, Sat. 8:45–4:45; closed Sun. Exhibit Hall, Labor Day–Mar., daily 10–5:30; Apr.–Labor Day, daily 10–9.

National Theatre. Mime, puppet, dance, magic, and theater shows for children ages four and up are performed at the Helen Hayes Gallery on Saturday mornings. Tickets are handed out in the lobby 30 minutes prior to the performance on a first-come, first-served basis. Similarly, on Monday evenings there are free performances for adults. Call for schedule of main stage productions. | 1321 Pennsylvania Ave. NW | 202/783–3372 or 202/628–6161. | www.nationaltheatre.org | Free | Sept.–Apr. Sat. 9:30–11 AM.

Old Executive Office Building. Among the city's most intricate pieces of architecture, this immense gray edifice houses many of the president's and vice president's staff. The modern interior is not nearly as interesting as the exterior, with its meticulously executed stone work and balconies, though some rooms dating from 1871 to 1888 have been restored. Guided tours take 90 minutes and must be scheduled well in advance. | Pennsylvania Ave. and 17th St. NW | 202/395–5895 | Free | Sat. mornings, by appointment only.

Old Stone House. Built in 1765, this is the oldest building in D.C. (and it looks it). Learn how the people of Georgetown lived when it was a major tobacco seaport. | 3051 M St. NW | 202/426–6851 | www.nps.gov/rocr/oldstonehouse | Free | Wed.–Sun. 12–5; reservations required for tours.

Petersen House. The 4-story brick town house where Lincoln died—across the street from Ford's Theatre—contains a replica of the bed in which Lincoln expired but the pillow and pillowcase are the originals. | 516 10th St. NW | 202/426–6924 | www.nps.gov | Free | Daily 9–5; closed Dec. 25.

Senate Office Buildings. The Russell, Dirksen, and Hart senate office buildings offer a wide range of architectural styles and eras, from the grand marble layout of the first-built Russell to the modernistic, open-atrium design of the Hart. You can drop in on your senator or just have a look around. All three are within one block of each other. | Russell: Constitution and Delaware Aves.; Dirksen: Constitution Ave. and 1st St.; Hart: Constitution Ave. and 2nd St. | 202/224–2341 | www.senate.gov | Free | Weekdays 9–6.

Shakespeare Theatre. Works of the renowned English playwright are the focus of programming at this pleasantly decorated theater | 450 7th St. NW | 202/547–1122 | www.shakespearedc.org | $17.50–$56 | Tues.–Fri. evenings, weekend matinees.

Supreme Court of the United States. Tours of this ornate and impressive court include lectures (when the court is not sitting), exhibits featuring all higher courts throughout the U.S., historical documents, and a theater showing a 24-minute film. You can also stop in at the cafeteria, snack bar, and gift shop. The longer line out front is for people who want to be present for a whole argument versus just part of one; it's a fascinating experience and worth the wait. | 1st St. NE at Maryland Ave. | 202/479–3211 | www.supremecourtus.gov | Free | Weekdays 9–4:30; guided tours 9:30–3:30; 20-min. lectures every hour on the ½ hr.

Tudor Place. This neoclassical house, designed by William Thornton for Martha Custus Peter, granddaughter of Martha Washington, lies on 5.5 acres of manicured grounds and gardens, in the middle of Georgetown. Artifacts and items on display represent six generations of the same family, from 1805 to 1984. | 1644 31st St. NW | 202/965–0400 | www.tudorplace.org | $6 (suggested) | Guided tours Tues.–Fri. 10, 11:30, 1, 2:30; Sat. hourly 10–3; reservations advised.

Washington Chamber Symphony. The performances are interactive and provide workbooks, sing-alongs, orchestras marching down the aisles, and bringing kids on stage. Family Series programs are for kids four and older; the Concerts for Young People series is for ages six and up. Most performances are at the Kennedy Center. | 2700 F Street, NW | 202/452–1321 | www.wcsymphony.org/.

★ **White House.** America's most famous residence is accessible to the public via guided and self-guided tours. Self-guided walk-through tours, which take 15 to 20 minutes, include the first and second floors, with views of numerous rooms. There are no public rest rooms or phones in the building. Tickets, limited to four per person, are necessary and are distributed at the visitors center at 15th and E streets NW (look for the three U.S. flags and blue awning), on a first come, first served basis starting at 7:30. Get there early! There are also weekend house and garden tours scheduled for April and October (one weekend each), no tickets necessary. Tours occasionally are delayed or canceled because of official events, so check the morning you plan to go. | 1600 Pennsylvania Ave. NW | 202/456–7041 | Free |

Self-guided walk-through tours Tues.–Sat. 10–noon; garden and house tours Mon.–Sat. 9–noon and 2–5, Sun. 1–5.

Woodrow Wilson House. The preserved home of the late U.S. president contains his furniture, clothes, and some documents. Tours are fully guided and take an hour. Tours are ongoing, with two or three departing each hour. | 2340 S. St. NW | 202/387–4062 | www.woodrowwilsonhouse.org | $5 | Tues.–Sun. 10–4.

PARKS, GARDENS, NATURAL AREAS, RECREATION

Anacostia Park. This 1,200 acres along the Anacostia River is one of the city's largest parks and enjoyed by the surrounding diverse population. There are three marinas, softball fields, basketball and tennis courts, picnic facilities, and a roller-skating rink in the Anacostia Park Pavilion. | Between S. Capitol St. and Benning Rd. SE | 202/690–5185 | www.nps.gov/nace/anacostia.htm | Free | Daily dawn to dusk.

Constitution Gardens. In a lovely area, with paths winding through groves of trees, a small lake was established here in 1976 to honor the bicentennial of the American Revolution. An island in the middle displays the names of the 56 signers of the Declaration of Independence. | Constitution Ave. between 17th and 23rd Sts. NW | 202/426–6841 | www.nps.gov/coga/index.htm | Free | Daily dawn to dusk.

Fort Stevens Park. This park within Rock Creek Park contains the restored remains of a historic fort, the site of the only civil war battle that occurred in D.C. Much of it is 1930s reconstruction. It's part of a system of forts that protected D.C. during that war. For more information call the Rock Creek Nature Center, 202/426–6828. | 13th and Quackenbos Sts. NW | 202/282–1063 | www.nps.gov/rocr | Free | Daily.

Fort DuPont Ice Arena. This indoor NHL-size ice rink has more than 450 pairs of skates for rent. | 3779 Ely Pl. | 202/584–5007 | $4, plus $1.50 skate rental | Daily Fri. noon–2, weekends 2:30–4:30.

Great Falls of the Potomac. Impressively strong falls blast through rock chasms about 20 miles north of the city. Sturdy walkways lead to overlook points from the Maryland and Virginia sides of the river, though the Maryland overlook is more dramatic. | Great Falls Park, 9200 Old Dominion Dr. | 703/285–2965 | www.nps.gov/gwnp/grfa | $4 per vehicle | Daily dawn to dusk.

Kahlil Gibran Memorial Garden. The limestone benches engraved with Gibran's quotes, which encircle a fountain and a bust of the Lebanese-born poet, are great for reflection in this small urban garden dedicated in 1991. | 3100 block of Massachusetts Ave. NW | 202/282–1063 | Daily dawn to dusk.

Kenilworth Aquatic Gardens. These 12-acre, all-outdoor gardens have 44 ponds stacked with water lilies, lotus, and other aquatic plants. They're pretty during all the warm months, but peak season is in July. | Anacostia Ave. and Douglas St. NE | 202/426–6905 | www.nps.gov/nace/keaq | Free | Daily 8–4.

Lafayette Square. In this 1-block-square public park across the street from the White House you can see daily demonstrations ranging from long-running anti-nuclear protests to issue-of-the-day rants. | Pennsylvania Ave. at 16th St. | Free | Daily dawn to dusk.

Meridian Hill Park. Also known as Malcolm X Park (after the speech he made here in the 1970s), this lovely space has an upper level designed to resemble a French garden and a lower level to resemble an Italian Renaissance garden. It's a great escape from the nearby urban neighborhood. | Between 15th, 16th, Euclid, and W Sts. NW | 202/282–1063 | www.nps.gov/rocr/cultural/merid.htm.

Potomac Park (East and West). These huge grassy expanses give you ample space to picnic, throw a frisbee, or pick up a volleyball game (there's a handful of sand pits and nets). And it all offers great views of surrounding memorials and the Potomac River. | NW and SE of the Jefferson Memorial | 202/619–7222 | Free | Daily dawn to dusk.

DISTRICT OF
COLUMBIA

INTRO
ATTRACTIONS
DINING
LODGING

Rock Creek Park. Among the largest urban parks in the world at 1,750 acres, Rock Creek is a dense, forested National Park bisected by Rock Creek and veined with 29 mi of hiking trails and more than 10 mi of equestrian trails, as well as a paved bike path, a golf course, and numerous picnic groves. A large portion of its main artery—Beach Drive—is closed to motorized traffic on weekends and holidays to accommodate bicyclists, in-line skaters, joggers, and walkers. A few hours in Rock Creek makes you forget you are anywhere near a big city. | 3545 Williamsburg Ln. NW | 202/282–1063 | www.nps.gov/rocr | Free | Daily, dawn to dusk.

A small **Nature Center** holds a wealth of information on local flora and wildlife, including live critters (Rock Creek Park has more species diversity than you'd think) as well as a planetarium, auditorium, and educational displays and programs for children. Two trails circle the center, one with handicapped access. Events such as planetarium and nature shows and animal feedings are usually at 4 Wednesdays through Fridays and twice daily on weekends. | 5200 Glover Rd. NW | 202/426–6829 | www.nps.gov/rocr | Free | Wed.–Sun. 9–5. S

Built in the 1820s and operated commercially until 1897, **Pierce Mill** was restored to working order in 1936. It became famous as the only 19th-century gristmill operating full time in the National Park Service system and was used off and on until April 1993, when it was determined that the wooden waterwheel and attached mechanical components were too deteriorated to run safely. | Tilden St. NW, at Beach Drive | 202/426–6908 | www.nps.gov/rocr/piercemill | Free | Sat. 9–noon.

U.S. Botanic Garden. The conservatory, which usually houses azaleas, lilies, cacti, citrus, orchids, chrysanthemums, and tropical and subtropical plants, is closed for renovations and will not reopen until the fall of 2001. In the meantime, you can wander through a few streetside gardens. | 1st St. and Maryland Ave. SW. | 202/225–8333 | www.nationalgarden.org | Free | Daily dawn to dusk.

U.S. National Arboretum. This beautiful property of 446 acres has numerous exhibits, including bonzai, azaleas, rhododendrons, roses, and herbs, as well as a huge meadow containing the Capitol Columns (where presidents used to take the oath of office). You can drive the 9.5 miles of paved road or, on weekends, take a tram tour for about 40 minutes. | 3501 New York Ave. NE | 202/544–8733 | www.fona.org | Free; tram tours $3 | Daily 8–5.

MUSEUMS, MONUMENTS, AND MEMORIALS

Anacostia Museum. This community-based museum, dedicated to increasing awareness of the rich African-American experience through research, programs, and exhibitions, is closed and projected to reopen in fall 2001. In the meantime, the museum's holdings are being managed by the Museum of Arts and Industries. | 1901 Fort Pl. SE | 202/357–2700 and 202/357–2627 | Free | Daily.

Art Barn. Works of local artists, in changing monthly exhibits and a permanent display, grace this vintage 1808 building. On view are paintings and crafts—jewelry, fabric, stationery—in two stories of gallery space. | Tilden St. and Beach Dr. NW | 202/244–2482 | Free | Thurs.–Sun. noon–6; summer hours vary.

Art Museum of the Americas. Part of the Organization of American States, this comparatively small museum in a two-story building houses a permanent collection of 20th-century Latin American and Caribbean art, one of the most important of its kind in the U.S. There are also special rotating Latin American art exhibits and related educational programs. | 201 18th St. NW | 202/458–6016 | www.OAS.org | Free | Tues.–Sun. 10–5.

B'nai B'rith Klutznick Museum. The permanent collection includes original, folk, and archeology exhibits, plus paintings, textiles and documents on Jewish tradition. The museum also has changing exhibits, such as architecture of the synagogue. | B'nai B'rith International Center, 1640 Rhode Island Ave. NW | 202/857–6583 | www.bnaibrith.org | Free | Sun.–Fri. 10–5.

Christian Heurich Mansion. This stunningly preserved house of beer brewer Christian Huerich contains his furniture and possessions. | 1307 New Hampshire Ave. NW | 202/785–2068 | $3 | Wed.–Sat. 10–4.

Corcoran Gallery of Art. The ornate building holds three floors of world-class art, with permanent and changing exhibits. | 17th St. between New York Ave. and E St. NW | 202/639–1700 | www.corcoran.org | $3 (suggested) | Wed. and Fri.–Mon. 10–5, Thurs. 10–9.

DAR Headquarters. This Beaux Arts building contains a decorative arts museum covering the colonial period to the mid-1800s, a world-famous quilt collection, an Americana room with papers, diaries, and letters of historical figures, and a geneological library. | 1776 D St. NW | 202/628–1776 or 202/879–3239 | www.dar.org | Free | Weekdays 8:30–4, Sun. 1–5. Closed Sat.

Decatur House Museum. Presidents have chatted in the parlors of this National Trust historic site. Nearly two centuries of powerful and famous people have left their mark here. Designed in 1817, the house tells the story of naval hero Stephen Decatur and his wife, Susan. Tours are guided. | 748 Jackson Pl. NW | 202/842–0920 | www.decaturhouse.org | $4 | Tues.–Fri. 10–3, last tour 2:30; weekends noon–4, last tour 3:30.

Fondo Del Sol Visual Arts & Media. Established in 1970, this nonprofit art museum showcases work that relates to the various cultures of Latin America and the Caribbean. | 2112 R St., at Florida Ave. NW | 202/483–2777 | $3 | Weds.–Sat. 12:30–6.

★ **Franklin Delano Roosevelt Memorial.** Just as FDR would have wanted, this memorial is a stone block the size of his desk. You can walk through four outdoor "rooms" intended to signify his four terms in office. Groups of statues and quotes from speeches convey the rough waters of the Depression. A ranger patrols the site from 8 AM until midnight. | Tidal Basin, West Potomac Park, W Basin Dr. | 202/426–6841 | Free | Daily 24 hrs.

Hillwood Museum. This former estate of Marjorie Merriweather Post, of Post Cereal, contains probably the largest collection of Russian decorative art outside Russia, including icons, tapestries, Sévres porcelain, and Fabergé eggs. There's a 40-room mansion, greenhouse, and gardens; to see them, reservations are essential. | 4155 Linnean Ave. NW | 202/686–5807, reservations 877/445–5966 | www.hillwoodmuseum.org | $10 | Mar.–Jan., Tues.–Sat.; closed Mon. and Feb.; guided tours 9:30 and 1:30; self-guided tours 11 and 3.

Kreeger Musuem. Designed by Philip Johnson, this former home of Washington philanthropists Carmen and David Kreeger displays highlights of the couple's painting and sculpture collection, including works by Monet, Picasso, Miró, Moore, and Stella. Reservations are required for the 90-minute tour. | 2401 Foxhall Rd. NW | 202/337–3050 or 202/338–3552 | $5 (suggested) | Tours Tues.–Sat. 10:30, 1:30. Closed Aug. No children under 12.

★ **Lincoln Memorial.** Completed in 1922, this most majestic and moving of Washington monuments honors President Abraham Lincoln. Its grand staircase spilling down to the Reflecting Pool. | Independence Ave. and 23rd St. NW | 202/426–6841 | Free | Daily 24 hrs; park ranger tours, daily 8 AM–midnight.

Mary McLeod Bethune Memorial. The famous African-American political activist of the New Deal era resided in this Victorian town house for six years, where she housed black women who weren't permitted in the city's segregated hotels. The museum and memorial museum celebrate her accomplishments and African-American women's history. There are also lectures, workshops, exhibitions, a photo library, films, plays, and concerts. | 1318 Vermont Ave NW | 202/673–2402 | www.nps.gov/mamc | Free | Mon.–Sat. 10–4.

MCI National Sports Gallery. A mecca of family sports entertainment, with interactive games, memorabilia, as well as the American Sportscasters Hall of Fame. | MCI Center, 601 F St. NW | 202/661–5133 | www.mcicenter.com | $5 | Hours vary.

★ **National Gallery of Art.** D.C.'s crown jewel of art museums, this imperial stone building is on the Mall and houses the city's most voluminous permanent collection of art ranging from prehistoric times, through the renaissance period, and into the modern art era. There's also a massive and impressive sculpture garden with rotating exhibitions, as well as cafeterias and gift shops. | Constitution Ave. between 3rd and 9th Sts. NW | 202/737–4215 | www.nga.gov | Free | Mon.–Sat. 10–5, Sun. 11–6.

DISTRICT OF
COLUMBIA

INTRO
ATTRACTIONS
DINING
LODGING

National Museum of Health and Medicine. A hidden gem of information on the D.C. museum circuit, this building offers displays relating to U.S. medical history and development from the Civil War (surgical kits, etc.) and exhibits such as Living in the World of AIDS. There are photos of amputations (no details spared), bone fragments, medical illustrations, and personal accounts. You can also see the bullet that killed President Lincoln, a lock of his hair, and skull fragments. | Bldg. #54, Walter Reed Army Medical Center, 6900 Georgia Ave., at Elder St. NW | 202/782–2200 | www.natmedmuse.afip.org | Free | Daily 10–5:30.

National Museum of Women in the Arts. It's the only museum in the world dedicated exclusively to recognizing the contributions of women artists, with a permanent collection containing works from the Renaissance to modernism. The museum also presents also special exhibitions, conducts education programs, maintains a library and research center, and supports a network of national and international chapters, as well as serving as a center for the performing arts and other creative disciplines in which women excel. | 1250 New York Ave. NW | 202/783–5000 | www.nmwa.org/ | Free | Mon.–Sat. 10–5, Sun. noon–5.

Navy Yard. These shipbuilding facilities were set ablaze in 1814 by the British and were later rebuilt. It's the Navy's oldest shore establishment and now operates as a supply and administrative center. In building 58, near the yard's M Street gate, is the Marine Corps Historical Center, where you can see the actual flag depicted in the famed Iwo Jima photo. | M St. between 1st and 11th Sts. SE | 202/433–2218 | www.ndw.navy.mil | Free | Weekdays 9–4, weekends 10–5.

Tour the exterior of the **Marine Barracks,** which have been on the site for almost 200 years. The Marine Band is stationed here. Also see the outside of the house of the Marine Commandant and his family, the oldest continuously used building in D.C. and a national historic landmark. | G St. between 8th and 9th Sts. SE | 202/433–4173 | www.usmc.mil | Free | Weekdays 7–4:30; guided tours Mon.–Thurs. 10, 2; Fri. tour hours vary.

In the Navy Yard, the **Marine Corps Museum** holds collections of the corps from 1775 to the present, including uniforms, some small arms, and educational and history displays. | 1254 Charles Morris St. SE | 202/433–3840 or 202/433–3841 | www.usmc.mil | Free | Mon. and Weds. 10–4, Fri. 10–8, Sun.12–5.

Young and old salts alike find lots to see and do at the **Navy Museum,** part of the Navy Yard. There are ship models, uniforms, medals, and photographs in an appropriate setting— the old Naval Gun Factory. With gun mounts to climb on and periscopes to look through, the museum affords many opportunities for interactive learning. | Bldg. 76, Washington Navy Yard, 805 Kiddler Breese St. SE | 202/433–6897 or 202/433–4882 | www.history.navy.mil | Free | Labor Day–Memorial Day, weekdays 9–4; Memorial Day–Labor Day, weekdays 9–5; year-round, weekends 10–5.

Octagon Museum. This Federal-period mansion served as the Executive Mansion when the British torched the White House in 1814 (James and Dolley Madison sheltered here). The structure's shape (it's really only six-sided) reflects the creativity of architect William Thornton, who was initially confounded by the angle of the building lot. See the remarkable oval central staircase and the Treaty Room, a circular second-floor study with the desk at which Madison signed the treaty ending the War of 1812. Old bedrooms have been converted and now show design and architecture exhibits. There are guided tours. | 1799 New York Ave. NW, at 18th and E Sts. NW | 202/638–3105 | $5 | Tues.–Sun. 10–4.

Organization of American States (OAS). The headquarters of this organization, composed of nations from all the Americas, has a patio with a fountain and tropical plants, a nice respite from D.C.'s summer heat. The upstairs Hall of the Americas is lined with busts of statesmen from OAS member nations along with their flags. There is also the Columbus Memorial Library, on 19th Street, holding the world's most complete collection of unique publications, archives, and records documenting the history of the OAS from 1889 to the present. | OAS, 1889 F St. NW; library, 19th St. and Constitution Ave. NW | 202/458–3000 | www.oas.org | Free | Weekdays 9–5:30.

★ **Phillips Collection.** America's first museum of modern art, dating from 1921, includes in its permanent collection works by Renoir, Cezanne, Van Gogh and Georgia O'Keeffe. | 1600 21st St. NW | 202/387–2151 or 202/387–0961 | www.phillipscollection.org | $7.50 | Tues.– Weds., Fri–Sat. 10–5, Thurs. 10–8:30, Sun. noon–5.

Renwick Gallery. The richness and diversity of American crafts are displayed through changing exhibitions as well as a selection of objects from the museum's permanent collection, spanning the development of American studio crafts after World War II. The Grand Salon has been restored and furnished in the styles of the 1860s and 1870s. The building, designed in 1859 by James Renwick Jr., architect of the Smithsonian Castle, was Washington's first art gallery. Summer hours vary. | Pennsylvania Ave. at 17th St. NW | 202/357–2700 | nmaa-ryder.si.edu/collections/renwick/main.html | Free | Daily 10–5:30.

Sewall-Belmont House. This museum is dedicated to the women's suffrage movement and serves as the headquarters of the National Woman's Party. See Susan B. Anthony's desk, where she drafted the 19th Amendment, and a statue of Joan of Arc. Admission by guided tour only. | 144 Constitution Ave. NE | 202/546–1210 | www.natwomanparty.org | $3 (suggested) | Tues.–Fri. 11–2, Sat. noon–3; tours hourly.

Smithsonian Institution. Completed in 1855, this original Smithsonian Institution Building, popularly known as the Castle, was designed by architect James Renwick Jr., whose other works include St. Patrick's Cathedral in New York City and the Smithsonian's Renwick Gallery in D.C. This landmark is constructed of red sandstone from Seneca Creek, Maryland, in the Norman style (a 12th-century combination of late Romanesque and early Gothic motifs). Summer hours vary. | 202/357–2700 | www.si.edu | Free | Daily 10–5:30.

The residence built in 1905 for diplomat Larz Anderson and his wife, Isabel, is now the ornate **Anderson House Museum,** which is part of the Smithsonian Institution and showcases decorative arts of Asia collected by the couple. It also contains a Baccarat crystal eagle, Revolutionary War-era weapons, Japanese screens, and an extensive war-related library. The museum is run by the Society of the Cincinnati. | 2118 Massachusetts Ave. NW | 202/785–2040 | Free | Tues.–Sat. 1–4; guided tours.

The Smithsonian's **Arthur M. Sackler Gallery** is devoted to education and research on the arts of Asia, from ancient times to the present. The museum sponsors changing exhibitions of paintings, sculptures, ceramics, and other art forms that express the diversity of Asian art. Summer hours vary. | 1050 Independence Ave. SW | 202/357–4880 | www.si.edu/asia/ | Free | Daily 10–5:30.

Opened in 1881, the **Arts and Industries Building** has been a repository for special exhibitions, from first ladies' gowns to the *Spirit of St. Louis,* now displayed elsewhere in the Smithsonian. The museum was partially restored in 1976 to its original appearance for the nation's bicentennial. In the Rotunda, a working fountain surrounded by seasonal plants provides a quiet respite, and off the west hall is the Discovery Theater, which showcases programs for young children most of the year. Summer hours vary. | 900 Jefferson Dr. SW | 202/357–2700 | www.si.edu/ai | Free | Daily 10–5:30.

Kids can find a wealth of hands-on interactive sites at the Smithsonian's **Capital Children's Museum,** where activities range from blowing bubbles and negotiating a maze to "driving" a bus, using a computer, and performing experiments in a lab. | 800 3rd St. NE | 202/675–4120 | www.ccm.org | $6, half-price Sun. before noon | Easter–Labor Day, 10–6, Labor Day–Easter, 10–5.

Opened in 1923, the **Freer Gallery,** part of the Smithsonian Institution, is home to one of the world's finest collections of Asian art, including Japanese screens, Korean ceramics, Chinese paintings, and Islamic metalware. Also see works of such American artists as Sargent, Dewing, and Whistler and enjoy the famous Whistler-designed Peacock Room, an elaborate dining room moved from London to the U.S. Summer hours vary. | Jefferson Dr. at 12th St. SW | 202/357–2700 | www.si.edu/organiza/museums/freer/start.htm | Free | Daily 10–5:30.

An outstanding collection of modern art, much of it donated by financier Joseph H. Hirshhorn, is on view at the Smithsonian's **Hirshhorn Museum and Sculpture Garden,** where changing exhibitions focus mostly on established contemporary masters and emerging artists. Also, works by such sculptors as Henry Moore, Rodin, and Giacometti can be seen indoors as well as on the lawns, fountain plaza, and in the sunken Sculpture Garden. Summer hours vary. | Independence Ave., between 7th and 9th Sts SW | 202/357–3091 | www.si.edu/hirshhorn/ | Free | Daily 10–5:30.

★ The Smithsonian's **National Air and Space Museum,** opened in 1976, documents major air and space achievements, and unless otherwise specified, all the aircraft and most of the spacecraft on display in the 23 galleries were actually flown or used as backup vehicles. See the suspended Wright brothers' 1903 *Flyer* and Charles Lindbergh's *Spirit of St. Louis,* touch the moon rock collected by the *Apollo* astronauts and walk through *Skylab.* Other popular attractions include IMAX films and daily planetarium presentations. Make reservations two weeks in advance by writing to Tour Scheduler, Office of Volunteer Services, National Air and Space Museum, Smithsonian Institution, Washington, DC 20560. | Independence Ave. and 6th St. SW | 202/357–1400 or 202/357–1686 | www.nasm.si.edu | Free | Daily 9:30–5:30; reservations necessary.

Dedicated to exploring and celebrating design, architecture, building arts, and urban planning, the Smithsonian's **National Building Museum** has engaging exhibitions and education programs. The Great Hall is 316 feet by 116 feet and towers 159 feet high. | Old Pension Building, F St. between 4th and 5th Sts NW | 202/272–2448 | www.nbm.org/ | Free | Mon.–Sat. 10–5, Sun. noon–5.

The only museum in the country devoted to the study, collection, and exhibition of African art, the Smithsonian's **National Museum of African Art.** Exhibits of sculpture, photography, pottery, archaeology, and modern art rotate at this museum, and storytelling and workshops are usually held on Saturdays. The museum is also home to the Warren M. Robbins Library and the Eliot Elisofon Photographic Archives and also stages films, festivals, and hands-on workshops. Summer hours vary. | 950 Independence Ave. SW | 202/357–4600 | www.si.edu/nmafa/nmafa.htm | Free | Daily 10–5:30.

Opened in 1964 as the National Museum of History and Technology, the Smithsonian's **National Museum of American History** has exhibits related to the cultural, scientific, and technological growth of the U.S. and interprets the American experience from early times to the present. Collections include agricultural implements, clothing and household furnishings, coins, cars, and musical and scientific instruments, as well as ships, trains, and ceramics. You can see the original Star-Spangled Banner and the John Bull locomotive, and such memorabilia as Archie Bunker's chair and the Fonz's jacket. Summer hours vary. | Constitution Ave. between 12th and 14th Sts. NW | 202/357–2700 | www.si.edu/nmah/ | Daily 10–5:30.

★ Recognized as one of the world's great centers for the study of humankind and our natural surroundings, the Smithsonian's **National Museum of Natural History** is the home of the Hope Diamond, an insect zoo, dinosaurs, a popular Discovery Room where you can touch and examine museum specimens, and a record 8-ton stuffed African bush elephant. | Constitution Ave. between 9th and 12th Sts. NW | 202/357–2700 | www.mnh.si.edu/nmnhweb.html | Free | Daily 10–5:30; summer hours vary.

Textile Museum. Founded in 1925, the museum has over 15,500 rugs and textiles as well as rotating exhibitions ranging from pre-Columbian textiles and Kashmir embroidery to Oriental carpets and contemporary fiber art. Try your hand at the Textile Learning Center. | 2320 South St. NW | 202/667–0441 | www.textilemuseum.org | $5 (suggested) | Mon.–Sat. 10–5, Sun. 1–5.

Thomas Jefferson Memorial. Construction of this memorial to our third president, completed in 1943, was designed by architect John Russell Pope and incorporated Jefferson's classical architectural tastes into the design. Based on the Roman Pantheon, the neoclassical marble memorial is wonderfully situated to overlook the Tidal Basin. | Tidal Basin, S. bank | 202/426–6841 | www.nps.gov/nacc | Free | Daily 24 hrs, ranger on duty 8AM–midnight.

★ **U.S. Holocaust Memorial Museum.** This museum offers a haunting and stark look at the Holocaust, sparing little detail in conveying the horrific tragedy of World War II. The permanent exhibit covers three floors; you start at the top and walk down. Visits are timed;

make a reservation in advance. | Entrances at 100 Raoul Wallenberg St. SW and 14th St. SW | 202/488–0400 | www.ushmm.org | Free | Daily 10–5:30.

United States Navy Memorial. This outdoor memorial includes a 100-foot replica map of the world in two shades of granite and has as its centerpiece a 7-foot bronze statue, *The Lone Sailor.* The Navy Memorial Foundation manages events such as Navy Band concerts (on Tuesdays from Memorial Day through Labor Day) and also oversees the Naval Heritage Center, which houses exhibits, displays, artifacts, and a gift shop. | Pennsylvania Ave. at 7th and 9th Sts. NW | 202/737–2300 | www.lonesailor.org | Free | Mon.–Sat. 9:30–5.

The Naval Heritage Center has a theater where you can view the film **At Sea,** covering modern-day aircraft carrier operations with the U.S. Navy. Screened continuously, the 70-millimeter award-winning film runs 35 minutes. | Arleigh and Roberta Burke Theater, Pennsylvania Ave. at 7th St. NW | 202/737–2300 | www.lonesailor.org | $3 | Mon.–Sat. 2PM.

★ **Vietnam Veterans Memorial.** A sad and powerful memorial, sited west of the Mall, this long, polished black-granite wall, completed in 1982, is engraved with the names of the 58,191 American casualties of the Vietnam War. | Constitution Ave. between Henry Bacon Dr. and 21st St. NW | 202/634–1568 or 202/393–0090 | Free | Daily 24 hrs., staffed by a ranger 8:30 AM–midnight.

Washington Dolls' House & Toy Museum. In six small galleries this two-story house/museum contains a carefully researched collection of dolls, houses, toys, and games, most of them Victorian and all of them antique. There is also an Edwardian tea room, as well as two small shops and a consignment center. | 5236 44th St. NW | 202/244–0024 | $4 | Tues.–Sat. 10–5, Sun. noon–5.

Washington Monument. Finished in 1884, this 555-foot-high obelisk is the tallest masonry structure in the world. Its marble exterior gleams anew, thanks to a three-year-long renovation. After an elevator ride to the top you'll see nonpareil views of the city. Tickets are necessary; the ticket office is at the base of the monument and opens at 8:30. | Mall at 15th St. NW | 202/426–6839 or 202/426–6841 | www.nps.gov | Free | Daily 9–5.

RELIGION AND SPIRITUALITY

Basilica of the National Shrine of the Immaculate Conception. The eighth-largest church in the world and the largest Catholic church in the Western Hemisphere, it has 60 chapels (most in mosaic) and 6 oratories. | 400 Michigan Ave. NE 20017 | 202/526–8300 | www.nationalshrine.com | Free | April–Oct., daily 7–7; Nov.–April, daily 7–5; guided tours Mon.–Sat. 9–11 and 1–3, Sun. group tours available by special arrangement.

Franciscan Monastery. This Byzantine-style monastery holds facsimiles of Holy Land shrines, such as the Grotto of Bethlehem and the Holy Sepulchre, as well as extensive gardens and a gift shop. Guided tours are given of the underground reproductions of the catacombs of Rome. | 1400 Quincy St. NE | 202/526–6800 | www.pressroom.com/~fransciscan | Free | Daily 9–4; Sun. afternoons only; tours on the hour from 1 Mon.–Sat., Sun. 1–4.

Islamic Center. This center offers prayer services and provides help to the community. See the elaborate and colorful two-room mosque inside. | 2551 Massachusetts Ave. NW | 202/332–8343 | Free | Daily 10–5, guided tours except during Fri. prayer service.

National Presbyterian Church and Center. Moved to this site in the 1960s, this large house of worship with a congregation of 2,000 is notable for its Chapel of the Presidents—among others, Eisenhower and Bush knelt there—its evocative stained-glass windows, and a bell tower overlooking the city. | 4101 Nebraska Ave. NW | 202/537–0800 | www.natpresch.org | Free | Daily 8–5, tours after 11 Sun. service.

New York Ave. Presbyterian Church. John Quincy Adams and Abraham Lincoln worshiped at this church, which has been rebuilt but still contains Lincoln's pew, as well as a handwritten Emancipation document (preceding the actual Proclamation). One of the stained-glass windows shows Lincoln standing in prayer. | 1313 New York Ave., at H St. NW | 202/393–3700 | www.nyapc.org | Free | Daily; services Sun. 8:45 and 11.

DISTRICT OF
COLUMBIA

INTRO
ATTRACTIONS
DINING
LODGING

St. John's Church. The oldest Episcopal church in Georgetown (1796), it has a Federal-style exterior and a gothic interior with colonial accents as a result of a 1950s renovation. Its stained-glass windows are worth a look. | 3240 O St. NW | 202/338–1796 | Free | Weekdays 9–noon and 1–4. Closed Sat.; Sun. services 9 and 11.

★ **Washington National Cathedral.** This landmark is among D.C.'s most awesome buildings, with a central tower that stands 676 feet above sea level, making it the highest point in the city. The sixth-largest cathedral in the world, and the second largest in U.S., at one tenth of a mile long, it boasts 215 stained-glass windows and many gargoyles (special gargoyle tours are available). Summer hours vary. | Massachussets and Wisconsin Aves. NW | 202/537–6207, 202/537–6247, or 202/537–6200 | www.cathedral.org | $3 (suggested donation) | Daily 10–4:30. Tours Mon.–Sat. 10–11:30 and 12:45–3:15, Sun. 12:30–2:45.

SHOPPING

Chinatown. This vibrant though fairly small neighborhood is full of Chinese restaurants and shops but it's being encroached on by the growing business district. | G and H Sts. between 6th and 8th Sts. NW | No phone.

Eastern Market. The last existing old food market in D.C., this block becomes a bustling farmers' market on Saturdays (with some arts and crafts) and an eclectic, culturally diverse flea market on Sundays. | 225 7th St. SE | 202/546–2698 | Free | Tues.–Sat. 7–6, Sun. 8–4.

Shops at National Place. This large atrium contains a variety of shops—jewelry, clothing, music, books, newsstand, and more—as well as a food court. Its in the heart of downtown, so if you can't find what you want at the shops, hit nearby neighborhoods for more options. | National Press Building, F St. between 13th and 14th Sts. | Free, parking at meters or a garage | Daily | No phone.

Union Station. D.C.'s train station, this hulking yet graceful structure has been hip since its renovation in the 1980s. It contains numerous restaurants and quick-stop eateries, as well as shops and movie theaters, and is very popular with teenagers. | Massachusetts Ave. between 1st NW and 1st St. NE | 202/371–9441 | Free | Daily.

SIGHTSEEING TOURS

Gold Line/Gray Line bus tours. Among the numerous city tours are an all-day tour of public buildings (monuments, museums, the Smithsonian Institution), an embassy row tour, a ride to Mount Vernon, Virginia, an after-dark excursion, and a multilingual tour. Tours vary in length; most have early morning departures, about 8:30. | Union Station, 50 Massachusetts Ave. NE | 301/386–8300 or 800/862–1400 | www.graylinedc.com | $25–$73 | Daily.
Tourmobile Sightseeing. Extensive bus tours of the city, with guided commentary, cover all major attractions on the Mall, the White House, Ford's Theatre, the FBI building, the Capitol, Smithsonian Museum, presidential memorials, and more. Twilight tours (3 hours) start from Union Station. You can board at any stop and get on and off as often as you want in one day. The bus stops along the Mall and at all major attractions marked with blue-and-white signs. | The Mall | 202/554–7950 | www.tourmobile.com | $16 | Daily 9–6:30.

SPECTATOR SPORTS

The NFL's **Washington Redskins** play at FedEx Field. | Arena Dr., Landover, MD | Redskin offices at 21300 Redskin Park Drive, Ashburn, VA | 703/478–8900; 301/276–6050 for tickets | www.redskins.com.

The **Washington Wizards,** a painfully bad NBA team, has one plus: Their low popularity makes it easy for you to score tickets to see your favorite team in D.C. | MCI Center, 601 F St. NW | 202/432–7328 | www.nba.com/wizards | $19–$75.

Exciting and unpredictable, the **Washington Capitals** went to the NHL Stanley Cup finals in 1998, then failed to make the playoffs in 1999. Tickets are rarely hard to acquire. | MCI Center, 601 F St. NW | 202/661–5050 | www.washingtoncaps.com.

OTHER POINTS OF INTEREST

If you're in the area for more than, say, five or six days, you should consider a day trip or an overnight to one of the nearby towns or outdoor attractions that are within easy striking distance of the city. To the west, out on Interstate 66, lie **Shenandoah National Park, Sky Meadows Park,** and, farther south, off Interstate 81, the **Blue Ridge Parkway.** To the east are the Naval Academy home and exclusive sailing community of **Annapolis** and the rest of the **Chesapeake Bay,** as well as the **Atlantic Ocean beaches** of Delaware, Maryland, and Virginia (they're unremarkable but can be a soothing respite from Washington's summer heat).

Just 45 minutes north of town is **Baltimore,** with its spectacular aquarium (in the lively Inner Harbor), bustling evening action on Fell's Point, and pro sports teams—the Orioles (baseball) and Ravens (football).

Chesapeake and Ohio Canal Boat Rides. Take a 1-hour (about 1 mile) mule-driven boat ride, including a lift through a lock, with narration by costumed staff as well as music and history. Boats run only between Memorial Day and Labor Day. | 1057 Thomas Jefferson St. NW | 202/653–5190 | $7.50 | Daily.

National Aquarium. See 250 species of fish, invertebrates, amphibians, and reptiles during your self-guided 45-minute tour. | Commerce Department Building, 14th St. between Constitution and Pennsylvania Aves. NW | 202/482–2826 | $3 | Daily 9–5.

National Zoological Park. On 163 rolling acres in Rock Creek Park, this zoo has a wide variety of fauna including elephants, giraffes, primates, bison, a komodo dragon, big cats, birds of prey, and a panda. There are also educational exhibits, such as a re-creation of an Amazon rain forest, as well as food stands on site. | 3001 Connecticut Ave. NW | 202/673–4800 | www.si.edu/natzoo/ | Free; charge for parking | May–Sept. 15, daily 6 AM–8 PM (animal buildings 10–6); Sept. 16–Apr., daily 6–6 (animal buildings 10–4:30).

Pavilion at the Old Post Office. Saved from the wrecking ball by city activists in the 1960s, this 19th-century, long-defunct post office headquarters now offers tours of the observation tower and its bells. Downstairs are eateries and shops. | Pennsylvania Ave. between 11th and 12th Sts. NW | 202/606–8691 or 202/289–4224 | Free | Old Tower mid-Apr.–Labor Day, daily 8 AM–10:45 PM; Labor Day–early Apr., daily 10–5:45; shops and eateries daily 7:30 AM–9 PM.

Voice of America. Tour the newsrooms and studios of this international radio broacaster, which brings America's voice to the world in 53 languages. Hear it in Swahili, if you like, and check out the outfit's two TV studios. Tours last about 45 minutes. | 330 Independence Ave. SW between 3rd and 4th Sts SW; enter on C St. | 202/619–3919 | Free | Weekdays 2:30; reservations required.

Washington Harbour. This is one of D.C.'s places to be seen on sunny weekends and balmy nights, as diners, partyers and river walkers pack the bars, restaurants, and promenade to enjoy other people and the aquatic view. Boaters frequently dock at the wooden promenade. Establishments include the River Front, Sequoia, and Tony & Joe's. | 30th & K Sts NW | No phone | Free | Daily.

Dining

INEXPENSIVE

Aditi. Indian. A red carpet and plants adorn this two-level restaurant, connected by a spiral staircase, and mirrors reflect the mellow lighting of this Georgetown favorite. Specialties include chicken tikka massala (boneless chicken with tomato sauce) and tandoori meat and fish. | 3299 M St. NW | 202/625–6825 | $6–$15 | AE, D, DC, MC, V.

Armand's Chicago Pizzeria. Pizza. Eat inside, in this old-fashioned space with wood floors and an open kitchen, or outside in the semi-enclosed patio. As its name indicates, the eatery, in Chinatown, is known for its deep-dish pizza and also serves sandwiches and salads. | 4231 Wisconsin Ave. NW | 202/686–9450 | $3–$14 | AE, D, MC, V.

Austin Grill. Tex-Mex. This bright, lively, three-level space in the Northwest section has a bar at the entrance and dining areas with music-themed artwork. It's the place to go for tacos, burritos, and the special enchiladas with three sauces. Saturday and Sunday brunch. | 2404 Wisconsin Ave. NW | www.austingrill.com | 202/337–8080 | $9–$13 | AE, D, DC, MC, V.

Bua. Thai. Three blocks from Dupont Circle, this elaborate restaurant with subdued lighting has a balcony patio upstairs and a bar downstairs. Specialties are pad thai and curry. Open-air patio dining. | 1635 P St. NW | 202/265–0828 | www.buathai.com | $7.95–$12.95 | AE, D, DC, MC, V.

C. F. Folks. American. If you're in a retro mood midday, drop into this Dupont Circle 1950s-style lunch counter for a burger, sandwich, or salad. The menu, which changes daily and seasonally, also has Cajun food on Monday, Mexican on Tuesday, and so forth. Outdoor dining. | 1225 19th St. NW | 202/293–0162 | Closed weekends. No dinner | $7–$11 | No credit cards.

Café Mozart. German. Traditional is the word for this restaurant two blocks from the White House. It's behind a deli and boasts white tablecloths and red napkins at dinner, and such specialties as Viennese veal schnitzel and sauerbraten (marinated beef). There's entertainment Fridays and Saturdays. | 1331 H St. NW | 202/347–5732 | www.cafemozart-germandeli.com | Breakfast also available | $9–$23 | AE, D, DC, MC, V.

City Lights of China. Chinese. This Art Deco spot at Dupont Circle makes the top restaurant critics' list every year. Mint-green booths and elegant silk-flower arrangements conjure up breezy spring days, even in the midst of a frenzied rush. The traditional Chinese fare is excellent. Try lamb in tangy peppery sauce, and shark's fin soup. | 1731 Connecticut Ave. NW | 202/265–6688 | www.citylightsofchina.com | $8–$15 | AE, D, DC, MC, V.

Fio's. Italian. Copper pots and Italian prints adorn this casual spot in a 1950s building overlooking Rock Creek Park. The restaurant is known for softshell crabs in season as well as Southern Italian preparations of squid, lamb, veal, and pasta. | 3636 16th St. NW | 202/667–3040 | Closed Mon. and last 3 weeks in Aug. No lunch | $7–$16 | AE, D, DC, MC, V.

4912. Thai. You can enjoy intimate dining in this small room, with low, romantic lighting and carpeted floors, as well as on an outdoor patio overlooking Wisconsin Avenue, in the area between the Friendship Pike and Tenleytown metro stations. Try the ginger chicken with basil and chili, and spicy bean curd. | 4912 Wisconsin Ave. NW | 202/966–4696 | $9–$13 | AE, D, DC, MC, V.

Guapo's. Mexican. Sip a margarita in this festive well-lit dining room or alfresco among youthful aficionados at umbrella-shaded tables in front of the restaurant, near the Tenleytown metro stop. Popular dishes include camarones (shrimp) tequilla, and mariscados (seafood). | 4515 Wisconsin Ave. NW | 202/686–3588 | www.guaposrestaurant.com | $5–$10 | AE, D, MC, V.

Haad Thai. Thai. This bright and beachy Capitol city restaurant has depictions of all things islandy adorning the walls, adding to the enjoyment of such dishes as ginger chicken, spicy bean curd, and duck with garlic sauce. | 1100 New York Ave. NW | 202/682–1111 | No lunch Sun. | $9–$15 | AE, DC, MC, V.

★ **Jaleo.** Spanish. Colorful murals lend a festive air to the dining room and busy raised bar area in this downtown tapas spot. With only three true entrées on the menu, you're encouraged to make a meal of such enticing tapas as skewered garlic shrimp and grilled chorizo. Sevillian dancers entertain on Wednesday nights. | 480 7th St. NW | 202/628–7949 | tapas $3.50–$8 | AE, D, DC, MC, V.

Jandara. Thai. Enjoy fish, chicken, and seafood combinations in this unpretentious Woodley Park space amid colorful American-style surroundings, or eat outdoors in front of the restaurant. | 2606 Connecticut Ave. NW | 202/387–8876 | $5–$13 | AE, DC, MC, V.

Mr. Yung's. Chinese. This cozy room, softened by burgundy and almond shades, is a quiet and elegant Chinatown enclave. Among Cantonese favorites, try baked jumbo shrimp sautéed with garlic, butter, and spicy sauce; eggplant with seafood; or steamed lobster in garlic sauce. | 740 6th St. NW | 202/628–1098 | $6.50–$29.95 | AE, D, DC, MC, V.

Park Bench Pub. American/Casual. This typical American café in Cleveland Park, adorned with photos of D.C. benches (hence the name), serves oversize sandwiches and salads. Downstairs there's a smoky bar with comfortable lounge seating and occasional live music. | 3433 Connecticut Ave. NW | 202/686–9235 | $7–$15 | AE, D, DC, MV, V.

Pizzeria Paradiso. Italian. You'll find such family-friendly fare as pizzas plain and fancy (with potatoes and pesto), salads, and sandwiches at this casual, bright eatery in Dupont Circle. Beer and wine only. No smoking. | 2029 P St. NW | 202/223–1245 | $6.95–$15.95 | DC, MC, V.

Saigon Gourmet. Vietnamese. Try the shrimp Saigon, pork on skewer, or Saigon-roasted noodles either in the simply designed interior or on the patio, across the street from National Zoo in Woodley Park. | 2635 Connecticut Ave. NW | 202/265–1360 | $7–$11 | AE, D, DC, MC, V.

Saigonnais. Vietnamese. Pictures of political luminaries and celebrities adorn the walls in this bright, modern space in Adams Morgan. Fare includes grilled lemon chicken and ginger duck. | 2307 18th St. NW | 202/232–5300 | No lunch Sun. | $9–$15 | AE, MC, V.

Sholl's Colonial Cafeteria. American. You walk through the line at this large basement cafeteria with a friendly staff, choosing such standbys as chicken, roast beef, and stew, and you seat yourself. It's often busy at lunch but the crowd turns over quickly. Early dinner ends at 8 weekdays. | 1990 K St. NW | 202/296–3065 | Breakfast also available. No dinner Sun. | $1.85–$5.95 | No credit cards.

Thai Kingdom. Thai. In this Farragut West gallery-style space with elaborate paintings, you can enjoy ginger chicken, curry chicken, noodles, and squid. Open-air dining. | 2021 K St. NW | 202/835–1700 | $9–$14 | AE, DC, MC, V.

The Tombs. American. This basement pub and resturant is a Georgetown neighborhood and university institution, with a lively bar in front and a sunken dining section in the rear. Known for its fabulous burgers. Sunday brunch. | 1226 36th St. NW | 202/337–6668 | $10–$20 | AE, D, DC, MC, V.

MODERATE

Anna Maria's. Italian. Quaint and cozy, with low lighting, linen tablecloths, and a 100-seat balcony, this old-fashioned place in Dupont Circle specializes in satisfying homemade pastas and has a 50-bottle wine list. | 1737 Connecticut Ave. NW | 202/667–1444 | www.washingtonpost.com | No lunch weekends | $9.95–$28.95 | AE, DC, MC, V.

Bistrot Lepic. French. This pleasant, casual sidewalk bistro in Georgetown has a dark interior with yellow and green accents and eclectic art. You can choose among salmon or veal dishes as well as typical bistro classics. | 1736 Wisconsin Ave. NW | 202/333–0111 | Closed Mon. | $13.95–$19.95 | AE, D, DC, MC, V.

Bombay Club. Indian. Only a block from the White House, this airy room has white linen tablecloths and attentive service befitting the high-powered clientele, including U.S. presidents. There's green-chili chicken, tandoori salmon, and tandoori lamb chops, as well as an extensive vegetarian menu. You can also eat at the sidewalk café, where the tables are attractive with tablecloths, flowers, and umbrellas. Pianist nightly. Sunday brunch. | 815 Connecticut Ave. NW | 202/659–3727 | No lunch Sat. | $13–$19 | AE, DC, MC, V.

Bombay Palace. Indian. The subdued burgundy-colored interior of this downtown restaurant, with original artworks, comfortable chairs, and etched glass, is just right for dining on tandoori prawns or chicken, lamb pilaf, or pungent vegetable curries. No smoking. | 2020 K St. NW | 202/331–4200 | $8–$25 | AE, DC, MC, V.

Burma. Burmese. Surrounded by tapestries, oil paintings, wood carvings, and puppets in this downtown spot, you can dine exotically on tamarind fish, mango pork, and fried eggplant and squash in a peppery sauce. | 740 6th St. NW | 202/638–1280 | No lunch weekends | $15 | AE, D, DC, MC, V.

DISTRICT OF
COLUMBIA

INTRO
ATTRACTIONS
DINING
LODGING

Busara. Thai. This retro spot in Cobble Park recalls a Hollywood diner. You can also eat in the garden with a fountain. | 2340 Wisconsin Ave. NW | 202/337–2340 | www.busara.com | $12–$24 | AE, D, DC, MC, V.

Clyde's of Georgetown. American. You can opt for pan-roasted Alaskan salmon, crab cakes, or rotisserie chicken in this wood-and-tile homey restaurant, the flagship place of a popular local chain, which serves until 2 AM weekdays, 3 AM weekends. Kids' menu. | 3236 M St. NW | 202/333–9180 | www.clydes.com | $13–$25 | AE, D, DC, MC, V.

Coppi's Vigorelli. Italian. The long, narrow, low-lit room in Cleveland Park has a small bar with framed posters of Italian bicycle-racing glory. Specialties include pasta, tuna, and catfish cakes. Kids' menu. | 3421 Connecticut Ave. NW | 202/244–6437 | No lunch Sun. | $14–$18 | AE, D, DC, MC, V.

Etrusco. Italian. This Mediterranean-style space in Dupont Circle, with bright colors and tiled floors, also has sidewalk dining, amid trees and shrubs. The restaurant is known for its fresh seafood. | 1606 20th St. NW | 202/667–0047 | Closed Sun. No lunch | $11–$17 | AE, DC, MC, V.

Garrett's. American. Once the residence of Maryland's governor T. S. Lee (1794), this popular party spot for young adults in Georgetown has three bars and four dining rooms and is known for barbecued ribs, steaks, and pasta. | 3003 M St. NW | 202/333–1033 | $12–$18 | AE, D, DC, MC, V.

Guards. Continental. This old- English country-style pub with three fireplaces serves up veal, Angus beef, and fresh seafood, and has been a Georgetown institution for more than 30 years. The attached dance bar, the Griffin Room, is open weekends until 2 AM. Sunday brunch. | 2915 M St. NW | 202/965–2350 | $13–$23 | AE, D, DC, MC, V.

The Grill From Ipanema. Brazilian. The restaurant is in Adams-Morgan but you can imagine yourself in Brazil in this evocative place, festive with bright oranges, yellows, and palm-tree greens. Try the seafood, grilled specials, and spiced paella. Live music. Saturday and Sunday brunch. | 1858 Columbia Rd. NW | 202/986–0757 | www.thegrillfromipanema.com | No lunch weekdays | $11–$22 | AE, D, DC, MC, V.

Hunan Chinatown. Chinese. You'll find nicer than average Chinese adornments and oriental art in this modern two-floor restaurant. Try one of the Hunan or Szechwan specialties. | 624 H St. NW | 202/783–5858 | $10–$20 | AE, D, DC, MC, V.

J. Paul's. Contemporary. A Georgetown institution in the heart of the action, this saloon-style 1892 building has a 65-foot mahogany bar and an equally long selection of beers and scotches. Raw bar. Kids' menu. Saturday and Sunday brunch. | 3218 M St. NW | 202/333–3450 | www.capitalrestaurants.com | $12–$22 | AE, D, DC, MC, V.

Johnny's Half Shell. Seafood. Opened in 1999, this Dupont Circle space in a turn-of-the-century building has clean lines and muted colors. It's lively and fun and is known for its raw bar and fresh seafood. | 2002 P St. NW | 202/296–2021 | Closed Sun. | $12–$22 | MC, V.

Kramerbooks and Afterwords. American. This hip, artsy bookstore-cum-café with both counter and table service is a haunt of the young Dupont Circle crowd, especially on weekends until the wee hours. Fare includes steak, seafood, salad, and pasta, which you can also enjoy at tables on the sidewalk. Entertainment Thursday through Sunday. Sunday brunch. | 1517 Connecticut Ave. | 202/387–1462 | Breakfast also available. Open 24 hrs. weekends | $13–$16 | AE, D, MC, V.

Krupin's. Kosher. Here in the quiet neighborhood of Tenleytown, with its network of quaint alleyways, you'll find this superb Jewish deli in 1950s diner surroundings, with the owner's personal photos on the walls. Known for their matzoh ball soup, corned beef sandwiches, and potato pancakes. Kids' menu. | 4620 Wisconsin Ave. NW | 202/686–1989 | Breakfast also available | $12–$15 | AE, DC, MC, V.

La Chaumiére. French. A Georgetown favorite, this romantic, rustic country restaurant (the name means "thatch-roof cottage") has a fireplace in the middle of the dining room. Dishes include quenelles of pike, rabbit stew, calf's brains, and wild game. | 2813 M St. NW | 202/338–1784 | Reservations essential | Closed Sun. No lunch Sat. | $14–$28 | AE, DC, MC, V.

La Colline. French. At this Capitol Hill restaurant you'll find attentive service in a cheerful comfortable setting, with murals and glass dividers and surrounded by windows. It's known for seasonal selections that include soft-shell crab, as well as fowl and other game. | 400 N. Capitol St. NW | 202/737–0400 | Breakfast also available. Closed Sun. No lunch Sat. | $13–$24 | AE, DC, MC, V.

La Fourchette. French. It's in Adams-Morgan but it looks like a Left Bank bistro, with exposed brick walls and large murals of the owner/chef's native France. Daily specials might include grilled salmon, lobster, duck, or rack of lamb in addition to the usual bistro fare. Outdoor patio dining. | 2429 18th St. NW | 202/332–3077 | No lunch weekends | $13–$25 | AE, DC, MC, V.

Lavandou. French. Provencale in spirit and fare, this sunny place in residential Cleveland Park has a large bay window, exposed wood beams, French artwork and murals, and colorful tablecloths. It's known for its huge menu. Try the mussel preparations, chicken liver, grilled meats, and soups. | 3321 Connecticut Ave. NW | 202/966–3002 | Reservations essential | No lunch weekends | $7–$19 | AE, DC, MC, V.

Lebanese Taverna. Middle Eastern. This bright, relaxing space in Woodley Park, an area rich in international restaurants, is simple but elegant with a touch of Lebanese history and culture. Fare includes shish kebab, shrimp, salmon, and Arabic bread baked in a wood-burning oven. | 2641 Connecticut Ave. NW | 202/265–8681 | No lunch Sun. | $14–$17 | AE, D, DC, MC, V.

Les Halles. French. At this downtown restaurant you will find French dining—with American touches—on three levels, ranging from light and lively to romantic and cozy. There are also cloth-covered tables and umbrellas on a patio out front. Selections include steak and great fries. Kids' menu. Sunday brunch. | 1201 Pennsylvania Ave. NW | 202/347–6848 | $14–$24 | AE, D, DC, MC, V.

Maggiano's Little Italy. Italian. This homey restaurant near Chevy Chase serves up such family-style fare as homemade lasagna and chicken parmigiana. There's also a café area up front. | 5333 Wisconsin Ave. NW | 202/966–5500 | www.maggianos.com | $14–$18 | AE, MC, V.

Market Inn. Seafood. Off Capitol Hill, this romantic 1959 restaurant with white tablecloths and candles also has 19th-century nude portraits and sheet music lining the walls The restaurant is known for she-crab soup and lobster, as well as soft-shell crabs called "whales," jumbo shrimp, and crab gumbo. The patio is open for lunch. Live music nightly. Jazz Sunday brunch. Kids' menu. | 200 E St. SW | 202/554–2100 | www.marketinnrestaurant.com | No lunch Sat. | $14–$25 | AE, D, DC, MC, V.

Marrakesh. Moroccan. This restaurant is an exotic anomaly in the downtown part of the city better known for auto-supply shops. Meals are served in shared containers at your table and are eaten without silverware (flat bread is used as a scoop). The first dish is chicken with lemon and olive, followed by beef or lamb, then vegetable couscous, fresh fruit, mint tea, and pastries. | 617 New York Ave. NW | 202/393–9393 | Reservations essential | Lunch only for groups of 10 or more by reservation | $25 per person for dinner | No credit cards.

McCormick and Schmick's. Seafood. With an old-fashioned yet shimmering interior (think wood and brass), this downtown restaurant has an open grill and a dark-wood bar area. Fresh fish is the specialty but there's also steak and pasta. Kids' menu. | 1652 K St. NW | 202/861–2233 | www.mccormickandschmicks.com | No lunch weekends | $12–$24 | AE, D, DC, MC, V.

Melrose. Eclectic. In Foggy Bottom, this restaurant is sunny, light, and airy by day, romantic and candle-lit by night. Enjoy dinner on the patio near the antique garden fountain in season. The food ranges from Thai calamari salad with lemongrass and mint to lobster risotto with fresh asparagus and sautéed spinach. Pianist nightly, big band Friday and Sat-

DISTRICT OF
COLUMBIA

INTRO
ATTRACTIONS
DINING
LODGING

urday. Kids' menu. Sunday brunch. | 1201 24th St. NW | 202/955–3899 | Breakfast also available | $13–$30 | AE, D, DC, MC, V.

Meskerem. Ethiopian. This cheery restaurant in the Adams-Morgan district is bright and colorful with skylights and Ethiopian art. You eat on leather cushions on the floor at tables like large woven baskets. Dishes include stews made with spicy berbere chili sauce and kitfo (a buttery beef dish served raw like steak tartare or very rare), all scooped up with homemade bread. Live Ethiopian music Friday and Saturday. | 2434 18th St. NW | 202/462–4100 | $10–$15 | AE, D, DC, MC, V.

Monocle on Capitol Hill. Seafood. Maroon carpeting, white tablecloths, raspberry walls, white beams, and political quotes in gold letters set the scene for the politicians who gravitate here. Homey dishes include fish, crab, and steak. Kids' menu. | 107 D St. NE | 202/546–4488 | Closed weekends except for special events | $12–$25 | AE, DC, MC, V.

Mr. Smith's. American. This old dark-wood tavern in Woodley Park has a brighter dining area and small garden patio on the lower level. There is piano music nightly and bands play on weekends. Sunday brunch. | 3104 M St. NW | 202/333–3104 | www.mrsmiths.com | $12–$20 | AE, DC, MC, V.

Murphy's of DC. Irish. Drop into this standard-issue Woodley Park pub (lots of wood, fireplace) for a beer and some Irish stew, steak, a burger, or seafood. Outdoor patio dining. Kids' menu. Beer and wine only. | 2609 24th St. NW | 202/462–7171 | $10–$15 | AE, DC, MC, V.

Music City Roadhouse. Southern. With brick walls, exposed beams, pool tables, and a jukebox, this funky joint serves up fried chicken, pot roast, and ribs. Kids' menu. Sunday brunch. | 1050 30th St. NW | 202/337–4444 | Closed Mon. No lunch Tues.–Sat. | $12–$18 | AE, D, DC, MC, V.

Old Ebbitt Grill. American/Casual. This downtown brightly lit, bustling old-fashioned saloon with raised bar is in an early 1900s former theater (though only the facade remains). The fare includes pasta, steak, and seafood, which can also be eaten outdoors in a covered patio. Sunday brunch. | 675 15th St. NW | 202/347–4801 | www.clydes.com | Breakfast also available | $13–$25 | AE, D, DC, MC, V.

Paolo's. Italian. This bustling Georgetown hangout has marble floors and earth tones; the back dining area is darker and cozier than the bright and lively café. The place is known for gorgonzola and pesto tortellini, grilled filet mignon, and pastas. There's open-air dining in a patio on the sidewalk in view of Wisconsin Street. Live jazz Sunday afternoon. Saturday and Sunday brunch. | 1303 Wisconsin Ave. NW | 202/333–7353 | $12–$27 | AE, D, DC, MC, V.

Primi Piatti. Italian. Italian-themed with murals and low lighting, this spot in Foggy Bottom is known for such northern-style dishes as tuna carpaccio. In season there's outdoor dining on a sidewalk patio surrounded by plants. | 2013 I St. NW | 202/223–3600 | www.primipiatti.com | Closed Sun. No lunch Fri.–Sat. | $13–$25 | AE, DC, MC, V.

Raku. Pan-Asian. A retro bustling spot in Dupont Circle, and reminiscent of a real Asian diner, this place draws a young crowd for its noodles and dumplings, which can also be eaten outdoors at the sidewalk tables shaded with umbrellas. | 1900 Q St. NW | 202/265–7258 | $10–$15 | MC, V.

Sushi-Ko. Japanese. Blurring of American 1950s-style and modern Japanese accents creates a clean and understated interior. This Georgetown favorite is known for its sushi bar, as well as traditional and modern Japanese dishes. | 2309 Wisconsin Ave. NW | 202/333–4187 | www.sushiko.com | No lunch weekends, Mondays | $13–$18 | AE, MC, V.

Tony Cheng's Mongolian Barbecue. Pan-Asian. There's a barbecue station in the center of this Chinatown eatery, where chefs cook the raw ingredients you hand-pick. It's an impressive operation with a genuine Mongolian staff. Try your selections stir-fried, grilled, or steeped tableside. | 619 H St. NW | 202/842–8669 | $14.95 for all–you–can eat buffet at dinner | AE, MC, V.

EXPENSIVE

Asia Nora. Pan-Asian. The soft light illuminating this two-level space, adorned with Asian artifacts, sets a romantic tone for the healthful East-meets-West variations on Asian cuisine. It's in the West End, between Foggy Bottom and Dupont Circle metro stops. | 2213 M St. NW | 202/797–4860 | www.noras.com | Closed 2 weeks before Labor Day and Sundays. No lunch | $19–$26 | AE, MC, V.

Bacchus. Middle Eastern. You can start a meal in this Dupont Circle basement spot with stuffed grape leaves and follow with a flavorful chicken dish or lamb shish kebab. | 1827 Jefferson Pl. NW | 202/785–0734 | No lunch Sat. Closed Sun. | $16–$20 | AE, MC, V.

Billy Martin's Tavern. American. Attractive with its shiny dark-wood bar, Tiffany lamps, and country accents, this casual Georgetown restaurant has an attentive staff and serves up crispy crab cakes, grilled salmon, and prime rib. Outdoor patio dining. Saturday and Sunday brunch. | 1264 Wisconsin Ave. NW | 202/333–7370 | www.billymartinstavern.com | Breakfast also available | $20–$35 | AE, D, DC, MC, V.

Bistro Français. French. If you're a late diner, you'll find yourself in the company of chefs who dine on steak frites and rotisserie chicken at this Georgetown bistro until the wee hours. Daily special might include duck confit or roast pork. Open weekends until 4 AM. Saturday and Sunday brunch. Early-bird dinners. | 3128 M St. NW | 202/338–3830 | $17–$25 | AE, DC, MC, V.

Café Atlantico. Caribbean. In this spacious three-floor restaurant downtown you can face the neighborhood or the kitchen, and there are cloth-covered tables with blue umbrellas for open-air dining. The place is known for guacamole and Jamaican jerk chicken. The bar is active on weekends. | 405 8th St. NW | 202/393–0812 | Reservations essential | No lunch Sun. | $25–$40 | AE, DC, MC, V.

Café Milano. Italian. The hip Euro scene at this Georgetown café is more fitting for a fun night out than for romantic dining but the cooking is sophisticated and good. Try the roasted veal chop, roasted duck breast, pasta, or light-crusted pizza. There's a streetside patio for alfresco dining. | 3251 Prospect St. NW | 202/333–6183 | www.cafemilano-dc.com | $15–$25 | AE, DC, MC, V.

The Capitol Grill. Steak. Upscale and opulent, this New York-style steak house downtown has large stuffed chairs, personal wine lockers, a cigar bar, and a lounge area. D.C.'s who's who flock here for you-know-what, as well as seafood. | 601 Pennsylvania Ave. NW | 202/737–6200 | www.thecapitolgrill.com | No lunch weekends | $18–$30 | AE, D, DC, MC, V.

Cashion's Eat Place. American. In Adams-Morgan, this modern, bustling place with a mirrored dining room and a raised bar area is one of D.C.'s "in" restaurants for all ages. You can eat such popular fare as roasted chicken or halibut inside or at an umbrella-shaded table on the patio. Sunday brunch. | 1819 Columbia Rd. NW | 202/797–1819 | Closed Mon. No lunch Tues.–Sat. | $16–$22 | MC, V.

Coco Loco. Brazilian. This hip Latin place downtown entices with its bright colors, abundant plants, and a rocking dance floor from Thursday to Saturday. Carnivores go for the churrasqueria (a variety of rotisserie-grilled meats) carved tableside and served with fried potatoes and unlimited salad from the buffet. There is also an extensive tapas menu and alfresco dining in a small courtyard garden. Entertainment Thursday through Saturday. | 810 7th St. NW | 202/289–2626 | No lunch Sat. Closed Sun. | $23 buffet | AE, DC, MC, V.

DC Coast. Contemporary. A 9-foot mermaid stands sentry over you at this downtown hot spot in a 1929 building. The 35-foot ceilings and a balcony open up the main dining room, which mixes Art Deco and contemporary accents. The restaurant is known for seafood dishes from the Atlantic, Pacific, and Gulf Coasts. | 1401 K St. NW | 202/216–5988 | www.dccoast.com | No lunch Sat. Closed Sun. | $15–$26 | AE, D, DC, MC, V.

Donatello. Italian. In a rustic turn-of-the-century townhouse near Foggy Bottom, you can enjoy such popular dishes as lobster-stuffed ravioli, veal chops, and fresh seafood, including calamari. There is also outdoor dining under a canopy with glass windows, year-round. | 2514 L St. NW | 202/333–1485 | www.donatello-dc.com | No lunch weekends | $20–$32 | AE, D, DC, MC, V.

Filomena Ristorante. Italian. Relax in this plant-filled homey restaurant with large windows overlooking the canal in Georgetown as you enjoy ravioli and other pastas and veal parmesan. Saturday and Sunday brunch. | 1063 Wisconsin Ave. NW | 202/338–8800 | $17–$26 | AE, D, DC, MC, V.

Fran O'Brien's. Steak. The surroundings in this cigar-friendly place two blocks from the White House include a lounge and a sports bar, plastered with the requisite memorabilia. Carnivores go for the array of steaks but there are also some vegetarian dishes and seafood, including lobster, crab cakes, and salmon. Kids' menu. | 1001 16th St. NW | 202/783–2599 | No lunch weekends | $19–$44 | AE, D, DC, MC, V.

Gabriel. Latin. Lots of wood, earth tones, low lighting, and candle-lit tables make for cozy dining in this Dupont Circle downstairs space. Dishes are prepared with an innovative touch, and there's a full tapas menu. Sunday brunch. | 2121 P St. NW | 202/956–6690 | www.gabriel.com | Breakfast also available | $17–$27 | AE, D, DC, MC, V.

★ **Galileo.** Italian. An exhibition-style kitchen is the focal point of this downtown 30-seat contemporary dining room with enormous floral arrangements and regional Italian artwork. The outdoor terrace, holding tables under a canopy, seats 75. Selections include Piedmontese ravioli, white truffle risotto, and rack of veal with wild mushrooms. | 1110 21st St. NW | 202/293–7191 | www.robertodonna.com | Reservations essential weekends | No lunch weekends | $22–$31 | AE, D, DC, MC, V.

Georgia Brown's. Southern. Designed by Adam Tihany, this casual but upscale downtown restaurant is great for spotting D.C.'s power elite while you tuck into meat loaf, crispy fried chicken livers, or the popular fried green tomatoes. In fine weather, you can dine alfresco in a small garden-like space. Live jazz/blues Sunday brunch. | 950 15th St. NW | 202/393–4499 | www.capitalrestaurants.com | $15–$21 | AE, D, DC, MC, V.

★ **Gerard's Place.** French. This cozy, romantic downtown space has modern artworks adorning warm terra cotta walls, as well as tables with flowers and umbrellas on the outdoor terrace. The restaurant is known for its sophisticated contemporary cooking; try the scallops with parsley mousse, an appetizer, and follow up with lobster with ginger and mango. | 915 15th St. NW | 202/737–4445 | No lunch Sat. Closed Sun. | $20–$41 | AE, DC, MC, V.

Goldoni. Italian. Enjoy a good meal in this downtown two-story Venetian-style establishment with tile flooring. A full-service bar is downstairs, while upstairs sets a quaint and romantic tone for daily seafood specials and such pastas as agnolotti (round, veal-stuffed pasta). Free parking. | 1120 20th St. NW | 202/293–1511 | No lunch weekends | $15–$30 | AE, D, DC, MC, V.

Hogate's. Seafood. Popular among theatergoers (it's across the street from the Arena stage in Waterfront), this old mariner-themed restaurant has seven dining rooms and two outdoor decks with a view of the Potomac marina. Dishes include pasta, steak, and chicken, as well as seafood. Live jazz Sunday brunch. Kids' menu. | 800 Water St. SW | 202/484–6300 | $17–$37 | AE, D, DC, MC, V.

I Matti Trattoria. Italian. This two-story Adams-Morgan spot falls between fancy and casual, with original Italian artworks and wall murals. It's known for traditional Tuscan cooking. | 2436 18th St. NW | 202/462–8844 | No lunch Sun. Closed Mon. | $30–$35 | AE, DC, MC, V.

★ **I Ricchi.** Italian. Terra-cotta tiles, cream-color archways, and floral frescoes make this a pretty, airy dining room in Dupont Circle. It's a favorite of critics and upscale crowds for its hearty Tuscan cuisine, often prepared on the wood-burning grill or oven. Try rolled pork roasted in wine and fresh herbs or grilled lamb chops. | 1220 19th St. NW | 202/835–0459 | No lunch Sat. Closed Sun. | $19–$30 | AE, DC, MC, V.

The Jefferson. Contemporary. Original Jeffersonian-era documents dot the entrance to this small, softly lighted downtown dining spot with brown leather chairs and white linen tablecloths. The room has Native American artworks, and there's a fireplace in the lounge area. Try the grilled rare ahi tuna with roasted fennel, mushroom-crusted Chilean sea bass, or the pepita-crusted lamb chop. You can also take tea from 3 to 5 daily. Sunday brunch. | 1200 16th St. NW | 202/833-6206 | www.camberleyhotels.com | Reservations essential | Jacket and tie | Breakfast also available | $23–$30 | AE, D, DC, MC, V.

Kinkead's. Seafood. Among D.C.'s hottest restaurants, this Foggy Bottom favorite is comfortable yet elegant and slightly formal, with spacious booths, muted green and beige tones, cherry wood, and an exhibition kitchen. There's a more relaxed café area downstairs and a tiny outdoor front patio. The kitchen turns out New England-style seafood with Asian and Latin accents. Live jazz nightly. Sunday brunch. | 2000 Pennsylvania Ave. NW | 202/296–7700 | www.kinkead.com | $21–$28 | AE, D, DC, MC, V.

Lauriol Plaza. Latin. This hip, two-story restaurant has lots of windows, high ceilings, and views of the Adams-Morgan neighborhood from all tables. Outdoor seating options include rooftop or streetfront. Try the fajitas, masitas del puerco (pork), paella, pollo (chicken) asado, and the daily seafood specials. Sunday brunch. | 1835 18th NW | 202/387–0035 | $20 | AE, D, DC, MC, V.

Luigino. Italian. Enjoy contemporary cooking with Piedmont (northern) accents in a bright room with an open kitchen, large windows, and cathedral ceilings. This downtown restaurant is known for ravioli with spinach and ricotta, baked and grilled fish (including imported rockfish), game in winter (including suckling pig and venison), and brick-oven pizza. There's also open-air dining at cloth-covered tables with umbrellas in the patio. Kids' menu. | 1100 New York Ave. NW | 202/371–0595 | www.luigino.com | No lunch weekends | $15–$26 | AE, D, DC, MC, V.

Morrison-Clark. American. This beautiful 1864 Victorian inn downtown is perfect for intimate dining. In season there's a courtyard in back with cloth-covered tables and umbrellas. Try numerous variations of rabbit, and for dessert, the lemon chess pie. Sunday brunch. | 1015 L St. NW | 202/898–1200 | www.morrisonclark.com | No lunch Sat. | $18–$25 | AE, D, DC, MC, V.

Nathans. American/Casual. The saloon-style bar, stocked with more than 270 kinds of liquor, has sailing-themed prints and teak floors, which contrasts with the English country-hunt dining room. This Georgetown restaurant is known for risotto, basil fettuccine with lobster, and a double-thick barbecued pork chop. DJ on weekends. Saturday and Sunday brunch. | 3150 M St. NW | 202/338–2000 | $16–$28 | AE, DC, MC, V.

New Heights. Eclectic. The upstairs dining room of this Woodley Park restaurant is bright and airy, with lively watercolors and a wall of windows overlooking Rock Creek Park. Specialties include black bean paté, buttermilk fried oysters, and *palak paneer* (Indian vegetarian dish). In season you can eat alfresco underneath two cherry trees. Sunday brunch. | 2317 Calvert St. NW | 202/234–4110 | No lunch Mon.–Sat. | $18–$29 | AE, D, DC, MC, V.

Occidental Grill. American. A downtown Washington institution since 1906, this spot is oldschool politico, underscored by stately, dark wood and myriad images of prominent 20thcentury Americans. The kitchen is known for New York strip steak and North Atlantic salmon. | 1475 Pennsylvania Ave. NW | 202/783–1475 | www.occidental.com | $19–$34 | AE, D, DC, MC, V.

Old Europe Restaurant and Rathskeller. German. Come to this classical Old World European restaurant in Glover Park for such hearty fare as sauerbraten (marinated beef) served with potato dumplings and red cabbage, and wiener schnitzel (breaded veal) with fried potatoes and house salad. The downstairs rathskeller is available for large parties. Pianist Thursday, Friday, and Saturday. Kids' menu. | 2434 Wisconsin Ave. NW | 202/333–7600 | No lunch Sun. | $19–$21 | AE, DC, MC, V.

The Oval Room. American. The meticulously done-up cream-color dining room downtown is rich and presidential, with glimmering chandeliers and a bar. Selections change sea-

DISTRICT OF
COLUMBIA

INTRO
ATTRACTIONS
DINING
LODGING

sonally; the restaurant is known for seafood, including excellent crab cakes and shrimp, as well as rack of lamb. There's outdoor dining in a flower garden. Pianist Wednesday through Saturday. | 800 Connecticut Ave. NW | 202/463–8700 | Closed Sun. No lunch Sat. | $15–$25 | AE, DC, MC, V.

Palm. Steak. This topnotch downtown steak house, part of a small nationwide chain, is a favorite of Washington power-brokers, and its walls are covered with caricatures of the famous who have dined here. If you don't fancy a huge steak you can opt for seafood. | 1225 19th St. NW | 202/293–9091 | www.thepalm.com | No lunch weekends | $15–$31 | AE, DC, MC, V.

Pesce. Seafood. This casual, bustling spot in Dupont Circle has renditions of colorful fish gracing the wall. The menu changes daily, and well-prepared seafood is what you get. | 2016 P St. NW | 202/466–3474 | No lunch Sun. | $19–$20 | AE, D, DC, MC, V.

Prime Rib. Steak. Black lacquer walls and high-back leather chairs lend a clubby tone to this 1950s New York-style steak house downtown. It's known for blue ribbon sirloin steak, and crab imperial. Live music nightly. | 2020 K St. NW | 202/466–8811 | www.primerib.com | Jacket and tie | Closed Sun. No lunch Sat. | $18–$39 | AE, DC, MC, V.

Saveur. Contemporary. You'll find a blend of French and California cuisines in this fairly casual Foggy Bottom spot with warm colors and moderate lighting. Fare includes tilapia (a mild white fish), bouillabaisse, and rack of lamb. Sunday brunch. | 2218 Wisconsin Ave. NW | 202/333–5885 | Reservations essential weekends | $18–$25 | AE, D, DC, MC, V.

Sea Catch. Seafood. This casual spot is in an 1890s building (purportedly where the computer was invented), with candle-lit tables and a patio overlooking the Georgetown canal. The restaurant is known for its fresh seafood, especially lobster and crab cakes, which have been voted the best in D.C. by *Washingtonian* magazine. | 1054 31st St. NW | 202/337–8855 | Closed Sun. | $15–$25 | AE, D, DC, MC, V.

Sequoia. American. A view of the Potomac is the main attraction of this Georgetown spot. The large, high-ceilinged atrium allows two levels in one room and there's also an extensive outdoor terrace perfect for brunch in season. Saturday and Sunday brunch. | 3000 K St. NW | 202/944–4200 | $10.95–$49.95 | AE, D, DC, MC, V.

Senses Restaurant and Bakery. French. This carpeted establishment, accented with modern art, is light and intimate. You might want to start with an appetizer of slow-braised rabbit and then move on to risotto with duck confit or exotic mushrooms, or the Moroccan chicken tangine. All desserts are made in-house. Try the decadent chocolate mousse dome. | 3206 Grace St. NW | 202/342–9083 | Breakfast also available. No dinner Sun. Closed Mon. | $18–$31 | AE, DC, MC, V.

701 Pennsylvania Avenue. Continental. Sweeping columns and etched glass frame views of outdoor fountains and give this rich space an understated elegance. Downtown near the Shakespeare Theatre, it's convenient for a meal before or after. There's also an outdoor patio with a view of the Navy Memorial. Pianist Sunday through Thursday, jazz combo weekends. | 701 Pennsylvania Ave. NW | 202/393–0701 | No lunch weekends | $18–$24 | AE, DC, MC, V.

Tony and Joe's. Seafood. This nautical-themed Georgtown spot is best for outdoor eating in fine weather, with its wide patio and bar overlooking the Potomac. Fare includes lobster, soft-shell crab, and stuffed salmon steak. Entertainment Tuesday through Saturday. Sunday brunch. | 3000 K St. NW | 202/944–4545 | $17–$30 | AE, D, DC, MC, V.

Two Quail. Contemporary. In this quaint restaurant, unusual for Capitol Hill, you'll be reminded of an eccentric grandmother's house—with overstuffed armchairs and lots of candles in a small, romantic dining area. Known for its vegetarian dumplings and old-fashioned double-stuffed pork chops. Sunday brunch. | 320 Massachusetts Ave. NE | 202/543–8030 | www.washingtonpost.com | No lunch weekends | $16–$24 | AE, D, DC, MC, V.

Vidalia. Southern. With such country farmhouse accents as harvest displays, this Dupont Circle folksy spot in a medium-lit basement is named for a Georgia onion; onions are indeed prominent on the menu in season. Try the crab cakes, sweetbreads, and lemon chess pie. | 1990 M St. NW | 202/659–1990 | Closed Sundays in summer. No lunch weekends | $24–$29 | AE, D, DC, MC, V.

VERY EXPENSIVE

Aquarelle. Eclectic. This bright, 80-seat restaurant in the Watergate complex of the Watergate Hotel has fabulous views of the Potomac and waterfront Georgetown. Try the caviar and corn soup with lobster for appetizers and then the swordfish or the Angus steak with garlic vegetables. Early-bird dinner. Sunday brunch. | 2650 Virginia Ave. NW | 202/298–4455 | Breakfast also available | $40 | AE, D, DC, MC, V.

Be Du Ci. Mediterranean. There's a lot to fill the eye in this Dupont Circle glass-enclosed room, which incorporates white tablecloths, banquettes, and stuffed heavy chairs plus high-end contemporary art (there's an attached deli, too). It's known for seafood, including shellfish, as well as paella. | 2100 P St. NW | 202/223–3824 | Closed late Aug. No lunch Sun. No lunch Sat. in winter | $30–$45 | AE, D, DC, MC, V.

Jockey Club. Continental. This Dupont Circle establishment is old money and clubby, with dim lighting, dark-paneled wood, and red-and-white-checkered tablecloths—reserved, yet down-to-earth. It's known for Nancy Reagan's chicken salad and rack of lamb. | 2100 Massachusetts Ave. NW | 202/835–2100 | Jacket and tie | Breakfast also available | $25–$40 | AE, D, DC, MC, V.

Lafayette. Continental. Visiting dignitaries and assorted power brokers flock to this extremely formal upscale dining establishment, across the street from the White House. While the fish dishes are the hottest items on the menu, don't overlook the duck breast, veal chops, or the bison. Pianist nightly. Sunday brunch. | 800 16th St. NW | 202/638–2570 | Reservations essential | Jacket and tie | Breakfast also available | $45 | AE, D, DC, MC, V.

Lespinasse. French. This is a grand, elegant space downtown with museum-quality paintings, two huge chandliers, and a hand-carved ceiling. Try the shellfish bouillon with quinoa, sorrel, and fenugreek; cauliflower-sweet pea papadum croustade with tamarind; or squab breast with potatoes and périgord truffles. | 923 16th St. NW | 202/879–6900 | Reservations essential | Jacket required | Closed Sun. and Mon. | $26–$34 | AE, D, DC, MC, V.

Marcel's. French. There's a bright Mediterranean look to the stone walls and tile floors of this restaurant's two dining rooms—one overlooking Pennsylvania Avenue and the other facing L Street—and there's also a bar. The cooking is Provençal. | 2401 Pennsylvania Ave. NW | 202/296–1166 | Closed Sun. No lunch Sat. | $26–$34 | AE, DC, MC, V.

★ **Michel Richard Citronelle.** French. Five-star chef Michel Richard heads this classy Georgetown restaurant, with its glassed-in exhibition kitchen and an extensive wine cellar. There's also a mood wall, which changes color every 59 seconds. Try the tuna tartare, terrine of smoked salmon, shiitake mushroom napoleon, shrimp wrapped in kataife, and crunchy apricot napoleon with ginger sauce for dessert. | 3000 M St. NW | 202/625–2150 | www.citronelledc.com | No lunch weekends | $65 prix–fixe | AE, D, DC, MC, V.

Morton's of Chicago. Steak. The Georgetown branch of this high-end chain is a bright, lively and upscale space serving enormous steaks, such as double filet mignon and New York strip sirloin. You can also opt for whole baked lobster as well as lamb, chicken, and fish. | 3251 Prospect St. NW | 202/342–6258 | www.mortons.com | No lunch | $23–$33 | AE, DC, MC, V.

Nora. Contemporary. This converted Dupont Circle carriage house adorned with antique Amish quilts makes for romantic dining. On the changing menu you might find soft-shell crabs in season as well as rockfish, grilled lamb chops, risotto, and organically grown greens. No smoking. | 2132 Florida Ave. NW | 202/462–5143 | Closed 2 weeks before Labor Day and Sundays. No lunch | $22–$30 | AE, MC, V.

Obelisk. Italian. Light cream-gray tones, natural wood accents, and large floral arrangements create an understated elegance in this small restaurant on the second floor of a Dupont Circle townhouse. The 5-course prix-fixe menu changes daily and the dishes—from pasta to meat, fish, and poultry—are simply and elegantly prepared. No smoking. | 2029 P St. NW | 202/872–1180 | Closed Sun.–Mon. No lunch | $47–$49 prix fixe | DC, MC, V.

Red Sage. Contemporary. Rich and warm with Southwestern accents, the multimillion-dollar interior of this downtown spot is a pseudo-adobe warren of dining rooms, with lizards and barbed wire enhancing the theme. The kitchen serves up pecan-crusted chicken, buffalo tenderloin, and pheasant sausage-stuffed quail. [For cheaper fare, try the Tex-Mex at the chili bar and café upstairs.] | 605 14th St. NW | 202/638–4444 | www.redsage.com | No lunch Sun. Closed Sun. in summer | $21–$37 | AE, D, DC, MC, V.

Sam and Harry's. Steak. This lavishly decorated Dupont Circle spot with wine displays, stuffed chairs, and a large dark-wood bar specializes in Kansas City strip steak and Maine lobster. | 1200 19th St. NW | 202/296–4333 | www.samandharrys.com | Closed Sun. No lunch Sat. | $25–$35 | AE, D, DC, MC, V.

1789. American. The five dining rooms in this restored Georgetown mansion have different themes (colonial, Civil War, etc.), and the food is unpretentious and tasty. Try black bean soup with unsweeted chocolate and the seafood stew. | 1226 36th St. NW | 202/965–1789 | Jacket required | No lunch | $24–$36 | AE, D, DC, MC, V.

Taberna del Alabardero. Spanish. This traditional, dimly lit Basque-style room downtown has Spanish paintings on the walls and the occasional Flamenco dancer. Start with tapas and go on to gazpacho and paella. Open-air dining. | 1776 I St. NW | 202/429–2200 | www.alabardero.com | Jacket required | Closed Sun. No lunch Sat. | $24–$36 | AE, D, DC, MC, V.

Lodging

INEXPENSIVE

Adams Inn. This is the only bed-and-breakfast in Adams-Morgan, D.C.'s lively multicultural neighborhood. The inn, with a private garden, occupies three Victorian houses two blocks from the National Zoo. Rooms vary in size. | 27 rooms. Complimentary Continental breakfast. No TV, cable TV in common area. Laundry services. Business services, parking (fee). | 1744 Lanier Pl. NW | 202/745–3600 or 800/578–6807 | fax 202/319–7958 | www.adams-inn.com | $65–$80 | AE, D, DC, MC, V.

Best Western Downtown Capitol Hill. It's a small European-style branch of a chain between downtown and Capitol Hill, with easy access to the Mall and Metro. | 58 rooms. Restaurant, bar with live jazz Tues.,Thurs., room service. Cable TV. Free parking. | 724 3rd St. NW | 202/842–4466 or 800/842–4831 | fax 202/842–4831 | www.bestwestern.com/downtown-capitolhill | $120–$130 | AE, D, DC, MC, V.

Braxton Hotel. Six blocks from the White House, this hotel draws mostly young backpackers. Room sizes vary (some are tiny) and all have private baths. | 60 rooms. Complimentary breakfast. Some microwaves, some refrigerators. Cable TV. Parking (fee). | 1440 Rhode Island Ave. NW | 202/232–7800 or 800/350–5759 | fax 202/265–3725 | $50–$90 | AE, MC, V.

Brickskeller Inn. A quaint, no-frills inn with shared baths, it's in a 1912 building convenient to downtown and Georgetown. The bar has an extensive beer selection and a bar menu. | 1523 22nd St. NW | 202/293–1885 | fax 202/293–0996 | 40 rooms. Bar. No TV. | $66 | AE, D, DC, MC, V.

Capitol Hill Suites. It's an all-kitchenette-suite hotel with basic American design in a historic residential neighborhood behind the Library of Congress. The lobby is cozy and the rooms are comparatively large. | 152 rooms. Complimentary Continental breakfast. Refrigerators. Cable TV. Business services, parking (fee). | 200 C St. SE | 202/543–6000 or 800/424–9165 | fax 202/547–2608 | $125 | AE, D, DC, MC, V.

Center City Hotel. This former Travelodge sits between the old (and still active) business center and the new office buildings and sports arena of Chinatown. The lobby is spacious, with vending machines. | 100 rooms. Restaurant, complimentary Continental breakfast. In-room data ports. Laundry facilities. Business services. Parking (fee). | 1201 13th St. NW | 202/682–5300 | fax 202/371–9624 | www.centercityhotel.com | $99 | AE, D, DC, MC, V.

Days Inn Gateway. This chain property is 4 mi away from the White House, the Capitol, and the Vietnam Memorial, 2 mi north of Howard University, and 3 mi northeast of Union Station. Restaurant. Cable TV. Outdoor pool. Exercise equipment. Laundry facilities, laundry service. Free parking. | 2700 New York Ave. NE | 202/832–5800 or 800/544–8313 | fax 202/269–4317 | www.daysinn.com | 193 | $49–$99 | AE, D, DC, MC, V.

Embassy Inn. In Dupont Circle, amid old churches, homes, and office buildings, this small four-story hotel (no elevator) originally built as an eight-unit apartment building in 1910, maintains some of its original accents, such as mosaic entrance tiles and marble staircase. Afternoon sherry is served in the lobby lounge. | 38 rooms. Complimentary Continental breakfast. Cable TV. | 1627 16th St. NW | 202/234–7800 or 800/423–9111 | fax 202/234–3309 | $89–$129 | AE, D, DC, MC, V.

Embassy Suites. Conveniently just west of downtown (toward Georgetown), this all-suite chain hotel is a home away from home, with a large lobby enlivened with fountains and waterfalls. | 318 suites. Restaurant, bar, complimentary breakfast, room service. In-room data ports, microwaves, minibars, refrigerators. Cable TV. Indoor pool. Hot tub. Exercise equipment. Business services, parking (fee). | 1250 22nd St. NW | 202/857–3388 | fax 202/293–3173 | www.embassy-dc.com | $119–$300 | AE, D, DC, MC, V.

Hotel Harrington. Family-owned and operated since 1914, this downtown hotel is in an older brick building with a cozy, contained lobby and is ideal for families and students. | 250 rooms, 40 deluxe rooms (2 adjoining rooms). Three restaurants, bar. Cable TV. Laundry facilities. Business services, parking (fee). Some pets allowed. | 436 11th St. NW | 202/628–8140 or 800/424–8532 | fax 202/343–3924 | reservations@hotel-harrington.com | www.hotel-harrington.com | $85, $125 deluxe rooms | AE, D, DC, MC, V.

Hotel Sofitel. This chain property, in a tastefully refurbished 1904 apartment building, sits at the juncture of upper downtown and the tony Kalorama neighborhood. | 104 rooms, 40 suites. Restaurant, bar, room service. In-room data ports, minibars. Cable TV. Exercise equipment. Business services, parking (fee). Some pets allowed. | 1914 Connecticut Ave. NW | 202/797–2000 or 800/424–2464 | fax 202/462–0944 | www.sofitel.com | $99–$159, $119–$259 suites | AE, D, DC, MC, V.

Howard Johnson. Just outside downtown, this chain hotel is a 10-minute walk from the White House and the Metro. | 184 rooms. Restaurant, bar. In-room data ports, some kitchenettes. Cable TV. Pool. Exercise equipment. Laundry facilities. Business services, parking (fee). | 1430 Rhode Island Ave. NW | 202/462–7777 | fax 202/332–3519 | $119 | AE, D, DC, MC, V.

Kalorama Guest House at Kalorama Park. The property, with a private garden, is on a residential side street two blocks from Adams-Morgan and a 10-minute walk from the Metro. Only three parking spaces are available, so ask about them when you reserve your room. | 30 rooms (some with shared baths), 5 suites. Complimentary Continental breakfast. Some room phones, no TV in some rooms, TV in common area. Business services, parking (fee). | 1854 Mintwood Pl. NW | 202/667–6369 | fax 202/319–1262 | www.washingtonpost.com/yp/kgh | $90, $120 suites | AE, D, DC, MC, V.

Kalorama Guest House at Woodley Park. Around the corner from the National Zoo and a five-minute walk from the Metro, this low-key facility in two converted turn-of-the-century townhouses has an antique-accented sitting room. Only two parking spaces are available, so ask about them when you reserve your room. | 19 rooms (7 with shared baths), 2 suites. Complimentary Continental breakfast. No room phones, TV in common area. Laundry services. Parking (fee). No kids under 5. No smoking. | 2700 Cathedral Ave. NW | 202/328–0860 | fax 202/328–8730 | www.washingtonpost.com/yp/kgh | $85, $105 suites | AE, D, DC, MC, V.

DISTRICT OF
COLUMBIA

INTRO
ATTRACTIONS
DINING
LODGING

Lincoln Suites. A modern studio-suite hotel with a quaint lobby, it's centrally located downtown. A king or two double beds are available. | 99 rooms. In-room data ports, some kitchenettes, microwaves, refrigerators. Cable TV. Business services, parking (fee). | 1823 L St. NW | 202/223–4320 or 800/424–2970 | fax 202/223–8546 | www.lincolnhotels.com | $109–$179 | AE, D, DC, MC, V.

Quality Hotel Downtown. This basic chain branch is five blocks north of the White House and convenient to Dupont Circle and the rest of downtown. | 113 kitchenette units, 22 junior suites. Restaurant, bar, room service. In-room data ports, kitchenettes, microwaves, refrigerators. Cable TV. Exercise equipment. Laundry services. Business services, parking (fee). | 1315 16th St. NW | 202/232–8000 | fax 202/667–9827 | qualityht@erols.com | www.quality-suite.com/online/quality.html | $109–$139, $139–$199 junior suites | AE, D, DC, MC, V.

St. James Suites. This all-suite luxury property has a mix of antique and modern art and European-style furniture. There are full kitchens with irons and ironing boards, hair dryers, king or queen beds, and pull-out sofa beds. | 195 suites. Complimentary Continental breakfast. In-room data ports. Cable TV. Pool. Exercise equipment. Laundry facilities. Business services, parking (fee). | 950 24th St. NW | 202/457–0500 or 800/852–8512 | fax 202/659–4492 | www.stjamessuiteswdc.com | $119–$179 | AE, D, DC, MC, V.

State Plaza Hotel. This all-suite facility, with two rooftop sun decks, is near the U.S. State Department, DAR Constitution Hall, and the National Academy of Sciences, as well as within close walking distance of the Mall. Amenities include hair dryers, ironing boards, and full baths. | 223 suites. Restaurant, bar. In-room data ports, kitchenettes, microwaves. Cable TV. Exercise equipment. Laundry facilities. Business services, parking (fee). | 2117 E. St. NW | 202/861–8200 or 800/424–2859 | fax 202/659–8601 | www.stateplaza.com | $89–$130 | AE, D, DC, MC, V.

Taft Bridge Inn. Antique art fills the small, neoclassic-style guest house in a converted 1905 mansion near Dupont Circle, and within walking distance to the Zoo. Each room is slightly different. | 12 rooms (7 with shared baths, 3 with showers only). Complimentary breakfast. In-room data ports, no TV in some rooms. Laundry service. Parking (fee). No smoking. | 2007 Wyoming Ave. | 202/387–2007 | fax 202/387–5019 | tbi@pressroom.com | www.pressroom.com/~taftbridge | $99–$120 | MC, V.

Windsor Inn. This large bed-and-breakfast, all with private bath, is east of Dupont Circle, below Adams-Morgan and above downtown, convenient to much of the city center. | 45 rooms, 9 suites. Complimentary Continental breakfast. Some refrigerators. Cable TV. Business services. | 1842 16th St. NW | 202/667–0300 or 800/423–9111 | fax 202/667–4503 | www.bedandbreakfast.com | $109, $129–$179 suites | AE, DC, MC, V.

Windsor Park. An old-fashioned hotel in a quiet neighborhood surrounded by embassies, it has a small, pleasantly decorated lobby and a 15-seat conference room. It's two blocks from the Washington Hilton and a few blocks from downtown. | 43 rooms, 6 suites. Complimentary Continental breakfast. Refrigerators. Cable TV. Business services. | 2116 Kalorama Rd. NW | 202/483–7700 or 800/247–3064 | fax 202/332–4547 | www.windsorpark.com | $112, $155 suites | AE, D, DC, MC, V.

MODERATE

Best Western. This all-suite representative of the chain is six blocks from the White House and two blocks from the Metro. The hotel provides à la carte service from the many neighborhood eateries. | 76 suites. Complimetary Continental breakfast. Microwaves, refrigerators. Cable TV. Parking (fee). | 1121 New Hampshire Ave. NW | 202/457–0565 or 800/762–3777 | fax 202/331–9421 | www.bestwestern.com | $169 | AE; D, DC, MC, V.

The Canterbury Hotel. Small yet elegant, this boutique-style hotel, with 18th-century European reproduction furnishings and interiors, is just above the heart of downtown, near the metro and shops. | 99 rooms. Restaurant, bar, complimentary Continental breakfast. In-room data ports, kitchenettes, microwaves, refrigerators. Cable TV. Business services, parking (fee). | 1733 N. St. NW | 202/393–3000 or 800/424–2950 | fax 202/785–9581 | dccantbry2@aol.com | www.canterburydc.com | $185–$255 | AE, D, DC, MC, V.

Channel Inn. The only hotel on D.C.'s marine waterfront, it overlooks the Washington Channel, the marina, and the Potomac River. There's a nautical theme in the public areas. | 100 rooms, 2 suites. Restaurant, bar with entertainment, room service. In-room data ports. Cable TV. Outdoor pool. Parking (free). | 650 Water St. SW | 202/554–2400 or 800/368–5668 | fax 202/863–1164 | www.channelinn.com | $135, $150 business suites | AE, D, DC, MC, V.

Courtyard by Marriott. This European boutique-style chain property is four blocks north of Dupont Circle and the Metro, and is convenient to downtown, Adams-Morgan, and Woodley Park. | 147 rooms. Restaurant, bar. In-room data ports, some minibars. Cable TV. Outdoor pool. Exercise equipment. Laundry facilities. Business services, parking (fee). | 1900 Connecticut Ave. NW | 202/332–9300 or 800/842–4211 | fax 202/328–7039 | www.courtyard.com | $185 | AE, D, DC, MC, V.

Doubletree Park Terrace. This chain hotel, three blocks from downtown and six blocks from the White House, has a small lobby and European furnishings. | 220 rooms, 40 suites. Restaurant, bar, room service. In-room data ports, microwaves. Cable TV. Exercise equipment. Laundry facilities. Business services, parking (fee). | 1515 Rhode Island Ave. NW | 202/232–7000 | fax 202/332–7152 | www.doubletreehotels.com | $185, $225 suites | AE, D, DC, MC, V.

Embassy Square Suites. This all-suites chain hotel, in a lively neighborhood one block off Dupont Circle, attracts a mixed clientele of domestic and international professionals. The rooms are basic yet comfortable, and most have kitchenettes. | 278 suites. Complimentary Continental breakfast. In-room data ports, microwaves. Cable TV. Outdoor pool. Exercise equipment. Laundry facilities. Business services, parking (fee). | 2000 N. St. NW | 202/659–9000 or 800/424–2999 | fax 202/429–9546 | emsgreserv@staydc.com | www.staydc.com | $134–$209 | AE, D, DC, MC, V.

George Washington University Inn. This full-service boutique hotel in the heart of Foggy Bottom is a few blocks from the Kennedy Center and has Williamsburg-style furnishings. | 55 rooms, 40 suites. Restaurant, bar, room service. In-room data ports. Cable TV. Business services, parking (fee). | 824 New Hampshire Ave. NW | 202/337–6620 or 800/426–4455 | fax 202/337–2540 | www.gwuinn.com | $169, $209 suites | AE, D, MC, V.

Georgetown Suites. In a brick courtyard one block south of M Street, in the heart of Georgetown, the property has ample suites of various shapes, all with full kitchens, voice mail, hair dryers, irons, and ironing boards. | 234 suites. Kitchenettes, in-room data ports. Gym. Laundry service. Parking (fee). | 1111 30th St. NW | 202/298–7800 or 800/348–7203 | fax 202/333–5792 | www.georgetownsuites.com | $175–$195 | AE, DC, MC, V.

Holiday Inn Georgetown. This full-service Holiday Inn conveys a modern style, with a marble front desk and floors. It's in Georgetown, a few blocks north from the heart of the action and accessible from the Wisconsin Avenue exit off I–495. Rooms have irons, ironing boards, and hair dryers. | 296 rooms, 4 suites. Restaurant, bar, room service. In-room data ports. Cable TV. Outdoor pool. Exercise equipment. Laundry facilities. Business services, parking (fee). | 2101 Wisconsin Ave. NW | 202/338–4600 | fax 202/333–6113 | www.hospitalityonline.com/profiles/202500 | $179–$209, $250 suites | AE, D, DC, MC, V.

Holiday Inn on the Hill. This modern-style Holiday Inn with a cozy lobby is just two blocks from the Capitol and Union Station. The hotel caters to families. Kids under 19 stay free; kids under 12 eat free. | 342 rooms. Restaurant, bar. In-room data ports. Cable TV. Outdoor pool. Exercise equipment. Children's programs (age 4–14). Business services, parking (fee). | 415 New Jersey Ave. NW | 202/638–1616 | fax 202/638–0707 | www.holiday-inn.com/was/onthehill | $189 | AE, D, DC, MC, V.

Hotel George. One of D.C.'s hot spots, this contemporary boutique hotel on Capitol Hill is very modern and stylish with original pop art and the occasional celebrity sighting. The lobby and furnings are light and airy, and the restaurant, Bis, is among the hippest in the city. There's also a poolroom and cigar lounge. | 139 rooms. Restaurant, bar, room service.

DISTRICT OF
COLUMBIA

INTRO
ATTRACTIONS
DINING
LODGING

In-room data ports. Cable TV. Gym. Parking (fee). | 15 E St. NW | 202/347–4200 or 800/576–8331 | fax 202/347–4213 | www.hotelgeorge.com | $169–$265 | AE, D, DC, MC, V.

Hotel Lombardy. Convenient to Georgetown, downtown, and George Washington University, this European-style hotel has antique furniture and a helpful staff. Rooms are lavishly done up with imported German and Italian fabrics, Oriental rugs, and art by local artists. | 127 rooms, 44 suites. Restaurant. In-room data ports, minibars, refrigerators. Cable TV. Business services, parking (fee). | 2019 Pennsylvania Ave. | 202/828–2600 or 800/424–5486 | fax 202/872–0503 | www.hotellombardy.com | reservations@hotellombardy.com | $179, $199–$209 suites | AE, D, DC, MC, V.

Hotel Tabard Inn. Three Victorian town houses make up this quaint, popular hotel in Dupont Circle, with old Victorian and American Empire furniture, fireplaces, and outdoor patio. Rooms vary in size, and some share bathrooms. | 40 rooms, 25 with bath. Restaurant. In-room data ports, no TV in some rooms. Business services, parking (fee). | 1739 N St. NW | 202/785–1277 | fax 202/785–6173 | www.tabardinn.com/home.htm | $140–$175 | AE, D, DC, MC, V.

Jurys Normandy Inn. This small inn sits amid numerous embassies in a leafy neighborhood five minutes from downtown. There's a fireplace in the lobby, a small library, a conservatory—and complimentary wine and cheese are served on Tuesday evenings. Rooms are smoking and nonsmoking with French-European-style furnishings. Amenities include a desk, coffee/tea maker, hair drier, and an iron and ironing board. | 75 rooms. In-room data ports, refrigerators. Cable TV. Laundry facilities. Parking (fee). | 2118 Wyoming Ave. NW | 202/483–1350 or 800/424–3729 | fax 202/387–8241 | www.jurysdoyle.com | $150 | AE, D, DC, MC, V.

Jurys Washington Hotel. Formerly the Dupont Plaza and Doyle's, the hotel takes its Irish motif to the hilt, adorning its spacious lobby with art and artifacts from the Emerald Isle. You'll find a typical Irish pub on the premises of this Dupont Circle locale. | 314 rooms, 9 suites. Restaurant, bar. In-room data ports, minibars, refrigerators. Cable TV. Gym. Business services, parking (fee). | 1500 New Hampshire Ave. NW | 202/483–6000 or 800/423–6953 | fax 202/328–3265 | www.jurysdoyle.com | $185, $250 suites | AE, D, DC, MC, V.

Marriott Wardman Park Hotel. This three-building compound, part of the chain, sits on a rolling hill in Woodley Park, between the National Zoo and downtown. There are some modernized rooms but a number of antique-style rooms remain. | 1,206 rooms, 125 suites. Restaurant, bar. Some refrigerators. Cable TV. Outdoor pool. Exercise equipment. Business services, parking (fee). Some pets allowed. | 2660 Woodley Rd. NW | 202/328–2000 | fax 202/234–0015 | www.marriotthotels.com | $139, $350 suites | AE, D, DC, MC, V.

CAR RENTAL TIPS

- ❏ Review auto insurance policy to find out what it covers when you're away from home.
- ❏ Know the local traffic laws.
- ❏ Jot down make, model, color, and license plate number of rental car and carry the information with you.
- ❏ Locate gas tank—make sure gas cap is on and can be opened.

- ❏ Check trunk for spare and jack.
- ❏ Test the ignition—make sure you know how to remove the key.
- ❏ Test the horn, headlights, blinkers, and windshield wipers.

*Excerpted from *Fodor's: How to Pack: Experts Share Their Secrets*
© 1997, by Fodor's Travel Publications

Melrose. This boutique-style hotel with European furnishings (including English art) is conveniently located between the White House and Georgetown. | 223 rooms, 16 suites. Restaurant, bar, room service. In-room data ports, kitchenettes. Cable TV. Exercise equipment. Business services, parking (fee). | 2430 Pennsylvania Ave. NW | 202/955–6400 | fax 202/955–5765 | www.windham.com | $179–$358, $279–$358 suites | AE, D, DC, MC, V.

Monticello Hotel. Formerly the Georgetown Dutch Inn, this Georgian-style all-suites hotel is in a quiet area off M street. The one-bedroom suites have separate living areas and sofa beds, and TV in the bedroom and living room. The hotel provides free passes to a nearby gym. | 9 kitchen suites; 38 suites. Complimentary Continental breakfast. In-room data ports. Cable TV. Parking (fee). | 1075 Thomas Jefferson St. NW | 202/337–0900 or 800/388–2410 | fax 202/333–6526 | www.hotelmonticello.com | $169–$300 | AE, DC, MC, V.

★ **Morrison-Clark Inn.** A Victorian town house downtown, the inn has fireplaces in its club rooms, antique furnishings, and an outdoor courtyard for dining as part of its restaurant. Guest rooms have either neo-classical, French-country, or Victorian furnishings. | 43 rooms, 11 suites. Restaurant, complimentary Continental breakfast, room service. In-room data ports, minibars. Cable TV. Exercise equipment. Parking (fee). | 11th St. and Massachusetts St. NW | 202/898–1200 or 800/332–7898 | fax 202/289–8576 | www.morrisonclark.com | $165, $175 suites | AE, D, DC, MC, V.

River Inn. Filled with old country art and furnishings, the quaint all-suite boutique hotel is in a quiet townhouse-lined neighborhood close to Georgetown and George Washington University, only a short Metro ride from downtown. King and queen beds are available. All suites (some efficiency, some one-bedroom) have full kitchens. | 126 suites. Restaurant, bar. In-room data ports, microwaves. Cable TV. Health club. Business services, parking (fee). Some pets allowed (fee). | 924 25th St. NW | 202/337–7600 or 800/424–2741 | fax 202/337–6520 | riverinn@erols.com | www.theriverinn.com | $175–$245 | AE, DC, MC, V.

Washington Hilton and Towers. This chain property, with a grand, spacious lobby, adorned with chandeliers and modern carpeting, hosts numerous conventions, large meetings, and banquets. It's a true full-service hotel, a few blocks north of Dupont Circle. | 1,103 rooms, 15 suites. Restaurant, bar with pianist. In-room data ports, some minibars. Cable TV. Outdoor pool, wading pool. Three outdoor tennis courts. Gym. Business services, parking (fee). Some pets allowed. | 1919 Connecticut Ave. NW | 202/483–3000 | fax 202/232–0438 | www.washington-hilton.com | $175–$250, $350 suites | AE, D, DC, MC, V.

Washington Suites Georgetown. Between Georgetown and downtown, nine blocks from the White House and a few blocks from the heart of the business district, this all-suite hotel has a small, cozy lobby decorated with photos of D.C. monuments and the C&O Canal. | 124 kitchen suites. In-room data ports, microwaves. Cable TV. Business services, Parking (fee). Pets allowed (fee). | 2500 Pennsylvania Ave. NW | 202/333–8060 | fax 202/338–3818 | www.washingtonsuiteshotel.com | $129–$219 | AE, D, DC, MC, V.

Westin Grand Hotel. Rooms at this hotel, halfway between Georgetown and Foggy Bottom, are done in natural colors and have spacious work desks. There's a bright, airy atrium with meeting space encircling a private couryard, and black-and-white photos of D.C. landmarks grace the walls. The suites have hot tubs. | 262 rooms, 8 suites. Restaurant, bar, room service. In-room data ports, minibars. Cable TV. Outdoor pool. Exercise equipment. Business services, parking (fee). | 2350 M St. NW | 202/429–0100 | fax 202/857–0127 | www.starwoodhotels.com | $155–$390, $350–$550 suites | AE, D, DC, MC, V.

EXPENSIVE

Clarion Hampshire. Close to Dupont Circle, this hotel has 18th-century European furniture, though the plain room carpeting reminds you that you're in the U.S. | 82 rooms. Restaurant, bar, room service. In-room data ports, microwaves, minibars, refrigerators. Cable TV. Business services, parking (fee). | 1310 New Hampshire Ave. NW | 202/296–7600 or 800/368–5691 | fax 202/293–2476 | www.clarioninn.com | $209 | AE, D, DC, MC, V.

Georgetown Inn. In the heart of Georgetown, this redbrick boutique hotel is reminiscent of a gentleman's sporting club and provides upscale full service. The large rooms have colonial-style furnishings and rooms are done in burgundy and gray hues. | 96 rooms, 10 suites. Restaurant, bar, room service. In-room data ports. Cable TV. Gym. Business services, parking (fee). | 1310 Wisconsin Ave. NW | 202/333–8900 or 800/424–2979 | fax 202/625–1744 | $195, $205 suites | AE, D, DC, MC, V.

Governor's House. This well-appointed, traditional hotel has a casual elegance and is a couple of blocks from the city's main business center, yet in a comparatively quiet neighborhood. The suites have kitchenettes. | 139 rooms, 10 suites. Restaurant, bar, room service. In-room data ports. Cable TV. Outdoor pool. Exercise equipment. Business services, parking (fee). | 1615 Rhode Island Ave. | 202/296–2100 or 800/821–4367 | fax 202/331–0227 | www.governorshousewdc.com | $195, $225 suites | AE, D, DC, MC, V.

Grand Hyatt Washington. This chain hotel is downtown between the Capitol and the White House. It has a fanciful interior–a massive atrium containing a lagoon and an island holding a piano. It also boasts cigar and sports bars that were rated best in D.C. by *Washingtonian* magazine. | 842 rooms, 58 suites. Three restaurants, three bars with entertainment, room service. In-room data ports, minibars. Cable TV. Business services, parking (fee). | 1000 H St. NW | 202/582–1234 | fax 202/637–4781 | www.washingtongrandhyatt.com | $255–$305, $500 suites | AE, D, DC, MC, V.

Henley Park. Reminiscent of an English country house, this hotel is quaint and small and promises everything you need at your fingertips. It's eight blocks from the Smithsonian Museums, five blocks from the MCI Sports Arena. | 96 rooms, 10 suites. Restaurant, bar with entertainment, room service. In-room data ports, minibars (in suites), refrigerators. Cable TV. Business services, parking (fee). | 926 Massachusetts Ave. NW | 202/638–5200 or 800/222–8474 | fax 202/638–6740 | www.henleypark.com | $195, $245 suites | AE, D, DC, MC, V.

Hilton–Embassy Row. Well situated for business downtown or within the embassy community, this European-boutique-style hotel is also convenient to the restaurants and shops of Dupont Circle. | 193 rooms. Restaurant, bar with entertainment, room service. In-room data ports, microwaves, some refrigerators. Cable TV. Outdoor pool. Exercise equipment. Laundry service. Business services, parking (fee). | 2015 Massachusetts Ave. NW | 202/265–1600 | fax 202/328–7526 | www.hilton.com | $230–$265 | AE, D, DC, MC, V.

Holiday Inn–Capitol. One block from both the Air and Space Museum and the L'Enfant Metro station, this chain hotel has a rooftop pool that overlooks the Capitol. Rooms have green and tan color schemes, mahogany furniture, and paisley bedspreads, as well as irons, ironing boards, and hair dryers. | 529 rooms, 13 suites. Restaurant, bar. In-room data ports. Cable TV. Outdoor pool. Gym. Laundry facilities. Business services, parking (fee). | 550 C St. SW | 202/479–4000 | fax 202/479–4353 | www.holiday-inn.com | $199, $239 suites | AE, D, DC, MC, V.

Holiday Inn–Central. Hotel and Bass Resorts has ranked this as one of the top Holiday Inns in D.C. five years' running. It's also among the top Holiday Inns worldwide. The inn is centrally located and convenient to the White House and the Convention Center. | 210 rooms. Restaurant, bar, room service. In-room data ports, some refrigerators. Cable TV. Outdoor pool. Exercise equipment. Laundry facilities. Video games. Business services, parking (fee). | 1501 Rhode Island Ave. NW | 202/483–2000 | fax 202/797–1078 | holiday@inn-dc.com | www.inn-dc.com | $199 | AE, D, DC, MC, V.

★ **Hotel Washington.** This historic downtown property dating from 1918, has a popular rooftop bar with extensive views and is within walking distance of most major attractions. Rooms have various color schemes but all have painted walls and mahogany furniture. | 344 rooms, 16 suites. Restaurant, bar. In-room data ports. Cable TV. Exercise equipment. Business services, parking (fee). Some pets allowed. | 515 15th St. NW | 202/638–5900 or 800/424–9540 | fax 202/638–4275 | www.hotelwashington.com | $205 | AE, D, DC, MC, V.

Hyatt Regency Washington on Capitol Hill. Within a short walking distance of the Capitol, museums, and the Mall, this chain site has a huge atrium and is a popular spot for large conferences and other gatherings. The rooms have modern furnishings and king or two double beds, irons and ironing boards, and hair dryers. | 834 rooms, 32 suites. Restaurants, bar, room service. In-room data ports, minibars, some refrigerators. Cable TV. Indoor pool. Beauty salon. Gym. Business services, parking (fee). | 400 New Jersey Ave. NW | 202/737–1234 | fax 202/737–5773 | pr@hyattdc.com | www.hyatt.com | $250, $450 suites | AE, D, DC, MC, V.

Latham Hotel. Boasting an award-winning restaurant, Citronelle, and the only hotel swimming pool in Georgetown, this full-service European-style boutique property, elegantly appointed, is in the heart of D.C.'s most chic shopping district. | 143 rooms, 16 suites. Restaurant, bar, room service. In-room data ports. Cable TV. Outdoor pool. Business services, parking (fee). | 3000 M St. NW | 202/726–5000 or 800/368–5922 (800/528–4261 in D.C.) | fax 202/337–4250 | www.staywashingtondc.com | $215, $315 suites | AE, D, DC, MC, V.

Loews L'Enfant Plaza. Amid some government and private sector offices—and close to other Federal agencies—this French-themed hotel, in the center of L'Enfant Plaza, is within walking distance of the scenic Tidal Basin. The plaza's underground shops, eateries, and Metro add to the convenience. The rooms, on the top four floors, have views of monuments, the Potomac, or the Capitol. Amenities include 2 double beds or a king, hair dryers, irons and ironing boards, and coffeemakers. | 370 rooms, 21 suites. Restaurant, bar, room service. In-room data ports, minibars, refrigerators. Cable TV. Indoor/outdoor pool. Gym. Business services, parking (fee). Some pets allowed. | 480 L'Enfant Plaza SW | 202/484–1000 | fax 202/646–4456 | www.loewshotels.com/lenfanthome.html | $259, $375 suites | AE, D, DC, MC, V.

Marriott. This chain hotel representative is within walking distance of Georgetown and downtown. The lobby is spacious, and there are off-site restaurants and bars close by, to complement those in-house. | 418 rooms, 4 suites. Restaurant, bar. In-room data ports. Cable TV. Indoor pool. Hot tub. Exercise equipment. Business services, parking (fee). | 1221 22nd St. NW | 202/872–1500 | fax 202/872–1424 | www.marriott.com/marriott/waswe | $214, $300 suites | AE, D, DC, MC, V.

Marriott at Metro Center. The full-service chain hotel is atop the Metro Center subway station, next to the convention center and four blocks from the MCI Center. Rooms are done in beige and are accented with floral print bedspreads. | 456 rooms, 3 suites. Restaurant, bar, room service. In-room data ports. Cable TV. Indoor pool. Hot tub, sauna. Gym. Business services, parking (fee). | 775 12th St. NW | 202/737–2200 | fax 202/347–5886 | www.marriott.com | $209, $750 2-bedroom hospitality suites | AE, D, DC, MC, V.

Omni Shoreham. This elegant 11-acre grand dame has hosted the rich and famous since 1930. In Woodley Park, it's a 10-minute walk to downtown. Traditional guest rooms have cherry furniture and floral bedspreads, and and some rooms overlook Rock Creek Park. Amenities include hair dryers, irons and ironing boards, and coffeemakers. | 834 rooms, 60 suites. Restaurant, bar, room service. Cable TV. Indoor pool. Health Club. Business services, parking (fee). Shops. Some pets allowed. | 2500 Calvert St. NW | 202/234–0700 | fax 202/332–1373 | www.omnishoreham.com | $209, $399 suites | AE, D, DC, MC, V.

One Washington Circle. An all-suite, well-appointed European style hotel with a small cozy lobby, it's in Foggy Bottom, about eight blocks from the White House and convenient to Georgetown and George Washington University. There are four types of suites, from efficiency apartments to one-bedroom "supreme suites." Built in 1959, it is refurbished every two years. | 151 kitchen suites. Restaurant, bar with entertainment, room service. In-room data ports. Cable TV. Outdoor pool. Business services, parking (fee). | One Washington Circle NW | 202/872–1680 or 800/424–9671 | fax 202/887–4989 | sales@onewashcirclehotel.com | www.onewashcirclehotel.com | $229 | AE, DC, MC, V.

Radisson Barcelo. The large rooms at this luxury hotel located in the Dupont Circle area are especially suited for families. It's convenient to attractions and historic sites. | 301 rooms, 76 suites. Restaurant, bar, room service. In-room data ports. Cable TV. Outdoor pool. Exercise equipment. Business services, parking (fee). | 2121 P St. NW | 202/293–3100 | fax 202/857–0134 | www.radisson.com | $225, $425 suites | AE, D, DC, MC, V.

DISTRICT OF
COLUMBIA

INTRO
ATTRACTIONS
DINING
LODGING

Renaissance Washington. It's a convention hotel, big bright and airy, located directly across the street from the Convention Center's main entrance. Rooms are individually furnished, some in antique style, some modern; all the furniture is custom-made. | 801 rooms, 14 suites. Restaurant, bar, room service. In-room data ports, minibars. Cable TV. Indoor pool. Hot tub. Gym. Business services, parking (fee). Some pets allowed. | 999 9th St. NW | 202/898–9000 | fax 202/289–0947 | www.renaissancehotel.com | $199, $229 suites | AE, D, DC, MC, V.

Washington Court on Capitol Hill. A waterfall cascades in the lobby of this spacious luxury hotel, with its airy atrium lobby and abundant marble. It's just off of Capitol Hill. Room furnishings are modern, and amenities include hair dryers, irons and ironing boards, and coffeemakers. | 250 rooms, 15 suites. Restaurant, bar with pianist, room service. In-room data ports, refrigerators. Cable TV. Exercise equipment. Business services, parking (fee). | 525 New Jersey Ave. NW | 202/628–2100 or 800/321–3010 | fax 202/879–7918 | www.washingtoncourthotel.com | $259, $365 suites | AE, D, DC, MC, V.

Wyndham City Center. In the heart of D.C., midway between the White House and Georgetown and near the Foggy Bottom metro station, this chain property is within walking distance of the city's power corridor and convenient to attractions. The bright, spacious lobby has a lounge area and the bar carries the East Coast's largest collection of single malt scotch. | 351 rooms, 9 suites. Restaurant, bar, room service. In-room data ports. Cable TV. Exercise equipment. Business services, parking (fee). | 1143 New Hampshire Ave. NW | 202/775–0800 | fax 202/331–9491 | www.wyndham.com | $208, $350 junior suites | AE, D, DC, MC, V.

VERY EXPENSIVE

Capital Hilton. In the heart of downtown, this full-service, well-appointed hotel has a lobby with a raised bar area, TVs, and airline and Amtrak offices. The hotel hosts banquets, large meetings, and special events. The rooms are decorated with modern furniture and wallpaper. Amenities include hair dryers, irons, ironing boards, 2 double beds or king size beds. | 544 rooms, 41 suites. Two restaurants, bar with entertainment, room service. In-room data ports, minibars, some refrigerators. Cable TV. Barbershop, beauty salon. Exercise equipment. Business services, parking (fee). | 16th and K Sts NW | 202/393–1000 | fax 202/639–5784 | www.hilton.com | $295, $650 suites | AE, D, DC, MC, V.

Crowne Plaza Washington. This hotel is centrally located downtown, at Franklin Square on the K Street business corridor, one block from the Metro and close to the MCI Center, and National, Warner, and Ford's theaters. The rooms are contemporary in style and many have commanding views of the city skyline. The restaurant has a daily breakfast buffet. | 318 rooms, 17 king corner suites. Restaurant, bar, room service. In-room data ports. Cable TV. Gym. Business services, parking (fee). | 1375 K St. NW | 202/682–0111 or 800/637–3788 | fax 202/682–9535 | www.CrownePlazaWashington.com | $272, $369 suites | AE, D, DC, MC, V.

Four Seasons Hotel. This brick hotel at the east end of Georgetown overlooks Rock Creek Park from the back. The restaurant is superb, the lobby is inviting and comfortable, and the rooms are spacious and bright. Some have sunken tubs and all have an extensive array of amenities. | 260 rooms. Restaurant, bar, room service. In-room data ports, minibars. Cable TV. Indoor pool. Spa. Gym. Business services, parking (fee). Some pets allowed. | 2800 Pennsylvania Ave. NW | 202/342–0444 | fax 202/944–2076 | www.fourseasons.com | $410 | AE, D, DC, MC, V.

★ **Hay-Adams.** At this stately, historical, luxury property, with antiques and renaissance art, the motto is "Nothing is overlooked but the White House." The architecture is vintage Italian, and the rooms have elaborately carved moldings and marble bathrooms. The downtown spot is a favorite of visiting dignitaries. | 143 rooms, 42 suites. Restaurant, bar, room service. In-room data ports, minibars, some refrigerators. Cable TV. Business services, parking (fee). Some pets allowed. | 800 16th St. NW | 202/638–6600 or 800/424–5054 | fax 202/638–2716 | www.hayadams.com | $375–$570 | AE, D, DC, MC, V.

J. W. Marriott. No expense was spared at this flagship hotel of the chain, near the White House and next to the National Theatre, in creating an opulent environment for business or pleasure. Plush guest rooms have overstuffed chairs, thick carpets, and muted color schemes, while the marble and mirrored hallways display extensive artworks. | 772 rooms, 34 suites. Restaurant, two bars with entertainment, room service. In-room data ports, refrigerators (in suites). Some cable TV. Indoor pool. Hot tub, massage. Gym. Shops. Business services, parking (fee). | 1331 Pennsylvania Ave. NW | 202/393–2000 | fax 202/626–6991 | www.marriott.com/marriott/dc-042.htm | $269, $700 suites | AE, D, DC, MC, V.

★ **Jefferson Hotel.** This downtown hotel has elegant 18th-century European furnishings. Some rooms have fireplaces and partial views of monuments and The White House. | 100 rooms, 32 suites. Restaurant, bar, room service. In-room data ports, some microwaves. Cable TV, in-room VCRs (and movies). Business services, parking (fee). | 1200 16th St. NW | 202/347–2200 or 800/368–5966 | fax 202/331–7982 | jeffersonres@compuserve.com | www.camberleyhotels.com | $279, $349–$589 suites | AE, D, DC, MC, V.

The Madison Hotel. A luxury hotel frequented by foreign diplomats and high-octane business types, it is one block from the heart of downtown. Each European-style room is differently furnished. | 311 rooms, 30 suites. Restaurant, bar, room service. In-room data ports, minibars, refrigerators. Cable TV. Gym. Business services, parking (fee). | 1177 15th St., at M St. NW | 202/862–1600 or 800/424–8577 | fax 202/785–1255 | dcmadisonhotel@erols.com | www.dcmadisonhotel.com | $295, $435 suites | AE, DC, MC, V.

Park Hyatt. Modern art graces the lobby and common rooms of this upscale hotel about four blocks from the eastern end of Georgetown. The modern rooms have luxurious European-style furnishings. | 111 rooms, 113 suites. Restaurant, bar with pianist, room service. In-room data ports, refrigerators. Cable TV. Indoor pool. Beauty salon, hot tub, massage. Gym. Business services, parking (fee). | 24th & M Sts. NW | 202/789–1234 | fax 202/457–8823 | www.hyatt.com | $330, $390 suites | AE, D, DC, MC, V.

Phoenix Park Hotel. This classically furnished building, with its small lobby and foyer area and European flavor, is in the shadow of the Capitol and a short subway ride from downtown. | 148 rooms, 4 penthouse suites. Restaurant, bar with entertainment, room service. In-room data ports, minibars, some refrigerators. Cable TV. Exercise equipment. Business services, parking (fee). | 520 N. Capitol St. NW | 202/638–6900 or 800/824–5419 | fax 202/393–3236 | phoenixpark@worldnet.att.net | www.phoenixparkhotel.com | $299, $575 suites | AE, D, DC, MC, V.

Renaissance Mayflower. A very upscale, full-service National Historic Landmark hotel in the center of downtown, it draws a high-powered international clientele. | 660 rooms, 76 suites. Restaurant, bar with entertainment, room service. In-room data ports, refrigerators. Cable TV. Exercise equipment. Business services, parking (fee). | 1127 Connecticut Ave. NW | 202/347–3000 | fax 202/775–5895 | www.renaissancehotels.com | $275, $375 suites | AE, D, DC, MC, V.

St. Regis Hotel. This elegant luxury hotel, near the White House, is among the city's preferred spots for the business elite and visiting dignitaries. There's a roomy lobby, and the rooms, with desk and chair, have antique furniture and Italian marble bathrooms. | 194 rooms, 14 suites. Restaurant, bar, complimentary afternoon tea, room service. In-room data ports, minibars, refrigerators. Cable TV. Exercise equipment. Business services, parking (fee). Some pets allowed. | 923 16th St. NW | 202/638–2626 | fax 202/638–4231 | www.starwood.com | $460, $800 suites | AE, D, DC, MC, V.

Swissotel Washington–The Watergate. Rising up from the banks of the Potomac River, this hotel is part of the fashionable shopping district in Georgetown and is next to the Kennedy Center. The luxurious rooms, furnished in modern European style, have marble baths, irons and ironing boards, coffeemakers, and hair dryers. | 250 rooms, 89 suites. Restaurant, bar with pianist, room service. In-room data ports, minibars. Cable TV. Indoor pool. Beauty salon, hot tub, massage. Gym. Business services, parking (fee). Some pets allowed. | 2650 Virginia Ave. NW | 202/965–2300 or 800/424–2736 | fax 202/337–7915 | www.swissotel.com | $400, $475 suites | AE, D, DC, MC, V.

Washington Monarch Hotel. A high-ceilinged atrium with massive windows and sunken lounge area greets you at this upscale hotel (formerly the Ana) two blocks from downtown. It's a frequent site of major industry conferences. | 406 rooms, 9 suites. Restaurant, bar with entertainment, room service. In-room data ports, minibars, some refrigerators. Cable TV. Indoor pool. Hot tub, massage. Gym, racquetball, squash. Business services, parking (fee). Some pets allowed. | 2401 M St. NW | 202/429–2400 or 877/222–2266 | fax 202/457–5010 | $289, $600 suites | AE, D, DC, MC, V.

Westin Fairfax Hotel. This upscale chain hotel is just one block from Dupont Circle, near numerous shops and restaurants, as well as the Metro. The rooms have old English furnishings and marble baths. | 206 rooms, 30 suites. Restaurant, bar with entertainment, room service. In-room data ports, minibars. Cable TV. Massage. Gym. Business services, parking (fee). | 2100 Massachusetts Ave. NW | 202/293–2100 or 800/937–8461 | fax 202/293–0641 | www.westinfairfax.com | $279, $550 suites | AE, D, DC, MC, V.

★ **Willard Inter-Continental.** Two blocks from the Mall and the White House in the heart of the downtown government area, this stately, grand hotel is a specimen of turn-of-the-century architecture, with huge marble columns and opulent comfort. Rooms have king or two double beds, writing desks, lounge chairs, sofas, marble baths, bathrobes, hair dryers, and in-room video games. | 265 rooms, 38 suites. Restaurant, bar, room service. In-room data ports, minibars, some microwaves. Cable TV. Gym. Business services, parking (fee). Some pets allowed. | 1401 Pennsylvania Ave. NW | 202/628–9100 | fax 202/637–7326 | www.inter-conti.com | $425, $550 junior suites, $1,000 suites | AE, D, DC, MC, V.

Eating Well Is the Best Revenge

Start at the top By all means take in a really good restaurant or two while you're on the road. A trip is a time to kick back and savor the pleasures of the palate. Read up on the culinary scene before you leave home. Check out representative menus on the Web—some chefs have gone electronic. And ask friends who have just come back. For big-city dining, reserve a table as far in advance as you can, remembering that the best establishments book up months ahead. Remember that some good restaurants require you to reconfirm the day before or the day of your meal. Then again, some really good places will call you, so make sure to leave a number where you can be reached.

Adventures in eating A trip is the perfect opportunity to try food you can't get at home. So leave yourself open to try an ethnic food that's not represented where you live or to eat fruits and vegetables you've never heard of. One of them may become your next favorite food.

Beyond guidebooks You can rely on the restaurants you find in these pages. But also look for restaurants on your own. When you're ready for lunch, ask people you meet where they eat. Look for tiny holes-in-the-wall with a loyal following and the best burgers or crispiest pizza crust. Find out about local chains whose fame rests upon a single memorable dish. There's hardly a food-lover who doesn't relish the chance to share a favorite place. It's fun to come up with your own special find—and asking about food is a great way to start a conversation.

Sample local flavors Do check out the specialties. Is there a special brand of ice cream or a special dish that you simply must try?

Have a picnic Every so often eat al fresco. Grocery shopping gives you a whole different view of a place.

Beyond T-Shirts and Key Chains

Budget for a major purchase If souvenirs are all about keeping the memories alive in the long haul, plan ahead to shop for something really special—a work of art, a rug or something else hand-crafted, or a major accessory for your home. One major purchase will stay with you far longer than a dozen tourist trinkets, and you'll have all the wonderful memories associated with shopping for it besides.

Add to your collection Whether antiques, used books, salt and pepper shakers, or ceramic frogs are your thing, start looking in the first day or two. Chances are you'll want to scout around and then go back to some of the first shops you visited before you hand over your credit card.

Get guarantees in writing Is the vendor making promises? Ask him to put them in writing.

Anticipate a shopping spree If you think you might buy breakables, bring along a length of bubble wrap. Pack a large tote bag in your suitcase in case you need extra space. Don't fill your suitcase to bursting before you leave home. Or include some old clothing that you can leave behind to make room for new acquisitions.

Know before you go Study prices at home on items you might consider buying while you're away. Otherwise you won't recognize a bargain when you see one.

Plastic, please Especially if your purchase is pricey and you're looking for authenticity, it's always smart to pay with a credit card. If a problem arises later on and the merchant can't or won't resolve it, the credit-card company may help you out.

© Artville

Maryland

The Chesapeake Bay is the heart and soul of Maryland. To some it's their livelihood; to others their playground. But for all Marylanders it's their history. The bay's waterways brought the English settlers here centuries ago and its bounty fed them.

Though the importance of the Chesapeake can not be overestimated, there is so much more to this diverse little state. Maryland has been dubbed "America in Miniature." Maryland may be small and oddly shaped, but its landscape is as varied as the nation's. The Free State stretches from the sandy shores of the Atlantic Ocean to the rugged peaks of the Allegheny Mountains. Between the ocean and the mountains lie the flatlands of the coastal plains, the expansive Chesapeake Bay, and the rolling hills of the piedmont. The tales of its thriving cities—Baltimore, Annapolis, and Frederick—are interwoven with the nation's colonial history. Explore Maryland and you'll find there is so much, so close together.

Baltimore, the state's largest city, lures visitors with its lively Inner Harbor, a waterfront promenade with something for everyone. The Inner Harbor's star attraction, the National Aquarium in Baltimore, is not to be missed. Restaurants, shops, and museums line the waterfront. The city's distinctive neighborhoods, impressive museums and monuments, historic sites, parks, and horse racing could leave a sightseer breathless. Baseball fans can see the Orioles play in Camden Yards or visit the birthplace of Babe Ruth.

To the west, Frederick entices travelers with its historic district—50 blocks of tree-shaded streets, parks, fountains, and grand Federal- and Georgian-style buildings. Take the time to browse among its many antiques shops or visit some of its unusual museums. Supreme Court Justice Roger Brooke Taney, Francis Scott Key, and Civil War heroine Barbara Fritchie called Frederick home at one time.

South of Baltimore, Annapolis beckons sailors and history buffs alike. The state capital, Annapolis is a busy sailing port and the center of Maryland government as well as the home of the U.S. Naval Academy. Its well-preserved streets provide glimpses of

CAPITAL: ANNAPOLIS	POPULATION: 5,094,000	AREA: 9,838 SQUARE MI
BORDERS: VA; WV; PA; DE; WASHINGTON, D.C.	TIME ZONE: EASTERN	POSTAL ABBREVIATION: MD
WEB SITE: WWW.MDISFUN.COM		

America's pre-Revolutionary past. Three of Maryland's signers of the Declaration of Independence lived here, and their homes are open to the public.

Despite increasing urbanization, outdoor diversions abound in Maryland. The Chesapeake and Ohio Canal National Historic Park, a nearly 185-mi linear park that begins in Washington D.C.'s Georgetown, veers westward to Cumberland in the Allegheny Mountains. The canal, built in the 19th century, moved goods by mule-drawn barges. Today, its towpath is popular with bikers, hikers, and runners. The famous Appalachian Trail cuts a path through 40 mi of Maryland mountains. It begins with a dramatic rise from the Potomac River near Harpers Ferry, West Virginia, and ends near the rugged, wooded Pennsylvania border. The thousands of acres of hardwoods and mountainous terrain of the Green Ridge State Forest hug the winding north branch of the Potomac River in western Maryland. Nature lovers come to the park to hunt in the fall and hike and camp in the spring and summer. Farther west, Maryland's largest lake, Deep Creek Lake, attracts boating and fishing enthusiasts. The state's only alpine ski resort, Wisp, touches the shores of the lake.

Maryland has witnessed some dramatic events in American history. In 1649 the state, which was founded as a Catholic colony in 1634, became the first to tolerate the practice of various religions. During the War of 1812, Francis Scott Key penned "The Star-Spangled Banner" as the British bombarded Baltimore. Fifty years later, Confederate and Union troops clashed near Sharpsburg in the Battle of Antietam in what became known as the single bloodiest day of the Civil War. Tucked away in the Catoctin Mountains, Camp David was the backdrop for the 1978 peace accords between Egypt and Israel. Though the presidential retreat is hidden from the public, the national park surrounding the site is open for hiking, camping, and pursuing other outdoor activities.

The geographic center—if not the heart—of Maryland is the Chesapeake Bay, the nation's largest estuary. For centuries scores of Marylanders—crabbers, oystermen, and fishermen—have drawn their livelihood from its bountiful waters. The bay, which divides the state in two, touches the state's major cities and ports. The Chesapeake serves as a recreational outlet for hundreds of thousands, who sail, boat, water-ski, fish, crab, and swim. One of the best vantage points to see the bay is the William Preston Lane Jr. Memorial Bridge, which spans the bay at its narrowest—4½ mi—and connects mainland Maryland with the Eastern Shore. However, the 17½-mi Chesapeake Bay Bridge-Tunnel, which goes over and under its waters, can give you a sense of the bay's breadth.

History

The influence of Maryland's English settlers is still evident. Streets in Annapolis—Duke of Gloucester, for instance—and many towns and counties across the state still bear royal names. Prince Frederick, Prince George's, and Queen Anne are a few examples.

English settlers arrived in Maryland in 1631, establishing the first permanent trading post and farming community on what is now Kent Island, the largest island in the Chesapeake Bay. A year later, King Charles I granted the Maryland Charter to Cecil Calvert, the second Lord Baltimore. In 1634 passengers on the ships *Ark* and *Dove*, who had departed from the Isle of Wight, landed at St. Clements Island in the Potomac River,

MD Timeline

1631	1634	1649	1694
The first permanent English settlement in Maryland is established at Kent Island.	English settlers on the *Ark* and *Dove* land at St. Clements Island in the Potomac River and buy land from Native Americans.	Virginia Puritans are invited to settle in Maryland; the colony's assembly passes An Act Concerning Religion, later known as the Toleration Act.	Anne Arundel Town, later Annapolis, replaces St. Marys City as the capital.

INTRODUCTION
HISTORY
REGIONS
WHEN TO VISIT
STATE'S GREATS
RULES OF THE ROAD
DRIVING TOURS

now a state park. They eventually settled on the mainland, building a fort at St. Marys City, the fourth permanent British settlement in the New World.

St. Marys City, near the southern tip of the state, became Maryland's first capital and the birthplace of religious toleration. In 1694, the General Assembly designated Anne Arundel Town—later renamed Annapolis—as the capital. In 1788, following the American Revolution, Maryland became the seventh state to ratify the U.S. Constitution. Three years later, Maryland ceded land to the Federal Government for the creation of the District of Columbia.

During the War of 1812, after the British burned Washington, D.C., they turned their attention to Baltimore, hoping to inflict similar damage. The British guns, however, were repulsed by the armaments of Fort McHenry. The bombardment inspired Maryland lawyer Francis Scott Key to pen the words to "The Star-Spangled Banner."

After the war, Maryland looked westward, seeking ways to expedite the flow of goods from the east to the Ohio Valley and beyond. The nation's first federally funded road, the National Pike, crossed the Appalachian Mountains into the Ohio Valley. Later came the canals—the Chesapeake and Ohio and the Chesapeake and Delaware. Even as the C and O Canal was being built, Baltimore and Ohio Railroad was laying tracks across the region. Although the railroad and other technology would doom the canal, the network of man-made waterways lasted into the 20th century.

Maryland's people stood divided during the Civil War. The state remained officially loyal to the Union, largely because of the presence of federal troops and political maneuvers by President Abraham Lincoln. However, the first casualties of war occurred on the streets of Baltimore, where an angry mob confronted Massachusetts volunteers en route to Washington, D.C. The state also was the site of several major battles, including the bloody Battle of Antietam, in western Maryland.

Following the war, Baltimore emerged as a major manufacturing center, most notably of iron, steel, chemical fertilizer, and textiles. The city also became the oyster capital of the world, packing more of those mollusks than any other place. Baltimore was also a major immigration center for Europeans in the 19th century. In 1904, a fire destroyed 1,500 structures in Baltimore. The city rebuilt and rode the economic roller coaster of two world wars and the Great Depression. The city experienced a rebirth in the 1970s and 1980s with the major refurbishment of the much-touted Inner Harbor.

Regions

1. BALTIMORE AND METRO AREA

Despite its large size, Baltimore has all the charms of a small city—maybe that's why residents have dubbed it "Charm City." It's easily navigable by car, foot or, along the waterfront, and by water taxi. Its bustling Inner Harbor symbolizes the city's revitalization. Shopping pavilions, museums, and restaurants now crowd the waterfront in an area that was once an urban wasteland. The renaissance

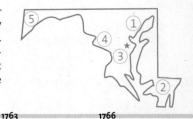

1727	1729	1731	1763	1766
The *Maryland Gazette*, the first newspaper in the Chesapeake Bay area, is published.	Baltimore Town is established.	Baltimore Company begins ironmaking on the Patapsco River.	Charles Mason and Jeremiah Dixon begin surveying the Pennsylvania-Maryland boundary, which is finalized four years later and named the Mason-Dixon line.	Sons of Liberty organize in Baltimore County.

continues today with even more museums and hotels, an expanded convention center, and the twin stadiums: Oriole Park at Camden Yards and the PSINet Stadium, home of the city's NFL team the Ravens.

Baltimore is a city of neighborhoods. The city's elegant past echoes in the stately homes and shops of Mount Vernon. Its seafaring history—and now its nightlife—can be found along the cobblestone streets of Fells Point. Throughout the city, row houses line the streets, and many still have marble front steps, a Baltimore trademark. For decades, Baltimore was one of the nation's major points of entry for European immigrants, and their influence is still noticeable in neighborhoods like close-knit Little Italy, near the Inner Harbor. The metropolitan area consists of Baltimore City proper plus five counties: Anne Arundel, Howard, Baltimore, Carroll, and Harford. They are all accessible by major interstates and, in some cases, light rail, commuter trains, and subway.

Towns listed: Aberdeen, Baltimore, Cockeysville, Columbia, Ellicott City, Havre de Grace, Pikesville, Taneytown, Towson, Westminster

2. EASTERN SHORE

Most of the Delmarva Peninsula, Maryland's Eastern Shore, is a gentle landscape of farmland, tidal waters, and woods. Bounded by the Chesapeake Bay and the Atlantic Ocean, the peninsula is teeming with beaches and small resort towns. Sailing, boating, fishing, and swimming are the big pastimes here. The Eastern Shore also is a popular place to bird-watch. The Blackwater National Wildlife Refuge near Cambridge is the winter home of many waterfowl.

Towns listed: Berlin, Cambridge, Chesapeake Bay Bridge Area, Chestertown, Crisfield, Easton, Elkton, Grasonville, North East, Ocean City, Oxford, Pocomoke City, Salisbury, Stevensville, Snow Hill, St. Michaels, Tilghman Island

3. SOUTHERN MARYLAND

The western shore of the Chesapeake Bay includes Annapolis and southern Maryland, a region rich in pre-Revolutionary War history. The tobacco fields of Calvert and Charles counties are lingering reminders of another era. The state's first capital was established at St. Marys City nearly four centuries ago at the mainland's southernmost point. Long stretches of beaches, imposing cliffs, and bayside scenery are among the region's natural attractions.

Towns listed: Annapolis, Chesapeake Beach, La Plata, Leonardtown, Port Tobacco, Solomons Island, St. Marys City, Waldorf

4. CAPITAL REGION

Millions of visitors find their way to Maryland's suburban counties around Washington, D.C.—Frederick, Prince George's, and Montgomery. Though many come to see Washington, venturing into Maryland is a pleasant side trip. Shopping abounds in Montgomery County's Rockville, Bethesda, and Gaithersburg. Historic Frederick and environs offer

1767	1772	1791	1796	1806
Annapolis merchants send Charles Willson Peale to London to study painting.	Work begins on new statehouse; Methodists build first house of worship in the colonies near New Windsor in Carroll County.	Maryland cedes land for creation of the District of Columbia.	The city of Baltimore is incorporated. Maryland law prohibits import of slaves for sale and allows voluntary slave emancipation.	Benjamin Henry Latrobe begins building America's first Roman Catholic cathedral, in Baltimore.

INTRODUCTION
HISTORY
REGIONS
WHEN TO VISIT
STATE'S GREATS
RULES OF THE ROAD
DRIVING TOURS

respite from the hustle and bustle. Even the president heads this way to escape Washington. Camp David, the presidential retreat, is north of Frederick deep in the Catoctin Mountains.

Towns listed: Bethesda, Bowie, Chevy Chase, College Park, Greenbelt, Emmitsburg, Frederick, Gaithersburg, Laurel, New Market, Rockville, Silver Spring, Thurmont

5. WESTERN MARYLAND

The state's best-kept secret is, perhaps, its mountainous western end, once the frontier of the new nation. Westward settlers passed through a narrow gap in the Appalachian Mountains to reach the Ohio Valley. Later, the Baltimore and Ohio Railroad and the first federally funded highway crossed through the same gap in the westward march. With its expansive forests and ample state parks, western Maryland is a playground for outdoor adventurers. The state's highest summit, the 3,360-ft Backbone Mountain, is tucked away in the extreme southwestern corner of Maryland. Winter activity flourishes in and around Deep Creek Lake with ice fishing and sailing, cross-country and alpine skiing, and snowshoeing. The summer months bring boaters, hikers, campers, and—along the north-flowing Youghiogheny River—kayakers and white-water rafters.

Towns listed: Boonsboro, Cumberland, Frostburg, Grantsville, Hagerstown, McHenry, Oakland, Sharpsburg

When to Visit

Overall, Maryland enjoys a moderate climate. Winter days rarely dip too far below freezing, though summer temperatures climb into the 90s. Winter arrives slowly; fall lingers, sometimes into November with unusually warm days. Snow is not uncommon but rarely lasts long. The average snowfall is a modest 26½ inches, while the rainfall is 41½ inches.

The state's Appalachian region, however, endures a winter more like that of its northern counterparts, with colder temperatures and much snow. The average snowfall in the Maryland mountains is 82 inches. Most Marylanders do their downhill and cross-country skiing here.

Summers are generally hot and humid, making outdoor activities uncomfortable. That weather, though, is perfect for days at the sandy beaches of Ocean City. Temperatures are cooler in the mountains in far western Maryland.

Spring and fall tend to be the best seasons to visit. In the spring, hundreds of thousands of tulips, azaleas, pansies, and blossoming trees bloom at Sherwood Gardens in Baltimore. In the fall, the foliage is breathtaking along the ridges of Baltimore and Carroll counties, the Catoctin Mountains, and the Appalachians. In most areas of the state, fall foliage peaks in mid- to late October.

1814	1818	1827	1833	1834
Francis Scott Key writes "The Star-Spangled Banner."	National Road opens between Cumberland and Wheeling, West Virginia.	"Jew Bill" passes legislature, enabling Jews to hold public office. Oyster canning begins in Baltimore.	Edgar Allan Poe's "Ms. Found in a Bottle" is published in Baltimore.	The Baltimore and Ohio Railroad reaches Harpers Ferry, West Virginia.

CLIMATE CHART

Average High/Low Temperatures (°F) and Monthly Precipitation (in inches)

	JAN.	FEB.	MAR.	APR.	MAY	JUNE
BALTIMORE	40/23	44/26	54/34	64/43	74/53	83/62
	3	3.1	3.4	3	3.7	3.7

	JULY	AUG.	SEPT.	OCT.	NOV.	DEC.
	87/67	86/66	79/58	67/46	57/37	45/28
	3.7	4	3.4	3	3.3	3.4

FESTIVAL AND SEASONAL EVENTS

WINTER

Nov.–Jan. **Winterfest of Lights** in Ocean City. Thousands of lights, hundreds of outdoor lighted displays, and animated pieces twinkle throughout the seaside resort drawing nearly 300,000 people from mid-November through January. | 410/289–8181.

Jan. **Annapolis Heritage Antiques Show** in Annapolis. One of the major mid-Atlantic events of its kind, this antiques show lasts three days. | 410/222–1919.

SPRING

Apr. **Sugar Loaf Craft Festival** in Gaithersburg. Held at the Montgomery County Fairgrounds, this unique marketplace features 300 to 500 top artisans, displaying and selling fine arts and contemporary crafts. It is considered one of the East Coast's largest retail crafts festivals. | 301/990–1400 | www.sugarloafcrafts.com.

May **Maryland Preakness Celebration** in Baltimore. More than 100 events make up this weeklong festival. Parades, street parties, and hot-air balloon races are just a few. The celebration culminates in the annual running of the Preakness Stakes at Pimlico Racetrack on the third Saturday in May. | 410/837–3030.

SUMMER

July **Artscape** in Baltimore. Held in the city's Mount Royal Cultural Corridor, this festival of the arts includes music and crafts, indoor and outdoor visual arts exhibits, and an outdoor musical performance with national and international acts. | 410/396–4575.

1838
Frederick Douglass escapes Baltimore slavery.

1849
Harriet Tubman, born on Maryland's Eastern Shore, escapes slavery.

1861
Mob attacks Massachusetts Civil War volunteers changing trains in Baltimore while en route to Washington.

1862
Battle of Antietam is fought.

1876
Johns Hopkins University opens.

INTRODUCTION
HISTORY
REGIONS
WHEN TO VISIT
STATE'S GREATS
RULES OF THE ROAD
DRIVING TOURS

Aug. **Rocky Gap Music Festival** in Cumberland. National country music entertainers often headline this three-day festival at the Allegany College of Maryland. Music workshops, children's activities, and food are all part of the fun. | 888/762–5942 | www.rockygapfestival.com.

Aug.–Sept. **Maryland State Fair** in Timonium (*see* Towson). This fun-filled event at the Maryland State Fairgrounds is 11 days of horse races, livestock contests, live entertainment, agricultural displays, and plenty of food and amusement rides. | 410/252–0200.

AUTUMN

Sept. **Maryland Seafood Festival** in Annapolis. This three-day event celebrates the bounty of the Chesapeake Bay with seafood, continuous entertainment, beach activities, regional arts and crafts, and more at Sandy Point State Park. | 410/268–7682.

Maryland Wine Festival in Westminster. This weekend event on the grounds of the Carroll County Farm Museum celebrates Maryland's up-and-coming wineries with food, entertainment, and, of course, wine. | 410/876–2667.

Oct. **U.S. Sailboat and Powerboat Shows** in Annapolis. These two events, each the world's largest of its kind, take place during separate weekends in October at the self-proclaimed sailing capital of the nation. Water and shore exhibits as well as companies touting boating services, accessories and equipment are on display. | 410/268–8828.

Nov. **Waterfowl Festival** in Easton. More than 500 prestigious national wildlife exhibitors attend this weekend event. Decoy displays, carving demonstrations, duck-calling contests, and retriever exercises are some of the activities. | 410/822–4567.

State's Greats

From the beauty of the expansive Chesapeake Bay and the coastal plains of the Eastern Shore to the rolling farmland of the piedmont and the worn Appalachian Mountains, Maryland lays claim to one of the most diverse landscapes of any state.

Many of the wonders of outdoor Maryland—from the rugged, forested mountains of the west to the sterling beaches of its Atlantic coastline—are within a four-hour drive of Baltimore. Nature lovers are drawn to Maryland's abundance of state and national parks. Hikers follow the nearly 185-mi footpath that parallels the Potomac River and

1886	1904	1914	1919	1929
Enoch Pratt Free Library opens in Baltimore.	Fire destroys much of downtown Baltimore.	Baltimore native Babe Ruth begins his pro baseball career with the International League Orioles.	H.L. Mencken publishes his first book.	Baltimore Museum of Art opens.

Maryland's 40-mi share of the famed Appalachian Trail. Its sprawling forests offer camping, hiking, hunting, and other outdoor activities.

Boating is a beloved hobby in the Free State. The Chesapeake Bay and its tributaries deliver ample opportunities for boating, sailing, fishing, and swimming. The Severn River near Annapolis and the Choptank on the Eastern Shore are popular with sailors, as is the bay. A tumultuous stretch of the Potomac River near Maryland's suburban Washington is a choice kayaking location. In extreme western Maryland, kayakers and whitewater rafters run the north-flowing Youghiogheny River.

The state's cultural and economic center remains Baltimore. Its urban landscape features countless museums, historic homes, shopping centers, and waterfront areas, all of which attract millions of tourists annually. In recent years, the area surrounding the Inner Harbor has been undergoing a continuing renaissance with new hotels, restaurants, a children's museum, and two new sports stadiums. The National Aquarium in Baltimore, the jewel of the Inner Harbor, is a must-see. Take the time to explore some of the city's remarkable neighborhoods. Many of them provide glimpses of not only the city's colorful past but shades of the nation's as well. The waves of European immigrants who settled in Baltimore in the 19th century left behind traces of their culture in the neighborhoods—even as a new group replaced them.

Outside Baltimore small towns welcome visitors with well-kept main streets lined with shops, boutiques, restaurants, and bed-and-breakfasts. Westminster, Havre de Grace, New Market, Emmitsburg, Easton, Cambridge, and North East are just a few of those towns. Many of them have small but unique museums, historic sites, or access to state parks, forests, or waterways.

Beaches, Forests, and Parks

Despite its miles of shoreline, Maryland has few stretches of beaches. Its best beaches are along its short Atlantic coastline in the summer resort of **Ocean City,** which boasts 10 mi of well-maintained sandy beaches. Its less-developed neighbor, **Assateague Island,** a state and national park, has pristine beaches that are home to a band of wild ponies. On the Chesapeake side, the best beaches include those at **Sandy Point State Park** near the Bay Bridge and **Calvert Cliffs State Park** in southern Maryland—where the adventurous can also hunt fossils. Maryland has no natural lakes, but several state parks have man-made lakes with beaches, including western Maryland's **Deep Creek Lake,** the state's largest. Maryland has preserved forests throughout the state, and some of the most popular include **Green Ridge State Forest** and **Savage River State Forest** in western Maryland. Many state parks are within a short drive of Baltimore, including **Gunpowder Falls State Park,** just north of the city. Baltimore's city parks include **Druid Hill Park,** home of the **Baltimore Zoo,** and **Patterson Park,** a favorite spot of picnickers, joggers, and others.

1939	1952	1959	1980	1992
The C and O Canal opens as a national park.	The Chesapeake Bay Bridge opens.	Interstate 83 links Baltimore and Harrisburg, Pennsylvania.	Harborplace opens in Baltimore, symbolizing the city's renaissance.	Oriole Park at Camden Yards opens in Baltimore.

Culture, History, and the Arts

Maryland is steeped in history, from the re-created colonial settlement at **St. Marys City** to the well-kept colonial streets of **Annapolis.** The state capital since the late 17th century, Annapolis plays host to one of the nation's largest concentration of pre–Revolutionary War buildings, many of them still in use as restaurants, stores, and inns. The restored homes of prominent Marylanders, including signers of the Declaration of Independence, welcome visitors. St. Marys, the re-created settlement of some of the area's first Europeans, includes a replica of one of the ships that brought them to Maryland from England.

In Baltimore, history buffs roam the grounds of **Fort McHenry,** which successfully defended the city during the War of 1812. That bombardment of the city inspired Francis Scott Key to write "The Star-Spangled Banner." The city also maintains the homes of horror writer **Edgar Allan Poe, St. Elizabeth Ann Seton,** the first American-born saint, and baseball great **Babe Ruth.** The country's first Roman Catholic cathedral, the **Basilica of the National Shrine of the Assumption,** and the **Washington Monument,** the nation's first formal monument to the first president, are among the city's treasures. The **Maryland Historical Society's** museum has a vast collection of Baltimore and Maryland memorabilia.

Baltimore's fine museums, concert halls, and theaters make it the cultural center of the state. The **Morris A. Mechanic Theatre,** near Charles Center, stages the latest touring Broadway productions. The **Joseph Meyerhoff Symphony Hall** is home to the renowned **Baltimore Symphony Orchestra.** The **Lyric Opera House** showcases Maryland opera and ballets. Many smaller theaters, including **CenterStage** in downtown Baltimore, put on first-rate productions. At the **Peabody Conservatory of Music,** students and guest artists perform symphonies, operas, and recitals. The historic **Senator Theater** premieres many of the movies filmed in Maryland.

In western Maryland, **Frederick** boasts a well-kept historic district. The homes of the state's first governor, **Thomas Johnson,** Civil War heroine **Barbara Fritchie,** and U.S. Supreme Court justice **Roger Brooke Taney** are in Frederick. Civil War buffs will find lots to see in the area. Just outside Frederick is the **Monocacy National Battlefield,** a little-known clash that historians believe saved Washington, D.C., from a Confederate invasion. In neighboring Washington County, **Antietam National Battlefield** is one of the best-preserved battlefields in the country. On July 4th the battlefield is the backdrop for the Maryland Symphony Orchestra's annual "Salute to Independence," a performance of light classical and patriotic music with cannon fire and fireworks.

Sports

Maryland may be a small state, but its sports activities are as diverse as its larger neighbors. Hikers ramble the hundreds of miles of trails throughout the state, including the **Appalachian Trail,** the towpath of the **Chesapeake and Ohio Canal National Historic Park,** and the countless trails at many state parks. Bicyclists peddle on some of the state's bike trails, including the 22-mi **Baltimore and Annapolis Trail** and the **North Central Railroad Trail,** which follows an old railroad bed from Baltimore to Pennsylvania. Many state parks have trails for mountain biking.

Several small companies offer guided biking, camping, and other excursions in the Maryland mountains. On the Eastern Shore, guided hunting expeditions are available.

Obviously fishing—both for business and pleasure—is a major pastime in this waterlogged state. Fishermen, crabbers, and others have plied the waters of the **Chesapeake Bay** and its tributaries for centuries. Marinas and charter services cater to the seafaring crowd in bayside and oceanfront communities. Sailing enthusiasts come ashore in Maryland's quaint ports, which offer everything from marinas and inns to shops and restaurants. Canoeists will enjoy the placid waters of the **Potomac** and **Pocomoke**

rivers. Kayakers will find thrills on the **Lower Potomac, Youghiogheny,** and **Savage rivers** in western Maryland.

Winter activities are limited to the western mountains of Maryland, where the state's only alpine ski resort, **Wisp** is located. Cross-country skiers will find groomed trails at two nearby state parks, **New Germany** and **Herrington Manor.** Snow permitting, cross-country skiing is also available at other state parks, including **Cunningham Falls State Park,** north of Frederick. In the winter the Inner Harbor's **Rash Field** converts to an ice-skating rink.

With more than 150 golf courses in Maryland, golfers will find a green playground in most every corner of the state. Many of the newest courses are near Ocean City. In western Maryland one of the newest is an 18-hole course at **Rocky Gap Lodge and Golf Resort,** near Cumberland, which was designed by Jack Nicklaus.

Rules of the Road

License Requirements: To drive in Maryland you must be at least 16 years old and have a valid driver's license. Residents of Canada and most other countries may drive as long as they have valid licenses from their home countries.

Right Turn on Red: Everywhere in Maryland you may make a right turn on red after a full stop, unless otherwise indicated.

Seat Belt and Helmet Laws: All drivers and front-seat passengers must wear seat belts. Children under 4 must only ride in a federally approved child safety seat. Bicyclists and motorcylists—of all ages—must wear helmets when riding on Maryland roads.

Speed Limits: In urban areas, particularly around Baltimore and heavily traveled I–95, the speed limit is 55 mph. On the interstates away from metropolitan area, the speed limit is 60 mph or 65 mph.

For More Information: Contact the Maryland Motor Vehicle Administration. | 6601 Ritchie Hwy. NE, Glen Burnie, MD | 410/768–7274 | www.mva.state.mb.us.

Baltimore and Annapolis Driving Tour

MARYLAND'S MAJOR CITIES

Distance: 73 mi   Time: 3 days
Breaks: Stay overnight in Baltimore or Annapolis.

This tour highlights Baltimore and historic Annapolis, with a quick trip over the Chesapeake Bay to the Eastern Shore. The landscape south of Baltimore is largely flat. The Annapolis area is a maze of creeks and tributaries flowing into the Chesapeake Bay. Your best bet is to visit in the spring and fall, when the temperatures are cooler and humidity is low.

❶ Begin the tour in Baltimore at the **Inner Harbor** (Access from I–95, exits 52–55; I–83 ends at Inner Harbor). The city's bustling waterfront is an urban Disneyland, with museums, water taxis and boat cruises, famous restaurants, and shops, all within walking distance of one another and rarely out of sight of the water. For a shopper's paradise be sure to visit **Harborplace** and its sister complex across the street the multilevel Gallery. The **National Aquarium in Baltimore** is a must-see for first-time visitors. The **World Trade Center** is Baltimore's scaled-down version of its more-famous New York landmark. Though it's only 30 stories high, the view from the 27th floor is unmatchable and provides a geographic and architectural sense of the city. Follow with a ride on a water taxi, which offers yet another spectacular view of the city.

2 When you're ready to leave the Inner Harbor area, head up to the **Baltimore Museum of Art** (Go one block north to Lombard then west to Charles. Proceed north on Charles Street to Art Museum Drive, just north of 29th Street) to see works by Rodin, Matisse, Picasso, Cézanne, Renoir, and Gauguin.

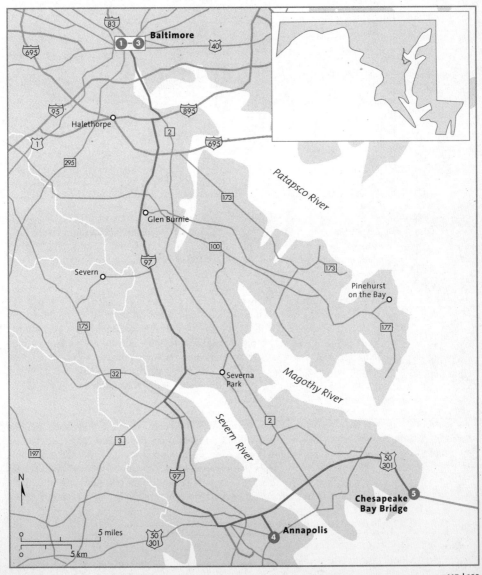

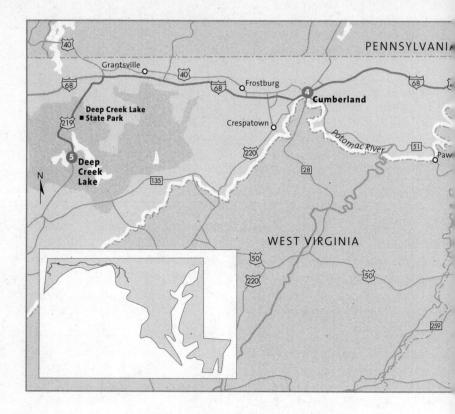

❸ On your way out of the city, stop at the **American Visionary Art Museum** in the southwestern corner of the Inner Harbor. (Take St. Paul south until it turns to Light Street then into Key Highway.) It showcases the eclectic and innovative art of everyday Americans in seven galleries.

❹ In **Annapolis** (leave Baltimore on I–97 S and proceed for 29 mi to U.S. 50/301) there's something for everyone—historic homes and mansions, colonial streets, boat rides, and the U.S. Naval Academy. Start at the Visitors Bureau and join a guided walking tour of the city. Visit the historic **Maryland State House** and one of the many restored mansions of the colonial era. The **Hammond-Harwood House,** the only verified full-scale example of the work of William Buckland, colonial America's most prominent architect, is a sure winner. Tours of the **United States Naval Academy** give visitors a glimpse of the daily life of midshipmen.

❺ The **Chesapeake Bay Bridge** (9 mi east of Annapolis on U.S. 50/301) connects Maryland's mainland with the Eastern Shore. Shoppers will enjoy the many outlet stores along U.S. 50, and seafood lovers won't be disappointed with any of the restaurants in Grasonville. St. Michaels is a popular sailing and tourist town with museums, boutiques, and restaurants. The **Chesapeake Bay Maritime Museum** traces the history of the bay and its traditions of boat building, commercial fishing and waterfowling.

To return to Baltimore backtrack west on U.S. 50/301 to Rte. 2 and head north into the city limits.

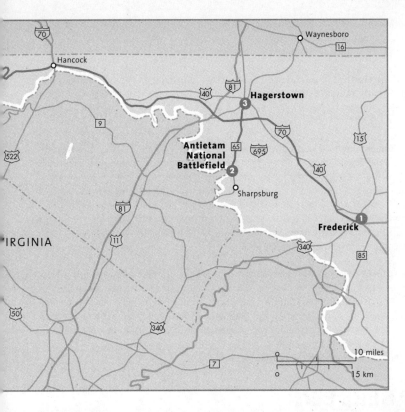

INTRODUCTION
HISTORY
REGIONS
WHEN TO VISIT
STATE'S GREATS
RULES OF THE ROAD
DRIVING TOURS

Western Maryland Driving Tour

ALONG INTERSTATES 70 AND 68

Distance: 160 mi   Time: 4 days

Breaks: Frederick offers the most varied overnight accommodations. Cumberland is a good midway point between Frederick and Garrett County.

This tour focuses on the state's mountainous region, home to historic Frederick, Civil War battlefields, and countless small towns. From Frederick, the rolling hills evolve into rugged mountains. The colors are breathtaking in the fall. In the winter, the westernmost county, Garrett, becomes a winter playground with downhill and cross-country skiing, ice fishing, and sledding. Summer temperatures are much cooler in Garrett County than in the rest of the state.

❶ Begin your tour in **Frederick** (47 mi west of Baltimore on I–70, exits 52–56). The city's lovely 50-block historic district features 18th- and 19th-century buildings, many still in use as homes, stores, and restaurants. Begin with a self-guided walking tour originating at the **Frederick Visitor Center.** If you arrive on a weekend, look for the costumed tour guides. The **Barbara Fritchie House and Museum** recounts the legend of Dame Fritchie, who reportedly waved a Union flag at passing Confederates during the Civil War. For a different kind of medical history, check out the **National Museum of the Civil War Medicine.** If time permits, visit **Mount Olivet Cemetery,** the resting place of Fritchie, Francis Scott Key, and Union and Confederate soldiers.

❷ **Antietam National Battlefield** (west approximately 22 mi on I–70, then south 9 mi on Rte. 65) is one of the nation's best-preserved battlefields. Antietam (in Sharpsburg) was the site of the bloodiest day of the Civil War.

❸ In **Hagerstown** (approximately 10 mi north of Sharpsburg on Rte. 65), the **Washington County Museum of Fine Arts** has an impressive collection of 18th- and 19th-century American art. The museum is within the boundaries of the **City Park,** a 27-acre wooded and landscaped haven.

❹ In **Cumberland** (take I–70/68 west 68 mi to exits 41–45) take a ride on the **Western Maryland Scenic Railroad.** Passengers enjoy a 16-mi mostly uphill trek to Frostburg where a 90-minute layover leaves just enough time for shopping and dining along the town's old-fashioned Main Street. Cumberland also was the western terminus of the C and O Canal. Efforts are under way to restore the canal; in the meantime, visitors can walk a stretch of the towpath, which meanders southeast of the city. **George Washington's Headquarters** during the French and Indian War was originally a cabin built in 1755. It is now in Riverside Park.

❺ **Deep Creek Lake** (proceed approximately 30 mi west on I–68, then 15 mi south on U.S. 219), Maryland's largest man-made lake, is a boater's paradise. Marinas rent boats and Jet-Skis. **Deep Creek Lake State Park** has a boat ramp, beach, hiking trails, and camping facilities. To the southwest of the lake **Swallow Falls State Park** offers a spectacular view of Muddy Creek Falls, Maryland's highest waterfall, and a stand of 300-year-old hemlocks.

To return to Frederick backtrack east on I–68/70.

ABERDEEN

MAP 4, G2

(Nearby towns also listed: Elkton, Havre de Grace, Towson)

An artillery testing site since 1917, Aberdeen is home to one of the world's largest military research and development centers, the Aberdeen Proving Ground. Despite its proximity to major highways, which have brought huge distribution centers for Frito-Lay, Saks Fifth Avenue, and Pier 1, Aberdeen has retained its small-town charm. Many neighborhoods boast spacious yards, and restored Victorian houses are common on some of the city's older streets. The nearby Chesapeake Bay has boating, fishing, and sailing.

Information: Discover Harford County Tourism Council Inc. | 121 N. Union Ave., Suite B, Havre de Grace, MD 21078 | 410/939–3336 or 800/597–2649 | www.harfordmd.com.

Attractions

The Ripken Museum. Memorabilia and other exhibits tell the story of Baltimore Orioles ironman Cal Ripken, Jr., his father, the late Cal Ripken, Sr., and brother, Bill. The museum is inside Aberdeen's City Hall. | 3 Bel Air Ave. | 410/273–2525 | fax 410/273–2609 | www.ripkenmuseum.com | $3 | Memorial Day–Labor Day, daily 11–3; Labor Day–Memorial Day, Fri., Mon. 11–3, Sat. 11–4, Sun. noon–3:30, closed Tues.–Thurs.

U.S. Army Ordnance Museum. One of the largest collections of armored fighting vehicles in the country—225 at last count—is here. Some are one-of-a-kind inventions, such as the "Christie," which was designed in 1934 to run at speeds up to 60 mph; its competitors could go no faster than 8 mph. The museum also has a collection of small arms on display. | Building 2601, Aberdeen Proving Ground, Rte. 22 | 410/278–3602 or 410/278–2396 | fax 410/278–7473 | www.ordmusfound.org | Free | Daily 10–4:45.

SEPT.: *Aberdeen Heritage Day.* On the last Saturday in September, the whole town celebrates its history with children's activities, food, crafts, and hayrides at Hall's Crossing. | 410/272–1600.

Dining

Colonel's Choice Ballroom. American. Named after a customer from the nearby army base, this is one of the town's higher-end dining options. Variety is its hallmark, with local southern dishes and crab cakes mixed in with steaks and more complicated fish and meat dishes. | U.S. 40 and Caro Ave. | 410/272–6500 | $9–$24 | AE, MC, V.

Durango's Grill. Mexican. This family-friendly cantina's design—steer skulls, dusty desert colors, and exposed wooden beams—points south of the border. The chicken fajitas and enchiladas doused in cheese sauce are popular choices. If you shy from spices, order a burger or grilled chicken sandwich. Lunch buffet weekdays. | 980 Hospitality Way | 410/273–6300 | $6–$12 | AE, D, MC, V.

New Ideal Diner. American. This 1931 roadside diner with its shiny steel siding, red neon sign, and all-vinyl booths is the real thing. Claiming to serve Maryland's best crab cakes, it does give competitors a run for their money. However, its old-fashioned comfort food—burgers, meatloaf, and homemade pies—is what draws crowds. | 104 S. Philadelphia Blvd. (Rte. 40) | 410/272–1880 | $5–$10 | AE, D, MC, V.

Lodging

Budget Inn. The motel is 1½ mi south of downtown Aberdeen, on Rte. 40 near a shopping center and fast-food restaurants. | 24 rooms. Complimentary Continental breakfast. Cable TV. Business services. Some pets allowed. | 1112 S. Philadelphia Blvd. | 410/272–2401 | fax 410/297–8906 | $35–$50 | AE, D, DC, MC, V.

Days Inn. The motel is in a quiet suburban area, 3 mi west of downtown Aberdeen, 2 mi from the Cal Ripken Museum and 3 mi from Aberdeen Proving Ground. | 49 rooms. Complimentary Continental breakfast. Cable TV. Pool. Pets allowed (fee). | 783 W. Bel Air Ave. | 410/272–8500 | fax 410/272–5782 | www.daysinn.com | $53–$60 | AE, D, DC, MC, V.

Holiday Inn–Chesapeake House. This hotel is 2 mi east of the Aberdeen Proving Grounds and downtown Aberdeen. | 122 rooms. Restaurant, bar. Cable TV. Indoor heated pool. Gym. Some pets allowed. | 1007 Beards Hill Rd. | 410/272–8100 | fax 410/272–1714 | www.basshotels.com/holiday-inn | $104–$114 | AE, D, DC, MC, V.

Quality Inn. Close to interstate I–95, this hotel is in downtown Aberdeen and is less than 3 mi from Aberdeen Proving Ground. | 110 rooms. Restaurant, bar, full breakfast buffet. Cable TV. Pool. Laundry facilities. Business services. | 793 W. Bel Air Ave. | 410/272–6000 | fax 410/272–2287 | www.qualityinn.com | $55–$75 | AE, D, DC, MC, V.

Sheraton Four Points. This hotel, just off exit 85 of I–95, has an inviting lobby with high ceilings, a brick fireplace, and attractive throw rugs on a tile floor. Rooms contain antique reproductions, greenery and tasteful art. | 134 rooms. Restaurant, bar. In-room data ports, cable TV. Pool. Gym. Business services. | 980 Beards Hill Rd. | 410/273–6300 or 800/346–3612 | fax 410/575–7195 | www.sheraton.com | $99–$130 | AE, D, DC, MC, V.

ANNAPOLIS

MAP 4, F3

(Nearby towns also listed: Baltimore, Bowie, Stevensville Grasonville)

Few cities charm as Annapolis does. With its tree-lined streets, brick roadways, elegant homes, and thriving seaport, Annapolis, the Maryland state capital, beckons tourists and sailors alike.

Part of the city's appeal lies in its history: Few cities have such a high concentration of 18th-century architecture, more than 50 pre–Revolutionary War structures (many of them still in use), restaurants, bed-and-breakfasts, and shops. Some of Maryland's prominent patriots lived here, including William Paca and Samuel Chase, both signers of the Declaration of Independence. Their stately homes are open to the public. Overlooking the city, the Maryland State House, the oldest state capitol in continuous legislative use, is topped by the largest wooden dome in the United States.

Annapolis traces its founding to the late 17th century. Puritan settlers relocating from Virginia in 1649 established the town of Providence at the mouth of the Severn River, a tributary of the Chesapeake Bay. Anne Arundel Town was established in 1684 on the south side of the Severn, across from Providence. Ten years later, the town became Annapolis, the colonial capital. For a brief time—1783 to 1784—Annapolis served as the nation's capital, too, the young country's first peacetime capital.

More than two centuries later, Annapolis remains a city steeped in tradition. Many of the customs and traditions that define life at the Navy's undergraduate college, the U.S. Naval Academy, have become part of Annapolis. The Navy's football team plays its home games at the Navy-Marine Corps Memorial Stadium. In mid-summer, Annapolis bustles with the arrival of the new class of plebes.

With its serene and accessible harbor, and 17 miles of shoreline, Annapolis is inviting to sailors and recreational boaters. In 1998, the city served as a port for a major yacht-racing event—the 32,000-mi Whitbread Around the World Race. The city's seafaring history dates back two centuries to when Annapolis was a port of call for merchant ships from around the world. Even well into the 20th century, the city's harbor was a working waterfront with paddle steamers and a great fleet of bay oyster and fishing boats. Today, some of the world's foremost racing and cruising yacht designers have bases in Annapolis.

Annapolis's charms are easily accessible. Its streets, laid out in 1695, fan out from Church and State circles. Today, stores, restaurants, and bed-and-breakfasts line the streets. Self-guided audio tours, narrated by Walter Cronkite, and costumed guides share Annapolis's history with you.

Away from its Colonial-era streets, Annapolis has become much like any other American community, home to countless fast-food and chain restaurants, discount stores, and shopping malls. They're a convenience for 24,000 who call Annapolis home but a detraction from the city's beauty. They're easily avoided by following Rowe Boulevard (off U.S. 50/301) in the historic district.

For More Information: Annapolis and Anne Arundel County Conference and Visitors Bureau | 26 West St., Annapolis, MD, 21401 | 410/280–0445 | www.visit-annapolis.org.

A NEIGHBORHOOD TO EXPLORE

Center City. The center of Annapolis, on the south side of the Severn River, is home to one of the highest concentrations of 18th-century architecture in the United States. There are more than 50 buildings that date from before the Revolutionary War. Redbrick houses, churches, and museums fill the area, complemented by quaint shops and restaurants on Main and West streets. Against this backdrop, motorboats and sailboats crowd the City Dock when the weather's warm. Next to the dock is Market Square, filled with relaxing places to grab a bite to eat and watch uniformed midshipmen from the U.S. Naval Academy, an ever-present feature of the neighborhood, walk to and from the school, which occupies some 300 acres at the eastern corner of the downtown area not far from St. John's College.

WALKING TOURS

Historic Homes and Museums (approximately 2½ hours)
Begin at Church Circle in front of **St. Anne's Church.** The Romanesque Revival–style church is the third to stand on the site; construction was begun in 1859. Notice the St. Anne's Win-

dow, given to the church in 1839. Follow State Circle past Duke of Gloucester Street, where you'll notice the angular **Maryland Inn,** originally built as an inn during the late 1700s and still operating as an inn and restaurant today. Continue along the circle to School Street. Turn right and follow the road to State Circle, the site of the **Maryland State House,** with its regal wooden dome. Maryland's legislative building is the oldest state capital in continuous use in the United States. From State Circle head east along East Street. Turn left onto Prince George's Street. On your right-hand side is the **William Paca House and Garden.** The Georgian mansion was built between 1766 and 1773 for Paca, one of the signers of the Declaration of Independence. The home is also noted for its lovely garden. Continue along Prince George's Street and turn right onto Maryland Avenue. On the right, at the corner of Maryland Avenue and King George Street, is the **Hammond-Harwood House,** the home of a patriot and planter, Mathias Hammond. The home, designed by renowned architect William Buckland, is an outstanding example of Colonial American architecture. Turn left on King George Street, pass College Avenue, and walk along the campus of **St. John's College.** On your left is another elegant 18th-century home, the **Charles Carroll Barrister House,** which serves as the admissions office of the college. You can walk through campus to the main building, **McDowell Hall.** It was built in 1742 for the colonial governor. The building was the first classroom for the college when it opened in 1789. The campus was also the home of the famous **Liberty Tree,** a more than 300-year-old tulip tree that marked the meeting places of the Sons of Liberty before the Revolutionary War. It was removed in 1999 due to severe storm damage. From the college campus, turn right on College Avenue and head back to Church Circle.

ANNAPOLIS

INTRO
ATTRACTIONS
DINING
LODGING

WATERWORLD

The Chesapeake Bay not only defines Maryland geographically, but recreationally as well. This expansive body of water provides the state with an ample playground for some of its favorite pastimes: boating, sailing, fishing, and crabbing.

Once crowded by practical working vessels like the traditional skipjack and bugeye, the bay—and many of its tributaries—is now primarily the preserve of pleasure boats and yachts. From Baltimore to Annapolis, from North East to Solomons Island, marinas and docks sparkle with rows of gleaming white fiberglass hulls. Annapolis, the self-proclaimed sailing capital of the country, also hosts the annual U.S. Sailboat and Powerboat Shows, on separate weekends every fall.

Maryland's reputation for outstanding sailing began in the 1800s, when Baltimore was the center of the maritime trades, home to builders of skipjacks and clippers. Today, you can explore Baltimore's waters on clippers, water taxis, paddleboats, cruiseships, and sailboats. Water taxis, by the way, are a convenient means of seeing some of the historic sites and communities that dot the city's harbor. In Annapolis, St. Michaels, Baltimore, Ocean City, and other shore towns, boats can be chartered for cruising, sailing, or fishing.

More than 200,000 boaters are registered in Maryland, and hundreds of sailboat races and regattas are held each season. The world's most famous sailboat race, the Whitbread Round the World Race, passed through Baltimore and Annapolis in 1998, attracting throngs of enthusiasts. The event will return to Maryland in 2002.

© Artville

City Dock and U.S. Naval Academy (approximately 2 hours)
Begin at **City Dock,** which has been the center of Annapolis's maritime life for three centuries. At the head of the dock a plaque marks the 1767 arrival in Annapolis of Kunte Kinte, who was immortalized by Alex Haley, one of his descendants, in the book *Roots.* Turn right along Randall Street. On the opposite side you'll notice the **Market House,** which dates back to 1858. The first market on the site was built in 1784. Step inside for refreshments. At the corner of Randall and Pinkney streets stands **Middleton Tavern,** where Samuel Horatio Middleton and his family operated one of the city's most successful taverns before the American Revolution. The tavern remains a restaurant today. Continue along Randall Street to Gate 1 of the **U.S. Naval Academy,** which was established here at the site of Fort Severn in 1845. The campus includes Beaux Arts buildings designed in the early 1900s by Ernest Flagg. The **Naval Academy Chapel,** built in 1904, is on the highest point of ground in the yard. On the far northwest side of the campus is the **U.S. Naval Academy Museum,** which contains more than 30,000 objects from Naval history. Exit at Gate 3 and follow Maryland Avenue. Turn right on King George Street. At the corner of King George Street and College Avenue is the **Ogle Hall/Alumni House,** built between 1735 and 1739. Visitors to the house have included George Washington and the Marquis de Lafayette. The USNA Alumni Association uses the house for its functions. Turn left on College Avenue and follow to Prince George Street. Turn left and follow Prince George back to the City Dock.

TRANSPORTATION INFORMATION

Driving around Town. Annapolis is really a town for walking, as its downtown Colonial layout and its narrow and angled streets make driving a challenge. The main thoroughfare, Main Street, runs between the City Dock and Church Circle and is bisected by many one-way streets. Rush hour is almost non-existent, though you might be delayed a few minutes in early evening. Perhaps the most convenient way to get downtown is to park at the Navy-Marine Corps Memorial Stadium, off U.S. 50 Exit 24, and take a shuttle to downtown. The price for parking an entire day is $4 and the shuttle ride costs less than a dollar. Alternatively, you can take Rowe Boulevard, to Church Circle and find metered parking on the street for 50 cents an hour, up to 2 hours, and in parking garages near the Visitor Center and the Naval Academy. Garage rates vary; some city lots allow you to park for free for the first hour, and then charge $1 for each additional hour.

Airports: Baltimore-Washington International Airport, about 30 mi north of Annapolis, has scheduled daily flights by most major airlines. | 800/I–FLY–BWI | www.bwiairport.com.
Bus Lines: Mass Transit Administration (MTA). Regularly scheduled bus service runs from Baltimore to Annapolis. | 410/263–7964.
Intra-City Transit: Annapolis Dept. of Parking and Transportation. Regular bus service operates throughout the city. | 410/263–7964.

Attractions

ART AND ARCHITECTURE

Aurora Gallery. Hand-blown glass, pottery, soft sculpture, and jewelry are among the contemporary works by local and regional artists on display at this museum. | 67 Maryland Ave. | 410/263–9150 | Donation accepted | Mon.–Sat., 10–5, Sun. 1–5.

Government House. The official home of Maryland's governor was built in 1868 during the Victorian period; seven rooms are open to the public and have a collection of Maryland art and antiques. | 101 School St. | 410/974–3531 | www.mdarchives.state.md.us | Free | Tours by appointment only.

Hammond-Harwood House. Built in 1774, this magnificent Georgian mansion is the only verified full-scale example of the work of William Buckland, colonial America's most prominent architect at the time of his death in 1774. The house also is known for its fine collection of 18th- and early 19th-century furniture and paintings. | 19 Maryland Ave. | 410/263–4683 | hammondharwood@annapolis.net | www.annapolis.net/hammondharwood | $5 | Mon.–Sat. 10–4, Sun. noon–4.

★ **Maryland State House.** Maryland's state capitol, built in 1780, is one of the oldest state capitols still in use today. Its dome, the largest wooden one in the country, was built without nails. The building once housed the U.S. Congress. | State Circle | 410/974–3400 | www.mdarchives.state.md.us | Free | weekdays 9–5, weekends 10–4.

William Paca House and Gardens. This 37-room redbrick mansion was the home of a wealthy planter and signer of the Declaration of Independence. Begun in 1763 and finished in 1765, the home contains authentic period furnishings, many of them from England, and has two acres of lovely gardens. | 186 Prince George St. | 410/263–5553 ext. 17, or 800/603–4020 | www.annapolis.org/paca | House $5, garden $4, both $7 | Jan.–Feb., Fri.–Sat. 10–4, Sun. noon–4, closed Mon.–Thurs.; Mar.–Dec., Mon.–Sat. 10–4, Sun. noon–4.

CULTURE, EDUCATION, AND HISTORY

Historic London Town and Gardens. The South River flows beside this 23-acre park and National Historic Landmark. Archaeologists from the Lost Towns Project have been excavating the area, looking at the late-17th and early 18th-century town of London. The **William Brown House** is a National Historic Landmark house museum on the grounds. An 8-acre woodland garden and the Richard Hill Garden of medicinal plants are also here. | 839 Londontown Rd., Edgewater | 410/222–1919 | www.historiclondontown.com | $5 | Tues.–Sat. 10–4, Sun. noon–4, closed Mon.

St. John's College. The college was begun as King William's School in 1696; it is known today for its Great Books curriculum and its most famous alumnus, Francis Scott Key, author of "The Star-Spangled Banner." | 600 College Ave. | 410/263–2371 or 800/727–9238 | www.sjca.edu | Free | Daily.

The **Elizabeth Myers Mitchell Art Gallery** has traveling art exhibits, demonstrations, tours, and lectures year-round. | St. John's College campus | 410/626–2556 | www.sjca.edu/college/tour/mitchell.phtml | Free | Tues.–Sun. noon–5, closed Mon.

Begun in 1742 as home for Maryland's colonial governor, **McDowell Hall** was never used for that purpose. The exterior of McDowell has not been altered since it was finished in 1789. Until 1837, McDowell was the single building on campus. | St. John's College campus | www.sjca.edu/college/tour/mcdowell.phtml.

The home of Dr. Charles Carroll (circa 1723), a signer of the Declaration of Independence, the **Charles Carroll Barrister House** was moved a few blocks to the St. John's campus in 1955 and serves as the college's admissions office. | St. John's College campus | www.sjca.edu/college/tour/carrbarr.phtml | Free | Weekdays 9–5, closed weekends.

United States Naval Academy. Founded in 1845, the academy was built on the site of a U.S. Army fort. You can view a 12-minute film and join a one-hour guided tour or explore independently. The most prominent building on the grounds is the **U.S. Naval Chapel,** which contains the crypt of Revolutionary War hero John Paul Jones. | 121 Blake Rd. | 410/263–6933 | www.navyonline.com/tours.htm | Free | Jan.–Feb. daily 9–4; Mar.–Dec. daily 9–5.

MUSEUMS

Banneker-Douglass Museum of African-American Life and History. In a former life, the museum was the first African Methodist Episcopal Church of Annapolis, founded in 1803. Today, the redbrick building houses changing exhibits, lectures, and films that present a picture of African-American life in Maryland. | 84 Franklin St. | 410/974–2893 | fax 410/216–6180 | Free, tours $3 | Tues.–Fri. 10–3, Sat. noon–4, closed Sun.–Mon.

Chesapeake Children's Museum. This small museum invites children to explore the hands-on activities, computer lab, and art room. | 25 Silopanna Rd. | 410/222–1608 | fax 410/266–7790 | www.theccm.org | $3 | Thurs.–Tues. 10–4; closed Wed.

Shiplap House Museum. Built in 1715, this museum is in one of the city's oldest buildings. Originally a sailor's tavern, it's now devoted to maritime art and artifacts as well as local history. | 18 Pinkney St. | 410/267–7619 | Free | weekdays 10–5, closed weekends.

PARKS, NATURAL AREAS, AND OUTDOOR RECREATION

Sandy Point State Park. On the western shore of the Chesapeake Bay near the Bay Bridge, this state park has a mile-long beach for swimming and fishing, boat ramps, and a fishing pier. | 1100 E. College Pkwy. | 410/974–2149 | www.dnr.state.md.us/publiclands/southern/sandypoint.html | Mon.–Tues., Thurs.–Fri. $2; Wed. $1; weekends $3 | Daily.

RELIGION AND SPIRITUALITY

St. Anne's Church. The third church by this name on this site, the current St. Anne's was built in 1858. The Episcopalian parish was founded in 1692, and the communion silver from that era is still in service. | Church Cir | 410/267–9333 | www.stannes-annapolis.org | Free | Daily 8–5:30.

SHOPPING

Historic Annapolis Foundation Museum Store. The former site of a Continental army storehouse during the War of Independence, the building is the starting point of a walking tour of early Annapolis, hosted on tape by Walter Cronkite. | 77 Main St. | 410/268–5576 | www.hafmuseumstore.com | Free | Mon.–Thurs. 10–9; Fri.–Sat. 10 AM–10 PM; Sun. 10–6.

SIGHTSEEING TOURS

Boat trips. Chesapeake Marine Tours and Charters has narrated 40-minute and 90-minute tours of the Annapolis harbor and nearby creeks on enclosed river boats. | City Dock | 410/269–6776 or 410/268–7600 | www.watermarkcruises.com | 40-minute tour $7, 90-minute tour $14 | Weekdays 1–3, weekends 11–6.

Historic Annapolis Foundation. The Foundation has self-guided, 45-minute taped tours narrated by Walter Cronkite. | 77 Main St. | 410/268–5576 | www.annapolis.org | $5 | Sat. 10–8, Sun.–Mon. 10–5, closed Tues.–Fri.

Sailing Tours. *Woodwind*, a 74-ft schooner, makes two-hour sailing excursions on the bay. Tours depart from the Annapolis Marriott Waterfront Hotel dock. | 80 Compromise St. | 410/263–7837 | www.schooner-woodwind.com | Day sail $24, sunset sail $27 | Mid-May–Sept., Tues.–Sun. 4 trips daily, Mon. sunset sail only; Apr., Oct., 12:30 and 3.

Three Centuries Tours of Annapolis. Organized walking tours are conducted by guides dressed in Colonial attire. You can learn the history of Annapolis and the U.S. Naval Academy. | 26 West St., City Dock, and 110 Prince George St. | 410/263–5401 | fax 410/263–1901 | www.annapolis-tours.com | $9 | Apr.–Oct., daily 10:30, 1:30; Nov.–Mar., Sat. 2:30.

OTHER POINTS OF INTEREST

Fordham Brewery. Named for the city's first brewery founded in 1703, this incarnation of Fordham produces beers for all occasions. Its Blue Point Oyster stout was created to go down easy with the area's famous shellfish. The brewery hosts special tasting events throughout the year. Tours are available by appointment. | 33 West St. | 410/268–4545 | Free | By appointment only.

William Preston Lane Jr. Memorial Bridge. The twin spans of this bridge—known to everyone as the Bay Bridge—cross the bay at its narrowest point, with 4 mi between shores. The bridge connects mainland Maryland with the Eastern Shore and provides motorists with a sweeping view of the beautiful Chesapeake Bay. | $2.50 toll | Daily.

ON THE CALENDAR

JAN.: *Annapolis Heritage Antiques Show.* One of the major mid-Atlantic events of its kind, this antique show is held at the National Guard Armory on Hudson St. and lasts for three days. | 410/222–1919 | $6.

MAY: *Bay Bridge Walk.* On the first Sunday in May, walkers cross the 4.3-mi-long bridge spanning Chesapeake Bay. Participants gather at the Naval Marine Stadium or at one of two other parking locations and a shuttle bus transports them to the eastern end of the bridge. | 410/288–8405 or 877/BAYSPAN | www.mdta.state.md.us/text/bridgewalktxt.html.

MAY: *Blue Angels Demonstration.* Spectators gather at Andrews Air Force Base to watch the Navy's precision flying team perform in the third week of May. | 410/268–7600.

JUN.: *Annapolis Waterfront Arts Festival.* Concerts by local bands, arts and crafts exhibits, a food court, and several dance troupes bring crowds to this annual event on St. John's College Campus. | 410/268–8828.

AUG.–OCT.: *Maryland Renaissance Festival.* From the last weekend of August to the third weekend of October, you can transport yourself to a 16th-century English festival with jousting, crafts, food, and entertainment. | 1821 Crownsville Rd. | 410/266–7304 | www.rennfest.com/mrf.

SEPT.: *Maryland Seafood Festival.* Sandy Point State Park hosts this celebration of Maryland seafood with food, entertainment, and arts and crafts. The festivities are typically held on the weekend after Labor Day. | 410/268–7682 | www.mdseafoodfestival.com.

OCT.: *U.S. Sailboat Show.* The nation's largest and oldest sailboat show is held in the first week of October at City Dock; you can see new sailboats, accessories, and equipment. | 410/268–8828 | www.usboat.com/shows/sbhomes.htm.

OCT.: *U.S. Powerboat Show.* In the second week of October, the powerboats take over at City Dock. New boats, accessories, and equipment are displayed at the nation's largest in-water powerboat show. | 410/268–8828 | www.usboat.com/shows/pbhomes.htm.

NOV.: *Annapolis by Candlelight.* Candlelight tours begin the first week in November of historic sites, private homes, and churches. | 410/267–7619 | www.annapolis.org.

NOV.–DEC.: *Christmas in Annapolis.* Caroling, tree lighting, parades, house tours, and Santa's arrival at City Dock mark the holiday season all over Annapolis. The fun starts on Thanksgiving and runs through New Year's Day. | 410/268–8687.

DEC.: *The Governor's Holiday Open House.* On one day in December, the governor's mansion is decked in its holiday best and open to celebrate the yuletide season. Light refreshments are served; if you come, the governor will greet you personally. | 101 School St. | 410/974–3531.

Dining

MODERATE

49 West. Eclectic. This European-style bistro is filled with art, music, books, and sometimes live classical music. The menu contains a variety of breakfast dishes, fresh baguettes, sandwiches, and traditional *filets de beouf.* | 49 West St. | $6–$22 | AE, MC, V.

Cafe Normandie. French. The wood-beam ceilings and rough plastered walls make this romantic retreat reminiscent of a French country inn. Among the dining choices are veal scallopini, crepes, and homemade pastas. A house specialty is salmon with blueberries and beurreblanc sauce. Kid's menu. | 185 Main St. | 410/263–3382 | $12–$27 | AE, D, DC, MC, V.

Griffins. American. Two stories of brick mark this eatery with marble accents, framed masks on the walls, and a granite-topped mahogany bar. Signature dishes include Griffin's seafood pasta and tuna randelle. Salad bar. Kids' menu. Sun brunch. | 24 Market Space | 410/268–2576 | www.griffins-citydock.com | $10–$22 | AE, D, DC, MC, V.

India's Restaurant. Indian. Paintings from India hang on the walls here. The dining area has a bar in the center, surrounded by wooden tables with white tablecloths. The lounge area has large comfortable couches. The restaurant is known for its vegetarian, rice, and chicken dishes. | 257 West St. | 410/263–7900 | $15–$20 | AE, MC, V.

★ **McGarvey's Saloon and Oyster Bar.** Seafood. This nautical eatery attracts locals, tourists, and occasionally a few real sailors to its low-key, rustic dining area. Of course, the ubiquitous Maryland crab cakes are on the menu. You can also find steaks, seafood, and burgers. For the true McGarvey's experience, try the oysters prepared nearly a dozen different ways. | 8 Market Space | 410/263–5700 | $12–$32 | AE, MC, V.

Ram's Head Tavern. Seafood. Rickety tables and a scarred wooden floor give this English-style pub, adjacent to the Fordham Brewing Company, a sense of being on a well-travelled ship. Try the crab cakes, the spicy shrimp salad or tender, crunchy beer-battered shrimp. Choose from the 170 beers on the menu, 26 of which are on tap. Relax to live jazz, blues, or folk music. | 33 West St. | 410/268–4545 | $10–$20 | AE, D, DC, MC, V.

EXPENSIVE

Cafe Bretton. French. The cafe, in front of the Bretton Gardens, is modeled after a French chateau. The restaurant grows its own herbs and vegetables. You might try the free-range chicken, osso buco, or beef Bourguignon. No smoking. | 849 Baltimore-Annapolis Blvd., Severna Park | 410/647–8222 | www.cafebretton.baweb.com | Closed Sun.–Mon. | $17–$25 | DC, MC, V.

Chart House. Seafood. This restaurant is part of a chain, but you'd never guess it. In a historic building that once sheltered World War II-era vessels, it is filled with nautical memorabilia. Wooden yacht models hang from the rafters, and a huge copper fireplace warms the scene. No surprise that seafood is the specialty here. Try the herb-crusted salmon with onion fronds. Sunday Brunch. | 300 2nd St. | 410/268–7166 | Reservations essential | $15–$32 | AE, D, DC, MC, V.

The Corinthian. Continental. This eatery is reminiscent of an old Maryland home, with padded armchairs, oil lamps, and flowers. The restaurant is 5 mi east of downtown in the Loews Annapolis Hotel. The crab cakes, sea bass, and pistachio-crusted rockfish are all popular. Kids' menu. Sunday brunch. | 126 West St. | 410/263–1299 | $18–$40 | AE, D, DC, MC, V.

Fergie's Waterfront. American. At the water's edge, this two-story restaurant has a phenomenal vista. Tinted windows cut the glare to allow an unimpeded view at sunset. The dining room is relaxed but elegant with a wood floor, white table linens, and crystal. For dinner, start with the hickory shrimp—four massive crustaceans in a thick barbecue sauce on baby greens—then move on to the southwestern salmon steak, which is slightly blackened and dusted with cilantro. Kids' menu. | 2840 Solomon Island Rd., Edgewater | 410/573–1371 | Reservations essential on weekends | $15–$25 | AE, D, DC, MC, V.

Lewnes' Steakhouse. Steak. This two-story building has operated as a restaurant since 1921. Inside black-and-white photographs hang on the walls, depicting early area residents and former owners of the restaurant. Three dining areas hold padded wood tables covered with white tablecloths as well as cozy booths. The restaurant has a reputation for serving generous-size portions of all its dishes, including prime rib, lamb chops, and salmon. | 401 4th St. | 410/263–1617 | Reservations essential | $15–$30 | AE, DC, MC, V.

Middleton Tavern. American. This 1750-era restored restaurant is nestled amid the hustle and bustle of City Dock. Antiques and nautical artifacts give the rooms cozy charm. The awning outside overhangs bare wood tables. It's known for seafood and crab dishes. Kid's menu. Raw bar. Entertainment. Sunday brunch. | 2 Market Space | 410/263–3323 | www.middletontavern.com | $18–$50 | AE, MC, V.

Northwoods. Continental. The 1940 house has been converted into a cozy, rustic restaurant. There are impressionist paintings on the walls, and candles and flowers add to the feeling of intimacy. You might try the beef Wellington, zuppa de pesce, or veal Sorrentina. Dining is available in the garden. | 609 Melvin Ave. | 410/268–2609 | Reservations essential | $19–$23; $27 prix fixe (not avail. Sat.) | AE, D, DC, MC, V.

Treaty of Paris. Continental. The restaurant at the Maryland Inn, built in 1776, has reproduction furniture in its handsome 18th-century dining room, along with a fireplace, old brick walls, and low ceilings with dark wooden beams. House specialties include the grilled chicken St. Michelle, veal Oscar, or the Treaty of Paris combo of shrimp, fish, mussels, and clams. Sunday brunch. | 58 State Cir | 410/263–2641 | Reservations essential Fri.–Sat. | $18–$30 | AE, D, DC, MC, V.

Carrol's Creek Cafe. American. The deck of this waterfront restaurant is right on the marina, and patrons may sit on the bare wood or at plastic shaded tables for a casual meal. Specialties include the rockfish, roasted free-range chicken, jumbo shrimp, and Maryland crab cakes. Sun. brunch. | 410 Severn Ave., Eastport | 410/263–8102 | Reservations essential on holidays | $20–$35 | AE, D, DC, MC, V.

Fred's Restaurant. Continental. The plain, white-stucco exterior of the restaurant belies the elegant Victorian interior with stained-glass windows, antiques, and Tiffany lamps. You will have to travel a bit, 12 mi east of downtown to get here. Crab cakes, stuffed lobster tails, steaks, and veal Parmesan are menu highlights. Kids' menu. | 2348 Solomons Island Rd. (Rte. 2) | 410/224–2386 | $25–$40 | AE, DC, MC, V.

Harry Browne's. Continental. Across from the Maryland State House, this elegant dining room is popular with the Annapolis business crowd. The main dining area has dark woods, white tablecloths, and art deco prints. Overhead is a hammered tin ceiling graced with unusual zodiac globe chandeliers. The front has an awning under which patrons may dine at the seasonal sidewalk cafe. Specialties include filet mignon, Maryland crab cakes, and New York strip steak. | 66 State Cir. | 410/263–4332 | www.annearundelcounty.com/dining/brownes.htm | $20–$30 | AE, D, DC, MC, V.

La Piccola Roma. Italian. This eatery's sophisticated black-and-white color scheme is a fitting backdrop for the kitchen's masterful renditions of classics like lasagna and fettucine alfredo. Also well worth trying are the risotto, osso buco, and freshly made desserts. | 200 Main St. | 410/268–7898 | Reservations essential | $24–$34 | AE, D, DC, MC, V.

O'Leary's. Seafood. This formal spot with views of Spa Creek has mustard-colored walls hung with photos of old Annapolis. In 2000 *Baltimore* magazine O'Leary's was voted Best Seafood Restaurant. The menu includes rockfish, crab cakes, and paella. Kids' menu. | 310 3rd St. | 410/263–0884 | www.olearys-seafood.com | $20–$32 | AE, DC, MC, V.

Lodging

Best Western. Best Western's Annapolis representative is 10 minutes from the historic areas, 2 mi west of downtown. | 142 rooms. Complimentary Continental breakfast. Cable TV. Pool. Gym. Laundry facilities. Business services. | 2520 Riva Rd. | 410/224–2800 | fax 410/266–5539 | www.bestwesternannapolis.com | $99–$139 | AE, D, DC, MC, V.

Comfort Inn. This chain motel is 4 mi west of the U.S. Naval Academy, 3 mi east of City Dock, and 2 mi west of downtown. | 60 rooms. Complimentary Continental breakfast. Cable TV. Pool. Laundry facilities. Business services. | 76 Old Mill Bottom Rd. N. | 410/757–8500 | fax 410/757–4409 | www.comfortinn.com | $89–$109 | AE, D, DC, MC, V.

Courtyard by Marriott. The Courtyard is about 2 mi from Annapolis Mall and 4 mi from the waterfront district and the Maryland State House. | 149 rooms. Restaurant, bar. In-room data ports, cable TV. Indoor pool. Hot tub. Exercise equipment. Laundry facilities. Business services. | 2559 Riva Rd. | 410/266–1555 | fax 410/266–6376 | www.marriott.com | $92–$152 | AE, D, DC, MC, V.

The Flower Box. Antiques, Oriental rugs, wicker furniture, and family photos abound in this ranch-style B&B, just 4 mi from downtown. Enjoy the 3 acres of gardens and wooded hollows on foot or from multiple decks and screened porches. The innkeepers welcome families. There's even a hand-built play area in the back. The rooms have botanical themes with lots of natural light, fresh and dried flowers, and a blend of antique and modern furnishings. | 3 rooms (2 with private baths). Complimentary breakfast. Cable TV. Pool. Play-

ground. | 1601 St. Margaret's Rd. | 410/757–3081 | www.bnbweb.com/flowerbox.html | $80–$100 | No credit cards.

Gibson's Lodgings. Three detached houses next to the U.S. Naval Academy were built in 1786, 1861, and 1890. Today they make up a quaint inn, with rooms reflecting the owner's eclectic taste in antiques. | 20 rooms (8 with shared bath) in 3 buildings. Complimentary Continental breakfast. Cable TV in some rooms, phones in some rooms. Business services. No smoking. | 110 Prince George St. | 410/268–5555 | www.avmcyber.com/gibson | $79–$149 | AE, MC, V.

Hampton Inn and Suites. Just 3 mi from the historic district, this chain hotel offers spacious rooms and even larger suites. The Galleria Shopping Mall is less than 1 mi away. Complimentary Continental breakfast. In-room data ports, cable TV, some refrigerators, some microwaves. Outdoor pool. Fitness center. Laundry facilities. No pets. | 124 Womack Dr. | 410/571–0200 | fax 410/571–0333 | www.hampton-inn.com | 70 rooms | $65–$119 | AE, D, DC, MC, V.

Historic Days Inn & Suites. This suburban Days Inn is close to Annapolis Mall and 3 mi west of downtown. | 68 rooms. Complimentary Continental breakfast. Cable TV. Business services. Some pets allowed. | 2451 Riva Rd. | 410/224–4317 | fax 410/224–6010 | www.daysinn.com | $75–$109 | AE, DC, MC, V.

Loews Annapolis Hotel. Four stories of redbrick surround an atrium at this luxury chain hotel six blocks from busy City Dock. The top two floors have a view of the water. Each suite has a private balcony. Parking (fee). | 217 rooms, 11 suites. Restaurant, bar. In-room data ports, minibars, refrigerators, cable TV. Beauty salon. Gym. Business services. Some pets allowed. Gift shop. Complimentary local shuttle. | 126 West St. | 410/263–7777 | fax 410/263–7813 | info@loewsannapolis.com | www.loewsannapolis.com | $109–$209 | AE, D, DC, MC, V.

Meadow Gardens Bed and Breakfast. This waterfront B&B, 2 mi from downtown, is nestled on more than 6 acres of gardens, orchards, vegetable patches, and a vineyard. Paddle a kayak from its private dock. Or, if you're looking for less strenuous pursuits, soak in the outdoor hot tub or snooze in the large, comfortable chairs on the front porch. Polished wood and wicker give this place a stately yet cozy air. | 2 rooms. Complimentary breakfast. Cable TV. Outdoor hot tub. | 504 Wilson Rd. | 410/266–6840 | fax 410/266–7293 | $85 | No credit cards.

Prince George Inn. This bed and breakfast was built in 1884 and has a romantic look. The rooms are done in East Lake style and have oriental area rugs covering the dark-wood floors. The beds have dark-wood headboards; the wallpaper varies to suit the look of each room. | 4 rooms (2 with shared bath). Complimentary breakfast. Cable TV, in-room VCRs, in-room refrigerators. No smoking. | 232 Prince George St. | 410/263–6418 | fax 410/626–0009 | www.princegeorgeinn.com | $100–$115 | DC, MC, V.

Radisson. You can walk from the Radisson to the nearby Annapolis Mall and restaurants, ½ mi north of the hotel. | 219 rooms. Restaurant, bar, room service. In-room data ports, cable TV. Pool. Gym. Business services. Some pets allowed. | 210 Holiday Ct | 410/224–3150 | fax 410/571–1123 | www.radisson.com/annapolis | $79–$179 | AE, D, DC, MC, V.

MODERATE

55 East. Antiques, paintings, fireplaces, and several porches add to the charm of this 1864 townhouse, now a B&B in the historic district. Rooms have views of the harbor and the Old Statehouse. Complimentary breakfast. Cable TV. No pets. No children under 12. No smoking. | 55 East St. | 410/295–0202 | fax 410/295–0203 | www.annearundelcounty.com/hotel/55east.htm | 3 rooms | $125–$135 | AE, MC, V.

Chesapeake Bay Lighthouse. These accommodations are inside an actual working lighthouse, the Sharps Point Light, 6 mi east of the historic district and Naval Academy. The bed and breakfast is a hexagonal cottage-style lighthouse, built of cherry wood. The third floor has 6 dormers, and its rooms have unpainted cherry walls with light bedspreads. | 5 rooms. Complimentary Continental breakfast. No room phones, TV in common area. No kids under 12. No smoking. | 1423 Sharps Point Rd. | 410/757–0248 | $125–$179 | D, MC, V.

Georgian House. Built in 1747, this two-story stone house with black shutters and white trim is one of the older houses in town. Find quiet repose on its garden patio after a day of traipsing around Annapolis. The rooms—with sleigh beds, private decks, claw-foot tubs, and gas fireplaces—are similarly soothing. | 4 rooms. Complimentary breakfast. Cable TV. No pets. No kids. No smoking. | 170 Duke of Gloucester St. | 410/263–5618 or 800/557–2068 | fax 410/263–5618 | $95–$165 | AE, MC, V.

Governor Calvert House. Built in 1727, this Gregorian building has a gambrel roof and each room has a Victorian theme. The rooms have antique furniture and vary in colors; some rooms have dark wood floors while others are carpeted. The Inn also has a unique atrium, and faces the Colonial Gardens. | 51 rooms. In-room data ports, cable TV. Business services, parking (fee). | 58 State Cir. | 410/263–2641 or 800/847–8882 | fax 410/268–3613 | historicinns@erols.com | www.annapolisinns.com/calverthouse.html | $169–$189 | AE, D, DC, MC, V.

Marriott Waterfront. This waterfront chain hotel has many rooms overlooking the Chesapeake Bay and the city's historic district. | 150 rooms. Restaurant, bar. In-room data ports, cable TV. Gym. Business services, parking (fee). | 80 Compromise St. | 410/268–7555 | fax 410/269–5864 | www.marriott.com | $154–$279 | AE, D, DC, MC, V.

Maryland Inn. This vintage Victorian building was built in 1776 and has porches and a marble tiled lobby. Some rooms are reminiscent of the Revolutionary era; all have antique furniture or reproductions. The rooms are Williamsburg colors, some with wallpaper and others with texture paint. | 44 rooms. Restaurant, bar. In-room data ports, cable TV. Business services. | Church Cir. and Main St. | 410/263–2641 or 800/847–8882 | fax 410/268–3613 | historicinns@erols.com | www.annapolisinns.com/marylandinn.html | $169–$189 | AE, D, DC, MC, V.

Robert Johnson House. The Robert Johnson House has views of the Governor's mansion and State House, and is actually made up of three houses which have been integrated, restored, and artfully furnished. Each room is filled with early 19th-century furniture. | 29 rooms. In-room data ports, refrigerators, cable TV. Business services. | 23 State Cir. | 410/263–2641 or 800/847–8882 | fax 410/268–3613 | historicinns@erols.com | www.annapolisinns.com/johnsonhouse.html | $169–$189 | AE, D, DC, MC, V.

Sheraton Barcelo. Close to U.S. 50/301 and about 4 mi from downtown Annapolis is this chain hotel. | 197 rooms. Restaurant, bar. In-room data ports, room service. Indoor pool. Hot tub. Gym. Business services. | 173 Jennifer Rd. | 410/266–3131 | fax 410/266–6247 | www.sheraton.com | $109–$210 | AE, D, DC, MC, V.

William Page Inn. The cedar-shingle, wood-frame structure was built in 1908. The antique furniture in each room adds to its Victorian charm. Each of the five rooms is named to reflect its theme. For example, the Marilyn Suite is a light and airy room complete with dormer windows, skylight, and whirlpool tub. | 5 rooms (2 with shared bath), 1 suite. Complimentary breakfast. Business services. No smoking. | 8 Martin St. | 410/626–1506 or 800/346–4160 | fax 410/263–4841 | wmpageinn@aol.com | www.williampageinn.com | $105–$195 | MC, V.

BALTIMORE

MAP 4, F2

(Nearby towns also listed: Cockeysville, Pikesville, Towson)

Though it's the 13th largest city in the country—and one that traces its history back to the early 1700s—Baltimore is often overshadowed by Washington, DC and Philadelphia. In fact, it has experienced an incredible rebirth over the past 20 years, redeveloped its waterfront and sports facilities, and become an underrated yet intriguing destination with a down-to-earth personality.

The Inner Harbor is an ideal starting point to explore Baltimore, often called "Charm City." Nowhere else is the city's success more evident than around the Inner Harbor, where new museums, restaurants, stores, and hotels are under construction almost all the time. The newer structures complement already well-known establishments such as the wonderful National Aquarium, the Maryland Science Center, and the Gallery at Harborplace. From the harbor, water taxis give great skyline views and access to historic landmarks and neighborhoods, including the lively, sometimes boisterous waterfront neighborhood of Fells Point.

Away from the waterfront, Baltimore is an amalgam of distinct neighborhoods that better tell the city's history than the sparkling Inner Harbor. There are neighborhoods of white marble steps, row houses, tree-shaded streets, and impressive history and architecture. Mount Vernon, for example, is often called one of the nation's most beautiful neighborhoods because of its distinctive 19th-century architecture and the impressive 178-ft Washington Monument. The city's elite once lived here; today, Mount Vernon is a cultural mecca with formidable museums, churches, and the Peabody Conservatory of Music.

Baltimore has its roots in Maryland's farming past. With its natural harbor on the Chesapeake Bay, the town evolved to become a convenient port for farmers to ship their produce overseas. Baltimore quickly became a seafaring and trading community.

© Artville

AMERICA'S OLDEST GAME

Never mind that Maryland's official state sport is jousting: Lacrosse is the unofficial one. Thousands of youths and adolescents—not to mention adults—from the flatlands of the Eastern Shore to the western mountains compete in the sport.

This unusual game involving sticks with mesh pouches at one end and a ball the size of an orange was first introduced to Europeans by the Iroquois Confederacy in the late 1600s. It is the oldest game native to North America, and one of the fastest-growing team sports in the nation.

Lacrosse has been a Maryland pasttime for well over a century. About 4,000 spectators showed up for the first formal lacrosse exhibition by the Baltimore Club in November 1878—about the same time the nation's first college team formed at New York University. Johns Hopkins University represented the United States in lacrosse exhibitions in the 1928 Summer Olympic Games in Amsterdam and the 1932 Olympic Games in Los Angeles. Today, there are more than 500,000 current and former players living in Maryland. More than 1 million people attend lacrosse games in the state each year.

Home to the headquarters of U.S. Lacrosse, the game's governing body, the Lacrosse Museum, the National Hall of Fame, and STX, Inc., one of the largest manufacturers of lacrosse equipment in the world, Maryland also hosts the National Junior Lacrosse Festival at Towson University. The festival attracts more than 11,000 players and their parents each year.

Its proximity to the nation's capital, too, assured Baltimore a colorful role in American history. During the War of 1812, the British, having burned Washington, DC, attacked Baltimore by land and sea. On the water, they were held off by the guns of Fort McHenry. The 25-hour bombardment of the city inspired Francis Scott Key, a Maryland lawyer who was detained aboard a ship after obtaining the release of a friend, to write a poem that eventually became the national anthem, "The Star-Spangled Banner." The first bloodshed of the Civil War occurred on the streets of Baltimore. When the 700-member 6th Massachusetts Regiment arrived at President Street Station and began marching along Pratt Street to catch a train at another station, a mob of Southern sympathizers began throwing stones. Nine civilians and three soldiers died in the ensuing fight.

The riches of the Chesapeake Bay helped the city to flourish in the late 1800s, with canning industries that preserved and shipped goods to other parts of the country. Shipbuilding and transportation were viable industries at this time, and the city was an active port of entry for European immigrants and rural residents of the upper South.

Like other cities, Baltimore suffered "suburban flight" in the 1960s, but a renaissance began in the 1970s with building efforts downtown and at the Inner Harbor. The rejuvenation continues today with the opening of newer museums, like Port Discovery, the Baltimore children's museum, which opened in December 1998; the restoration of the city's old Power Plant into a sports and entertainment complex; the expansion of the Baltimore Convention Center; and the opening of a stadium for Baltimore's pro football team, the aptly named Ravens. Away from the Inner Harbor, neighborhoods like Fells Point, Federal Hill, Canton, Mount Vernon, Mount Royal, Little Italy, and Roland Park continue to flourish.

Information: Baltimore Area Convention and Visitors Association. | 100 Light St., Baltimore 21202 | 410/659–7300 or 800/343–3468 | fax 410/727–2308 | www.baltimore.org.

NEIGHBORHOODS

Federal Hill. Jubilant Baltimoreans celebrating Maryland's ratification of the U.S. Constitution in 1788 marched to the top of a hill in this area and named it for their new government. The waterfront neighborhood became home to both merchants and laborers employed at Baltimore's port. Named a national historic district in 1970, Federal Hill benefits from its location adjacent to the Inner Harbor and its charming 18th- and 19th-century row houses.

Fells Point. This maritime community, led by Quaker shipbuilder William Fell, was settled in 1730. Today it is known for its nightlife. Every Friday and Saturday night, swarms of bar hoppers fill the cobblestone streets. Even so, Fells Point—with its narrow lanes and redbrick buildings—retains the charm of an 18th-century seafaring village. The old recreation pier once served as the set for the NBC television drama *Homicide: Life on the Street.*

Canton. Once a run-down collection of canneries, factories and working-class row houses, Canton is today a thriving community with an eclectic mix of restaurants. The canneries are now up-scale condominiums and shops. The row houses are being restored to their original 19th-century appearances. Its O'Donnell Square, flanked by a stone church and an old fire station, is a smorgasbord of eateries and bars. Canton is accessible to Fells Point and the Inner Harbor by water taxi.

Little Italy. Just east of the Inner Harbor, the 12-block enclave is dominated by Italian families, whose ancestors arrived in the mid-19th century with the promise of railroad jobs. By 1900, every home in the neighborhood was owned by Italians. Today, you'll find plenty of trattorias and bakeries.

Mount Vernon. Perhaps the loveliest and most fashionable neighborhood in Baltimore, Mount Vernon is just north of downtown. Well-planned squares, classic architecture, bronze statues, and marble fountains evoke another era. You can climb the 228 steps of the Washington Monument for an enticing view of the city or visit the Peabody Conservatory of Music and the Walters Art Gallery.

WALKING TOURS

Literary and Cultural Baltimore (approximately 2 hours)

Begin at the **Washington Monument** at Mount Vernon Place. Climbing the 228 steps to the top affords not only a spectacular view of the Mount Vernon neighborhood but of downtown Baltimore too. Across from the monument on West Mount Vernon Place is the **Peabody Library and the Peabody Conservatory of Music.** If the library is open, it's worth a peek inside. Skylights illuminate the marble-floor court, framed by six stories of balconies; it's called the most beautiful room in Baltimore. Walk to the opposite side of the park, at the corner of East Mount Vernon Place and South Washington Place, you'll find **Mount Vernon Place Methodist Church.** Built in 1873, the church sits on the site where Francis Scott Key, the author of "The Star-Spangled Banner," died in 1843. A plaque on the church marks his death there. In the plaza across South Washington Place is a sculpture of Key's brother-in-law and law partner, U.S. Chief Justice Roger Brooke Taney, author of the controversial Dred Scott Decision. Follow East Mount Vernon Place around the monument and turn right on North Washington Place, on the opposite side of the park. On North Washington Place near Madison Street a plaque marks the former hotel where F. Scott Fitzgerald and his wife, Zelda, stayed while she was being treated at Johns Hopkins University. Fitzgerald later lived in a town house on nearby Park Avenue, where he finished the classic *Tender Is the Night.* Nearly three blocks west at 12 Madison Street is the 19th-century home of congressman and Navy secretary John Pendleton Kennedy, a best-selling novelist of the 1820s, who, many believe, created the myth of the Old South. A block south of the Kennedy home is the **Maryland Historical Society Museum and Library of Maryland,** which contains the original manuscript of "The Star-Spangled Banner." East of the historical society, as you head back toward Mount Vernon Place, are two noteworthy residences. At 704 Cathedral Street, H.L. Mencken, one of the most influential journalists of the early 20th century, lived on the third floor with his wife, Sara Haardt. Next door, in a private home at 702 Cathedral Street, President Abraham Lincoln spent a night away from the White House. Continue back to the Washington Monument.

Inner Harbor (approximately 2 hours)

Begin at the Harborplace Amphitheater, where you can board a water taxi and take in the view of Baltimore's waterfront. As the taxi ferries you to places like Fells Point, the city's historic maritime neighborhood, you'll be able to see some of the harbor's landmarks from a unique vantage. Leave the water taxi at Landing 4, on the harbor's west side. You'll see the unusually shaped restaurant **Rusty Scupper** at the water's edge. On land, head back toward the Inner Harbor. To the left, the imposing hill is **Federal Hill Park,** once the site of Civil War fortifications. Directly in front of you, at the corner of Key Highway and Covington Street, is the extraordinary **American Visionary Art Museum,** which showcases the creations of self-taught artists. As you continue along the promenade, past Rash Field, you'll see the oddly shaped building with the neon sign; it's the **Maryland Science Center,** which has an IMAX movie theater. The throngs of people ahead of you are probably shopping or dining at the Light Street and Pratt Street pavilions. Step inside for refreshments or find an empty bench along the waterfront. Berthed along the promenade will most likely be the *Patriot III,* which has narrated cruises from enclosed decks, and *Clipper City,* a 158-ft clipper ship. On the other side of the Pratt Street Pavilion is the **Gallery,** a five-story shopping mall. The most imposing building on the waterfront is the 32-story **World Trade Center.** If time permits, take the elevator to the 27th-story observation deck to enjoy a sweeping view of the harbor and the city. Just east is the lively **Power Plant,** the city's former power station, home to the Hard Rock Cafe, Barnes and Noble, and ESPN Zone, a sports-themed restaurant and entertainment center. Along Pier 3 are the floating historic vessels of the **Baltimore Maritime Museum.** At the edge of the pier is the popular **National Aquarium in Baltimore,** home to more than 10,000 fish, dolphins, sharks and other forms of aquatic life. On Pier 5 is the **Seven-Foot Knoll Lighthouse.**

TRANSPORTATION INFORMATION

Driving around Town: You can reach downtown area via two main thoroughfares: from the north via I–83, the Jones Falls Expressway; and from the south via I–395, which branches off I–95. Congestion on these routes, as well as on the Baltimore Beltway, I–695, will slow your travel in the morning and even more in the evening. Most downtown streets run one-way. The streets are identified as east or west based on their orientation to Charles Street, or as north or south based on their orientation to Baltimore Street. Complicating travel within the city, traffic lights are often not properly synchronized, meaning that you're often left waiting at long red lights. Be patient. The speed limit for most streets is 25 mph. Parking can be difficult to find downtown. Meters cost $1 per hour, and fines run $20 or more for expired meters. Parking garages are a good alternative; they're easy to find along Pratt Street between Camden Yard and the Inner Harbor. Daily prices average $15. Many downtown attractions are within easy walking distance of these garages and many of those that are not are accessible via a water taxi.

Airports: About 10 mi south of Baltimore off Route 295 (Baltimore-Washington Parkway), the **Baltimore-Washington International Airport** has scheduled daily flights by most major airlines. | 800/I–FLY–BWI | www.bwiairport.com.

Rail: Daily service to Baltimore is via **Amtrak.** Departs from **Penn Station,** 1500 N. Charles St. | 800/872–7245 | www.amtrak.com.

Bus Lines: Greyhound extends to Baltimore and many Maryland communities. Service from **Trailways-Greyhound Bus Terminal,** 210 W. Fayette St. | 800/231–2722 | www.greyhound.com.

Intra-City Transit: The **Mass Transit Administration,** known as the MTA, runs light rail, metro subway, and bus service around metropolitan Baltimore; commuter trains run to Washington, D.C. | 6 St. Paul St., Baltimore | 410/539–5000 | fax 410/333–3289.

Attractions

ART AND ARCHITECTURE

★ **American Visionary Art Museum.** The national museum in Federal Hill is dedicated to the self-taught or "outsider" artist. Seven galleries contain an eclectic mix of unusual creations. Unconventional materials including rags, household wares, and toothpicks are among the media used. Parking (fee). | 800 Key Hwy. | 410/244–1900 | www.avam.org | $6 | Tues.–Sun. 10–6, closed Mon.

Baltimore Museum of Art. Works by Matisse, Picasso, Cézanne, Gaugin, van Gogh, and Monet are among the 100,000 paintings, sculptures, and decorative arts on display. The museum, just south of Johns Hopkins, also has the world's second-largest collection of Andy Warhol pieces. | 10 Art Museum Dr. | 410/396–7100 or 410/396–7101 | www.artbma.org | $6 | Wed.–Fri. 11–5, weekends 11–6, closed Mon.–Tues.

City Court House. This downtown hall of justice contains an expanse of columns and classical ornament in Beaux Arts style. The interior was used in the Hollywood film *And Justice for All.* | 111 N Calvert St. | 410/396–3100 | www.ci.baltimore.md.us/government/court.html | Free | Weekdays 8–4:30, closed weekends.

City Hall. Mansard roofs and a gilt dome over a 110-ft rotunda make this impressive structure a standout in downtown Baltimore. City Hall contains exhibits on Baltimore's history. | 100 N. Holliday St. | 410/396–3100 | www.baltimorecity.gov | Free | Weekdays 8–4:30, closed weekends.

Mount Clare Museum House. One of the oldest homes in Baltimore, this elegant Georgian mansion in Carroll Park predates the American Revolution (it was completed in 1760). The home was owned by the noted barrister Charles Carroll, one of the major landowners in the state, a signer of the Declaration of Independence, and a member of the Continental Congress. | 1500 Washington Blvd. | 410/837-3262 | fax 410/837-0251 | users.erols.com/mountclaremuseumhouse | $6 | Tues.–Fri. 11–4, weekends 1–4, closed Mon.

★ **Walters Art Gallery.** More than 30,000 artworks spanning 5,000 years are on exhibit in two wings of this Mount Vernon museum. The older wing, built in 1904, contains Renaissance and Baroque paintings. Also on display are medieval armor and artifacts, jewelry, and decorative works. Parking (fee). | 600 N. Charles St. | 410/547-9000 | www.thewalters.org | $5 | Tues.–Fri. 10–4, weekends 11–5, closed Mon.

CULTURE, EDUCATION, AND HISTORY

Battle Monument. The first war memorial erected in the country honors Marylanders who lost their lives during the War of 1812 while defending the City of Baltimore. Italian sculptor Antonio Capellano sculpted the downtown monument out of pure white marble. | Calvert and Fayette Sts. | Free | Daily dawn–dusk.

Baltimore Center for the Performing Arts–Morris A. Mechanic Theater. Baltimore's Broadway has the latest touring musicals, dramas, and dance performances. | 25 Hopkins Plaza | 410/625-4230 | www.themechanic.org | $35–$65.

Baltimore Opera Company. Opened in 1894, the Lyric Opera House is known for its fine interior and splendid acoustics. It is home to the Baltimore Opera Company and various traveling musical and stage productions. | 140 W. Mt. Royal Ave. | 410/727-6000 | www.baltimoreopera.com | $37–$130.

Baltimore Symphony Orchestra. The renowned orchestra plays out the season at Joseph Meyerhoff Symphony Hall near the University of Baltimore. | 1212 Cathedral St. | 410/783-8000 or 410/783-8100 | www.baltimoresymphony.com | $25–$65 | Sept.–Jun.

Center Stage. This regional theater group, founded in 1963, presents a six-play main stage season along with solo performances from their Off Center division. | 700 N. Calvert St. | 410/332-0033 | fax 410/727-2522 | www.centerstage.org.

© Corbis

BEACONS OVER THE BAY

Lighthouses have brightened the shores of Maryland's Chesapeake Bay for more than a century. Although most are no longer operating, many have been preserved within state parks.

The first Maryland lighthouse was built in 1822, the last in 1910. Maryland's shoreline of the Chesapeake Bay was once home to 44 lighthouses; today, about 25 remain. Perhaps the most famous is the Drum Point Lighthouse, built in 1883. An example of the screwpile architecture, its base screws into the sandy depths of the bay. It's now part of the Calvert Marine Museum in Solomons Island.

Maryland also has plenty of more familiar-looking lighthouses, simple masonry towers built on pieces of land that jut into the water. Examples include the Concord Point Lighthouse in Havre de Grace, open for tours on weekends during the warm months, and Turkey Point Lighthouse at Elk Neck State Park near the town of North East. The latter is not open to the public but is accessible by a footpath.

Once tools for guiding sailors at sea, lighthouses today are popular tourist attractions. And if the tourists can't come to them, sometimes lighthouses are brought to the tourists: The Seven-Foot Knoll Lighthouse, now part of the Baltimore Maritime Museum, was relocated to the Inner Harbor.

Cockpit in Court Summer Theatre. Summer community theater at Essex Community College, just east of Baltimore, gives theater lovers an outdoor option. | 7201 Rossville Blvd., Essex | 410/918–4023 | $10–$15.

Edgar Allan Poe Grave. The grave of the "Master of the Macabre" is in one of the city's oldest cemeteries, Westminster Cemetery and Catacombs, just west of downtown. Other famous Marylanders are buried here as well. Tours are given for the entire cemetery (fee). | Fayette and Greene Sts. | 410/706–2072 | www.eapoe.org/balt/poegrave.htm | Daily 8–dusk.

Edgar Allan Poe House. Poe lived in this tiny row house, west of downtown, for three years and wrote his first horror story, "Berenice," in the tiny garret. Changing exhibits and a video about Poe's short, tempestuous life are featured. | 203 N. Amity St. | 410/396–7932 | www.eapoe.org/balt/poehse.htm | $3 | Apr.–Jul., Wed.–Sat., noon–3:45; Aug.–Sept., Sat., noon–3:45; Oct.–Dec., Wed.–Sat., noon–3:45.

Enoch Pratt Free Library. One of the country's largest libraries, it has rooms devoted to the works of Edgar Allan Poe and H.L. Mencken. | 400 Cathedral St. | 410/396–5430 | fax 410/396–1441 | www.pratt.lib.md.us | Free | Mon.–Wed. 10–8, Thurs. and Sat. 10–5, closed Fri. and Sun.

★ **Fort McHenry National Monument and Historic Shrine.** The star-shaped, brick-and-earth structure, built in 1803, is most famous for its role in the War of 1812. In September 1814, Maryland lawyer Francis Scott Key was inspired to write the words to "The Star-Spangled Banner" during the 25-hour battle in which the fort defended the city. The visit includes a 15-minute history film. | East Fort Ave. | 410/962–4290 | fax 410/962–2500 | www.nps.gov/fomc | $5 | Daily 8 AM–8 PM.

Holocaust Memorial. Erected in 1980, the downtown memorial and sculpture stands as a stark reminder of the 6 million Jews and others murdered by the Nazis in Europe between 1933 and 1945. | Lombard St., at Gay St. | 410/542–4850 | Free | Daily dawn–dusk.

Johns Hopkins University. The 140-acre Homewood campus is the heart of Johns Hopkins University (founded in 1876), and home to nearly 4,000 undergraduates and more than 1,300 full-time graduate students. The university sponsors lectures and performances year-round. | Charles and 34th Sts. | 410/516–8000 | www.jhu.edu | Free | Daily.
Twentieth-century artist Benjamin Bufano created the works in the **Bufano Sculpture Garden,** 10 pieces of sculpture depicting various animals. | Dunning Park, behind Mudd Hall | 410/396–7100 | www.jhu.edu/tour/bufano.html | Free | Daily.
Built in the 1850s, the 48-room Italianate mansion known as **Evergreen House** was the home of John Work Garrett, whose grandfather of the same name was president of the Baltimore and Ohio Railroad. The house and its large collection of books, prints, and paintings, belong to Johns Hopkins University. Tours are given on the hour. | 4545 N. Charles St. | 410/516–0895 | www.jhu.edu/~evrgreen | $6 | Weekdays 10–4, weekends 1–4.
Homewood House Museum was the home of Charles Carroll, Jr., the son of Charles Carroll of Carrollton, a signer of the U.S. Declaration of Independence. The home has been restored to its appearance of 1801. | 3400 N. Charles St. | 410/516–5589 | www.jhu.edu/news_info/to_do/homewood | $6 | Tues.–Sat. 11–4, Sun. noon–4, closed Mon.

Maryland Institute, College of Art. The nation's oldest four-year independent college of art has changing exhibits by students, faculty, and regional and national artists. | 1300 Mt. Royal Ave. | 410/669–9200 | www.mica.edu | Free | Daily.

Morgan State University. The predominantly African-American college was founded in 1867 with a mission to educate men and women as teachers. | 1700 E. Cold Spring Ln. | 443/885–3333 | www.morgan.edu | Free | Weekdays; weekends by appointment.

Mother Seton House. St. Elizabeth Ann Seton, the first American-born saint, founded a girls school and took her first vows in this modest row house. | 600 N. Paca St. | 410/523–3443 | Free | Weekends 1–4 or by appointment.

Peabody Conservatory of Music. The Conservatory is affiliated with Johns Hopkins University. The Miriam Friedberg Concert Hall seats 800. The Conservatory holds orchestra concerts, recitals, and operas. | 17 E. Mount Vernon Pl. | 410/659–8179 | www.peabody.jhu.edu | Most shows free.

The **Peabody Library** is a fine example of neo-Renaissance architecture and the masterpiece of architect Edmund G. Lind. Especially impressive are the cast-iron balconies towering above a black-and-white marble floor. More than a quarter of a million books, the oldest dating back to 1470, line the shelves. | 17 E. Mount Vernon Pl | 410/659–8179 | Free | Weekdays 9–3, closed weekends.

Pier 6 Concert Pavilion. Major recording artists perform at the canopy-covered outdoor amphitheater on the Inner Harbor. | Pier 6 | 410/752–8632 | $25–$55 | May–Sept.

Senator Theatre. Built around 1939, the 900-seat movie house in northern Baltimore is listed on the National Register of Historic Places. You can enjoy the art deco styling, velvet curtains, retro lobby, and a great selection of new and classic films. The theater also hosts film festivals and musical performances. | 5904 York Rd. | 410/435–8338 | www.senator.com | Daily.

Shot Tower. One of the few remaining structures of its kind, the 215-ft shot tower was built in 1829 from a million bricks. The tower was used to manufacture lead-shot ammunition: Molten lead was dropped from the top of the tower into a vat of water at the bottom; the lead droplets would form into perfect spheres as they fell into the cooling water below. The tower has been closed since 1970. | Fayette and Front Sts. | www.cr.nps.gov/nr/travel/baltimore/b29.htm | Free | Daily 9–5.

University of Baltimore More than 4,500 students—most of them part-time—are earning graduate and undergraduate degrees at this college in the Mount Royal neighborhood. The university's library holds collections of more than 300,000 volumes, including books, periodicals, CD-ROM indexes, microforms, government documents, and audio-visual materials. | Maryland Ave., at Charles St. | 410/837–4756 | www.ubalt.edu | Free.

Vagabond Theater. Players perform recent Broadway hits throughout the year at this Fells Point theater. | 806 S. Broadway | 410/563–9135 | www.bcpl.lib.md.us/~djelliot/vag.html | $10–$12.

Washington Monument. Erected in 1829, the marble Doric column is arguably the oldest formal monument to the nation's first president. The 178-ft monument was designed by Robert Mills, who also designed the more famous Washington Monument in the nation's capital. You may climb 228 steps to its top for a bird's-eye view of the city. On a hill 100 ft above sea level, it was once a landmark for ships sailing into harbor. The four lovely gardens surrounding the monument form a Greek cross. This park also was the first planned open space in the city. | N. Charles St. | 410/396–0929 | www.wam.umd.edu/~jlehnert/welcome.html | $1 | Wed.–Sun. 10–4, closed Mon.–Tues.

MUSEUMS

★ **B and O Railroad Museum.** The birthplace of the famous Baltimore and Ohio Railroad, the museum, just west of Camden Yards, contains more than 120 full-size locomotives and a collection of railroad memorabilia. | 901 W. Pratt St. | 410/752–2490 | www.borail.org | $7 | Daily 10–5.

Babe Ruth Birthplace/Baseball Center. This modest brick row house, just three blocks from Oriole Park at Camden Yards, was the birthplace of "The Bambino." The museum is devoted to Ruth's life and the local Orioles baseball club. | 216 Emory St. | 410/727–1539 | www.baberuthmuseum.com | $6 | Apr.–Oct., daily 10–5 and until 7 on the days of Orioles home games; Nov.–Mar., daily 10–4.

Baltimore Civil War Museum. The museum at the eastern edge of the Inner Harbor is housed in the former President Street Station, where Union troops en route to Washington began their ill-fated walk across town along Pratt Street. The ensuing riot resulted in the first deaths of the Civil War. | 601 President St. | 410/385–5188 | fax 410/385–5189 | www.civilwarinbaltimore.org | $2 | Apr.–Dec., Tues.–Sun. 10–5 closed Mon.; Jan.–Mar., Wed.–Sun. 10–5, closed Mon.–Tues.

Baltimore Maritime Museum. Three docked vessels, including the Coast Guard cutter *Taney*, the lightship *Chesapeake*, and the submarine USS *Torsk*—credited with sinking the last two Japanese warships of World War II—are along Pier 4 in the Inner Harbor. | Pier 4 | 410/396–3453 | www.baltomaritimemuseum.org | $6 | Spring–Fall, Sun.–Thurs. 10–5:30, Fri.–Sat. 10–6:30; Winter, Fri.–Sun. 10:30–5.

Baltimore Museum of Industry. Housed in a 1865 oyster cannery in Federal Hill, this unusual museum has a fascinating glimpse of the city's industrial and labor histories. You can help operate functional re-creations of a machine shop, print shop, and garment work room. | 1415 Key Hwy. | 410/727–4808 | www.charm.net/~bmi | $6 | Tues.–Sat. 10–5, Sun. noon–5, closed Mon.

Baltimore Public Works Museum. The oldest of its kind in the nation, this unusual museum is in the ornate, redbrick Eastern Avenue Sewage Pumping Station on the eastern edge of the Inner Harbor. Exhibits tell the story of city services, including trash removal. Many exhibits are designed for kids to crawl in and around. | 751 Eastern Ave. | 410/396–5565 | $2.50 | Tues.–Sun. 10–4; closed Mon. Call for summer hours.

Baltimore Streetcar Museum. The museum, located ½ north of downtown, documents the evolution of streetcars, which once dominated the streets of Baltimore; you can ride a restored streetcar. | 1901 Falls Rd. | 410/547–0264 | www.baltimoremd.com/streetcar | $5 | June–Oct., weekends and holidays noon–5; Nov.–May, Sun. noon–5; closed weekdays.

Great Blacks in Wax Museum. This is the nation's first black-history wax museum, containing more than 100 life-size wax figures in dramatic historical scenes. | 1601–03 E. North Ave. | 410/563–3404 or 410/563–6416 | fax 410/675–5040 | www.greatblacksinwax.org | $6 | Weekdays 9–6, weekends noon–6.

Dr. Samuel D. Harris National Museum of Dentistry. On the campus of the University of Maryland at Baltimore, this unusual museum has exhibits on the anatomy and physiol-

BOUNTY OF THE BAY

A visit to Maryland would not be complete without stepping into a crab house in Baltimore or along the bay for a feast of steamed blue crabs. One of the culinary delights of the Chesapeake Bay, blue crabs are smaller than their counterparts elsewhere in the United States, not to mention tastier, according to many Baltimoreans.

At a typical Maryland crab house, tables are covered in brown paper and littered with mallets, picks and, most importantly, pitchers of beer. The crabs are steamed in Maryland's favorite spice mixture—Old Bay—until they turn red. There's a bit of a trick to cracking the shell and tearing the crab apart to find the sweet meat. For locals, this ritual is as much a part of summer as watching the Orioles or spending a week at the beach in Ocean City.

If steamed crabs aren't your style, try them in soup—cream of crab or tomato-based Maryland crab soup. Most places also serve crab cakes, a mixture of crab, bread crumbs, and spices. Many restaurants claim to have the best crab cakes—and you'd do well not to argue. But there is some truth to the local adage: The closer to the bay, the better the crabs and the seafood. Also try crab imperial, deep-fried crab, and a crab dip appetizer.

© Artville

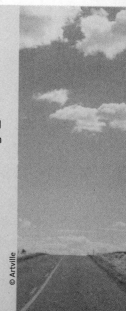

ogy of human and animal teeth and the history of dentistry. Among the artifacts are George Washington's wooden dentures. | 31 S. Greene St. | 410/706–0600 | fax 410/706–8313 | www.dentalmuseum.umaryland.edu | $4.50 | Wed.–Sat. 10–4, Sun. 1–4, closed Mon.–Tues.

Jewish Museum of Maryland. Founded in 1960, the museum, located about 8 blocks northwest of the Inner harbor, has changing exhibits related to Jewish history in Baltimore, Maryland, the nation, and the world. The museum incorporates the adjoining *Lloyd Street Synagogue*, built in 1845, the first in Maryland and third in the nation, and the B'nai Israel Synagogue. | 15 Lloyd St. | 410/732–6400 | www.jhsm.org | $4 | Sun. and Tues.–Thurs. noon–4; closed Mon., Fri.–Sat., and Jewish holidays.

Lacrosse Museum and National Hall of Fame. The only national museum dedicated to lacrosse, it's a showplace for equipment, uniforms, and other memorabilia relating to lacrosse and its history, including its Native American origins. This museum near Johns Hopkins' main campus includes the national hall of fame. | 113 W. University Pkwy. | 410/235–6882, ext. 122 | www.lacrosse.org/museum.html | $3 | Jun.–Jan., weekdays 10–3; Feb.–May, Tues.–Sat. 10–3.

Maryland Historical Society. This downtown museum depicts Maryland's heritage and the history and culture of the Chesapeake Bay through displays of its more than 200,000 cultural artifacts and everyday objects including paintings, furniture, costumes, toys, sports memorabilia, period furniture and the Radcliffe Maritime Collection. The museum also contains the original manuscript of "The Star-Spangled Banner." | 201 W. Monument St. | 410/685–3750 | fax 410/385–2105 | www.mdhs.org | $4 | Tues.–Fri. 10–5, Sat. 9–5, Sun. 11–5, closed Mon.

Maryland Science Center. Housed in a contemporary building on the west side of the Inner Harbor, the museum includes changing and stationary hands-on exhibits, a planetarium, an IMAX movie theater, and an astronomical observatory. | 601 Light St. | 410/685–5225 | www.mdsci.org | $13 | Weekdays 10–5; weekends 10–6.

Port Discovery. This hands-on museum for children in downtown has a three-story, enclosed climbing structure at its center, a room dedicated to toddlers, and a re-created Nile River and pyramids. The 80,000-square-ft facility was designed by Disney and immerses children in learning fun. McDonald's on site. | 34 Market Pl | 410/727–8120 | www.portdiscovery.org | $10 | Tues.–Sun. 10–5:30; closed Mon.

Star-Spangled Banner Flag House and 1812 Museum. Built in 1793, this Federal home on the edge of Little Italy, was where Mary Pickersgill hand-sewed the 15-star, 15-stripe flag that survived the British bombardment of Fort McHenry and inspired Francis Scott Key. | 844 E. Pratt St. | 410/837–1793 | www.flaghouse.org | $4 | Tues.–Sat. 10–4, closed Sun.–Mon.

PACKING IDEAS FOR HOT WEATHER

- ❏ Antifungal foot powder
- ❏ Bandanna
- ❏ Cooler
- ❏ Cotton clothing
- ❏ Day pack
- ❏ Film
- ❏ Hiking boots
- ❏ Insect repellent
- ❏ Rain jacket
- ❏ Sport sandals
- ❏ Sun hat
- ❏ Sunblock
- ❏ Synthetic ice
- ❏ Umbrella
- ❏ Water bottle

*Excerpted from *Fodor's: How to Pack: Experts Share Their Secrets*
© 1997, by Fodor's Travel Publications

PARKS, NATURAL AREAS, AND OUTDOOR RECREATION

Cylburn Arboretum. Local businessman Jesse Tyson began building the Cylburn Mansion in 1863, and completed it in 1888. Gardens, trails, and a hands-on nature center are on the 176-acre estate in the Coldspring area. The grounds are a popular stopping place for migratory birds. The mansion houses a nature museum with extensive bird exhibits. | 4915 Greenspring Ave. | 410/367–2217 | Free | Grounds open daily 6 AM–9 PM; Mansion and nature museum open weekdays 7:30–3:30.

Druid Hill Park. The 744-acre park has a reservoir, Victorian-era picnic shelters, and a Chinese pagoda. The park also contains miles of bridle, jogging, and bicycle paths, plus tennis courts. | 2700 Druid Hill Lake Dr. | 410/396–7931 | Free | Daily dawn–dusk.

The third-oldest zoo in the nation, the **Baltimore Zoo** spans more than 150 acres and has more than 2,000 animals, including elephants, lions, tigers, giraffes, and penguins. A re-created barnyard has a petting zoo, and the Maryland Wilderness exhibit contains animals native to the state. | Druid Hill Park | 410/366–LION | fax 410/243–8691 | www.baltimorezoo.org | $9.50 | Daily 10–4; 10–5:30 summer weekends.

The **City of Baltimore Conservatory** contains acres of gardens and flowers. It was built in 1888 and is known to locals as "The Palm House" because of its large collection of tropical plants. | 3100 Swan Dr. | 410/396–0180 | Free | Thurs.–Sun. 10–4, closed Mon.–Wed.

Federal Hill Park. To the southwest of the Inner Harbor, the park was named to commemorate Maryland's ratification of the U.S. Constitution. Later, the park was the site of Civil War fortifications. The summit provides an excellent view of Rash Field, the Inner Harbor, and beyond. | 300 Warren Ave. | 410/396–7931 | Free | Daily dawn–dusk.

Patterson Park. The 155-acre park in southeast Baltimore has a Chinese pagoda, a duck pond, playground equipment, tennis and basketball courts, indoor ice skating rink (fee), ball fields, swimming pool (fee), and walking, jogging, and cycling paths. | 1741 N. Patterson Park Ave. | 410/732–1609 | Free | Daily dawn–dusk.

Rash Field. This scenic park is on the south side of the Inner Harbor. Jogging and biking paths are available. Outdoor ice skating center (fee). | 201 Key Hwy. | 410/752–8632 park; 410/385–0675 ice skating | Free | Daily dawn–dusk, ice-skating center Oct.–Mar.

Sherwood Gardens. If you come in spring you'll see 80,000 tulips bloom in a 7-acre park. Other plants include acres of azaleas, wisteria, flowering cherries, English boxwoods, dogwoods, magnolias, and more. | 711 W 40th St. | 410/323–7982 | Free | Daily dawn–dusk.

RELIGION AND SPIRITUALITY

Basilica of the National Shrine of the Assumption. The oldest Catholic cathedral in the United States was begun in 1806 and completed in 1821. Benjamin Latrobe, architect of the U.S. Capitol, designed this masterpiece of neo-Classical architecture. | Cathedral and Mulberry Sts. | 410/727–3564 | fax 410/539–0407 | www.archbalt.org/parishes/urban/harborwest/basilica.htm | Free | Daily 7:30–5.

First Unitarian Church. Founded in 1817, this Mount Vernon church is on the National Register of Historic Places. It is the oldest building continuously occupied and used by a Unitarian Universalist congregation. A terra-cotta "Angel of Truth" sculpture sits above the entrance. The stained-glass windows were made by Louis Comfort Tiffany. | Charles and Franklin Sts. | 410/685–2330 | www.toad.net/~firstubalt | Free | Services, Sun. 10 AM.

Lovely Lane United Methodist Church. The church is called "The Mother Church of American Methodism" after the original congregation, which was founded in 1784. The current building housing Lovely Lane was built in 1884 and is on the National Register of Historic Places. The stained-glass windows are excellent examples of Italianate mosaics. | 2200 St. Paul St. | 410/889–1512 or 800/368–2520 | www.gbgm-umc.org/lovelylaneumc | Free | Weekdays 9–4; Sun. after 11 AM services or by appointment.

Mount Vernon Place United Methodist Church. The American Institute of Architects named this Victorian Gothic building as the most significant in the city of Baltimore. Built

in 1872, the church sits on the site where Francis Scott Key, author of "The Star-Spangled Banner," died in 1843. His death here is noted on a plaque on the church. | 10 E. Mount Vernon Pl | 410/685–5290 | www.gbgm-umc.org/mtvernonplumc | Free | Weekdays 9–3; services, Sun. 11 AM.

Old Otterbein United Methodist Church. The oldest ecclesiastical building in Baltimore, the church was built in 1785; today it stands in the shadow of the Baltimore Convention Center. The sanctuary is made of ballast discarded by ships in the nearby harbor, and all of the nails used in the building's construction were handmade. | 112 W. Conway St. | 410/685–4703 or 410/256–4987 | www.southbaltimore.com/church/otterbein | Free | Services, Sun. 11 AM; Apr.–Oct., Sat. 10–4.

SHOPPING

The American Can Company. Once just another abandoned factory marring Canton's waterfront, this redbrick and glass building is now home to offices, restaurants, a wine shop, a bakery, travel agent and more. Bibelot, a local chain bookstore, is its anchor. | 2400 Boston St. | 410/276–9700.

Harborplace and The Gallery. More than 100 specialty shops and restaurants flourish at two waterside pavilions in the Inner Harbor; a skywalk across Pratt Street leads to a five-story shopping mall. Street entertainers perform regularly at an outdoor amphitheater between the two pavilions. | 280 E. Pratt St. | 410/332–4191 or 800/HARBOR–1 | www.harborplace.com | Mon.–Sat. 10–9, Sun. 11–7.

Lexington Market. Founded in 1782, Lexington Market is the oldest, largest, and most famous of the city-owned markets. More than 130 vendors sell fresh meat, seafood, produce, take-out meals, and baked goods. | 400 W. Lexington St. | 410/685–6169 | www.lexingtonmarket.com | Mon.–Sat. 8:30–6, closed Sun.

Power Plant. The city's former power plant has been reborn as a restaurant and entertainment complex. Hard Rock Cafe, the first-ever ESPN Zone (a sports-themed entertainment and dining complex), and a Barnes and Noble bookstore are the inhabitants. | 601 E. Pratt | 410/752–5444 | Daily.

SIGHTSEEING TOURS

Clipper City **Tall Ship Cruises.** The *Clipper City* hosts two-hour cruises of the Inner Harbor, including Fort McHenry. The ship is a replica of a 19th-century schooner. The main deck has a custom canopy in case of poor weather conditions. Evening and Sunday brunch cruises are also available. | Light St., next to Maryland Science Center | 410/539–6227 | www.sailingship.com | $12 | Mon.–Sat. noon and 3; Sun. 3 and 6.

Harbor Cruises' *Lady Baltimore* **and** *Bay Lady.* Narrated tours of the Inner Harbor, including Fells Point, Fort McHenry, and Patapsco River are available. Lunch and dinner cruises are aboard fully enclosed decks; the top deck is open air. | 301 Light St. | 410/727–3113 or 800/695–BOAT | www.harborcruises.com | $12.50–$54 | Daily.

Minnie V. The *Minnie V* is a skipjack, a Chesapeake sailing craft designed to dredge oysters. At the peak of Baltimore's oyster industry (in the late 19th century), more than 1,000 of these vessels were on the bay. The cruises cover such topics as harbor landmarks, the history of the U.S. Naval Academy, Baltimore's maritime heritage, the great Baltimore fire, and much more. The ship is owned by Living Classrooms, a nonprofit group. | Pier 1 | 410/685–0295 | Reservations required | Mar.–Nov., Tues. and Thurs. evenings.

SPECTATOR SPORTS

Baltimore Orioles. The American League's Orioles play at Oriole Park at Camden Yards, a beautiful 1992 baseball-only stadium that harks back to the ballparks of baseball's early years; the stadium is open for tours daily. | Camden Yards, 333 W. Camden St. | Tickets 410/685–9800; tour info 410/547–6234 | www.theorioles.com | Games $9–$35 | Apr.–Oct.

Baltimore Ravens. The Ravens—named after Poe's famous work—play the National Football League season at PSINet Stadium at Camden Yards. | Camden Yards, 1101 Russell St. | 410/230–8010 | www.baltimoreravens.com | Games $20–$200 | Games Sept.–Jan.; tours daily 10–2.

Pimlico Race Course. The race course in northeast Baltimore is home to the Preakness, the second jewel of horse racing's Triple Crown (*see On the Calendar*). | 5201 Park Heights Ave. | 410/542–9400 | www.pimlico.com/pimfacts.html | $3 (stands) and $5 (box) except during Preakness | Mar.–Jun., Wed.–Fri. 2:05 (post time), weekends 1:05. No races Mon.–Tues.

OTHER POINTS OF INTEREST

★ **Fells Point.** A maritime neighborhood and historic district that dates back to the early 1700s is 1½ mi east of the Inner Harbor; it includes homes built before the War of 1812. The quaint neighborhood contains antiques shops, boutiques, restaurants, and inns. It is a popular nightlife destination. | Gough St.–waterfront, between Caroline and Chester Sts. | www.baltimorefellspoint.org.

★ **National Aquarium in Baltimore.** One of the most popular attraction in Baltimore, the contemporary-looking aquarium is home to more than 14,000 creatures, including mammals, fish, birds, reptiles, and amphibians. The top floor contains a re-created Amazon rain forest. Dolphin shows are staged at regular intervals in the Marine Mammal Pavilion. | 501 E. Pratt St. | 410/576–3800 | www.aqua.org | $15 | Mar.–June and Sept.–Oct., Sat.–Thurs. 9–5, Fri. 9–8; July–Aug., daily 9–8; Nov.–Dec., Sat.–Thurs. 10–5, Fri. 10–8.

World Trade Center. Baltimore's World Trade Center in the Inner Harbor affords a sweeping view of the city from the observation deck, Top of the World. At 423 ft, it is the world's tallest pentagonal building. Observation-deck exhibits focus on Baltimore's history and growth. | 401 E. Pratt St. | 410/837–8439 | www.bop.com/topworld | $3 | Mon.–Sat. 10–5, Sun. noon–5, extended summer hours.

ON THE CALENDAR

FEB.: *ACC Crafts Fair.* More than 800 exhibitors showcase wares in three days of trading in late February. The show is produced by the American Craft Council. | 1 W. Pratt St. | 800/836–3470 | www.craftcouncil.org.

APR.–MAY: *Maryland House and Garden Pilgrimage.* This nonprofit organization, established in 1937, puts together yearly tours of gardens and homes in Baltimore and six counties. The tours raise funds for historic preservation and restoration of significant and historic architectural treasures. | 410/821–6933 or 410/516–5589.

MAY: *Maryland Preakness Celebration.* The annual mid-May running of the Preakness Stakes at Pimlico is celebrated with hot air balloon launches, parades, and concerts. | 5201 Park Heights Ave. | 410/837–3030 | www.preaknesscelebration.com.

JUNE–SEPT.: *Showcase of Nations Ethnic Festivals.* Celebrations are held across the city, with each week's festival honoring a different nationality. The showcases include regional dances, foods, crafts, and music. | 800/282–6632 | www.baltimore.org.

JULY: *Artscape.* Visual, literary, and performing arts are celebrated in the Mount Royal neighborhood. A wine tasting, children's activities, street theater, and concerts round out the event. | 410/396–4575 | www.artscape.org.

SEPT.: *Baltimore Book Festival.* A celebration of literary arts arrives in late September with author signings, book publishers, children's activities, and walking tours. | Mt. Vernon Pl., off Charles St. | 410/837–4636 | www.bop.org/calendar/events/book_index.html.

NOV.: *Thanksgiving Parade.* Santa Claus receives his official holiday welcome as floats and bands fill the streets along the Inner Harbor. The parade starts off at Eutaw and Pratt streets, travels along Pratt Street, and disbands at Market Place. | 410/837–4636.

DEC.: *Country Christmas Craft Fair.* Unique crafts and handmade items are all for sale at this holiday fair at the Maryland State Fairgrounds. | 301/984–5950.

DEC.: *Zoolights.* This annual safari through the Baltimore Zoo is highlighted by the light displays and holiday cheer. | 410/366–LION.

DEC.: *New Year's Eve Extravaganza.* The non-alcoholic celebration has fireworks, parades, music, and themed parties for all ages. | Inner Harbor | 410/837–4636 or 800/282–6632 | www.bop.org/calendar/events/newyears.html.

DEC.: *Night of 100 Elvises.* Elvis may be gone, but he's still the King. This annual event at Lithuanian Hall, just west of downtown, pays him homage with live bands, dancing, and a dozen or so "tribute artists." There's even a life-sized Elvis ice sculpture. You can show up in a tux or a rhinestone jumpsuit—it's all allowed in the name of a good time. Drinks and food are available, and all proceeds benefit local charities. | 851 Hollins St. | 410/494–9558 or 888/494–9558.

Dining

INEXPENSIVE

An Poiton Stil. Irish. Salads, sandwiches, and local fish round out this pub-style restaurant's menu, which is heavy with traditional dishes such as colcannon (Irish mashed potatoes with cabbage), shepherd's pie, and fish and chips. A full bar is available, as are a few wines. | 2323 York Rd., Timonium | 410/560–7900 | www.thestill.net | $7–$21 | AE, D, MC, V.

Cafe Hon. American. In a former hardware store, this restaurant looks like a 1950s kitchen with its old porcelain tables, colorful tablecloths, and Hoosier cabinet. Homestyle cooking includes crab cakes, lasagna, and meat loaf. Kids' menu. Saturday and Sunday brunch. No smoking. | 1002 W. 36th St. | 410/243–1230 | $10–$20 | AE, DC, MC, V.

Ikaros. Greek. Owned and operated by an immigrant family since 1967, this Greektown institution was voted the Best Greek Restaurant for 15 years in a row by *Baltimore* magazine. Greek paintings and photos adorn the walls, and the waitstaff wear Cleopatra-design dark blue uniforms imported from Greece. Traditional dishes include moussaka, fried calamari, lamb in wine and tomato sauce, and eggplant salad. | 4805 Eastern Ave. | 410/633–3750 | Closed Tues. | $8–$16 | AE, D, MC, V.

Nacho Mama's. Mexican. A wooden statue of Elvis marks the entrance to this Canton bar and restaurant. Inside a funky mixture of local sports and Elvis memorabilia hang from the ceiling and walls. Share a margarita-filled hubcap with friends as you wait for a table. Look for south-of-the-border fare plus burgers and salads. The spinach salad with feta, roasted red peppers and avocado dressing is especially good. | 2907 O'Donnell St. | 410/675–0898 | $6–$14 | AE, MC, V.

Needful Things. American. Large front windows brighten this Canton eatery as well as provide a backdrop for imaginative window displays that change with the season. Breakfast and lunch—and on Fridays and Saturdays dinner—are served by the fireplace in this cozy cafe. Hearty omelets and pancakes with your choice of fillings are breakfast favorites. For lunch or dinner, try the chicken pot pie or turkey meatloaf. | 2921 O'Donnell St. | 410/675–0595 | Closed Mon. | $4–$12 | MC, V.

Papermoon Diner. American. In a rather unassuming little house near the Charles Village neighborhood, the Papermoon has mismatched furniture and high ceilings crisscrossed with vibrantly painted pipes and ducts. Lava lights bubble, and mannequins in various stages of undress strike poses. Old-fashioned comfort foods like meatloaf with mashed potatoes and gravy and mac and cheese are on the menu along with dishes like angel hair pasta with garlic, lemon herb seasoning, and basil sauteed in butter. | 227 W. 29th St. | 410/889–4444 | Reservations essential for groups of 5 or more | Open 24 hrs | $6–$12 | MC, V.

Wayne's Bar-B-Que. Barbecue. This Pratt Street Pavilion eatery in the Inner Harbor caters to crowds. The dining area has chairs made of logs, red-and-white checkered tablecloths, and recorded country music in the background. There is a patio area with a view of the harbor for more scenic dining. You might want to try the BBQ ribs, pork, or chicken sandwich. Kids' menu. | 201 Pratt St. | 410/539–3810 | $7–$21 | AE, D, MC, V.

MODERATE

Angelina's. Italian. This neighborhood restaurant has an Irish pub downstairs and two dining rooms with casual booths. Specialties include crab cakes and lasagna. Kids' menu. | 7135 Harford Rd. | 410/444–5545 | www.crabcake.com | Closed Mon. | $10–$33 | AE, D, MC, V.

The Bay Cafe. American. This Canton eatery's position as a water taxi stop makes it a popular watering hole, especially in the summer when a large outdoor dining section is landscaped with palms and tropical flowers. In the winter some of its waterfront tables are converted for indoor use, yet they still retain the panoramic views. The menu includes seafood, steaks, pasta, stir fry and sandwiches. Shrimp cocktail is the kitchen's specialty. | 2809 Boston St. | 410/522–3377 | $14–$18 | AE, MC, V.

Bertha's. Seafood. Originally a seaman's bar dating to the 19th century, this Fells Point institution has been operating as a family business since 1972. Its two dining rooms have a nautical flavor. Best known for its steamed mussels, Bertha's also serves crab cakes, Spanish rice dishes, and more. Kids' menu. Live jazz Tuesday to Saturday nights. | 734 S. Broadway | 410/327–0426 | $14–$20 | MC, V.

Chiapparelli's. Italian. Family pictures and scenes of Baltimore landscapes line the walls of this two-level restaurant. A Little Italy favorite, this restaurant has white tablecloths and redbrick walls, with coordinating brick-red carpeting in the dining area. Menu choices include spinach ravioli, osso buco, and veal saltimbocca. Kids' menu. | 237 S. High St. | 410/837–0309 | fax 410/783–7985 | www.chiapparellis.com | $12–$28 | AE, D, DC, MC, V.

City Lights. Seafood. Only a glass wall separates you from the harbor, making the view unforgettable. This second-floor, Inner Harbor restaurant has a cozy patio where you can dine under the canopy. Crab cakes, crab dip, lobster, and fresh fish are popular here. Kids' menu. | 301 Light St. | 410/244–8811 | $15–$24 | AE, D, DC, MC, V.

Dalesio's of Little Italy. Italian. Bare wood tables and chairs are accented by the dining room's hunter-green color scheme, but it's the view of the harbor that gets attention. The outdoor balcony is reminiscent of a European cafe, with quaint marble tables and wrought-iron chairs. The veal chop, shrimp marinara, and duck ravioli are among the northern Italian menu's offerings. | 829 Eastern Ave. | 410/539–1965 | www.dalesios.com | No dinner Sun. | $14–$24 | AE, MC, V.

ESPN Zone. American. Not surprisingly, televisions—all airing different games—are in every nook of this sports-themed dining and entertainment complex. Upstairs you'll find a wide range of high-end, sports-related arcade games. It's known mostly for easy fare such as burgers and pasta. Kids' menu. | 601 E. Pratt St. | 410/685–3776 | espn.go.com/espn-inc/zone/baltimore.html | $10–$22 | AE, D, MC, V.

Hard Rock Cafe. American. Music memorabilia all over the walls—the trademark of this chain eatery—plus a bar shaped like a Les Paul guitar, make this restaurant, est. July 1997, an attraction unto itself. Burgers, steaks, and pasta are popular choices. Entertainment. | 601 E. Pratt St. | 410/347–7625 | $9–$18 | AE, MC, V.

Henninger's Tavern. Contemporary. An antique china closet and an eclectic display of photos fill this 200-year-old building in Fells Point. White tablecloths mute the effect of the bright green and pink sponge-painted walls. Look for crab cakes and filet mignon; they're usually offered although the menu changes biweekly. No cell phones. | 1812 Bank St. | 410/342–2172 | Reservations not accepted | Closed Sun.–Mon. | $14–$20 | AE, DC, MC, V.

John Steven, LTD. Contemporary. This restaurant takes its name from the owner's son's Teddy bear, hence the logo (a Teddy bear in a suit, playing the cello). The restaurant is done in old stone with 18th- to 20th-century paintings, and bare dark-wood tables. The brick courtyard has intimate dining in the open air. You might try the steamed shrimp, Cajun crawfish pie, or something from the sushi menu. | 1800 Thames St. | 410/327–5561 | fax 410/327–0413 | www.johnstevenltd.com | $11–$20 | AE, D, DC, MC, V.

Joy America Cafe. Southwestern. Despite its artsy location, this eatery atop the American Visionary Art Museum has few decorative accents. A large half-moon window in the dining room overlooks the harbor. For an even better view choose a table on the terrace. Specialties include roasted chicken, Caribbean lobster stew, and grilled whole fish. Kids' menu. Sun. brunch. No smoking. | 800 Key Hwy. | 410/244–6500 | Closed Mon. | $11–$26 | AE, DC, MC, V.

Kawasaki. Japanese. Amid art galleries and shops on Mount Vernon's North Charles Street, Kawasaki's private rooms provide dining in true Japanese style seated on the floor. For the long-legged there are tables and booths in the main dining area. Most famous for its sushi, this restaurant also serves salmon teriyaki or tonkatsu (pork tenderloin). | 413 N. Charles St. | 410/659–7600 | Closed Sun. | $10–$21 | AE, MC, V.

Lista's. American. Unmistakably Southwestern, this Fells Point eatery has dark-wood tables, padded chairs, and Native American decorations on the walls. House specialties are margaritas, New Mexican dishes, and chile Colorado. Accessible by water taxi. Dock space. | 1637 Thames St. | 410/327–0040 | www.onlinedining.com/diningout/listas/listas.html | $11–$17 | AE, DC, MC, V.

Louie's Cafe. Contemporary. Original art hangs in the busy two-story dining room and adjoining lounge. You might try the baked mahi-mahi, Spanish pork, or the shrimp and salmon linguine. Live jazz Tuesday to Sunday. Sunday brunch. | 518 N. Charles St. | 410/230–2998 | $12–$30 | AE, MC, V.

Obrycki's. Seafood. This famous Baltimore crab house has no frills. Eating crabs properly is a messy business and the operators know it. The building in Fells Point dates from 1851 and has pictures of old Baltimore adorning the walls. The windows and oak for the bar top came from a monastery. Choices include backfin crab cakes, shrimp in garlic butter, and sea scallops. Kids' menu. | 1727 E. Pratt St. | 410/732–6399 | www.obryckis.com | Closed mid-Dec.–Mar. | $15–$30 | AE, D, DC, MC, V.

Ruby Lounge. Contemporary. The lounge in this Mount Vernon bistro is an inviting ruby color while the dining area is canary yellow. The romantic surroundings make it a great place to bring a date or even to propose to that special someone. The eclectic cuisine includes green chili wontons, smoked trout quesadillas, and Cajun prime rib. | 802 N. Charles St. | 410/539–8051 | Closed Sun.–Mon. | $12–$25 | AE, MC, V.

Rusty Scupper. Seafood. The restaurant looks just like the inside of a ship, complete with portholes, exposed pipe work, wood posts, and white-painted wood walls. It also has great views of the harbor. It's known for fresh seafood, chicken, and pasta. | 402 Key Hwy. | 410/727–3678 | Reservations essential | $15–$23 | AE, MC, V.

Spike & Charlie's. Contemporary. A century-old building is home to this chic Mount Vernon restaurant and wine bar. The quaint dining room has mahogany tables and chairs and interesting paintings from local artists. The menu changes seasonally, but there are often unusual pizzas, pastas, or seafood to choose from. There is also a lengthy wine list. | 1225 Cathedral St. | 410/752–8144 | www.spikeandcharlies.com | Reservations recommended | Closed Mon. | $10–$29 | AE, MC, V.

Velleggia's. Italian. The Vellegia family has run this busy Little Italy restaurant since 1937. The dining area has an old Italy influence. There are smaller private dining areas for special occasions, a bar, and a lounge. Among the menu choices are beef, seafood, and chicken dishes. Kids' menu. | 829 E. Pratt St. | 410/685–2620 | www.onlinedining.com/diningout/velleggiasdir/velleggias.html | $13–$21 | AE, DC, MC, V.

EXPENSIVE

Boccaccio. American. This 1870 Victorian mansion on the edge of Little Italy is now a Mediterranean-style restaurant with five dining rooms, filled with carved teak furniture, a Tiffany skylight, and marble fireplaces. The Dover sole, seared scallops, or angel hair pasta are solid menu choices. | 925 Eastern Ave. | 410/234–1322 | $22–$27 | AE, DC, MC, V.

Brass Elephant. Contemporary. Classical music fills this grand 1850 town house in Mount Vernon. Hand-carved fireplaces, Tiffany skylight and windows, Waterford crystal chandeliers, and parquet floors give it its elegance. Known for fresh seafood, grilled foie gras, and seared scallops. | 924 N. Charles St. | 410/547–8480 | Reservations essential | $18–$34 | AE, DC, MC, V.

Germano's Trattoria. Italian. From this informal dining room, you can watch people on the bustling streets of Little Italy. Osso buco, arista (roasted loin of pork), and taglierini are house specialties. | 300 S. High St. | 410/752–4515 | www.littleitalybaltimore.com | $16–$29 | AE, D, DC, MC, V.

Helen's Garden. Eclectic. Original art on the exposed brick walls, earth tones and a worn wooden floor give this Canton bistro a casual elegance. Choose from seating in one of the three dining rooms or the backyard patio. Dishes range from pecan-crusted brook trout with horseradish potatoes to Asian pesto shrimp, sauteed with peanuts, basil, lime, and garlic. Wine and beer only. Take out available. | 2908 O'Donnell St. | 410/276–2233. | fax 410/675–8132 | Closed Mon. | $13–$27 | D, MC, V.

Jeannier's. French. Quiet dining rooms face Johns Hopkins University. The cafe has casual hardwood floors, while the main dining area has French paintings, lace curtains, and vases throughout the room. Specials include rack of lamb, quenelle (classic mousse of pike fish), and seafood Catalane. Early-bird suppers. | 105 W. 39th St. | 410/889–3303 | Closed Sun. | $18–$32 | AE, DC, MC, V.

La Scala. Italian. Mahogany chairs, multi-colored tablecloths, and tile floors give this family-owned restaurant in Little Italy its upscale appearance. Dishes include the veal chop, grilled Caesar salad, and shrimp Luana. | 1012 Eastern Ave. | 410/783–9209 | www.lascala-dining.com | Reservations recommended | $15–$30 | AE, D, DC, MC, V.

Mt. Washington Tavern. American. The tavern in this building is more than 150 years old. Lacrosse and hunting objects accent the dining rooms, which are lined with tables and booths. There is a glass-enclosed atrium with a retractable roof for more scenic dining. Seafood choices include soft-shell crab, crab cakes, and rockfish. Entertainment. Kids' menu. Sun. brunch. | 5700 Newbury St. | 410/367–6903 | www.mtwashingtontavern.com | $17–$30 | AE, DC, MC, V.

Pierpoint. Contemporary. A bistro look with contemporary furnishings, this Fells Point eatery has faux marble walls, marble chairs, and cushioned booths. You might try the smoked Maryland crab cakes or the soft-shell stack. Sun. brunch. | 1822 Aliceanna St. | 410/675–2080 | Closed Mon. No lunch Sat. | $18–$26 | AE, D, DC, MC, V.

★ **Polo Grill.** Contemporary. Wood and brass furnishings underscore this eatery's warm, comfortable character. It's north of downtown in the Doubletree Inn at the Colonnade. Specialties include grilled aged filet mignon, rockfish with cellophane noodles, and crab cakes. | 4 W. University Pkwy. | 410/235–8200 | www.polo-grill.com | $15–$45 | AE, D, DC, MC, V.

Rocco's Capriccio. Northern Italian. In the heart of Little Italy, this elegant dining room has a Mediterranean flair. Flambe dishes are cooked at your table. Your options include the veal chop a la Toscana, seafood ravioli, or stuffed calamari. | 846 Fawn St. | 410/685–2710 | $15–$31 | AE, D, DC, MC, V.

Ruth's Chris Steak House. Steak. Just a few blocks from the Inner Harbor, the two-story dining room here is accented in greens and florals. Ruth's Chris is known for aged steaks, salmon, lobster, and homemade desserts like chocolate sin cake. Free valet parking. | 600 Water St. | 410/783–0033 | www.serioussteaks.com | Reservations essential Fri.–Sat. | $17–$35 | AE, D, DC, MC, V.

Tio Pepe. Spanish. One of Mount Vernon's busiest restaurants, this basement-level restaurant with seven dining rooms resembles a cave. Each table is candlelit for a romantic look. Traditional foods include paella, lenguada molinera and zarzuela de mariscos. | 10 E.

Franklin St. | 410/539–4675 | Reservations essential | Jacket required | $17–$29 | AE, D, DC, MC, V.

VERY EXPENSIVE

Hamilton's. American. This small, intimate dining room inside the Fells Point landmark The Admiral Fell Inn has a wine cellar for private dining. It's known for its grilled beef tenderloin, wild rockfish, and pastries. Sunday brunch. | 888 S. Broadway | 410/522–2195 | $30–$42 | AE, DC, MC, V.

★ **Hampton's.** American. This elegant restaurant at the Harbor Court Hotel has panoramic views of the Inner Harbor and the National Aquarium. Wing-back chairs, candelabras, and red draperies give it a formal but romantic air. You might try the grilled dry aged beef tenderloin, Maine lobster gratinee, or the pan-seared Atlantic halibut. Vegetarian prix-fixe menu available. Sunday brunch. No smoking. | 550 Light St. | 410/234–0550 | www.harborcourt.com/restrnt | Reservations essential | Jacket and tie required | Closed Mon. | $32–$42 | AE, D, DC, MC, V.

★ **The Prime Rib.** American. Low lighting and black-lacquer walls create an intimate look at this restaurant modeled after a 1940s supper club. Naturally the house specialty is beef, but you might also try the crab cakes and seafood. Pianist. | 1101 N. Calvert St. | 410/539–1804 | www.theprimerib.com | Reservations essential | Jacket required | $27–$32 | AE, DC, MC, V.

Lodging

INEXPENSIVE

Abacrombie Badger Bed & Breakfast. This four-story gray stone row house dates to 1890. The rooms all are done in Victorian style, though each room is distinctive. Some have four-poster beds. The inn is across the street from Symphony Hall and two blocks from the Lyric Opera House. | 12 rooms. Restaurant, bar, complimentary Continental breakfast. Cable TV. Business services. | 58 W. Biddle St. | 410/244–7227 | fax 410/244–8415 | info@badger-inn.com | www.badger-inn.com | $115–$155 | AE, D, DC, MC, V.

Aunt Rebecca's Bed & Breakfast. This small Victorian home in Mount Vernon is within 1 mi of the Joseph Meyerhoff Symphony Hall, Lyric Opera House, Penn Station, and several museums and restaurants. Complimentary breakfast. Some VCRs. No Smoking. | 106 E. Preston St. | 410/625–1007 | fax 410/625–1007 | auntrebecca@aol.com | 4 rooms | $80–$119 | AE, D, MC, V.

Beltway Motel and Restaurant. Primarily the haunt of business travelers, this motel's rooms are basic but have large desks and in-room coffeepots for all-nighters. | 110 rooms. Restaurant, bar. In-room data ports, cable TV. Business services. | 3648 Washington Blvd. | 410/242–2363 | fax 410/242–2363 | $49–$70 | AE, D, MC, V.

Best Inn And Suites. Directly across the street from a mall full of stores and restaurants, this chain hotel is 7 mi from the Inner Harbor. | 147 rooms. Cable TV. Pool. Hot tub, sauna. Laundry facilities. Business services. Pets allowed (fee). | 5701 Baltimore National Pk. (Rte. 40) | 410/747–8900 | fax 410/744–3522 | $73–$83 | AE, D, DC, MC, V.

Best Western Hotel and Conference Center. About 4 mi east of the Inner Harbor, this hotel has shuttle service available to downtown. | 175 rooms. Restaurant, bar, room service. In-room data ports, cable TV. Indoor pool. Gym. Game room. Laundry facilities. Business services. | 5625 O'Donnell St. | 410/633–9500 | fax 410/633–4314 | $109–$119 | AE, D, DC, MC, V.

Christlen. This no-frills, family-owned motel built in 1965 is 7 mi east of downtown. The look is quite simple with basic furniture in each room and white wallpapered walls. | 28 rooms. Cable TV. Pets allowed. | 8733 Pulaski Hwy. (U.S. 40) | 410/687–1740 | fax 410/391–1847 | $51–$60 | AE, D, DC, MC, V.

Comfort Inn–Airport. The motel, 8 mi south of downtown, is 3 mi from the airport and light rail. | 188 rooms. Restaurant, bar, complimentary breakfast. In-room data ports, cable TV. Sauna. Gym. Video games. Business services, airport shuttle. Some pets allowed. | 6921 Baltimore-Annapolis Blvd. (Rte. 648) | 410/789–9100 or 800/228–5150 | fax 410/355–2854 | www.comfortinn.com | $89–$109 | AE, D, DC, MC, V.

Courtyard Baltimore Airport. A residential area, 8 mi south of downtown and 2½ mi from the airport, hosts this chain representative. | 149 rooms. Restaurant, bar. Cable TV. Indoor pool. Hot tub. Gym. Laundry facilities. Business services, airport shuttle. | 1671 W. Nursery Rd., Linthicum | 410/859–8855 | fax 410/859–5068 | www.courtyard.com | $79–$109 | AE, D, DC, MC, V.

Days Inn–West. Close to the Baltimore Beltway and 6 mi west of downtown, this chain motel is directly across the street from the Westview Mall. | 94 rooms. Restaurant, complimentary Continental breakfast. Refrigerators, cable TV. Pool. Laundry facilities. Business services. | 5801 Baltimore National Pk. (U.S. 40), Catonsville | 410/744–5000 | fax 410/788–5197 | www.daysinn.com | $69–$99 | AE, D, DC, MC, V.

Embassy Suites Hunt Valley. Just off I–83, this hotel is less than ¼ mi from the city's light rail system. It has a large tropical atrium, and rooms are all suites with balconies. The Inner Harbor is about 15 mi away. Restaurant, bar, room service. In-room data ports, cable TV, some in-room VCRs, refrigerators, some microwaves, some in-room hot tubs. 2 pools. Exercise equipment. Laundry facilities. Business services, free parking. Pets allowed. | 213 International Circle, Hunt Valley | 410/584–1400 | www.embassy-suites.com | 223 rooms | $99–$229 | AE, D, DC, MC, V.

Glenda's Bed and Breakfast. In a 3-story Italianate brownstone in the Mount Royal neighborhood, this inn is a great stopover point for those touring the historic sites downtown or antique shopping. Antiques culled from several different periods accent the rooms, and copious greenery fills the sun-room dining area. Complimentary breakfast. No room phones, no TV. Some private baths. No kids under 12. | 2028 Park Ave. and 601 Reservoir St. | 410/383–8535 or 800/899–2533 | fax 410/383–1773 | 3 rooms in 2 buildings | $80–$90 | No credit cards.

Hampton Inn. Across the street from the White Marsh Mall is this chain representative, 10 mi east of Baltimore's central business district, and 14 mi northeast of Inner Harbor. | 127 rooms, 16 suites. Complimentary Continental breakfast. In-room data ports, some refrigerators, cable TV. Pool. Exercise equipment. Video games. Business services. | 8225 Town Center Dr. | 410/931–2200 | fax 410/931–2215 | www.hamptoninn.com | $99–$119 | AE, D, DC, MC, V.

Holiday Inn Baltimore West. About 10 mi southwest from the Inner Harbor, this chain motel is close to the Baltimore Beltway. | 135 rooms. Restaurant, bar. In-room data ports, cable TV. Pool. Business services. Some pets allowed. | 1800 Belmont Ave. | 410/265–1400 or 800/465–4329 | fax 410/281–9569 | www.basshotels.com/holiday-inn | $69–$79 | AE, D, DC, MC, V.

Hopkins Inn. One block from the Johns Hopkins campus, this pale yellow stucco building dates to the late 1920s. The rooms reflect a wide range of influences such as art deco, Federal, and Victorian. | 25 rooms. Complimentary Continental breakfast. No smoking. Business services. Parking (fee). | 3404 St. Paul St. | 410/235–8600 or 800/537–8483 | fax 410/235–7051 | www.bichotels.com/hopkinsinn | $99–$129 | AE, D, DC, MC, V.

Inn at Government House. This city-owned, 1889 Victorian structure in Mount Vernon has a library, music rooms, and several parlors. These redbrick and brownstone connecting town homes have reproductions of antique furniture in each room. The Inn is 14 blocks from the Inner Harbor and 1½ mi from Johns Hopkins University. | 19 rooms. Complimentary Continental breakfast. Business services, free parking. No smoking. | 1125 N. Calvert St. | 410/539–0566 | fax 410/539–0567 | $125–$145 | AE, D, DC, MC, V.

Mr. Mole Bed & Breakfast. Dating back to the 1860s, this redbrick building in the Bolton Hill neighborhood was owned by a series of merchants. Each room has a unique theme, one of which is African. All rooms have fireplaces and some have canopy beds. The inn is 4 blocks from the Maryland Institute, College of Art. | 5 rooms, 2 suites. Full breakfast. In-room data ports. Business services. No kids under 10. No smoking. | 1601 Bolton St. | 410/728–1179 | fax 410/728–3379 | www.mrmolebb.com | $115–$175 | AE, D, DC, MC, V.

Mount Vernon Hotel. Currently run by students at a local hospitality school, this tan brick building, built in 1908, was originally a YMCA. There is European influence evident in the antique-furnished lobby and rooms. | 133 rooms. Restaurant. In-room data ports, cable TV. Business services. | 24 W. Franklin St. | 410/727–2000 or 800/245–5256 | fax 410/576–9300 | www.bichotels.com/mtvernon | $109 | AE, D, DC, MC, V.

Quality Inn. Within 4 blocks of Camden Yards and 1 mi of the Inner Harbor, this hotel is often packed with baseball fans coming in for a game at the stadium. Some in-room data ports, cable TV, some refrigerators, some microwaves. Outdoor pool. Pets allowed. | 1701 Russell St. | 410/727–3400 | fax 410/547–0586 | 52 rooms | $79–$119 | AE, D, DC, MC, V.

Quality Inn & Suites at the Carlyle. Inside a 15-story apartment building, this hotel is within 1 mi of Johns Hopkins. It is 3 mi from the zoo and 8 mi from the Inner Harbor. | 80 rooms. Restaurant, bar. Some refrigerators, cable TV. Pool. Sauna. Gym. Laundry service. Business services, parking (fee). | 500 W. University Pkwy. | 410/889–4500 | fax 410/467–1645 | www.qualityinn.com | $110–$125 | AE, D, MC, V.

Sheraton International at BWI Airport. This chain representative is on airport grounds, 6 mi from Marley Station Mall. | 203 rooms. Restaurant, bar, room service. In-room data ports, cable TV. Pool. Exercise equipment. Business services, airport shuttle. | 7032 Elm Rd. | 410/859–3300 | fax 410/859–0565 | www.sheraton.com | $85–$219 | AE, D, DC, MC, V.

Star Motel. This small and independent motel caters to the budget-minded traveler. Rooms here are basic but spacious and clean. The commercial strip surrounding the motel is home to a number of fast-food eateries, and the Inner Harbor area is about 20 minutes away. Cable TV. | 9619 Pulaski Hwy. | 410/687–3169 | fax 410/687–3169 | 17 rooms | $30–$40 | AE, D, MC, V.

MODERATE

★ **Admiral Fell Inn.** In Fells Point near the busy nightlife, this hotel consists of eight buildings dating back to the 1700s and 1800s. The rooms are furnished with 19th-century Federal pieces as well as antique reproductions. | 80 rooms. 3 restaurants, 3 bars, complimentary Continental breakfast. In-room data ports, some in-room hot tubs, cable TV. Business services. Free parking. Pets allowed. | 888 S. Broadway | 410/522–7377 or 800/292–4667 (outside MD) | fax 410/522–0707 | info@admiralfell.com | www.admiralfell.com | $139–$199 | AE, DC, MC, V.

Biltmore Suites. This 19th-century Victorian brownstone is in Baltimore's historic Mount Vernon neighborhood. Rooms are graced with elegant contemporary pieces that stand in refreshing counterpoint to the ornate original moldings and huge fireplaces. Walls are sponge-painted for a textured effect. Many rooms have views of downtown. Complimentary Continental breakfast. In-room data ports, cable TV, some kitchenettes. Business services. | 205 W. Madison St. | 410/728–6550 or 800/868–5064 | fax 410/728–5829 | 25 rooms | $99–$149 | AE, D, DC, MC, V.

BWI Airport Marriott. Five minutes from the airport, this hotel has shuttle service available every 20 minutes. The hotel is 9 mi south of the Inner Harbor and 15 mi from Pimlico Race Course. | 310 rooms. Restaurant, bar. Cable TV. Indoor pool. Hot tub. Health club. Business services, airport shuttle. | 1743 W. Nursery Rd., Linthicum | 410/859–8300 | fax 410/691–4555 | www.marriott.com | $99–$279 | AE, D, DC, MC, V.

Clarion at Mount Vernon Square. In the heart of Mount Vernon, this restored hotel was built in 1928. It is 12 blocks from Inner Harbor, and four blocks from several antique shops. Parking (fee). | 103 rooms. Restaurants, bar. In-room data ports, some in-room hot tubs, cable TV. Video games. | 612 Cathedral St., Mount Vernon | 410/727–7101 or 800/292–5500 | fax 410/789–3312 | www.clarioninn.com | $139–$160 | AE, D, DC, MC, V.

Cross Keys Inn. This redbrick building with French country charm was built in 1960. It's about 5 minutes north of downtown in a village complex surrounded by woods. | 146 rooms. Restaurant, bar, room service. In-room data ports, cable TV. Pool. Beauty salon. Video games. Business services, free parking. | 5100 Falls Rd. | 410/532–6900 or 800/532–5397 | fax 410/532–2403 | sales@crosskeysinn.com | www.crosskeysinn.com | $135–$185 | AE, DC, MC, V.

Days Inn–Inner Harbor. This redbrick building is three blocks from the Inner Harbor, across the street from the convention center. | 250 rooms. Restaurant, bar. Some refrigerators, room service, cable TV. Pool. Business services. Video games. Parking (fee). | 100 Hopkins Pl. | 410/576–1000 | fax 410/659–0257 | www.daysinn.com | $159–$299 | AE, D, DC, MC, V.

Doubletree Inn at the Colonnade. The Victorian-influenced building is across the street from Johns Hopkins University and 3½ mi north of the Inner Harbor. | 125 rooms, 31 suites. Restaurant, bar, room service. In-room data ports, cable TV. Indoor pool. Beauty salon, hot tub. Exercise equipment. Business services. Some pets allowed. | 4 W. University Pkwy. | 410/235–5400 | fax 410/235–5572 | www.doubletreehotel.com | $109–$350 | AE, D, DC, MC, V.

BALTIMORE

INTRO
ATTRACTIONS
DINING
LODGING

Embassy Suites. About 20 minutes from the Inner Harbor and 1 mi from airport and light rail is this chain hotel. | 251 suites. Restaurant, bar. In-room data ports, refrigerators, cable TV. Indoor pool. Hot tub. Exercise equipment. Business services. Airport shuttle. | 1300 Concourse Dr., Linthicum | 410/850–0747 | fax 410/850–0895 | www.embassy-suites.com | $179–$199 | AE, D, DC, MC, V.

Gramercy Mansion Bed and Breakfast. This stately 1902 Tudor-style mansion commands a lovely view of its own 45-acre estate in Greenspring Valley about 10 mi west of downtown. Stroll through the wooded grounds and gardens or ramble around inside and admire the Persian carpets, massive stone fireplaces, and the gleam of polished hardwood. One-of-a-kind French antiques, original oil paintings, and the occasional small potted tree fill the guest rooms. For breakfast, you can savor the Gramercy's signature shiitake mushroom omelettes on the terrace or in the dining room. Complimentary breakfast. Some room phones, cable TV. Pool. No kids. | 1400 Greenspring Valley Rd., Stevenson | 410/486–2405 or 800/553–3404 | fax 410/486–1765 | 7 rooms | $100–$295 | AE, D, DC, MC, V.

Holiday Inn Baltimore–Inner Harbor. Some rooms have panoramic views of the city in this hotel near Camden Yards and 4 blocks from the Inner Harbor. | 375 rooms. Restaurant, bar. Cable TV. Indoor pool. Gym. Video games. Business services, parking (fee). | 301 W. Lombard St. | 410/685–3500 | fax 410/727–6169 | www.holiday-inn.com/bal-downtown | $179–$219 | AE, D, DC, MC, V.

Hilton Baltimore and Towers. This Art Deco redbrick building, built in 1928, has been restored to its original appearance. The entrance is particularly impressive, with its marble columns, hand-carved artwork, brass fixtures, and massive central chandelier. It has been designated a Historic Landmark and is 4 blocks north of the harbor. | 439 rooms. 2 restaurants, bar. In-room data ports, cable TV. Gym. Business services. | 20 W. Baltimore St. | 410/539–8400 | fax 410/332–4229 | www.hilton.com | $165–$195 | AE, D, DC, MC, V.

The Inn at Henderson's Wharf. This waterfront redbrick building in Fells Point was built in 1895. There is a country look in the rooms, and an interior English garden courtyard. Some rooms have feather beds. | 38 rooms. Complimentary Continental breakfast. In-room data ports, cable TV. Gym. Dock. Laundry facilities. Business services. Free parking. | 1000 Fell St. | 410/522–7777 or 800/522–2088 | fax 410/522–7087 | gm@hendersonswharf.com | www.hendersonswharf.com/the-inn.htm | $139–$259 | AE, D, DC, MC, V.

Omni Inner Harbor. Baltimore's largest hotel has rooms in twin towers, and is 5 blocks east of the Inner Harbor. | 707 rooms in 2 buildings. Restaurant, bar. In-room data ports, mini-bars, refrigerators, cable TV. Pool. Gym. Video games. Business services, parking (fee). Pets allowed. | 101 W. Fayette St. | 410/752–1100 | fax 410/727–6223 | $169–$269 | AE, D, DC, MC, V.

Scarborough Fair. Two blocks from Inner Harbor, this Georgian brick house is in the quaint Federal Hill neighborhood. Built in 1801, the house—which is one of the oldest in the area—sports gabled roofs and Flemish-bonded brickwork. Rooms are done with a blend of contemporary and Colonial-era furnishings. Complimentary breakfast. No room phones, cable TV. No kids. | 1 E. Montgomery St. | 410/837–0010 | fax 410/783–4635 | 6 rooms | $129–$159 | AE, D, MC, V.

Sheraton Inner Harbor. One block from Harborplace and two blocks from Camden Yards, this hotel offers Orioles and Ravens ticket packages. Most rooms have city views. | 337 rooms. 2 restaurants, bar. In-room data ports, minibars, cable TV. Indoor pool. Exercise equipment. Video games. Business services, parking (fee). | 300 S. Charles St. | 410/962–8300 | fax 410/962–8211 | www.sheraton.com | $149–$290 | AE, D, DC, MC, V.

★ **Tremont Plaza Hotel.** This 13-story brown-brick building was converted to a small European-style hostelry in 1985. The hotel is 5 blocks from the Inner Harbor. All rooms are suites with kitchens; the large suites provide comfort to couples and the business traveler. | 60 suites. Restaurant, bar, complimentary Continental breakfast. Cable TV. Business services, parking (fee). Some pets allowed. | 222 St. Paul Pl. | 410/727–2222 or 800/873–6668 | fax 410/244–1154 | www.tremontsuitehotels.com | $135–$155 | AE, D, DC, MC, V.

EXPENSIVE

Brookshire Suites. This black marble building, built in 1984, has an Art Deco look in its lobby, which is accented in violet and gold. It is one block from the Inner Harbor and downtown. The rooms have cherry-wood furniture and earth-tone colors. | 97 rooms, 70 suites. Complimentary full breakfast. Minibars, refrigerators, cable TV. Exercise equipment. Business services, parking (fee). | 120 E. Lombard St. | 410/625–1300 or 800/647–0013 (outside MD) | fax 410/625–0912 | www.brookshiresuites.com | $209–$289 | AE, D, DC, MC, V.

Celie's Waterfront Bed & Breakfast. A roof deck affords spectacular views of the harbor at this three-story B&B on Fells Point waterfront avenue. A lush garden patio is a lovely retreat. Most rooms have a view of the harbor; all rooms have large windows, skylights, and antiques. | 7 rooms. Complimentary Continental breakfast. In-room data ports, some in-room hot tubs, cable TV. Business services. No kids under 10. No smoking. | 1714 Thames St. | 410/522–2323 or 800/432–0184 | fax 410/522–2324 | celies@aol.com | www.celieswaterfront.com | $192–$220 | AE, D, MC, V.

Hyatt Regency. Connected by skywalk to Inner Harbor, this hotel's lobby has glass elevators and the chain's trademark atrium. It is 3 blocks from Camden Yards. | 486 rooms. 2 restaurants, bar. In-room data ports, minibars, cable TV. Pool. Hot tub. Putting green, tennis courts. Basketball, gym. Business services, parking (fee). | 300 Light St. | 410/528–1234 | fax 410/685–3362 | quality@bwirbpo.hyatt.com | www.hyatt.com | $255–$280 | AE, D, DC, MC, V.

Marriott Inner Harbor. One of the city's largest hotels, this Marriott has a quiet public area; some rooms have views of Inner Harbor and Camden Yards. The hotel is a ½ mi from downtown. | 524 rooms, 17 suites. Restaurant, bar. In-room data ports, cable TV. Indoor pool. Hot tub. Exercise equipment. Business services, parking (fee). | 110 S. Eutaw St. | 410/962–0202 | fax 410/625–7892 | www.marriott.com | $224–$244 | AE, D, DC, MC, V.

Pier 5 Hotel. At the Inner Harbor on Pier 5, this unusual hotel has modern, funky furniture, which adds to the overall contemporary, colorful, hip look of the rooms. | 65 rooms. 2 restaurants, 1 lounge. In-room data ports, cable TV. Business services. | 711 Eastern Ave. | 410/539–2000 or 877/207–9047 | fax 410/783–1469 | www.thepier5.com | $229–$239 | AE, D, DC, MC, V.

Renaissance Harborplace. The hotel occupies a prime spot in the Inner Harbor. Rooms are light and cheerful. There is a coffee bar in the lobby and a shopping mall next door. | 622 rooms. Restaurant, bar, room service. In-room data ports, minibars, cable TV. Indoor pool. Hot tub. Exercise equipment. Shops. Business services, parking (fee). Pets allowed. | 202 E. Pratt St. | 410/547–1200 | fax 410/539–5780 | www.renaissancehotels.com/bwish | $199–$259 | AE, D, DC, MC, V.

VERY EXPENSIVE

★ **Harbor Court Hotel.** This redbrick hotel, built in 1986, has a modern exterior, while the interior has the charm of an English country manor. A grand winding staircase and crystal chandelier are highlights of the lobby. | 202 rooms, 25 suites. Restaurant, bar. In-room data ports, refrigerators, room service, cable TV. Pool. Hot tub, massage. Tennis. Gym, racquetball. Business services, airport shuttle, parking (fee). | 550 Light St. | 410/234–0550 or 800/824–0076 | fax 410/659–5925 | reservations@harborcourt.com | www.harborcourt.com | $289–$500 | AE, D, DC, MC, V.

BALTIMORE/WASHINGTON INTERNATIONAL AIRPORT AREA (SEE BALTIMORE)

BERLIN

MAP 4, I5

(Nearby towns also listed: Ocean City, Pocomoke City, Salisbury)

A short drive from the beaches, Berlin is a pleasant respite from the hustle and bustle of Ocean City. Its turn-of-the-century business district contains many well-kept Federal and Victorian buildings. Distinctive architectural elements, including stamped metal cornices and awnings, contribute to Berlin's pleasing streetscape.

Information: Worcester County Tourism | 113 Franklin St., Snow Hill, MD 21863 | 800/852–0335 | www.berlinmdcc.org.

Attractions

Calvin B. Taylor House. This early 19th-century house on the National Registry of Historic Places currently houses a Colonial-era museum in the east wing. The west wing illustrates local history and commemorates the area's World War II veterans. | 208 Main St. | 410/641–1019 or 410/641–4775 | $2 | Memorial Day–Labor Day 10–4.

ON THE CALENDAR

AUG.: *Berlin Summer Celebration.* The town celebrates summertime during this three-day event on Main Street. Good music, sidewalk sales, children's events, and more are on tap. | 410/641–4775.

SEPT.: *Berlin Fiddlers' Convention.* Win cash prizes showing off your talent at playing banjo, guitar, and, of course, the fiddle at this two-day event. Or, if you prefer, just listen while you grab some chow at the many food vendors. | 410/641–4775.

Dining

Firehose Tavern. American/Casual. The restaurant is in an old firehouse and sports rustic wooden floors, huge exposed beams, and museum-quality displays of firefighting equipment—hats, hooks, boots, and so forth. It serves basic, hearty fare like burgers and wings. | 500 S. Baltimore Ave. | 410/289–5893 | $5–$10 | AE, MC, V.

Lodging

Atlantic Hotel. The rooms in this lovely Victorian, built in 1895, are furnished with period antiques. The front porch, dotted with rockers, spans the length of the hotel. | 16 rooms. Restaurant, bar, complimentary breakfast. Cable TV. | 2 N. Main St. | 410/641–3589 | fax 410/641–4928 | www.atlantichotel.com | $95–$175 | AE, MC, D, V.

Holland House. This small, 2-story house was built in 1915 and is sprinkled with Victorian reproductions throughout. The common area is stocked with games, puzzles, and current magazines and is a good place to socialize with other guests, as is the large front porch. | 6 rooms. TV/VCR in common area, no room phones. No pets. No kids under 10. No smoking. | 5 Bay St. | 410/641–1956 | $70–$95 | No credit cards.

Merry Sherwood Plantation. This Italianate B&B, built in 1859, is ringed by impeccably maintained topiaries and rose gardens. Exquisite Victorian furnishings accent its rooms. | 8 rooms (2 with shared bath). Complimentary breakfast and afternoon snacks. No room phones, no TV. No kids under 8. No smoking. | 8909 Worcester Hwy. (Rte. 113) | 410/641–2112 or 800/660–0358 | fax 410/641–3605 | www.merrysherwood.com | $150–$175 | MC, V.

BETHESDA

MAP 4, E3

(Nearby towns also listed: Chevy Chase, Rockville, Silver Springs, Washington, D.C.)

The upscale business area in this trendy suburb of Washington, D.C., is home to a variety of shops and restaurants. For those looking for an indoor shopping experience, Montgomery Mall, which houses more than 200 specialty stores and eateries, is nearby as well. Accessible by subway on the Washington Metro system's red line, Bethesda is just a short trip to the District's monuments.

Information: Conference and Visitors Bureau of Montgomery County, Inc. Bethesda Urban Partnership Inc. | 7906 Woodmont Ave., Bethesda, MD 20814 | 301/215–6660 | fax 301/428–9705 | www.cvbmontco.com.

Attractions

Chesapeake and Ohio Canal National Historical Park. Built in the early 19th century to move goods westward, the 184-mi Chesapeake and Ohio Canal runs from Georgetown to Cumberland in the western Maryland mountains. Remnants of the canal, made obsolete by the railroads in the 1920s, and the path that runs beside them are a favorite of bicyclists, runners, and hikers. The National Park Service gives mule-drawn barge rides on a stretch of the old waterway. The site also contains a small museum. The highlight for most people, though, is a short trek to the Great Falls, a stretch of steep cascades that churn through a narrow gorge. | 11710 MacArthur Blvd., Potomac | 301/299–3613 or 301/767–3714 | www.nps.gov/choh | $4 per vehicle | Daily 9–5.

Clara Barton National Historic Site. The house, built in 1891, was the final home of Clara Barton, founder of the American Red Cross. It served as her home, her headquarters, and a warehouse for disaster relief supplies. | 5801 Oxford Rd., Glen Echo | 301/492–6245 | www.nps.gov/clba | Free | Daily 10–4.

ON THE CALENDAR

APR.: *Landon Azalea Garden Festival.* Stroll through an array of azaleas, flourishing gardens, and wildflowers at Landon School or buy some greenery for your own garden. | 301/320–3200.

Dining

Andalucia de Bethesda. Spanish. Enjoy the culinary treats of southern Spain. On Sunday through Thursday evenings, dine to the sounds of classical guitar. | 4931 Elm St. | 301/907–0052 | Reservations essential Fri.–Sat. | No lunch Sun. | $16–$23 | AE, D, DC, MC, V.

Austin Grill. Tex-Mex. A popular suburban Washington chain eatery with colorful walls, this restaurant serves up Mexican entrees such as enchiladas. Take your meal under blue skies in the open-air dining area. Kids' menu. Sunday brunch. No smoking. | 7278 Woodmont Ave. | 301/656–1366 | $7–$14 | AE, D, DC, MC, V.

Bacchus. Lebanese. Walls blanketed with vivid tapestries add to a relaxed charm. Tasty treats include a variety of meat kabobs and humus. In temperate weather, dine on the outdoor patio. | 7945 Norfolk Ave. | 301/657–1722 | No lunch weekends | $13–$16 | AE, MC, V.

Bethesda Crab House. Seafood. Pick at those tasty crustaceans at paper-covered tables inside this rustic crab house or at the umbrella-shaded tables on the front patio. Beer and wine only. | 4958 Bethesda Ave. | 301/652–3382 | $28–$40 | MC, V.

Bombay Dining. Indian. Though this elegant restaurant specializes in Tandoori meats, it also has a well-stocked salad bar. | 4931 Cordell Ave. | 301/656–3373 | $10–$22 | AE, D, DC, MC, V.

Buon Giorno. Italian. Portraits of Italian landscapes and silver tablecloths brighten Buon Giorno's two dining rooms. Look for fresh fish and imported pastas and cheeses on the menu. | 8003 Norfolk Ave. | 301/652–1400 | Closed Mon. mid-Aug.–mid-Sept. | $17–$27 | AE, D, DC, MC, V.

Cafe Bethesda. French. Impressionist paintings and copious greenery give this bistro its homey appeal. Patio dining available. Beer and wine only. No smoking. | 5027 Wilson La. | 301/657–3383 | Reservations essential Fri.–Sat. | $20–$27 | AE, DC, MC, V.

Cafe Europa. Contemporary. Soft peach walls and black banquettes set the stage for the food. In summer the big front windows are flung open for the breeze and the view. In winter the wood-burning pizza oven warms the place. Individual pizzas have fresh toppings. For dinner try the steak Parisienne, a top-grade sirloin with a crust of crushed black pepper, cognac, shallots, and a whisper of tomato sauce. Finish with a torte, mousse, or cheesecake. | 7820 Norfolk Ave. | 301/657–1607 | Reservations recommended | $9–$20 | AE, D, DC, MC, V.

Cottonwood Cafe. Southwestern. With Mexican rugs and chili peppers on the walls, it's no surprise to find margaritas on the menu. They go great with the seafood paella. Open-air dining available on the covered patio in the front. | 4844 Cordell Ave. | 301/656–4844 | $13–$17 | AE, MC, V.

Faryab. Afghan. Photos of Afghanistan and its people line the walls in this small restaurant. The air is full of pungent, often unfamiliar scents. Try a serving of Afghanistan's national dish, aushak—flat dumplings stuffed with chopped scallions then steamed and topped with ground beef, yogurt, and mint. Finish with a slab of flaky baklava drizzled with honey. | 4917 Cordell Ave. | 301/951–3484 | Reservations recommended | Dinner only on weekends | $6–$15 | MC, V.

Foong Lin. Chinese. Share a family-style meal at this tony, contemporary eatery. No smoking. | 7710 Norfolk Ave. | 301/656–3427 | $7–$24 | AE, MC, V.

Frascati Ristorante Italiano. Italian. Sup beside a mural of Rome inside or under a vine-draped arbor outside at this family-run restaurant. Kids' menu. No smoking. | 4806 Rugby Ave. | 301/652–9514 | Closed Mon. No lunch weekends | $9–$17 | AE, D, DC, MC, V.

Haandi. Indian. Floral paintings accent this formal but not stuffy restaurant, which specializes in northern Indian cuisine. Buffet lunch. No smoking. | 4904 Fairmont Ave. | 301/718–0121 | $17–$22 | AE, DC, MC, V.

Jean-Michel. French. Despite its location in a shopping center, this restaurant serves up French provincial charm in its cozy dining room. Specialties include venison, soft-shell crab, and lobster cooked in whiskey. | 10223 Old Georgetown Rd. | 301/564–4910 | Closed Sun. July–Aug. | $30–$40 | AE, DC, MC, V.

La Miche. French. Baskets suspended from wooden beams, lace curtains and white table-cloths give this place a rustic yet graceful appeal. Feast on hearty French country-style cuisine such as filet mignon, duck *a l'orange,* and Cornish hen. No smoking. | 7905 Norfolk Ave. | 301/986–0707 | $15–$25 | AE, DC, MC, V.

Le Vieux Logis. French. Eye-catching outdoor murals draw you into this romantic restaurant accented with fresh flowers and candlelight. Open-air dining. | 7925 Old Georgetown Rd. | 301/652–6816 | Reservations essential Sat. | $35–$40 | AE, DC, MC, V.

Matuba Japanese. Japanese. Sample the sushi and tempura beneath a Japanese flag in the expansive dining area. Beer and wine only. No smoking. | 4918 Cordell Ave. | 301/652–7449 | $9–$15 | AE, MC, V.

Montgomery's Grille. American. You can savor the pastas, soups, and sandwiches either beneath a twinkling chandelier in the dining room or under the starry skies in the outdoor seating area. Stop in for Sunday brunch. Kids' menu. No smoking. | 7200 Wisconsin Ave. | 301/654–3595 | $4–$22 | AE, D, DC, MC, V.

O'Donnell's. American. Each dining room is dominated by a theme, including nautical and garden motifs. A large patio sheltered by trees also makes a pleasant backdrop for your meal. Expect to find sauteed shellfish and crab cakes on this seafood-heavy menu. Live music. Kids' menu. | 8301 Wisconsin Ave. | 301/656–6200 | $13–$33 | AE, D, DC, MC, V.

Oodles & Noodles. Pan-Asian. The kitchen dishes up authentic Asian cuisine minus the fierce peppers and fiery sauces. The dining area is bright and modern, with lots of blond wood and greenery. The clientele ranges from downtown business people to emigres looking for a taste of home. Try the savory Thai noodle bowl with peanut sauce and crunchy chow mein. | 4907 Cordell Ave. | 301/986–8833 | $6–$10 | AE, D, MC, V.

Original Pancake House. American. Wake up to an old-fashioned, stick-to-your-ribs breakfast at this restaurant distinguished by checkered floors and brightly colored walls. Choose from pancakes, bacon and eggs, waffles, and more. Kids' menu. | 7700 Wisconsin Ave. | 301/986–0285 | No dinner | $5–$9 | AE, MC, V.

Rio Grande Cafe. Mexican. Part cantina, part loading dock, this eatery's walls are lined with crates of Mexican beer, and 50-pound sacks of rice slump in the corner. While you wait, and you will, you can watch the perpetual-motion machine making fresh tortilla dough. Though the Rio Grande serves unusual dishes like quail and roasted baby goat, there are more familiar favorites like cheesy enchiladas and fajitas. The large portions make it a good bet for families. | 4919 Fairmont Ave. | 301/656–2981 | $7–$18 | AE, D, DC, MC, V.

Tastee Diner. American. This 24-hour greasy spoon is popular with students and other night owls, more for its classic diner atmosphere than for its food. The sandwich counter and cracked vinyl booths make you feel like you're in an Edward Hopper painting. A serving of meatloaf and mashed potatoes or a sandwich will cost you less than five bucks. | 7731 Woodmont Ave. | 301/652–3970 | $3–$6 | MC, V.

Thai Leela. Thai. Done in shades of green with Thai art dressing up the walls, this eatery has a casual flair. Outdoor dining is available at tables on the lawn. Kids' menu. No smoking. | 4733 Bethesda Ave. | 301/654–0262 | Closed Sun. | $7–$19 | MC, V, DC, AE.

Raku. Pan-Asian. Oversized chopsticks on the walls and umbrella-shaped lamps give this eclectic dining room an Asian flair. Start off this culinary experience with the miso soup or the sesame-crusted shrimp cocktail. The front sidewalk provides an outdoor dining area. Kids' menu. No smoking. | 7240 Woodmont Ave. | 301/718–8681 | $3–$20 | AE, MC, V.

Red Tomato Cafe. Italian. Richly colored tiles, low-hanging lights and vintage Italian paintings make this a cozy spot to share its trademark brick-oven pizzas with a friend. No smoking. | 4910 St. Elmo Ave. | 301/652–4499 | $6–$17 | AE, D, DC, MC, V.

Rock Bottom Brewery. American. The first East Coast venture of this Colorado-based chain, this brew pub is just the place for knocking back a few beers while watching a game. Try the foot-long tortillas stuffed with smoked chicken and jack cheese, then fried crisp and served with salsa cruda and guacamole. Entertainment Friday and Saturday. | 7900 Norfolk Ave. | 301/652–1311 | $8–$17 | AE, DC, MC, V.

Ruth's Chris Steak House. Steak. Part of an upscale chain, this clubby restaurant is known for steaks, ribs, and other meaty dishes. A piano player serenades diners Monday through Saturday. No smoking. | 7315 Wisconsin Ave. | 301/652–7877 | $24–$48 | AE, DC, MC, V.

Tara Thai. Thai. Murals of sea creatures set a watery tone at this place known for its spicy dishes. Pad Thai and crispy flounder are just two of the house specialties. No smoking. | 4828 Bethesda Ave. | 301/657–0488 | $8–$13 | AE, D, DC, MC, V.

Tel-Aviv Cafe. Middle Eastern. People-watch from a street-side window seat or turn your attention inside to the Jewish artwork as you await your meal. The menu includes a spicy, Black Angus filet mignon, red snapper stuffed with crab meat, and a lamb T-bone. Outdoor dining is available on the large enclosed patio. Entertainment Tuesday and Saturday. | 4867 Cordell Ave. | 301/718–9068 | $9–$20 | AE, D, DC, MC, V.

Thai Place. Thai. Images of Thailand adorn the walls at this two-level restaurant, giving the large dining area a Southeast Asian flair. Fresh flowers on tables add a nice touch. Chicken basil leaf is a good examples of the zesty fare. | 4828 Cordell Ave. | 301/951–0535 | $8–$13 | AE, D, MC, V.

Thyme Square. Eclectic. Sleek and modern, this brick building sports murals of vegetables in bright colors and an open kitchen, making its design as eclectic as its food. Try the Moroccan pad Thai or Brazilian shellfish. Sunday brunch. No smoking. | 4735 Bethesda Ave. | 301/657–9077 | Reservations essential Thurs.–Sun. | $9–$22 | AE, MC, V.

Tragara. Italian. Fresh flowers and soft lighting contribute to Tragara's formal elegance. Fresh fish, lobster and pasta are staples of its sophisticated northern Italian menu. | 4935 Cordell Ave. | 301/951–4935 | Reservations essential Fri.–Sat. | $10–$28 | AE, DC, MC, V.

Lodging

American Inn of Bethesda. A sunlit atrium is the highlight of this small European-style hotel, a few blocks from the subway. | 76 rooms. Restaurant, complimentary Continental breakfast. Pool. In-room data ports, cable TV. Business services. | 8130 Wisconsin Ave. | 301/656–9300 or 800/323–7081 | fax 301/656–2907 | innkeeper@american-inn.com | www.american-inn.com | $115 | AE, D, DC, MC, V.

Holiday Inn Bethesda. This large hotel is 8 miles from Washington, D.C. and 2 blocks from a Metro stop. It specializes in kosher catering. | 270 rooms. Restaurant, complimentary Continental breakfast. In-room data ports, cable TV. Pool. Exercise equipment. Business services. No pets. | 8120 Wisconsin Ave. | 301/652–2000 or 877/888–3001 (reservations) | fax 301/652–4525 | www.basshotels.com/holiday-inn | $179 | AE, D, DC, MC, V.

Hyatt Regency of Bethesda. This hotel, favored by business travelers, is only 6 mi from downtown D.C. and 5 mi from the National Zoo. | 382 rooms, 10 suites. Restaurant, bar. In-room data ports, cable TV. Indoor pool. Exercise equipment. Business services, parking (fee). | 1 Bethesda Metro Center | 301/657–1234 | fax 301/657–6453 | www.hyatt.com | $140–$160 | AE, D, DC, MC, V.

Marriott Suites. About 20 mi from downtown Washington and a ½ mi from Montgomery Mall, this 11-story hotel has spacious suites. | 274 suites. Restaurant, bar. Complimentary Continental breakfast. In-room data ports, cable TV. Indoor-outdoor pool. Hot tub. Exer-

cise equipment. Laundry. Business services, free parking. No pets. | 6711 Democracy Blvd. | 301/897–5600 | fax 301/530–1427 | www.marriott.com | $199–$219 | AE, D, DC, MC, V.

BOONSBORO

MAP 4, D2

(Nearby towns also listed: Frederick, Hagerstown, Sharpsburg, Thurmont)

Brothers George and William Boone, relatives of famed frontiersman Daniel Boone, founded this community more than two centuries ago. Its early residents built the first monument to George Washington on a mountain overlooking the town and valley. The jar-shaped, stone monument—dedicated July 4, 1827—stands in what is today a state park. Boonsboro is the largest Maryland community near Antietam National Battlefield. Stroll down Main Street and you'll find a handful of restaurants, pubs, and shops.

Information: Hagerstown/Washington County Convention and Visitors Bureau | 6 N. Potomac St., Boonsboro, MD 21740 | 301/791–3246 or 800/228–STAY | www.marylandmemories.org.

Attractions

Boonsboro Museum of History. An eclectic museum tracing the area's history with artifacts from the Civil War, arrowheads, weapons, china, porcelain, and pressed glass. | 113 N. Main St. | 301/432–6969 | $3 | May–Sept., Sun. 1–5.

Crystal Grottoes Caverns. One of the largest solution caves in the world, this is Maryland's only commercially run cavern. | 19821 Shepherdstown Pike (Rte. 34) | 301/432–6336 | $8.50 | Apr.–Oct., daily 10–5; Nov.–Mar., weekends 11–4.

Gathland State Park. A large stone monument dedicated to war correspondents stands near Civil War journalist George Alfred Townsend's home, now a museum. The Appalachian Trail runs through the park. | 21843 National Pike | 301/791–4767 | www.dnr.state.md.us | Free | Daily dawn–dusk.

Greenbrier State Park. This 1,288-acre park with a 42-acre man-made lake is a favorite of swimmers and boaters. Campers and daytrippers enjoy the hiking trails and campsites. No pets. | 21843 National Pike, Boonsboro | 301/791–4767 | www.dnr.state.md.us | $3 weekends, May–Sept. | Daily 8–sunset.

Washington Monument State Park. Local residents claim the jar-shaped stone structure, built in 1827, was the first monument to the nation's founding father. The Appalachian Trail cuts through the park's 147 acres. | 21843 National Pike | 301/791–4767 | www.dnr.state.md.us | Free | Daily dawn–dusk.

ON THE CALENDAR

SEPT.: *Boonsboro Days*. Watch period entertainment or browse for antiques at this two-day early American arts-and-crafts festival in Shafer Park. | 301/432–5889.

Dining

Old South Mountain Inn. American. After a day trekking through the nearby state parks, stop in here for some pampering. Built in the 1700s, this three-story colonial is home to an upscale dining establishment. Try the prime rib or beef Wellington. Kids' menu. Sunday brunch. No smoking. | 6132 Old National Pike (U.S. 40A) | 301/371–5400 | Reservations essential weekends | Closed Mon. | $15–$26 | AE, DC, MC, V.

Town Center Sub & Pizza. Italian. This local favorite serves pizza, sandwiches, and subs. You can get takeout or eat in one of the red, green, and white dining rooms or on the brick patio. Try the steak and cheese sub. | 20 S. Main St. | 301/432–2743 | $4–$7 | MC, V.

BOWIE

(Nearby towns also listed: Bethesda, Chevy Chase, College Park, Silver Spring, Washington, D.C.)

Once a railroad stop, Bowie is the largest municipality in Prince George's County, a suburban enclave of Washington, D.C. Historically, the area surrounding Bowie has been associated with thoroughbred horses and railroading. Originally named Huntington, the community traces its roots back to 1870, when developers created the town at a major junction of the Baltimore and Potomac Railroad. Today, Bowie is a community of 44,000 people covering about 16 square mi. At the crossroads of Route 3/U.S. 301 and U.S. 50/301, Bowie is easily accessible to Baltimore and Annapolis.

Information: Prince George's County Conference and Visitors Bureau Inc. | 9200 Basil Ct., Suite 101, Largo, MD 20774 | 301/925–8300 | www.mybowie.com.

Attractions

Belair Mansion. The original mansion, built in the 1740s, was the home of Samuel Ogle, a three-term colonial governor of Maryland. | 12207 Tulip Grove Dr. | 301/262–6200 | www.cityofbowie.org | Free | Thurs.–Sun. 1–4, closed Mon.–Wed.

Belair Stable. More than 200 years of American thoroughbred racing history is told by exhibits of memorabilia and artifacts. | 2835 Belair Dr. | 301/262–6200 | www.cityofbowie.org | Free | May–June and Sept.–Oct.; Sat.–Sun. 1–4.

Marietta Manor. Built by U.S. Supreme Court Justice Gabriel Duvall in 1812, the Federal brick mansion houses Duvall family heirlooms, antiques from the late-18th and 19th century, and reproductions. | 5626 Bell Station Rd. (off Rte. 193) Glenn Dale | 301/464–5291 | www.pgheritage.org | $3 | Mar.–Dec., Fri–Sun. noon–4.

Port Tobacco Players. Housed in a renovated movie theater, this local performing group has a half-dozen shows each year and countless performances on the road. | 11704 Fenno Road, Upper Marlboro | 301/932–6819.

Six Flags America. This massive amusement park has more than 100 rides (roller coasters, go carts, and much more) as well as shows and water attractions with in excess of 1 million gallons of water. Summer hours vary. | Central Ave. (Rte. 214), Mitchellville, MD | 301/249–1500 | $30 | Daily 10:30–9.

ON THE CALENDAR

MAY: *Heritage Day.* Citizens of Bowie celebrate their history on the third Sunday in May. Bring the family for period reenactments, colonial life demonstrations, and children's activities. | 301/809–3088.

SEPT.: *City of Bowie Arts Expo.* Local and regional performing and visual artists–such as dancers, musicians, and painters–show their stuff at this one-day event in Allen Pond Park. | 301/262–6200.

Dining

New China Restaurant. Chinese. Cantonese favorites are served at this family restaurant. Try the chicken with lobster. | 3544 Crain Hwy. | 301/352–4061 | $5–$15 | AE, D, MC, V.

Vince's Italian Deli. Delicatessen. Inexpensive and plentiful entrees make this a good place for a quick bite. You can build your own sandwich from the wide selection of cheeses, cold cuts, and toppings or try a bowl of Vince's soup of the day. Danish and bagels are made fresh daily. | Rte. 3, Crofton | 410/721–2017 | $5–$8 | AE, D, MC, V.

Lodging

Comfort Inn and Conference Center Bowie. Just 17 mi from Washington, this six-story motel has marble floors in the lobby and spacious, well-appointed rooms. | 186 rooms. Restaurant and bar. Complimentary Continental breakfast. Some in-room data ports, some microwaves, some refrigerators, some in-room hot tubs, cable TV. Pool. Laundry. Business services. No pets. | U.S. 301 and U.S. 50 | 301/464–0089 | fax 301/805–5563 | www.comfortinn.com | $87 | AE, D, DC, MC, V.

Forest Hill Motel. This motel, 8 mi south of Bowie, is near the county courthouse and a handful of Upper Marlboro businesses. | 13 rooms. Some refrigerators. Some pets allowed. | 2901 U.S. 301, Upper Marlboro | 301/627–3969 or 800/793–2828 | fax 301/627–4058 | $55 | AE, D, DC, MC, V.

CAMBRIDGE

MAP 4, G4

(Nearby towns also listed: Easton, Salisbury)

On the southern shore of the Choptank River, Cambridge has a rich history as Maryland's second-largest port. Besides being a shipbuilding and canning center, Cambridge was a mill town and a stop on the Underground Railroad. Its historic district reflects its prosperous past with Georgian and Federal buildings clustered on High Street. Mansions, many in the Queen Anne and Colonial Revival styles, line Oakley and Locust streets. Though its good fortune has waned, Cambridge remains an important port with vessels still seen on scenic Cambridge Creek.

Information: Wicomico Convention and Visitor Bureau | 8480 Ocean Hwy., Delmar, MD 21875 | 410/548–4914 or 800/332–TOUR | www.wicomicotourism.org.

Attractions

Blackwater National Wildlife Refuge. Nearly 24,000 acres of marshland, forests, open water, and farmland provide a winter haven for migratory birds, water fowl and songbirds. Canada geese are prominent during the winter months. | 2145 Key Wallace Rd. | 410/228–2677 | $3 per vehicle, $1 per bike | Visitor center weekdays 8–4, weekends 9–5; nature drive and grounds daily dawn–dusk.

Old Trinity Church, Dorchester Parish. Built in 1675 but altered in the 19th century, this Episcopal church, one of the denomination's oldest in continuous operation, has been restored to its original appearance. | Rte. 16, near Cherry Creek | 410/228–2940 | Free | Mon., Wed., Fri.–Sat. 10–4; Sun. 1–4; closed Tues., Thurs.

Spocott Windmill. This post windmill for grinding grain is the only one in Maryland today, though they were common in the 1700s. This mill is a replica of one destroyed in the blizzard of 1888. | 1610 Hudson Rd. (Rte. 343) | 410/228–7090 | Free | Mon.–Sat. 10–5, closed Sun.

ON THE CALENDAR

FEB.: *National Outdoor Show.* Friendly rivalry prevails at this competition in Golden Hill School in South Dorchester. Trappers, hunters, and watermen show off skills such as muskrat skinning and cooking. | 410/397–8535 or 800/522–TOUR.

MAY: *Antique Aircraft Fly-In.* Aviation buffs touch down in antique aircraft for a day of exhibition and judging. | 1904 Horns Point Rd. | 410/228–5530, 410/228–1899, or 800/522–TOUR.

JULY: *Bay Country Festival.* This three-day event in Sailwinds Park celebrates the heritage and history of Cambridge with nightly live entertainment, a carnival, children's games and activities, and boat rides on the Choptank River. | 800/522–8687.

Dining

McGuigan's Pub and Restaurant. English. This elegant yet family-friendly establishment is outfitted like an old English pub, with hardwood floors, coats of arms, and antique tankards lining the walls. McGuigan's specialty is "pub pies"—hot, deep-dish individual pies with pastry crusts filled with meat, veggies, and other tasty bits. Try the seafood version, with shrimp, scallops, and fish topped with seafood sauce, hard-boiled egg, and creamed potatoes. | 411 Muse St. | 410/228–7110 | $6–$17 | AE, D, MC, V.

Lodging

Cambridge House. A refurbished redbrick apartment house on a tree-lined residential street, this B&B's interior is done in high Victorian style, with a blend of antique and reproduction pieces. The guest parlor has crimson walls, fringed lamps, gold-trimmed curtains, and a cherub motif. Guest rooms have carved oak four-poster beds, wingback armchairs, and tile baths, and some have private decks overlooking the inn's gardens. | 6 rooms. Complimentary breakfast. | 112 High St. | 410/221–7700 | $120 | AE, MC, V.

Glasgow Inn. Built in 1760, this riverside colonial plantation house is surrounded by 7 acres of grounds. Wingback chairs and fireplaces give it a formal yet comfy air. | 7 rooms (4 with shared bath). Complimentary breakfast. No phones, no TV. Playground. No smoking. | 1500 Hambrooks Blvd. | 410/228–0575 or 800/373–7890 | fax 410/221–0297 | glasgow@shorenet.net | www.glasgowinn.com | $100–$150 | No credit cards.

CHESAPEAKE BEACH

MAP 4, F4

(Nearby towns also listed: Annapolis, Solomons, Waldorf)

Earlier this century, thousands of visitors would ride the train from Washington, D.C., or the steamboat from Baltimore to this seaside resort. They would flock to its boardwalk and go fishing or crabbing from a pier that extended 1 mi into the bay. In 1933 a hurricane did irreparable damage to many of the resort's amenities, and in 1935 the last train left Chesapeake Beach. Today, remnants of the resort remain visible, and new throngs of tourists are discovering the town's charms. The Chesapeake Beach Railway station is now a museum and a water park opened along the shoreline in 1995. The town's biggest appeal, though, remains its panoramic view of the Chesapeake Bay.

Information: Calvert County Department of Economic Development | 175 Main St., Prince Frederick, MD 20678 | 410/535–4583 or 800/331–9771.

Attractions

Battle Creek Cypress Swamp Sanctuary. The northernmost stand of bald cypress trees in the nation can be inspected from an elevated boardwalk. A nature center contains exhibits focusing on the natural and cultural history of the area. | Grays Rd., off Rte. 506 | 410/535–5327 | Free | Tues.–Sat. 10–4:30, Sun. 1–4:30.

Calvert Cliffs State Park. Rising from the edge of the Chesapeake, the 100-foot-high Calvert Cliffs encase more than 600 species of fossils dating back 15 million to 20 million years. A 2-mi trail from the parking lot leads to the cliffs' base. | Rte. 2/4, Lusby | 301/872–5688 | www.dnr.state.md.us | $3 | Fri.–Sun. 10–6, call for weekday hours.

Chesapeake Beach Railway Museum. This railroad station, circa 1898, houses a collection of relics and memorabilia from the town's brief heyday as a seaside resort. | 4155 Mears Ave. (Rte. 261) | 410/257–3892 | Free | May–Sept., daily 1–4; Apr. and Oct., weekends 1–4; and by appointment.

AUG.: *BayFest*. This weekend festival on the town's waterfront promenade in North Beach attracts over 100 craft vendors. Other attractions include food booths (crab cakes!), kids' activities, pony rides, and an antique car show. | 410/257–9618.

Dining

Rod and Reel. Seafood. At this century-old, family-owned seafood restaurant you can enjoy a view of the water from a linen-draped table in the main dining area or sit outside at the open-air bar. Of course the Rod and Reel serves crab cakes, but don't miss the rockfish filet stuffed with crab imperial and roasted shrimp. | Rte. 261 and Mears Ave. | 410/257–2735 | Reservations recommended | $13–$46 | AE, D, MC, V.

Lodging

Tidewater Treasures. This two-story contemporary B&B is a refreshing departure if you're tired of Victorian fussiness. Half the guest rooms have Chesapeake views. The house sits on several wooded acres on a tidewater basin. | 4 rooms, 2 with private bath. TV/VCR in common room. No room phones. | 7315 Bayside Rd. | 410/257–0785 | $87–$115 | No credit cards.

CHESTERTOWN

MAP 4, G3

(Nearby town also listed: Grasonville)

One of the loveliest towns on the Eastern Shore, Chestertown has a historic district that's easily traveled by foot, affording glimpses of well-maintained Federal townhouses, Georgian mansions, and a stone house reportedly built from a ship's ballast. This river town grew elegant, prosperous, and daring by the time of the American Revolution. In 1774, angered by the Boston Port Act, residents staged their own tea party in broad daylight. The event is commemorated each May at the Chestertown Tea Party. Today, tourists, sailors, and boat enthusiasts still flock to Chestertown, the seat of Kent County. The town is also home to Washington College, chartered in 1782 and named for the country's first president.

Information: Kent County Tourism | 100 N. Cross St., Suite 3, Chestertown, MD 21620 | 410/778–0416 | www.kentcounty.com.

Attractions

Washington College. Founded in 1782, this is the 10th oldest liberal arts college in the country. George Washington gave his name and 50 guineas to the college, in appreciation of Kent County's aid to his soldiers. An easy walk from downtown, the college is on 112 acres, some along the Chester River, and is home to 1,200 students. | 300 Washington Ave. | 410/778–2800 or 800/422–1782 | Free.

MAY: *Chestertown Tea Party Festival*. Townsfolk commemorate the 1774 Tea Party in Chestertown with a reenactment, parade, art show and other entertainment at this day-long festival. | 410/778–0416.
JULY: *Chestertown Fireworks*. These fireworks light up the sky every Independence Day. Grab a lawn chair and view them from the edge of the Chester River. | 410/778–0416.

Dining

Blue Heron. Seafood. In the historic district near the Chester River, this light and airy restaurant is home to a collection of pottery by local artists. Regional cuisine—such as local rockfish, oyster fritters, and Maryland jumbo lump crab cakes—dominates the menu. | 236 Cannon St. | 410/778–0188 | Closed mid-Feb.–mid-Mar. Closed Sun.–Mon. No lunch | $17–$24 | AE, D, MC, V.

Old Wharf Inn. American. This relaxed, waterfront eatery at the edge of Chestertown is known for its crab bisque. Kids' menu. Sunday brunch. | 98 Cannon St. | 410/778–3566 | Reservations not accepted | $10–$20 | AE, MC, V.

Waterman's Crab House. American. Boaters can dock right at this waterfront restaurant known for its steamed crabs and barbecued ribs. Listen to the water lap against the boats as you eat in the open-air dining area. Kids' menu. | 21055 Sharp St. Wharf, Rock Hall | 410/639–2261 | Closed Dec.–Feb. | $9–$33 | AE, D, DC, MC, V.

Lodging

Comfort Suites of Chestertown. A five-minute drive from the historic district, this three-story hotel has cascading ivy and comfortable burgundy chairs in the lobby. Each room has separate living rooms and sleeping areas. | 53 suites. Complimentary Continental breakfast. Refrigerators, cable TV. Indoor pool. Laundry facilities. Business services. | 160 Scheeler Rd. | 410/810–0555 | www.comfortinn.com | $80–$119 | AE, D, DC, MC, V.

Huntingfield Manor. Built in 1850, this B&B is in the center of 70 acres of farmland bordering the Eastern Shore. | 6 rooms, 1 cottage. Complimentary Continental breakfast. No room phones. Some pets allowed. | 4928 Eastern Neck Rd., Rock Hall | 410/639–7779 | fax 410/639–2924 | www.huntingfield.com | $95–$145 | AE, MC, V.

★ **Imperial Hotel.** Nestled in the heart of the historic district, this brick, three-story hotel, built in 1903, is fronted by two-levels of wide balconies supported by white columns. | 11 rooms, 2 suites. Dining room, complimentary Continental breakfast and afternoon tea. Cable TV. Business services. | 208 High St. | 410/778–5000 | fax 410/778–9662 | www.imperialchestertown.com | $95–$200 | AE, MC, V.

Inn at Mitchell House. This 18th-century manor house on 10 acres overlooking a pond has wide highly polished floorboards and fireplaces in some of the rooms. | 6 rooms (1 with shared bath). Complimentary breakfast. No room phones, TV in common area. Tennis. Beach. No smoking. | 8796 Maryland Pkwy. | 410/778–6500 | fax 410/778–2861 | innatmitch@friend.ly.net | www.chestertown.com/mitchell | $90–$110 | MC, V.

The Parker House. This 1876 farm house is in Chestertown's historic district, a few blocks from downtown. Guest rooms, with names like the Queen's Room and the Lincoln Room, are furnished with antiques. There is a sitting porch off the kitchen and flower gardens all around the one-acre plot. | 4 rooms. Complimentary Continental breakfast. TV in common area. Some pets allowed. | 108 Spring Ave. | 410/778–9041 | fax 410/778–7318 | parkerbb@dmv.com | $110–$125 | No credit cards.

★ **White Swan Tavern.** Restored to its 1793 appearance, this B&B is furnished with antiques and has a room displaying the many artifacts found during the renovation. | 6 rooms, 2 suites. Complimentary Continental breakfast. Refrigerators, no room phones, TV in common area. | 231 High St. | 410/778–2300 | fax 410/778–4543 | www.chestertown.com/whiteswan | $120–$200 | MC, V.

CHEVY CHASE

INTRO
ATTRACTIONS
DINING
LODGING

CHEVY CHASE

MAP 4, E3

(Nearby towns also listed: Bethesda, Rockville, Silver Springs, Washington, D.C.)

Chevy Chase, an affluent suburb of Washington, D.C., is an upscale shopping mecca. Along Wisconsin Avenue, shoppers will find the urban sophistication of New York in the national and international jewelers, clothiers, and the like. Also the city is home to or near four shopping malls. Chevy Chase also is known for its historic homes and churches.

Information: Montgomery County Conference and Visitors Bureau | 12900 Middlebrook Rd., Suite 1400, Germantown, MD 20874 | 301/428–9702 or 800/925–0880 | www.cvb-montco.com.

Attractions

Mazza Gallerie. This shopping mall, at the Friendship Heights Metro stop, has 20 stores, including Saks Fifth Avenue, Nieman Marcus, Filene's Basement, and Williams-Sonoma. There is also a General Cinema and The R Room Restaurant. | 5300 Wisconsin Ave. | 202/966–6114 | Weekdays 10–8, Sat. 10–7, Sun. noon–5.

ON THE CALENDAR

AUG.: *Montgomery County Agricultural Fair.* For over 50 years folks have been celebrating the area's agricultural roots here, with livestock shows, tractor-pulls, bull-riding, music, and carnival rides. | 301/926–3100.

Dining

La Ferme. French. Whether dining among the art, fresh flowers, and tinkling piano indoors or on the patio amid flowers and dangling grapevines, elegance is tantamount here. Ingredients such as venison, fish and rabbit give dishes a hearty rustic flavor. | 7101 Brookville Rd. | 301/986–5255 | www.lafermerestaurant.com | Reservations essential Fri.–Sat. | Closed Mon. No lunch weekends | $30–$40 | AE, DC, MC, V.

Clyde's. American. Clyde's decor takes you back to the '20s and '30s with model trains, cars, and memorabilia. Try the burgers or any of the fresh seafood, pasta, and vegetable dishes. The Race Bar downstairs has a 1955 Jaguar parked inside. | 70 Wisconsin Cir. | 301/951–9600 | $6–$22 | D, DC, MC, V.

Lodging

Embassy Suites Chevy Chase Pavilion. Hotel suites share the building with an uptown shopping mall and the Friendship Heights Metro station. The 45 shops are arranged in a circle around a huge atrium. | 198 suites. Complimentary breakfast, room service. Refrigerators, minibars, microwaves. Cable TV. Indoor pool. Gym. Laundry facilities. Business services, parking (fee). | 4300 Military Rd. NW | 202/362–9300 | fax 202/686–3405 | www.embassy-suites.com | $269 | AE, D, DC, MC, V.

Holiday Inn–Chevy Chase. Two blocks from the District's border, this 12-story hotel, built in 1975, is on tony Wisconsin Avenue amid world-renowned shops. | 213 rooms. Restaurant, bar, complimentary Continental breakfast. In-room data ports, cable TV. Pool. Gym. Business services. Some pets allowed. | 5520 Wisconsin Ave. | 301/656–1500 | fax 301/656–5045 | cornel@pop.net | www.basshotels.com/holiday-inn | $169 | AE, D, DC, MC, V.

COCKEYSVILLE

MAP 4, F2

(Nearby towns also listed: Baltimore, Pikesville, Towson)

Cockeysville, a northern suburb of Baltimore off I–83, is a mix of shopping plazas, restaurants, motels, and offices. The Oregon Ridge Nature Center, a habitat for wildflowers, birds, and other wildlife, is nearby. The Hunt Valley Mall and its more than 100 stores and restaurants are also in the near vicinity.

Information: Baltimore County Conference and Visitors Bureau | 118 Shawan Rd., Hunt Valley, MD 21030 | 800/570–2836 | www.visitbacomd.com.

Attractions

Gunpowder Falls State Park. Outdoor enthusiasts canoe, hike, cycle and fish along the two creeks—Big Gunpowder Falls and Little Gunpowder Falls—that are at the heart of this sprawling park. More than 100 mi of trails in four unspoiled natural areas run along the creeks, which converge at Days Cove to become Gunpowder River. Visitors' center. | 7200 Graces Quarters Rd. | 410/592–2897 | www.dnr.state.md.us | $2 | Daily dawn–dusk.

Ladew Topiary Gardens. Stroll through a rose garden, cottage garden, water garden, berry garden, and by some of America's finest sculpted trees—all designed by the late Harvey Smith Ladew. English antiques fill the house, which is also open for tours. | 3535 Jarrettsville Pike | 410/557–9466 | www.harfordmd.com/attractn.htm | $12 | Mid-Apr.–late Oct., Tues.–Fri. 10–4, weekends 10:30–5, closed Mon.

Northern Central Railroad Hike and Bike Trail. This scenic 21-mi trail extends along the old railroad bed all the way to the Maryland-Pennsylvania border. | 1820 Monkton Rd. | 410/592–2897 | Free | Daily dawn–dusk.

ON THE CALENDAR

MAR.: *Maryland Day.* During the third week of March, Loyola College honors Father Andrew White, who led the first Catholic Mass in the colony in 1634. The week-long celebration includes films, art exhibits, talks, and museum tours. The college is 8 mi south of town on I-83. | 410/617–2000.

APR.–MAY: *Point-to-Point Steeplechase.* These three well-known equestrian events— My Lady's Manor in Monkton, Grand National in Butler, and Maryland Hunt Cup in Glyndon—are held on consecutive weekends. | 410/557–9466 My Lady's Manor; 410/666–7777 Grand National and the Maryland Hunt Cup.

Dining

The Milton Inn. Continental. Reminiscent of places in Colonial Williamsburg, this two-level restaurant has an English country style. Specialties include rack of lamb, shellfish crabs, and jumbo lump crab cakes. Open-air dining. No smoking. | 14833 York Rd., Sparks | 410/771–4366 | Jacket required | $22–$28 | AE, D, DC, MC, V.

York Inn. Continental. This dimly lit New York–style supper club has stone walls and somber wallpaper. Order the veal, chicken, or seafood off the menu or choose from one of the five daily specials. Kids' menu. Sunday brunch. | 10010 York Rd. | 410/666–0006 | Closed Mon. | $14–$25 | AE, D, DC, MC, V.

Lodging

Chase Suites. Just 3 mi from the state fairgrounds and within 1 mi of restaurants and shops, this hotel's suites range from one room to two bedrooms. It serves a complimentary dinner Monday through Thursday. | 96 rooms, 24 suites. Complimentary Continental breakfast. In-room data ports, some kitchenettes, cable TV. Pool. Business services. Some pets allowed. | 10710 Beaver Dam Rd. | 410/584–7370 or 800/331–3131 | fax 410/584–7843 | $169 | AE, D, DC, MC, V.

Econo Lodge. On a busy north-south route from Baltimore, this motel is 12 mi from the Inner Harbor. | 80 rooms. Restaurant. Cable TV. Pool. Business services. | 10010 York Rd. | 410/667–4900 | fax 410/666–2666 | www.econolodge.com | $44 | AE, D, DC, MC, V.

Marriott Hunt Valley Inn. On 18 landscaped acres, this three-story hotel is just 3 mi from the light rail, which travels to downtown Baltimore. Rooms in this property, built in 1970, have easy chairs, ottomans, and floral bedspreads. | 390 rooms, 2 suites. Restaurant, bar, room service. In-room data ports, cable TV. Indoor pool, wading pool. Hot tub. Tennis. Exercise equipment. Laundry facilities. Business services, free parking. Some pets allowed. | 245 Shawan Rd., Hunt Valley | 410/785–7000 | fax 410/785–0341 | www.marriott.com | $169 | AE, D, DC, MC, V.

COLLEGE PARK

MAP 4, F3

(Nearby towns also listed: Bowie, Greenbelt, Silver Spring)

Founded more than 150 years ago, College Park is home to the main campus of the University of Maryland. Students add a vitality to this town, patronizing its eclectic mix of stores and ethnic restaurants. College Park is also home to the nation's oldest continuously operating airport, where the Wright brothers once trained military officers to fly. Nearly two centuries ago, distinguished stagecoach travelers, including George Washington, visited the town, the first stage stop after Washington, D.C.

Information: Prince George's County Conference and Visitors Bureau Inc. | 9200 Basil Ct., Suite 101, Largo, MD 20774 | 301/925–8300.

Attractions

College Park Aviation Museum. Overlooking the runway at the nation's oldest continuously operating airport, this museum exhibits a 1911 Wright B Aeroplane, a 1918 Curtiss Jenny, and the National Air & Space Museum's Berliner helicopter. The building's curved roofline is reminiscent of an early Wright airplane. | 1985 Corporal Frank Scott Dr. | 301/864–6029 | $4 | Daily 10–5.

Oxon Hill Farm. Unlike many D.C. area attractions, this National Park Service site doesn't preserve the past but gives demonstrations in cow milking, egg collecting, corn husking, and animal grooming. Seasonally, you can witness sheep shearing, wheat threshing, tobacco harvesting, and cider pressing. There are also hayrides, animal petting, a nature trail. | Oxon Hill Rd., Oxon Hill, MD | 301/839–1177 | www.nps.gov/nace/oxhi | Free | Daily 8–4:30.

University of Maryland. With more than 24,000 undergraduates, the university teems with activities, from sports to the arts. Established in 1862, it is on 1,500 rolling acres in the Baltimore-Washington corridor. | 7603 Baltimore Ave. | 301/405–1000 | fax 301/314–6693 | www.inform.umd.edu | Free.

KODAK'S TIPS FOR PHOTOGRAPHING WEATHER

Rainbows
- Find rainbows by facing away from the sun after a storm
- Use your auto-exposure mode
- With a SLR, use a polarizing filter to deepen colors

Fog and Mist
- Use bold shapes as focal points
- Add extra exposure manually or use exposure compensation
- Choose long lenses to heighten fog and mist effects

In the Rain
- Look for abstract designs in puddles and wet pavement
- Control rain-streaking with shutter speed
- Protect cameras with plastic bags or waterproof housings

Lightning
- Photograph from a safe location
- In daylight, expose for existing light
- At night, leave the shutter open during several flashes

From Kodak Guide to Shooting Great Travel Pictures © 2000 by Fodor's Travel Publications

Washington Redskins. Once the athletic glue that held Washington together, the Redskins have slid in recent years and, perhaps appropriately, moved out of their urban stadium to a leviathan new home in Landover, Maryland. | 21300 Redskins Park Dr., Landover, MD | 703/478–8900 | www.redskins.com | For tickets, 301/276–6050 | Call for kick-off times.

ON THE CALENDAR
MAY: *International Music Competitions.* Every year at the end of May, world-famous musicians compete at the Clarice Smith Performing Arts Center at the University of Maryland. The competition focuses on one instrument or voice per year. | 301/405–8174.

Dining
Alamo. Mexican. Mexican-style paintings enliven the walls of this eatery. You'll find the San Antonio dinner and Loghorn plate among the house specialties. Entertainment on Friday and Saturday. Kids' menu. | 5510 Kenilworth Ave., Riverdale | 301/927–8787 | $4–$20 | AE, D, DC, MC, V.

Calvert House Inn. American. Stop in Friday and Saturday for some live jazz. Steak and seafood are the menu specialties. Kids' menu. | 6211 Baltimore Ave. Riverdale | 301/864–5220 | Reservations essential Fri.–Sat. | No lunch weekends | $18–$35 | AE, D, DC, MC, V.

Moose Creek Steak House. Contemporary. One mile south of the university in the Holiday Inn, Moose Creek specializes in grilled steaks and burgers, salads, and a full kids' menu. | 10000 Baltimore Ave. | 301/345–6700 | Breakfast available | $13–$18 | AE, D, DC, MC, V.

Santa Fe Cafe. Southwestern. Sink your teeth into a Texas rib-eye. If you're in the mood for something lighter try the jerk chicken pita. Check out the collection of pottery by local artists inside or have your meal in the outdoor seating area. Entertainment Tuesdays and Thursday through Saturday. | 4410 Knox Rd. | 301/779–1345 | Closed Sun. | $6–$14 | AE, D, DC, MC, V.

Lodging
Comfort Inn and Suites. Less than 1 mi south of the university, this hotel has both rooms and suites. | 125 rooms. Complimentary Continental breakfast. Cable TV. Pool. Exercise equipment. No pets. | 9020 Baltimore Ave. | 301/ 441–8110 | fax 301/474–7725 | $90–$170 | AE, D, DC, MC, V.

Holiday Inn–College Park. Spread out in two buildings, this property is just 2 mi from the University of Maryland and 15 mi from downtown Washington, D.C. | 222 rooms, 1 suite. Restaurant, bar. In-room data ports, some refrigerators, cable TV. Outdoor pool. Hot tub. Exercise equipment. Laundry facilities. Business services. | 10000 Baltimore Ave. (U.S. 1) | 301/345–6700 | fax 301/441–4923 | www.basshotels.com/holiday-inn | $159 | AE, D, DC, MC, V.

The New Carrollton Courtyard by Marriott. Convenient to I–95, shopping, and restaurants, this four-story hotel caters mostly to business travelers. | 150 rooms. Restaurant, bar. In-room data ports, cable TV. Indoor pool. Hot tub. Gym. Business services. Laundry facilities. Free parking. | 8330 Corporate Dr., Landover | 301/577–3373 | fax 301/577–1780 | cy.wasld.gm@marriott.com | $128 | AE, D, DC, MC, V.

COLUMBIA

MAP 4, E4

(Nearby towns also listed: Baltimore, Ellicott City)

Columbia, created in 1966 as a large-scale planned community, was intended to be an alternative to the sprawl associated with many suburbs. Home to more than

88,000 people, the city is made up of nine self-contained villages as well as Town Center, the central downtown area. The largest city in Howard County, it has many recreational areas and an array of shopping facilities.

Information: Howard County Tourism Council | Box 9, Ellicott City, MD 21041 | 800/288–TRIP | www.howardcountymdtour.com.

Attractions

Maryland Museum of African Art. Browse the exhibits or listen to a lecture focusing on traditional and contemporary art from African societies. | 5430 Vantage Point Rd. | 410/730–7105 | $2 | Tues.–Fri. 10–4, Sun. noon–4, closed Mon., Sat.

Merriweather Post Pavilion. This outdoor concert venue with a grassy seating area is in a shady grove. Regional and national musical acts perform in season. | 10475 Little Patuxent Pkwy. | 301/596–0660 | www.mppconcerts.com | Prices vary | June–mid-Sept., call for performance schedule.

ON THE CALENDAR

MAY: *Wine in the Woods*. Sample wines from all over Maryland at this event on the third weekend in May at Symphony Woods. Take home your glass as a souvenir. | $15 | 410/313–7275.

MAY–OCT.: *Courtyard Concert Series*. Concerts for adults and kids are held throughout the eight village centers of Columbia during lunch and dinner hours. | 410/992–3600.

JUNE: *Columbia Festival of Arts*. Ten days of performances by local and national artists, gallery openings, master classes, workshops, fine and traditional arts and crafts, and hands-on activities make this an event for the whole family. | 410/715–3044.

NOV.–JAN.: *Symphony of Lights*. Bundle up the kids and meander through this exhibit of more than 50 animated and stationary holiday light displays at the Merriweather Post Pavilion. | 410/740–7645.

Dining

Clyde's of Columbia. American. Unwind amid the hanging plants and checkered tablecloths in the dining room or at the umbrella-shaded wooden tables on the side patio. Kids' menu. Sunday brunch. No smoking. | 10221 Wincopin Cir. | 410/730–2828 | $6–$24 | AE, D, DC, MC, V.

King's Contrivance. American. This rambling turn-of-the-century mansion on 4 acres houses seven dining rooms on two floors. Oil paintings of flowers and hunting scenes give it an easy mix of Victorian elegance and country flavor. You'll find venison, duck, and potato-crusted crab cakes on its sophisticated menu. | 10150 Shaker Dr. | 410/995–0500 | Closed Jan. | $18–$30 | AE, D, DC, MC, V.

Old Hickory Grille. Contemporary. In the Hickory Ridge Village Center, this restaurant is known for its barbecued ribs and smoked foods but also serves pastas and salads. | 6420 Freetown Rd. | 410/531–0326 | $7–$16 | AE, D, DC, MC, V.

Lodging

Columbia Sheraton Hotel. Entertainment of all sorts is easily available when staying at this hotel across the street from the Columbia Mall and just 1 mi from the Merriweather Post Pavilion. It's also just 16 mi from BWI airport. | 288 rooms. Restaurant, bar. In-room data ports, refrigerators, cable TV. Pool. Business services. Some pets allowed. | 10207 Wincopin Cir. | 410/730–3900 or 800/638–2817 | fax 410/730–1290 | sales@columbiainn | www.columbiainn.com | $99–$169 | AE, D, DC, MC, V.

Hilton Columbia. An atrium and glass-enclosed elevators give guests an impressive view of the lobby. Catch a shuttle from this property in an office park to malls and shopping centers. It is 15 mi to BWI Airport. | 152 rooms. Restaurant, bar. In-room data ports, refrigerators, cable TV. Indoor pool. Hot tub. Exercise equipment. Business services. | 5485 Twin Knolls Rd. | 410/997–1060 | fax 410/997–0169 | www.hilton.com | $89–$144 | AE, D, DC, MC, V.

CRISFIELD

MAP 4, G6

(Nearby town also listed: Pocomoke City)

An unpretentious community on the Chesapeake's Eastern Shore, Crisfield was the principal center of Maryland's seafood industry from the mid-1800s to the early 1900s. Oysters were once such a dominant bounty that part of the town is built on a foundation of discarded oyster shells. Today, Crisfield is famous for its hard- and soft-shell blue crabs. Watermen still bring their catch to the town docks. The docks also are the departure point for day excursions via ferry to Smith Island, which is only accessible by boat.

Information: Somerset County Tourism | Box 243, Princess Anne, MD 21853 | 410/651–2968 or 800/521–9189 | www.skipjack.net/le_shore/visitsomerset.

CRISFIELD

INTRO
ATTRACTIONS
DINING
LODGING

Attractions

Janes Island State Park. This park, nearly surrounded by the Chesapeake Bay and its inlets, has miles of isolated shorelines and marshes. Canoeing, fishing and crabbing are popular activities. Boat and cabin rentals available. | Alfred Lawson Rd. | 410/968–1565 | www.dnr.state.md.us | Free | Daily dawn–dusk.

Smith Island. Many natives of this isolated fishing community, accessible only by boat, have not lost the accents of their 17th-century English ancestors. Islanders take pride in their local cuisine—soft-shell crabs, crab cakes, oysters, and clam fritters. Visit the Smith Island Center and watch a 20-minute film to get a glimpse of island life. | 20915 Summers Road, Ewell | 410/425–3351 | www.intercom.net/npo/smithisland/ | $2 visitors center | Apr.–Oct., daily noon–4.

Tyler's Cruises. This passenger ferry from Crisfield to Smith Island departs from Summers Cove Marina in Crisfield and docks in Ewell, Smith Island's main community. | 4065 Smith Rd. | 410/425–2771 | $20 | Memorial Day–Oct., departs daily at 12:30, returns at 5.

ON THE CALENDAR

SEPT.: *Hard Crab Derby and Fair.* Marylanders do take their crabs seriously. On Labor Day weekend at the Somer's Cove Marina, enjoy crab races, skiff races, a boat-docking contest, kids' rides, and the Miss Crustacean beauty pageant. | 800/782–3913.

Dining

Watermen's Inn. Seafood. Paisley linens, flowers, and soft lighting make for pleasant dining at Watermen's. The crab cakes and crab soup are locally famous, as are the homemade cakes, pies, and pastries. Try the soft-shell crab with artichoke, with key lime pie for dessert. | 901 W. Main St. | 410/968–3970 | Mon. | $9–$20 | AE, D, MC, V.

Lodging

The Pines Motel. Just 1 mi from the waterfront, this two-story motel is a short hike to the water's edge for fishing or crabbing. | 40 rooms. Pool. Cable TV. | 127 N. Somerset Ave. | 410/968–0900 | carson@shore.intercom.net | www.intercom.net/biz/pines | $70 | AE, MC, V.

CUMBERLAND

MAP 4, B2

(Nearby towns also listed: Grantsville, Frostburg, McHenry, Oakland)

Cradled in the Allegheny Mountains of western Maryland, Cumberland was the young nation's gateway to the West. A 1-mi natural pass in the mountains—the Narrows—allowed wagon trains, later locomotives, and eventually motorists to make their way westward. The National Pike—the first federally funded highway—the Chesapeake and Ohio Canal, and the Baltimore and Ohio Railroad all converged in Cumberland, a once-prosperous industrial town. Today, Cumberland is tapping into its rich transportation heritage to lure tourists. Millions of dollars are being spent to repair a stretch of the canal; a restored steam locomotive chugs along a rugged mountainside to Frostburg; and a new $54-million resort has opened east of the city at the breathtaking Rocky Gap State Park.

Information: Allegany County Convention and Visitors Bureau | Western Maryland Station Center, 13 Canal St., Cumberland, MD 21502 | 301/777–5905 or 800/50–VISIT | www.mdmountainside.com.

Attractions

Allegany College of Maryland. Two miles east of town, this rural liberal arts community college is home to 2,200 students. Music festivals, pedigree dog shows, and craft fairs are some of the events held here. | 12401 Willowbrook Rd. | 301/784–5000 | www.ac.cc.md.us | Free.

Dans Mountain State Park. This 481-acre day-use park with an Olympic-size pool and rugged, isolated mountain terrain is perfect for swimming, picnicking, bicycling, and hiking. | Water Station Run Road, off Rte. 36 | 301/777–2139 | www.dnr.state.md.us | Free, pool $1 | Mon.–Fri. 8–4.

Fort Cumberland Trail. Take a self-guided walking tour of the boundaries of Fort Cumberland, built during the French and Indian War. Plaques mark notable spots. | Riverside Park | 301/722–2000 | Free | Daily dawn–dusk.

George Washington's Headquarters. A small portion of original log structure of Washington's headquarters during the French and Indian War and Whiskey Rebellion remains standing. An audio tape tells its stories. | Riverside Park | 301/777–8678 | Free | Presidents' Day, 2nd weekend in June or by appointment.

Green Ridge State Forest. Wildlife is plentiful in this 43,000-acre forest with a stunning view of the Potomac and mountain valleys. Camping, hiking, bicycling, and hunting—in season—are favored activities. | I–68, off exit 64 | 301/478–3124 | Free | Daily 8–4:30.

History House. A Second Empire house built in 1867 by the president of the Chesapeake and Ohio Canal is now home to a local historical society and museum. | 218 Washington St. | 301/777–8678 | $3 | May–Oct., Tues.–Sat. 11–3, Sun. 1:30–4, closed Mon.

La Vale Toll Gate House. This toll building, erected in 1836 along the Old National Highway just outside of Cumberland, is the only remaining one in Maryland. | Old National Hwy. (U.S. 40A) | 301/729–1681 | Free | May–Oct., weekends 1:30–4:30, closed weekdays or by appointment.

Rocky Gap State Park. This lovely natural haven is nestled between Evitts and Martin mountains. Popular with hikers, campers, boaters, and swimmers, this park has a man-made lake. | 12500 Pleasant Valley Rd., off I–68 | 301/777–2139 or 301/777–2138 | www.dnr.state.md.us | Free | Daily dawn–dusk; campground year-round.

The Narrows. This dramatic mile-long natural mountain pass, used by westward travelers in the 19th century, is accessible today via U.S. 40 or on board the Western Maryland Scenic Railroad.

Western Maryland Scenic Railroad. This 3-hour round-trip ride to Frostburg traverses rugged mountains with panoramic vistas. A 1916 Baldwin locomotive, once used in Michigan's Upper Peninsula, does the heavy work. | 13 Canal Pl. | 301/759–4400 or 800/TRAIN–50 | www.wmsr.com | $17.50; $19.50 in Oct. | May–Sept., Tues.–Sun. 11:30, closed Mon.; Oct., Mon.–Thurs. 11, Fri.–Sun. 11 and 4; Nov.–mid-Dec., weekends 11:30, closed weekdays.

Western Maryland Station Center. This restored 19th-century train station is the departure point for the Western Maryland Scenic Railroad. Inside you'll find exhibits on history of the C and O Canal. | 13 Canal St. | 301/759–4400 | www.wmsr.com | Free | May–mid-Dec., weekdays 9–5, weekends 9–4; Mar.–Apr., weekends 9–4, closed weekdays.

ON THE CALENDAR
JULY: *Agricultural Expo and Fair.* Carnival rides, livestock exhibits and shows make this good old-fashioned country event fun for the whole family. | 301/729–1200.
JULY: *Drum and Bugle Corps Competition.* International drum and bugle corps compete for top honors as they show off their fancy footwork and rhythmic compositions on the last Saturday in July. | 301/777–8325.
AUG.: *Rocky Gap Music Festival.* Regional and national country stars headline this event during the first week in August. Crafts and food vendors ply their wares at booths. | 888/762–5942.
SEPT.: *Western Maryland Street Rod Roundup.* Check out the more than 1,000 souped-up, pre-1949 cars exhibited at this Labor Day weekend event. Plus, enjoy music and crafts. | 301/729–5555.
OCT.: *Maryland Railfest.* A celebration of Maryland's transportation heritage, this event includes a kids' festival, music, a train show, train rides, historic walking tours, and more. | 301/759–4400.

Dining

Fred Warner's German Restaurant. German. Top off a hearty meal of sourbeef and homemade bread with one of Fred's rich desserts, such as chocolate tortes and Black Forest cake. Dine outside on the garden patio. Kids' menu. No smoking. | Rte. 220 Cresaptown | 301/729–2361 | Closed Mon. | $9–$13 | AE, D, DC, MC, V.

Mason's Barn. American. This barn-like restaurant is accented with antique farm equipment. Try the steaks, ribs, or crab cakes, but don't miss the homemade jams, jellies, and candy in the adjacent shop. | 12801 Ali Ghan Rd. | 301/722–6155 | Breakfast available | $8–$17 | AE, D, MC, V.

When Pigs Fly. American. Six blocks west of Baltimore Street, this restaurant and lounge is chock full of pig paraphernalia. It's famous for its barbecued ribs. | 18 Valley St. | 301/722–7447 | $8–$17 | AE, D, MC, V.

Lodging

Best Western Braddock Motor Inn. Convenient to I–68 and near several restaurants, gas stations, and shopping centers this motel, built in 1989, is five minutes west of Cumberland and 2 mi from a mall. | 108 rooms, 11 suites. Restaurant, bar, room service. In-room data ports, cable TV. Indoor pool. Hot tub, sauna. Gym. Business services. Airport shuttle. | 1268 National Hwy. (U.S. 40) La Vale | 301/729–3300 | fax 301/729–3300 | www.bestwestern.com | $69–$110 | AE, D, DC, MC, V.

The Castle. Surrounded by a 12-foot wall, this Gothic Revival stone house, built in 1840, is on a 2-acre estate. Victorian-style furnishings, brass fixtures, and mahogany furniture exude a stately air. | 6 rooms. Complimentary Continental breakfast. | Rte. 36 Mount Savage | 301/

264–4645 | fax 301/264–3136 | castlecraig@mindspring.com | www.noomoon.com/castle | $95–$130 | AE, D, MC, V.

Holiday Inn. Built in 1972, this six-story hotel is in downtown Cumberland and within 1 mi of the train station and an antiques mall. | 130 rooms, 2 suites. Restaurant, bar. In-room data ports, room service, cable TV. Outdoor pool. Gym. Business services. Airport shuttle. Some pets allowed. | 100 S. George St. | 301/724–8800 | fax 301/724–4001 | www.basshotels.com/holiday-inn | $109–$159 | AE, D, DC, MC, V.

Inn at Walnut Bottom. Two buildings make up this country inn, built in 1820. Each is accented by antiques, pine floors and oriental rugs. Area state parks and a historic center are just a short drive away. | 12 rooms (4 with shared bath), 2 suites. Complimentary breakfast. Cable TV. Bicycles. Business services. | 120 Greene St. | 301/777–0003 or 800/286–9718 | fax 301/777–8288 | girvin@hereintown.net | www.iwbinfo.com | $135–$190 | AE, D, MC, V.

Oak Tree Inn. Five miles west of La Vale, this motel has a 24-hour diner and three meeting rooms. | 82 rooms. Restaurant. In-room data ports, microwaves, refrigerators, cable TV, VCRs. Laundry facilities. Pets allowed (fee). | 12310 Winchester Rd., La Vale | 301/729–6706 | www.hereintown.com | $69 | AE, D, DC, MC, V.

Rocky Gap Lodge & Golf Resort. This lakeside resort on 243 acres is inside one of Maryland's most spectacular state parks. Its wood paneling and rustic furniture are reminiscent of a country cabin. | 218 rooms, 4 suites. 2 restaurants, bar. In-room data ports, cable TV. Indoor pool. Hot tub. 18-hole golf course, tennis. Gym, volleyball. Beach, boating, fishing, bicycles. Video games. Business services. | 16701 Lakeview Rd. NE | 301/784–8400 or 800/724–0828 | fax 301/784–8408 | www.rockygapresort.com | $155–$325 | AE, D, DC, MC, V.

Super 8. On the main road between Cumberland and Frostburg, this motel is close to plenty of restaurants and stores as well as Rocky Gap State Park. It is 6 mi from Frostburg State University and 10 mi from the airport. | 63 rooms. Complimentary Continental breakfast. Cable TV. Business services. | 1301 National Hwy. (U.S. 40), La Vale | 301/729–6265 | fax 301/626–4500 | www.super8.com | $53–$76 | AE, D, DC, MC, V.

EASTON

MAP 4, G4

(Nearby towns also listed: Cambridge, St. Michaels, Tilghman)

On Maryland's Delmarva Peninsula, Easton is a busy stopover for hundreds of thousands of beachgoers on their way to Ocean City. About halfway to the ocean from Baltimore, Easton's stretch on U.S. 50 is home to countless fast-food restaurants, gas stations, and discount stores. The business of the highway belies the gentility of the city's downtown. Many of its buildings, dating from the late 19th and early 20th centuries, are cradled by large shade trees. The downtown boasts small specialty shops and elegant Victorian homes. Of particular interest are the restored Avalon Theatre, the Talbot County Courthouse, and the Tidewater Inn. Each fall, thousands of people flock to Easton for the renowned Waterfowl Festival.

Information: Talbot County Conference and Visitors Bureau | 210 Marlboro Ave., Suite 3, Easton, MD 21606-1366 | 410/822–4606 or 888/BAY–STAY | www.eastonmd.org.

Attractions

The Academy of the Arts. This museum exhibits works by regional and national artists. It also sponsors lectures, trips, and classes. | 106 South St. | 410/822–0455 or 410/822–ARTS | www.art-academy.org | $2 (suggested) | Mon.–Sat. 10–4, Wed. 10–9, closed Sun. Closed Aug.

Avalon Theatre. Built in 1921, this vaudeville and movie palace was at the time "The Showplace of the Eastern Shore." Lovingly restored in 1989, this Art Deco venue hosts touring, national performing artists. | 40 E. Dover St. | 410/822–0345 | www.avalontheatre.com | Prices vary | Call for performance times.

Historical Society of Talbot County. The society, which leads walking tours of downtown, runs a museum with exhibits depicting local history. | 25 S. Washington St. | 410/822–0773 | www.hstc.org | $3 | Tues.–Fri. 11–3, Sat. 10–4; closed Sun.–Mon.

Third Haven Friends Meeting House. Built by Quakers in 1682, this meeting house occasionally played host to William Penn, the denomination's most famous member. | 405 S. Washington St. | 410/822–0293 | Free | Daily 9–5.

Tuckahoe State Park. A quiet country stream, bordered by wooded marshlands, runs the length of this 3,498-acre park. Its 60-acre lake is ideal for boating and fishing. | Off Rte. 404 via Rte. 480 | 410/820–1668 | www.dnr.state.md.us | Free | Daily dawn–dusk, campgrounds late Mar.–late Oct.

ON THE CALENDAR

JUNE: *Eastern Shore Chamber Music Festival.* Local and visiting artists perform classical music for two weekends at various historical sites. | 888/889–0980.
JULY: *Tuckahoe Steam and Gas Show and Reunion.* Antique steam engines, blacksmith demonstrations, a horse pull, and an auction are among the highlights. | 410/822–9868.
NOV.: *Waterfowl Festival.* More than 500 prestigious national wildlife exhibitors attend this weekend event. Decoy displays, carving demonstrations, duck-calling contests, and retriever exercises are some of the activities. | 410/822–4567 | $10.

Dining

Hunter's Tavern. American. This restaurant's signature dish is a snapper soup served with a jigger of sherry. The rest of the menu emphasizes regional cuisine as well. Sunday brunch. Open-air dining | 101 E. Dover St. | 410/822–1300 | $18–$35 | AE, MC, V.

The Inn at Easton. Mediterranean. The dining room has a working fireplace, hand-carved molding, and original artwork by Russian Impressionist painter Nikolai Timkov. On the menu are roasted duck breast, New York strip steak, and tempura of yellowfin tuna. | 28 S. Harrison St. | 410/822–4910 | fax 410/822–4910 | $22–$30 | AE, MC, V.

Legal Spirits. American. This Prohibition-themed eatery romanticizes the 1920s and '30s with table-top pictures of Elliot Ness, juke-joint raids, and Bonnie and Clyde. Steaks, burgers, lamb, calamari, quiche, and sesame-crusted salmon are on the menu. | 42 E. Dover St. | 410/820–0033 | Closed Sun. in Aug. | $14–$22 | AE, D, DC, MC, V.

Restaurant Columbia. Contemporary. In a Federal brick townhouse dating from 1795, this restaurant serves roast rack of lamb as one of its specialties. | 28 S. Washington St. | 410/770–5172 | $22–$28 | AE, MC, V.

Lodging

★ **Ashby 1663.** This Colonial-style building with a columned portico is now a B&B. Heart-of-pine floors complement the tall windows and fireplaces. An antique Waterford crystal chandelier and a grand piano add to the opulence. | 13 rooms, 6 suites. Complimentary breakfast, evening cocktails. Cable TV. Pool. Hot tub. Tennis. Exercise equipment, volleyball. No smoking. | 27448 Ashby Dr. | 410/822–4235 | fax 410/822–9288 | info@ashby1663.com | www.ashby1663.com | $215; suites $595 | AE, MC, V.

Bishops House. Three blocks from the town center, this romantically furnished Victorian house (circa 1880) is now a B&B. | 5 rooms. Complimentary breakfast. Some in-room hot tubs, some TVs. No kids under 13. | 214 Goldsborough St. | 410/820–7290 or 800/223–7290 | fax 410/820–7290 | bishopshouse@skipjack.bluecrab.org | www.traveldata.com/inns/data/bishop.html | $110–$120 (2–night minimum stay, 3 nights on weekends) | No credit cards.

Chaffinch House. In the historic district, this cream-and-burgundy Victorian dates from 1893. It has a wraparound porch in front and a porch, patio, and garden in back. Inside there are period furnishings and a working fireplace in the parlor. You can walk to shops and restaurants in town. | 6 rooms, with baths. No pets. No smoking. | 132 S. Harrison St. | 410/822–5074 or 800/861–5074 | $90–$120 | MC, V.

Comfort Inn. On a busy highway to Ocean City, this two-story motel is 5 minutes from the historical district and 20 minutes from St. Michael's area restaurants. Complimentary newspaper. | 84 rooms. Complimentary Continental breakfast. In-room data ports, refrigerators, cable TV. Pool. Hot tub. Business services. | 8523 Ocean Gateway (U.S. 50) | 410/820–8333 | fax 410/820–8436 | bsdiggs@ix.netcom.com | www.comfortinn.com | $100 | AE, D, DC, MC, V.

Days Inn. Floor-to-ceiling windows brighten the lobby of this motel on a busy strip near shops and restaurants. | 80 rooms. Complimentary Continental breakfast. Some refrigerators, cable TV. Pool, wading pool. Some pets allowed. | 7018 Ocean Gateway (U.S. 50) | 410/822–4600 | fax 410/820–9723 | bsdiggs@ix.netcom.com | www.daysinn.com | $103–$115 | AE, D, DC, MC, V.

Holiday Inn Express. This four-story hotel, built in 1995, is just 3 mi from the historic downtown section. Marble floors and tasteful paintings are a nice touch. | 73 rooms. Complimentary Continental breakfast. Cable TV. Indoor pool. In-room data ports, in-room safes. Hot tub. Exercise equipment. Business services. | 8561 Ocean Gateway (U.S. 50) | 410/819–6500 | fax 410/819–6505 | www.basshotels.com/holiday-inn | $109 | AE, D, DC, MC, V.

The Inn at Easton. This upscale inn is a 1790 Federal-style mansion in the historic district. Each room has original artwork, featherbeds, down comforters, Egyptian cotton towels, cotton waffle robes, and Aveda body care products. Suites have private sitting rooms and clawfoot bathtubs. | 3 rooms, 4 suites. Complimentary breakfast. No pets. No kids under 9. | 28 S. Harrison St. | 410/822–4910 | fax 410/822–4910 | www.theinnateaston.com | $100–$160 rooms, $150–$300 suites | AE, MC, V.

Tidewater Inn. The elegantly appointed, Victorian-style rooms, and its proximity to St. Michael's—just 20 minutes—make the Tidewater Inn a great lodging choice. | 114 rooms, 8 suites. Restaurant, bar. In-room data ports, in-room safes, cable TV. Pool. Business services, airport shuttle. | 101 E. Dover St. | 410/822–1300 or 800/237–8775 | fax 410/820–8847 | www.tidewaterinn.com | $120–$185 | AE, D, DC, MC, V.

ELKTON

MAP 4, G2

(Nearby town also listed: Havre de Grace)

Just south of the Delaware border, Elkton is the largest municipality in Cecil County. It's also one of the fastest-growing areas of the state and a major industrial center. The city is easily accessible by I–95 and U.S. 40.

Information: Cecil County Tourism | 129 E. Main St., Room 324, Elkton, MD 21921 | 410/966–5303 or 800/CECIL–95 | www.seececil.org.

Attractions

Elk Neck State Park. This 2,188-acre park, 25 mi north of town, has sandy beaches, woodlands, campgrounds, and the Turkey Point Lighthouse on the North East River, as well as five 2-mi hiking trails. | Rte. 272 | 410/287–5333 | $2.

ON THE CALENDAR

SEPT.–OCT.: *Milburn Orchards.* On weekends bring the kids to enjoy pony, carriage, and hayrides, or to explore the corn maze, straw crawl, boo barn, and bale trail. | 410/398–1349.

Dining

Chesapeake Inn Restaurant and Marina. Mediterranean. You can enjoy the view of Back Creek Basin and the Chesapeake and Delaware Canal from this waterfront restaurant, 5 mi south of town. Of course, its specialty is crab cakes, but the menu is full of surf and turf choices. You can dine on the deck in summer, when there is a more casual menu of pizza and sandwiches. | 605 2nd St., Chesapeake City | 410/885–2040 | $18–$29 | AE, D, DC, MC, V.

Granary. American. This top-notch eatery has two dining areas, one with a rustic deck. Both areas have a dramatic view of the Sassafras River and beautiful wooded areas. It's primarily known for its seafood and steaks. Entertainment Friday and Saturday (seasonal). Kids' menu available. | George St., Georgetown | 410/275–1603 | Closed Mon.–Tues. from Nov.–Mar. | $20–$35 | AE, D, MC, V.

Schaefer's Canal House. American. This place, which is nearly 100 years old, will bring you back to another era. One wall is an oversized window that gives diners an impressive view of Schaefer's Canal. There's also an outdoor terrace for when the weather allows. Crab cakes are the specialty here. Live entertainment on weekends. Kids' menu. Sunday brunch. | 208 Bank St., Chesapeake City | 410/885–2200 | $20–$26 | AE, MC, V.

Lodging

Elkton Lodge. Well located, the lodge is just 10 minutes from the malls and only 2 mi from Elkton and Newark, Del. | 32 rooms. Microwave, refrigerators, cable TV. | 200 Belle Hill Rd. | 410/398–9400 | fax 410/398–9579 | $48 | AE, D, DC, MC, V.

Inn at the Canal. This quaint stopover displays 19th-century furnishings, antique quilts, and old baking and cooking implements. The Inn, also known as the Brady-Rees House, is close to several horse farms and a canal museum. | 7 rooms, 1 suite. Complimentary breakfast. Cable TV. Business services. No kids under 10. No smoking. | 104 Bohemia Ave., Chesapeake City | 410/885–5995 | fax 410/885–3585 | www.chesapeakecity.com/innatthecanal/inn.htm | $80–$130 | AE, D, DC, MC, V.

Knights Inn. You can walk to shops and restaurants from this economical in-town motel. | 119 rooms. Cable TV. Pool. Pets allowed. No smoking. | 262 Belle Hill Rd. | 410/392–6680 | fax 410/392–0843 | $49–$75 | AE, D, MC, V.

Sutton Motel. This family-owned motel is within 5 mi of Meadow Park. | 11 rooms. No room phones. Some pets allowed. | 405 E. Pulaski Hwy. (U.S. 40) | 410/398–3830 | $34–$36 | No credit cards.

Sinking Springs Herb Farm. This 130-acre farm is the home of the Bristoll Sycamore, a 400-year-old tree. It's immensely quiet, a truly romantic place to spend the night. The main entrance is on Elk Forest Road. | 1 room. Complimentary breakfast. Pets allowed (fee). | 234 Blair Shore Rd. | 410/398–5566 | www.cecilcounty.org | $93 | MC, V.

ELLICOTT CITY

MAP 4, F3

(Nearby towns also listed: Baltimore, Columbia)

Once a summer destination for Baltimore residents who came by way of the Baltimore and Ohio Railroad, Ellicott City today is still popular with tourists who patronize the antiques stores, boutiques, and restaurants along its sloping streets. Ellicott City, a well-preserved 19th-century mill town on the Patapsco River, resembles an English industrial village with its sturdy granite buildings. One of the town's most interesting structures is the granite stone train station, now the Ellicott City B & O Railroad Museum. It served as the terminus of the original 13 mi of track between Baltimore and Ellicott's mills. The nation's first steam engine, the *Tom Thumb*, made its debut on these tracks in 1830.

Information: Howard County Tourism Council | 2367 Main St., Ellicott City, MD 21401 | 410/313–1900 or 800/288–TRIP | www.howardcountymdtour.com.

Attractions

Cider Mill Farm. Today you can buy apples by the bushel and cider by the gallon at this old mill and farm established in 1916. Turn the kids loose in the petting zoo, then lunch in the picnic area. Pony rides and hayrides are available. | 5012 Landing Rd., Elkridge | 410/788–9595 | www.farmmd.com | Free, petting zoo $1.50, pony rides $2, hayride $1.25 | Sept.–Nov., daily 9–6, Apr.–May, daily 9–3.

Ellicott City B and O Railroad Station Museum. This granite stone station, built in 1830 as the terminus of the original 13 mi of track between Baltimore and Ellicott City, is now home to a museum showcasing the area's railroad history. The *Tom Thumb*, the first steam engine, is here. | 2711 Maryland Ave. | 410/461–1945 | $4 | Weekdays 11–3, weekends noon–4.

Patapsco Valley State Park. Five recreational areas along 32 mi of the Patapsco River make up this outdoor enthusiast's haven. Bicycling, camping, canoeing, fishing, hiking, and horseback riding are common activities in the 12,699-acre park. | 8020 Baltimore National Pike | 410/461–5005 | www.dnr.state.md.us | $2 | Daily dawn–dusk.

University of Maryland at Baltimore County. This large college on 500 rural acres is home to 10,000 students. It's about 10 mi west of town. | 1000 Hill Top Cir. | 410/455–1000 | umbc.edu | Free.

ON THE CALENDAR

SEPT.–NOV.: *Haunting of Ellicot Mills.* Every Friday and Saturday you can relive ghostly events that actually happened in this old town. | 410/313–1900.

Dining

Crab Shanty. Seafood. Not everything on the menu at this Maryland crab house comes in a shell or even from the water. Besides tasty crustaceans, you can order fresh fish, shrimp, crab cakes, and prime beef. Kids' menu. | 3410 Plumtree Dr. | 410/465–9660 | $14–$26 | AE, D, DC, MC, V.

Sidestreets. American. This old mill converted to a restaurant has seating on two floors. The menu includes crab cakes, beef, veal, pasta, and chicken. Sunday brunch. No smoking. | 8069 Tiber Alley | 410/461–5577 | $13–$19 | AE, D, MC, V.

Sorrentos. American. You can't beat the prices and convenience of this family-style restaurant. It serves pizza and sandwiches in the center of town and is open seven days a week. | 8167 Main St. | 410/465–7489 | $3.50–$6 | AE, D, MC, V.

Tersiguel's. French. Each of the six dining rooms celebrates a different region of France. Look for shrimp, scallops, veal, and duck on the French country menu. No smoking. | 8293 Main St. | 410/465–4004 | $20–$28 | AE, D, DC, MC, V.

Lodging

Turf Valley Resort. Originally a horse farm, this family-owned resort on 1,000 attractively landscaped acres is 25 minutes from Baltimore and an hour from Washington, D.C. The bright, cheery rooms have floral motifs. | 223 rooms, 28 suite, 6 villas. Restaurant, bar. In-room data ports, cable TV. Indoor pool. Hot tub, sauna. Driving range, 54-hole golf course, putting green, tennis. Basketball, exercise equipment, volleyball. Business services. | 2700 Turf Valley Rd. | 410/465–1500 or 800/666–8873 | fax 410/465–8280 | tvrcc@aol.com | www.turfvalley.com | $149–$215, villas $650 | AE, D, DC, MC, V.

The Wayside Inn. This impressive Federal-style B&B, built in 1780, has 20-inch-thick granite walls. A generous breakfast is served in the sunroom, overlooking the 2-acre grounds and pond, home to wood ducks, geese, turtles, fish. A blue heron sometimes visits in the morning. Most rooms and suites have hot tubs and fireplaces, and one has two fireplaces and a shower that doubles as a steam room. One of the Wayside's most endearing traditions is the innkeeper's habit of leaving a lit candle in the downstairs window at night to indicate a vacancy. | 5 rooms with baths, 3 suites with baths. Complimentary breakfast. In-room data ports, some in-room hot tubs, cable TV, in-room VCRs. Library. No pets. No smoking. | 4344 Columbia Rd. | 410/461–4636 | www.waysideinnmd.com | $85–$200 | AE, D, MC, V.

EMMITSBURG

MAP 4, E2

(Nearby towns also listed: Frederick, Hagerstown, Thurmont)

In the foothills of the Catoctin Mountains, Emmitsburg's well-preserved Main Street is lined with Federal, Georgian, and Victorian homes and accented by shade trees and antique streetlights. The small but growing town is home to the National Fire Academy, a national training center for firefighters, and Mount St. Mary's College, one of the nation's oldest Catholic colleges. In the early 19th century, Elizabeth Ann Seton, the first American-born saint, made her home in Emmitsburg, where she founded the country's first parochial school and the Sisters of Charity. Her restored home is open to visitors as part of the National Shrine of St. Elizabeth Ann Seton.

Information: Tourism Council of Frederick County, Inc. | 19 E. Church St., Frederick, MD 21701 | 301/663–8687 or 800/999–3613 | www.visitfrederick.org.

Attractions

Mt. St. Mary's College and Seminary. Founded in 1808 on a mountainside south of town, this college has been a repository of cultural artifacts of the Catholic Church in America for nearly two centuries. | 16300 Old Emmitsburg Rd. | 301/447–6122 | www.msmary.edu | Free | Weekdays 9–5, closed weekends.

Goucher College. Founded in 1885, this private coeducational liberal arts school located 8 mi from downtown Baltimore awards bachelors degrees in 18 departments and 6 interdisciplinary areas. Postbaccalaureate and graduate programs include a Post-Baccalaureate Premedical Program, Master of Arts in Arts Administration and Historic Preservation, Master of Fine Arts in Creative Nonfiction, Master of Arts in Teaching, and Master of Education, as well as short courses and certificate programs. | 1021 Dulaney Valley Road, Baltimore | 410/337–6000 or 800/468–2437 | www.goucher.edu | Free | Daily.

National Fallen Firefighters Memorial. This bronze memorial, in the shape of a Maltese cross, has an eternal flame honoring all firefighters who have died in the line of duty. | 16825 S. Seton Ave. | Free.

National Shrine Grotto of Lourdes. If you can't make a trip to France, visit this replica of the famous grotto where a peasant girl saw visions of the Virgin Mary. Sunrise Easter Mass draws a large crowd. | 16300 Old Emmitsburg Rd. | 301/447–5318 | Free | Daily dawn–dusk.

National Shrine of St. Elizabeth Ann Seton. The restored home of the first American-born saint and her gravesite are part of the shrine. Pope John Paul II designated the chapel at the shrine a minor basilica. | 333 S. Seton Ave. | 301/447–6606 | Free | Daily 10–4:30. Closed late Jan., Mondays in Dec.

SEPT.: *The Emmitsburg Mason–Dixon Line Fall Festival.* This town celebration happens on a weekend in mid-September. You can tour local horse farms, see a rugby match or softball tournament, play a round of bingo, or join the bike tour, and end the day with a delicious chicken dinner. Bring the kids for the horse and pony rides, the clowns, and face painting. | 301/447–2771.

Dining

Carriage House Inn. Contemporary. This family-run restaurant in the heart of town serves steaks and seafood. The dining room is done in an elegant country style. | 200 S. Seton Ave. | 301/447–2366 | $12–$30 | AE, D, DC, MC, V.

Lodging

Stonehurst Inn. A summer mansion (circa 1875) once owned by the first National Episcopal Bishop, The Right Reverend John G. Murray, this bed and breakfast is centrally located in the beautiful Catoctin mountains 1 mi from downtown Emmitsburg's fine restaurants, wineries, and interesting shops and 8 mi south of the Gettysburg and Antietam Battlefields. You can relax with a complimentary beverage on the wrap-around porches or on the sofa-filled solarium overlooking views of the rolling hills and gardens. For recreation on the property you can stroll around the fishing pond or visit the meditation chapel in the woods. | 5 rooms, 1 suite. Complimentary breakfast, air conditioning, TV in common area. Pond, fishing, library. No pets, no kids under 12, no smoking. | 9436 Waynesboro Rd. | 301/447–2880 or 800/497–8458 | www.emmitsburg.net/lodging | $65, $95 suite | AE, MC, V.

FREDERICK

MAP 4, E2

(Nearby towns also listed: Boonsboro, Hagerstown, Sharpsburg, Thurmont)

Less than an hour from Baltimore and Washington, Frederick is a choice destination with daytrippers. It boasts a 50-block historic district with tree-lined streets, historic homes, museums, restaurants, and more than a dozen churches—not to mention the countless antiques shops and boutiques. Though Frederick played a role in the Revolutionary War and the War of 1812, the town's Civil War history is what the public has embraced. And no wonder. Confederate and Union troops passed through frequently en route to famous battles like Antietam in western Maryland. The city was a major medical center during the war, and many of the buildings that served as hospitals remain today. Barbara Fritchie, a gray-haired widow, reportedly waved a Union flag in defiance of passing Confederate troops. Today, a replica of her home is one of the city's most visited attractions.

Information: Tourism Council of Frederick County, Inc. | 19 E. Church St., Frederick, MD 21701 | 301/663–8687 or 800/999–3613 | www.visitfrederick.org.

Attractions

Barbara Fritchie House and Museum. A replica of the redbrick cottage where the elderly Dame Fritchie waved a flag defiantly in front of passing Confederate troops during the Civil War. | 154 W. Patrick St. | 301/698–0630 | www.fredericktoday.com/html/barbara_fritchie_house.html | $2 | Call for hours.

Brunswick Museum. Near a 1907 brick roundhouse and 1891 train station, this transportation museum is home to an extensive model railroad. | 40 W. Potomac St., Brunswick | 301/834–7100 | $4 | June–Dec., Thurs.–Sun. 10–4, closed Mon.–Wed. Call for Jan.–May hours.

Evangelical Reformed Church. Confederate general Stonewall Jackson worshiped at this 1848 Greek Revival church in 1862 the Sunday before the Battle of Antietam. | 15 W. Church St. | 301/662–2762 | Free | Mon.–Thurs. 8–3.

Frederick National Historic District Tour. Take a 90-minute, guided walking tour of the 50 blocks of restored and protected Victorian and Federal architecture. | 19 E. Church St. | 301/663–8687 or 800/999–3613 | fax 310/663–0039 | www.visitfrederick.org | $4.75 | Weekends 1:30 and by appointment.

Frederick Tour and Carriage Company. Wend your way through the historic downtown in the slow clippity-clop of a horse-drawn carriage ride. | 301/694–RIDE. | Daily by appointment.

Gambrill State Park. West of Frederick, this 1,100-acre day-use park, a favorite of hikers, overlooks the Frederick and Middletown valleys. | Gambrill Park Rd., off Rte. 40 W | 301/271–7574 | www.dnr.state.md.us | $2 per vehicle | Apr.–Oct., daily dawn–dusk.

Historical Society of Frederick County Museum. Artifacts and documents tracing the history of the county are displayed in this lovely mansion built in 1820. | 24 E. Church St. | 301/663–1188 | www.fwp.net/hsfe | $2 | Tues.–Sat. 10–4, Sun. 1–4.

Monocacy National Battlefield. Many historians believe this little-known Civil War battle between Confederate Gen. Jubal T. Early and Union Gen. Lew Wallace hastened a Union victory by thwarting the Confederate invasion of Washington. | 4801 Urbana Pike | 301/662–3515 | www.nps.gov/mono/home.htm | Free | Apr.–Oct., weekdays 8–4, weekends 8–5:30; Nov.–Mar., Wed.–Sun. 8–4:30, closed Mon.–Tues.

Mt. Olivet Cemetery. This graveyard is the final resting place of local heroine Barbara Fritchie, Francis Scott Key, and many Union and Confederate soldiers. | 515 S. Market St. | 301/662–1164 | Free | Daily.

National Museum of Civil War Medicine. More than 3,000 artifacts are exhibited, including the only known surviving Civil War surgeon's tent. A multimedia exhibit uses photographs, artifacts, and videos to draw a picture of Civil War medical techniques. The museum is a starting point for a walking tour of the city's Civil War history. | 48 E. Patrick St. | 301/695–1864 | www.civilwarmed.org | $6.50 | Weekdays 10–5, weekends 11–5.

Roger Brooke Taney Home. Two-story Federal house once belonged to the famed Supreme Court Justice and author of the Dred Scott Decision. One room is dedicated to his brother-in-law, Francis Scott Key. | 121 S. Bentz St. | 301/663–8687 | Free | By appointment.

Rose Hill Manor Park and Children's Museum. Children love the hands-on exhibits depicting life in the 19th century in this period home of Thomas Johnson, Maryland's first governor. Several outbuildings, including a log cabin, also are worth a look. | 1611 N. Market St. | 301/694–1648 or 301/694–1650 | $3 | Apr.–Oct., Mon.–Sat. 10–4, Sun. 1–4.

Schifferstadt. A stone house built by German immigrants in 1756. Barren rooms allow you to observe structural details. | 1110 Rosemont Ave. | 301/663–3933 | $2 (suggested) | Apr.–mid-Dec., Tues.–Sat. 10–4, Sun. noon–4, closed Mon.

Trinity Chapel. A stone tower is all that remains of the original church, built in 1763. The steeple, built in 1807, is the oldest of the city's famed clustered spires. | 10 W. Church St. | Free | Daily.

ON THE CALENDAR

SEPT.: *The Great Frederick Fair.* This weeklong agricultural fair in mid-September has livestock shows, a petting farm, harness racing, and carnival rides. | 301/633–5895.

Dining

Barbara Fritchie Candystick Restaurant. American. Enjoy old-fashioned food at this restaurant, which has been around since 1920. The owner recommends the creamed chipped beef on toast, and the homemade pies, apple dumplings, or cakes for dessert. | 1513 W. Patrick St. | 301/662–2500 | $6–$12 | No credit cards.

Barley and Hops Grill and Microbrewery. Contemporary. You can watch beer-making in progress while you dine here, 2 mi south of town. Try the Georgia peach bourbon barbecued ribs. | 5473 Urbana Pike | 301/668–5555 | fax 301/668–5550 | $9–$15 | AE, D, DC, MC, V.

Brown Pelican. Continental. Pictures of pelicans line the walls at this elegant restaurant. White linens and candlelight add a romantic touch. Fresh seafood, duck, and veal are menu staples. | 5 E. Church St. | 301/695–5833 | Reservations essential Fri.–Sat. | No lunch weekends | $13–$25 | AE, D, DC, MC, V.

Comus Inn. Contemporary. Amid flower gardens overlooking Sugar Loaf Mountains, this eatery's cuisine includes seafood, steaks and a salad bar. Kids' menu. Sunday brunch. No smoking. | 23900 Old Hundred Rd., Comus | 301/428–8593 | Closed Mon. | $16–$24 | AE, DC, MC, V.

Gabriel's. French. Four dining rooms with French country interiors serve up traditional cuisine. | 4730 Ijamsville Rd., Ijamsville | 301/865–5500 | Closed Mon.–Wed. No lunch | $17–$35 | AE, DC, MC, V.

Province Restaurant. American. Homemade quilts and crafts, lit by sconce lamps, adorn the walls, and the seats are Vermont snowshoe chairs. The garden room overlooks the kitchen's herb garden. The Province is known for its crab cakes, quiche, pies, cakes, and cobblers, which it sells in a bakery down the road. | 129 N. Market St. | 301/663–1441 | $16–$24 | AE, DC, MC, V.

Tauraso's. Italian. Whatever your mood, this restaurant in a 19th-century building has a place for you–a formal dining room with mirrors and elegant paintings, a casual pub, or tables in the garden. Steak, pasta and pizza are on the menu. | 6 East St. | 301/663–6600 | $12–$24 | AE, D, DC, MC, V.

Lodging

Catoctin Inn. Built in 1780, this inn's antiques give it both an 18th- and 19th-century flavor. With meeting space and a computer available, the inn attracts business travelers as well as vacationers. | 19 rooms, 1 suite, 3 cottages. Restaurant, complimentary breakfast. Cable TV. Hot tub. Laundry service. Business services. | 3613 Buckeystown Pike (Rte. 85), Buckeystown | 301/874–5555 or 800/730–5550 | fax 301/874–2026 | catoctin@fred.net | www.catoctininn.com | $109–$129, cottages $159 | AE, D, DC, MC, V.

Days Inn–Frederick. South of downtown on Rte. 85, this two-story motel, built in 1981, has plenty of stores, restaurants, and other conveniences nearby. | 119 rooms. Complimentary Continental breakfast. Refrigerators, cable TV. Outdoor pool. Playground. Business services. | 5646 Buckeystown Pike (Rte. 85) | 301/694–6600 | fax 301/831–4242 | www.daysinn.com | $72 | AE, D, DC, MC, V.

Fairfield Inn by Marriott–Frederick. In a corporate park near a shopping mall and restaurants, this three-story property, built in 1996, is about an hour from Baltimore and Washington, D.C. | 105 rooms. Complimentary Continental breakfast. In-room data ports, refrigerators, cable TV. Pool. Hot tub. Exercise equipment. Business services. | 5220 Westview Dr. | 301/631–2000 | fax 301/631–2100 | www.fairfieldinn.com | $80 | AE, D, DC, MC, V.

Hampton Inn. This hotel 1 mi south of town is convenient to shopping plazas and restaurants. The health club across the street is free to guests. | 161 rooms, 2 suites. Restaurant, bar. Complimentary Continental breakfast. In-room data ports, cable TV. Pool. Exercise equipment. Pets allowed (fee). | 5311 Buckeystown Pike | 301/698–2500 | fax 301/695–8735 | $89 rooms, $150 suites | AE, D, DC, MC, V.

Hill House Bed and Breakfast. This three-story, cream-colored brick B&B dates from 1875. It's just a few blocks from shops and restaurants. There is a balcony and garden. The third-floor Chesapeake Suite has a bedroom, kitchen, and bath. | 4 rooms with baths, 1 suite. Some in-room TVs. No pets. No kids under 13. No smoking. | 12 W. 3rd St. | 301/682–4111 | hillhouseent@starpower.net | $105–$125 room, $150 suite | No credit cards.

Holiday Inn—FSK Mall. Next to a mall and restaurants and within driving distance of historic sites, this hotel is 45 minutes from Washington, D.C. | 155 rooms, 2 suites. Restaurant, bar. In-room data ports, refrigerators, cable TV. Pool. Mini-golf. Hot tub, sauna. Gym. Business services. | 5400 Holiday Dr. | 301/694–7500 | fax 301/694–0589 | www.basshotels.com/holiday-inn | $109–$250 | AE, D, DC, MC, V.

Inn at Buckeystown. Magnificent chandeliers and working fireplace add romance to the rooms as well as the common areas of this 19th-century inn just 10 minutes south of Frederick. | 5 rooms. Restaurant. Some microwaves. Business services. No kids under 12. No smoking. | 3521 Buckeystown Pike (Rte. 85), Buckeystown | 301/874–5755 or 800/272–1190 | fax 301/831–1355 | www.innbrook.com/buckeystown | $110–$165 | AE, MC, V.

Morningside Inn. This country B&B in a renovated dairy barn has striking views of the 300 rolling acres of grounds. | 10 rooms. Complimentary breakfast. Gym. Hot tub. Business services. | 7477 McKaig Rd. | 301/898–3920 or 800/786–7403 | fax 301/898–1815 | www.bbonline.com/md/morningside | $125–$135 | D, MC, V.

Red Horse Motor Inn. This local institution is easily distinguished by a red horse on the roof. Less than a mile east of town, it is convenient to shopping centers, restaurants, and movie theaters. | 72 rooms. Restaurant, bar. In-room data ports, cable TV, microwaves. Business services. | 998 W. Patrick St. (U.S. 40 W) | 301/662–0281 | $54–$67 | AE, D, DC, MC, V.

Spring Bank Bed and Breakfast. Frescoed ceiling, original wallpaper, and faux-marble mantles are just some of the lovely touches in this restored Victorian B&B. Just 2 mi north of town, it is surrounded by 10 landscaped acres. | 1 room with bath, 4 rooms share bath. Complimentary breakfast. TV in common area. No pets. No kids under 12. No smoking. | 7945 Worman's Mill Rd. | 301/694–0440 | fax 301/694–5926 | www.bbonline.com/md/springbank | $95–$110 | MC, V.

Stone Manor. Built in 1760 this B&B's 114 acres of farmland, gardens, lawns, and forest make it a lovely country retreat. Fireplaces, mahogany furnishings and balconies can be found in many of the rooms. | 6 suites. Restaurant, complimentary Continental breakfast, room service. No room phones, TV/VCR in common area. Business services. No smoking. | 5820 Carroll Boyer Rd., Middletown | 301/473–5454 | fax 301/371–5622 | themanor@stonemanor.com | www.stonemanor.com | $150–$275 | AE, D, MC, V.

Turning Point. If browsing this farmhouse-turned-B&B's lovely antique furnishings isn't enough, there are antique shops and restaurants nearby. | 5 rooms, 2 cottages. Restaurant, bar, complimentary breakfast. Cable TV. Business services. | 3406 Urbana Pike | 301/831–8232 | fax 301/831–8092 | $125–$150 | AE, D, DC, MC, V.

FROSTBURG

MAP 4, B2

(Nearby towns also listed: Cumberland, Grantsville, Oakland, McHenry)

Once a major stopover on the National Highway (U.S. 40) today Frostburg is a sleepy college town in the western Maryland mountains. Frostburg State University provides cultural and recreational activities for an otherwise isolated community. When the weather warms up, Washington Redskins fans flock here for the team's summer practice session at FSU. The city also is the western terminus of the Western Maryland Scenic Railroad. Passengers explore the shops and restaurants along Main Street during a 90-minute layover in the city.

Information: Allegany County Convention & Visitors Bureau Western Maryland Station Center | 13 Canal St., Frostburg, 21502 | 301/777–5905 or 800/50–VISIT | www.mdmountainside.com.

Attractions

Western Maryland Scenic Railroad. *See* Cumberland *above.*

AUG.: *FSU Block Party.* To celebrate the first week of classes at Frostburg State University, the town closes off Main Street and throws a bash downtown with live bands, karaoke competitions, local business information booths, food, and prizes. | 301/689–6000.

Dining

Au Petit Paris. French. An art-filled passageway greets patrons of this popular restaurant, and the three intimate dining areas are hung with art depicting all things Parisian. For dinner, try the lamb tenderloins in Madeira wine sauce. Top it off with either the bananas foster or cherry jubilee. An extensive wine list includes both European and Californian vintages. | 86 E. Main St. | 301/689–8946 | Reservations essential | Closed Sun.–Mon. | $19–$41 | AE, D, DC, MC, V.

Lodging

Fallinger's Hotel Gunter. Built in 1896, the original Hotel Gunter had a jail cell in the basement for criminals on their way to the state penitentiary. When the current owners painstakingly restored the dilapidated hotel, they left the jail cell right in place but added some displays of artifacts found while renovating. The hotel boasts pressed-tin ceilings, a grand oak staircase, and guest rooms all done differently in period furnishings. Cable TV, in-room VCRs. | 11 W. Main St. | 301/689–6511 | fax 301/689–6034 | www.hotelgunter.com | 17 rooms | $75–$90 | AE, D, DC, MC, V.

Frostburg Mountain Side Inn. Just off I–68 about a mile from Frostburg's main drag, this rustic inn has small, cozy rooms brightened by artwork from local artists. | 100 rooms. Complimentary Continental breakfast. In-room data ports, cable TV. Gym. Business services. | 11100 New George's Creek Rd. | 301/689–2050 or 800/221–2222 | fax 301/689–2050 | $51–$63 | AE, D, DC, MC, V.

GAITHERSBURG

MAP 4, E3

(Nearby towns also listed: Rockville, Washington, D.C.)

Once a tiny, rural settlement called Log Town, Gaithersburg is now a sprawling suburb of Washington, D.C. Although the town was established in 1765, it took local leaders nearly 100 years to agree to the name Gaithersburg. The city is named for Benjamin Gaither, who built a house in 1802 near a large oak tree, which eventually grew to be more than 300 years old. Just 12 mi from the northwestern border of Washington, the city is accessible by the D.C. Metro's red line and I–270. Within an hour's drive of the area's major airports, Gaithersburg is a major regional location for high-tech companies, including IBM, Lockheed Martin, Federal Systems, and Hughes.

Information: Conference and Visitors Bureau of Montgomery County | 12900 Middlebrook Rd., Suite 1400, Germantown, 20874 | 301/428–9702 or 800/925–0880 | www.cvbmontco.com.

Attractions

Corner Kick. A bar and restaurant overlook two playing fields in this indoor recreational sports arena. You can have a burger while taking in a soccer tournament or visit the video arcade. Spaces are also available for racquetball, volleyball, and lacrosse. | 18707 N. Fredrick Rd. | 302/840–5425 | $2–$15, depending on group size and activity | Daily 9–7.

Seneca Creek State Park. Boat rentals on this park's 90-acre lake make for a day of fun in the sun. An 18-hole flying disc golf course, a historic mill, and an old schoolhouse provide recreation for those who like to keep their feet dry. | Clopper Rd. (Rte. 117), 2 mi west of I–270 | 301/924–2127 | www.dnr.state.md.us | $1 weekends, free weekdays | Daily 8–sunset.

ON THE CALENDAR
APR.: *Sugar Loaf Craft Festival.* One of the East Coast's largest retail crafts festivals, this annual marketplace at the Montgomery County Fairgrounds spotlights as many as 500 top artisans. All display and sell fine arts and contemporary crafts. | 301/990–1400.
SEPT.: *Olde Towne Gaithersburg Day.* The history and heritage of Gaithersburg is the focal point of this yearly celebration in Olde Towne. Seven different stages host concerts throughout the day, with a choice of salsa, jazz, oldies cover bands, and folk acts. For kids, there's giant bubble machines, sidewalk chalk mural-making, sand painting, craft workshops, and supervised activities for pre-schoolers. | 301/258–6350.

Dining

Chris' Steak House. Steak. Redskins memorabilia dominates this friendly family restaurant with hearty fare like cheese fries, New York strip steaks, and prime rib. Kids' menu. | 201 E. Diamond Ave. | 301/869–6116 | Closed Sun. | $3–$20 | AE, D, MC, V.

Flaming Pit. Continental. A pianist lightens the mood in this cozy eatery with brick fireplace and stucco walls. Locals favor the stuffed salmon, crabcakes, and prime rib. Kids' menu. | 18701 N. Frederick Ave. | 301/977–0700 | Reservations essential Fri.–Sat. | $14–$40 | AE, DC, MC, V.

Golden Bull Grand Cafe. American. Chandeliers illuminate the roomy dining area in this restaurant known for various styles of prime rib, crabcakes, and local seafood. Kids' menu. Early-bird suppers. | 7 Dalamar St. | 301/948–3666 | $22–$33 | AE, D, DC, MC, V.

House of Chinese Delights. Chinese. Depictions of stylistic dragons give this large dining room a traditional Chinese character, just like its cuisine. Sample the fish in hot bean sauce or hot crispy beef. No smoking. | 16240 S. Frederick Ave. | 301/948–9898 | $8–$11 | AE, MC, V.

Il Forno. Italian. This family-oriented eatery is almost a cliche with its red-checkered tablecloths and pictures of Italy on the walls. Its specialty, brick-oven pizzas with premium ingredients, can be topped off perfectly with a cannoli. In fair weather, dine on the small patio with umbrellas and greenery. Beer and wine only. | 8941 Westland Dr. | 301/977–5900 | $7–$17 | MC, V.

Jenny's. Chinese. Paper lanterns, greenery, and a collection of silk animals give this place its funky appeal. Try the crispy Szechuan-style beef. Buffet lunch. | 608 Quince Orchard Rd. | 301/977–0057 | $10–$15 | AE, D, DC, MC, V.

Julliano's. Italian. Watch from the open, spacious dining room as your pizza bakes in a brick oven. Or if you prefer, order the calzone or stromboli. Finish with a chocolate pizza. Outdoor seating is available on the small deck with lush greenery. Kids' menu. Beer and wine only. No smoking. | 6840 Olney-Laytonsville Rd., Laytonsville | 301/921–0199 | $13–$20 | AE, D, MC, V.

New Fortune Restaurant. Chinese. This huge restaurant is in what used to be a Rite-Aid drug store, and the lighting is still clinically bright. The extensive menu actually has chapters, and the kitchen tackles everything from standard favorites like lemon chicken to more exotic fare like frog, sea cucumbers, and fish-throat. | 16515 S. Fredrick Ave. | Weekdays until 1 AM; weekends 2 AM | 301/926–8828 | $5–$14 | AE, D, MC, V.

Peking Cheers. Chinese. Traditional Oriental art and lanterns brighten this large, well-established eatery, known for Peking duck, sesame chicken, and seafood. No smoking. | 519 Quince Orchard Rd. | 301/216–2090 | $10–$15 | AE, D, MC, V.

Roy's Place. American. This place's vintage photos from the 1930s and '40s, Tiffany-style lamps and small tables put you in the mind of a speakeasy. Burgers and creative sandwiches like the Pocohantas, a pile of crab and ham topped with a golden sauce, are favorites on the extensive menu. | 2 E. Diamond Ave. | 301/948–5548 | $5–$18 | AE, D, DC, MC, V.

Sir Walter Raleigh. American. Brick walls and mirrors create intimacy in the otherwise spacious dining room of this chain restaurant. Prime rib, slow-roasted choice beef, and Eastern Shore crab cakes are among its menu selections. Salad bar. Kids' menu. | 19100 Montgomery Village Ave. | 301/258–0576 | $17–$28 | AE, D, DC, MC, V.

Summit Station. American. This quaint two-story brew pub is in the old section of town. Brewery and beer memorabilia hang on walls along with vintage photographs of the area. This relaxed eatery's menu includes beef, pasta, and seafood. Kids' menu. No smoking. | 227 E. Diamond Ave. | 301/519–9400 | $12–$22 | AE, DC, MC, V.

Lodging

Comfort Inn–Shady Grove. Every room is different in this chain motel, which exhibits the work of local artists in the lobby. Restaurants and stores are close at hand, and a Washington subway stop is just a ½ mi away. | 127 rooms. Complimentary breakfast. In-room data ports, refrigerators, cable TV. Pool. Exercise equipment. Laundry facilities. Business services, free parking. Some pets allowed. | 16216 Frederick Rd. | 301/330–0023 | fax 301/258–1950 | www.comfortinn.com | $99–$119 | AE, D, DC, MC, V.

Courtyard by Marriott–Gaithersburg. On a busy highway next to the Lake Forest Mall, this hotel is convenient to shopping plazas, offices, and restaurants. A desk in every room as well as its location make it a favorite of business travelers. | 203 rooms. Restaurant, bar. In-room data ports, refrigerators, cable TV. Pool. Hot tub. Tennis courts. Exercise equipment. Laundry facilities. Business services, free parking. | 805 Russell Ave. | 301/670–0008 | fax 301/948–4538 | www.marriott.com | $69–$115 | AE, D, DC, MC, V.

Econo Lodge. Two miles northwest of downtown, this chain property is also 1 mi away from Lake Forest Mall and Seneca Creek State Park. | 97 rooms. In-room data ports, cable TV. | 18715 N. Frederick Ave. | 301/963–3840 | fax 301/947–7924 | www.econolodge.com | $48–$68 | AE, D, MC, V.

Hampton Inn–Germantown. Fresh flowers as well as paintings of boats, lakes, and woodland scenes dress up the lobby and rooms of this motel, which is just 3 mi from the Lake Forest Mall. | 178 rooms, 16 suites. Restaurant, bar, complimentary Continental breakfast. In-room data ports, cable TV. Pool. Hot tub. Exercise equipment. Laundry facilities. Business services, free parking. | 20260 Goldenrod La., Germantown | 301/428–1300 | fax 301/428–9034 | www.hamptoninn.com | $89–$129 | AE, D, DC, MC, V.

Hilton–Gaithersburg. Directly across from the Lake Forest Mall and near a busy commercial corridor, this rustic-looking hotel is geared toward business travelers. | 301 rooms. Restaurant, bar. In-room data ports, cable TV. Indoor pool. Exercise equipment. Business services. Some pets allowed. | 620 Perry Pkwy. | 301/977–8900 | fax 301/869–8597 | www.hilton.com | $99–$109 | AE, D, DC, MC, V.

Holiday Inn–Gaithersburg. This property on I–172 is near a busy shopping area. If you don't have time to check out the local scenery, don't worry. The rooms have panoramic paintings of local lakes and woods. | 301 rooms. Restaurant, bar, room service. In-room data ports, refrigerators, cable TV. Indoor pool. Hot tub. Exercise equipment. Video games. Laundry facilities. Business services. Some pets allowed. | 2 Montgomery Village Ave. | 301/948–8900 | fax 301/258–1940 | www.basshotels.com/holiday-inn | $99–$124 | AE, D, DC, MC, V.

Red Roof Inn. This chain establishment is 26 mi northwest of Washington, DC. | 115 rooms. Restaurant. In-room data ports, cable TV. | 492 Quince Orchard Rd. | 301/977–3311 | fax 301/990–1053 | $56–$79 | AE, D, MC, V.

Springhill Suites. The rooms here are everything you'd expect from a budget hotel, only a lot bigger. Spacious sitting areas are separated from sleeping quarters by arched doorways, and adjacent kitchenettes have bar counters and stools. | 162 suites. Cable TV. Pool, hot tub. Excercise equipment. | 9715 Washingtonian Blvd. | 301/987–0900 | fax 301/987–0500 | $69–$109 | AE, D, DC, MC, V.

GRANTSVILLE

(Nearby towns also listed: Cumberland, Frostburg, McHenry, Oakland)

Just south of the Mason-Dixon line on the National Highway (U.S. 40), Grantsville was a heavily traveled stagecoach stopover in the 19th century. Not much has changed in the ensuing years. The Casselman Hotel, built in 1824 for the drovers and farmers traveling westward, is still in operation today. Penn Alps, originally a stagecoach stop, is a restaurant and crafts shop adjacent to the Spruce Forest Artisan Village, where artists demonstrate their skills every summer. East of town, the Casselman River Bridge was the largest single-span stone arch bridge when it was built in 1813. Today, the bridge—no longer in use—is a popular picnic spot.

Information: Garrett County Chamber of Commerce | 15 Visitors Center Dr., McHenry, 21541 | 301/387–6171 | www.garrettchamber.com.

Attractions

Casselman River Bridge State Park. America's largest single-span stone arch bridge in 1813, the Casselman River Bridge is now a top-notch picnic site in this 4-acre state park. | U.S. 40, just east of Grantsville | 301/895–5453 | www.dnr.state.md.us | Free | Daily 8–sunset.

Savage River State Forest. Enjoy whitewater canoeing, camping, bicycling, hiking, and fishing at Maryland's largest state forest. New Germany and Big Run state parks are within its borders. | Savage River Rd., 8 mi south of New Germany State Park | 301/895–7559 | Free | Daily dawn to dusk.

New Germany State Park. Within the boundaries of the 52,000-acre Savage River State Forest, New Germany has hiking and cross-country skiing trails, cabins, and a 13-acre lake. | 349 Headquarters La. | 301/895–5453 | www.dnr.state.md.us | $2 weekends and holidays, Mar.–Oct.; free Nov.–Feb. | Daily 8–sunset.

Spruce Forest Artisan Village. A rustic museum village where the artisans of Upper Appalachia show off their talents. | 125 Casselman Rd. | 301/895–3332 | Free | Memorial Day–Oct., Mon.–Sat. 10–5, closed Sun.

ON THE CALENDAR

JULY: *Summer Fest and Quilt Show.* Hundreds of quilts, both new and heirloom, are on display among the restored log cabins of the Spruce Forest Artisan Village, alongside booths from 100 other juried artisans, musicians, and storytellers. Children's activities and food booths are manned by volunteers from local church groups. | 301/895–5985.

Dining

Penn Alps. American. Built around an 1818 stagecoach stop, this quaint wood-and-stone structure is divided into small adjoining rooms restored to their original style. Smoked sausage, prime rib and a steamed shrimp buffet keep customers coming back. Kids' menu. Sunday brunch. No smoking. | 125 Casselman Rd. | 301/895–5985 | Breakfast also available. No supper Sun. | $12–$20 | AE, D, MC, V.

Lodging

Elliot House Victorian Inn. Three private cottages on 7 acres make up this charming river-side property. Each cottage has its own deck overlooking the river. CD players and binoculars are provided in all the cottages and the beds have handmade Amish quilts. You can lounge about in a hammock or borrow a mountain bike from the Inn to explore the surrounding woods. No smoking, pets, or kids under 10. TV, VCRs. Massage. Hiking, water sports, fishing, bicycles. | 146 Casselman Rd. | 800/272–4090 or 301/895–4250 | 3 cottages | $87–$150 | AE, MC, V.

Holiday Inn–Grantsville. A fireplace in the lobby and woodland scenes in the rooms give this place a woodsy charm much like the nearby state parks. | 100 rooms. Restaurant, bar. In-room data ports, cable TV. Pool. Sauna. Health club. Business services. Some pets allowed. | 2541 Chestnut Ridge Rd. | 301/895–5993 | fax 301/895–3410 | www.basshotels.com/holiday-inn | $59–$69 | AE, D, DC, MC, V.

GRASONVILLE

MAP 4, G3

(Nearby towns also listed: Annapolis, Chestertown, Easton)

Home to some of the best seafood on the Eastern Shore, Grasonville was once lined with seafood-packing houses and shanties. Today they've been replaced by antiques stores, furniture shops and other small retailers. The town has changed its name three times. Originally it was Ford's Store after one of its grocers. Later, the name was changed to Winchester. Finally, the townsfolk settled on the current name in honor of Gov. Grason. Outlet stores, wildlife areas, and marinas are nearby.

Information: Queen Anne's County Office of Tourism | 425 Piney Narrows Rd., Chester, 21619 | 410/604–2100 | www.qac.org.

Attractions

Mears Point Marina. In addition to boat-docking, the marina has a ship store with boating supplies and accessories, souvenirs, T-shirts, and other items. Adjacent to the marina is a swimming pool and Red Eye's Dock Bar, which offers live entertainment and lots of salty local color. The Kent Narrows Yacht Club conducts cruises from Mears Point. | 428 Kent Narrows Way N | 410/827–8888 | Free | Daily.

Wye Oak State Park. The Wye Oak is the largest white oak, Maryland's state tree, in the U.S. Estimated to be more than 460 years old, it is over 100 ft tall. This 4-acre park, popular with picnickers, also has a colonial one-room schoolhouse. | Rte. 662, 1 mi from junction of Rte. 50, Rte. 404 | 410/820–1668 | www.dnr.state.md.us | Free | Daily dawn to dusk.

ON THE CALENDAR

JUNE: *Queen Anne County Watermen Festival.* Docking contests, rowing competitions, an anchor-throw, and scores of kid's games are just a few of the events at this festival on Kent Narrows that celebrates the seafood industry of the Chesapeake Bay. The festival also has educational exhibits of fishing boats and equipment, food booths, and lots of live music. | 410/827–8861.

Dining

Annie's Paramount Steak and Seafood House. Seafood. Several large dining areas accommodate the crowds that descend on this restaurant in Mears Point Marina. Try a massive 24-oz. Porterhouse steak, or a succulent cold-water lobster tail stuffed with crab imperial, broiled and sided with greens and rice. | 428 Kent Narrows Way N | 410/827–7103 | $8–$18 | AE, D, MC, V.

Fisherman's Inn & Crab Deck. American. Immense, wall-to-wall windows that afford a striking view of the bay and walls covered with maps, fish hooks and other seafaring gizmos make up the overall nautical backdrop of this restaurant and seafood market. Specialties are the crab imperial and prime rib. The Crab Deck, right on the water, serves fresh seafood, including steamed shrimp and, of course, crabs. Live music on weekends. | 3116 Main St. | 410/827–8807 | Deck closed Nov.–Apr. | $11–$30 | AE, D, MC, V.

Harris Crab House. Seafood. This maritime-themed restaurant, on the mainland side of Kent Narrows, is a favorite of boaters who can dock right outside. Open-air dining is available on a deck overlooking the water. The menu focuses on crab dishes, including crab imperial, steamed crabs, and crabcakes. | 433 Kent Narrows Way N | 410/827–9500 | $15–$40 | MC, V.

Narrows. Seafood. Open and airy, this brick-and-wood restaurant has large windows overlooking the water. Menu favorites include cream of crab soup, crabcakes, and a selection of grilled fish. Kids' menu. Sunday brunch. | 3023 Kent Narrows Way S | 410/827–8113 | $13–$30 | AE, D, DC, MC, V.

Lodging

Comfort Inn–Kent Narrows. Right off U.S. 50, this motel is within a ½ mi of a marina and boat charter company. | 86 rooms, 9 suites. Complimentary Continental breakfast. Refrigerators, cable TV. Indoor pool. Hot tub. Exercise equipment. Laundry facilities. Business services. | 3101 Main St. | 410/827–6767 | fax 410/827–8626 | www.comfortinn.com | $95–$150 | AE, D, DC, MC, V.

Sleep Inn. This two-story cement-and-stucco building is surrounded by a few flower beds and a lot of concrete. The guest rooms are modern-looking, with recessed track lighting, abstract wall art, and vivid, color-block bedspreads and window dressings. | 59 rooms. Restaurant. In-room data ports, cable TV. | 101 VFW Ave. | 410/827–5555 | fax 410/827–8801 | $56–$76 | AE, D, MC, V.

GREENBELT

MAP 4, F3

(Nearby towns also listed: Bowie, College Park, Laurel, Washington, D.C.)

The U.S. government built Greenbelt, a planned community, during the Great Depression. The project provided work for many unemployed in the 1930s and created homes for modest-income families during a severe housing shortage. Its planners attempted to create a small utopia, using the principles of garden city planning: Many homes face large garden courts with abundant trees and shrubs. Greenbelt, which hugs the Washington Beltway, became a National Historic Landmark in 1997.

Information: Prince George's County Conference and Visitors Bureau | 9200 Basil Ct., Suite 101, Largo, 20774 | 301/925–8300 or 888/925–8300.

Attractions

Greenbelt Museum. This original home built in 1937 as part of Roosevelt's New Deal has been restored to its original Depression-era appearance with period furnishings. | 10-B Crescent Rd. | 301/474–1936 | www.otal.umd.edu/~vg | $2 | Sun. 1–5, closed Mon.–Sat.

NASA/Goddard Visitor Center. The Hubble Space Telescope and the Cosmic Background Explorer are among the projects that can be experienced through interactive educational exhibits. Tours daily. | Soil Conservation Rd., off exit 22A of I-495 | 301/286–8981 | www.pao.gsfc.nasa.gov | Free | Daily 9–4.

SEPT.: *Labor Day Festival.* Held in and around the Roosevelt Center in downtown Greenbelt, this festival offers live music (mostly jazz and folk), arts and crafts exhibits, and a photography show. Also on the roster is a beauty pageant, kid's pet show, a parade, talent show, and carnival. | 301/345–9605.

Dining
The New Deal Cafe. American. Housed in a brick building in the heart of Old Greenbelt, this is a small but hip cafe and espresso house run as a co-op. The interior is furnished with local art, comfy old couches, and small bistro tables and chairs. You can get a pre-made deli sandwich or sample one of the delicious desserts like cheesecakes, tortes, and cookies. | 113 Centerway | 301/474–5642 | $3–$5 | AE, MC, V.

Siri's Chef's Secret. Thai. Fresh flowers accent the tables at this elegant establishment. Try the chicken ginger or shrimp paradise. | 5810 Greenbelt Rd. | 301/345–6101 | $7–$9 | AE, D, DC, MC, V.

Lodging
Courtyard by Marriott. You'll find contemporary rooms with landscape paintings and a lush courtyard in this hotel, which is near restaurants and stores and just 4 mi from the University of Maryland. | 152 rooms, 12 suites. Restaurant, bar, room service. In-room data ports, refrigerators, cable TV. Indoor pool. Hot tub. Exercise equipment. Laundry facilities. Business services, free parking. | 6301 Golden Triangle Dr. | 301/441–3311 | fax 301/441–4978 | www.marriott.com | $124–$139 | AE, D, DC, MC, V.

Holiday Inn. This seven-story chain hotel is only a mile or so from the headquarters of NASA and the Secret Service Training Facility in Washington. Restaurant, bar. Outdoor pool. In-room data ports, cable TV and movies. Volleyball. Business services. | 7200 Hanover Dr. | 301/982–7000 or 800/280–4188 | fax 301/345–8271 | 160 rooms | $149–$159 | AE, D, DC, MC, V.

HAGERSTOWN

MAP 4, D2

(Nearby towns also listed: Boonsboro, Frederick, Sharpsburg, Thurmont)

Formerly a well-heeled railroad hub and manufacturing center, Hagerstown today is a major retail center in western Maryland, most noticeably with the expansive Outlet Village of Hagerstown. The Association for the Preservation of Civil War Battlefields is just one of the tenants in the many downtown buildings that the city has spent millions of dollars to refurbish. The city's historic district reflects a more prosperous era—1880 to 1920. The centerpiece is the lovely City Park with a man-made, spring-fed lake, islands, picnic areas, a neoclassical band shell, and the Washington County Museum of Fine Arts.

Information: Hagerstown/Washington County Convention and Visitors Bureau | 16 Public Sq, Hagerstown, 21740 | 301/791–3246 or 800/228–STAY | www.marylandmemories.org.

Attractions
C&O Canal Museum. Operated by the National Park Service, this small museum runs slide presentations on the history of the canal system. A replica of a canal boat is on display, in addition to photos, artifacts, and books. | 326 E. Main St., Hancock | 301/678–5463 | Free | Tours by appointment.

Ft. Frederick State Park. One of the few surviving stone forts from the French and Indian War. It houses war artifacts in a small museum dedicated to Civilian Conservation Corps. Hiking, camping, canoeing, and cross-country skiing are among the activities in this 550-

acre park. | 11100 Ft. Frederick Rd., off exit 12 of Rte. 56, Big Pool | 301/842–2155 | www.dnr.state.md.us | $2 | Daily dawn to dusk; visitor center Apr.–Oct., daily 8–4; call for hours Nov.–Mar.

Hagerstown Roundhouse Museum. Exhibits depict the history of the Western Maryland Railroad and six other lines that made Hagerstown the "Hub City." | 300 S. Burhans Blvd. E | 301/739–4665 | $3 | Fri.–Sun. 1–5, closed Mon.–Thurs.

Jonathan Hager House and Museum. The original home of Hagerstown's founder was built in 1739. | 110 Key St. | 301/739–8393 | $4 | Tues.–Sat. 10–4, Sun. 2–5, closed Mon.

Mansion House Art Center. Built in 1846, this Georgian house in the center of City Park is now used for rotating exhibits of local art. | City Park | 301/797–6813 | Free | Thurs.–Sat. 10–4, Sun. 1–5.

Miller House. Built in 1818, this house is now an eclectic museum with collections of dolls and clocks as well as a turn-of-the-century general store. | 135 W. Washington St. | 301/797–8782 | $3 | Mid-Apr.–mid-Dec., Tues.–Sat. 1–4, closed Sun.–Mon.

Washington County Museum of Fine Arts. This small museum boasts an impressive collection of American paintings, drawings, prints, and sculpture from the 18th century to present. | 91 Key St. | 301/739–5727 | www.washcomuseum.org | $1 (suggested) | Tues.–Sat. 10–5, Sun. 1–5, closed Mon.

HAGERSTOWN

INTRO
ATTRACTIONS
DINING
LODGING

ON THE CALENDAR

JUNE: *Western Maryland Blues Fest.* Every summer, this celebration of the blues draws thousands of people to downtown Hagerstown to hear nationally and internationally recognized talent. Free picnics, multiple concerts, and kid's activities round out the weekend's roster. Venues may vary. | 301/739–8577 ext. 546.

Dining

Crazy Horse Steak House. Steak. With its plank floors, wood beams, and low lighting, this eatery is so casual you can flick your peanut shells while waiting for your grub. The latter includes BBQ chicken, baby back ribs, and generous side dishes. A live roadhouse band performs on Friday nights. | 104 Railway Ln | 301/791–2611 | $12–$20 | AE, D, DC, MC, V.

Junction 808. American. Home-style comfort food served up in a fun, family place. Try the spaghetti with homemade sauce, fresh roast turkey, and the barbecue ribs. Kids' menu. No smoking. | 808 Noland Dr. | 301/791–3639 | Closed Sun. | $8–$15 | MC, V.

Red Horse Steak House. American. Easy to spot by the red horse on the roof, this cozy, quiet dining room has a fireplace and early-American furnishings. This place is known for prime rib and jumbo seafood cocktails. Kids' menu. | 1800 Dual Hwy. (U.S. 40) | 301/733–3788 | Breakfast available. No lunch | $14–$29 | DC, MC, V.

Richardson's. American. Greenery and railroad memorabilia abound in this relaxed, woodsy eatery. Crab cakes, prime rib, and Richie's special ham sandwich are some of the menu's best bets. Salad bar. Kids' menu. | 710 Dual Hwy. (U.S. 40) | 301/733–3660 | $9–$15 | D, MC, V.

Lodging

Beaver Creek House. Built in 1905, this country Victorian B&B with a mountain view has a wraparound screened porch, elegantly appointed dining room, country gardens, and a fish pond. | 5 rooms. Complimentary Continental breakfast. No kids under 10. No smoking. | 20432 Beaver Creek Rd. | 301/797–4764 or 888/942–9966 | fax 301/797–4978 | www.bbonline.com/md/beavercreek | $75–$95 | AE, MC, V.

Days Inn–Hagerstown. Civil War-era portraits grace the lobby as well as the quaint, country-style rooms in this motel that is 10 mi from the airport. | 140 rooms. Restaurant, bar, complimentary breakfast. Cable TV. Pool. Laundry facilities. Playground. Business services.

| 900 Dual Hwy. (U.S. 40) | 301/739–9050 | fax 301/739–8347 | www.daysinn.com | $49–$65 | AE, D, DC, MC, V.

Econo Lodge. This squat, brick chain establishment, 6 mi from downtown, has budget antique reproductions and floral chintz in the rooms. Cable TV. | 18221 Mason-Dixon Rd. | 301/791–3560 | fax 301/791–3519 | www.econolodge.com | 57 rooms | $45–$65 | AE, D, MC, V.

Four Points by Sheraton. Just off exit 32 of I-70, this hotel—with contemporary stylings such as soft lighting, mirrors and tiled floors—is only 8 mi from the airport and Antietam. | 108 rooms. Restaurant, bar, complimentary Continental breakfast, room service. Cable TV. Pool. Exercise equipment. Business services, airport shuttle, free parking. Some pets allowed. | 1910 Dual Hwy. (U.S. 40) | 301/790–3010 | fax 301/790–0633 | www.sheraton.com | $89–$99 | AE, D, DC, MC, V.

Plaza Hotel. Directly across the street from a shopping center and a ½ mi from industrial parks, this 5-story hotel makes up what it lacks in charm by its convenience. | 164 rooms. Restaurant, bar, room service. Refrigerators, in-room data ports, cable TV. Indoor pool. Hot tub. Exercise equipment. Business services, airport shuttle, free parking. | 1718 Underpass Way | 301/797–2500 | fax 301/797–6209 | www.plazahotelhagerstown.com | $65–$88 | AE, D, DC, MC, V.

Ramada Inn Convention Center. Despite its location on a busy commercial strip, this property retains a countrified charm. The indoor pool area is lush with tropical plants. | 200 rooms. Restaurant, bar, room service. In-room data ports, cable TV. Indoor pool. Health club. Laundry facilities. Business services, airport shuttle. | 901 Dual Hwy. (U.S. 40) | 301/733–5100 | fax 301/733–9192 | www.ramada.com | $79–$89 | AE, D, DC, MC, V.

Super 8. This three-story, budget chain hotel is just 12 mi from the historic Antietam Battlefield. In-room data ports, cable TV. Business services. | 1220 Dual Hwy. | 301/739–5800 | fax 301/739–5800 Ext. 465 | 61 | $35–$55 | AE, D, DC, V.

Venice Inn. Convenient to downtown, shopping centers and restaurants, this property was remodeled in 1984 to slightly resemble a Venetian inn. The light-filled lobby is colorful with pillars that go to the second floor. | 222 rooms. Restaurant, bar, room service. Refrigerators, cable TV. Pool. Exercise equipment. Business services, free parking. Some pets allowed. | 431 Dual Hwy. (U.S. 40) | 301/733–0830 | fax 301/733–4978 | $60–$70 | AE, D, DC, MC, V.

Wingrove Manor Inn. Pruned shrubs and brick walkways encircle this lovely Victorian perched on a hill. Guest rooms have ornate, Queen Anne-style oak furnishings and rich window dressings. Terrycloth robes and luxury linens are provided. Cable TV. No pets. No kids. No smoking. | 635 Oak Hill Ave. | 301/733–6328 | 4 rooms | $75–$140 | AE, D, MC, V.

HAVRE DE GRACE

MAP 4, G2

(Nearby towns also listed: Aberdeen, Elkton, North East)

Havre de Grace's location at the point where the Susquehanna River flows into Chesapeake Bay has made it an important commercial and transportation center since the 1700s. Laid out by a French architect in 1795, its streets still bear names like Bourbon and Lafayette. While many homes and buildings date from the 19th century, the Queen Anne mansions on Union Street are particularly impressive sights. Havre de Grace hosts festivals celebrating the arts, decoys, and seafood and is home to museums devoted to decoys, boat building, and maritime heritage. Its Concord Point Lighthouse has been a beacon for sailors and boaters in the upper Chesapeake Bay for more than 160 years.

Information: Discover Harford County Tourism Council | 121 N. Union Ave., Suite B, Havre de Grace, 21078 | 410/939–3336 or 800/597–2649 | www.thatharfordsite.com/visitor.

Attractions

Concord Point Lighthouse. This lighthouse, the oldest continuously operated one on the Chesapeake, has shined its light for sailors since 1827. | Concord St. | 410/939–9040 | Free | Apr.–Oct., Sat.–Sun. 1–5, closed Mon.–Fri.

Decoy Museum. This converted power plant houses 1,500 facsimiles of ducks, geese, and swans made from wood, iron, cork, and other materials. Carvers demonstrate their art on weekends. | 215 Giles St. | 410/939–3739 | www.decoymuseum.com | $4 | Daily 11–4.

Steppingstone Museum. Artisans demonstrate their crafts in this private, non-profit 10-acre complex of seven restored turn-of-the-century farm buildings inside Susquehanna State Park. | 461 Quaker Bottom Rd. | 410/939–2299 | $2 | May–Sept., weekends 1–5, closed weekdays.

Susquehanna State Park. This sprawling 2,500-acre park has all the typical outdoor activities—hiking, biking, horseback riding, fishing, bird-watching and camping—plus a few historical ones. The Steppingstone Museum and a working mill are within the parks' boundaries. On weekends between May and September, Rock Run Grist Mill grinds corn into meal, which is given away to visitors. There also is a self-guided historical walking tour. | Rte. 155, 3 mi north of Havre de Grace, Jarrettsville | 410/836–6735 | www.dnr.state.md.us | Free | Daily 9–sunset.

Susquehanna Museum. A restored 1836 lockhouse, swing bridge, and canal lock make up this museum complex on the Susquehanna River. Period rooms illustrate local history through photos, old documents, artifacts, and model boats. | Erie St., at Conesto St. | 410/939–5780 | Free | Open May–Oct. By appointment only.

ON THE CALENDAR

MAY: *Civil War Living History Day.* Costumed reenactments tell the story of Havre de Grace's role in the Civil War, along with a dramatic restaging of the attack on the town during the Battle of 1812. Food and music add to the fun at this event at the Steppingstone Museum. | 410/939–2299.

Dining

Bayou. Seafood. The owner's collection of locally made decoys are a feast for the eyes. For the stomach there's crab cakes, fried oysters, and a seafood sampler. Kids' menu. | 927 Pulaski Hwy. (U.S. 40) | 410/939–3565 | $11–$25 | AE, DC, MC, V.

Crazy Swede. Continental. A nautical motif dominates this former hotel on a tree-lined avenue. Seafood, prime rib, and crab cakes are menu highlights. Kids' menu. Sunday brunch. | 400 N. Union Ave. | 410/939–5440 | $15–$30 | AE, DC, MC, V.

MacGregors. Seafood. In a bank building built in 1928, this two-level restaurant has glass walls on three sides and a phenomenal view of the Chesapeake Bay. The two dining rooms are decorated with carved wooden duck decoys, mounted guns, and vintage images of the town. In fine weather, you can eat on the outdoor deck or in the gazebo, sampling the likes of crab cakes, fillet of sole in lemon butter, or deep-fried shrimp in beer batter. | 331 St. John's St. | 410/939–3003 | $20–$30 | AE, D, DC, MC, V.

Vandiver Inn. Continental. A glass-enclosed sun porch and two interior dining rooms sporting colorful stained-glass windows and snowy linens await you at this lovely Victorian mansion, now a restaurant and B&B. Opt for one of the fixed-price meals, which change nightly, or order king crab legs, oysters, or lobster off the menu. The Chambord raspberry cheesecake with chocolate crust is divine. | 410 S. Union Ave. | 410/939–5200 | Reservations essential | Closed Sun.–Thurs. No Lunch | $20–$35 | AE, D, MC, V.

Lodging

Currier House Bed and Breakfast. This charming two-story farmhouse overlooks the junction of the Susquehanna with Chesapeake Bay. Built circa 1861, it has a wraparound porch

set about with potted flowers; inside, antiques, family heirlooms, and mementos add to the coziness. All guest rooms have antique furnishings, some have water views, and one has a private veranda. No smoking or pets. | 4 rooms. Cable TV and phones in common area. | 800 S. Market St. | 410/939–7886 or 800/827–2889 | $85–$115 | AE, D, MC, V.

Vandiver Inn. The guest rooms and common spaces in this rambling Victorian B&B, built in 1886, are rife with period furnishings made with dark mahogany and rich fabrics. Relax on the inn's spacious front porch or settle in by one of its fireplaces for a quiet evening. | 17 rooms. Restaurant, complimentary breakfast. Cable TV. | 410 S. Union Ave. | 410/939–5200 | fax 410/939–5202 | $85–$160 | AE, D, MC, V.

LA PLATA

MAP 4, F4

(Nearby towns also listed: Waldorf, Washington, D.C.)

This Charles County community grew from its origins as a train stop of the same name during the late 1800s. The Chapman family, which donated land when the town was laid out, once owned a farm originally named Le Plateau but later changed to La Plata. More than a century later, this county seat retains its small-town charm, though you will find motels and other amenities on U.S. 301 and Rte. 6.

Information: Charles County Tourism | Box 2150, La Plata, 20646 | 301/645–0558 or 800/766–3386 | www.charlescounty.org/tourism.

Attractions

Doncaster Demonstration Forest. This state-owned, 1,445-acre forest provides areas for hunting, picnicking, and hiking. | Rte. 1 Indian Head | 301/934–2282 | www.dnr.state.md.us | Free | Daily dawn to dusk.

Port Tobacco. One of the oldest communities on the East Coast, Port Tobacco first existed as an Indian settlement then was colonized by the English in 1634. By the end of the 17th century it was a major seaport. Historic sites include a 19th-century courthouse with displays of artifacts, a restored one-room schoolhouse and Catslide House, a restored 18th-century home. | Rte. 6, 3 mi west of La Plata, Port Tobacco | 301/934–4313 | $2 | Apr.–mid-Oct., Wed.–Sun. 11–4, closed Mon.–Tues.

Smallwood State Park. This park is home to the restored plantation home of Revolutionary War general and Maryland governor William Smallwood. The marina has 50 boat slips; outdoor activities include fishing, hiking, picnicking, and camping. | Chicamuxen Road, 4 mi east of Rte. 225 | 301/888–1410 | www.dnr.state.md.us | $2 weekends, May–Sept., free weekdays | Daily dawn to dusk.

ON THE CALENDAR

SEPT.: *Charles County Fair.* Food and live music punctuate exhibits at the county fairgrounds by area businesses and displays by craft merchants and artisans. | 8440 Fairground Rd. | 301/932–1234.

Dining

Casey Jones Pub. American. With duck decoys, rope knots, and lanterns hanging from the walls and ceilings, this eatery has a decidedly nautical appeal. Casey Jones offers a full range of pub fare, from seafood (crab cakes and oysters) to steak, prime ribs, or pub sandwiches sided with thick french fries. Live music on Thursday nights. | 417 Charles St. | 301/932–6226 | $8–$15 | AE, D, MC, V.

Lodging

Best Western. On a busy highway to Washington, D.C., this contemporary motel is near several restaurants. | 73 rooms, 8 suites. Complimentary Continental breakfast. In-room data ports, cable TV, microwaves, refrigerators. Pool. Exercise equipment. Laundry facilities. Business services. | 6900 Crain Hwy. S (U.S. 301) | 301/934–4900 | fax 301/934–5389 | www.bestwestern.com | $73–$81, suites $100–$110 | AE, D, DC, MC, V.

Pawtuxent Inn. Rooms in this basic, independently-run motel are furnished with functional motel furniture in various shades of wood veneer. Cable TV. | 9400 Chesapeake St. | 800/500–1484 | 45 rooms | $38–$60 | AE, D, DC, MC, V.

LAUREL

MAP 4, F3

(Nearby towns also listed: Bethesda, Bowie, College Park, Greenbelt, Silver Spring, Washington, D.C.)

Laurel owes its existence to a prosperous stone grist mill near the banks of the Patuxent River that flourished in the early 1800s. Originally Laurel Factory, named after the area's mills and abundant mountain laurel, the town's name later was shortened to Laurel. When the railroad came to town, Laurel became a major station on the Baltimore and Ohio Railroad. The train paralleled U.S. 1, once a stagecoach route and today a major highway through the region. The town's Main Street contains many historic buildings, including mills, factories, churches, homes, and the train station. The downtown also has many specialty shops and restaurants.

Information: Prince George's County Conference and Visitors Bureau | 9200 Basil Ct., Suite 101, Largo, 20774 | 301/925–8300.

Attractions

Laurel Park Racetrack. Built in 1911, this thoroughbred racetrack was considered the finest on the east coast in the '20s and '30s. The main event here is the Maryland Million, held in October. When no live races are scheduled, the clubhouse screens horse races from other tracks. | Racetrack Rd. and Route 198 | 301/725–0400 | $3–$5 | Wed.–Mon. 11:30 AM–11 PM.

Montpelier Mansion. One of the finest examples of 18th-century Georgian architecture in the state, this was once the home of prominent Marylander "Major" Thomas Snowden. | Murkirk Road, off U.S. 197 | 301/953–1376 | $3 | Mar.–Nov., Sun. noon–3, Dec.–Feb., Sun. 2–3; closed Mon.–Sat.

National Wildlife Visitors Center. Get close to nature the old-fashioned way by rambling down a trail or take a high-tech tack with state-of-the-art wildlife exhibits and a guided tram tour of the woodlands area. | 10901 Scarlet Tanager Loop | 301/497–5760 | Free | Daily 10–5:30.

ON THE CALENDAR

MAY: *Main Street Festival.* Sponsored by the Laurel Board of Trade, the festival has three entertainment stages, lots of food, and local vendors selling clothing, crafts, jewelry, and artwork. The event kicks off in the morning with a parade down Main Street. | 301/604–0808 | Free.

Dining

Cafe du Paris. French. Hardwood floors, country tiles, and French memorabilia lend a provincial charm to this bistro. Try the house-cured salmon or French onion soup for starters, followed by rib-eye steak, venison, or pork medallions. For dessert, don't miss the profiteroles, ice-cream-filled puff pastry topped with warm chocolate sauce. | 14252 Baltimore Ave. | 301/490–8111 | $18–$23 | AE, D, DC, MC, V.

Lodging

Comfort Suites Laurel Lakes. Near restaurants, shopping centers, and movie theaters, this hotel has large rooms with pull-out sofas. | 119 suites. Complimentary Continental breakfast. Refrigerators, microwaves, cable TV. Indoor pool. Hot tub. Exercise equipment. Laundry facilities. Business services. Some pets allowed. | 14402 Laurel Pl. | 301/206–2600 | fax 301/725–0056 | www.comfortinn.com | $99–$129 | AE, D, DC, MC, V.

Holiday Inn–Laurel. This motel has large rooms done in beige with floral patterns. It is 12 mi from BWI Airport and 15 mi from downtown Washington D.C. | 115 rooms. Restaurant, bar, room service. In-room data ports, refrigerators, cable TV. Pool. Exercise equipment. Laundry facilities. Business services. | 3400 Ft. Meade Rd. | 301/498–0900 | fax 301/498–0900 | www.basshotels.com/holiday-inn | $119–$149 | AE, D, DC, MC, V.

Quality Inn & Suites. This chain hotel is just 1 mi from the Laurel Center Mall. The guest rooms, all done in a maroon-and-green color scheme, contain coffeemakers, irons, and ironing boards. Complimentary Continental breakfast. Some kitchenettes, some microwaves, some refrigerators, some in-room hot tubs, cable TV. Outdoor pool. Gym. Laundry facilities. No pets. | 1 Second St. | 301/725–8800 | fax 301/725–7874 | www.qualityinn.com | 96 rooms | $90 | AE, D, DC, MC, V.

LEONARDTOWN

MAP 4, F5

(Nearby towns also listed: St. Marys City, Waldorf, Washington, D.C.)

One of the oldest county seats in the United States, Leonardtown, which can trace its history back to the mid-18th century, is a busy government, education, and medical center in St. Marys County. Despite military intrusions during the late 20th century, Leonardtown is one of the few Maryland towns to have an intact town square. Residents claim that the town was invaded twice: once by the British during the War of 1812 and then by the Yankee army in search of Confederate weapons and supplies during the Civil War.

Information: St. Mary's County Division of Travel and Tourism | Box 653, Governmental Center, Washington Street, 2nd floor, Leonardtown, 20650 | 301/475–4411 or 800/327–9023 | www.stmarys-countymd.com.

Attractions

Old Jail Museum. Built in 1858 this granite and brick building served as a jail until 1942. Today it's a museum as well as the headquarters and library of St. Mary's County Historical Society. | 41625 Courthouse Dr. | 301/475–2467 | www.somd.lib.md.us/smchs | Free | Weekdays noon–4, closed weekends.

St. Clement's Island State Park–Potomac River Museum. A small museum on the mainland depicts the history of St. Clement's Island, the landing place of English settlers in 1634. The island in the mouth of the Potomac is accessible only by boat. | 38370 Point Breeze Rd., Colton's Point | 301/769–2222 | $1 | Apr.–Sept., weekdays 9–5, weekends noon–5, tour boat weekends 12:30, 2:30.

Sotterley Plantation. Surrounded by the only working 18th-century plantation in Maryland, this house, built in 1727, is one of the earliest post-in-ground structures in the U.S. | 44300 Sotterley Main Rd. (U.S. 245), Hollywood | 301/373–2280 | www.sotterley.com | $7 | May–Oct., Tues.–Sun. 10–4, closed Mon.

Tudor Hall. This 1756 Georgian mansion overlooking Breton Bay boasts a beautiful hanging staircase in the main hall and a valuable research library. Of the many influential people who have called Tudor Hall home, the most well known may be Francis Scott Key, composer of the "Star-Spangled Banner." | Camalier Dr. and Tudor Hall Pl. | 301/475–2467 | Free, library use $2.50 | Thurs.–Fri. noon–4, Sat. 10–4.

ON THE CALENDAR

OCT.: *National Oyster Festival.* This unusual festival, staged the third weekend in October at the county fairgrounds, has been held annually since 1967. The winner of the National Oyster Shucking Contest here goes to the international competition in Ireland. Don't know how to shuck an oyster? Free lessons are offered. An oyster cook-off, square dancing, clown shows, bands, and carnival rides are all part of the nonstop entertainment. | 301/863–5015 | $5.

Dining

Cafe des Artistes. French. You'll find flowers on the tables and vintage cameras and musical instruments on the walls of this casual cafe. Start with shrimp bisque or escargot, then enjoy tenderloin Wellington, rack of lamb, or chicken cordon bleu. Crème brûlée and baked apple tart make dessert a difficult decision, unless you order them both! | 4165 Frederick St. | 301/997–0500 | $15–$20 | AE, D, MC, V.

Lodging

Best Western. You're a 10-min drive from Point Lookout and the boardwalk at this chain hotel. The spacious rooms contain coffeemakers, irons, and ironing boards. Restaurant, complimentary Continental breakfast. In-room data ports, some kitchenettes, some microwaves, some refrigerators, cable TV. Outdoor pool. Laundry facilities. No pets. No smoking in some rooms. | 22769 Three Notch Rd. | 301/862–4100 or 800/528–1234 | fax 301/862–4673 | www.bestwestern.com | 120 rooms | $70–$85 | AE, D, DC, MC, V.

MCHENRY

MAP 4, A2

(Nearby towns also listed: Cumberland, Frostburg, Grantsville, Oakland)

McHenry, a western Maryland mountain town, is a year-round destination. The community—a scattering of gas stations, restaurants, and small shopping plazas—serves skiers visiting the Wisp Ski Area in the winter and boaters who enjoy the cool waters of Deep Creek Lake in the summer. Outdoor enthusiasts come here to hike, camp, bike, raft, and kayak. The community was named for Col. James McHenry of Baltimore, an aide to George Washington during the American Revolution. Interestingly, the settlement was initially named "Buffalo Marsh" after the first Europeans in the area found a buffalo carcass in the mud.

Information: Garrett County Chamber of Commerce | 15 Visitors Center Dr., McHenry, 21541 | 301/387–6171 | www.garrettchamber.com.

Attractions

Deep Creek Lake State Park. Covering 6 square mi, Deep Creek Lake is the state's largest man-made lake. Outdoor enthusiasts flock to the 1,800-acre park for its beach, camping, hiking trails, boating, and other outdoor activities. | 898 State Park Rd., off U.S. 219 | 301/387–4111 | www.dnr.state.md.us | $2, Mar.–Oct. | Daily dawn to dusk.

Wisp Ski Area. Atop the 3,080-ft Marsh Mountain and on the shores of Deep Creek Lake, this ski area—the only downhill ski resort in the state—affords skiers lovely views as they schuss down its 23 slopes and 80 acres of skiable terrain. | 290 Marsh Rd. | 301/387–4911 | www.gcnet.net/wisp | Lift ticket $35 | Late Nov.–early Apr.

SEPT.: *Western Maryland Brew Fest.* Bikes, blues, and brews abound at this annual event begun in 1999. After the morning's benefit bike tour around Deep Creek Lake, rehydrate with unlimited samples of over 30 local and national beers. Enjoy the outdoor blues festival during the day or the band at the Deep Creek Brewing Company later in the evening. | 301/387–2182.

Dining

Deep Creek Brewing Company. American. Best bets here are the pub's own Quarryman Pale Ale and the beer-battered portabello-mushroom appetizer. Dinner menu highlights include the Buffalo chicken wrap and grilled chicken Deep Creek with feta cheese, artichokes, and roasted red peppers. Live acoustic music in the bar on Saturday night. | 75 Visitor's Center Dr. | 301/387–2182 | Closed Sun. | $12–$18 | AE, D, MC, V.

McClive's. American. Overlooking Deep Creek Lake and the Wisp Ski Area, McClive's is one of the area's busier restaurants. Masks and lingerie dangling from the chandeliers in one dining room suggest Bourbon Street, while another dining area resembles a ski chalet. House favorites include the prime rib, fresh bay seafood, and pasta. In the summer, the courtyard lounge offers patio dining and weekend entertainment. | 1375 Deep Creek Dr. | 301/387–6172 | No lunch | $12–$20 | AE, D, DC, MC, V.

Point View Inn. Continental. Dine under the stars aside the lake or in the cozy lodge-style building with country antiques. Though much of the menu is German influenced, the veal cordon bleu and prime rib are other favorites. Entertainment Thursday to Saturday. Kids' menu. Sunday brunch. | Deep Creek Dr. | Breakfast available | 301/387–5555 | Reservations not accepted | $9–$18 | AE, MC, V.

Lodging

Comfort Inn–Deep Creek Lake. Off U.S. 219 and about ¼ mi from Deep Creek Lake, this motel is just a short drive from area restaurants. Country furnishings give the rooms a cozy charm. | 76 rooms. Complimentary Continental breakfast. Some in-room hot tub, cable TV. Some pets allowed. | 2704 Deep Creek Dr. | 301/387–4200 | fax 301/387–4204 | www.comfortinn.com | $60–$80 | AE, D, DC, MC, V.

Innlet Motor Lodge. Enjoy the soothing gentle breezes from Deep Creek Lake and a ski-slope view at this relaxed, friendly motel. Some rooms have fireplaces, and all balconies face the lake. | 20 rooms. Picnic area. Cable TV. Lake. Fishing. No pets. | 2001 Deep Creek Dr. | 301/387–5596 or 800/540–0763 | $78 | Closed Nov.–Apr. | AE, D, MC, V.

Lake Pointe Inn. In summer catch the soft lake breezes while relaxing on the wraparound porch of this restored 1890 farmhouse just steps from Deep Creek Lake. In the winter cozy up by the living room fireplace after a day at the slopes. Some of the country-style rooms have lake views, and all have down comforters and pillows. | 9 rooms. Complimentary breakfast, evening snacks. No smoking. | 174 Lake Pointe Dr. | 301/387–0111 or 800/523–5253 | fax 301/387–0190 | www.deepcreekinns.com | $133–$168 | D, MC, V.

Point View Inn. A private beach and dock on Deep Creek Lake make this old-fashioned, restful inn a perfect stopover for boaters. Antiques accent the small but homey rooms. | 19 rooms. Restaurant, bar, complimentary Continental breakfast. Cable TV. Pool. Some pets allowed (fee). | 21541 Deep Creek Dr. | 301/387–5555 | fax 301/387–5335 | $40–$85 | AE, MC, V.

Savage River Inn. This former farmhouse built in 1934 is nestled among towering pines and lily ponds in Savage River State Forest off Highway 495. Professionally decorated, the inn offers guest rooms with fireplaces, decks, and patios. Complimentary breakfast. No room phones. Outdoor pool, pond. Outdoor hot tub. Hiking, boating, bicycles. No pets. No smoking. | Dry Run Rd. | 301/245–4440 | sri@iceweb.net | www.savageriverinn.com | 4 rooms | $110–$150 | MC, V.

Wisp Resort Hotel & Conference Center. At the base of ski slopes, this mountain lodge with its country antiques, fireplace, and board games is an ideal place to unwind after a day on the slopes. An 18-hole golf course and its proximity to Deep Creek Lake keep people coming back year-round. | 168 rooms. 2 restaurants, 2 bars. In-room data ports, cable TV. Pool. Hot tub. 18-hole golf course, tennis. Gym. Downhill skiing. Ski shop. Business services. | 290 Marsh Rd. | 301/387–5581 or 800/462–9477 | fax 301/387–4127 | www.wisp-resort.com | $119–$159 | AE, D, DC, MC, V.

NEW MARKET

MAP 4, E2

(Nearby towns also listed: Boonsboro, Frederick)

Once a stop on the National Pike (Rte. 144), New Market is now the self-proclaimed antiques capital of Maryland. Its 19th-century Main Street, unparalleled almost anywhere else in the state, has escaped modern intrusion. Lined with 18th- and 19th-century homes—many still occupied—the quaint thoroughfare is the heart of the antique district. The town also has a handful of restaurants and inns. Modern conveniences, including gas stations and fast-food restaurants, can be found outside town near I–70.

Information: Tourism Council of Frederick County | 19 E. Church St., Frederick, 21701 | 301/663–8687 or 800/999–3613.

Attractions
National Pike Antique Market. At the end of the 18th century, the banks built a road that eventually crossed five states, connecting Baltimore with Vandalia, Illinois. The half-mile stretch through New Market, which was once home to button factories, wagon shops, and taverns, now sustains 30 antique shops and a general store that sells modern goods. | Main Street | 301/865–6313 | www.newmarketmd.com | Free | Daily.

ON THE CALENDAR
SEPT.: *New Market Days.* For one weekend in autumn, New Market turns the clock way back. Meander through the colonial crafts festival, take a horse-and-buggy ride, or enjoy old-time entertainers such as barbershop quartets and banjo players. | 301/865–5544 | www.newmarketmd.com.

Dining
Mealey's. Contemporary. A large stone fireplace dominates Mealey's spacious main dining room furnished with antiques. The menu keeps changing, but try the salmon Wellington in phyllo pastry topped with crab and beurre blanc or the Caribbean grilled jumbo shrimp served with pureed sweet potatoes and mango relish. | 8 Main St. | 301/865–5488 | No lunch Sun.–Thurs. | $13–$27 | AE, D, DC, MC, V.

Lodging
Strawberry Inn. The rooms are surprisingly large in this small renovated 1840 farmhouse. Though you may be tempted to stay inside to admire all the Victorian antiques, the grounds—which include a porch, gazebo and flower gardens—are just as delightful. | 5 rooms. Complimentary breakfast. | 17 W. Main St. | 301/865–3318 | newmarketmd.com/ straw.htm | $95–125 | No credit cards.

NORTH EAST

(Nearby towns also listed: Aberdeen, Elkton, Havre de Grace)

North East, a charming town on the upper banks of the Chesapeake, is largely without touristy attractions. Its genteel appeal lies in its small business district—a smattering of eateries, shops, and antiques stores—and a lovely bayside park. Elk Neck State Park, which offers campgrounds, hiking trails, and beaches, is nearby.

Information: Cecil County Tourism | One Seahawk Dr., Suite 114, North East, 21901 | 410/966–6292 or 800/CECIL–95 | www.seececil.org.

Attractions

Elk Neck State Park. Sandy beaches, marshlands, and wooded bluffs make this park on the North East River a favorite of nature lovers. Turkey Point Lighthouse can be seen from one of the bluffs. Camping and shooting range available. | 4395 Turkey Point Rd. (Rte. 272) | 410/287–5675 | www.dnr.state.md.us | $2 Mar.–Oct. | Daily dawn to dusk.

ON THE CALENDAR

DEC.: *Dickens Weekend*. Celebrate the holiday season with Santa Claus, carolers, traditional music, and a Christmas parade. The festivities center around the shop displays on Main Street, and merchants dress in Victorian costumes for the occasion. | 410/287–2658.

Dining

Woody's Crab House. Seafood. Woody's claims to have the best crab cakes in Cecil County, which may explain the weekend crowds in the two nautically themed dining rooms. Other house specialties include the Alaskan snake crabs, steamed shrimp, and jumbo crab salad. Landlubbers can choose steak or pasta from the menu. | 29 S. Main St. | 410/287–3541 | Closed Mon. | $8–$30 | AE, D, MC, V.

Lodging

Crystal Inn. This hotel sits at the top of Center Drive off I–95 north of town. Large windows, comfy chairs, and flowers welcome you to the lobby. The spacious rooms favor a burgundy color scheme and provide irons and ironing boards. Picnic area, complimentary Continental breakfast. In-room data ports, microwaves, refrigerators, cable TV, in-room VCRs. Indoor pool. Hot tub. Gym. Laundry facilities, laundry service. Business services. Pets allowed. | 1 Center Dr. | 410/287–7100 or 800/631–3803 | fax 410/287–7109 | www.crystal-inns.com | 92 rooms | $129 | AE, D, DC, MC, V.

OAKLAND

(Nearby towns also listed: Cumberland, Frostburg, Grantsville, McHenry)

The main line of the Baltimore and Ohio Railroad came through Oakland in 1851, boosting the town's efforts to become a commercial center. In the late 18th century, the railroad was responsible for bringing throngs of Baltimore and Washington residents to summer resorts in the cool mountain communities of Deer Park and Oakland, which is situated on a plateau 2,650 ft above sea level. Oakland is the county seat of

Garrett County, the state's westernmost county, and is near popular state parks—Herrington Manor and Swallow Falls—which offer camping, hiking, and more.

Information: Garrett County Chamber of Commerce | 15 Visitors Center Dr., McHenry 21541 | 301/387–6171 | www.garrettchamber.com.

Attractions

Backbone Mountain. The highest point in Maryland, 3,360 ft, is noted by a historical marker. | Rte. 219 | Free | Daily.

B&O Railroad Station. This lovely Queen Anne–style train station with incised brick and a slate roof is one of the oldest in the country. Now listed on the National Registry, the 1884 station was restored to its former glory in 2000. | Second Ave. and Liberty St. | 301/334–1948 | Free | Daily.

Garrett State Forest. Mountain forests, streams, and valleys make up this nearly 8,000-acre forest. For the adventurous, primitive camping is available. | Entrances from U.S. 219 and U.S. 135 | 301/334–2038 | www.dnr.state.md.us | Free | Daily dawn to dusk.

Herrington Manor State Park. One of the few state parks with rustic cabins, Herrington Manor has a 53-acre man-made lake, hiking, and cross-country skiing trails, mountain biking, fishing, and swimming. | 222 Herrington La. (Rte. 20) | 301/334–9180 | www.dnr.state.md.us | $2 Mar.–Oct. | Daily dawn to dusk.

Potomac State Forest. This rugged mountain forest with remote trout streams is a good place for whitewater canoeing. | 1431 Potomac Camp Rd., off Rte. 135 | 301/334–2038 | www.dnr.state.md.us | Free | Daily dawn to dusk.

Swallow Falls State Park. A 54-ft waterfall surrounded by tall hemlocks is the jewel of this park, which counts camping, hiking, and canoeing among its outdoor activities. | Rte. 20., 9 mi NW of Oakland | 301/387–6938 | www.dnr.state.md.us | $2 Mar.–Oct. | Daily dawn to dusk.

ON THE CALENDAR

OCT.: *Autumn Glory Festival.* The state banjo and fiddle championships, a tournament of bands, and a firefighters parade are all part of Oakland's Octoberfest celebration. | 301/334–1948.

Dining

Cornish Manor. French. The owners' flair with sauces and cutesy names shows in dishes like "sweet talk" orange roughy, "hanky panky" fettucine, and "flirtation" filet mignon in a "say yes" sauce. The original 1868 woodwork in the casual dining rooms is set off with lace curtains and stained glass. | 830 Memorial Dr. | 301/334–6499 | Closed Sun. and Mon. | $12–$27 | AE, D, MC, V.

Four Seasons Dining Room. Continental. Wood and stone contribute to the rustic grandeur of the dining room, which overlooks Deep Creek Lake. The seasonal menu capitalizes on local ingredients in dishes such as Flounder Four Seasons, sautéed flounder and shrimp with a rich cream-and-Vermouth sauce. | 20160 Garrett Hwy. | 301/387–5503, ext. 2201 | $10–$18 | AE, D, DC, MC, V.

Silver Tree. Italian. After trying this busy waterfront restaurant's seafood and other fare, you can top it off with an ice cream sundae. Kids' menu. | 19638 Garrett Hwy. | 301/387–4040 | $15–$35 | AE, D, DC, MC, V.

Lodging

Alpine Village. Country-style furnishings, including beds with locally made quilts, brighten this mountain lodge. If you stay in one of the rooms, you'll be treated to breakfast. | 29 rooms, 8 suites, 14 chalets. Restaurant, bar, complimentary Continental breakfast, picnic area.

Some kitchenettes, cable TV. Pool, wading pool. | 19638 Garrett Hwy. | 301/387–5534 or 800/343–5253 | www.alpine/silvertree.com | $35–$80 | AE, D, DC, MC, V.

The Board Room Motel. The tiled bathrooms, mauve carpet, and tan painted walls lend a freshness to the guest rooms. A family restaurant and health club are adjacent to the motel. Some refrigerators, cable TV. Laundry facilities. Pets allowed (fee). | 12678 Garrett Hwy. | 301/334–2126 | 13 rooms | $50–$55 | AE, D, DC, MC, V.

Carmel Cove Inn. Once a monastery of the Carmelite friars, this hidden country inn on 2 wooded acres is decidedly more fun today. Now the single-story blue building has an English great room with a pool table, TV, and fireplace. Rooms are small, but some have fireplaces. It's just a few minutes from the lake and restaurants. | 10 rooms. Restaurant, complimentary breakfast. Hot tub. Tennis courts. TV in common area. | 105 Monastery Way | 301/387–0067 | fax 301/387–2394 | carmelcove@aol.com | www.carmelcoveinn.com | $100–$160 | D, MC, V.

The Oak and Apple Bed & Breakfast. This 1915 house presides over a lovely lawn with apple, oak, pine, cherry and maple trees. Relax on the enclosed sun porch, in the parlor by a warming fire, or in the cozy gathering room. Whitewater rafting is nearby. Complimentary Continental breakfast. Some in-room hot tubs. No pets. No smoking. | 208 N. Second St. | 301/334–9265 | oakandapplebb@mail2.gcnet.net | www.oakandapple.com | 5 rooms | $75–$105 | MC, V.

Oak-Mar Motel. This sparsely furnished but well-kept motel is in the heart of Oakland near the small downtown shopping area. | 21 rooms. Restaurant. Cable TV. | 208 N. 3rd St. | 301/334–3965 | $45–$60 | AE, D, DC, MC, V.

Will o' the Wisp. Along the shoreline of Deep Creek Lake, this development's condominiums reflect the tastes of their individual owners. | 54 condos. Restaurant, bar, picnic area. Cable TV. Indoor pool. Hot tub, sauna. Gym, racquetball, beach. Pool table, table tennis, video games. Playground. | 20160 Garrett Hwy. (U.S. 219) | 301/387–5503 | fax 301/387–4999 | www.willothewisp.com | $86–$300 | AE, D, DC, MC, V.

OCEAN CITY

MAP 4, I5

(Nearby towns also listed: Belin, Pocomoke City, Salisbury, Snow Hill)

This 10-mi, narrow peninsula swells with crowds every summer as sun-seekers flock to its well-maintained beaches along the Atlantic. The Coastal Highway (Hwy. 1), which bisects town, is packed with hotels, motels, condos, restaurants, shops, and amusements. Tourists swarm the city on summer weekends to take advantage of the area's outdoor activities: swimming, sailing, boating, bodysurfing, parasailing, fishing, tennis, and golf, just to name a few. Most of those weekend warriors eventually find their way to the carnival-like scene on the city's 3-mi boardwalk, home to a small amusement park, surf and T-shirt shops, fudge and saltwater-taffy stores, and countless other amenities. For a more tranquil boardwalk experience, bicycling is permitted in the morning and evening hours.

Information: Ocean City Convention and Visitors Bureau, Town of Ocean City Tourism Division | 4001 Coastal Hwy., Ocean City, 21842 | 410/289–8181 or 800/626–2326 | www.oceancity.org.

Attractions

★ **Assateague Island National Seashore.** This pristine, untamed 37-mi-long barrier island, just south of the excitement of Ocean City, provides a haven for those seeking a little peace and quiet. Swimming, biking, camping, surf fishing, hiking, and picnicking are permitted. | 7206 National Seashore La. | 410/641–1441 | www.nps.gov | $5 per vehicle, $2 per pedestrian | Park daily, visitor center daily 9–5.

Assateague State Park. The state's only oceanside park is home to a band of wild ponies. Camping, swimming, boating, and fishing are permitted. | 7307 Stephen Decatur Hwy. | 410/641–2120 | www.dnr.state.md.us | $2 Mar.–Oct. | Daily dawn to dusk.

Boardwalk. This beachfront institution, with its shops, pubs, restaurants, hotels, fishing pier, and amusement park, is the city's hub of all tourist activities. Thrasher's french fries and saltwater taffy from Dolles and Candy Kitchen are local goodies. | Free | Daily.

Jolly Roger Amusement Park. Two miniature-golf courses, a water park, a roller coaster, kid's rides, petting zoo, and miniature racing cars make this a busy summer attraction. | Coastal Hwy, at 30th St. | 410/289–3477 | Rides and golf priced individually | May–Sept., daily noon–midnight; Easter–Apr., weekends noon–midnight, closed weekdays.

Trimper's Amusement Park. At the south end of the boardwalk, this small park has more than 100 rides, games and amusements. Some of the highlights include a carousel dating from 1902, double-loop roller coaster, an arcade and miniature golf. While most of the rides are outdoor, an indoor amusement park has rides for littler kids. | Boardwalk, at S. 1st St. | 410/289–8617 | www.beach-net.com/trimpers | Rides priced individually | Memorial Day–Labor Day, 1–midnight, Labor Day–May, indoor park weekends noon–4, closed weekdays.

OCEAN CITY AND ASSATEAGUE ISLAND

The Atlantic Ocean makes up only about 20 miles of Maryland's shoreline, all of it along a thin peninsula that attracts hundreds of thousands of beachgoers. They come for the sandy, well-kept beaches in Ocean City, its fabled 3-mile boardwalk, and numerous hotels, motels, inns, and restaurants.

Ocean City has long been the traditional summer vacation spot for thousands of Baltimoreans who head "downey ocean" to escape the city heat. On any summer weekend the population of 7,500 swells to 250,000 to 300,000. At times like this the Coastal Highway often resembles the Beltway in rush hour.

At Trimper's Amusement Park on the boardwalk, you can ride a 19th-century carousel, eat saltwater taffy, fudge and Thrasher's french fries, and buy T-shirts and souvenirs.

Ocean City's uninhabited neighbor to the south, Assateague Island, lies partly in Virginia and is home to a state park and a national seashore. Unspoiled beaches fringe the island, and wild ponies roam freely. Far from the glitzy bustle of Ocean City, Assateague has no homes or permanent structures other than those owned by the National Park Service. You can camp, fish, canoe, hike, or bike in designated areas by the bay or ocean. *National Geographic* named Assateague among the top national parks in the nation.

Just a few miles from the beaches are the well-preserved historic mainland towns of Snow Hill and Berlin. You can also birdwatch further inland—the region is home to more than 350 species—or hike the Beach to Bay Indian Trail, a national recreation trail that follows a path similar to one the Algonquin Indians used.

© Corbis

NOV.–JAN.: *Winterfest of Lights.* Nearly 300,000 people come to see the thousands of lights twinkle on stationary and animated displays throughout the seaside resort. | 800/626–2326.

Dining

Angelo's. Italian. Murals in the spacious open dining room provide a Mediterranean backdrop. Order the veal, seafood, or pasta with homemade sauce. Kids' menu. | 2706 Coastal Hwy. | 410/289–6522 | Closed Nov.–Jan. | $7–$21 | AE, D, DC, MC, V.

Bonfire. American. Expect large crowds lining up at the seafood and prime rib buffet. Menu favorites include the crab cakes and the Chesapeake steak, a sirloin stuffed with crab imperial. Kids' menu. Early-bird suppers. | 7009 Coastal Hwy. | 410/524–7171 | Closed Oct.–Mar., weekdays. No lunch | Reservations essential Fri.–Sat. | $15–$28 | AE, DC, MC, V.

Charlie Chiang's Restaurant. Chinese. Specializing in spicy Hunan and Szechuan dishes, this restaurant offers eat-in, carry-out, and delivery service. Among the house favorites are crispy hot beef, three-flavor chicken, and Hong Kong–style seafood. Full bar. | 5401 Coastal Hwy. | 410/723–4600 | $8–$22 | AE, D, DC, MC, V.

Embers. American. This large-scale dining operation, close to the boardwalk, is ready to serve the sunburned masses. In addition to a seafood buffet, the menu offers Cajun prime rib, Eastern Shore–style crab cakes, and flounder almondine. Kids' menu. | Philadelphia Ave., at 24th St. | 410/289–3322 | Closed Dec.–Feb. | $17–$26 | AE, MC, V.

Fager's Island. Seafood. This bayside restaurant's tropical spirit extends to the food as well as the environment. Pacific Rim–influenced dishes include curried coconut scallops, roast duckling with Grand Marnier sauce, and pecan-crusted mahi mahi. Dine on the wooden deck that stretches out over the bay and enjoy the nightly entertainment. Raw bar. Early-bird suppers. Sunday brunch. | 201 60th St. | 410/524–5500 or 888/371–5400 | $18–$28 | AE, DC, MC, V.

Hanna's Marina Deck. American. The view of the sun melting into Assateague Bay is just one thing that makes this place a favorite with the locals. The cuisine—with dishes including stuffed flounder and crab imperial—is another. Open-air dining is available on a small deck overlooking the water. Kids' menu. | 306 Dorchester St. | 410/289–4411 | Closed mid-Oct.–Easter | $7–$28 | AE, D, MC, V.

Harrison's Harbor Watch. Seafood. This two-story restaurant on an inlet overlooking Assateague Island skirts the edge of the boardwalk. The extensive menu has a variety of seafood platters and the ubiquitous Maryland crab cakes. Kids' menu. | 806 S. Boardwalk | 410/289–5121 | Closed Nov.–Mar., Mon.–Thurs. No lunch | $15–$25 | AE, D, DC, MC, V.

Hobbit. French. Murals and carved lamps in the dining rooms portray J.R.R. Tolkien's characters. Specialties include chicken flamed in applejack brandy, prime rib, and crab imperial. An outdoor deck overlooks the water. Early-bird suppers. Kids' menu. | 81st St., at the bay | 410/524–8100 | $18–$26 | AE, D, MC, V.

Little Italy on the Shore. Italian. This upscale restaurant is the only place in town to find osso buco, veal shank roasted with olive oil, tomato, and rosemary. Other specialties include the tender calamari and the tortellini la nonna with prosciutto, peas, and mushrooms in a light white sauce. Warm, earthy colors and house wine on each table make this a romantic dining spot. Open-air dining on the terrace. | 215 S. Baltimore | 410/289–0505 | No lunch | $15–$23 | AE, D, DC, MC, V.

Lombardi's. American. Seat yourself at a cozy wooden booth or table to sample this casual eatery's thin-crust pizza, cheese steaks, or cold-cut sandwiches. | 9203 Coastal Hwy. | 410/524–1961 | No lunch mid-Sept.–mid-May. Closed mid-Sept.–mid-May, Wed. | $7–$15 | MC, V.

Macky's Bayside Bar Grill. American. Behind Chauncey's Surf-O-Rama, you'll find Macky's, a restaurant that serves soups, salads, pizzas, fried chicken, and seafood. Try the seafood au gratin, a baked casserole of crabmeat, shrimp, and scallops topped with jack cheese and seasoned bread crumbs. You can amuse yourself in the bayfront game room before or after dinner. | 54th St., at Coastal Hwy. | 410/723–5565 | Closed Nov.–Feb. | $9–$23 | AE, D, DC, MC, V.

Mario's. Italian. White tablecloths and linen napkins as well as the scenes of Italy dominating the walls add a touch of elegance to this restaurant, which is known for steak and seafood. Kids' menu. | 2204 Philadelphia Ave. | 410/289–9445 | Closed Jan.–mid-Feb. No lunch | $13–$25 | AE, DC, MC, V.

Ocean Club. American. You can spy the ocean through the oval windows in the ample dining room with wooden pillars and wicker furnishings. Look for a diverse menu of seafood, chicken, beef, and veal dishes. A palm-shaded beach provides a restful outdoor dining spot. Early-bird suppers. Entertainment daily. | 49th St., at the ocean | 410/524–7500 | Closed Nov.–Mar., Tues. No lunch weekdays Sept.–May | $19–$25 | AE, D, DC, MC, V.

Phillips Seafood. Seafood. Chandeliers, gold linens, and red carpets give this ornate eatery a baroque sort of charm. Tiffany-style lamps illuminate the piano bar and lounge area. While it focuses on all seafood, this restaurant's strong point is its crab dishes. Kids' menu. | 1301 Atlantic Ave. | 410/289–9121 or 800/492–5834 | $15–$40 | AE, D, DC, MC, V.

Reel Inn Grille. American. Trophy fish and nautical pictures line the walls of this popular spot above the White Marlin Club. Sport fishermen come for the 30-ounce porterhouse steak and the 8-ounce center-cut filet with mushrooms and shallots. The seared ahi tuna appetizer and the jumbo lump crab cakes are other favorites. | 12902 Kelly Bridge Road, West Ocean City | 410/213–1618 | Closed Tues. No lunch | $8–$24 | AE, D, MC, V.

Rio Grande Cafe and Tiki Bar. American. This seasonal restaurant with both indoor and outdoor seating is known for its overstuffed sandwiches, salads, and grilled tuna. Other popular selections include the boneless pork chops with cranberry and the chicken Rio Grande, topped with bacon, provolone, and barbecue sauce. | 145th St., at Coastal Hwy. | 410/250–0409 | Breakfast also available. No dinner Sept.–May. Closed Sept.–May, weekdays | $7–$14 | AE, D, MC, V.

Windows on the Bay. Contemporary. Fine picture windows, hanging plants, and tables set with linens and flowers greet you in the dining room here. Sample baked duck with peach and burgundy sauce or wienerschnitzel while gazing at expansive views of the bay, perhaps the best in Ocean City. | 6103 Sea Bay Dr. | 410/723–3463 | No lunch | $15–$25 | AE, DC, MC, V.

Lodging

Atlantic House Bed and Breakfast. Take a break and head to "your house at the beach," as the owners call their charming 1923 home. It's a short walk to the town's attractions. In the afternoon, take in the ocean view from the front porch while enjoying complimentary cookies and lemonade. Picnic area, complimentary breakfast. Cable TV, no room phones, TV in common area. Outdoor hot tub. Bicycles. No pets. No kids under 6. No smoking. | 501 N. Baltimore | 410/289–2333 | fax 410/289–2430 | ocbnb@atlantichouse.com | www.atlantichouse.com | 11 rooms | $75–$145 | AE, D, MC, V.

Beachmark Motel. On the peninsula's ocean side and nestled amid high-rise condominiums, this three-story, family-friendly motel is close to many restaurants. The rooms, which have beach-style furnishings, all have private balconies with an ocean or pool view. | 96 rooms. Restaurant. Kitchenettes, cable TV. Pool. Beach. | 73rd St., at the ocean | 410/524–7300 or 800/638–1600 | www.beachmarkmotel.com | $116–$126 | Closed Oct.–May | MC, V.

Best Western Flagship. At the terminus of the boardwalk, this motel is just a stroll to restaurants and shops. The rooms, all with a beige-and-white color scheme, have private balconies overlooking the pool or ocean. | 93 rooms. Some kitchenettes, cable TV. 2 pools (1 indoor), wading pool. Hot tub. Tennis. Exercise equipment. Video games. Playground. Laundry service. Business services. | 2600 Baltimore Ave. | 410/289–3384 or 800/837–3585 | fax 410/289–1743 | www.bestwestern.com | Closed Jan., weekdays | $189–$209 | AE, D, DC, MC, V.

Castle in the Sand. This family-oriented place, which wraps around a courtyard and pool, is just 200 yards from the convention center. The hotel also rents out privately owned condominiums as well as rooms, cottages and efficiencies. Units range from oceanfront to bayside to within 1 block of the beach. | 145 units. Restaurant, bar. Refrigerators, cable TV. Pool. Video games. Kids' programs. | 3701 Atlantic Ave. | 410/289–6846 or 800/552–7263 | fax 410/289–9446 | www.castleinthesand.com | $159–$230, $775–$1170 cottages, efficiencies, condominums (weekly) | Closed Nov.–Mar. | AE, D, DC, MC, V.

Coconut Malorie. The blue stone facade and palm trees give this hotel on Isle of Wight Bay a Caribbean flavor. Antique sculptures and carvings, a traditional English library and an art gallery make it like no other place in town. Hawaiian art and eclectic pieces from around the world accent the custom furnishings in the rooms. | 23 rooms, 85 suites in 2 buildings. Restaurant, bar. In-room data ports, refrigerators, cable TV. Pool. Business services. | 200 59th St. | 410/723–6100 or 800/767–6060 | fax 410/524–9327 | www.coconut-malorie.com | $128–$196 | AE, D, DC, MC, V.

Comfort Inn Boardwalk. Every room in this six-story pink building, right in the thick of the boardwalk scene, has a balcony with an ocean view. The rooms are done in blue floral motifs and plaid patterns. | 84 rooms. Complimentary Continental breakfast. Kitchenettes, cable TV. Pool. Beach. | 50th St., at the boardwalk | 410/289–5155 or 800/282–5155 | fax 410/289–6547 | www.comfortinn.com | $205–$239 | Closed Dec.–Jan. | AE, D, DC, MC, V.

Commander Hotel. This boardwalk hotel was built in 1998 on the site of the 1930 Ocean City mainstay of the same name. All suites and efficiencies have private balconies and marble vanities in the bathrooms; many have canopy beds. Cabanas and apartments are also available. | 109 rooms. Restaurant, bar. In-room data ports, in-room safes, microwaves, refrigerators, cable TV. Indoor and outdoor pools. Golf privileges. Beach. Laundry facilities. No pets. | 14th St., at the boardwalk | 410/289–6166 or 888/289–6166 | fax 410/289–3998 | cmdrhotel@aol.com | www.commanderhotel.com | $218–$229 | MC, V.

Days Inn Boardwalk. A large garden connects these two former motels combined into one beachside property. The southwestern style rooms have a teal-and-beige color scheme. | 95 units. Restaurant. Some kitchenettes, refrigerators, microwaves, cable TV. Two pools, wading pool. Business services. | 23rd St., at the boardwalk | 410/289–7161 or 800/926–1122 | fax 410/289–6525 | www.daysinnboardwalk.com | $139, $159 efficiencies, $189–$259 suites | MC, V.

Dunes Manor Hotel. A Victorian sensibility permeates this large beachfront hotel. All the rooms, colored in pink and green, have an ocean view. | 170 rooms, 11 suites. Restaurant, bar, complimentary afternoon tea, room service. In-room data ports, microwaves, refrigerators, cable TV. Indoor-outdoor pool. Gym. Beach. Business services. | 2800 Baltimore Ave. | 410/289–1100 or 800/523–2888 | fax 410/289–4905 | www.dunesmanor.com | $199–$239 | AE, D, DC, MC, V.

Dunes Motel. This motel at the north end of the boardwalk has oceanfront efficiencies and rooms. Its other rooms overlook the courtyard around the pool. Rooms are done in green and peach and have floral patterns and wicker furniture. | 103 rooms. Restaurant. Pool, wading pool. | 27th St., at the boardwalk | 410/289–4414 | fax 410/289–0891 | www.ocean-city.com/dunes.htm | $99–$159, efficiencies $149–$199, suites $189–$239 | Closed mid-Oct.–mid-Feb. | AE, MC, V.

Executive Motel. This small place on busy Baltimore Avenue is just a few blocks from the boardwalk. Rooms are in pastel colors with beach paintings and ceramic-tiled baths. | 47 rooms. Refrigerators, cable TV. | Baltimore Ave., at 30th St. | 410/289–8334 or 800/638–1600 | www.executivemotel.com | $98–$108 | MC, V.

Gateway. Simple contemporary furnishings accent the rooms of this three-story property. Some rooms have ocean views. | 59 units. Restaurant, bar, room service. Kitchenettes, cable TV. Pool, wading pool. Hot tub. Beach. Laundry facilities. Business services. | 48th St., at the ocean | 410/524–6500 or 800/382–2582 | fax 410/524–5374 | www.gatewayoc.com | $155–$210, $1224 efficiencies (weekly) | AE, D, DC, MC, V.

Holiday Inn Oceanfront. Near the convention center and convenient to the bridge to the mainland, this eight-story building with a contemporary flair has oceanfront rooms. | 216 rooms. Restaurant, bar, room service. In-room data ports, kitchenettes, cable TV. Pools. Hot tub. Tennis courts. Gym, beach. Video games. Kids' programs, laundry service. Business services. | 66th St., at the ocean | 410/524–1600 or 800/837–3588 | fax 410/524–1135 | www.basshotels.com/holiday-inn | $209–$269 | AE, D, DC, MC, V.

Howard Johnson Oceanfront Inn. Rooms in this four-story motel near the boardwalk have balconies and contemporary furnishings, including a sleeper sofa in every room. | 72 rooms. Restaurant. Some kitchenettes, refrigerators, microwaves, cable TV. Pool. Hot tub. Business services. | 2401 Atlantic Ave. | 410/289–6401 or 800/926–1122 | www.hojoexpress.com | $135–$205 | Closed Nov.–Mar. | AE, D, DC, MC, V.

Inn on the Ocean. Small, elegant and romantic, this beachfront B&B has a fireplace in the living room to warm you up and a wraparound veranda to cool you off. Wood and wicker furnishings give it a relaxed charm. Afternoon refreshments available. | 6 rooms. Complimentary Continental breakfast. In-room hot tubs, cable TV. Bicycles. Beach. | 1001 Atlantic Ave. | 410/289–8894 or 888/226–6223 | fax 410/289–8215 | www.bbonline.com/md/ontheocean | $185–$290 | AE, D, DC, MC, V.

Lighthouse Club Hotel. Reached by a wooden bridge, this three-story octagonal house on Fager's Island is encircled by wetlands and waterfowl. Many rooms have private decks, perfect for taking in the spectacular sunset views. All suites have custom furnishings and marble baths, and some have fireplaces. | 23 suites. Restaurant, complimentary Continental breakfast, room service. Refrigerators, in-room hot tubs, cable TV. Business services, airport shuttle. | 201 60th St. | 410/524–5400 or 888/371–5400 | fax 410/524–3928 | www.fagers.com/lghtmain.htm | $184–$295 | AE, D, MC, V.

The Marylander Hotel/Condominium. A company rents out these privately owned condominiums at attractive rates. Each three-room apartment has one bedroom and a private balcony. Kitchens, microwaves, refrigerators, in-room hot tubs, cable TV. Indoor pool. Hot tub. Golf privileges. Laundry facilities. | 6 127th St. | 410/250–1518 or 800/750–9516 | 26 apartments | $120–$185 | D, MC, V.

Nassau Motel. You can choose between a room in the oceanside or poolside building. The spacious rooms have balconies and are done in floral patterns. | 63 rooms in 2 buildings. Many kitchenettes, refrigerators, microwaves, cable TV. Pool. Volleyball, beach. | 60th St., at the ocean | 410/524–6451 (summer) or 410/641–1323 | www.ocean-city.com/nassau.htm | $85–$128 | Closed mid-Oct.–mid-Mar. | AE, D, MC, V.

Paradise Plaza Inn. Just steps from the boardwalk, this oceanfront hotel has a great location close to restaurants and local amusements. Most rooms have balconies, and terry bathrobes are provided. Restaurant, room service. In-room data ports, microwaves, refrigerators, some in-room hot tubs, cable TV. Outdoor pool. Golf privileges. Beach. Shops. No pets. | 9th St., and the boardwalk | 410/289–6381 or 888/678–4111 | fax 410/289–1301 | ddouglas@paradiseplazainn.com | www.paradiseplazainn.com | 88 rooms | $200–$270 | AE, D, MC, V.

Park Place Hotel. Enjoy the sunrise from your oceanfront balcony at this modern family-run hotel right on the boardwalk. Restaurant, bar, room service. Kitchenettes, microwaves, cable TV. Outdoor pool. | 208 N. Atlantic Ave. | 410/289–6440 or 888/212–7275 | fax 410/289–3389 | parkplace@beachin.net | www.ocparkplacehotel.com | 90 rooms | $220–$240 | AE, D, DC, MC, V.

Phillips Beach Plaza. This oceanfront hotel is near everything you'd expect from Ocean City—restaurants, shops, beach and the boardwalk. Victorian-style furnishings add to its retro charm as one of the older hotels on the strip. | 96 units. Restaurant, bar. Some kitchenettes, cable TV. Beach. Business services. | 13th St., at the boardwalk | 410/289–9121 or 800/ 492–5834 | fax 410/289–3041 | www.ocean-city.com/phillips/beachplaza/index.html | $129– $164, $1,025–$1,220 efficiencies weekly, $1,095–$1,450 apartments weekly | Closed Jan.– Feb.; weekdays in Mar. | AE, D, DC, MC, V.

Plim Plaza. On the boardwalk near shopping, the beach, and an amusement park, this yellow four-story building has a tropical appeal. The front porch overlooks the ocean, and the rear sundeck is beside an Olympic-size pool. | 181 rooms. Two restaurants, bar. Cable TV. Pool. Hot tub. Business services. | 2nd St., at the boardwalk | 410/289–6181 or 800/837–3587 | fax 410/289–7686 | www.ocmdhotels.com/plimplaza/ | $125–$179 | Closed Nov.–Mar. | D, DC, MC, V.

Princess Royale. This oceanside, 10-story hotel has five levels of condos, an ocean deck, a private boardwalk, and an Olympic-size heated pool in a four-story atrium. Warm colors and beach paintings make the suites, each with a living room and private balcony, a relaxing place to kick off your sandals after a long day at the beach. Some have heart-shaped hot tubs. | 310 units. Restaurant, bar. In-room data ports, kitchenettes, microwaves, cable TV. Indoor pool. Beauty salon, hot tub. Tennis court. Exercise equipment, beach. Video games. Laundry facilities. Business services. | 91st St., at the ocean | 410/524–7777 or 800/ 476–9253 | fax 410/524–7787 | www.princessroyale.com | $149–$299, $2,599–$3,099 condos weekly | AE, D, DC, MC, V.

Quality Inn Oceanfront. It feels like summer all year in this inn's five-story atrium filled with tropical birds and exotic plants. The rooms, which have a beige-and-red color scheme and floral designs, have private balconies. Video cameras are available for free loan during your stay, and there is a tanning bed on the premises. | 126 units. Restaurant, bar. In-room data ports, kitchenettes, cable TV. 2 pools (1 indoor), wading pool. Hot tub. Tennis. Exercise equipment, beach. Video games. Laundry service. Business services. | 54th St., at the ocean | 410/524–7200 | fax 410/723–0018 | www.ocmdhotels.com/qioceanfront/ | $189–$234 | AE, D, DC, MC, V.

Ramada Limited Oceanfront. This small hotel is just 2 blocks from restaurants and an amusement park and 6 blocks from the action of the boardwalk. | 76 rooms. Complimentary Continental breakfast. Kitchenettes, cable TV. Pool, wading pool. Beach. Volleyball, bicycles. Laundry service. | 3200 Baltimore Ave. | 410/289–6444 | fax 410/289–0108 | www.ocmdhotels.com/ ramada.htm | $199–$229 | AE, D, DC, MC, V.

Safari. Two yellow brick buildings, one with four floors and the other with three, make up this family-friendly motel on the boardwalk. | 46 rooms. Cable TV. Some pets allowed. | 13th St., at the boardwalk | 410/289–6411 or 800/787–2183 | $135–$170 | Closed Nov.–Mar. | AE, D, DC, MC, V.

Sahara. Though its name may put you in mind of a desert, the only sand around here is tracked in from the beach, which is just steps away. Some rooms in this property on the boardwalk have private porches with ocean views. | 161 rooms in 4 buildings. Restaurant. Some kitchenettes, refrigerators, cable TV. 2 pools. | 19th St., at the ocean | 410/289–8101 or 800/638–1600 | www.saharamotel.com | $98–$150 | Closed Nov.–Apr. | MC, V.

Santa Maria Hotel. This three-story white-concrete hotel is right on the boardwalk, minutes away from shopping, amusements, and the convention center. Each cheerful room has its own balcony. Restaurant. Refrigerators, cable TV. Outdoor pool. Beach. No pets. | 15th St., at the boardwalk | 410/289–7191 | fax 410/289–8609 | santa@shore.intercom.net | www.santamariahotel.com | 102 rooms | $90–$167 | Closed Nov.–mid-Apr. | AE, D, DC, MC, V.

Sheraton Fontainebleau. This highrise hotel is on Ocean City's "Golden Mile." The rooms, some with ocean views, are done in floral patterns. | 250 rooms. 3 restaurants, bar. In-room data ports, some kitchenettes, microwaves, refrigerator, cable TV. Indoor pool. Beauty salon, hot tub. Gym, beach. Video games. Business services, airport shuttle. Some pets allowed (fee). | 10100 Coastal Hwy. | 410/524–3535 | fax 410/524–3834 | www.sheratonoc.com | $249– $309 | AE, D, DC, MC, V.

Tides Motel. The rooms in this three-story stucco motel on the ocean side of the island have a nautical style. | 54 rooms. Kitchenettes, cable TV. Pool. Beach. | 71st St., at the ocean | 410/524–7100 or 800/638–1600 | www.tidesmotel.com | $102–$108 | Closed Oct.–Apr. | MC, V.

Tidelands Caribbean Hotel. Palm trees and tropical flowers point up the Caribbean theme at this blue-and-white oceanfront hotel with spacious rooms. Take a dip in the rooftop pool, or hang out on your private balcony. Some kitchenettes, microwaves, refrigerators, cable TV. Outdoor pool. Golf privileges. Beach. Shops, video games. No pets. | 5th St. and the Boardwalk | 410/289–9455 | fax 410/289–4355 | 67 rooms | $160–$200 | AE, D, MC, V.

OXFORD

(Nearby towns also listed: Easton, St. Michaels, Tilghman)

Founded in 1683, Oxford is one of Maryland's oldest communities. Once the state's largest port of call, it is now a favorite side-trip from St. Michaels. Many visitors make the 7-mi journey across the Tred Avon River aboard the Oxford–Bellevue Ferry, one of the oldest ferries in the United States. Although Oxford dates to 1683, few of its buildings constructed before the mid-1800s survive today. A notable exception is the Robert Morris Inn, which has expanded gradually from a four-room house built in 1710 to a 35-room lodge.

Information: Talbot County Conference and Visitors Bureau | 210 Marlboro Ave., Suite 3, Easton, 21601 | 410/822–4606 or 888/BAY–STAY | www.oxfordmd.com/oba.

Attractions
Oxford–Bellevue Ferry. One of the country's oldest privately owned ferries in continuous operation, it has been running across the Tred Avon River to the St. Michaels area since 1683. | N. Morris St., at the Strand | 410/745–9023 | www.oxfordmd.com/obf | $5 per car one-way, $8 same-day round-trip | Closed Dec.–Feb., call for schedule.

Oxford Museum. Browse this maritime museum's exhibits, which include sailboat models, a lamp from a nearby lighthouse, a sail-maker's bench, and an oyster-shucking stall. | Morris and Market Sts. | 410/226–0191 | Free | Apr.–Oct., Fri.–Sun. 3–5, closed Mon.–Thurs.

ON THE CALENDAR
APR.: *Oxford Day.* This town-wide event celebrates what Oxford is all about: history, community and crabcakes! You can take a historical tour of town, eat and shop your way along the waterfront and catch a parade in the afternoon. | 410/226–5730.

Dining
Latitude 38. Continental. At this stylish bistro, polished hardwood floors gleam under linen-draped tables and painted vines spiral up the walls. When the weather's warm, you can eat outside on wrought-iron cafe tables in the bricked courtyard. The brief menu includes local fare like veal scalloppini topped with crab imperial and peppercorn hollandaise sauce, or the crab and Dijon ravioli with herbed cream sauce. | 26342 Oxford Rd. | 410/226–5303 | Reservations recommended | $23–$33 | AE, MC, V.

Lodging
Combsberry. On the banks of Island Creek amid magnolias and willow trees, this inn, built as a private residence in the 1730s, has eight arched fireplaces, floral chintz sofas, polished wood floors and a formal garden. All rooms have water views and private baths; some have

whirlpool tubs. Cable TV. | 4837 Evergreen Rd. | 410/226–5353 | 4 rooms, 2 suites, a cottage and a carriage house | $295–$395 | AE, MC, V.

Robert Morris Inn. This early 18th-century waterfront lodge has grown considerably from its humble beginnings as a four-room house. The innkeeper's easygoing hospitality and a private beach make it a relaxing retreat. All rooms have quaint country furnishings, and some have private porches overlooking the water. | 35 rooms. Restaurant, bar. No TV, no room phones. Beach. Business services. No kids under 10. No smoking. | 314 N. Morris St. | 410/226–5111 | fax 410/226–5744 | www.robertmorrisinn.com | $110–$190 | Closed Dec.–mid-Feb. | AE, MC, V.

PIKESVILLE

MAP 4, F2

(Nearby towns also listed: Baltimore, Towson)

Northwest of Baltimore, Pikesville is a community with history stretching back 200 years. Straddling both sides of the Baltimore Beltway (I–695), it is accessible to upscale shops, hotels, and restaurants as well as the busy Owings Mills Mall. Much of the streetscape along Reisterstown Road (Rte. 140) has been reconstructed with trees and benches to be more pedestrian-friendly.

Information: Baltimore County Conference and Visitors Bureau | 435 York Rd., Towson, 21204 | 410/583–7313 or 800/570–2836 | www.visitbacomd.com.

Attractions

Soldiers Delight Natural Environment Area. The 1,800-acre park contains the Serpentine Grasslands, the state's largest undisturbed expanse of prairie grasses, which were once prevalent in this area. | 5100 Deerpark Rd., Owings Mills | 410/922–3044 | www.dnr.state.md.us/publiclands | Free | Daily dawn to dusk, visitors center Wed.–Sun. 9–4, closed Mon.–Tues.

ON THE CALENDAR

JUNE–AUG.: *Summer Concert Series.* Throughout the summer, the Beth El Synagogue hosts musicians from all over Maryland and around the country to entertain with performances ranging from jazz to blues to Jewish folk music. Admission varies depending on the entertainment. | 801 Park Heights Ave. | 410/484–2337.

Dining

Due. Italian. Mahogany furniture gives this eatery the air of a northern Italian villa. Locals come for the osso buco, veal chops, pizzas, and lobster tail with white wine sauce. | 25 Crossroads Dr., Owings Mills | 410/356–4147 | Reservations essential Fri.–Sat. | $12–$29 | AE, DC, MC, V.

Linwood's Cafe. American. This restaurant is graced with elegant charcoal etchings and mahogany trim. The imaginative Californian-style menu emphasizes seafood and healthy fare. | 25 Crossroads Dr., Owings Mills | 410/356–3030 | Reservations essential Fri.–Sat. | $31–$50 | AE, DC, MC, V.

Puffins. American. This neighborhood place, with its chrome trim and color scheme of electric blue and violet, is as funky as any of the artworks it displays. The pieces rotate bimonthly and are for sale. The menu offers several vegetarian dishes plus crabcakes, seafood, and meat dishes. No smoking. | 1000 Reisterstown Rd. (Rte. 140) | 410/486–8811 | $11–$19 | AE, DC, MC, V.

Stixx Cafe. Pan Asian. Murals of the Mediterranean create a relaxing mood in a small dining room with comfy armchairs and expansive windows. Grilled salmon teriyaki, crispy veal, or the lotus seafood udon are just some of the dishes on the eclectic menu. Other options are Chinese dishes, sushi, salads, and pastas. You can dine outside on a small garden patio shaded by umbrellas. No smoking. | 1500 Reisterstown Rd. (Rte. 140) | 410/484–7787 | $9–$17 | AE, D, DC, MC, V.

Lodging

Comfort Inn–Northwest. This motel is about 12 mi from Baltimore's Inner Harbor and 2 mi from shopping centers and movie theaters. | 103 rooms. Complimentary Continental breakfast. Pool, wading pool. In-room data ports, cable TV. Laundry facilities. Business services. | 10 Wooded Way | 410/484–7700 | fax 410/653–1516 | www.comfortinn.com | $65–$95 | AE, D, DC, MC, V.

Hilton Garden Inn. Built in 1999, the hotel is adjacent to the Owens Mills Restaurant Park. The structure is six stories high but effort has been made to make guests feel at home rather than in a chain hotel. Rooms include large desks for business travelers; bedspreads and chairs have been upholstered in deep, jewel-tone fabrics. Restaurant, pool. Gym. Business services, laundry services. | 4770 Owings Mills Blvd., Owings Mills | 410/654–6030 | fax 410/654–0269 | 140 rooms | $89–$124 | AE, D, MC, V.

Ramada Inn. A courtyard that runs both indoors and out distinguishes this motel from its run-of-the-mill brethren. Many of the large rooms have a pool view. This property is about 15 minutes by car to Baltimore's Inner Harbor. | 108 rooms. Restaurant, complimentary Continental breakfast. Pool. In-room data ports, refrigerators, cable TV. Business services. Some pets allowed. | 1721 Reisterstown Rd. | 410/486–5600 | fax 410/484–9377 | www.ramada.com | $79–$89 | AE, D, DC, MC, V.

POCOMOKE CITY

MAP 4, H5

(Nearby town also listed: Crisfield)

Located on the banks of the Pocomoke River on Maryland's Eastern Shore, this bustling community is just north of the Virginia state line. Settled in the 1600s, the downtown still retains some remnants of its past, including a 1920s Art Deco theater and the Costen House Museum, an example of Italianate Victorian architecture. Pocomoke State Forest and Park and the Viewtrail, a 100-mi bike trail through Worcester County's countryside, are nearby. Hotels and restaurants can be found along U.S. 13 and U.S. 113.

Information: Worcester County Tourism | 113 Franklin St., Snow Hill, 21863 | 410/632–3110 or 800/852–0335 | www.atbeach.com/cities/snowhill/.

Attractions

Viewtrail 100. This marked 100-mi biking circuit through Worcester County uses secondary roads between Berlin and Pocomoke City. You can pick it up in the town center off Market Street. | 410/632–1972 | Free | Daily.

ON THE CALENDAR

FEB.: *East Coast Jazz Festival.* This 5-day event kicks off at Walter Johnson High School in Bethesda with a senior citizens concert but then moves to the Doubletree Hotel in Rockville for the remainder of the 21 ticketed concerts. Emerging artists, school groups and other amateurs peform free concerts on three stages in the hotel. | 301/933–1822.

APR.: *Maryland International Kite Festival.* This three-day festival on the beach between Division and 7th streets is a riot of color and activity, with kite enthusiasts from around the world converging to test their skills and show off their fabulous flyers. Kids' kite-making workshops are also available. | 410/289–7855.

Dining

Bonanza. American. This chain buffet may not be the pinnacle of culinary expression, but it could be just the thing if you've been on the road with the kids all day and just need to sit down and have some mashed potatoes and pudding. The food is what you might expect—roast beef, ham and chicken, along with a host of whipped-cream desserts—and the prices are reasonable. | 1621 Ocean Hwy. | 410/957–4292 | $6–$12 | AE, D, MC, V.

Upper Deck. American. Antiques elegantly accent this dining room and lounge, which is popular for its corn bread and local seafood, particularly its crabcakes. Entertainment Thursday through Saturday. Kids' menu. No smoking. | 1245 Ocean Hwy. (U.S. 13) | 410/957–3166 | $10–$18 | MC, V.

Lodging

Days Inn. On a busy highway, this motel is near several restaurants. Inside the stucco building, the large rooms are furnished in a contemporary style. | 87 rooms. Complimentary Continental breakfast. In-room data ports, cable TV. Pool. Business services. Some pets allowed. | 1540 Ocean Hwy. (U.S. 13) | 410/957–3000 | fax 410/957–3147 | www.daysinn.com | $53–$79 | AE, D, DC, MC, V.

Littleton's Bed and Breakfast. This stately 1860 home is decked out with both contemporary and Victorian furniture and accessories. The parlor sports an unusual Lincrusta frieze, and guest rooms are opulent. Some have fireplaces, all have private baths. Breakfast is served each morning in the elegant parlor. Cable TV. No room phones. | 407 Second St. | 410/957–1645 | 4 rooms | $50–$80 | No credit cards.

Quality Inn. This motel, 3 mi south of downtown Pocomoke, has large rooms with a muted beige-and-white color scheme. | 64 rooms. Pool, wading pool. In-room data ports, cable TV. Refrigerators, microwaves in some rooms. Business services. Some pets allowed. | 825 Ocean Hwy. (U.S. 13) | 410/957–1300 | fax 410/957–9329 | www.qualityinn.com | $67–$72 | AE, D, DC, MC, V.

ROCKVILLE

MAP 4, E3

(Nearby towns also listed: Gaithersburg, Silver Springs, Washington, D.C.)

The county seat of populous Montgomery County, Rockville is a busy suburban community, home to corporate offices, shopping malls and plazas, hotels, and restaurants. Though this city on the Washington Metro's red line is entrenched as a bedroom community, Rockville traces its history back to the late 1700s. Today, visitors can follow a self-guided walking tour that highlights the buildings from the last three centuries. Of particular interest is the redbrick courthouse built in 1891, and the burial place of F. Scott and Zelda Fitzgerald at St. Mary's Church Cemetery.

Information: Conference and Visitors Bureau of Montgomery County | 12900 Middlebrook Rd., Suite 1400, Germantown, 20874 | 301/428–9702 or 800/925–0880.

Attractions

Beall-Dawson House. This elegant Federal-style townhouse, built in 1815, is now a museum depicting the daily life of the Beall family, their household, and slaves. | 103 W. Montgomery Ave. | 301/762–1492 | www.montgomeryhistory.org | $3 | Tues.–Sun. noon–4, closed Mon.

Cabin John Regional Park. This park delivers family fun in any season. A year-round ice rink, tennis courts, hiking trails, picnic area, playground, and miniature train provide something for everyone. The nature center features classes and exhibits. | 7400 Tuckerman La. | 301/299–4555 | Free | Daily dawn to dusk.

Glenview Mansion. Part of the Rockville Civic Center, this 19th-century home with a grand staircase, marble-floor conservatory, and acres of parks and gardens is an art gallery with rotating exhibits. Judge Richard Johns Bowie, a U.S. Congressman and chief judge of the Maryland Court of Appeals, constructed the house in 1838. | 603 Edmonston Dr. | 301/309–3007 | Weekdays 9–4:30, closed weekends.

Dining

A & J. Chinese. Cafe tables and Oriental carpets give this restaurant, known for its dim sum, a cozy charm. No smoking. | 1319-C Rockville Pike (Rte. 355) | 301/251–7878 | $10–$13 | No credit cards.

Addie's. Contemporary. Reminiscent of a European cafe, this bistro has small tables, hardwood floors and a colorful collection of contemporary clocks. A small, umbrella-shaded patio in front provides open-air dining. Locals come here for the grilled Black Angus steak, seared tuna with orange-mango sauce, and steamed mussels. Kids' menu. | 11120 Rockville Pike (Rte. 355) | 301/881–0081 | $18–$23 | AE, DC, MC, V.

Andalucia. Spanish. The murals of Seville as well as the food make it as if you have stepped into a small restaurant in the south of Spain. The menu focuses on seafood dishes like paella and linguine with clam sauce. Flamenco dancers take to the floor on some nights. Call for schedule. No smoking. | 12300 Wilkens Ave. | 301/770–1880 | Reservations essential Fri.–Sat. dinner | Closed Mon. No lunch Sat.–Sun. | $13–$20 | AE, D, DC, MC, V.

Back Streets Cafe. American. This diner-style restaurant serves American favorites—charbroiled burgers, fries and shakes. | 12352 Wilkins Ave. | 301/984–0394 | $5–$10 | AE, MC, V.

Barbeque Country. American. This place has the feel of an upscale but pleasant roadhouse. You can bring the family for no-frills, no-surprises fare. Though barbecue is the specialty here, they also serve burgers and steaks. | 1321 Rockville Pike #C | 301/309–3740 | $8–$15 | AE, D, MC, V.

Bombay Bistro. Indian. This casual neighborhood restaurant is highlighted by displays of Indian art and metalwork. The extensive menu focuses on Tandoori-style chicken and seafood. Buffet lunch. Beer and wine only. | 98 W. Montgomery Ave. | 301/762–8798 | $10–$16 | AE, D, DC, MC, V.

Copeland's of New Orleans. Cajun/Creole. Take your taste buds on a trip south. Crawfish, shrimp and redfish Creole, and blackened chicken are among the New Orleans–inspired dishes at this restaurant. Kids' menu. | 1584 Rockville Pike (Rte. 355) | 301/230–0968 | $10–$14 | AE, D, DC, MC, V.

Hard Times Cafe. American. Cattle horns on the walls and an antique Wurlitzer jukebox stocked with old Western tunes gives this chili parlor the appeal of the American West. Chili styles range from the spicy Texas version to the savory-sweet Cincinnati type to the meatless variety. Kids' menu. | 1117 Nelson St. | 301/294–9720 | $5–$7 | AE, MC, V.

Hautam Kebobs. Middle Eastern. This small, unassuming restaurant serves traditional Iranian fare, specializing in grilled kebobs—chunks of seasoned meat slow-grilled on a stick with vegetables and then served on a bed of rice with a side of flatbread. The lamb kebobs are particularly popular. | 785-D Rockville Pike | 301/984–0394 | $6–$12 | AE, MC, V.

Normandie Farm. French. Bone up on your French as you dine in one of this restaurant's four fireside dining rooms. The cathedral ceilings are inscribed with 19th-century French quotations. Choose from menu specialties such as tournados of beef with truffle sauce, filet mignon with crab imperial, and swordfish steak with shrimp butter. On the first and third Wednesday of each month high tea is served. Entertainment Thursday through Saturday. Sunday brunch. | 10710 Falls Rd., Potomac | 301/983–8838 | Closed Mon. | $14–$32 | AE, D, MC, V.

Old Angler's Inn. Contemporary. This relaxed dining spot has English country elegance. A slate terrace with a fountain and small waterfall overlooking a wooded area provides a lovely outdoor dining experience. Specialties range from Maryland softshell crabs with local corn to organic rib-eye with black truffles. | 10801 MacArthur Blvd., Potomac | 301/299–9097 | Reservations essential Fri.–Sat. | Closed Mon. | $23–$32 | AE, DC, MC, V.

Red, Hot and Blue. American. A Memphis theme permeates the dining room, thanks to the blues memorabilia and Elvis records everywhere. Memphis-style barbecue, served as a pork sandwich and as ribs, is on the menu. A small deck out back, dressed up with a few plants, provides open-air dining. Kids' menu. | 16811 Crabbs Branch Way | 301/948–7333 | $12–$17 | AE, MC, V.

Seven Seas. Pan Asian. Though traditional Chinese wall ornaments dominate this restaurant, both Japanese and Chinese cuisine are on the menu. Try the chicken, beef, and shrimp dishes, or sample the sushi and sashimi. | 1776 E. Jefferson St. | 301/770–5020 | $10–$25 | AE, D, MC, V.

Silver Diner. American. You can do more than just eat in this classic diner. Take a lesson in the history of diners in America from the murals on the wall. Though typical favorites such as shakes and malts are on the menu, some dishes, such as the Cajun chicken, are decidedly more upscale. Kids' menu. Early-bird supper. | 11806 Rockville Pike (Rte. 355) | 301/770–4166 | $7–$15 | AE, D, DC, MC, V.

Taste of Saigon. Vietnamese. This stylish dining room is trimmed with black lacquer, marble and glass. Whole fish bathed in spices and scallions, various soups, and stir fries are on the menu. Outdoor patio with umbrellas. | 410 Hungerford Dr. | 301/424–7222 | $11–$18 | AE, D, DC, MC, V.

That's Amore. Italian. Low ceilings and low lighting hang over a collection of family photos and famous Italian-Americans. Menu favorites include fried calamari and spicy grilled sausage. | 15201 Shady Grove Rd. | 301/670–9666 | $10–$30 | AE, D, DC, MC, V.

Wurzburg Haus. German. Mirrors do their best to brighten the dark beer-hall look of this place, and paintings of German towns add a touch of authenticity. Patrons come here for the wienerschnitzel, sausage platters, Black Forest chicken, and, of course, German draft beers. An accordionist livens up the place on Friday and Saturday. Oktoberfest celebration. Kids' menu. Beer and wine only. | 7236 Muncaster Mill Rd. | 301/330–0402 | $9–$16 | AE, D, DC, MC, V.

Lodging

Best Western Inn. Guest rooms in this salmon-colored brick building on the outskirts of town have large work spaces designed for business travelers. It is about 15 mi from Washington, DC. Pool, exercise equipment. Cable TV, in-room data ports. Business services. | 1251 W. Montgomery Ave. | 301/424–4940 | 162 rooms | $60–$115 | AE, D, DC, MC, V.

Courtyard by Marriott–Rockville. Just off Rte. 355 in an office park, this hotel is convenient to shopping centers and restaurants. Its small rooms have contemporary furnishings. | 147 rooms, 13 suites. Restaurant, bar. In-room data ports, room service, cable TV. Indoor pool. Hot tub. Exercise equipment. Laundry facilities. Business services. | 2500 Research Blvd. | 301/670–6700 | fax 301/670–9023 | www.marriott.com | $79–$129, $89–$139 suites | AE, D, DC, MC, V.

Doubletree. The eight-story atrium is the highlight of this hotel, an additional complement to its rooms with Victorian reproductions. The hotel is adjacent to a Metro stop. | 315 rooms. Restaurant, bar. In-room data ports, refrigerators, cable TV. Indoor pool. Beauty salon, hot tub. Exercise equipment. Video games. Business services. | 1750 Rockville Pike (Rte. 355) | 301/468–1100 | fax 301/468–0163 | www.doubletree.com | $89–$169 | AE, D, DC, MC, V.

Quality Suites. This three-story hotel surrounds a garden and atrium. Two miles from a D.C. Metro stop, it is also convenient to restaurants, stores, and a mall. | 127 units. Complimentary breakfast. In-room data ports, some kitchenettes, refrigerators, cable TV. Pool. Exercise equipment. Laundry facilities. Business services, free parking. | 3 Research Ct. | 301/840–0200 | fax 301/258–0160 | www.qualityinns.com | $109–$159 | AE, D, DC, MC, V.

Ramada Inn. This inn is just 2 blocks from a Metro stop, making it only about 30 minutes from the nation's capital by public transportation. The seven-story hotel has an unremarkable brick facade resembling an office building. The interior is cozy, however, with brightly colored spreads and window treatments in spacious, well-lit guest rooms. Cable TV, refrigerators. Free parking. | 1775 Rockville Pike | 301/881–2300 | fax 301/881–9047 | 160 rooms, 4 suites | $65–$120 | AE, D, DC, MC, V.

Woodfin Suites. Tucked in an office park near I–270, this hotel is 1 mi from D.C. Nearby, there's a Metro stop, restaurants, stores, and theaters. Three floors overlook an open lobby with country furnishings and a fireplace. | 203 suites. Restaurant, bar, complimentary breakfast. In-room data ports, refrigerators, cable TV. Pool. Hot tub. Exercise equipment. Business services. | 1380 Piccard Dr. | 301/590–9880 or 800/237–8811 | fax 301/590–9614 | www.woodfinsuitehotels.com | $89–$159 | AE, D, DC, MC, V.

ST. MARYS CITY

MAP 4, F5

(Nearby towns also listed: Leonardtown, Waldorf, Washington, D.C.)

Every Maryland school kid learns that St. Marys was the first state capital and one of the first permanent settlements in the English colony. The original St. Marys is being painstakingly re-created on the shores of the Patuxent River as a living history museum. St. Marys is home to St. Mary's College, a state-supported liberal arts institution, and of the finish line of the Governor's Cup, the largest overnight race on the East Coast.

Information: St. Marys County Division of Travel and Tourism | Box 653, Governmental Center, Washington St., 2nd floor, Leonardtown, MD 20650 | 301/475–4411 or 800/327–9023 | www.co.saint-marys.md.us.

Attractions

★ **Historic St. Marys City.** Several notable buildings, like the State House of 1676, have been restored or re-created as part of this living history museum dedicated to 17th century life in Maryland's birthplace. | Rte. 5 and Rosecroft Rd. | 301/862–0990 or 800/SMC–1634 | www.smcm.edu/hsmc/ | $7.50 | Late Mar.–late Nov., Wed.–Sun. 10–5, closed Mon.–Tues.

Leonard Calvert Monument. This obelisk in Trinity Episcopal Church cemetery celebrates the vision of religious tolerance advocated by Maryland's first governor, Leonard Calvert. | Off Rte. 5 S | 301/862–4597 | Free | Daily.

Margaret Brent Memorial. A gazebo and gardens make up this memorial to Mistress Margaret Brent, who requested the right to vote nearly three centuries before American women received suffrage. | Rte. 5, at Rosecroft Rd. | Daily.

Point Lookout State Park. Site of a Union prison during the Civil War, the park is at the end of a scenic peninsula and is a popular area for boating, fishing, hiking, and camping. | Rte. 5 | 301/872–5688 | www.dnr.state.md.us | $3 weekends | Daily dawn–dusk; camping Apr.–Oct. | 301/872–5688.

St. Mary's College. This four-year, coeducational school is home to a diverse student body of more than 6,000 graduate and undergraduate students. The college hosts dozens of special events each year from concerts to lecture series. The campus is composed of modern brick buildings separated by wide, grassy lawns and shade trees. | 18952 E. Fisher Rd. | 301/862–0200 | Free.

ON THE CALENDAR

OCT.: *Grand Militia Muster.* Each fall, Revolutionary War re-enactors gather to compete in skills such as muzzle-loading and sharpshooting. You can wander through the Living History Encampment, sample Colonial-era camp cooking, and purchase period crafts from artisans and merchants. One highlight is the recreation of the Revolutionary War's Battle of Severn.

Dining

Aloha. Pan Asian. The Aloha has traditional Oriental trimmings like hanging lanterns. Try the sizzling scallop and shrimp with vegetables and a brown sauce.Sunday buffet. Sushi bar. Kids' menu. | 23415 Wildewood Center, California | 301/862–4838 | $7–$13 | AE, D, MC, V.

Broome-Howard Inn. Continental. Two intimate dining areas—one in the formal parlor and one in the foyer—make up this elegant, 19th century-style restaurant. Fine crystal and white linens adorn antique tables. The kitchen produces tasty dishes, often using unexpected or unorthodox ingredients. For example, you may want to try the lean and juicy grilled bison seasoned with cracked black peppercorns. | 18281 Rosecroft Rd. | 301/866–0656 | Reservations essential | No lunch | $15–$30 | AE, D, MC, V.

Evans Seafood. Seafood. Pictures of oystermen at work and old crab traps pack this bar and restaurant overlooking both the Potomac and St. Marys rivers. Choose any seat downstairs; they all face the water. Upstairs has an outdoor deck. Try the crab cakes. Kids' menu. | 16680 Piney Point Rd., St. George Island, Piney Point | 301/994–2299 | Closed Mon. No lunch | $9–$30 | MC, V.

Lodging

Best Western. Despite its dull exterior, the burgundy-and-green lobby is surprisingly cozy inside, with coffee brewing throughout the day. It's about 15 minutes from St. Marys City. | 120 rooms. Complimentary Continental breakfast. In-room data ports, some refrigerators, cable TV. Pool, tennis courts. Laundry facilities. Business services. | 22769 Three Notch Rd., California | 301/862–4100 | fax 301/862–4673 | www.bestwestern.com | $79 | AE, D, DC, MC, V.

Broome-Howard Inn. This elegant Victorian home sits on 30 acres of manicured grounds and gardens. The 19th-century house was once part of a tobacco plantation. Guest rooms are decorated with original family furnishings. Big porches and a patio provide you with quiet space for relaxing and gazing at the St. Marys River, which flows past not 200 feet away. The inn's grounds are crisscrossed with hiking trails, and there are bicycles you can use to explore the surrounding countryside. Cable TV, hiking, bicycling. | 18281 Rosecroft Rd. | 301/866–0656 | 3 rooms, 1 suite | $95–$160 | AE, D, MC, V.

Days Inn. Rooms are standard, and the lobby is filled with plants. There's a movie theater next door, and shops in walking distance. | 165 rooms. Complimentary Continental breakfast. Refrigerators, cable TV. Pool. Laundry facilities. Some pets allowed. | 21847 Three Notch Rd., Lexington Park; Rte. 235 | 301/863–6666 | fax 301/863–4691 | www.daysinn.com | $67–$71 | AE, D, DC, MC, V.

ST. MICHAELS

MAP 4, G4

(Nearby towns also listed: Annapolis, Easton, Oxford)

Today one of the Eastern Shore's most popular sailing destinations, St. Michaels made its name first in 1778 as a shipbuilding center. The town, which is surrounded by tributaries of the Chesapeake Bay, came under attack during the War of 1812, and in one battle, residents diverted British fire by adroitly placing lanterns in the fog. The aptly named Cannonball House, was struck during the shelling. Built in 1805, the house is private, but you can see it from the outside, as you can other historic Federal-period houses dating to the early 1800s. Specialty shops, restaurants, and small museums line the streets, and a steamboat wharf and canning plant at Navy Point have been turned into the impressive Chesapeake Maritime Museum.

Information: Talbot County Conference and Visitors Bureau | 210 Marlboro Ave., Suite 3, Easton, MD 21601-1366 | 410/822–4606 or 888/BAY–STAY | www.talbotcounty.md.

Attractions

★ **Chesapeake Bay Maritime Museum.** A complex of 10 buildings on 17 acres contains the history of the bay and its boat-building traditions. Exhibits include a restored skipjack and a racing log canoe. | Navy Point, Mill St. | 410/745–2916 | www.cbmm.org | $7.50 | Apr.–May. and Sept.–Oct. daily 9–5; June–Aug. daily 9–6; Nov.–Feb. daily 9–4.

Country Comfort Farm. At this equine center, you can ride a horse, take riding lessons or stable your own horse. The farm maintains indoor and outdoor arenas augmented by 70 acres of wooded countryside for trail riding. The experienced staff is on hand to instruct and act as guides. | 23720 St. Michaels Rd. | 410/745–3160 | Varies | Mon.–Fri. 9–6.

The Footbridge. The one remaining footbridge of three that once connected Navy Point and Cherry Street. It provided the only link between the town and the harbor. | Navy Point, at Cherry St. | Free | Daily.

The *Patriot*. Narrated cruises of the Miles River depart from the Chesapeake Bay Maritime Museum. | Navy Point, Mill St. | 410/745–3100 | $9.50 | Apr.–Oct., departs 11, 12:30, 2:30, 4.

St. Mary's Square. Originally laid out along with the town in 1778, the square once contained a public market house, which stored the guns and cannons used in the Battle of St. Michaels. | Free | Daily.

St. Mary's Square Museum. Local historical artifacts include a shipyard bell that still rings at the start of the work day, at lunch, and at quitting time. | St. Mary's Square | 410/745–9561 | Free | May–Oct., weekends 10–4; closed weekdays.

ON THE CALENDAR

AUG.: *Crab Days*. This event, held at the Chesapeake Maritime Museum, is a weekend-long bash to honor the Maryland blue crab. Experience chicken-necking and trot-lining, and bet on your favorite crustacean in a crab race. The festival also includes live music, boat rides, kid's activities, and—of course—mountains of crabcakes. | Navy Point, Mills Rd. | 410/745–2916.

Dining

★ **208 Talbot.** Continental. Built in 1870, the restaurant still serves food in its original brick building, now comprised of four antique-filled dining rooms. Try the oysters with prosciutto, pistachios, and champagne cream sauce and the crispy soft shell crabs with green tomato butter, green beans and corn. | 208 N. Talbot St. | 410/745–3838 | Reservations essential weekends | Closed Mon.–Tues. | $23–$29 | D, MC, V.

Ashley Room. Continental. If the Laura Ashley trimmings views aren't to your taste, console yourself with the waterfront views while you munch on a crab spring roll filled with pink grapefruit, avocado, and toasted almonds. For dinner try the honey-and-tarragon glazed shank of lamb served with sun-dried tomato sauce. A prix-fixe menu changes daily, and all spices come straight from the herb garden out back. | 308 Watkins La. | 410/745–2200 or 800/722–2949 | $70 | AE, DC, MC, V.

Harbour Lights. Seafood. Blonde wood paneling and captain's chairs give a bright, contemporary look to this nautically themed restaurant. Big windows and an outdoor deck provide an excellent view of activity in the marina below. Specialties include onion-encrusted rockfish, diver scallops, and medallions of venison. | 101 N. Harbor Rd. | 410/745–5102 | Reservations recommended | $12–$25 | AE, DC, MC, V.

St. Michaels Crab House. Seafood. A typical Maryland crab house, this restaurant built in the 1830s overlooks the harbor. Sit on the patio (built of bricks kilned in the 1880s), and get messy on steamed crabs. Kids' menu. | 305 Mulberry St. | 410/745–3737 | www.stmichaelscrabhouse.com | Closed mid-Dec.–mid-Mar. | $10–$19 | D, MC, V.

Town Dock. American. The only wall here is the one separating the kitchen from the dining room. Glass panels give every seat a view of the water—where most of the fish at your table was caught. Specialties include a local rock fish topped with sauteed shrimp and green tomato piccalilli. Kids' menu. Sunday brunch. | 125 Mulberry St. | 410/745–5577 | Closed Jan.–Mar., Tues.–Wed. | $18–$24 | AE, D, DC, MC.

Lodging

Best Western. On the main road to St. Michaels, 1 mi south of the harbor, the hotel occupies a former colonial private home. | 93 rooms. Complimentary Continental breakfast. Cable TV. 2 pools. Business services. | 1228 S. Talbot St. (Rte. 33) | 410/745–3333 | fax 410/745–2906 | www.bestwestern.com | $98–$125 | AE, D, DC, MC, V.

Harbourtowne. About 1½ miles outside town, at the mouth of the Miles River, each room at this modern hotel has a waterfront view. | 111 rooms. Restaurant. In-room data ports, cable TV. Pool. Driving range, 18-hole golf course, putting green, tennis courts. Exercise equipment, paddle boats, bicycles. Business services. | Rte. 33, Miles River | 410/745–9066 or 800/446–9066 | fax 410/745–9124 | www.harbourtowne.com | $169–$259 | AE, D, DC, MC, V.

Harris Cove Cottages. Billed as a "Bed & Boat" rather than a "Bed & Breakfast," this lodging is actually a collection of six small efficiencies ranged along a stretch of wooded waterfront property. The cottages are charming and spotless, surrounded by picnic tables, a screened gazebo, and comfortable lounge furniture. This is a non-fussy, non-pampering place to stay. You can cook your own fish and crabs on outdoor grills, play horseshoes on the lawn or fish in the cove off nearby Harris Creek. Fishing, swimming, boating. | 8080 Bozman-Neavitt Rd. (Rte. 579) | 410/745–9701 | 6 cottages | $125–$175 | No credit cards.

★ **Inn at Perry Cabin.** Built right after the War of 1812, this white colonial mansion is perched on the banks of the Miles River. Each room is distinct. Some have Laura Ashley fabrics and wallpaper, while others are furnished with English and early-American antiques. The hotel gets its name from Commodore Oliver Hazard Perry, the War of 1812 veteran who designed it after his own cabin on the USS Niagara. | 35 rooms, 6 suites. Restaurant, complimentary breakfast, afternoon tea, room service. In-room data ports, cable TV. Pool. Hot tub, sauna, massage. Tennis courts. Exercise equipment. No kids under 10. Some pets allowed. Business services, free parking. | 308 Watkins La. | 410/745–2200 or 800/722–2949 | fax 410/745–3348 | www.perrycabin.com | $295–$795 | AE, DC, MC, V.

Parsonage Inn. This 1883 brick Victorian inn at the colonial seaport has nine rooms, all decorated differently with country floral patterns and Queen Anne reproductions. | 8 rooms, 1 suite. Complimentary breakfast. No room phones, TV in sitting room and in 2 guest rooms. | 210 N. Talbot St. | 410/745–5519 or 800/394–5519 | fax 410/745–6869 | www.bestinns.net/usa/md/parsonage | $100–$185 | MC, V.

St. Michaels Harbour Inn and Marina. A favorite of bay boaters, this Victorian inn has paneled and wallpapered walls and rooms with large windows. Picnic tables and a 60-slip marina provide ample outdoor diversions. | 46 rooms, 38 suites. Restaurant, bar. Refrigerators in suites, cable TV. Pool. Hot tub. Exercise equipment. Laundry facilities. Business services. | 101 N. Harbor Rd. | 410/745–9001 or 800/955–9001 | fax 410/745–9150 | www.harbourinn.com | $189–$339 | AE, D, DC, MC, V.

Tilghman Island Inn. In a quiet residential neighborhood at the confluence of the Chesapeake Bay and the Choptank River, this inn offers a charming setting and loads of activities. Explore the area by boat or join your fellow guests in a rousing game of horseshoes on the back lawn. The inn provides bicycles for the quiet roads surrounding the property. It is furnished in a comfortable, contemporary style, with the emphasis on relaxation rather than a lot of fussy antiques. The inn's kitchen has received numerous awards for its culinary efforts, and its wine list is extensive. | 20 rooms. Pool. Tennis. Fishing, boating, biking, hiking, croquet. | 21384 Coopertown Rd. | 410/886–2141 | $130–$210 | AE, D, DC, MC, V.

Victoriana Inn. An old four-story house with a mansard roof, this inn is right on the harbor, across the footbridge from the Maritime Museum. The sloping lawns are punctuated with well-tended gardens and dotted with Adirondack chairs. Rooms have four-poster beds, handwoven rugs, and late-18th and early-19th century antiques. Some have fireplaces. | 5 rooms. Cable TV. | 205 Cherry St. | 410/745–3368 | $169–$189 | No credit cards.

Wades Point Inn on the Bay. Rooms in each of the three buildings are decorated differently. The modern "Mildred T. Kemp" annex, named after the B&B's original owner, has private porches and waterfront views; in the "Country Farm House," rooms are appropriately rustic, and some have four-poster beds. | 24 rooms. Complimentary Continental breakfast. Some kitchenettes, no room phones, TV in common area. No smoking. | End of Wades Point Rd., McDaniel | 410/745–2500 or 888/923–3466 | fax 410/745–3443 | www.wadespoint.com | $115–$230 | MC, V.

SALISBURY

MAP 4, H5

(Nearby towns also listed: Berlin, Cambridge, Ocean City, Snow Hill)

As the largest Maryland city on the Eastern Shore (population 20,000), Salisbury has become a bustling highway community, with shopping centers, malls, fast-food restaurants, and discount retailers along U.S. 50 and its major arteries. Primarily an industrial city, Salisbury has a 6-block historic district with Victorian homes; a brochure with a walking tour is available. The city has a small zoo and an impressive museum dedicated to wildfowl art.

Information: Wicomico Convention and Visitor Bureau | 8480 Ocean Hwy., Delmar, MD 21875 | 410/548–4914 or 800/332–TOUR.

Attractions

Mason-Dixon Line Marker. Built between 1763 and 1767, this crown stone marker, made in England, marks the line separating the southern and northern United States, as well as the borders of Maryland and Delaware. | Rte. 54 near Mardela Springs | Free | Daily.

Poplar Hill Mansion. Built in 1805, and one of the few structures to survive a fire in 1886, this Federal house has a large Palladian window and a 12-foot wide arched front hallway. | 117 Elizabeth St. | 410/749–1776 | $1.50 | Sun. 1–4, closed Mon.–Sat.

Princess Anne. Settled in the early 18th century, this town is named after the eldest daughter of King George II. The historic district has many elegant 18th- and 19th-century homes along its tree-lined streets. Tunstall Cottage, built in 1755, is the oldest existing house in town; Teackle Mansion is the grandest home, built in 1802. | 14 mi south of Salisbury on Rte. 13.

Salisbury State University. This is a four-year, liberal-arts university that is home to some 6,000 students from around the country and all over the world. Established in 1922, the school's 20 or so buildings—a few dating back to the university's founding—are arranged around well-maintained grounds. | 1101 Camden Ave. | 410/543–6000.

Salisbury Zoological Park. The 12-acre park has animals native to Maryland, in addition to monkeys, prairie dogs, lions, panthers, alligators, and bison. | 750 S. Park Dr. | 410/548–

3188 | www.salisburyzoo.org | Free | Memorial Day–Labor Day, 8–7:30; Labor Day–Memorial Day, weekdays 8–4:30, weekends 8–7.

★ **Ward Museum of Wildfowl Art.** Learn all about the history of decoy carving, and tour a re-created studio of the Ward brothers, the first people to bridge the gap between hunter and artist. | 909 S. Schumaker Dr. | 410/742–4988 | www.wardmuseum.org | $7 | Mon.–Sat. 10–5, Sun. noon–5.

ON THE CALENDAR

MAY: *Dogwood Festival.* Held each year on the downtown plaza in conjunction with the blooming of the area's dogwood trees, this festival features craft merchants, food booths, a carnival and an antique car show. The weekend culminates with a city-wide block party with live music and much food and drink. | 410/749–0144.

Dining

Golden Dragon. Chinese. Fans, small lanterns and the odd smiling Buddha give this place a generic Chinese-restaurant look. However, the food at the Golden Dragon is not run of the mill. Try the chicken-fried rice, which is refreshingly non-greasy, or the moo goo gai pan, with crunchy greens and savory mushrooms. Finish off with a hot cup of jasmine tea. | 1314 S. Salisbury Blvd. | 410/742–7087 | $5–$10 | AE, D, MC, V.

Legends. American/Casual. Festooned with NFL, NBA and baseball pennants and other sports memorabilia, this downtown sports bar and grill has multiple television screens. Food here is what you might expect and then some—thick, juicy burgers, prime rib and other hearty fare. The hot buffalo wings are also popular. | Salisbury Downtown Plaza | 410/742–7087 | $6–$15 | AE, D, MC, V.

Lombardi's Pizza. Italian. The oldest continuously operating restaurant in town, this place has a big, family-friendly dining area decked out in red, white and green. Pictures of Italian landmarks hang on the walls. Lombardi's specialty is authentic, stone-baked pizza. They also make strombolis big enough to share. | 315 Civil Ave. | 410/749–0522 | $5–$12 | AE, D, MC, V.

Lodging

Comfort Inn. On the main road through the Delmarva Peninsula, this landscaped hotel is surrounded by shops and restaurants. | 96 rooms, 34 suites. Complimentary Continental breakfast. Some refrigerators, cable TV. Business services. Some pets allowed. | 2701 N. Salisbury Blvd. (U.S. 13) | 410/543–4666 | fax 410/749–2639 | www.comfortinn.com | $70–$140 | AE, D, DC, MC, V.

Days Inn. Rooms are basic, and each has an outdoor entrance on the first or second floor. | 100 rooms. Complimentary Continental breakfast. Cable TV. Pool. Business services. | 2525 N. Salisbury Blvd. (U.S. 13) | 410/749–6200 | fax 410/749–7378 | www.daysinn.com | $89–$139 | AE, D, DC, MC, V.

Howard Johnson. On busy U.S. 13, minutes from The Centre at Salisbury mall, this motel has standard rooms. | 123 rooms. Restaurant, complimentary Continental breakfast. Cable TV. Pool. Laundry facilities. Business services. Some pets allowed. | 2625 N. Salisbury Blvd. (U.S. 13) | 410/742–7194 | fax 410/742–5194 | www.hojosalisbury.com | $65–$120 | AE, D, DC, MC, V.

Ramada Inn and Conference Center. Pillars and a lobby piano uplift the otherwise chain-hotel atmosphere of this hotel, a two-minute drive from Salisbury State University. | 156 rooms. Restaurant, bar, room service. In-room data ports, cable TV. Indoor pool. Exercise equipment. Business services, airport shuttle. | 300 S. Salisbury Blvd. (U.S 13B) | 410/546–4400 | fax 410/546–2528 | www.ramadasalisbury.com | $120–$145 | AE, D, DC, MC, V.

SHARPSBURG

(Nearby towns also listed: Boonsboro, Frederick, Hagerstown, Thurmont)

As the site of the Battle of Antietam, Sharpsburg is an important stop for Civil War buffs. On September 17, 1862 more than 23,000 were killed or wounded in the woods north and east of Sharpsburg. It would come to be known as the bloodiest single day of the war. Following the Union victory at Antietam, President Abraham Lincoln issued the Emancipation Proclamation, freeing all slaves in the Confederacy and infusing the Union's cause with moral power. The remains of 4,776 Union soldiers, including 1,836 unknown, are buried in Antietam National Cemetery in town. Most of the Confederate dead are buried in nearby towns like Frederick and Hagerstown.

Information: Hagerstown/Washington County Convention and Visitors Bureau | 16 Public Square, Hagerstown, MD 21740 | 301/791–3246 or 800/228–STAY | www.maryland-memories.org.

Attractions

★ **Antietam National Battlefield.** The corn fields and woods surrounding Sharpsburg were the site of the bloodiest single day of the Civil War. Landmarks include Burnside Bridge, Dunkard Church, and Bloody Lane. | Sharpsburg Pike (Rte. 65), 10 mi south of I–70 | 301/432–5124 | www.nps.gov/anti | $2 | Sept.–May 8:30–5, June–Aug. 8:30–6.

ON THE CALENDAR
JULY: *Salute to Independence.* Cannon fire and fireworks highlight the annual Independence Day performance by the Maryland Symphony Orchestra at Antietam National Battlefield in the woods north and east of Sharpsburg. | 301/797–4000.
SEPT.: *Sharpsburg Heritage Festival.* This quintessential Civil War festival on the town's Main Street includes battle reenactments, walking tours, workshops, and military band concerts. | Weekend closest to Sept. 17 | 800/228–7829 | www.nps.gov/anti.

Dining
Red Byrd Restaurant. American. The kitschy but charming dining area hasn't changed a bit since the '50s. Old photos line the walls above booths and tables. Dinner offerings include country-style ham steak, grilled liver, and homemade pie. | Hwy. 34, 1 mi north of Sharpsburg | 301/791–5915 | $4–$8 | MC, V.

Lodging
Ground Squirrel Holler. On the main road to the Antietam, the inn is surrounded by shade trees and flower gardens. The pottery-filled lobby has a tin ceiling. | 3 rooms. Complimentary Continental breakfast. | 6735 Sharpsburg Pike (Rte. 65) | 301/432–8288 | $70–$80 | No credit cards.

Jacob Rohrbach Inn. This pale-yellow, three-story Victorian home is 1 1/2 mi from Antietam National Park. The guest rooms in the 1830 inn are furnished with period antiques. The largest one was once a ballroom; others have porches or sitting rooms. | 4 rooms (2 with shared bath). Complimentary breakfast. No room phones. Hot tub. No kids under 10. No smoking. | 138 W. Main St. | 301/432–5079 or 877/839–4242 | fax 413/473–1797 | www.jacob-rohrbach-inn.com | $75–$155 | MC, V.

SILVER SPRING

(Nearby towns also listed: Bethesda, Chevy Chase, Rockville, Washington, D.C.)

Just off the Washington Beltway, Silver Spring is one of the city's oldest suburbs. Easily accessible by Metro, its downtown area has plenty of restaurants and shops, and a few hotels. Silver Spring is home to the National Oceanic and Atmospheric Administration.

Information: Conference and Visitors Bureau of Montgomery County, Inc. | 12900 Middlebrook Rd., Suite 1400, Germantown, 20874 | 301/428–9702 or 800/925–0880.

Attractions

Brookside Gardens. Changing floral displays brighten 11 specialty gardens. There's also a conservatory, a Japanese tea house, and educational programs. | 1500 Glenallan Ave., Wheaton | 301/949–8230 | Free | Daily. Gardens dawn–dusk; conservatory 10–5.

National Capital Trolley Museum. The history of Washington streetcars is told here in story form, as well as with films and dioramas. Many of the 17 trolleys run on the 1-mi demonstration railway. | 1313 Bonifant Rd., Layhill | 301/384–6088 | www.dctrolley.org | Free, trolley rides $2.50 | Jan.–Nov. weekends noon–5; Dec. noon–9, call for weekday hrs.

Silver Spring Stage. Occupying the lower level of a shopping center, this theater gives aspiring local actors a chance to take the stage. The group performs a wide range of dramatic

USEFUL EXTRAS YOU MAY WANT TO PACK

- ❏ Adapters, converter
- ❏ Alarm clock
- ❏ Batteries
- ❏ Binoculars
- ❏ Blankets, pillows, sleeping bags
- ❏ Books and magazines
- ❏ Bottled water, soda
- ❏ Calculator
- ❏ Camera, lenses, film
- ❏ Can/bottle opener
- ❏ Cassette tapes, CDs, and players
- ❏ Cell phone
- ❏ Change purse with $10 in quarters, dimes, and nickels for tollbooths and parking meters
- ❏ Citronella candle
- ❏ Compass
- ❏ Earplugs
- ❏ Flashlight
- ❏ Folding chairs
- ❏ Guidebooks
- ❏ Luggage tags and locks
- ❏ Maps
- ❏ Matches
- ❏ Money belt
- ❏ Pens, pencils
- ❏ Plastic trash bags
- ❏ Portable TV
- ❏ Radio
- ❏ Self-seal plastic bags
- ❏ Snack foods
- ❏ Spare set of keys, not carried by driver
- ❏ Travel iron
- ❏ Travel journal
- ❏ Video recorder, blank tapes
- ❏ Water bottle
- ❏ Water-purification tablets

and musical works each year. | 10145 Colesville Rd. | 301/593–6036 | Varies | Call for performance schedule.

ON THE CALENDAR
JUNE: *Ethnic Heritage Festival and Taste of Silver Spring.* Townsfolk dedicate this weekend to celebrate their cultural diversity at this event in downtown's Jessup Blair Park. Music, dance, international food, and sales of traditional arts and crafts from around the world are all part of the fun. | 301/565–7300.

Dining

Blair Mansion Inn. Continental/American. This antique-filled Victorian mansion hosts a murder-mystery dinner on the weekends. Its imperial crab is a popular dish. | 7711 Eastern Ave. | 301/588–1688 | Closed Mon. | $10–$20 | AE, D, DC, MC, V.

Crisfield at Lee Plaza. American. You'll know you're in Maryland as you dine among the Chesapeake Bay pictures and decoys lining the walls. Try the baked stuffed shrimp. Kids' menu. | 8606 Colesville Rd. (U.S. 29) | 301/588–1572 | Reservations recommended Fri.–Sat. | $13–$25 | AE, D, DC, MC, V.

Mrs. K's Toll House. American. Built in 1850, this antique-filled eatery was Montgomery County's last-operating toll house. Mrs. K's specialties include angel hair pasta tossed in a light cream sauce with shrimp and andouille sausage, and shrimp with tomatoes and feta cheese over tri-color orzo. Sunday brunch. | 9201 Colesville Rd. (U.S. 29) | 301/589–3500 | Closed Mon. | $20–33 | AE, D, DC, MC, V.

Tastee Diner. American. A local favorite, this classic steel-and-vinyl diner is friendly and casual, with intimate booths and a long lunch counter. The food is homey fare—juicy burgers, old-fashioned meatloaf with mashed potatoes, and oven-fresh pie—and you can't beat the price. | 8516 Georgia Ave. | 301/589–8171 | $3–$6 | AE, MC, V.

Vicino. Italian. This casual, mid-size restaurant serves a variety of homemade raviolis, filled with anything from portobella mushrooms, to sun-dried tomatoes, to spinach. Eat outside on a patio overlooking the gardens. Kids' menu. Beer and wine only. | 959 Sligo Ave. | 301/588–3372 | $6–$17 | AE, MC, V.

Lodging

Courtyard by Marriott. A courtyard with gazebos and gardens offsets the hotel's otherwise drab commercial park setting. Rooms are basic and comfortable. | 146 rooms, 12 suites. Restaurant, bar. In-room data ports, some refrigerators, cable TV. Indoor pool. Hot tub. Exercise equipment. Laundry facilities. Business services. Free parking. | 12521 Prosperity Dr. | 301/680–8500 | fax 301/680–9232 | www.marriott.com | $129–$169 | AE, D, DC, MC, V.

Town Center Hotel. Marble and mahogany make for an elegant lobby, but rooms are more basic and contemporary, with modular furnishings and big desks. Mere blocks from downtown and a Metro stop, this hotel's location is its key asset. | 228 rooms, 28 suites. 2 restaurants, bar, room service. Cable TV. Indoor pool, sauna, exercise room. | 8727 Colesville Rd. | 301/589–5200 | $104–$124 | AE, D, DC, MC, V.

SNOW HILL

MAP 4, H5

(Nearby towns also listed: Berlin, Ocean City, Pocomoke City)

Although it's nothing like its glory days as a shipping center in the 18th and 19th centuries, Snow Hill still welcomes floating vessels. These days, cruiseships and canoes sail up and down the Pocomoke River all summer. The 300-year old town has brick sidewalks, tree-lined streets, and a small historic district, with more than 100 homes built a century ago. Two small museums depict life in bygone times, and nearby Furnace Town recreates a 19th-century industrial village.

Information: Worcester County Tourism | 105 Pearl St., Snow Hill, MD 21863 | 410/632–3617 or 800/852–0335.

Attractions

Furnace Town. The recreated 19th-century industrial village recalls the years 1820–1870, when the Nassawango Iron Furnace was the town's number one employer. The village has a blacksmith shop, smokehouse, print shop, broom house, church, and the Paul Leifer Nature Trail. | Old Furnace Rd. | 410/632–2032 | www.dol.net/~ebola/ftown.htm | $3 | Apr.–Oct., daily 11–5.

Pocomoke Cypress Swamp. This swamp within the Pocomoke River State Forest and Park is home to many bird species, including screech owls, red tail hawks, great horned owls, and a growing population of bald eagles. It's 4 mi south of Snow Hill and 30 mi south of Ocean City. | 3461 Worcester Hwy. (U.S. 113), Snow Hill | 410/632–2566 | Free | Daily dawn–dusk.

Pocomoke River Canoe Company. Rent a canoe or kayak and paddle the calm, cypress swamps of the Pocomoke River and Nassawango Creek. | 312 N. Washington St. | 410/632–3971 | www.atbeach.com/amuse/md/canoe | Weekdays $35 canoe, $30 kayak per day; $50 canoe and $40 kayak per weekend. Shuttle-service rates vary | Apr.–Nov., daily.

Pocomoke River State Forest and Park. Meandering through thick cypress swamps, the Pocomoke River has only a few access points. One of the easiest to find is at this state park's Shad Landing, which has campsites, a marina, hiking trails, and rowboat and canoe rentals. Farther downriver, Milburn Landing also has camping and a launching ramp. | 3461 Worcester Hwy. (U.S. 113) | 410/632–2566 | www.dnr.state.md.us/publiclands/eastern/pocomokeriver.html | Daily.

ON THE CALENDAR

AUG: *Worcester County Fair.* The fun at this old-fashioned county fair at Furnace Town includes live music, kids' activities, livestock, craft vendors, business and organization exhibits, and lots of tasty food. | 410/632–2032.

Dining

Snow Hill Inn and Restaurant. American. Low lighting and a laid-back attitude make this eatery in the heart of Snow Hill a relaxed spot for can't-miss favorites like burgers, steaks, and prime rib. | 104 E. Market St. | 410/632–2102 | $12–$20 | AE, DC, MC, V.

Lodging

The Mansion House. You won't find lace doilies and other fussy knickknacks at this unpretentious 1835 B&B. All rooms have stone fireplaces, and most also have splendid views of Chincoteague Bay. Launch your kayak from the private pier, or bird-watch on the large front porch while enjoying afternoon refreshments. Pets and kids welcome by prior arrangement. | 4 rooms. Complimentary breakfast. No room phones. Hiking, boating. | 4436 Bayside Rd. | 410/632–3189 | fax 410/632–1980 | www.bestinns.net/usa/md/mansionhouse.html | $140–$160 | MC, V.

SOLOMONS

MAP 4, F5

(Nearby towns also listed: Leonardtown, St Marys City)

A popular sailing destination, Solomons extends across a tiny peninsula where the Patuxent River flows into the Chesapeake Bay. Marinas, B&Bs, restaurants, and boutiques dot the shoreline. The Calvert Marine Museum recounts the history of the area.

Information: Department of Economic Development | 175 Main St., Calvert County Courthouse, Prince Frederick, MD 20678 | 410/535–4583 or 800/331–9771.

Attractions

★ **Calvert Marine Museum.** Re-created blacksmith and ship's carpenter shops and the restored 1883 Drum Point Lighthouse host exhibits and artifacts that chronicle the history of the Chesapeake Bay and the Patuxent River. Kids' activities. | Rtes. 2/4, at Solomons Island Rd. | 410/326–2042 | www.calvertmarinemuseum.com | $5 | Daily 10–5.

Joseph C. Lore and Sons Oyster House. Formerly a seafood packinghouse, this museum, now on the National Register of Historic Places, houses tools and gear of the area's water trades. Find the boatbuilding exhibit on the second floor. | 14430 Solomon Island Rd. | 410/326–2878 | Free | Jun.–Aug. and for special occasions.

ON THE CALENDAR
SEPT.: *Artsfest*. This juried art show is held each year at the beautiful Annmarie Garden alongside St. John's Creek. Food, music, ballet performances, storytelling, and art demonstrations are all part of the event. | 410/326–4640.

Dining

CD Cafe. Eclectic. Overlooking the Patuxent River, this cozy bistro serves a limited but expertly prepared menu with inventive dishes such as pan-seared chicken breast with pecans, apples, onions, and Schnapps. Don't miss the freshly made desserts. | 14350 Solomons Island Rd. | 410/326–3877 | No lunch Mon. | $12–$20 | MC, V.

Lodging

Back Creek Inn. Built in 1880 at the creek's edge, the wood-frame inn is bright and airy, and furnished with antiques. You can make use of the boat slips to ply the creek. | 4 rooms, 2 suites. Complimentary breakfast. Hot tub. Bicycles. | 210 Alexander St. at Calvert St. | 410/326–2022 | fax 410/326–2946 | www.bbonline.com/md/backcreek | $95–$145 | AE, MC, V.

Holiday Inn Select. Every room in this five-story bayfront hotel has a water view—if you count the swimming pool. Rooms either face the courtyard, the bay, or the creek. All rooms have large desks and lots of natural light. Restaurant, 2 bars. In-room data ports, some in-room hot tubs, cable TV. Pool. Sauna. 2 tennis courts. Excercise equipment. | 155 Holiday Rd. | 410/326–6311 or 800/356–2009 | slmmd@olg.com | www.basshotels.com/holiday-inn | 326 rooms | $89–$149 | AE, D, DC, MC, V.

Solomons Victorian Inn. Period antiques fill this white wood-frame house built by a sea magnate in 1906. Rooms have views of either Solomon Harbor or the surrounding gardens. | 7 rooms, 1 suite. Complimentary breakfast, afternoon snacks. Some in-room hot tubs, room phones, cable TV. | 125 Charles St., at Maltby St. | 410/326–4811 | fax 410/326–0133 | www.chesapeake.net/solomonsvictorianinn | $90–$175 | AE, MC, V.

STEVENSVILLE

MAP 4, G3

(Nearby towns also listed: Annapolis, Grasonville)

Once a center of steamboat-related trade, Stevensville today is the largest town on Kent Island, the largest island in the Chesapeake Bay. The town is accessible by the twin-arched William Preston Lane Jr. Memorial Bridge. Though the town was founded in 1850, the island has been a thriving outpost since 1631, when it became the first permanent English settlement in Maryland. Stevensville's six-block historic district has 19th- and early 20th-century frame commercial buildings and bungalow homes. Along U.S. 50/301, you'll find restaurants, marina services, and stores.

Information: Queen Anne's County Office of Tourism | 425 Piney Narrows Rd., Chester, MD 21619 | 410/604–2100.

Attractions

Cray House. This wooden, gambrel-roof house built in 1809 is on the National Register of Historic Places. The rooms inside, with their unusual post-and-plank walls and period furnishings, offer a glimpse into upper-crust life in pre-Victorian Maryland. | Cockey's Ln. | 410/643–5969 | Free | May–October, Sat. 1–4 by appointment.

ON THE CALENDAR

MAY: *Kent Island Days.* This annual festival celebrates the history and industry of the region. Browse the food booths and arts-and-crafts exhibits, then tour the Cray House, the old Stevensville train depot, and the post office. Kids' activities are also scheduled. | 410/643–5969 | Free.

Dining

Tavern on the Bay. Seafood. The tavern has two dining areas: the cathedral-ceiling bar can become smoky and raucous on weekend nights, and the more formal, smoke-free dining room is set with linens and crystal. Menu highlights are the fresh lump crabmeat cakes and the hearty seafood pies. Try the one with oysters, shrimp, lobster, and scallops in a flaky, thyme-seasoned crust. | 500 Marina Club Rd. | 410/604–2188 | $15–$25 | D, MC, V.

Lodging

★ **Kent Manor Inn.** This Kent Island mansion, circa 1820, boasts lavish rooms with Italian marble baths, fireplaces, four-poster beds, private porches, and fresh flowers. Nature trails crisscross its 226 acres of manicured grounds, which slope gently into Thompson's Creek. | 24 rooms. Cable TV. Pool. Hiking, volleyball, boating. Laundry service. Business services. No pets. | 500 Kent Manor Dr. | 410/643–5757 | $130–$235 | AE, D, MC, V.

Stillwater Inn. This upscale B&B with breezy wraparound porches, polished pine floors, and crown molding was built in 1904. It's a pleasant stroll to the peaceful Queenstown Creek, where you can watch for wildlife or relax amid the tall grass. Complimentary breakfast. No room phones, no TV. Library. No kids under 12. No smoking. | 7109 Second Ave., Queenstown | 410/827–9362 | stillwtr@shore.intercom.net | www.bbonline.com/md/stillwater | 3 rooms | $100–$115 | MC, V.

TANEYTOWN

(Nearby towns also listed: Emmitsburg, Hagerstown, Thurmont, Westminster)

About an hour northwest of Baltimore, Taneytown sits amid the pastoral farmland of Carroll County. Founded in 1754, it's the oldest municipality in the county. A popular misconception is that the town was named after Roger Brooke Taney, the former Supreme Court chief who authored the controversial Dred Scott Decision before the Civil War. But the name actually comes from Raphael Taney, a resident of St. Mary's County who laid out plans for the town but never lived there. Five miles west of Taneytown lies Terra Rubra, the birthplace of Francis Scott Key, the author of "The Star-Spangled Banner." Key taught Sunday School in Taneytown.

Information: Carroll County Office of Tourism | 224 N. Center St., Room 100, Westminster, MD 21157 | 410/857–2983 or 800/272–1933.

Attractions

St. Joseph's Church. Built in 1764, this English-style wooden church with adjacent cemetery is one of the oldest in the state. | 44 Frederick St. | 410/756–2500 | Free | Daily.

ON THE CALENDAR

AUG.: *Celebrate Taneytown.* This weekend's festivities pays homage to the rich history of the area. The main event is a Civil War reenactment involving some 200 costumed participants and an Abraham Lincoln look-alike. In addition to the battle, there are Civil War–era crafts and food, a historical encampment, and lots of activities for kids. | 410/751–1100.

Dining

Antrim 1844. Continental. During the warmer months, dinner is served on the veranda. When the season turns chilly, dinner guests adjourn to a cozy building with a brick floor and large fireplaces. Dinner is usually six courses of dishes like a tulip stuffed with goat cheese served on brown butter spinach with a beet aioli or pheasant breast stuffed with spinach and pine nuts. | 30 Trevanion Rd. | 410/756–6812 or 800/858–1844 | Reservations essential | $55–$62 prix fixe | AE, D, DC, MC, V.

Bear Creek Inn. American. The dining room here is an eclectic blend of antiques, old signs, and bare wood. The basic, no-frills menu of roast chicken, steaks, crab cakes, and homemade desserts makes the inn a good option for families with finicky kids. | 5525 Taneytown Pike | 410/756–1503 | $11–$15 | MC, V.

Lodging

Antrim 1844. Once a sprawling 2,500-acre agriculture plantation, the 1844 manor house, now a B&B, sits on a mere 23 acres today. Rooms have amenities that include fireplaces, canopy feather beds, marble baths and double jacuzzis. | 22 rooms, 12 suites. Restaurant, bar, complimentary breakfast. No room phones. Pool. Some hot tubs. Putting green, tennis. Croquet. Business services. No smoking. | 30 Trevanion Rd. | 410/756–6812 or 800/858–1844 | fax 410/756–2744 | www.antrim1844.com | $225–$375 | AE, D, DC, MC, V.

THURMONT

MAP 4, E2

(Nearby towns also listed: Boonsboro, Frederick, Hagerstown, Sharpsburg)

Dubbed the "Gateway to the Mountains," Thurmont is the closest town to Camp David, the secluded presidential retreat in Catoctin Mountain Park that hosted the peace accords between Egypt and Israel in 1978. However, presidents staying at Camp David rarely venture into town. Also in the vicinity is Cunningham Falls State Park, a popular spot for hiking and camping. Thurmont is at the crossroads of Route 77 and U.S. 15, an intersection overflowing with shopping centers, motels, and restaurants.

Information: Tourism Council of Frederick County, Inc. | 19 E. Church St., Frederick, MD 21701 | 301/663–8687 or 800/999–3613.

Attractions

Catoctin Mountain Park. Rocky outcroppings, thick forests, scenic mountain vistas, and miles of hiking trails make this 6,000-acre national park a nature lover's dream. The park is also home to Camp David, the presidential retreat. The visitor center has a small wildlife museum and gift shop. Picnic and camping facilities are available. | Rte. 77, 3 mi west of Rte. 15 | 301/663–9330 | www.nps.gov/cato | Free | Weekdays 10–4:30, weekends 8:30–5.

Catoctin Wildlife Preserve and Zoo. More than 300 animals, including tigers, macaws, monkeys, and boas, live in this 26-acre zoo. Kids love the petting zoo and tree-lined winding paths. | 13019 Catoctin Furnace Rd. (Rte. 15) | 301/271–3180 | www.cwpzoo.com | $9.95 | Daily. May–Sept., 9–6; Apr., Oct., 10–5; March and Nov., 10–4; Closed Dec.–Feb.

Cunningham Falls State Park. Home to a 78-ft waterfall, Maryland's tallest, this state park is a favorite of daytrippers. In season, you can swim or boat in a man-made lake. Campsites are also available. | 14039 Catoctin Hollow Rd. at Rte. 77 | 301/271–7574 | www.dnr.state.md.us | $2 weekdays year-round; $3 weekends May–Sept. | Daily dawn–dusk.

ON THE CALENDAR
OCT.: *Boo in the Zoo*. Lights and luminaries lead the way to holiday activities for kids such as mask making, snake petting, and hayrides in this decidedly unscary event in the Catoctin Wildlife Preserve. | 301/271–4922 | $8.

Dining
Cozy. American. Tour-bus groups can fill up this cavernous restaurant with an all-you-can-eat buffet. Each of the themed dining areas—including the Presidential Room, the Old-Time Parlour Room, and the North and South Catoctin Rooms—have a fireplace and views of a fish pond. Kids' menu. | 105 Frederick Rd. (Rte. 806) | 301/271–7373 | $8–$15 | AE, MC, V.

Lodging
Cozy Country Inn. Each room is named for a U.S. president and done in the spirit of his times. The Kennedy Room, for example, has 1960s furnishings, and the Clinton Room has a step-up bed and a jacuzzi. | 21 rooms, 5 cottages. Restaurant, complimentary Continental breakfast. In-room data ports, cable TV. Business services. | 103 Frederick Rd. (Rte. 106) | 301/271–4301 | fax 301/271–4301 | cozyvillage@aol.com | www.cozyvillage.com | $43–$150 | AE, D, MC, V.

Ole Mink Farm. Stone fireplaces warm up the cabins on this primitive campground high atop the Catoctin Mountains. The cabins have outdoor picnic tables and comfortable, contemporary furnishings. Unlike the campsites, the only thing primitive about the cabins are the logs used for their construction. Kitchenettes. No room phones. No TV. | 12806 Mink Farm Rd. | 301/271–7012 | fax 301/271–4856 | 9 cabins | $250 (2–night minimum) | MC, V.

Rambler Motel. This locally owned establishment close to downtown isn't your average motel. A local artisan crafted the walnut and cherry room furnishings, and the proprietor offers friendly service. Moderate-size rooms have large windows and tiled baths. Cable TV. | U.S. 15 and 550 | 301/271–2424 | fax 301/271–2425 | 30 rooms | $42–$72 | AE, D, DC, MC, V.

Super 8. Near state and national parks and 5 minutes from Mount St. Mary's College, this motel has basic rooms. | 46 rooms. In-room data ports, cable TV. Some pets allowed. | 300 Tippin Dr. | 301/271–7888 | $53–$68 | AE, D, DC, MC, V.

TILGHMAN

MAP 4, G4

(Nearby towns also listed: Easton, Oxford, St. Michaels)

Unlike popular Eastern Shore destinations like St. Michaels, Oxford, and Easton, Tilghman remains largely untouched by commercial development. The community is really nothing more than a fishermen's village. In spring, you can find skipjacks (oyster boats) ready and waiting for the beginning of the oyster season. Geared primarily toward hunters and outdoor enthusiasts, the popular Harrison's Chesapeake House, Country Inn and Sportfishing Center is a short drive beyond the Knapps Narrows Bridge.

Information: Talbot County Conference and Visitors Bureau | 210 Marlboro Ave., Suite 3, Easton, MD 21601-1366 | 410/822–4606 or 888/BAY–STAY.

Attractions

Skipjack H. M. Krentz. Set sail on this 49-ft, oyster-dredging skipjack. You can either bring your own provisions or arrange with the skipper for picnic fare or cocktails and hors d'oeuvres to be served on board. | Dogwood Harbor | 410/745–6080 | www.oystercatcher.com/index.html | $30 | Daily.

ON THE CALENDAR

OCT.: *Tilghman Island Day.* Skipjack cruises, a workboat race, and oyster-shucking, crab-picking, jigger-tossing, and rowing contests are all part of the fun at this annual event to benefit the town's fire department. Arts-and-crafts exhibits, a raffle, and live music at Kronsberg Park round out the day's activities. | 410/822–4606.

Dining

The Bridge. Continental. Locals and tourists alike congregate at this nautically themed eatery with a patio and outdoor bar to enjoy dishes such as grilled chicken topped with a broiled crab cake and rich cream sauce or duck a l'orange. The crème brûlée and key lime cheesecake are made fresh daily. | 6136 Tilghman Rd. | 410/886–2330 | $10–$20 | AE, D, DC, MC, V.

The Gallery Dining Room. Contemporary. This warm, sophisticated dining room, which overlooks the Knapps Narrows, has bay-themed art on the knotty-pine walls and white linen and candles on the tables. Menu standouts include the gnocchi with Chesapeake shad roe, romano cheese, and pancetta-chive vinaigrette, the black-eyed pea cakes, and lamb chops with mint jelly. | Coopertown Rd. | 410/886–2141 | $27–$39 | AE, D, DC, MC, V.

Lodging

Black Walnut Point. Surrounded by a 57-acre wildlife preserve this B&B is all about relaxation. Snooze in a hammock or while away the day on the veranda. Many rooms have sitting areas or screened porches. | 7 rooms. Picnic area, complimentary Continental breakfast. No room phones, TV in sitting room. Pool, hot tub. Tennis. Business services. No kids under 12. | End of Black Walnut Point Rd. (Rte. 33) | 410/886–2452 | fax 410/886–2053 | www.tilghmanisland.com/blackwalnut | $120–$150 | D, MC, V.

Chesapeake Wood Duck Inn. In its past lives, this 1890 Victorian inn was a boarding house, bordello, and private home. These days, you can relax on the porch or by the fire or simply retire to your antique-furnished room. | 7 rooms. Complimentary breakfast. No room phones, TV and VCR in main room. Sailing. Business services. No kids under 14. No smoking. | 21490 Dogwood Harbor Rd. | 410/886–2070 or 800/956–2070 | fax 410/886–2263 | www.woodduckinn.com | $145–$219 | MC, V.

Lazyjack Inn. This 1855 waterfront home has antique quilts and furnishings, and views of the water. | 4 rooms. Complimentary breakfast. Some in-room hot tubs, no room phones, TV in common room. No kids under 12. No smoking. | 5907 Tilghman Island Rd. | 410/886–2215 or 800/690–5080 | fax 410/886–2635 | www.lazyjack.com | $130–$215 | MC, V.

The Moorings Bed & Breakfast. Just a few minutes north of town you'll find this pale-yellow Victorian on a 40-acre waterfront expanse. Go crabbing, launch a canoe from the private dock, or take a leisurely stroll around the well-tended grounds. The rooms, some of which look out onto the bay, have nautical or country themes. The innkeepers can arrange for a fishing charter or in-house massage. Picnic area, complimentary breakfast. Some in-room hot tubs, no room phones. Pool. Dock, boating, fishing. | 7857 Tilghman Island Rd., Sherwood | 410/745–6396 or 800/316–6396 | fax 410/745–2329 | www.mooringsbb.com | 5 rooms | $85–$110 | AE, MC, V.

Sinclair House. Embellished with nautical memorabilia from the innkeeper's days as a Chesapeake Bay waterman, this B&B has a big front porch with comfortable wicker furniture. Both antiques and contemporary furniture in the guest rooms set a casual country tone. Complimentary breakfast. No room phones. Tennis. | 5718 Black Walnut Point Rd. | 410/886–2147 or 888–859–2147 | www.tilghmanisland.com/sinclair | 4 rooms | $75–$125 | AE, D, DC, MC, V.

TOWSON

MAP 4, F2

(Nearby towns also listed: Baltimore, Pikesville)

William and Thomas Towson founded this community in 1750 when they began farming the area. In 1768 Thomas' son, Ezekiel built a large tavern at the crossroads of York and Joppa roads, which is still a major intersection, and the small village of "Towsontown" began to grow around it. In 1854 Towson became the Baltimore County Seat. Towson has grown rapidly since World War II. Today it is a center for education, medicine, county government and law, and more recently a retail destination. Easily accessible off I–695, Towson is home to Goucher College, a small private liberal arts college, and Towson University, a state university.

Information: Baltimore County Conference and Visitors Bureau | 435 York Rd., Towson, 21204 | 410/583–7313 or 800/570–2836 | www.visitbacomd.com.

Attractions

Asian Art Center. This museum on Towson University houses an extensive collection of Japanese, Chinese, Indian, and Nepali artwork, as well as armor and musical instruments. The center regularly hosts tours, concerts, and workshops. | Towson University Fine Arts Building, Rm. 236 | 410/830–2807 | fax 410/830–4032 | Free | Mon.–Fri. 11–4, Sat. 2–4:30.

Fire Museum of Maryland. Peruse a collection of antique firefighting apparatus, including more than 40 fire trucks dating from 1804. | 1301 York Rd. (Rte. 45), Lutherville | 410/321–7500 | www.firemuseummd.org | $5 | July–Aug. Tues.–Sat. 11–4, May, Nov. Sat. 11–4.

Hampton National Historic Site. When it was completed in 1790, Hampton was the largest house in the United States. Once the site of a self-contained community of artisans, skilled laborers, and slaves, the Georgian mansion now provides a glimpse of the life of the Ridgely family, who occupied the estate for more than 160 years. | 535 Hampton La. | 410/823–1309 | www.nps.gov/hamp | $5 | Daily 9–4.

Towson University. Founded in 1866 as State Normal School in Baltimore it moved to Towson in 1915. The largest comprehensive university in metropolitan Baltimore, the school has about 11,000 full-time students.
The Asian Arts and Culture Center hosts arts and cultural events. | Towsontown Blvd., at Osler Dr. | 410/830–2000, university; 410/830–ARTS arts center | www.towson.edu | Free.

ON THE CALENDAR

AUG.–SEPT.: *Maryland State Fair.* This 19-day event on the fairgrounds in Timonium has horse races, livestock contests, live entertainment, agricultural displays, farm implements, and plenty of food and amusement rides. | 410/252–0200.

Dining

An Poiton Stil. Irish. Salads, sandwiches, and local fish round out this pub-style restaurant's menu, which is heavy with traditional dishes such as colcannon (Irish mashed potatoes

ONE LAST TRAVEL TIP:

Pack an easy way to reach the world.

Wherever you travel, the MCI WorldCom Card℠ is the easiest way to stay in touch. You can use it to call to and from more than 125 countries worldwide. And you can earn bonus miles every time you use your card. So go ahead, travel the world. MCI WorldCom℠ makes it even more rewarding. For additional access codes, visit **www.wcom.com/worldphone**.

EASY TO CALL WORLDWIDE

1. Just dial the WorldPhone® access number of the country you're calling from.
2. Dial or give the operator your MCI WorldCom Card number.
3. Dial or give the number you're calling.

Canada	1-800-888-8000
Mexico	01-800-021-8000
United States	1-800-888-8000

EARN FREQUENT FLIER MILES

6 "I'm thirsty"s, 9 "Are we there yet"s, 3 "I don't feel good"s,
1 car class upgrade.
At least something's going your way.

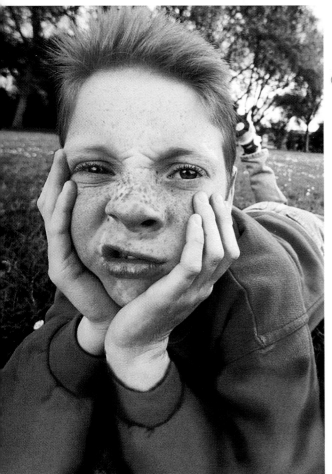

Hertz rents Fords and other fine cars. ® REG. U.S. PAT. OFF. © HERTZ SYSTEM INC., 2000/005-00

Make your next road trip more comfortable with a free one-class upgrade from Hertz.

Let's face it, a long road trip isn't always sunshine and roses. But with Hertz, you get a free one car class upgrade to make things a little more bearable. You'll also choose from a variety of vehicles with child seats, Optional Protection Plans, 24-Hour Emergency Roadside Assistance, and the convenience of NeverLost, the in-car navigation system that provides visual and audio prompts to give you turn-by-turn guidance to your destination. In a word: it's everything you need for your next road trip. Call your travel agent or Hertz at **1-800-654-2210** and mention PC# **906404** or check us out at **hertz.com** or AOL Keyword: **hertz**. Peace of mind. Another reason nobody does it exactly like Hertz.

Hertz
exactly.®

with cabbage), shepherd's pie, and fish and chips. A full bar is available, as are a few wines. | 2323 York Rd., Timonium | 410/560–7900 | www.thestill.net | $7–$21 | AE, D, MC, V.

Cafe Troia. Italian. Stone floors, fireplaces, and a terrace add to the Tuscan flavor of Cafe Troia. The menu changes seasonally, but regular favorites include osso buco and risotto. | 28 W. Allegheny Ave. | 410/337–0133 | No lunch Sat. and Sun. | $14–$22 | AE, DC, MC, V.

Liberatore's Ristorante. Italian. Murals and frescoes with plenty of cherubs give this upscale eatery a Mediterranean flavor. Try the 22-oz. veal chop marinated in extra virgin olive oil and topped with rosemary and garlic. Entertainment on weekends. | 9515 Deereco Rd., Timonium | 410/561–3300 | $11–$37 | AE, D, DC, MC, V.

Peerce's Plantation. Continental. In a mid-20th-century building, the restaurant overlooks Loch Raven Reservoir. Try its trademark super-thin, house-cured smoked salmon or french bread smothered in lump crabmeat, shrimp, scallops, and a creamy dill sauce. Open-air dining. Kids' menu. Sun. brunch. | 12460 Dulaney Valley Rd., Phoenix | 410/252–3100 | Jacket required | $35–$50 | AE, D, DC, MC, V.

Rothwell's Grille. American. Feast on wild rock fish with crabmeat, capers, and wild mushrooms at the bar shaped like a baseball diamond or on the open-air patio. | 106 W. Padonia Rd., Timonium | 410/252–0600 | $10–$22 | AE, D, DC, MC, V.

That's Amore. Italian. Pictures of the Italian countryside adorn the walls, and an open-air patio looks out onto a fountain. Known for serving huge portions, the restaurant makes a popular veal Caprese in Marsala wine with a wheel of mozzarella and spinach topped with prosciutto. | 720 Kenilworth Dr. | 410/825–5255 | fax 410/825–3147 | No lunch weekends | $11–$23 | AE, D, DC, MC, V.

Lodging

Burkshire Guest Suites. Adjacent to historic Towson University, this all-suites Marriott property is popular among collegiate sports fans and visiting parents. All suites have living rooms furnished with comfortable contemporary couches and most have balconies. Restaurant, bar. In-room data ports, kitchenettes, cable TV. Beauty salon. Exercise equipment. Laundry service. Business services. | 10 W. Burke Ave. | 410/324–8107 or 800/435–5986 | fax 410/324–8199 | burkshire@towson.edu | www.conferencecenters.com/bwibu | 119 suites | $129–$144 | AE, D, DC, MC, V.

Days Inn. Half a mile from the light rail that leads to downtown Baltimore, this inn was renovated in 1998. | 145 rooms. Restaurant, complimentary Continental breakfast. In-room data ports, refrigerators, cable TV. Pool. Exercise equipment. Laundry service. Business services. | 9615 Deereco Rd., Timonium | 410/560–1000 | fax 410/561–3918 | www.daysinn.com | $89–$94 | AE, D, DC, MC, V.

Holiday Inn Select. This comfortable hotel has a five-level atrium in the lobby. Easy access to I-83 and I-695 make the hotel convenient for business travelers. | 250 rooms. Restaurant, 2 bars. In-room data ports, cable TV. 2 pools (1 indoor), hot tub. Exercise equipment. Free parking. Laundry facilities. | 2004 Greenspring Dr., Timonium | 410/252–7373 | fax 410/561–0182 | www.basshotels.com/holiday-inn | $119–$149 | AE, D, DC, MC, V.

Ramada Inn. This two-story hotel off the Baltimore Beltway is less than 2 mi from Towson University. The rooms are furnished with modular, wood-veneer furniture, and the grounds here are well-kept. Restaurant, bar, room service. Some refrigerators, some microwaves, cable TV. Outdoor pool. Tennis courts. Laundry service. Business services. Pets allowed. | 8712 Loch Raven Blvd. | 410/823–8750 | fax 410/823–8644 | 122 rooms | $52–$82 | AE, D, DC, MC, V.

Sheraton Baltimore North. Connected to the Towson Town Center mall, and 3 mi from Goucher College and Towson State University, the hotel has the largest lobby in town. | 284 rooms. Restaurant, bar. In-room data ports, cable TV. Indoor pool. Hot tub. Exercise equipment. Business services. | 903 Dulaney Valley Rd. (Rte. 146) | 410/321–7400 | fax 410/296–9534 | www.sheraton.com | $110–$180 | AE, D, DC, MC, V.

TOWSON

INTRO
ATTRACTIONS
DINING
LODGING

WALDORF

(Nearby towns also listed: La Plata, Washington, D.C.)

Once a farming community, Waldorf is now the largest commercial shopping area in Charles County, a fast-growing suburb of Washington, D.C. The Baltimore and Ohio Railroad built a station here in 1872, but the community appeared as a town on a post office map even before then. The completion of the Potomac River Bridge contributed to the town's prosperity, as did slot-machine gambling before it was outlawed in Maryland.

Information: Charles County Tourism | Box B, La Plata, MD 20646 | 301/645–0558 or 800/766–3386.

Attractions

American Indian Cultural Center. Learn about the life of the region's Piscataway Indians through exhibits and artifacts. | 16816 Country La. | 301/372–1932 | Free | Closed Mon., Wed., and Fri.–Sun. Call for hrs.

Cedarville State Forest. Hike, fish, and check out the state's only warm-water fish hatchery. | Cedarville Rd. off Rte. 301 | 301/888–1410 | www.dnr.state.md.us/publiclands/southern/cedarville.html | $2 per vehicle | Daily dawn–dusk.

Dr. Samuel A. Mudd House Museum. This home of a country doctor who made a splint for Lincoln's assassin and lent him a room during his escape is still in the Mudd family. See the room where John Wilkes Booth slept. | Dr. Samuel Mudd Rd. (Rte. 232) | 301/934–8464 or 301/645–6870 | www.surratt.org | $3 | Apr.–Nov., weekends. noon–4 and Wed. 11–3, closed Mon.–Tues., Thurs.–Fri.

Fort Washington National Park. This National Park was a military installation from 1808 to 1946, and exhibits early 19th-century fortifications as well as turn-of-the-century gun batteries. Tours are guided. | Fort Washington Rd. in Fort Washington | 301/763–4600 | www.nps.gov | $4 per vehicle | Daily dawn to dusk.

Friendship House. Now part of the Charles County Community College campus, this small, tidewater-style house with brick interior was built around 1680, making it one of the oldest structures in the county. In 1968, it was dismantled, moved from its original site and reassembled eight years later on the CCCC campus. | Charles County Community College | 301/870–3008 ext. 7110 | Free | Sat.–Sun. noon–4, and by appointment.

John Wilkes Booth Escape Route Tour. Each spring and fall history buffs retrace the the original escape route through southern Maryland to Virginia of President Lincoln's assassin, John Wilkes Booth. Booth, a young actor, fatally shot Lincoln while he was watching a play at Ford's Theater in Washington. He fled Washington to the Surratt Tavern in Clinton, then to the home of Dr. Mudd. He eventually crossed the Potomac into Virginia, where he was shot and killed by federal troops. Proceeds benefit the preservation of the Surratt House Museum. | 9118 Brandywine Rd., Clinton | 301/868–1121 | www.surratt.org | $50 | Apr.–May; Sept.–Oct.; call for dates.

National Colonial Farm. This full-scale working farm, founded in 1958, is a replica of a typical 18th-century middle-class farm and gives you the opportunity to understand what life in the region was like 200 years ago for the great majority of people. Part of the National Park Service's Piscataway Park, the farm is managed by the Maryland-based Accokeek Foundation and has livestock and a tobacco barn as well as special events. | Bryan Point Rd., Accokeek | 301/283–2113 | www.accokeek.org | $2 | Tues.–Sun. 10–5.

Surratt House and Tavern. Built in 1852 as a private home, the tavern also served as a hostelry and post office. It was made famous when Lincoln's assassin, John Wilkes Booth, stopped here during his escape from Washington, D.C. | 9110 Brandywine Rd., Clinton | 301/868–1121

| www.surratt.org | $3 | Mid-Jan.–mid-Dec., Thurs.–Fri. 11–3, weekends noon–4, closed Mon.–Wed.

ON THE CALENDAR
NOV.: *Annual Fall Craft Fair.* This gathering attracts dozens of area artisans and craftspeople, who exhibit and sell their wares just before the holiday season. | 301/870–8707.

Dining

Lefty's BBQ Unlimited. Barbecue. Far from limiting itself to just barbecue, this rustic restaurant also serves burgers and spicy wings. Lefty's is a particularly good option if you're traveling with kids and sticking to a budget. | 2064 Crain Hwy. | 301/870–8998 | $6–$10 | AE, D, MC, V.

Shoney's. American. While somewhat short on charm, this chain restaurant does have an extensive menu that's sure to satisfy everyone in your party. Seating in the dining area is either in booths or at large tables, and dishes range from taco salads served in crunchy tortilla-shell bowls to steak and eggs. | 3315 Crain Hwy. | 301/932–8587 | $6–$10 | AE, D, MC, V.

Wall's Wigwam Bakery. Café. Though not a restaurant in the strict sense, Wall's is famous throughout the area for baking some of the best éclairs and French pastries around. The building that now houses the bakery was once a swanky nightclub. | 2805 Crain Hwy. | 301/645–2833 | $1–$5 | MC, V.

Lodging

Colony South Hotel. In a quiet community, just 10 minutes from the Waldorf Mall and theaters, the hotel has a sunken lobby and exposed rafters. | 197 rooms. Restaurant, bar, room service. Some refrigerators, cable TV. Indoor pool. Beauty salon, hot tub. Tennis courts. Gym, racquetball. Business services, airport shuttle. | 7401 Surratts Rd., Clinton | 301/856–4500 or 800/537–1147 | fax 301/868–1439 | www.colonysouth.com | $130–$175 | AE, D, DC, MC, V.

Comfort Suites. This three-story, white stucco building with a covered circle drive is popular with business travelers. Rooms are pleasant and well lit, with large windows and work desks. Complimentary breakfast. In-room data ports, cable TV. Indoor pool. Laundry service. Business services. | 11765 Business Park Dr. | 301/932–4400 | fax 301/932–7566 | 69 rooms | $75–$129 | AE, D, DC, MC, V.

Days Inn. Just off Rte. 301 this hotel is near shopping plazas. | 99 rooms. Complimentary Continental breakfast. In-room data ports, cable TV. Business services. Some pets allowed. | 11370 Days Ct. | 301/932–9200 | fax 301/843–9816 | www.daysinn.com | $55–$80 | AE, D, DC, MC, V.

Holiday Inn. This three-story hotel is directly across from a shopping mall and 10 mi from the Port Tobacco historical site. | 192 rooms, 10 suites. Restaurant, bar, room service. In-room data ports, some kitchenettes, cable TV. Pool. Laundry facilities. Business services. | 45 St. Patrick's Dr. | 301/645–8200 | fax 301/843–7945 | www.basshotels.com/holiday-inn | $50–$80 | AE, D, DC, MC, V.

Howard Johnson Express Inn. This single story hotel with pink interior is cozy, and you're ½ mi from restaurants and a shopping mall. | 109 rooms. Picnic area, complimentary Continental breakfast. In-room safes, cable TV. Pool. Business services. Some pets allowed. | 3125 S. Crain Hwy. (U.S. 301 and Rte. 228) | 301/932–5090 | fax 301/932–5090 | www.hojo.com | $64–$80 | AE, D, DC, MC, V.

Mastersuites. This all-suite property is an economical choice for families or other travelers who need extra space. All suites have sitting areas and are equipped with unremarkable but comfortable contemporary furniture. | 60 suites. Picnic area, complimentary

breakfast. Kitchenettes, cable TV. Sauna. Exercise equipment. | 2228 Old Washington Rd. | 301/870–5500 | fax 301/843–0821 | $60–$70 | AE, D, MC, V.

WESTMINSTER

MAP 4, E2

(Nearby towns also listed: Baltimore, Frederick, Taneytown)

Westminster's Main Street, a tree-lined avenue with restaurants, antique shops, boutiques, and well-maintained 19th-century homes, is one of the state's most attractive. Its founder, William Winchester purchased the town's first 100 acres in 1754 and named it after his birthplace in England. Westminster is the county seat and the major commercial hub of Carroll County. Many of the city's first settlers were Germans from Pennsylvania and Scotch-Irish from the state's Eastern Shore. The city therefore resembles some of the German-influenced towns of central and eastern Pennsylvania.

Information: Carroll County Office of Tourism | 224 N. Center St., Room 100, Westminster, MD 21157 | 410/857–2983 or 800/272–1933 | www.carr.org/visit.

Attractions

Carroll County Farm Museum. A 19th-century farmhouse with restored outbuildings, including a general store and barn, the museum displays farm equipment, and hosts the annual Maryland Wine Festival. | 500 S. Center St. | 410/848–7775 | ccpl.carr.org/tourism/todo/things.htm | $3 | Call for seasonal hrs.

Union Mills Homestead and Gristmill. The 1797 estate of the Shriver family, who lived here for six generations, was a stopover for Civil War soldiers. Listed on the National Register of Historic Places, the mill produces stone-ground corn meal, wheat, and buckwheat flour. | 3311 Littlestown Pike (Rte. 97), Union Mills | 410/848–2288 | ccpl.carr.org/tourism/todo/things.htm | $5 | Call for seasonal hrs.

ON THE CALENDAR

SEPT.: *Maryland Wine Festival.* This weekend event at the Carroll County Farm Museum celebrates Maryland's up-and-coming wineries with wine, food, and entertainment. | 410/876–2667.

Dining

Baugher's. American. The Baugher family owns nearby orchards, so it's no surprise that the walls here are covered in apple-related prints. Sit at a vintage 1950s table or booth and try the popular fried chicken. | 289 W. Main St. | 410/848–7413 | $5–$12 | D, MC, V.

Chameleon. Contemporary. Try the veal chop with wild mushroom sauce or the steak with blue cheese, grapes, and walnuts. Tables have white linens, and a small oak bar has live entertainment. | 32 W. Main St. | 410/751–2422 | Closed Mon. | $21–$35 | AE, D, DC, MC, V.

Johansson's. Continental. Five dining rooms and a glass-enclosed parlor set the scene at this microbrewery known for veal, beef, and fresh seafood. Entertainment Fri.–Sat. Kids' menu. | 4 W. Main St. | 410/876–0101 | Reservations essential Fri.–Sat. | $14–$23 | AE, D, MC, V.

Paradiso Italian Restaurant. Italian. Originally part of a distillery, this restaurant's walls are almost all windows. Nightly specials might include rack of lamb, veal tenderloin with Gorgonzola wine sauce, filet mignon, or breast of chicken in lemon butter sauce topped with crab. | 20 Distillery Dr. | 410/848–1419 | No lunch Sun. | $8.50–$23 | AE, D, DC, MC, V.

Rudy's 2900. Continental. White linen tablecloths lend a formal country club ambience to Rudy's. Grouper in a potato crust is a popular dish. Fresh salmon, rack of lamb and sirloin steak are great items to try. | 2900 Baltimore Blvd., Finksburg | 410/833–5777 | fax 410/526–2201 | Reservations essential Fri.–Sat. | Closed Mon. | $25–$41 | AE, D, DC, MC, V.

Lodging

Boston Inn. On 4 acres of land and in five buildings, this cozy inn is on Route 140 near shopping centers, restaurants. | 118 rooms. Complimentary Continental breakfast. In-room data ports, cable TV. Business services. | 533 Baltimore Blvd. (Rte. 140) | 410/848–9095 or 800/634–0846 | fax 410/848–9326 | www.boston-inn.com | $48–$60 | AE, D, DC, MC, V.

Bowling Brook Country Inn. Ten mi west of Westminster, this 1837 Georgian manor house sits on 225 acres of pasture and meadow. Some rooms have hot tubs and fireplaces. | 8 rooms. Complimentary breakfast. Some in-room hot tubs, no room phones, no TV. Hiking. No pets. No kids under 6. No smoking. | 6000 Middleburg Rd., Middleburg | 410/876–2893 | $110–$175 | AE, D, DC, MC, V.

Best Western. A fireplace in the lounge makes this chain motel cozier than usual. Both Western Maryland College and a golf course are across the street; a shopping center and restaurants are next door. | 101 rooms. Complimentary Continental breakfast. Cable TV. Pool, hot tub. Business services. Some pets allowed. | 451 Western Maryland College Dr. | 410/857–1900 | fax 410/857–9584 | www.bestwesternwestminster.com | $69–$179 | AE, D, DC, MC, V.

Days Inn. Behind a shopping center, this three-story motel is in a busy commercial area just off Rte. 140. | 96 rooms. In-room data ports, some refrigerators, cable TV. Pool. Business services. Some pets allowed. | 25 S. Cranberry Rd. | 410/857–0500 or 800/336–DAYS | fax 410/857–1407 | www.daysinn.com | $65–$92 | AE, D, DC, MC, V.

Westminster Inn. Furnished with antiques, this B&B is in a renovated school built in 1899. Each room has a hot tub. | 24 rooms. Complimentary breakfast. In-room data ports. Indoor pool. Exercise equipment. Business services. | 5 S. Center St. | 410/876–2893 | fax 410/876–2893 | www.westminsterinn.com | $145–$195 | AE, D, DC, MC, V.

Winchester Country Inn Bed and Breakfast. This 1760s Colonial home once belonged to William Winchester, Westminster's founder. In keeping with that heritage, the rooms, which have canopy beds and quilts, are named after Winchester's five children. | 5 rooms. Complimentary breakfast. No room phones, TV in common area. No pets. No kids under 6. No smoking. | 111 Stoner Ave. | 410/876–7373 or 800/887–3950 | fax 410/848–7409 | $85 | AE, D, MC, V.

WESTMINSTER

INTRO
ATTRACTIONS
DINING
LODGING

Pennsylvania
Welcomes You
TOM RIDGE, GOVERNOR
1 - 800 - VISIT PA
www.state.pa.us

Pennsylvania

Pennsylvania, a sprawling state stretching some 300 mi from New Jersey to Ohio, is a microcosm for the history, growth, and development of the United States. Nicknamed the Keystone State, this moniker is apt: The Commonwealth has played a critical role in the creation and development of the nation, from Colonial days, when it was the seat of the Revolution and Philadelphia served as the first capital, through the Industrial Revolution, when its mighty coal mines and factories supplied fuel and goods to the nation, through today, when the state serves as an important center for education, research, and development of lifesaving drugs.

Pennsylvania has fascinating contrasts. A mostly rural state, it is home to two large cities: Philadelphia, the nation's fifth largest and the regional center for the eastern portion of the state, and Pittsburgh, the focus for the western portion. Both cities are enjoying a resurgence. Considered the birthplace of our nation, Philadelphia is experiencing a development boom that, in the next few years, will bring a dozen more hotels, a performing arts complex that will house the world-class Philadelphia Orchestra and other ensembles, an entertainment center with a Disney interactive game center as its centerpiece, and scores of shops and restaurants. Meanwhile, Pittsburgh has reimagined itself through the redevelopment of its downtown and the creation of cultural attractions like the Andy Warhol Museum and the Mattress Factory.

Within a few hours' drive of the the worldliness and sophistication of these cities, you can return to a simpler way of life. The winding country lanes and now silent battlefields conjure up images of the Civil War, while, in Lancaster, the horse and buggy is still a viable means of transportation, as today's Pennsylvania Dutch hew to the traditions of their ancestors.

As one of the earliest colonized regions of the United States, many families can trace their roots back to William Penn, yet the Commonwealth is also a place where

CAPITAL: HARRISBURG	POPULATION: 12,001,451 (1998)	AREA: 45,888 SQUARE MI
BORDERS: NJ, NY, OH, WV, MD, DE	TIME ZONE: EASTERN	POSTAL ABBREVIATION: PA
WEB SITE: WWW.STATE.PA.US/VISIT		

recent immigrants, notably from Russia and Vietnam, have traveled thousands of miles to claim their own freedom.

History

The first recorded contact between Europeans and Pennsylvania's Native American residents occurred in 1608 when Captain John Smith of Virginia traveled up the Susquehanna River and encountered the Susquehannock. From then, it was only a matter of time before Pennsylvania would gain its first settlers. Before there was a colony, various explorers made preliminary forays into this vast unknown territory: in 1609, Englishman Henry Hudson, working for the Dutch, entered what is now known as the Delaware Bay; in 1610, Capt. Samuel Argall of Virginia named the bay after Lord de la Ware, governor of his colony; in 1615, Etienne Brule became the first white man to make his way to the interior of Pennsylvania; and in 1616, Capt. Cornelius Henderson, a Dutchman, sailed up the Schuylkill River and claimed the land.

The first recorded settlement was built some seven years later by the Dutch, who raised Fort Nassau on the New Jersey side of the Delaware River. The Swedish West India Company would follow suit by constructing Fort Christiana, near what is now the city of Wilmington. A 1641 settlement from Connecticut failed, but two years later, Gov. John Printz successfully established the capital of New Sweden—the first Swedish settlement in Pennsylvania—on Tinicum Island. Over the next 30 years, the settlement changed hands several times, as first the Dutch, led by Gov. Peter Stuyvesant, took Pennsylvania from the Swedes, only to be thrown out by the English, who were overturned by the Dutch, but took permanent control in 1674 under the Treaty of Westminster.

Some six years later, William Penn petitioned King Charles II for a land grant. The king was only too happy to give Penn a parcel of land across the Atlantic to settle a debt. Penn, who had been imprisoned for his Quaker beliefs, was considered a troublemaker in his native country. Penn distinguished himself from other settlers of the era in two key ways: As a Quaker, a persecuted religious group in England, he included freedom of religion as a central tenet of his First Frame of Government, which was approved by the General Assembly in 1682. He also recognized the land rights of the Indians and made sure they were compensated for lands taken from them by settlers.

What of these Indians? The native inhabitants at the time of Penn's arrival were descended from Stone Age people who came to the Americas from Asia sometime between 8000 and 6000 BC, traveling over a land bridge across the Bering Strait. Mostly hunter-gatherers, the three most important tribes were the Delaware, also known as Leni Lenape, the Susquehannock, and the Shawnee. Despite Penn's best intentions, though, the Indians and the colonists did not learn to live together peacefully. The cultural gaps were too large and often centered on land ownership. The common Native American belief was that the air, land, and water were owned by all people; they thought by coexisting together, they were sharing the land, not parceling it out.

PA Timeline

1643	1655	1674	1681
Governor John Printz establishes the capital of New Sweden in Pennsylvania.	The Dutch, urged on by New Amsterdam Director General Peter Stuyvesant, take over New Sweden.	The Treaty of Westminster ends hostilities between the Dutch and the English and turns Dutch colonies, including Pennsylvania, over to the English.	To settle a $40,000 loan from Admiral William Penn, the king gives a parcel of land in the colonies to his son, William, who soon sets sail to inspect his new property. The land grant also

INTRODUCTION
HISTORY
REGIONS
WHEN TO VISIT
STATE'S GREATS
RULES OF THE ROAD
DRIVING TOURS

Arriving in the new land, Penn was also a visionary with respect to how his settlement would look. Establishing the city of Philadelphia (Greek for "City of Brotherly Love") on a peninsula between the Delaware and Schuylkill Rivers, Penn designed a "green countrie towne," a series of streets and squares laid out in a grid pattern. His thinking was that the openness of the design would serve practical and aesthetic purposes, helping to avoid the disastrous fires and outbreaks of contagious diseases in England and allowing for trees and common greens.

Penn's territory began at the Delaware but did not have western borders; this caused great conflict with Pennsylvania's neighbors—namely Maryland, Virginia, and Connecticut—for nearly a century. The solution proved to be boundaries set by three men, whose names are still well known: Charles Mason and Jeremiah Dixon, who, in 1767, established the eastern border, known as the Mason-Dixon Line, a demarcation that would figure prominently in the Civil War as the dividing line between North and South, and free states and slave states; and David Rittenhouse (namesake of Philadelphia's Rittenhouse Square) set the western boundary in 1784.

The Colonial period was a time of great turmoil in Pennsylvania. In 1753, the French and Indian War—a conflict over the possession of the Ohio Valley and control of the Ohio River as a transportation route to the Mississippi River and French-held New Orleans—broke out. The British military eventually drove the French out, establishing several important military forts and a presence in the western portion of Pennsylvania. By the 1770s, Pennsylvania and the other original colonies had made many of the settlers wealthy, and Britain, wanting a share of the bounty, imposed a series of taxes. These unpopular tariffs led to the formation of the First Continental Congress in 1774 in Philadelphia, and the seeds for a revolution were planted.

The following year, the Second Continental Congress met, again in Philadelphia, and appointed George Washington commander-in-chief. In 1776, the Congress adopted the Declaration of Independence, and war officially broke out. The seven-year conflict included significant local victories by both the revolutionary forces—Washington defeated the British at Trenton—and the British—who subsequently defeated the upstarts in Brandywine and the Germantown section of Philadelphia—and the occupation of Philadelphia by the British. After the war ended, Philadelphia became the fledgling nation's capital, a position of power it would hold until 1800. In 1787, the U.S. Constitution, the nation's lasting blueprint, was ratified in Philadelphia; Pennsylvania was the second state to vote for this landmark document.

Although no longer the site of the nation's capital, Pennsylvania in the 19th century was a leader in mining and manufacturing. The shaping of the earliest versions of the state highway system, coupled with the development of mighty railroads like the Philadelphia and Reading lines, helped Philadelphia and Pittsburgh become important centers for the production of coal and manufacture of steel. Meanwhile, the Quakers were quietly laying the groundwork for the battle over slavery that would result in the Civil War; its members formed the Underground Railroad, a conduit to move slaves to freedom

solves the problem of what to do about William, a vocal and outspoken proponent of Quakerism, a religion that challenged the king's rule of divine right and England's rigid class structure.

1682
Penn found the city of Philadelphia—the Greek word for brotherly love—after an ancient Syrian city, site of one of the earliest and most venerated Christian churches. Penn's plan for the

city called for a "green countrie towne."

1751
Pennsylvania Hospital, the first in America, receives its charter in Philadelphia.

1758
General John Forbes captures Fort Duquesne, which was destroyed by the French as they retreated. He names the site Pittsburgh; Fort Pitt, the largest in America, is constructed here.

in Canada. During the Civil War, Pennsylvania manufactured many of the Union's guns and ships, and the battle fought in the town of Gettysburg proved to be the bloodiest and most pivotal conflict; the Union forces made sure Gettysburg was the farthest north the Confederate forces would reach.

Following the war, the last decades of the 19th century saw Pennsylvania at the forefront of the Industrial Revolution. The demand for goods and materials to help the nation's move west fueled tremendous growth in the state; the end of the century saw the state's population reach six million, as the state continued to serve as a mighty industrial engine for much of the nation. During the first half of the 20th century, it was business as usual for Pennsylvania. The two world wars served as economic stimulants for the state's major industries. But after World War II, Pennsylvania began to suffer some difficult times as many of its bread-and-butter industries slowed considerably.

Today, the state is in the process of retooling itself for the millennium, with an emphasis on tourism, service-sector jobs, medical advancements, and pharmaceutical research.

Regions

1. PHILADELPHIA

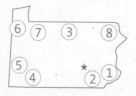

In Philadelphia, Pennsylvania's largest city, you'll find modern skyscrapers rubbing elbows with quaint brick row houses, cars and buses sharing tree-lined streets with horses and carriages, and, in certain areas, statesman and inventor Benjamin Franklin strolls the brick sidewalks. For the history buff, there is America's most historic square mile, site of the Liberty Bell, Independence Hall, and the Betsy Ross house. Less than an hour from the city is Valley Forge National Historical Park, where Washington and his troops were based during the winter of 1777; more Revolutionary War battles were waged in the Philadelphia region than in all of the New England states combined.

But Philadelphians don't just live in the past; they also celebrate a present that includes a vibrant downtown with one of the nation's most exciting restaurant scenes, and a lively cultural scene that includes world-class institutions like the Philadelphia Orchestra and the Philadelphia Museum of Art, as well as dozens of theater and dance companies. Restaurants are a major pleasure here, from the simple repast of the hoagie and cheese steak to a world of inexpensive ethnic eateries to the upscale creations of nationally known chefs and celebrity restaurateurs.

Sports are also a big deal in this town, and the city's natives are vocal in their likes and dislikes. They avidly follow professional teams in baseball, football, basketball, hockey, and lacrosse, as well as the many college squads, and spend many hours jogging, bicycling, and in-line skating along the drives of the Schuylkill River in Fairmount Park, the nation's largest urban park.

1774	1775	1776	1780	1783
The First Continental Congress meets in Carpenter's Hall in Philadelphia.	The Second Continental Congress meets and appoints George Washington as commander-in-chief of the Continental Army.	The Declaration of Independence is adopted. Washington crosses the Delaware River from Bucks County to Trenton to defeat the British on Christmas night.	The state passes the Gradual Emancipation Act, mandating the end of slavery in a generation.	The Revolutionary War ends.

INTRODUCTION
HISTORY
REGIONS
WHEN TO VISIT
STATE'S GREATS
RULES OF THE ROAD
DRIVING TOURS

Towns listed: Bristol, Chadds Ford, Chester, Downingtown, Fort Washington, Frazer, Jenkintown, Kennett Square, King of Prussia, Media, Norristown, Philadelphia, West Chester, Willow Grove

2. PENNSYLVANIA DUTCH COUNTRY

In the rolling countryside just over an hour from cosmopolitan Philadelphia, it's possible to return to a simpler way of life: Here, Amish and Mennonites follow time-honored traditions, traveling in horse-drawn buggies, building barns by hand, and stitching quilts using patterns handed down over generations. Ephrata Cloister goes back even farther in time, showing the introspective life of this 18th-century cloister—a reminder of the tenet of religious tolerance central to the founding of Pennsylvania.

The vast, unspoiled beauty of nearby Gettysburg belies its importance as the site of the Civil War's most violent confrontation, and later the inspiration for Lincoln's famous—and famously brief—address. The state capitol is also in this region, as well as the marvelous chocolate world of Hershey, with its thrilling roller coasters and lights shaped like chocolate kisses. Commerce is important here. You can shop 'til you drop in Reading, home to over 300 factory outlets, or peruse the wares of hundreds of dealers in the Adamstown area, known as America's antiques capital.

Towns listed: Allentown, Bethlehem, Bird-in-Hand, Boiling Springs, Camp Hill, Carlisle, Chambersburg, Cornwall, Denver/Adamstown, Doylestown, Easton, Ephrata, Erwinna, Fogelsville, Gettysburg, Hamburg, Hanover, Harrisburg, Hershey, Holicong, Kutztown, Lahaska, Lancaster, Lebanon, Limerick, Lititz, Mechanicsburg, Middletown, New Hope, Pottstown, Quakertown, Reading, Shartlesville, Skippack, Strasburg, Wrightsville, York

3. SUSQUEHANNA RIVER VALLEY

Considered by many to be the heart and soul of Pennsylvania, the valley surrounding this mighty river has some of the most scenic areas of the state. For example, Shavers Creek Environmental Center in the Stone Valley Recreation Area boasts turkey and other game birds and a sparkling display of wildflowers, while the Montour Preserve in Turbotville is a 148-acre refuge that attracts more than four dozen species of migrating birds.

There are also many signs of the state's mighty industrial past, from the Bellefonte Historical Railroad to the Eagle Ironworks, a restored iron-making plant open for tours. And a giant in science, Joseph Priestly, considered the father of modern chemistry, hails from Northumberland. The glories of the present include a stopover in State College, where the Nittany Lions have dominated the gridiron for decades and where the freshest of ice cream can be sampled—and taken home packed in dry ice—in the creamery. Looking for some high-flying adventure? You'll find that in the Phoenix, ranked by buffs as one of the 10 best roller coasters in the United States, and dozens of other rides at the old-fashioned Knoebel's Amusement Resort in Elysburg.

Towns listed: Clearfield, Galeton, Lock Haven, Mansfield, State College, Wellsboro

1787	**1790**	**1800**	**1829**	**1857**
Pennsylvania is the second state to ratify the Constitution in Philadelphia.	Philadelphia is named capital of the United States.	The nation's capital is moved from Philadelphia to Washington, D.C.	The Stourbridge Lion, the first locomotive in America, begins operations between Honesdale and Carbondale.	James Buchanan, the only Pennsylvanian elected president, is inaugurated.

4. LAUREL HIGHLANDS/SOUTHERN ALLEGHENIES

The Allegheny Mountains provide an inspired backdrop for this section of the state. You can take part in many outdoor activities, notably the 71-mi trail through Ohiopyle State Park and along the Youghiogheny River, and daring ski trails at Blue Knob, Hidden Valley, and Seven Springs. Once upon a time, pioneers headed west along Route 40; it's also the route President George Washington traveled to put down the Whiskey Rebellion of 1794—a protest by western Pennsylvania farmers against a tax on distilled spirits. For man-made beauty, stop by Fallingwater, the landmark residential design by the great 20th-century American architect, Frank Lloyd Wright. Fans of the simple pastime of baseball can enjoy the intimate 6,000-seat home of the Pittsburgh Pirates' AA affiliate, the Altoona Curve.

Towns listed: Altoona, Bedford, Bellefonte, Breezewood, Connellsville, Donegal, Ebensburg, Farmington, Huntingdon, Johnstown, Ligonier, Loretto, Orbisonia, Somerset, Uniontown

5. PITTSBURGH

In the last three decades, Pittsburgh has reimagined itself, from a polluted city to a new city for the '90s. Built around three rivers, this city on seven hills provides drama and the warmth of its residents, many of whom have roots here spanning generations. Art and history come together in interesting ways. The seven-story Andy Warhol Museum is the largest single-artist museum in the United States, and a fitting homage to a native son who also left his mark on 20th-century art, while the Carnegie Museums of Art and Natural History has excellent collections of French Impressionist art, dinosaurs, and gems.

There is plenty of life on the streets of Pittsburgh, where former warehouses have been turned into restaurants and many street fairs are held in trendy neighborhoods like the South Side, Shadyside, and The Strip. Rising above it all is the Duquesne Incline, a restored rail car that carries passengers up Mount Washington for some fabulous views. Sports fans can enjoy the city's rich tradition of football, baseball, and hockey.

Towns listed: Ambridge, Coraopolis, Greensburg, Monroeville, New Stanton, Pittsburgh, Washington

6. LAKE ERIE REGION

Home to one of the country's five great lakes, Erie is a place where water rules. Boating and fishing are major activities, as is the preservation of wildlife. Gull Point on Presque Isle is considered a major stop on the "Atlantic Flyway" during spring and fall migration. History is important, too. Erie is home to the restored U.S. brig *Niagara*, the tallest of six ships built on the lake during the War of 1812. This was where Commodore Oliver Hazard Perry defeated the British. Oil boomed here once, a period captured at

1863	1876	1903	1920	1926
The Battle of Gettysburg is fought from July 1 to 3. Lincoln makes his historic Gettysburg Address on November 19 at a ceremony dedicating the battlefield as a National Cemetery.	The Centennial International Exposition in Philadelphia celebrates 100 years of independence.	Milton Hershey begins the mass production of chocolate and plans his namesake community.	Radio station KDKA in Pittsburgh produces the first scheduled radio broadcast in the world, announcing the results of the Harding-Cox presidential election.	Philadelphia holds a sesquicentennial celebration.

the Drake Well Museum, while a drive along Route 6 is sure to reward—it was ranked "one of America's most scenic drives" by *National Geographic*.

Towns listed: Edinboro, Erie, North East

7. ALLEGHENY NATIONAL FOREST REGION

One of the least populated and most scenic parts of the Commonwealth, your neighbors are more likely to be elk than a guy named Ed. This is also where an animal of his own stripe named Punxsutawney Phil gives hope—or dashes it—to millions feeling oppressed by Old Man Winter. The numbers behind the forest itself—Pennsylvania's only national forest—also tell the story of this region: 500,000 acres, 120 mi of pristine trout streams, 300-year-old stands of towering trees.

Other natural delights here include Kinzua Dam, a nature and recreation area with a 91-mi shoreline, much used for boating and fishing. The Allegheny Reservoir has 12,000 acres of fishable, boatable, and water skiable waterways. Hunting is also popular on some 250,000 acres of gamelands, plus skiing on the steepest slope in the East. While it's not quite as grand as its western counterpart, many consider the 1,000-ft drop of the Pine Creek Gorge, a.k.a. the Grand Canyon of Pennsylvania, just as inspiring.

Towns listed: Beaver Falls, Bradford, Brookville, Butler, Clarion, Conneaut Lake, Du Bois, Franklin, Harmony, Indiana, Kane, Meadville, Mercer, New Castle, Oil City, Port Allegany, Punxsutawney, St. Mary's, Sharon, Titusville, Warren, West Middlesex

8. POCONO MOUNTAINS/ENDLESS MOUNTAINS

On the opposite side of the state sits some of its most scenic land. This is the place to witness the Technicolor splendor of fall foliage, or to schuss your way downhill in winter at dozens of resorts. In spring and summer, there is great hiking, and for the adventurous, the chance to drop some 300 ft into a mine shaft at the Lackawanna Coal Mine. The Steamtown National Historic Site in Scranton presents a fascinating history of the American railroad, while the family-owned Yuengling Brewery gives an insider's glimpse of how the nation's oldest brewery plies its craft. Waterfalls abound, including 22 alone in Ricketts Glen State Park, while speedsters can enjoy their moment at the Pocono International Raceway, site of NASCAR races.

Towns listed: Ashland, Bloomsburg, Bushkill, Canadensis, Carbondale, Cresco, Danville, Delaware Water Gap, Hawley, Hazleton, Honesdale, Jim Thorpe, Lewisburg, Lewistown, Milford, Mt. Pocono, Pottsville, Scranton, Shamokin Dam, Shawnee on Delaware, Stroudsburg, Tannersville, Towanda, Tunkhannock, Union Dale, White Haven, Wilkes-Barre, Williamsport

INTRODUCTION
HISTORY
REGIONS
WHEN TO VISIT
STATE'S GREATS
RULES OF THE ROAD
DRIVING TOURS

1933
As Prohibition is repealed, the state takes control of all wine and liquor stores, a practice that continues today.

1940
The first section of the Pennsylvania Turnpike, the first interstate highway in the country, opens between Irwin and Carlisle.

1952
The first black state police officer is hired.

1953
The Salk vaccine, developed by Dr. Jonas Salk of the University of Pittsburgh, is formally approved to prevent polio, and mass inoculations begin.

1954
WQED, the nation's first public television station, begins broadcasting in Pittsburgh.

When to Visit

The weather in Pennsylvania varies from region to region, but, overall, is typical of the northeastern United States. In general, the spring and fall months are the most pleasant, while winter temperatures, particularly in January and February, often hover around the freezing mark, and in summer, particularly in Philadelphia and the vicinity, heat waves are common in which the thermometer can soar well into the 90s.

CLIMATE CHART

Average High/Low Temperatures (°F) and Monthly Precipitation (in inches)

	JAN.	FEB.	MAR.	APR.	MAY	JUNE
PHILADELPHIA	38/23	41/25	52/33	63/42	73/53	82/62
	2.3	2.8	3.5	3.6	3.8	3.7
	JULY	AUG.	SEPT.	OCT.	NOV.	DEC.
	86/67	85/66	78/59	66/47	55/38	43/28
	4.3	3.8	3.4	2.6	3.3	3.4

	JAN.	FEB.	MAR.	APR.	MAY	JUNE
PITTSBURGH	34/19	37/20	49/30	60/39	71/48	79/57
	2.5	2.4	3.4	3.2	3.6	3.7
	JULY	AUG.	SEPT.	OCT.	NOV.	DEC.
	83/62	81/60	74/54	63/42	50/34	39/24
	3.8	3.2	3	2.4	2.9	2.9

FESTIVALS AND SEASONAL EVENTS

WINTER

Dec. **Army–Navy Football Game.** Annual game in Philadelphia promotes one of the oldest rivalries in college football. | 215/636–3417.

Dec. **The Crossing.** Reenactment of Washington's 1776 crossing of the Delaware River into Trenton, where he defeated the British. | 215/493–4076.

Jan. **Pennsylvania State Farm Show.** State fair held in Harrisburg. | 717/787–5373.

Feb. **Chocolate Lovers' Extravaganza.** All things chocolate are celebrated at the Hotel Hershey in Hershey. | 800/533–3131.

SPRING

May **Devon Horse Show.** One of America's leading equestrian events is held on Philadelphia's Main Line. More than 1,200 horses compete. | 610/964–0550.

1962
A massive fire in an abandoned coal mine in Centralia defies the efforts of firefighters, and the town is gradually abandoned; the fire continues to burn underground today.

1970
The Pittsburgh Steelers win the first of their four Super Bowls.

1971
The General Assembly approves the first state income tax, a graduated tax, in March, repeals it in August, and replaces it with a flat income tax.

1974
The Philadelphia Flyers win their first Stanley Cup, a feat they would repeat the following year.

1979
The Three Mile Island nuclear power plant malfunctions; radiation is released into the air, but a major disaster is averted. The incident raises national awareness of the dangers of nuclear power.

June **Elfreth's Alley Fete Days.** Philadelphia celebrates the nation's oldest continuously occupied street with house tours, demonstrations of Colonial crafts, food, and entertainment. | 215/574–0567.

June **Three Rivers Arts Festival.** A host of music, dance, and performance art events, as well as a juried visual art show with works by local and national artists are the high points of this major Pittsburgh festival. | 412/281–8723.

June **First Union U.S. Pro Cycling Championship.** At 156 mi, this is the longest single-day cycling event in the country. | 215/636–1666.

June–July **Civil War Heritage Days.** Commemorates the anniversary of the battle of Gettysburg; events include lectures by historians, memorabilia collectors' shows, entertainment, a firefighters' festival, and fireworks. | 717/334–6274.

Aug. **Das Awkscht Fest.** Auto show, every first weekend in August, in Allentown featuring some 2,500 antique, classic, and special-interest cars, antique toys, arts and crafts, and entertainment. | 610/967–2317.

Aug. **Musikfest.** Nine-day festival celebrating Bethlehem's musical and ethnic heritage; includes more than 600 national and local performers of all types of music. | 610/861–0678.

FALL

Sept. **Fringe Festival.** Dozens of theater troupes, dance companies, and performance artists take the stage in Philadelphia at this festival modeled on Edinburgh's fringe festival. | 215/413–1318.

Sept. **Highland Games and Gathering of the Clans of Scotland in Ligonier.** Celebration of Scottish culture has massed pipe bands, Highland dancing competitions, Scottish fiddling, wool spinning and weaving demonstrations, and a genealogy booth. | 412/851–9900.

Sept. **Wine Country Harvest Festival.** Wine festival in North East includes arts and crafts, wine tastings, bands, and buses to area wineries. | 814/725–4262.

1980	**1985**	**1995**
The Philadelphia Phillies win their first World Series.	Philadelphia police bomb MOVE headquarters in a private home, killing 11, including five children, and destroying 60 homes over a three-block area.	The Philadelphia Naval Shipyard closes.

State's Greats

From the dramatic hills of Pittsburgh across rolling farmland and majestic forest to the narrow streets of Colonial Philadelphia, Pennsylvania provides a wide range of experiences. The state reflects a rich history—from halcyon days as the seat of the American Revolution and a fledgling nation's first capital through its role as a leader in the country's transformation into an industrial powerhouse—and its role today as a leader in the health-care and pharmaceutical industries, a center for the arts, and a burgeoning tourist destination.

Still mainly a rural state, Pennsylvania exhibits the culture and sophistication of its two largest cities, Philadelphia and Pittsburgh, as well as the tranquility of its many charming towns and villages. The countryside boasts plenty to do outdoors—including hiking, fishing, skiing, and rafting—or plenty of nothing for those who prefer to laze by a quiet river or take a peaceful walk through unspoiled woods. Whether you're wishing for the thrill of the big city or the simple pleasures of country life, Pennsylvania embodies the best of both.

Parks, Natural Areas, and Outdoor Recreation

Pristine forests and scenic parks abound throughout Pennsylvania, which has some 4.5 million acres of public land.

In the eastern part of the state, birders flock to **Hawk Mountain Sanctuary** during the spring and fall migrations when thousands of hawks, eagles, and falcons travel through. The **Delaware Water Gap Recreation Area** covers some 70,000 acres and includes a part of the famous Appalachian Trail, while **Bushkill Falls,** considered by many the "Niagara of Pennsylvania," is a series of eight waterfalls in the Pocono Mountains.

Close to Philadelphia is **Delaware Canal State Park,** which runs along the former towpath of the Delaware River, and the 89-acre **Bowman's Hill Wildflower Preserve,** while Philadelphia has **Fairmount Park,** the nation's largest urban park. West of the City of Brotherly Love is **Valley Forge National Historical Park,** the headquarters of the Revolutionary Army in 1777–78 and now a sprawling recreation area.

The former coal-mining towns of southwestern Pennsylvania form the fascinating backdrop for the **Ghost Town Trail** along an abandoned rail line. In the Laurel Highlands, **Ohiopyle State Park** is the site of the dramatic 1,700-ft-deep **Youghiogheny Gorge,** and a popular spot for whitewater rafting. The Grand Canyon of Pennsylvania, officially known as the **Pine Creek Gorge,** is 50 mi long and 1,000 ft deep, and is surrounded on its east and west sides by two state parks.

Pennsylvania's only national forest, the **Allegheny National Forest,** spans four counties and boasts stands of virgin beech-hemlock forest that are among the oldest in the eastern United States. Near the city of Erie is **Presque Isle State Park,** a 7-mi-long peninsula that is a popular spot to witness bird migration.

With much of Pennsylvania still rural, outdoor activities are plentiful. Camping, fishing, hunting, hiking, whitewater rafting, horseback riding, and skiing are popular throughout the state.

Campers can find more than 7,000 sites in state parks, as well as hundreds of private campgrounds. The fish are usually plentiful, too, with trout, bass, pike, and perch among the more common underwater creatures in the state's lakes and waterways. With one of the nation's largest populations of white-tailed deer, Pennsylvania is a prime destination during hunting season.

For hikers, the Appalachian Trail beckons, following the mountain ridges across the state from the Maryland border in the Laurel Highlands east to New Jersey and the Delaware Water Gap. Some of the best rafting in the region is in the **Youghiogheny River,** while equestrians treasure the **Horse Shoe Trail,** which runs some 130 mi from

Valley Forge to the Appalachians. The **Poconos** and the **Alleghenies** are popular draws for downhill skiers who flock to the slopes during the cold-weather months.

INTRODUCTION
HISTORY
REGIONS
WHEN TO VISIT
STATE'S GREATS
RULES OF THE ROAD
DRIVING TOURS

Culture, Education, and History

The early history of the United States comes alive in Philadelphia, site of **Independence National Historical Park,** as well as the gracious redbrick town homes of the **Society Hill Historic District.** The **Philadelphia Museum of Art,** the nation's third largest, displays a comprehensive sampling of art through the ages, while other institutions—such as the **Franklin Institute,** a science museum that honors Ben Franklin, the **Barnes Foundation,** which specializes in post-Impressionist art, and the **Pennsylvania Academy of the Fine Arts,** considered the nation's first museum and a treasure trove of American artists—take a more focused approach.

In Pittsburgh, contemporary art shines through the site-specific installations at the **Mattress Factory,** and at the **Andy Warhol Museum,** which celebrates the late pop artist's work, while the **Carnegie Museum of Art** and **Frick Art Museum** present rich holdings of European masterpieces and decorative arts. The **Gettysburg National Military Park** is a reminder of the tremendous sacrifice made to preserve these United States. Other cultural centers in the state commemorate the unique contributions of craftsmen and architects, notably the **Wharton Esherick Studio** in Chester County, the **Pearl S. Buck House** in Dublin, and Frank Lloyd Wright's **Fallingwater** in Fayette County near Pittsburgh. The state's key role in the early history of the petroleum industry is shown at the **Drake Well Museum** near Titusville, and one of Pennsylvania's native sons has his day in his hometown of Indiana, where the **Jimmy Stewart Museum** presents memorabilia from the star of *It's a Wonderful Life.*

Spectator Sports

Spectator sports, both professional and at the college level, are a passion among Pennsylvanians. Key cross-state rivalries among professional teams include the **Philadelphia Eagles** and **Pittsburgh Steelers** for football, the **Philadelphia Flyers** and **Pittsburgh Penguins** for hockey, and the **Philadelphia Phillies** and **Pittsburgh Pirates** for baseball. The **Penn State Nittany Lions** are usually a college football powerhouse, while **Temple University's Owls** men's basketball squad makes a regular run in the NCAA tournament. Auto racing also has a following at the **Pocono International Raceway** and the **Jennerstown Speedway.**

Rules of the Road

License requirements: To drive in Pennsylvania, you must be at least 16 years old and have a valid driver's license. Residents of Canada and most other countries can drive as long as they have valid driver's licenses issued in their home countries.

Right turn on red: Everywhere in Pennsylvania, you can make a right turn on red after coming to a complete stop, unless a sign is posted prohibiting it.

Seatbelt and helmet laws: Seatbelts are required for all passengers in the front seats. Children under four years must be in an approved passenger restraint everywhere in the vehicle and must use an approved safety seat in the front seat; ages one to three can use a regulation seatbelt in the back seat only; under age one, an approved safety seat must be used everywhere in the vehicle. Children aged four and older can use a regulation seatbelt. For more information, contact the State Department of Motor Vehicles at 717/787–6853.

Speed limit: The speed limit is 65 mph on rural interstate highways and 55 mph on heavily congested highways in and around urban areas.

Bucks County Driving Tour

RIVER RAFTING, ANTIQUES, AND COVERED BRIDGES

Distance: Approx. 50 mi (one way)   Time: 4 days (3 nights)
Breaks: Point Pleasant, New Hope, Doylestown

About an hour's drive northeast of Philadelphia and a short drive from New York City, Bucks County was unspoiled countryside until the 1930s, when weekend escapees from nearby cities built country retreat homes in the area. This slice of the Delaware River valley has, indeed, experienced the effects of urban sprawl and development, but many small-town communities, historic towns, and pastoral landscapes continue to make Bucks County the classic weekend getaway for Philadelphians. The area is known for antiques shops, many of which fall along a 4-mi stretch of U.S. Highway 22 between Lahaska and New Hope and on intersecting country roads. Eleven covered bridges remain in the area—the **Bucks County Tourist Commission** has a good map with concise details and information about the sites. There are also many charming inns and restaurants in the area.

Summer and fall weekends are very busy, so you need to make reservations well ahead and be ready for some crowds; a weekday trip could be more relaxing. Winter has its appeal here, too, especially around the holidays; the snow-covered buildings and fields are lovely.

❶ Begin your tour in **Point Pleasant** (on Route 32/River Road, approximately 8 mi north of New Hope). If you want a more scenic route take the Delaware Canal towpath (which

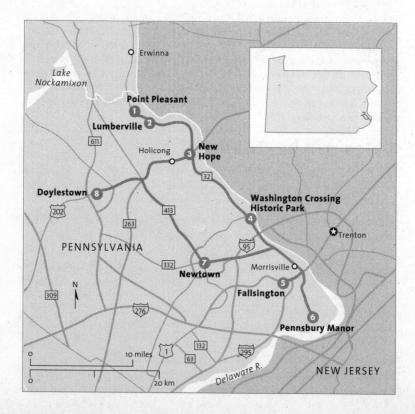

INTRODUCTION
HISTORY
REGIONS
WHEN TO VISIT
STATE'S GREATS
RULES OF THE ROAD
DRIVING TOURS

runs parallel to River Road). This is the section of Bucks County that is reminiscent of the Cotswolds of England, with bridge-keeper-lodges, corkscrew bends in the road, and gorgeous vistas (drivers, beware of the artists often painting at easels by the side of the road).

Point Pleasant is a popular base for exploring the Delaware River. More than 100,000 people a year—from toddlers to senior citizens—negotiate the Delaware on inner tubes or in canoes from **Bucks County River Country Canoe and Tube.** Rafts and kayaks are also available from April through October. If you get tired from all the fresh air and outdoor activity, head back to Point Pleasant and stay the night; otherwise south on Route 32/River Road for approximately 2 mi into Lumberville.

❷ Tiny **Lumberville** is centered around the Lumberville Store, established in 1770. This is the place to open your mail, pick up groceries, or rent a bicycle for a ride on the pastoral riverfront towpath.

❸ From Lumberville, drive south on Route 32/River Road for 3 mi to **New Hope.** The cosmopolitan village of New Hope is a mecca for artists, shoppers, and lovers of old homes—and hordes of day-trippers and backpackers on summer weekends. The town, listed on the National Register of Historic Places, is easy to explore on foot. The most interesting sights and stores are clustered along four blocks of Main Street and on the cross streets—Mechanic, Ferry, and Bridge—which lead to the river. The **Parry Mansion,** a stone house built in 1784, displays furnishings that reflect decorative changes from 1775 to the Victorian era—including candles, whitewashed walls, oil lamps, and wallpaper. The **New Hope Canal Boat Company** provides one-hour narrated barge excursions that take you past Revolutionary-era cottages, gardens, and artists' workshops. Have dinner and stay the night in New Hope.

❹ From New Hope continue south on Route 32/River Road for approximately 7 mi to **Washington Crossing Historic Park.** It was here on Christmas night in 1776 that General George Washington and 2,400 of his men crossed the Delaware River, surprised the mercenary Hessian soldiers, and captured Trenton. A tall granite shaft surrounded by 13 cedar trees marks the point from which the soldiers embarked that snowy night. Spend half a day exploring the park and then continue south on Route 32/River Road to Interstate 95 south to Route 1 into Morrisville and the nearby attractions of Fallsington and Pennsbury Mansion.

❺ The pre-Revolutionary village of **Fallsington** is where William Penn attended Quaker meetings. Exhibits at the village cover 300 years of American architecture, from a simple 17th-century log cabin to the Victorian excesses of the late 1800s. Ninety period homes surround the village, which is listed on the National Register of Historic Places. Three buildings, including a log cabin, have been restored and opened for guided tours by **Historic Fallsington, Inc.**

❻ **Pennsbury Manor,** on a slope 150 yards from the Delaware River, is a reconstruction of the Georgian-style mansion and plantation William Penn built as his country estate. Formal gardens, orchards, an icehouse, a smokehouse, a bake-and-brew house, and collections of tools attest to the self-sufficient nature of Penn's early community, and living-history demonstrations provide a glimpse into daily life in 17th-century America.

❼ From Pennsbury Manor, take Interstate 95 north to Route 332 west into **Newtown** (approximately 10 mi), with its many 18th- and 19th-century homes and inns. Downtown Newtown is on the National Register of Historic Places. The **Newtown Historical Association** has regional antiques and paintings by the late local artist Edward Hicks. An association brochure provides a walking tour of the town.

❽ Continue north on Route 413 for approximately 12 mi to U.S. Highway 202 west, and proceed for 3 mi into **Doylestown,** the county seat. The town is a showcase of American architecture, with stately Federal brick buildings, and gracious Queen Anne, Second Empire, and Italianate homes. The historic district includes nearly 1,200 buildings and is listed on the National Register of Historic Places. Stop at the **Central Bucks Chamber of Commerce** for a map highlighting three walking tours of the area. A main feature of Doylestown is Mercer Mile, consisting of three National Historic Landmark buildings—Fonthill, Mercer Museum, and the Moravian Pottery and Tile Works—conceived by talented resident Henry Chapman Mercer in the early 1800s. **Fonthill** is Henry Chapman Mercer's storybook home and surely one of the most unique abodes in the country. Built in 1910, and designed after a 13th-century Rhenish castle, the stone mansion bristles with turrets and balconies on the outside while the inside is a veritable maze of Gothic doorways, sudden stairways, and dead ends. The **Moravian Pottery and Tile Works** still produces unique Arts and Crafts–style picture tiles, with scenes from mythology, the Bible, and history. These "Mercer" tiles adorn such structures as Graumann's Chinese Theater in Hollywood, the Pocantico Hills residence of John D. Rockefeller, and the Harvard Lampoon Building. The **Mercer Museum** opened in 1916 and displays Mercer's collection of tools and more than 50,000 objects from before the age of steam. The **James A. Michener Art Museum** focuses on 19th- and 20th-century American art and Bucks County art. It was endowed by the late best-selling author, a Doylestown native. Have dinner and stay overnight in Doylestown before heading back to Erwinna or Point Pleasant.

To return to Point Pleasant, drive east on Route 202 for about 10 mi, then north on Route 32/River Road for another 10 mi.

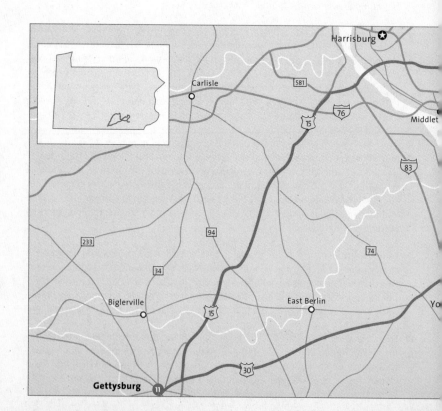

Lancaster County Driving Tour

FROM COLUMBIA TO GETTYSBURG

INTRODUCTION
HISTORY
REGIONS
WHEN TO VISIT
STATE'S GREATS
RULES OF THE ROAD
DRIVING TOURS

Distance: Approx. 175 mi (one way)   Time: 6 days (5 nights)

Breaks: Strasburg (lunch and overnight), Lancaster (lunch and overnight), Lititz (overnight), Hershey, Gettysburg

Lancaster County can be hectic, especially on summer weekends and in October, when the fall foliage attracts crowds and farmers markets and family-style restaurants overflow with people. Its main arteries, U.S. Highway 30 (also known as the Lincoln Highway and Lancaster Pike) and Route 340 (sometimes called the Old Philadelphia Pike), are lined with gift shops and outlets. If possible, plan your trip for early spring, September, or Christmas season, when it is less crowded. You should note that although many restaurants, shops, and farmers markets close Sunday for the Sabbath, commercial attactions remain open.

❶ Begin your tour in **Strasburg** (Routes 741 and 896), the railroad center of eastern Pennsylvania. The **Strasburg Rail Road** provides a scenic 9-mi round-trip excursion from Strasburg to Paradise on a rolling antique train originally chartered in 1832 to carry milk, mail, and coal. The train has wooden coaches and is pulled by an iron steam locomotive. You can buy a box lunch at the station and have a picnic at Groff's Grove along the way. Across the road from the Strasburg Rail Road is the **Railroad Museum of Pennsylvania,** which includes 12 railroad cars, including a Pullman sleeper that operated from 1855 to 1913, sleighs, and railroad memorabilia documenting the history of Penn-

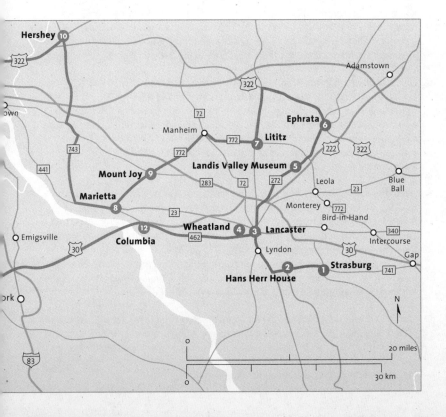

sylvania railroading. The **National Toy Train Museum** includes huge moving setups and hundreds of locomotives and cars on display, and the **Choo-Choo Barn, Traintown USA,** has a 1,700-sq-ft display of Lancaster County in miniature, with 16 trains and 140 figures and vehicles. Stay the night in Strasburg and head out next morning toward Lancaster.

❷ From Strasburg head west on Route 741 for about 2 mi and then south on U.S. Highway 222 to the **Hans Herr House.** This is the oldest in Lancaster County, considered the best example of medieval-style German architecture in North America.

❸ From the Hans Herr House, return to Route 741 and drive west for approximately 5 mi to Route 272, then north on Route 272 for 6 or so mi to **Lancaster** (on Route 272 just south of Route 283). In the early 1700s this was one of the largest inland cities in the 13 colonies. Today it is the heart of Pennsylvania Dutch Country. To get a good feel for the town, take the 90-minute **Historic Lancaster Walking Tour,** led by costumed guides and covering a 6-block radius filled with points of architectural and historical interest. One of the stops on the tour is the **Central Market,** which began with open-air stalls in 1742. You'll find everything from shoo-fly pie and sticky buns to fresh-grown produce from area farms.

❹ After you've had your tour and maybe a snack or lunch from the market, head to **Wheatland,** home of the only president from Pennsylvania, James Buchanan. The restored 1828 Federal mansion displays the 15th president's furniture just as it was during his lifetime.

❺ From Wheatland return to Lancaster and continue north for approximately 4 mi on Route 272 to the **Landis Valley Museum,** an outdoor museum of Pennsylvania's German rural life and folk culture before 1900. There are more than 15 structures on the grounds, from a farmstead to a country store, and from May through October there are demonstrations of crafts of the era. Head back to Lancaster for dinner and overnight.

❻ Next day, drive to **Ephrata** (12 mi northeast of Lancaster, on Route 501 to Route 272 into town). Visit the popular **Green Dragon Farmers Market and Auction.** The market, one of the largest in the state, occupies 30 acres of land, and includes a flea market and auction as well, and plenty of goods from local Amish and Mennonite farmers. Be sure to see the remains of the 18th-century **Ephrata Cloister.** There's a 45-minute tour of three restored buildings, after which you can wander unescorted through the stable, print shop, and craft shop.

❼ From the Cloister, drive west on Route 772 for approximately 8 mi to **Lititz.** Lititz was founded in 1756 by Moravians who settled in Pennsylvania to do missionary work among the Native Americans. Its tree-shaded main street, lined with 18th-century cottages and shops selling antiques, crafts, clothing, and gifts, is a fine place for a walk. Around the main square are the Moravian communal residences, a church dating from 1787, and a hospital that treated the wounded during the Revolutionary War. You can pick up a Historical Foundation walking tour brochure at the **General Sutter Inn** or at the **Johannes Mueller House**. Plan to stay overnight in Lititz.

❽ From Lititz, drive west on Route 772 for approximately 15 mi to **Marietta.** Close to half of the buildings in this restored river town, ranging in architectural style from log cabins to Federal and Victorian homes, are listed on the National Historic Register. In recent years it has become an artists' community, and is a nice place for a stroll past well-preserved facades, art galleries, and antiques shops.

➒ When you're tired of walking or just ready for a break, head to **Mount Joy** (5 mi northeast of Marietta on Route 772) for lunch or a snack. If you're interested in beer and beer-making, be sure to take the tour of **Bube's Brewery.** It will take you 43 ft below the street into the brewery's vaults and passages, which were built in a cave and served as part of the Underground Railroad.

➓ From Mount Joy, drive west on Route 230 for approximately 2 mi to Route 743 and proceed north for about 10 mi to the "chocolate town" of **Hershey.** Founded in 1903 by confectioner Milton S. Hershey, the town flaunts streetlights shaped like foil-wrapped kisses and avenues named Chocolate and Cocoa. At **Hershey's Chocolate World,** a 10-minute automated ride takes you through the steps of producing chocolate—from picking the cocoa beans to making candy bars. It also serves as the town's official visitor center. Taste-testing is a favorite part of the tour. Be sure to visit the **Hershey Museum of American Life,** which preserves the history of the town and its founder as well as that of Pennsylvania Germans and the Native Americans of the area. Have dinner and stay overnight in Hershey.

⓫ From the fanciful "World of Chocolate," drive 20 mi west on U.S. Highway 322 to U.S. Highway 15 south and proceed for 30 mi to the stark battlefields and monuments of **Gettysburg,** jarring testimonials to a darker chapter in American history. On this site, from July 1-3, 1863, 51,000 Americans were killed, wounded, or counted as missing in the bloodiest battle of the Civil War. The Gettysburg National Military Park **Visitor Center** provides a free map with a driving tour through the battlefield, as well as an orientation program, Civil War exhibits, and current schedules of ranger-conducted programs and talks. Free walking-tour maps, outlining short 1-mi loops that include the sites of some of the battle's most pivotal engagements, are available at the center. Spend at least a day exploring the park and stay overnight in Gettysburg.

⓬ From Gettysburg, drive approximately 45 mi east on U.S. Highway 30 to the once-bustling river town of **Columbia.** Today Columbia is tranquil, with several museums worth exploring. The **Watch and Clock Museum of the National Association of Watch and Clock Collectors** displays a large and varied collection of timepieces, specialized tools, and related items from the primitive to the modern. There's a 19th-century Tiffany globe clock, a German Black Forest organ clock with 94 pipes, and the showstopper Engle Clock—an 1877 clock of Strasbourg, France, that took clock-maker Stephen D. Engle 20 years to complete. It has 48 moving figures. You can capture a bit of the state's history at **Wright's Ferry Mansion,** the former residence of English Quaker Susanna Wright. The 1738 stone house showcases period furniture in the Philadelphia William and Mary and Queen Anne styles and a great collection of English needlework, ceramics, and glass, all predating 1750. Before heading back to Lancaster, stop for lunch and a bit of shopping at the **Market House and Dungeon,** one of the oldest continuously operating farmers markets in the state.

To return to Lancaster, drive west on U.S. Highway 30 for approximately 10 mi.

ALLENTOWN

MAP 7, K5

(Nearby towns also listed: Bethlehem, Easton, Erwinna, Kutztown, Quakertown)

Originally called North Hampton Town, the city was first settled by German immigrants in the 1720s. It was where the Liberty Bell was hidden when British troops began melting church bells in Philadelphia for additional ammunition. In 1829, the name was changed to Allentown in honor of William Allen, who first settled the village. Today, the city has transformed itself from an iron town to a tourist destination with its numerous historic sites and museums.

Information: **Lehigh County Chamber of Commerce** | 462 Walnut St., 18102 | 610/437–9661 | fax 610/437–4907 | www.lehighcountychamber.org.

Attractions

Allentown Art Museum. The library collection of architect Frank Lloyd Wright is here, along with permanent collections spanning 200 years of Early American paintings and sculpture. | 35 North St. (5th and Court) | 610/432–4333 | www.allentownartmuseum.org | $4; free Sun. | Tues.–Sat. 11–5, Sun. noon–5.

Cedar Crest College. A private liberal arts college for women established in 1867 with 35 majors and preprofessional programs. Many weekly events throughout the school year including live band performances, comedy nights, theater and dance productions, lectures, and casino nights. | 100 College Dr. | 610/437–4471 or 800/360–1222 | fax 610/606–4647 | www.cedarcrest.edu | Free | Daily.

Clover Hill Vineyards and Winery. Taste and buy local wines here, and go on a special tour during July through September. You can also buy special non-grape wines, including a warm spiced-apple wine that's perfect for Pennsylvania's crisp fall weather. | 9850 Newtown Rd., Breinigsville | 610/395–2468 | fax 610–366–1246 | www.cloverhillwinery.com | Free | Mon.–Sat. 10–5:30, Sun. noon–5.

Dorney Park and Wildwater Kingdom. A 200-acre amusement and water park with over 100 rides and attractions, four world-class roller coasters, and water slides. Rides include The Dominator, twin towers that rocket 160 ft up and plummet 17 stories; Steel Force, the tallest and fastest roller coaster on the East Coast; and Hercules, a wooden roller coaster with a 157-ft drop. Wildwater Kingdom has more than 11 water slides including the world's largest elevated water slide. | 3830 Dorney Park Rd. | 610/395–3724 or 800/551–5656 | fax 610/391–7685 | www.dorneypark.com | $31.10, special rates for senior citizens and children, parking $6 | Dorney Park, May–Oct., Sun.–Fri. 10 AM–10 PM, Sat. 10 AM–11 PM; Wildwater Kingdom, Memorial Day–mid-Sept., daily 10 AM–7 PM.

Frank Buchman House. The home of Frank Buchman, founder of the international Moral Re-Armament movement. You can learn how the ordained Lutheran pastor traveled throughout the world during the early 19th century as an emissary for peace. | 117 N. 11th St. | 610/435–4664 | fax 610/435–9812 | www.voicenet.com/~lchs | $2 | May–Sept., Sat. 1–4 and by appointment, closed Sun.–Fri.

Game Preserve. Founded in 1909 as a sanctuary to preserve various wildlife species. Animals from all over the world roam free among the preserve's 1,108.4 acres. There is a petting area for kids, a nature study building, and a picnic area along Jordan Creek, where fishing is allowed. | 5150 Game Preserve Rd., Schnecksville | 610/799–4171 | fax 610/799–4170 | www.gamepreserve.org | $6, special rates for senior citizens, children, and groups | Late Apr.–Oct., daily 10–5.

George Taylor House and Park. Home of George Taylor, a signer of the Declaration of Independence. The home was built in 1768 in the Georgian style and includes period furnishings. | Lehigh and Poplar Sts., Catasauqua | 610/435–4664 | fax 610/435–9812 | www.voicenet.com/~lchs | $2 | June–Oct., weekends 1–4 and by appointment, closed weekdays.

Haines Mill Museum. A water turbine–driven gristmill built before the American Revolution as a service to local farmers. The mill ceased operations in 1956 due to national competition. | 3600 Dorney Park Rd. | 610/435–4664 | fax 610/435–9812 | Free | May–Sept., weekends 1–4 and by appointment, closed weekdays.

Lehigh County Museum. Houses permanent and changing exhibits on Lehigh County history including geology, immigration, and industrial growth. The building, constructed in

1814–1817, also houses a research library and the office of the Lehigh County Historical Society. | 501 W. Hamilton St. | 610/435–4664 | fax 610/435–9812 | www.voicenet.com/~lchs | Free | weekdays 9–5, Sat. 10–4, Sun. 1–4.

Liberty Bell Shrine. The shrine occupies the exact spot where the Liberty Bell was hidden from the British when they came through Philadelphia in 1776. The museum has changing exhibits on the Revolutionary War and the Colonial era. A 46-ft mural depicts in six scenes the important area events during the Revolutionary War. | 622 Hamilton St. | 610/435–4232 | fax 610/435–5667 | www.geocities.com/athens/ithaca/1760 | Free | Mar.–Apr. and Nov.–Dec., Thurs.–Sat. noon–4, closed Sun.–Wed.; May–Oct., Mon.–Sat. noon–4, Sun. by appointment.

Lil'le'hi Trout Nursery. Ask anyone in town to point the way to this hatchery, which houses about 65,000 brook, brown, and rainbow trout. You can buy food to feed the eager fish. | Fish Hatchery Rd. | 610/437–7656 | Free | Daily 9–3.

Lock Ridge Furnace Museum. Two anthracite coal-burning iron furnaces built by the Thomas Iron Company in 1868 are the focus of this museum. The furnaces turned Alburtis into an industrial powerhouse, providing material for railroads and other industries. Exhibits illustrate how iron was made over 100 years ago. You also can tour the rebuilt furnace room, engine house, and cast house. | 525 Franklin St., Alburtis | 610/435–4664 | fax 610/435–9812 | www.voicenet.com/~lchs | Free | May–Sept., weekends 1–4 and by appointment; closed weekdays.

Muhlenberg College. An independent undergraduate coed institution affiliated with the evangelical Lutheran Church. It was founded in 1848 to provide a liberal arts education in the Christian humanistic tradition. | 2400 Chew St. | 484/664–3230 | fax 484/664–3477 | www.muhlenberg.edu | Free | Daily.

Saylor Park Cement Industry Museum. The nation's only historic site devoted to the people and processes that made "liquid rock," a vital building material for the industrial revolution. | 245 N. 2nd St., Coplay | 610/435–4664 | fax 610/435–9812 | www.voicenet.com/~lchs | Free | May–Sept., weekends 1–4 by appointment.

Skiing. With 27 runs and seven lifts, **Blue Mountain** provides the highest vertical drop in Pennsylvania at 1,082 ft. The mountain has a terrain park, a half pipe, and snow tubing. Snowboarding, snowblades, and ski rentals are available. | 1660 Blue Mt. Dr., Palmerton | 610/826–7700 or 877/SKI–BLUE | fax 610/826–7828 | www.skibluemt.com | $35 weekdays, $42 weekends and holidays | Dec.–Apr., weekdays 8:30AM–10 PM, weekends and holidays, 7:30 AM–10PM. **Doe Mountain** has 790 acres of skiable terrain, an 1,100-ft summit, and a 500-ft vertical drop. With a total of 15 trails, the longest run measures 7,920 ft. There are seven lifts, a terrain park, and a half pipe. Snow tubing and equipment rental are available. | 101 Doe Mountain La., Macungie | 610/682–7100 | fax 610/682–7110 | www.doe-mountain.com | $25 weekdays, $33 weekends | Dec.–mid-Mar.

Trexler Memorial Park. The park covers 134 acres, with 71 acres of spacious landscaped lawns and gardens and two ponds. Two trails are available for hiking: a 1.2-mi trail and a 1.5-mi trail. Bicycling is allowed on Tuesday, Thursday, and Saturday. | Cedar Crest Blvd. and Parkway Blvd.; Take Rte.22W to Cedar Crest Blvd. exit. Make a left off to the exit going toward Allentown. Take Cedarcrest Blvd. to intersection of Parkway Blvd. and Certonia Rd. Turn right onto Certonia and follow to Spring House. Make a right onto Spring House and the entrance to the park will be ½ mi on the right | 610/437–7628 | fax 610/437–7685 | Free | Daily dawn to dusk.

Trout Hall. Allentown's oldest surviving home, built in 1770 by James Allen, a member of an elite British-American family and son of the founder of Allentown. | 414 Walnut St. | 610/435–4664 | fax 610/435–9812 | www.voicenet.com/~lchs | $2 | Apr.–Nov., Tues.–Sat. noon–3, Sun. 1–4 and by appointment; closed Mon.

Troxell–Steckel House and Farm Museum. Built in 1755–1756, this Colonial stone farmhouse has German medieval-style architecture. Exhibits of farm implements and craft tools are on display in the barn. On 31.4 acres open to picnicking and fishing in Coplay Creek, which is stocked with trout from the Cedarbrook hatchery. | 4229 Reliance St., Egypt | 610/435–4664 | fax 610/435–9812 | www.voicenet.com/~lchs | $2 | June–Oct., weekends 1–4 and by appointment, closed weekdays.

ON THE CALENDAR

MAY: *Mayfair.* Family-oriented arts festival presents more than 220 free musical performances over five days and includes crafts and food. | 2020 Hamilton St. | 610/437–6900 | fax 610/437–6904 | www.mayfairfestival.org | Free | Memorial Day weekend.

AUG.: *Das Awkscht Fescht.* You can spend three days enjoying one of America's largest antique, classic, and sports car exhibits with food, entertainment, crafts, music, an antique auto flea market, kids' shows, and an antique toy show. | Macungie Memorial Park | 610/967–2317 | www.awkscht.com | $6.

AUG.: *Drum Corps International—Eastern Regional Championship.* Nearly two dozen world-class drum corps compete in this annual event. Skilled musicians combine showmanship with precision marching, competing over five days. | J. Birney Crum Stadium, 21st and Linden Sts. | 610/966–5344 | www.dci.org | Call for prices.

AUG.–SEPT.: *Great Allentown Fair.* The staples of the country fair are all here for one week: farm and commercial exhibits, games, food, entertainment, and rides. | Fairgrounds | 610/435–SHOW | fax 610/433–4005 | www.allentownfair.com | $4.

AUG.–DEC.: *Hawk Mountain Sanctuary Official Fall Hawk Watch.* On the Kittatinny Ridge on North Lookout, 30 mi south of Allentown. Annual 123-day census of migrating raptors includes golden eagles, peregrine falcons, and several kinds of hawks. Established in 1934 as the first refuge for raptors, census takers note some 18,000 birds each fall. | 610/756–6000.

SEPT.: *Super Sunday.* An annual one-day event includes craft booths, food, and entertainment. | Hamilton Street Mall | 610/437–7616 | Free.

NOV.–JAN.: *Lights in the Parkway.* Light sculptures illuminate a 1.7 mi stretch of the Lehigh Parkway in the City of Allentown. You can take a 25-minute drive through eight major displays while listening to a customized holiday music soundtrack on a targeted radio station. A trip to Santa's workshop, a gift shop, and refreshment barn complete the experience. | 610/437–9661 | Free.

Dining

Appennino. Italian. Showcasing a 19th-century stone dining room, with tapestry-covered chairs, this restaurant is only 5 mi northwest of town. Specialties include Gnocchi Appenino, homemade potato dumplings with fresh tomato basil sauce; spaghetti a la Genovese, which is served with pesto of basil pine nuts and fresh mint; and for dessert, Appennino cheesecake. | 3079 Willow St. | 610/799–2727 | Closed Sun. No lunch Sat. | $16–$30 | AE, D, MC, V.

Cab Frye's. Continental. An 1830s tavern that has been used as such since it was built. About 10 mi south of town on Rte. 29, the three-story brick building includes an interior with antiques and period furniture. Known for veal Oscar and Scottish lobster. | 914 Gravel Pike, Palm | 215/679–9935 | www.cabfryes.com | Closed Sun. No lunch Mon., Tues. | $20–$35 | AE, D, MC, V.

Inn at Perkiomen Creek. Continental. Once a barbershop, speakeasy, and general store before being renovated into a restaurant, this 1846 building has been in constant use since it was built. The interior has exposed stone walls and fireplaces, and the inn is known for its chicken and beef dishes. Live music on Thursday; Sunday brunch. | 1840 Perkiomenville Rd., Perkiomenville; 20 mi south of town on Rte. 29 | 215/234–2292 | www.innatperkiomen-creek.com | $12–$22 | AE, D, DC, MC, V.

Portabellos. Italian. On the first floor of the Globe Hotel, this restaurant has dark wood chairs, all in different designs, and glass top tables, all in the Victorian style. Known for pasta and seafood. Sunday brunch. | 326 4th St., East Greenville; 12 mi south of town on Rte. 29 | 215/679–5948 | No lunch | $15–$30 | AE, MC, V.

Shanty Restaurant. Seafood. On the west side of Allentown, this popular restaurant has a formal sit-down area and lounge with live music. Hear blues to pop music most Thursdays through Saturdays. | 617 N. 19th St. | 610/437–5358 | Reservations essential | $15–$27 | AE, D, DC, MC, V.

Lodging

Allenwood. Built in 1962 out of cinder block and wood, this small motel in west Allentown is 2 mi from Dorney Park. It is one story high with outside room entrances and some studio units. Microwaves, refrigerators. Cable TV. Some pets allowed. | 1058 Hausman Rd. | 610/395–3707 | fax 610/530–8166 | www.aaa.com | 21 rooms | $50–$120 | AE, D, MC, V.

Comfort Suites. Popular with families, this upscale, four-story hotel is across from Dorney Park. It has a lobby with atrium and contemporary furniture, interior corridors, and spacious suites with sofa beds. Restaurant, bar (with entertainment), complimentary Continental breakfast, room service. In-room data ports, microwaves, refrigerators. Cable TV. Exercise equipment. Business services, airport shuttle. | 3712 Hamilton Blvd. | 610/437–9100 | fax 610/437–0221 | www.comfortinn.com | 122 suites | $110–$130 suites | AE, D, DC, MC, V.

Days Inn Conference Center. Built in 1957 on 27 acres, this single-story motor hotel is about 3 mi outside Allentown, only 5 min. from Dorney Park. Restaurant, bar. Some refrigerators. Cable TV. Pool. Volleyball. Video games. Laundry facilities. Business services, airport shuttle. | 1151 Bulldog Dr. | 610/395–3731 | fax 610/395–9899 | www.daysinnallentown.com | 285 rooms in 5 buildings | $49–$140 | AE, D, DC, MC, V.

Econo Lodge. Like many of the Allentown hotels, this lodge is near the commercial district. You can smell the baked goods from the Pillsbury factory nearby. Complimentary breakfast. | 2115 Downy Flake La. | 610/797–2200 | fax 610/797–2818 | www.econolodge.com | 49 | $50–$80, suites $95–$150 | AE, D, DC, MC, V.

Hampton Inn. Convenient to I–78 and Rte. 100, this five-story hotel is 10 mi west of downtown Allentown. It was built in 1987 on highway property and is only 9 mi from Doe Mountain Ski Area. Picnic area, complimentary Continental breakfast. Cable TV. Exercise equipment. Business services, airport shuttle. | 7471 Keebler Way | 610/391–1500 | fax 610/391–0386 | www.hamptoninn.com | 124 rooms, 10 suites | $69–$134, $109–$164 suites | AE, D, DC, MC, V.

Hilton. An elegant lobby is one of the highlights of this upscale, eight-story hotel. It was built in 1981 and is within walking distance of the Lehigh County Museum and many restaurants in downtown Allentown. Restaurant, bar. In-room data ports. Cable TV. Pool. Exercise equipment. Business services, airport shuttle. | 904 Hamilton St. | 610/433–2221 | fax 610/433–1077 | www.hilton.com | 224 rooms, 7 suites | $145–$165 | AE, D, DC, MC, V.

Holiday Inn Express. Completely renovated in 1999, this relatively small hotel was built in 1980 and is in the heart of downtown. It has four stories with interior corridors and it's only 8 mi from Dorney Park. Complimentary Continental breakfast. In-room data ports. Cable TV. Business services. Some pets allowed (fee). | 1715 Plaza La. | 610/435–7880 | fax 610/432–2555 | www.humphreyhospitality.com | 82 rooms | $79–$110 | AE, D, DC, MC, V.

Howard Johnson Inn and Suites. This hotel is on a busy commercial strip, close to local highways. It was built in 1989 and has two floors with interior corridors and elevators. Complimentary breakfast. Indoor pool. Hot tub. Some pets allowed ($30 deposit). | 3220 Hamilton Blvd. | 610/439–4000 | fax 610/438–8947 | www.hojo.com | 58 | $62–$140 | AE, D, DC, MC, V.

Mcintosh Inn of Allentown. Less than 1 mi from Lehigh International airport, this inn is directly across the street from a shopping center. Continental breakfast. Cable TV. | 1701 Catasauqua Rd.; Rte.22 and Airport Rd. | 610/264–7531 | fax 610/264–5474 | www.mcintoshinn.com | 107 | $65–$74 | AE, D, DC, MC, V.

Sheraton Inn Jetport. This full-service, three-story hotel is next to the airport in the Lehigh Valley Industrial Park, about 5 mi from both Allentown and Bethlehem. Restaurant, bar (with entertainment), room service. In-room data ports. Cable TV. Indoor pool. Hot tub, sauna. Exercise equipment. Business services, airport shuttle. Some pets allowed. | 3400 Airport Rd. | 610/266–1000 | fax 610/251–5717 | www.sheraton.com | 147 rooms, 30 suites | $99–$119, $119–$145 suites | AE, D, DC, MC, V.

ALTOONA

MAP 7, E6

(Nearby town also listed: Ebensburg)

One of the first towns to be dubbed the gateway to the West, Altoona became a focal point in western expansion with the completion of Horseshoe Curve in the Allegheny Mountains. At one time, the city produced most of the nation's railroad cars. Today it remains a destination point for railroad buffs who visit its active railroad yards.

Information: Blair County Chamber of Commerce | 1212 12th Ave., 16601 | 814/943–8151 | fax 814/943–5239 | www.blairchamber.com.

Attractions

Allegheny Portage Railroad Historic Site. Learn about the history of the local rail connection, built in 1834 and operational until 1854. The rail used stair-step locks connected by track that hauled barges up one side of the mountain and down the other. See reconstructed dioramas of equipment, horses, and local folk as they might have looked in days gone by. | 110 Federal Park Way, Gallitzin | 814/886–6150 | www.nps.gov/alpo | $2 | Daily 9–5 except major holidays.

Baker Mansion Museum. A Greek Revival–style mansion finished in 1849 by Elias Baker, owner of the Allegheny Iron Furnace. The Baker family lived there until 1914. The rooms of the mansion have period furnishings and antiques, depicting the lifestyle of the Baker family, and exhibits display local history. The Blair County Historical Society maintains a research library at the mansion. | 3500 Oak La. | 814/942–3916 | fax 814/942–7078 | www.alleghenymountains.com | $4, special rates for students, senior citizens, and children; research library $3 | Memorial Day–Labor Day, Tues.–Sun. 1–4:30, closed Mon.; April 15–Memorial Day and Labor Day–Oct., weekends 1–4:30, closed weekdays.

Benzel's Pretzel Factory. Self-guided tours illustrate the pretzel-making process. You can buy some fresh pretzels at the the outlet store at the end of the tour. | 5200 Sixth Ave. | 814/942–5062, 800/344–4438 | www.benzel.com | Free | Mon.–Fri. 9–5, Sat. 9–1, closed Sun.

Bland's Park. The park consists of mostly water rides, but there's also miniature golf and many kids' rides. | Old Rte. 220 Box 235, Tipton | 814/684–3538 | fax 814/684–9820 | www.blandspark.com | Free to enter park; daily pass for rides and water park $6.95–$11.95 | May, weekends noon–dusk, closed weekdays; June–Aug., daily 10–9; Sept., weekends noon–dusk, closed weekdays.

Canoe Creek State Park. Remnants of the Blair County Limestone Company operations are in this 958-acre park, which also has a 155-acre lake that provides fishing, swimming, and boating. There are eight modern cabins available to rent, an extensive trail system for hiking and horseback riding, and several picnic tables. Hunting is allowed on 550 acres of the park and winter activities include ice skating, sledding, and cross-country skiing. | R.R. 2, Hollidaysburg 16648 | 814/695–6807 or 888/PA-PARKS | fax 814/696–6023 | www.dcnr.state.pa.us | Free | Daily 8 AM–sunset; cabins and lake, 24-hour access.

Fort Roberdeau. Reconstruction of a 1778 fort originally built to protect settlers and miners producing bullet lead for Washington's troops during the initial stages of the Revolutionary War. On the National Register of Historic Places, the stockade and cabins were rebuilt in 1976. The 45 acres include picnic facilities, a visitor center, a museum shop, an 1858 barn, and nature trails. | R.R. 3 Box 391 | 814/946–0048 | fax 814/943–5074 | www.alleghenymountains.com | $3, special rates for senior citizens, children, and groups | May–Oct., Tues.–Sat. 11–5, Sun.–Mon. 1–5.

Horseshoe Curve Visitors Center. A National Historic Landmark, the visitor center interprets the story of how trains scaled the Allegheny Mountains—one of the gateways to the West—for the first time on February 15, 1854. You can walk the steps to the track elevation or ride the funicular. | 1300 9th Ave. | 814/946–0834 | fax 814/946–9457 | www.railroad-city.com | $3.50, special rates for senior citizens, children, and groups | Apr.–Oct., daily 10–7; Nov.–Dec., Tues.–Sun. 10–4, closed Mon.

Lakemont Park. Opened in 1894, Lakemont Park is the eighth oldest park in the country and is home to the world's oldest standing wooden roller coaster, Leap the Dips, which was built in 1902. The roller coaster has been restored and reopened in 1999. The park includes more than 30 other rides. | 700 Park Ave. | 814/949–7275 or 800/434–8006 | fax 814/949–9207 | www.lakemontparkfun.com | Free to enter park, day pass for rides $7.95 | May–Sept., daily 11–9.

Prince Gallitzin State Park. The 6,249-acre park includes 437 campsites, 10 cabins, several picnic tables, a 9-mi trail network for hiking, horseback riding trails, 7 mi of cross-country ski trails, more than 3,000 acres for hunting, and a 1,600-acre lake that provides boating, fishing, and swimming. The park is open to snowmobiling in the winter. | 966 Marina Rd., Patton | 814/674–1000 814/674–1007, or 888/PA–PARKS | fax 814/674–1010 | www.dcnr.state.pa.us | Free | Daily 8 AM–sunset.

Railroader's Memorial Museum. You can learn the story of the men and women of the Pennsylvania Railroad through interactive exhibits and movies at this museum, which opened in 1980. It also includes model trains, rolling stock, and a film tribute to the people who built the Horseshoe Curve. Housed in the former Pennsylvania Railroad master mechanics building, the facility documents the technological development of the largest railroad in the world. A computer database provides information about the men and women who worked for the railroad. | 1300 9th Ave. | 814/946–0834 or 888/425–8666 | fax 814/946–9457 | www.railroadcity.com | $8.50, special rates for senior citizens, children, and groups | Apr.–Oct., daily 9–5; Nov.–Mar., Tues.–Sun. 10–5, closed Mon.

KODAK'S TIPS FOR NIGHT PHOTOGRAPHY

Lights at Night
· Move in close on neon signs
· Capture lights from unusual vantage points

Fireworks
· Shoot individual bursts using a handheld camera
· Capture several explosions with a time exposure
· Include an interesting foreground

Fill-In Flash
· Set the fill-in light a stop darker than the ambient light

Around the Campfire
· Keep flames out of the frame when reading the meter
· For portraits, take spot readings of faces
· Use a tripod, or rest your camera on something solid

Using Flash
· Stay within the recommended distance range
· Buy a flash with the red-eye reduction mode

From *Kodak Guide to Shooting Great Travel Pictures* © 2000 by Fodor's Travel Publications

ON THE CALENDAR

MAY: *Blair County Arts Festival.* Held on the campus of Penn State University, this annual celebration of visual and performing arts lasts two days and features music, food, student music, crafts, and a fireworks show. | 814/949–2787.

SEPT.: *Keystone Country Festival.* A 3-day event that celebrates local specialties with country crafts, food, and live music. | Lakemont Park | 814/943–418 or 800/84–ALTOONA | $3, special rates for children and seniors.

OCT.: *Railfest.* This weekend event commemorates Altoona's rail heritage with shop tours, excursions around the Horseshoe Curve and through the Gallitzin Tunnels, and dozens of exhibits. | 1300 9th Ave. | 814/946–0834 | fax 814/946–9457 | www.railroadc-ity.com | $5, train ride $14, weekender pass $25.

Dining

Jethro's. Continental. A long oak bar, fireplace, and a large patio facing nearby woods enhance the rustic warmth of this restaurant. It's by the Ramada, less than a mile south of Logan Valley Mall. Known for prime rib and steaks. Kids' menu. Sunday brunch. | 417 Parkview La. | 814/942–2178 | No lunch Sun. | $7–$16 | AE, D, MC, V.

U.S. Hotel. Continental. This 1835 building once housed a hotel popular with disembarking train passengers, and still has many of those original fixtures and furnishings. The hotel's tavern next door still has its original booths. The restaurant is separated into four dining sections. Specialties include Maryland crab cakes, veal Santa Monica, and stuffed rainbow trout. | 401 S. Juniata St., Hollidaysburg; 6 mi south of town on Rte. 36 | 814/695–9924 | www.theushotel.com | No lunch Sat. | $12–$20 | AE, D, DC, MC, V.

Lodging

Days Inn. An up-to-date, two-story chain hotel, built in 1985 and close to the Altoona Rail-roaders Museum. It is less than a mile from Lakemont Park and 3.5 mi from the Rail-roader's Memorial Museum. In-room data ports, microwaves, refrigerators. Cable TV. Hot tub. | 3306 Pleasant Valley Blvd. | 814/944–9661 | fax 814/944–9557 | www.daysinn.com | 111 rooms | $76.50 | AE, D, DC, MC, V.

Hampton Inn–Altoona. Built in 1998, this hotel is adjacent to Logan Valley Mall. Indoor pool. Hot tub. | 180 Charlotte Dr. | 814/941–3500 | fax 814/941–0968 | www.hamptoninn.com | 110 | $79–$92 | AE, D, DC, MC, V.

Holiday Inn. Built in 1960, this hotel is 2 mi from downtown Altoona, 1 mi from Lakemont Park, and within 15 mi of Horseshoe Curve. Some rooms have mountain and valley views. Restaurant, bar (with entertainment). In-room data ports, refrigerators, some in-room hot tubs. Cable TV. Laundry facilities. | 2915 Pleasant Valley Blvd. | 814/944–4581 or 800/465–4329 | fax 814/943–4996 | www.innaltoona.com | 149 rooms, 2 suites | $79–$99, $129 suites | AE, D, DC, MC, V.

Motel 6. Large rooms have king and queen beds at a reasonable price. This one-story motel was built in 1987 and is only 7 mi from Horseshoe Curve. Outdoor pool. Laundry facil-ities. Pets allowed (no fee). | 155 Sterling St. | 814/946–7601 | fax 814/946–5162 | www.motel6.com | 112 rooms | $50–$55 | AE, D, DC, MC, V.

Ramada. The only full-service hotel in town, this three-story chain hotel offers ski pack-ages to Blue Knob Ski Area (20 mi southwest of town). It is only 2 mi from downtown, 3 mi from the Railroader's Memorial Museum, and 10 mi from Horseshoe Curve. 3 Restau-rants, bar, complimentary Continental breakfast, room service. In-room data ports. Cable TV. Indoor pool, wading pool. Hot tub. Gym. Business services, airport shuttle. Some pets allowed. | 1 Sheraton Dr. | 814/946–1631 | fax 814/946–0785 | www.ramada.com | 215 rooms | $75–$90 | AE, D, DC, MC, V.

AMBRIDGE

(Nearby towns also listed: Beaver Falls, Pittsburgh)

One of Pennsylvania's younger boroughs, Ambridge was established in 1903 when the Harmony Society, a band of people who came to America in search of religious freedom, sold more than 2,500 acres of land as a site for a bridge-building plant. It took its name from the American Bridge Company, the area's first big industry. The borough is only 15 minutes from Pittsburgh International Airport and 20 minutes from downtown Pittsburgh.

Information: Ambridge Chamber of Commerce | 422 Merchant St., 15003 | 724/266–3040 | fax 724/266–3096 | www.beavercounty.net/aacc.

Attractions

Laughlin Memorial Library. Alexander Laughlin built this library for his son in 1929. The building has unusual monolithic columns made of solid Italian marble. | 11th Street and Maplewood Avenue | 724/266–3857 | www.co.beaver.pa.usa/library/ambridge.html | Free | Mon.–Thur. 10–7, Fri. 10–4, Sat. 9–4, closed Sun.

Old Economy Village. Third and final home of the Harmony Society (1804–1905), one of America's most successful Christian communal societies. Guides wearing Harmonist dress take you through the museum, cabinet shop, community kitchen, baker house, store, and the George and Frederick Rapp houses, all built between 1824 and 1830. More than 16,000 Harmonist-owned objects are displayed in the 17 original buildings. | 14 Church St. | 724/266–4500 | fax 724/266–7506 | www.oldeconomyvillage.org | $5, special rates for senior citizens, children, and families | Mar.–Dec., Tues.–Sat. 9–5, Sun. noon–5, closed Mon.

Raccoon Creek State Park. A 7,323-acre park includes a 101-acre lake, available for boating, swimming, fishing, ice skating, and ice fishing. There are hiking trails, 16 mi of equestrian trails, 172 campsites, 11 cabins, several picnic tables, hills for sledding, and more than 5,000 acres for hunting. The historic Frankfort Mineral Springs, site of a nationally known health spa in the 1800s, is in the park. Thousands of people who believed in the healing powers of the mineral water were attracted to this area until the spa was destroyed by fire in 1932. | 3000 Rte. 18, Hookstown | 724/899–2200 or 888/PA–PARKS | www.dcnr.state.pa.us | Free | Daily 8 AM–dusk.

ON THE CALENDAR

MAY: *Nationality Days.* This three-day festival celebrates ethnic pride with local foods, entertainment, crafts, and kids' attractions. | Merchant St. | 724/266–3040 | free.
DEC.: *Christmas Open House.* You can enjoy horse and carriage rides and carolling during this two-day annual event. Many free hand-outs from the local businesses create holiday fun for the whole family. | 724/266–3040.

Dining

House of Hunan. Chinese. An oriental-style sign greets and leads you inside, where Asian music fills the air, the walls are adorned with Chinese wall coverings, and each table has a Chinese lantern. Try General Tso's chicken or sesame chicken. BYOB. Only 1 mi north of downtown. | 2316 Duss Ave. | 724/266–5778 | Closed Mon. No lunch weekends | $7–$13 | No credit cards.

Lodging

Sewickley Country Inn. Families with children and pets are welcome at this inn, 4 mi from Ambridge. It was built in the 1940s. There are six individual buildings: three 1-story, two 2-story, one 3-story. 1 restaurant. Outdoor pool. Laundry. | 801 Ohio River Blvd., Sewickley | 412/741–4300 | fax 412/741–1908 | www.sewickleycountryinn.com | 149 | $82 | AE, D, DC, MC, VI.

ASHLAND

MAP 7, I5

(Nearby town also listed: Hazelton)

In the valley between Mahoney and Logan Mountains, Ashland was named for Henry Clay's estate in Lexington, Kentucky, by Samuel Lewis in 1847. The town was settled as a result of mining. Today, its vast forests and mountains make ideal hunting and fishing grounds and provide hiking and camping.

Information: Schuylkill County Chamber of Commerce | 91 S. Progress Ave., Pottsville, PA 17901 | 570/622–1942 | fax 570/622–1638 | www.schuylkillchamber.com.

Attractions

Knoebels Grove Amusement Park. At the turn of the century, people who took hayride trips to places like this original family farm and park for relaxation were called "tally-hos." Today the park has amusements both old and new with rollercoasters and an original carousel from 1913. | 45 East Valley Ave. Elysburg | 800/487–4386 | fax 570/672–3293 | www.knoebels.com | Free | Varies (11-10 summer).

Museum of Anthracite Mining. The museum contains a diverse collection of tools, machinery, and photos that depict the mining of hard coal. Exhibits and equipment provide a unique glimpse of the work in and around the anthracite mines and explore the dangers of mining hard coal. | 17th and Pine Sts. | 570/875–4708 | fax 570/875–3732 | www.state.pa.us | $3.50; special rates for senior citizens, children, families, and groups | Apr.–Nov., daily 10–6; Dec.–Mar., by appointment.

Pioneer Tunnel Coal Mine and Steam Lokie Ride. Mine cars rebuilt and electrically powered take you into the Pioneer Tunnel, which ceased operation as an anthracite coal mine in 1931. The temperature inside the mine averages 52 degrees year-round. The other main attraction is a narrow-gauge steam train ride aboard the Lokie Henry Clay, which was used years ago to haul coal cars. Now it pulls passengers in the cars 3,000 ft along the side of Mahanay Mountain. | 19th & Oak Sts. | 570/875–3850 or 570/875–3301 | fax 570/875–3301 | www.pioneertunnel.com | Coal mine $6.50; steam ride $4.50; special rates for kids and groups | Daily 10–6.

ON THE CALENDAR

AUG.: *Pioneer Day.* You can tour the coal mines, ride the steam train, and visit a large craft fair with live music and lots of activities for kids. You can also eat open-pit chicken BBQ and a variety of ethnic foods, cooked to honor the pioneers. | 570/875–3850 | Coal Mine tour $7, special rates for children; Steam Train Tour $5, special rates for children.

Dining

Henry's Fine Dining. American. You can order anything from hotdogs to lobster and dress in blue jeans or fancy clothes in this row-home type town building. The original building once housed a variety of businesses from a supermarket to a dress factory. | 1120 Centre St. | 570/875–1234 | $7.95–$15.95 | AE, DC, MC, V.

Lodging

Holiday Inn Express Hotel & Suites. This three-story hotel is adjacent to a small shopping center, 10 min from downtown. Complimentary Continental breakfast. Outdoor pool. Sauna. No pets. | 956 Schuykill Mall, Frackville | 570/874–1700 | fax 570/874–2700 | www.holiday-inn.com | 61 North | 65 | $89 | AE, D, MC, V.

BEAVER FALLS

(Nearby towns also listed: Ambridge, Harmony)

Approximately 30 mi west of Pittsburgh, Beaver Falls, originally called Brighton, is a popular destination for the falls that form on the west bank of the Beaver River. The name was changed by the Harmony Society in 1866. Today the borough is home to Geneva College, founded by the Presbyterian Church in 1880.

Information: Beaver County Chamber of Commerce | 250 Insurance St., Ste. 300, 15009 | 724/775–3944 | fax 724/728–3666 | www.bcchamber.com.

Attractions

Air Heritage Museum. The museum houses the active Aircraft Restoration Facility, which collects, restores, and preserves historically significant aircraft, aeronautical materials, and artifacts. You can see several authentic flight suits and aviation tools. Tour a full-sized plane in the hangar. | Beaver County Airport | 724/843–2820 | fax 724/847–4581 | www.trfn.clpgh.org/ah | 7 mi northwest | free | Mon.–Sat. 10–5, Sun. 11–6.

ON THE CALENDAR
JUNE: *Garrison Days.* Held on the last weekend of June in Irvine Park in downtown Beaver Falls, you can browse through the crafts, collectibles and antiques, listen to music, see entertainment, and taste the local food. | 724/775–3944 or 724/775–0189.

Dining

Giuseppe's Italian Restaurant. Italian. This stone and brick building's warm interior has exposed brick walls, Italian statuary and art, wine bottles, and grape vines. Known for fresh seafood on weekends. Try the chicken and broccoli a la Guiseppe or the seafood scoglio. Kids' menu. | R.R. 18 | 724/843–5656 | $8–$18 | AE, D, DC, MC, V.

Wooden Angel. Contemporary. A covered carport and red brick lobby floor lead into the dining area, with its high cathedral ceilings, exposed wood beams, plaid carpeting, and high-backed booths. Wine tastings are held in a secluded room off the wine cellar. The Casual Cafe next to the main dining room is more relaxed with smaller portions of food and a bar. Try the American rack of lamb and the fresh fish available every day. Jazz Thurs., pianist Fri. Kids' menu. Next to the railroad tracks, just 4 blocks from the river, with dock space available. | 308 Leopard La. | 724/774–7880 | www.wooden-angel.com | Closed Sun., Mon. No lunch Sat. | $15–$28 | AE, D, DC, MC, V.

Lodging

Beaver Valley Motel. This small motel is near Exit 2 of the Pennsylvania Turnpike Exit. Built in 1954, this one-story building is 4 mi north of downtown Beaver Falls. Cable TV. Business services. | 7257 Big Beaver Blvd. | 724/843–0630 or 800/400–8312 | fax 724/843–1610 | www.bvmotel.com | 27 rooms | $40–$60 | AE, D, DC, MC, V.

Conley's Motor Inn. Just off Exit 2 of the Pennsylvania Turnpike, this two-story, budget motel is 3 mi outside of Beaver Falls. You're just a 20-mi drive away from Pittsburgh. Restaurant, bar. Some kitchenettes, refrigerators. Cable TV. Spa. Business services. Some pets allowed. | 7099 Rte. 18 | 724/843–9300 or 800/345–6819 | fax 724/843–9039 | 58 rooms in 2 buildings | $55–$60 | AE, D, DC, MC, V.

Holiday Inn. Only 4 mi from downtown Beaver Falls, this midpriced, two-story chain hotel is near Exit 2 of the Pennsylvania Turnpike. It is 18 mi from New Castle and within 5 mi of Geneva College. Restaurant, bar, room service. In-room data ports. Indoor pool. Hot tub, sauna. Video games. Business services. Some pets allowed. | 7195 Eastwood Rd. | 724/846–3700 | fax 724/846–7008 | www.crownamericanhotels.com | 156 rooms | $89–$104 | AE, D, DC, MC, V.

McKinley Place Bed & Breakfast. A white colonial home with blue shutters and English country appeal. You can relax here on its private three-acre property. Each of the four bedrooms has lots of pillows and early 1900s antiques. Hardwood floors and a spiral staircase are original to the house. Families welcome. Massage. No pets. No smoking. | 132 McKinley Rd. | 724/891–0300 | www.mckinleyplace.com | Rte. 51 | 4 rooms | $75–$105 | AE, MC, V.

Todd House. This two story white with gray-roof house is full of turn-of-the-century antiques, except for a large guest room reserved for families with children. Built in 1875, the house is on the main street of town, with other similar period homes as neighbors. Local businesses and ecletic shops are nearby. Complimentary breakfast. | 330 Third St. | 724/775–1424 | fax 724/775–1424 | 6 rooms | $80 | AE, D, MC, V.

BEDFORD

MAP 7, E7

(Nearby towns also listed: Breezewood, Somerset)

At the intersection of Route 220 and Interstate 76, Bedford is a mix of modern conveniences and a working historic village. The downtown is dotted with antiques and Art Deco shops. The city is a gateway to 14 covered bridges and served as George Washington's headquarters during the Whiskey Rebellion.

Information: Bedford County Chamber of Commerce | 37 E. Pitt St., 15522 | 814/623–2233 | fax 814/623–6089 | www.bedfordcountychamber.org.

Attractions

Bedford County Courthouse. Built in 1828, this is the oldest functioning courthouse in Pennsylvania. The unsupported circular stairway is one of the architectural highlights of the building, which was designed and constructed by Solomon Filler. | 230 S. Juliana St. | 814/623–4807 | fax 814/624–0488 | Free | Weekdays 8:30–4:30, closed weekends.

Blue Knob Ski Area. At 3,146 ft, with a 1,072-ft vertical drop, Blue Knob is the highest skiable mountain in Pennsylvania. The longest run is about 2 mi. There are 36 trails, seven lifts, a tubing park, a terrain park, an area for cross-country skiing, a French restaurant, and mountainside condominium lodging. During warmer months, you can play golf or go mountain biking, hiking, tennis, and swimming. | Overland Pass, Claysburg | 814/239–5111 or 800/458–3403 | fax 814/239–8754 | www.blueknob.com | $39, special rates for senior citizens and children | Nov.–Mar., daily 9 AM–10 PM.

Blue Knob State Park. The park has 5,614 acres of woodland on Blue Knob Mountain, the second highest point of land in the state at 3,146 ft. The park includes a guarded swimming pool, 17 mi of hiking trails, 45 campsites, several picnic tables, and trails for horseback riding, mountain biking, snowmobiling, and cross-country skiing. More than 5,000 acres are open to hunting and fishing. | 124 Park Rd., Imler | 814/276–3576 or 888/PA–PARKS | fax 814/276–9142 | www.dcnr.state.pa.us | Free | Daily 8 AM–dusk.

Covered Bridges. The Bedford County Visitors Bureau has a map of covered bridges, including a 24-mi tour, which is popular during the first two weeks of October when the leaves change color. | 141 South Julina St. | 814/623–1771 | free | Mon.–Fri. 9-5.

Fort Bedford Park and Museum. On the site of the original Fort Bedford, which was built in 1758 by the British during the French-Indian War to keep the British supply line open along the Forbes Trail. The museum houses a large-scale model of the original fort, Native American artifacts, early period wagons, the original Fort Bedford flag, and thousands of household items from the 1700s and 1800s. | Fort Bedford Dr. | 814/623–8891 or 800/259–4284 | www.bedfordcounty.net | $3, special rates for senior citizens, children, families, and groups | June–Aug., daily 10–5; May and Sept.–Oct., Wed.–Mon. 10–5, closed Tues.

Old Bedford Village. More than 40 structures on a 42-acre site that have been collected from the surrounding area or reconstructed to create a typical mid-1790s village of the area, with residences, schools, farms, a church, and shops. Costumed interpreters and crafters man the buildings, reenacting the daily activities of pioneer life. Upon entering the village, you cross the Claycomb Covered Bridge. | 220 Sawblade Rd. | 814/623–1156 or 800/238–4347 | fax 814/623–1158 | www.bedford.net/village | $6.95, special rates for senior citizens and children | Memorial Day weekend–mid-Sept., Thurs.–Tues. 9–5, closed Wed.; mid-Sept.-Oct., Thurs.–Tues. 10–4, closed Wed.

Shawnee State Park. The park encompasses 3,983 acres in the state's Ridge and Valley province. You can go boating, fishing, swimming, ice fishing, ice boating, and ice skating on the 451-acre lake. There are 293 campsites, a 12-mi trail system, more than 3,000 acres for hunting, picnic tables, hills for sledding, and trails for snowmobiling. Gen. Forbes camped his troops within the boundaries of the park while building the Forbes Trail in the 1758 Campaign against the French at Fort Duquesne. You can still walk on remnants of the Forbes Trail within the park. | 132 State Park Rd., Schellsburg | 814/733–4218 | fax 814/733–2544 | www.dcnr.state.pa.us | Free | Daily 8 AM–dusk.

Warriors Path State Park. A 334-acre park that lies near the famous path used by the Iroquois in raids and wars with the Cherokee and other Native American tribes of southern Pennsylvania. Recreational activities available at the park include boating and fishing on the Raystown Branch of the Juniata River, hiking, picnicking, hunting, and cross-country skiing. | R.R. 1, June's Creek | 814/658–3847 or 888/PA–PARKS | fax 814/658–2973 | www.dcnr.state.pa.us | Free | Daily 8 AM–dusk.

ON THE CALENDAR

OCT.: *Fall Foliage Festival Days.* The fall season is celebrated during this four-day annual event with 350 craft booths, entertainment, ethnic foods, and an antique car display. | Downtown | 814/623–1771 or 800/765–3331 | www.bedfordcounty.net/fall | Free.
OCT.: *PA Guild of Craftsmen Indoor Craft Show.* Local craftspeople show their talents and sell their wares. Woodworking, pottery, and more are showcased at this craft show held in St. Thomas School Hall the first two weeks of October. | 814/623–1771 | Free.

Dining

Gamble Mill Tavern. American. Locals come to this tavern because it's cozy. The remains of the old mill are long gone, but this tavern has lots of brick and hardwood floors. Dishes are a traditional mix of beef, chicken, and pasta. Desserts are creative and plentiful. | 160 Dunlop St. | 814/355–7764 | Closed Sun. | $15–$22 | MC, V.

Jean Bonnet Tavern. Continental. Filled with antiques and period furnishings, this old Colonial inn (built in 1762) is on the National Register of Historic Places. Guest rooms are available. Known for prime rib and crab cakes. Kids' menu. Sunday brunch. | 6048 Lincoln Hwy; 3 mi west of Bedford on Rte. 30 | 814/623–2250 | fax 814/623–2264 | www.bedfordcounty.net/bandb/jbt | $12–$21 | AE, D, DC, MC, V.

Oralee's Golden Eagle. Continental. This Colonial tavern serves lunch and dinner to the public, and breakfast for overnight guests of the inns. The menu is ever-changing, but usually includes lamb, quiche, salmon, and pasta dishes. | 131 E. Pitt St | 814/624–0800 | Closed Mon. | $9.95–$18.95 | MC, V.

Lodging

Best Western Bedford Inn. Only 3 mi from Old Bedford Village and downtown Bedford, this medium-sized, full-service motel is near Exit 11 of the Pennsylvania Turnpike. The one-story building is designed around a central courtyard. Rooms are in both a one- and two-story building. Restaurant, bar. Cable TV. Pool. Exercise equipment. Video games. Some pets allowed (fee). | 4517 Business 220 | 814/623–9006 | fax 814/623–7120 | www.bestwestern.com/best.html | 105 rooms in 2 buildings | $54–$65 | AE, D, DC, MC, V.

Econolodge. Built in the late 1960s, this relatively modern, two-story motel has interior corridors and is 2 mi from Old Bedford Village and 25 mi from Blue Knob Ski Resort. A small, budget motel that's easily accessible from Exit 11 of the Pennsylvania Turnpike. Bar. Cable TV. Some pets allowed. | 141 Hillcrest Dr. | 814/623–5174 | fax 814/623–5455 | www.econolodge.com/hotel/pa182 | 32 rooms | $42–$65 | AE, D, DC, MC, V.

Jean Bonnet Tavern. Filled with antiques and period furnishings, this old Colonial inn dates back to 1762. There are thick fieldstone walls, large fireplaces, and chestnut-beamed ceilings. Guest rooms are on the third floor. Restaurant. Bar. No room phones, no TV. | 6048 Lincoln Hwy | 814/623–2250 | www.bedcounty.net/bandb/jbt | 4 rooms | $54.99 | AE, D, DC, MC, V.

Oralee's Golden Eagle. Built in 1794, this federal-style tavern is in a walking section of Bedford. Rooms are filled with Colonial antiques. A full breakfast, often a stack of Belgian waffles, is included in the price. Restaurant. Complimentary breakfast. No smoking. | 131 E. Pitt St. | 814/624–0800 | fax 814/623–9020 | oralee@bedford.net | www.bedford.net/oralee | 16 rooms | $79.99–$99.99 | MC, V.

Quality Inn. Less than ½ mi from Old Bedford Village, this reasonably priced motel is near fishing in Blue Knob State Park (15-min drive), golfing, and 20 mi from Blue Knob Ski Resort. The two-story inn with interior corridors underwent a major renovation in 1990. Restaurant, bar. Cable TV. Pool. Business services. Some pets allowed. | 4407 Business Rte. 220 | 814/623–5188 | fax 814/623–0049 | www.qualityinn.com | 66 rooms, 2 suites in 3 buildings | $60–$69, $80 suites | AE, D, DC, MC, V.

BELLEFONTE

MAP 7, F4

(Nearby town also listed: State College)

Former home of seven Pennsylvania governors, by far the most in the state, Bellefonte's Victorian downtown is just 10 min from Penn State University in State College and 3 mi from Interstate 80. While other towns demolished many of their Victorian buildings from the 1950s to 1970s, Bellefonte remained largely unscathed. Today, its museum sits in the center of the town's National Historic District.

Information: **Bellefonte Intervalley Area Chamber of Commerce** | 320 W. High St., 16823 | 814/355–2917 | fax 814/355–2761 | www.iul.com/bellefonte.

Attractions

Black Moshannon State Park. The park's 3,394 acres includes a 250-acre lake, on which you can go boating and fishing. Other recreational activities include hunting, picnicking, bicycling, camping, snowmobiling, cross-country skiing, and a 16-mi network of hiking trails. | R.R. 1, Phillipsburg | 814/342–5960 or 888/PA–PARKS | fax 814/342–5964 | www.dcnr.state.pa.us | Free | Daily 8 AM–dusk.

Centre County Library and Historical Museum. Houses exhibits of state and local history, including a gown worn to President Abraham Lincoln's inaugural ball and a large genealogy collection. | 203 N. Allegheny St. | 814/355–1516 | fax 814/355–0334 or 814/355–2700 | www.countrystore.org | Free | weekdays 9–5, Sat. 9–noon and 1–5, closed Sun.

ON THE CALENDAR

DEC.: *Victorian Christmas.* This small-town, three-day celebration includes sleigh rides and period decorations. | Downtown | 814/355–2917 | fax 814/355–2761 | www.bellefonte.org | Free.

Dining

Schnitzels Tavern. German. In the basement of an old downtown hotel, this tavern has stone walls, a wooden bar, high-backed booths, and uses decorative beer steins from Germany. You can sit outside under umbrella-covered tables on the patio overlooking Spring Creek and watch the ducks, fish, and kayakers. Known for schnitzel and a large selection of imported beer. Open-air dining. | 315 W. High St. | 814/355–4230 | $10–$15 | AE, D, DC, MC, V.

Lodging

Reynolds Mansion Bed and Breakfast. Built in 1885, this mansion is in Bellefonte's National Historic District, 10 mi from Penn State. The inn has a marble vestibule, handcrafted woodwork, stained glass windows, detailed moldings, and unique inlaid parquet floors. Brandy and non-alcoholic beverages are served complimentary. Minimum stay is two nights. Complimentary breakfast. No kids under 12. No pets. | 101 W Linn Street | 814/353–8407 | www.bedandbreakfast.com | 6 | $95–$175 | AE, MC, V.

BETHLEHEM

(Nearby towns also listed: Allentown, Easton, Erwinna, Quakertown)

Restored 18th-century industrial buildings and homes highlight this popular Christmas destination as attested by its nickname "Christmas City USA." An hour north of Philadelphia, Bethlehem was founded in 1741 by members of a Protestant denomination known as the Moravians, from Moravia, Czechoslovakia, who came here to bring the Gospel to the American Indians. A veritable "who's who" has visited Bethlehem including George and Martha Washington. Today, the city remains culturally diverse.

Information: Bethlehem Area Chamber of Commerce | 509 Main St., 18018 | 610/867–3788 | fax 610/758–9533 | www.bethlehemchamber.org.

Attractions

Brethren's House. Built in 1748 when the Bethlehem community was founded and in continuous use ever since. According to Moravian tradition, the single men and single women lived in separate buildings. This was the building where the single men were housed. On the National Register of Historic Places, the building was used as a hospital for Revolutionary War soldiers in 1776. | 1200 Main St. | 610/868–1513 or 800/360–TOUR | fax 610/865–9251 | www.moravian.edu | Free | Daily. 8–4

Central Moravian Church. At one time the largest place of worship in Pennsylvania. Built in 1803 and in continuous use ever since, it is the site where the world-renowned Bach Choir formed 100 years ago. | 73 West Church St. | 610/866–5661 | fax 610/866–7256 | www.enter.net/~cmc | Free | By appointment.

God's Acre. The oldest cemetery in Bethlehem, dating back to 1742. In keeping with the Moravian belief that all people are equal in death, all the headstones are flat. Buried in the cemetery are Native Americans, Europeans, and Afro-Caribbeans. The most notable of the 56 Native Americans buried here is Tschoop, characterized as Uncas in James Fenimore Cooper's *The Last of the Mohicans*. | On first block of West Market St. | 610/867–0173 | www.moravianmuseum.org | Free | Daily dawn to dusk.

Historic Bethlehem Inc.'s Colonial Industrial Quarter. Dates to 1741, when members of the Moravian Church immigrated to the New World to bring the Gospel to Native Americans. By 1748, when Bethlehem's population was only 395, 38 industries were in full swing. The buildings that made up the industrial quarter still stand today. Self-guided walking tour brochures are available at the gristmill. | 459 Old York Rd. | 610/691–0603 | fax 610/882–0460 | www.historicbethlehem.org | $2 | Weekdays 8:30–5, summer Sat. noon–4.

Goundie House. Built in 1810, the Georgian Federal–style Goundie House is perhaps Bethlehem's first brick residence. It was the home of John Sebastian Goundie, a prominent Moravian brewer and community leader. In keeping with Historic Bethlehem's Colonial Industrial Quarter, the home has been restored to its early 1800s appearance, complete with period furnishings in the rooms. | 501 Main St. | 610/691–0603 | fax 610/882–0460 | www.historicbethlehem.org | $3 | Christmas season noon–5; July and August, Sat. noon–4.

Luckenbach Mill. Standing on the site of the first (1743) and second (1751) gristmills in Bethlehem, the Luckenbach Mill was built in 1869. It now houses an exhibit area of working scale models of the waterworks and the mill, artifacts, and a history of the Quarter. | 459 Old York Rd. | 610/691–0603 | fax 610/882–0460 | www.historicbethlehem.org | $2 | Christmas season noon–5; July and Aug., Sat. noon–4.

Springhouse. A reconstruction of the 1764 log structure that at one time protected the spring, the Springhouse provided the Colonial Industrial Quarter with drinking water and cold storage for food. | 459 Old York Rd. | 610/691–0603 | fax 610/882–0460 | www.historicbethlehem.org | $2 | Christmas season noon–5; July and Aug., Sat. noon–4.

Tannery. Restored in 1971, the Tannery now houses exhibits on early leather production, Colonial crafts, and trades. This limestone structure in the Colonial Industrial Quarter, built in 1761, is where animal hides were converted to leather from 1761 to 1870. | 459 Old York Rd. | 610/691–0603 | fax 610/882–0460 | www.historicbethlehem.org | $2 | Christmas season noon–5; July and Aug., Sat. noon–4.

Waterworks. On the National Register of Historic Places, the 1762 Waterworks is the oldest municipal waterworks in the United States. It was used in the Colonial Industrial Quarter to pump water from the creeks up to the town. It served as Bethlehem's pumping station until 1832. | 459 Old York Rd. | 610/691–0603 | fax 610/882–0460 | www.historicbethlehem.org | $2 | Christmas season noon–5; July and Aug., Sat. noon–4.

Kemerer Museum of Decorative Arts. Originally established through bequests from Annie S. Kemerer, who collected rare antiques that reflected the Victorian era. The collection represents the best examples of fine, folk, and decorative arts from the past 250 years. There is a formal 7,500-square-ft garden at the rear of the building. | 427 N. New St. | 610/691–0603 or 610/868–6868 | fax 610/882–0460 | www.historicbethlehem.org | $5, special rates for children and families | Tues.–Sun. noon–4, closed Mon.

Lehigh University. Founded in 1865 by Asa Packer, an entrepreneur and railroad magnate who wanted students to be ready for the technological revolution of the 20th century. The three campuses make up 1,600 acres; half is preserved as open space. The main campus is on the wooded northern slope of South Mountain. | 27 Memorial Drive West | 610/758–3000 | www.lehigh.edu | Free | daily.

Lost River Caverns. Discovered in 1883 and opened to the public in 1930, this natural limestone cavern has five chambers with a lot of stalactites and stalagmites, crystal formations, and fluorescent minerals. The temperature inside the cave is a constant 52 degrees year-round. Guided tours are given every half hour. Outside the cavern is a picnic grove, a natural history rock and mineral museum, and an indoor tropical garden. | 726 Durham St., Hellertown | 610/838–8767 | fax 610/838–2961 | www.lostcave.com | $8, special rates for children and groups | Memorial Day–Labor Day, daily 9–6; Labor Day–Memorial Day, daily 9–5.

Moravian Museum of Bethlehem (Gemein Haus). The 1741 Gemein House is Bethlehem's oldest building and a National Historic Landmark. You can explore the city's rich heritage and discover what life was like in 18th-century Moravian Bethlehem. | 66 W. Church St. | 610/867–0173 | fax 610/882–0460 | www.historicbethlehem.org | $5, special rates for kids | Feb.–Dec., Tues.–Sun. noon–4, closed Mon.

Old Chapel. This stone structure is often referred to as the Indian Chapel because so many Native Americans were baptized here. Notables such as Benjamin Franklin and George Washington visited the chapel. It is still used today for services and weddings. | 73 W. Church St. | 610/866–5661 | fax 610/866–7256 | www.enter.net/~cmc | Free | By appointment (call Moravian Museum at 610/867–0173).

1752 Apothecary and Medicinal Herb Garden. One of the oldest pharmacies in the United States. There are displays of early medical equipment, including Delft apothecary jars purchased from Holland in 1743; many still retain residue from the ointments and herbs that were once stored in them. Herbs grown in the Medicinal Herb Garden are dried and stored in apothecary drawers just as they would have been more than 250 years ago. | 424 Rear Main St. | 610/867–0173 | www.moravianmuseum.org | $3, special rates for children | By appointment.

Philadelphia Eagles Summer Training Camp. Held on the campus of Lehigh University every August, you can join fellow fans to watch the Eagles prepare for football season. Stick around after practice and grab a few autographs. | 27 Memorial Drive West | 610/758–3000 | Free | August.

Zoellner Arts Center. Part of Lehigh University campus in Bethlehem, this art center has the 1,000-seat Baker Hall, the 300-seat Diamond Theater, and the 100-seat Black Box Theatre. A three-story lobby and visual art galleries have permanent and rotating collections. Plus, there's a museum shop. | 27 Memorial Drive West | 610/758–3000 | www.lehigh.edu | Free | Daily 9–5; longer during school year.

ON THE CALENDAR

MAY: *Bach Festival.* This three-day festival spotlights choral music. | Packer Church, Lehigh University campus on Packer Ave. | 610/866–4382 | fax 610/866–6232 | www.bach.org | $16–$45.

JUNE: *Moravian College Art Auction.* Framed art ranging in price from $35 to $4,000 is sold to benefit Reeves Library during this one-night auction. | Harper Union Building, Moravian College | 610/861–1540 or 888/743–3100 | $15, or 2 for $25.

JULY: *Blueberry Festival.* The local blueberry harvest is the centerpiece of this two-day event, which also includes crafts, farm animals, and entertainment. | Burnside Plantation | 610/691–0603 | $5, special rates for children and families, cap of $15.

AUG.: *Musikfest.* This nine-day festival presents some 600 musical acts in a broad range of styles, from Bach to gospel to jazz to the Village People. | Various locations | 610/861–0678 | Free.

NOV.–JAN.: *Christmas.* For about 4 weeks, you can enjoy walking tours, a huge "Star of Bethlehem" hanging on South Mountain, and presentations of Moravian "putzes," or nativity scenes, just some of the activities at this traditional celebration. | Various locations | 610/868–1513 or 800/360–8687 | Call for individual tour prices.

NOV.–JAN.: *Christkindlmarket.* Named after a German festival, this holiday-oriented market boasts more than 80 vendors and lasts for about three weeks. | Downtown | 610/868–1513 or 800/360–8687 | $4, special rates for children.

DEC.: *Live Bethlehem Christmas Pageant.* During two nights, you can see and hear the retelling of the nativity story with actors dressed in biblical costumes and live animals, performed outdoors. | Christian Education Building, 140 West Church St. | 610/867–2893 | Free.

Dining

Bethlehem Brew Works. Contemporary. In this industrial-themed restaurant, the booths and the bar are made of steel. Murals and photographs of the Bethlehem Steel mills adorn the walls. The dining area is surrounded by 10 huge brewing tanks, and tours of the brewing operation are available upon request. Many menu items incorporate handcrafted beer into their recipes, such as golden ale hummus, beer and cheese soup, and porter chicken. Kids' menu. Sunday brunch. | 569 Main St. | 610/882–1300 | www.thebrewworks.com | Reservations essential for 8 or more | $8–$17 | AE, D, MC, V.

Candlelight Inn. Contemporary. The chandelier and brass staircase in the lobby prepare you for elegance, yet the dining room has a more eclectic look, with remnants of a southwestern theme. Try Chesapeake steak, chicken with broccoli and cheese. Buffet. Kids' menu. Sunday brunch. Banquet facilities are available. | 4431 Easton Ave.; 5 mi northeast of downtown, just west of Farmersville | 610/691–7777 | No lunch Sat. | $10–$39 | AE, D, DC, MC, V.

Minsi Trail Inn. Contemporary. The ancient Roman-style entrance gives way to a neo-classical, entirely peach-and-cream-colored interior. Six dining rooms are available, some of which have no windows and are more intimate. There is a bar and lounge area next to the restaurant. Known for prime rib, lobster tail, and crab cakes. Buffet. Kids' menu and early-bird suppers. Sunday brunch. Dock space. Smoking only in bar. | 626 Stefko Blvd.; 2 blocks north of the river and railroad tracks, ½ mi from downtown | 610/691–5613 | No lunch | $13–$60 | AE, MC, V.

Spring Valley Inn. Seafood. Built and operated as a restaurant since 1860, the dining room overlooks a trout pond, which runs through the basement of the building. Try the trout, which is caught fresh from the same spring-fed pond. Open-air, screened and roofed, dining. Magician Sat., harpist Sun., guitarist Mon., Wed. Kids' menu. Sunday brunch. | 1355 Station Ave., about 8 mi southeast of town, in the village of Spring Valley | 610/838–6767 | $15–$20 | AE, D, DC, MC, V.

Vineyard Restaurant. Italian. The split-level dining area has brick walls, candles on each table, and, true to its name, hanging grape vines. Known for its marinara sauce. Strolling musicians Fri., Sat. | 605 Fiot St., about 3 mi southwest of downtown | 610/867–2441 | No lunch | $9–$20 | AE, MC, V.

Lodging

Comfort Inn. A standard, budget-oriented motel is just off U.S. 22. Built in 1984, this two-story inn with interior corridors is 6 mi north of downtown Bethlehem. Bar (with entertainment), complimentary Continental breakfast. Cable TV, in-room VCRs (and movies). Business services, free parking. Some pets allowed. | 3191 Highfield Dr. | 610/865–6300 | fax 610/865–5074 | www.comfortinnbethlehem.com | 116 rooms | $75–$95 | AE, D, DC, MC, V.

Holiday Inn. This midpriced chain hotel is about 5 mi from downtown Bethlehem and the Colonial Industrial Quarter. This two-story hotel has a courtyard in front and a nightclub. Restaurant, bar, room service. In-room data ports, cable TV. Pool, wading pool. Exercise equipment. Business services, airport shuttle. | Rte. 512 and 22 | 610/866–5800 | fax 610/867–9120 | www.holiday-inn.com | 192 rooms | $89–$139 | AE, D, DC, MC, V.

Sayre Mansion Inn. Built in 1858, this English brick country tudor was extensively restored in 1993 and is listed on the National Register of Historic Places. A large conference room is available to accommodate up to 40 guests in complete privacy. Indoor receptions can also take place in a pair of elegant parlors, each with its own fireplace. A minimum stay required. Children are welcome. Complimentary breakfast. Laundry facilities. Business services. No pets. No smoking. | 250 Wyandotte St. | 610/882–2100 | fax 610/ 882–1223 | jmfattell@earthlink.net | www.sayremansion.com | 19 rooms | $90–$135, Penthouse $165 | AE, D, DC, MC, V.

BIRD-IN-HAND

MAP 7, 17

(Nearby towns also listed: Ephrata, Lancaster, Lititz)

Founded in 1734, Bird-in-Hand is listed on the National Register of Historic Places and is said to have gotten its name from the phrase "a bird in the hand is worth two in the bush." Established when the Old Philadelphia Pike was built as a gateway to the West, Bird-in-Hand has a population of less than 300 and is dotted with antiques dealers and farm markets.

Information: **Pennsylvania Dutch Convention and Visitors Bureau** | 501 Greenfield Rd., Lancaster, PA 17601 | 717/299–8901 | fax 717/299–0470 | www.padutchcountry.com.

Attractions

Sightseeing tours. Lancaster County has many small, off-the-beaten-path roads and one of the best ways to discover them, as well as the people who created and reside alongside them, is to tour with a local. Various touring companies have tour packages from bus and automobile to authentic Amish carriages. One touring company is **Abe's Buggy Rides.** They'll take you on a 2-mi tour of Amish country in an Amish buggy. The tour takes you by farms, schoolhouses, and homes while discussing the Amish lifestyle and traditions. | 2596 Old Philadelphia Pike, | 717/392–1794 | www.800padutch.com/abes | $10 | Weekdays 9 AM–dusk, Sat. 9–6, closed Sun.

Take a bus or minivan tour for 2-4 hour Amish farmland trips from **Amish Country Tours.** | Route 340 between Bird-in-Hand and Intercourse | 717/768–8400 | www.amishexperience.com/cotour.html | $19.95 | daily April–Oct., Mon–Sat, 10:30–2:00; Sun., 11:30 AM only. Nov., daily, 11:30. Dec.- Mar., weekends only at 11:30 AM. May–Oct.,Wed. only, the Philadelphia Tour departs at 8:30 AM returning at approximately 5 PM.

Bird-in-Hand Farmers' Market. The standholders in the market have a variety of foods, quilts, hand-carved items, and home-baked goods. The market also includes a glass factory, clothing discounters, and oak and pine furniture makers. | Rte. 340 & Maple Ave. | 717/393–9674 | fax 717/393–6718 | www.goodnplenty.com | Free | Fri.–Sat. 8:30–5; Apr.–Nov., Wed. 8:30–5; Jul.–Oct., Thurs. 8:30–5.

Folk Craft Center and Museum. The museum presents an overview of the lifestyles and culture of the Pennsylvania Germans, including exhibits of Pennsylvania German antiques and folk art. Three shops sell locally handmade wares. | 441 Mt. Sidney Rd., Witmer | 717/397–3609 | fax 717/397–3989 | www.folkcraftcenter.com | Donations accepted | Mon.–Sat. 10–5, Sun.noon–4.

★ **The People's Place.** Answers the most asked questions about the Amish and Mennonites. It includes photography, music, and poetry. A 30-minute documentary, *Who Are the Amish,* illustrates the life of the Amish. There is a gallery displaying the work of Mennonite-related artists throughout North America, a gallery devoted to the work of nationally known artist P. Buckley Moss, and a bookshop selling books about the Amish, Mennonite, and Hutterite lifestyles. | 3513 Old Philadelphia Pike, Intercourse | 717/768–7171 or 800/390–8436 | fax 717/768–3433 | www.thepeoplesplace.com | $5, special rates for children and groups | June–Aug., Mon.–Sat. 9:30–8, closed Sun.; Sept.–May, Mon.–Sat. 9:30–5, closed Sun.

Weavertown One-Room Schoolhouse. A one-room schoolhouse, built in 1877, that held classes for nearly 100 years until May 1969. Today it demonstrates a lifestyle that still exists among Lancaster County's plain people. Through the use of audio-Animatronics, the schoolhouse comes to life with 30 animated students and their teacher, showing what it's like to go to school where grades 1 through 8 are in the same room. | Rte. 340 East | 717/768–3976 or 717/291–1888 | fax 717/291–1595 | www.800padutch.com/wvrtown.html | $3, special rates for senior citizens and children | Apr.–Oct., daily 10–5; Mar. and Nov., weekends 10–5.

ON THE CALENDAR

SEPT.: *Heritage Days.* A three-day hometown celebration of the town's roots includes country foods, crafts, and lots of people. Special concerts, a country auction, and a hymn sing get the crowd hopping. | 717/299–8901 | Free.

Dining

Amish Barn. Contemporary. You can dine in a rustic barn or on the enclosed courtyard patio, both overlooking the vegetable and flower gardens. Plants also grace the Amish interior of this Pennsylvania Dutch restaurant. Try chicken pot pie for dinner and apple dumplings for dessert. Salad bar. Family-style service geared toward high-volume tourist traffic. Kids' menu. No smoking. | 3029 Old Philadelphia Pike | 717/768–8886 | www.amishbarnpa.com | Closed Jan.–mid-Feb. and weekdays in late Feb. Breakfast available | $8–$15 | AE, D, MC, V.

★ **Good 'N Plenty.** American. This family-style restaurant is set in a redesigned Amish farm-house, big enough to serve 650 people. Expect to share a table here with at least a dozen other people while servers bring out large portions of Pennsylvania Dutch food (menu changes daily). Bring your appetite and a good story to share with your fellow diners. | Rte. 896, Smoketown | 717/394–7111 | Closed Sun. and entire month of Jan. | $16 | MC, V.

Plain and Fancy Farm. Contemporary. Traditional Pennsylvania Dutch food served in an Amish homestead. The buildings also house a variety of specialty shops. Buggy rides are available from 8AM to dusk. Try the shoofly pie. Family-style service to accommodate the large number of tourists. No smoking. | 3121 Old Philadelphia Pike | 717/768–4400 | www.plainandfancyfarm.com | $15.95 | AE, D, MC, V.

Lodging

Amish Country Motel. Here you can see the neighboring Amish farmlands, but during summer nearby traffic is busy. Most rooms are on ground level. This is a no-frills motel that offers inexpensive rooms. Outdoor pool. | 3013 Old Philadelphia Pike | 717/768–8396 | www.birdinhand.com/amishcountry | 25 | $53–$79 | Closed Dec.–Mar. Open weekends only Mar.–May | AE, D, MC, V.

Bird-in-Hand Family Inn. Right in the middle of Bird-in-Hand, this inn caters to families visiting Lancaster area attractions. It consists of one motel- and one hotel-style building that were both built in 1960. In the heart of Amish country, it's surrounded by craft shops and outlet malls. Restaurant, picnic area. In-room data ports, refrigerators. Cable TV. Indoor-outdoor pool. Miniature golf, tennis courts. Playground. Laundry facilities. Business services. | 2740 Old Philadelphia Pike. (Rte. 340) | 717/768–8271 or 800/537–2535 | fax 717/768–1117 | smucker@bird-in-hand.com | www.bird-in-hand.com | 125 rooms in two buildings, 8 suites | $80–$95, $124–$159 suites | AE, D, DC, MC, V.

Greystone Manor. A manor house built in the mid-1880s and extensively restored by the Treier family. Upon entering, you are greeted with original stained-glass windows, double leaded-glass doors, and an exquisite three-story carved stairway with walnut handrail and landing newel. The inn, on 2 acres of lawn and gardens, is just a short walk from the Farmers Market in town. Picnic area, complimentary breakfast. No room phones. Kids in Carriage House only. No smoking. | 2658 Old Philadelphia Pike | 717/393–4233 | fax 717/393–0616 | www.greystonemanor.com | 18 rooms | $80–$100 | Closed mid-Dec.–mid.-Feb. | MC, V.

Mill Creek Homestead B&B. Built in 1790, this Georgian fieldhouse has a covered front porch, complete with rocking chair. Sample local wines, or partake of afternoon tea, free daily. Rooms vary in style, from the Shaker furniture in one room, to a room that explodes with a violet-laced garden theme. Minimum stay is two nights. Complimentary breakfast. No air-conditioning in some rooms. No room phones. TV in common area. Pool. Library. Business services. No pets. No kids under 10. No smoking. | 2578 Old Philadelphia Pike | 717/291–6419 or | fax 2171 | valfone@concentric.net | www.bbhost.com/millcreekhomestead | 4 rooms | $99–$129 | D, MC, V.

The Village. Once a stop for 18th-century travelers using the Old Philadelphia Pike, this Victorian inn is right in the middle of Bird-in-Hand. Originally built in 1734, this three-story brick building was rebuilt in 1852. It is in the heart of Amish country and surrounded by outlet malls. Complimentary Continental breakfast. Cable TV. | 2695 Old Philadelphia Pike | 717/293–8369 or 800/914–2473 | fax 717/768–1117 | www.yourinfo.com/lanco/smucker/bird-hand.html | 11 rooms, 6 suites | $89–$99, $119–$149 suites | Closed early Dec.–early Feb. | AE, D, MC, V.

BLOOMSBURG

(Nearby town also listed: Danville)

The only city in Pennsylvania that is an incorporated town, Bloomsburg was formed in 1870 as a means to create a local governing body. Set on the Susquehanna River, the town has more than 650 buildings that depict a variety of architectural styles and many downtown buildings are registered as National Historic Sites.

Information: Bloomsburg Chamber of Commerce | 238 Market St., 17815 | 570/784–2522 | fax 570/784–2661 | www.bloomsburg.org.

Attractions

Bloomsburg University of Pennsylvania. Founded in 1839, the 282-acre campus contains a museum of fine art with a permanent sculpture collection and gardens that surround the traditional red brick. The university has over 7,000 students enrolled in 63 undergraduate and 19 graduate programs. | 400 E. 2nd St. | 570/389–4000 | fax 570/389–2095 | www.bloomu.edu | Free | Daily.

Historic District. Downtown Bloomsburg, which is part of a National Historic District, has more than 650 buildings that depict a variety of architectural styles. Laid out in 1802, Bloomsburg and the surrounding area grew rapidly during the 19th century as the iron industry flourished. | 301 E. 2nd St. | 570/784–7703 | fax 570/784–1518 | www.bafn.org | Free | Daily, hours vary.

Ricketts Glen State Park. A 13,050-acre park that has 120 campsites, 10 modern cabins, a 9-mi trail network for horseback riding, 26 mi of hiking trails, and picnic facilities. You can swim, boat, fish, and ice fish in Lake Jean and Mountain Springs Lake, and there are about 9,000 acres for hunting and trails for cross-country skiing and snowmobiling. | 695 State Rte. 487, Benton | 570/477–5675 or 888/PA–PARKS | www.dcnr.state.pa.us | Free | Daily 8 AM–dusk.

Twin covered bridges. The Twin Bridges—East Paden and West Paden—were constructed in 1884 for $720 and are the only twin covered bridges in the United States. They are named after John Paden, who operated a nearby sawmill. | Village of Forks, Benton | 570/784–8279 or 800/847–4810 | fax 570/784–1166 | www.columbiapa.org/coveredbridges | Free | Daily.

ON THE CALENDAR

SEPT.: *Bloomsburg Fair.* Held since 1854, this eight-day fair includes agricultural exhibits, food, entertainment, and harness racing. | Fairgrounds | 570/784–8279 or 800/847–4810 | www.bloomsburgfair.com | $3, parking $3.

OCT.: *Covered Bridge and Arts Festival.* A two-day celebration of the rich heritage and expert craftsmanship of nine covered bridges in Washington and Greene counties. | Knoebels Amusement Resort, Rte. 487, Elysburg | 570/784–8279, 800/847–4810 | fax 570/784–1166 | www.cmtpa.org | Free.

OCT.–JUNE: *Bloomsburg Theatre Ensemble.* The company presents productions of classic and contemporary works. | Alvina Krause Theatre, 226 Center St. | 570/784–8181 or 800/282–0283 | Call for prices.

DEC.: *TreeFest.* Held the first two weekends after Thanksgiving in the town's Mason house, this is an indoor winter wonderland of more than 100 decorated Christmas trees, live entertainment, arts and crafts sales, a holiday auction, gingerbread house displays, and general holiday cheer. The proceeds benefit the local theater, and trees are donated to needy families. | 717/784–2522 | $3.

Dining

Harry's Grille. Continental. Large green awnings outside this brick building make it easy to locate right downtown. Known for pot roast (served on Sat. and Sun.) and their bread bowl cheese steak. | 20 W. Main St. | 570/784–3500 or 800/331–9815 | www.magees.com | Breakfast also available | $12–$20 | AE, MC, V.

Inn at Turkey Hill. American. The dining rooms overlook the inn's gardens. The dining room walls are covered with a mural painted by a local artist. House speciality is a grilled chicken and herb dish. The menu changes every other month with innovative items like Thai-grilled ostrich. | 991 Central Rd. | 570/387–1500 | Reservations essential | No lunch | $16–$23 | AE, D, DC, MC, V.

Lodging

Budget Host Patriot Inn. About 6 mi north of downtown Bloomsburg and the university, this small motel has some of the most affordable rates in the area. Built in 1989, the one-story building has two wings. Bar. Refrigerators, some in-room hot tubs. Cable TV. Business services. | 6305 Columbia Blvd. | 570/387–1776 | fax 717/387–9611 | www.budgethost.com | 48 rooms, 2 suites | $50–$65, $85 suites | AE, D, DC, MC, V.

Econo Lodge at Bloomsburg. This motel sits on the edge of a mall parking lot that also connects to a truck stop at Rte. 80. Cable TV. Business services. Pets allowed ($10). | 189 Columbia Mall Dr. | 570/387–0490 | fax 570/387–0893 | www.econolodge.com | 80 | $65–$119 | AE, D, DC, MC, V.

Inn at Turkey Hill. Built in 1839, this homestead has elegant rooms and pretty, landscaped grounds. The privately owned home was turned into an inn in 1984 and includes a gazebo and pond. It is 5 mi south of downtown Bloomsburg. Bar, dining room, complimentary breakfast, room service. In-room data ports, some in-room hot tubs. Cable TV. Business services, airport shuttle. Some pets allowed (fee). | 991 Central Rd. | 570/387–1500 | fax 570/784–3718 | www.innatturkeyhill.com | 23 rooms, 2 suites | $95–$100, $150–$190 suites | AE, D, DC, MC, V.

Inn of Buckhorn. Just off Exit 34 of I–80, right near Columbia Mall, this moderately sized, two-story hotel is about 2 mi from the middle of downtown Bloomsburg. Bar. Business services. Some pets allowed. | 5 Buckhorn Rd. | 570/784–5300 | fax 570/387–0367 | www.pavisnet.com/innatbuckhorn | 120 rooms in 2 buildings | $55–$68 | AE, D, DC, MC, V.

Log Home Bed and Breakfast. A log cabin that sits atop a hill on nine acres with a 270-degree view. From the porch you can view the sunsets. Accommodations are limited. A Queen size bed is on the first floor and a full size bed is in the loft, which has a private half bath. You share the shower on the first floor. Bloomsburg is 12 mi away. Complimentary breakfast. No pets. No kids. | 289 Sult Road, Millville | 570–458–6654 | 2 rooms | $45–$75 | V.

Magee's Main Street. Originally built in 1855 and purchased by James Magee in 1911, this small, two story hotel is right in the heart of downtown Bloomsburg, 1 mi from the Bloomsburg Fairgrounds. Bar, dining room, complimentary breakfast. Cable TV. Business services. Some pets allowed. | 20 W. Main St. | 570/784–3200 or 800/331–9815 | fax 570/784–5517 | www.magees.com | 43 rooms, 5 suites | $70–$90, $84 suites | AE, D, DC, MC, V.

BOILING SPRINGS

MAP 7, H6

(Nearby towns also listed: Camp Hill, Hershey, Mechanicsburg, Middletown)

At the heart of Boiling Springs is Children's Lake, which earned its name because the wildlife surrounding the area draws kids. The town earned its name from the nearby subterranean springs that give the appearance that they are boiling. Boiling Springs is also known for the caves near Children's Lake, which were a stop on the Underground Railroad.

Information: **The Penn. Capital Regents Vacation Bureau** | 660 Boas St., Ste. 1419, Harrisburg, PA 17102 | 717/231–7788 | fax 717/231–7790 | www.pacapitalregents.com.

Attractions

Allenberry Playhouse. Since 1949, the Allenberry Playhouse has offered live professional theatre, starting in April and running through November. | 1559 Boiling Springs Rd. | 717/258–6120 | www.allenberry.com/info.html | $20 (varies with performance). | March–Dec.

ON THE CALENDAR

JUNE: *Foundry Day Arts and Crafts Festival.* Celebrate over 250 years of Cumberland County History at this annual one-day festival. Exhibits are by 100 juried craftspeople and artists who show their designer crafts and fine art. Fill up at a food court and enjoy the entertainment. | 717/240–8048.

Dining

Boiling Springs Tavern. Continental. A Colonial building from 1832, originally an inn, this tavern's interior is highlighted with period furnishings and fixtures. The menu focuses on seafood and veal dishes, with some chicken and beef. Specialties include salmon Rockefeller and veal pillows. Kids' menu. | 1 East 1st St. | 717/258–3614 | www.sccis.org/main/entrepwebs/bstavern | Closed Sun., Mon. | $15–$25 | AE, MC, V.

Highlands Pub. American. On the edge of a popular golf course, this pub has an outdoor patio for use during much of the year. Come for the wings and large sandwiches. The menu specials change often. | 1 Mayapple Dr, Carlisle | 717/258–1800 | $3.75–$9.95 | MC, V.

Lodging

Allenberry. Bordering Yellow Breeches Creek, this resort consists of renovated structures from around 1800. Set on 57 acres, the resort includes a professional playhouse and a convention center. Bar, 2 dining rooms. Pool, wading pool. Hot tub. Tennis courts. Business services, airport shuttle. | 1559 Boiling Springs Rd. | 717/258–3211 | fax 717/960–5293 | www.allenberry.com | 69 rooms in 7 lodges, 1 cottage | $105–$225; $340 cottage | AE, D, MC, V.

Yellow Breeches House. A fly-fisher's delight, this 1870 three-story Colonial with wrap-around porch is furnished with many fly fishing antiques and memorabilia. Minimum 2 night stay. Innkeepers host fly-fishing instruction and outings. Guest kitchen. Complimentary breakfast. Bathrooms out of room. Library. No pets. No kids under 9. | 213 Front St. | 717/258–8344 | flyfish@pa.net | www.pa.net/flyfish | 4 rooms | $90–$175 | October through April | AE, MC, V.

BRADFORD

MAP 7, E2

(Nearby towns also listed: Kane, Warren)

Home of the Zippo lighter factory, Bradford is also home to one of America's first oil discoveries in 1859. John D. Rockefeller and other turn-of-the-century millionaires made their fortunes in this town before moving west after the wells went dry. A father-and-son team managed to resurrect the wells and today the town continues to extract oil from its soil.

Information: **Bradford Area Chamber of Commerce** | 10 Marilyn Horn Way, 16701 | 814/368–7115 | fax 814/368–6233 | www.bradfordpa.com.

Attractions

Bradford Landmark Society. The Herbig location houses the society's offices as well as photographs, records, books, newspapers, and information on early pioneers and settlers. The

Crook Farm location is a living history museum. | 45 E. Corydon St. | 814/362–3906 | www.bradfordlandmark.org | Free | Mon., Wed., Fri. 11–2; closed Tues., Thurs., and weekends.

Crook Farm. The site of one of the first oil well strikes in Bradford. On the National Register of Historic Places, the farm dates to the 1840s. Interpreters dressed in period costume man the buildings, some of which are original to the farm, including the farmhouse and oil-well powerhouse. The old barn was moved from down the road. Also on site are a schoolhouse that was moved there and a replica of the first bank in Bradford. | 45 E. Corydon St. | 814/362–3906 or 814/362–6730 | $2 | May–Sept., Tues.–Fri. 1–4, Sat. by appointment, closed Sun.–Mon.

Built in 1849 and restored up until the 1880s, the **farmhouse** is the centerpiece of Crook Farm. There are period furnishings authentic to the 1880s and interpreters in period costumes. | 45 E. Corydon St. | 814/362–3906 or 814/362–6730 | $2 | May–Sept., Tues.–Fri. 1–4, Sat. by appointment, closed Sun.–Mon.

Moved from down the road to Crook Farm, the **barn** was built in 1890. Interpreters dressed in period costume are on hand. | 45 E. Corydon St. | 814/362–3906 or 814/362–6730 | $2 | May–Sept., Tues.–Fri. 1–4, Sat. by appointment, closed Sun.–Mon. Built in 1859, the **Old One-Room Schoolhouse #8** operated until 1929. It has been refurbished to its origins including period desks and chairs. | 45 E. Corydon St. | 814/362–3906 or 814/362–6730 | $2 | May–Sept., Tues.–Fri. 1–4, Sat. by appointment, closed Sun.–Mon.

Penn-Brad Oil Museum. Experience the town's oil-drilling days by viewing a 72-ft-tall wooden drilling rig and a 100-year-old player piano. | US 219 | 814/362–1955 | www.bradford-online.com/pennbrad | $4 | Memorial Day–Labor Day, Mon.–Sat. 10–4, Sun. noon–5.

ON THE CALENDAR

AUG.: *Crook Farm Country Fair.* This two-day event includes arts and crafts, farm exhibits, homemade pies and relishes, and entertainment. | Seaward Ave. extension | 814/362–3906 | www.bradfordlandmark.org | $3.

SEPT.: *Taste of Bradford.* Sponsored by the Downtown Merchants, this one-day festival has the finest examples of local food from a variety of restaurants and vendors. | 814/368–7115.

Dining

Beefeaters. Contemporary. Once a library, this 1829 building has a Victorian interior with oak and marble accents throughout. Known for roast beef and prime rib. Kids' menu. | 27 Congress St. | 814/362–9717 | Closed Sun. No lunch Sat. | $5–$20 | AE, D, MC, V.

Downbeat Restaurant. Italian. The musical notes on the outside of the building make this an easy restaurant to find. No live music, but you can see lots of pictures of jazz greats lining the walls. Try one of the rich dishes like fetticine alfredo. | 29 Main St. | 814/362–3710 | Sun. | $6–$12 | AE, D, DC, MC, V.

Lodging

De Soto Holiday House. Built in 1966, this small, three story hotel is 1 mi from downtown Bradford. It is a mile from the Zippo visitor's center and a 30-minute drive to Kinzua Dam. Restaurant, bar (with entertainment). Cable TV. Pool. Hot tub. sauna. Driving range, miniature golf. Playground. Business services. | 515 South Ave. | 814/362–4511 | fax 814/362–1699 | 70 rooms | $50–$55 | AE, D, DC, MC, V.

Fisher Inn at Bradford. Original home of sawmill owner William R. Fisher, constructed in 1847, this inn's rooms are renovated, but still retain their historical roots. The smell of fresh baked bread fills the air, and you can relax on the back porch with white wicker furniture. Complimentary breakfast. No pets. | 253 E. Main St. | 814/368–3428 | fax 814/368–7053 | www.bradford-online.com/fisherinn | 8 | $60–$90 | AE, DC, MC, V.

Glendorn. Built in 1929, the buildings of this full-service resort are constructed out of redwood in the Adirondak style. About 4 mi outside of Bradford, the 1,280 acres include trout streams, lakes, and forests. Some refrigerators. Pool. Tennis courts. Exercise equipment, hiking. Water sports, fishing, bicycles. Cross-country skiing. Business services. No kids under 12 in main lodge. | 1032 W. Corydon St. | 814/362–6511 or 800/843–8568 | fax 814/368–9923 | glendorn@glendorn.com | www.glendorn.com | 24 rooms (main lodge), 2 suites; 6 cabins | $475–$495, $600–$715 suites and cabins (2–night min. stay cabins and on weekends for suites) | Closed Jan. | AP | AE, MC, V.

Howard Johnson. With three stories built around a courtyard, this standard chain motel is off U.S. 219, close to the University of Pittsburgh as well as the Zippo Visitor's Museum. The Kinzua Dam and Allegheny National Forest are also within a 30-min drive. Restaurant, bar. Cable TV. Gym. Business services. | 100 S. Davis St. | 814/362–4501 | fax 814/362–2709 | www.hojobradford.com | 112 rooms, 5 suites | $89–$119 | AE, D, DC, MC, V.

Mountain Laurel Inn. An 1894 inn with Greek and Colonial Revival architecture, the building shows craftmanship throughout. There is a circular staircase, period moldings, Gothic doors, and large planked oak floors. Complimentary breakfast. No pets. No kids under 16. No smoking. | 136 Jackson Ave. | 814/362–8006 | fax 814/362–4208 | www.bradford-online.com/mountainlaurel | 7 | $85–$100 | AE, MC, V.

BREEZEWOOD

MAP 7, E7

(Nearby towns also listed: Bedford, Chambersburg)

Dubbed the "Town of Motels," Breezewood is a traveler's haven with numerous gas stations and hotels ready to serve those traveling on Interstate 76. It also serves as a gateway to Maryland and Washington, D.C., as Interstate 79 intersects with Interstate 76 in this town.

Information: **Bedford County Chamber of Commerce** | 37 E. Pitt St., Bedford, PA 15522 | 814/623–2233 | fax 814/623–6089 | www.bedfordcountychamber.org.

Attractions
Jackson's Mill Covered Bridge. Named for M.J. Jackson, owner of the nearby grist and sawmill, this bridge is now 300 yards downstream of its original location when a flood in 1889 moved the bridge. The bridge is a 95-ft Burr Truss bridge with a shallow gable roof and high exterior sides. To find the bridge, cross Brush Creek 3½ mi south of Breezewood on Township Route 412. | Jackson's Mill Road (call for directions) | 800/765–3331 | www.bedfordcounty.net/bridges/jacksons.htm | Free | daily.

ON THE CALENDAR
SEPT.: *Breezewood Town Parade.* This firemen's parade has small-town appeal. Plenty of games, cookouts, and activities all day long. All the locals show up, but anyone can join in the fun. | 814/623–2233.

Dining
Gateway Restaurant. Contemporary. A popular, 24-hour truck stop for people traveling I–70 and I–76, with gift shop, general store, and fueling and repair facilities available. Salad bar. Kids' menu. | 16563 Lincoln Hwy. | 814/735–4011 | Reservations not accepted | $5–$12 | AE, D, DC, MC.

Prime Rib Restaurant. American. Just like the name implies, there are no surprises here. Main dishes include prime rib, steaks, seafood. Part of the Ramada Inn, this restaurant is often booked with hotel guests. | 1 Rte. 30 | 814/735–4005 | $10–$14 | AE, D, DC, MC, V.

Lodging

Best Western Plaza Motor Lodge. Eight miles from the beautiful Down River and the Down River Golf Course, this motel is off Exit 12 of the Pennsylvania Turnpike. Two of the buildings were built in 1970 while the third was constructed in 1985, all one story with exterior corridors. Restaurant. Cable TV. Outdoor pool. | 16407 Lincoln Hwy. | 814/735–4352 | fax 814/735–3036 | www.bestwestern.com/best.html | 89 rooms in 3 buildings | $45–$55 | AE, D, DC, MC, V.

Quality Inn Breeze Manor. Right in the middle of Breezewood, this midpriced motel is off Exit 12 of the Pennsylvania Turnpike. It's 64 mi from Gettysburg and only 17 mi from Old Bedford Village. Many of the rooms have been renovated over the past two years. Cable TV. Pool, wading pool. Playground. Laundry facilities. Business services. | 16621 Lincoln Hwy. | 814/735–4311 | fax 814/735–3433 | www.qualityinn.com | 50 rooms in 2 buildings | $50–$80 | AE, D, DC, MC, V.

Ramada Inn. A full-service, two-story hotel that was remodeled in 1981. It is in the scenic mountains of south central Pennsylvania, giving you easy access to many outdoor activities year-round. Restaurant, bar, picnic area, room service. In-room data ports. Cable TV. Indoor pool. Hot tub, sauna. Exercise equipment. Playground. Business services. Some pets allowed. | 16602 Lincoln Hwy. | 814/735–4005 | fax 814/735–3228 | www.bedford.net/ramada | 125 rooms, 6 suites | $49–$89, $129–$169 suites | AE, D, DC, MC, V.

Wiltshire Motel. Popular because of the low prices, often traveling workers live here. No on-premise facilities, but the owner will point out the local laundromat or store. Some pets allowed. | 140 Breezewood Rd. | 814/735–4361 | 12 | $41–$44 | AE, D, MC, V.

BRISTOL

MAP 7, L7

(Nearby towns also listed: Chadds Ford, Chester, Philadelphia)

As the third oldest city in Pennsylvania, Bristol's residential and commercial sections include the entire original town as it was laid out in 1697. Once known as the premier spa in the United States, it grew into a major shipbuilding town and then into a city that embraces a variety of textile and carpet mills.

Information: **Lower Bucks County Chamber of Commerce** | 409 Hood Blvd., Fairlesshills, PA 19030 | 215/943–7400 | fax 215/943–7404 | www.lbcc.org.

Attractions

Fallsington. Historic Fallsington was founded by Quakers who came to America with William Penn in the late 1600s. Guided tours are given of three buildings in the 300-year-old village. The Burges–Lippincott House, built in 1807, was a doctor's residence and office until the middle to late 1800s. The Stagecoach Tavern, which originally was built as a house and later leased as a tavern in 1794, operated as a tavern until prohibition. The Moon–Williamson log house, built in the 1700s, is the oldest log house still standing on its original site in Pennsylvania. | 4 Yardley Ave., Fallsington | 215/295–6567 | fax 215/295–6567 | www.buckscountycvb.org | $3.50, special rates for senior citizens, children, and groups | May–Oct., Mon.–Sat. 10–4, Sun. 1–4.

Neshaminy State Park. The 330-acre park has three swimming pools: the main pool, diving pool, and kids' pool. Other activities include boating and fishing on the Delaware River, picnicking, and hiking. | 3401 State Rd., Bensalem | 215/639–4538 or 888/PA–PARKS | fax 215/639–7712 | www.dcnr.state.pa.us | Free. pool fee | Daily 8 AM–dusk.

Pennsbury Manor. Re-created 17th-century home of William Penn, America's foremost Quaker, the founder of Pennsylvania, a statesman and diplomat. The manor house is reconstructed on the foundations of the original structure and is furnished with items Penn owned or might have owned. Also on the 43-acre plantation, you can see Penn's barge, many outbuildings, kitchen gardens, formal gardens, animals and a barn, bake and brew house, cemetery, orchard, and vineyard. | 400 Pennsbury Memorial Rd., Morrisville | 215/946–0400 | fax 215/295–2936 | www.pennsburymanor.org | $5, special rates for senior citizens, children, and families | Tues.–Sat. 9–5, Sun. noon–5, closed Mon.

Sesame Place. What kid could resist climbing a giant bag of marbles or discovering Ernie's Bed Bounce? For years, young fans of the popular TV show "Sesame Street" have enjoyed this recreation park especially designed for them. The wee ones splash around at Rubber Duckie Pond, while older kids can run free in Twiddlebug Land, the larger-than-life attractions themed around the tiny creatures in the flower box outside Ernie and Bert's window. | 100 Sesame Rd. | 215/752–7070 | www.sesameplace.com | $31.95, special rates for senior citizens and groups | May–Labor Day, daily 9–8; after Labor Day–late Oct., weekends 9–8, closed weekdays.

ON THE CALENDAR

JUNE–AUG.: *Summer Concerts.* Held at the Bristol Lions Park Gazebo, the concert series showcases a variety of free musical performances from Celtic music to jug band country. | 215/943–7400.

OCT.: *Fallsington Day.* This one-day outdoor fair at a restored Colonial-era village highlights period craft demonstrations, food, and entertainment. | 4 Yardley Ave., Fallsington | 215/295–6567 | fax 215/295–6567 | www.buckscounty.org | $6.

Dining

Mill Street Cafe. American. Open for breakfast and lunch, locals come here for every type of imaginable omelet and interesting grilled sandwiches, like crab-meat melt. The cafe's interior is simple and is on a main street with lots of little shops to explore. | 407 Mill St. | 215/785–2110 | No supper (Open daily 7–3) | $3.45–$6.95 | No credit cards.

Lodging

Villager Lodge. This lodge also has efficiency units that can be rented out weekly or monthly. Traffic is at times noisy on this major highway. | 5361 Rte. 13 | 215/788–9272 | fax 215/788–7822 | www.villagerlodge.com | 40, 20 efficiencies | $41–$175 | AE, D, MC, V.

BROOKVILLE

MAP 7, D4

(Nearby town also listed: Clarion)

Off Interstate 80 between Youngstown, OH, and Clarion, Brookville once served as one of the links for the Underground Railroad in western Pennsylvania and is credited as the town where embalming was first practiced.

Information: **Brookville Chamber of Commerce** | 70 Pickering St., 15825 | 814/849–8448 | fax 814/849–8455 | www.penn.com/bacc.

Attractions

Clear Creek State Park. Encompassing 1,676 acres, the park has 53 campsites, 22 cabins, 15 mi of hiking trails, several picnic tables, and more than 677 acres for hunting. Other activities include canoeing, fishing, swimming, and sledding. | R.D. 1 Box 82, Sigel | 814/752–2368 or 888/PA-PARKS | fax 814/752–6302 | www.dcnr.state.pa.us | Free | Daily 8 AM–dusk.

Jefferson County Historical and Genealogical Society. The Brady Craig House, built in the late 1830s, houses the museum. Displays include Victorian furniture, maps, diaries, and photographs. Local docents are on hand to answer questions. There is also a genealogical library with a collection of historical reference materials for research enthusiasts. | 232 Jefferson St. | 814/849–0077 | Free | Tues.–Sun. 2–5.

ON THE CALENDAR

JULY: *Jefferson County Fair.* Dating to the early 1800s, this week-long event includes the staples of country fairs—livestock displays, hundreds of homemade pies, and carnival rides. | Rte. 28 north of I–80 exit 14 | 814/849–8448 | fax 814/265–8577 | www.jeffco-fairgrounds.tripod.com | $6.

DEC.: *Victorian Christmas Celebration.* Walk through historic homes and buildings, attend a Victorian Ball, take horse and buggy rides at this annual five-day festival. There is also a doll and dollhouse show, living windows, and a live nativity procession. | 814/849–8448.

Dining

Golden Eagle Restaurant. Continental. The inside of this country restaurant is covered in a rustic barn motif. Rooms and walls showcase horse equipment from tackles to sleigh bells. Local business folk come here often to enjoy the prime rib. | 250 W. Main St. | 814/849–8251 | Lunch | $7–$12 | AE, D, MC, V.

Meeting Place. Continental. Restaurant in Victorian mode with full service bar. It is in downtown historic Brookville. Try the New York strip and the stuffed chicken. Kids' menu. | 209 Main St. | 814/849–2557 | www.meetingplace-icehouse.com | Closed Sun. | $8–$14 | AE, D, MC, V.

Lodging

Days Inn. Off Exit 13 of I–80, this affordable, three story motel is 16 mi from Cook Forest State Park, but only 1 mi from historic Brookville. Bar. Cable TV. Pool. Spa. Video games. Laundry facilities. Business services. Some pets allowed. | 230 Allegheny Blvd. | 814/849–8001 | fax 814/849–9647 | www.daysinn.com | 124 rooms | $50–$70 | AE, D, DC, MC, V.

Golden Eagle Inn. This budget hotel has some unique style with its wooden paneling and white-wash walls. A short drive into town, or to the Cook Forest State Park. 1 restaurant. Complimentary Continental breakfast. Some pets allowed. | 250 W. Main St. | 814/849–7344 | fax 814/849–7345 | budgethost.com | 29 | $34–$60 | AE, D, MC, V.

Holiday Inn Express. Only 1 mi from historic Brookeville, this budget chain hotel is near Exit 13 of I–80 and it's only 30 mi to the Smicksburg Amish community. Originally built in 1969, this three-story hotel was renovated 2 years ago. It has an interior corridor but no elevators. Complimentary Continental breakfast. Cable TV. Laundry facilities. Business services. Some pets allowed (fee). | 235 Allegheny Blvd. | 814/849–8381 | fax 814/849–8386 | www.hiexpress.com/brookevillepa.com | 68 rooms, 2 suites | $60–$75, $89–$99 suites | AE, D, DC, MC, V.

BUSHKILL

MAP 7, L4

(Nearby town also listed: Milford)

The name may mean "little river" in Dutch, but the falls that are nearby have been dubbed the "Niagara of Pennsylvania." Today, it's a popular tourist destination because of its scenic gorges and falls and the area's numerous hiking trails.

Information: **Pike County Chamber of Commerce** | Box 883, Milford, PA 18337 | 570/296–8700 | fax 570/296–3921 | www.pikechamber.com.

Attractions

Bushkill Falls. Called "the Niagara of Pennsylvania," these eight waterfalls are on more than 300 acres in the Pocono Mountains. The main falls drop 100 ft. There are exhibits of Pennsylvania wildlife and Native Americans, paddleboat rides, miniature golf, a network of hiking trails, and fishing and boating on Twin Lakes. | Bushkill Falls Rd. | 570/588–6682 | fax 570/588–9060 | www.visitbushkillfalls.com | $8, special rates for senior citizens, children, and groups | Apr.–Oct., daily 9–5.

Bushkill Visitors Center. Pick up maps, guidebooks, and other books describing the local areas. The center is on one of many trails that lead to the scenic waterfalls nearby. | US Route 209 | 570/588–7044 | www.nps.go/dewa | free | July – Oct. Daily 9-5.

Delaware Water Gap National Recreation Area. The Delaware Water Gap is one of the most significant and interesting geologic formations in the northeastern United States. The Delaware River has carved a gap nearly 1,500 ft high in the Kittatinny Ridge of the Appalachian Mountains. The park is along approximately 40 mi of the Delaware River in both Pennsylvania and New Jersey and covers almost 70,000 acres of land. A focal point of the area is the natural 2-mi gorge carved by the Delaware River, with 1,200-ft cliffs on each side. There are historic 19th-century houses and waterfalls on site.

The area provides a wide range of recreational activities including fishing, canoeing, swimming, hiking, bicycling, hunting, and horseback riding. Cross-country skiing and snowmobiling are popular winter sports in the area. Nearly five million people visit the park where they can admire the wide range of plant and animal life and enjoy a picnic. Camping is available in various places throughout the Recreation Area. | River Rd. | 570/588–2435 or 570/588–2451 | fax 570/588–2780 | www.nps.gov/dewa | Free to enter park; Smithfield and Milford Beach $5; Bushkill and Dingmans Ferry Access $5 | Daily 24 hours, though some facilities may be closed during the winter.

Pocono Indian Museum. The history of the Delaware Indians is shown through displays of ancient artifacts, weapons, and tools. You can use a recorded tour to help guide you step-by-step through the museum. | Rte. 209; 5 mi north of Marshall Creek | 570/588–9338 or 570/588–9164 | fax 570/588–2502 | www.pocoindianmuseum.com | $4, special rates for senior citizens, children, and groups | Weekdays 10–6, Sat. 9:30–6:30, Sun. 10–6.

ON THE CALENDAR

SEPT.: *Pike County Agricultural Fair.* The six-day fair is held at Magic Valley in Bushkill. Activities include games, rides, contests, and many food vendors. Admission is around $6 per person, which includes rides and most entertainment, cheerleading, and demolition derby events. Farm animals are also on display. | 570/588–4601.

Dining

Pocmont Resort and Conference Center Dining Room. American. Hear live dance music and singers, and laugh with the on-stage comedians on the third floor of this resort. Dinners include seafood and meat entrees. | Bushkill Falls Rd. | 570/588–6671 | www.pocmont.com | $21–$24 | AE, D, DC, MC, V.

Lodging

Fernwood Resort and Country Club. All recreational possibilites are on the premises. Grounds and buildings are well-maintained, and staff is abundant. Two-night minimum stay on weekends May–Oct. 2 restaurants. Indoor pool, wading pool. Hot tub, sauna. 18-hole golf course, miniature golf, 7 tennis courts. Volleyball. Fishing. Cross-country skiing, downhill skiing, snowmobiling. | Rte. 209 | 570/588–9500 | fax 570/588–0403 | www.fernwoodhotel.com | 177 | $118–$198 | AE, D, DC, MC, V.

BUTLER

MAP 7, B5

(Nearby towns also listed: Harmony, Pittsburgh)

Named after Richard Butler, a lieutenant colonel with Morgan's Rifles of 1777 and a major general in the St. Clair expedition, in which he was killed. Today, Butler is a center for banking and is bisected by the Conoquenessing Creek.

Information: **Butler County Chamber of Commerce** | 201 S. Main St., 16003 | 724/283–2222 | fax 724/283–0224 | www.butlercountychamber.com.

Attractions

Butler County Historical Society. The mission of the Society is to collect, preserve and interpret the historical documents and artifacts of the county, for the educational benefit of the public. Through its four museums (Little Red Schoolhouse, Shaw House, Cooper Cabin, Butler County Heritage Center) the Society keeps local history alive. | 106 S. Main St. | 724/283–8116 | fax 724/283–2505 | butlercounty.com | Free | Mon.–Fri. 9–4.

Jennings Environmental Education Center. A state park environmental education center on 300 acres with environmental programs and 5½ mi of trails. An endangered species of rattlesnake as well as deer and several species of birds can be viewed. | 2951 Prospect Rd., Slippery Rock | 724/794–6011 | fax 724/794–1367 | Free | Daily dawn to dusk.

Moraine State Park. Containing 3,225-acre Lake Arthur, the park has two beaches for swimming, a 7-mi paved trail for bicycling, a 6-mi mountain bike trail, 11 cabins, and 20 mi of snowmobile trails. Fishing, boating, windsurfing, hiking, picnicking, ice skating, cross-country skiing, ice boating, ice fishing, and sledding are other possibilities. | 225 Pleasant Valley Rd., Portersville | 724/368–8811 or 888/PA–PARKS | fax 724/368–3417 | www.dcnr.state.pa.us | Free | Daily 8 AM–dusk.

Dining

Dingbats. American. Pizza to filet mignon is a sample of what this restaurant serves. The dining room has booths and tables and there are two enclosed patios, although the view is a car dealership and a hotel. Locals come here to meet with friends after work. | 100 Fairfield La. | 724/285–5222 | fax 724/285–5044 | $6.95–$13.95 | AE, D, MC, V.

Dream Spinners Restaurant and Dairy Bar. American. Decorated as an "oldies" restaurant, this restaurant has over 50 menu items and an authentic jukebox. Specials of the house are meatloaf, creamed chicken and biscuits, and "rodeo steaks" (lots of meat with onions and bbq sauce). | 781 New Castle Rd. | 724/283–9287 | $6.95–$11.95 | AE, D, MC, V.

Michael's Restaurant. American. Lots of brown wood paneling and artificial flowers like a country home with dishes to match. Lasagna and stuffed chicken top the menu. | 970 New Castle Rd. | 724/865–9838 | $5.95–$11.95 | AE, D, MC, V.

Lodging

Applebutter Inn. Both floors of this circa-1844 brick farmhouse inn are filled with antiques and flowers from the gardens. There are also rooms available in a 1988 addition. In the heart of Pennsylvania-Dutch Country, it's within 15 mi of Moraine and McConnells Mills State Parks, and a 10-min drive from Prime Outlets mall. Complimentary breakfast. No smoking. Massage. | 666 Canterville Pike, Slippery Rock | 724/794–1844 | fax 724/794–3319 | www.pathway.net/applebutterinn.com | 11 rooms, 1 suite | $62–$132, $100–$132.50 suites | AE, MC, V.

Comfort Inn. The hotel is on a hill a bit away from traffic, five mi south of town. It's one of the newest hotels in Butler, built in 1996. Complimentary Continental breakfast. Indoor pool. Exercise equipment. | 1 Comfort Lane | 724/287–7177 | fax 724/287–1497 | www.comfortinn.com | 70 | $55–$85 | AE, D, DC, MC, V.

Conley's Resort Inn. With a waterpark on site, this small, full-service resort is popular with families. The three-story hotel is nestled in western Pennsylvania's rolling hills, about 10 mi from downtown Butler. Restaurant, bar, room service. Some kitchenettes. Indoor pool. Hot tub, sauna. 18-hole golf course, putting green, tennis courts. Video games. Business services. | 740 Pittsburgh Rd. | 724/586–7711 or 800/344–7303 | fax 724/586–2944 | www.conleyresort.com | 56 rooms | $90–$109 | AE, D, DC, MC, V.

Days Inn. Only 2.5 mi from downtown, this midpriced, two-story motel was built in 1986. It's 7.5 mi from Suncrest and Rittswood Golf Courses and 5.2 mi from the Mansion, a well-known local restaurant. Restaurant, bar (with entertainment), room service. Cable TV. Indoor pool. Hot tub. Laundry facilities. Business services. | 139 Pittsburgh Rd./Rte. 8 | 724/287–6761 | fax 724/287–4307 | 139 rooms | $69–$89 | AE, D, DC, MC, V.

Fairfield Inn. At the north end of town, this hotel is about 10 min from downtown and state parks. It attracts many business travelers and families, and is often sold out, so make reservations well in advance. Complimentary Continental breakfast. Some refrigerators. Indoor pool. Hot tub. Exercise equipment. | 200 Fairfield La. | 724/283–0009 or 800/228–2800 | fax 724/283–1045 | www.fairfieldinn.com | 64 | $69 | AE, D, DC, MC, V.

McKee's. Because it's 4.5 mi north of town, this small, ranch style motel, built in 1960, has some of the least expensive rates in the area. It is only 10 mi to Moraine State Park and beautiful Lake Arthur. Some kitchenettes. Cable TV. | 930 Newcastle Rd./U.S. 422 | 724/865–2272 | 23 rooms | $34–$45 | AE, D, MC, V.

CAMP HILL

MAP 7, H6

(Nearby towns also listed: Boiling Springs, Harrisburg, Hershey, Mechanicsburg, Middletown)

Supposedly named after the New York National Guard unit that made camp in the area to defend it in 1863. Today it is home to Peace Church, the country's early Reformed and Lutheran congregations.

Information: Greater West Shore Chamber of Commerce | 4211 Trindale Rd., 17011 | 717/761–0702 | fax 717/761–4315 | www.wschamber.org.

Lodging

Radisson Penn Harris. Constructed in the late 1960s but furnished in a Colonial style, this two-story chain hotel is 1 mi from downtown Camp Hill. It's also about 5 mi from Exit 17 of the Pennsylvania Turnpike, 20 mi west of Hershey, and 40 mi from Gettysburg. Restaurant, bar, room service. In-room data ports. Cable TV. Pool. Exercise equipment. Business services, airport shuttle, free parking. Some pets allowed. | 1150 Camp Hill Bypass | 717/763–7117 or 800/333–3333 | fax 717/763–4518 | www.radisson.com | 250 rooms, 6 suites | $89–$135, $195–$395 suites | AE, D, DC, MC, V.

CANADENSIS

MAP 7, K4

(Nearby towns also listed: Cresco, Mt. Pocono, Stroudsburg, Tannersville)

Taken from the Latin name of the hemlock, Canadensis is in the Pocono Mountains of eastern Pennsylvania and is just 15 mi north of Stroudsburg. With a permanent population of about 800, Canadensis nearly triples in size in the summer months. Near several ski resorts and the many attractions in the Pocono Mountains, it's a place that caters to vacationers.

Information: Pocono Mountains Visitors Bureau Inc. | 1004 Main St., Stroudsburg, PA 18360 | 570/424–6050 | fax 570/421–6927 | www.800poconos.com.

Attractions

Holley Ross Pottery. Demonstrations of pottery making, showing how a piece is made from clay through all the steps to the final product. There's a large showroom selling factory products, as well as a variety of other giftware. Also on site is a woodland park with a swing-

CANADENSIS

INTRO
ATTRACTIONS
DINING
LODGING

ing bridge, sawdust trails, and a 5-acre lake. | R.R. 2, Cresco; midway between Cresco and Newfoundland | 570/676–3248 | www.hollyross.com | Free | May–mid-Dec., Mon.–Sat. 9:30–5:30, Sun. 1–5:30.

Promised Land State Park. Surrounded by state forest and a natural area, the 3,000-acre park is on the Pocono Plateau, 1,800 ft above sea level. There are two lakes, 422-acre Promised Land Lake and 173-acre Lower Lake, that you can use for swimming, fishing, boating, ice fishing, and ice skating. There are 487 campsites, cabins for rent, picnic facilities, more than 30 mi of hiking trails, a 6½-mi bike route around Promised Land Lake, 450 acres for hunting, more than 27 mi designated for snowmobiling, snowshoeing, and cross-country skiing. | R.R. 1, Greentown | 570/676–3428 or 888/PA–PARKS | www.dcnr.state.pa.us | Free | Daily 8 AM–dusk.

ON THE CALENDAR

OCT.: *Balloon Festival.* Every year during the weekend after Columbus Day, about 15 mi south of Canadensis in Shawnee On Delaware, you can join hot air balloonists from across the globe in celebrating and promoting their balloons. There is food, entertainment, rides and even a petting zoo at this event. | 570/421–4433 | Sat. and Sun. $10, special rates for seniors and children. $5 for parking. On Fri., tickets are half price.

Dining

Calico Kitchen. American. Dinners such as barbecued pork chops, house-smoked salmon, spaghetti, and roast duckling are served with potato, vegetables and salad at this restaurant popular with locals and vacationers. | Rte. 390, I–80 to Exit 52 to 447. Follow to 390 and turn right at the light | 570/595–3444 | $7–$15 | MC, V.

The Forks. American/Italian. One-quarter mile south and just up the hill from downtown Canadensis in Mountain Home, this restaurant serves such fare as pork chops with sauteed onions and garlic. No lunch. | Rte. 30, Mountain Home | 570/595–7335 | Closed Mon. | $14 | MC, V.

Frog Town Inn. American. In a country inn, this eatery serves its own smoked salmon and roast duckling to locals and travelers. | Rte. 390, I–80 to Exit 52 to 447. Follow to 390 and make a right and the restaurant is ⅓ mi down the road | 570/595–6282 | Closed Mon.–Wed. | $14–$22 | AE, MC, V.

Lodging

Brookview Manor. Built in 1911 for a wealthy Scranton family, this cream-colored home and carriage house overlooks Broadhead Creek and sits on four acres of property which includes a trail that leads to a waterfall. Every room has a view of the countryside at this small inn. It's 1 mi north of town. Picnic area, complimentary breakfast. Some in-room hot tubs, no room phones. No kids under 12. No smoking. | Rte. 447 | 570/595–2451 or 800/585–7974 | fax 570/595–5065 | www.travelassist.com/reg/pa111s.html | 10 rooms | $120–$165 | AE, D, DC, MC, V.

Hillside Lodge and Resort. On 30–acres of woods and trails, this rustic resort has many red and white buildings. The main building has a wrap-around porch and houses the dining room and two of the guest rooms. Full breakfast and dinner on weekends. Microwaves, refrigerators, some in-room hot tubs. Cable TV, in-room VCRs. Outdoor pool. Playground. Laundry facilities. No pets. | Rte. 390, I–80 to exit 52, which will put you on 447. Follow 447 to 390 | 570/595–7551 | fax 570/595–3050 | dkline@ptdprolog.net | www.hillsidelodge.com/ | 23 suites, 8 cottages | $195–$260 | D, MC, V.

Merry Inn. When proprietor Chris Huggard suggested the name for this inn he did not know that, as a child, his wife Meredyth was known as Merry. The name, and the irony, has become part of the legend of this blue-and-white inn in the Pocono Mountains. Full breakfast. Cable TV, in-room VCR. Hot tub. Some pets allowed. No smoking. | Rte. 390; I–80 to exit 52 which will put you on 447. Follow 447 to 390 | 570/595–2011 or 800/858–

4182 | Merryinn@ezaccess | www.pbcomputerconsulting.com/themerryinn | 6 rooms | $95 | MC, V.

Overlook Inn. A rambling, country-style farmhouse built in 1880, this inn is on 20 acres right in the middle of the Poconos, about 2 mi from downtown Canadensis. All three stories are filled with area antiques and there's a large porch for relaxing or dining. Horseback riding and ski facilities are nearby. There are also many antiques stores and shopping outlets close by. Restaurant, bar. TV in common area. Pool. Cross-country skiing. | R.R. 1 | 570/595–8550 | www.theoverlookinn.com | overlook1@noln.com | 20 rooms, 2 suites | $110–$175 | AE, D, MC, V.

Pine Knob. Decorated with 19th-century antiques, this charming inn, about ½ mi from downtown Canadensis, dates to 1847. Horseback riding facilities and an antique store are close by. No room phones, TV in common area. Tennis courts. | ½ mi from Candensis on Rte. 447 | 570/595–2532 or 800/426–1460 | fax 570/595–6429 | innkeepers@pineknob.com | 28 rooms (10 with shared bath) | $165–$195 | AE, D, DC, MC, V.

Pump House. Built as a stagecoach stop in 1842, this small, three-story inn is furnished with country antiques. Golfing, hiking, and horseback riding facilities are all within 15 minutes. Restaurant, complimentary Continental breakfast. | 390 Skytop Rd. | 570/595–7501 | 8 rooms | $60 | DC, MC, V.

Skytop Lodge. It's a huge, four-story building that resembles multiple barns combined into one building. This full-service resort was built in 1928, and is now on 5,500 acres. It is 3 mi from downtown Canadensis with shopping outlets and antiques stores nearby. Bar, 2 dining rooms, picnic area, room service. Refrigerators (in cottages). 2 pools (1 indoor), wading pool. Hot tub, massage. Driving range, 18-hole golf course, putting green, tennis courts. Gym, hiking, boating, fishing, bicycles. Cross-country and downhill skiing, sleigh rides, tobogganing. Video games. Children's programs (4–10, younger ages welcome when accompanied by baby-sitter or guardian), playground. Business services, free parking. | 1 Skytop, Skytop | 570/595–7401 | fax 570/595–9618 | www.skytop.com | 185 rooms, 40 cottages | $240–$400; $240–$400 cottages | AE, DC, MC, V.

CARBONDALE

(Nearby towns also listed: Hawley, Scranton)

Nestled within the Scranton metropolitan area, Carbondale's origins can be traced to the mining of anthracite. By the mid-1820s, camps of Irish men and Welshmen dominated the landscape to mine hard coal. Like most suburbs, Carbondale is home to many of Scranton's working families and has kept many of its original buildings and landmarks.

Information: Carbondale Chamber of Commerce | 1 N. Main St., Carbondale, PA 18407 | 570/282–1690 | fax 570/282–1690 | www.ci.carbondale.pa.us.

Attractions

Elk Mountain Ski Center. With 27 runs for skiing, the longest one is 1¾ mi. Summit elevation is 2,693 ft with a 1,000-ft vertical drop. There are six lifts. | R.R. 2 Box 3328, Uniondale | 570/679–4400 or 800/233–4131 | fax 570/679–4409 | www.elkskier.com | Call for prices | Dec.–Mar.

Merli–Sarnoski Park. A 844-acre park that includes a 33-acre lake that is stocked with trout for fishing. There is also swimming, a 7-mi trail system for bicycling or hiking, a playground, and picnic facilities. In the winter, you can cross-country ski, ice skate, and ice fish. | 570/876–1714 | Free | mid-Apr.–Sept., daily 8–8; Oct.–mid-Apr., daily 8–4:30.

Mount Tone Ski Resort. This ski area has 10 trails, the longest one being 2,640 ft, and three lifts. The summit elevation is 1,930 ft with a 450-ft vertical drop. | Wallerville Road, Lake Como | 717/798–2707 | www.mttone.com | Dec.–Mar.

Salt Spring State Park. Virgin hemlock trees estimated to be between 600 and 700 years old are the focal points of this 400-acre park. Also in the park are the waterfalls of Fall Brook, a stream that flows into Silver Creek. Activities include picnicking, fishing, hiking, and hunting on more than 300 acres. | R.R. 1 Box 230, Dalton | 570/945–3239 or 888/PA–PARKS | fax 570/945–7097 | www.dcnr.state.pa.us | Free | Daily 8 AM–dusk.

ON THE CALENDAR

DEC.: *Christmas in a Small Town.* Usually held the first Sunday in December, this family celebration includes a visit from Santa, who comes riding in on a little train, and games and prizes for children. | 570/282–1690 | Free.

Dining

Ben-Mar Restaurant. Italian. The most popular restaurant in town, Ben–Mar serves American–Italian favorites such as steak, scampi, veal, and chicken parmesan. | 89 N. Main St. | 570/282–5970 | $6–$16 | AE, D, MC, V.

Lodging

Heritage House on the Park. In the morning you are treated to a candlelight breakfast, and if you'd like to explore during the day you can arrange for a picnic basket. This B&B is full of Victorian antiques and lace. Each bed has extra large pillows and the two-room Ivy suite has French doors that separate a marble tiled step–up garden tub framed with full wall–to–wall mirrors and over–sized windows from the full poster bed, wicker chairs, Cheval free standing mirror, bay window, and fireplace. TV in common area. No pets. No smoking. | 5 Park Place | 570/282–7477 | fax 570/282–7477 | www.users.erols.com/ltorehek/bandb.htm | 3 rooms | $115 | No credit cards.

CARLISLE

MAP 7, G6

(Nearby town also listed: Harrisburg)

Laid out in 1751, Carlisle is steeped in history from the Revolutionary and Civil Wars to one of the nation's greatest athletes. Mirroring its namesake in England, the city is home to the country's second oldest army post, the Carlisle Barracks, which was the home of Molly Pitcher, Revolutionary War heroine. Many of the town's buildings were built to resemble similar buildings in England. Currently home to various antiques shops and artist galleries in restored 18th- and 19th-century buildings, Carlisle is between Interstate 76 and Interstate 81 just east of Harrisburg.

Information: **Carlisle Chamber of Commerce** | 212 N. Hanover St., 17013 | 717/243–4515 | fax 717/243–4446 | www.carlislechamber.org.

Attractions

Carlisle Barracks. Home of the former Carlisle Indian Industrial School where famous athlete Jim Thorpe went to school and the second oldest Army post in the United States. The Hessian Magazine Museum, which is the last remaining building from the Revolutionary period on site, was used during the Revolution as a prison and for weapons storage. The Omar Bradley Museum is housed in Upton Hall. Bradley was a general in World War II and personal items such as his uniforms are here. The barracks are also home to the U.S. Army War College. | U.S. 11 | 717/245–3611 | fax 717/245–4370 | carlisle-www.army.mil | Free | Grounds daily; museums daily 10–4.

Colonel Denning State Park. The park includes 273 acres of woodland and a 3½-acre lake. There are 52 campsites and you can go swimming, fishing, hiking, picnicking, hunting, cross-county skiing, and ice skating. | 1599 Doubling Gap Rd., Newville | 717/776–5272 or 888/PA–PARKS | fax 717/776–4640 | www.dcnr.state.pa.us | Free | Daily 8 AM–dusk.

Fowler's Hollow State Park. The park has 18 campsites, picnic facilities, fishing on Fowler Hollow Run, and 2 mi of cross-country ski trails. The area is a trailhead for a variety of hiking trails within and connecting to the trail system of the Tuscarora State Forest. | 1599 Doubling Gap Rd., Newville | 717/776–5272 or 888/PA–PARKS | fax 717/776–4640 | www.dcnr.state.pa.us | Free | Daily 8 AM–dusk.

Cumberland County Historical Society and Hamilton Library Association. Founded in 1874, the Cumberland County Historical Society is one of the country's oldest historical societies. It maintains a museum on Cumberland County history that includes artifacts, a folk art gallery, photo archives, books, maps and county historical records, items from the Carlisle Indian Industrial School, household items, and the oldest American-made printing press. | 21 N. Pitt St. | 717/249–7610 | fax 717/258–9332 | www.historicalsociety.com | Free | Mon. 7 PM–9 PM, Tues.–Fri. 10–4, Sat. 10–1, closed Sun.

Dickinson College. On the recommendation of Benjamin Franklin, a grammar school built in 1773 was transformed into Dickinson College by 1783. Old West, the school's first building, was finished in 1804 by the architect of the Capitol building in Washington, D.C. The campus is on 104 acres with an 18-acre recreation area close by | W. High St. | 717/243–5121 | fax 717/245–1937 | www.dickinson.edu | Free | Grounds daily dawn to dusk, buildings weekdays 9–5, closed weekends.

The **Trout Gallery** has changing exhibits including selections from Dickinson College's collection of about 600 pieces. The college has an extensive African collection. | W. High St. | 717/243–5121 | fax 717/245–1937 | www.dickinson.edu | Free | Weekdays 9–5, closed weekends.

Evansburg State Park. In this park, you'll find an eight-arch stone bridge spanning Skippack Creek on the Germantown Pike, constructed in 1792, that is the oldest bridge in continuous, heavy use in the nation. The park is a quiltwork of cropland, meadows, old fields, and mature woodlands providing fishing on Skippack Creek, more than 1,000 acres for hunting, a mountain bike trail, more than 6 mi of hiking trails, picnic facilities, horseback riding, an 18-hole golf course, four softball fields, and cross-country skiing. Also in the park is the Friedt Visitor Center, housed in a home built in the early 1700s, where you can learn about the lifestyles of the German Mennonite families who owned the home for 190 years. An exhibit room in the house is devoted to the natural history of the area. | 851 May Hall Rd., Collegeville | 610/409–1150 or 888/PA–PARKS | www.dcnr.state.pa.us | Free | Daily 8 AM–dusk.

Grave of "Molly Pitcher." Mary Ludwig Hays McCauley was an artillery wife who shared the rigors of Valley Forge with her husband. Her actions during the Battle of Monmouth on June 28, 1778, became legendary. She earned the name Molly Pitcher by bringing pitcher after pitcher of water to the exhausted and thirsty men on the battlefield. She also tended the wounded and watched her husband fall wounded. When that happened, she took the rummer staff from her husband's hands and for the second time on an American battlefield a woman manned a gun. George Washington himself issued her a warrant as a noncommissioned officer. A flagstaff and cannon stand at her grave site. | Old Graveyard, E. South St. | Free | Daily dawn to dusk.

Huntsdale Fish Hatchery. One of more than a dozen fish hatcheries operated by the Pennsylvania Fish and Boat Commission. Established in 1932, it is one of the largest in the United States. The tour is self-guided (although guided tours can be arranged), where you can witness nearly every aspect of raising fish in volume. The visitors center's living stream closely approximates the natural habitat of trout. There are ponds displaying various warm-water fish. Other displays trace the history of fish culture in Pennsylvania. | 195 Lebo Rd., Huntsdale | 717/486–3419 | fax 717/486–4040 | www.fish.state.pa.us | Free | Daily 8–3:30.

Kings Gap Environmental Education and Training Center. The park contains 1,454 acres of forest on South Mountain. There are 16 mi of hiking trails, several hundred acres for hunting, and a permanent orienteering course. | 500 Kings Gap Rd. | 717/486–5031 or 888/PA–PARKS | fax 717/486–3736 | www.dcnr.state.pa.us | Free | Daily 8 AM–dusk.

Pine Grove Furnace State Park. A 696-acre park is in the mountains with two lakes—25-acre Laurel Lake and 1.7-acre Fuller Lake—that can be used for boating, fishing, swimming, and ice skating. There are 74 campsites, 75 acres for hunting, and trails for bicycling, hiking, and cross-country skiing. The remains of the Pine Grove Iron Furnace site date back to 1764, and for over 100 years the company manufactured cast-iron products. | 1100 Pine Grove Rd., Gardners | 717/486–7174 or 888/PA–PARKS | fax 717/486–4961 | www.dcnr.state.pa.us | Free | Daily 8 AM–dusk.

ON THE CALENDAR

JULY: *Summerfair*. This annual July 4 event includes a 5K race, a parade, and an arts festival at Dickinson College. | 717/243–4515 | Some events have fees while others are free. Call for more info.

OCT.: *Art Festival and Octubafest*. More than 200 crafters, free activities for kids, and a gathering of tuba players are in the spotlight at this one-day event. | West High St. | 717/245–2648 | Free.

Dining

California Cafe. Contemporary. Soft lighting and a variety of French and local artworks are stunning for dinners by candlelight. The restaurant is a renovated fire house right in downtown Carlisle. Try the shrimp scampi and the coq au vin, or fricassee chicken in wine sauce. | 38 W. Pomfret St. | $8–$22 | AE, D, DC, MC, V.

Fay's Country Kitchen. American. Only breakfast and lunch are served at this eatery, a favorite of local residents. You can have waffles, sandwiches and other breakfast classics. | 203 S. Hanover St. | 717/243–5510 | $4 | No credit cards.

Market Cross Pub. . This restaurant and pub with traditional English fare such as burgers, shepherd's pie, and fish–n–chips serves more than 200 micro–brewed and imported ales and lagers, and continually wins awards for best beer menu in central Pennsylvania. | 113 N. Hanover St. | 717/258–1234 | $5–$7 | AE, D, MC, V.

Piatto. Italian. In Carlisle's historic district in a Victorian home, this restaurant serves dishes including pizza, risotto and linguine with pesto, from all 20 of Italy's regions. Outdoor seating is available in the summer. You can come for family pasta nights Tuesday through Thursday or for the five-course tasting menu on Friday and Saturday. | 22 W. Pomfret St. | 717/249–9580 | Closed Sun.–Mon. | $5–$12 | MC, V.

Sunnyside Restaurant. Mediterranean. Owned and operated by the Mallios family since 1948, this restaurant, across from the U.S. Army War College, serves seafood, pasta and western cut steaks in rooms with themes such as Greece. | 850 N. Hanover St. | 717/243–5712 | Closed Sun. | $12–$28 | AE, D, MC, V.

Lodging

Appalachian Trail Inn. Built in 1990, right next to the Appalachain Trail, this large, two-story affordable hotel is convenient to Exit 17E off I–81 South. It's only 3 mi south of Carlisle. Restaurant, picnic area. Cable TV. Exercise equipment. | 1825 Harrisburg Pike/Rte. 11 | 717/245–2242 or 800/445–6715 | fax 717/258–4881 | 200 rooms, 3 suites | $50–$60, $125 suites | AE, D, DC, MC, V.

Best Western Inn Carlisle. Just off I–81, this hotel has four wings, the main wing with three stories, and the others single-stories. It was built over the course of 20 years, from the 1960s–1980s and remodeled in 1998. It's about 2 mi from Carlisle Barracks, 4 mi from Dickinson College and downtown, and 15 mi northeast of Kings Gap State Park. Restaurant, bar.

cable TV Pool. | 1245 Harrisburg Pike/Rte. 11 | 717/243–5411 | fax 717/243–0778 | 130 rooms | $65–$80 | AE, D, DC, MC, V.

Clarion Hotel and Convention Center. A full-service, one-story hotel that was renovated in 1999. It's about 4 mi from downtown and Dickinson College and 2 mi to Carlisle Barracks. Restaurant, bar, room service. In-room data ports, refrigerators, cable TV. Indoor pool, wading pool. Hot tub, sauna. Exercise equipment. Business services, airport shuttle, free parking. Some pets allowed. | 1700 Harrisburg Pike/U.S. 11 | 717/243–1717 or 800/692–7315 | fax 717/243–6648 | sales@clarioncarlisle.com | 273 rooms | $75–$85 | AE, D, DC, MC, V.

Days Inn. A midpriced chain hotel, about 2 mi south of Carlisle, is just off Exit 13 of I–81. Originally built in 1989, additions were made to this two-story building with interior corridors in 1995. About 35 mi from Hershey, 30 mi from Gettysburg, but within 5 mi of Dickinson College and the Army War College. Complimentary Continental breakfast. Some refrigerators, cable TV. Pool. Exercise equipment. Video games. Laundry facilities. Business services. | 101 Alexander Spring Rd. | 717/258–1207 | fax 717/258–4147, ext. 501 | www.daysinn.com | 136 rooms, 3 suites | $65–$89, $95–$129 suites | AE, D, DC, MC, V.

Holiday Inn. Built in 1983, this moderately priced, two-story chain hotel is at Exit 17 of I–81. It's about 2 mi from downtown Carlisle, the Carlisle Fairgrounds, and the Army War College. Restaurant, bar, room service. In-room data ports, cable TV. Pool. Gym. Laundry facilities. Business services, free parking. Some pets allowed. | 1450 Harrisburg Pike/U.S. 11 | 717/245–2400 | fax 717/245–9070 | www.lodgingincarlisle.com | 100 rooms | $89–$99 | AE, D, DC, MC, V.

Jacob's Resting Place. Built in 1790 as a tavern and inn called the Sign of the Green Tree, this classic five-bay brick Georgian home still has its original architecture including floors, doors, and seven fireplaces. The colonial innkeeper, Jacob Matter, named the land and the trout stream surrounding the inn after himself. You can relax in a hot tub in a log house adjacent to the inn. Full breakfast. Outdoor pool. Hot tub. Exercise equipment. Library. No pets. No kids under 12. | 1007 Harrisburg Pike | 717/243–1766 | fax 717/241–5010 | Jacobsrest@pa.net | www.bbhost.com/restingplace.com | 5 rooms | $85 | AE, D, MC, V.

Line Limousin Farm House. Built in 1864, this B&B is on a 110–acre farm and borders a golf course which leaves balls you can find and use on the driving range. You can tour the beef farm (Limousin is a French breed of beef cattle), hike, cross-country ski, play croquet and bocce ball, or picnic under the giant sugar maple trees. Traveling horses and cattle are welcome in the barn. Full breakfast. Room phones. TV in common area. No kids under 18. No smoking. | 2070 Ritner Hwy. | 717/243–1281 | fax 717/249–5537 | bline@planetcable.net | www.pafarmstay.com/line/index.html | 4 rooms, 2 with bath | $75–$85 | No credit cards.

Pheasant Field. This Federal red brick farmhouse, built in 1800, across the street from a three-acre pond, used to be on a pheasant farm (the present owners are hoping to re-introduce the birds to the area). Its summer kitchen, once separate because of heat and in case of fire, has a hiding place that was used for the underground railroad. Full breakfast. Cable TV, room phones. Some pets allowed. No kids under 8. No smoking. | 150 Hickorytown Rd. | 717/258–717 or 877/258–0717 | fax 717/258–0717 | pheasant@pa.net | www.pheasantfield.com/ | 5 rooms | $85–110 | AE, MC, V.

Quality Inn. An affordable, two-story motel with interior corridors is at Exit 17 of I–81. It's close to the Carlisle Fairgrounds, Dickinson University, and the Army War College. It is 4 mi from downtown Carlisle and about 30 mi from Gettysburg and Hershey. Bar, complimentary Continental breakfast. Cable TV. Pool, wading pool. Laundry facilities. Business services, free parking. Some pets allowed. | 1255 Harrisburg Pike/U.S. 11 | 717/243–6000 | fax 717/258–4123 | www.qualityinn.com | 96 rooms | $65–$125 | AE, D, DC, MC, V.

Super 8. Built in the late 70s to early 80s, this three-story motel with interior corridors is about 3 mi from downtown Carlisle. This affordable motel is near Exit 17 of I–81, within 30 mi of Gettysburg and Hershey Park. Some kitchenettes. Cable TV. Laundry facilities. | 1800 Harrisburg Pike/U.S. 11 | 717/249–7000 | fax 717/249–9070 | www.super8.com | 112 rooms, 1 suite | $50–$120, $175 suite | AE, D, DC, MC, V.

CHADDS FORD

MAP 7, K7

(Nearby towns also listed: Bristol, Chester, Downington, Doylestown, Holicong, Jenkintown, King of Prussia, New Hope, Philadelphia, Quakertown, Willow Grove)

Center of the Battle of Brandywine along the east bank of Brandywine Creek in 1777, a major defeat for the Colonials as British troops defeated General George Washington's troops en route to Philadelphia, the nation's capital at the time. Chadds Ford was named for John Chadds, the man who helped the country expand westward by establishing a ferry service across the treacherous Delaware River. Today many people visit the area to go skiing in the winter and visit the battlefield, John Chadd's house, and various other historical buildings.

Information: **Delaware County Chamber of Commerce** | 602 E. Baltimore Pike, Media, PA 19063 | 610/565–3677 | fax 610/565–1606 | www.delcochamber.org.

Attractions

Barns–Brinton House. Early tavern authentically restored as a living history museum. Costumed guides take you back in time with a tour of the museum and by demonstrating hands-on crafts. | 630 Baltimore Pike | 610/388–7376 | fax 610/388–7480 | www.voicenet.com/~cfhs | $5 | May–Sep., weekends noon–5 and by appointment, closed weekdays.

Brandywine Battlefield. Fought on September 11, 1777, the Battle of Brandywine was the largest engagement of the Revolutionary War between the Continental Army led by George Washington and the British forces headed by Gen. William Howe. The battle was fought for control of territory near Philadelphia. The site includes Washington's headquarters, tours of houses, and a visitors center with exhibits and dioramas. | U.S. 202 | 610/459–3342 | fax 610/459–9586 | www.ushistory.org/brandywine | $3.50 | Tues.–Sat. 9–5, Sun. noon–5, closed Mon.

★ **Brandywine River Museum.** Home to one of the largest and most comprehensive collections of works by N.C., Andrew, and Jamie Wyeth, three generations of artists who embody the family's distinctive artistic legacy. Other works on display are from Maxfield Parrish, Charles Dana Gibson, Rockwell Kent, Rose O'Neill, William Trost Richards, Jasper Cropsey, George Cope, William Michael Harnett, John F. Peto, Horace Pippin, and J.D. Chalfant. Housed inside a Civil War–era gristmill that was converted into a modern museum. | Rtes. 1 & 100 | 610/388–2700 | fax 610/388–1197 | www.brandywinemuseum.org | $5, special rates for students, senior citizens, children, and groups | Daily 9:30–4:30.

Chaddsford Winery. An 18th-century barn houses an intimate winery that hosts events, festivals, and concerts in the summer. Testing and tours are available. | 632 Baltimore Pike | 610/388–6221 | fax 610/388–0360 | www.chaddsford.com | $5 for logo glass and tasting 7–8 different wines | Apr.–Dec., Tues.–Sun. noon–6; Jan.–Mar., Tues.–Sun. noon–6, closed Mon.

John Chad's House. Built in 1725, the house pays tribute to the man who the town is named after. John Chad was a ferryman who built a business of taking people across the Brandywine River. | 630 Baltimore Pike | 610/388–7376 | fax 610/388–7480 | www.voicenet.com/~cfhs/chads.htm | $5 | May–Sept., weekends noon–5 and by appointment, closed weekdays.

ON THE CALENDAR

OCT.: *Great Pumpkin Event.* Held the Thursday, Friday, and Saturday before Halloween, this community event showcases the work of local artists who carve their own pumpkins. Come view the pumpkins, eat the food, take a hay ride, and listen to the music. | $2 | 610/280–6145 | $2.

Dining

Barnaby's of America. American. Part restaurant, part sports bar, this place, 1 mi south of Rte. 1 in Chadds Ford, is self-identified as "where good sports come to eat." You can have Barna-b-qued baby back ribs, sandwiches, salads, and more for lunch, dinner, or a late-night snack while watching the game on the two giant TVs. Kids menu. | Rte. 202, 1 mi south of Rte 1 | 610/789–1885 | open daily | $7–$17 | D, MC, V.

Copper Kettle. Contemporary. Once a private home, this brick building (built in 1897) is 2 mi east of downtown. Now renovated, the front of the building serves as a spacious dining area, and early American antiques highlight the interior. Specialties include prime rib, steaks, and seafood. Kids' menu. | 1049 Lincoln Way E/U.S. 30 | 717/264–3109 | Reservations essential | No lunch. Closed Sun. | $15–$36 | AE, D, DC, MC, V.

Lodging

Brandywine River Hotel. This small, two-story hotel was built in 1985 and has a Victorian interior, including some rooms with fireplaces. It is close to the Art History and Gardens, right in downtown Chadds Ford. Complimentary Continental breakfast. Refrigerators (in suites). Cable TV. Exercise equipment. Shops. Business services. Some pets allowed. | Routes 1 and 100 | 610/388–1200 | fax 610/388–1200 | www.virtualcities.com/pa/brh.htm | 40 rooms, 10 suites, 1 cottage | $125–$169, $149–$169 suites | AE, D, DC, MC, V.

Pennsbury Inn. Originally built in 1714 this inn, on land purchased from William Penn's commissioners, was later enlarged by a stone and brick addition and later still with a clapboard extension. Visitors claim to have seen the ghost of Joseph Lancaster, the first innkeeper, around the coachmen's quarters and there is a trap door entrance to the basement hiding a stop on the underground railroad. Full breakfast. In-room data ports. Cable TV, room phones. Library. Some pets allowed. No kids under 12. No smoking. | 883 Baltimore Pike | 610/388–1435 | fax 610/388–1436 | www.bbchannel.com/bbc/ph601510.asp | 7 rooms | $150–225 | AE, DC, MC, V.

CHAMBERSBURG

MAP 7, G7

(Nearby towns also listed: Breezewood, Gettysburg)

At the heart of Chambersburg is a site that made the town's founder, Benjamin Chambers, end his journey west and build his home and gristmill. Settlers quickly surrounded the Falling Springs and Chambers's mill and the town was officially established in 1756. In 1864, the town was held for ransom by Confederate troops; when the townspeople refused to pay the $100,000 bounty, troops burned and looted all 537 buildings. Chambersburg has rebuilt itself into a town of antiques shops.

Information: Chambersburg Chamber of Commerce | 75 S. 2nd St., 17201 | 717/264–7101 | fax 717/267–0399 | www.chambersburg.org.

Attractions

Caledonia State Park. The Appalachian Trail traverses the central portion of this 1,125-acre park on the Blue Ridge. It has 184 campsites, two cottages available to rent, picnic facilities, a swimming pool, 740 acres open to hunting, and you can go fishing, golfing, and hiking. Also on site is the Totem Pole Playhouse, which has daily performances during the summer. | 40 Rocky Mountain Rd., Fayetteville | 717/352–2161 or 888/PA–PARKS | www.dcnr.state.pa.us | Free | Daily 8 AM–dusk.

Old Jail. Built in 1818, the former jail now houses Franklin County artifacts and a genealogical library. The gallows that were once used are on display in the excercise yard. The building was a station on the Underground Railroad. | 175 E. King St. | 717/264–6364 or 717/264–1667 | Free | May–Oct., Thur.–Sat. 9:30–4, closed Sun.–Wed.

Walking Tour. You can pick up a brochure and map at the visitor's center and take yourself on a walking tour to see the homes, churches, former jail, and learn the history of Chambersburg. | 75 South Second St. | 717/264–7101 or 717/261–1200 | fax 717/267–0399 | chamber@chambersburg.org | www.chambersburg.org | Free | Mon.–Fri., 8–5.

ON THE CALENDAR

JUNE–AUG.: *Totem Pole Playhouse.* A range of productions, including comedies, dramas, and musicals, are performed in a 453-seat theater. | 40 Rocky Mountain Rd., Fayetteville | 717/352–2164 | $18–$27.

JULY: *ChamberFest.* This annual, three-day Civil War festival includes a market day, a Civil War seminar, a pet parade, games, and battle reenactments. | Various locations | 717/264–7101 | some fees, variable.

AUG.: *Franklin County Fair.* The state turkey-calling contest, a tractor pull, and needlework displays are among the highlights at this traditional, two-day county fair. | Fairgrounds | 717/369–4100 | some fees.

Dining

Dodie's Restaurant. American. Sit inside or take advantage of the drive-up window at this casual restaurant, open until 9 every night. Try the roasted chicken, roast beef sandwiches, burgers, or the combination meals. | 2019 Lincoln Way E | 717/264–2563 | $5–$7 | Daily, 11 AM–9 PM | No credit cards.

Mercersburg Inn. Contemporary. An inn and restaurant with antique saws, brooms, and even old tennis rackets hung artfully on the walls, along with more typical antiques. Only a 20-mi drive southwest of Chambersburg, you can try specialties like rack of lamb with Dauphinoise potatoes, asparagus, and a red wine demi-glaze or Chesapeake style crab cakes with corn tortilla basket, fried corn salad, and roasted red pepper couli. Kids' menu. | 405 S. Main St., Mercersburg | 717/328–5231 | www.mercersburginn.com | Reservations required | Closed Sun.–Thurs. | $10–$21 | D, MC, V.

Schoenberger's. American. You can select stuffed pork chops, Weiner schnitzel, seafood, or pasta at this restaurant in the heart of downtown Chambersburg. | 346 Lincoln Way E | 717/263–1137 | $15–$16 | No lunch | AE, D, DC, MC, V.

Lodging

Days Inn. An affordable, three-story motel that is at Exit 6 of I–81. Built in 1984, it's less than 2 mi from downtown with Whitetail Ski Resort less than 25 mi away. Complimentary Continental breakfast. Cable TV. Some pets allowed. | 30 Falling Spring Rd. | 717/263–1288 | fax 717/263–6514 | www.daysinn.com | 99 rooms | $55–$70 | AE, D, DC, MC, V.

Four Points by Sheraton–Chambersburg. Just 3 mi east of Wilson College, this three-story tan hotel is at the intersection of I–81 and Route 30. Some rooms have a view of Falling Spring Duck Pond. Restaurant, bar room service. In-room data ports, Some refrigerators. Cable TV. Indoor Pool. Sauna. Health club. Laundry facilities, laundry service. Business services, free parking. No pets. | 1123 Lincoln Way E | 717/263–9191 | fax 717/263–4752 | www.sheraton.com | 125 rooms, 3 suites | $85–$140 | AE, D, DC, MC, V.

Hampton Inn. Built in 1993, this three-story building is right in downtown Chambersburg. You can easily access it from I–81 and it's only 20 mi west to Cowans Gap State Park. Complimentary Continental breakfast. In-room data ports, refrigerators. Cable TV. Exercise equipment. Business services. | 955 Lesher Rd. | 717/261–9185 | fax 717/261–1984 | www.hamptoninn.com | 124 rooms | $68–$73 | AE, D, DC, MC, V.

Mercersburg Inn. The grand double-staircase and mahogany paneling in the entry hall set the tone for this elegant inn. This Georgian inn was constructed in 1909 right in downtown Chambersburg on 6.5 acres of terraced, landscaped lawns. It is less than 10 mi from the Whitetail Ski Resort. Restaurant, complimentary breakfast. TV in common area. No smoking. | 405 S. Main St., Mercersburg | 717/328–5231 | fax 717/328–3403 | www.mercers-burginn.com | 15 rooms | $130–$250 | D, MC, V.

Penn National Inn. The Federal-style manor house, built around 1850, provides Georgian period charm, but most guest rooms are in a 1989 addition. It's only 10 mi southeast of Chambersburg. Restaurant, complimentary breakfast. Refrigerators. Cable TV. Pool. Driving range, 18-hole golf course, putting green, tennis courts. Playground. Some pets allowed. | 3809 Anthony Hwy., Mont Alto | 717/352–2400 or 800/231–0080 | fax 717/352–3926 | www.penngolf.com | 40 rooms in 2 buildings | $100–$120 | AE, D, MC, V.

Quality Inn. This full-service hotel is near Exit 5 of I–81. The two-story building was built in 1984 and is 5 mi north of downtown Chambersburg. Restaurant, bar, room service. Some in-room data ports. Cable TV. Pool. Exercise equipment. Business services, free parking. Some pets allowed. | 1095 Wayne Ave. | 717/263–3400 | fax 717/263–8386 | www.qualityinn.com | 139 rooms, 32 suites | $70–$75, $97 suites | AE, D, DC, MC, V.

Shultz Victorian Mansion Bed and Breakfast. On a tree-lined street this Victorian brick home, full of antiques, has an onion-topped turret and is half a block north of Wilson College. Built by the Craig family in 1880, it remained in the family until 1975 and is now owned by the Shultz family. You can sit on the porch or balcony, request a room with a fireplace, and try the baked French toast with sticky topping for breakfast. Full breakfast. Some in-room hot tubs. Cable TV. No pets. No smoking. | 756 Philadelphia Ave. | 717/263–3371 | fax 717/263–8902. | www.bedandbreakfast.com/bbc/p204624.asp | 7 rooms | $85–$125 | AE, D, MC, V.

Travelodge. Only 1 mi from downtown Chambersburg, this afforable, three-story motel at Exit 6 of I–81 was built in 1964 and all of its rooms were remodeled in 2000. It is within 25 mi of Gettysburg and 33 mi of Carlisle. Restaurant, bar, room service. Cable TV. Some pets allowed. | 565 Lincoln Way East/U.S. 30 | 717/264–4187 | fax 717/264–2446 | www.travelodge.com | 49 rooms | $55–$65 | AE, D, DC, MC, V.

CHESTER

MAP 7, K7

(Nearby towns also listed: Bristol, Chadds Ford, Downington, Doylestown, Fort Washington, Frazer, Holicong, Jenkintown, King of Prussia, Limerick, Media, New Hope, Norristown, Philadelphia, Pottstown, Quakertown, Willow Grove)

Chester was founded by the Swedish Trading Company in the mid 1600s. William Penn came to the area in the later part of that century and named the town Chester after a Quaker settlement in Cheshire, England. Today this bustling suburb of Philadelphia is a busy port and shipbuilding center.

Information: **Delaware County Convention and Tourist Bureau** | 200 E. State St., Ste. 100, Media, PA 19063 | 610/565–3679 or 800/343–3983 | fax 610/565–0833 | www.brandywinecvb.org.

Attractions

Caleb Pusey Home, Landingford Plantation. A cottage built in 1683 for Caleb Pusey, a friend and business partner of William Penn. The two-room cottage has been in continuous use since it was built. It is furnished with 17th-century English pieces. | 15 Race St., Upland | 610/874–5665 | www.delcohistory.org/FCPH | Free | May–Oct., weekends 1–4 and by appointment, closed weekdays.

Morton Homestead. This 18th-century Swedish log house was the home of John Morton, signer of the Declaration of Independence. The house is typical of the early Swedish log buildings built by early settlers of the New Sweden Colony, which was established in 1638 along the Delaware River. | 100 Lincoln Ave., Prospect Park | 610/583–7221 | Free | Apr.–Oct.,

Wed.–Thurs., Sat. 9:30–3:30 and Sun. by appointment, closed Mon.–Tues.; Jun.–Aug., Fri. 9:30–5 and Sun. by appointment, closed Mon.–Tues.

Swarthmore College. Founded in 1864 as a private liberal arts college, the campus has a total undergraduate enrollment of 1,370. Prominent alumni include Pulitzer Prize winner James Michener and former governor of Massachusetts Michael Dukakis. The campus is on more than 330 wooded acres with more than 5,000 plants. | 500 College Ave., Swarthmore | 610/328–8000 or 610/328–8001 | www.swarthmore.edu | Free | Daily.

Widener University. A private college founded in 1821 by John Bullock with an enrollment of 7,500. The 100-acre campus has 82 buildings with a mixture of modern and Victorian architecture. The university is composed of eight schools and colleges that provide 124 programs of study. | 1 University Pl. | 610/499–4000 or 800/870–6481 | www.widener.edu | Free | Daily.

ON THE CALENDAR
MAY: *Mother's Day Parade.* Every year the mayor and the city council lead the Boy Scouts, school bands, the Masons, and other groups on a parade through town to honor and celebrate motherhood. | 610/447–7723 | Free.

Dining
Edgemont Diner. American. Next to the Airport Inn, this diner has an extensive menu including fried shrimp, crab cakes and salads. Breakfast served all day. | 1300 Providence Rd. | 610/872–9100 | $8 | D, MC, V.

Lodging
Airport Inn. Major renovation is underway at this seven-story motel that was once a Howard Johnson's and is now a Days Inn 2 mi south of the Philadelphia airport. Cable TV. Indoor pool. Exercise equipment. Laundry facility. Airport shuttle. No pets. | 1300 Providence Rd. | 610/876–7211 | fax 610/874–5210 | www.daysinn.com | 60 rooms | $70 | AE, D, DC, MC, V.

CLARION

MAP 7, C4

(Nearby towns also listed: Brookville, East Brady)

Named after the Clarion River, the borough of Clarion was settled as a result of lumbering for companies from Pittsburgh. Today, the borough is popular as a rest stop for weary travelers on Interstate 80 and for its vast acres of forests and streams, which provide fertile hunting and fishing grounds.

Information: **Clarion County Chamber of Commerce** | 41 S. 5th Ave., 16214 | 814/226–9161 | www.clarionpa.com.

Attractions
Cook Forest State Park. One of only eight Commonwealth parks to possess a National Natural Landmark, the Forest Cathedral, which has stands of virgin timber measuring as much as 5 ft in diameter and towering 200 ft into the air. The 7,443-acre park has nearly 30 mi of hiking trails; canoeing, fishing, or inner tubing on the Clarion River; bicycling; horseback riding; camping; cabin rentals; picnic facilities; a swimming pool; playgrounds; more than 4,000 acres for hunting; ice skating; cross-country skiing; snowmobiling; and sledding. More than 90 species of birds have been identified at the park. Also on site is the Sawmill Center for the Arts, with more than 125 classes, and the Vera Leith Sawmill Theatre. | Box 120, River Rd., Cooksburg | 814/744–8407 or 888/PA–PARKS | fax 814/744–8253 | www.penn.com/cforest | Free | Daily 8 AM–dusk.

Sutton–Ditz House Museum and Library. A late Victorian home in its original condition, complete with a Victorian parlor, bedroom, and kitchen with period furnishings. Permanent exhibits illustrate the iron, lumber, and glass industries; an old country store; and the Clarion County military. The museum also houses a library and changing exhibits on the history of Clarion County. | 18 Grant St. | 814/226–4450 | fax 814/226–7106 | www.cson-line.net/cchs | $1.50 (suggested) | Tues.–Sat. 10–4, closed Sun.–Mon.

ON THE CALENDAR

MAY: *Spring Fling.* This week-long event welcomes the warm weather with concerts, games, and food booths. | Downtown | 814/226–9161 | Free.

JULY: *Clarion County Fair.* Each year for one week in June the county gets together, 17 mi south of Clarion in New Bethlehem, to show-off livestock, vegetables, and candy and other foods. Live music. | 814/849–5197 | $5.

SEPT.–OCT.: *Autumn Leaf Festival.* This nine-day event includes an antique car show, a motorcycle display, a craft show, and a parade. | Downtown | 814/226–9161 | Free.

Dining

Captain Loomis Inn. American. Named for a Civil War captain, this restaurant serves prime rib. Open for breakfast on the weekends. | 540 Main St. | 814/226–8400 | $10 | AE, D, MC, V.

Vinny's. Italian. Open until midnight, Vinny's serves veal Parmesan, sausage dishes, shrimp, and more. | 518 Main St. | 814/226–5421 | $9–$14 | D, MC.

Lodging

Clarion House B&B. This turn–of–the–20th– century white Victorian home, built by the granddaughter of the Cooks, for whom Cook Forest is named, takes up an entire city block. It is even made with timber from the Cook forest. Located 1 ½ blocks west of Clarion University. Inside, there's rare leaded and stained glass doors, a stained glass skylight, and an original hardwood stairway. Full breakfast. TV in common area. No pets. No kids under 14. No smoking. | 77 South 7th Ave. | 814/226–4996 or 800/416–3297 | fax 800/416–3217 | www.chouse.com | www.chouse.com | 5 rooms | $75 | AE, D, MC, V.

Comfort Inn Clarion. From this two-story hotel you can walk just down the hill, to the Clarion mall. Complimentary Continental breakfast. Some refrigerators, some in-room hot tubs. Cable TV. Laundry facilities, laundry service. No pets. | 129 Dolby St. | 814/226–5230 or 800/252–7466 | fax 814/226–5231 | www.comfortinn.com | 81 rooms | $74 | AE, D, DC, MC, V.

Days Inn. A full-service hotel with two floors and interior corridors. It is at Exit 9N of I–80. Built in 1983, this hotel is 22 mi from Cook Forest State Park and only 1 mi from downtown Clarion. Restaurant, bar (with entertainment), complimentary Continental breakfast, room service. Cable TV. Pool. Laundry facilities. Business services. Some pets allowed. | Rte. 68 and I–80 | 814/226–8682 | fax 814/226–8372 | www.daysinn.com | 150 rooms, 1 suite | $60–$70, $100 suite | AE, D, DC, MC, V.

Holiday Inn. Indoor balconies on two floors overlook a central courtyard in this midpriced chain hotel, near Exit 9 of I–80. It's only a mile from downtown and the Sutton-Ditz House Museum and Library. Restaurant, bar, room service. In-room data ports. Cable TV. Indoor pool. Sauna. Putting green. Exercise equipment. Video games. Business services, airport shuttle. | 45 Holiday Inn Rd. | 814/226–8850; 250 | fax 814/226–9055, ext | www.holidayinn.com | 122 rooms | $79–$94, $149 suite | AE, D, DC, MC, V.

Super 8. This midpriced motel is near Exit 9 of I–80. Its rooms are all on one floor with exterior corridors. It's only 1 mi from downtown and 22 mi from Cook Forest State Park. Complimentary Continental breakfast. In-room data ports, some kitchenettes. Cable TV. Outdoor pool. Some pets allowed. | Rte. 3 at Rte. 68 | 814/226–4550 | fax 814/227–2337 | www.super8.com | 99 rooms, 2 suites | $60–$66, $150 suites | AE, D, DC, MC, V.

CLEARFIELD

MAP 7, E4

(Nearby towns also listed: Du Bois, St. Mary's)

Like many boroughs in northern Pennsylvania, Clearfield was founded because of its timber and coal deposits. Many of the nation's great ships and schooners were made from wood from this area. Today, Interstate 80 connects the borough with major cities to the east and west, while acres of forest and Curwensville Lake bring adventure seekers and hunters to the area.

Information: Clearfield County Chamber of Commerce | 125 E. Market St., 16830 | 814/765–7560 | fax 814/765–6948.

Attractions

Parker Dam State Park. Covering 968 acres, this park is the western trailhead of the Quehanna Trail system. There are 110 campsites and 16 cabins. Activities include hiking, boating, swimming, hunting, picnicking, snowmobiling, ice skating, and sledding. | R.D. 1, Penfield | 814/765–0630 or 888/PA–PARKS | fax 814/765–0633 | www.dcnr.state.pa.us | Free | Daily 8 AM–dusk.

S.B. Elliott State Park. This 318-acre park has picnicking, fishing in the small mountain streams, hunting, hiking, cross-country skiing on more than 4 mi of trails, and snowmobiling. There are 25 campsites and six cabins. | R.D. 1 Box 165, Penfield | 814/765–0630 or 888/PA–PARKS | fax 814/765–0633 | www.dcnr.state.pa.us | Free | Daily 8 AM–dusk.

Walking Tour. See Victorian homes as you take a self-guided walking tour along Front Street. | Front St. | 814/765–7560 | fax 814/765–6948 | clearfieldchamber@penn.com | Free | Mon.–Fri., 8:30–4:30.

ON THE CALENDAR
MAR.: *Central Counties Concerned Sportsmen Annual Show.* This three-day event includes wildlife displays, vendors, and educational seminars. | Expo II Building, Clearfield County Fairgrounds. Driving Park Rd. | 814/765–9495 | $3.
JUNE: *Clearfield County Gospel Music Festival.* This weekend event attracts more than three dozen gospel groups and soloists. | Clearfield County Fairgrounds, Driving Park Rd. | 814/765–7567 | Free.
JUNE: *Riverfront Festival.* Summer is welcomed with three days of entertainment, food, crafts, and fireworks. | Front St. | 814/765–7567 | Free.
JULY: *High Country Arts and Crafts Fair.* A one-day annual event that includes crafters and a barbecue. There are also three bands that play live music. | S.B. Elliott State Park, Rte. 153 | 814/422–8207 | Free.
JULY–AUG.: *Clearfield County Fair.* For six days this fair provides livestock displays, home-baked goods, entertainment, and rides. | Clearfield County Fairgrounds, Mill Rd. | 814/765–4629 | fax 814/765–2186 | $2.

Dining

Moena. Italian. Named for the Italian village where the DellAntonio family originated, their restaurant brings a taste of Italy to Pennsylvania. You can order from an extensive menu of Italian dishes including pasta and salads, as well as steaks. | 211 E. Market St. | 814/765–1564 | $10–$16 | Closed Sun., Mon. No lunch Sat. | AE, D, MC, V.

Lodging

Christopher Kratzer House. The oldest house in Clearfield, built in 1828, this yellow with green shutters classic Revival mansion is full of antiques and artwork by co-owner Ginny Baggett. There are views of the river and park. The house has white picket fences, a big yard, and large old trees. It is near shops, a public library, restaurants, a movie theater, and the Clearfield County Historical Museum. The B&B is 3 mi south of I–80. Full breakfast. Cable TV, room phones. Some pets allowed. | 101 E. Cherry St. | 814/765–5024 or 888/252–2632 | fax / | bbagget@uplink.net | www.virtualcities.com/pa/kratzerhouse.htm | 3 rooms, 2 with bath | $65–85 | D, MC, V.

Days Inn. An affordable chain motel near Exit 19 of I–80, 2 mi from downtown Clearfield and less than 5 mi from Moshannon State Forest. The two-story building with interior corridors was built in the late 70s. There are shopping outlets less than a mile away. Bar, complimentary Continental breakfast. In-room data ports. Pool. Exercise equipment. Business services. Some pets allowed. | R.R. 1 | 814/765–5381 | fax 814/765–7885 | www.daysinn.com | 118 rooms, 4 suites | $55–$85, $65–$95 suites | AE, D, DC, MC, V.

COLUMBIA

(Nearby towns also listed: Lancaster, Lititz, Wrightsville)

It's a quiet town now, but Columbia and other river communities were very important in the days when rivers were one of the easiest means of transportation. Eighteenth-century Quaker missionary John Wright worked in this area, and two of his sons set up a ferry that became an important transportation point for settlers moving west. Today museums and the tranquil countryside are diversions.

Information: **Susquehanna Valley Chamber of Commerce** | 445 Linden St., P.O. Box 510, 17512 | 717/684–5249 | www.parivertowns.com.

Attractions

The Market House and Dungeon. Built in 1869, this is one of the oldest continuously operating farmers' markets in the state. The basement of the market used to be a dungeon, and you can still see the ground-level windows through which the prisoners were shoved down a chute into the darkness. | 308 Locust St., off Rte. 441 | 717/684–2468 | Farmers' market: Fri. 7-4, Sat. 7-noon. Dungeon by appt. only: contact Susquehanna Heritage Visitors Center, 3rd and Linden Sts., 717/684-5249.

National Watch and Clock Museum. Take an entertaining trip through the history and future of timekeeping. The museum displays more than 10,000 timepieces and time-related items, including early sundials; a 19th century Tiffany globe clock; and the showstopper, the Engle Clock, an 1877 timepiece designed to resemble the famous astronomical cathedral clock of Strasburg, France. | 514 Poplar St. | 717/684–8261 | www.nawcc.org | $6 | Tues.-Sat. 10-5, Sun. noon-4.

Wright's Ferry Mansion. This 1738 stone house was the residence of English Quaker Susanna Wright, a silkworm breeder whose family helped open Pennsylvania west of the Susquehanna River. The collection showcases period furniture in the Philadelphia William & Mary and Queen Anne styles and a great collection of English needlework, ceramics, and glass, all predating 1750. | 38 S. 2nd St. | 717/684–4325 | $5 | May-Oct., Tues., Wed., Fri. 10-3.

Dining

Columbia Family Restaurant. American. This casual eatery specializes in the kind of meals Mom used to make–roasted chicken, broiled haddock, and homemade coconut cream pie. | 960 Lancaster Ave. | 717/684–7503 | $6–$10 | No credit cards.

Hinkle's Pharmacy Restaurant. American. Operating continuously since 1893, this old-fashioned restaurant and soda fountain is inside a traditional, small town pharmacy. The menu offers such fare as chicken pot pie and chicken with waffles, home-baked pies and luscious ice cream sundaes. | 261 Locust St. | 717/684–2888 | No dinner on Sun.; restaurant closes at 3 p.m | $6–$8 | AE, D, MC, V.

Prudhomme's Lost Cajun Kitchen. Cajun. Transplanted southerners and other Cajun food fans come from as far away as Philadelphia and Baltimore to dine at the only restaurant for mi where you can taste crawfish étouffée, fried alligator, and other specialties. They are prepared as hot as you like them by David Prudhomme, whose famous Uncle Paul perfected these flavors. | Rte. 462 and Cherry St. | 717/684–1706 | No dinner Sun., no lunch Mon. | $20–$25 | AE, D, MC, V.

Lodging

Clock Tower Bed & Breakfast. The rooms at this cozy bed and breakfast are named after famous clock makers like Seth Thomas, Waltham, and Hamilton. This is the sister property to The Columbian. | 441 Chestnut St. | 717/684–5869 or 800/422–5869 | www.columbiapa.com/clocktower | 3 rooms | $60–$70 | D,MC,V.

The Columbian. In this Victorian mansion in the heart of the village, a tiered staircase leads to rooms filled with antiques. Several rooms have fireplaces, and the rate includes an ample country breakfast. Playground. | 360 Chestnut St. | 717/684–5869 | www.columbian.com | 6 rooms, 2 suites | $75–$125 | D,MC,V.

CONNEAUT LAKE

MAP 7, B3

(Nearby towns also listed: Franklin, Meadville, Oil City)

Pennsylvania's largest natural lake is a haven for boating and fishing enthusiasts. It's nestled on Route 6 between Pittsburgh and Erie. The community was established in 1880 for hunters and fishermen, then dubbed a resort area with the establishment of the Conneaut Lake Exposition Park in 1892.

Information: Crawford County Convention and Visitors Bureau | 211½ Chestnut St., Meadville, PA 16335 | 814/333–1258 | fax 814/333–9032 | www.visitcrawford.org.

Attractions

Conneaut Cellars Winery. A country-style winery in the heart of a family resort area with guided tours and tastings of the winery's 23 different wines. | 12005 Conneaut Lake Rd. | 814/382–3999 or 877/CCW–WINE | fax 814/382–6151 | www.ccw-wine.com | Free | Daily 10–6.

Pymatuning State Park. Some of the sites in the park are the dam, spillway, fish hatchery, and waterfowl museum. The park includes Pymatuning Lake, which provides boating, fishing, swimming, ice fishing, ice skating, and ice boating. Other activities include picnicking, hiking, hunting, sledding, cross-country skiing, and snowmobiling. There are 657 campsites and cabins for rent. | 2660 Williamsfield Rd., Jamestown | 724/932–3141 | fax 724/932–3724 | www.dcnr.state.pa.us | Free | Daily 8 AM–dusk.

Pymatuning Spillway. A favorite site in Pymatuning State Park to feed fish and ducks. The spillway flows off the Pymatuning dam, dedicated on August 17, 1934. Pymatuning Lake's main purpose is the conservation of water entering the Pymatuning swamp and the regulation of water flow in the Shenango and Beaver Rivers. The fish being fed in the spillway are so crowded that ducks walk on their backs to compete for the food being thrown by visitors. | 2660 Williamsfield Rd., Jamestown | 724/932–3141 | fax 724/932–3724 | www.dcnr.state.pa.us | Free | Daily 8 AM–dusk.

Pymatuning Visitors Center. A wildlife visitors center with several stuffed animals preserved through taxidermy. There are wildlife education programs and eagles nesting on site you can view through a telescope. | 12590 Hartstown Rd., Linesville | 814/683–5545 | Free | Mar.–Oct., daily 9–4.

CONNELLSVILLE

(Nearby towns also listed: Donegal, Farmington, Uniontown)

Connellsville is 40 mi southeast of Pittsburgh in the Allegheny Mountains. The town provides some of the best whitewater rafting and kayaking in the country.

Information: Connellsville Chamber of Commerce | 923 W. Crawford Ave., 15425 | 724/628–5500 | fax 724/628–5676 | www.greaterconnellsville.org.

Attractions

Fallingwater (Kaufmann Conservation on Bear Run). Famous architect Frank Lloyd Wright designed the home in 1936 for the family of Edgar J. Kaufmann, a Pittsburgh department store owner. The house was completed with a guest and service wing in 1939. Built over a waterfall and constructed of sandstone quarried on the property, the home exemplifies Wright's desire to join architecture with nature and is perhaps his most famous work. The Kaufman family used it as a weekend home from 1937 to 1963, until the house, its contents, and grounds were presented to the Pennsylvania Conservancy by Edgar Kaufman Jr. A National Historic Landmark, the home was opened to the public in 1964. | Rte. 381, Mill Run | 724/329–8501 | fax 724/329–0553 | www.paconserve.org | $10 Tue.–Fri., $15 weekends and holidays, special rates for children | mid-Mar.–Nov., Tues.–Sun. 10–4, closed Mon.; Dec. and first 2 weeks of Mar., weekends 10–4, closed weekdays. Closed Jan.–Feb.

Laurel Hill State Park. The 13,625-acre park stretches along Laurel Mountain from the Youghiogheny River at Ohiopyle to the Conemaugh Gorge near Johnstown, spanning five counties. The main highlight of the park is the 70-mi hiking and backpacking trail. Other park activities include hunting, more than 70 mi for snowmobiling, and about 35 mi of cross-country ski trails. | 1117 Jim Mountain Rd., Rockwood | 724/455–3744 | fax 814/926–4532 | www.dcnr.state.pa.us | Free | Daily 8 AM–dusk.

Linden Hall. On the National Register of Historic Places, the mansion, dedicated on December 25, 1913, was built for Sarah Cochran, widow of coke and coal pioneer Philip Cochran, at the cost of $2 million. With 8,720 square ft on each of its four floors, the mansion contains 35 rooms, 27 fireplaces, 13 baths, and a finished basement. The Tiffany windows, an indoor bowling alley, and an Aeolian pipe organ—one of three in the world—that can be heard throughout the mansion emphasize its uniqueness. Also on the 785-acre estate there are overnight accommodations, a restaurant, a picnic area, and facilities for swimming, golfing, tennis, and fishing. | R.D. 1 Linden Hall, Dawson | 724/529–2882, 724/529–7543, or 800/944–3238 | fax 724/529–0529 | www.lindenhallpa.com | $8, special rates for senior citizens, children, and groups | Mar.–Oct., weekdays 11–3, weekends by appointment.

Youghiogheny Station Glass and Gallery. This factory has a blown glass studio with vases, candlesticks, paperweights, and jewelry. It also manufactures large sheets of stained glass bought by artists to make windows, lampshades, and other art. | 900 W. Crawford Ave. | 724/628–0332 | yough@cvzoom.net | www.youghioghenyglass.com/ | Free | Thu. 10–7, Sun. noon–4, other days 10–5.

Dining

R and R Stations Restaurant and Inn. Continental. During its 115-year history, this hotel provided housing for railroad workers, and was once struck by a runaway trolley. The restaurant and the inn's 17 rooms all contain railroad memorabilia, and there's also a tearoom with a coal-burning stove. Known for its baked pork chops and baked chicken dishes as well as its cabbage rolls. | 19 W. Main St. | 724/547–7545 | $15–$22 | MC, V.

Lodging

Melody Motor Lodge. A one-story motel with exterior corridors has some of the lowest rates in the region. It's only 4 mi from downtown and 15 mi from Fallingwater. Bar, picnic area. Cable TV. Some pets allowed. | 1607 Morrell Ave./U.S. 119 | 724/628–9600 | 46 rooms | $40–$50 | AE, D, MC, V.

Newmyer House. This B&B is right in the middle of downtown Connellsville and within an 11-mi drive of Frank Lloyd Wright's Fallingwater. It's a large, brick Queen Anne Mansion, built in the 1890s, with large porches. There are whitewater rafting outfitters 30 minutes away at Ohio Pyle, Seven Springs Ski Resort is less than 20 mi away, and the Yough Bike trails are ½ mi away. Complimentary breakfast. No room phones, TV in common area. No kids under 12. | 507 S. Pittsburgh St. | 724/626–0141 | www.bbonline.com/pa/newmyer | 4 rooms (1 with shower only) | $80–$90 | MC, V.

CORAOPOLIS

MAP 7, B5

(Nearby towns also listed: Ambridge, Beaver Falls, Butler, Harmony, Monroeville, Pittsburgh)

Coraopolis was incorporated as a borough in 1886 and is named for the Greek word meaning "Maiden City." Prior to its incorporation, the borough was known as Middletown and was a hub of railroad and oil activity.

Information: Greater Pittsburgh Convention and Visitors Bureau, Inc. | Regional Enterprise Tower, 425 6th Ave., 30th Fl., Pittsburgh, PA 15219 | 412/281–7711 or 800/366–0093. www.visitpittsburgh.com

ON THE CALENDAR
MAY: *Memorial Day Parade.* This annual parade runs down 5th and 4th Avenues and has drill teams, bands, floats and, of course, fire trucks. | 412/264–0940.

Dining
Hyeholde. Contemporary. Located on four acres of lawns and gardens, this castle-like Tudor mansion built in 1938 is only three mi from town. The chef's table seats two to six in the kitchen, where you can watch the dinner preparation. Known for rack of lamb and roasted elk. Open-air dining with picnics in summer. Jacket required. Free parking. | 190 Hyeholde Dr. | 412/264–3116 | Closed Sun. No lunch Sat. | $20–$36 | AE, D, DC, MC, V.

Pizzeria. Italian. Eat all pizza all the time at this casual local spot. You can try the special 16–topping or buy one slice at a time. | 1225 4th Ave. | 412/264–8735 | Closed Sun., Mon. | $1–$13 | No credit cards.

Lodging
Airport Plaza. Happy hour with free beer and wine, along with affordable rates, entices travelers to stay at this two-story motel. It's only 8 mi from the airport. Complimentary Continental breakfast. In-room data ports, some refrigerators. Cable TV. Exercise equipment. Business services, airport shuttle, free parking. | 1500 Beers School Rd. | 412/264–7900 or 800/542–8111 | fax 412/262–3229. www.plazaairport.com | 193 rooms | $50–$70 | AE, D, DC, MC, V.

Clarion-Royce. Only 16 mi from downtown Coraopolis, this upscale, nine-story hotel is 5 mi from the airport and 10 mi to downtown Pittsburgh. Restaurant, bar (with entertainment). In-room data ports. Cable TV. Pool. Exercise equipment. Business services, airport shuttle. Some pets allowed. | 1160 Thorn Run Rd. Ext. | 412/262–2400 | fax 412/264–9373. www.lodgian.com | 193 rooms | $79–$149 | AE, D, DC, MC, V.

Embassy Suites. A waterfall and river run through the center atrium of this hotel within the Cherrington Corporate Center and next to Pittsburgh International Airport. Restaurant, bar, complimentary breakfast. Cable TV, in-room VCRs. Indoor pool. Hot tub, sauna.

Gym. Shops. Laundry facilities, laundry service. Business services, airport shuttle. Pets allowed. | 550 Cherrington Pkwy. | 412/269–9070 or 800/EMBASSY | fax 412/262–4119 | www.embassy-suites.com | 223 suites | $109–$189 | AE, D, DC, MC, V.

Hampton Inn–Northwest. You can take advantage of the affordable rates at this five-story chain motel, 13 mi from downtown Coraopolis. It's 13 mi northwest of Pittsburgh's Golden Triangle and 7 mi from the airport. Complimentary Continental breakfast. Cable TV. Business services, airport shuttle, free parking. Some pets allowed. | 1420 Beers School Rd. | 412/264–0020 | fax 412/264–3220 | www.hamptoninn.com | 129 rooms | $69–$79 | AE, D, DC, MC, V.

La Quinta. Another affordable three-story chain motel, 2 mi from downtown Coraopolis. It's 7½ mi to the airport, 15 mi to downtown Pittsburgh, and a short drive to two malls. Complimentary Continental breakfast. In-room data ports. Cable TV. Pool. Exercise equipment. Laundry facilities. Business services, airport shuttle, free parking. Some pets allowed. | 1433 Beers School Rd. | 412/269–0400 | fax 412/269–9258. www.laquinta.com | 128 rooms | $69–$89 | AE, D, DC, MC, V.

Pittsburgh Airport Marriott. It's the tallest building in the area, with views of the Ohio River from its 14 floors. This upscale, full-service hotel is 5 mi from downtown Coraopolis and 7 mi from the airport. Restaurant, bar. In-room data ports, some refrigerators. Cable TV. Indoor-outdoor pool. Hot tub, sauna. Exercise equipment. Business services, airport shuttle. Some pets allowed. | 777 Aten Rd. | 412/788–8800 | fax 412/788–6299. www.marriott.com | 314 rooms | $89–$179 | AE, D, DC, MC, V.

Red Roof Inn. Convenient to the airport (4 mi), this 3-story motel has reasonable rates. It's also within 5 mi of three golf courses: Montour Heights, Bon Air, and Scally's. Cable TV. Laundry facilities. Business services, airport shuttle, free parking. Some pets allowed. | 1454 Beers School Rd. | 412/264–5678 | fax 412/264–8034 | www.redroof.com | 119 rooms | $47–$63 | AE, D, DC, MC, V.

CORNWALL

MAP 7, I6

(Nearby towns also listed: Denver, Ephrata, Hummelstown, Lebanon, Manheim)

Named after a region in England, Cornwall played a major role in the development of the country's railroad system and Pennsylvania's coal-mining region.

Information: **Lebanon Valley Chamber of Commerce** | 252 N. 8th St., Lebanon, PA 17042 | 717/273–3727. www.lvchamber.org

Attractions

Cornwall Iron Furnace. One of the world's best-preserved 19th-century charcoal iron-making facilities. The massive stone furnace, steam-powered air-blast machinery, and several related buildings are intact. Used from 1742 to 1883 primarily as a producer of pig iron and domestic products, the furnace cast cannon barrels and ammunition for the American Revolution. | 717/272–9711 | fax 717/272–0450. www.phmc.state.pa.us | $3.50; special rates for senior citizens, children, and groups | Tues–Sat, 9–5, Sun, noon-5, closed Mon.

Eckley Miner's Village. A tract of coal workers' homes built in 1854, Eckley Miner's village is an original anthracite mining town which is now a museum devoted to the everyday lives of the anthracite miners and their families. There are guided tours available daily from Memorial Day week end to Labor Day weekend, for an additional charge. There are cultural artifacts, displays and exhibits. | 9 mi east of Hazleton off PA Route 940 | 570/636–2070 | $3.50, special rates for children and seniors; $8.50 for families | Mon.– Sat.,9–5 and Sun. noon–5.

Historic Schaefferstown. The oldest water company in the United States that is still in operation, built in the 1760s, is included in this historic area. The Alexander Schaeffer farm has a stone farmhouse built in the 1750s and a barn built in the 1800s with a display of antique farm implements. The Thomas R. Brendle Museum houses historical items and area artifacts from the 1700s, many of the items donated by Thomas Brendle. | Intersection 419 and 897 | 717/949–2244 | $5; special rates for children | Thur–Fri, 8–5, 2nd and 4th Sundays of each month, 1–4.

ON THE CALENDAR
JUNE: *Cherry Fair.* Cherry-flavored foods highlight this one-day annual event that also includes crafts and entertainment. | Historic Schaefferstown Farm | 717/949–2244. www.lvchamber.org | $3.
SEPT.: *Harvest Fair and Plowing Contest.* You can see rye-threshing, cider-making, and apple butter–making in action at this annual two-day event and sample fresh baked goods. | Historic Schaefferstown Farm | 717/949–2244 | www.lvchamber.org | $5.

Dining
Tony's Mining Company Restaurant. American. You can have steak, pork, lamb, vegetables and more in Tony's. It's a favorite place for locals. | 211 Rexmont Rd. | 717/273–4871 | Closed Sun., Mon. | $16 | AE, D, MC, V.

Lodging
Schoolhaus Inn. Bought by the school district in 1955, the first part of this three-story tan clapboard inn was built in 1890. Full of antiques, it has a dining room and many sitting rooms. Full breakfast. TV in common area. No pets. No smoking. | 25 Freeman Dr. | 717/273–4615 or 800/644–5946 | www.theschoolhausinn.com | 4 rooms, 2 with bath | $79–$89 | MC, V.

CRESCO

MAP 7, K4

(Nearby towns also listed: Bushkill, Canadensis, Mt. Pocono, Shawnee on Delaware, Stroudsburg, Tannersville)

Like most small boroughs in the Pocono region, Cresco's population of 500 can swell quickly in the summer months and when snow falls as you and others take advantage of its proximity to vast forests and high mountains. In Latin, Cresco means "am growing" and that certainly holds true for this resort town.

Information: Pocono Mountains Visitors Bureau, Inc. | 1004 Main St., Stroudsburg, PA 18360 | 570/424–6050 | www.800poconos.com.

Attractions
Holly Ross Pottery. You can watch the making of Weeping Gold products and shop for gifts at this pottery factory midway between Cresco and Newfoundland. | Rte. 191 Access from I–80 and I–84 | 570/676–3248 | www.holleyross.com | Free | Mon.–Sat. 9:30–5:30, Sun. 1–5:30.

Dining
Crescent Lodge. Continental. An exposed brick fireplace, dark wood paneling, chandeliers, and a view of the Pocono Mountains make this a cozy and romantic restaurant. Guest rooms are available. Classic dishes inlude roast duckling, beef Wellington, and lobster tail. Entertainment Sat. | Rte. 940 E. | 570/595–7486 or 800/392–9400. www.crescentlodge.com | Closed Mon., Tues. in Jan.–May. No lunch | $16–$24 | AE, D, DC, MC, V.

Homestead Inn Restaurant. Continental. About 100 Andrew Wyeth prints, including a signed one, are on the walls of this restaurant that also has a redwood bar, two aquariums, and a fireplace room. It serves filet au poivre, roast duckling, veal dishes, and seafood. | Sand

Spring Dr.; Off of 191-follow signs | 570/595–3171 | Closed Mon., Columbus Day–Memorial Day | $17 | AE, MC, V.

Lodging

Crescent Lodge Inn. Built in the 1950s on 100 acres, with gardens and hiking trails on the grounds. It's a rustic yet full-service, two-story inn with a fireplace in the lobby, only five minutes from Cresco proper. Restaurant, bar, picnic area, complimentary Continental breakfast. Some in-room hot tubs, some kitchenettes, some refrigerators, cable TV. Pool. Tennis courts. Business services. | Intersection of 191 and 940, Paradise Valley | 570/595–7486 or 800/392–9400 | fax 570/595–3452. www.crescentlodge.com | 12 rooms, 19 cottages | $120–$195, $135–$350 cottages | AE, D, DC, MC, V.

La Anna Guest House. This Victorian home, built in 1877 for proprietor Kay Gilpin Swingle's great-grandmother, was the original home in the homestead of La Anna. It has large rooms furnished in Empire and Victorian antiques and you can walk outside by waterfalls and see mountain views. Continental breakfast. TV in common area. No pets. No kids under 12. | Rte. 191; 8 mi from I–80 at Mt. Pocono | 717/676–4225 | fax 717/676–4225 | none | 4 rooms, 2 with bath | $45 | No credit cards.

DANVILLE

MAP 7, I4

(Nearby towns also listed: Bloomsburg, Lewisburg, Shamokin Dam, Williamsport)

Established in 1774 when William Montgomery built his cabin, the town took the name "Dan's Village" when William's son, Dan, began selling tracts of land and building homes on the site. By 1806, it officially was named Danville and became an industrial hub when iron ore was discovered. Today, the homes built by wealthy industrialists still stand and many are listed on the National Historic Register. The downtown has a variety of specialty stores and restaurants along the Susquehanna River.

Information: Danville Chamber of Commerce | 206 Walnut St., 17821 | 570/275–5200 | www.danvillepa.org.

Attractions

Knoebels Amusement Resort and Campground. Just 12 mi east of downtown Danville is this traditional, old-fashioned place. You can ride the roller coaster, the water slides and enjoy the food provided by the third generation of Knoebels. | Rte. 487, Elysburg, PA | 570/672–2572 | Info@Knoebels.com | www.knoebels.com/ | $17–$22 | Weekends May and Sept., Daily Memorial day–Labor day.

Joseph Priestley House. Built in 1794 by Joseph Priestley, a theologian and chemist who discovered oxygen. Priestley lived at this home until his death in 1804. The house is furnished with period antiques and has Priestley's laboratory as well as exhibits on the scientist. | 472 Priestley Ave., Northumberland | 570/473–9474 | fax 570/473–7901 | www.phmc.state.pa.us | $3.50; special rates for senior citizens, children, families, and groups. Tours available | Tues.–Sat. 9–5, Sun. noon–5, closed Mon.

ON THE CALENDAR

JULY: *Iron Heritage Festival.* Held each year to celebrate the history of the area this three-day festival, the largest in the town, includes re-enactments, rides, food, and crafts. | 570/275–5200.

Dining

BJ Ribs. BJ's place may be heavy on the steaks, but it also serves lobster, crab legs and, of course, surf and turf. | 291 Mill St. | 570/275–5110 | $15–$25. | AE, MC, V.

Pine Barn Inn. American. Five dining areas, including one with a rustic stone fireplace and antiques single out this restaurant. Its seasonal menu changes every four months, specializing in fresh seafood and grilled steaks. The in-house baker makes delicious desserts. Open-air dining on patio. Salad bar. Kids' menu. Sun. brunch. Some live entertainment. | 1 Pine Barn Pl. | 570/275–2071 or 800/627–2276. www.pinebarninn.com | $10–$25 | AE, D, DC, MC, V.

Lodging

Danville Motor Lodge. A two-story motel near Exit 33 of I–80. It has reasonable rates and it's only 2 mi from Danville center. In-room data ports. Cable TV. Pool. Laundry facilities. Business services. | 15 Valley West Rd. | 570/275–5100 | fax 570/275–1886 | 77 rooms | $60–$75 | AE, D, DC, MC, V.

Hampton Inn. There is cherry furniture in each of the rooms at this three-story hotel, just off exit 33 of I–80. It's 12 mi from the Buckhorn Mall (exit 34). Complimentary Continental breakfast. Some in-room data ports. Cable TV. Indoor pool. Spa. No pets. | 97 Valley School Rd. | 570/271–2500 or 800/HAMPTON | fax 570/271–9110 | www.hampton-inn.com | 71 rooms | $99 | AE, D, DC, MC, V.

Pine Barn Inn. Three separate buildings house this locally owned three-story hotel next to Geisinger Medical Center in a residential area of town. Restaurant, bar, room service. Cable TV. Exercise equipment. Business services, free parking. | 1 Pine Barn Pl. | 570/275–2071 or 800/627–2276 | fax 570/275–3248. www.pinebarninn.com | 102 rooms | $48–$95 | AE, D, DC, MC, V.

DENVER/ADAMSTOWN

MAP 7, J6

(Nearby towns also listed: Bird-in-Hand, Cornwall, Ephrata, Hummelstown, Lancaster, Lebanon, Manheim)

Dubbed the "Antique Capital" of the United States, Denver/Adamstown is filled with more than 3,000 dealers throughout the year and is home to the Old Order Amish. Located in the heart of Pennsylvania's Dutch Country, horse and buggy travel are as common as kids in plain clothes. Denver/Adamstown is 10 mi from Reading and 20 mi from Lancaster, two popular outlet-mall destinations.

Information: Pennsylvania Dutch Convention and Visitors Bureau | 501 Greenfield Rd., Lancaster, PA 17601 | 717/299–8901 | www.padutchcountry.com.

Attractions

Adams Antique Annex. With more than 100 showcases and 30 booths, Adams, a three-building market, is a complete antiques shopping experience. There's a 1930s diner on the premises. | 2400 N. Reading Rd. | 717/335–0001 | www.adamsantiques.com/ | Mon.–Sat. 10–5, Sun. 8–5.

Zinn's Park. This 32-acre park has batting cages, basketball, water rides, and miniature golf. | Rte. 272, 2270 N. Reading Rd. | 717/336–2210 | http://www.zinnsdiner.com/DOCS/park.html | $1.25–$5.25 | Memorial day–Labor day Sun.–Thur. 10–10, Fri.–Sat. 10–11. Labor day–Memorial day Mon.–Fri. 5–10, Sat. 10–11, Sun. 10–10.

ON THE CALENDAR

MAY, OCT.: *Spring and Fall Motorcycle Shows.* Motorcycle Monthly magazine sponsors this motorcycle and car show–a family event with competition among vehicle types and vendors. | 856/728–6699 | $5.

AUG.: _Bavarian Summer Fest._ Every weekend the whole month of August, and Sundays in October this Oktoberfest-type celebration boasts oompah bands, dance groups, and German foods. | Stoudts Brewery, Rte 272, Exit 21, Black Angus Bier Garten | 717/484–4385 | www.stoudtsbeer.com | $7, special rates for children.

Dining

Black Horse Inn. American. Only 3 mi from Denver, the Black Horse Inn, with its wood-paneled, plant-filled dining room, is renowned for its certified Black Angus beef, fresh seafood, and local poultry. The tavern next door provides 350 spirits, 100 wines, 100 beers, smoking allowed. Kids' menu. Sun. brunch. | 2170 N. Reading Rd., Denver | 717/336–6555. www.blackhorselodge.com | Closed Christmas | $15–$40 | AE, D, DC, MC, V.

Zinn's Diner. American. The Zinn family opened this diner in 1950 and has been serving Pennsylvania Dutch meals ever since. Sit at the counter and have a cup of coffee or a full meal. Daily specials. Breakfast served. Kids menu. | Rte. 272, 2270 N. Reading Rd., Denver | 717/336–2210 | $7 | open 6 AM–11 PM daily. Breakfast served | D, MC, V.

Lodging

Adamstown and Amethyst Inns. Two charming, three-story Victorian bed and breakfasts, dating from 1925 and 1871, respectively, in the center of Adamstown. Both inns have a 7-color exterior paint scheme, and are filled with antiques, lace curtains, oriental rugs and family heirlooms. Picnic area, complimentary Continental breakfast. Some in-room hot tubs. Cable TV. No kids under 12. No smoking. | 62 W. Main St., Adamstown | 717/484–0800 or 800/594–4808 | fax 717/484–1384 | info@adamstown.com | www.adamstown.com | 8 rooms (2 with shower only) | $69–$159 | MC, V.

Black Horse Lodge. Five two- and single-story buildings stand on 10 acres of landscaped property only 3 mi from Denver. This full-service hotel, built in 1959, is at Exit 21 of the Pennsylvania Turnpike and its rooms were remodeled many times since. Restaurant, bar, picnic area, complimentary breakfast. Some refrigerators. Cable TV. Pool. Playground. Laundry facilities. Business services. Some pets allowed. | 2180 N. Reading Rd., Denver | 717/336–7563 | fax 717/336–1110. www.blackhorselodge.com | 74 rooms | $79–$189 | AE, D, DC, MC, V.

Holiday Inn. An expensive chain hotel that is only 3 mi from Denver and Adamstown. This two-story hotel was built in the 1970s near Exit 21 of the Pennsylvania Turnpike for easy access to the area. Restaurant, bar, room service. In-room data ports. Cable TV. Pool. Laundry facilities. Business services. | 1 Denver Rd., Denver | 717/336–7541 | fax 717/336–0515. www.holidayinnlancaster.com | 110 rooms | $99–$109 | AE, D, DC, MC, V.

DONEGAL

MAP 7, C7

(Nearby towns also listed: Connellsville, Farmington, Greensburg, Ligonier, Somerset)

Donegal is a small town off Exit 9 on I–76 that owes its existence to vacationers on their way to the Laurel Mountains. The town is home to a petting zoo, an amusement park, and is a popular destination for railroad buffs who scour the area for remnants of the old South Penn Continental Railroad.

Information: Laurel Highlands Visitors Bureau | Town Hall, 120 E. Main St., Ligonier, PA 15658 | 724/238–5661 | www.laurelhighlands.org.

Attractions

Kentuck Knob. You can explore a house built by Frank Lloyd Wright 20 mi south of Donegal. An early settler heading for Kentucky fell in love with the area and gave this town the name Kentuck Knob. That name was later bestowed on Wright's house, built in 1953 from tidewater red cypress and native fieldstone. The house overlooks the Youghiogheny River Gorge. Although privately owned, it's open to the public. | Kentuck Knob Rd. | 724/329–1901 | fax 724/329–0977 | www.kentuckknob.com | $15 | Tues.–Sun. 10–4, closed Mon.

Seven Springs Mountain Resort. This is Pennsylvanis's largest ski resort, with 540 acres of slopes, 18 lifts, 31 trails, one with a drop of 6,600 ft. The mountain has a summit elevation of 2,990 ft and a 750-ft vertical drop. In warmer months, there's an Alpine slide, golf, tennis courts, horseback riding, chairlift rides, outdoor pool, and miniature golf. | Champion-Trent Rd. | 814/352–7777 or 800/452–2223 | www.7springs.com | $40 weekends | Dec.–Mar., weekdays 9 AM–10 PM, weekends 9 AM–10:30 PM; May–Sept., daily 9–5.

ON THE CALENDAR
DEC.: *Holiday Tours at Kentuck Knob.* For the entire month of December, by appointment only, you can visit this fine example of a Frank Lloyd Wright house decorated for the holidays in a wash of festive lights. While you're there, you can relax in the visitors center with a cup of hot spiced cider. | 724/329–1901.

Dining
Lesley's. Contemporary. Housed in a restored chestnut barn that's part of a country inn, Lesley's serves updated versions of classic American fare. The menu changes frequently, but can include farm-raised trout, beef Wellington or penne pasta. | 10 Mountain View Rd. | 800/392–7773 | fax 724/593–6345 | Reservations essential | No breakfast. No lunch. Sun.–Tue | $24–$36 | AE, D, DC, MC, V.

Nino's. Italian. Antiques, Tiffany shades, and other memorabilia highlight this 100-year-old building, with three dining rooms on two floors. Specialties include the broiled seafood platter, chicken Marsala, imported pastas with homemade sauces, and a spaghetti and meatball dinner on Sundays. In nice weather, you can eat outside on the patio. Kids' menu. Salad bar. DJ on Thurs. Sun. brunch. | Rte. 31, Mt. Pleasant; 9 mi northwest on Rte. 31 | 724/547–2900 | Closed Mon. | $8–$24 | AE, D, DC, MC, V.

Lodging
Days Inn. An affordable, 2-story chain motel near Exit 9 of the Pennsylvania Turnpike. It's 10 mi to Seven Springs, 20 mi to Idlewild Park, and 20 min to Frank Lloyd Wright's Fallingwater. Picnic area, complimentary Continental breakfast. Cable TV. Pool. | Rte. 31 | 724/593–7536 | fax 724/593–6165 | www.daysinn.com | mtviewbb@westol.com | 51 rooms | $79–$89 | AE, MC, V.

Mountain View Bed & Breakfast. Established as a bed-and-breakfast in 1987, this 1850s farmhouse overlooks the Laurel Mountains. The parlor has a piano, fireplace, and television. Guest rooms have private baths. From here you can hike, ski, or go white-water rafting. The property has a converted barn with a public restaurant and wine bar. Complimentary breakfast, some refrigerators, some in-room hot tubs, TV in common area. | 10 Mountain View Rd. | 724/593–6349 or 800/392–7773 | fax 724/593–6345 | www.shol.com/mtviewbb | 8 rooms | $150–$210 | AE, D, DC, MC, V.

Seven Springs. Only 10 mi from Donegal, this resort has a rustic main lodge with conference center and many smaller buildings scattered on the grounds. Built in 1932, you can spend any and all of the four seasons on the resort's 5, 000 acres. Bar, dining room. 2 pools. Barbershop, beauty salon, hot tub. Driving range, 18-hole golf course, miniature golf, putting green, tennis courts. Bowling, exercise equipment, horseback riding. Bicycles. Downhill skiing. Shops. Kids' programs (18 mos.–12), playground. Laundry facilities. Business services, airport shuttle. | R.R. 1, Champion | 814/352–7777 or 800/452–2223 | fax 814/352–7911 | www.7springs.com | 385 rooms, 238 condos, 16 chalets, 5 cabins, 10 dorms | $160–$175; $540–$950 (2–day minimum stay) cabins; $525 (2–day minimum stay) chalets | D, MC, V.

DOWNINGTOWN

(Nearby towns also listed: King of Prussia, West Chester)

Midway between Philadelphia and Lancaster, Downingtown was first known as Milltown because it was home to the last mill on the edge of the unsettled western frontier. John Downing moved to the area, where he opened a tavern and helped develop an industrial complex. The village was named after him during the American Revolution when the town was used as a storage location for food.

Information: Downingtown Chamber of Commerce | 38 W. Lancaster Ave., 19335 | 610/269–1523.

Attractions
Hibernia County Park. Hibernia is a 1,000-acre wooded area with multiple hiking trails, a 90-acre lake for fishing and boating, and 40 campsites. | 1 Park Rd. | 610/383–3812 | fax 610/384–1898 | www.chesco.org/ccparks | Free | Daily dawn to dusk.

Historic Yellow Springs. Take a self-guided walking tour of mineral springs, hospital ruins, and historic buildings, including houses and the Inn at Yellow Springs. The Cultural Arts Center hosts many programs throughout the year. | 1685 Art School Rd., Chester Springs | 610/827–7414 | fax 610/827–1336 | Free | Mon.–Fri. 9–4.

Marsh Creek State Park. The 1,705-acre park has a 535-acre lake that can be used for boating, fishing, ice skating, ice fishing, and ice boating. There's also a pool for swimming, picnic facilities, a 6-mi hiking trail system, 6 mi of horseback riding trails, about 900 acres for hunting, and 7 acres for sledding. | 675 Park Rd. | 610/458–5119 or 888/PA–PARKS | www.dcnr.state.pa.us | Free | Daily 8 AM–dusk.

Valley Forge National Historical Park. *See* Norristown.

ON THE CALENDAR
AUG.: *Old Fiddlers' Picnic.* You can hear a range of amateur musicians, visit craft vendors and food booths, and go on a hayride at this one-day event on the second Saturday of the month. | Hibernia County Park | 610/383–3812 | www.chesco.org/ccparks | $5 per car.
DEC.: *Hibernia Mansion Christmas Tours.* For 3 days around the holiday, you can take tours of the 19th-century mansion decorated for the holidays, complete with Christmas carols and refreshments. | Hibernia County Park | 610/383–3812 | www.chesco.org/ccparks | $4.
DEC.–JAN.: *Victory Brewery Tours.* You can tour this 23,000-square-ft brewery and brewhouse in an abandoned Pepperidge Farm factory. After the tour, given on Saturdays at noon and 3 and Sundays at 2, you can relax at the 70-ft bar with one of Victory's many brews. | 420 Acorn La. | 610/873–0881 | Weekends only.

Dining
Vickers Tavern. Continental. In a building that was once an Underground Railroad stop, this restaurant is filled with crystal chandeliers, rustic mirrors, and antiques. Steaks, seafood, and game are on the menu, and specialities are twin Chesapeake crab cakes, Atlantic salmon, and veal and beef dishes with Chester County mushrooms and herbs from the garden. Open-air dining in garden. Live music, pianist, Wed., Fri., Sat. Free parking. | Gordon Drive, Lionville; 3 mi northeast of town | 610/363–7998 | fax 610/524–2445 | www.vickerstavern.com | Closed Sun. | $18–$27 | AE, MC, V.

Victory Brewing Company. American. The Victory has the feeling of a cozy inn. There's a big wood-fired brick oven in the center of the pub and a bar made from wooden crates. The brewery was built as part of an old Pepperidge Farm complex, 1 mi from downtown. Try the wood-fired pizzas and calzones. Live music Fri., Sat. Kids' menu. | 420 Acorn La. | 610/873–0881 | www.victorybeer.com | Closed Mon. | $15–$26 | AE, D, DC, MC, V.

Lodging

Best Western–Exton Hotel and Conference Center. Only 4 mi from town, this hotel is off U.S. Highway 30, in the center of Chester County. Built in the 1970s, the 5-story hotel is less than 5 mi from Marsh Creek State Park and 15 mi from Valley Forge National Historic Park. Restaurant, bar (with entertainment), picnic area, room service. In-room data ports, refrigerators, cable TV. 2 pools. Laundry facilities. Business services, airport shuttle, free parking. Pets allowed. | 815 N. Pottstown Pike, Exton | 610/363–1100 | fax 610/524–2329 | www.bestwestern.com | 225 rooms | $99–$109 | AE, D, DC, MC, V.

Glen Isle Farm Country Inn. Built in the 1730s, this home has several common rooms filled with comfy chairs and couches. You can roam through eight acres of shaded gardens, adjacent woods, and meadows. The inn is smokefree, gay-friendly, and welcomes older kids. TV in common area. Hiking. | 130 S. Lloyd Ave. | 610/269–9100 or 800/269–1730 | fax 610/269–9191 | $60–$90 | MC, V.

DOYLESTOWN

MAP 7, L6

(Nearby towns also listed: Philadelphia, Quakertown)

Doylestown is 12 mi west of New Hope and 25 mi northeast of Philadelphia in the heart of Bucks County.

Information: **Central Bucks County Chamber of Commerce** | 115 W. Court St., 18901 | 215/348–3913 | www.centralbuckschamber.com.

Attractions

Covered bridges. Bucks County has 12 covered bridges. The oldest bridges were built in 1832. The longest bridge—Schofield Ford Covered Bridge—is 170 ft long. Only two of the bridges have no vehicle access: South Perkasie Covered Bridge and Schofield Ford Covered Bridge. | 215/345–4552 or 800/836–BUCK | www.bccvb.org | Free | Daily. Uhlerstown Bridge is closed during the winter.

James A. Michener Art Museum. Named in honor of the Pulitzer Prize–winning author and Doylestown native, the museum has the James Michener exhibit, which showcases his career as a writer, public servant, art collector, and philanthropist. Other exhibits include Bucks County regional art from Colonial times to the present; the *Garber Mural*, part of the sesquicentennial exposition in Philadelphia in 1926; and a multimedia exhibition with displays on 12 Bucks County natives. Cafe on premises. | 138 S. Pine St. | 215/340–9800 | fax 215/340–9807 | www.michenerartmuseum.org | $5 | Tues., Thurs.–Fri. 10–4:30, Wed. 10–8, weekends 10–5, closed Mon.

Mercer Mile. The three National Historic Landmarks here—Mercer Museum, Fonthill Museum, and Moravian Pottery and Tile Works—were the work of Henry Chapman Mercer, a historian, archaeologist, collector, and ceramist. | Various locations | 215/345–0210 (Mercer Museum), 215/345–6722 (Moravian Pottery and Tile Works), or 215/348–9461 (Fonthill) | fax 215/230–0823 | www.libertynet.org | Daily.

★ Built entirely of hand-mixed concrete in 1908–1910, the **Fonthill Museum** is the former home of Henry Mercer. It has 44 rooms, 18 fireplaces, at least 32 stairwells, more than 200 windows, and more than 900 prints and other objects that Mercer gathered throughout the world. Dubbed by Mercer as "a concrete castle for the New World," he left it as "a museum of decorative tiles and prints." | East Court St. | 215/348–9461 | fax 215/348–9462 | www.mercermuseum.org | $5 | Mon.–Sat. 10–5, Sun. noon–5.

In 1913–16, Henry Mercer built the **Mercer Museum of the Bucks County Historical Society** to contain his boundless collection of early American everyday objects and ancient artifacts. The museum's expanding collection has furnishings, folk art, and implements of early

America. The building rises seven stories and also has the Spruance Library, a research library with more than 20,000 volumes, including Mercer's papers. | 84 S. Pine St. | 215/345–0210 | fax 215/230–0823 | www.mercermuseum.org | $5 | Mon., Wed., Thurs., Fri., Sat. 10–5, Tues. 10–9, Sun. noon–5.

The **Moravian Pottery and Tile Works** produced tiles and mosaics for floors, walls, and ceilings. Henry Mercer's tiles adorn buildings throughout the world, including the Pennsylvania Capitol. Built in 1912, the tile works today is a living history museum, making reproductions of Mercer's original line of tiles. Self-guided tours offered every half hour following a brief video and welcome. | 130 Swamp Rd. | 215/345–6722 | fax 215/345–1361 | www.mercermuseum.org | $3 | Daily 10–4:45.

Pearl S. Buck House. Here you can take a guided tour of this National Historic Landmark. The 1835 farmhouse of author Pearl S. Buck, whose book *The Good Earth* won the Pulitzer Prize and the Nobel Prize, making her the first American woman to receive both awards for literature. She moved to Green Hills Farm in 1934 and lived there for 38 years until her death in 1973, two months before her 81st birthday. She is buried on the 60-acre farm. Buck published more than 70 books, was active in the American Civil Rights and women's rights movements, and founded the Pearl S. Buck Foundation, which provides sponsorship funding for thousands of children in Asian countries. | 520 Dublin Rd., Dublin | 215/249–0100 or 800/220–BUCK, ext. 170 | fax 215/249–9657 | www.pearl-s-buck.org | $5 | Call for hours.

ON THE CALENDAR
SEPT. OR OCT.: *Doylestown Arts Festival.* See live entertainment and an array of craft and food vendors at this two-day event. | Downtown | 215/340–9980 | Free.
OCT.: *Bucks County Wine and Food Festival.* During this celebration, you can sample the cuisine of local chefs and wines from local vineyards. | Downtown | 215/230–7533.

Dining

★ **Café Arielle.** French. A restored livery built in the 1800s, Café Arielle has original artwork, white linen tablecloths, fresh flowers, and an open kitchen. Only 1 ½ mi from downtown, it's known for duck and seafood. | 100 S. Main St. | 215/345–5930 | fax 215/345–5932 | No lunch weekends. Closed Mon., Tues. | $18–$32 | AE, DC, MC, V.

Inn on Blueberry Hill. Contemporary. You can eat in the cozy, fireplace-heated dining room or on the enclosed porch at this Victorian manor listed on the National Register. Specials are steak, pasta, and seafood. | 1715 S. Easton Rd. | 215/491–1777 | Reservations essential | No breakfast. No lunch. Closed Mon. | $20–$30 | AE, DC, MC, V.

Los Sarapes. Mexican. The surroundings are simple and the menu has fileta mignon with shrimp and chipotle sauce and fileta huachinango (red snapper) cooked in garlic oil. No smoking. | 17 Moyer Rd., Chalfont; 2 mi south of town | 215/822–8858 | No lunch Sun. Closed Mon. | $18–$27 | AE, D, MC, V.

Sign of the Sorrel Horse. French. There are six dining rooms in this converted 1714 mill about 2 mi from town. You can dine in the Chandelier Room with its wide open windows overlooking the grounds, or the Beard Room with seating for eight at a single table surrounded by an original mural, or by the fireplace in the Escoffier Room. Guest rooms available. The menu has bear, wild boar, and ostrich, filet mignon topped with crab cakes, and a swordfish and salmon pairing. Try the pheasant or other game dishes. You can eat outside overlooking the grill "race." | 4424 Old Easton Rd. | 215/230–9999 | fax 215/230–8053 | www.sorrelhorse.com | Reservations essential | Jacket required | No lunch. Closed Mon., Tues. and early Mar. | $20–$30 | AE, DC, MC, V.

Lodging

Best Western. Full-service, 3-story hotel at Exit 31 of the Northeast Extension of the Pennsylvania Turnpike for convenient access to Philadelphia. Built in 1975, it's 15 mi to Doylestown's Mercer Mile. Restaurant, bar (with entertainment), room service. In-room data ports, cable TV. Pool. Exercise equipment. Business services, airport shuttle, free parking. Pets allowed.

| 1750 Sumneytown Pike, Kulpsville | 215/368–3800 | fax 215/368–7824 | www.bestwestern.com | 183 rooms | $89–$99 | AE, D, DC, MC, V.

Comfort Inn. A chain motel 6 mi southwest of the downtown, next door to a Bennigans restaurant, and less than a mile to the Montgomeryville Mall, this 3-story motel was built in 1992 and has interior corridors and an elevator. Complimentary Continental breakfast. In-room data ports, some refrigerators, cable TV. Laundry facilities. | 678 Bethlehem Pike/Rte. 309, Montgomeryville | 215/361–3600 | fax 215/361–7949 | www.comfortinn.com | 84 rooms | $100–$135 | AE, D, DC, MC, V.

Courthouse Motor Inn. Here's a no-frills motel in the heart of town. Restaurant. Refrigerators, cable TV. | 625 N. Main St. | 215/348–9222 or 888/673–8683 | fax 215/345–5072 | 45 rooms | $54–$65. AE, D, MC, V

★ **Highland Farms.** This 3-story mansion, built in the 1800s, was once home to famed Broadway lyricist Oscar Hammerstein II. Today, the inn, 1 mi from downtown, is elegantly furnished with antiques and Hammerstein family memorabilia. Picnic area, complimentary breakfast. In-room data ports, TV in common area. Pool. Tennis. No kids under 12. No smoking. | 70 East Rd. | 215/340–1354 | www.web-comm.com/highland | 4 rooms (2 with shared bath), 2 suites | $145–$185, $225–$295 suites | MC, V.

Inn at Fordhook Farm. The Burpee family's (of seed catalog fame) country estate is now a B&B on 60 acres. It's ½ mi from town, and there's still a working farm here, with trial and show gardens. Picnic area, complimentary breakfast. Some room phones, no TV. Business services. No kids under 12. No smoking. | 105 New Britain Rd. | 215/345–1766 | fax 215/345–1791 | www.fordhook.com | 6 rooms (2 with shower only) | $175–$295 | AE, MC, V.

Maplewood Farm. This farmhouse in nearby Gardenville dates to the late 18th century. You can relax under shade trees on the spacious grounds or watch farm animals graze on nearby meadows. Hearty breakfasts often include homemade granola, French toast, or omelettes. Complimentary breakfast. Outdoor pool. Hiking. | 5090 Durham Rd., Gardenville | 215/766–0477 | maplewoodfarm@rcn.com | www.bbhost.com/maplewoodfarm | 5 rooms | $105–$175 | AE, D, MC, V.

Pine Tree Farm. A solarium highlights this Colonial farmhouse dating back to 1730s. The inn, less than 3 mi from town, has antiques in light and airy rooms. Complimentary Continental breakfast. Pool. No kids under 16. No smoking. | 2155 Lower State Rd. | 215/348–0632 | 4 rooms | $155–$185 | No credit cards.

Sign of the Sorrel Horse. The building here was once a grist mill in the early 1700s that supplied flour for Washington's army and lodged Lafayette. The inn, about 2 mi from town, is now styled after a French auberge, with gardens and elegant dining. Restaurant, picnic area, complimentary Continental breakfast. No room phones. Business services, airport shuttle. | 4424 Old Easton Rd. | 215/230–9999 | fax 215/230–8053 | www.sorrelhorse.com | 5 rooms (2 with shower only), 2 suites | $85–$125, $150–$175 suites | AE, DC, MC, V.

Stone Ridge Farm. You can stay in a converted barn built in 1818 on this 10-acre working horse farm. Some rooms have decks that overlook pastures. All rooms have private baths. Complimentary breakfast. Outdoor pool. Hiking. Business services. | 956 Bypass Rd., Dublin | 215/249–9186 or 877/855–2276 | fax 215/249–9185 | innkeeper@stoneridge-farm.com | www.stoneridgefarm.com | 6 rooms, 2 cottages | $95–$225 | AE, MC, V.

DU BOIS

MAP 7, D4

(Nearby town also listed: Clearfield)

When John Du Bois exhausted his timber supply in the Williamsport area, he moved his operation to Rumberger in Clearfield County. The area's rich supply of white pine timber provided years of business. During that time, Du Bois built more than 100 homes and a post office for his employees. As a result, the town was renamed Du Bois in his honor. Today, much of the area's timber remains and Du Bois is a central location for people to enjoy the great outdoors.

Information: Du Bois Chamber of Commerce | 3 S. Brady St., #205, 15801 | 814/371–5010 | www.duboispachamber.com.

Attractions

Penn State–DuBois. You can stroll through the attractive grounds of this branch of the main Penn State campus in State College. About 1,100 students attend the DuBois branch, which opened in 1935. | College Pl. | 800/346–7627 | www.ds.psu.edu | Free | Daily.

ON THE CALENDAR

JUNE: *Festival of the Arts.* Held each year in downtown, the 1-day festival showcases the work of area artists and craftspeople. You can purchase locally made art, take an art lesson, or listen to live music. | 814/371–5010.

Dining

Buster's Sports Bar. American. Buster's is not the place for a quiet, intimate dinner, but if you want a burger, sandwich, or fries while you catch up on the latest sports score, you can get both here. Big TVs are usually turned to sports stations. | 318 W. DuBois Ave. | 814/375–2727 | $5–$8 | D, MC, V.

Central Restaurant. Continental. Probably the most upscale restaurant in DuBois, this place specializes in seafood, pasta, and steak dishes. | 1120 S. Brady St. | 814/371–0458 | $12–$20 | AE, MC, V.

Krach's Original Hoagie Shop. American. Along with the standard ham-and-cheese, turkey breast, and roast beef subs, you can also order hot sandwiches made to order here. | 2 S. Main St. | 814/375–0201 | $4–$7 | No credit cards.

Lodging

Best Western Inn and Conference Center. Built in 1980, this affordable, 3-story chain hotel is off I–80, less than a mi from Du Bois Mall and 6 blocks from downtown. Picnic area, complimentary Continental breakfast. Cable TV. Gym. Playground. Business services. | 82 N. Park Pl. | 814/371–6200 | fax 814/371–4608 | www.bestwestern.com | 52 rooms | $58–$64 | AE, D, DC, MC, V.

DuBois Manor Motel. This '60s-era drive-up motel has no frills, but is 3 mi from the interstate and just a short walk from a park. Cable TV. | 525 Liberty Blvd. | 814/371–5400 | fax 814/371–4694 | 45 rooms | $35–$48 | AE, D, MC, V.

Hampton Inn. Next to the Du Bois Mall, this reasonably priced, 5-story chain hotel is 2 mi from downtown. Complimentary Continental breakfast. Cable TV. Indoor pool. Hot tub. Gym. | RR 8 | 814/375–1000 | fax 814/375–4668 | www.hamptoninn.com | 96 rooms | $65–$75 | AE, D, DC, MC, V.

Holiday Inn. At Exit 16 of I–80, this midpriced, 2-story chain hotel is 5 mi to Du Bois Mall and 4 mi to downtown. Restaurant, bar, room service. In-room data ports, cable TV. Pool, wading pool. Laundry facilities. Business services, airport shuttle. Pets allowed. | Rte. 219 and I–80 | 814/371–5100 | fax 814/375–0230. www.holiday-inn.com | 160 rooms | $80–$90 | AE, D, DC, MC, V.

Ramada Inn. A large lobby with a fireplace highlights this midpriced, 3-story chain hotel. Built in 1973, this hotel is off Exit 17 of I–80. Restaurant, bar (with entertainment), room service. Cable TV. Indoor pool. Business services, airport shuttle. Pets allowed. | Rte. 255 N and I–80 | 814/371–7070 | fax 814/371–1055. www.ramada.com | 96 rooms | $65–$80 | AE, D, DC, MC, V.

Towne House Inn. Eight 3-story Victorian and Tudor homes, built for wealthy families in the early 20th century make up this inn. Two buildings are on the National Register of Historic Places. Although it's 30 mi northeast of Du Bois, it's only 11 mi to the Allegheny National Forest and 7 mi to Bendigo State Park. Restaurant, picnic area, complimentary Continental breakfast, room service. In-room data ports, cable TV. Exercise equipment. Business services. | 138 Center St., St. Marys | 814/781–1556 | fax 814/834–4449 | www.towne-houseinn.com | 60 rooms in 8 buildings | $60–$100 | AE, D, DC, MC, V.

Yesterday's Inn. This one-story drive-up motel is about 3 mi from downtown. A restaurant on the premises has diner-style breakfast, lunch, and dinner. Cable TV, room phones. | Blinker Pkwy. at intersection of Rte. 219 and 322; Take I–80 to exit 16 or 17 to 322. Follow to 219 and the motel will be at the intersection of 219 and 322 | 814/371–6110 | fax 814/371–6058 | 18 rooms | $26–$40 | MC, V.

EASTON

MAP 7, K5

(Nearby towns also listed: Allentown, Bethlehem, Erwinna)

Settled by Thomas Penn, son of the colony's original proprietor William Penn, in 1752, the town was named Easton after Thomas Penn's father-in-law's estate in England. Similar to Philadelphia, the town is laid out around a great square where officials met with Native Americans to come up with a peace treaty. By the 19th century, the borough had become one of the country's earliest industrial centers.

Information: **Two Rivers Chamber of Commerce** | 1 S. 3rd St., 18044 | 610/253–4211 | www.eastonareachamber.org.

Attractions

Crayola Factory. You can see how Crayola crayons and markers are made and learn about the history of the Crayola brand. Kids can participate in interactive projects that change each month. Admission includes the factory and the National Canal Museum. | 30 Centre Sq. | 610/515–8000 | fax 610/559–6690 | www.crayola.com | $7 | Sept.–May, Tues.–Sat. 9:30–5, Sun. noon–5, closed Mon.; Memorial Day–Labor Day, Mon.–Sat. 9:30–6, Sun. 11–6.

National Canal Museum. You can go back in time to the early 1800s before railroads, highways, and airplanes to see how canals helped create the anthracite coal and iron industry. You can also learn how canals are still relevant today. See exhibits such as operating a lock model and piloting a boat through a lock, artifacts, photomurals, and life-size figures of canal life. Admission includes both the museum and the Crayola Factory. | 30 Centre Sq. | 610/515–8000 | fax 610/559–6690 | www.canals.org | $7 | Sept.–May, Tues.–Sat. 9:30–5, Sun. noon–5, closed Mon.; Memorial Day–Labor Day, Mon.–Sat. 9:30–6, Sun. 11–6.

Delaware Canal State Park. The 60-mi-long towpath parallels the Delaware River between Easton and Bristol and includes the historic canal and towpath, many miles of river shoreline, and 11 river islands. The Delaware Canal is the only remaining continuously intact canal of the great towpath canal-building era of the early and mid-19th century. The Delaware River is the longest free-flowing river east of the Mississippi River. You can canoe on the river. | 11 Lodi Hill Rd., Upper Black Eddy | 610/982–5560 or 888/PA–PARKS | www.dcnr.state.pa.us | Free | Daily 8 AM–dusk.

Hugh Moore Park. Locks, canal structures, the restored Lehigh Canal, 19th-century industrial ruins, the Locktender's House Museum, and the mule-drawn boat *Josiah White II* are all here. The park parallels 6 mi of the Lehigh River, and canoe and pedalboat rentals are available. There's a playground, picnic facilities, and areas for fishing and hiking. | Lehigh Drive at Lehigh River | 610/515–8000 | fax 610/559–6690 | www.canals.org | Free | Daily dawn to dusk.

Lafayette College. Founded as a men's college in 1826, Lafayette College became coed in 1970. The church-affiliated liberal arts college has a total undergraduate enrollment of 2,185. The campus has about 100 acres of land and more than 50 buildings. | High St. | 610/250–5000 or 610/330–5120 | fax 610/330–5127 | www.lafayette.edu | Free | Weekdays 9–5.

Northampton County Historical Society. Northhampton County Museum, Illick Memorial Library, Nicholas House Children's Museum, Northampton County Historic Resource Survey, and the History Learning Center of Northampton County are all part of the Historical Society. | 101–107 S. 4th St. | 610/253–1222 | fax 610/253–4701 | Free | Weekdays 9–4, closed weekends.

ON THE CALENDAR

SEPT.: *Riverside Festival of the Arts.* Riverside Park on the Delaware River comes alive when more than 40 regional artists display their work for show and purchase. Poetry readings, jazz concerts, and demonstrations take place throughout the day. | 610/330–5361.

Dining

Mandarin Tang. Chinese. Artifacts and photographs of China's landscape hang on the walls here. Typical fare includes moo shu pork with rice patties, and garlic chicken. | 25th Street Shopping Ctr. | 610/258–5697 | Reservations not accepted | $6–$15 | AE, DC, MC, V.

Pearly Baker's Ale House. American. In the heart of downtown, this pub and restaurant can be crowded during Friday afternoon happy hours or when there's a show at the nearby State Theatre. A crystal chandelier lights the dining room. Food is standard American fare accompanied by piped-in jazz. | 11 Center Sq. | 610/253–9949 | $6–$12 | D, MC, V.

Lodging

Best Western Easton Inn. This hotel is 1.2 mi from downtown, next to Delaware River State Park, and within walking distance to restaurants and shopping. Restaurant, bars, room service. Indoor pool. Laundry facilities. Business services. | 185 S. 3rd St. | 610/252–9131 or 800/882–0113 | fax 610/252–5145 | www.bestwestern.com | 85 rooms | $75–$95 | AE, D, DC, MC, V.

Lafayette Inn. Though you'd never know it now, this 1895 mansion on College Hill was a frat house before the building was renovated and established as an inn. There's a common library. Some guest rooms have fireplaces and four-poster beds; all have antiques and private baths. Complimentary Continental breakfast. Some in-room hot tubs. | 525 W. Monroe St. | 610/253–4500 | fax 610/253–4635 | www.lafayetteinn.com | 16 rooms | $99–$150 | AE, D, DC, MC, V.

EBENSBURG

MAP 7, D6

(Nearby towns also listed: Altoona, Johnstown)

Founded in the early 1800s by a religious dissenter and leader of Welsh immigrants, Ebensburg was named the county seat when it was determined that it was the geographical center of Cambria County. Ebensburg has the distinction of being at the crossroads of two of the area's major highways, to the east I–99 (U.S. Highway 220) and to the west U.S. Highway 219. North on I–99, you can go to Altoona and State College; south on U.S. 219 takes you to Johnstown.

Information: **Greater Johnstown/Cambria County Chamber of Commerce** | 111 Market St., Johnstown, PA 15901 | 814/536–5107 | www.johnstownchamber.com.

Attractions

Allegheny Portage Railroad National Historic Site. The Lemon House Tavern is on site here, and the Engine House Interpretive Shelter, which houses full-scale models and hands-on exhibits. You can see a 20-minute film, exhibits, models, and displays at the visitor center. Also, there are trails along the railroad route, a picnic area, and cross-country ski trails. | 110 Federal Park Rd., Gallitzin | 814/886–6150 | fax 814/886–6117 | www.nps.gov/alpo | $2 | Memorial Day–Labor Day, daily 9–6; Labor Day–Memorial Day, daily 9–5.

Cambria County Historical Society and Museum. Housed in an 1890 Queen Anne Victorian, the museum exhibits artifacts and displays about early settler life and the development of regional business and industry. You can also look through a document collection. | 615 N. Center St. | 814/472–6674 | Free | Tue.–Fri. 10–4:30, Sat. 9–1.

Dining

Noon-Collins Restaurant. Continental. Housed in the Noon-Collins Inn, this restaurant has grills, pastas, and an occasional seafood dish. | 114 E. High St. | 814/472–4311 | fax 814/472–6946 | Reservations essential | Closed Sun. and Mon. | $12–$20 | AE, D, MC, V.

Lodging

Comfort Inn. Only 3 mi to the Ebensburg Airport, a golf course, the fairgrounds and strip malls, this midpriced hotel was built in 1991. Cable TV. Indoor pool. Spa. Business services. | 111 Cook Rd. | 814/266–3678 or 800/228–5150 | comfortjohnstown@ aol.com | www.comfortinn.com | $59–$68 | AE, D, DC, MC, V.

EDINBORO

MAP 7, B2

(Nearby towns also listed: Erie, Meadville)

Named after the Scottish town, Edinboro overcame three fires in the early 1900s that destroyed many of its downtown buildings to become a popular summer resort town today. On the edge of Edinboro Lake, Edinboro has two beaches, several public and private docking areas, and many parks on its 250 acres of publicly owned lakeshore.

Information: Erie Area Chamber of Commerce | 109 Boston Store Place, Erie, PA 16501 | 814/454–7191 | www.eriepa.com.

Attractions

French Creek Canoe and Kayak. You can take a float trip along French Creek in a kayak or canoe. Here's how it works: a crew transports you and your boat to the water, then picks you up downstream a few hours later and brings you back to your car. | Box 575 | 814/796–3366 | fax 814/734–1026 | www.frontpage.erie.net/budd.

Mountain View Ski Area. The ski area has a summit elevation of 1,550 ft with a 320-ft vertical drop. There are three lifts and nine trails, the longest trail is 2,500 ft. There's also a tubing park with four chutes. Snowboarding. | 14510 Mt. Pleasant Rd. | 814/734–1641 | www.skimtview.org | $12 weekdays, $20 weekends | Dec.–Mar.

ON THE CALENDAR

SEPT.–NOV.: *Fighting Scots Football.* If you are so inclined, you can wear your tartan to cheer on the Edinboro University Fighting Scots football team. Home games are almost always on Saturday afternoons at Sox Harrison Stadium. | 814/732–2000.

Dining

Uncle Charlie's Pizza Pub. Pizza. You can eat white, rye, or wheat-crust pizzas with the usual toppings, as well as hoagies, calzones, hot dogs, salads, and bagel sandwiches. | 606 Erie St. | 814/734–1715 | No breakfast | $3–$6 | MC.

Lodging

Abplanalp's Rooster Ridge Bed and Breakfast. This 1840 Colonial house has rooms with private baths and all have large windows overlooking the countryside. The hosts greet your arrival with fresh-baked ginger cookies and serve a large country breakfast on one of three porches or in the dining room. Complimentary breakfast. | 8520 Pageville Rd. | 814/756–5135 | weaera@juno.com | www.bedandbreakfast.com | 5 rooms | $50–$60 | No credit cards.

Ramada Inn and Conference Center. Built in downtown in 1972, this 2-story hotel is only 2 mi from the Mount Pleasant Ski Resort next to the Culberston Hills golf course, and ½ mi from Edinboro University. Restaurant, bar, room service. Indoor pool. Sauna. Putting green. Laundry facilities. Business services. | 401 W. Plum St. | 814/734–5650 | fax 814/734–7532 | www.ramada.com | 105 rooms | $90–$100 | AE, D, DC, MC, V.

Riverside. In operation since 1885, this 3-story Victorian building sits on a bank of French Creek. There's a dinner theater weekends, with matinees weekdays. Bar, dining room, complimentary breakfast. No TV in some rooms, TV in common area. Pool. Business services. | 1 Fountain Ave., Cambridge Springs; 7 mi southeast | 814/398–4645 or 800/964–5173 | fax 814/398–4647 | www.theriversideinn.com | 74 rooms | $65–$105 | Closed Jan.–mid Apr. | D, MC, V.

EPHRATA

(Nearby towns also listed: Adamstown, Bird-in-Hand, Cornwall, Denver, Lancaster, Lebanon, Lititz, Reading)

Ephrata is the hub of northeastern Lancaster County and is one of the few places where you can see the rich traditions of the Amish mesh with New World offerings. In spring, summer, and fall, festivals dot the landscape; the most popular is a Christmas light show. Today, residents of Ephrata perform full-scale musicals in summer, telling the story of their village through a live stage show. There are a number of arts-and-crafts shops in town.

Information: Ephrata Area Chamber of Commerce | 77 Park Ave., Ste #1, 17522 | 717/738–9010 | www.ephrata-area.org.

Attractions

Ephrata Cloister. Founded in 1732 by Conrad Beissel, the Ephrata Cloister was one of America's earliest communal societies. The membership declined after the Revolution, following Beissel's death in 1768. By 1800, the celibate orders were nearly extinct, and in 1814, the remaining householders incorporated with the Seventh Day German Baptist Church. Today you can see many of the medieval-style buildings, and there's a slide show and exhibits about the religious order at the visitor center. | 632 W. Main St. | 717/733–6600 | fax 717/733–4364 | www.state.pa.us | $6 | Mar.–Dec., Mon.–Sat. 9–5, Sun. noon–5; Jan.–Feb., Tues.–Sat. 9–5, Sun. noon–5, closed Mon.

★ **Green Dragon Farmers Market and Auction.** Here at one of the state's largest traditional agricultural markets on 30 acres, local Amish and Mennonite farmers tend to many of the 400 indoor and outdoor stalls, selling meats, fruits, vegetables, fresh-baked pies, and dry goods. | 955 N. State St. | 717/738–1117 | www.greendragonmarket.com | Free | Fri. 9 AM–10 PM.

Museum and Library of the Historical Society of Cocalico Valley. A three-story Victorian home with antiques, the house also has a library for local historians and genealogy research. | 249 W. Main St. | 717/733–1616 | Free; library $3 | Mon., Wed., Thurs. 9:30–6, Sat. 8:30–5; closed Tues., Fri., Sun.

ON THE CALENDAR

JUNE–JULY: *Summer Evening Tours of Ephrata Cloister.* On Saturday nights in June and July you can arrange, by reservation, a special dinner at the Doneckers restaurant followed by a guided tour of the cloister. | 717/738–9501 | $28 for dinner (plus tax and gratuity), $6 for the tour.

Dining

Doneckers. French. Housed in a former shoe factory downtown, the five dining rooms have French artifacts and paintings. The bistro serves simple French fare such as onion soup and three-cheese fondue. The formal dining menu has creative French dishes like Maine lobster rougai and pan-seared apricot glazed breast of duck. Live music, piano, Fri., Sat. Kids' menu. | 333 N. State St. | 717/738–9501 | fax 717/735–9512 | www.doneckers.com | Closed Wed, Sun. | $13–$19, bistro, $20–$30, formal dining | AE, D, DC, MC, V.

Olde Lincoln House. American. So named because it was originally a log cabin and because of the Lincoln memorabilia placed throughout, this place has pub grub in the bar and a formal menu of steak and pasta in the dining room. | 1398 W. Main St. | 717/733–3490 | No breakfast | $5–$10 | AE, DC, MC, V.

Stoudt's Black Angus. American/German. Prime rib cut from certified Angus beef is the specialty of this Victorian-style restaurant, adjacent to the Black Angus Antiques Mall. Also notable are its raw oyster bar and German dishes such as Wiener (veal) and Schwabian (pork) schnitzel. Stoudt's beer, brewed right next door, is on tap. On weekends from August through October, a Bavarian Beer Fest with German bands, a pig roast, and ethnic food takes over Brewery Hall. There are brewery tours Saturday at 3 and Sunday at 1. The restaurant is 6 mi northeast of Ephrata. | Rte. 272, Adamstown | 717/484–4385 | $19–$35 | AE, DC, MC, V | No lunch Mon.–Thurs.

Whispers, Inc. American. You can join the locals at this popular neighborhood pub, which serves standard American fare. | 548 S. State St. | 717/733–9926 | $8–$12 | D, MC, V.

Lodging

Clearview Farm B&B. This restored limestone house on 200 acres of countryside, adjacent to a swan-filled pond and landscaped yard, is filled with a mix of antiques and country furniture. Guest rooms have private baths. Complimentary breakfast. Tennis. | 355 Clearview Rd. | 717/733–6333 | www.clearviewfarms.com | 5 rooms | $95–$140 | AE, D, MC, V.

Doneckers Guest House. A comfortable, more modern alternative in the Doneckers community built between the 1920s and 1930s, this 3-story inn is downtown. Restaurant, complimentary Continental breakfast. | 318-324 N. State St. | 717/738–9502 | fax 717/738–9554 | www.doneckers.com | 19 rooms | $75–$99 | AE, D, DC, MC, V.

★ **Historic Smithton Inn.** This rustic Colonial bed and breakfast founded in 1763 has working fireplaces, a sitting area, and Pennsylvania Dutch quilts in each room. Complimentary breakfast. No room phones, no TV. | 900 W. Main St. | 717/733–6094 | www.historicsmithtoninn.com | 8 rooms | $75–$175 | MC, V.

Martin House. You can relax on a large open deck or in the common TV and reading rooms in this modern home on Ephrata Mountain. Guest rooms have private baths. A family suite has its own kitchen and sleeps up to six. Complimentary breakfast. Some in-room hot tubs, TV in common area. | 265 Ridge Ave. | 717/733–6804 or 888/615–8418 | fax 717/733–8038 | www.virtualcities.com | 3 rooms, 1 suite | $80–$120 | MC, V.

1777 House. Filled with European antiques, this cozy, 3-story bed-and-breakfast is in an 18th-century building with gardens outside. Complimentary Continental breakfast. No TV in rooms, TV in common area. | 301 W. Main St. | 717/738–9502 | fax 717/738–9552 | www.doneckers.com | 12 rooms, 2 suites (in carriage house) | $75–$99, $195–$210 suites | AE, D, DC, MC, V.

ERIE

(Nearby towns also listed: Edinboro, North East)

Erie is Pennsylvania's only port town on the Great Lakes and its northernmost city. Its history is rich with stories about battles with the English in the War of 1812 and Native Americans during the Pontiac Uprising. Despite its lakeside location, the town, in the early years, was inhabited by less than 100 people. However, with the dawn of the steam engine and the use of ships, the town's population exploded. Its rich maritime history includes the building of boats to fend off the British and the large number of boats that sank during rough weather. Today, the area remains a popular summer destination and, during hot days, its beaches at Presque Isle are filled.

Information: Erie Area Chamber of Commerce | 109 Boston Store Place, 16501 | 814/454–7191 | www.eriepa.com.

Attractions

Erie Art Museum. The two-story building houses changing art exhibits of local artists and traveling exhibits. The museum's programming also includes shows, classes, workshops, concerts, kids' programs, and lectures. | 411 State St. | 814/459–5477 | fax 814/452–1744 | www.erieartmuseum.org | $2 | Tues.–Sat. 11–5, Sun. 1–5, closed Mon.

Erie Historical Museum and Planetarium. Here you can see exhibits of different topics in history, including local history. Planetarium shows illustrate the movement of the sun, moon, planets, and stars. | 356 W. 6th St. | 814/871–5790 | fax 814/879–0988 | $4; Planetarium shows: Sun. at 2, 3, separate admission | Tues.–Fri. 10–5, weekends 1–5.

Erie Maritime Museum. This is the home port for the reconstructed U.S. Brig *Niagara,* the warship that won the Battle of Lake Erie in the War of 1812. There are multimedia exhibits on area maritime life and an exhibit about the Great Lakes ecosystem. | 150 E. Front St. | 814/452–2744 | www.brigniagara.org/museum.htm | $6 | Mon.–Sat. 9–5, Sun. noon–5.

Erie Zoo. The zoo has 111 species and 377 specimens from all over the world. There's a train, carousel ride, and a picnic area. | 423 W. 38th St. | 814/864–4091 | fax 814/864–1140 | www.eriezoo.org | $5.50 | Daily, 10–5.

Firefighters Historical Museum. A two-bay, two-story fire station built in 1903, the building is now full of firefighter memorabilia, such as 1823 fire apparatus, a steamer, and hand-pull pumpers. You can pull the fire alarm box to hear the alarm, and watch fire safety films. | 428 Chestnut St. | 814/456–5969 or 814/864–2156 | www.geocities.com/soho/museum/7606 | $2 | May–Oct., Sat. 10–5, Sun. 1–5, and by appointment; closed weekdays.

Gridley's Grave. Charles Vernon Gridley (1844–1898) was a captain in the Philippines during the Spanish-American War. He was the commander of the *Olympia,* the flagship of Commodore Dewey's Asiatic squadron, at the Battle of Manila Bay. At his grave are historical cannons from the ship. | 1718 E. Lake Rd. | 814/459–8200 | fax 814/459–6601 | Free | Daily dawn to dusk.

Land Lighthouse. The lighthouse was built in 1818, replaced in 1858, and again in 1867. You can view the lighthouse from the exterior. | 2 Lighthouse St. | 814/452–3937 | Free | Daily 24 hours, 7 days a week.

Misery Bay. This spot is named for the hardship suffered by the sailors under the command of Commodore Oliver Hazard Perry in the winter of 1813–1814 immediately following the Battle of Lake Erie. It's a popular fishing spot and a site for pleasure watercraft. The bay is popular for ice fishing. | End of Presque Isle State Park at Perry Monument | 814/454–7191 | fax 814/459–0241 | Free | Daily 5 AM–Sunset.

Presque Isle State Park. This is the sandy peninsula at Lake Erie that creates Presque Isle Bay, a wide and deep harbor. Presque Isle is a National Natural Landmark, containing more endangered, threatened, and rare species than any other area of comparable size in the state. Stull Interpretive Center has exhibits and displays about the park and its wildlife. In the park is the 1873 Presque Isle Lighthouse, towering 74 ft into the air. There are 15 mi of hiking, bicycle, and cross-country ski trails, swimming, boating, fishing, picnicking, ice fishing, and ice boating. | Peninsula Dr.; Rte. 832 | 814/833–7424 or 888/PA–PARKS | fax 814/833–0266 | www.dcnr.state.pa.us | Free | Daily 8 AM–dusk.

Waldameer Park and Water World. More than 75 rides, slides, pools, and games are here at Waldameer, the 11th oldest continuously operating amusement park in the country. Ali Baba takes you seven stories high before falling back to Earth. Waterworld has 11 slides, five kiddie slides, and three pool areas. | 220 Peninsula Dr. | 814/838–3591 | fax 814/835–7435 | www.waldameer.com | Waldameer $13.50; Waterworld $11.50; combination pass $16 | Water World, 11–7, Waldameer, 1–10, closed Mon.

Wayne Memorial Blockhouse. Built in 1861 to defend Fort Presque Isle, the blockhouse has been restored. It was named in honor of General Anthony Wayne, who died in the blockhouse, next to the Veterans Memorial Cemetery. | 560 E. 3rd St. | 814/454–1813 | Free | Daily.

ON THE CALENDAR

JULY: *Harborfest.* The U.S. Navy SEAL's skydiving team makes an appearance at this annual, 4-day midsummer celebration that also includes hot-air balloons, musical entertainment, and an arcade. | Community Park, Harbor Creek | 814/899–9173.

Dining

Damon's. Barbecue. This is a casual restaurant with several TVs always tuned to sports. You can eat prime rib, chicken steaks, barbecue ribs, or their specialty – an onion ring loaf that looks like it sounds. | 7165 Peach St. | 814/866–7427 | $8–$15 | MC, V.

JR's Last Laugh Comedy Club and Restaurant. American. Would you like a hamburger with that one-liner? It's an option at JR's, where touring comics deliver jokes while you feast on salads, sandwiches, and burgers. | 1402 State St. | 814/461–0911 | Sun.–Tue. No lunch | $5–$10 | AE, D, MC, V.

Maximilian's. Continental. Fresh flowers, original paintings, and candlelight offset the Mediterranean-style colors and maroon tables and booths in this downtown restaurant. Known for beef and chicken, specials are filet Oscar, a 6-oz beef filet wrapped in bacon and topped with crab meat, and the Chilean sea bass. Live music, piano, Tues.–Sat. Kids' menu. Sun. brunch. Free parking. | 2800 W. 8th St. | 814/838–9270 | www.bel-airehotel.com | $10–$25 | AE, D, DC, MC, V.

McGarrey's Oakwood Cafe. Contemporary. On the southwest end of downtown, long banquet tables and chairs fill the interior here, and the outside is just as simple. If you like soup this is your place – it's popular for its homemade soups. | 1624 W. 38th St. | 814/866–0552 | $5–$11 | AE, MC, V.

Porters Restaurant and Tap Room. American. Dark green paint, beige marble counters, and dark wood paneling fill this old railroad station, formerly called Hoppers Brewpub, in the northwest section of the city. Hoppers moved, but their brews are all still served here. Try oysters Rockefeller and raspberry duck in the dining rooms, or order pasta and burgers in the tap room. Known for steak and pasta. Kids' menu. | 123 W. 14th St. | 814/452–2787 | www.portersrestaurant.com | $12–$30 | AE, D, DC, MC, V.

Pufferbelly. American. Named for the steam pumpers and engines that were here when it was a fire station in the early 20th century, this downtown restaurant has original fire fighting equipment, drawings, and photographs of firemen on the walls. The menu has stuffed Portabello mushroom appetizer, steak Madagascar cooked in a mushroom sauce, and salmon salad. You can eat outside on a patio overlooking the street. Buffet. Sun. brunch. | 414 French St. | 814/454–1557 | www.thepufferbelly.com | $10–$18 | AE, D, MC, V.

Lodging

Avalon Hotel. In the heart of the downtown, this modern six-story hotel was built in 1970. You can walk to the Civic Center and the local semi-pro baseball stadium. Restaurant, bar. Some refrigerators, cable TV. Business services. | 16 W. 10th St. | 814/459–2220 or 800/822–5011 | fax 814/459–2322 | www.avalonerie.com | 193 rooms | $79–$104 | AE, D, DC, MC, V.

Bel Aire. An upscale downtown hotel, it's near Presque Isle State Park, shops, and restaurants. Restaurant, bar. In-room data ports, cable TV. Indoor pool. Hot tub, sauna. Exercise equipment. Free parking. | 2800 W. 8th St. | 814/833–1116 or 800/888–8781 | fax 814/838–3242 | www.bel-airehotel.com | 151 rooms | $125–$175 | AE, D, DC, MC, V.

Comfort Inn. This midpriced hotel won a Choice Hotels Gold Award. It's near Exit 6 of I–90, south of downtown and less than 2 mi from the Millcreek Mall shopping and restaurants. The 2-story hotel was built in 1990, and its rooms were remodeled in 1998. Complimentary Continental breakfast. In-room data ports, some refrigerators, cable TV, in-room VCRs (and movies). Pool. Hot tub. Exercise equipment. Business services, airport shuttle. | 8051 Peach St. | 814/866–6666 | fax 814/866–6666 | www.comfortinn.com | 110 rooms | $100–$130 | AE, D, DC, MC, V.

Econo Lodge. Winner of a Choice Hotels Gold Award, this midpriced motel is 5 mi south of downtown, near Exit 6 of I–90 and the Millcreek Mall. Complimentary Continental breakfast. In-room data ports, some refrigerators, cable TV. Indoor pool. Hot tub. Exercise equipment. Business services, airport shuttle. | 8050 Peach St. | 814/866–5544 | fax 814/866–5544, ext. 142 | www.erieinns.com | 97 rooms | $89–$129 | AE, D, DC, MC, V.

Glass House Inn. Here's a classic 50s motel with a Colonial design and affordable rates. The third generation owners continue the family tradition with a bed- and breakfast-style inn, southwest of downtown with easy access to Presque Isle. Complimentary Continental breakfast. In-room data ports, cable TV. Pool. Free parking. | 3202 W. 26th St. | 814/833–7751 or 800/956–7222 | fax 814/833–4222 | www.glasshouseinn.com | 30 rooms | $49–$95 | AE, D, DC, MC, V.

Hampton Inn. Built in the mid-1920s, this 5-story chain hotel is 2 mi southwest of downtown. Staying here, you have easy access to shops, restaurants, and Presque Isle. Complimentary Continental breakfast. Cable TV. Pool. Business services, free parking. | 3041 W. 12th St. | 814/835–4200 | fax 814/835–4200 | www.hampton-inn.com | 100 rooms | $85–$110 | AE, D, DC, MC, V.

Holiday Inn–Downtown. Right in downtown, this hotel is within walking distance to restaurants and shops. It was built in 1962 and has 4 stories. Restaurant, bar (with entertainment), complimentary Continental breakfast, room service. In-room data ports, cable TV. Pool. Laundry facilities. Business services, airport shuttle, free parking. | 18 W. 18th St. | 814/456–2961 | fax 814/456–7067 | holidinn@erie.net | www.holiday-inn.com | 131 rooms | $99–$140 | AE, D, DC, MC, V.

Lakeview on the Lake. On the shore of Lake Erie about 10 mi from downtown, the inn's grounds are parklike. You can stroll along Lake Erie and hike around the grounds. Microwaves, refrigerators, cable TV, room phones. Outdoor pool, dock. | 8696 E. Lake Rd. | 814/899–6948 | www.lakeviewerie.com/ | lakeview@erie.net | 12 rooms in inn, 3 cottages, 2-bedroom mobile home | $70–$110 | MC, V.

Motel 6 Erie. An affordable motel at Exit 6 of I–90, the motel is 3 mi south of downtown, across the street from Erie Downs and fast food. Renovated in 1997, this 2-story motel has interior corridors. Cable TV. Indoor pool, wading pool. Sauna. Laundry facilities. Business services, free parking. | 7575 Peach St. | 814/864–4811 | fax 814/864–4396 | www.erieinns.com | 83 rooms | $59–$99 | AE, D, DC, MC, V.

Quality Inn. Near Exit 7 of I–90, this hotel is 5 mi south of downtown. The 2-story hotel was built in 1960 and gives you easy access to downtown via Perry Highway. Restaurant, bar, room service. In-room data ports, cable TV. Pool. Airport shuttle, free parking. | 8040 Perry Hwy./Rte. 97 | 814/864–4911 | fax 814/864–3743 | www.qualityinn.com | 110 rooms | $59–$100 | AE, D, DC, MC, V.

Ramada Inn. On Route 8, 4 mi south of downtown, this hotel is just a few minutes' drive to restaurants and shopping. Restaurant, bar, room service. In-room data ports, cable TV. Pool, wading pool. Video games. Business services. | 6101 Wattsburg Rd. | 814/825–3100 | fax 814/825–0857 | 120 rooms | $88–$99 | AE, D, DC, MC, V.

Residence Inn. You can find rooms here with hot tubs, fireplaces, and two national newspapers delivered complimentary each morning. Suites have kitchenettes, a living room with sofa. Cable TV, room phones. Laundry facilities, laundry service. Business services. | 8061 Peach St. | 814/864–2500 | fax 814/864–0688 | www.residenceinn.com | 89 | $119–$129 | AE, D, MC, V.

Spencer House Bed and Breakfast. Your hosts at this Victorian downtown inn speak English and Hebrew. Built in 1876 and listed on the National Register of Historic Places, the inn is filled with antiques. Complimentary breakfast, cable TV, in-room VCRs. Business services. | 519 W. 6th St. | 814/454–5984 or 800/890–7263 | fax 814/456–5019 | www.erie.net/~spencer | 5 rooms | $85–$135 | AE, D, MC, V.

Vineyard Bed and Breakfast. You can watch beautiful sunsets over Lake Erie from this farmhouse, built in 1900 and remodeled into a bed and breakfast in 1993. Rooms have private baths. Complimentary breakfast. Pets allowed. | 10757 Sidehill Rd. | 814/725–5307 or 888/725–8998 | www.lakeside.net/vineyardbb | 5 rooms | $65–$75 | AE, D, MC, V.

ERWINNA

MAP 7, L5

(Nearby towns also listed: Allentown, Bethlehem, Easton, Quakertown)

Erwinna is a quaint town along the twists of River Road on the Delaware River in scenic Bucks County. Great for a getaway, it's a place where you can relax and take in the river view from the porch of one of several bed-and-breakfasts.

Information: **Bucks County Convention and Visitors Bureau** | 152 Swamp Rd., Doylestown, PA, 18901 | 215/345–4552 or 800/836–2825 | www.buckscountycvb.org.

Attractions

Tinicum Park. At this 126-acre park, you can picnic, hike, and fish. You can also tour (by appointment) the Erwin Stover House, an 1800 Federal-style home with 1840 and 1860 additions. | River Rd. | 215/757–0571 or 215/348–6114 | Free | Daily 8AM–Sunset.

Sand Castle Winery. Take a tour of the vineyard and underground wine cellar and do a little wine tasting here. Ask about special, 2½ hour VIP tours, and wine and food courses. | 755 River Rd. | 610/294–9181 or 800/722–9463 | www.sandcastlewinery.com | $3 | Weekdays 9–6, Sat. 10–6, Sun. 11–6.

Erwinna Covered Bridge. One of many covered bridges in Bucks County, this one dates to either 1832, according to county records, or 1871, according to the National Register of Historic Places. | Geigel Hill Rd. | Free.

Dining

★ **Evermay-on-the-Delaware.** Contemporary. In a Victorian mansion-turned-inn once frequented by the Barrymores, the chef here serves an impressive prix-fixe six-course dinner. The nightly menu has a choice of two entrees, such as coriander-seared yellowfin tuna with shaved fennel, preserved lemon and sundried tomatoes, and loin of lamb with summer ratatouille and jus provençal. Dinner includes champagne, hors d'ouevres, and a cheese course. | River and Headquarters Rds | 610/294–9100 | Reservations essential | Closed Mon.-Thurs. | $68 | MC, V.

★ **Golden Pheasant Inn.** Contemporary. At one of the prettiest places along the Delaware Canal, the chef prepares culinary creations such as filet mignon with Béarnaise sauce and poached salmon in a lobster-and-champagne sauce. You can dine under the stars in a renovated greenhouse, or the cozy tavern room with working fireplace and pierced tin chandeliers. | 763 River Rd. | 610/294–9595 | Mon.-Tues.; Sun, brunch only | $20–$25 | AE, D, DC, MC, V.

Lodging

★ **Evermay-on-the-Delaware.** Guest rooms at this Victorian mansion, where the Barrymores once played croquet, are filled with fine antiques and fresh flowers. Be sure to ask for a room with a river view or the more private carriage house or cottage. You can take a predinner sherry or afternoon tea in the parlor warmed by twin fireplaces. | River and Headquarter Rds. | 610/294–9100 | www.evermay.com | 18 rooms | $135–$350 | MC.

★ **Golden Pheasant Inn.** This 1857 landmark has been restored as a rustic yet elegant French auberge with a fine restaurant serving contemporary American cuisine. The six guest rooms are furnished with four-poster beds and have river or canal views. Some rooms face River Road, a sometimes heavily trafficked road. Restaurant. | 763 River Rd. | 610/294–9595 | www.goldenpheasant.com | 6 rooms | $95–$125 | CP | AE, D, DC, MC, V.

Isaac Stover House. An 1837 Federal-Victorian mansion, rooms here have views of the Delaware River and historic Stover's Mill and are furnished with antiques, treasures collected from around the world, and a bit of whimsy. You're welcomed with afternoon tea or a glass of sherry. | 5 River Rd. | 610/294–8044 | fax 610/294–8132 | www.isaacstoverhouse.com | 4 rooms | $130–$160.

FARMINGTON

MAP 7, C7

(Nearby towns also listed: Connellsville, Donegal, Uniontown)

The small town of Farmington lies just north of the West Virginia border and is close to three of Pennsylvania's most famous sites: Fort Necessity Battlefield, the field where General George Washington experienced his one and only defeat; Braddock Grave, within a short drive of Farmington.

Information: Fayette County Chamber of Commerce | 65 W. Main St., Uniontown, PA 15401 | 724/437–4571 or 800/916–9365 | www.fayettecountypa.net.

Attractions

Laurel Caverns. Also known as Dulaney's Cave, Laurel Caverns are rumored to contain the lost treasure of a local gang of thieves who lost their buried loot somewhere in the maze of caverns. Take a 45-minute guided tour as an introduction to the dark, chilly cave, or roam the caverns unguided. You can expect a constant temperature of 52 degrees within the cave. | 200 Caverns Park Rd. | 724/438–3003 | $8 | Jan–Oct, 9–5.

ON THE CALENDAR

SEPT.: *Chili Cook-Off and Harvest Festival.* You can sample some of the region's best chili at the Christian W. Klay Winery during this 1-day celebration. | 412 Fayette Springs Rd. | 724/439–3424.

Dining

Stone House Restaurant and Inn. Continental. Dine on rich, hearty, old-world food such as New York strip, roasted duck, dumplings, and locally harvested trout in this historic brick home with a wraparound front porch. | 3023 National Pike | 724/329–8876 | $7–$20 | AE, D, MC, V.

Lodging

Nemacolin Woodlands. An equestrian center offering surrey rides all year is but one highlight of this sprawling resort. Its 60-or-so buildings were built in 1988 on 15,000 acres, in the heart of Farmington. The 5-story French-style Chateau Lafayette has elegant rooms, while the 4-story lodge has a more casual and rustic appeal. Bar (with entertainment), dining room, room service. In-room data ports, minibars, some microwaves, some refrigerators, cable TV. 4 pools (2 indoor). 5 hot tubs, massage. Driving range, 2 18-hole golf courses, miniature golf, 2 putting greens, tennis. Gym, hiking. Boating, bicycles. Cross-country and downhill skiing, sleigh rides, tobogganing. Video games. Kids' programs (4–12), playground. Laundry facilities. Business services. | 1001 LaFayette Dr. | 724/329–8555 or 800/422–2736 | fax 724/329–6198 | www.nemacolin.com | 220 rooms in 3 buildings, 54 1- to 2-bedroom apartments | $250–$350; $315–$550 apartments | AE, DC, MC, V.

Quiet House B & B. There are only three guest rooms in this 1860 Georgian farmhouse, but you can stay in one of the more private cottages scattered over the inn's 264 acres. The innkeepers can arrange in-room massages, and Kentuck Knob, Fallingwater, Laurel Caverns, and Nemacolin Woodlands are all within a 10-mi drive. Complimentary breakfast. Hiking. | 667 Elliotsville Rd. | 724/329–8120 | fax 724/329–0797, ext. 51 | www.quiethousebnb.com | 3 rooms, 4 cottages | $79–$248 | D, MC, V.

Summit Inn. A 19th-century building with original Stickley furniture, this mini-resort has commanding views from its perch on Chestnut Ridge in the Laurel Highlands. It's only 3 mi from downtown Uniontown, 3 mi east from Fort Necessity National Battlefield, and Braddock Grave. Bar, dining room, picnic area, room service. Cable TV. Indoor-outdoor pool. Hot tub. 9-hole golf course, putting green, tennis. Exercise equipment. Business services. | 101 Skyline Dr. | 724/438–8594 | fax 724/438–3917 | www.hhs.net/summit | 94 rooms | $129–$179 | Closed from Nov.–Apr. | AE, D, MC, V.

FOGELSVILLE

MAP 7, J5

(Nearby towns also listed: Allentown, Bethlehem, Hamburg, Kutztown)

Fogelsville is a popular stop along I–78, west of Reading.

Information: **Lehigh County Chamber of Commerce** | 462 Walnut St., Allentown, PA 18102 | 610/437–9661 | www.lehighcountychamber.org.

Attractions

Bushkill Falls. Known locally as the "Niagara of Pennsylvania," you can see a series of eight waterfalls secluded within the forests of the Pocono Mountains. Make sure to wear your walking shoes. The falls are down a series of trails and bridges in the midst of dramatic scenery. | Bushkill Falls Rd., off Route 209 Bushkill | 570/588–6682 or 888/628–7454 | fax 570/588–9060 | $8 | Apr.–Oct., 9–7.

ON THE CALENDAR

JUNE: *Schnecksville Community Fair.* For one week at the fairgrounds on Route 309 in nearby Schnecksville, you can walk the midway, eat local foods, take a carnival ride, and see local arts and crafts. You can also watch livestock demonstrations and competitions, and hear live music. | 610/799–9467.

Dining

Orient Express. Chinese. Choose from Chinese classics and a few American dishes here. The wonton soup is a specialty. | Rte. 100 and Old 22 | 610/391–9130 | $6–$10 | AE, D, MC, V.

Lodging

Glasbern. A late 1800s farmhouse, barn, gate house and carriage house have been converted into a small inn filled with antiques. It's only 1 and ½ mi from downtown Fogelsville. Dining room, complimentary breakfast. Cable TV, in-room VCRs (and movies). Pool. Business services. | 2141 Pack House Rd. | 610/285–4723 | fax 610/285–2862 | www.glasbern.com | 39 rooms | $125–$360 | AE, MC, V.

Hawthorn Suites Ltd.–Fogelsville. This hotel has standard rooms, suites and kitchenettes, 4 mi from the Dorney Wild Water Kingdom. Some kitchenettes, some minibars, some in-room hot tubs, cable TV. Exercise equipment. Laundry service. Business services. | 7720 Main St. | 610/366–9422 or 800/527–1133 | fax 610/366–9445 | www.hawthorn.com | 64 rooms | $65–$104 | AE, D, DC, MC, V.

FORT WASHINGTON

(Nearby towns also listed: King of Prussia, Limerick, Norristown, Willow Grove)

Named after General George Washington's encampment during the Revolutionary War, Fort Washington is a suburb of Philadelphia. You can see many period buildings here.

Information: Montgomery County Chamber of Commerce | 1341 Sandy Hill Rd., Norristown, PA 19401 | 610/277–9500 | www.montcocc.org.

Attractions

Fort Washington State Park. The 493-acre park has a softball field, 3½ mi of hiking trails, an observation deck, fishing in Wissahickon Creek, picnic facilities, a 400-ft slope for sledding, and a 1.7-mi loop for cross-country skiing. | 500 Bethlehem Pike | 215/591–5250 or 888/PA–PARKS | fax 215/591–5249 | www.dcnr.state.pa.us | Free | Daily 8 AM–dusk.

The Highlands. Built by Anthony Morris, Speaker of the Pennsylvania Senate in 1793–1794, the 18th-century, late Georgian–style mansion is on 44 acres of land. The estate has a 2-acre formal garden and nine outbuildings, including a barn and a springhouse built in 1799. | 7001 Sheaff La. | 215/641–2687 | fax 215/641–2556 | $4 | Weekdays 10–4; June–Aug. Sun. by appointment.

Hope Lodge. An 18th-century mansion that was occupied until the 1950s, the lodge has its original Colonial form and was never modernized. A perfect example of Georgian architecture, the home was built between 1743 and 1748 by Samuel Morris, a Quaker businessman. Revolutionary troops camped on the estate in 1777 on their way to Valley Forge. | 553 Bethlehem Pike | 215/646–1595 | fax 215/628–9471 | www.ushistory.org/hope | $3.50 | Wed.–Sat. 9–5, Sun. noon–5, closed Mon., Tue.

Mennonite Heritage Center. Designed to look like an early Mennonite Meeting House, this heritage center has rotating and permanent exhibits illustrating Mennonite life in the 20th century. | 565 Yoder Rd., Harleysville, | 215/256–3020 | fax 215/256–3023 | info@mhep.org | www.mhep.org | Free | Tue.–Fri. 10–5, Sat. 10–2, Sun. 2–5.

ON THE CALENDAR

JAN.: *Greater Philadelphia Sport, Travel and Outdoor Show.* Held at the Fort Washington Expo Center, this 4-day show highlights the latest boats, fishing gear and hunting equipment, cooking exhibits, and informational booths describing area resorts and travel destinations. | 215/641–4500 | $9.

Dining

Harvey's. Continental. In the Holiday Inn, Harvey's offers hearty Continental cuisine with an emphasis on pasta dishes. You can choose your ingredients at the breakfast omelette bar. The lounge has live music Wed. through Sat. nights. | 432 Pennsylvania Ave. | 215/643–3000 | $8–$15 | AE, D, DC, MC, V.

Palace of Asia. Indian. Traditional Indian music and unique Indian artwork decorate the interior. There's a full bar and the menu has chicken tandoori, chicken tikka masala, lamb, and vegetarian dishes such as cooked okra. Weekend brunch. | 285 Commerce Dr. | 215/646–2133 | Reservations essential | $9–$20 | AE, D, DC, MC, V.

Lodging

Holiday Inn Fort Washington. One mile from Fort Washington State Park, this hotel has rooms in varying degrees of luxury and a babysitting service. Restaurant, room service. Cable TV, Outdoor pool. Exercise equipment. Video games. Laundry service. Business services. | 432 Pennsylvania Ave. | 215/643–3000 | 224 rooms | $92–$115 | AE, D, DC, MC, V.

FRANKLIN

MAP 7, B3

(Nearby towns also listed: Meadville, Oil City, Titusville)

One of two boroughs in Pennsylvania with the name Franklin, this Franklin is in Venango County on the banks of the Allegheny River and near Oil City. Called the "Victorian City," Franklin takes pride in its many elegant homes in the heart of the city. It played a major role during the French and Indian War and in the discovery of oil. Just a 25-min drive from I–80, the town has many antiques stores and a 15-mi scenic trail along the Allegheny River.

Information: **Oil Heritage Region Tourist Promotion Agency** | 206 Seneca St., 4th Fl., Oil City, PA 16301 | 814/677–3152 or 800/4–VENANGO | www.usachoice.net/oilregiontourist.

Attractions

DeBence Antique Music World. You can take a guided tour of the collection of more than 100 antique, automated music machines from the Roaring Twenties to the 1990s, nickelodeons, Swiss and German music boxes, merry-go-round band organs, pipe organs, and player pianos. | 1261 Liberty St. | 814/432–8350 or 814/432–5668 | fax 814/437–7193 | www.debencemusicworld.com | $8 | Dec.–Mar., Fri.–Sat. 11–4, Sun. 12:30–4, closed Mon.–Thurs.; Apr.–Nov., Tues.–Wed. and Fri.–Sat. 11–4, Sun. 12:30–4, closed Mon. and Thurs.

Hoge–Osmer House. The house has displays of local history and furnishings from the early 1900s, plus there's a genealogy research library. | 301 S. Park St. | 814/437–2275 | Free | May–Dec., Tues.–Thurs. and Sat. 10–2, closed Sun.–Mon. and Fri.; Jan.–Apr., Sat. 10–2, closed Sun.–Fri.

Two Mile Run County Park. You can camp, rent a cabin, hike, cross-country ski, or ride a horse on 26 mi of trails that run along the foot of the Alleghenys. The park also has a swimming beach, a fishing area, and picnic pavillions. | R.D. 5 | 814/676–6116 | fax 814/678–1190 | www.twomile.org | Free | Park, daily sunrise–sunset; family campground, Mid-Apr.–Mid-Oct.; Crosby Beach, Memorial Day–Labor Day, daily 11–7.

Venango County Court House. The red-brick courthouse, built in the 1860s, is the third courthouse to be built on the same site. The first courthouse had to be rebuilt and the second one was destroyed by fire. | 1168 Liberty St. | 814/432–9500 | Free | Weekdays 8:30–4:30, closed weekends.

MAY: *Memorial Day Celebration.* This 2-day event marks the beginning of summer at Two Mile Run County Park. You can watch the Ya Gotta Regatta, the opening of Crosby Beach, and fishing contests. | 814/676–6116.

JULY: *Rocky Grove Fair.* A traditional 7-day fair is sponsored by the local fire company. | Rocky Grove Fire Company, 29 Wood St. | 814/432–3962 | Free.

OCT.: *Applefest.* A 2-day festival that has more than 350 vendors of arts, crafts, and food, as well as entertainment, a 5K race, theater, and an antique auto show. Apple-related events are an apple pancake breakfast, and an apple pie baking contest. | Downtown | 814/432–5823 | www.franklin-pa.org/appleevents | Free.

Dining

Cauvel's Diner. American. You can eat breakfast all day at this roadside diner, or choose from burgers, sandwiches, and other dishes. The homemade cinnamon rolls and pies are the specialties. | 408 12th St. | 814/437–6518 | $4–$8 | AE, D, MC, V.

Primo Barones. Italian. This brewpub and restaurant has balloons, props, and other flying gear on display. At the Franklin County Airport, you can get a complete view of small engine planes coming and going while you try house specialties like filet Italian style or the Tour of Italy, veal and chicken parmigiano with fettuccini alfredo. | 1564 Airport Rd. | 814/432–2588 | www.primabarones.com | $6–$18 | AE, MC, V.

Rosalee's Parkside Restaurant. American. The restaurant is known locally for home-cooked meals and large portions. It's heavy on deep-fried food, but you can also order salads and low-fat dishes. | 1234 Liberty St. | 814/432–3525 | $4–$7.

Lodging

Idlewood Motel. This one-story, drive-up hotel at the top of the hill overlooks downtown Franklin. An efficiency-style room is also available with a small kitchen area. Some kitchenettes, cable TV. | R. R. 62 & Hwy. 8 | 814/437–3003 | 18 rooms | $42 | AE, MC, V.

Inn at Franklin. Modern lodgings in a historic district, the 6-story inn is right downtown, within easy walking distance to restaurants and shopping. This hotel was built in 1965 and is on Route 8. Restaurant, bar, complimentary Continental breakfast. Cable TV. Beauty salon. Business services, airport shuttle. | 1411 Liberty St. | 814/437–3031 or 800/535–4052 | fax 814/432–7481 | www.innatfranklin.com | 100 rooms | $65–$70 | AE, D, DC, MC, V.

Lamberton House. A 3-story Victorian home built in 1874, this bed and breakfast is on the National Register of Historic Places. It's right in downtown Franklin 2 blocks from the business district and 2 blocks to DeBence Antique Music World and the Court House. Complimentary breakfast. No room phones, TV in common area. | 1331 Otter St. | 814/432–7908 | www.bedandbreakfast.com | 6 rooms (2 with shared bath, 3 with shower only) | $65–$85 | MC, V.

Quo Vadis. A Queen Anne-style bed and breakfast, built in 1867, and accented with terra cotta tile, this 3-story inn is in the historic district of Franklin. Complimentary breakfast. TV in common area. No smoking. | 1501 Liberty St. | 814/432–4208 | www.travelassist.com | 6 rooms | $70–$90 | AE, MC, V.

Red Brick Inn. You can stay on this working beef cattle farm in a restored pre-Civil War farmhouse adjacent to the owners' home. While here, you can explore 100 acres of farmland, relax on the front porch, or pet the cows. Complimentary breakfast. Hiking. | R.D. 1, Emlenton | 814/498–2659 | redbrickinn@pafarmstay.com | www.pafarmstay.com | 4 rooms | $40–$50 | No credit cards.

GALETON

(Nearby town also listed: Wellsboro)

Galeton started when lumbering was in its heyday in the 1880s, and soon had lumber mills, a tannery, and businesses to provide services to residents. Some of that 1880s architecture remains and is a reminder of the lumbering heritage this borough enjoys. Today, Galeton is popular with anglers and hunters, who come for the whitetail deer. The community is a gateway town to Pennsylvania's Grand Canyon.

Information: **Galeton Chamber of Commerce** | Box 176, 16922. | 814/435–2302.

Attractions

Lyman Run State Park. The park has 595 acres of forested mountain land where you can hike, hunt, stream fish, camp, and picnic. There are 50 campsites and 505 acres for hunting. | 454 Lyman Run Rd. | 814/435–5010 or 888/PA–PARKS | www.dcnr.state.pa.us | Free | Daily 8 AM–dusk.

Ole Bull State Park. The 125-acre park is along the Kettle Creek Valley. The area is referred to as the Black Forest because of its dense tree cover, mountainous terrain, and wilderness habitat. The park has 81 campsites and one cabin. There's swimming and fishing in Kettle Creek, picnicking, hunting on 25 acres, hiking, and cross-country skiing. | HCR Box 9, Cross Fork | 814/435–5000 or 888/PA–PARKS | fax 814/435–5002 | www.dcnr.state.pa.us | Free | Daily 8 AM–dusk.

Pennsylvania Lumber Museum. A gallery for lumbermen from the late 1800s and early 1900s, you can see equipment, photos, a Civilian Conservation Corps cabin, and a replica of a logging camp including a sawmill. | 5660 U.S. Rte. 6W | 814/435–2652 | www.lumbermuseum.org | $3.50 | Apr.–Nov., daily 9–5.

Ski Denton/Denton Hill. The mountain has a 650-ft vertical drop with a 66-degree incline. There are 20 runs, a tube slide, snowboard park with 2 mi of high-banked quarter walls, five cabin chalets and a ski school. | U.S. Rte. 6 | 814/435–2115 | www.skidenton.com | Dec.–Mar., Fri.–Sun, 9–9; Tue.–Thur., 1–9; Mon., 10–9.

ON THE CALENDAR

JULY: *Bark Peeler's Convention.* This 2-day woods festival has sawmilling and woodhick demonstrations, contests in birling (log-rolling), fiddling, tobacco spitting, and frog jumping. A woodhick, by the way, is a lumberworker. | Pennsylvania Lumber Museum | 814/435–2652.

JULY: *Red Suspender Weekend.* Held the same weekend as the Bark Peeler's Convention, this event marks the important work of firefighters with games, live music, and food. | Centertown Park, Park La. | 814/435–5010.

AUG.: *Bowhunter's Festival.* Bowhunters compete in many contests during this 3-day festival. | Denton Hill State Park, U.S. 6 | 814/435–2115.

AUG.: *Woodsmen's Carnival.* You can watch horse-pulling and wood-cutting competitions, see related displays, and visit food vendors at this annual event. | Branch Rd., Cherry Springs State Park | 814/435–5010.

SEPT.: *Germania Old Home Day.* Food, dancing, games, and entertainment are part of this celebration. | Pigeon Hill Rd. | 814/435–8881.

Dining

Ox Yoke Inn. Eclectic. You can order American classics, Tex-Mex, Asian, and Middle Eastern meals here. | 29 U.S. Hwy. 6 W | 814/435–6522 | Reservations essential | $12–$20 | AE, D, MC, V.

Lodging

Handwerk House. Operated with the romantic weekend getaway in mind, this inn serves candlelit breakfasts. The inn is one block from Center Lake, a year-round recreation center. Complimentary breakfast. In-room data ports. | 25 Prospect Ave. | antiques@penn.com | www.handwerkhouse.com | 814/435–8827 | 3 rooms | $95 | AE, D, MC, V.

GETTYSBURG

MAP 7, G7

(Nearby towns also listed: Hanover, York)

Known for the turning-point battle of the Civil War, Gettysburg has a national military park and you can see more than 1,300 monuments dedicated to those who died during the Battle of Gettysburg. Many of the buildings and homes built during the 1860s remain. The town and surrounding area has more than 25 museums and attractions.

Information: Gettysburg–Adams County Chamber of Commerce | 18 Carlisle St., Ste. 203, 17325 | 717/334–8151 | www.gettysburg-chamber.org.

Attractions

A. Lincoln's Place. A one-man performance, about 45 minutes long, shows President Abraham Lincoln's life from birth through the Gettysburg address. Actor Jim Getty depicts Lincoln and there are photo and question-and-answer sessions after the performances. | Battle Theater, 571 Steinwehr Ave. | 717/334–6049 or 717/334–8003 | fax 717/334–4932 | www.gettysburg.com/gcvb/lincoln.html | $7 | Mar. 1–Nov. 30, call for showtimes.

★ **Eisenhower National Historic Site.** You can visit the only place President and Mrs. Dwight D. Eisenhower ever owned as a home. In 1951, the Eisenhowers, looking forward to retirement, purchased the Allen Redding farm adjoining Gettysburg National Military Park. During Eisenhower's presidency, the 230-acre country estate was used as a weekend retreat and as a meeting place for world leaders. There is an 11-minute video and exhibits on Eisenhower's life. | 250 Eisenhower Farm La. | 717/338–9114 | fax 717/338–0821. | www.nps.gov/eise | $5.25. | Apr.–Oct., daily 9–4; Jan. and Nov.–Mar., Wed.–Sun. 9–4, closed Mon.–Tues.

Historic Round Barn and Farm Market. Built in 1914, this Adams County landmark 8 mi west of Gettysburg off Route 30 really is round. Regional arts and crafts are sold and in summer you can buy locally grown produce and flowers. | 298 Cashtown Rd. | 717/334–1984 | Free | June–Oct.

Jennie Wade House. Jennie Wade was the only civilian casualty in the Battle of Gettysburg, and her home and its furnishings have been preserved. The museum tells the story of Jennie and shows a snapshot of life in the Civil War era. | 758 Baltimore St. | 717/334–4100 | $5.75 | Daily 9–5:45.

Schriver House. George Washington Schriver was a local hero during the Civil War. His home has been restored to show what civilian life was like in the battle of Gettysburg. The home tour showcases an area where sharpshooters perched (and were killed), as well as Schriver's Saloon, operated out of the basement. | 309 Baltimore St. | 717/337–2800 | www.schriverhouse.com | $6 | Apr.-Nov. Mon.–Sat. 10–5, Sun. 12–5; Dec., Feb. and March, Sat.–Sun. 12–5; closed Jan. Groups of 10 or more with advance reservation, Tues.–Sun. 10–5.

Land of Little Horses. The largest herd of Falabella miniature horses lives at this amusement park. Daily events include pig races, carousel rides, saddle rides, train rides, and an arena show. There's also a museum and nature area with more than 100 animals. | 125 Glenwood Dr. | 717/334–7259 | www.landoflittlehorses.com | $7 | Memorial Day–late Aug., Mon.–Sat. 10–5, Sun. noon–5; Apr., May, and Sept.–Oct., Sat. 10–5, Sun. noon–5, closed weekdays.

GETTYSBURG

INTRO
ATTRACTIONS
DINING
LODGING

General Lee's Headquarters. Gen. Robert E. Lee established his personal headquarters in this old stone house, which dates from the 1700s. On July 1, 1863, Lee made plans for the Battle of Gettysburg in this house. The home now holds a collection of Civil War artifacts. | 401 Buford Ave. | 717/334–3141 | fax 717/334–1813 | www.civilwarheadquarters.com | $3 | Mid-Mar.–mid-Apr. and mid-Oct.–Nov, daily 9–5; mid-Apr.–mid-Oct., Sun.–Thurs. 9–7, Fri.–Sat. 9–8:30, closed Dec.–mid-Mar.

Gettysburg Battle Theatre. Orient yourself to the important sites in the Battle of Gettysburg by looking at a 50-ft diorama and an electronic wall map. Then you can watch a half-hour documentary film on the three-day Battle of Gettysburg. | 571 Steinwehr Ave. | 717/334–6100 | www.gettysburg.com | $5.75 | May–Labor Day, daily 9–9; Sep.–Oct. 15, daily 9-7; Oct.15–Nov. and Mar.–Apr., daily 9-5; closed Dec.–Feb.

Gettysburg College. Founded in 1832, this church-affiliated liberal arts college has a 200-acre campus with an undergraduate enrollment of 2,243. The administration building is

PENNSYLVANIA HISTORY

Traveling through Pennsylvania is a lesson in history. Battlefields, monuments, and steel towns are scattered across the state, and, it seems, every little town has its historic buildings and centuries-old graveyards. Historical landmarks dot the landscape and are, in general, well kept and preserved. In large cities and small towns, historical buildings have been restored and renovated for modern-day use, so don't be surprised to find yourself dining in a 250-year-old barn or sipping suds in a 100-year-old church.

A stop in Philadelphia alone can fill your head with facts and figures about the founders of our country. Venture outside the city and you'll learn more in almost every town you visit, from King of Prussia, where an inn that Washington frequented still stands next to the country's second largest shopping mall, to Lancaster where for one day the nation's capital rested following the fall of Philadelphia to the British.

If you tire of Revolutionary War history, travel to Gettysburg and view the fields that turned the tide in the War Between the States. Every year Gettysburg draws millions, but one weekend a year the city explodes with visitors. The Fourth of July is celebrated as thousands of people help to reenact the three-day battle. Visitors can spend one or several days walking the fields and buildings with trained guides who explain every aspect of the battle that raged from July 1-3, 1863.

Head farther west and you'll end up in Pittsburgh, a town that helped change America's landscape with the production of steel. Today, the steel town lives up to its reputation and honors its most respected citizen, Andrew Carnegie, with museums, galleries, libraries, and a college bearing his name.

Much of the state's history is well known, but there are undiscovered tidbits as well. For instance, did you know that the very first discovery of oil in the United States occurred in Titusville or that the western expansion of the railroad didn't hit full stride until a little engineering marvel, known as the Horseshoe Curve, was completed in the foothills of the Allegheny Mountains near Altoona.

So, if you're looking for history, Pennsylvania's a good place to start.

listed on the National Register of Historic Places. It served as a hospital for the wounded of both sides during the Battle of Gettysburg. | 300 N. Washington St. | 717/337–6000 or 800/431–0803 | fax 717/337–6145 | www.gettysburg.edu | Free | Daily.

★ **Gettysburg National Military Park.** There are few landmarks showing the history of the United States as touching as the field where troops from the North and South met and decided the fate of the Civil War. More than 51,000 soldiers were killed, wounded, or captured at the Battle of Gettysburg, making it the bloodiest battle of the Civil War. The park has more than 6,000 acres, and 1,300 monuments to state units. There are markers and memorials scattered throughout the park. Cannons stand along the 35 mi of scenic battlefields and avenues. You can visit 20 museums and attractions dedicated to the battle. In the first week of July, thousands of volunteers dress in period uniforms and reenact the three-day battle, which started July 1, 1863. | 97 Taneytown Rd. | 717) 334–1124 | fax 717/334–1891 | www.nps.gov/gett | Park grounds and roads open daily, 6 AM –10 PM.

The **Visitor Center** contains the Gettysburg Museum of the Civil War, with one of the world's largest collections of Civil War items, Gettysburg-related memorabilia, and the electric map battle orientation program. The audiovisual program, displayed on a giant relief map of the battlefield, gives you an overview of the field, three days of battle, and who the major combatants were. | Museum free; Electric Map $3 | mid-June–mid-Aug., daily 8–6; mid-Aug.–mid-June, daily 8–5.

It was on **East Cemetery Hill** that Gen. Winfield Scott Hancock rallied beaten Union troops on July 1, 1863. Some Federal troops took up positions behind the stone walls that border the hill while artillerymen dug barricades for their guns. By the morning of July 2, 1863, Cemetery Hill was one of the most heavily fortified positions on the field. That night, the "Louisiana Tigers" broke the Union line here and charged up the slope to attack the cannon on top of the hill. Both Union and Confederate armies had severe losses in that fighting.

Little Round Top, on the southern end of Cemetery Ridge, is another key area of the battlefield. Strewn with loose rocks and large boulders, the hill was a natural position from which to defend this important end of the Union line. Several soldiers from both sides died in battle here on July 2, 1863.

Devil's Den marks the Union position on the second day of battle, July 2, 1863. The Confederate troops pushed the Union forces from this area.

Charge and countercharge on the afternoon of July 2, 1863 left the **wheatfield** and nearby woods strewn with more than 4,000 dead and wounded. The thousands of troops that fought in this area compared the fighting to a whirlpool, a stream of eddies and tides that flowed around the 19 acres of George Roses's wheatfield.

Culp's Hill was the important anchor for the right flank of the Union line at Gettysburg. The battle fought here July 3, 1863 ended with the Confederate Army retreating across Rock Creek, leaving the woods filled with dead and wounded. For the next 50 years, the dying trees on Culp's Hill bore scars of the battle.

Seminary Ridge was the primary Confederate position west of Gettysburg for the final two days of the battle. Confederate batteries still stand here.

The Angle marks the Union position on July 3, 1863 where the Federal soldiers stopped Confederate Gen. George E. Pickett's charge.

Troops destroyed the **peach orchard,** owned by Joseph Sherfy, during the battle. In the fighting, troops ransacked his house, tore apart fences, burned his barn to the ground, and in the process covered his fields with the dead.

The **Eternal Light Peace Memorial,** dedicated in 1938 by President Franklin Delano Roosevelt, memorializes the coming together of the union.

The **Gettysburg National Cemetery** contains more than 7,000 interments including more than 3,500 from the Civil War. It is also where President Abraham Lincoln delivered the Gettysburg Address in the dedication ceremonies on Nov. 19, 1863. | daily, dawn–dusk.

The **Cyclorama Center** contains the Gettysburg Cyclorama, a 360-ft-long circular oil-on-canvas painting depicting *Pickett's Charge,* the climactic moment of the three-day battle. Completed and exhibited in 1884, it is one of the last surviving cycloramas in the United States. There is a 20-minute film on the battle and exhibits. | Free | Daily 6 am–10 pm.

Gettysburg Railway. You can take 90-minute and four-hour trips on a diesel train. The theme rides include Civil War raids, a ride with Lincoln, dinner trips, fall foliage, a Santa train, an Easter bunny train, and a Halloween ghost train. | 106 N. Washington St. | 717/334–6932 or 888/94–TRAIN | fax 717/334–4746 | www.gettysburgrail.com. | $10 | Thur.–Sun., 10–3.

Ghosts of Gettysburg Candlelight Walking Tours. Guides take you on one of three different evening tours through sections of Gettysburg—outside houses and buildings where it's not as quiet as it should be and to cemeteries where the dead lie, though sometimes not so peacefully. Tours are on foot, but guides can be arranged to accompany private tour bus groups. | 271 Baltimore St. | 717/337–0445 | fax 717/337–9673 | www.gettysburg.com | $6.50 | Memorial Day–Labor Day, daily noon–8; Mar.–May and Oct., daily 2–8.

Hall of Presidents and First Ladies. The U.S. presidents are meticulously reproduced in wax and tell the story of America in their own voices. The wax replicas of the first ladies wear copies of their inaugural gowns. | 789 Baltimore St. | 717/334–5717 or 800/447–8788 | fax 717/334–6913 | www.gettysburgbattlefieldtour.com | $5.75 | Memorial Day–Labor Day daily 9–9., Mar. and Oct. 15–Thanksgiving daily 9-5; Apr. and Labor Day–Oct.15 daily 9-7.

Lincoln Room Museum. The Willis House is where Abraham Lincoln stayed and completed his Gettysburg Address on November 18, 1863. The furnishings in the home are original. | 12 Lincoln Sq | 717/334–8188 | fax 717/338–9491 | www.gettysburg.com | $3.50 | Memorial Day–Labor Day, daily 9–8; Labor Day–Memorial Day, Sun.–Thur., 10-5; Fri. and Sat., 10-8.

Lincoln Train Museum. You can ride and listen to reporters and distinguished people reenact their roles as they take the same route the president took from Washington, D.C., to Gettysburg where he ultimately gave his famous address. You can also visit an 1890 caboose, model train display, and military rail collection. | 425 Steinwehr Ave. | 717/334–5678 or 717/334–6296 | fax 717/334–6913. | www.gettysburgaddress.com | $5.75 | Daily Memorial Day–Labor Day 9–9, Mar. 10–5, Apr. and Sept. 9–7, Oct.–Nov. 9–5. Closed Dec.–Feb.

Lutheran Theological Seminary. Founded in 1826, this is the oldest Lutheran seminary on the continent. In 1863, during the Battle of Gettysburg, the buildings on the 52-acre campus played a role first as an observatory for Union soldiers, then as a signal station for the Confederates, and finally as a hospital for the wounded of both armies. | 61 Seminary Ridge | 717/334–6286 or 800/M–LUTHER | fax 717/334–3469 | www.ltsg.edu | Free | Mon.–Fri. 8:30–4:30.

National Civil War Wax Museum. The Civil War audiovisual presentation has more than 200 life-size figures in 30 scenes including a battle-room auditorium, a reenactment of the Battle of Gettysburg, and an animated Abraham Lincoln giving the Gettysburg Address. | 297 Steinwehr Ave. | 717/334–6245 | fax 717/334–9686 | www.e-gettysburg.cc | $4.50 | daily Memorial Day–Labor Day 9-9, Mar.–Apr. and Labor Day–Dec. 9-5, Jan.–Feb. weekends 9–5, weather permitting.

Ski Liberty. The 1,410-ft mountain has a 600-ft vertical drop, 16 trails, and eight lifts. The longest run is 5,200 ft. | 78 Country Club Trail, Carrol Valley | 717/642–8282 | www.skiliberty.com | $27–$42 | Dec.–Mar., weekdays 9–10 PM, weekends 8–10 PM.

Soldiers' National Museum. The headquarters for Union General Oliver O. Howard during the Battle of Gettysburg, this building became the Soldiers National Orphanage after the war and now has 60 displays of more than 5,000 Civil War items. | 777 Baltimore St. | 717/334–4890 or 717/334–6296 | fax 717/334–9100 | www.gettysburgaddress.com | $5.75 | Daily Jun.–Labor Day, 9–9; Mar.–Apr. and mid-Oct.–Thanksgiving 9-5, May and Sept.–mid-Oct. 9–7.

ON THE CALENDAR

MAR.: *Gettysburg Ghost Conference.* The International Ghost Hunters Society, which sponsors this event, says Gettysburg is "one of the most concentrated haunted spots in America." You can hear the stories at this annual conference, including seminars, lectures, walking ghost tours, and battlefield inspections. | 541/548–4418 | $80.

MAY: *Apple Blossom Festival.* You can take an orchard tour, eat apple foods, buy hand-made crafts, and watch various performers entertain during the 3 days of this festival at South Mountain Fairgrounds in Biglerville. | 717/677–7444.

JULY: *Civil War Heritage Days.* Rides, a carnival midway, and fireworks are part of this multiple-day event. There's also a reenactment of the Battle of Gettysburg. | 717/334–6274.

OCT.: *Apple Harvest Festival.* The emphasis is on apples and products like apple cider, caramel apples, and apple butter. There are free hayrides, scarecrow making, and crafts all at South Mountain Fairgrounds in Biglerville. | 717/677–9413.

Dining

Altland House. American. *Central Pennsylvania* magazine voted the Altland House the finest restaurant in Adams County. Twenty minutes east of downtown, this 1790 public tavern was supposedly President Eisenhower's favorite restaurant. The menu has seafood and meat, or lighter fare in the bar area. | Rte. 30 | 717/259–9535 | $12–$20 | AE, D, MC, V.

Blue Parrot Bistro. Eclectic. Here's a great place to take a party of friends with dissimilar eating tastes. White linen tablecloths cover each table, but the food ranges from pita pizza and creative homemade soups and salads to eggs benedict, fried rice with vegetables, pan-fried catfish, and porterhouse steaks. As the name suggests, parrot decorations fill a main dining room and a smaller side room. Both rooms have bars and there's also a pool table. | 35 Chambersburg St. | 717/337–3937 | Closed Mon.–Sun. | $10–$25 | AE, D, DC, MC, V.

Dobbin House. Continental. Listed on the National Register of Historic Places, this tavern and inn has servers wearing period clothing. The building is the oldest in Gettysburg. It was a stop on the Underground Railroad and a hospital during the Civil War. You can order a meal like those eaten in the 1700s and eat it while reclining under a bed canopy, part of the restaurant's seating area. Choose from prime rib, roast duck over apples with a cit-rus–orange sauce, or a pork tenderloin with raspberry sauce. For dessert there's apple pie and pecan pie. Kids' menu. | 89 Steinwehr Ave. | 717/334–2100 | fax 717/334–6905 | No lunch | $16–$34 | Reservations required | AE, D, MC, V.

Dunlap's Restaurant and Bakery. American. This casual spot is owned by a couple who fell in love with the town and bought the restaurant after visiting their son at Gettysburg College. You can get burgers, sandwiches, and salads, but save room for a piece of freshly baked cake or pie. | 90 Buford Ave. | 717/334–4816 | $5–$10 | D, MC, V.

★ **Farnsworth House Inn.** Southern. You can eat like a Civil War soldier: wild game pie, peanut soup, pumpkin fritters, and spoon bread. The historic home has more than 100 bullet holes from the war. You are invited to tour the attic full of Civil War memorabilia and see the sharpshooter's post. Kids' menu. | 401 Baltimore St. | 717/334–8838 | Reserva-tions essential | $8–$15 | AE, D, MC, V.

General Pickett's All-U-Can-Eat Buffet. American. Here "all you can eat" takes on new meaning. You can fill up on homemade soups, bread, pies, and cakes as well as American buffet mainstays like fried chicken and roast beef. | 571 Steinwehr Ave. | 717/334–7580 | $8–$12 | AE, DC, MC, V.

Gettysbrew Restaurant and Brewery. Contemporary. Housed in a building that was used as a field hospital by the Confederate Army during the Civil War, Gettysbrew has a patio overlooking the surrounding farmland where many Civil War battles took place. There are no fried items or hamburgers on the menu, but you can order steaks or seafood focaccia (shrimp, blue crab with cheese and herbs on Italian flatbread). Kids' menu. | 248 Hunter-stown Rd. | 717/337–1001 | No lunch weekdays | $10–$15 | D, MC, V.

Gingerbread Man. American. There are brass fixtures, exposed brick walls, and pho-tographs and prints of the Civil War and Battle at Gettysburg. Fresh crab cakes and large salads are popular choices. Known for New York-style deli sandwiches. Kids' menu. | 217 Stein-wehr Ave. | 717/334–1100 | $9–$18 | AE, D, DC, MC, V.

Herr Tavern and Publick House. Continental. Built in 1815, this tavern survived a direct hit on its second floor from artillery during the Battle of Gettysburg and it served as the first Confederate hospital. The dining room has a view of the Gettysburg Battlefield. You can choose from roast duck, blackened prime rib, and chicken Chesapeake (breast stuffed with crabmeat and topped with supreme sauce). End your meal with homemade cheesecake, pecan pie, or apple dumplings. Eat on the porch overlooking nearby farmland. Kids' menu. | 900 Chambersburg Rd. | 717/334–4332 | No lunch Sun. | $14–$26 | D, MC, V.

Hickory Bridge Farm. American. Meals in the 150-year-old barn with antiques and knick-knacks are home-cooked and large, often served family-style. | 96 Hickory Bridge Rd. | 717/642–5261 or 800/642–1766 | Reservations essential | Closed Mon.–Thu. No lunch Fri., Sat. No dinner Sun. | $7–$15 | MC, V.

Historic Cashtown Inn. Continental. This meat-and-potato menu is reminiscent of home-cooked food from the Civil War era. The restaurant is in an old building with walk-up porch, 8 mi west of downtown Gettysburg. | 1325 Old Rte. 30 | 717/334–9722 or 800/367–1797 | Closed Mon. No lunch Sun. | $8–$15 | AE, D, MC, V.

Lincoln Diner. American. Locals flock to the Lincoln Diner for its cheesecake, as well as cakes, pies, and Greek pastries. Menu choices include the anytime-of-day breakfast and a daily special. | 32 Carlisle St. | 717/334–3900 | Open 24 hours | $4–$8 | No credit cards.

Pub and Restaurant. Eclectic. A casual, friendly downtown restaurant with an extensive menu ranging from Tex-Mex to pitas to burgers. Try the chicken marsala, broiled scallops, or sausage jambalaya. | 20-22 Lincoln Sq. | 717/334–7100 | fax 717/334–8081 | $7–$20 | AE, MC, V.

Stonehenge. Continental. If you're tired of Civil War history, try this restaurant where photographs and prints from the early rock-and-roll era line the walls. The menu has New York strip steak, and a large platter of crab legs, shrimp, clams, and broiled fish. For dessert, there's apple-walnut-raisin cake. Kids' menu. Live entertainment, karaoke, Tues.–Sun. | 985 Baltimore Pike | 717/334–9227 | fax 717/334–5044 | $6–$20 | AE, D, DC, MC, V.

Lodging

Baladerry Inn. On four acres with a gazebo, the brick Federal home was built in 1812. You can stay in the original home or a newer addition. Some rooms have private patios and fireplaces. Complimentary breakfast. No TV, TV in common area. Tennis. No kids under 14. | 40 Hospital Rd. | 717/337–1342 | fax 717/337–1342 | 8 rooms (7 with shower only) | $110–$160 | AE, D, DC, MC, V.

Baltimore Street Bed and Breakfast. Central to town and within easy walking distance of the Gettysburg National Military Park Visitors Center, the Gettysburg National Cemetery, and a host of small museums and shops, this Gothic Revival Victorian was built in 1868. You can borrow one of the 500 Civil War-related books in the library and grab a seat in a rocking chair on the front porch for a relaxing, yet educational hour or two of reading. Complimentry Continental breakfast. No pets. No smoking. | 449 Baltimore St. | 717/334–2454 or 888/667–8266 | tannery@cvn.net | www.baltimorestreetbandb.com | 7 rooms, 3 suites | $100 | MC, V.

Battlefield. Here you can stay in an 1809 stone farmhouse on 46 acres with a pond facing the South Cavalry Battlefield of the Battle of Gettysburg. Rooms are named for generals or infantry divisions that fought here or fired upon the property. You can take a carriage ride from here. Complimentary breakfast. No room phones, no TV in rooms, TV in common area. Kids' programs (5 and up), playground. No smoking. | 2264 Emmittsburg Rd. | 717/334–8804 | fax 717/334–7330 | www.gettysburgbattlefield.com | 8 rooms | $135–$185 | AE, D, DC, MC, V.

★ **Best Western Gettysburg Hotel.** In the center of town, this 1797 white brick building served as the summer White House during the Eisenhower administration. Restaurant, bar, room service. In-room data ports, some refrigerators, some in-room hot tubs, cable TV. Pool. Hot tub. Laundry service. Business services. | 1 Lincoln Sq | 717/337–2000 | fax 717/337–2075 | www.webscaper.com/getty | 83 rooms, 23 suites | $105–$165 rooms, $110–$165 suites | AE, D, DC, MC, V.

Brafferton. The original townhouse here, a half block from Lincoln Square, was built in stone in 1786 with a brick addition added in 1815. You can find bullet holes from the Battle of Gettysburg in some walls. The townhouse once served as a chapel. Complimentary breakfast. No room phones, no TV in some rooms. | 44 York St. | 717/337–3423 | fax 717/334–8185 | www.braffertoninn.com | 12 rooms | $90–$150 | AE, D, MC, V.

Brickhouse Inn Bed and Breakfast. Guest rooms in this 1898 brick Victorian are furnished with antiques and reproductions. You can relax in one of two formal parlors. Complimentary breakfast. | 452 Baltimore St. | 717/338–9337 or 800/864–3464 | fax 717/338–9265 | www.brickhouseinn.com | 7 rooms | $90–$140 | AE, D, MC, V.

College Motel. This small one-story motel across the street from Gettysburg College caters to parents and others visiting the college. Cable TV. Pool. | 345 Carlisle St. | 717/334–6731 or 800/367–6731 | www.gettysburg.com | 21 rooms | $85–$140 | AE, MC, V.

Colonial Motel. This small motel is near Gettysburg College and two blocks north of the square. Cable TV. | 157 Carlisle St. | 717/334–3126 | www.gettysburg.com | 30 rooms | $75–$85 | AE, D, MC, V.

Comfort Inn. National Military Park is near this hotel, 1 mi east of downtown. Complimentary Continental breakfast. Some refrigerators, some in-room hot tubs, cable TV. Indoor pool. Hot tub. | 871 York Rd. | 717/337–2400 | fax 717/337–2400 | www.comfortinn.com | 81 rooms, 3 suites | $95–$105 rooms, $120 suites | AE, D, DC, MC, V.

Cross Keys Motor Inn. This moderately priced motor hotel is 10 mi east of Gettysburg. Restaurant, bar, room service. Some in-room hot tubs, cable TV. Business services. | 6110 York Rd./U.S. 30, New Oxford | 717/624–7778 | fax 717/624–7941 | 64 rooms | $49–$83 | AE, D, MC, V.

Days Inn. It's only a mile from downtown and the National Military Park to this motel. There's a family-style restaurant next door to this motel. Complimentary Continental breakfast. In-room data ports, some microwaves, some refrigerators, cable TV. Outdoor pool. Exercise equipment. Video games. Laundry facilities. Business services, free parking. | 865 York Rd./U.S. 30 | 717/334–0030 | fax 717/337–1002 | 112 rooms | $90–$100 | AE, D, DC, MC, V.

Doubleday Inn Bed and Breakfast. This B&B is on Oak Ridge overlooking the battlefield. Decorated in English country fashion, the inn has two patios, several common rooms, a library, and dining room. Complimentary breakfast. No smoking. | 104 Doubleday Ave. | 717/334–9119 | www.bedandbreakfast.com | 9 rooms | $84–$104 | D, MC, V.

★ **Farnsworth House Inn.** This inn is an early 19th-century Federal brick house that Confederate sharpshooters occupied during the Battle of Gettysburg. You can take a tour of the house and cellar, rumored to be haunted. Rooms have Victorian furnishings and some have claw-foot bathtubs. An art gallery and bookstore are on the premises. Restaurant, complimentary breakfast. No room phones, TV in common area. Shops, library. Business services. | 401 Baltimore St. | 717/334–8838 | fax 717/334–5862 | farnhaus@mail.cvn.net | www.farnsworthhousedining.com | 9 rooms | $95–$160 | AE, D, MC, V.

Gaslight. Many original details from this 1872 mansion are intact, including its Italianate front. The gardens provide an oasis in the heart of Gettysburg. Some rooms have fireplaces, and several of the showers are 5-ft stalls with steam spas. Off-street parking. Dining room, complimentary breakfast. Some in-room hot tubs, cable TV, some in-room VCRs. No kids under 12. Business services. | 33 E. Middle St. | 717/337–9100 | fax 717/337–9616 | www.thegaslight.com | 9 rooms (7 with shower only) | $110–$150 | AE, D, MC, V.

Gettysburg Pond View Farm Inn. You can eat breakfast in bed at this Civil War-era brick farmhouse in the country about 15 min from Gettysburg. Guest rooms have queen beds and private baths. Complimentary breakfast. | 530 Carr Hill Rd. | 717/642–9493 | smutans57@aol.com | www.bbonline.com/pa/pondview/ | 3 rooms | $75–$85 | D, MC, V.

Gettystown Inn. Across from the National Cemetery, this inn is on the grounds of the Dobbin House restaurant. The rooms have Victorian furnishings. Restaurant, complimentary breakfast. Some kitchenettes, refrigerators, some room phones, no TV in some rooms. No kids under 5. No smoking. | 89 Steinwehr Ave. | 717/334–2100 | fax 717/334–6905 | info@dobbinhouse.com | www.dobbinhouse.com | 4 rooms, 3 suites | $95–$110 rooms, $125–$150 suites | AE, D, MC, V.

Herr Tavern and Publick House. Antiques set the scene in this antebellum tavern and inn 1 mi from town square. All rooms have fireplaces. You can sit on the front porch and see a pond with a watergarden. Restaurant, complimentary breakfast, room service. Some microwaves, some refrigerators, some in-room hot tubs, cable TV, some in-room VCRs. No kids under 12. No smoking. | 900 Chambersburg Rd. | 717/334–4332 or 800/362–9849 | fax 717/334–3332 | info@herrtavern.com | www.herrtavern.com | 12 rooms | $100–$180 | D, MC, V.

Holiday Inn Express. Next to a family fun center with miniature golf, this hotel is 3 mi from the National Military Park and less than a mile from downtown. Picnic area, complimentary Continental breakfast. In-room data ports, some microwaves, some refrigerators, cable TV. Indoor pool. Hot tub. No pets. | 869 York Rd./U.S. 30 | 717/337–1400 | fax 717/337–1400, ext. 301 | www.hiexpress.com | 51 rooms | $89–$119 | AE, D, DC, MC, V.

Home Sweet Home Motel. You can walk to the Battlefield Visitors Center from this motel or take advantage of its free shuttle service. Complimentary Continental breakfast. Cable TV, room phones. | 593 Steinwehr Ave. | 717/334–3916 or 800/440–3916 | 40 rooms | $65 | AE, D, MC, V.

Homestead Motor Lodge. You have moderate rates and easy access to and from the Route 15 bypass at this small motel. It's only 3 mi from downtown Gettysburg. Picnic area. Cable TV. Laundry facilities. No pets. No smoking. | 1650 York Rd./U.S. 30 | 717/334–3866 | 10 rooms | $59–$79 | Closed Dec.–Mar. | AE, D, MC, V.

James Gettys Hotel. All rooms are suites in this hotel, established in 1804. You can enjoy high tea in the British-sytle tea room, a half block from town square. Restaurant, complimentary Continental breakfast. Kitchenettes, microwaves, refrigerators, cable TV. Laundry service. Business services. No smoking. | 27 Chambersburg St. | 717/337–1334 | fax 717/334–2103 | 11 suites (1 with shower only) | $125–$145 | AE, D, MC, V.

Keystone Inn Bed and Breakfast. A three-story, late Victorian, built in 1913, with leaded glass windows, polished wood floors, and lots of lace and flowers. You can relax on the huge wraparound porch outfitted with wicker furniture. Complimentary breakfast. Cable TV. | 231 Hanover St. | 717/337–3888 | 6 rooms | $69–$109 | D, MC, V.

Lightner Farmhouse Bed and Breakfast. On 19 acres of countryside, this farmhouse served as a hospital for Union troops during the battle of Gettysburg. You can relax in the common room filled with oak furniture. The owner here is likely to ask you to sample one of his home brews. Complimentary breakfast. TV in common area. | 2350 Baltimore Pike | 717/337–9508 | lightner@cvn.net | www.cvn.net/~lightner | 4 rooms | $95–$115.

Quality Inn. Next door to the Gettysburg National Park Visitor's Center, this hotel is 1 mi south of downtown. Bar. In-room data ports, some kitchenettes, some in-room hot tubs, cable TV. 1 outdoor pool, 1 indoor pool. Hot tub, sauna. Putting green. Exercise equipment. Laundry facilities. | 380 Steinwehr Ave. | 717/334–1103 | fax 717/334–1103 | gburgqi@mail.cvn.net | www.qualityinn.com | 109 rooms | $79–$110 | AE, D, DC, MC, V.

Quality Inn Larson's. Next to General Lee's headquarters near Seminary Ridge, this Colonial-style motel is only eight blocks from downtown. Restaurant, bar, complimentary Continental breakfast. Some microwaves, some refrigerators, some in-room hot tubs, cable TV. Pool. Business services. | 401 Buford Ave. | 717/334–3141 | fax 717/334–1813 | www.qualityinn.com | 43 rooms | $79–$99 | AE, D, DC, MC, V.

Red Carpet Inn Perfect Rest. At the edge of the National Military Park, this motel is 1 mi from the Battlefield and 4½ mi from downtown. There are several restaurants nearby. Picnic area. Cable TV. Pool. | 2450 Emmitsburg Rd. | 717/334–1345 or 800/336–1345 | fax 717/334–5026 | www.gettysburg.com | 25 rooms | $45–$89 | AE, D, DC, MC, V.

GREENSBURG

(Nearby towns also listed: New Stanton, Ligonier, Donegal)

Named in honor of General Nathanial Green, today Greensburg is a growing city with many shopping centers, hotels and restaurants. Its downtown includes a tavern that was frequented by General Green during the Whisky Rebellion. Seton Hall University and the University of Pittsburgh–Greensburg are here.

Information: **Central Westmoreland Chamber of Commerce** | R.D. 1, Box 240, PA 15601 | 724/834–2900 | info@westmorelandpa.com | www.westmorelandpa.com.

Attractions

Bushy Run Battlefield. This is the site of a key battle between the British and Native Americans in Pontiac's Rebellion on Aug. 5–6, 1763. Pontiac, an Ottawa chief, led warriors from various tribes against the British to protest strict regulations that limited provisions for Native American people. One of the few British victories in the rebellion prevented Fort Pitt from being captured. The British troops were able to withstand a seige and Pontiac subsequently dissolved his Indian confederacy. You can see exhibits and educational programs at the visitor center. The 183-acre area has 3 mi of hiking trails, picnic areas, and there are guided and self-guided tours of the battlefield. | Rte. 993, Jeannette | 724/527–5584 | fax 724/527–5610 | $2 | Apr.–Oct. 31, Wed.–Sun. 9–5. Closed Mon.–Tues.

Historic Hanna's Town. The first county seat west of the Allegheny Mountains, this 18th-century town was destroyed on July 13; 1782, but has been reconstructed. Costumed guides give tours of the courthouse-tavern, log fort, Klingensmith House, and archaeological excavations. You can see demonstrations of Colonial skills and crafts. | On Forbes Road; Between U.S. Rte. 819/119 | 724/836–1800 | history@wchspa.com | $3 | May–Sep., Tue.–Sat. 10–4, Sun. 1–4; Apr. and Oct., Sat. 10–4, Sun. 1–4.

Keystone State Park. The 1,200-acre park has a 78-acre lake where you can boat, swim, fish, ice skate, and ice fish. Or you can picnic, bicycle, hike, hunt, sled, and cross-country ski. There are 100 campsites and 11 modern cabins. | R.R. 2, Derry 15627 | 724/668–2939, 724/668–2566, or 888/PA–PARKS | www.dcnr.state.pa.us | Free | Daily 8 am–dusk.

Lincoln Highway Heritage Corridor. At the turn of the 20th century, a group of automotive businessmen came up with a plan to build a national system of paved roads. That idea led to construction of the Lincoln Highway (now Route 30), the nation's first transcontinental highway. A 150-mi stretch of the highway through Westmoreland, Somerset, Bedford, Fulton, and Franklin counties has been designated as a heritage corridor. | Box 386 | 724/837–9750 | fax 724/837–9751 | www.lhhc.org | Free | Mon.–Fri., 8–5.

Westmoreland County Courthouse. Built in 1906, the four-story building is one of the region's Beaux Arts buildings. It has a 175-ft high central dome and is one of only two in the world designed by the courthouse's original architect, William Kauffman. | 2 N. Main St. | 724/830–3000 | Free | Weekdays 8:30–4.

Westmoreland Museum of American Art. This museum preserves, exhibits, and interprets American works of art and toys from the late 18th century to the present, with an emphasis on southwestern Pennsylvania art. There are educational programs for kids and adults. | 221 N. Main St. | 724/837–1500 | fax 724/837–2921 | info@wmuseumaa.org | www.wmuseumaa.org | Free | Wed., Fri.–Sun. 11–5, Thurs. 11–9, closed Mon.–Tues.

ON THE CALENDAR

JUNE–JULY: *Westmoreland Arts and Heritage Festival.* More than 100,000 people attend this annual four-day festival at Twin Lakes Park, featuring crafts and entertainment from near and far. Check out the live entertainment on the floating stage on the lake, or stroll past the booths set up under the trees. | 724/834–7474 ext.4.

Dining

Carbone's. Italian. In a single-story brown building, this restaurant has been serving patrons since 1938. It is also a popular nightspot. The look is Mediterranean with archways, stucco, and Italian tile. The beef braciole (rolled stuffed steak in a tomato sauce) and the Italian sampler (gnocchi and homemade pastas) are always popular. Kids' menu. | Rte. 119, Crabtree | 724/834–3430 | fax 724/836–2501 | No lunch. Closed Sun. | $5–$18. | AE, D, DC, MC, V.

Fatz Zackel's Fish House. Seafood. Here's a simple diner with a nautical look and a huge fish sandwich. Order the Big Fish (one pound!) and you'll be asking where the bun is. | 2001 Main St. | 724/744–2907 | Reservations not accepted | Closed Sun. | $6–15 | AE, MC, V.

Jioio's. Italian. White-and-red-checkered tablecloths and candles in wine bottle candleholders cover the tables here. The homemade sauces are so popular that they are sold independently. Family-style service. Try the cavatelli or pizza. | 939 Carbon Rd. | 724/836–6676 | $11–$22 | Reservations not accepted | MC, V.

Red Star Brewing. Cajun/Creole. Here in the city's old railroad station you can still catch a train on one end or have a freshly brewed beer at the other end, in the station's former lobby. The two-tiered dining area overlooks the large square oak bar and the station's orig-

PENNSYLVANIA SUDS

Mention northern California businesses to a traveler and invariably thoughts of the area's wine regions come to mind. Ask that same person about Pennsylvania businesses and thoughts of steel and railroads might enter the conversation. But, there's more to Pennsylvania's business sector than factories and steel.

Beer has long played a part in Pennsylvania's history. In a time when microbreweries are popping up all over the country, Pennsylvania's Yuengling Brewery holds the distinction of being the oldest brewery in America. Straub Brewery is the smallest pre-prohibition brewery in the nation. Nearly every large town, and even some smaller towns, have a brewery within its limits. And, except for Latrobe's Rolling Rock, none of the state's breweries mass-produce their beer. The breweries cater to a loyal Pennsylvania following.

There are more than 50 brewing establishments in the state, more than in any state in the country and many of those are in the brewpub category. Unlike their big brothers, brewpubs cater to the restaurant crowd as well as to lovers of suds. Their locations range from the traditional roadside restaurant to pubs in a small commercial airport, a converted church, factory buildings, and old movie theaters.

So while in northern California you can sip some of the world's greatest wines, in Pennsylvania you can enjoy some suds with history and tour facilities that have been around since before the turn of the 20th century.

inal clock. Specials are Kentucky roasted back ribs, gumbo, and homemade warm ginger-bread stout cake. | 101 Ehalt St. | 724/850–7245 | $10–$25 | AE, D, DC, MC, V.

Rialto Cafe. Italian. Built in 1796, this was the first stone structure in the area, once a popular stagecoach stop and now on the National Register of Historic Places. The brick dining room has the original oak bar. It's known for homemade lasagna, chicken parmesan, and their very own spumoni. | 25 W. Otterman St. | 724/834–8010 | $7–$15 | AE, MC, V.

Lodging

Comfort Inn. This hotel is near Exit 7 of the Pennsylvania Turnpike, east of Greensburg. Complimentary Continental breakfast. Some refrigerators, some in-room hot tubs, cable TV. Pool. Exercise equipment. Laundry service. Business services, airport shuttle. | 1129 E. Pittsburgh St. | 724/832–2600 | fax 724/834–3442 | www.comfortinn.com | 77 rooms | $85–$120 | AE, D, DC, MC, V.

Four Points by Sheraton. This hotel is near Exit 7 of the Pennsylvania Turnpike. Restaurant, bar with entertainment. Some refrigerators, cable TV. Indoor pool. Gym, volleyball. Business services, airport shuttle. Pets allowed (fee). | 100 Sheraton Dr./U.S. 30 E | 724/836–6060 | fax 724/834–5640 | www.sheraton.com | 146 rooms | $80–$95 | AE, D, DC, MC, V.

Hampton Inn Greensburg. A 5-story hotel in the middle of town. It's 3 mi from the county courthouse and the art museum. Complimentary Continental breakfast. In-room data ports, some hot tubs, cable TV. Outdoor pool. Exercise equipment. Laundry service. | 1000 Towne Sq. Dr. | 724/838–8800 | www.hamptoninns.com | 69 rooms | $85 | AE, D, DC, MC, V.

Holiday Inn Express Greensburg. This three-story hotel is about 2 mi from the town center, with Westmoreland Mall less than 1 mi away. Restaurants are within walking distance. Complimentary Continental breakfast. In-room data ports, cable TV. Indoor pool. Laundry service. | R.R. 7, Rte. 30 E | 724/838–7070 | fax 724/838–8136 | brygadr@aol.com | 57 rooms | $80 | AE, D, DC, MC, V.

Knights Inn. This motel is 1 mi from downtown and near Bushy Run. In-room data ports, some microwaves, some refrigerators, cable TV. Outdoor pool. Laundry facilities. Business services. | 1215 S. Main St. | 724/836–7100 or 800/843–5644 | fax 724/837–5390 | www.knightsinn.com | 108 rooms | $60–$70 | AE, D, DC, MC, V.

Mountain View Inn. This wood and brick inn dates to the 1920s, and has views of the Chestnut Ridge Mountains. Restaurant, bar, complimentary Continental breakfast, room service. In-room data ports, some microwaves, some refrigerators, some in-room hot tubs, cable TV. Pool. Exercise equipment. Laundry service. Business services. | 1001 Village Dr. | 724/834–5300 | fax 724/834–5304 | www.mountainviewinn.com | 93 rooms | $79–$145 | AE, D, DC, MC, V.

HAMBURG

MAP 7, J5

(Nearby towns also listed: Fogelsville, Kutztown, Shartlesville, Reading)

Founded in 1779, Hamburg lies on the east bank of the Schuylkill River and is just 17 mi north of Reading. Its name comes from German immigrants who settled in the area. Today it's a popular destination for travelers on I–78 and for people heading to the Hawk Mountain Sanctuary.

Information: **Berks County Chamber of Commerce** | 601 Penn St., Reading, PA 19601 | 610/376–6766 | www.berkschamber.org.

Attractions

Blue Rocks. A river of boulders and rocks that glaciers left as part of a moraine, Blue Rocks cascades down over the mountain. Also on site are 190 campsites and two hiking trails. |

341 Sousley Rd., Lenhartsville | 610/756–6366 | $3 | Apr.–Nov. 1, Mon.–Thur. 9–7, Fri.–Sat. 9–11, Sun. 8–7.

Hawk Mountain Sanctuary. You can see thousands of raptors at this 2,400-acre nature observation area, where an average of 18,000 hawks, eagles, and falcons pass through during raptor migration between August 15 and December 15. Ospreys and thousands of hawks arrive in September. October brings the greatest variety of species. A total of 235 species of birds have been seen near this area, where you can see the Appalachian Mountains. There are wildlife programs, workshops, and lectures, a rugged 8-mi trail sytem, and a native plant garden. | 1700 Hawk Mountain Rd., Kempton | 610/756–6000, 610/756–6961 or 610/756–6961 | fax 610/756–4468 | www.hawkmountain.org | $6 | Trails, daily dawn to dusk. Visitor Center, daily Dec.–Aug. 9–5, Sept.–Nov. 8–5.

Kersher Creek Park. Less than a mile east of Hamburg on Route 22, this 40-acre park has a lake, a kids' play area, and hiking trails. Fishing is available. | Rte. 78 | 610/374–8839. | Free | 9–dusk.

Wanamaker, Kempton and Southern Inc. Travel on the tourist railroad with a steam locomotive that gives 6½-mi round-trip rides through Berks and Lehigh Counties along Maiden Creek. | Turn off Route 22 (I–78) at Krumsville (Exit 12/Rt. 737) or Lenhartsville (Exit 11/Rt. 143) and travel north to Kempton and the WK&S Railroad | 610/756–6469 | www.wknsrr.com | $5 | May–Oct. weekends 1–4.

ON THE CALENDAR

MAY: *Family Festival.* Held every Memorial Day weekend in Hamburg Boro Park, the festival is a small-town fair with rides, food vendors, and local musicians. | 610/562–4403 | $3.

Dining

Jack D's. Contemporary. This family-style restaurant is housed in a large brick warehouse that used to be a knitting factory. Eat outside at their sidewalk cafe, or indoors surrounded by art. The veal and chicken dishes are popular, or try the piccata and pasta parmigiana. On Saturdays choose prime rib, and for dessert, tiramisu or cappuccino eclairs. | 202 S. Third St. | 610/562–1488 | Sun.–Thurs. 11–10, Fri.–Sat. 11–11 | $6–$17 | D, MC, V.

Lodging

Fort Motel. About a 10-minute drive north of Hamburg in Orwigsburg, this small, independently run hotel is the closest hotel to Hamburg. Cable TV. No pets. | 1223 Rte. 61, Orwigsburg | 570/366–2091 | 12 rooms | $40 | MC, V.

HANOVER

MAP 7, H7

(Nearby towns also listed: Gettysburg, York)

Known as "no man's land" when it was settled in 1731, Hanover used to be a hiding place for outlaws from all over the region. Today the borough is home to shoemakers, potato chip producers, and pretzel vendors. The town center has many homes of Federal, Queen Anne, Victorian, Georgian Revival, and Art Deco styles. Hanover, Pennsylvania, is named for Hanover, Germany, and today is known as the Black Rose Community because members of the royal family of the house of Hannover in Germany wore a Hannover Black Rose insignia to indicate their lineage. The insignia was adopted as the local community insignia in 1978.

Information: **Hanover Chamber of Commerce** | 146 Carlisle St., 17331 | 717/637–6130 | chamber@hanoverchamber.com | www.hanoverchamber.com.

Attractions

Codorus State Park. The 3,326-acre park includes 1,275-acre Lake Marburg, with 26 mi of shoreline and fishing, boating, and ice skating. The park has 198 campsites, swimming and wading pools, a 5-mi hiking system, a 7-mi horseback trail, picnic facilities, boat rentals, hunting on 2,900 acres, 100 acres for snowmobiling, 300 acres for cross-country skiing, and a 2½–acre slope for sledding. | 1066 Blooming Grove Rd. | 717/637–2816, 717/637–2418, or 888/PA-PARKS | fax 717/637–4720 | www.dcnr.state.pa.us | Free; pool $4. | Daily 8 am–dusk.

Conewago Chapel. On the National Register of Historic Places, the log chapel built in 1741 on this site was destroyed to be replaced by the present chapel in 1787. In 1962 the church was named a basilica. Prince Demetrius Gallitzin, the first Catholic priest to receive all of his orders in the United States, was the priest here until moving to Loretto. | 30 Basilica Dr. | 717/637–2721 | www.dioceseofharrisburg.org | Free | Daily dawn to dusk.

Fire Museum. You can find old pumps and other pieces of firefighting equipment dating back to 1770 at this museum, owned and operated by the Hanover Fire Department. | 201 N. Franklin St. | 717/637–6671 | Free | Daily 10–8.

Neas House Museum. The home of Mathias Neas and Hanover's first burgess, the Georgian mansion was built about 1783. It's furnished from the 1815 estate inventory. The museum has items of local culture and crafts from the late 18th and early 19th centuries. | 113 W. Chestnut St. | 717/632–3207 | fax 717/632–5199 | www.hellohanover.com. | $1 | May–Oct., Tues.–Fri. 10–1, closed Sat.–Mon.

Utz Quality Foods, Inc. This potato chip company was started in 1821 by Bill and Salie Utz, who were dissatisfied with the quality of chips being produced at the time. You can take a self-guided tour at an observation tower to see how to make potato chips, and receive a bag of potato chips when you finish your tour. An outlet store sells Utz products. | 900 High St. | 717/637–6644 or 800/367–7629 | fax 717/637–1058 | www.utzsnacks.com | Free | Mon.–Thurs. 8–4, closed Fri.–Sun.

ON THE CALENDAR

JULY: *Hanover Dutch Festival.* One of the largest single-day outdoor craft fairs on the East Coast, this annual festival was founded to promote community awareness and pride in Hanover's Dutch heritage. Browse the 280 craft and food stands (try the bratwurst and funnel cakes), or listen to Dutch and German performers. Open-house tours, an antique car show, a Pennsylvania Dutch worship service, and a kids' carnival are other attractions. The festival is held the last Saturday in July in downtown Hanover. | 717/637–6130 | $80.

Dining

Patty & John's Restaurant. Continental. Originally a barn built in 1887, this restaurant overlooks a golf course 3 mi outside of Hanover. The original wood beams and floors are intact; there's also local artwork, a huge fireplace, an enclosed porch, and a patio. Popular dishes are the veal piccata and chicken with crab meat, asparagus tips, and béchamel sauce. Try a chocolate torte for dessert. | 1161 Westminster Ave. | 717/637–2200 | fax 717/637–1322. | Sun.–Mon. | Tues.–Sat. 4–10. | $17 | AE, MC, V.

Lodging

Beechmont. This small bed-and-breakfast is in an early 19th-century Federal home furnished with antiques. You can sit on benches in the gardens or view them from the front porch and parlor. Some rooms have fireplaces. Complimentary breakfast. Some refrigerators, cable TV. Library. Business services. No kids under 12. | 315 Broadway | 717/632–3013 or 800/553–7009 | www.thebeechmont.com | 4 rooms, 3 suites | $90–$105 rooms, $115–$145 suites | AE, MC, V.

Sheppard Mansion Bed & Breakfast. Built in 1913, this neoclassical Greek Revival home was where the Sheppard family once entertained prestigious guests, "from princesses to politicians." Each room is designed in a different style, from Art Deco and Rococo to French

Provincial and Mission-style. Call before-hand if you have kids. Complimentary breakfast. Cable TV. No pets. | 117 Frederick St. | 717/633–8075 | fax 717/633–8074. | reservations@sheppardmansion.com | www.sheppardmansion.com | 9 rooms | $160–$210 | MC, V.

HARMONY

MAP 7, B5

(Nearby towns also listed: Beaver Falls, Butler, Gibsonia, New Castle)

The site of the first communal settlement in the region is at the heart of Harmony's history. Led by George Rapp, the Harmony Society came to the area to live what they called primitive Christianity. Many of the frame houses built by the Harmony Society remain undisturbed, as does Rapp's thronelike rock that overlooks the city from high on a hill and is dubbed "Father Rapp's Seat."

Information: **Butler County Chamber of Commerce** | 201 S. Main St., Butler, PA 16003 | 724/283–2222 | info@butlercountychamber.com. | www.butlercountychamber.com.

Attractions

Harmonist Cemetery. There are no headstones here, as was the Harmonist custom. You can find this cemetery on Route 68 just east of town. A massive revolving stone gate marks the entrance; it's inscribed in German with "Here rest 100 members of the Harmony Society, who died from 1805 to 1815." The cemetery is enclosed in a stone wall built by Mennonites in 1869. | Off West Street | 724/452–7341 | Free. | Daily, all hours.

Harmony Museum. A National Historic Landmark, this was the first home of the Harmonists and the beginning of Father George Rapp's religious society in 1804. Rapp had 600 followers who came here from Germany for religious freedom. They set up a community on 5,000 acres where they lived for 10 years. The homes are intact and have period furnishings. | 218 Mercer St. | 724/452–7341 and 888/821–4822 | $3.50 | Tues.–Sun. 1–4, closed Mon.

ON THE CALENDAR

AUG.: *Dankfest.* Costumed artisans demonstrate 18th-century crafts and provide museum and National Historic District tours of the first American homes of the German Communal Harmony Society. | Harmony Museum, 218 Mercer St. | 724/452–7341 or 888/821–4822.

DEC.: *Christmas Open House.* Candelight tours of the Harmony Museum and Ziegler Log House are part of this holiday event. | 724/452–7341 or 888/821–4822.

Dining

Harmony Inn. Eclectic. Built in 1856, the Harmony Inn has retained much of its original design. The inn is next door to the Harmony Museum and serves a combination of Continental, American, and Mexican cuisine; meats are smoked in the backyard. You can try barbecue ribs with campfire beans and coleslaw, or cracked-peppercorn T-bone steak with garlic mashed potatoes and vegetables. Other specials are German potato salad with bratwurst on rye, spicy Creole-style crab, shrimp, and chicken with red beans and rice. You can eat inside or out on the patio. | 230 Mercer St. | 724/452–5124 | Mon.-Thurs. 11:30–9, Fri.–Sat. 11:30–10, Sun. 11:30–8 | $9 | AE, D, DC, MC, V.

Log Cabin Inn. Contemporary. This is a real log cabin with memorabilia and antiques, including old logging tools and farming implements. Known for its seafood and prime rib. | 430 Perry Hwy. | 724/452–4155 | $12–$20 | AE, MC, V.

Lodging

Zelienople Motel. About ¼ mi out of town on 6 acres of open land, this old brick ranch-style motel offers quiet and simple lodging. There's a creek on the property. Cable TV. Pets allowed (fee). | 238 Perry Hwy. | 724/452–7900 | fax 724/452–7900 | 27 rooms | $40–$60 | AE, D, DC, MC, V.

HARRISBURG

(Nearby towns also listed: Boiling Springs, Camp Hill, Carlisle, Hershey, Mechanicsburg, Middletown)

The Capital City is also the heart of the state with nearly all major roadways meeting in this one place. Its importance to travelers can be traced back to the days of riverboats that traveled along the Susquehanna River. Because of its location on the river and its placement in the center of the state, Harrisburg became the capital in 1812.

The city played a large part in the early development of the Pennsylvania canal system and the local railroads, highways, and airlines. Today, it is one of the most important commercial centers and distribution points in the East because of its relatively short distance from Baltimore, Washington, D.C., Philadelphia, and Pittsburgh.

In Colonial days, John Harris operated a ferry along the Susquehanna, and he and his son first laid out the city in 1785. The duo eventually gave the land to the Commonwealth of Pennsylvania for later use as the site of the capitol building.

Harrisburg has two popular parks, Riverfront Park and City Island, with activities along the banks of the Susquehanna. You can take a leisurely stroll or bike ride and enjoy the view, cruise the river on the *Pride of the Susquehanna* paddlewheeler, or get a wetter perspective from a canoe, paddleboat, or jet ski. City Island has many restaurants, quaint shops, miniature golf, a restored carousel, and train and carriage rides.

Because of its location, Harrisburg is a hub location for many one-day trips including Gettysburg, Carlisle, and York.

Information: Harrisburg Regional Chamber of Commerce | 3211 N. Front St., Ste. 201, 17110 | www.visit hhc.com | 717/232–4099.

TRANSPORTATION

Airport: You will fly into **Harrisburg International Airport.** | 217 Fifth St., Middletown | 717/948–3901.

Rail: Harrisburg's Transportation Center is served by **Amtrak** (717/232–5241). Service from Philadelphia is operated by the **Southeastern Pennsylvania Transportation Authority** (215/580–7852).

Bus Travel: Service into the Harrisburg Transportation Center is provided by **Capitol Trailways** (717/232–4251) and **Greyhound Bus Lines** (717/232–4251).

Intra-city Transport: Local bus service is provided by **Capital Area Transit** (CAT). | 901 N. Cameron St., Box 2945 | 717/238–8304.

Driving around Town: Parking meters are plentiful and cost 25 cents per minute, but those around the state offices downtown are usually taken. Try Walnut and Forster streets, which are near the Capitol and downtown attractions, or spring for a garage (about $12 for a full day): If you do park at a meter and overstay your welcome, you'll be given a parking ticket that will cost $7 ($10 if you don't pay within 96 hours). There are no parking facilities for RVs downtown; head for Island City. East-west streets are named, while north-south streets are numbered. Keep in mind that Harrisburg has three rush hours: between 7 and 9 in the morning, again at lunchtime, between 11:30 and 1:30, and finally between 4:30 and 5:30 in the afternoon.

NEIGHBORHOODS

Shipoke. Coal miners once filled this 3½-square-block neighborhood, now one of Harrisburg's historic districts, one of the handsomest sections of the city. Three-story

row-houses dating back to the start of the twentieth century and now completely refurbished, line the streets, and there are nice restaurants; the historic Peace Church is here as well.

Capitol Complex. The State Capitol Building is the focal point of these 65 acres. The Italianate building cost an eye-popping $13 million to build in the 1920s. The surrounding area, which used to get pretty sleepy after offices closed, is coming back to life with the addition of theaters, restaurants, a cyber café, and hotels, including the Hilton Towers and the remodeled Marriott Crown, which has a Titanic theme. In summer, Front Street park is lively with festivals, people, activities, and food vendors. Shops and eateries fill nearby Strawberry Square, a mall. Next door is the Whitaker Center, which includes an IMAX Theatre, the Museum of Science and Discovery, and the Sunoco Performing Arts Theatre. Cross the Susquehanna River on the nearby Walnut Street footbridge, and you are on City Island, home to Harrisburg's baseball and soccer teams, the City Island Miniature Railroad, Riverside Village Park, and other attractions.

KODAK'S TIPS FOR PHOTOGRAPHING THE CITY

Streets
- Take a bus or walking tour to get acclimated
- Explore markets, streets, and parks
- Travel light so you can shoot quickly

City Vistas
- Find high vantage points to reveal city views
- Shoot early or late in the day, for best light
- At twilight, use fast films and bracket exposures

Formal Gardens
- Exploit high angles to show garden design
- Use wide-angle lenses to exaggerate depth and distance
- Arrive early to beat crowds

Landmarks and Monuments
- Review postcard racks for traditional views
- Seek out distant or unusual views
- Look for interesting vignettes or details

Museums
- Call in advance regarding photo restrictions
- Match film to light source when color is critical
- Bring several lenses or a zoom

Houses of Worship
- Shoot exteriors from nearby with a wide-angle lens
- Move away and include surroundings
- Switch to a very fast film indoors

Stained-Glass Windows
- Bright indirect sunlight yields saturated colors
- Expose for the glass not the surroundings
- Switch off flash to avoid glare

Architectural Details
- Move close to isolate details
- For distant vignettes, use a telephoto lens
- Use side light to accent form and texture

In the Marketplace
- Get up early to catch peak activity
- Search out colorful displays and colorful characters
- Don't scrimp on film

Stage Shows and Events
- Never use flash
- Shoot with fast (ISO 400 to 1000) film
- Use telephoto lenses
- Focus manually if necessary

From *Kodak Guide to Shooting Great Travel Pictures* © 2000 by Fodor's Travel Publications

WALKING TOUR

Begin your tour at the **State Museum of Pennsylvania,** a modern, circular building that also houses a planetarium. Continue south-east, and cross State Street to the **Capitol Building** and the **Capitol Complex.** Here you will find all of the legislative, judicial, and executive buildings. Continue east on Third Street. The street makes a slight turn as you cross South Street to Walnut Street. Go north here, to visit **Strawberry Square,** loaded with shopping, and the Science Center, housed in the **Whitaker Center,** where you can see over 200 interactive exhibits. Head back south down Walnut, and walk east to Market Street; continue south. At Second Street, go east to the **John Harris Mansion.** One of Harrisburg's designated landmarks, it was the home of the city's founder. Head south to Front Street, and go west to visit the **Dauphin County Courthouse.** Go south across the Market Street Bridge, to **City Island,** where the Kipona Festival takes place in September, featuring boating, water and land activities, and a plethora of food vendors.

Attractions

ART AND ARCHITECTURE

The Capitol. The Capitol, covering more than 3 acres, was dedicated in 1906 after fire destoyed an earlier building in 1897. The capitol is an Italian Renaissance–style statehouse and has a collection of art and sculpture. On the floor of the main hallway, tiles show Pennsylvania's history, symbols, and animals. You can take a 30–min tour that includes the rotunda, the state chamber, the house chamber, and the supreme court room. If you request a tour in advance, you can see the Governor's reception room. The capitol's welcome center has interactive displays about the people and events that helped shape Pennsylvania. | State St. and 3rd St. | 717/787–6810 or 800/868–7672 | www.lwgis.state.pa.us | Free | Weekdays 8:30–4, weekends 9–3.

State Museum of Pennsylvania. Four floors of exhibits showcase Pennsylvania's story from its beginning to the present. There are changing exhibits, workshops, performances, fine art displays, and a planetarium. Curiosity Corner, the museum's hands-on learning center for kids, has a general store, Victorian parlor, and Colonial kitchen with historical settings where you can learn about life in the past. | 3rd St. and North St. | 717/787–4978 or 717/787–4979 | fax 717/783–4558 | www.statemuseumpa.org | Museum, free. Planetarium $2. Curiosity Corner $1.50 | Museum, Tues.–Sat. 9–5, Sun. noon–5, closed Mon.; Curiosity Corner, Tues., Thurs.–Sun. 1–4, closed Mon. and Wed.; planetarium shows, weekends 1 and 2 PM.

Dauphin County Courthouse. Built in 1942, the neoclassical building has an interior clad with marble. The front of the building has a fountain and a statue of *Youth Crushing Evil.* | Front St. and Market St. | 717/257–1596 | Free | Weekdays 8:30–5, closed weekends.

BEACHES, PARKS, AND NATURAL SIGHTS

Fort Hunter Park. Here you can see a mansion, tavern house, springhouse, dairy, barn, and stable. There are picnic facilities, a playground, and a riverfront walk. | 5300 N. Front St. | 717/599–5751 | fax 717/599–5838 | Free | Daily 8 am–dusk.
The Federal **Fort Hunter Mansion** is at Fort Hunter. Built in three sections, the front stone portions were built in 1786 and 1814; the back was added later in the 1800s. Take a guided tour of the restored mansion to see what sophisticated country living was like in the early 19th century. The mansion has period furnishings that belonged to the family who lived here. | $4 | May–Dec., Tues.–Sat. 10–4:30, Sun. noon–4:30, closed Mon.)

Little Buffalo State Park. Inside the park is 88-acre Lake Holman and Little Buffalo Creek, where you can fish, boat, ice fish, and ice skate. There's a half-acre swimming pool, two picnic areas, about 300 acres for hunting, 8 mi of hiking trails, cross-country ski trails, and sledding. | R.R. 2, Newport; From PA Rte. 322, take the Newport Exit and follow PA Rte. 34 S through the town of Newport. One mi from town turn right onto Little Buffalo State Park

Rd. to the park. From PA Rte. 322 to the park entrance is 4.6 mi | 717/567–9255 or 888/PA–PARKS | www.dcnr.state.pa.us | Free | Daily 8 am–dusk.

Memorial Lake State Park. The 230–acre park has an 85–acre lake for boating and year-round fishing. You can also hike, picnic, and cross-country ski. | R.R.1, Grantville; The park is 30 min east of Harrisburg. From I–81 at Exit 29 (Fort Indiantown Gap), take PA Rte. 934 North and follow the signs to the park | 717/865–6470 or 888/PA–PARKS | www.dcnr.state.pa.us | Free | Daily 8 AM–dusk.

CULTURE, EDUCATION, AND HISTORY

John Harris Mansion. On the National Register of Historic Places, this home was built in 1766 by John Harris Jr., founder of Harrisburg. It later became the home of U.S. Senator Simon Cameron, Abraham Lincoln's Secretary of War. The museum has exhibits on folk art and esteemed past residents, a genealogy library, and is headquarters for the local historical society. | 219 S. Front St. | 717/233–3462 | fax 717/233–6059 | $7 | Weekdays 10–4, and by appointment; closed weekends.

The **Science Center,** a part of the Whitaker Center, has over 200 interactive exhibits. The flagship exhibit "Bodies in Motion: The Physics of Human Movement," explores the physics of dance, ice-skating, and gymnastics. | 222 Market Street, | 717/221–8201 | www.whitaker-center.org/science | $6.75 | Mon.–Sat., 9:30–5, Sun. 11:30–5.

Whitaker Center for Science and the Arts. The first facility in the country to house a science center, a performing arts theater, and an IMAX theater in one complex, this complex explores science through the arts, combining education and entertainment into one experience. There's also a theater that mounts performances of music, theater, and dance, and an art gallery, among other components | 222 Market St., | 717/221–8201 ext. 2513 or 2504 | www.whitakercenter.org.

SHOPPING

Strawberry Square. This retail complex is part of an immense mixed-use facility in downtown Harrisburg. With its atrium, shops, eateries, and offices, it is one of the hot spots of downtown Harrisburg. | Third St. and Walnut St., | 717/236–5700 | www.strawberrysquare.com/facts.htm | Free | Daily.

ON THE CALENDAR

JAN.: *Pennsylvania State Farm Show.* Some 5,000 animals are on display in this event that celebrates Pennsylvania agriculture, with hundreds of commmerical stands, a food court, and demonstrations and lectures. | 2301 N. Cameron St. | 717/787–5373.

JULY: *American Musicfest.* Held at Riverfront Park and City Island, this 5-day event is the largest Fourth of July celebration in central Pennsylvania. You can see dozens of local, regional, national, and international artists and performers, international foods, and a kids' theater, educational activities, arts and crafts, and rides. Boat races, sporting events, and other family activities, including a fireworks display. | 717/255–3020 | Free | Daily 10–10.

SEPT.: *Fort Hunter Day Festival.* The 1800s are recreated at 35-acre Fort Hunter Park. Crafts show, bake sale, carriage and hay rides, and more. | Free.

SEPT.: *Kipona.* Boating and other watersports on the Susquehanna River are part of this Labor Day weekend event held at City Island and Riverfront Park. | 717/231–7788.

OCT.: *Pennsylvania National Horse Show.* This 10-day event has competitions in 200 classes. | State Farm Show Building, 11th and Maclay Sts. | 717/975–3677.

Dining

INEXPENSIVE

Angie's Family Restaurant. American. Open 24 hours a day, seven days a week, this family-owned restaurant is about 2 mi from downtown. The walls are lined with old pictures of movie stars; there's a wood dance floor for live entertainment on the weekends. Try the turkey platter, lasagne, or steak, and for dessert there's Angie's baklava or honey semolina cake. | 1360 Eisenhower Blvd. | 717/939–0417 | $5–$15 | AE, D, MC V.

Appalachian Brewing Company. American. Formerly an 1890 print shop, this building has hardwood floors, high ceilings, and more than 20,000 square ft of dining and entertainment. There are pool tables, darts, pinball games, and a sports pub with televisions. Though known for stone-oven pizza, steaks, and pasta, you can also choose ginger tuna. Eat outside on a deck overlooking the Capitol building. Live music Fri. and Sat. | 50 N. Cameron St. | 717/221–1080 | $7–$17 | AE, DC, MC, V.

Fisherman's Wharf. Seafood. Five miles outside of Harrisburg, this restaurant can seat up to 200 people and serves seafood with a Greek flair. Two dining areas look like a Greek tavern, complete with stucco walls. Sharks, barracudas, and mahi mahi are mounted on the walls. Buffalo wings, crab cake platters, and homemade rice pudding and baklava are popular choices. | 6852 Derry St. | 717/564–9920. | Mon.–Sat. 11–midnight, Sun. 11–9. | $5–$12 | AE, D, MC, V.

North Street Café. American. An old brick building is the backdrop of this coffee shop and art gallery. Local photographers and artists hang their work on the walls and most pieces are for sale. Writers and poets speak on Wednesdays. Known for vegetarian food and specialty sandwiches. No alcohol. | 231 North St. | 717/233–7194 | fax 717/233–2470 | $5–$10 | Reservations not accepted | MC, V.

MODERATE

Cantone's. Italian. Locals come here for southern Italian food including the homemade pasta served under cathedral ceilings. Cantone's is known for its homemade sauces, soups, and stromboli. Kids' menu. | 4701 Fritchey St. | 717/652–9976 | Closed Sun. | $11–$22 | AE, D, MC, V.

Doc Holliday's. American. Named after the gambler, lawmaker, and dentist famous for his fight at the OK Corral, this steakhouse can seat up to 300 people and has two dining rooms and a saloon. Stuffed game is mounted on the barnlike walls. You can order from a selection of USDA steaks, or try crab cakes or a rib platter. It's in Harrisburg's hotel district, on the outskirts of town. | 469 Eisenhower Blvd. | 717/564–4448 | fax 717/564–5763 | $6–$25 | AE, D, DC, MC, V.

Manada Hill Inn. Continental. This antiques-filled, 130-year-old farmhouse serves roast duckling a l'orange, steak au poivre, and almond chicken, fresh seafood, and prime rib. Kids' menu. Sun. brunch. | 128 N. Hershey Rd. | 717/652–0400 | No lunch Mon.–Sat. | $9–$20 | AE, D, DC, MC, V.

Pagliaros Trattorias. Italian. Between Harrisburg and Hershey, this restaurant is as popular with locals as it is with tourists. While the menu is small, the pastas and sauces are made fresh daily; popular dishes are minestrone soup, pasta alfredo, calamari, and Caesar salad. You can eat indoors or out. | 6301 Grayson Rd. | 717/561–4610 | Mon.–Thurs. 4–9, Fri.–Sat. 11–10, Sun. noon–8 | $12 | AE, MC, V.

Passage to India. Indian. Indian artwork and crafts blend well with contemporary fixtures and chairs, offset by a view of the Susquehanna River outside. Sun. brunch. | 525 Front St. | 717/233–1202 | fax 717/233–1202 | $11–$16 | AE, D, DC, MC, V.

EXPENSIVE

Maverick. Continental. A popular establishment among Harrisburg's politicians, the elegant interior here has antique chairs, glass partitions, and dark wood accents. Menu choices are seafood and steaks, prime rib, crab cakes, and fresh lobster. Dishes often have creative sauces. Kids' menu. Free parking. | 1851 Arsenal Rd. | 717/233–7688 | fax 717/232–2701 | Closed Sun. | $16–$31 | AE, D, DC, MC, V.

Lodging

INEXPENSIVE

Friendly Inn. This is a small, privately run downtown motel. Facilities are basic. Cable TV. No pets. | 8004 Allentown Blvd. | 717/652–2634 | 15 rooms | $30–$40 | AE, D, DC, MC, V.

Greenlawn Motel. Built in the 1950s, this motel complex of three brick and stone buildings is 8 mi from Harrisburg, 5 mi from Hershey Park. Rooms have porches with lawn chairs, and there's a garden full of groundhogs and squirrels. Picnic Area. | 7490 Allentown Blvd. | 717/652–1530 | 12 rooms | $35–$45 | MC, V.

MODERATE

Abide with Me Bed and Breakfast. Built in the 1880s, this bed and breakfast is a mile from downtown and has Second Empire architecture, oak parquet, random plank hardwood floors, and rooms filled with period furniture. There's also a front porch, a swing, and a parlor; games, puzzles, television, and reading materials are in the common area. Smoking is allowed on the porch. Complimentary breakfast. No pets. No kids under 12. No smoking. | 2601 Walnut St. | 717/236–5873 | 3 rooms | $55 | No credit cards.

Red Roof Inn. This midsize motel is near downtown and 15 mi from Hershey. In-room data ports, cable TV. Pets allowed. | 400 Corporate Circle | 717/657–1445 | fax 717/657–2775 | www.redroof.com | 110 rooms | $55–$70 | AE, D, DC, MC, V.

EXPENSIVE

Baymont Inn. Midway betwen Harrisburg and Hershey, this hotel is 12 mi from Hershey Park Chocolate World and outlets and 8 mi from Penn National Race Track. Rooms have cream colored walls, with dark green drapes and spreads. Restaurants within 1 mi. Complimentary Continental breakfast. In-room data ports, some microwaves, some refrigerators, cable TV. Laundry facilities. Business services. Pets allowed. | 200 N. Mountain Rd. | 717/540–9339 | fax 717/540–9486 | www.baymontinn.com | 67 rooms | $75–$85 | AE, D, DC, MC, V.

Best Western Harrisburg–Hershey Hotel and Suites. This hotel is near Exit 26B of I–81, between Harrisburg and Hershey. It is near downtown Harrisburg and the center of Hershey. Restaurant, bar. In-room data ports, some refrigerators, some microwaves, cable TV. Indoor pool. Hot tub, sauna. Exercise equipment. Laundry facilities. Business services. Pets allowed. | 300 N. Mountain Rd. | 717/652–7180 | fax 717/541–8991 | www.bestwestern.com | 101 rooms | $89–$95 | AE, D, DC, MC, V.

Comfort Inn. You receive complimentary passes to a nearby gym and all rooms have coffee makers and irons at this hotel near Exit 29 of I–83. Complimentary Continental breakfast. Some microwaves, some refrigerators, cable TV. Outdoor pool. Laundry facilities. Business services, airport shuttle. Pets allowed. | 4021 Union Deposit Rd. | 717/561–8100 | fax 717/561–1357 | www.comfortinn.com | 115 rooms | $89–$119 | AE, D, DC, MC, V.

Crowne Plaza Harrisburg-Hershey Area. Opened in June 2000, the rooftop patio here gives you a birds-eye view of downtown. It's 4 blocks to the Capital Complex and near the waterfront and City Island. Restaurant, bar, room service. In-room data ports, some microwaves, some refrigerators, cable TV. Indoor pool. Exercise equipment. Laundry facilities. Business services. | 23 S. 2nd St. | 717/234–5021 or 800/2–RAMADA | fax 717/234–2347 | crwnplzhbg@aol.com | www.basshotels.com | 254 rooms | $105–$145 | AE, D, DC, MC, V.

Days Inn. At Exit 22N of I–81, 3 mi from downtown, this motel has hair dryers and ironing equipment in all rooms. Picnic area, complimentary Continental breakfast. Some microwaves, some refrigerators, cable TV. Outdoor pool. Exercise equipment. Playground. Laundry facilities. Business services. | 3919 N. Front St. | 717/233–3100 | fax 717/233–6415 | www.travelweb.com/daysinn.html | 116 rooms | $89–$99 | AE, D, DC, MC, V.

Hampton Inn. This five-story chain hotel is near Exit 29 of I–83. Complimentary Continental breakfast. Cable TV. Pool. Hot tub. Exercise equipment. Laundry facilities. Business services, free parking. | 4230 Union Deposit Rd. | 717/545–9595 | fax 717/545–6907 | www.hampton-inn.com | 145 rooms | $75–$85 | AE, D, DC, MC, V.

Howard Johnson. There's a rental car agency on the premises of this chain motel near Exit 1 of I–283. Restaurant, bar. Microwaves, refrigerators, cable TV. Pool, wading pool. Exercise equipment. Business services, airport shuttle, free parking. | 473 Eisenhower Blvd. | 717/564–4730 | fax 717/564–4840 | gmhersheyhotels@earthlink.com | www.hersheyhotels.com | 175 rooms | $72–$99 | AE, D, DC, MC, V.

Marriott. This hotel at I–283/83 and Route 441 is a 10-min drive to downtown. Restaurant, bar (with entertainment), complimentary Continental breakfast, room service. In-room data ports, cable TV. Indoor-outdoor pool. Hot tub. Exercise equipment. Video games. Laundry service. Business services, airport shuttle, free parking. Pets allowed ($50 fee). | 4650 Lindle Rd. | 717/564–5511 | fax 717/564–6173 | www.marriott.com | 348 rooms | $90–$169 | AE, D, DC, MC, V.

Towne House Suites Hotel. The 20-story building is right in downtown. The rooms all have balconies; there's a public pool next door. Complimentary breakfast. In-room data ports, kitchenettes, some in-room hot tubs, cable TV. Barbershop, beauty salon. Exercise equipment. Shops. Laundry service. Airport shuttle. No pets. | 660 Boas St. | 717/232–1900 or 888/532–1900 | www.townehousesuites.com | 60 rooms | $99 | AE, D, DC, MC, V.

VERY EXPENSIVE

Hilton and Towers. Three blocks from the State Capitol, this high-rise hotel is next to a retail complex with more than 50 specialty shops and restaurants. On its concierge level you get separate registration, a bathrobe, built-in hair dryer, extra towels, and a private lounge serving hors d'oeuvres, beverages, and a complimentary Continental breakfast. 3 restaurants, bar (with entertainment). In-room data ports, minibars, refrigerators, cable TV. Indoor pool. Exercise equipment. Shops. Business services, airport shuttle, parking (fee). | 1 N. 2nd St. | 717/233–6000 | fax 717/233–6271 | www.hilton.com | 341 rooms | $109–$179 | AE, D, DC, MC, V.

Holiday Inn. This chain hotel is near Harrisburg Airport and downtown Harrisburg. Restaurant, bar (with entertainment), picnic area, room service. In-room data ports, some microwaves, some refrigerators, cable TV. Indoor pool. Hot tub. Exercise equipment. Video games. Laundry facilities. Business services, airport shuttle, free parking. Pets allowed (fee). | 148 Sheraton Dr., New Cumberland | 717/774–2721 | fax 717/774–2485 | www.holiday-inn.com | 196 rooms | $109–$129 | AE, D, DC, MC, V.

Holiday Inn East. On the eastern shore of the Susquehanna River, this motel is 3 mi from downtown. All rooms have coffee pots, hair dryers, and irons. There's an outdoor deck overlooking the pool and shuffleboard court. Restaurant, bar, room service. In-room data ports, some in-room hot tubs, cable TV. 2 pools (1 indoor). Hot tub. Putting green, tennis. Basketball, exercise equipment, volleyball. Video games. Laundry service. Business services, airport shuttle, free parking. | 4751 Lindle Rd. | 717/939–7841 | fax 717/939–9317 | www.holiday-inn.com | 299 rooms | $149–$161 | AE, D, DC, MC, V.

Inn of the Dove. A mile out of town, this hotel is surrounded by gardens and trees. One room has a private, indoor pool. Complimentary breakfast. In-room data ports, microwaves, refrigerators, some in-room hot tubs, cable TV. No pets. No kids. | 2225 Kohn Rd. | 717/540–5540 | fax 717/540–9318 | www.innofthedove.com | 40 rooms | $120–$325 | AE, D, DC, MC, V.

Sheraton Harrisburg East. A dramatic, skylit lobby draws attention at this hotel 5 mi from downtown. Restaurant, bar, room service. In-room data ports, some microwaves, some refrigerators, some in-room hot tubs, cable TV. Indoor pool. Hot tub. Gym. Video games. Laundry facilities, laundry service. Business services, free parking. | 800 East Park Dr. | 717/561–2800 | fax 717/561–8398 | www.sheraton.com | 174 rooms | $105–$125 | AE, D, DC, MC, V.

Wyndham Garden. You can get freshly baked cookies, coffee, and a newspaper in your room, and even a choice of foam or feather pillows at this downtown hotel near Exit 1 of I–283/

83, 9 mi from Hershey. Restaurant, bar, room service. In-room data ports, some microwaves, some refrigerators, cable TV. Pool. Hot tub, sauna. Exercise equipment. Laundry facilities, laundry service. Business services, airport shuttle, free parking. Pets allowed. | 765 Eisenhower Blvd. | 717/558–9500 | fax 717/558–8956 | www.travelweb.com | 167 rooms | $99–$129 | AE, D, DC, MC, V.

HAWLEY

MAP 7, K3

(Nearby towns also listed: Carbondale, Honesdale, Milford, Scranton)

What started as a lumber town near Scranton in 1827 has become a popular resort village today. On the northern tip of Lake Wallenpaupack, Pennsylvania's largest manmade lake, formed by the damming of the Lackawaxen River, Hawley has many outdoor activities including boating, fishing, hunting, and camping. The Lake Region of northeastern Pennsylvania is an area of year-round natural beauty and historical interest. The surrounding area includes the Pocono Plateau, 1,800 ft above sea level, where you can canoe, raft, kayak, or go tubing on the Delaware River.

Information: **Hawley–Lake Wallenpaupack Chamber of Commerce** | Box 150, 18428 | 570/226–3191.

Attractions

Claws 'N Paws Wild Animal Park. Here you can see a rare white tiger and a snow leopard, and more than 100 other rare and exotic species. | Rte. 590, 4 mi east of Hamlin in the Pocono Mountains | 570/698–6154 | fax 570/698–9257 | www.clawsnpaws.com | $9.95 | May–Oct., daily 10–6.

Lake Wallenpaupack. The 5700-acre lake has 52 mi of shoreline for fishing, boating, swimming, and more than 300 campsites around the lake, plus hiking trails, picnic facilities, and a public beach. | Rte. 6 (adjacent to dam) | 570/226–2141 or 570/226–3702 | www.pplinc.com/landman | Free; beach $2.50 | Daily dawn to dusk.

Promised Land State Park. About 3,000 acres, the park has two lakes (the 422-acre Promised Land Lake and the 173-acre Lower Land Lake) and several streams, 487 campsites, 12 cabins, more than 30 mi of hiking trails, a 6½-mi bike trail around Promised Land Lake, 27 mi of snowmobile trails, and 450 acres for hunting. | Rte. 390, Greentown; In Pike County, 10 mi north of Canadensis | 570/676–3428 or 888/PA–PARKS | fax 570/676–5043 | www.dcnr.state.pa.us | Free | Daily 8 AM–dusk.

Ritz Company Playhouse. A 1930s Comerford movie theater, the playhouse is now home to a nonprofit theater ensemble that performs plays and Broadway shows. | 512 Keystone St. | 570/226–9752 | Call for ticket prices | June – Labor Day weekend.

Skiing Tanglewood. With nine trails, five lifts, and a designated mogul area, this skiing mountain has a peak elevation of 1,750 ft and a vertical drop of 415 ft. | Tafton | 717/226–7669 or 888/226–SNOW | Dec.–Mar.

ON THE CALENDAR

DEC.: *Winterfest.* Held on the main street of downtown Hawley, this festival has a Victorian-era parade, a house and tree decorating contest, carols, and bonfires. There's also a special train ride through town, food, and performances. A fee is charged for some events; most are free or by donation. | 570/226–3191.

Dining

Boat House. American. This former 1950s diner is about a mile out of Hawley on Lake Wallenpaupack. There's live local music every Friday; you can watch Monday night football while enjoying a buffet. Murals and historic photos of Hawley fill the walls. Try the crab cakes and the prime rib. Eat indoors or on the covered patio. | HC 6, Rte. 507 | 570/226–5027 | Mon.–Fri. 11–9, Sat.–Sun. 8–10 | $10–$20 | AE, D, DC, MC, V.

Ehrhardt's Lakeside. Contemporary. You can see Lake Wallenpaupack from every angle of Ehrhardt's all-windows dining room. The menu has surf and turf and shrimp scampi. Kids' menu. Sun. brunch. | Rte. 507, Tafton | 570/226–2124 | fax 570/226–3417 | $15–$23 | AE, D, MC, V.

Gresham's Chop House. American. Whether you're seated inside the glass-walled dining room or outside on the patio, you can see the lake at this multitiered family restaurant. The chicken français and the prime rib are popular items, along with the fudge brownie with ice cream, caramel, peanuts, and chocolate syrup. | 6150 HC 6 | 570/226–1500 | Tues. | Mon., Wed.–Fri. 5–9, weekends noon–10 | $14 | AE, D, DC, MC, V.

Restaurant at the Old Mill Stream. American. At the edge of Paupack Falls, this restaurant is in an 1890 mill. You can sit out on the deck among the remains of old stone foundations, or dine inside in the turbine room. Two decks, one enclosed with screens, extend from the main building into the gorge. The specials are sea scallops with saffron, Thai red curry shrimp, escargot, pork chops with apple cider sauce, and the Yucatan-style burrito grande. For dessert, choose from three different kinds of cheesecake. Less than a mile from town. | 120 Falls Ave. | 570/226–1337 | Mon. | Tues.–Sun. 5–9 | $12–$19 | AE, D, MC, V.

Lodging

Academy Street Bed and Breakfast. Once the manor of Captain Joseph Atkinson and later home to the first sheriff of Wayne County, this Italianate Victorian home sits on the edge of town near Lake Wallenpaupack. The wraparound porch has swings and rocking chairs, and rooms have period antiques. Complimentary breakfast. Cable TV. No pets. No kids under 12. | 528 Academy St. | 570/226–3430 | www.academybb.com | 6 rooms | $85–$105 | Nov.–Apr. | MC, V.

Caesars Cove Haven. Built in 1958 on 300 acres of land at Lake Wallenpaupack, this Ceasars resort is built in pseudo-Roman style complete with Roman arches and sandstone colors. Bars (with entertainment). Refrigerators. Indoor-outdoor pools, lake. Hot tub. Driving range, miniature golf, tennis. Exercise equipment, racquetball, water sports, boating. Ice-skating, snowmobiling. Video games. Laundry facilities. No kids allowed. | Rte. 590, Lakeville | 717/226–4506 or 800/233–4141 | fax 717/226–4697 | 282 rooms | $205–400 | AE, D, DC, MC, V.

Falls Port Inn. A 1902 Victorian brick building downtown near many antique shops, this inn is less than a mile from hiking, horseback riding, and a lake. Restaurant, complimentary Continental breakfast, room service. No room phones, no TV in some rooms. | 330 Main Ave. | 570/226–2600 | fax 570/226–4906 | 9 rooms (5 with shared bath) | $75–$120 | AE, MC, V.

Gresham's Lakeview. Ultra modern two-story motel, it's minutes from horseback riding, golf, tennis, swimming, and skiing. Cable TV. | HC 6 | 570/226–4621 | fax 570/226–4621 | 21 rooms | $78–$83 | AE, D, MC, V.

Old Mill Stream Country Inn. This 1890 stone mill has been converted into a restaurant and inn with day activities nearby in the area, from boating and riding to having a cookout. Ask about the inn's "dinner mystery"–"Eat, Drink, and Be Married." There are three golf courses a half-hour drive away. TV, in-room VCRs (and movies). No pets. | 120 Falls Ave. | 570/226–1337 | fax 570/226–8419 | www.medresorts.com | 22 rooms | $75–$139 | AE, D, MC, V.

Roebling Inn on the Delaware. A two-story white country house with black shutters and a large front porch with rocking chairs, this 1870 bed & breakfast inn is close to the Zane Grey Museum and Roebling Bridge, a precursor to Roebling's Brooklyn Bridge, which spans New York Harbor, linking Brooklyn to Manhattan. Complimentary breakfast. Some kitchenettes, refrigerators, cable TV. Business services. | 155 Scenic Dr., Lackawaxen | 570/685–7900 | fax 570/685–1718 | 6 rooms (4 rooms with shower only) | $75–$140 | AE, D, MC, V.

Settlers Inn. A three-story 1920s Tudor building, this inn is across the street from Bingham Park, along a river bank, and a few miles from Lake Wallenpaupack. A golf course, as well as cross-country and downhill skiing are close by. The inn has quiet spots for reading, playing chess and other games, and you can play croquet or horseshoes on the lawn. Restaurant, complimentary breakfast. In-room data ports. Business services, airport shuttle. No smoking. | 4 Main Ave. | 717/226–2993 or 800/833–8527 | fax 717/226–1874 | 18 rooms, 5 suites | $95–$150 | AE, D, MC, V.

HAZLETON

MAP 7, J4

(Nearby towns also listed: Ashland, Bloomsburg, Jim Thorpe, Wilkes-Barre)

Who would have thought that a deer pawing the earth would create a town like Hazleton. According to legend, that is exactly what occurred in the forming of Hazleton. Named for Hazel Creek, the town had tremendous amounts of anthracite under it. The name was changed to Hazleton when an attorney misspelled the name on papers incorporating the borough.

Information: **Hazleton Chamber of Commerce** | 1 S. Church St., 18201 | 570/455–1508.

Attractions

Eckley Miners Village. Settled in 1854, Eckley is a monument to the immigrants who worked in the coal fields at the height of the anthracite boom. Covering 100 acres, the village is home to more than 17 residents, some retired miners and their families. Its 58 buildings are surrounded by black-silt ponds and strip-mining pits. | Weatherly, 8 mi north of Hazleton, 6 mi off I-80, and 8 mi off I-81 | 570/636–2070 or 570/636–2071 | fax 570/636–2938 | $3.50 | Mon.–Sat. 9–5, Sun. noon–5.

Hazleton Historical Society Museum. Three floors of photographs and memorabilia highlight Hazleton's history, starting in the 1700s. | 55 N. Wyoming St. | 570/455–8576 | $4 | Weekdays 9:30–1, closed weekends.

National Shrine of the Sacred Heart. On 40 acres, this is the largest outdoor shrine in North America dedicated to the Sacred Heart. The whole story of Christ from his birth to his death is told here. | 1 Church Pl. | 570/455–1162 | fax 570/455–0306 | Free | Daily.

ON THE CALENDAR
SEPT.: *Funfest.* This celebration is held in downtown, with free entertainment, a craft show, a car show, a fireworks display, and a parade. | 570/455–1508 | Free.

Dining
Byorek's Knotty Pine Restaurant. Barbecue. This casual family-style restaurant is practically a local institution, starting out as a tiny drive-in. Although it's grown since, almost no changes were made to the original interior and design. Paintings of Hazleton line the walls. | 27 R.R. 2 | 570/455–3211 | Mon.–Sat. 7–11, Sun. 8–11 | $8–$10 | AE, DC, MC, V.

Scatton's. Italian. Inside, you can eat surrounded by antique prints, earth tones, fresh flowers, and plants. The musketeri tortelli alberto and fresh fish are house specialties. | 1008 N. Vine St. | 570/455–6630 | Closed Sun. | $13–$26 | AE, D, DC, MC, V.

Lodging
Best Western Genetti Motor Lodge. On 60 wooded acres in Luzerne County, this motel is a mile from shopping and the Sacred Heart Shrine, and 5 mi from golf and Eckley Historic Village. Complimentary Continental breakfast. Cable TV. Outdoor pool. Hot tub. Gym. Play-

ground. Laundry facilities. Business services, free parking. | 32nd St. and Rte. 309 | 570/454–2494 | fax 570/455–7793 | 89 rooms | $65–$75 | AE, D, DC, MC, V.

Hampton Inn. At the highest point of Hazleton, this three-story hotel overlooks Cunningham Valley. It's 5 minutes from town center, on I–81 and Route 93. A restaurant behind the hotel has room service. Complimentary breakfast. In-room data ports, cable TV. Outdoor pool. Exercise equipment. Laundry service. | 273A R.R. 1 | 570/454–3449 | fax 570/454–3396 | www.hamptoninn.com | 123 rooms | $99 | AE, D, DC, MC, V.

Ramada Inn. You can see a spectacular view of Hazelton from this motel, less than a mile from downtown and close to ski resorts and golf courses. Restaurant, bar, room service. In-room data ports, cable TV. Pool. Business services. Laundry services. Pets allowed. | Rte. 309 | 570/455–2061 | fax 570/455–9387 | 107 rooms | $65–$70 | AE, D, DC, MC, V.

HERSHEY

(Nearby towns also listed: Boiling Springs, Camp Hill, Cornwall, Harrisburg, Lebanon)

The "sweetest place on earth," the borough of Hershey is home to the Hershey Chocolate factory. Since 1905, when Milton S. Hershey's factory opened, Hershey has contributed so much to the community that today it bears his name. Whether you're visiting the chocolate factory or doing some outlet shopping, the number of Hershey Kisses that adorn the top of lampposts throughout downtown are a constant reminder that you are in chocolate heaven.

Information: Harrisburg–Hershey–Carlisle Tourism and Convention Bureau | 25 N. Front St., Ste. 100, Harrisburg, PA 17101 | 717/231–7788 or 800/995–0969.

Attractions

Adventure Sports. Three miles south of Hershey, this entertainment center has go-carts, miniature golf, bumper boats, a batting range, a driving range with grass tees, an arcade, and an ice cream parlor. | 3010 Elizabeth Town Rd. | 717/533–7479 | www.adventure-hershey.com | Pay per activity | Memorial Day – Labor Day, Mon.–Sun. 10–10; other months, weekends only 10–10.

Hershey Gardens. Started in 1937 as a 3½-acre rose garden, the garden has expanded to more than 20 acres, with a rose garden, rock garden, Japanese garden, and a memorial garden dedicated to veterans. Many of the flowers were grown by Catherine Hershey. | 170 Hotel Rd. | 717/534–3492 or 800/HERSHEY | www.hersheypa.com | $6 | May–Oct., daily 9–5; Apr.–Sept., 9–6.

★ **Hershey Museum.** You can hear the story of Milton Hershey's world of candy making here. There are exhibits of Pennsylvania German furniture, folk art, and Hershey's Native American doll collection. | 170 W. Hersheypark Dr. | 717/534–3439 or 800/HERSHEY | www.hersheymuseum.org | $6 | Memorial Day–Labor Day, 10–6; Labor Day–Memorial Day, 10–5.

Hersheypark. What began in 1907 as picnic and baseball grounds has grown to include more than 50 rides, seven roller coasters, six water rides, more than 20 kiddie rides, and three arcades. | Hersheypark Dr. | 800/HERSHEY | www.hersheypa.com | $32.95 | Call for hrs The 11-acre **ZooAmerica** has plants and animals native to North America, with gray wolves, prairie dogs, bison, deer, black bear, owls, and animals of the desert. | 100 W. Hersheypark Dr. | 717/534–3860 or 800/HERSHEY | $6 | Daily 10–8.

Hersheypark Arena. Built during the Depression, the monolithic structure has been home to the Hershey Bears, a minor league hockey team, since 1938. The arena, with unobstructed views from every seat, also hosts circuses, ice shows, and concerts. | 100 W. Hersheypark Dr. | 717/534–3911 or 800/HERSHEY | www.hersheypa.com | Prices vary with shows | Call for schedule.

Hersheypark Stadium. The site of President Dwight D. Eisenhower's 1953 birthday gala, the 25,000-seat stadium is home to the Hershey Wildcats, a professional outdoor soccer team, and also hosts summer concerts. | 100 W. Hersheypark Dr. | 717/534–3911 or 800/HERSHEY | www.hersheypa.com | Prices vary with shows | Call for schedule.

★ **Hershey's Chocolate World.** Hershey's chocolate experience is told through a tour ride that shows how chocolate is made and also gives some company history. There's a gift shop and restaurants featuring Hershey products. | 800 Park Blvd. | 717/534–4900 or 800/HERSHEY | www.hersheypa.com | Free | Daily 9–5.

Indian Echo Caverns. Take a tour through natural underground geological formations of stalactites, stalagmites, columns, flowstone, and crystal clear lakes. The caverns are 3 mi outside of Hershey. | 368 Middletown Rd. | 717/566–8131. | www.indianechocaverns.com | $9 | Memorial Day–Labor Day, daily 9–6; Mar.–May, Sept., and Oct. daily 10–4; Nov.–Feb., call for hrs.

Milton Hershey School and Founders Hall. A 22-minute film tells the story of the school and how it got started by Milton and Catherine Hershey in 1909 as an orphan school. No longer an orphan school, it now has 1,100 students. The second largest unsupported dome in the world, 137 ft, 3 inches high, is on the school's campus. | Governor Road (Rte. 322) | 717/520–2000 or 800/322–3248 | www.hershey.pvt.k12.pa.us | Free | mid-Mar.–Dec., daily 10–4; Jan.–mid-Mar., daily 10–3.

Seltzer's Lebanon Bologna Co. A video tour shows the entire process of making Lebanon bologna from the meat's arrival to the packaging of the final product. The retail store sells their products and gives free samples. | 230 N. College St., Palmyra | 717/838–6336 or 800/282–6336 | fax 717/838–5345 | www.seltzerslebanonbologna.com | Free | Store room weekdays 7–5, Sat. 7–1; video weekdays 8–4:30.

ON THE CALENDAR

DEC.: *Christkindlmarkt.* Held at the Hershey Museum, this German Christmas market has handicrafts, entertainment, and German food. | 717/534–3439.

Dining

Al Mediterraneo. Mediterranean. You can see murals, copper work, and terra cotta tiles in this restaurant, which has live music Wednesday nights and outdoor patio dining. Try pasta, veal, steak, lamb, or the Mediterranean stew of vegetables and seafood with saffron rice. | 228 E. Main St. | 717/566–5086. | Business casual (no jacket required) | Sun. | Mon.–Thurs. 5–10, Fri.–Sat. 5–11 | $16 | AE, D, DC, MC, V.

Bob Evans. American. Burgers, salads, and other specials are popular at this chain restaurant, which began in the 1960s in Ohio. Try the wildfire chicken salad or the country fried steak served with white country gravy and mashed potatoes. | 650 Walton Ave. | 717/566–1545 | Mon.–Thurs. 6–10, Fri.–Sat. 6–11 | $7 | AE, MC, V.

Catherine's at Spinners Inn. American. Housed in the 50-year-old Spinners Inn, this candlelit restaurant has fine china and linen-covered tables, and walls lined with portraits of Catherine and Milton Hershey. Try the beef medallions stuffed with crab meat and sun-dried pesto, followed with tiramisu for dessert. | 845 E. Chocolate Ave. | 717/533–9157 | Sun.–Mon. | Tues.–Sat. 5–10 | $20–$40 | AE, D, DC, MC, V.

Chocolate Town Cafe. Connected to Chocolate World, this kids' cafe is painted in bright colors with Hershey's characters on the walls, and a starry carpet on the floor. The half-pound burger and the chicken fingers are popular; try the milkshakes, which the cafe claims are the world's thickest. | 800 Park Blvd. | 717/533–2917 | Daily 11–5 | $7–13 | AE, D, MC.

Circular Dining Room. Continental. On the first floor of the Hotel Hershey, this glassed-in formal dining room overlooks the gardens at the back of the hotel. Entrees are lobster, filet of salmon, grilled filet mignon, and roast leg of lamb. The restaurant is famous for its chocolate cream pie, creme caramel, and white-chocolate honey cheesecake. | 400 Hotel Rd. | 717/533–2171 | Jacet and tie required. Daily 7–10, 11:30–2, 5:30–9. | $25–$37 | AE, D, DC, MC, V.

Giddy Ap Cafe. American. Less than a mile from Hershey, this cafe serves soups and deli sandwiches. It gets very busy around lunchtime. | 709 Fishburn Rd. | 717/533–3003 | Sun. | Mon.–Sat. 3 AM–7 PM | $6 | AE, D, DC, MC, V.

Hershey Pantry. American. Famous for winning the best breakfast award in the area since 1990, this family restaurant is about a mile from Hershey in a 1930s building. Awnings line the interior and exterior of the restaurant. You can eat outdoors on the enclosed porch. The stuffed French toast is popular here. | 801 E. Chocolate Ave. | 717/533–7505 | Sunday | Mon.–Thurs. 6:30–9, Fri.–Sat. 6:30–10 | $12 | No credit cards.

Isaac's. American. There are exposed ceilings, aquariums, and paintings of wildlife in this roadside restaurant, off Highway 422 and about a mile from downtown. Try the Whooping Crane (turkey, onions, and spinach grilled with Swiss cheese and honey-dijon dressing) or the Jamaican Today (grilled chicken breast seasoned with Caribbean jerk spices on pumpernickel with ranch dressing, pineapple, melted cheddar, and lettuce). | 1201 W. Chocolate Ave. | 717/533–9665 | $7 | AE, D, MC, V.

Union Canal House. Continental. A rustic inn from 1751, this restaurant's specialties are roasted duckling and broiled crab cakes. Kids' menu. | 107 S. Hanover St., S. Hanover | 717/566–0054 | fax 717/566–5867 | Closed Sun. No lunch | $15–$30 | AE, D, DC, MC, V.

Lodging

Addey's. A 1920s brick farm house on a hill overlooking the Hershey valley, this inn has 12 rooms, one for each month of the year. Hersheypark, the Hershey Library, and Zeigler's Antique Mall are all close by, as well as a large playground, tennis courts, a softball field, and track. Picnic area, complimentary Continental breakfast. Cable TV. Playground. No smoking. | 150 E. Governor Rd./U.S. 322 E | 717/533–2591 | addeysinn@aol.com | www.go2pa.com/addeys_inn | 12 rooms | 78–$99, suites $199 | AE, D, MC, V.

Best Western Inn. A two-story modern concrete and limestone building, this hotel is only minutes from Hersheypark, Hershey's Chocolate World Visitor's Center, Hershey Gardens, ZooAmerica North American Wildlife Park, Hersheypark Arena and Stadium, Hershey Museum of American Life, and Founder's Hall. Complimentary Continental breakfast. In-room data ports, refrigerators, cable TV. Outdoor pool. Spa. Laundry facilities. Business services, free parking. | Rte. 422 and Sipe Ave. | 717/533–5665 | fax 717/533–5675 | www.bestwestern.com | 123 rooms | $109–$169 | AE, D, DC, MC, V.

Days Inn. You can walk or drive a couple minutes to Hershey Amusement Park, Chocolate Factory, Reeses Factory, and Hershey Stadium from this four-story brick building constructed in 1989. Complimentary Continental breakfast. Some refrigerators, cable TV. Free parking. | 350 W. Chocolate Ave. | 717/534–2162 | fax 717/533–6409 | www.daysinn.com | 75 rooms | $69–$169 | AE, D, DC, MC, V.

Hen-Apple Bed and Breakfast. In Palmyra, about 3 mi outside of Hershey, this 1825 Georgian-style farmhouse is furnished with antiques, reproductions, and flea market finds. There's a parlor, a wicker room, and in the backyard, a hammock under old fruit trees. Complimentary breakfast. No kids. | 409 S. Lingle Ave. | 717/838–8282 | www.visithhc.com/henapple.html | 6 rooms | $75 | AE, D, DC, MC, V.

Hershey Lodge. This modern five-level lodge and convention center is 2 mi from Hersheypark (free shuttle provided) and across the road from Hershey Medical Center. The Hersey School is just down the road. Restaurant, bar (with entertainment), dining room. In-room data ports, cable TV. 2 pools (1 indoor), wading pool. Hot tub. Miniature golf, tennis. Exercise equipment. Playground. Business services, airport shuttle, free parking. | West Chocolate Ave. and University Dr. | 717/533–3311 or 800/533–3131 | fax 717/533–9642 | www.800hershey.com | 457 rooms | $199 | AE, D, DC, MC, V.

Holiday Inn Harrisburg-Hershey. Near Hershey Park and Penn Down Race Track, and 10 mi from downtown Harrisburg, this modern stucco hotel is designed to accommodate families and business travelers. Restaurant, bar (with entertainment), room service. In-room data ports, cable TV. 2 pools, wading pool. Hot tub. Exercise equipment. Shops. Laundry facilities. Business services, airport shuttle, free parking. Pets allowed. | 604 Station Rd., Grantville | 717/469–0661 | fax 717/469–7755 | info@stayholiday.com | www.stayholiday.com | 195 rooms | $139–$199 | AE, D, DC, MC, V.

★ **Hotel Hershey.** The grand dame of Hershey hotels, this is a luxurious eight-story Mediterranean style building with formal gardens and woods on its grounds. Restaurants, bar (with entertainment), room service. Cable TV. 2 pools, wading pool. Hot tub, massage. 9-hole golf course, putting green, tennis. Exercise equipment. Bicycles. Business services, airport shuttle, free parking. | 1 Hotel Rd. | 717/533–2171 or 800/533–3131 | fax 717/534–8887 | www.hershey.com/~herco | 241 rooms | $299–$360 | AE, D, DC, MC, V.

Milton. A two-story brick motel, it's 1½ mi from Hershey Park, Hershey's Chocolate World, Hershey Museum, ZooAmerica, and Hershey Gardens. If you have a little time, take day trips to Amish Country (30 mi away in Lancaster), Reading outlets (40 mi away), or Gettysburg (55 mi away). In-room data ports, some microwaves, some refrigerators, cable TV. Pool. Business services. | 1733 E. Chocolate Ave. | 717/533–4533 | fax 717/533–0369 | www.miltonmotel.com | 34 rooms | $69–$149 | AE, D, DC, MC, V.

Ogden's Country Bed & Breakfast. Less than 1 mi from downtown, this two-story colonial in the historic village of Union Deposit, has rooms furnished with 1940s furniture. There's a deck, a porch, and a big back yard. Children under 12 can stay for free. Complimentary breakfast. Cable TV. No pets. | 407 N. Hanover St. | 717/566–9238 | members.aol.com/ogdenbbher/ | 3 rooms | $55–$75 | No credit cards.

Pinehurst Inn Bed & Breakfast. The closest bed and breakfast to Hershey Park, this inn sits on three acres. The 1930 building has a big front porch and large common rooms. Complimentary breakfast. No pets. | 50 Northeast Dr. | 717/533–2603 | fax 717/534–2639 | www.bedandbreakfast.com | 15 rooms | $49–$75 | Dec.–Apr. | MC, V.

Rodeway Inn. In a quiet residential area surrounded by woodlands and near Hershey Park, this inn is 15 mi from Hershey and Lancaster at PA Turnpike Exit #20. In-room data ports, cable TV. Pool. Business services. | 43 W. Areba Ave. | 717/533–7054 | fax 717/533–3405 | www.rodeway.com | 22 rooms, 4 suites | $139–$240, suites $240 | Closed Dec.–Mar. | AE, D, DC, MC, V.

Simmons. Family operated by the original owners since 1958, this brick and cobblestone motel is within walking distance of Hershey Park. Picnic area. Cable TV. Business services. | 355 W. Chocolate Ave. | 717/533–9177 | fax 717/533–3605 | www.simmonsmotel.com | 35 rooms | $75–$105 | AE, D, MC, V.

Spinner's Inn. This two-level country-style brick inn is 1 mi from Hershey Park. Restaurant, bar, picnic area, complimentary Continental breakfast, room service. Some microwaves, some refrigerators, cable TV. Pool. Video games. Business services, free parking. | 845 E. Chocolate Ave. | 717/533–9157 | fax 717/534–1189 | www.spinnersinn.com | 52 rooms (4 with shower only) | $79–$139 | AE, D, DC, MC, V.

Strawberry Patch Bed & Breakfast. Fifteen miles from Hershey, this modern log cabin is on 10 acres, with peacocks, a pygmy goat, and two rabbits on the grounds. The rooms have floral patterns and four-poster beds, handmade quilts, and fireplaces. There's a formal dining room for breakfast and afternoon tea. Complimentary breakfast. In-room data ports, in-room hot tubs, cable TV. Laundry service. No pets. No kids. | 115 Moore Rd., Lebanon | 717/865–7219 or 888/246–8826 | www.strawberrypatchbnb.com | 7 rooms | $95–$149 | MC, V.

White Rose. This small motel is 1 mi east of Hershey Chocolate Factory and a 5-min drive from Hersey's Chocolate World, Hershey outlets, and Hershey Park. Picnic area. In-room data ports, refrigerators, cable TV. Pool. Business services. No smoking. | 1060 E. Chocolate Ave. | 717/533–9876 | fax 717/533–6923 | whiterose@worldnet.att.net | www.whiterosemotel.com | 24 rooms | $59–$122 | AE, D, MC, V.

HOLICONG

(Nearby towns also listed: Doylestown, Lahaska, New Hope, Quakertown)

Once a favorite destination for New York's entertainment people, Holicong is a suburb east of Philadelphia. Before being named Holicong, it was called Greenville in honor of Revolutionary War hero Nathaniel Green. Many of the borough's original homes still stand and can be traced back to the early 1700s. Just to the east of Holicong is the art colony of New Hope. Here, you can also travel the Delaware canal by mule barge or ride a real old-fashioned steam train. You can browse in antique shops, sifting through the past of a region with a rich history. If you like performing arts, you can enjoy dramas, musicals, and comedies by the theaters and playhouses in New Hope, Doylestown, Buckingham, and Newtown. You can tour country estates along the Delaware River, visit Washington Crossing Historic Park, or the 300-year-old colonial village of Fallsington. If you like active leisure, take a hot-air balloon ride, or go boating, tubing, fishing, jogging, biking, or horseback riding.

Information: Bucks County Conference and Visitors Bureau | 152 Swamp Rd., Doylestown, PA 18901 | 215/345–4552.

ON THE CALENDAR
SEPT.: *Concours d'Elegance.* Every year, you can see a collection of the most elegant vintage automobiles on display at Holicong Park. | 215/598–0882. $5.

Dining
Black Bass. American. Three miles from Holicong in Lumberville, Black Bass is on the Delaware River in a 1745 building that now doubles as a restaurant and inn. Take your pick of places to sit; there are four dining areas, a porch overlooking the river, a stone room, and a room lit entirely by lanterns. The Charleston Meeting Street Crab—a cheese, crab, noodle, and vegetable casserole—has been a popular dish for more than 50 years. For dessert, try the deep-dish apple pie with cinnamon ice cream. | 3774 River Rd. | 215/297–5770 | Mon.–Sat. 11:30–3, 5:30–9:30; Sun. 11–2:30, 4:30–8 | $25 | AE, D, DC, MC, V.

Lodging
Ash Mill Farm Bed and Breakfast. This bed and breakfast is in a 1790 manor house with a patio and a wraparound porch. Period and faux antiques fill the house, which sits on 11 acres where sheep and goats graze. As you enter the house, you can see a massive mural of the house, grounds, and Bucks County landscape painted by a local artist. Complimentary breakfast. Cable TV in some rooms. No pets. No kids. | 5358 York Rd. | 215/794–5375 | 5 | $100–$160 | MC, V.

★ **Barley Sheaf Farm.** Once the home of Pulitzer Prize-winning playwright George S. Kaufman, author of *Dinner at Eight* and *You Can't Take It With You.*, this 1740 stone mansion has views of horse farms and meadows. Complimentary breakfast. In-room data ports, TV in common area. Pool. Business services. No smoking. | 5281 York Rd./Rte. 202, Holicong | 215/794–5104 | fax 215/794–5332 | barleysheaf@netreach.net | www.barleysheaf.com | 12 rooms | $150–$265 | AE, MC, V.

HONESDALE

(Nearby towns also listed: Hawley, Scranton)

The first locomotive in the United States arrived in Honesdale. In 1829, Horatio Allen made a short trip between Honesdale and Seelyville on the new engine and thus the railroad was born in America. Today, the borough blends history with music, art, and commerce. The area is host to dozens of historic sites and museums from the home of Zane Grey to the Dorflinger Glass Museum. It's surrounded by 112 lakes with 52 mi of unspoiled shoreline.

Information: Wayne County Chamber of Commerce | 303 Commercial St., 18431 | 570/253–1960 or 800/433–9008.

Attractions

Gravity Coach. You can visit this original passenger car from the Gravity Railroad, built in 1850, and learn about the history of the Gravity Coach. | Wayne County Historical Society, 810 Main St. | 570/253–3240 | $3 | Wed.–Sat. 10–4, closed Sun.–Tues.

Replica of the *Stourbridge Lion*. America's first railroad train, this was made to duplicate the *Stourbridge Lion* locomotive in England, built in 1829. The replica was made in 1933 for the Century of Progress Exposition in Chicago. | Wayne County Historical Society, 810 Main St. | 570/253–3240 | $3 | Wed.–Sat. 10–4, closed Sun.–Tues.

Stourbridge Rail Excursions. You can ride from Honesdale through Hawley along the Lackawaxen River in one of the 1940s diesel and vintage passenger cars. The trip has on-board entertainment and a stopover to tour the Zane Grey Museum and Roebling Aqueduct. | 303 Commercial St. | 570/253–1960 or 800/433–9008 | fax 570/253–1517 | www.waynecountycc.com | Admission varies | Call for hours.

Triple W Riding Stable. On about 200 acres and with more than 50 horses, this working horse farm gives scenic trail rides, private lessons, sleigh rides, and hayrides, and also runs overnight camping trips on horses. | R.R. Box 1514 | 570/226–2620 or 800/540–2620 | www.triplewstables.com | Prices vary depending on activity | Daily 9–5.

Wayne County Historical Society Museum. Permanent exhibits include the history of the Delaware and Hudson Canals and Native American exhibits. The museum also has a research library and changing exhibits on topics of Wayne County history. | 810 Main St. | 570/253–3240 | fax 570/253–5204 | $3 | Mar.–Dec., Wed.–Sat. 10–4, closed Sun.–Tues.; Jan.–Feb., Sat. 10–4, closed Sun.–Fri.

ON THE CALENDAR

FEB.: *Winter Carnival.* Every year, the second week in February, Honesdale celebrates its winter carnival with everything from ice carvings at the Main Street pavilion to Winter Olympics at the local YMCA. Local stores are involved too. | 570/253–1960.

AUG.: *Wayne County Fair.* This is a traditional country fair with farm and livestock exhibits, horse racing, entertainment, and food. | Wayne County Fairgrounds, 3 mi out of Honesdale | 717/253–1960 or 800/433–9008.

Dining

Maple City. American. Right in downtown, this family-style restaurant is named for the maple trees that line the main street. The restaurant is in a brick 1940s building and is furnished with wood paneling, tables, and chairs. The country chicken and biscuits is the most popular dinner item; for dessert, choose from at least 10 different pies, including the ever-popular lemon meringue. | 734 Main St. | 570/253–2462 | Sun. | Mon.–Sat., 6 AM–8 PM. | $7 | No credit cards.

Lodging

Double W Ranch Bed and Breakfast. Ten miles south of Honesdale, this ranch-style bed and breakfast is on a 183-acre farm at the end of a 1½-mi road. Relax in the outdoor hot tub, hike around the property, or ride horses to your heart's content—the Double W also has a public riding stable. Bears, coyote, deer, and other Pocono Mountains wildlife have been sighted, and there are cats and dogs closer to the house. Lake Wallenpaupak is about 10 min away. Complimentary Breakfast. Pond. Hiking, horseback riding, volleyball. Cross-country skiing, sleigh rides. No pets. | R.R. 2 | 570/226–3118 | doublew@ptd.net | www.doublewranchbnb.com | 10 rooms | $100–$200 | D, MC, V.

HUNTINGDON

(Nearby towns also listed: Altoona, Orbisonia)

In south-central Pennsylvania among ridges of the Appalachian Mountains, Huntingdon is known as the land of 1,000 hills. Rev. William Smith founded the area in 1767; today it follows much of the plan developed by Smith when he laid it out. The Juniata River, which runs through the borough, provides fertile fishing grounds for trout, bass, and other species. The town is near three state parks and Raystown Lake, the largest manmade lake in the state.

Information: **Huntingdon County Business and Industry** | 241 Mifflin St., 16652 | 814/643–1110.

Attractions

Indian Caverns. As far back as 1500, Native Americans used the cave as a winter shelter and council chamber. You can take a tour through nearly a mile of the cave's illuminated concrete and gravel walks and also see the more than 500 Native American relics unearthed in 1929. | Spruce Creek; Rte. 45, 11 mi east of Tyrone, between Water St. and State College | 814/632–7578 or 814/632–8333 | www.indiancaverns.com | $8.50 | Memorial Day–Labor Day, daily 9–6; April–May and Sept.–Oct., daily 9–4.

Lincoln Caverns. Discovered in 1930, these two caverns have massive flowstones, stalactites, calcite, and sparkling crystals. | Rte. 22, 3 mi west of Huntingdon | 814/643–0268 | fax 814/643–1358 | www.lincolncaverns.com | $8.50 | Apr.–Nov., daily 9–6; Mar. and Dec., weekends 9–5, closed weekdays; Jan.–Feb., by appointment.

Raystown Lake. This is Pennsylvania's largest manmade lake, with 8,300 acres of water, 11 launch ramps, and three tour boats. There's camping, hiking trails, picnic areas, and two large marinas. | Hesston; on Rte. 26, 8 mi south of Huntingdon, east of Lewistown, south of State College, and east of Altoona | 814/658–3405 or 877/444–6777 | fax 814/658–3313 | www.nab.usace.army.mill or www.reserveusa.com | Free; $2 launch fee | Reservations recommended | Daily.

Swigart Auto Museum. Established in 1920 by the late W. Emmert Swigart, this automobile collection began as a private passion of the present owner's father, with numbers in the hundreds and 40 to 50 on display at a time. You can see two Tucker autos and "Herbie the Love Bug." The license plate and radiator emblem collections might be the largest worldwide. | Rte. 22, 3 mi east of Huntingdon | 814/643–0885 or 814/643–2024 | fax 814/643–2857 | www.swigartmuseum.com | $4 | Memorial Day–Oct., daily 9–5.

Trough Creek State Park. On a scenic gorge, which cuts through Terrace Mountain and empties into Raystown Lake, the 554-acre park has 12 mi of hiking trails, 32 campsites, Trough Creek Lodge (which can be rented), five picnic areas, about 100 acres for hunting, and fishing on Great Trough Creek. | 6 mi on Rte. 26 from town, park on left | 814/658–3847 or 888/PA–PARKS | fax 814/658–2973 | www.dcnr.state.pa.us | Free | Daily 8 AM–dusk.

AUG.: *Huntingdon County Fair.* Held at the Huntingdon County Fairgrounds, this is a week-long event with performing artists, art exhibits, craft displays, livestock, local produce, food vendors, and stock car racing. | 814/643–4452 | $4.

OCT.: *Hartslog Day.* A celebration of local heritage features crafts, games, music, and food in Alexandria. | 7 mi west of Huntingdon | 814/643–3577.

Dining

Donna's Family Restaurant. American. In a mall that's less than a mile from Huntingdon, this restaurant serves roast beef, pork chop platters, and meatloaf. Choose from Wisconsin cheese soup and, for desert, coconut cream pie. | Rte. 22, Mat Plaza | 814/643–6113 | Sun.–Thurs. 6–10, Fri.– Sat. 24 hrs | $6–$10 | No credit cards.

Lodging

Days Inn. This two-story brick motel is just minutes away from Raystown Lake and 1 mi from town. Restaurant, bar. In-room data ports, cable TV. Business services, free parking. No Pets. | Rte. 22 and S. 4th St. | 814/643–3934 | fax 814/643–3005 | www.daysinn.com | 76 rooms | $59–$70 | AE, D, DC, MC, V.

Huntingdon Motor Inn. In a quiet residential neighborhood, this two-story brick motel is a short car ride from most Huntingdon attractions. Bar. In-room data ports, cable TV. Gym. Business services. Pets allowed. | Junction of Rte. 22 and 26, Rd. #1 | fax 814/643–1331 | www.huntingdon.net/lodging.htm | 48 rooms | $50–$65 | AE, D, DC, MC, V.

Inn at Solvang. Four miles north of Huntingdon on Route 26 and surrounded by forests and lawns, this 1938 three-story brick Colonial home has columns, balconies, and balustrades. The rooms are furnished with antiques, and chandeliers are everywhere. There's a private trout stream on the property, and a golf course nearby. Complimentary breakfast. Some in-room hot tubs, no TV in some rooms. Hiking. Fishing. Library. No pets. No kids under 15. | R.R. #4, Rte. 26N | 814/643–3035 or 888/814–3035 | fax 814/641–7306 | Innkeeper@solvang.com | www.solvang.com | 6 rooms | $95–$135 | AE, MC, V.

INDIANA

MAP 7, D5

(Nearby towns also listed: Ford City, Johnstown)

While the surrounding county is called the "Christmas Tree Capital of the World," Indiana is best known as the home of actor Jimmy Stewart, who grew up in this borough. The town, established in 1861, grew along with the lumber industry and eventually became a coal town. Today, with a population of 29,331, the downtown area remains largely unchanged from when it was laid out and you can see its 19th-century buildings, as well as pay homage to the man who gave us *It's a Wonderful Life.*

Information: **Indiana County Chamber of Commerce** | 1019 Philadelphia St., 15701 | 724/465–2511.

Attractions

Blue Spruce County Park. This park has a 12-acre lake and 6 mi of trails for hiking or cross-country skiing, a playground, a volleyball court, a softball field, and a hill for sledding. | 1128 Blue Spruce Park Rd. | 724/463–8636 | fax 724/463–8740 | www.indiana-co-pa-tourism.org | Free | Daily 7 AM–dusk.

Eliza Furnace. Near the border of Cambria and Indiana counties, Eliza Furnace (1850) is one of the best-preserved iron furnaces in Pennsylvania–and one of the only ones to still have its hot-blast coils intact. It's believed that the furnace was named after the daughter of a wealthy patron who used to buy iron from the mill—or after the wife of one of the owners. Nobody knows for sure, but most agree that the furnace is haunted; you'll hear plenty of stories if you visit. | R.D. 2 | 724/463–8636 | fax 724/463–8740 | Free | Daily, sunrise–sunset.

Jimmy Stewart Museum. You can learn about the life and accomplishments of Indiana's most famous native here. There are photographs, old movie posters, books, and gifts presented to the movie star. | 845 Philadelphia St. | 724/349–6112 | fax 724/349–6140 | www.jimmy.org | $5 | Apr.–Dec., Mon.–Sat. 10–5, Sun. noon–5; Jan.–Mar., Wed.–Sat. 10–5, Sun. noon–5, closed Mon.–Tues.

Yellow Creek State Park. The 2,981-acre park has a 720-acre lake with a beach and swimming area. Here you can go fishing, boating, ice skating, ice fishing, picnicking, hunting, hiking, cross-country skiing, sledding, and snowmobiling. | 170 Rte. 259, Penn Run | 724/357–7913 or 888/PA–PARKS | fax 724/357–7956 | www.dcnr.state.pa.us | Free | Daily 8 AM–dusk.

ON THE CALENDAR
JULY: *Hoodlebug SummerFest.* A family-oriented day, with ethnic food booths, crafts, a kids' alley, a duck race, a 5K run/walk, a parade, game booths, and informational displays. | 724/479–9759 | Free.

Dining
Coney Island. Irish. The walls of this 1933 pub are covered with photographs of and articles about Ireland. The restaurant, with an outdoor covered patio, is known for seafood, soups, and hot dogs. Live music Thurs.–Sat. | 642 Philadelphia St. | 724/465–8082 | $8–$17 | AE, D, MC, V.

Rouki's Restaurant. American. A dining tribute to Jimmy Stewart, this restaurant serves sandwiches with names like George Bailey, Vertigo, and the Man Who Knew Too Much. A 1900s Super Simplex theater projector is on display in the dining room, along with autographed pictures and memorabilia from the cast of *It's A Wonderful Life*. Breakfast. | 665 Philadelphia St. | 724/465–7200 | $8–$15 | MC, V.

Lodging
Best Western University Inn. One mile from Indiana University's campus and the Jimmy Stewart Museum and birthplace, this Best Western is 5 mi from several golf courses, downtown shops, two local malls, and 9 mi from Yellow Creek State Park. Restaurant, bar, room service. In-room data ports, cable TV. Pool. Pets allowed ($15 fee). | 1545 Wayne Ave. | 724/349–9620 | fax 724/349–2620 | www.bestwestern.com | 107 rooms | $70–$80 | AE, D, DC, MC, V.

4 Sisters Bed & Breakfast. Named in honor of two generations of four sisters, this 100-year-old three-story red brick building is on the west side of town. Today, the house has a women's resource library and art gallery dedicated to women from the past 100 years. Outside, there's a sprawling backyard with a stream. Indiana University of Pennsylvania is five blocks away. You can get a cheaper rate if you don't want breakfast. Cable TV. No smoking. | 1500 Philadelphia St. | 724/349–3623 | cathompson@yourinter.net | 4 rooms | $30–$60 | MC, V.

Holiday Inn. A modern two-story stucco building, this hotel is 1 mi from downtown and a short drive from the Jimmy Stewart Museum, Indiana University of Pennsylvania, Challenger Raceway, Yellow Creek State Park, Blue Spruce County Park, Saltsburg Canal, Smicksburg Amish Village, Windgate Vineyards, Indiana Mall, and Punxsutawney. Restaurant, bar (with entertainment), complimentary breakfast, room service. In-room data ports, cable TV. Indoor pool. Hot tub, sauna. Miniature golf. Business services. Pets allowed. | 1395 Wayne Ave. | 724/463–3561 | fax 724/463–8006 | 159 rooms | $89–$99 | AE, D, DC, MC, V.

JENKINTOWN

(Nearby towns also listed: Fort Washington, Philadelphia, Willow Grove)

Settled in 1697 by William Jenkins, the town became Jenkintown in 1759. Today, although it's better known as a suburb of Philadelphia, Jenkintown has many Victorian-style houses and historical sites.

Information: **Eastern Montgomery County Chamber of Commerce** | Box 172, 19046 | 215/887–5122.

Attractions

Beth Shalom Synagogue. The last architectural work of Frank Lloyd Wright, Beth Shalom Synagogue was dedicated in 1959. The hexagonal shape of the building represents two outstretched hands and the dome that rests within represents Mt. Sinai. | 8231 Old York Rd., Elkins Park | 215/887–1342 | fax 215/887–6605 | www.bethshalomcongregation.org | Free | Mon.–Thurs., 10 and 2, and by appointment.

Wall House. Built in 1682 by Richard Wall, one of the first two original settlers in Cheltenham Township, the house is now a museum owned and operated by Cheltenham Township, 2 mi south of Jenkintown. | 1 Wall Park Dr. | 215/887–1000 | By donation | Sun. 1–4, or by appointment.

ON THE CALENDAR

OCT.: *Best of the Burbs.* Held during the first two weeks of October, this town festival has a jazz festival, international foods, crafts, performances, cultural events, rides, and games. | 215/887–5122.

Dining

Deetrick's Cafe and Jazz Bar. Continental. The sleek bar and dimly lit room make it perfect for good food and live jazz performances on Mondays and Sundays. The bar has a large selection of international liquors and beers. The restaurant is known for the crab cakes and salmon. Sun. brunch. | 211 Old York Rd. | 215/576–7690 | Reservations essential | No lunch | $16–$28 | AE, D, DC, MC, V.

Stazi Milano. Italian. A 100-ft high ceiling hung with mobiles, a chandelier, a collection of Andy Warhol prints, and a miniature train set add to this Art Deco restaurant. Specials are chicken lasagna, rack of lamb, and crab cakes. Live music Fri. Kids' menu, early-bird suppers. | Township Line Rd. and Greenwood Ave. | 215/885–9000 | fax 215/885–9353 | weekends | $9–$17 | AE, DC, MC, V.

Lodging

Cherry Tree Hotel. There's no lodging in Jenkintown, but you can find a place to stay in Washington, 5 mi north. This hotel is a modern, six-story building surrounded by chain hotels and motels, close to the Expo center, used for conventions, and exhibitions. Restaurant, bar, complimentary Continental breakfast. In-room data ports, cable TV. Outdoor pool. | 530 Pennsylvania Ave. | 215/643–1111 or 800/249–4648 | fax 215/653–0115 | www.cherrytreehotel.com | 135 rooms | $69 | AE, D, DC, MC, V.

JIM THORPE

(Nearby town also listed: Hazleton)

Named after the legendary Native American athlete, the borough of Jim Thorpe was, for much of its history, known as "Old Mauch Chunk," a Native American term for Bear

Mountain. The borough became a prominent rail transfer point for coal in the 1920s. With the decline of the coal industry, Mauch Chunk, Upper Mauch Chunk, and East Mauch Chunk were offered the opportunity to rename the area Jim Thorpe after the famous athlete's widow presented her husband's name and remains as a uniting symbol in exchange for a proper memorial.

Information: **Carbon County Tourist Promotion Agency** | Railroad Station, Box 90, Jim Thorpe, PA 18229 | 570/325–3673 or 888/546–8467.

Attractions

Asa Packer Mansion. Built between 1859 and 1861 by artisans from Switzerland for industrialist and philanthropist Asa Packer, founder of the Lehigh Valley Railroad and Lehigh University in Bethlehem, this Victorian mansion has 18 rooms with original furnishings. Constructed for approximately $14,000, the house and estate were valued at $54 million at the time of Asa Packer's death. | 30 Elk Dr. | 570/325–3229 | www.jimthorpe.com | $5 | June–Oct., daily 11–4:15; Apr.–May and Nov., weekends 11–4:15, closed weekdays.

Jim Thorpe Memorial. This tomb honors the Sac and Fox Indian who won gold medals in the pentathlon and decathlon in the 1912 Olympics in Sweden, played on the 1911 and 1912 All-American football teams and, in 1920, became the first president of the American Professional Football Association (now the National Football League). The Associated Press in 1950 named Thorpe the greatest football player and greatest all-around athlete for the first 50 years of the 20th century. | Rte. 903 N, near the Carbon County Vo-Tech School; along Rte. 903 | 570/325–3673 or 888/JIM–THORPE | fax 570/325–5584 | www.visitcarboncounty.org | Free | Daily.

Lehigh Gorge State Park. The 4,548 acres of parkland are along 25 mi of the Lehigh River, running from White Haven to Jim Thorpe. Here you can fish, go whitewater boating, and view the thick vegetation, rock outcroppings, and many waterfalls in the park. About 26 mi of abandoned railroad grade follow the river, making this a great place for hiking, biking, cross-country skiing, and snowmobiling. There's an overnight charge and reservations are suggested. | From I–80 take Exit 40 (Hickory Run State Park), and drive east on PA 534 for 6 mi | 570/443–0400, 570/427–5000, or 888/PA–PARKS | www.dcnr.state.pa.us | Free | Daily 8 AM–dusk.

Mauch Chunk Opera house. Built in 1879, this ornate Victorian building used to be a farmer's market on the first floor and a concert hall on the second. Later it became a regular stop for traveling vaudeville performers. Musicals and plays are still performed here. | 14 W. Broadway | 570/325–4439 | Call for ticket prices.

Old Jail Museum. An active prison until January 1995, this was the site of the hanging of nearly 100 Molly Mcguires, coal miners who fought for the rights of miners. The old jail is listed on the National Register of Historic Buildings. | 128 W. Broadway | 570/325–5259 | fax 570/325–8380 | www.jimthorpe.com | $4 | May–Oct., daily noon–4:30, closed Wed. Sept.–Oct. weekends only.

St. Mark's Episcopal Church. This Gothic Revival church was designed by Richard Upjohn Sr. in 1869. The interior has early Tiffany windows, an ornate baptismal font, and the original English minton tile floor. | 21 Race St. | 570/325–2241 | fax 570/325–2241 | Free | Tue.–Fri. 2–5, and by appointment.

Stone Row. Built for Lehigh Valley Railroad personnel, these three-story houses were individualized by variations in dormers, bay windows, doors, and window trim. Today Stone Row is being revitalized for studio, display, and living space. | 27–57 Race St. | 570/325–3673 or 888/JIM–THORPE | fax 570/325–5584 | www.jimthorpe.org | Free | Daily.

Whitewater rafting. There are three rafting outfitters in the area that give guided whitewater rafting trips down the Lehigh River and through the Lehigh River Gorge. | 570/325–3673 or 888/JIM–THORPE | fax 570/325–5584 | www.jimthorpe.com | Mar.–Oct.
Jim Thorpe River Adventures Inc. has guided rafting trips on the Lehigh River with

transportation to and from the river. Paddles, life preservers, and waterproof lunch containers are provided. You can also rent mountain bikes here. | 1 Adventure La. | 570/325–2570, 570/325–4960, or 800/424–RAFT | fax 570/325–2688 | www.jtraft.com | $47 | Mar.–Oct., daily 8–6.

Pocono Whitewater Adventures leads rafting trips that last from 4½ to 5½ hours on 8 to 12 mi of the Lehigh River through the Lehigh River Gorge. The outfitter also has mountain biking, paintball, and guided hikes. | Rte. 903 | 570/325–3655, 570/325–8430, or 800/WHITE-WATER | fax 570/325–4097 | www.whitewaterrafting.com or www.skirmish.com | $50 | Mar.–Oct., daily 10–8.

Whitewater Challengers Inc. has whitewater rafting, biking, kayaking clinics, orienteering, camping, and rafting. The guided whitewater trips can last from 3 to 5 hours and range in difficulty. | 288 North Stage Coach Rd., Weatherly | 570/443–9758 | fax 570/443–9727 | www.wcrafting.com | $30–$50 | Mar.–Oct., call for hrs.

ON THE CALENDAR
MAY: *Jim Thorpe Birthday Weekend.* Every year James Francis Thorpe is honored with slide presentations, kids' activities, food and craft stands, music, and a huge birthday cake. Held the last weekend in May. | 570/325–3673.

JUNE: *Laurel Blossom Festival.* An early summer festival with steam train rides, crafts, food, and entertainment. | Downtown, East Packer Park | 570/325–3673.

OCT.: *Fall Foliage Festival.* This event has food, entertainment, crafts, and scenic train rides. | Downtown | 570/325–3673.

Dining
Black Bread Cafe. Continental. Not much has changed in this restaurant in two 1850 Victorian stone houses in an area known as Stone Road. The original wood and plasterwork remains, and the walls are lined with local artwork. Entrees include salmon puttanesca, rabbit with baby lima beans, honey-roasted half duckling, and Key lime chicken. | 47 Race St. | 570/325–8957 | Reservations essential | Tues. | Wed.–Mon. 11–9 | $12–$21 | D, MC, V.

Lodging
Inn at Jim Thorpe. Built in the 1840s, this New Orleans-style inn in the historic district has hosted General Grant, President Taft, Buffalo Bill, Thomas Edison, and John D. Rockefeller. Restaurant, bar (with entertainment), dining room, complimentary Continental breakfast. Some microwaves, some refrigerators, cable TV, some in-room VCRs. Business services. | 24 Broadway | 717/325–2599 or 800/329–2599 | fax 717/325–9145 | www.innjt.com | 29 rooms, 8 suites | $85–$115, suites $165–$250 | AE, D, DC, MC, V.

Victoria Ann's Bed & Breakfast. Part of Jim Thorpe's "Millionaire Row" on Broadway, this 1860 Victorian town house is close to Pocono Mountain ski resorts, whitewater rafting, hiking, biking, and camping. Relax on the patio or wander through the English garden in the back. Cable TV. No kids under 12. No pets. | 68 Broadway | 570/325–8107 | www.thevictoriann.com | 8 rooms | $65–150 | AE, D, MC, V.

JOHNSTOWN

MAP 7, D6

(Nearby towns also listed: Ebensburg, Ligonier)

Johnstown, with its long history as a steel town, is most famous for the Johnstown Flood of 1889. On May 31 a wall of water thundered 14 mi down the mountain and roared into town at 40 mi per hour, killing 2,209 men, women, and children. That fateful day is remembered with a museum where you can walk a portion of the flood's path. Today, Johnstown is known for many industries and is part of Hollywood history as the movies *All the Right Moves* and *Slap Shot* were filmed on its streets.

Information: Greater Johnstown/Cambria County Chamber of Commerce | 111 Market St., 15901 | 814/536–5107.

Attractions

Conemaugh Gap. The deepest gorge east of the Mississippi River, this gap extends for 7 mi through a 1,350-ft gorge of the Laurel Mountain Ridge, which was cut by the Conemaugh River. | Haws Pike (off of Rte. 56) in Armagh, 13 mi from Johnstown | Free | Daily.

Grandview Cemetery. Many of the 2,209 people who died in the Johnstown Flood are buried at this cemetery, where there is also a monument to the 777 unidentified victims of the flood. | 801 Millcreek Rd. | 814/535–2652 | fax 814/539–5508 | Free | Mon.–Sat. 8–4:30, closed Sun.

Inclined Plane Railway. Opened in 1891, the world's steepest incline plane capable of carrying vehicles, the railway, and its 38-ton cars can haul 8 tons of payload up 500 vertical ft at a grade of 71.9 percent. The whole Johnstown Valley can be viewed from an observation deck at the top. | 711 Edgehill Dr. | 814/536–1816 | fax 814/536–4328 | www.incline-plane.com | $3 | Mon.–Fri. 6:30 AM–midnight; Sat. 7:30 AM–midnight; Sun. 9 AM–midnight.

Johnstown Chiefs. A member of the Eastern Coast Hockey League, the Chiefs play their games at Cambria County War Memorial Stadium, which was used for the movie *Slap Shot*. | 326 Napoleon St. | 814/536–5156 | www.johnstownchiefs.com | $8–$15 | Oct.–Apr.

Johnstown Flood Museum. The museum tells the story of the 1889 flood through exhibits, an Academy Award–winning documentary film, a lighted and sound-animated relief model of the path of the flood, video presentations, objects, and photos. | 304 Washington St. | 814/539–1889 or 888/222–1889 | fax 814/535–1931 | www.jaha.org | $4 | May–Oct., Sun.–Thurs. 10–5, Fri.–Sat. 10–7; Nov.–Apr., daily 10–5.

Johnstown Flood National Memorial. Established in 1964 to commemorate the flood victims, the memorial is near the site of the former South Fork dam, which was breached after heavy rains, leading to the Johnstown Flood. You can see many exhibits and a 35-minute film on the flood, and remains of the dam. | 733 Lake Rd., South Fork | 814/495–4643 | fax 814/495–7181 | www.nps.gov/jofl/ | $2 | Memorial Day–Labor Day, daily 9–6; Labor Day–Memorial Day, daily 9–5.

Windber Coal Heritage Center. You can travel back to an early 20th-century bituminous coal town to experience the life of a miner and his family through three interactive exhibits, including getting coal grit on your face. | 501 15th St. | 814/467–6680 | fax 814/467–8715 | www.allegheny.org/windber | $3.50 | Apr.–Oct., Fri. and Sat. 10–5; Nov.–Mar., by appointment.

ON THE CALENDAR

SEPT.: *FolkFest.* This free three-day event draws more than 120,000 people each year to see performers from all over the United States. The festival is held in the Cambria City National Historic District, which used to be a working-class neighborhood for immigrants who came to Johnstown to work in the coal and steel mills during the 19th and early 20th centuries. Guided tours of houses and churches in the neighborhood run throughout the festival. | 814/539–1889 or 888/222–1889.

Dining

Baker's Loaf Eatery. Café. Eight different kinds of freshly baked bread are the main draw at this cafe, in a brick building in the middle of town. Eat inside at one of the old wooden tables surrounded by plants and bay windows, or on the outdoor sidewalk patio. You can choose from sandwiches, salads, soups, and strawberry, blueberry, and chocolate-filled croissants. | 1073 Franklin St. | 814/539–0788 | Sun. | $5–10 | AE, MC, V.

Santoyos Mexican Food. Mexican. Right in the center of town, this restaurant has inexpensive Mexican dishes. Try the enchiladas or the tacos, both popular. You can eat outside at one of the sidewalk tables, or inside, surrounded by colorful Mexican ornaments. | 207 ½ Market St. | 814/539–7056 | Closed weekends | Weekdays 9–5 | 5–10 | No credit cards.

Lodging

Comfort Inn. The Johnstown Flood Museum is 5.2 mi northwest of this two-story stucco motel. Picnic area, complimentary Continental breakfast. In-room data ports, refrigerators, cable TV, in-room VCRs (and movies). Indoor pool. Hot tub. Exercise equipment. Laundry facilities. Business services, airport shuttle. Pets allowed (fee). | 455 Theatre Dr. | 814/266–3678 | fax 814/266–9783 | www.comfortinn.com | 117 rooms, 27 suites | $65–$70, $95 suites | AE, D, DC, MC, V.

Holiday Inn–Downtown. This six-story hotel made of mostly brick is downtown and within walking distance of the central park, Cambria County Community College, shopping, the Johnstown Flood Museum, and Inclined Plane Railway. Restaurant, bar. In-room data ports, cable TV. Indoor pool. Hot tub, sauna. Exercise equipment. Business services, airport shut-

JOHNSTOWN FLOOD

On a stormy evening in 1889 the steel mill town of Johnstown was awakened by the sound of thunder, but not thunder from the heavens. The rumbling was coming from the ground and was growing in intensity every minute. On that fateful night, the town would be turned to rubbish and more than 2,000 men, women, and children would lose their lives. The famous Johnstown flood would enter the annals of American history.

The history of the flood began some years before it actually occured when the area's wealthy residents decided to create a lake for their own recreational purposes. A local stream, on a hilltop above Johnstown, was dammed and the wealthy got their playground, but Mother Nature had something else in store for them.

Although the dam was built to withstand a large rain, on May 31, 1889, there was more rain than the dam could handle. After hours of rain and no way of relieving the pressure on the dam, the dam broke and released a wall of water, down the gorge, heading straight for Johnstown. As the water rushed down the hill, it uprooted large trees and boulders. Johnstown had no warning and was slammed with a wall of water that caused millions of dollars in damage to property and many casualties. To make matters worse, the debris carried along with the raging flood caught fire in the town, creating a firestorm that further ravaged the city.

Like most cities that go through disasters, the citizens rebuilt and moved on with life. However, it is said that every family in the town lost at least one family member and in some cases children were not only left without parents, but without grandparents and aunts and uncles as well.

To get a better understanding and more detailed story of how the events of this night transpired, visit the Johnstown Flood Museum in downtown Johnstown. The museum houses actual photographs and artifacts from the disaster as well as a three-dimensional model that shows a path of the flood. The movie shown in the museum won an Academy Award and is considered one of the best documented short subject films ever made.

tle. Pets allowed. | 250 Market St. | 814/535–7777 | fax 814/539–1393 | www.holidayinn.com | 164 rooms | $82–$99 | AE, D, DC, MC, V.

Sleep Inn. In the business district, this three-story motel is 5 mi northwest of the Johnstown Flood Museum. Complimentary Continental breakfast. In-room data ports, cable TV. Business services, airport shuttle. Pets allowed (fee). | 453 Theatre Dr. | 814/262–9292 | fax 814/262–0486 | www.sleepinn.com | 62 rooms (59 with shower only) | $60–$65 | AE, D, DC, MC, V.

Towne Manor Motel. Built in the 1940s, this two-story downtown motel is next to a park, a stadium, and the Inclined Plane Railway. Different sizes of rooms and suites are available, with some for a family of four. Complimentary Continental breakfast. Cable TV. Pets allowed. | 155 Johns St. | 814/536–8771 | 55 rooms | $30–$60. | AE, D, DC, MC, V.

Windmill Bed & Breakfast. Five minutes from downtown, this small house on the east side of town has just one suite available. There's a large wraparound porch, and a pond in the backyard. Cable TV. | 145 Hostetler Rd. | 814/269–4625 | 1 room | $75 | No credit cards.

KANE

MAP 7, D3

(Nearby towns also listed: Bradford, St. Mary's, Warren)

Named after the first man in Pennsylvania to volunteer his service in the Civil War, Kane was established in 1887. Although Kane is known as the Black Cherry Timber Capital of the World, some call it the Icebox of Pennsylvania because more than 107 inches of snow falls here every year. It's an ideal place for snowmobiling, cross-country skiing, and ice fishing at the Allegheny Reservoir of the Kinzua Dam. The Allegheny National Forest surrounds Kane on three sides and offers an abundance of outdoor recreation. Tionesta Scenic National Historic Landmark and North Country National Scenic Trail are nearby.

Information: **Kane Chamber of Commerce** | 14 Greeves St., 16735 | 814/837–6565.

Attractions

Bendigo State Park. The 100-acre park on a bank of the East Branch of the Clarion River has a swimming pool, picnic facilities, and sledding. | Glen Hazel Rd., Jones Township, Johnsonburg | 814/965–2646 or 888/PA–PARKS | fax 814/965–3161 | www.dcnr.state.pa.us | Free | Daily 8 AM–dusk.

Kane Railroad Depot & Museum. The old Pennsylvania Railroad Depot, constructed in the late 1800s, has been transformed into a community museum and cultural center to preserve the town's transportation heritage. You can board the Knox, Kane, Kinzua Excursion Train in Kane for a 32-mi round-trip to the Kinzua Bridge (including a half-hour layover). | S. Fraley St., U.S. 6 at Rte. 66 | 814/837–8752 or 814/837–6565 | Free | By appointment.

Kinzua Bridge State Park. The 316-acre park is the site of the 2,053-ft Kinzua Railroad Bridge, which has been designated as a National Engineering Landmark. The highest railroad bridge in the world at the time of its construction in 1882, it rises 301 ft. The park has a scenic overlook, picnic facilities, hunting on 306 acres, fishing in Kinzua Creek, and organized group camping. | Johnsonburg; 4 mi north of U.S. 6 at Mt. Jewett on Rte. 3011 | 814/965–2646 or 888/ PA–PARKS | fax 814/965–3161 | www.dcnr.state.pa.us | Free | Daily 8 AM–dusk.

Thomas L. Kane Memorial Chapel. Memorabilia from the family of General Thomas L. Kane, including a tea set used by Thomas Jefferson, can be seen here. General Kane is buried on site between the two sets of steps at the chapel. | 30 Chestnut St. | 814/837–9729 | Free | Tues.–Sat. 9–5, closed Sun.–Mon.

KANE

INTRO
ATTRACTIONS
DINING
LODGING

Twin Lakes. Once the site of factories, stores, and company row houses, Twin Lakes has 50 campsites. The Black Cherry National Recreation Trail runs past the lake. | 8 mi SE of Kane on Rte. 321 in the Alleghney National Forest | 814/723–5150 | Free | Daily dawn to dusk.

ON THE CALENDAR

JAN.: *Winterfest.* This two-day event features a snow sculpture contest, ice skating, horse-drawn sleigh rides, an ice-sculpting demonstration, and a children's carnival. | Throughout town of Marienville | 814/837–6565 | Free.

Dining

Texas Hot Lunch. American/Casual. Locals who travel can hardly wait to return home for a Texas Hot—a hot dog with onions, mustard, and the house special sauce—from this popular eatery, which also serves Greek dishes such as souvlaki. It's two blocks from the old railroad depot, and has a pub, a no–smoking room, and an ATM. Serves breakfast. | 24 Field St. | 814/837–8122 | $0.99–$6.50 | No credit cards.

Lodging

Kane Manor Country Inn. In 1897 General Kane built this three-story Greek Revival house in the foothills of the Alleghenies. His wife, Dr. Elizabeth Kane, named it Anoatok, an Eskimo word meaning "wind loved spot." Bordered by the Allegheny National Forest, the inn is 1½ blocks from Rte. 6 and 25 minutes west of the Kinzua Bridge. The house is full of furniture, portraits, paintings, books, and Civil War memorabilia. Bar, dining room, complementary Continental breakfast. Cable TV, some room phones. Library. No pets. No smoking. | 230 Clay St. | 814/837–6522 | fax 814/837–6664 | info@kanemanor.com | www.kanemanor.com | 10 rooms (6 with private bath) | $99–$149 | AE, D, MC, V.

KENNETT SQUARE

MAP 7, J7

(Nearby towns also listed: Chadds Ford, West Chester)

Kennett Square was settled by Francis Smith, who came to the area in 1686 to look for mushrooms for a large mushroom cannery he owned in Kennett, a village in England. Today the town doesn't send mushrooms back to England, but it does ship a large amount of roses around the country.

Information: **Southern Chester County Chamber of Commerce** | 206 E. State St., 19348 | 610/444–0774.

Attractions

★ **Longwood Gardens.** Here you can stroll 1,050 acres of woodlands, meadows, 20 outdoor gardens, and 20 indoor gardens with 4 acres of greenhouse with 11,000 different types of plants, and illuminated fountains. Longwood dates back to 1700, when George Pierce acquired 402 acres from William Penn. Pierce's descendants farmed the land and in 1798 began planting an arboretum. The farm was purchased in 1906 by Pierre S. du Pont, who personally designed most of what is enjoyed today. | U.S. 1, 3 mi northeast | 610/388–1000 or 800/737–5500. | www.longwoodgardens.org | $12 | Apr.–Oct., daily 9–6; Nov.–Mar., daily 9–5.

Phillips Mushroom Museum. The museum explains the history, love, and mystique of mushrooms through film, dioramas, slide presentations, and exhibits. You can see mushrooms in all stages of their development at the museum. | 909 E. Baltimore Pike | 610/388–6082 or 800/243–8644 | $1.25 | Daily 10–5:30 | www.mushroomfest.com.

White Clay Creek Park and Preserve. The 1,253-acre park has 3 mi of hiking trails, fishing in White Clay Creek, 1,240 acres for hunting, and an 8-mi trail for horseback riding. You can also find here the Yeatman Mill House, the hub of a very prosperous milling and agricultural complex in the 18th and 19th centuries, and the 1729 London Tract Baptist Meeting House, with a stone-walled cemetery where many of the area's earliest settlers are buried. | 425 Wedgewood Road, Newark, DE 19711 | 610/274–2900 or 888/PA–PARKS | www.dcnr.state.pa.us | Free | Daily 8 AM–dusk.

ON THE CALENDAR

SEPT.: *Mushroom Festival.* Held in downtown, usually two weeks after Labor Day, this festival celebrates the local mushroom industry with tastings, contests, and mushrooms for sale – also a golf tournament. | 610/793–3202 or 610/444–0774.

Dining

Kennett Square Inn. Contemporary. Built in the 1700s, this inn is known for its crab cakes and the steak Diane. Live music Wed., Sat. | 201 E. State St. | 610/444–5687 | No lunch Sun. | $13–$22 | AE, D, MC, V.

The Terrace. Continental. With plants and flowers hanging from the ceiling and sunlight filling the room, this restaurant's dining area is surrounded by large glass windows overlooking Longwood Gardens. You can eat outdoors on the patio at one of the tables shaded by umbrellas. Popular dishes include mushroom soup and crab cakes. Kids' menu. | Rte. 1, Kennett Square, PA 19348 | 610/388–6771 | fax 610/388–7064 | Closed Jan.–Mar. | $12–$22.

Trumpets. Contemporary. Opened in April 1999, this restaurant serves regional fare such as grilled salmon with mole verde. The menu changes seasonally. Trumpets is on the former site of the Kennett Hotel in the downtown historic district. | 114 E. State St. | 610/444–9644 | Lunch Tues.–Fri. Closed Mon. | $16.95–$22.95 | AE, D, DC, MC, V.

Lodging

B&B; at Walnut Hill. Less than 2 mi south of downtown, this white clapboard and fieldstone millhouse is full of country antiques, with writing desks in the bedrooms, and dried flowers and herbs. The family who built this pre-Civil War home ran a grist mill on the premises. Complimentary breakfast. Some room phones, no TV in some rooms. No pets. No smoking. | 541 Chandler's Mill Rd. | 610/444–3703 | fax 610/444–6889 | millsjt@magpage.com | 2 rooms | $95 | No credit cards.

Fairville Inn. A bed and breakfast in the heart of the Brandywine Valley in Chadds Ford, just 8 mi north of Wilmington, Delaware. Surrounded by magnificent homes, estates, and mi of back roads, the Inn has three different buildings: the Main House (built in the 1820s), the Carriage House, and the Springhouse. Most rooms have a canopy bed and fireplace. You can enjoy afternoon tea with home-baked cookies and pastries daily. | 15 rooms. Complimentary breakfast. Cable TV. Business services. No kids under 12. No smoking. | 506 Kennett Pike, Mendenhall | 610/388–5900 | fax 610/388–5902 | www.fairvilleinn.com | $145–$205 | AE, D, MC, V.

Meadow Spring Farm. This 1836 brick colonial farmhouse, about 3 mi north of downtown, is bursting with red-coated Santas—or cows— depending on the season. You can walk the 120-acre farm, visit the animals in the barn, or play pool and ping-pong in the game room. Complimentary breakfast. Cable TV. Outdoor pool. Hot tub. No pets. No smoking. | 201 E. Street Rd. | 610/444–3903 | fax 610/444–7859 | 5 rooms | $85–$95 | No credit cards.

Scarlett House. Gracing the historic district of Kennett Square, this house was built in 1910 by a prominent Quaker businessman for his son Robert, who resided here until the 1960s. Many of the music boxes, teapots and miniatures that fill the house were collected by the hosts, who have traveled extensively. Complimentary breakfast. Cable TV. No pets. No smoking. | 503 W. State St. | 610/444–9592 or 800/820–9592 | www.traveldata.com/inns/data/scarlett | 4 rooms (2 with private bath), 1 suite | $95–$139 | AE, D, DC, MC, V.

Mendenhall Hotel and Conference Center. A step inside this three-level stucco building reveals refreshing floral arrangements, marble floors, smooth Persian rugs, and cozy sitting areas. Restaurant, bar, complimentary Continental breakfast, room service. In-room data ports, minibars, cable TV. Exercise equipment. Business services, airport shuttle. | Rte. 52, Mendenhall | 610/388–2100 | fax 610/388–1184 | www.brandywinevalley.com | 70 rooms | $125 | AE, D, DC, MC, V.

KING OF PRUSSIA

MAP 7, K7

(Nearby towns also listed: Norristown, Philadelphia, West Chester)

Originally named Reeseville for the Welsh family that owned the land, this suburb of Philadelphia is known for its shopping malls and the nearby Valley Forge Historical National Park.

Information: **King of Prussia Chamber of Commerce** | 1150 1st Ave., 19406 | 610/265–1776.

Attractions

Harriton House. Built in 1704, this two-story stone house is one of the few representing early American architecture in Philadelphia. Originally called Bryn Mawr, the home is furnished with 18th-century pieces. | 500 Harriton Rd., Bryn Mawr | 610/525–0201 | $2.50 | Tues.–Sat. 10–4, Sun. by appointment, closed Mon.

Mill Grove. This is the only true Audubon house still standing. The house was built in 1762 and was home to Jean Audubon, father of naturalist and artist John James Audubon. You can see a restored studio where Audubon used to paint and do taxidermy. | Pawlings Rd. and Audubon Rd., Audubon | 610/666–5593 | Free | Grounds, Tues.–Sun. 7 AM–dusk, closed Mon.; museum, Tues.–Sat. 10–4, Sun. 1–4, closed Mon.

The Plaza and the Court at King of Prussia. This is the largest shopping center on the East Coast, with nine department stores, 365 specialty shops, and 59 restaurants. | Rte. 202 at Mall Blvd. | 610/265–5727 | www.shopking.com | Free | Mon.–Sat. 10–9:30, Sun. 11–6.

Swiss Pines. You can see butterflies in August at the 17-acre Japanese garden with winding paths, a waterfall, and pool. The area is not recommended for people with walking difficulties, groups, or children under age 12. | RD 1, Charlestown Rd., Malvern, PA | 610/933–6916 or 610/935–8795 | fax 610/935–8795 | $5 | mid-May–Nov., Wed.–Fri. 10:30–3:30, Sat. 9–1, closed Sun.–Tues.

Valley Forge National Historical Park. After losing Philadelphia to the British, General George Washington retreated to Valley Forge tired and ill equipped. More than 2,000 soldiers lost their lives in an extremely harsh winter. In addition to Washington's headquarters, the park has 50 reconstructed huts and many memorials. | Rte. 23 (Valley Forge Rd.) and Rte. 252 (Valley Creek Rd.) | 610/783–1077 | www.nps.gov/vafo/ | Free | Daily dawn to dusk.

ON THE CALENDAR

DEC./JUNE: *March into Valley Forge.* Each year on December 19, Pennsylvanians commemorate the 1777 march of George Washington and his 12,000 troops into Valley Forge by reenacting the event at Valley Forge National Historic Park. Experience the glowing campfires, an encampment, living history demonstrations, and tours of the park. If you return to the park in June, on the weekend nearest the 19th, you can celebrate surviving the winter as the troops march out. The festivities, with the firing of muskets, last longer than the march. | 610–783–1077.

Dining

Bertolli's Authentic Trattoria. Italian. The sauces and pasta here keep people coming back. Characteristic dishes are the favzoletto con funghi and the tagliolini al frutti di mare. | 160 N. Gulph Rd. | 610/265–2965 | $9–$19 | AE, DC, MC, V.

Blue Grotto Restaurant. Continental. Soft lighting and candlelit tables make this hotel restaurant, known for its seafood, perfect for romance. Kids' menu. Sun. brunch. | 160 1st Ave. | 610/337–2825 | Closed Sun. No lunch | $15–$22 | AE, D, DC, MC, V.

Brew Moon. Contemporary. Large circular steel kettles greet you as you walk through the door. Inside, the contemporary interior has black and tan tables and fixtures. The Maine lobster and cornmeal-crusted catfish are specialties. Live music, jazz, Sun. Kids' menu. Sun. brunch. | 160 N. Gulph Rd. | 610/230–BREW | www.brewmoon.com | $12–$22 | AE, DC, MC, V.

Chumley's Restaurant. Continental. With its soft light, the lounge is an intimate place to talk or listen to live music on Friday or Saturday. The restaurant in this 18th-century brick building has dark wooden tables and chairs and the windows are draped with curtains. Choose from certified Angus beef and stuffed lobster tail with crab meat. Kids' menu. | 1160 1st Ave. | 610/337–2000 | No lunch weekends | $18–$25 | AE, DC, MC, V.

General Warren Inn. Continental. You can choose to dine or you can stay the night at the inn, housed in an 18th-century stone building. Salads are prepared at tableside. Dine by candlelight indoors, or outdoors overlooking the vegetable garden. The restaurant is known for its beef and chicken dishes, and beef Wellington salad. | Old Lancaster Hwy, Malvern | 610/296–3637 | Closed Sun. No lunch Sat. | $20–$26 | AE, DC, MC, V.

Kimberton Inn. Continental. Stroll through the 4½ acres of gardens on the grounds of this 1796 tavern, known for its fresh seafood, rack of lamb, and crab cakes. Live music every night but Mon. Sun. brunch. | Kimberton and Hares Hill Rd., Kimberton | 610/933–8148 | No lunch | $20–$27 | AE, D, DC, MC, V.

Lily Langtry's Restaurant and Showplace. Continental. You can enjoy a real 90-minute Broadway spectacular with amphitheater-style seating and candlelit dining. Costumes and sets are lavish and dancers come from New York City and Los Angeles. The interior has lots of velvet and a 30-foot high garden skylight. Known for their chicken Saltimbocca and filet mignon. Kids' menu. Live entertainment, Broadway show, Tues.–Sun. | 1160 1st Ave. | 888/267–1500 | Reservations essential | Closed Mon. | $15–$20 | AE, D, DC, MC, V.

Taquet. French. Formerly a 1909 hotel, the bistro side of this restaurant is casual, while the main dining room is formal. Both dining rooms have Victorian interiors, with white linen tablecloths, fresh flowers, and candles. Choose from rack of lamb or braised veal chops. You can eat on a patio near the lobby of the Wayne Hotel. | 139 E. Lancaster Ave. | 610/687–5005 | fax 610/687–5292 | Closed Sun. | $15–$30 | AE, D, DC, MC, V.

Valley Forge Brewing Company. Contemporary. Housed in the old movie theater of a shopping center, this Colonial-style restaurant has an authentic covered bridge in the center of the dining room. Inside, you can see wood grain paneling with murals hanging on the walls. Also, the restaurant claims to have the state's largest bar. Known for many dishes made with beer, the reuben sandwich, and the salmon. Kids' menu. | 267 E. Swedesford Rd., Wayne | 610/687–8700 | fax 610/687–8549 | $12–$21 | AE, DC, MC, V.

Villa Strafford. Continental. Though set in a Colonial revival-style building with large robust columns, the restaurant's interior has white linen tablecloths and fresh flowers. Try the Weiner schnitzel or the rack of lamb. Live music, jazz, Fri., Sat. | 115 Strafford Ave. | 610/964–1116 | fax 610/964–9086 | Closed Sun. | $17–$35 | AE, D, DC, MC, V.

Wild Onion. Contemporary. The outside here looks like an English pub with old gas lights lining the walkway, and the inside has small wooden booths with floral curtains, hardwood floors, and brass rails. Upstairs you can sit at a sports bar with large-screen TVs. House specials are brasserie salad and the beef stew. Kids' menu. No smoking. | 900 Conestoga Rd., Rosemont | 610/527–4826 | $10–$19 | AE, D, DC, MC, V.

Lodging

Best Western. On five landscaped acres with a beautiful outdoor pool and courtyard, all rooms offer patios or balconies with the majority overlooking the pool and courtyard. It

caters to both the leisure and corporate traveler, directly across from The Plaza and Court (second largest shopping mall in the U.S.) and convenient to major traffic arteries and local Fortune 500 corporations. | 168 rooms. Restaurants nearby, complimentary Continental breakfast. In-room data ports, cable TV. Pool. Laundry facilities. Business services. Airport shuttle. | 127 S. Gulph Rd. | 610/265–4500 | fax 610/337–0672 | www.bestwestern.com | $89–$115 | AE, D, DC, MC, V.

Comfort Inn–Valley Forge. The five-story stucco hotel is in the center of one of the country's premier, high tech business and recreational corridors. Nearly every key corporate park and major highway is close by. The King of Prussia Mall (the second largest in the country) is adjacent to the hotel, and historic Valley Forge National Park is just 1 mi away. Center City Philadelphia is only 25 mi north. | 121 rooms. Complimentary Continental breakfast. Some minibars, cable TV. Exercise equipment. Laundry facilities. Business services. Airport shuttle. | 550 W. DeKalb/U.S. 202 N | 610/962–0700 | fax 610/962–0218 | www.comfortinn.com | $95–$149 | AE, D, DC, MC, V.

Courtyard by Marriott. A midpriced, six-story stucco building, this chain hotel is just outside of King of Prussia. Close attractions are Devon Horseshow & Fairgrounds (3 mi), Downtown Historic Philadelphia (3 mi), King of Prussia Shopping Malls (1 mi), Lancaster & Amish Country (45 mi), Longwood Gardens (25 mi), Valley Forge National Park (0.3 mi), and Villanova University (4 mi). | 150 rooms. Restaurant, bar. In-room data ports, refrigerator, cable TV. Indoor pool. Hot tub. Exercise equipment. Laundry facilities. Business services. | 1100 Drummers La., Wayne | 610/687–6700 | fax 610/687–1149 | www.marriott.com | $89–$150 | AE, D, DC, MC, V.

Fairfield Inn– Valley Forge. Across the street from the King of Prussia malls, this five-story hotel is next to a health club, which guests are allowed to use. Complimentary Continental breakfast. Cable TV. Indoor pool. Laundry service. Pets allowed. | 258 Mall Blvd. | 610/337–0700 or 800/228–2800 | fax 610/337–7027 | www.fairfieldinn.com | 80 rooms | $79 | AE, D, DC, MC, V.

Hilton Valley Forge. Overlooking Valley Forge National Park, this nine-story concrete hotel is in the center of the King of Prussia/Valley Forge business district just 19 mi west of Center City Philadelphia and the Convention Center. It has easy access to local attractions including the famed Court at King of Prussia, the 2nd largest shopping mall in the country; Longwood Gardens; the casinos of Atlantic City; and Sesame Place. | 340 rooms. Restaurants, bars (with entertainment). In-room data ports, cable TV. Indoor-outdoor pool. Hot tub. Exercise equipment. Business services. Airport shuttle. | 251 W. DeKalb Pike/Rte. 202 N | 610/337–1200 | fax 610/337–2224 | www.hilton.com | $120–$149 | AE, D, DC, MC, V.

Holiday Inn. Directly across from the world famous Court & Plaza at King of Prussia Shopping Complex, this midpriced, full-service, six-story hotel is also near Valley Forge National Historical Park. | 225 rooms. Restaurant, bar. In-room data ports, room service, cable TV. Beauty salon. Business services. | 260 Mall Blvd., Valley Forge | 610/265–7500 | fax 610/265–4076 | www.holiday-inn.com | $145 | AE, D, DC, MC, V.

Mainstay Suites. There's a Sleep Inn here (for shorter stays) on the same property. Both hotels supply a free newspaper on weekdays. Complimentary Continental breakfast. In-room data ports, kitchenettes, microwaves, refrigerators, cable TV. Indoor pool. Hot tub. Exercise equipment. Laundry service. No pets. | 440 American Ave. | 484/690–3000 | fax 484/690–2001 | Mainstay@nni.com | www.comfortinn.com | 63 rooms | $109 | AE, D, DC, MC, V.

Radisson Valley Forge Hotel/Scanticon Hotel. These two hotels share a 15-story building overlooking Valley Forge National Historic Park. Some of the suites have "fantasy" themes such as Gilligan's Island and Hollywood. A variety of room, dinner and show, or business packages are available. 3 restaurants, room service. In-room data ports, some in-room hot tubs, cable TV. Outdoor pool. Hot tub, sauna, spa, steam room. Gym, health club. Laundry service. Business services. No pets. | 1160 First Ave. | 610/337–2000 or 800/267–1500 | fax 610/337–2564 | www.radissonvalleyforge.com | 328 rooms; Radisson 39 suites, Scanticon 160 suites | $179–$399 | AE, D, DC, MC, V.

Wyndham Valley Forge. In the Chesterbrook Corporate Center, this all-suites hotel's guest rooms feature distinct living areas including a spacious living room and separate bedroom, mini-bar and wet bar. It's just 25 min from many of Philadelphia's attractions and the King of Prussia Shopping Complex, Valley Forge National Park, and Longwood Gardens are all just minutes away. | 229 suites. Restaurant, bar. In-room data ports, refrigerators, cable TV. Indoor pool. Hot tub, sauna. Exercise equipment. Business services. Airport shuttle. | 888 Chesterbrook Blvd., Wayne | 610/647–6700 | fax 610/889–9420 | www.wyndham.com | $189 | AE, D, DC, MC, V.

McIntosh Inn. An affordable, modern stucco seven-story inn that is adjacent to the world famous King of Prussia Mall and the Court at King of Prussia. It is also next to two restaurants, one family style and one restaurant and lounge and within a few minutes drive of historic Valley Forge National Park. | 212 rooms. In-room data ports, cable TV. Business services. | 260 N. Gulph Rd. | 610/768–9500 or 800/444–2775 | fax 610/768–0225 | www.mcintoshinn.com/ | $65–$85 | AE, DC, MC, V.

Radisson Valley Forge Inn. Overlooking Valley Forge National Park, this 13-floor circular tower Radisson is nestled between all major highways: I-476, I-76, and the Pennsylvania Turnpike. It's just 20 min to historic downtown Philadelphia and the Philadelphia International Airport. | 489 rooms. Restaurants (*see* the Blue Grotto, Chumley's and Lily Lonatra's Restaurant and Showplace), bars (with entertainment). In-room data ports, cable TV. Pool. Hot tub. Exercise equipment. Business services. Airport shuttle. | 1160 First Ave. | 610/337–2000 | fax 610/768–3222 | www.radisson.com | $150–$190 | AE, D, DC, MC, V.

Wayne. The first thing you notice about the Tudor-style Wayne Hotel is the wrap-around porch, where you can enjoy the morning paper over a sampling of the hotel's complimentary Continental breakfast, in warm weather. This turn-of-the-century building is in the heart of a charming Main Line town. | 40 rooms. Restaurant, bar, complimentary Continental breakfast. In-room data ports, cable TV. Pool. Business services. Airport shuttle. | 139 E. Lancaster Ave., Wayne | 610/687–5000 or 800/962–5850 | fax 610/687–8387 | www.waynehotel.com | $135–$169 | AE, D, DC, MC, V.

KUTZTOWN

MAP 7, J5

(Nearby towns also listed: Allentown, Hamburg, Reading)

In the Pennsylvania Dutch countryside, Kutztown pays homage every year to those who settled the borough at its annual German festival.

Information: **Kutztown Chamber of Commerce** | 276 W. Main St., 19530 | 610/683–8860.

Attractions

Crystal Cave Park. You can take guided tours of the many geologic formations, check out the gift shops, rock shop, and museum, play miniature golf, or hike the 125-acre trail. The tour is 45 minutes long and the temperature inside the cave is a constant 52 degrees. | 963 Crystal Cave Rd. | 610/683–6765 | www.crystalcavepa.com | $8 | Mar.–Nov., weekdays 9–6, weekends 9–7. Sept.–Feb., Mon.–Sun. 9–5.

Kutztown University Cultural Center. Preserves the Pennsylvania German language dialect and stores over 10,000 artifacts, including numerous historical documents from the 18th and 19th centuries. | The Pennsylvania German Cultural Heritage Center @ Kutztown University, Luckenbill Road (at the end of the lane, adjacent to the University) | 610/683–1330. 610/683–4638 | www.kutztown.edu/community/pgchc/home.html | $5, special rates for children | Mon.–Fri., 10 AM–4 PM, and by appointment.

Renninger's Farmer's Market and Antiques. This gigantic marketplace has indoor and outdoor shopping and a flea market. It's a popular stop for travelers passing through Kutz-

KUTZTOWN

INTRO
ATTRACTIONS
DINING
LODGING

town. Watch out for the annual Antiques Extravaganza in September. | Rte. 222 | 610/683–6848 | Fri. 10–7, Sat. 8–4.

ON THE CALENDAR

JUNE–JULY: *Folk Festival.* A 10-day celebration of Pennsylvania Dutch culture that boasts demonstrations of traditional crafts, including basket- and rug-making, as well as displays of quilts, music, dancing, and food. | Festival grounds | 610/683–8707.

AUG.: *First Union Betsy King Classic.* Held at the Berkleigh Country Club less than 10 mi south of Kutztown, this is one of the tournaments where LPGA players can earn Solheim Cup points. Usually held between late August and mid-October, the event benefits kids' charities, including Easter Seals and the Bethany Children's Home. | 610/683–8311 or 800/443–6610 | www.firstunionbetsyking.com.

Dining

Bowers Hotel. American. You can order seafood, pork, vegetables, veal, and many more traditional dishes from this 75-item menu. Look for the green roof, 1½ mi from Kutztown. It's the largest building for miles | Bowers Rd., Bowers | 610/682–2900 | Closed Mon. | $14 | AE, D, MC, V.

New Smithville Country Inn. Continental. The antiques and farmhouse implements show you that this country farmhouse used to be a general store. Popular dishes are the crab meat Colorado and the chicken Olivia. Kids' menu. | 10425 Old 22 Rd. | 610/285–2987 | No lunch Mon. | $12–$26 | AE, MC, V.

Lodging

Die Bauerei. This restored red-brick 1867 farmhouse (bauerei means farmhouse in the Pennsylvania-German dialect), is 2 mi northwest of Kutztown University. Filled with Pennsylvania Dutch quilts and artwork, it has a walk-in fireplace. Complimentary breakfast. Some room phones, no TV in some rooms. Pets allowed. No smoking. | 187 Sharadin Rd. | 610/894–4854 | bauerei@juno.com | www.bauerei.com | 5 rooms (4 with bath) | $85 | AE, MC, V.

LAHASKA

MAP 7, L6

(Nearby towns also listed: Doylestown, Holicong, New Hope)

This popular Philadelphia suburb is known for Peddler's Village and a host of antiques shops in and around town. Shopping is the most popular pastime in this town, 40 minutes northwest of downtown Philadelphia.

Information: **Bucks County Conference and Visitors Bureau** | 152 Swamp Rd., Doylestown, PA 18901 | 215/345–4552.

Attraction

Peddler's Village. This village is a replica of an old English village, with more than 65 specialty craft, gift, and clothing shops, plus a handful of restaurants. The town hosts 18th-century-style festivals and craft shows year-round. Laid out on 42 acres, walking paths wind throughout. | Rte. 263 downtown | 215/794–4000 | www.peddlersvillage.com | Free | Sun.–Thurs. 10–6, Fri.–Sat. 10–9.

The park includes **Carousel World,** a turn-of-the-20th-century Philadelphia-style amusement park. More than 60 antique carousel animals are on display, along with miniature amusement rides and other displays from the last century. | Rte. 263 downtown | 215/794–4000 | www.peddlersvillage.com | Free | Sun.–Thurs. 10–6, Fri.–Sat. 10–9.

Penn's Purchase Factory Outlet. Adjacent to Peddler's Village, this outlet has Coach, G. H. Bass, Izod, Jones New York, and Osh Kosh B'Gosh. | 5861 York Rd. | 215/794–0300 | Mon.-Fri. 10-8, Sat. 9-8, Sun. 9–6.

ON THE CALENDAR

NOV.: *Apple Festival and Grand Illumination Celebration.* On the first weekend of November at Peddler's Village you can participate in a pie-eating contest, listen to live music, watch (and taste) apple butter being made over an open fire, and see the crafts and skills of local artists. On the third weekend of the month, starting Friday at dusk, you can witness the seasonal debut of the village's holiday lights' display while drinking cider, eating toasted marshmallows, and joining in a sing-along. The village green is the center for many special events throughout the year. | 215/794–4000.

Dining

Buckingham Mountain Brewing Corporation. American/Casual. Serving mostly pub food—burgers, roast beef, blue corn nachos, mountain onion soup—this busy restaurant, next to Peddler's Village, has a view of the mountain and valley from the upstairs dining room. You can sample the seasonal beer and see where it's brewed. | 5775 Rte. 202 | 215/794–7302 | $12.95–$15.95 | AE, MC, V.

Jenny's Bistro. Continental. From the large front windows in this country French bistro you can watch what's going on in Peddler's Village. The Victorian building has stained-glass windows and unique columns. Specials are the filet Chesterfield, filet mignon with homemade cheddar cheese horseradish sauce served with fresh steamed asparagus and herbed mashed potatoes. Live music, piano bar, Fri., Sat. Sun. brunch. | Corner of Rte. 202 and Street Rd. | 215/794–4020 | fax 215/794–4008 | $17–$24 | AE, D, DC, MC, V.

Lodging

Golden Plough Inn. Within Peddler's Village, this inn has 18th-century Colonial-style architecture and is filled with antiques. A split of champagne, soft beverages, and a snack basket when you check in can refresh and revive. Its rooms are throughout Peddler's Village. You can stroll along winding brick walkways through colorful gardens and lush landscaping. Restaurant, complimentary Continental breakfast. In-room data ports, in-room hot tubs, cable TV. Business services. | U.S. 202 and Street Rd. | 215/794–4004 | fax 215/794–4008 | www.goldenploughinn.com | 60 rooms in 6 buildings, 19 suites | $115–$335, $235–$325 suites | AE, D, DC, MC, V.

Inn at Lahaska. This renovated 1880 country house across from Peddler's Village offers a $150 brews-and-snooze package that includes a night at the inn plus dinner and a beer sampler at the Buckingham Mountain Brewing Corp. Complimentary Continental breakfast. No room phones, no TV. No pets. No smoking. | 5775 Rte. 202 | 215/794–0440 | fax 215/794–3732 | 6 rooms | $75–$125 | AE, MC, V.

LANCASTER

MAP 7, I7

(Nearby towns also listed: Bird-in-Hand, Columbia, Ephrata, Lititz, Manheim, Wrightsville)

During the Revolutionary War, Lancaster was the largest inland city in the Colonies and for one day was the nation's capital after the American Congress fled Philadelphia and convened here. Today, its rich heritage is captured in many historic districts and in the Central Market at Penn Square.

Information: **Lancaster Chamber of Commerce** | 100 S. Queen St., 17603 | 717/397–3531.

LANCASTER

INTRO
ATTRACTIONS
DINING
LODGING

Attractions

Amish Farm and House. You can take a guided tour through an Amish house on a 25-acre farm. The house was built in 1805 and is a replica of an "Old Order" Amish home. The farm dates back to 1715 and has a stone-lined well, a windmill, a stone barn built in 1803, a water-wheel, a tobacco shed, a blacksmith shop, and other buildings. | 2395 Lincoln Hwy. E. | 717/394–6185 | www.amishandhouse.com | $6.50 | Daily 8:30–6.

Anderson Pretzel Company. The company has been making pretzels in the area for more than 100 years and the self-guided tour shows you how the pretzels are made from beginning to end. A free sample is available after the tour. | 2060 Old Philadelphia Pike | 717/299–2321 | www.andersonpretzel.com | Free | Weekdays 8:30–4, closed weekends.

Bube's Brewery. A 19th-century brewery complex that includes a museum, three restaurants, outdoor biergarten, art gallery, and a brewery store, it's the only surviving intact brewery from the 1800s. | 102 N. Market St., Mount Joy | 717/653–2056 | Free | museum daily 4–10.

★ **Central Market.** In the heart of town, the market began as open-air in 1742 and is now in an 1889 Romanesque building. It's one of the oldest covered markets in the country and a good place to pick up everything from bologna to shoofly pie. | Penn Sq.(William Penn Way) | 717/291–4723 | Free | Tues. and Fri. 6–4, Sat. 6–2.

Dutch Wonderland. The 48-acre park has two roller coasters, a water coaster, log flume shows, botanical gardens, and 19th-centruy paddleboats. Also, you can see Acapulco cliff divers who plummet 90 ft, and listen to Chief Halftown, a Seneca Native American, tell stories every weekend in summer. | 2249 Rt. 30 E. | 717/291–1888 | www.dutchwonderland.com | $22.50 | Memorial Day–Labor Day, daily 10–7; Other times, call for hrs.

Franklin and Marshall College. Founded in the late 1700s, the college was called Franklin College and was the first and only bilingual college in the country. The first class was 78 men and 36 women, but the next time a woman would attend class was 1969. In 1853, Marshall College and Franklin merged, saving both institutions during hard times. | College Ave. | 717/291–3911 | www.fandm.edu | Free | Daily.

North Museum. The museum has exhibits of natural history and science collections, plus a planetarium. The planetarium is the third largest in Pennsylvania. | 400 College Ave. | 717/291–3941 | www.northmuseum.org | $2 | Tues.–Sat. 9–5, Sun. noon–5, closed Mon.

Fulton Opera House. Built in 1852, the building is one of only three theaters designated a National Historic Landmark. W. C. Fields, Mark Twain, and Al Jolson played here. The lobby has a large staircase, a crystal chandelier, and period furnishings. | 12 N. Prince St. | 717/397–7425 | www.fultontheatre.org | Free | Daily 10–5.

Hands-on House. The museum is for kids ages 2 to 10 and has eight self-directed exhibits, including a corner grocery section, a space voyage point, and a factory. | 721 Landis Valley Rd. | 717/569–KIDS | www.handsonhouse.org | $5 | Labor Day–Memorial Day, Tue.–Thurs., 11–4, Fri.–Sun., 11–8, closed Mon.

★ **Hans Herr House.** Built in 1719, it is the oldest building in Lancaster County and the oldest remaining site of Mennonite worship in North America. The stone house also has a reconstructed blacksmith shop, an outdoor baking oven, and a smokehouse. | 1849 Hans Herr Dr., Willow Street, PA | 717/464–4438 | $3.50; special rates for children | Apr.–Nov., Mon.–Sat. 9–4, closed Sun.

Heritage Center of Lancaster County. A museum with more than 300 years of Lancaster history on display, the buildings show every major architectural style from 18th-century Georgian to Art Deco. The Mason Lodge Hall was once visited by General LaFayette and President James Buchanan. A hands-on museum classroom offers a chance for you and your kids to learn about Lancaster County's history. | Penn Sq., intersection of King and Queen Sts. | 717/299–6440 | Free | Apr.–Dec., Tue.–Sat., 10–5.

Historic Lancaster Walking Tour. This company conducts 90-minute narrated tours through the 6-block heart of the old city. Costumed guides touch on the points of architectural and historical interest. Tours depart from the Visitor Center downtown. | 100 S. Queen St. at Vine St., near Penn Sq. intersection | 717/392–1776 | $5 | Apr.–Oct., Tues and Fri.–Sat. at 10 and 1, Sun.–Mon. and Wed.–Thurs. at 1; Nov.–Mar., by reservation only.

Historic Rock Ford Plantation. Built in 1794, the Georgian-style manor has original rails, shutters, doors, and a large center hall with four rooms surrounding it. You can stroll through an herb garden, orchards, and landscaped grounds. | 881 Rock Ford Rd. | 717/392–7223 | www.padutchcounty.com | $5 | Apr.–Oct., Tues.–Fri. 10–4, Sun. noon–4, closed Mon.

Kauffman Museum. In a reconstructed 18th-century barn, the museum exhibits illustrate life during that period, with the work of fraktur, pewter, copper, brass, and crafts, period furnishings and firearms. | 881 Rock Ford Rd. | 717/392–7223 | $4.50 | by appointment only.

Discover Lancaster County History Museum. The museum blends animation and state-of-the-art audio to bring 32 in-depth scenes to life. You can relive moments from the country's past, beginning with Native Americans, William Penn, Robert Fulton, and James Buchanan. | 2249 Rte. 30 E. | 717/393–3679 | www.800padutch.com/museum | $6.50 | Memorial Day–Labor Day daily 9–5; Apr.–May., Sun.–Fri., 9–5, Sat. 9–8; Sept.–Oct., Sun.–Fri., 9–5, Sat. 9–8; all other times daily 9–5.

Landis Valley Museum. Here you can experience the rural lifestyle of the Pennsylvania Germans by exploring 15 historic buildings with craft demonstrations, a mid-1800s country hotel, and a museum shop. | 2451 Kissel Hill Rd. | 717/569–0401 | fax 717/560–2147 | $7 | May–Oct., Mon.–Sat. 9–5, Sun. noon–5.

Mennonite Information Center. The gift shop here has inspirational books and Mennonite history, and a video on Mennonite and Amish struggles in Europe, plus a 20-minute film that answers questions about the Mennonite and Amish lifestyles. | 2209 Millstream Rd. | 717/299–0954 | www.mennoniteinfoctr.com | Free | Apr.–Oct., Mon.–Sat. 8–5, closed Sun.; Nov.–Mar., 8:30–4:30.

Furnishings designed from biblical description as given to Moses and the Israelites are on display at the **Hebrew Tabernacle Reproduction.** A lecture tour explains the construction, history, and significance. A wax high priest figure and Ark of the Covenant are

YOUR CAR'S FIRST-AID KIT

- ❏ Bungee cords or rope to tie down trunk if necessary
- ❏ Club soda to remove stains from upholstery
- ❏ Cooler with bottled water
- ❏ Extra coolant
- ❏ Extra windshield-washer fluid
- ❏ Flares and/or reflectors
- ❏ Flashlight and extra batteries
- ❏ Hand wipes to clean hands after roadside repair
- ❏ Hose tape

- ❏ Jack and fully inflated spare
- ❏ Jumper cables
- ❏ Lug wrench
- ❏ Owner's manual
- ❏ Plastic poncho—in case you need to do roadside repairs in the rain
- ❏ Quart of oil and quart of transmission fluid
- ❏ Spare fan belts
- ❏ Spare fuses
- ❏ Tire-pressure gauge

*Excerpted from *Fodor's: How to Pack: Experts Share Their Secrets*
© 1997, by Fodor's Travel Publications

featured. | 2209 Millstream Rd. | 717/299–0954 | www.mennoniteinfoctr.com | $5 | Apr.–Oct., Mon.–Sat. 8–4, closed Sun.; Nov.–Mar., Mon.–Sat., 11, 1, 3.

Muddy Run Recreation Park of Philadelphia Electric Co. The park has a 100-acre lake for boating and fishing, many hiking trails, softball fields, basketball courts, picnic areas, and camping. Displays on how the Philadelphia Electric Company provides energy to the community, as well as wildlife displays, are here at the information center. | 172 Bethesda Church Rd. West, Holtwood | 717/284–2538 | Free | Daily dawn to dusk | Info. Center, Daily 10–4.

National Wax Museum of Lancaster County Heritage. The history and culture of Lancaster County is captured here. Some of the scenes show the early settlers of Penns Woods, the Hospital of the Ephrata Cloister during the Revolution, the signing of the Great Indian Treaty in 1744, the Lititz Pretzel House, and an animated Amish barn raising. The narrated tour is presented by life-size wax figures of historical events. | 2249 Rte. 30 E | 717/393–3679 | fax 717/291–1595 | $6.50 | Call for hrs.

Robert Fulton Birthplace. Many of Robert Fulton's activities, including inventing the steamboat, are recounted here. View life in the 1800s complete with period furnishings and artifacts. | Robert Fulton Hwy., Quarryville; 20 mi south of Lancaster | 717/548–2679 | $1 | Memorial Day–Labor Day, Sat. 11–4, Sun. 1–5, closed weekdays.

Twin Brook Winery. This 20-acre vineyard with a 19th-century barn is equipped with winemaking facilities. Wine tasting from dry to sweet, sales, and tours available. | 5697 Strasburg Rd. | 717/442–4915 | Free | Apr.–Dec., Mon.–Sat. 10–6, Sun. 1–5; Jan.–Mar., Tues.–Sun. noon–5.

★ **Wheatland.** Here you can see the former home of James Buchanan, the 15th president of the United States. The 4½-acre, 1828 national historic landmark, part of the Civil War Discovery Trail, is also the place where Buchanan wrote his inaugural address. | 1120 Marietta Ave. | 717/392–8721 | $5.50 | Apr.–Nov., daily 10–4.

ON THE CALENDAR

APR.: *Sheep Shearing.* You can watch this 2-day rite of fall as it's demonstrated on a typical Lancaster County farm. | Amish Farm and House, U.S. 30 | 717/394–6185 | $6.50, special rates for children.
MAY: *Wheels Wheels Wheels.* More than 200 antique cars and cycles line the streets of downtown Lancaster during this annual event, usually held the weekend after Mother's Day. You can taste food from various vendors and listen to live music. | 717/291–4758.
JUNE–SEPT.: *Music at Gretna.* Nationally known artists perform chamber music and jazz in two different locations, once a week from June through September. Mount Gretna Playhouse, corner of Pennsylvania and Carnagie Rd., Mount Gretna, 17064 and Leffler Performance Center, 1 Alpha Dr., Elizabethtown, 17022 | 717/964–3836 | $15–$20.
OCT.: *Harvest Days.* Every Columbus Day weekend more than 80 crafts and harvest activities are demonstrated during this celebration of the fall harvest. | Landis Valley Museum | 717/569–0401 | $7, special rates for children and seniors.
DEC.: *Victorian Christmas Tours.* Each year, between Christmas and New Year's, Wheatland is dressed in Victorian Christmas finery for the holiday season. Day and candlelight tours are available. | Wheatland, 1120 Marietta Ave. | 717/392–8721 | $6.50, special rates for children and seniors.

Dining

Akron Restaurant. Continental. In a simple building with wooden beams, this 1970s home-style restaurant, has breakfast everyday but Sunday. It's a Dutch restaurant filled with candles and quilts, and the gift shop next door sells Amish and Dutch crafts. Dishes are homebaked chicken pie and pies and cakes. Kids' menu. | 33 S. 7th St. | 717/859–1181 | Reservations not accepted | $6–$14 | MC, V.

Belvedere Inn. Contemporary. Built in 1872, this restaurant is named for the belvedere or widow's walk that projects above its roof. Specials are crab cakes, New York strip steak with mango chutney, and salmon. The favorite item on the menu, though, is the Caesar salad, made with grilled lettuce. | 402 N. Queen St. | 717/394–2422 | $11–$24 | AE, D, DC, MC, V.

The Catacombs/Alois's/The Bottling Works. Continental. You can dine in the original dining rooms of this 19th-century brick brewery or its cellars. The hotel dining room is Victorian, while the cellar has a staff dressed in clothing resembling the Middle Ages. You can take a guided tour of the old bottling works. The restaurant menu has shrimp, roast duck, and other favorites. Open-air dining on a patio. Live entertainment, acoustic guitar, Fri., Sat. | 102 N. Market St., Mount Joy | 717/653–2056 | No lunch Sun. | $20–$30 | AE, D, MC, V.

Doc Holliday's Steakhouse. Steak. At this western-style saloon, you can have steak any way you like it any day of the week. | 931 Harrisburg Pk. | 717/397–3811 | $12–$30 | AE, D, MC, V.

Ellington's. Contemporary. Named for Duke Ellington (the business cards read "off Duke on Orange") this restaurant serves blackened tuna with Brazilian spices and a sake plum-tomato sauce, vegetarian dishes, and steak. You can also try chocolate or blueberry pasta. Listen to live jazz and try a cigar. | 37 E. Orange St. | 717/509–1818 | Closed Sun. | $16–$25 | AE, D, MC, V.

Gimmies Sports Bar. Continental. With a race car suspended from the ceiling and large-screen TVs throughout, there's no mistaking that this is a sports bar. There are also many signed memorabilia and photographs on display. The burgers are famous. | 650 Pinkerton Rd. | 717/653–2048 | $6–15 | D, MC, V.

Groff's Farm. Continental. Decorated with antiques and period lanterns, this restaurant in a 1756 stone farmhouse is separated into several dining rooms, with one room ideal for large parties. Chicken Stoltzfus is a house specialty. Kids' menu. Sun. brunch. | 650 Pinkerton Rd. | 717/653–2048 | Reservations essential | Jacket required | Closed Sun.–Mon. | $12–$36 | AE, D, DC, MC, V.

Lancaster Malt Brewing Company. Contemporary. Opened in 1995 in a renovated tobacco warehouse, this brewpub has wood floors, massive wood beams, a high brick ceiling, and copper accents. The bar and casual dining area wrap around an open drop to the brewhouse below. Known for fresh brewed beer, Porter float, and LMB's Oyster Shooter. Try the crab cakes or brewers plate. Kids' menu. | 302 N. Plum | 717/391–MALT | $11–$24 | AE, D, MC, V.

★ **Log Cabin.** Continental. This log cabin, built during Prohibition, is filled with 18th- and 19th-century original paintings and has a cozy hearth. The steak here is popular, but fresh seafood and poultry are also top notch. Live music, piano, Sat. Kids' menu. | 11 Lehoy Forest Dr. | 717/626–1181 | No lunch | $18–$30 | AE, DC, MC, V.

The Meritage Restaurant. Contemporary. Named for the wine term meaning "blended," this eatery has salmon, rack of lamb, and gingered scallops. Look for the giant awning above the front door. | 51 N. Market St. | 717/396–1189 | $15–$26 | AE, D, MC, V.

Olde Greenfield Inn. Continental. In a 1780 Pennsylvania stone farmhouse, this inn is filled with antiques and early American furnishings. You can take advantage of its romantic dining in its wine cellar or on a balcony overlooking the lounge where you can hear live piano music Friday and Saturday nights. Get breakfast, lunch, and dinner here. The menu has all-lump crab cakes and fresh salmon filet, baked or broiled with a compound butter sauce or chef's choice. Kids' menu. Sun. brunch. | 595 Greenfield Rd. | 717/393–0668 | Reservations essential | No lunch Mon. | $22–$38 | AE, D, DC, MC, V.

The Press Room. American/Casual. Named for the owner's other business, the Lancaster newspaper, this restaurant serves pizza, burgers, salads, and other informal fare. It's ½ block from the main square. | 26 W. King St. | 717/399–5400 | Closed Sun. | $16.95 | AE, D, DC, MC, V.

Rainbow Dinner Theatre. Contemporary. This is America's only all-comedy dinner theatre, with shows year-round. The tiered seating ensures a good seat, and there are chandeliers, candlelight, and contemporary furnishings. Known for pasta. Live entertainment, comedy shows, Tues.–Sun. Kids' menu. | Rte. 30 E, Paradise | 800/292–4301 | Reservations essential | Closed Mon. No supper Tues.–Thurs. No lunch. Fri., Sat. | $30–$35 | D, MC, V.

Revere Tavern. Continental. This 1740s stone building, formerly called "Sign of the Spread Eagle," was considered one of the state's best inns in its day. Today it's owned by Best Western and has 5 rooms for dining. House specialties include filet mignon and South Atlantic lobster tails. Kids' menu. Sun. brunch. | 3063 Lincoln Hwy. | 800/429–7383 | $10–$25 | AE, D, DC, MC, V.

Stockyard Inn. American. Next to real stockyard pens, this 1750 farmhouse was once home to President James Buchanan. The menu has prime rib and other American classics. | 1147 Lititz Pk. | 717/394–7975 | Closed Sun. | $21 | AE, D, MC, V.

Lodging

1725 Historic Witmer's Tavern Inn & Museum. This pre-Revolutionary hostelry, about 1½ mi east of downtown, is the oldest and most complete Pennsylvania inn still lodging travelers in its original building. The bathrooms have been refurbished in Victorian style, and there's an 1890's icebox in the hall you can use. The innkeeper has a collection of the many antiques found buried on the property, including coins, teeth, and bottles of mysterious potion. Complimentary Continental breakfast. No pets. No smoking. | 2014 Old Philadelphia Pk. | 717/299–5305 | www.800padutch.com/1725histwit/ | 7 rooms (2 with bath) | $110 | No credit cards.

The Australian Walkabout. An Australian-style bed and breakfast in the heart of the Amish country, the house is a 22-room, 1925 brick Mennonite farmhouse with large wraparound porches and wicker furniture. There's a fountain and wildflower gardens, and a lily pond with waterfall. Picnic area, complimentary breakfast. No room phones, cable TV. Hot tubs. No smoking. | 837 Village Rd., Lampeter | 717/464–0707 | fax 717/464–2501 | www.bbonline.com/pa/walkabout | 8 rooms | $99–$145 | AE, MC, V.

★ **Best Western Eden Resort Inn.** In the heart of Dutch Country, this two-level modern brick lodging has a detailed garden and lawn. Restaurant, bar (with entertainment), room service. In-room data ports, cable TV. 2 pools (1 indoor). Hot tub. Tennis. Exercise equipment. Playground. Business services, airport shuttle. Pets allowed. | 222 Eden Rd. | 717/569–6444 | fax 717/569–4208 | eden@edenresort.com | www.edenresort.com | 276 rooms, 42 suites | $159 | AE, D, DC, MC, V.

Cameron Estate. Formerly the home of Simon Cameron, who was a member of Abraham Lincoln's cabinet, this mansion was built in 1805. | 17 rooms (2 with shared bath). Restaurant, complimentary breakfast. No room phones. No kids under 12. Business services. | 1855 Mansion La., Mount Joy | 717/653–1773 or 888/722–6376 | fax 717/653–8334 | www.getawaysmag.com | $135–$200 | AE, D, DC, MC, V.

Country Living. A small, 3-story motel that was built in 1989. It is 5 mi from Lancaster center. | 34 rooms. In-room hot tub (in suite); cable TV. | 2406 Old Philadelphia Pike | 717/295–7295 | fax 717/295–0994 | www.800padutch.com/ctryliv.html | 34 rooms | $72–$135 | MC, V.

Days Inn. Standard chain accommodations are available at this 3-story motel half a mile away from downtown Lancaster. | 193 rooms. Restaurant, bar. Some refrigerators, cable TV. 2 pools (1 indoor), wading pool. Tennis courts. Playground, laundry facilities. Business services. | 30 Keller Ave. | 717/299–5700 | fax 717/295–1907 | www.padutch.com/daysinnl.html | $76–$108 | AE, D, DC, MC, V.

Flowers and Thyme B&B. Named for the extensive flower beds surrounding it, this 1941 two-story red-brick house was built by an Amish carpenter and is 4 mi east of downtown. Complimentary breakfast. Some in-room hot tubs. TV in common area. No pets. No kids under 12. No smoking. | 238 Strasburg Pk. | 717/393–1460 | fax 717/399–1986 | www.membersaol.com/padutchbnb | 3 rooms | $85–$120 | MC, V.

Gardens of Eden. Outside, wildflowers, perennials, and trails surround this Federal-style house overlooking the Conestoga River. Inside, the house is filled with dried flowers, handmade quilts, baskets, and country furnishings. Complimentary breakfast. In-room data ports, some microwaves, some refrigerators, no room phones, TV in common area. No pets. No smoking. | 1894 Eden Rd. | 717/393–5179 | fax 717/393–7722 | www.gardens-of-eden.com | 3 rooms, 1 cottage | $100–$150 | MC, V.

Garden Spot. A family operated, one-level brick and stucco building, this small motel offers affordable rates. It's AAA and Mobil approved. You can walk to Dutch Wonderland, Lancaster Host Resort, American Music Theatre, outlet malls, movies, and restaurants. | 18 rooms. Restaurant. Cable TV. | 2291 U.S. 30 E | 717/394–4736 | fax 717/299–6339 | www.padutch.com | $50–$65 | Closed Dec.–Mar. | AE, D, MC, V.

Hershey Farm Motor Inn. In the heart of Amish Country, this inn is also on 23 acres of beautiful Lancaster County farmland, minutes from all the leading area attractions. There is a half-mile long walking trail flowing through shaded wooded areas, beautiful flower, fruit and vegetable gardens, with views of the adjoining creek and Amish farmland. | 59 rooms. Complimentary breakfast. Some in-room hot tubs, cable TV. Pool. Playground. Business services. | Rte. 896S, Ronks | 717/687–8635 or 800/827–8635 | fax 717/687–8638. | www.hersheyfarm.com | $69–$124 | D, MC, V.

Hilton Garden Inn. In the Granite Run Corporate Center, the hotel is just 5 mi from downtown Lancaster and 20 mi to Hershey. This full-service, one-level modern brick chain hotel was built in 1989. | 155 rooms. Restaurant, bar, complimentary Continental breakfast. In-room data ports, cable TV. Indoor pool. Hot tub. Exercise equipment. Laundry facilities. Business services. | 101 Granite Run Dr. | 717/560–0880 | fax 717/560–5400 | www.hilton.com | $135–$165 | AE, D, DC, MC, V.

Holiday Inn Visitors Center. Dominated by two large Amish figures and a very large sign, this two-level brick inn is hard to miss. It's right next to the Pennsylvania Dutch Convention and Visitor's Bureau in the heart of Pennsylvania Dutch Country, just minutes from some of the most popular Amish attractions, farmers' markets, and historic downtown Lancaster. | 189 rooms. Restaurant, bar. In-room data ports, room service, cable TV. 2 pools (1 indoor). Tennis courts. Business services. | 521 Greenfield Rd. | 717/299–2551 | fax 717/397–0220 | www.holiday-inn.com | $89–$119 | AE, D, DC, MC, V.

Hotel Brunswick. In historic downtown Lancaster, this full-service hotel is in a large 10-story brick building on a city street corner. It's within walking distance of the famous Central Market, Fulton Opera House, and numerous shops and art galleries. Complimentary enclosed parking is provided in the adjacent parking deck. | 222 rooms. Restaurant, bar (with entertainment). Cable TV. Indoor pool. Exercise equipment. Laundry facilities. Business services. Some pets allowed. | Corner of Chestnut and Queen St. | 717/397–4801 or 800/233–0182 | fax 717/397–4991 | hblanc@lancnews.info.net | www.hotelbrunswick.com | $80–$95 | AE, D, DC, MC, V.

Howard Johnson. An oddly-shaped, modern two-story stucco building with an orange-colored roof, the hotel has interior corridors with electronic locks on all entrance doors. It's centered in Pennsylvania Dutch country, yet 5 min to major outlet malls. | 112 rooms. Restaurant, bar. Cable TV. Indoor pool. Business services. | 2100 Lincoln Hwy. E | 717/397–7781 | fax 717/397–6340 | www.hojo.com | $109 | AE, D, DC, MC, V.

★ **King's Cottage.** Built in 1913, this hotel is listed on the National Register of Historic Places and has been honored with the C. Emlen Urban Award for historic preservation. This elegant, Spanish-style mansion has been beautifully restored, down to the fireplace in the library. It's only 1½ mi from downtown. | 9 rooms. Complimentary breakfast. No smoking, no TV in rooms, TV in common area. No kids under 12. | 1049 E. King St. | 717/397–1017 or 800/747–8717 | fax 717/397–3447 | www.kingscottagebb.com | $110–$145 | D, MC, V.

Lincoln Haus. Built in 1915, this white stucco house, 2 mi east of downtown, is named after the Lincoln Highway and Abe Lincoln himself. Breakfast often includes wheat pancakes, scrapple, and quiche. Complimentary breakfast. Some kitchenettes. No pets. No kids under 12. No smoking. | 1687 Lincoln Hwy. E. | 717/392–9412 | 6 rooms | $67–$83 | No credit cards.

O'Flaherty's Dingeldein House. The former residence of the Armstrong family of the floor tile fortune, this is a two-story bed-and-breakfast. Since its original construction in 1912, portions have been added, and other owners include the Leath family, founders of the Strasburg Railroad. Complimentary breakfast. No room phones, TV in common area. Playground. Airport shuttle. No smoking. | 1105 E. King St. | 717/293–1723 or 800/779–7765 | fax 717/293–1947 | oflahbb@lancnews.infi.net | www.800padutch.com/ofhouse.html | 6 rooms, (2 with shared bath) | $90–$110 | D, MC, V.

Quality Inn. This one-story brick hotel, 3 mi north of downtown, used to be the Olde Hickory Inn. It's across the street from the Landis Valley Museum. Restaurant, complimentary Continental breakfast. Some kitchenettes, some in-room hot tubs, cable TV. Pool. Hot tub. Laundry service. No pets. | 2363 Oregon Pike. | 717/569–0477 or 800/228–5151 | fax 717/569–6479 | 82 rooms, 18 suites | $160 | AE, MC, V.

Ramada Inn. A long one-story (made of brick), built in 1968, this full-service hotel is just minutes away from Pennsylvania Dutch Country and outlet mall shopping. | 160 rooms. Restaurant, bar. In-room data ports, some refrigerators, room service, cable TV. Pool. Business services. | 1492 Lititz Pike/Rte. 501 | 717/393–0771 | fax 717/299–6238 | www.ramada.com | $95–$105 | AE, D, DC, MC, V.

Ramada Inn. Built in 1967, this one-level brick hotel is directly across from Dutch Wonderland Family Park. The Strasburg Railroad is 5 mi away and Hershey Park and Chocolate World, 40 mi. | 166 rooms. Picnic area. In-room data ports, refrigerators, cable TV. 2 pools (1 indoor). Sauna. Driving range, putting green, Tennis courts. Video games. Playground. Laundry facilities. Business services. Airport shuttle. Some pets allowed. | 2250 Lincoln Hwy. E | 717/393–5499 | fax 717/293–1014 | www.ramada.com/ramada.html | $90–$129 | AE, D, DC, MC, V.

Rockvale Village Inn. At the center of the Rockvale Square Outlets, this is a two-level inn made of brick on a nice green and grassy lot. The building encloses the outdoor pool. It's only 5 mi to downtown Lancaster. | 113 rooms. Restaurant, bar. Cable TV. Pool. Business services. | 24 S. Willowdale Dr. | 717/293–9500 or 800/524–3817 | fax 717/293–8558 | $79–$119 | AE, D, MC, V | www.rockvale.com.

Westfield Inn. A two-level brick building, built in 1985, this inn is only 20 min from the PA Turnpike. It's only 6 mi from downtown. | 84 rooms. Complimentary Continental breakfast. Refrigerators, cable TV. Pool. Laundry facilities. Business services. | 2929 Hempland Rd. | 717/397–9300 or 800/547–1395 | fax 717/295–9240 | $59–$89 | AE, D, DC, MC, V | www.westfieldinn.com.

Willow Valley Resort and Conference Center. Built in 1987, this is a family-oriented resort near Amish countryside. Free guided tours of Amish areas conducted Monday thru Saturday. The hotel has 2 indoor pools, 1 outdoor pool, 2 saunas, 2 whirlpools, kiddie pool, fitness room, tennis courts, 9-hole executive golf course, and playground. The hotel is a five-story white stone building on a green, grassy, tree-lined property with a lake and fountain. 2 restaurants. Cable TV. Hot tub, sauna. Putting green, tennis. Exercise equipment. Laundry facilities. Business services, airport shuttle. | 2416 Willow St. Pike | 717/464–2711 or 800/444–1714 | fax 717/464–4784 | www.travelweb.com/thisco/willow/5081/5081_b.html | 352 rooms | $119–$159 | AE, D, DC, MC, V.

LEBANON

MAP 7, I6

(Nearby towns also listed: Cornwall, Denver, Hershey, Hummelstown, Manheim, Myerstown)

In the center of Pennsylvania's iron ore fields, most of Lebanon's history and development is tied to the production of iron. Bethlehem Steel Company has a plant that stretches almost the whole length of the city. One of the city's unique attractions is the Union

Canal Tunnel, the oldest existing tunnel in the nation. It was built in 1825 and goes through solid rock 80 feet below the summit of the hill.

Information: Lebanon Valley Chamber of Commerce | 252 N. 8th St., 17042 | 717/273–3727 | www.lebanononline.org.

Attractions

Coleman Memorial Park. The park offers something for everyone. It has a miniature golf course, an ice-cream place, an amphitheater, a 500,000-gallon swimming pool that can hold up to 1,000 people, a picnic area, fields, and sporting venues. | W. Maple St. | 717/272–7271 | Free | Daily dawn to dusk.

Stoevers Dam Recreational Area. A nature center with wildlife exhibits, movies, educational programs, and a 36-acre lake for fishing and boating. Here you can also picnic, go camping, walk nature trails, walking paths, and ride horses. | 749 Miller St. | 717/228–4470 | Free | Mar.–Nov., daily 8–3.

Stoy Museum of the Lebanon County Historical Society. You can wander through three floors and a half city block of German furniture, quilting, fraktur, and redware. A one-room school house, toy shop, general store, and dentist office are filled with period furnishings. | 924 Cumberland St. | 717/272–1473 | $3 | Sun. 1–4:30, Mon. 1–8, Tues.–Thurs. 10–4:30, Wed. and Fri. 10–4:30.

Swatara State Park. The park consists of 3,515 acres of rolling fields and woodlands. One of the focal points is the 8 mi of Swatara Creek that winds through the park, which can be used for fishing and boating. The Appalachian National Scenic Trail, which stretches from Georgia to Maine, traverses 2 mi of the southern portion of the park. There are also other hiking trails within the park. Most of the park is open to hunting, and horseback riding is permitted on the public roads throughout the park. | Swatara State Park is located in Lebanon and Schuylkill counties, 14 miles north of Lebanon and 3 miles west of Pine Grove. The park is easily accessible from I-81: at Exit 30, Lickdale, take Route 72 N; at Exit 31, take PA Route 443 W; Rt. 443, 15 mi north of Lebanon | 717/865–6470 or 888/PA–PARKS | www.dcnr.state.pa.us | Free | Daily 8 AM–dusk.

Dining

Inn 422. Contemporary. In a maybe-haunted building dating back to 1880, this restaurant's 1900 Miller organ is a handsome addition to its high ceilings, sturdy floors, and candles, and the staff works in an open kitchen. Dine at the chef's back door table, on the porches, patios, or terraces, or relax in any of the three dining rooms. The menu has many appetizers, and main dishes such as land and sea, a filet and haddock, and veal steak parmesan over vermicelli. Guest rooms available. Breakfast, lunch, and dinner. | 1800 W. Cumberland St. | 717/274–3651 | No supper Mon.–Thur. | $12–$47 | AE, D, MC, V.

The Cedar Grill. American. This Lebanon Valley eatery is popular with locals as well as tourists for its homestyle cooking. Crab cakes and other fish are the favorites on its extensive Pennsylvania Dutch menu. | 1800 E. Cumberland St. | 717/279–7210 | $6.95–$15.95 | MC, V.

Lodging

Lantern Lodge. Built on the site of a 200-year-old farm, surrounded by the homes and farms of the Amish, this two-story, white brick hotel has fine Pennsylvania House cherry furnishings in all rooms. Suites each include a sitting area and working fireplace. Most rooms open onto private porches overlooking the glorious gardens. It's 10 mi to downtown Lebanon. | 80 rooms. Restaurant. Room service, cable TV. Tennis courts. Playground. Business services. Free Parking. | 411 N. College St., Myerstown | 717/866–6536 or 800/262–5564 | fax 717/866–6536, ext. 112 | $70–$100 | AE, D, DC, MC, V | www.thelanternlodge.com.

Quality Inn of Lebanon Valley. A five-story brick building that faces a courtyard with garden and pool, 1 mi from downtown. The Tourist Bureau is at the hotel, Cornwall Iron Furnace is 5 mi south, and Ephrata Cloister is 10 mi southeast. Restaurant, bar (with entertainment), room service. Cable TV. Pool. Business services. | 625 Quentin Rd. | 717/273–6771 | fax 717/273–4882 | 120 rooms in 2 buildings | $85–$125 | AE, D, DC, MC, V.

Quality Inn. This red-brick four-building complex, housing the Lebanon Tourist Bureau, was renovated in 1999. It's 12 mi east of Hershey Park. Restaurant, bar, room service. In-room data ports, some microwaves, some refrigerators, cable TV. Outdoor pool. Laundry service. Pets allowed (fee). | 625 Quentin Rd. | 800/626–8242 | fax 717/273–4882 | 130 rooms | $79–$110 | AE, D, DC, MC, V.

LEWISBURG

MAP 7, H4

(Nearby towns also listed: Danville, Williamsport)

Known primarily as a furniture and textiles borough, today Lewisburg is best known for having one of Pennsylvania's leading educational institutions. Bucknell University is on 200 acres in the borough's southern section and provides a wealth of opportunity to walk among Mother Nature or enjoy one of the school's programs.

Information: **Union County Chamber of Commerce** | 219 Hafer Rd., Room D, 17837 | 717/273–3727.

Attractions

Bucknell University. First called the University at Lewisburg, this school was founded by Philadelphia Baptists in 1846 and renamed for its post-Civil War benefactor, William Bucknell. Located on a 400-acre hillside campus, it overlooks the Susquehanna River and the town of Lewisburg. | Bucknell University | 570/577–2000 | www.bucknell.edu | Free | Daily.

Mifflinburg Buggy Museum. From the late 1800s to the early 1900s, William A. Heiss manufactured horse-drawn vehicles in his coach works. Tour guides explain the items and methods used in the manufacture of buggies and carriages. Also on site is the home of William Heiss and many of its original furnishings. | 523 Green St., Mifflinburg | 570/966–1355 | fax 570/966–9231 | www.lycoming.org/buggy | $5 | Thurs.–Sun. 1–5, closed Mon.–Wed.

Milton State Park. The park is an 82-acre island on the Susquehanna River, providing picnic facilities, hiking trails, a play area, a ballfield, soccer fields, and fishing and boating. The southern half of the park remains in a wooded state for hiking and nature study. Milton State Park is between the boroughs of Milton and West Milton, with access via PA Rte. 642 off PA Rte. 147 on the east and US Rte. 15 at West Milton. | 570/988–5557 or 888/PA–PARKS | fax 570/988–5557 | www.dcnr.state.pa.us | Free | Daily 8 AM–dusk.

Packwood House Museum. A guided tour of the house's 18 rooms over three floors includes 10,000 antiques from the 18th to 20th centuries. There are also artifacts from central Pennsylvania. | 15 N. Water St. | 570/524–0323 | fax 570/524–0548 | $4 | Tues.–Sat. 10–5, Sun. 1–5, closed Mon.

Raymond B. Winter State Park. The 695-acre park is within the Bald Eagle State Forest. There are 60 campsites, one modern cabin, 6.3 mi of hiking trails, hunting on 400 acres, and 5 mi of cross-country ski trails. Other activities include fishing, swimming, and picnicking. | R. B. Winter State Park is situated on 695 acres within the Bald Eagle State Forest. The park is in central Pennsylvania, Union County, on PA Rte. 192, 18 miles west of Lewisburg; 18 west of Lewisburg along PA 192 | 570/966–1455 or 888/PA–PARKS | www.dcnr.state.pa.us | Free | Daily 8 AM–dusk.

Slifer House Museum. This former home of Eli Slifer, built in 1861, still has period furnishings. Many of the items are Victorian and are from the Slifer family. | 1 River Rd. | 570/524–2245 | $4 | Apr.–late Dec., Tues.–Sun. 1–4, closed Mon.; late Dec.–Mar., Tues.–Fri. 1–4, closed Sat.–Mon.

DEC.: *Victorian Holiday Parade*. For just a moment, on the first Friday of December, the town of Lewisburg is completely silent and dark – then the holiday lights come on and signal the start of the seasonal celebration. The following day there's a parade with horse-drawn floats, giant puppets, Queen Victoria, Abe Lincoln, Kris Kringle, and local school bands. And on every Saturday from Thanksgiving to Christmas, kids whose parents are shopping can sit in a free matinee at the town's theater. | 570/523–3614.

Dining

Bull Run Inn. American/Casual. Full of students and locals, this restaurant serves stuffed mushrooms, Cajun chicken breast and other sandwiches, fish, and steak. In a century-and-a-half-old building next to Bull Run Creek, it's a good place to experience off-campus life in Lewisburg. | 605 Market St. | 570/524–2572 | $8.99–$13.99 | AE, MC, V.

Country Cupboard. Continental. This light blue-and-white-walled restaurant, which seats 650, shares its turf with a shopping center. Buffet, cafeteria service. Kids' menu. No alcohol. No smoking. | Hafer Rd. From I–80, go south on 15 to the first red light—you will see the restaurant across the street on Hafer road. No street number | 570/523–3211 | Reservations not accepted weekends | Closed Sun. | $13–$20 | D, MC, V.

The Inn at Olde New Berlin. Continental. An elegant dining room with large arched windows and rich, intricately carved woodwork distinguishes this restaurant's interior. Seafood and veal are popular here, but try the winter mango salad with tender field greens, enoki mushrooms, diced mango, and red grapefruit laced with candied pecans and honey croutons. Sun. brunch. Beer and wine only. | 321 Market St. | 570/966–0321 | Closed Mon., Tues. | $13–$28 | D, MC, V.

Lodging

Best Western Country Cupboard Inn. A Victorian style, three-story brick building, this motel is at Exit 30A of I–80. It's only 3 mi from Bucknell University, 13 mi from Fort Augusta, and 15 mi from Raymond B. Winter State Park. | 106 rooms, 9 suites. Complimentary Continental breakfast. Refrigerators (in suites), cable TV. Pool. Exercise equipment. Laundry facilities. Business services. | Rte. 15 N | 570/524–5500 | fax 570/524–4291 | $85–$115, $104–$149 suites | AE, D, DC, MC, V.

Days Inn–Lewisburg. A two-story motor hotel in a modern stucco building, this chain motel is a favorite for parents and others visiting Bucknell University. It's only 3 blocks from the downtown area. | 108 rooms. In-room data ports, cable TV Pool. Exercise equipment. Business services. | Rte. 15 | 570/523–1171 | fax 570/524–4667 | $61–$135 | AE, D, DC, MC, V.

Pineapple Inn. Located in the heart of Lewisburg 4 blocks from the Bucknell campus, this Federal-style house was built in 1857 by Philadelphia architect Louis Palmer. With its equestrian artifacts, Amish quilts, brass rubbings, and Victorian-style furnishings—including a bedroom suite that once belonged to the Archbishop of Canterbury—the inn has a hearty Pennsylvania Dutch breakfast and complimentary afternoon tea. Smoking permitted in parlor only. You need to call six months in advance to reserve peak college weekends. Complimentary breakfast. TV in common area. No pets. | 439 Market St. | 570/524–6200 | fax / | pineappl@jdweb.com | www.jdweb.com/pineappleinn | 6 rooms (2 with bath) | $85 | AE, D, DC, MC, V.

LEWISTOWN

(Nearby towns also listed: Bellefonte, Huntingdon, State College)

Named after William Lewis, owner of the Hopewell Furnace, this borough is popular today for its proximity to Harrisburg and the historic buildings that dot its downtown district. Much of central Pennsylvania travels through Lewistown to reach the state's capital and to enjoy the forest and hills that surround it.

Information: **Juniata Valley Chamber of Commerce** | 3 W. Monument Sq., #208, 17044 | 717/248–6713.

Attractions

Brookmere Farm Vineyards. A 16-year-old winery with guided tours and free tastings of their 22 wines, it's in a 19th-century stone and wood barn, with a vintner's loft with local artwork. | 5369 Rte. 655, Belleville | 717/935–5380 | fax 717/935–5349 | $1 | Mon.–Sat. 10–5, closed Sun.

Greenwood Furnace State Park. The park covers 423 acres and includes a 6-acre lake, 50 campsites, picnic areas, and hiking trails. It allows for hunting, fishing, and horseback riding. It is also the site of the Greenwood Furnace, a village that was built around an iron furnace in the 1800s. The works operated from 1834 to 1904 and six of the original buildings remain. | On PA Rte. 305, 30 min west of Lewistown | 814/667–1800 | www.dcnr.state.pa.us | Free | Daily 8 AM–dusk.

Poe Valley State Park. In a rugged mountain valley and surrounded by Bald Eagle State Forest, the 620-acre park has 77 campsites and picnic areas. The focal point of the park is 25-acre Poe Lake, used for boating, fishing, swimming, ice skating, and ice fishing. Other activities permitted in the park are hunting, hiking, cross-country skiing, and snowmobiling. | Off of Rte. 322 and Rte. 45, 30 mi north of Lewistown | 814/349–8778, 717/667–3622, or 888/PA–PARKS | www.dcnr.state.pa.us | Free | Daily 8 AM–dusk.

Reeds Gap State Park. A park that allows fishing in Honey Creek and a smaller mountain stream, hunting on 96 acres, and hiking, it has 14 campsites, two swimming pools, 5 mi of cross-country trails, and picnicking. | 1042 New Lancaster Valley Rd. | 717/667–3622 | fax 717/667–6086 | www.dcnr.state.pa.us | Free | Daily 8 AM–dusk.

ON THE CALENDAR
DEC.: *Festival of Ice.* Each year, during the first weekend of December, thousands of people gather in the center of Lewistown to rejoice in the early winter. Santa is there, and live reindeer and carolers. You can watch as two half-ton blocks of ice are carved into sculptures, take a carriage ride, or help decorate trees throughout the town in celebration of the weekend's free Festival of Trees. | 717/248–6713.

Dining

Green Inn. Continental. The renowned arched stone entryway of this 1800s inn and former stagecoach stop makes it hard to miss. The restaurant and tavern also have a ballroom. Sun. brunch. | 900 S. Main St. | 717/248–4242 | $10–$22 | AE, D, DC, MC, V.

Jack's Mountain Restaurant and Brewery. American. This is a simple spot both inside and out, with brew kettles right below the main dining area and long, cozy bar. Known for traditional country food. Wide array of original beers. Each weekend Jack's has a featured culinary masterpiece, such as Beer Battered Shrimp-batter made from Mountain Jack's Bold Lager, fried to a golden brown, which is exquisite. Kids' menu. | 9074 U.S. 522 S | 717/242–6483 | Closed Sun. | $12–$19 | AE, D, MC, V.

Lodging

Clarion Inn. Built in 1960, this two-story chain motel is 3 mi outside of Lewistown and 30 min west of State College. | 119 rooms. Restaurant, bar. In-room data ports, room service, cable TV. Pool. Some pets allowed. | 13015 Ferguson Valley Rd., Burnham | 717/248–4961 | fax 717/242–3013 | $69 | AE, D, DC, MC, V.

LIGONIER

(Nearby towns also listed: Donegal, Greensburg, New Stanton)

Isolated by two mountains, Laurel to the east and Chestnut Ridge to the west, Ligonier is in the heart of Ligonier Valley, which permits very few roadways. So the valley, in effect, is protected by two great walls 10 mi apart and 25 mi long. The town played an important role in the French and Indian War with Fort Ligonier being the heart and soul of the battles. Today, the borough's "Diamond" is the center of area shopping and dining and has been established since Ligonier was incorporated in 1834.

Information: Ligonier Valley Chamber of Commerce | 120 E. Main St., 15658 | 412/238–4200.

Attractions

Compass Inn Museum. A restored stagecoach stop that was built in 1799 with a stone addition in 1820. The inn is furnished with period pieces. The working kitchen, blacksmith shop, and barn are reconstructed on their original sites. | Laughlintown; On Rte. 30, 3 mi east of Ligonier | 724/238–4983 | $5; special rates for senior citizens | May–Oct., Tues.–Sat. 11–4, Sun. noon–4, closed Mon.

Fort Ligonier. A full-scale reconstruction of the original fort that sat on that site from 1758 to 1766. It offers living history activities including reenactments, folk crafts, and archaeological digs. It was a Colonial outpost that guarded the route to Pittsburgh and the West. | 216 S. Market St. | 724/238–9701 | May.–Oct., Mon.–Sat., 10–4:30, Sun. noon–4:30.

Idlewild Park. Founded in 1878, it is believed to be the oldest continuously operating amusement park in the country. With 410 acres, 15 major rides, a number of theme areas, and a picnic area, it offers something for everyone. Attractions include Storybook Forest, Mr. Rogers Neighborhood, H2-O Zone and water slides. | Rte. 30 E, 2 mi west of Ligonier | 724/238–3666 | www.idlewild.com | $17; special rates for senior citizens and children | May–Sept., Tues.–Sun. 10–9, closed Mon.

Within Idlewild Park, you can travel through **Mister Rogers Neighborhood of Make Believe** on its famous trolley car. Meet and talk to King Friday, Pussycat, and Daniel Striped Tiger among others.

In the **Story Book Forest** within Idlewild Park, favorite storybook characters come to life as paths take you from house to house to witness events and characters in action. Snow White, Jack-Be-Nimble, and the old woman in the shoe are among those appearing. | Rt. 30 east, 2 mi w of Ligonier | 724/238–3666 | www.idlewild.com | $17 | May–Sept., Tues.–Sun. 10–9, closed Mon.

Laurel Summit State Park. The 6-acre picnic area is 2,739 feet above sea level and is several degrees cooler than surrounding towns. The area provides trailhead parking for Spruce Flats bog and Wolf Rocks Trail. | Laurel Summit, 11 mi southeast of Ligonier | 724/238–6623 or 888/PA–PARKS | www.dcnr.state.pa.us | Free | Daily 8 AM–dusk.

Linn Run State Park. This 612-acre park is surrounded by Forbes State Forest. It has 10 rustic cabins, picnic facilities, and 5 mi of hiking trails. Other activities include fishing on Linn Run, hunting on more than 400 acres, horseback riding on Linn Run Road, and snowmobiling. | To reach the park from Ligonier, take U.S. Route 30 E for two miles. At the intersection of PA Route 381, turn south for two miles. Turn left on Linn Run Road at the small town of Rector; Linn Rd., 9 mi southeast of Ligonier | 724/238–6623 or 888/PA–PARKS | www.dcnr.state.pa.us | Free | Daily 8 AM–dusk.

St. Vincent Archabbey and College. The site of the first abbey in America founded by the Benedictine Order of the Roman Catholic Church, it was founded in 1846 and became a college in 1870. A gristmill built in 1854 is still used for grinding grain. St. Vincent's Museum has Native American relics and a fossil and mineral collection. | 300 Fraser Purchase Rd., Latrobe | 412/537–4560 or 412/537–8900 | www.stvincent.com | Free | Tues. and Thurs. 1:30–4, closed Fri.–Mon. and Wed.

ON THE CALENDAR

JAN.: *Ligonier Ice Fest*. This Presidents' Weekend event boasts dozens of ice sculptures created by professionals and amateurs. | Various locations | 724/238–4200 | Free.

MAY–OCT.: *Mountain Playhouse*. Broadway shows are presented in a restored grist-mill dating to 1805. | 7690 Summerset Pike, Jennerstown | 814/629–9201 | Prices vary according to performances.

SEPT.: *Ligonier Highland Games and Gathering of the Clans of Scotland*. A 3-day traditional Scottish celebration features massed pipe bands, fiddling, sheep dogs, wool spinning and weaving demonstrations, and dancing competitions. | Idlewild Park | 814/942–0077 | $10 adults, $5 kids 6-12, free for kids under 6.

OCT.: *Fort Ligonier Days*. This 3-day event commemorates the French and Indian War with a juried craft show, food, and battle reenactments. | Fort Ligonier, South Market St. | 724/238–9701 | $6, special rates for children.

Dining

Colonial Inn. Continental. Inside this large farmhouse, with its long porch and pond, you'll find a stone fireplace, chandeliers, and dark-toned walls. A cigar gallery with comfortable, large leather chairs, and cigars for sale is separate from the dining area. One house specialty is the walnut breaded chicken. | Rte. 30, W. Ligonier | 724/238–6604 | Closed Mon. No lunch | $15–$25 | AE, D, DC, MC, V.

Ligonier Tavern. Contemporary. Near the Diamond section of town, this three-story Tudor tavern-restaurant has four modern rooms and a large standout tower. Try homemade baked goods and pasta, and you can take a peek at its wild game selections on the menu. There's open-air dining on a balcony and a screened-in porch. Kids' menu. | 137 W. Main St. | 412/238–4831 | www.ligonier.com | $12–$22 | AE, MC, V.

Lodging

Colonial House. The least-lacy B&B in the state, this three-story red-brick house, built in 1906, was restored and renovated in 1999. It has four rocking chairs, complete with afghans, on the front porch, which is comfortable enough—say those who've spent some time there—to serve as an extra bedroom. Dining room. Complimentary breakfast. Cable TV. No room phones. Pets allowed. No kids under 16. No smoking. | 231 W. Main St. | 724/238–6804 | www.col-house.helicon.net | 4 rooms (sharing 2 baths) | $85 | No credit cards.

Ramada Inn-Historic Ligonier. In the heart of the beautiful Laurel Highlands, this hotel was completely renovated in 1999. With its great in-town location, you can walk to shopping, dining, and historic Fort Ligonier. Restaurant, bar, room service. In-room data ports, cable TV. Pool. Business services. | 216 W. Loyalhanna St. | 724/238–9545 | fax 724/238–9803 | 73 rooms | $72–$175 | AE, D, MC, V.

LIMERICK

MAP 7, K6

(Nearby towns also listed: Fort Washington, King of Prussia, Pottstown, Norristown)

On Route 363, the small town of Limerick is between Pottstown and Norristown. Its origins can be traced back to the early 1800s and many of its historic homes and buildings remain popular visitors' sites.

Information: **Montgomery Chamber of Commerce** | 420 W. Germantown Pike, Eagleville, PA 19403 | 610/277–9500.

Attractions

Limerick Golf Club. This 18-hole championship public golf course has weekend "nite" golf, event facilities, a bar, restaurant, and night club. You should call in advance for weekend tee times. From Expressway 422, take the Linfield/Limerick Exit. | 765 N. Lewis Rd. | 610/495–5567 | www.limerickgolfclub.com | $32 weekend greens fee | Daily 7AM–dark.

Spring Mountain Ski Area. With an elevation of 528 feet, the ski area offers skiing and snowboarding. Its top vertical drop is 420 feet and it has four lifts taking you to one of eight trails. The longest run is 2,200 feet and ski rentals are available. | Spring Mountian Rd., Spring Mount; on Rte. 29, northeast of Limerick | 610/287–7900 | $18–$25 | Jan.–Mar.

Dining

Gypsy Rose. Continental. You can dine in one of the dining rooms, on the outdoor brick terrace (open from April-October), or relax in the bar with a renowned wine list. Specialties of the house are Maryland crab cakes and California seafood symphony, grilled shrimp, tuna, salmon, and scallops with linguine tossed in a Chardonnay sauce. Kids' menu. Sun. brunch. | 505 Bridge Rd. | 610/489–1600 | $14–$21 | AE, D, DC, MC, V.

Airport Restaurant and Hotel. American. Across from the Limerick airport and next to a hotel that rents rooms by the week, this restaurant is a local favorite. Your can choose from homemade soup to lobster. According to one waitress, you'll leave full and satisfied. | 3347 W. Ridge Rd. | 610/495–7626 | Closed Sunday. No lunch weekends. No dinner Mon. | $12.95–$22.95 | Reservations essential | MC, V.

LITITZ

(Nearby towns also listed: Bird-in-Hand, Columbia, Ephrata, Lancaster, Manheim)

This town was founded in 1756 by Protestant Moravians who came to Pennsylvania with the hope of converting the "heathen" natives. Today, it is a charming small town of clean, shaded streets lined with stately 18th-century buildings of fieldstone and aged brick. Inside many of the buildings are antiques stores and crafts shops. Still, at the center of town life is Moravian Square, bordered by a 1787 Moravian church, Brethren and Sisters' houses, and Linden Hall, the oldest girls' residence school in the United States.

Information: **The Pennsylvania Dutch Convention and Visitors Bureau** | 501 Greenfield Rd., Lancaster, 17601 | 717/299–8901 | www.800padutch.com.

Attractions

Julius Sturgis Pretzel House. At the nation's oldest pretzel bakery, pretzels are twisted by hand and baked in brick ovens the same way Julius Sturgis did it in 1861. You can try your hand at the almost extinct art of pretzel twisting at the end of the 20-minute tour. | 219 E. Main St. | 717/626–4354 | www.sturgispretzel.com | $2 | Mon.-Sat.9-5.

Wilbur Chocolate Factory's Candy Americana Museum and Factory Outlet. The first thing you notice in Lititz is the smell of chocolate coming from the Wilbur Chocolate Factory, which produces 150 million pounds of the luscious product each year. There's a small museum of candy-related memorabilia and a large retail store. | 48 N. Broad St. | 717/626–3249 | www.wilburbuds.com | Free | Mon.-Sat. 10-5.

Lititz Museum Step back into late 18th-/early 19th-century Moravian life as you visit the restored 1792 home of tradesman Johannes Mueller. | 137-145 E. Main St. | 717/627–4636 | www.lititzmutual.com/historical/museum.asp.

Dining

1764 Restaurant. The restaurant in the historic General Sutter Inn's (see Lodging below) has pan-seared buffalo in a sauce with cumin, pine nuts, and caramelized onions, and crab cakes with a lemon-caper remoulade. | 14 E. Main St. | 717/626–2115 | fax 717/626–0992 | $16.50–$24.50 | AE, D, MC, V.

Zum-Anker Cafe. Contemporary. The historic General Sutter Inn's (see Lodging below) casual eatery serves up eggs with Canadian bacon, spinach, and Mornay sauce, and grilled cinnamon buns for breakfast, soups, stews, and salads for lunch, including garden penne pasta and broiled scallops and spinach salad. | 14 E. Main St. | 717/626–2115 | fax 717/626–0992 | No dinner | $6–$10 | AE, D, MC, V.

Chimney Corner Restaurant. American. This casual restaurant serves home-style items like traditional turkey dinner and chicken, as well as waffles and chocolate cake with peanut butter icing. | 707 Rothsville Rd. | 717/626–4707 | $6–$10 | MC, V.

Lodging

★ **General Sutter Inn.** Built in 1764, the oldest continuously operating inn in Pennsylvania was named after the man who founded Sacramento in 1839, 10 years before the discovery of gold on his property started the gold rush. Sutter retired in Lititz. The inn, a Victoriana lover's delight, is at the crossroads of the town, within walking distance of the historic district. | 16 rooms, 3 suites. Restaurant, bar, coffee shop. | 14 E. Main St.; corner of Rtes. 501 and 772 | 717/626–2115 | fax 717/626–0992 | http://www.generalsutterinn.com/ | Rooms:$65.00–$105; Suites:$105.–$140 | BP | AE, D, MC, V.

★ **Swiss Woods.** On the edge of 30-acres of woods overlooking Speedwell Forge Lake, this is an open and airy European-style bed and breakfast. Each room has its own balcony or patio. Hiking, boating, fishing. | 500 Blantz Rd. | 717/627–3358 or 800/594–8018 | fax 717/627–3483 | www.swisswoods.com | 6 rooms, 1 suite | $99–$175 | BP | AE, D, MC, V.

Alden House. This bed and breakfast offers period rooms with modern baths in an 1850 red brick Victorian/Colonial house in the heart of the historic district. | 62 E. Main St. | 717/627–3363 or 800/584–0753 | www.aldenhouse.com | 5 rooms | $90–$120 | BP | MC, V.

LOCK HAVEN

MAP 7, G4

(Nearby town also listed: Williamsport)

Lock Haven was established because one man saw its potential and decided to make it happen. When Jeremiah Church bought land along the west branch of the Susquehanna River, he immediately turned it into the county seat. Named after the canal that once had a lock there and was considered a haven for travelers on the river, many of Lock Haven's homes were built along the river. Today, these homes remain, and Lock Haven's downtown buildings draw antiques lovers, while its lush forests draw hunters and fishermen.

Information: Clinton County Chamber of Commerce | 151 Susquehanna Ave., Lock Haven, PA 17745 | 570/748–5782.

Attractions

Bald Eagle State Park. The 5,900-acre park was developed around Foster Joseph Sayers Dam and along Bald Eagle Creek. It has a 1,730-acre lake with 23 mi of shoreline, swimming, boating, and fishing. There's hiking, camping, hunting, and cross-country skiing. | 149 Main Park Rd., Howard | 814/625–2775 | www.dcnr.state.pa.us | Free | Daily 8 AM–dusk.

Fin, Fur and Feather Wildlife Museum. There are 450 mounted animals from all over the world. It all belongs to one man, Paul Asper, and is the largest private collection in the world. The animals that you can view include a walrus, an elephant, a white rhino, a kangaroo, a bear, an antelope, and a sheep. | Off of Rte. 664 (which turns into Rt. 44) 18 mi north of Lock Haven | 570/769–6482 | $5 | May–Dec. 10-4 daily, after Labor Day weekdays 10-4, Sat.–Sun., 12:30–5.

Heisey Museum. A Victorian home in the 1800s style, the house has many documents that tell the history of Clinton County. | 362 E. Water St. | 570/748–7254 | fax 570/748–7590 | www.kcnet.org/~heisey/ | $3 | Tues.–Fri. 10-4, closed Sat.–Mon.

Hyner Run State Park. Hang gliding is a very popular activity at this 6-acre park. Hang gliders take off from the scenic vista and sail over the west branch of the Susquehanna River. The focal point of the park is the overlook wall. There's a small picnic area. Hyner View is an overlook in the park, constructed in 1930. | Hyner Run Rd. | 570/923–6000 or 888/PA–PARKS | www.dcnr.state.pa.us | Free | Daily 8 AM–dusk.

Kettle Creek State Park. The park's 1,793 acres are along the Kettle Creek. It offers a 7-acre lake for boating and fishing. It also has 71 campsites, a 15-mile horseback riding trail, hiking trails, and a biking trail. There's hunting, swimming, picnicking, and snowmobiling. | The park is located along S.R. 4001, 7 miles north of Westport and PA Route 120; Rte. 4001, 43 mi northwest of Lock Haven | 570/923–6004 | www.dcnr.state.pa.us | Free | Daily 8 AM–dusk.

Piper Aviation Museum. William T. (Bill) Piper, who established the Piper Aircraft Corporation in 1937, dreamed that one day airplanes would be as common as cars. He built the Piper Cub, the aircraft that "taught the world to fly," from a miscellany of parts that included a ferris wheel and old barn rails—and sold it for $999. His factory, closed in 1984, is now home to a museum where armchair pilots can take a spin in a flight simulator. | 1 Piper Way | 570/748–8283 | fax 570/893–8357 | www.kcnet.org/~piper/ | $3 | Weekdays 9-4, Sat. 10-4, Sun. 12-4.

ON THE CALENDAR

MAY–AUG.: *Summer Concert Series.* Every Sunday from Memorial Day until the end of August, free concerts—mostly rock and rhythm-and-blues bands—are held in the 3,000-seat outdoor J. Doyle Corman Amphitheater and Floating Stage. | 570/893–5900. | www.lockhavencity.org/concert.

OCT.: *Flaming Foliage Festival.* You can join in this 2-day celebration of fall colors with a variety of events. | Renovo, 28 mi north of Lock Haven | 570/923–2411 | free.

Lodging

Best Western. One mile from the Piper Aviation Museum, this three-story brick hotel is 12 blocks from Lehigh University. Complimentary Continental breakfast. In-room data ports, some microwaves, some refrigerators, cable TV. Gym. Laundry facilities. Business services. Pets allowed (fee). | 101 E. Walnut St. | 570/748–3297 | fax 570/748–5390 | www.bestwestern.com/lockhaven | 67 rooms | $90 | AE, D, DC, MC, V.

Victorian Inn. Built in 1859, this 2-story bed-and-breakfast is only a block away from the Heisey Museum and downtown. As its name indicates, the hardwood, frame-house inn is filled with Victorian antique mirrors and artwork. There's a river runnning past the front, and a paved 3 mile jogging trail. | 13 rooms (2 with shower only, 2 with shared bath). Complimentary breakfast. No kids except by prior arrangement. | 402 E. Water St. | 570/748–8688 | fax 570/748–2444 | http://www.clintoncountyinfo.com/din_log.htm | $70–$75 | AE, D, DC, MC, V.

MANHEIM

MAP 7, 16

(Nearby towns also listed: Bird-in-Hand, Cornwall, Denver, Ephrata, Hershey, Hummelstown, Middletown)

Mennonite settlers made their way to the area, and when Henry William Stiegel built a glass factory and sold land for a church for the price of one red rose per year, it helped establish Manheim as a borough. A one-time center for glass and iron making, today Manheim is home to many farmers markets and gift shops. It's also near the heart of Amish country, with many of its dining and craft establishments following the Amish tradition in their daily operation.

Information: **Manheim Chamber of Commerce** | 210 S. Charlotte St., 17545 | 717/665–6330.

Attractions

Kreider Farms. Cows are the main attraction here, hundreds of them, all housed in a barn big enough to hold the Titanic. If you take the educational tour—created by teachers and based on the ages of those in the group—you can see 54 cows being milked at the same time on a high-tech computerized carousel, then watch as that milk is processed for market. After the tour, you're invited to enjoy a cone filled with the farm's own ice-cream. | 1461 Lancaster Rd. | 717/665–5039 | $4.50 | Mon., Wed., Fri. 9:30 and 11:30AM, reservations required.

Mt. Hope Estate and Winery. This pastoral locale is the site of the Pennsylvania Renaissance Faire, with a cast of over 100 colorfully costumed people in a re-creation of 16th-century Europe. A 35-acre Elizabethan village has a three-story re-creation of Shakespeare's Theater in the Round. Sixty shows appear on 12 stages daily, including jousting and hand-to-hand battles. | Rte. 72 and PA Tpk. | 717/665–7021 | www.parenaissancefaire.com | Free, except shows and events | Aug.–Oct., daily 10–6:30.

Zion Lutheran Church. This house of worship is also known as the Red Rose Church; each year church officials must present one red rose to a descendant of Henry William Stiegel, who donated the land on which the church was built. The church has been making the payment for the past 225 years. | 2 S. Hazel St. | 717/665–5880 | Free | Weekdays 8–4.

ON THE CALENDAR

JUNE: *Rose Festival.* In this traditional rite of early summer, a descendant of town founder Henry William Stiegel comes to the Zion Lutheran Church grounds to accept the annual rent of one red rose for their use. | 717/665–5880 or 717/665–6330.

AUG.:–OCT.: *Pennsylvania Renaissance Faire.* The grounds of the Mt. Hope Winery host this seasonal festival, complete with costumed lords and ladies, a medieval jousting tournament, and a human chess match. | 717/665–7021.

OCT.: *Manheim Community Farm Show.* Held each year during the first full week in October on Saturday, this is a true farm show, not a fair. Here animals, vegetables, plants, and crops are viewed and judged; tractors and other farm equipment are admired and appraised; and homemade food is consumed. The show is held in the town's Farm Show building, next to Manheim High School. | 717/665–5960.

Dining

The Cat's Meow. American/Casual. Flapper-style mannequins and photos from the Roaring '20s establish the theme of this restaurant, which serves hamburgers, crab and cheddar melts, chicken quesadillas, and salads. The kitchen is open from 11 AM until midnight Sunday through Tuesday and until 1 AM Wednesday through Saturday. | 215 S. Charlotte St. | 717/664–3370 | $11.95–$18.95 | AE, D, MC, V.

Lodging

Rose Manor Bed & Breakfast. About 20 mi south of Hershey, this bed and breakfast is in a 1905 stucco home. The parlor and dining room are furnished with original chestnut woodwork and cabinets; wicker and other period antiques fill the rooms. There's an herbal gift shop on the premises. Complimentary breakfast. Cable TV. No pets. No kids under 12. | 124 S. Linden St. | 717/664–4932 | fax 717/664–1611 | rosemanor@paonline.com | 5 rooms | $70–$120 | MC, V.

Rodeway Inn Penn's Woods. Formerly a Friendship Inn, this hotel is ½ mi north of Manheim on I–72, less than ½ mi north of the Mount Hope Winery. Picnic area. Indoor pool. Volleyball. Pets allowed (fee). | 2931 Lebanon Rd. | 717/665–2755 / | fax 717/664–2513 | www.choicehotels.com | 43 rooms | $70 | AE, D, MC, V.

MANSFIELD

(Nearby town also listed: Wellsboro)

In 1800, Asa Mann, an Englishman from Rhode Island, settled at the northern end of what is now the borough of Mansfield. He was the first person to clear any considerable amount of land, about 25 acres. His holdings became known as Mann's Field and hence became Mansfield. He soon divided his cleared land into building lots. The borough was incorporated in 1857. Mansfield celebrates the anniversary of the world's first night football game played under lights on September 28, 1892. The original match pitted Mansfield Seminary against Wyoming Seminary and was the highlight of the Great Mansfield Fair that year.

Information: Greater Mansfield Chamber of Commerce | 39 E. Wellsboro St., Suite A, 16933 | 570/662–3442 | www.mansfield.org.

Attractions

Cowanesque Lake. You can go boating or fishing at this 1,090-acre lake. The land around the lake can be used for camping, hiking, and hunting, and has trails for biking and snowmobiling. | Rte. 49 | 570/835–5281 | Free | May–Oct., daily dawn to dusk; Nov.–Apr., daily 8–4.

Hills Creek State Park. This 406-acre park has a 137-acre lake for boating, fishing, and swimming. Camping, hiking, skating, and picnicking are just a few of the other things you can do here. | Take Rte. 6 and follow signs for park | 570/724–4246 | www.dcnr.state.pa.us | Free | Daily 8 AM–dusk.

Tioga–Hammond Lakes. A 470-acre lake, Tioga, and a 680-acre lake, Hammond, are connected by a channel, and both park areas are havens for boating, fishing, hiking, swimming, camping, and hunting. The park offices have a garden display, wildlife display, and archery range. | Rte. 287 | 570/835–5281 | Free | May–Oct., daily dawn to dusk; Nov.–Apr., daily 8–4.

ON THE CALENDAR

SEPT.: *The Northern Appalachian Storytelling Festival.* This is the oldest storytelling festival (20 years) held at a U.S. university. You can listen as Native American, Irish, Jewish, African, Scottish, and Cajun storytellers take part in a tradition as old as mankind. | 570/662–3442 | director@wso.net | www.wso.net/storyfest/.

SEPT.: *The Fabulous 1890's Weekend.* This festival commemorates the world's first night football game, Mansfield University against Wyoming Seminary, played in Mansfield on September 28, 1892. You can enjoy the parade, hot air balloons, strolling banjo players, crafts, food, music, soccer games, fireworks, an old-fashioned square dance and, of course, a reenactment of the game. | 570/662–3442.

Dining

Farmer in the Dell. American/Casual. Across the river from the high school, this restaurant has hamburgers with beef grown at its dairy farm, 4 mi away. The owners even have some cows in downtown Mansfield. | 85 W. Main St. | 570/662–2494 | $5–$10 | No credit cards.

Lodging

Comfort Inn. Built in 1991, this hotel is within 15 mi of most local attractions, and its location on a hill gives it a gorgeous view of the mountains and Mansfield College. Complimentary Continental breakfast. Cable TV. Exercise equipment. Business services. Pets allowed (fee). | 300 Gateway Dr. | 570/662–3000 | fax 570/662–2551 | www.comfortmansfield.com | 100 rooms | $77–$105 | AE, D, DC, MC, V.

Oasis Motel. This motel in a modern building is on 6 ½ acres 2 ½ mi from the center of town. Wood paneling makes it homey inside. | R.R. 1, Box 90; Rte. 15 south of Mansfield | 570/659–5576 or 800/448–5576 | fax 570/659–5576 | 12 rooms | $45–$50 | D, MC, V.

West's Deluxe Motel. This one-story red-brick motel is 3½ mi south of downtown Mansfield, next to West's restaurant (not related, but recommended). Picnic area. Refrigerators, cable TV. Outdoor pool. Pets allowed. | R.R. 1, Rte. 15 | 570/659–5141 or 800/995–9378 | fax 570/659–5851 | www.westsdeluxe.com | 20 rooms | $50 | AE, D, MC, V.

MEADVILLE

MAP 7, B3

(Nearby towns also listed: Conneaut Lake, Franklin)

The county seat of Crawford County, Meadville is in the western foothills of the Allegheny Mountains on Route 6. You can see a number of local attractions including Conneaut Lake, the Erie National Wildlife Refuge, and many museums and historical homes.

Information: Meadville Chamber of Commerce | 211 Chestnut St., 16335 | 814/337–8030.

Attractions

Allegheny College. Founded in 1815, the college has 36 buildings on 72 acres of land. It also owns a 283-acre nature preserve full of flora and fauna. | N. Main St. | 814/332–3100 or 814/332–4365 | www.alleg.edu | Free | Daily.

Baldwin–Reynolds House Museum. Built in 1834 by Supreme Court Justice Henry Baldwin, the museum is on 3 acres overlooking the French Creek Valley. The grouping of the 19th-century house, museum, and 19th-century doctor's office is on the National Register of Historic Places. | 639 Terrace St. | 814/724–6080 | www.visitcrawford.org | $3 | May–Labor Day, Wed.–Sun. 1–5, closed Mon.–Tues.

Colonel Crawford Park. Picnic shelters guard outdoor snackers at this park, which was named after William Crawford, who surveyed and helped erect nearby Fort Crawford. The fort was used as a depot and headquarters during skirmishes with Native Americans. | Off Dixon Rd. | 814/724–6879 | Free | Daily dawn to dusk.

Erie National Wildlife Refuge. In Crawford County, the refuge is a habitat for waterfowl on 8,777 acres of beaver ponds, pools, marshlands, and grasslands. Here you can hike, fish, bird-watch, take scenic drives, hunt, and cross-country ski. | 11296 Wood Duck La. | 814/789–3585 | Free | Weekdays 7–4:30, weekends 8–6.

Pymatuning State Park. The Pymatuning Reservoir was once a huge swamp occupied by the Mound Builders, who buried their important dead in large mounds and eventually disappeared—only to be replaced by the Erie Nation, which was conquered by the Seneca Nation of the Iroquois Confederacy. Pymatuning is Iroquois for "the crooked-mouthed (deceitful) man's dwelling place." The park, 27 mi west of Meadville, is now a place where you can picnic, hike, camp, hunt, fish, and boat all year long. (In winter, fishing and boating become ice-fishing and ice-boating.) | 2660 Williamsfield Rd., Jamestown | 724/932–3141 | pymatuning@dcnr.state.pa.us | www.dcnr.state.pa.us/stateparks/parks/pyma | Free.

ON THE CALENDAR

FEB.: *Winter Fun Days.* Held the first weekend in February at Pymatuning State Park, this celebration is all about winter. You can ice-skate, ice-boat, snowmobile, see the chainsaw-cut wood figures, and eat wieners at the Friday night roast. | 724/932–3141.
AUG.: *Crawford County Fair.* Participants in this fair display livestock, sell home-baked goods, and provide rides and other entertainment on the Crawford County Fairgrounds. | $3 | 814/333–1258.

Dining

Hoss's Steak & Sea House. American. You can have steak, seafood, chicken, or sandwiches at this restaurant, a favorite with the locals. It's next to a bowling alley—look for the big brick sign. | 18817 Smock Hwy. | 814/333–4333 | $8.99 | AE, D, DC, MC, V.

Lodging

Days Inn. This motel is at Exit 36A of I–79, 30 min from the Grove City outlets. Restaurant, bar. Cable TV. Indoor pool. Hot tub. Laundry facilities. Business services. Pets allowed. | 18360 Conneaut Lake Rd. | 814/337–4264 | fax 814/337–7304 | www.daysinn.com | 163 rooms | $77–$86 | AE, D, DC, MC, V.

Wynken, Blynken & Nod. Opened January 2000, this two-story brown-brick house, two blocks east of Diamond Park (the center of Meadville), is named for the family's favorite sleepytime tale. Complimentary breakfast. No pets. No kids under 12. No smoking. | 468 Chestnut St. | 814/337–2018 or 814/683–4234 | fax 814/337–1148 | 3 rooms (sharing 2 baths) | $60 | No credit cards.

MECHANICSBURG

MAP 7, H6

(Nearby towns also listed: Boiling Springs, Camp Hill, Carlisle, Harrisburg)

Victorian homes, many with towers, are common in this borough that dates back to 1818. Historically, Mechanicsburg has been one of northeast Pennsylvania's largest towns and each summer draws more than 2,000 visitors a day for its Jubilee Day celebration.

Information: **Harrisburg–Hershey–Carlisle Tourism and Convention Bureau.** | 25 N. Front St., Ste. 100, Harrisburg, PA 17101 | 717/231–7788 or 800/995–0969 | www.cumberlink.com.

Attractions

Freight Station Museum. Also known as the Mechanicsburg Museum Association, this museum, in a freight station, has various exhibits—education, sports, seasonal displays—relating to the town's history. | 3 W. Allen St. | 717/697–6088 | Free | Tues.–Sat. 10–4.

ON THE CALENDAR

JUNE: *Jubilee Day.* Held each year on the third Thursday in June, this festival—the world's largest one-day street fair—began as Farmers and Merchants Day in 1923. Now visitors from as far away as Florida and California come to check out more than 400 vendors on Main Street and Market Street and to sample deep-fried pickles, deep-fried oreo cookies, and ostrich burgers. There are also crafts, rides, entertainers, and live bands. | 717/796–0811.

OCT.: *Mechanicsburg Halloween Parade.* This massive parade has more than 2,000 marchers, nine marching bands, and more than 10 floats. It draws a crowd from all over the state. | 717/795–8659 | www.mechparade.org.

Dining

Scottie's Beef and Reef. American. Recommended by locals, this downtown restaurant—named for its owner—offers combinations of filet mignon and fish (the crab cakes are reputed to be excellent), pasta, an aquarium platter (four types of broiled fish), and even veal. | 710 W. Main St. | 717/697–5024 | Closed Sundays | $11.95–$34.95 | AE, D, MC, V.

Lodging

Comfort Inn West. A four-story hotel, 2 mi east of downtown, it's across from Twin Pines Rink, where many skating competitions are held. Complimentary Continental breakfast. Cable TV. Exercise equipment. Laundry facilities, laundry service. No pets. | 6325 Carlisle Pike (U.S. 11) | 717/790–0924 or 800/228–5150 | fax 717/691–9385 | www.comfortinn.com | 125 rooms | $71 | AE, D, DC, MV, V.

Hampton Inn West. The landscaped gardens and a special walk for your pet give it suburban charm. This hotel is less than 3 mi west of Harrisburg. Complimentary Continental breakfast. In-room data ports, cable TV. Pool. Hot tub. Exercise equipment. Laundry facilities. Business services. | 4950 Ritter Rd. | 717/691–1300 | fax 717/691–9692 | www.hamptoninn.com | 129 rooms | $89–$112 | AE, D, DC, MC, V.

Holiday Inn–West. Pillars and a canopy surrounded by flowers and shrubs frame the entrance of this motel, 2 mi west of Harrisburg. Restaurant, bar (with entertainment), picnic area, room service. Some in-room hot tubs, cable TV. Indoor-outdoor pool. Miniature golf. Exercise equipment. Laundry facilities. Business services. Pets allowed (fee). | 5401 Carlisle Pike | 717/697–0321 | fax 717/697–7594 | www.holiday-inn.com | 218 rooms | $110–$125 | AE, D, DC, MC, V.

MEDIA

MAP 7, K7

(Nearby towns also listed: Chadds Ford, Chester, King of Prussia, Philadelphia)

Primarily a commuter borough for workers in Philadelphia, Media is also the center of Delaware County. The borough was settled by Quakers, but wasn't incorporated until 1848 when it was named the county seat.

Information: **Delaware County Chamber of Commerce** | 602 E. Baltimore Pike, 19603 | 610/565–3677.

Attractions

Colonial Pennsylvania Plantation. People in early-American costumes tending live animals give you a glimpse of life on a working farm in colonial times. Open on weekends, the farm is in—but not affiliated with—Ridley State Park, south of Media. Weekdays are reserved for educational workshops and group tours. | Ridley State Park | 610/566–1725 | $4 | Weekends 10–4, weekdays by appointment.

Franklin Mint Museum. The Franklin Mint has spent decades creating artistic pieces based on icons of our culture. Here you can see all the items the Franklin Mint has made over the years. Every two months there's a special exhibit. Dresses worn by Marilyn Monroe and Princess Diana are on permanent display, as are plates, china, jewelry, dolls, and Jackie Kennedy's famous triple-strand faux-pearl necklace. | U.S. Rte. 1, Franklin Center | 610/459–6168 | www.franklinmint.com | Free | Mon.–Sat. 9–4:30; Sun 1–4:30.

Newlin Mill Park. A double-structure gristmill built in 1704 is one of several restored historic features in this 150-acre park. | 219 S. Cheney Rd. | 610/459–2359 | Free | Daily 8 AM–dusk.

Ridley Creek State Park. The park is 2,606 acres of woodlands and meadows and is bisected by Ridley Creek. It also has the Colonial Pennsylvania Plantation. The Plantation, a working farm for more than 300 years, has a late 18th-century appearance complete with historical interpreters in period clothes. In other areas of the park, you can go fishing, hiking, bicycling, horseback riding, cross-country skiing, and picnicking. | Sycamore Mills Rd. | 610/892–3900 | fax 610/892–3906 | www.dcnr.state.pa.us | Free | Daily 8 AM–dusk.

Tyler Arboretum. Fields and forests here serve as habitat for a variety of plants and wildlife. There are 20 mi of marked trails and a fragrance garden and butterfly garden, greenhouse, and small museum. | 515 Painter Rd. | 610/566–5431 | www.sccs.swarthmore.edu | $5 | Daily 8AM to dusk.

ON THE CALENDAR

OCT.: *Media Business Authority Food Festival.* Each year during the first weekend in October Media's restaurants spill onto State Street, where local chefs serve up samples of their cuisine and share their joy in creating it. You can also enjoy craft displays, live music, and other entertainment. | 610/565–3677.

Dining

Brodeur's Country House Inn. American. A favorite of Media locals, this restaurant, south of Media next to the state police barracks and the Franklin Mint, serves steak, lobster, and veal Oscar—but most people come for the crab cakes. | 1330 W. Baltimore Pk. | 610/558–4111 | $20 | AE, D, DC, MC, V.

D'Ignazio's Towne House. American. This restaurant from 1950 is filled with antiques and memorabilia. Crab cakes and roast prime rib are house specialties. Kids' menu. | 117 Veterans Sq. | 610/566–6141 | No lunch Sun. | $12–$25 | AE, D, DC, MC, V.

Lodging

Media Inn. After a fire destroyed the original Media Inn in the 1950s, this red-brick two-story building went up directly across the street. It's on the edge of downtown. Complimentary Continental breakfast. Some kitchenettes, cable TV, room phones. Pets allowed. | 435 E. Baltimore Pk. | 610/566–6500 | fax 610/566–4173 | www.mediainn.com | 39 rooms | $69–$74 | AE, D, DC, MC, V.

MERCER

MAP 7, A4

(Nearby town also listed: Franklin)

Mercer is noted for its lovely tree-lined streets and Victorian homes. The borough has more than a dozen antiques shops within a 5-mi radius. For a better view of the area, visit the Mercer County Courthouse, built in 1911 on the highest point in the county. This Gothic structure features a grand stairway, murals, and a stained-glass dome.

Information: Mercer County Chamber of Commerce | Box 473, 16137 | 412/662–4185.

Attractions

Magoffin House Museum. The museum is home to the Mercer County Historical Society. It provides material for researchers of the Mercer area and has exhibits on Mercer history. | 119 S. Pitt St. | 412/662–3490 | www.pathway.net/mchs/ | Free | Tues.–Fri. 10–4:30, Sat. 10–3, closed Sun.–Mon.

Maurice K. Goddard State Park. A major attraction of the 2,856-acre park is 1,860-acre Lake Wilhelm, where you can go boating, fishing, ice skating, ice fishing, and ice boating. There are 21½ mi of hiking trails along the lake and throughout the wooded fields. Other activities such as picnicking, sledding, and hunting are also popular on more than 1,155 acres. | 684 Lake Wilhelm Rd., Sandy Lake | 724/253–4833 or 888/PA–PARKS | www.dcnr.state.pa.us | Free | Daily 8 AM–dusk.

Wendell August Forge, Inc. Since 1923 craftsmen here have made items in aluminum, bronze, pewter, and silver. You can watch the artisans at work and buy their hand-hammered collectibles in the forge gift shop. | 620 Madison Ave., Grove City | 412/458–8360 | www.wendell.com | Free | Mon.–Thurs. and Sat. 9–6, Fri. 9–8, Sun. 11–5.

ON THE CALENDAR

FEB: *Penn's Woods West Folk and Art Festival.* Each year during the third weekend of February more than 200 vendors flock to Mercer High School to show off their wares. You can see calligraphers at work, watch candy being made, have your face painted, and admire and buy quilts and other crafts. | 724/662–4185.

Dining

Chadagan's. American. Old farm tools and other authentic country items are on display in this former barn. Upstairs is a 45-ft bar with a limited menu; full meals are served downstairs, with different entrées nightly. Specials are steak, seafood, and pasta. Kids' menu. | 8399 Sharon-Mercer Rd. | 724/662–4533 | Closed Sun. | $8–$15 | AE, D, MC, V.

Iron Bridge Inn. Continental. From the outside it looks like a cabin, and the antiques, period tools, and rustic furniture on the inside complete the image of a country home. The restaurant is known for pasta and prime rib, but seafood specials are also available. Kids' menu. Sun. brunch. | 1438 Perry Hwy. | 724/748–3626 | $6–$23 | AE, D, DC, MC, V.

Springfield Grille. Continental. The unique half-circle doorway and the front porch that wraps around the outside can give you a mental flash of an Old West saloon. You can stroll through the gardens outside while you wait for your table. Inside you can see dark cherry wood, antiques, and a menu with chicken marsala stuffed with spinach and cheese, and a 24-oz. Porterhouse steak. The restaurant is known for its Certified Angus beef. Kids' menu. | 1226 Perry Hwy. | 724/748–3589 | $6–$22 | AE, D, DC, MC, V.

Lodging

Howard Johnson. Eight miles from Grove City factory outlets, this motel is popular with families visiting the area. The lobby is full of Amish furniture. Restaurant, bar, room service. Some in-room data ports, cable TV. Pool. Exercise equipment. Playground. Laundry facilities. Business services. Pets allowed. | 835 Perry Hwy. | 724/748–3030 | fax 724/748–3484 | www.hojo.com | 102 rooms | $78–$90 | AE, D, DC, MC, V.

Mehard Manor. This white Georgian-style home was built in 1913 for Samuel S. Mehard, a Mercer County judge and attorney. It's 1 block from the north side of the courthouse. You can enjoy a breakfast of soufflés, crêpes, or coffee cake at a table set with fine china, silver, and crystal stemware—-then retire to the sitting room or solarium to relax and plan your day. Dining room, complimentary breakfast. TV in common area. No pets. No smoking. | 146 N. Pitt St. | 888/606–2489 or 724/662–2489 | mehardmanor@pathway.net | www.pathway.net/mehardmanor | 4 rooms | $75–$85 | D, MC, V.

MIDDLETOWN

(Nearby towns also listed: Boiling Springs, Camp Hill, Harrisburg, Manheim, Mechanicsburg)

Halfway between Lancaster and Carlisle, Middletown was founded in 1755 and was one of the first steel producers in the United States. It was a favorite site of William Penn, and during the American Revolution it was a hub of boat building.

Information: Harrisburg–Hershey–Carlisle Tourism and Convention Bureau | 25 N. Front St., Suite 100, Harrisburg, PA 17101 | 717/231–7788 or 800/995–0969.

Attractions

Middletown and Hummelstown Railroad. You can climb aboard a 1920's-vintage coach for a narrated, 1¼-hour round-trip along the Swatara Creek and Union Canal to Indian Echo Caverns. Call for information about special Civil War reenactments, fall foliage tours, holiday rides, and dinner trains. | 136 Brown St. | 717/944–4435 | $10 | Memorial Day–Aug., Tues., Thurs., Sat., Sun.; Aug.–May, weekends only.

Three-Mile Island Visitors Center. On March 28, 1979, a combination of mechanical and human error caused the nuclear reactor on Three-Mile Island to fail. It was America's worst commercial nuclear accident—nearly a meltdown. The accident cost more than $1 billion and left a decade's worth of cleanup work, removing the damaged nuclear fuel. Exhibits and videotapes recapture the event, and visitor-center's staff will explain nuclear energy and answer your questions. | Hwy. 441 | 717/948–2087 | Free | June–Aug. Thurs.–Sun., Sept.–May Thurs.–Sat., 12–4:30, closed Jan., Feb. and major holidays.

ON THE CALENDAR

JUNE: *Crafts Festival* Each June the historical society of Middletown sponsors a festival to show off local arts and crafts. | 717/944–3420.

Dining

Alfred's Victorian Restaurant. Italian. There are five dining rooms here, each with different Victorian antiques and reproductions, plus unique fireplaces. Homemade pasta is on the menu, as are tournedos imperial, filet mignon medallions with a crab and shrimp mixture topped with melted cheese. You can eat outside on a patio in the herb garden. | 38 N. Union St. | 717/944–5373 | No lunch Sat.–Sun. | $12–$35 | AE, D, DC, MC, V.

Lodging

Best Western Inn and Suites. At I-76, Exit 19, this six-story hotel is 13 mi west of Hershey Park. Restaurant, bar, complimentary Continental breakfast. In-room data ports, some microwaves, some refrigerators, cable TV. Indoor pool. Sauna. Exercise equipment. Laundry facilities, laundry service. No pets. | 815 Eisenhower Blvd. | 717/939–1600 or 800/528–1234 | fax 717/939–8763 | 174 rooms, 50 suites | $99–$119 | AE, D, DC, MC, V.

MILFORD

(Nearby town also listed: Bushkill)

The small town of Milford lies along the Delaware River, just inside the northeast Pennsylvania border in Pike County. Sometimes called the gateway to the Poconos, Milford covers 1 square mile and holds 1,100 people, although the surrounding population density seems to inflate that number. A bustling community in mercantile trade during the late 19th and early 20th centuries, Milford was home to Gifford Pinchot, founder of the USDA Forest Service and later one of Pennsylvania's most popular governors.

Information: **Pike County Chamber of Commerce** | Box 883, 18337 | 717/296–8700.

Attractions

The Columns. This early 20th-century Greek Revival home was converted to a museum in 1983. Inside are exhibits on the Civil War, local history and culture, and a collection of pre- and early 19th-century vintage clothing. You can also see the Lincoln Flag, placed under President Lincoln's head—and stained with his blood—after he was shot in Ford's Theatre on April 14, 1865. | 608 Broad St. | 570/296–8126 | Free | Wed., Sat., Sun., 1–4.

Dingman's Falls and Silver Thread Falls. These two waterfalls are in the Delaware Water Gap National Recreation Area. A boardwalk trail winds through a hemlock ravine to the falls. Dingman's Falls is Pennsylvania's second largest waterfall, cascading 130 feet; Silver Thread is 80-ft high and provides a cooling mist in summer. | 209N to Johnny B Rd. | 570/588–2451 | www.nps.gov/dewa | Free | Daily dawn to dusk.

Grey Towers. Built in 1888, the mansion has gardens, walkways, and two outbuildings. It's the original summer estate of James Pinchot and Gifford Pinchot, America's first forester and founder of the USDA Forest Service. The estate was donated to the United States Department of Agriculture in 1963. | Rte. 6 | 717/296–6401 | www.pinchot.org | Closed for renovation until 2001.

ON THE CALENDAR

OCT.: *Black Bear Film Festival.* Independent, documentary, and short films that connect human experience with the natural world are highlighted at this weekend festival, held at the Milford Theater. The festival also focuses on Pike County's history as a filmmaking location and as the birthplace of American conservation. Awards are presented Sunday night. | 570/409–0909 | www.blackbearfilm.com.

Dining

Apple Valley Restaurant. American. A full-size canoe hangs from the dining room ceiling here, along with lobster catches, buoys, lanterns, and walls with life-size posters of Marilyn Monroe and Betty Boop. Besides a menu of burgers, sandwiches, and pastas, you can try a personal eight-inch pizza with Cajun chicken or a 13-ounce prime-grade sizzle steak. Kids' menu. | Rte. 6 | 570/296–6831 | $7–$17 | AE, MC, V.

The Cliff Park Inn. Contemporary. The wood-burning fireplace and lace-covered antique tables add to the Colonial style of the dining room here, where you can order veal chop Faulkner—a 9-oz veal chop covered in Dijon mustard and cracked black pepper, breaded, sauteed, and baked to medium. The Miali Tuscana—roasted boneless pork tenderloin with sausage and pesto stuffing, wrapped in bacon, and served with brown sauce—is also a house favorite, along with 4-oz Brazilian lobster tails. Breakfast also available. June–Thanksgiving, daily. Thanksgiving–May, weekends. | 155 Cliff Park Rd. | 570/296–6491 or 800/225–6535 | Reservations essential | Weekends Dec.–May | $18–$24 | AE, DC, MC, V.

Mount Haven Country Resort and Restaurant. Italian. Sample more than 50 items at the salad bar, including pasta, potato, bean, and carrot salads. The pasta bar has homemade tortellini, fettuccini, penne, and homemade sauces. The glass-enclosed dining room—with hanging plants, copper kettles, and a white-brick fireplace—features a piano player and candlelit tables for dinner. Breakfast also available. Kids' menu. | Log Tavern Rd. near Rte. 2001 | 570/296–8502 or 800/553–1530 | $14–$27 | AE, D, DC, MC, V.

Lodging

Best Western Inn at Hunts Landing. Sitting atop 30 acres and overlooking the Delaware River, this hotel has its own stocked trout pond. Restaurant, bar. In-room data ports, some in-room hot tubs, cable TV. Indoor pool. Sauna. Video games. Laundry facilities. Business services. Pets allowed (fee). | 120 Rte. 6/209, Matamoras | 570/491–2400 | fax 570/491–5934 | www.bestwesternpa.com | 108 rooms | $119–$129 | AE, D, DC, MC, V.

Black Walnut Bed and Breakfast and Country Inn. Built in 1897, this stone farmhouse has a European marble fireplace and rooms furnished with brass beds and other antiques, plus there's a deck with an outdoor hot tub. It's on 160 acres of pines, oaks, maples, and black walnut trees, and even has its own little petting zoo. Dining room. No air-conditioning, no TV in rooms, TV in common area. | R. D. 2, Firetower Rd. | 570/296–6322 | fax 570/296–7696 | www.theblackwalnutinn.com | 12 rooms (4 with shared bath) | $80–$190 | AE, MC, V.

Cliff Park Inn and Golf Course. The building is filled with heirlooms and antiques and retains its original 1820-era wide floorboards, cozy parlor, and working hearths. Many rooms have a view of the golf course. Dining room. 9-hole golf course, putting green. Hiking. Cross-country skiing. Business services. | 155 Cliff Park Rd. | 570/296–6491 or 800/225–6535 | fax 570/296–3982 | www.cliffparkinn.com | 19 rooms | $135–$200 | AE, D, DC, MC, V.

Dimmick Inn. A two-tiered wraparound porch and uniquely styled rooms add variety to this 1828 brick Connecticut Colonial revival; rooms include a Manhattan loft replica with an interior brick wall, a Victorian room with handmade curtains, bedspread, and a pale green and gold canopy, and an Americana-themed room with a pencil-post bed and depictions of scenes from American history. Restaurant, bar. Some in-room hot tubs, cable TV, no room phones. No smoking. | 101 Harford St. | 570/296–4021 | fax 570/409–1901 | 8 rooms (some with shared bath); 2 suites | $65–$85; $120–$135 suites | AE, D, DC, MC, V.

Myer Motel. This motel boasts "All the luxury of home but in a country-style cottage." Although all the cottages have wraparound porches out front, each one has a different color scheme and individualized touches. The cottages are on 4 acres with blue spruce and white pine trees lining the courtyard. Picnic area. Some kitchenettes, refrigerators, cable TV. Pets allowed. | 600 Rte. 6/209 | 570/296–7223 or 800/764–6937 | www.myermotel.com | 19 cottages | $60–$80 cottages | AE, D, DC, MC, V.

Parkview Hotel. With rooms over a bar and restaurant in a residential area, this hotel has plain rooms. Restaurant, bar. No air-conditioning in some rooms, some kitchenettes, cable TV, no room phones. Laundry facilities. | 197 Main St., New Milford | 570/465–7940 | 8 rooms | $35 | AE, D, MC, V.

MONROEVILLE

MAP 7, B6

(Nearby town also listed: Pittsburgh)

Monroeville is an eastern suburb of Pittsburgh. Its biggest draw is its shopping center and various other businesses on Old Route 220.

Information: **Monroeville Chamber of Commerce** | 2790 Mosside Blvd., Room 295, 15146 | 412/856–0622.

Attractions
Pittsburgh Expomart. This huge exhibit hall has 45,000 parking spaces and schedules many displays throughout the year. Shows and conventions here sell a wide variety of items, such as computer products, crafts and sewing items, bridal showcases, rare coins, militaria, and outdoorsman equipment. | 105 Mall Blvd. | 412/856–8100 | www.pghexpomart.com | $6–$7 | Daily.

ON THE CALENDAR
SEPT.: *The Pittsburgh Women's Show.* Come to the Philadelphia Expomart to put together affordable, fashionable outfits or try a new hairstyle or make-up technique at the event. See presentations on body-detox, weight loss, natural hormones, facial cos-

metic surgery, financial matters, cooking, and spirituality. Clothing, accessories, jewelry, and candles are on sale. | 412/373–0277.

Dining

John Harvard's Brew House. Continental. An English-style pub, a glassed-in room here shows tools and kettles that were once used to make beer. A recipe board hanging above the brewing kettles details beer recipes dating from the Revolutionary War period. Try the grilled meat loaf with garlic mashed potatoes, onion rings, and vegetables. | 3466 William Penn Hwy. | 412/824–9440 | $7–$11 | AE, D, DC, MC, V.

Lodging

William Penn Motel. The rooms in this 1950s motel are furnished with early-American oak or maple wood pieces, with landscape pictures on the walls. The block-long Miracle Mile Shopping Center is across the street. Complimentary Continental breakfast. Cable TV, some in-room VCRs. Pets allowed. | 4139 William Penn Hwy. | 412/373–0700 | fax 412/372–3814 | www.williampennmotel.com | 22 rooms | $52–$56 | AE, D, DC, MC, V.

MT. POCONO

MAP 7, K4

(Nearby towns also listed: Bushkill, Canadensis, Cresco, Stroudsburg, Shawnee on Delaware, Tannersville)

Considered the heart of the Poconos, Mount Pocono has spectacular views from its many hilltop parks. The community's primary popularity stems from its mountainous nature, which makes it a favorite location for builders of skiing and summer mountain resorts.

Information: **Pocono Mountains Chamber of Commerce** | 556 Main St., Stroudsburg, PA 18360 | 570/421–4433.

Attractions

Crossings Factory Stores. This huge outlet has more than 100 stores and, on peak weekends, stops traffic on I–80. Treat yourself at Ann Taylor Loft, Enzo Angiolini, Liz Claiborne, or Brooks Brothers and get bargains for the kids at Toy Liquidators. Other stores are Waterford Crystal, Mikasa, and London Fog. | I–80, Exits 44 and 45 | 717/629–4650 | Mon.–Sat. 10–9; Sun. 10–6.

Gouldsboro State Park. The park has a lake for boating, fishing, and swimming, and allows hunting, hiking, picnicking, and winter activities. In World War I the army used the area as an artillery training center, then as a tank and ambulance corps training center from 1918 to 1931. | Rte. 507 | 570/894–8336 | www.dcnr.state.pa.us | Free | Daily 8 AM–dusk.

Memorytown, USA This little village is full of unique shops, an inn, and restaurants. It's also home to a museum dedicated to old printing processes. | Grange Rd. | 570/839–1680 | Free | Daily 10–5.

Pocono Knob. The highest spot in Mt. Pocono is here at Pocono Knob. You can drive up the hill and walk to the point for a breathtaking view of the Pocono Mountains. | Knob Rd. | 570/421–5791 | Free | Daily dawn to dusk.

Tobyhanna State Park. The park has a lake for boating, fishing, and swimming, and also has 140 campsites, a picnic area, 12 mi of hiking trails, and winter activities. From about 1900 to 1936, the park and lake were sites of active ice industries. The ice was cut from the lake during the winter and stored, then later added to railroad boxcars hauling fresh produce and meats. | Rte 423, 2 mi. north of Tobyhanna | 570/894–8336 | www.dcnr.state.pa.us | Free | Daily 8 AM–dusk.

ON THE CALENDAR

AUG.: *Civil War Weekend.* Don't be surprised to see small skirmishes or even bar-room brawls adding to the realism of Memorytown's reenactment weekend, presented by over 150 players from both sides of the Mason-Dixon line. Amidst cannon fire, you can see graphic reproductions of surgeries involving gunshot wounds and amputations. There are also laundry demonstrations and an 1860s fashion show. | 570/839–1680.

Dining

Bailey's Steakhouse. Steak. American and British street signs decorate the softly lit dining room here. You can choose from many cuts of prime-grade steak, including prime rib, filet mignon, center-cut sirloin, and a whopping 16-oz T-bone. Or try hickory smoked baby-back ribs, or crabkey chicken–breast of chicken sautéed in white wine, topped with crab-meat, asparagus, and béarnaise sauce. Kids' menu. | 604 Pocono Blvd. | 570/839–9678 | fax 570/839–9310 | $10–$20 | AE, D, MC, V.

Big Daddy's. American/Casual. Here you can find inexpensive burgers and sandwiches as well as charcoal-grilled ribs, Alaskan snow crab legs, and shrimp in marinara sauce with cream and garlic. For dessert there's lemon torte, or mint chocolate chip ice cream cake in an oreo cookie shell, dolloped with whipped cream. Kids' menu. | Rte. 611 | 570/839–9281 | $5–$22 | AE, D, DC, MC, V.

Golden Dragon. Chinese. Quick, low-priced meals are available at this place. Expect standard Chinese kitchen fare–beef or chicken with broccoli and General Tso's Chicken. This is a popular stop for tour groups. No smoking. Alcohol-free. | 601 Rte. 940 | 570/839–9780 | $6–$8 | AE, D, MC, V.

POCONO MOUNTAINS

Before Patrick Swayze and Jennifer Grey tripped the light fantastic in the movie "Dirty Dancing" the Pocono resorts already were well known to most New Yorkers and the entertainment industry. The resorts have been popular summer destinations for generations because of their location in the cool Pocono Mountains and their all-inclusive accommodations.

But as times have changed so have the Pocono attractions. No longer does the area rely on summer or big-city folks looking for a country getaway. Today the Pocono region is a year-round attraction, with skiers hitting the slopes from December until March, and honeymooners coming throughout year. Outdoors, people enjoy the landscape with its rich fishing and hunting areas as well as its natural wonders such as Bushkill Falls and the Delaware Water Gap Recreation Area.

Whitewater rafting, bicycling, hot-air ballooning, golfing, and shopping also play a major role in attracting visitors to the region. Honeymooners still can enjoy the champagne flute-styled Jacuzzi at some resorts, while families can take their children to museums and zoos dedicated to their enjoyment.

Hampton Court Inn. Continental. Pictures of King Henry and etchings of scenes from British history dominate the wall space of the Hampton Court Inn, originally built as a farmhouse in 1890. The restaurant is divided into three separate dining rooms, including a flower-filled section with candle-lit tables. Specials are filet mignon au poivre, roast duck grand marnier with cranberry sauce, and jumbo shrimp stuffed with crabmeat. Bananas Foster—sauteed caramelized bananas with rum, cognac, banana liqueur, and vanilla ice cream—is the star dessert. | Rte. 940 | 570/839–2119 | Reservations essential | No lunch. Closed Tuesday | $16–$25 | AE, DC, MC, V.

Tokyo Teahouse. Japanese. This is an outstanding traditional Japanese restaurant, distinguished by bamboo accents and prints. The establishment is known for its sushi, shrimp tempura, and steak teriyaki. | Rte. 940, 1/2 mi west of I–380 | 570/839–8880 | Closed Tues. in July and August | AE, D, DC, MC, V.

Lodging

Caesars Paradise Stream. A couples-only resort that is designed to be a romantic getaway or honeymoon spot. The hotel has a neo-Roman theme and features big-name entertainment. There are fireplaces in some rooms, and hot tubs. Bar, room service. Cable TV. 2 pools (1 indoor). Hot tub. Miniature golf, tennis. Exercise equipment, hiking. Boating, bicycles. Snowmobiling. Business services. | Box 547, Scotrun | 570/839–8881 or 800/233–4141 | fax 570/839–1842 | www.caesarspoconoresorts.com | 164 rooms | $540–$700 | AE, D, DC, MC, V.

French Manor. This mansion perches atop Huckleberry Mountain. It's a unique stone chateau with an imported Spanish slate roof, cypress interiors, a great hall, a Romanesque arched entranceway, and massive stone fireplaces. Dining room, complimentary breakfast, room service. Cable TV. Hot tubs. Hiking. Massage, spa. Cross-country skiing. | Rte. 191 and Huckleberry Rd., South Sterling | 570/676–3244 or 800/523–8200 | fax 570/676–9786 | www.thesterlinginn.com | 9 rooms | $90–$385 | AE, D, MC, V.

Farmhouse Bed and Breakfast. The large-windowed dining room of this 1850s red and white farmhouse has a Hoosier Cabinet, an apothecary table, and a collection of Kentucky rifles from the early 1800s. Outside, the surrounding 6½ acres of grass and woods are home to a variety of wildlife. Cottages and suites have private entrances and baths, living rooms, and fireplaces. Dining room, picnic area, complimentary breakfast. Refrigerators, cable TV, no room phones. No smoking. | Grange Rd. | 570/839–0796 | fax 570/839–0795 | 4 suites; 1 cottage | $95–$115 (2–night minimum stay on weekend; 3–night minimum stay on holiday weekend) | D, MC, V.

Hampton Court Inn. This small motel has basic rooms at affordable rates. Restaurant. Cable TV, no room phones. Pool. | Rte. 940 east | 570/839–2119 | fax 570/839–6982 | 10 rooms | $65–$75 | AE, DC, MC, V.

Mount Airy Lodge. With 1,200 acres of grounds, the rooms have a view of either the woods, mountains, lake, or golf course. On the 35-acre lake, you can go fishing, boating, tubing, canoeing, and paddle boating. Some suites have private swimming pools, log burning fireplaces, canopy beds, king-size round beds, chandeliers, and private courtyards. Restaurant, bar, picnic area, room service. Some in-room safes, some in-room refrigerators, some in-room hot tubs, cable TV. Indoor-outdoor pool, lake. Massage, sauna, spa, steam room. Driving range, 18-hole golf course, miniature golf, putting green, 21 tennis courts. Basketball, health club, hiking, volleyball. Beach, dock, water sports, boating, fishing, bicycles. Ice-skating, cross-country skiing, downhill skiing, sleigh rides, snowmobiling. Shops, video games. Baby-sitting, kids' programs (ages 4–12), playground. | 42 Woodland Rd. | 800/441–4410 | fax 570/839–1464 | www.mountairylodge.com | 410 rooms | $190, $230–$290 suites | Breakfast and dinner included | AE, D, DC, MC, V.

Mt. Pocono Motel. With plenty of lawn space, large trees, and some views of the Pocono mountains, this motel is on a four-acre property one block from downtown. Outside, you can play shuffleboard or horseshoes. Restaurant, bar, picnic area. Some kitchenettes, some microwaves, some refrigerators, some in-room hot tubs, cable TV. Pool. Laundry facilities. | 25 Knob Rd. | 570/839–9407 | fax 570/839–7726 | www.mountpoconomotel.com | 28 rooms | $49–$55 | AE, D, MC, V.

Pocono Manor. Built in 1902, this resort is on 3,500 acres. In the lobby there are antique grandfather clocks, paintings, and a fieldstone fireplace. Rooms have mahogany furniture and ornate rugs. Some rooms have views of the Pocono mountains. You can find many extras here, including trapshooting and an artificial ice rink. Bar, dining room, room service. In-room data ports. Indoor-outdoor pool. Massage, sauna. Driving range, golf courses, putting green, tennis. Exercise equipment. Bicycles. Sleigh rides. Library. Kids' programs. Business services, airport shuttle. | Pocono Manor | 570/839–7111 or 800/233–8150 | fax 570/839–0708 | 257 rooms in 3 buildings | $109–$199 | AE, DC, MC, V.

Sterling Inn. All the rooms in this lakeside inn have country furnishings and antiques. The inn is parklike with many gardens. Dining room. Indoor pool. Hot tub, spa. Tennis. Hiking. Boating, fishing. Sleigh rides. Business services, airport shuttle. | Rte. 191, South Sterling | 570/676–3311 or 800/523–8200 | fax 570/676–9786 | 39 rooms, 27 suites, 10 cottages | $160–$180, $210–$240 suites, $240–$280 cottages | AE, D, MC, V.

Super 8. This one-level motel has lots of beautiful landscaping, lush gardens, and outside entrances. In-room data ports, cable TV. Pool. Hot tub. Playground. | Rte. 611, HCR 1, Box 115 | 570/839–7728 | fax 570/839–7729 | www.super8.com | 38 rooms | $65–$175 | AE, D, DC, MC, V.

NEW CASTLE

MAP 7, B4

(Nearby towns also listed: Beaver Falls, Harmony)

In the heart of Lawrence County, one hour north of Pittsburgh, New Castle serves as the county seat. The borough was once a center for iron ore manufacturing. Among its historic attractions are the county courthouse and the 100-year-old former Erie–Lackawanna Railroad Station, now occupied by the Lawrence County Chamber of Commerce. The city was laid out in 1802 and made a borough in 1825. It is not certain whether it was named after Newcastle, England, or New Castle, Delaware.

Information: Lawrence County Chamber of Commerce | 138 Washington St., 16101 | 412/658–1648.

Attractions

Greer House. The three-story Colonial Revival residence with a limestone foundation is the former home of George Greer, founder of the tin mill industry in the United States. It is currently the home of the Lawrence County Historical Society. | 408 N. Jefferson Rd. | 724/658–4022 | www.ilovehistory.com | Free | Weekdays 9–5, Sat. 10–4, closed Sun.

Hoyt Institute of Fine Arts. Two 1913 mansions here house an art museum and are furnished to match the period. As a nonprofit organization, the Institute has been dedicated to keeping the arts alive since 1965. The Hoyt East Mansion has three gallery rooms. | 124 E. Leasure Ave. | 724/652–2882 | fax 724/657–8786 | $2 | Tues.–Sat. 9–5, closed Sun.–Mon.

Lawrence County Historical Society Museum. An early 1900s mansion, the building has massive Greek columns and heavy wooden doors with beveled, leaded glass, and a main staircase of golden oak, a 7 sq ft stained glass window, and a grandfather clock made of Lawrence County hardwood. Inside are photographs, writings, and oral histories. You can also see an enormous collection of vitrified China and the reed organ of a local evangelist and gospel hymn composer. | 408 North Jefferson St. | 724/658–4022 | www.ilovehistory.com/.

Living Treasures Animal Park. This small zoo is home to tigers, llamas, monkeys, zebra, goats, deer, and elephants. It also has a petting zoo where you can hand-feed 90% of the animals. | Fox Rd. and Rte. 422 | 724/924–9571 | $6.50 | Daily 10–8.

McConnell's Mill State Park. The park has 2,529 acres of the Slippery Rock Creek Gorge, a National Natural Landmark. Pastimes here are whitewater boating, fishing, and hunting. You can also come for picnicking, hiking trails, and tours of the Thomas McConnell gristmill built in 1868. | Near the intersection of PA Rte. 19 and U.S. Rte. 422 | 724/368–8091 or 724/368–8811 | www.dcnr.state.pa.us | Free | Daily 8 AM–dusk.

Scottish Rite Cathedral. Built from 1924 to 1925, the neoclassical rectangular hall is 245-ft wide, 181-ft deep, and 110-ft high. It has a ballroom and a theater with two balconies, with seating capacity for 3,240. | 110 East Lincoln Ave. | 724/654–6683 | Free | Weekdays 10–4:30, closed weekends.

ON THE CALENDAR

MAY: *Giant Yard Sale.* More than 100 local families use the space at Rose Point Park Campground for their annual combined yard sale. At lunch time, you can share in a 10-ft-long banana split. A live auction follows in the evening. | 724/924–2415.

Dining

Crisci's Olde Library Inn. Italian. This was the town's library, and its history is now the theme of this restaurant, with book displays and old wooden tables and chairs. You can try Italian wedding soup, stuffed hot banana peppers, or shrimp scampi over angel hair pasta. Kids' menu. | 106 E. North St. | Closed Sun. No lunch Sat. | $15–$23 | AE, D, DC, MC, V.

Lodging

Beechwood Inn. This 1860s building has a second-floor covered balcony with wrought-iron tables where you can sit and watch the passing Amish buggies. Each of the three high-ceilinged bedrooms has a queen-size bed, a private bath, and a conversation area with a table and chairs. Choose from the Lady Grace room—cranberry and green, with an antique bed enlarged by an Amish artisan, the Captain Williams room—pink and blue, with a sunlight and shadows quilt and an Amish oak headboard with heart cut-outs, or the Angus McKay room—tan and white, with a crocheted bedspread, brass headboard, and Scottish tartan wallpaper. Seven mi north of Newcastle. Complimentary breakfast. No room phones, TV in common area. No kids under 12. No smoking. | 175 Beechwood Rd., New Wilmington | 724/946–2342 | 3 rooms | $61 | MC, V.

Comfort Inn. This motel has well-landscaped grounds and flower gardens and is 2 mi from the Hoyt Institute. Complimentary Continental breakfast. Some refrigerators, microwaves, cable TV. Sauna. Exercise equipment. Business services. | 1740 New Butler Rd. | 724/658–7700 | fax 724/658–7727 | www.comfortinn.com | 79 rooms, 13 suites | $68–$79, $108–$113 suites | AE, D, DC, MC, V.

NEW HOPE

MAP 7, L6

(Nearby towns also listed: Doylestown, Holicong, Lahaska)

William Penn owned the land that became New Hope and signed it over in 1681 to another owner. After the Revolutionary War, Benjamin Parry began operating two mills here, which burned down in 1790. When they were rebuilt they were called the "New Hope Mills," offering new hope to all of the town. An arts community made up of painters and other craftspeople has since spung up and has flourished here for decades.

Information: **New Hope Chamber of Commerce** | Box 633, 18938–0633 | 215/862–5880 | www.newhopepa.com.

Attractions

Bucks County River Country Canoe and Tube. The company has equipment for rafting, canoeing, tubing, and kayaking on the Delaware River. All tours are self-guided; the company takes you to the drop-off point and picks you up after the trip. | Rte. 32N. to Byram Rd.; follow signs | Pt. Pleasant | 215/297–5000 | www.rivercountry.net | $15–$33 | Apr.–Oct., daily 9–7.

New Hope Canal Boat Company. The one-hour narrated excursion travels past Revolutionary-era cottages, gardens, and artists' workshops. A barge historian/folk singer is aboard to entertain and educate. | 149 S. Main St. | 215/862–0758 | $7.95 | Apr., Fri.–Sun. 12:30, 3; May–Oct., daily noon, 1:30, 3, 4:30.

New Hope and Ivyland Rail Road. A vintage locomotive and restored 19th-century cars cover a 9-mi trip through the countryside of New Hope and Lahaska. The tour takes about one hour. | 32 W. Bridge St. | 215/862–2332 | www.newhoperailroad.com | $9.50 | Weekends Apr.–June 18; June 18–Nov. daily 11–4.

Parry Mansion Museum. The museum has decorative art from 1775 to 1900 and details the life of the Parry family, some of the area's original founders. | 45 S. Main St. | 215/862–5652 | $5 | May–Dec., Fri.–Sun. 1–5, closed Mon.–Thurs.

Washington Crossing Historic Park. On Christmas night 1776, George Washington and the Continental Army crossed the icy Delaware River here and assaulted the unsuspecting Hessians at Trenton. Every year on Christmas Day the town conducts a reenactment of this famous crossing. The 500-acre site has 13 historic buildings, 100-acre Bowman's hill, which is a wildflower preserve, and an observation tower. The site includes a number of homes used by Washington and his troops, including McKonkey's Ferry Inn, which served as a guard post during the Continental Army's encampment in Bucks County in December. According to traditional lore, this is where Washington and his aides ate their Christmas dinner prior to the crossing. Other buildings are Hibb's House, Frye House, and the Blacksmith's Shop. The restored 19th-century homes were built between 1820 and 1830 as part of the village of Taylorsville. Today, Colonial living demonstrations take place at these homes at various times year-round. The other significant building is the Durham Boat House, the 20th-century structure that houses the Durham boat replicas. These boats were originally used to haul iron ore and are an example of the kind of sturdy craft used by Washington and his men for the crossing. Today, these Durham boat replicas are used in the annual reenactment. | 1112 River Rd. | 215/493–4076 | fax 215/493–4820 | $4 | Tues.–Sat. 9–5, Sun. 12–5, closed Mon.

ON THE CALENDAR

JULY: *Teddy Bear Picnic.* Peddler's Village center hosts this celebration of the teddy bear with parades, competitions, vendors, and a clinic for "hurt" bears. | 215/794–4000.

SEPT.: *Scarecrow Festival.* This festival ushers in Halloween with a jack-o'-lantern contest, scarecrow-making, and pumpkin painting on the green in Peddler's Village. | 215/794–4000.

DEC.: *The Crossing.* Held in Washington Crossing Historic Park, this reenactment Christmas Day at 1 PM commemorates Washington's crossing of the Delaware River on Christmas night, 1776—an event that resulted in the capturing of Trenton by the Revolutionary Forces and proved to be a turning point in the war. | 215/493–4076.

Dining

★ **La Bonne Auberge.** French. While others crowd New Hope's busy Main Street looking for a spot to dine, those who know the area travel up the hill overlooking the city and dine in this stone farm house with a view of beautiful gardens. The interior is a mix of new and old, with Louis XIII chairs and tables and antique fixtures. The carré d'agneau roti Arlesienne, a tender rack of lamb, is a prominent entree. | Village 2; 1 Rittenhouse Cr. | 215/862–2462 | Reservations essential | Jacket required | Closed Mon., Tues. | $30–$40 | AE, MC, V.

Cock 'N Bull. American. The popular shopping district of Peddler's Village is the site of the Cock 'N Bull, a Colonial-style restaurant. At your table, you are surrounded by exposed brick, and meals are served on period plates. Crab cakes and chicken pot pie are two popular entrees. Salad bar Mon.–Wed. Sun. brunch. | U.S. 202 and Rte. 263 | 215/794–4000 | $14–$38 | AE, D, DC, MC, V.

Cuttalossa Inn. Continental. This stone building has a spectacular view and its interior is cozy, pastel-colored, and sunny. The restaurant is known for seafood, especially the crab imperial, which is like a crab soufflé. Open-air dining on a stone terrace gives a view of the waterfalls. Entertainment. | 3498 River Rd. (Rte. 32) | 215/297–5082 | Closed Sun. | $19–$28 | AE, MC, V.

Havana Bar and Restaurant. Continental. The restaurant serves an eclectic mix of foods, such as crab cakes, quesadillas, tropical plantains, and iron pan provolone. Exotic mixed drinks are a favorite here and the food is well-received, but it's the entertainment (with no cover charge) that makes this a popular night spot. Depending on the night you visit, you can find jazz, karaoke, or a comedy club. Entertainment Mon.–Sun. | 105 S. Main St. | 215/862–9897 | $10–$25 | AE, D, MC, V.

Hotel du Village. French. This restaurant provides a quiet dining experience with soft lights and dark room tones. The menu has a variety of sweetbreads. | 2535 N. River Rd./ Rte. 32 | 215/862–9911 | Closed Mon., Tues.; closed Sun.–Wed in Jan. No lunch Sun. | $16–$22 | AE, DC.

Inn at Phillips Mill. French. Fireplaces, candlelight, and a dark interior make this a romantic spot, and the inn's tiny bedchambers offer a good night's stay. You have the option of eating out on the patio with its view of a well-tended garden. You might choose the salmon served the chef's way or the beef filet served with a shallot demiglaze. Live music, Fri., Sun. | 2590 N. River Rd. | 215/862–9919 | Reservations essential | Closed Jan. | $15–$24 | No credit cards.

Jean Pierre's. French. Built in 1747, this home is filled with period antiques and French country knickknacks. The fireplaces and subtle light make it a cozy getaway. You can see a range of foie gras, caviar, and paté on the list of appetizers. The entree list has coulibiac of salmon, which is a lobster tail and claw, salmon filet, and salmon mousse wrapped in pastry and served with a champagne cream sauce. | 101 S. State St. | 215/968–6201 | Closed Sun.–Mon. | $25–$30 | AE, D, DC, MC, V.

Odette's. Continental. This restored 200-year-old building on the Delaware River pays homage to long-ago Broadway star Odette Myrtil Logan; memorabilia from her career is displayed throughout. The restaurant's pan-roasted beef tenderloin is served with horseradish gnocchi, grilled summer leeks, and finished with Italian truffle aioli. Live music, Wed.–Mon. Kids' menu. Sun. brunch. | S. River Rd. | 215/862–2432 | www.odettes.com | Reservations essential | $17–$29 | AE, D, DC, MC, V.

Spotted Hog. Continental. A mural in the Pasture room has information on the family that started this restaurant and their pet-like pig farm Barbi Q, for whom the establishment is named. There are four seating areas: Pig Pen, Pasture, Corn Crib, and the Tavern, where you can eat peanuts and toss the shells on the floor. A great sandwich is the Foxbriar chicken sandwich, a sauteed chicken breast served with a cherry wine sauce and mushrooms and onions on a French baguette. Kids' menu. | Rte. 202 and Street Rd., Lahaska | 215/794–4040 | Reservations not accepted | $9–$17 | AE, D, DC, MC, V.

Lodging

1740 House. This inn, in a hamlet north of New Hope, has an early American style, a large fireplace, and maple furniture throughout. The inn faces the river for a spectacular view. Complimentary breakfast. Pool. Business services. | River Rd., Lumberville | 215/297–5661 | 24 rooms | $80–$131 | No credit cards.

Aaron Burr House. Hardwood floors, tall arched windows, and a screened-in patio accent this circa-1854 bed-and-breakfast. Complimentary breakfast. TV in common area. Business services. Pets allowed. No smoking. | 80 W. Bridge St./Chestnut St. | 215/862–2570 | fax 215/862–3937 | www.new-hope-inn.com/aaron | 6 rooms, 2 suites | $90–$195, $150–$255 suites | MC, V.

Barley Sheaf Farm. Each suite in the main house here has a sitting area with a fireplace; in some rooms there are queen-sized sleigh beds, window seats, and views of the pool and pond. If you don't mind a smaller room, you can stay in the cottage overlooking the meadows and sheep pastures. One barn suite has a Vermont woodburning stove and a four-post bed, while the other has exposed wood beams, a poplar wood-floored living room, and a fully equipped open kitchen. Dining room, complimentary breakfast. Some in-room hot tubs. Cable TV. Pool, pond. No kids under 8. No smoking. | Rt. 202 | 215/794–5104 | fax 215/794–5332 | www.barleysheaf.com | 5 rooms and 2 suites in main house; 3 rooms in cottage; 2 suites in barn | main house rooms $150–$195; cottage rooms $140–$150; suites $195–$215; two–night minimum on weekends; three–night minimum on holiday weekends | AE, MC, V.

Best Western New Hope Inn. This motel is a few minutes from New Hope and 30 min from Sesame Place. Restaurant, bar. Cable TV. Pool. Exercise equipment. Tennis. Playground. Laundry facilities. Business services. Pets allowed. | 6426 Lower York Rd./US 202 | 215/862–5221 or 800/467–3202 | fax 215/862–5847 | www.bwnewhope.com | 152 rooms | $73–$100 | AE, D, DC, MC, V.

Centre Bridge Inn. You can find canopy beds and antiques in all the rooms of this Victorian-style building that sits beside the river. Restaurant, bar, complimentary Continental breakfast. No room phones. Cable TV. Business services. | 2998 N. River Rd. | 215/862–9139 | fax 215/862–9130 | 10 rooms | $135–$200 | D, MC, V.

Cordials Bed and Breakfast. Themed rooms in this white clapboard building vary from Gay '90s furnishing to art deco styles with burgundy, white, black, and gold coloring. From each room, you can access either a private balcony or deck overlooking large pines, hemlocks, annual flowers, and statuary. Wine and cheese are served on weekends. Dining room, complimentary Continental breakfast. Refrigerators, cable TV, in-room VCRs (and movies). Pool. Pets allowed. No kids under 16. No smoking. | 143 Old York Rd. | 215/862–3919 or 877/219–1009 | fax 215/862–3917 | www.cordialsbb.com | 6 rooms | $120–$130 (2–night minimum stay on weekend; 3–night minimum stay on holiday weekend) | AE, MC, V.

The Fox and Hound. This bed-and-breakfast, a half-mile out of New Hope, is a stone Victorian house that's on the banks of the Delaware River. Picnic area, complimentary Continental breakfast. Some in-room hot tubs, cable TV, some room phones. No kids under 12. Business services. | 246 W. Bridge St. | 215/862–5082 or 800/862–5082 | fax 215/862–5082 | www.foxhoundinn.com | 8 rooms | $130–$170 | AE, MC, V.

Hollileif Bed and Breakfast. This 18th-century farmhouse, outside of New Hope, was named for the 40-ft holly tree outside the entrance. Made of plaster and fieldstone, this home is on 5 ½ acres of parklike grounds. It has a blend of period furnishings, family antiques, and original artwork. Complimentary breakfast. No room phones, TV in common area. No smoking. | 677 Durham Rd./Rte. 413, Wrightstown | 215/598–3100 | www.hollileif.com | 5 rooms | $85–$165 | AE, D, MC, V.

Hotel du Village. An old stone boarding school has become a hotel with country furnishings to give it the feeling of an English manor house. Bar, dining room, complimentary Continental breakfast. No room phones. Pool. Tennis. | 2535 N. River Rd. | 215/862–9911 | fax 215/862–9788 | 20 rooms | $90–$110 | AE, DC.

Inn at Phillips Mill. Built in 1750 as a stone barn, this small inn is filled with antiques in a French Victorian style. Dining room (see Inn at Phillips Mill), room service. Pool. | 2590 N. River Rd. | 215/862–2984 | 4 rooms, 1 suite | $80–$90 | Closed Jan. | No credit cards.

Inn at Stoney Hill. This inn has a large wood-paneled kitchen and dining room, a two-story stone fireplace, and a deck with wrought-iron tables and chairs. Rooms have brass headboards with matching lamps, plants in wicker baskets, upholstered, wooden, or wicker chairs, and some have access to a private deck that overlooks six acres of woods and gardens. You even get a fluffy bathrobe to use during your stay. Dining room, picnic area, complimentary breakfast. Cable TV, in-room VCRs (and movies). Pond. No kids under 13. No smoking. | 105 Stoney Hill Rd. | 215/862–5769 | fax 215/862–0448 | www.innatstoneyhill.com | 7 rooms | $145–$225 | AE, MC, V.

Inn to the Woods. You can view the woods from this small inn on 7 acres of forest. Each room has a name and "tells a story." Complimentary breakfast. In-room data ports, cable TV, in-room VCRs (and movies, some room phones. Hiking. No kids under 10. Business services. No smoking. | 150 Glenwood Dr., Washington Crossing | 215/493–1974 or 800/982–7619 | fax 215/493–7592 | Mon.–Wed. | www.inn-bucks.com | 6 rooms (5 with shower only), 1 suite | $189–$245 | AE, MC, V.

The Logan. This lodge in the center of a historic district was built in 1722 and later placed on the National Register of Historic Buildings. The rooms today have original and reproduction Colonial and Victorian furnishings. Rooms have views of the canal. Restaurant, complimentary Continental breakfast. Cable TV. | 10 W. Ferry St. | 215/862–2300 | fax 215/862–3931 | www.loganinn.com | 16 rooms (10 with shower only) | $105–$165 | AE, D, DC, MC, V.

★ **Mansion Inn.** This 1865 inn is in the heart of downtown New Hope. It's designed with Baroque Victorian architecture of the 2nd French empire. Each room is different, with restored original moldings, fixtures, and woodwork. Some rooms have fireplaces. Complimentary breakfast. Cable TV. Pool. No kids under 16. Business services. No smoking. | 9 S. Main St. | 215/862–1231 | fax 215/862–0277 | www.themansioninn.com | 3 rooms, 5 suites | $195–$225, $245–$285 suites | AE, MC, V.

Maplewood Farm Bed and Breakfast. Towering maples surround this 1792 fieldstone farmhouse. You can sit on the porch to watch the grazing sheep, walk to the creek to see deer, owls, and blue heron, or go into the henhouse to pick fresh warm eggs. One room has a reproduction Shaker rope featherbed and a hand-painted garden mural on the walls; another has a hand-painted rocker and floral wallpaper. All rooms have canopy beds, colorful quilts, and fireplaces. The two-story loft suite has a living room, primitive murals, and exposed beams of natural oak and pine. Nine mi west of New Hope. Dining room, picnic area, complimentary breakfast. No room phones. No TV. Pool. Massage. No kids under 12. No smoking. | 5090 Durham Rd., Gardenville | 215/766–0477 | www.bbhost.com/maplewoodfarm/ | 4 rooms; 1 suite | $105–$165 (2–night minimum on weekends; 3–night minimum on holiday weekends) | AE, D, MC, V.

Mountainside Hotel. A few of the bedrooms here were part of the original 1689 structure; several more were added in 1737. Decorated with bold stripes and patterns in styles from English nautical to French country, rooms come with matching period china and crystal if you order room service. You can also have European feather mattresses, Egyptian cotton towels, and a quote of the day left on your pillow. The hotel owns 22 acres of property on the Delaware River. Six mi northwest of New Hope. Dining room, room service. Cable TV. | 4770 River Rd., Point Pleasant | 215/297–9900 | fax 215/297–0677 | www.mountainsidehotel.com | 6 rooms; 2 suites | $129–$149; suites $179–$249 (2–night minimum on weekends; 3–night minimum on holiday weekends) | AE, MC, V.

Pineapple Hill. This 1790 Colonial manor has views of the Delaware River from its 6 acres of land, plus a rose garden and many sitting areas. The Colonial-style furnishings and decorations match the exterior. Picnic area, complimentary breakfast. Cable TV. Pool. Business services. No smoking. | 1324 River Rd. | 215/862–1790 | fax 215/862–5273 | www.pineapplehill.com | 5 rooms (3 with shower only), 4 suites | $89–$160, $138–$230 suites | AE, D, MC, V.

Tattersall Inn. A plastered-stone 18th-century manor house in a small town north of New Hope, this antique-laden inn has several porches and is on 2 acres of landscaped grounds. Complimentary breakfast. Business services. No smoking. | Box 569, N. River Road, Point Pleasant | 215/297–8233 or 800/297–4988 | fax 215/297–5093 | www.tattersallinn.com | 6 rooms | $105–$145 | MC, V.

★ **Wedgwood Inn.** Three buildings, two Victorians and an 1840 Federal manor, make up this bed-and-breakfast. All buildings were renovated in 2000. There are Victorian antiques, flowers, original art, and Wedgwood china, and it's on 2 parklike acres with gazebos and wicker-sealed porches. Picnic area, complimentary breakfast. Some in-room hot tubs, some room phones. Business services. Pets allowed. No smoking. | 111 W. Bridge St. | 215/862–3996 | fax 215/862–3936 | www.new-hope-inn.com | 19 rooms, 6 suites | $90–$195, $150–$255 suites | MC, V.

The Whitehall Inn. Guest rooms at the 18th-century manor house of what was once a gentleman's horse farm are furnished with period antiques and canopy beds. Fireplaces abound. Picnic area, complimentary breakfast. No room phones. Pool. No kids under 12. Business services. No smoking. | 1370 Pineville Rd. | 215/598–7945 or 888/379–4483 | fax 215/598–0378 | www.innbook.com | 5 rooms | $140–$210 | AE, D, DC, MC, V.

The Woolverton Inn Bed and Breakfast. Most of the rooms in this 1792 stone manor house overlook rolling hills or pasture, and all have access to a large front porch and formal gardens. The two main house rooms have king-size canopy featherbeds and fireplaces; one has floor-to-ceiling bookshelves. The Garden Cottage is a large suite in a renovated 1860s carriage house, remodeled with a private entrance, private garden, fireplace, stained glass windows, sitting area with sofa, king size four-post featherbed, and oversized shower. Three mi north of New Hope. Dining room, complimentary breakfast. Some in-room hot tubs. No kids under 12. No smoking. | 6 Woolverton Road, Stockton, NJ | 609/397–0802 | fax 609/397–0987 | www.woolvertoninn.com | 9 rooms | rooms $115–$185; suites $225–$245; cottage $285; 2–night minimum on weekends | AE, MC, V.

NEW STANTON

MAP 7, C6

(Nearby towns also listed: Connellsville, Donegal, Greensburg, Ligonier)

New Stanton is the second busiest stop on I–76, mainly because it is also the point in the state where I–70 and Route 119 meet the Pennsylvania Turnpike. Thirty minutes from Pittsburgh, the town is experiencing a building boom with many new construction projects in progress or on the drawing board.

Information: Laurel Highlands Visitors Bureau | Town Hall, 120 E. Main St., Ligonier, PA 15658 | 724/238–5661.

Attractions
L.E. Smith Glass Co. See what the craftsmen are making for the day. The company hand-forges carved glass and other items. Management recommends that you go early in the day, as the heat builds up from the furnaces throughout the day and can make the afternoons too hot for tours. | 1900 Liberty St., Mt. Pleasant | 724/547–3544 | Free | Weekdays 9:30–3, closed weekends.

West Overton Museum. Here you can visit the birthplace of Henry Clay Frick, who became a millionaire by building ovens to turn coal into coke. Exhibits include a film describing the process of making coke, a restored wash house, several barns, a garden, a blacksmith shop, and the Overholt Mill/Distillery, which displays many household, farm, and industrial tools of the 19th century. Ten mi southwest of New Stanton. | Rte. 819, West Overton Village, Scottdale | 724/887–7910 | $1 | May 15–Oct. 15, Tues.–Sat. 10–4.

ON THE CALENDAR

AUG.:–SEPT.: *Greater Pittsburgh Renaissance Festival.* Partake in peasant story-telling, Celtic music, Middle Eastern dancing, magic, comedy, and juggling at this six-week re-creation of 16th-century life. Enter the Wooing Contest or the Wench Press while your kids go on a treasure hunt or march in the Royal Parade. Costumed artisans weave, blow glass, and even fashion medieval weapons. The market has 75 craft shops. | 724/872–1670 | www.pgh-renfest.com.

Dining

Eat'n Park Family Restaurant. American. The first Eat'n Park opened in 1949 as a drive-in restaurant with carhops. The chain now operates over 75 restaurants furnished with formica tables, wooden booths with cushioned seats, and blue-, green-, and brown-flecked carpeting. The New Stanton location is open 24 hours a day and has a breakfast and fruit buffet, a soup and salad bar, and a midnight buffet. Dinners include grilled bone-in pork chops, marinated and seasoned with a touch of garlic and onion, and oven-baked scrod, prepared with a buttery breadcrumb topping. Kids' menu. | 111 West Byers Ave. | 724/925–1060 | $6–$8 | AE, D, DC, MC, V.

Lodging

Days Inn. This motel has affordable rates and comfortable rooms. Restaurant, bar (with entertainment), room service. In-room data ports, cable TV. Pool. Exercise equipment. Laundry facilities. Business services. | 127 W. Byers Ave. | 724/925–3591 | fax 724/925–9859 | www.newstandondaysinn.com | 135 rooms | $48–$80 | AE, D, DC, MC, V.

Howard Johnson. This motel is in the picturesque Laurel Highlands ½ mi from Exit 8 of the Pennsylvania Turnpike. Complimentary Continental breakfast. In-room data ports, refrigerators, cable TV. Pool. Playground. Business services. | 112 W. Byers Ave. | 724/925–3511 | fax 724/925–3511 | www.hojo.com | 87 rooms | $39–$85 | AE, D, DC, MC, V.

New Stanton Motel. Rooms here have brown and gold carpeting and floral or solid-colored bedspreads with coordinated curtains. About 15 rooms have queen-size beds. The motel is in a commercial area three blocks from fast food restaurants. Laundry facilities. Pets allowed. No kids under 21. | 116 W. Pennsylvania Ave. | 724/925–7606 | 34 rooms | $25–$28 | AE, D, MC, V.

NORRISTOWN

MAP 7, K6

(Nearby towns also listed: King of Prussia, Kulpsville, Philadelphia)

Established in 1784 as the county seat of Montgomery County, Norristown is just 10 min north of downtown Philadelphia. Norristown was the terminus of the nation's first commuter railway to Philadelphia. The town had gaslights early on, courtesy of local inventor Thaddeus Lowe, and also had the first refrigerated brewery, the Adam Scheidt Brewing Company. The city was an important port on the Schuylkill River and Canal system, permitting the transport of anthracite coal from the mines at the headwaters of the river to the city of Philadelphia.

Information: **Central Montgomery County Chamber of Commerce** | Lafayette Place One, 19401 | 610/277–9500.

Attractions

The Barnes Foundation. View millionaire-inventor Dr. Albert Barnes' private collection of early French Modern and Post-Impressionist art. Early and late work of Renoir, Cezanne, and Matisse are on display, plus paintings by Picasso, Modigliani, Monet, Seurat, and Degas. You can also visit the arboretum to see over 1,500 woodland species and collections of lilacs and roses. Reservations should be made 60 days in advance to ensure your date.

Parking fee. 12 mi southeast of Norristown. | 300 N. Latch's Lane, Merion Station | 610/667–0290 | fax 610/664–4026 | www.barnesfoundation.org | $5 | Sept.–June, Fri., Sat., Sun. 9:30–5. July–Aug., Wed., Thurs., Fri. 9:30–5.

Elmwood Park Zoo. The Norristown Zoological Society has operated this zoo since 1924. The zoo's seven acres hold 145 animals and 45 species groups; it includes a sensorium, which is a museum of unique animal sense, and a barn petting zoo. | 1661 Harding Blvd. | 610/277–3825 | $4.50 | Mon.–Thurs. 10–4; Fri. 10–8; Sat.–Sun. 10–5.

Peter Wentz Farmstead. Volunteers at this 18th-century farm dress in period costumes and demonstrate how farming was done in the 1700s, tending to Morgan horses, cattle, and crops. | 2100 Shultz Rd., Worcester | 610/584–5104 | Free | Tues.–Sat. 10–4, Sun. 1–4, closed Mon.

Valley Forge National Historical Park. After losing Philadelphia to the British, General George Washington retreated to Valley Forge, tired and ill equipped. More than 2,000 soldiers lost their lives in an extremely harsh winter. The park has many historic sites including 50 reconstructed huts, various memorials, and Washington's headquarters.

A good place to start your tour of the park is at the **Visitor Center,** which has free maps and information on the park, bus tours, and audio tours. The building also houses exhibits, a bookstore, and an 18-minute film called *Valley Forge: A Winter Encampment.* | Rte. 23, Valley Forge Park | 610/783–1077 | www.nps.gov/vafo | Free | Daily 9–5.

The **Washington Headquarters** is part of the park's living history program. George Washington and his staff stayed here while at Valley Forge. Park volunteers dress in period costumes and discuss life at Valley Forge for Washington, his staff, and his troops. | $2 | Apr.–Nov., daily 9–5.

Built in 1904 as a tribute to George Washington, **Washington Memorial Chapel** is still used today. The church is famous for its carillon, one of the world's largest with 58 bronze bells that are played from a keyboard. It weighs over 26 tons and can cover nearly five octaves. The church also has a Patriots Tower and Veterans Wall of Honor. | 610/783–0120 | www.libertynet.org/chapel | Free | Weekdays 9–4; carillon concert Wed. evening.

The **Soldier Life Program,** in the park at stop number 2/Muhlenberg's Brigade, details a soldier's existence during the harsh Revolutionary War. The program has a demonstration of musket firing on Saturday afternoons. | Free | Daily dawn to dusk.

National Memorial Arch is a memorial to the soldiers who camped at Valley Forge from 1777 to 1778. A mile from the visitors center, it is part of the automobile and bus tour. | Free | Daily dawn to dusk.

You can visit Valley Forge Historical Park and tour it in different ways. A bus tour leaves the visitors center daily and includes a guide, or you can guide yourself in your own car. The **Auto Tape Tour** is a do-it-yourself tour with a tape of the events that took place at Valley Forge. The tapes can be picked up at the visitors center, and last about 60 minutes. Pull-off areas are available so you can walk through some of the sites. The tape is yours to keep. | 610/783–5788 | $8 | Daily 9–5.

A 45-minute **Bus Tour** with a taped narration leaves from the visitors center. Passengers can depart at various locations and pick up another bus as it passes by. Buses run every 30 minutes. | 610/783–5788 | $5.50 | June–Labor Day, daily 9–5; Labor Day–Oct., weekends 9:30–4:30, closed weekdays.

The Wharton Esherick Studio. This studio is also the home of the "dean of American wood sculpture," Wharton Esherick. The home is a work of art, with a red-oak spiral staircase that was exhibited at the 1939 World's Fair. Many sculptures and carvings are on display here, 7 mi west of Norristown. Call to reserve your spot for a one-hour tour. | Horseshoe Trail, Valley Forge | 610/644–5822 | $9 | Sat. 10–5, Sun. 1–5.

ON THE CALENDAR

AUG.: *Philadelphia Folk Festival.* Founded in 1962, this is one of the longest-running festivals in the country, attracting more than 20,000 people. Acts include Bluegrass, Irish, Cajun, Klezmer, blues, and cowboy performers; dancing, kids' activities and crafts are throughout the property. On-site camping is allowed. | 215/247–1300.

Dining

August Moon. Pan-Asian. Japanese decorations and Korean artifacts are fairly common in this type of restaurant, but the cooking method is unusual: a combination of Asian culinary styles come into play as the chefs cook your food right at the table. | 300 E. Main St. | 610/277–4008 | No lunch Sun. | $11–$25 | AE, DC, MC, V.

General Lafayette Inn and Brewery. American. A 1732 building that's been in constant use since it was built with little renovation (evidenced by its small rooms and low doorways) now is a brewpub, with kettles in full view from what used to be the porch. The interior is Colonial style with period antiques and furnishings. The menu has wild game, braised rabbit, and duck confit. Live music, bands, Wed.–Sat. Kids' menu. Sun. brunch. | 646 Germantown Pike, Lafayette Hill | 610/941–0600 | Reservations essential | $12–$24 | AE, DC, MC, V.

Gypsy Rose. Contemporary. Built in 1725, this farmhouse was once a hotel before it became a restaurant. Improvements have been made, but the look of the interior matches its his-

VALLEY FORGE

Following the fall of Philadelphia to the British, General George Washington retreated to Valley Forge, and along with his troops, endured one of the harshest chapters of the Revolutionary War. From December 1777 to June 1778 the tired, ill-equipped army of 12,000 endured blizzards, inadequate food and clothing, damp quarters, and disease. There were many deserters and, although there was no battle, over 2,000 soldiers lost their lives.

The men, from various parts of the country, set up camp quickly but the construction of shelters ranged from adequate to downright poor. Since troops were clothed and equipped by the states from which they came, some were better prepared for the harsh winter than others. In the month of February alone, the army dwindled to 6,000 men, the result of diseases caused by poor sanitary conditions and inadequate diet. Spring proved to be the only relief.

Valley Forge National Historical Park contains various historic sites, including 50 reconstructed huts, various memorials, and Washington's headquarters. A trip around the park begins at the visitors center, where you can pick up a map, and tour in one of four ways—automobile, bus, walking, or bicycling. While at the visitors center, be sure to take some time to view the actual weapons and tools used by Washington's troops (some quite rare), and watch an 18-minute video on what life was like during that winter.

The 10-mi auto tour takes you to the huts, Washington's headquarters, the Arch memorial, and various encampments and artillery fields. On hot and humid days, the automobile and bus tours are most popular and can be narrated by audio tape. The bus tour includes 10 stops, and passengers can disembark to take photographs or have a picnic and then catch the next bus that comes along. Buses run every 30 min. Only one stop, George Washington's cathedral, has food and beverages so people planning to make a day out of the visit may want to pack a picnic lunch and enjoy one of the many picnic areas. For visitors looking for a workout or a more leisurely tour of the area, a paved bike and walking path is the answer.

© Corbis

tory and features exposed brick and antiques. Daily specials are available. | 505 Bridge Rd., Collegeville | 610/489–1600 | $15–$28 | AE, D, DC, MC, V.

The Jefferson House. Contemporary. Once the Buckland estate, this restaurant is set on 11 acres of property; the three glass-enclosed rooms provide spectacular views. This establishment is known for its horseradish-crusted salmon served with a red wine sauce. Kids' menu, early-bird suppers. | 2519 DeKalb Pike | 610/275–3407 | Reservations essential | No lunch Sun. | $14–$35 | AE, DC, MC, V.

Kennedy-Supplee Mansion. Continental. The mansion, built in 1852 and since restored, has eight elegant Federal-style dining rooms. Specialties are tenderloins of bison and seared buffalo medallions with sauce medoc. | 1100 W. Valley Forge Rd./23W.; King of Prussia/Valley Forge National Park | 610/337–3777 | www.kennedysupplee.com | Reservations essential | Jacket required | Closed Sun. No lunch Sat. | $20–$30 | AE, DC, MC, V.

William Penn Inn. Continental. Early American accents surround you at this restaurant, which has a menu with snapper soup and veal oscar. The eatery has its own bakery on the premises, and also guest rooms. Harpist, pianist Tues.–Sat. Early-bird suppers. Sun. brunch. | Rte. 202 and Sumneytown Pike, Gwynedd | 215/699–9272 | $30 | AE, D, DC, MC, V.

Lodging
Budget Inn. Just look for the basics here—bed, dresser, and private bath. Three blocks from downtown. Cable TV. | 830 W. Main St. | 610/279–0150 | 40 rooms | $46 | MC, V.

William Penn Inn. Built in 1714, this inn has museum-quality antiques and marble bathtubs. Restaurant, complimentary Continental breakfast, room service. In-room data ports, minibars, refrigerators, cable TV. Business services. No smoking. | Rte. 202 and Sumneytown Pike, Gwynedd | 215/699–9272 | fax 215/699–4808 | www.williampenninn.com | 1 room, 3 suites | $125–$160, $150–$180 suites | AE, D, DC, MC, V.

NORTH EAST

MAP 7, B1

(Nearby town also listed: Erie)

In the Erie Triangle, North East was named for its location relative to Erie. One of only a handful of boroughs on the shore of Lake Erie, North East has a unique climate that is conducive to wine growing.

Information: **North East Chamber of Commerce** | 21 S. Lake St., 16428 | 814/725–4262.

Attractions
Heritage Wine Cellars. This vineyard started making wine in the area more than 150 years ago. It's owned by the Bostwick family, who own 150 acres of grapes and process them in an 18th-century barn. They offer free tastings and tours. | 12162 E. Main Rd. | 814/725–8015 | Free | Mon.–Sat. 9–6; Sun. 12–6.

Mazza Vineyards. One of Pennsylvania's oldest and largest wineries, its processing plant has a touch of Mediterranean architecture. You can take a free tour of it before enjoying a complimentary tasting. Try ice wine and French and American varietals. | 11815 E. Lake Rd. | 814/725–8695 | www.mazzawines.com | Free | Mon.–Sat. 9–5:30; Sun. 12–4:30.

Penn–Shore Vineyards and Winery. The vineyard grows a variety of grapes including Baco Noir, Chardonnay, and Riesling. The winery began in 1968 and has free tastings and tours. | 10225 E. Lake Rd. | 814/725–8688 | www.pennshore.com | Free | Mon.–Sat. 9–5:30, Sun. 11–4:30.

Railway Museum. See static locomotives, a dining car, a sleeper, and a caboose. Also on display are dishes from the dining car, maps, and tools. Out back you can join diehard train-watchers who set up chairs for a front-row view of the active yard, with over 80 daily trains. | Wall St. and Robinson St. | 814/825–2724 | $2 | Weekends, 1–5.

ON THE CALENDAR

JULY: *Cherry Festival.* This festival in downtown has a parade, rides, games, and food. | 814/725–4262.

SEPT.: *Community Fair.* Contests at this fair include pie-eating and apple-peeling (for the longest peel), plus there's a kids' toy-tractor race and a frog-jumping contest. Local fruits, vegetables, and handicrafts are judged and the produce is auctioned. | 814/725–4262.

SEPT.: *Wine Country Harvest Festival.* Crafts, food, and winery tours are the order of the day at this celebration, held in Gravel Pit Park and Gibson Park. | 814/725–4262.

Dining

Johnny B's. Italian. On Friday and Saturday evenings a piano player tickles a dark brown 1920s upright in this downtown restaurant, filled with beer-themed mirrors. Entrées range from a 24-oz prime-grade prime rib, to seafood alfredo with shrimp, crabmeat, and fettucine noodles, to veal or chicken parmigiana dishes. Kids' menu. Breakfast also available. | 37 Vine St. | 814/725–1762 | Closed Sun. | $6–$17 | AE, D, MC, V.

Lodging

Vineyard Bed and Breakfast. Vineyards, orchards, and Lake Erie are all in view of this 1900 country home, in a quiet rural area. A vine motif is present throughout the house; the blue concord suite even has vines draped over sheer-white curtains. Other rooms have pillows and wallpaper with grape designs to bring out the mauve, green, and cranberry color schemes. The owners make homemade juice from their own grapes. Dining room, complimentary breakfast. Cable TV, some room phones. Pets allowed. No smoking. | 10757 Sidehill Rd. | 814/725–8998 or 888/725–8998 | www.lakeside.net/vineyardbb | 5 rooms | $65–$75 | AE, D, MC, V.

OIL CITY

MAP 7, B3

(Nearby towns also listed: Franklin, Titusville)

Before becoming an oil boomtown, Oil City's largest resource was used for medicinal purposes by Native Americans. Edwin L. Drake built the first oil well and almost immediately other towns sprang out of nowhere and the area became known as the "Valley That Changed the World." At one time, the town produced more than one million barrels of oil a year. Although the boom has ended, many of the structures from that time remain.

Information: **Oil City Chamber of Commerce,** | Box 376, 16301 | 814/676–8521.

Attractions

Oil Creek State Park. The 7,096-acre park has more than 52 mi of hiking trails, canoeing and fishing on Oil Creek, about 6,250 acres for hunting, two picnic areas, a 9½-mile paved bicycle trail through Oil Creek Gorge, and 10 mi of cross-country skiing trails. The visitors center has displays and programs on Petroleum Centre, the focal point of the early oil boom. | SR-1007/SR-1004 | 814/676–5915 or 888/PA–PARKS | www.dcnr.state.pa.us | Free | Daily 8 AM–dusk.

Venango Museum of Art, Science, and Industry. Rotating exhibits show the history of this oil region with displays on the Allegheny River, artifacts from the Oil Well Supply Company, and examples of early Pennzoil and Quaker State product advertising. | 270 Seneca St. | 814/676–2007 | $2 | Tues.–Sat. 10–4, Sun. 12–4.

JULY: *Oil Heritage Festival.* This Oil City fair is one of the largest in northwestern Pennsylvania. You can go to rock, jazz, blues, country, and oldies concerts or watch the 5K race, volleyball, and tennis tournaments. An Erie trolley car even comes to Oil City to give guided tours of the neighborhood's Victorian homes. | 814/676–8521 or 800/264–5248.

Dining
Yellow Dog Lantern. Seafood. Named for the old lanterns used in local oil fields, this restaurant is filled with antique lamps and more than 100 sharpening stones of various sizes. House specials are oysters bingo–oysters dusted in flour, pan fried, and seasoned in herb garlic and white wine, and oysters Rockefeller–oysters served with spinach pernod, cream, parmesan cheese, and herbs. You can also choose from Maryland snow crab cakes, lobster, chicken fettucine, or veal marsala. Kids' menu. | 218 Elm St. | 814/676–1000 | Closed Sun. | $13–$32 | AE, D, DC, MC, V.

Lodging
Holiday Inn. This hotel is in the heart of oil heritage region and overlooks the Allegheny river. Restaurant, bar, room service. In-room data ports, cable TV. Pool. Exercise equipment. Business services. | 1 Seneca St. | 814/677–1221 | fax 814/677–0492 | 105 rooms | $59–$125 | AE, D, DC, MC, V.

Turtle Bay Lodge. Each guestroom at this lodge has a king-size bed, and one has a cannonball bed. You can use a completely furnished kitchen and a great room with a big-screen TV and stone fireplace, as well as the 55-ft front porch. Some rooms have loveseats, an antique gate-leg table, and an antique cedar chest. 15 mi northeast of Oil City. Dining room, picnic area, complimentary Continental breakfast. Some in-room hot tubs, cable TV. No smoking. | President Rd., Tionesta | 814/677–8785 | 5 rooms | $100–$150 | D, MC, V.

ORBISONIA

(Nearby towns also listed: Chambersburg, Huntingdon)

A former hub of railroad activity, Orbisonia today remains steeped in railroad history. The East Broad Top railway station shut down in 1956, but since then it has become a tourist location with rides along the rail line.

Information: Greater Huntingdon Chamber of Commerce | 500 Allegheny St., Huntingdon, PA 16652 | 814/643–1110.

Attractions
East Broad Top Railroad. The 33-mile coal and mineral hauling railroad closed in 1956, but you can still take a round trip on steam-powered trains from Orbisonia station to Colgate Grove. | U.S. 522; From Orbisonia go west on PA 994 and drive about half a mile to Rockhill Furnace. Look for Orbisonia Station on the north side of the road | 814/447–3011 | $9 | June–Oct., Sat.–Sun. 11 AM, 1 PM, 3 PM.

Juniata College. Visit Juniata's Museum of Art, where you can see historical photographs of the college from the 1870s to 1920, American and European paintings, works on paper, portrait miniatures, and Navajo textiles. The campus hosts an array of dance groups, choirs, jazz ensembles, and soloist musicians as part of a performing artist series. 18 mi northwest of Orbisonia. | 1700 Moore St., Huntingdon | 814/643–5031 | www.juniata.edu | Open daily.

Rockhill Trolley Museum. Ride a historic trolley or just view the collection of restored and unrestored trolleys. You can watch workers restore cars by hand here and learn about the history of the trolley. | U.S. 422 | 814/447–9576 | $3 | Memorial Day–Oct., daily 11:30–3:30.

ON THE CALENDAR
DEC.: *Madrigal Dinner.* Dinner and drink are served while performers wearing 14th-century Italian dress sing madrigals—festive compositions for two or more voice parts. | 814/641–3443.

Dining

Wooden Spoon Inn. American. The homemade vegetable-beef and chicken-corn soups here are favorites of the local hunters. You can get roast turkey, baked ham, deep-fried haddock tails, or steaks, such as a 20-oz porterhouse and a 16-oz T-bone. The horseshoe-shaped bar is filled with beer signs and photographs of drag car drivers and Harley riders who've visited the restaurant. 16 mi southwest of Orbisonia. | Star Route, Hustontown | 814/448–3211 | Closed Mon. | $6–$15 | No credit cards.

Lodging

Lane's Country Homestead. This grey and blue 1789 farm home is available as one unit, with three double beds, two single beds, a couch that pulls out to queen-size, and 2 ½ baths. You can use a fully furnished kitchen with a pedestal table, dishes and silverware, dishwasher, and a large pancake grill. There's a pond for fishing and one that freezes over for ice-skating. You can sit on a rocker on the front porch as you watch the kids on the swings, slide, and fireman's pole. Eight miles northwest of Orbisonia. Dining room, picnic area. Pool, pond. Hiking. Fishing, bicycles. Ice-skating, sleigh rides. Playground. Laundry facilities. No smoking. | Lane Rd., Cassville | 814/448–3351 | 1 unit | $75 | No credit cards.

PHILADELPHIA

MAP 7, L7

(Nearby towns also listed: Bristol, Chester, Jenkintown, King of Prussia, Media, Norristown)

The City of Brotherly Love is also the birthplace of the United States. It was here on July 4, 1776, that the Declaration of Independence was adopted.

Philadelphia has historic landmarks around every corner and some of the same cobblestone streets that the nation's Founding Fathers once strolled. In the heart of the city two of the nation's symbols of freedom, Independence Hall and the Liberty Bell, are in Independence National Historical Park. Originally built as the Pennsylvania Statehouse, Independence Hall is where the Declaration of Independence was adopted and the U.S. Constitution was written. The Liberty Bell rang from the top of Independence Hall on the day the Declaration of Independence was read publicly for the first time.

More than a dozen other historic attractions are within the park including Carpenter's Hall, where the First Continental Congress met in 1774; the First Bank of the United States; Franklin Court, where Benjamin Franklin's home once stood; Christ Church Burial Ground, where Benjamin Franklin is buried; and the Declaration House, where Thomas Jefferson drafted the Declaration of Independence.

The oldest continuously occupied residential street in the nation—Elfreth's Alley—is off Second Street between Arch and Race Streets. This National Historic Landmark consists of 33 Colonial- and Federal-style homes.

Some of the city's most famous residents besides Benjamin Franklin include Betsy Ross and Edgar Allan Poe. The home where Ross stitched together the first American flag is within walking distance of the Liberty Bell. Poe lived in Philadelphia for about six years. For the last 18 months of that time he lived at a home on Seventh Street, now the Edgar Allan Poe National Historic Site.

Philadelphia is more than just a city of history; it is also a city of restaurants with a large variety of ethnic eateries. Perhaps one of its most popular dishes also bears the city's name, the Philadelphia cheesesteak.

Included among the city's many parks is Fairmount Park, the nation's largest landscaped city park, encompassing 8,900 acres of winding creeks, lush green meadows, and 100 mi of trails. Nearby is the Philadelphia Zoo, the oldest zoo in the nation, which is home to more than 1,800 animals.

Philadelphia's diverse shopping districts include Jewelers Row, the nation's oldest diamond district and one of the largest; South Street, with 150 stores, boutiques, and galleries; and the Italian Market, the world's largest outdoor market.

Several museums within the city limits are sure to entertain and educate those who visit. The Philadelphia Museum of Art, the Franklin Institute Science Museum, the Natural Science Museum, the Philadelphia Doll Museum, and the Independence Seaport Museum are just a few of the many museums here.

Philadelphia is home to four professional sports teams: the Philadelphia Eagles, Phillies, 76ers, and Flyers.

Where the Schuylkill River flows into the Delaware River, Philadelphia has served as an important port from its beginnings.

The city is home to 27 colleges and universities including the University of Pennsylvania, which was founded by Benjamin Franklin in 1740 and was the first school in America to earn the title of "university" in 1779.

Information: Philadelphia Chamber of Commerce | 1234 Market St., Room 1800, 19107 | 215/545–1234.

NEIGHBORHOODS

Benjamin Franklin Parkway. From City Hall the Benjamin Franklin Parkway stretches northwest to a Greco-Roman temple on a hill—the Philadelphia Museum of Art. The parkway is the city's Champs-Elysées, a grand boulevard designed by French architects and alive with flowers, trees, and fountains. Along the way are many of the city's grandest buildings and finest cultural institutions: the Academy of Natural Sciences, the Franklin Institute, and the Rodin Museum. **Center City.** This is Philly's business district around City Hall and Market Street, anchored by Oz-like skyscrapers and solidly Victorian City Hall, including an enormous statue of William Penn. The term "Center City" refers to the entire area between the Delaware and Schuylkill rivers (east and west boundaries) and Vine and South streets (north and south). **Germantown and Chestnut Hill.** Germantown, an area north of Center City, was settled by Germans fleeing economic and religious turmoil. At the time of its founding it was far out in the country, linked to the city 6 mi away by a dirt road. Before long, the Germans' modest homes and farms became interspersed with the grand homes of affluent Philadelphians who hoped to escape the city's summer heat. Today Germantown is an integrated neighborhood prized for its large old homes; several of the historic houses that line Germantown Avenue are open for tours. Over the years, development continued outward from the city along the length of the avenue, culminating in Chestnut Hill, today one of Philadelphia's prettiest neighborhoods. **The Historic District.** No matter how you first approach Philadelphia, all things start at Independence National Historical Park, the focal point of "America's most historic square mile." Independence Hall, Congress Hall, Old City Hall, Carpenters' Hall, Franklin Court, Declaration House, and, of course, the Liberty Bell are all in this neighborhood. **Manayunk.** This old mill town, wedged between the Schuylkill River and some very steep hills 7 mi northwest of Center City, became part of the city in 1854. It's a designated historic district and has become the city's hottest neighborhood, filled with restaurants and boutiques. **Old City.** Long considered one of Society Hill's poorer neighbors and known as a melting pot for immigrants, Old City is associated with three historic monuments: Christ Church, Elfreth's Alley, and the Betsy Ross House. The area is known for its chic art galleries, cafés, and restaurants, and its reworked houses and residential lofts. Theater and dance companies, art workshops, and design firms add to the neighborhood's renewed vitality as a cultural, shopping, and dining district. **Rittenhouse Square.** Rittenhouse Square is one of the prettiest of the city's public squares and the heart of upper-crust Philly. Swank hotels and modern office buildings line the streets along with the vestiges of onetime grandeur on display in the many Victorian townhouses that remain in the area. **Society Hill.** Society Hill is Philadelphia as it has been for 200 years, with its old chimney pots, hidden courtyards, ornate door knockers, and cobblestone streets. Although many houses are trinity abodes (one room to a floor), others are numbered among America's Federal-style showplaces, including the Physick House and the Powel House. **South Philadelphia.** This is Philly's "Little Italy," the neighborhood that gave the world Rocky Balboa, as well as the less-fictional Bobby Rydell, Frankie Avalon, and Fabian. The neighborhood has the fabulous Italian Market and plenty of restaurants. **Southwark.** This old neighborhood, which stretches from Front to 6th streets and from South to Washington avenues, is undergoing renovation and gentrification at present. Some of the most charming streets in the city are here, including Hancock and Queen. **University City.** Philadelphia hosts an astonishing concentration of colleges and universities, a number nearly unrivaled in the country. Two of the larger institutions, the University of Pennsylvania and Drexel University, are in an area dubbed University City in West Philadelphia, west of the Schuylkill River. City buses travel along Walnut Street from Society Hill to University City; 34th and Walnut streets is the subway stop for UPenn.

TRANSPORTATION

Airports: Philadelphia International Airport is 8 mi from downtown in the southwest part of the city. Recent renovations have made the terminal more attractive. The airport is serviced by many major and minor carriers. (8900 Essington Ave. | 215/937–6800 or 215/937–6937).

Rail: Philadelphia's 30th Street Station is a major stop on the northeast corridor of **Amtrak** (215/824–1600 or 800/872–7245). **NJ Transit** stops at the Greyhound terminal and has service between Philadelphia and Atlantic City and other New Jersey destinations (215/569–3752).

Bus Lines: Greyhound operates long-haul service to Baltimore, Washington, DC, New York, Wilmington, and points beyond. The terminal is at 10th and Filbert streets, just north of the Market East commuter rail station (215/931–4075 or 800/231–2222).

Intra-City Transportation: Philadelphia's mass transit system, **SEPTA,** consists of buses, trolleys, and subways, with fares to be paid by exact change or token. Most of the system is in bus lines. There are 110 bus routes extending throughout the city and into the suburbs. The PHLASH vehicles, purple minivans that service Center City, make 33 stops in the loop that runs from the Philadelphia Museum of Art on the Benjamin Franklin

Parkway through Center City to Penn's Landing. There are a few remaining trolleys that you can ride in the summer, but only to limited Center City stops. (215/580–7800).

Driving around Town: The Schuylkill Expressway (I–76) runs east–west through the city, and I–95 runs north and south. To reach Center City, take I–95, which will take you to the Vine Street Expressway, right into the city. Streets are gridded, with the heart of the city at the intersection of Broad and Market streets, where City Hall stands. North–south streets are numbered, starting with Front Street, which is the same as 1st Street at the Delaware River, and going up as you head west. Where you should have 14th Street is Broad Street. The Ben Franklin Parkway runs diagonally, breaking the grid pattern, leading out from City Hall and Center City, to Fairmount Park. With the exception of a few wide streets, like the Ben Franklin Parkway, Broad Street, Vine Street, and Market Street, many streets downtown are narrow and one-way. Rush hours are challenging; I–76 can be tied up for miles. Parking is difficult in Center City. Meters are hard to find at cost 25 cents for 15 minutes; parking garages are numerous and charge about $20.00 a day. Plan to park and walk around town or take public transportation.

WALKING TOUR

When visiting Philadelphia a pair of good walking shoes can open your world to some of the country's richest history. Here is where the country was born. Buildings, taverns, and cobbled walks used by the nation's Founding Fathers are preserved and welcome a host of new visitors. No stroll in Philadelphia would be complete without touring the city's historic district, which includes Independence Hall, Congress Hall, Betsy Ross's House, and the site Benjamin Franklin used to call home.

Start at the **Welcome Park.** The park pays homage to the city's founder, William Penn, and is at the site of the house Penn rented. The park was named for the *Welcome*, the ship that brought Penn to America. Part of the park's design is a map depicting Penn's original layout for the city and in its center is a statue of Penn himself. Cross Walnut Street and you'll find yourself at **City Tavern** once the political, social, and business center of Philadelphia. It is the spot where the delegates from the first Continental Congress met before choosing to convene at Carpenter's Hall. Around the corner on Walnut St. is the **Philadelphia Merchant's Exchange.** Built between 1832 and 1834, it was the original gathering place for merchants to barter or sell their merchandise. Follow Walnut west to 3rd St. and head north a block and you can find the **First Bank of the United States.** This is the oldest bank in the country and was in use until 1811 when its charter lapsed. Over the years it has been occupied by other financial institutions and today remains remarkably intact. If you need a little more information about the area, stop at the **Visitor Center** directly across the street from the bank. Here you can find maps and guides to assist in your walk to the area's other attractions.

Having left the visitor center, travel south on 3rd St. toward Walnut Street and turn right; from there you can run into the **Bishop White House.** This is the former home of William White, who was chaplain of the Continental Congress and later filled the same office for the U.S. Senate. The first and second floors are open to the public and the furnishings displayed are all of the period and represent the social standing of White and his family. Walk a little further down Walnut Street and you're introduced to an 18th-century garden that re-creates many features of formal gardens of the 1700s. The row houses along this street are either restorations or reconstructions. When you reach 4th Street, you'll notice the headquarters of the **Philadelphia Contributionship for the Insurance of Houses from Loss by Fire.** This is the oldest fire insurance company in America and was founded by Benjamin Franklin and friends.

On the northeast corner of 4th and Walnut stands **Todd House,** home of Dolley Madison. The house was built in 1775 and occupied by Madison until 1793. Turn north on 4th Street and you can see **Carpenter's Hall.** This is where the first Continental Congress met in 1774. This landmark building was erected between 1770 and 1774 by the Carpenter's Company, the oldest building organization in the country. In the same complex as Carpenter's Hall you can find the **Military Museum at New Hall.** This is a reconstruction of a building built in 1790 and used by the War Department in 1791 and 1792. It now houses the Army–Navy Museum with flags, guns, swords, uniforms, and medals on display.

To view the place Benjamin Franklin called home, make a right onto Chestnut and turn north on the alley about midway down the block, where you come upon **Franklin Court.** This area consists of a skeleton-like structure depicting the area where Franklin's house used to sit. The house was taken down by his heirs and no one is sure what it looked like or its exact placement. This court is also home to a museum dedicated to Benjamin Franklin's life and accomplishments. Retrace your steps out of the alley, turn right toward 5th Street, and you can see the **Second Bank of the United States.** This Greek Revival structure was built between 1819 and 1824 and today houses more than 100 Revolutionary and Federal portraits. Adjacent to the Second Bank is **Library Hall.** This 1959 reconstruction of a 1790s building is now occupied by the library of the American Philosophical Society. Founded by Benjamin Franklin, the Philosophical Society's library contains a large collection of Franklin's books and papers as well as works by other great thinkers of the time.

Cross 5th Street and you are in the city's most famous historic district, **Independence Square.** There are three buildings in the square, with the center building being **Independence Hall.** To its left is **Old City Hall** and to the right is **Congress Hall.** Independence Hall is where the Second Continental Congress met and ratified the Constitution. It is also here on July 8, 1776, that the Declaration was first read to a crowd of nearly 3,000. Allow yourself 30 minutes to an hour to wait in line for entrance to Independence Hall. Inside, a ranger can discuss the history of the hall and reveal the rooms where much of Congress's discussions took place.

On leaving the square, walk to the corner of 7th and Market to the site of the **Jacob Graff House,** also known as Declaration House. It is here that the Declaration of Independence was actually written.

No trip would be complete without viewing the true symbol of democracy and our country's past, the **Liberty Bell,** housed in an air-conditioned facility on the corner of 6th and Market streets. Its most famous ring occurred on July 8, 1776, when it summoned the citizens of Philadelphia for the reading of the Declaration of Independence. However, its famous crack formed nearly 80 years later when in 1835 the bell was rung for the funeral of Chief Justice John Marshall. On the bell's outside face are the words "Proclaim liberty throughout all the land, unto all the inhabitants thereof."

Attractions

ART AND ARCHITECTURE

★ **City Hall.** The largest and most elaborate city hall in the country, with more than 700 rooms, sits here in the center of Philadelphia. Its tower soars 548 ft and is topped by a 37-ft bronze statue of William Penn. The interior tour at 12:30 includes the restored Conversation Hall and Council Chambers. | Broad and Market Sts. | 215/686–2840 | Free | Weekdays 9:30–4:30, closed weekends.

★ **Elfreth's Alley.** Elfreth's Alley claims to be the oldest residential street in America, with 30 houses dating from 1728 to 1836. Number 126 is a museum with period furnishings and changing exhibits. | Elfreth's Alley between Arch and Race | 215/574–0560 | Free | Daily dawn to dusk.

Japanese Exhibition House. This 17th-century mansion features authentic Japanese architecture and furnishings. The mansion is surrounded by genuine Japanese manicured gardens. | Horticulture Center, West Fairmount Park | 215/878–5097 | $2.50 | May–Labor Day, Tues.–Sun. 10–4, closed Mon.; Labor Day–Oct., weekends 10–4, closed weekdays.

★ **Pennsylvania Academy of the Fine Arts.** America's first art museum, which opened in 1876 to celebrate the centennial, is renowned for its American paintings and sculptures that span three centuries. It is a National Historic Landmark. | 118 N. Broad St. | 215/972–7600 | www.pafa.org | $5 | Mon.–Sat. 10–5, Sun. 11–5.

★ **Philadelphia Museum of Art.** America's third largest art museum has more than 300,000 paintings, sculptures, drawings, prints, decorative art objects, period rooms, and Oriental art. A permanent collection of arms and armor is also on display. | Benjamin Franklin Parkway and 26th St. | 215/763–8100 | www.philamuseum.org | $8 | Tues. and Thurs.–Sun. 10–5, Wed. 10–8:45, closed Mon.

Philip and Muriel Berman Museum of Art at Ursinus College. This museum has a collection of 18th-century works of art. The exhibits include American and European landscapes, portraits, and works by Impressionists and Pennsylvania German artists. | Main St., Collegeville | 610/409–3500 | Free | Tues.–Fri. 10–4, Sat.–Sun. 12–4:30, closed Mon.

★ **Physick House.** An imposing Federal-style townhouse built in 1786 by Henry Hill is now home to a romantic 19th-century garden and a collection of 18th-century and early 19th-century furniture, silver, and porcelain. | 321 S. 4th St. | 215/925–7866 | $3 | Thurs.–Sun. 1–4, closed Mon.–Wed.

★ **Powel House.** An elegant Georgian townhouse was built in 1765 for Samuel Powel, Philadelphia's first mayor after the American Revolution. Today you can visit its even more elegant 18th-century garden and fine collection of period furniture, silver, and porcelain. | 244 S. 3rd St. | 215/627–0364 | $3 | Thurs.-Sun. 12–4; reservation recommended.

★ **Rodin Museum.** This small museum has the largest collection of Rodin sculptures and drawings in the United States. Museum pieces include his famous *The Thinker*, *The Burghers of Calais*, and *The Gates of Hell*. | Benjamin Franklin Pkwy. and 22nd St. | 215/563–1948 | www.rodinmuseum.org | $3 | Tues.–Sun. 10–5, closed Mon.

Stenton House. Built in 1730 by James Logan, administrator of the colony of Pennsylvania, its interior is furnished in 18th- and 19th-century Philadelphia style, reflecting three generations of the Logan family. | 4601 18th St. | 215/329–7312 | $5 | Tues.–Wed., by appointment only; Thurs.–Sat. 1–4, closed Sun.–Mon.

CULTURE, EDUCATION, AND HISTORY

Arch Street Friends Meetinghouse. The meeting house was built on land that William Penn gave the Quakers in 1693. A receptionist is on hand to greet you, answer questions, and speak about Quaker history and beliefs, and tell the history of the meeting house and grounds. A 15-minute slide show is available as well as Quaker artifacts and six dioramas on Penn. | 320 Arch St. | 215/627–2667 | Free | Mon.–Sat. 10–4, closed Sun.

★ **Betsy Ross House.** This restored two-story Colonial home was built in 1740; Betsy Ross lived here when she was credited with making the first American flag. At this site you can read the story of Ross sewing the flag, learn about her life in general, and find out how to cut a five-point star in one snip. | 239 Arch St. | 215/627–5343 | www.libertynet.org/iha/betsy | Free | Daily 10–5.

★ **Cliveden.** The Georgian stone home on 6 acres was built in 1767 and was the site of the Battle of Germantown in 1777. One family occupied it continuously for two centuries; it is now Philadelphia's only National Trust museum property. | 6401 Germantown Ave. | 215/848–1777 | www.cliveden.org | $6 | Apr.–Dec., Thurs.–Sun. 12–4, closed Mon.–Wed.

Deshler–Morris House. This was George Washington's residence when he lived in Germantown. It has period furnishings and artifacts that tell the story of George Washington and his family. | 5442 Germantown Ave. | 215/596–1748 | $1 | Apr.–Nov., Tues.–Sat. 1–4, closed Sun.–Mon.

Edgar Allan Poe National Historic Site. Edgar Allan Poe lived in Philadelphia for about six years, spending his last year in the city in this house. An eight-minute film describes Poe's life, after which you can take a look through a room with biographical and critical information on Poe. | 532 N. 7th St. | 215/597–8780 | www.philadelphia.com | Free | June–Oct., daily 9–5; Nov.–May, Wed.–Sun. 9–5.

Fort Mifflin. The fort was the site of a pivotal seven-week Revolutionary War battle and served as a federal prison during the Civil War. It was an active military installation until 1959. Programs include guided tours, uniform and weapons demonstrations, and soldier life programs. | Fort Mifflin Rd. | 215/492–1881 | $5 | Apr.–Nov., Wed.–Sun. 10–4, closed Mon.–Tues.

Free Library. More than 6 million books, magazines, newspapers, recordings, and other materials are here. If you check the schedule, you can catch one of the feature films, concerts, lectures, or children's programs that are hosted regularly. Daily tours of the Rare Book Department are offered. | Logan Sq | 215/686–5322 | Free | Mon.–Wed. 9 AM–9 PM, Thurs.–Fri. 9–6, Sat. 9–5, closed Sun.

Haverford College. This college was founded in 1833 by members of the Religious Society of Friends (Quakers). It is not affiliated with any religious body today, but remains a private university. The 216-acre parklike campus has more than 400 species of trees and shrubs, a nature walk, and a duck pond. | 370 W Lancaster Ave., Haverford | 610/896–1000 or 610/896–1162 | www.haver.edu | Free | Daily.

Historical Society of Pennsylvania. Founded in 1824, it is one of the oldest historical societies in the country and holds many of the nation's most important historical documents. The Society is currently one of the nation's premier nongovernmental repositories of documentary materials. It's home to more than 500,000 books, 300,000 graphic works, and 15 million manuscripts. | 1300 Locust St. | 215/732–6200 | fax 215/732–2680 | www.hsp.org | $5 | Tues. and Thurs.–Sat. 10–4:45, Wed. 2–8:45, closed Sun.–Mon.

Independence National Historical Park. Often referred to as "The Birthplace of the Nation," it contains the Liberty Bell and Independence Hall, where the Declaration of Independence and the U.S. Constitution were created. The park's features provide education about the events and the lives of the diverse population when Philadelphia was the capital of the country from 1790 to 1800. Spanning approximately 45 acres, the park has about 20 buildings that are open to the public, including Carpenter's Hall, the Second Bank of the U.S., Old City Hall, and many historic homes. | 313 Walnut St. | 215/597–8974 | www.nps.gov/inde | Free | Daily 9–5.

The **Bishop White House,** with period furnishings and fixtures, was the home of the first Episcopal minister in Philadelphia. An interpretive tour explains the importance of the 1786-era house and its residents. | 309 Walnut St. | 215/597–8974 | $2 | Daily 9–5.

Carpenter's Hall was built just in time to host the First Continental Congress in September 1774, who met here to oppose British rule. Early tools and original chairs from the Carpenter's Company, which still owns the building, are on exhibit. | 320 Chestnut St. | 215/597–8974 | Free | Tues.–Sun. 9–5.

The newly formed Congress occupied **Congress Hall** when Philadelphia was the capital of the country. After the Congress departed, the hall became the Philadelphia County Courthouse. George Washington and John Adams were inaugurated here. It has been restored to the way it looked between 1793 and 1800. | 6th and Chestnut Sts. | 215/597–8974 | Free | Daily 9–5.

The first structure was torn down in 1883, but photographs of **Declaration House** enabled the National Park Service to build a faithful re-creation of the original building. This is the house where Thomas Jefferson wrote the Declaration of Independence. The exhibit includes a re-creation of the two rooms Jefferson rented on the second floor. | 701 Market St. | 215/597–8974 | Free | Daily 10–3.

The first charter of the **First Bank of the United States** was drafted in 1791 by Congress and signed by George Washington. In 1811 Congress voted to abandon the bank and its charter. It is the oldest bank in America, built from 1795 to 1797 at a cost of $110,168.05. | 3rd St. | 215/597–8974 | Not open to the public.

A tribute to Benjamin Franklin, **Franklin Court** features a print shop, a museum with a special film about Franklin, the B. Free Franklin Post Office, archaeological remains of a building Franklin owned, and the Robert Venturi-designed "Ghost House," depicting Franklin's home in a cutaway version with its steel skeleton showing through. | 3rd and 4th Sts. between Market and Chestnut | 215/597–8974 | Free | Daily 9–5.

The **Free Quaker Meeting House** has an unusual history. A small group of Quakers supported and fought for the Colonists during the Revolutionary War, and were expelled from their congregations for straying from the Quaker tenet of pacifism. This group formed their own congregation, the Free Quakers, and built their own meeting house in 1783. Betsy Ross was an active member of the group until 1834. The structure is used today as headquarters for the Junior League of Philadelphia. | Arch St. between 5th and 6th Sts. | Free | Memorial Day–Labor Day, Tues.–Sat. 10–4, Sun. Noon–4, closed Mon. .

Built from 1698 to 1700, **Gloria Dei Church National Historic Site ("Old Swedes")** is the oldest church in Pennsylvania. The Swedes preceded the English to this part of America, arriving in 1646. Primarily a mission of the Church of Sweden, the building became an Episcopal church in 1845. It is currently owned and maintained by its congregation and contains important historic relics and artifacts. | Columbus Blvd. near Christian St. | 215/389–1513 | www.nps.gov/glde | Free | By appointment.

★ **Independence Hall** was originally built in 1732 as the Pennsylvania State House. Within its walls the Declaration of Independence was adopted; here the Congress of the United States debated, drafted, and signed the historic document. | Chestnut St. | 215/597–8974 | Free | Daily 9–5.

The area south of Independence Hall, **Independence Square,** is where the newly drafted Declaration of Independence was read to the public on July 8, 1776. | Between Walnut and Chestnut Sts. and 5th and 6th St. | 215/597–8974 | Free | Daily.

On July 8, 1776, the Liberty Bell rang out from the tower of Independence Hall, summoning citizens to hear the first public reading of the Declaration of Independence. At **Liberty Bell Pavilion,** you can read the history of the bell, see pictures from its 1915 cross-country journey, and find out all the facts. | Market St. | 215/597–8974 | Free | Daily 9–5.

The first library in the country open to the public, and the forerunner of the Library of Congress, is **Library Hall.** Founded in 1731 by Benjamin Franklin and his friends, the actual building was erected in 1790. The original journals of the Lewis and Clark expedition are in this building, along with a copy of the Declaration of Independence in Jefferson's own handwriting. | 5th St. between Chestnut and Walnut Sts. | 215/597–8974 | Not open to the public.

With the interactive theater of **Lights of Liberty,** you can take a moonlit journey back to the American Revolution. Headsets and five-story projections in Independence National Park take you back in time to when the country was first being formed. | 150 S. Independence St. | 877/GO–2–1776 | www.lightsofliberty.org | $17.76 | Apr.–Oct. 31, dusk–11 PM; call for days.

A former Georgian mansion today houses a bookstore and the **Museum Shop (Pemberton House).** When Joseph Pemberton, a Quaker merchant, built his mansion, the First Continental Congress had just finished meeting in Carpenter's Hall in 1774. | Chestnut St. | 215/597–8974 | Free | Daily 9–5.

The **New Hall Military Museum** is a reconstructed 1790 building that served as headquarters for the U.S. Department of War from 1791 to 1792. It contains the early history of the Marines, Army, and Navy. | 4th and Chestnut Sts. | 215/597–8974 | Free | Daily 10–1.

Old City Hall, Philadelphia's second city hall, served as the home of the U.S. Supreme Court between 1791 and 1800. | 5th and Chestnut Sts. | 215/597–8974 | Free | Daily 9–5.

One of the most noted 19th-century architects, William Strickland, is credited with the design of the **Philadelphia Merchants Exchange,** constructed between 1832 and 1834. It was originally a gathering place where merchants met to barter or sell their cargo and merchandise. It is said to be a masterpiece of elaborate Greek Revival architecture. | 3rd and Walnut Sts. | 215/597–8974 | Not open to the public.

The organizers of the **Philosophical Hall** conceived of it as a home for thinkers about nature, machines, industry, and governance; it is now the headquarters for the oldest surviving learned organization in the country, the American Philosophical Society. Founded in 1743, it includes an armchair used by Thomas Jefferson during his writing of the Declaration of Independence. It also serves as a miniature art museum. | 5th and Chestnut Sts. | 215/597–8974 | Not open to the public.

The **Second Bank of the United States** was the first major example of Greek Revival architecture in Philadelphia. A portrait gallery of famous Americans and foreigners make up the exhibit "Portraits of the Capital City." | 420 Chestnut St. | 215/597–8974 | $2 | Daily 10–5.

The Polish patriot rented a room in this small townhouse during the winter of 1797–1798. What is now the **Thaddeus Kosciuszko National Memorial** has been restored as a tribute to his efforts for the American Revolutionary cause. | 3rd and Pine Sts. | 215/597–1785 or 215/597–8974 | Free | Daily 10–5.

Dolley Payne Todd, later Dolley Madison, lived in **Todd House.** This restored middle-class home was built in 1775. You can pick up tickets for the home at the visitors center. | 4th and Walnut Sts. | 215/597–8974 | $2 | Daily 9–5.

John Bartram House. This 18th-century farm has a house, a barn, and outbuildings such as the seedhouse and the stable and carriage shed. The house, built in 1728, includes period furnishings and the history of the Bartram family, a pioneering family of naturalists, botanists, and explorers. | 54th St. and Lindbergh Blvd. | 215/729–5281 | $3 | Apr.–Dec., daily 12–4; Jan.–Mar., Wed.–Fri. 12–4, closed Sat.–Tues.

Morris Arboretum of the University of Pennsylvania. The 92-acre public garden contains many of Philadelphia's newest, rarest, and largest trees in a romantic Victorian garden. It also has an English Park, a rose garden, a swan pond, and a Japanese garden. | Northwestern Ave. | 215/247–5777 | $6 | Mon.–Fri. 10–4, Sat.–Sun., 10–3.

National Archives Branch. This branch houses over 42,000 ft of federal records from Delaware, Maryland, Pennsylvania, Virginia, and West Virginia. Genealogical and court records are featured. | U.S. Courthouse, Room 1350 | 215/597–3000 | Free | Weekdays 8 AM–5 PM, closed weekends.

Old City Gallery and Cultural District. Once a busy commercial district, it's now an active cultural, dining, and shopping district. This area is home to numerous galleries, studios, and cooperatives, as well as architectural firms and restaurants. | 303 Cherry St. | 215/238–9576 | www.snyderman-works.com | Free | Tue.–Sat. 10–6.

The oldest college of pharmacy in the nation, **Philadelphia College of Pharmacy and Science,** was founded in 1821 at historic Carpenter's Hall. A fully accredited independent college, it houses more than 8,000 pharmaceutical containers, medicines, botanicals, and pieces of equipment dating back five centuries. | 600 S. 43rd St. | 215/596–8800 | Free | Daily.

Temple University. Founded in 1884, Temple is the 35th largest university in the country and the largest provider of professional education. It is in north Philadelphia on 95 acres. | 215/204–8551 | www.temple.edu | Free | Weekdays 9–5.

Tomb of the Unknown Soldier. This is the only tomb in the country erected to the memory of unknown Revolutionary War soldiers. An eternal flame was installed in 1976. | Washington Square, Walnut St. | Free | Daily dawn to dusk.

University of Pennsylvania. Founded in 1740 as a charity school for Philadelphia children, this West Philadelphia university was begun by Benjamin Franklin. The nation's first medical school, journalism program, and hospital teaching program got their starts here, as did the first liberal arts curriculum. The university is on 262 acres with various historic landmarks throughout. | 3451 Walnut St. | 215/898–5000 | www.upenn.edu | Free | Weekdays 9–5.

★ The archaeological and ethnographic collection housed at the **University of Pennsylvania Museum of Archaeology and Anthropology** is world-renowned. Exhibits pertaining to Native Americans, Egyptians, African-Americans, as well as galleries dedicated to many ethnic groups are all on display. Guided and self-guided tours are available. | 33rd and Spruce Sts. | 215/898–4000 | www.upenn.edu | $5 | Tues.–Sat. 10–4:30, Sun. 1–5, closed Mon.

Walnut Street Theatre. This nonprofit regional theater is dedicated to the preservation and development of the art of theater. It was built in 1827 and is the oldest theater in the country. | Walnut St. near 8th St. | 215/574–3550 | www.wstonline.org | Free, except for shows | Weekdays 9–4, closed weekends.

Washington Square. One of Philadelphia's five original squares, this was laid out in 1682 by William Penn's surveyor, Thomas Holme. Beginning in 1776, fallen troops from Washington's army were buried in the square. | Walnut to Locust Sts. between 6th and 7th Sts. | Free | Daily dawn to dusk.

MUSEUMS

Academy of Natural Sciences Museum. *Tyrannosaurus rex* and more than a dozen fellow dinosaurs populate this museum. Other exhibits include geology and gems, bears, and nature center activities. | 1900 Benjamin Franklin Pkwy. | 215/299–1000 | $8.50 | Weekdays 10–4:30, weekends 10–5.

Afro-American Historical and Cultural Museum. One of the nation's largest collections of African-American history and culture is here for you to see. The museum hosts both historical and fine art exhibits reflecting the experience of African-Americans. It also sponsors many cultural events focusing on the contributions and perspective of African-Americans. | 701 Arch St. | 215/574–0380 | $6 | Tues.–Sat. 10–5, Sun. 12–5, closed Mon.

American Swedish Historical Museum. Built on land granted to Swedish settlers in 1653 and designed in the style of Swedish manor houses, the museum has 14 galleries commemorating the art, artifacts, and contributions of Sweden and its people to America. Its changing exhibitions, educational programs, Swedish-language courses, and traditional Swedish festival help preserve Swedish culture and history. | 1900 Pattison Ave. | 215/389–1776 | www.americanswedish.org | $5 | Tues.–Fri. 10–4, weekends 12–4, closed Mon.

Athenaeum of Philadelphia. The Athenaeum is a nonprofit member-supported library and historic site museum founded in 1814. The building was constructed in 1845 from a design by John Notman in the Italianate Revival Style and is one of the first Philadelphia buildings made of brownstone. The museum is a repository of architectural records, and its objective is to collect materials "connected with the history and antiquities of America, and the useful arts." It was declared a National Historic Landmark in 1977. Early sketches of the U.S. Capitol and Independence Hall are here. | 219 S. 6th St. | 215/925–2688 | fax 215/925–3755 | www.philaathenaeum.org | Free | Weekdays 9–5, closed weekends.

Atwater Kent Museum—The History Museum of Philadelphia. More than 40,000 objects spanning the city's 300-year history are displayed here, with emphasis on the culture of urban life in the 1800s and 1900s. Exhibits on Colonial, Revolutionary, industrial, and urban archaeology are permanent; various other exhibits change throughout the year. | 15 S. 7th St. | 215/922–3031 | www.philadelphiahistory.org | $3 | Wed.–Mon. 10–5, closed Tues.

Balch Institute for Ethnic Studies. This small museum is dedicated to honoring Philadelphia's ethnic and cultural diversity. Words and photographs tell the story of Philadelphia's constant growth through immigration. | 18 S. 7th St. | 215/925–8090 | www.balchinstitute.org | $3 | Weekdays 10–4, closed weekends.

Civil War Library and Museum. The museum's exhibits and photographs depict Civil War events. Its library contains 15,000 volumes and numerous manuscripts. | 1805 Pine St. | 215/735–8196 | www.libertynet.org | $5 | Tues.–Sat. 11–4:30, closed Sun.–Mon.

Fireman's Hall Museum. This restored 1903 firehouse contains firefighting apparatus dating from 1731 to 1907. You can see all sorts of badges, fire marks, helmets, parade hats, tools, and a fireboat pilot house. | 149 N. 2nd St. | 215/923–1438 | Free | Tues.–Sat. 9–4, closed Sun.–Mon.

★ **Franklin Institute Science Museum.** The Franklin Institute was the museum that pioneered hands-on science activities. Today it has eight such exhibits dedicated to exploring the 21st century. The museum has the Fels Planetarium, the Mandell Futures Center, the Tuttleman Omniverse Theater, and the Benjamin Franklin National Memorial. | 222 N. 20th St. | 215/448–1200 | www.fi.edu | $9.75 | Daily 9:30–5.

★ **Independence Seaport Museum.** The museum, opened in 1995, celebrates Philadelphia's maritime history and is a waterfront educational and cultural center. It explores Philadelphia's waterfront and its impact on the nation. The centerpiece exhibit is called Home Port: Philadelphia, diving into a dozen different waterfront worlds including commerce and trade, naval defense, shipbuilding, and the immigrant experience. | 211 S. Columbus Blvd. | 215/925–5439 | www.libertynet.org/seaport | $7.50 | Daily 10–5.

Mario Lanza Institute and Museum. A tribute to Mario Lanza, the great Italian-American tenor from Philadelphia, was established at the place he received his first music lesson. A life-size bust, paintings, and photographs detail the rise to fame of this 1950s icon. Vintage films are also shown daily. | 416 Queen St. | 215/468–3623 | www.mario-lanza-institute.org | Free | Sept.–June, Mon.–Sat. 10–3:30, closed Sun.

Mummer's Museum. Exhibits highlight the historical tradition of the Philadelphia Mummers and the annual January 1st parade. Videotapes of the parades over the years play alongside the costume displays. | 1100 S. 2nd St. | 215/336–3050 | $2.50 | Tues.–Sat. 9:30–5, closed Sun.–Mon.

Mütter Museum. Over 20,000 medical objects are on display here, including fluid-preserved anatomical and pathological specimens, medical instruments, anatomical and pathological models, and memorabilia of famous scientists and physicians. The museum has both permanent and changing exhibits. | 19 S. 22nd St. | 215/563–3737 | $8 | Mon.–Sat. 10–4, Sun. 12–4.

National Museum of American Jewish History. This is the only museum in the nation dedicated exclusively to collecting, preserving, and interpreting artifacts pertaining to the American Jewish experience. The museum's collection has grown to more than 10,000 items acquired through donation and purchase, and has historic documents, ritual objects, artwork, clothing, and personal memorabilia. | 55 N. 5th St. | 215/923–3811 | $3 | Mon.–Thurs. 10–5, Fri. 10–3, Sun. 12–5, closed Sat.

Philadelphia Doll Museum. This museum chronicles how African-Americans were perceived throughout history through its collection of more than 300 African-American dolls. A large collection of Roberta Bell dolls are on exhibit here. The accumulated works also include African, European, and American folk art. | 2253 N. Broad St. | 215/787–0220 | fax 215/787–0226 | $4 | Thurs.–Sat. 10–4, Sun. 12–4, closed Mon.–Wed.

Please Touch Museum for Children. "Don't touch" is never heard at the first hands-on museum in the country designed specifically for children 7 and younger. Activities range from crafts to educational methods. On Sunday, you can take advantage of the pay-as-you-wish admission. | 210 N. 21st St. | 215/963–0667 | www.pleasetouchmuseum.org | $6.95 | Daily 9–4:30.

Rosenbach Museum. A magnificent 18th-century townhouse contains fine and decorative arts collections and world-renowned holdings of rare books and manuscripts. Original artwork by author Maurice Sendak and a manuscript of James Joyce's *Ulysses* are permanent displays. | 2010 DeLancey Pl | 215/732–1600 | www.rosenbach.org | $5 | Tues.–Sun. 11–4, closed Mon.

Wagner Free Institute of Science. This National Historic Landmark was founded in 1855 to be a natural history museum. The collection of natural science specimens is in the original Victorian building. Free adult education courses and museum lessons for school-age children are available. | 1700 W. Montgomery Ave. | 215/763–6529 | Free | Tues.–Fri. 9–4, closed Sat.–Mon.

Fairmount Park. The park, all 4,180 acres of it, is the largest landscaped park in the country. You can walk along its trails, bicycle, go in-line skating, and even drive along its outskirts. It was the site of the Centennial Exposition of 1876 and several buildings from that earlier fair still stand, most notably Memorial Hall. The park has several million trees, the oldest zoo in the country, and various gardens and historic buildings. | Runs North–South through Philadelphia between Broad St. and the Schuylkill River | 215/685–0000 | Free | Daily dawn to dusk.

Classic 19th-century Tudor structures form **Boat House Row,** which houses the Schuylkill Navy and Rowing Club. The buildings are noted for their hundreds of signature white lights. | Boathouse Row | 215/978–6919 | Free | Daily.

Cedar Grove Mansion is a Quaker farmhouse built as a country retreat in 1748. It was moved, stone by stone, to Fairmount in 1928. It has been restored with period furnishings from five generations of Quakers. | 215/763–8100 | $2.50 | Daily 10–5. Built in the mid-18th century, **Laurel Hill Mansion** has period and early 19th-century furnishings. It's next to the "medicine man" sculpture. | Eldegly and Fairmount Aves | 215/235–1776 | $2.50 | Tues.–Sat. 10–4, closed Sun.–Mon.

On the tour of mansions **Lemon Hill Mansion** is the starting point of the route. It's an 18th-century Federal mansion noted for its oval rooms with curved doors and fireplaces. | Kelly and Sedgely Drs | 215/232–4337 | $2.50 | Wed.–Sun. 10–4, closed Mon.–Tues.

John Adams once described this Georgian home as the most elegant seat in Pennsylvania. **Mt. Pleasant Mansion** was built by a wealthy Scottish privateer in 1763–1764 and has various ornate woodwork and Chippendale-style furniture. | 215/763–8100 | $2.50 | Wed.–Sun. 10–4, closed Mon.–Tues.

Open for tours only by appointment, **Ormiston** was built just after the American Revolution. It has been completely restored with furniture from the 18th and 19th centuries. | Reservoir Drive, E. Fairmount Park | 215/763–2222 | $2.50 | Appointments only, 10–5.

Built in 1797 by an owner who wanted to escape a yellow fever epidemic in the city, **Sweetbriar Mansion** is a Federal mansion that overlooks the Schuylkill River. It's furnished with period antiques and is known for its floor-to-ceiling windows. (Lansdowne Ave., W. Fairmount Park | 215/763–8100 | $2.50 | Wed.–Sun. 10–4, closed Mon.–Tues.

Strawberry Mansion is the largest mansion in the park. This spacious house features a Federal-style center section with Greek Revival wings containing a mixture of Federal and Empire furniture, Tucker porcelain, and an antique toy exhibit. | 33rd and Dauphin Sts. | 215/228–8364 | $2.50 | Wed.–Sun 10–4, closed Mon.–Tues.

Built in 1756, the Georgian mansion, **Woodford Estate,** was home to both Patriots and Tories. Today it is furnished with a superb collection of Colonial furniture and artwork. | 33rd and Dauphin Sts. | 215/229–6115 | $2.50 | Daily 10–5.

Historic Bartrams' Garden. The Bartrams were a pioneering family of naturalists, botanists, and explorers. The 44-acre park has botanical gardens, a meadow, parklands, and wetlands. An 18th-century house overlooks the property and the Schuylkill River. | 54th St. and Lindbergh Blvd. | 215/729–5281 | www.philadelphia.com | Bartram Mansion $3; grounds, free | Mansion, Tues.–Sun. 12–4, grounds dawn to dusk, closed Mon.

John Heinz National Wildlife Refuge at Tinicum. In the Tinicum Marsh, you can spot more than 280 birds and can even see the endangered red-bellied turtle and southern leopard frog. | 86th St. and Lindbergh Blvd. | 215/365–3118 or 610/521–0662 | Free | Daily dawn to dusk.

Penn's Landing. This area stretches along the Delaware River for about 10 blocks from Vine Street to South Street and encompasses the spot where William Penn first touched ground in Philadelphia. After his arrival, it quickly became the heart of the area's maritime center and the city's dominant commercial district. Today, it's a riverside park and the place where locals gather in the summer to hear concerts. | Vine St. to South St. | Free | Daily dawn to dusk.

Gazela of Philadelphia is a 177-ft square-rigged vessel built in 1883. The *Gazela* is still seaworthy and sets sail each year to visit ports of the world. It was the oldest tall ship to participate in the OpSail Tall Ship Festival in 1976, and also took part in the Statue of Liberty's 100th birthday celebration in New York Harbor in 1986. | Penn's Landing | 215/923–9030 | www.gazela.org | Donations | June–Sept., weekends 12–5, closed weekdays.

Built in 1892, the **USS *Olympia.*** became the flagship of the North Atlantic Squadron and protected American interests in many foreign countries. During the First World War, the *Olympia* served as an escort ship in the Atlantic Ocean. The historic ship's last assignment, in 1921, was bringing the body of the Unknown Soldier back from Europe and carrying him to his final resting place at Arlington National Cemetery. | Penn's Landing | 215/922–1898 | $7.50 | Daily 10–5.

★ **Philadelphia Zoo.** America's first zoo opened on July 1, 1874. You can see red kangaroos, vampire bats, elephants, and lions, and more than 100 mammals, 150 bird species, and 155 reptiles. | 3400 W. Girard Ave. | 215/243–1100 | www.phillyzoo.org | $10.50 | Apr.–Oct., weekdays 9:30–5, weekends 9:30–6; Nov.–Mar., daily 9:30–5.

Schuylkill Center for Environmental Education. This plot of land is Philadelphia's largest privately owned open area with 500 acres of forest, fields, streams, and ponds. There are 6 mi of hiking trails and numerous places to bird-watch. | 8480 Hagy's Mill Rd. | 215/482–7300 | Free | Daily 8:30–5.

RELIGION AND SPIRITUALITY

Blessed Katherine Drexel Shrine. The shrine is part of the motherhouse of the Sisters of the Blessed Sacrament founded in 1891. The burial site of Katherine Drexel was dedicated for her efforts to help Native and African-Americans by using her fortune, estimated at more than $20 million, for the cause. | 1663 Bristol Pike, Bensalem | 215/639–7878 | www.libertynet.org/sbs | Donations | Daily 1–5.

Burial Ground of the Congregation Mikveh Israel. There are 371 known grave sites, including some fascinating Revolutionary-era people, buried in this site established in 1740. British troops occupying Philadelphia in 1777 used the tombstones for target practice. Nathan Levy, the captain whose ship brought the Liberty Bell to America, is interred here. | Spruce St. between 8th and 9th | Free | Sun.–Thurs. 10–3, closed Fri.–Sat.

Christ Church. Organized in 1695 during the reign of William and Mary, this Episcopal church was built between 1727 and 1754 when George II was king. George Washington, Francis Hopkinson, Robert Morris, and Benjamin Franklin all worshipped here. Thomas Jefferson also worshipped here on occasion. The 600-year-old font in which Penn was baptized remains. | 2nd St. north of Market St. | 215/922–1695 | Free | Mar.–Dec., Mon.–Sat. 9–5, Sun. 12:30–5; Jan.–Feb., Wed.–Sat., 9–5, Sun. 12:30–5, closed Mon.–Tues.

Christ Church Burial Ground. Established in 1719, with the earliest tombstone dating back to 1720, five signers of the Declaration of Independence are buried here, including Benjamin Franklin. | Arch St. between 4th and 5th | 215/922–1695 | Free | By appointment.

Historic Olde St. Augustine's Church. Founded in 1796, its early contributors include George Washington, John Berry, and Thomas Fitzsimmons. It was the first foundation of the Augustine Friars in the country. | 243 N. Lawrence St. | 215/627–1838 | Free | Weekdays 11:30–1:30, Sun. 8–1:30, closed Sat.

National Shrine of St. John Neumann. The shrine contains the tomb of St. John Neumann, a Redemptorist priest who became the fourth bishop of Philadelphia. He promoted parochial education and the care of immigrants. | 1019 N. 5th St. | 215/627–3080 | Free | Daily dawn to dusk.

Old St. Joseph's Church. The site of Philadelphia's first Roman Catholic church is actually tucked away in an alley in Independence National Park. The original building was erected in 1733 by Jesuits; the current structure dates from 1838. | 321 Willings Alley | 215/923–1733 | fax 215/574–8529 | www.oldstjoseph.org | Free | Rectory hours: Mon.–Sat. 10–4, Sun. 8–3:30.

Old Pine St. Presbyterian Church. It is the only pre-Revolutionary Presbyterian structure still standing in Philadelphia. William Hurry, who rang the Liberty Bell the day the Declaration of Independence was read for the first time, is buried in the church's cemetery. | 412 Pine St. | 215/925–8051 | Free | By appointment.

Old St. Mary's Church. This Catholic church was the first procathedral, a parish church used as a cathedral, of the Archdiocese of Philadelphia. | 252 S. 4th St. | 215/923–7930 | Free | Daily 10–2.

★ **St. Peter's Church.** Founded in 1758 and first opened for services in 1761, it has remained largely unchanged since it was built. Scottish master carpenter Robert Smith gave it an unusual mid-Georgian design. The churchyard is an urban oasis and the resting place for many of the locals. | 313 Pine St. | 215/925–5968 | Free | Weekdays 8–4, closed weekends.

SHOPPING

Antique Row. Along Pine Street, six blocks from the Pennsylvania Convention Center, you can choose from a tremendous selection of period furnishings, antiques, and collectibles. You can also find estate jewelry and vintage clothing from around the world. | Pine St. | Daily.

The Bourse. Inside this landmark you can find a variety of shops for souvenirs and other gifts. The restaurants range from cafés serving Philadelphia cheesesteaks to Victorian dining with a view of the Liberty Bell. | 111 S. Independence Mall East | 215/625–0300 | Mon.–Sat. 10 AM– 6 PM, Sun. 11–5.

El Centro de Oro. A unique and festive district in the heart of Philadelphia's Latin community, el Centro has the city's greatest concentration of ethnic shops and sites. Authentic music, arts, and crafts, as well as hard-to-find tropical foods from the Caribbean and Central/South America can be purchased here. | North 5th St. from Huntingdon to Allegheny Aves., and Lehigh Ave. from Front to 8th St. | 215/426–4990 | fax 215/426–9122 | Free | Daily 10–6.

The Gallery. With more than 170 shops and 40 eateries, this mall is one of the nation's largest shopping centers. The complex spans four city blocks and is four levels high. | 901 E. Market St. | 215/925–7162 | Mon.–Sat. 10–7, Sun. 12–5.

Italian Market. The country's largest outdoor market has fresh produce, meats, and dry goods. You can get a behind-the-scenes tour to find out how it all comes together. | 9th and Wharton Sts. to 9th and Catherine St. | 215/592–1295 | Daily.

Jeweler's Row. The nation's second largest jewelry district has more than 50 dealers and America's oldest diamond district (est. 1851). Everything's here, from one-of-a-kind art pieces to costume jewelry. | Sansom St. between 7th and 8th, and on 8th St. between Chestnut and Walnut Sts. | 215/627–5284 | Mon.–Thurs. 10–6, Fri.–Sat. 9–7, Sun. 12–4.

Shops at the Bellevue. Restaurants and unique shops keep company in this landmark hotel. The structure is split in two with the Shops at the Bellevue and Downstairs at the Bellevue. | Broad and Walnut Sts. | 215/875–8350 | Mon.–Sat. 10–6, closed Sun.

South St. More than 75 restaurants, 150 stores, theaters, and nightclubs make this street the entertainment and nightlife capital of Philadelphia. People-watching here is as fun as window-shopping. | South St. between Front and 8th Sts. | 215/875–8350 | Daily 9 AM–2 AM.

SIGHTSEEING TOURS

American Trolley Tours. An authentic trolley bus is the platform for narrated area tours, which depart every 45 min from local hotels and the Visitor Center. | 215/333–2119 | $14 | Daily 9:45–3:45.

Chef's Tour of the Italian Market. Food and culture fans visit one of the country's oldest outdoor ethnic markets on this tour and learn about the roots and legends of Italian cooking—such as why southern Italians cook red sauce and northern Italians cook white sauce. You can also see the street Sylvester Stallone made famous in the movie *Rocky*. | 1817 Addison St. | 215/772–0739 | fax 215/772–0739 | $30 | Daily, 9:30 AM and 2 PM.

Ghost Tour of Philadelphia. This candlelit 1½-hour walk takes in said-to-be-haunted Philadelphia and regales you with chilling tales and legends. | 5th and Chestnut Sts. | 215/413–1997 | www.ghosttour.com | $10 | April–Oct., daily 7:30 PM.

Philadelphia Carriage Company. A private horse-drawn carriage takes you through Philadelphia's National Historic Park, Society Hill, and Old City for anywhere from 20 min to an hour. | 500 N. 13th St. | 215/925–TOUR | $20–$60 | Daily 10–6.

SPECTATOR SPORTS

Philadelphia Eagles. A member of the National Football League's Eastern Conference, the Eagles have been a part of the league since 1933. The team played in Super Bowl XV in the Pontiac Super Dome in 1981, where they lost to the Oakland Raiders. | 3501 S. Broad St. | 215/463–2500 | www.eaglesnest.com.

Philadelphia Flyers. One of the original members of the National Hockey League, the Flyers play in the league's Eastern Conference's Atlantic Division. The Flyers play their home games at the First Union Center and won a Stanley Cup in 1974. | 3601 S. Broad St. | 215/465–2000 | www.philadelphiaflyers.com.

Philadelphia Phantoms. Minor league affiliate of the Philadelphia Flyers and winner of the Calder Cup, this team was American Hockey League Champion for two years. | 1 Corestates Complex | 215/465–4522 | fax 215/952–5245 | www.phantomshockey.com | $8–$17 | Oct.–Apr.

Philadelphia Phillies. The Phillies are the city's second major-league baseball team (the Athletics, now on the west coast, were the first). The Phillies play their games in Veterans Stadium as part of baseball's National League East division. The team last won a World Series in 1980 with the help of Hall-of-Famers Steve Carlton and Mike Schmidt. | 3501 S. Broad St. | 215/463–6000 | fax 215/463–9878 | www.phillies.com.

Philadelphia 76ers. In 1966 Philadelphia welcomed a professional basketball team from Syracuse and changed their name to the 76ers. The organization plays its home games at the First Union Center and has had Hall-of-Famers Julius Erving, Wilt Chamberlain, and Bobby Jones play for them. Among the team's most famous accomplishments were Chamberlain's 100-point game and its championship wins in 1967 and 1983. | 3601 S. Broad St. | 215/339–7676 | www.nba.com/sixers.

OTHER POINTS OF INTEREST

Eastern State Penitentiary. During the 1820s social thinking postulated that solitary confinement was the way to rehabilitate criminals. This penitentiary was constructed at that time, with skylit vaulted ceilings. Some of the country's most notorious criminals spent time here, including Al Capone and Willie Sutton. It was abandoned in 1971. | 22nd St. and Fairmount Ave. | 215/236–3300 | fax 215/564–7926 | www.easternstate.com | $7 | May, weekends 10–5, closed weekdays; June–Aug., Wed.–Sun. 10–5, closed Mon.–Tues.; Sept.–Oct., weekends 10–5, closed weekdays.

Independence Brewing Company. This 32,000-square-ft brewery uses traditional recipes for its ales and lagers. You can view its 4-vessel, 40-barrel, stainless-steel system in operation. | 1000 E. Comly St. | 215/537–2337 | fax 215/537–4677 | Free | Sat. noon and 2 PM, closed Sun.–Fri.

Pennsylvania Hospital. This is the nation's first hospital, founded in 1751 by Benjamin Franklin and Dr. Thomas Bond. You can see the Pine Building, a cornerstone inscribed by

Franklin, a medical library founded in 1762, and North America's oldest surgical amphitheater for medical students. It also has a painting of Benjamin West, a museum dedicated to the history of nursing, and a medicinal garden. | 800 Spruce St. | 215/829–3971 | www.pahosp.com | Free | Weekdays 9–4:30, closed weekends.

Poor Henry's American Street Brew Pub. This Ortlieb brewery was built in 1869. You can see an Ortlieb family brewmaster as he brews and bottles lager and ales from generations-old recipes. | 829 N. American St. | 215/413–3500 | www.poorhenrys.com | Free | Mon.–Thurs. 11 AM–midnight PM, Fri.–Sun. 12–2 AM.

★ **Reading Terminal Market.** The market is nothing short of a historical treasure and a food heaven. One floor beneath the former Reading Railroad's 1891 train shed, the sprawling market has more than 80 food stalls and other shops. Some stalls change daily, offering items from hooked rugs and handmade jewelry to South American and African crafts. From Wednesday through Saturday the Amish from Lancaster County cart in their goodies, including Lebanon bologna, shoofly pie, and scrapple. If you want to cook, you can buy a large variety of fresh food from fruit and vegetable stands, butchers, fish stores, and Pennsylvania Dutch markets. The entire building is a National Historic Landmark, and the train shed is a National Engineering Landmark. | 12th and Filbert Sts. | 215/922–2317 | Closed Sun.

Sesame Place. The popular kid's morning show comes alive with Elmo, Big Bird, Bert, Ernie, and all the other popular characters at this amusement park loaded with water slides, pools, and other watery features. You can also find live shows, a roller coaster, a ball crawl, and other games. Count on spending a day and bring towels. | Oxford Valley Rd., Langhorne | 215/752–7070 or 800/ADVENTURE | www.sesameplace.com | $32 | May–Oct., daily 10–7.

U.S. Mint. The country's first mint, built in 1792, was two blocks from this structure. The Philadelphia Mint has the capacity to produce 1.8 million coins an hour, 32 million coins a day, and 13.5 billion coins a year. Besides coins it produces the Bronze Stars and Purple Hearts awarded to military heroes. The Philadelphia Mint is the largest mint in the world. | 151 N. Independence Mall E | 215/597–7350 | www.usmint.gov | Free | Weekdays 9–4:30, closed weekends.

ON THE CALENDAR

JAN.: *Mummers Parade.* The extravaganza goes on all day long in this New Year's Day gathering of costumed string bands, elaborate fancy brigades, and squads of comics in a parade down Broad Street. | 215/636–1666.

MAR.: *The Book and the Cook.* Nationally known cookbook authors get together with the finest chefs at restaurants across the city to create special meals. | 215/686–3662.

MAR.: *Philadelphia Flower Show.* Roam 10 acres of blooming gardens at the Pennsylvania Convention Center, home of this oldest and largest indoor flower show in the world. Join 250,000 international attendees in viewing professional displays of specimen plants, topiary, flower arrangements, and miniature garden scenes. It's possible to enter an exhibit of your own in any of 500+ artistic and horticultural classes, including rare plant specimens, Bonsai, roses, and orchids. You can also shop the Garden Marketplace with 130 vendors. | 215/988–8899.

APR.:–MAY: *Philadelphia Open House.* Some 150 Philadelphians open up their homes and gardens for tours, which usually include lunch, candlelight dinner, or high tea. | 215/928–1188.

MAY: *Devon Horse Show.* One of the nation's top equestrian events is held at the Horse Show Grounds in Devon on Memorial Day weekend. The show has more than 1,200 horses in competition, an antique carriage drive, and a country fair. | 610/964–0550.

MAY: *Philadelphia Festival of World Cinema.* This festival showcases independent and foreign films. | Prince Theater, 1412 Chestnut St., and other locations | 215/895–6593.

JUNE: *Elfreth's Alley Fete Days.* A celebration of Elfreth's Alley, the nation's oldest continuously occupied street, has food, entertainment, house tours, and demonstrations of Colonial crafts. | 215/574–0567.

JUNE: *First Union U.S. Pro Cycling Championship.* This 156-mile race is the nation's longest and highest-paying single-day cycling event. It begins and ends at the Benjamin Franklin Parkway. | 215/636–1666.

JUNE–AUG.: *Head House Open Air Craft Market.* Crafts and artwork are displayed and sold. | Head House Sq., Pine and 2nd Sts.

JUNE–SEPT.: *Mann Music Center.* The Philadelphia Orchestra and national pop and rock acts perform throughout the warm-weather months at this outdoor stage. | 52nd St. and Parkside Ave. | 215/567–0707.

JULY–AUG.: *Robin Hood Dell East.* Nationally known rhythm and blues, soul, and jazz acts perform at this open-air theater. | 33rd and Dauphin Sts. | 215/477–8810.

SEPT.: *Fringe Festival.* Modeled on Edinburgh's fringe festival, this Old City event showcases dozens of "the next wave" of performance artists, theater troupes, and dance companies. | 215/413–1318.

SEPT.:–JUNE: *Pennsylvania Ballet.* One of the nation's leading companies performs classic repertoire, including a holiday run of *The Nutcracker*. | Merriam Theater (250 S. Broad St.); Academy of Music (Broad and Locust Sts.) | 215/551–7000 | www.paballet.org.

SEPT.:–JUNE: *Philadelphia Orchestra.* The city's world-class orchestra performs a full season of classical music. | Academy of Music (Broad and Locust Sts. | 215/893–1900 | www.philorch.org.

OCT.:–APR.: *Opera Company of Philadelphia.* The city's leading opera company performs works from the classic repertoire. | Academy of Music (Broad and Locust Sts.) | 215/928–2100 | www.operaphilly.com.

NOV.: *Thanksgiving Day Parade.* This event ushers in the holiday season with giant floats and an appearance by Santa Claus. | 215/636–1666.

DEC.: *Fairmount Park Historical Christmas Tours.* The 18th-century mansions of Fairmount Park are decorated with period trimmings for these seasonal tours. | 215/684–7922.

Dining

INEXPENSIVE

Corned Beef Academy. Delicatessen. In the heart of restaurant row on Walnut Street, blond tables and chairs flank a counter filled with fresh home-cooked meats. This contemporary deli is a simple yet delicious alternative to more crowded eateries in the area. Sandwiches include the hand-carved turkey and fresh-cooked corned beef. | 1605 Walnut St. | 215/561–6222 | Reservations not accepted | Closed Sun. No supper | $5–$8 | AE, D, DC, MC, V.

Daēhlak. Ethiopian. You'll eat in the traditional Ethiopian manner with an injera, a large crepe that serves as both plate and spoon, surrounded by photographic posters of Ethiopia and traditional woven blankets. The restaurant has a large vegetarian menu and many lamb dishes. | 4708 Baltimore Ave. | 215/726–6464 | Reservations essential | $7–$11 | MC, V.

Elephant and Castle. English. Complete with wood-beamed walls, ceilings, and fireplace, it's a bit of London in Philadelphia. Traditional English food abounds, such as bangers and mash or shepherd's pie. A patio has open-air dining. Sun. brunch. | 1800 Market St. | 215/751–9977 | $9–$14 | AE, DC, MC, V.

Fisher's Seafood House. Seafood. This casual restaurant has two separate dining rooms and a sports bar. You might want to try the broiled and fried seafood combination. Kids' menu. | 7312 Castor Ave. | 215/725–6201 | Closed Sun., Mon. | $10–$12 | D, MC, V.

Isabella's. Contemporary. This quaint restaurant displays original artwork by Carmelo Adamo. The small bar adds to the coziness. Kids' menu. | 6516 Castor Ave. | 215/533–0356 | Reservations essential | Jacket required | Closed Mon. | $10–$20 | AE, DC, MC, V.

Jamaican Jerk Hut. Jamaican. A small storefront with limited seating, the "hut" has Jamaican oil paintings on its walls, and a bamboo curtain in front of the kitchen area. It's known for Jamaican curries and jerk dishes. You can eat out on the patio if you like. BYOB. | 1436 South St. | 215/545–8644 | $8–$20 | AE, D, MC, V.

Maccabbean. Israeli. Glatt Kosher food is served here in a space with an open kitchen. An individual with specialized training and credentials oversees the entire operation. The menu includes Israeli and Middle Eastern dishes, such as baba ghanoush and shawarma, sliced turkey off a rotisserie skewer. BYOB. | 128 S. 12th St. | 215/922–5922 | Closed Sat. No supper Fri. | $8–$20 | AE, D, MC, V.

New Mexico Grille. Southwestern. The brick walls, peppers, and huge cacti evoke New Mexico at this restaurant known for its grilled meats and seafood. | 50 S. 2nd St. | 215/922–7061 | $10–$20 | AE, DC, MC, V.

Pietro's Coal Oven Pizzeria. Italian. An offshoot of Patsy Grimaldi's pizza place in New York City, this pizzeria cooks its pies in coal-fired ovens. Corinthian columns and Roman murals surround you, and the ceiling is pressed tin. | 1714 Walnut St. | 215/735–8090 | $8–$19 | AE, D, DC, MC, V.

Rangoon. Burmese. Rangoon is the area's only Burmese restaurant and has Burmese artifacts and memorabilia. Specialties include chili shrimp and basil chicken with a tamarind fish sauce. No smoking. | 112 N. 9th St. | 215/829–8939 | Reservations not accepted | $9–$17 | MC, V.

River City Diner. American/Casual. Its sign reads "The Diner of Tomorrow." Of course, this is the "tomorrow" envisioned in the '50s, with stainless steel and lavender-and-turquoise neon lights. Deep fried calamari is one of the appetizers; daily blue plate specials head the entrees. Kids' menu. | 3720 Main St., Manayunk | 215/483–7500 | Reservations not accepted | $6–$15 | AE, D, DC, MC, V.

Samuel Adams Brew House. American/Casual. This was Philadelphia's first brewpub after Prohibition. It has a dart board, jukebox, pool tables, and two wraparound booths. The bar is small but cozy. The smoked fish platter is the order of choice. Live music, various bands, Thurs.–Sat. Kids' menu. | 1516 Sansom St. | 215/563–2326 | Closed Sun. | $7–$16 | AE, DC, MC, V.

Santa Fe Burrito. Mexican. Strings of dried peppers, ropes of dried corn, and New Mexican and Mexican crafts create a Southwestern style. Among the specialties are burritos and nachos, and there's a taco bar. Open-air dining is available streetside. BYOB. No smoking. | 227 S. 20th St. | 215/563–4468 | Reservations not accepted | $6–$10 | No credit cards.

Tony Luke's. American. There are few frills at this restaurant, although the outdoor patio is enclosed and heated in winter. But the portions are huge. Try the Steak Italian sandwich, a cheesesteak with broccoli rabe and sharp provolone, and the Italian pork sandwich. No alcohol. | 39 E. Oregon Ave. | 215/551–5725 | www.tonylukes.com | Reservations not accepted | $2–$7 | No credit cards.

MODERATE

Abbey Grill. Continental. In the Radnor Hotel, the Abbey Grill overlooks a formal garden and the interior follows suit with fresh flowers and bright colors. The restaurant is very good at making beef and seafood, especially dishes like the grilled gulf shrimp with mango pineapple cream sauce or the sauteed petit crab cakes with spicy Old Bay marinade. You can eat out on the patio overlooking the garden. Salad bar. Live music Fri. Kids' menu. Buffet (lunch). Sun. brunch. | 591 E. Lancaster Ave. | 610/341–3165 | $11–$25 | AE, D, DC, MC, V.

Arroyo Grille. Southwestern. Multicolored painted walls, lizard-shaped door handles, and plastic potted cacti make you feel like you're in a cantina at this faux adobe structure. Specialties include fried oyster nachos on blue chips as an appetizer, and the chicken fajitas for dinner. Open-air dining is on a pair of decks with views of the Schuylkill River. Live music Wed.–Sun. Kids' menu. Sun. brunch. | 1 Leverington Ave., Manayunk | 215/487–1400 | $16–$24 | AE, D, MC, V.

Azafran. Eclectic. This former storefront is now a traditional South American restaurant, with large colorful paintings, saffron-colored walls, handmade Mexican tiles, hand-painted tables, and a unique beehive oven and open kitchen. The flavors of Venezuela, Columbia, and Cuba come through in the food. The eatery is best known for its paella, but you might also try the mixed grill, which has lamb, pork, steak, and chorizo served on a wooden cutting board with traditional relishes, black beans, rice, and plantains. BYOB. No smoking. | 617 S. 3rd St. | 215/928–4019 | Reservations not accepted | No lunch | $10–$20 | AE, D, DC, MC, V.

Berlengas. Portuguese. There are two distinct dining areas: upstairs is less formal, a hangout with Portuguese neighbors gathering to talk; downstairs is more formal with wrought-iron accents and wine displays. Cancarne alentejana, pork cubes served with potatoes and clams, is a specialty of the house. | 4926 N. 5th St. | 215/324–3240 | Reservations essential | Jacket required | Closed Wed. | $10–$25 | MC, V.

Bistro Romano. Italian. The cellar of an 18th-century granary is a large space, but the tasteful Italian touches and soft piano music help make it romantic and a favorite destination for Philadelphians going out on the town. Kids' menu. Mystery Dinner Theater Fri.–Sat. | 120 Lombard St. | 215/925–8880 | No lunch | $10–$24; $35 show | AE, D, DC, MC, V.

Bridget Foy's South Street Grill. American. You can people-watch on the deck overlooking South Street, one of Philadelphia's most active, or dine inside, where walls are stylishly, starkly paneled. A house specialty is the java joint pork loin, a tenderloin with spiced marinade and papaya black bean salsa. Sun. brunch. | 200 South St. | 215/922–1813 | $12–$24 | AE, D, DC, MC, V.

Cafe Flower Shop. American. Flowers and plants are actually for sale in this shop, where the menu of homestyle cuisine and fresh seafood changes daily. Sun. brunch. BYOB. No smoking | 2501 Meredith St. | 215/232–1976 | $13–$21 | MC, V.

Coyote Crossing. Southwestern. During the day the restaurant lights up naturally via skylights in its cathedral ceiling, and at night traditional southwestern glassware and lighted plants magnify the artificial light. Both fajitas and daily fish specials can be had here. | 800 Spring Mill Ave., Conshohocken | 610/825–3000 | fax 610/828–4015 | No lunch weekends | $13–$22 | AE, D, DC, MC, V.

Dickens Inn. English. Styled after an old English pub with Dickens-related decorations, this restaurant has four bars specializing in ales and lagers to help you wash down the hearty English fare. Menu choices include roast beef with Yorkshire pudding and beef Wellington. Kids' menu. Sun. brunch. | 421 S. 2nd | 215/928–9307 | Closed Mon. | $13–$24 | AE, D, DC, MC, V.

Dinardo's Famous Crab. Seafood. It may be housed in an 18th-century building, but there's no Colonial bric-a-brac at Dinardo's—here it's all about the crab: Fishing lures and artwork designed around lures are everywhere. Unlike most local seafood places, the crabs are flown in from the Gulf of Mexico rather than from nearby Chesapeake Bay; the thinking is that Gulf crabs are meatier. The special sauce and large portions are legendary in Philadelphia. Kids' menu. | 312 Race St. | 215/925–5115 | No lunch Sun. | $13–$26 | AE, DC, MC, V.

Dmitri's. Mediterranean. A no-frills restaurant that has an extremely loyal following, Dmitri's regulars order dinner to go—it's just that crowded here. Each seafood item is prepared simply, often on an iron grill. All dishes come with escarole and wild rice. | 795 S. 3rd St. | 215/625–0556 | Reservations not accepted | No lunch | $12–$25 | No credit cards.

Ho Sai Gai. Chinese. A large photograph of the Chinese countryside and traditional Chinese artwork embellishes this popular Philadelphia restaurant, where Mandarin and Hunan cuisine are the specialties. | 1000 Race St. | 215/922–5883 | $15–$25 | AE, MC, V.

Jake & Oliver's House of Brews. Contemporary. Formerly a bank, then a church, this building is now a restaurant with an upstairs disco. A mural of blue skies and wheat fields presides over a serious beer selection: more than 60 kinds are available. The menu has pizza, generously sized steaks, and beer-battered cod filets. Kids' menu. | 22 S. 3rd St. | 215/627–4285 | $20 | AE, DC, MC, V.

Knave of Hearts. Continental. Simple, stylish, and warm, this is a nice romantic spot for supper. Entrees include filet mignon and roast duckling. Sun. brunch. | 230 South St. | 215/922–3956 | $15–$25 | AE, MC, V.

Meiji-En. Japanese. An indoor waterfall and a garden with a view of the Delaware River characterize this Asian favorite, which serves sushi, tempura, and teppanyaki-grilled items. Live music, jazz, Sat.–Sun. Sun. brunch. | 325 N. Columbus Blvd. | 215/592–7100 | Reservations essential | $15–$30 | AE, D, DC, MC, V.

Michael's Ristorante. Italian. A long oak bar greets you at this eatery, where you can sample homemade gnocchi or sea bass on a bed of lentils. Kids' menu. | 824 S. 8th St. | 215/922–3986 | Closed Mon., No lunch Sun. | $12–$25 | AE, D, DC, MC, V.

Pompano Grille. Caribbean. A Caribbean theme dominates with bright colors and a rum bar. At night, the rooftop decks are transformed into a nightclub. The specialty here is seafood. Live music, jazz, Fri., Sat. | 701 E. Passyunk Ave. | 215/923–7676 | fax 215/923–7348 | No lunch | $13–$22 | AE, D, DC, MC, V.

The Restaurant School. Continental. A culinary academy has to give its students a chance to practice, so this one opened several attached restaurants that are open to the public. You have your choice of several different themed restaurants to eat in. The School is best known for its baked goods. | 4207 Walnut St. | 215/222–4200 | www.therestaurantschool.com | Reservations essential | Jacket and tie | Closed Sun., Mon. and during student breaks | $15–$35 | AE, D, DC, MC, V.

Shiroi Hana. Japanese. This local hangout for businesspeople has photographs of Japanese landscapes on the walls and an extensive Japanese menu. You can choose sushi, tempura, sukiyaki, or other traditional favorites. Sushi bar. No smoking. | 222 S. 15th St. | 215/735–4444 | Reservations essential | No lunch Sat.–Sun. | $13–$25 | AE, D, DC, MC, V.

Sonoma. Continental. A wood burning oven and herb garden enhance the California style of this restaurant. Unusual menu items include honey-lavender salmon and secret roasted chicken, served with garlic mashed potatoes and broccoli rabe. The creme brûlée is a standout. The bar in the upstairs greenhouse is stocked with over 180 types of vodka. You can enjoy open-air dining in a garden courtyard. Kids' menu, early-bird suppers. Sun. brunch. | 4411 Main St., Manayunk | 215/483–9400 | $9–$22 | AE, D, DC, MC, V.

U.S. Hotel Bar and Grill. Continental. Original tiles and ceiling and a 30-foot mahogany bar set the scene in this 1903 restaurant, a favorite of Philadelphia's business crowd. It can be noisy but the steaks, pasta, or sauteed jumbo lump crab cakes are worth the noise. | 4439 Main St. | 215/483–9222 | $13–$23 | AE, D, DC, MC, V.

Vega Grill. Latin. Vivid southwestern colors bring this small smoke-free room to life. Try the quesadillas or the Chilean sea bass over boniato (sweet potatoes) with mushroom tamarind sauce. You can eat out on the patio in fine weather. Kids' menu. Sun. brunch. No reservations are accepted on Saturday. | 4141 Main St., Manayunk | 215/487–9600 | No lunch | $10–$20 | AE, DC, MC, V.

Victor Cafe. Italian. Opera memorabilia covers the walls in this restaurant in two townhouses, and many of the servers are opera students, who serenade you with great arias while you eat. A featured entrée is the Pearl Fisher linguine, linguine with lobster and shrimp in a champagne bisque sauce. Live music, opera, daily. No smoking. Parking (fee). | 1303 Dickenson St. | 215/468–3040 | Reservations essential | No lunch | $11–$21 | AE, DC, MC, V.

White Dog Cafe. Contemporary. Its deep wood grains, piano, and silk tapestries contribute to the experience in this restaurant known for its innovative cuisine and seasonal menu. There are tables outside as well as inside. Live music Wed.–Sun. Kids' menu. Sun. brunch. | 3420 Sansom St. | 215/386–9224 | $16–$24 | AE, D, DC, MC, V.

Zócalo. Mexican. Simple chairs and tables, offset by unique artwork infused with the colors of Mexico, create a charming interior for Zócalo's main attraction, its food. If you're adventurous, try the "Shrimp from Hell," head-on shrimp in a habanero butter sauce. Happy Hour Mon.–Sat. There's a patio for open-air dining. Smoking permitted at bar area only. | 3600 Lancaster Ave. | 215/895–0139 | No lunch weekends | $10–$20 | AE, D, DC, MC, V.

Zorba's. Greek. This restaurant serves ample portions of traditional Greek food, surrounded by fanciful murals of the stunning blue sky and water of a Greek island. It's across the street from the Quaker Landmark Prison. Gyros are a specialty. BYOB. | 2230 Fairmount Ave. | 215/978–5990 | Closed Mon. No lunch | $13–$20 | MC, V.

EXPENSIVE

Le Bar Lyonnaise. French. At this before- and after-theater spot downstairs from Le Bec-Fin, you can taste George Perrier's cuisine. The bookshelves and the antique oil paintings on the walls provide a sense of a French bistro. If you like seafood, try the black sea bass with oriental sauce or the galette de crabe, the signature crabcakes. | 1523 Walnut St. | 215/567–1000 | Reservations not accepted | Closed Sun. No lunch Sat. | $10–$26 | AE, D, DC, MC, V.

Bookbinder's 15th Street Seafood House. Contemporary. 106 years old, Bookbinder's looks like other fish places with its plain dark wooden floors, lobsters on the walls, and fishing nets, but decorative objects also recall the life of the Bookbinder family and the many famous people who have eaten here. The menu includes lobster, crab cakes, and, for dessert, homemade peanut butter pie. Kids' menu. | 215 S. 15th St. | 215/545–1137 | No lunch weekends | $18–$40 | AE, D, DC, MC, V.

Ciboulette. French. This restaurant sits on the second floor of the Park Hyatt at the Bellevue, amid grand staircases and ornate ceilings. Chef Lim's delectable appetizers include cauliflower soup and oysters in champagne and butter. Other offerings are mackerel tartare with a lemon-tinged olive oil and salmon caviar, and breast of duck with a sauce made of orange juice, stock, and green peppercorns. | 200 S. Broad St. | 215/790–1210 | fax 215/790–1209 | Reservations essential | Jacket and tie | Lunch Tues.–Fri. Noon–2PM; Dinner 5:30–9 Mon.–Thurs.; Dinner 5:30–10:30 Fri. and Sat. Closed Sun. No lunch Mon. | $20–$30 | AE, MC, V.

Circa. Contemporary. In this former bank building, traditional chandeliers hang from the high ceiling; the best tables are downstairs in the vault. Menu choices include Moroccan lamb sirloin, lamb with grilled fennel and tomato and chick pea puree, or the onion crusted mahi-mahi with a mustard aioli. After dinner the restaurant becomes a nightclub. | 1518 Walnut St. | 215/545–6800 | Reservations essential | No lunch Mon., weekends | $16–$27 | AE, DC, MC, V.

City Tavern. American. The signers of the Declaration of Independence are said to have stopped in this restored Colonial tavern. Food is served on china authentic to the period in 10 dining rooms. Try the Tavern lobster pie, a pie shell with lobster, scallops, and shrimp topped with a puff pastry. Kids' menu. You can eat outside on the patio. Live music Fri., Sat. | 138 S. 2nd St. | 215/413–1443 | $17–$40 | AE, D, DC, MC, V.

Cuvee Notredame. Belgian. White linen, Belgian fixtures, and photographs of life in Belgium fill this restaurant. Try the traditional mussels with pommes frites, the bouillabaisse, or the duck Chambord. Sun. brunch. | 1701 Green St. | 215/765–2777 | $16–$22 | AE, D, DC, MC, V.

Dock Street Brewery. American/Casual. Pride of place in this eatery goes to the brewery tanks. You can eat in comfortable leather booths or at tables, and there are homemade breads and grilled meats and fish. Live music, jazz, Wed., Fri. | 2 Logan Sq | 215/496–0413 | fax 215/496–0423 | $18–$30 | AE, D, DC, MC, V.

The Garden. Continental. Floral designs and fresh flowers set the scene in this vintage townhouse, with views of a garden. You can eat inside or, in season, outdoors, to munch Dover sole or soft shell crabs. Kids' menu, pre-theater menu. Valet parking (fee). | 1617 Spruce St. | 215/546–4455 | Closed Sun. No lunch Mon., Sat. | $20–$35 | AE, D, DC, MC, V.

Kansas City Prime. Steak. Soft colors lend a calm feeling to this Japanese-influenced steak house, which can be helpful when you see the Kobe steak on the menu for $100. The rest of the menu is more reasonably priced, with items such as grilled garlic veal chops and grilled tuna steak with your choice of sauces. Valet parking (fee). | 4417 Main St., Manayunk | 215/482–3700 | No lunch | $20–$35 | AE, D, DC, MC, V.

The Marker. Contemporary. This eatery is a popular after-work destination for business-people. The sauteed jumbo lump crab cakes are a favorite, as are the pecan and rosemary crusted baby rack of lamb. Live music, pianist. Sun. brunch. | 4000 City Ave. | 215/581–5010 | No lunch Sat. | $20–$30 | AE, D, DC, MC, V.

Opus 251. Continental. The Philadelphia Art Alliance has this gracious dining room with a terrace overlooking a traditional European garden. The seasonal menu varies depending on when you visit, but you can always choose from favorites such as wood-grilled Angus beef and homemade sausage. Baked goods and ice cream are made on the premises. Open-air dining is available on the terrace. Sun. brunch. | 251 S. 18th St. | 215/735–6787 | Reservations essential | $19–$28 | AE, DC, MC, V.

★ **Overtures.** Contemporary. This restaurant has oversized tiles on the floor, an antique walnut bar, and 19th-century European artwork on the walls. On the menu: crab cakes in lobster bisque, smoked pheasant salad with walnut-sherry dressing, ravioli with savory shrimp, and desserts such as lemon tarts and flan. | 609 E. Passyunk Ave. | 215/627–3455 | Closed Mon. No lunch | $20–$30 | AE, DC, MC, V.

Ristorante Panorama. Italian. This bustling trattoria with murals of the Delaware River and exposed brick walls claims to have the largest wine bar in the country—some 120 wines are served by the glass. Dinner options are the pasta misto trio, a homemade lobster ravioli, homemade gnocchi with a fontina sauce, and penne arrabiata, or grilled calamari with virgin olive oil and lemon. Kids' menu. | Front and Market Sts. | 215/922–7800 | Reservations essential | No lunch Sat., Sun. | $15–$30 | AE, DC, MC, V.

Rococo. Continental. In the former Corn Exchange Bank building, this restaurant is divided into little sections, including a large dining room and cigar lounge. Specials include jumbo lump crab cakes and fire-grilled filet mignon. | 123 Chestnut St. | 215/629–1100 | No lunch | $18–$29 | AE, DC, MC, V.

★ **Susanna Foo.** Chinese. Chinese antiques arranged with flair distinguish this elegant two-story restaurant with refined and unusual cuisine. Try the lobster dumplings with emulsified coconut lobster sauce, an appetizer, and grilled wild striped bass with caramelized sweet and sour sauce, an entrée. No smoking. | 1512 Walnut St. | 215/545–2666 | Reservations essential | Jacket required | No lunch Sun. | $20–$34 | AE, DC, MC, V.

★ **Tequila's.** Mexican. As authentic a Mexican restaurant as you can find in Philadelphia— and the traditional furnishings are a fitting prelude to the excellent cuisine. Try the fowl in mole sauce, the chiles rellenos, or the pozole, a pork and hominy dish. | 1511 Locust St. | 215/546–0181 | Closed Sun. No lunch Sat. | $20–$35 | AE, DC, MC, V.

Treetops at the Rittenhouse. American. The large windows of this second-story eatery overlook the treetops of the nearby park here. The garlic-encrusted Chilean sea bass with roasted onion, one favorite, comes with purple mashed potatoes and baby vegetables. Kids' menu. Sun. brunch. Valet parking (fee). | 210 W. Rittenhouse Sq | 215/790–2533 | fax 215/546–9858 | Reservations essential | $20–$30 | AE, D, DC, MC, V.

Zanzibar Blue. Continental. Steps down from street level, pictures of greats who performed here adorn the walls of a room where you can hear some of today's best young jazz musicians. American seafood dishes like crab cakes and grilled fish make up most of the menu, but you can also get more exotic entrees like Moroccan spiced filet mignon or pollo pan-do, a West Indian curried chicken. Live music daily. | 200 S. Broad St. | 215/732–4500 | Reservations essential | No lunch | $17–$25 | AE, DC, MC, V.

VERY EXPENSIVE

★ **Le Bec-Fin.** French. Georges Perrier presides over this restaurant, one of the best in the country. The dining room is Louis XVI style with crystal chandeliers, red silk wallpaper, and gilt mirrors, and the fare is just as sumptuous—smoked salmon in pistachio crust, escargots in champagne and hazelnut sauce, and venison sauteed in caramelized chestnuts with cranberry relish. | 1523 Walnut St. | 215/567–1000 | www.lebecfin.com | Reservations essential | Jacket and tie | Closed Sun. No lunch Sat. | $120 prix fixe dinner, $38 prix fixe lunch |. AE, D, DC, MC, V.

★ **Brasserie Perrier.** Contemporary. The silver-leafed ceiling and dramatic lighting draw a smart crowd to this elegant restaurant, Georges Perrier's second Philadelphia operation after the ultra-posh Le Bec-Fin. Here French food reflects Asian and Italian culinary styles. Entrees include smoked salmon with potato pancakes and crème fraiche, and rack of lamb with sundried tomato pearl pasta and thyme jus. No smoking. | 1619 Walnut St. | 215/568–3000 | Reservations essential | Jacket required | $25–$40 | AE, D, DC, MC, V.

La Buca Ristorante. Italian. A long flight of stairs takes you down to this restaurant embellished with tapestries, ceramics, and Italian furnishings. Look for good seafood—langostini, whole red snapper, and shrimp. | 711 Locust St. | 215/928–0556 | Closed Sun. No lunch Sat. | $30–$40 | AE, DC, MC, V.

Deux Cheminées. French. Two adjoining brownstone townhouses designed by Frank Furness house this restaurant, a longtime local favorite. Antiques, oriental rugs, and six working fireplaces keep things cozy and romantic. Crab marguerite, a cream-based crab soup laced with scotch, and rack of lamb with a truffle sauce are two of signature dishes. Pre-theater menu. No smoking. | 1221 Locust St. | 215/790–0200 | Reservations essential | Jacket required | Closed Sun., Mon. No lunch | $55–$80; prix fixe | AE, DC, MC, V.

La Famiglia. Italian. In this anchor in Old City, marble covers nearly every surface: stairs, fireplaces, floors, walls, etc. The wine cellar is one of the largest on the East coast, with more than 11,000 bottles. Specials are the penne àla famiglia, with caramelized onions, prosciutto and Parmesan; and veal papa sena, veal picante, involtino, and capri served together on one plate. | 8 S. Front St. | 215/922–2803 | Reservations essential | Jacket required | Closed Mon. No lunch weekends | $25–$45, $20 prix fixe lunch | AE, DC, MC, V.

The Founders. French. If you want dinner with a view, head for the top floor of the Park Hyatt at the Bellevue. A 42-ft domed ceiling with stained glass panel provides the drama, while city views and candlelight provide the romance. Entrees include lobster Thermidor and roast veal over tricolor lentils with wild mushrooms. Jazz, weekends. Pre-theater menu. Sun. brunch. | 200 S. Broad St. | 215/790–2814 | fax 215/893–9865 | Reservations essential | Jacket required | $30–$35 | AE, D, DC, MC, V.

★ **Fountain Restaurant.** Continental. Decorations at the entrance of this lovely, polished restaurant in the Four Seasons Hotel change with the seasons. Try the rack of lamb, the sautéed snapper, or the venison medallions in red wine sauce. Save room for a lavish dessert. Entertainment. Kids' menu. Sun. brunch. | 1 Logan Sq | 215/963–1500 | Reservations essential | Jacket required | $28–$42; $80–$95 prix fixe | AE, D, DC, MC, V.

★ **Monte Carlo Living Room.** Northern Italian. High-backed chairs and mirrors enhance this large room. Upstairs, you can dance the night away in the building's nightclub. Downstairs, you can dine on veal loin medallions in Madeira foie gras sauce or Dover sole in white sauce. DJ Wed.–Sat. Parking (fee). | 150 South St. | 215/925–2220 | Reservations essential | Jacket required | No lunch | $30–$65 | AE, DC, MC, V.

Old Original Bookbinder's. Seafood. This famous restaurant is renowned in Philadelphia for its generous portions. It's a big draw for dignitaries, tourists, and locals, with the seals of the original 13 colonies adorning the walls. Seafood and steaks are the specialty here. Kids' menu. Valet parking (fee). | 125 Walnut St. | 215/925–7027 | No lunch weekends | $25–$40 | AE, D, DC, MC, V.

The Palm. Steak. Dark mahogany and pictures of celebrity patrons adorn the walls of this branch of the New York original. Most people come for the steak, but the lobster is famous as well. | 200 S. Broad St. | 215/546–7256 | No lunch weekends | $25–$35 | AE, DC, MC, V.

The Saloon Restaurant. Italian. Large portions of traditional Italian food are the norm at this classic spot in South Philadelphia, which is warm and romantic with its dark paneling. Locals prize the steaks. | 750 S. 7th St. | 215/627–1811 | Closed Sun. | $20–$40 | AE.

Serrano. Eclectic. This long-standing neighborhood diner is home to a music club, Tin Angel. Purple walls, burgundy drapes, and a fireplace create a little drama. The menu ranges from chicken Hungarian and Malaysian pork chops to Korean rolled bulgogi. Live music upstairs Wed.–Sat. | 20 S. 2nd St. | 215/928–0770 | Reservations essential | No lunch | $30–$40 | AE, D, DC, MC, V.

Spirit of Philadelphia. American. Travel down the Delaware River on this dinner-cruise ship while servers pay a musical tribute to Broadway. There's dancing on the deck after dinner. Seafood is the star of the menu. Live music, jazz daily. Sun. brunch. | Penn's Landing, Delaware and Market Sts. | 215/923–1419 | Reservations essential | Jacket and tie | $25–$45 | AE, D, DC, MC, V.

★ **Striped Bass.** Seafood. This former brokerage house is glamorous yet intimate with its 28-ft ceilings, marble columns, an open kitchen, and muslin-draped windows; a 16-ft sculpture of a leaping striped bass dominates the room. The menu changes weekly, but Chilean sea bass with braised corn, oven-dried tomatoes, and chorizo oil shows up regularly, along with salmon tartare with capers, dill, and dijon mustard. Sunday brunch, prix fixe lunch. | 1500 Walnut St. | 215/732–4444 | Reservations essential | No lunch Sat. | $18–$48, $26 prix fixe lunch | AE, D, DC, MC, V.

Swann Lounge and Cafe. Contemporary. This sedate, genteel space in the Four Seasons Hotel is great for late night brasserie-style dinners or for tea—when caviar is served, along with sandwiches and cakes. Open-air dining is available on a courtyard patio. Lunch buffet. Live music, jazz, weekends. Sun. brunch. Parking (fee). | 1 Logan Sq | 215/963–1500 | fax 215/963–9507 | $28–$42 | AE, DC, MC, V.

Lodging

INEXPENSIVE

Adam's Mark. Built in 1975, this large, 23-floor modern hotel has some rooms with views of the downtown skyline and others with a view of Fairmount Park. It's within walking distance of good shopping and restaurants, and within 6 mi of Center City and Manayunk. Restaurant, bar (with entertainment). In-room data ports, some refrigerators, cable TV. Indoor-outdoor pool. Beauty salon. Gym. Business services, airport shuttle. | 4000 City Ave. and Monument Rd. | 215/581–5000 or 800/444–2326 | fax 215/581–5069 | www.adamsmark.com | 515 rooms | $90–$195 | AE, D, DC, MC, V.

Anam Cara Bed and Breakfast. Floral-patterned rooms with lace curtains and queen-sized, antique beds, including a four-poster bed, are accompanied with plush towels, scented soaps, and fresh flowers in this B&B. You can have a cordial nightcap by the fireplace in the living room. Dining room, picnic area, complimentary breakfast. In-room data ports, cable TV, some room phones. Massage. No smoking. | 52 Wooddale Ave. | 215/242–4327 | www.anamcarabandb.com | 3 rooms | $90–$110 | D, MC, V.

Bed and Breakfast Man. Choose the fourth floor Italian-styled room for a view of the Philadelphia skyline or try the smaller Lowlands, with artwork and furnishings inspired by Belgium and the Netherlands. Downtown Philly is three blocks away. Full complimentary breakfast on weekends. Dining room, complimentary Continental breakfast. In-room data ports, cable TV, no room phones. No smoking. | 218 Fitzwater Street | 215/829–8951 | fax 215/829–0933 | http://www.bedandbreakfastman.com/ | 4 rooms | $85–$125 | AE, MC, V.

Best Western–Center City. This chain hotel has reasonable rates and a location less than four blocks from the museums on Benjamin Franklin Parkway. It's 2 mi from Center City attractions. Restaurant, bar. In-room data ports, cable TV. Exercise equipment. Pool. Business services, free parking. Pets allowed. | 501 N. 22nd St. | 215/568–8300 | fax 215/557–0259 | www.bestwesternpa.com | 183 rooms | $107–$154 | AE, D, DC, MC, V.

Best Western Hotel Philadelphia Northeast. This hotel is in the northeastern part of Philadelphia. It's 12 mi to historic Philadelphia, 8 mi to Sesame Place, and even closer to outlet shopping. You can walk from the hotel to area restaurants. Bar, picnic area, complimentary Continental breakfast. Cable TV. Pool. Exercise equipment. Playground. Laundry facilities. Business services. | 11580 Roosevelt Blvd. | 215/464–9500 | fax 215/464–8511 | 100 rooms | $99–$145 | AE, D, DC, MC, V.

A City Garden Bed and Breakfast. The lower-priced garden suite in this 1850 Greek Revival building has a private entrance in the courtyard garden, an eat-in kitchen, a black and white checkerboard couch, and a queen-size bed. Additionally, there's a 600-square-ft, high-ceiling Casablanca suite, which also has a private entrance, an eat-in kitchen, and queen-size bed, but adds a wicker double-bed futon. Both suites are available for extended stays at reduced rates. Complimentary Continental breakfast. Kitchenettes, cable TV. Laundry facilities. | 1103 Waverly Street | 215/625–2599 | 2 suites | $100–$140; 2–night minimum on weekends | AE, MC, V.

Clarion Suites Convention Center. The former Heywood Brothers Furniture Company has been transformed into a modern all-suites hotel in the heart of Chinatown. Boasting its original exposed brick walls and wood-beam cathedral ceilings, this hotel is within a block of the convention center, and eight blocks from the Liberty Bell. Complimentary Continental breakfast. In-room data ports, kitchenettes, cable TV. Gym. Business services. | 1010 Race St. | 215/922–1730 or 800/CLARION | fax 215/922–6258 | www.clarionsuitesphilly.com | 96 suites | $90–$185 suites | AE, D, DC, MC, V.

Comfort Inn. This motel is north of Philadelphia city limits, and 5 mi from the Northeast Philadelphia Airport. Bar (with entertainment), complimentary Continental breakfast. In-room data ports, some in-room hot tubs, cable TV. Exercise equipment. Laundry services. Business services. Pets allowed. | 3660 Street Rd., Bensalem | 215/245–0100 | fax 215/245–1851 | www.comfortinn.com | 141 rooms | $95–$160 | AE, D, DC, MC, V.

Comfort Inn Penn's Landing. Overlooking the Delaware River and the Philadelphia skyline, this 10-story hotel is a few blocks from the Liberty Bell, Betsy Ross House, and Penn's Landing. It's also 3 mi from Drexel University. Bar, complimentary Continental breakfast. In-room data ports, cable TV. Business services, airport shuttle. | 100 N. Christopher Columbus Blvd. | 215/627–7900 | fax 215/238–0809 | www.comfortinn.com | 185 rooms | $80–$160 | AE, D, DC, MC, V.

Doubletree Club Hotel. This 5-story hotel is north of Center City. You can get to the Glenford Mansion with a short walk, and 9 mi separate you from the Liberty Bell and the Franklin Institute. Restaurant, bar. In-room data ports, some refrigerators, cable TV. Indoor pool. Exercise equipment. Laundry facilities. Business services, free parking. | 9461 Roosevelt Blvd. | 215/671–9600 | fax 215/464–7759 | www.doubletree.com | 188 rooms | $89–$149 | AE, D, DC, MC, V.

Four Points Hotel Philadelphia Airport. This reasonably priced hotel has a convenient—and surprisingly quiet—location 5 min from Philadelphia International Airport. Built in 1986, this 5-story hotel is well appointed. Restaurant, bar, room service. In-room dataports, cable TV. Pool. Laundry facilities. Business services, airport shuttle, free parking. | 4101 Island Ave. | 215/492–0400 | fax 215/365–6035 | www.fourpoints.com | 177 rooms | $99–$179 | AE, D, DC, MC, V.

Gables Bed and Breakfast. This 1889 red-brick Queen Anne Victorian has a wrap-around porch and a perennial garden, with a large Norway maple, a blossoming dogwood, a Japanese cherry, a crab apple, and a magnolia tree. You can find a brass or wrought-iron bed along with oak, mahogany, and walnut furnishings in most rooms. Dining room, complimentary Continental breakfast. Cable TV. No kids under 6. No smoking. | 4520 Chester Ave. | 215/662–1918 | www.gablesbb.com/ | 10 rooms (some with shared bath) | $80–$115 | AE, D, MC, V.

Holiday Inn Express Midtown. The contemporary rooms are larger-than-average here, and the location is two blocks from the Merriam Theater, shopping, restaurants, and the subway. Complimentary Continental breakfast. In-room data ports, cable TV. Pool. Business services, free parking. | 1305 Walnut St. | 215/735–9300 | fax 215/732–2682 | www.holiday-inn.com | 166 rooms | $105–$165 | AE, D, DC, MC, V.

Holiday Inn–Independence Mall. The Colonial-style rooms at this hotel reflect its prime location next to Independence National Historical Park. The hotel was renovated in 1999 and is a short walk from the Liberty Bell, Penn's Landing, Gallery mall, and many restaurants. Restaurant, bar, dining room, room service. Cable TV. Pool. Exercise Equipment. Laundry facilities. Business services. | 400 Arch St. | 215/923–8660 | fax 215/923–4633 | www.holiday-inn.com | 364 rooms | $95–$175 | AE, D, DC, MC, V.

La Reserve. This small inn has a classic 19th-century French and English style. It's right in the heart of Rittenhouse Square. In warm weather, you can relax in the private garden. Complimentary breakfast. No room phones, TV in common area. Business services. No smoking. | 1804 Pine St. | 215/735–1137 or 800/354–8401 | fax 215/735–0582 | www.centercitybed.com | 8 rooms (5 with shared bath), 3 suites | $70–$95, $110 suites | AE, MC, V.

Radisson-Northeast. This upscale hotel is north of the city, at Exit 24 of I-95. It's within 8 mi of Sesame Place and Bucks County. Restaurant, bar (with entertainment, room service. Some refrigerators, cable TV. Indoor-outdoor pool. Beauty salon. Laundry facilities. Business services. | 2400 Old Lincoln Hwy., Trevose | 215/638–8300 | fax 215/638–4377 | 282 rooms | $99–$149 | AE, D, DC, MC, V.

Rodeway Inn. This hotel has Colonial-style rooms in an 1890s building, with four-poster beds in each. It's within four blocks of the Pennsylvania Convention Center, restaurants, shopping, and Jeweler's Row. Complimentary Continental breakfast. In-room data ports, cable TV. Business services. | 1208 Walnut St. | 215/546–7000 or 800/887–1776 | fax 215/546–7573 | www.rodewayinn.com | 25 rooms (22 with shower only), 6 suites | $89–$125, $145–$195 suites | AE, D, DC, MC, V.

Sheraton Rittenhouse Square Hotel. The first "environmentally smart" facility from Starwood Hotels and Resorts Worldwide, this hotel has eco-friendly features such as fresh, filtered air, organic cotton linens, and a bamboo garden designed to oxygenate air in the lobby. The panoramic views of Rittenhouse Square and the city skyline are another draw. From here, you only have to take a quick walk to Restaurant Row and the Franklin Institute. Restaurants, bar, room service. In-room data ports, minibars, some refrigerators, cable TV. Massage. Gym. Business services. Pets allowed. | 227 S. 18th St. | 215/546–9400 or 800/854–8002 | www.sheratonphiladelphia.com | 193 rooms | $129–$200 | AE, D, DC, MC, V.

Shippen Way Inn. Two 18th-century houses have been restored into a charming period inn with a Colonial-style herb and rose garden. This bed-and-breakfast is a block away from South Street attractions, and five blocks from Penn's Landing. Complimentary Continental breakfast. Some room phones. TV in common area. | 416-418 Bainbridge St. | 215/627–7266 or 800/245–4873 | fax 215/627–7781 | 9 rooms | $90–$110 | AE, MC, V.

Silverstone Bed & Breakfast. Room looks vary from mint-colored walls, pink floral bedspreads, and large white-laced windows to blue and gold motifs with dark curtains. The backyard is home to both a kid's play area and an herb and vegetable garden. Dining room, complimentary breakfast. Cable TV, in-room VCRs (and movies). Laundry facilities. | 8840 Stenton Avenue | 215/242–1471 | fax 215/242–1471 | www.silverstonestay.com | 5 rooms | $60–$140 | AE, D, MC, V.

Spring Garden Manor. Rooms at this B&B have antique and restored furniture. You can choose the Ben Franklin room for its oval canopy bed, bay window, dining table, fireplace, and a local artist's large abstract painting of a sunset. The Falcon room has a four-post bed and private deck overlooking the Japanese garden and teahouse. Dining room, complimentary breakfast. In-room data ports, refrigerators, cable TV. No smoking. | 2025 Spring Garden St. | 215/567–2484 | fax 215/567–2484 | www.members.aol.com/naim43/springbb/spring1.htm | 3 rooms | $119–$149 | AE, DC, MC, V.

Spruce Hill Manor. In the deluxe suite, you can find a hand-carved walnut queen-size bed, an oversized dressing room, a large sitting room, and a bathroom with a hot tub, a shower for two, a pedestal sink, and stained glass windows. The double suite has a double bed with china lamps, oriental rugs, two lounge chairs, and a sofa. Dining room, complimentary breakfast. Kitchenettes, microwaves, refrigerators, some in-room hot tubs, cable TV, in-room VCRs (and movies). No kids under 10. | 331 South 46th St. | 215/472–2213 | fax 215/472–5885 | www.sprucehillmanor.com | 2 suites | $100–$125; 2–night minimum | AE, MC, V.

★ **Ten Eleven Clinton.** Built in 1836, this all-suites bed-and-breakfast spans two adjoining townhouses on one of the city's most charming blocks, within a mile of the city's cultural and historic areas. Complimentary Continental breakfast. Some kitchenettes, TV in common area. Business services. | 1011 Clinton St. | 215/923–8144 | fax 215/923–5757 | 1011@concentric.net | 8 suites | $125–$175 suites | AE, MC, V.

Thomas Bond House. Once the home of the cofounder of the nation's first hospital, this four-story, circa-1769 house has rooms with marble fireplaces and four-poster beds—and 20th-century hot tub baths. Many of the decorations are antiques. This inn is actually inside Independence National Historic Park. The Liberty Bell, as well as restaurants and shopping, are within easy walking distance. Complimentary Continental breakfast. Cable TV. Business services. No smoking. | 129 S. 2nd St. | 215/923–8523 or 800/845–2663 | www.winston-salem-inn.com/philadelphia | fax 215/923–8504 | 12 rooms | $95–$175 | AE, D, DC, MC, V.

MODERATE

Best Western Independence Park Hotel. Placed on the National Register of Historic Places, this building is a former dry goods warehouse dating to 1856. The hotel has high-ceiling rooms with Colonial-style touches and modern amenities. It's 8 mi to the airport and within half a block of Independence Park. Penn's Landing is less than four blocks away. Complimentary Continental breakfast. In-room data ports, cable TV. | 235 Chestnut St. | 215/922–4443 or 800/624–2988 | fax 215/922–4487 | www.bestwestern.com | 36 rooms | $135–$165 | AE, D, DC, MC, V.

Crowne Plaza–Center City. A former Holiday Inn has been renovated into an upscale property. Rooms have irons and ironing boards, coffee makers, and hair dryers. This hotel in the heart of downtown is less than 2 mi from Independence Mall, the Historic District, the Philadelphia Museum of Art, and Penn's Landing. Restaurant, bar. In-room data ports, cable TV. Pool. Exercise equipment. Laundry facilities. Business services, airport shuttle. | 1800 Market St. | 215/561–7500 | fax 215/561–4484 | www.holiday-inn.com | 445 rooms | $169–$230 | AE, D, DC, MC, V.

Embassy Suites Center City. Housed in an unusual, round 28-story tower, this hotel has modern, upscale suites. It's within a few blocks of the Academy of Natural Science, the "Please Touch" Museum, and the Rodin Museum. Restaurant, bar. In-room data ports, minibars, refrigerators, cable TV. Exercise equipment. Laundry service. Business services. | 1776 Benjamin Franklin Parkway. | 215/561–1776 or 800/EMBASSY | fax 215/963–0122. www.embassy-suites.com | 288 suites | $119–$249 suites | AE, D, DC, MC, V.

Hilton–Philadelphia Airport. This hotel has a unique pool just off the lobby. Many of the guest rooms are oversized. It's 1 mile to Philadelphia International Airport. Restaurant, bar, room service. In-room data ports, cable TV. Indoor pool. Hot tub. Exercise equipment. Laundry service. Business services, airport shuttle. Pets allowed. | 4509 Island Ave. | 215/365–4150 | fax 215/937–6382 | 330 rooms | $125–$205 | AE, D, DC, MC, V.

The Latham. This small, classic European-style hotel puts an emphasis on personal service. Wood paneling and floors, plus a crystal chandelier, add elegance to the lobby. It's within a block of Rittenhouse Square and four blocks of the theater district. Restaurant. In-room data ports, some minibars, cable TV. Pool. Exercise equipment. Business services. | 135 S. 17th St. | 215/563–7474 or 800/LATHAM–1 | fax 215/563–4034 | www.lathamhotel.com | 138 rooms | $169–$239 | AE, D, DC, MC, V.

Penn's View. In a refurbished 19th-century commercial building, this cosmopolitan little hotel is at the intersection of the city's gallery and historic districts. You can relax amid the Chippendale-style furniture and floral wall coverings. Dining room (*see* Ristorante Panorama), complimentary Continental breakfast. In-room data ports, some in-room hot tubs, cable TV. Business services, airport shuttle, parking (fee). | Front and Market Sts. | 215/922–7600 or 800/331–7634 | fax 215/922–7642 | www.pennsviewhotel.com | 40 rooms | $125–$195 | AE, DC, MC, V.

Philadelphia Marriott. This 23-story convention hotel—the biggest in Pennsylvania—takes up an entire city block. A short walk takes you to the Franklin Institute, Penn's Landing, or the Liberty Bell. Restaurant, bar, room service. In-room data ports, some refrigerators, cable TV. Indoor pool, wading pool. Beauty salon, hot tub. Exercise equipment. Laundry facilities. Business services, parking (fee). Pets allowed. | 1201 Market St. | 215/625–2900 | fax 215/625–6000 | 1,408 rooms, 76 suites | $129–$290, $350–$1100 suites | AE, D, DC, MC, V.

Radnor. Built in 1950 and renovated in 1999, this hotel is filled with plants and floral designs that make it seem more like an inn. The Radnor is on the Main Line to the west of Philly proper. Restaurant, bar (with entertainment), room service. In-room data ports, cable TV. Pool, wading pool. Exercise equipment. Video games. Business services. | 591 E. Lancaster, St. Davids | 610/688–5800 or 800/537–3000 | fax 610/341–3299 | www.radnorhotel.com | 170 rooms | $119–$249 | AE, D, DC, MC, V.

Renaissance Hotel – Philadelphia Airport. This hotel has a glass-and-concrete look and is in a quieter spot than many of the airport hotels. It's about 15 min from Center City. Restaurant, bars. In-room data ports, cable TV. Indoor pool. Hot tub. Exercise equipment. Video games. Business services, airport shuttle. | 500 Stevens Dr. | 610/521–5900 | fax 610/521–4362 | www.renaissancehotel.com | 353 rooms | $155–$175 | AE, D, DC, MC, V.

★ **Sheraton Suites Philadelphia Airport.** Renovated in 1997, this all-suites property is considered one of the finest among the airport hotels. It caters to the business traveler. Restaurant, bar. In-room data ports, minibars, refrigerators, cable TV. Indoor pool. Hot tub. Exercise equipment. Business services, airport shuttle. | 4101 Island Ave. | 215/365–6600 | fax 215/492–8471 | www.sheraton.com | 251 suites | $150–$200 suites | AE, D, DC, MC, V.

EXPENSIVE

Doubletree Philadelphia. The 26-story hotel has a view of Center City in the common area, while the hotel's sawtooth design results in guest rooms with 180-degree views. Across the street are the Academy of Music and Merriam Theater. Restaurant, bar. In-room data ports, cable TV. Indoor pool. Hot tub. Exercise equipment. Sauna. Laundry service. Business services. | Broad St. at Locust | 215/893–1600 | fax 215/893–1663 | www.doubletree.com | 434 rooms | $129–$250 | AE, D, DC, MC, V.

Doubletree Guest Suites Plymouth Meeting. This all-suites property is about 30 min west of Center City Philadelphia and 8 mi from Valley Forge. Built in 1986, the atrium-style hotel is in a natural wooded landscape. Restaurant, bar. In-room data ports, refrigerators, cable TV. Indoor pool, wading pool. Hot tub. Exercise equipment. Laundry facilities. Business services. | 640 W. Germantown Pike, Plymouth Meeting | 610/834–8300 | fax 610/834–7813 | www.doubletreeplymouth.com | 252 suites | $179–$199 suites | AE, D, DC, MC, V.

PHILADELPHIA

INTRO
ATTRACTIONS
DINING
LODGING

Korman Suites. Topped by an abstract neon sign, this upscale, business-oriented, all-suites hotel has fully equipped kitchens and washer/dryers in most accommodations. In 2 buildings, the furniture is cherry wood and soft oak. The Rodin Museum and the Franklin Institute are three blocks away. Restaurant, bar (with entertainment). In-room data ports, kitchenettes, microwaves, cable TV. Pool. Barbershop, beauty salon, hot tub. Exercise equipment. Laundry facilities. Business services. | 2001 Hamilton St. | 215/569–7000 | fax 215/496–0138 | www.kormansuiteshotel.com | 608 suites | $189–$229 suites | AE, D, DC, MC, V.

Marriott Philadelphia West. This upscale hotel is at Exit 29 of I–76. Valley Forge National Park is 4 mi away, and 13 mi away is Center City. Restaurant, bar. In-room data ports, cable TV. Pools. Hot tub. Exercise equipment. Laundry service. Business services, airport shuttle. | 111 Crawford Ave., West Conshohocken | 610/941–5600 | fax 610/941–4425 | www.marriott.com | 286 rooms | $199–$229 | AE, D, DC, MC, V.

Omni Hotel at Independence Park. This elegant hotel has a cozy lobby-bar area with floor-to-ceiling views of Independence National Historical Park, as well as spacious, well-appointed guest rooms. The pool, spa, and health club have been renovated for luxury and comfort. You can walk from here to Penn's Landing and the Liberty Bell. Restaurant, bar (with entertainment), room service. In-room data ports, minibars, cable TV. Indoor pool. Hot tub, massage, spa. Exercise equipment, health club. Laundry facilities. Business services. | 401 Chestnut St. | 215/925–0000 | fax 215/925–1263 | www.omnihotels.com | 150 rooms | $189–$300 | AE, D, DC, MC, V.

Park Hyatt Philadelphia at the Bellevue. The "Grand Dame of Broad Street," and of Philadelphia hotels, this Beaux Arts-style landmark has luxurious accommodations. It sits in the heart of Center City theaters, shopping, and restaurants. Guest rooms are spacious and pleasant. Restaurant (see Ciboulette, The Founders), bar (with entertainment), room service. In-room data ports, minibars, cable TV, in-room VCRs (and movies). Beauty salon, hot tub, massage, sauna. Shops. Laundry service. Business services. | 200 S. Broad St. | 215/893–1776 or 800/233–1234 | fax 215/893–9868 | www.hyatt.com | 172 rooms | $300–$425 | AE, D, DC, MC, V.

Penn Tower Hotel. On the eastern edge of the University of Pennsylvania campus, this former Hilton is now run by UPenn. Built in 1976, the hotel is mainly brick and wood, has a garden lobby and traditional provincial furniture throughout the hotel. Restaurants, bar, room service. In-room data ports, cable TV. Laundry facilities. Business services. | 34th St. and Civic Center Blvd., University City | 215/387–8333 or 800/356–PENN | fax 215/386–8306 | www.upenn.edu/penntower | 175 rooms, 7 suites | $225–$285, $325–$425 suites | AE, D, DC, MC, V.

★ **Rittenhouse Bed and Breakfast.** A stay here is like stepping into a country manor house—but you're actually in the heart of Center City, close to the best shopping, dining, and elegant Rittenhouse Square. This B&B is loaded with pampering touches, TVs with VCR. Some rooms have whirlpool baths, balconies, or fireplaces. Complimentary Continental breakfast. Breakfast room, in-room data ports, concierge. | 1715 Rittenhouse Sq., 19103 | 215/545–1755 | fax 215/546–6500 | 8 rooms, 2 suites | $209 | AE, D, DC, MC, V | CP.

Sheraton Society Hill. This neo-Colonial hotel, with a four-story atrium and traditionally furnished rooms, is in the heart of the city's historic district. Restaurant, bar, room service. In-room data ports, minibars, some refrigerators, cable TV. Indoor pool, wading pool. Hot tub, massage, sauna. Gym. Business services. Pets allowed. | 1 Dock St. | 215/238–6000 | fax 215/922–2709 | www.sheraton.com | 362 rooms; 17 suites | $189–$299 | AE, D, DC, MC, V.

The Warwick. First opened in 1924, this 23-story hotel in English Renaissance style has completed a thorough renovation, which added a new restaurant and made guest rooms from former apartments. The hotel is across the street from Rittenhouse Square. 3 Restaurants, 2 bars. In-room data ports, cable TV. Beauty salon. Exercise equipment. Business services. Pets allowed. | 1701 Locust St. | 215/735–6000 or 800/523–4210 (outside PA) | fax 215/790–7766 | www.warwickhotels.com/phil | 550 rooms; 17 suites | $189–$269 | AE, D, DC, MC, V.

The Westin Philadelphia. This is one of Center City's most upscale properties. The hotel prides itself on impeccable service and discreet personal attention. The chain is well known for its "Heavenly Bed," with pillowtop mattresses and down-filled duvets. You can walk easily to Restaurant Row, shopping, and theaters. Restaurant, bar (with entertainment), room service. In-room data ports, minibars, cable TV. Massage. Exercise equipment. Business services, airport shuttle. | 17th and Chestnut Sts. | 215/563–1600 or 800/WESTIN–1 | fax 215/567–2822 | www.westin.com | 290 rooms | $155–$275 | AE, D, DC, MC, V.

Wyndham Franklin Plaza. A popular hotel for conventions, it has full-length mirrors, coffee makers, and hair-dryers in the rooms. It's within a few blocks of the Franklin Institute and a mile from Independence Hall. Restaurant, bars. In-room data ports, some refrigerators, cable TV. Indoor pool. Beauty salon, hot tub, massage. Tennis. Gym. Laundry service. Business services. | 2 Franklin Plaza | 215/448–2000 | fax 215/448–2864 | www.wyndham.com/franklinplaza | 758 rooms | $200–$260 | AE, D, DC, MC, V.

VERY EXPENSIVE

★ **Four Seasons Hotel Philadelphia.** Considered the city's finest, this hotel has one of the city's best restaurants (The Fountain), luxuriously appointed guest rooms, and a stunning location on Logan Circle across from Swann Fountain. Restaurant, bar (with entertainment), room service. In-room data ports, minibars, cable TV. Indoor pool. Hot tub, massage. Gym. Laundry service. Business services. Pets allowed. | 1 Logan Sq. | 215/963–1500 | fax 215/963–9506 | www.fourseasons.com/locations/philadelphia | 365 rooms | $335–$470 | AE, D, DC, MC, V.

★ **The Rittenhouse Hotel.** This small luxury hotel has condominium residences on other floors of the building. It takes full advantage of its Rittenhouse Square location and boasts some of the city's most plush guest rooms, with marble bathrooms and mahogany accents. Restaurants, bar (with entertainment), room service. In-room data ports, minibars, cable TV. Indoor pool. Beauty salon, massage. Gym. Laundry service. Business services. Pets allowed. | 210 W. Rittenhouse Sq. | 215/546–9000 or 800/635–1042 | fax 215/732–3364 | www.rittenhousehotel.com | 98 rooms; 28 suites | $345–$410, $575–$1500 suites | AE, D, DC, MC, V.

PITTSBURGH

MAP 7, B6

(Nearby town also listed: Ambridge, Coraopolis, Monroeville)

PITTSBURGH

INTRO
ATTRACTIONS
DINING
LODGING

The steel capital of the United States has undergone a subtle change. No longer a purely blue-collar working town, Pittsburgh today has a real sense of fun, with various outdoor activities on its rivers and parks, unique shopping downtown and in the suburbs, and dining in some of the state's most interesting locales.

Pittsburgh was home to steel magnate Andrew Carnegie and you can find his moniker attached to some of the city's best attractions. From Carnegie Mellon University and Carnegie Music Hall to the Carnegie Free Library and Carnegie Museum of Art, the tycoon had as much influence on Pittsburgh's economic and cultural development as the three rivers that converge at its heart had on the local geography.

The Monongahela River, from the west, and Allegheny River, from the east, meet and form the Ohio River in Pittsburgh. The peninsula formed on the eastern side of this convergence grew into the downtown area, often referred to as the Golden Triangle. The city chose to put a park at its very tip, fittingly referred to as the Point; the stadium across the Allegheny also bears the geographical imprint in its name—Three Rivers Stadium.

Although visiting the park allows for an up-close view of the rivers, for the best view you can use one of Pittsburgh's two 19th-century inclines and travel up Mt. Washington, which locals call "the mount." The views are breathtaking from the overlooks and restaurants up here. You can see the rivers flowing together, appreciate the city's unique skyline, and take in the stadium, home to the Pittsburgh Pirates and Pittsburgh Steelers.

Information: Greater Pittsburgh Convention and Visitors Bureau Inc. | Regional Enterprise Tower, 425 6th Ave., 15219 | 412/281–7711 or 800/366–0093 | fax 412/644–5512 | www.pittsburgh-cvb.org | Mon.–Fri. 9–5, Visitors Bureau Mon.–Sun. 8–8.

TRANSPORTATION

Airport: Greater Pittsburgh International Airport Pittsburgh International, served by most major airlines, is 18 mi north of downtown. A cab ride from the city should cost about $30. | Rte. 60 N | 412/472–3525 | fax 412/472–3636 | www.pitairport.com | Office Mon.–Fri. 8:30–4:30. **Port Authority Transit** operates daily bus service among the airport, downtown, and Oakland. | 345 6th Ave. | 412/442–2000 | fax 412/566–5358 | www.ridegold.com | Mon.–Fri. 7–7, Sat.–Sun. 8–6. Cost is $1.95.

Rail: Amtrak runs daily service to Pittsburgh from Chicago and Philadelphia. | 1100 Liberty Ave. | 412/471–6171 or 800/872–7245 | www.amtrak.com | Office Mon.–Sun. 8–1AM.

Bus: Greyhound has service into the Pittsburgh area. | 11th St. and Liberty Ave. | 800/231–2222 | fax 412/392–6511 | www.greyhound.com | 24 hrs.

Intra-City Transportation: Daily bus and trolley service around Pittsburgh is operated by **Port Authority Transit.** Within the central business district, the subway, called the T, is always free, and buses are free during the day. Two funiculars–the *Duquesne Incline,* from West Carson Street on the Ohio River to the restaurant area of Grandview Ave., and the *Monongahela Incline,* from Station Square on the Monongahela to Grandview Ave.–carry passengers from river level to the top of Mt. Washington, which has a magnificent view. | 345 6th Ave. | 412/442–2000 | fax 412/566–5358 | www.ridegold.com | Weekdays 7–7, weekends 8–6. Cost is $1.95.

Driving around Town: Small and tourist-friendly Pittsburgh is easy to explore both on foot and by car, though some streets zigzag, and climb hills so steep that the sidewalks are stepped. Watch out for the occasional street name change as well. Major highways travel through tunnels and over bridges, of which there are many all over town. Ongoing construction makes for a maze of detours. If you drive, it's best to put your car in a garage when you park. Garages are plentiful, though residents complain that there are still not enough; you pay between $8 and $11 in Parking Authority garages, between $12 and $16 in other privately owned garages. If you do manage to find a meter, you pay 25 cents for 15 minutes. Fines for overstaying your welcome at a meter are between $10 and $15. Many streets are one-way; it is okay to make a turn from one one-way street onto another one-way street at a red light. Rush hours run from 6AM to 9AM and from 3PM to 6PM; traffic slows downtown and you can easily sit in traffic for 5 to 10 minutes. Rainy weather increases your travel time by 20 to 25 minutes.

NEIGHBORHOODS

The Strip. Wonderful aromas fill this 15-block-long, three-block-wide produce and wholesale district just outside the Golden Triangle northeast of downtown; old warehouse buildings have been turned into luxurious condos. A stroll takes in the scents of fresh flowers and grilling ginger chicken, cooked by Vietnamese immigrants; coffee brewing at the various coffee emporiums perfumes the air. In the early morning, the Strip is lined with tractors unloading fresh foods from local farms and vendors. Later on, shoppers crowd the streets, hunting for great deals on bulk goods, like full-pound cuts of fine cheeses at Pennsylvania Macaroni Co. on Penn Ave. In the evening, people come for the restaurants and clubs along Penn Avenue and Smallman Street.

Oakland. Fine century-old row houses line the streets in this old, prestigious neighborhood; Grand Boulevard is home to some of Pittsburgh's best-known art institutions. There are three university campuses, and bordering Schenley Park, the four-block, L-shaped complex houses the Carnegie Museum of Art, the Carnegie Museum of Natural History, the Carnegie Free Library, and the Carnegie Music Hall. You will also see the University of Pittsburgh's towering Cathedral of Learning, a gothic building where 26 classrooms were designed to represent Pittsburgh's diverse ethnic community.

WALKING TOUR
Begin your tour at the Flemish-Gothic Two Mellon Bank Center building. Walk inside to view the stunning stained-glass dome over the lobby. Opposite, on Grant Street, visit the Romanesque "Allegheny County Courthouse and Jail," which was designed by Henry Hobson Richardson and completed in 1888. Continue north on Grant Street to the "Pennsylvanian," once the Daniel Burnham Union Station, now an apartment building. Continue north on Grant Street, which turns into Liberty Avenue. Follow Liberty to 16th Street and go north to the "John Heinz Pittsburgh Regional History Center," to brush up on your western Pennsylvania history and learn about glassmaking. Go west on Smallman Street then south to Penn Avenue. Follow Penn west to 7th Street, then go North on 7th Street over the bridge. Once over the bridge, this street will be Sandusky; it's the site of the 7-story Andy Warhol Museum, devoted to exploring the life and work of the 1960s pop artist, who grew up in Pittsburgh.

Attractions

ART AND ARCHITECTURE
Alcoa Building. One of the most prominent of Pittsburgh's high-rise structures, it's a 32-story skyscraper designed as a showpiece for the aluminum used in creating it. Aluminum was used wherever possible, from shanks to utilities. The Alcoa company has since left, giving this building over to the city's economic development. | 425 6th Ave. | Free | Weekdays 8AM–10PM, closed weekends.

Allegheny County Courthouse. Architect Henry Hobson Richardson's masterpiece was built in 1884–1888 of granite, with castle-like towers. For a true view, enter on the Grant Street side and look at the flight of stairs that opens to cavernous vault space defined by Romanesque arches. | 436 Grant St. | 412/350–5313 | Free | Weekdays 9–5, closed weekends.

Andy Warhol Museum. The late Andy Warhol, a Pittsburgh native, was one of the most influential artists of the 20th century. The museum houses a collection of drawings, prints, paintings, sculptures, film, and audiotapes. Much of the collection details the artist's life. Many temporary exhibits, which can include work of other artists, are often presented. The Warhol Museum is one of the Carnegie Museums. | 117 Sandusky St. | 412/237–8300 | fax 412/237–8340 | www.warhol.org | $7 | Wed.–Thu and Sat. 10–5, Fri. 10–10, closed Mon.–Tues.

Byham Theatre's Dance Alloy. The works of this contemporary dance company have dealt with gender issues, love and death, and the tension between organized religion and personal faith. The company sometimes partners with local students and independent artists to bring fresh perspectives and talent to their performances. | 101 6th St. | 412/363–4321 | fax 412/363–4320 | www.dancealloy.org.

Carnegie Museum of Art. More than 500 pieces of original art are on permanent display here. Changing exhibits appear regularly and can include themes such as contemporary landscape and medieval work. | 4400 Forbes Ave. | 412/622–3131 | fax 412/622–3112 | www.cmoa.org | $6 | Tues.–Sat. 10–5, Sun. 1–5, closed Mon.

Gateway Center. More than 23 acres of land is home to a complex of several office buildings, a hotel, and restaurants. In the summer it's filled with activities ranging from festivals to concerts. | 603 Stanwix St., Suite 400 | 412/392–6000 | fax 412/392–6090 | Free | Weekdays 8–5.

Harris Theater. Foreign and independent films can be seen at this high, narrow theatre, full of older, plush red seats. | 809 Liberty Ave. | 412/471–9700 | $6.

Mattress Factory. Artists perform their research and development in labs in this museum of contemporary art. Newly commissioned site-specific art and permanent exhibits in two buildings are on display. | 500 Sampsonia Way | 412/231–3169 | fax 412/322–2231 | www.mattress.org | $6 | Tues.–Sat. 10–5, Sun. 1–5, closed Mon.

Mellon Arena. The home of the Pittsburgh Penguins also hosts live concerts and events. Built in 1961 to be the home of the opera, it has the largest retractable roof of any arena and was a featured part of the movie *Sudden Death*. | 500 Mario Lemieux Pl. | 412/642–1800 | fax 412/642–1925 | www.mellonarena.com | Free | Office weekdays 9–5.

Pittsburgh Playhouse. Here you can see performances of ballet, modern, and jazz dance, and plays on subjects such as Joan of Arc, King Arthur, and the Balkan conflicts. | 222 Craft Ave. | 412/621–4445 | www.ppc.edu/playhouse | $12–$22 | Wed.–Sun.

USX Tower. The former headquarters of U.S. Steel has a triangular cross-section and 64 floors, each about one square acre in area. At 841 ft, it's the tallest building between NYC and Chicago. You can ride to the top for the commanding view from the observation deck, or dine in style at the posh Top of the Triangle restaurant. | 600 Grant St. | 412/433–1121 or 800/366–0093 | fax 412/433–1598 | Free | Daily 9–5.

CULTURE, EDUCATION, AND HISTORY

Benedum Center for the Performing Arts. A $42 million restoration and expansion of the Stanley Theatre, built in 1928 as a "movie palace version of Versailles," has created the Benedum Center. Every detail from the 500,000-piece crystal chandelier to the gilded plasterwork has been restored or replicated. | 719 Liberty Ave. | 412/456–2600 | fax 412/456–2645 | Free | Daily 10–6.

Block House of Fort Pitt. Built by Colonel Henry Bouquet in 1764, this is the only remaining structure of the original Fort Pitt, making it the oldest structure in western Pennsylvania. | 101 Commonwealth Pl | 412/281–9284 | fax 412/281–1417 | $4 | Wed.–Sat. 10–4:30, Sun. 12–4:30, closed Mon.–Tues.

Carnegie Mellon University. Founded in 1900 by Andrew Carnegie in an attempt to create the Carnegie Technical School, its vision was to be a vocational training school for the children of Pittsburgh's working class. The name changed in 1912 to the Carnegie Institute of Technology and the school merged with Mellon Institute in 1967. The university today has seven colleges and schools; there are about 8,000 students and 3,800 faculty and staff. | 5000 Forbes Ave. | 412/268–2000 or 412/268–5052 | fax 412/268–7838 | www.cmu.edu | Free | Daily.

Fort Pitt Museum. The museum is in the Monongahela Bastion, one of the five original bastions of old Fort Pitt, and focuses on frontier days. During summer, the Royal American Regiment, a volunteer reenactment group of the British army of the 18th century, performs on Sunday afternoons. | 101 Commonwealth Pl | 412/281–9284 | fax 412/281–1417 | www.pmhc.state.pa.us | $4 | Wed.–Sat. 10–4:30, Sun. 12–4:30, closed Mon.–Tues.

Hunt Institute for Botanical Documentation. A facility for research in botanical history, it has a continuous program of exhibitions based on various aspects of botanical art and illustration. | 5000 Forbes Ave. | 412/268–2434 | fax 412/268–5677 | www.library.cmu.edu | Free | Mon.–Thurs. 8 AM–11 PM, Fri. 8–6, Sat. 10–5, Sun. 12–5.

University of Pittsburgh. Founded in 1787 as a small private school and originally known as the Pittsburgh Academy, it was housed in a log cabin near Pittsburgh's Three Rivers Stadium. In 1908 the name was changed to the University of Pittsburgh. By 1910, it had bought 43 acres of land in Oakland to expand. | 4200 5th Ave. | 412/624–4141 | fax 412/628–8815 | www.pitt.edu | Free | Daily.

On 14 acres at the university, the **Cathedral of Learning** is a 42-story Gothic stone tower, the only collegiate skyscraper in the nation. On the first floor are 26 classrooms, each reflecting the ethnic origins of the different nationalities that helped build the city. | 4200 5th Ave. | 412/624–6000 | fax 412/624–4214 | www.pitt.edu | Free | Mon.–Sat. 9:30–3, Sun. 11–3.

Erected in memory of Henry J. Heinz and his mother, **Heinz Chapel** is an interfaith chapel with high-pitched vaults, pointed arches, and attenuated stone buttresses. Its stained-glass windows, among the tallest in the world, depict 391 sacred and secular figures. | 5th and Bellefield Ave. | 412/624–4157 | fax 412/624–4155 | www.pitt.edu/~chapel | Free | Weekdays 9–5, Sun. 1–5.

Built in an Italian Renaissance style, the **Henry Clay Frick Fine Arts Building** has an art gallery and cloistered garden. | 1 Schenley Plaza | 412/648–2400 | fax 412/648–2792 | www.pitt.edu | Free | Sep.–mid-Apr., daily 10–4.

The **Stephen Foster Memorial** is home to the university's theater department. It also has the Center for American Music and the Stephen Foster Museum, and acts as a repository for much of Foster's music. | 4301 Forbes Ave. | 412/624–4100 | www.pitt.edu | Free | Mon.–Fri. 9–4, Closed on Weekends.

MUSEUMS

Carnegie Library of Pittsburgh. In 1895 Andrew Carnegie presented the library to Pittsburgh with the stipulation that it be maintained by the citizens and funded through public tax money. Today, it remains free and houses an enormous selection of books, magazines, and periodicals. | 4400 Forbes Ave. | 412/622–3114 | fax 412/622–6278 | www.clpgh.org/clp | Free | Mon.–Thurs. 9–9, Fri.–Sat. 9–5:30, Sun. 1–5.

The 200-seat **Music Hall** is inside the Carnegie Library of Pittsburgh. The stage curtain depicts Skibo Castle, Andrew Carnegie's Scottish home. Seats are mahogany. | 300 Beechwood Ave. | 412/276–3456 | www.clpgh.org | Tue.–Thu. 12–8, Fri. 12–5, Sat. 10–2.

Carnegie Museum of Natural History. A dinosaur hall and Egyptian hall provide a lot of hands-on activities, while other exhibits tell the history of humankind. The museum's interactive aspects make it a hit with younger audiences. | 4400 Forbes Ave. | 412/622–3131 | fax 412/622–3112 | www.clpgh.org/cmnh | $6 | Tues.–Sat. 10–5, Sun. 1–5, closed Mon.

Carnegie Museums of Pittsburgh. Four museums make up the Carnegie museums group, including the Andy Warhol Museum, Carnegie Museum of Art, Carnegie Museum of Natural History, and Carnegie Science Center. The Art and Natural History Museums are in the same building. | 4400 Forbes Ave. | 412/622–3360 | fax 412/622–6278 | www.clpgh.org/Carnegie.html | Museum closed Mon.

Carnegie Science Center. The four floors of exhibits here include a real beehive, working robots, Omnimax Theater, and an authentic World War II submarine. | 1 Allegheny Ave. | 412/237–3400 | fax 412/237–3375 | www.carnegiesciencecenter.org | $10 | Sun.–Fri. 10–5, Sat. 10–9.

Frick Art and Historical Center. A mansion and art gallery fill the six manicured acres here. The grounds are open to the public at no cost from dawn to dusk. | 7227 Reynolds St. | 412/371–0600 | fax 412/241–5393 | www.frickart.org | $8 | Tues.–Sat. 10–5, Sun. 12–6, closed Mon.

Clayton, the Henry Clay Frick Home, began its life as an 11-room Italianate structure, but as the Frick family grew the house needed to grow with them. The Fricks hired architect Frederick Osterling to modify and expand the house into the 23-room chateau-style mansion that still stands today. This is one of America's most meticulously documented Victorian residences, and the model of a well-appointed Victorian home. More than 90 percent of the artifacts here are original to the house. | 7227 Reynolds St. | 412/371–0600 | fax 412/241–5393 | www.frickart.org | $8 | By appointment. Helen Frick, daughter of Henry Clay Frick, collected this group of French and Italian Renaissance paintings, and generations after her can enjoy it here in the **Frick Art Museum.** A low, sleek white building has the original artwork as collected by Helen Frick. A portrait by Rubens is the pride of the museum. | 7227 Reynolds St. | 412/371–0600 | fax 412/241–5393 | www.frickart.org | Free | Tues.–Sat. 10–5, Sun. 12–6, closed Mon.

Photo Antiquities. The museum displays 19th-century photographs and all of the equipment with which they were created. See Civil War photos, vintage Pittsburgh pictures, and 3,000 other images. | 531 E. Ohio St. | 412/231–7881 or 800/474–6862 | fax 412/231–1217 | www.photoantiquities.org | $4 | Mon.–Sat. 10–5.

Pittsburgh Children's Museum. Kids are encouraged to climb, finger-paint, and explore the many hands-on activities in this two-story museum. | 1 Landmarks Sq | 412/322–5058 | fax 412/322–4932 | www.pittsburghkids.org | $5 | Tues.–Sat. 10–5, Sun. 12–5.

Senator John Heinz Pittsburgh Regional History Center. The museum documents the history of Pittsburgh and western Pennsylvania. An old trolley car sits on the first floor, and you can explore the area's ethnic culture on the second floor. Kids can enjoy the special exhibits on the third floor, and the fourth floor displays a glass exhibit and memorabilia from the Heinz family. | 1212 Smallman St. | 412/454–6000 | fax 412/454–6031 | www.pghhistory.org | $6 | Daily Mon.–Sun. 10–5.

Society for Contemporary Crafts. This visual art organization has been presenting artists who use traditional crafting methods for more than 20 years. Exhibits include ceramic, wood, glass, metal, and fiber pieces. | 2100 Smallman St. | 412/261–7003 | fax 412/261–1941 | www.contemporarycrafts.org | Free | Tues.–Sat. 10–5, closed Sun.–Mon.

Soldiers and Sailors Memorial Hall and Military History Museum. Built between 1908 and 1910, the building is modeled after the Mausoleum of Halicarnassus, one of the Seven Wonders of the Ancient World. Although it was begun as a monument to Union veterans of the Civil War, today it commemorates all veterans of all wars and conflicts. | 4141 5th Ave. | 412/621–4253 | fax 412/683–9339 | www.soldiersandsailorshall.org | $4 | Tue.–Sun. 9–4, Closed on Mon.

PARKS, NATURAL AREAS, AND OUTDOOR RECREATION

Frick Park. The 150-acre reserve has gardens filled with native Pennsylvania plants and trees. It's open every day for nature walks, and has extensive trails. | 2005 Beechwood Blvd. | 412/422–6538 | fax 412/422–6532 | Free | Daily dawn to dusk.

Hartwood Acres. A former horse-lover's estate is now a park that's free and open to the public dawn to dusk. You can enjoy the park's bike trails and horse trails, or just watch the cultural events hosted here such as the summer concert series and outdoor theater. The mansion has been turned into a museum featuring 16th-century and 17th-century furniture. | 2000 Saxonburg Blvd. | 412/767–9200 | fax 412/767–0171 | $5 house tours | Wed.–Sat. 10–3, Sun. 12–4.

Mt. Washington. You can take one of the two inclines to the top for a moving view of Pittsburgh's Golden Triangle. The mountain's top has homes and streetside restaurants, and views of the city skyline and Three Rivers area. | Station Sq | Free | Daily dawn to dusk.

National Aviary in Pittsburgh. More than 500 individual birds representing over 200 different species live in this sanctuary. Tours include information on how birds live, their function in the ecosystem, and their environment. You can walk through the birds' natural environment. | Allegheny Commons West | 412/323–7235 | fax 412/323–4346 | www.aviary.org | $5 | Daily 9–5.

Pittsburgh Zoo and Aquarium. The zoo has created large, walk-through naturalistic habitats for its many denizens. Kids Kingdom is the children's zoo, with lots of interactive exhibits; the Aquarium has a large saltwater tank with a communication system so you can talk to the divers as they work inside it. | 1 Wild Pl | 412/665–3639 | fax 412/665–3661 | www.zoo.pgh.pa.us/home | $8 | Daily 9–5.

Point State Park. At the tip of Pittsburgh's Golden Triangle, the park preserves the strategic and historic heritage of the area from the French and Indian Wars. The Point was the site of four different forts, all built within 10 years. Designated as a National Historic

Landmark, the park also has a 200-ft wide fountain. | 101 Commonwealth Pl | 412/471–0235 | www.dcnr.state.pa.us | Free | May–Labor Day, daily 7 AM– 11 PM.

Riverview Park. North of downtown, the 251-acre park has four major picnic facilities and views of the Ohio River. At its center is an observatory run by the University of Pittsburgh's department of astronomy. | Rte. 19 | 412/255–2135 | fax 412/255–2821 | Free | Apr.–Nov., daily dawn to dusk; May–Sept., permit required.

A two-hour tour of the **Allegheny Observatory** includes a slide presentation and lecture. If weather permits, you can take a gander at whatever the telescope reveals. Call ahead for reservations. | 159 Riverview Ave. | 412/321–2400 | Free | Apr.–Oct., Thurs.–Fri. 8 PM.

Rodef Shalom Biblical Botanical Garden. Thoughtful presentations on the plant world of the Bible distinguish this place from your everyday backyard garden. You can see more than 100 varieties of plants, including special program plantings (such as "Fragrance Through the Ages" and "King Tut's Vegetable Garden") that are designed to provoke questions about the world of the Biblical era. | 4905 5th Ave. | 412/621–6566 | fax 412/687–1977 | www.rodefshalom.org | Free | June–mid-Sept., Sun.–Thurs. 10–2, Sat. 12–1, closed Fri.

Schenley Park. In this 456-acre park, you can bike and hike, swim and skate, and bring a picnic of your own or buy fresh produce at a farmer's market in summer. In winter, you can go sledding, ice skating, or cross-country skiing. The park was designed by New York's Central Park designer. | Overlook Dr. | 412/422–6523 | Free | Daily 6 AM–11 PM.

The **Phipps Conservatory,** once a giant Victorian greenhouse, has become a botanical garden and conservatory with seasonal flowers. The 13 rooms and outdoor gardens have a butterfly room, a desert room, and a Victorian room with orchids. | 1 Schenley Park | 412/622–6914 | fax 412/622–7363 | www.phippsconservatory.org | $6 | Tues.–Sun. 9–5, closed Mon.

SHOPPING

Fifth Avenue Place. A 31-story structure with a pyramid cap and mast serves as an ornate shopping plaza. It has many upscale shops and dining spots. | 120 5th Ave. | 412/456–7800 | fax 412/456–7810 | Free | Mon. and Thurs. 10–7:30, Tues.–Wed. and Fri. 10–6, Sat. 10–5:30, closed Sun.

Market Square. Once a farmer's market, today it's a public square that is often used as an entertainment venue. It's surrounded by restaurants and shops, and is also the site of the 635-ft PPG Place Tower. | Off 5th Ave., between Stanwix and Wood Sts. | 412/232–0751 | www.marketsquare.org | Free | Daily.

Station Square. An outdoor museum, buggy rides and restaurants abound here on the shores of the Monongahela River. The area was originally the Pittsburgh and Lake Erie Railroad yards, which were converted into a shopping mall with 40 shops on 52 acres. | 450 Landmarks Building, 1 Station Sq | 412/261–2811 | fax 412/261–2825 | www.stationsquare.com | Free | Mon.–Sat. 10–9, Sun. 12–5.

SIGHTSEEING TOURS

Gray Line. Bus tours in and around Pittsburgh have narrators aboard to discuss key aspects of Pittsburgh and the surrounding area. Five tours are available ranging from two to seven hours. | 110 Lenzer Ct | 412/761–7000 or 888/565–3963 | www.coachusa.com | $18–$40 | Office Mon.–Sun. 8–6.

SPECTATOR SPORTS

Pittsburgh Penguins. The Penguins joined the National Hockey League in 1967 and won two Stanley Cups in the 1990s. They play their home games in the Civic Arena and are a part of the Eastern Conference's Atlantic Division. | 1 Chatham Center | 412/642–1300 | fax 412/642–1859 | www.pittsburghpenguins.com | $15–$50.

Pittsburgh Pirates. The Pirates have been a part of major league baseball for 113 years and play in the National League East conference. Home games are played in Three Rivers Stadium. The Pirates last won a World Series in 1979 and prior to that they won it in 1909,

1925, 1960, and 1971. | 600 Stadium Circle | 412/323–5000 | fax 412/323–5009 | www.pirate-ball.com | $6–$20.

Pittsburgh Steelers. The fifth oldest franchise in the National Football League is also one of its most successful, with four Super Bowls to their credit. They play their home games in Three Rivers Stadium and a bronze statue of Art Rooney graces the stadium entrance. Hall-of-Famers include Terry Bradshaw, "Mean" Joe Green, and Chuck Knoll. | 300 Stadium Circle | 412/323–0300 or 412/432–7800 | fax 412/432–7878 | www.pittsburghsteelers.com | $15–$40.

OTHER POINTS OF INTEREST

Kennywood Park. Out in West Mifflin, 10 mi southeast of downtown, you can find one of the last of America's great traditional amusement parks; admission is cheap, parking is free, and you pay for rides individually (or get an all-day ride pass for $22.95). The roster of 31 major rides includes three bone-jangling wooden roller coasters, 14 kiddie rides, and three water rides. | 4800 Kennywood Blvd., West Mifflin | 412/461–0500 | fax 412/461–1825 | www.kennywood.com | $7.50 + $0.25 per ride ticket | Daily 10:30–12.

Inclines. The city has two working inclines you can take from river level up to Mt. Washington where breathtaking views of the city await. Each incline looks like a cable car, but it's attached to a solid, inclined base that keeps the car level as it travels upward. They were built to help the city's workers travel up and down the mountain, which remains their primary role to this day. | 1220 Grandview Ave. | 412/381–1665 | $1 | Daily 5:30 AM–12:45 AM.
The **Duquesne Incline** climbs Mt. Washington to view the Pittsburgh skyline. Built in 1877, the incline can take you up to some of the city's best restaurants. | 1220 Grandview Ave. | 412/381–1665 | www.trfn.clpgh.org/incline | $1 | Daily 5:30 AM–12:45 AM.
If you've been visiting Station Square and are tired of shopping, you can get relief by taking the **Monongahela Incline** up to Mt. Washington. This used to be a popular incline for workers on the river before the square was turned into a shopping center. | E. Carson St. and Smithfield St. | 412/237–7000 or 412/442–2000 | www.portauthority.org/ride/incline.html | $1 | Daily 5:30 AM–12:45 AM.

Sandcastle Water Park. You can really beat the heat at this major water park with 15 large water slides, a wave pool, and many rides for kids. Parking is free. | 1000 Sandcastle Dr. | 412/462–6666 | fax 412/462–0827 | www.sandcastlewaterpark.com | $16.95 | June–Aug., daily 11–6.

Tour-Ed Mine and Museum. Tour-Ed was an active mine in use from 1920 until the late 1980s. Today you can travel down the mine in an actual mining car for a half-hour tour that explains the life of miners. The mine stays at a constant 52 degrees. | 748 Bull Creek Rd., Tarentum | 724/224–4720 | www.tour-edmine.com | $6 | May–Labor Day, daily 1–4.

ON THE CALENDAR

MAY: *Folk Festival.* At this multicultural event in Station Square you can sample foods from around the world, visit crafts booths, dance, and, of course, enjoy the folk music over Memorial Day weekend. | 412/278–1267 | www.pghfolkfest.org.
JUNE: *Three Rivers Arts Festival.* Local and national artists contribute to the visual arts show, held along Penn Avenue in the Golden Triangle area. You can compare your opinions of these works with the jury's. The festival has a host of music, dance, and performance art events. | 412/281–8723 | fax 412/281–8722 | www.artsfestival.net.
JULY–AUG.: *Pittsburgh/Shop-N-Save Three Rivers Regatta.* This is the world's largest inland display of powerboat races, water-skiing demonstrations, and sailboat parades. Spectators should make their home base in Point State Park. | 412/875–4853 | fax 412/928–8833 | www.pghregatta.com.
SEPT.: *Pittsburgh Irish Festival.* On the second weekend of September you can celebrate Irish culture even as you learn more about it. The festival, held in Station Square, has authentic food, dance, and other entertainment. | 412/422–1113 | www.pghirishfest.org.

SEPT.:–MAY: *Pittsburgh Symphony Orchestra Concerts.* The nationally acclaimed ensemble performs the classic repertoire. | 600 Penn Ave. | 412/392–4900 | www.pittsburghsymphony.org.

NOV.: *Three Rivers Film Festival.* This 14-day festival, held in the Pittsburgh Filmmakers' three art houses, features foreign, independent, documentary, and classic films from famous directors as well as up-and-coming filmmakers. | 412/682–4111.

Dining

British Bicycle Club. American. British-style fixtures and bicycles, hang from the ceiling, and walls are accented with photographs and prints of bikes and bike riders. You can order steak and chicken salad, fish, burgers, baked stuffed chicken, or one of many other dishes at this casual dining spot. | 923 Penn Ave. | 412/391–9623 | Closed weekends | $9–$18 | AE, D, DC, MC, V.

Cheese Cellar. Continental. In a former freight house that has been turned into the Station Square Mall, the restaurant overlooks the Monongahela River. Beer and cheese flounder, grilled swordfish, and chicken Mediterranean pasta are just a few examples from the menu. Kids' menu. | #25 Freight House Shops | 412/471–3355 | fax 412/281–0549 | Reservations not accepted | $5–$14 | AE, D, DC, MC, V.

Dave & Andy's Homemade Ice Cream. Cafe. Old milk cans serve as the stools for a real old-fashioned ice-cream parlor. You can have yogurt sorbets or good old homemade ice cream, with flavors like chocolate chip, mocha espresso, and honey apple cinnamon granola. | 207 Atwood St. | 412/681–9906 | $2–$17 | No credit cards.

Jimmy Tsang's. Chinese. The traditional Chinese artwork and sculpture in the main dining room are similar to what you see in other Chinese restaurants, but Jimmy Tsang's distinguishes itself with reliable, tasty fare like honey chicken, Chinese flank steak, and authentic eggrolls. The Chinese style courtyard has a piano. Romantic private dining is available for you and your sweetie. | 5700 Centre Ave. | 412/661–4226 | fax 412/661–8659 | No lunch Sun. | $6–$11 | AE, DC, D, MC, V.

Max's Allegheny Tavern. German. Tiffany lamps above wooden booths and old mosaic tile floors give this tavern an aura of late-1800s authenticity. Here you can enjoy sausage and schnitzel. Dinner is a bit more formal. Sun. brunch. | 537 Suisman St. | 412/231–1899 | fax 412/231–5099 | www.maxsalleghenytavern.com | $5–$15 | AE, D, DC, MC, V.

Max and Erma's. American. The surrounding woodwork lends a homey warmth to a meal taken in this unpretentious, contemporary restaurant. Pictures of old Pittsburgh hang on the walls, and other memorabilia is also on display. Specials are portobello mushroom chicken and penne pasta, Laredo steak, and 10-oz burgers. | 5533 Walnut St. | 412/681–5775 | fax 412/681–5137 | www.maxandermas.com | No breakfast | Reservations not accepted | $10–$15 | AE, D, DC, MC, V.

Penn Brewery. German. This 1848-era restored brewery in the city's German district has long wooden tables and benches. Try the schweinebraten, Wiener schnitzel, and sauerbraten. Biergarten. Kids' menu. | 800 Vinial St., Troy Hill | 412/237–9402 | fax 412/237–9406 | www.pennbrew.com | Reservations not accepted | No lunch Sun. | $9–$17 | AE, D, MC, V.

Pizzeria Uno. Italian. Chicago deep-dish pizza is the specialty here and Old Country memorabilia is hung on the walls. Menu choices are chicken and portobello mushroom, spinoccoli numero uno, and thin crust pizza. Sun. brunch. | 333 Penn Center Blvd., Monroeville | 412/824–8667 | fax 412/824–8455 | www.pizzeriauno.com | $6–$12 | AE, D, MC, V.

Primanti Bros. Italian. The home of "The Almost Famous" sandwich is a true Pittsburgh icon. Whether it's after the bars close or during the lunch rush, Primanti Brothers is always filled with locals enjoying their peerless sandwiches. Sandwich specials include the Primanti cheesesteak, the deluxe double egg and cheese, or the "Almost Famous" with everything on it, including coleslaw and french fries. Open 24 hours. | 46 18th St. | 412/263–2142 | www.primantibros.com | Reservations not accepted | $3–$11 | No credit cards.

Seventh Street Grille. Continental. A popular downtown pre-theater hangout rewards you for sampling each of its 42 beers by engraving your name on the wall. Filet Zimmermann, chicken Geradi, and grilled marlin are just a few of the entree choices. Pre-theater menu. | 130 7th St. | 412/338–0303 | fax 412/281–0577 | No breakfast | $5–$22 | AE, D, DC, MC, V.

Sushi Two. Japanese. A glass block facade leads to an entrance with a mirrored rock garden, bronzed cranes, and a big white Japanese drum. The inside is quaint and small with traditional Japanese artwork. You can get beef and chicken in addition to seafood. | 2122 E. Carson St. | 412/431–7874 | fax 412/431–7864 | www.sushi2-too.com | $5–$16 | AE, D, DC, MC, V.

Tessaro's. Contemporary. If you love a good burger, you want to visit this winner of Citysearch's "Best of Pittsburgh" award for best hamburger, 2000. Steak filets, pork chops, and other options are also available for those not in a burger mood. | 4601 Liberty Ave. | 412/682–6809 | Reservations not accepted | Closed Sun. | $5–$19 | AE, D, DC, MC, V.

Thai Place. Thai. Glass-paned windows, pale cherry walls, pink tablecloths, and traditional artwork make a pleasant, informal surrounding for your meal. Sample dishes are emerald chicken and tiger prawns. | 809 Bellefonte St. | 412/687–8586 | fax 412/687–7970 | No lunch Mon. | $7–$16 | AE, D, DC, MC, V.

Vermont Flatbread Co. Contemporary. This place may remind you of a ski lodge. The wood interior is accented with warm lights and dark fabrics. Entrees include flatbread pizza, sandwiches made with homemade breads, soups, and homemade desserts. Kids' menu. Wide selection of handcrafted beers, wine, and alcohol. | 2701 Penn Ave. | 412/434–1220 | fax 412/434–0973 | Closed Sun. | $6–$14 | D, DC, MC, V.

MODERATE

Asiago. Contemporary. Try puff pastry filled with artichoke hearts and mushrooms in a Madeira garlic cream sauce, or Asiago's special asparagus ravioli with tomato basil concasse. Examples of entrees are chicken au miel—pan-seared chicken breast medallions served with grapes and toasted almonds in a honey and vinegar glaze; veal tenderloin Normande, served with apples, mushrooms, and walnuts in a Calvados and apple cider sauce; and crabcake Valencia–a mixture of lightly sauteed jumbo lump crabmeat, tangy seasonings, and a Spanish scarlet orange sauce. Even with all of the choices, the menu states that you can request your favorite dish if it's not on the menu. | Oxford Centre | 412/392–0225 | Jacket and tie | Closed Sun. | $14–$26 | AE, D, MC, V.

Benihana. Japanese. A traditional Japanese garden complete with koi pond graces the outdoor dining area, while Japanese sculptures and prints highlight the inside. "Land and Sea," "Rocky Choice," and "Benihana Marina" are just a few of the menu selections. Kids' menu. | 2100 Greentree Rd. | 412/276–2100 | fax 412/276–1584 | www.benihana.com | No lunch weekends | $13–$30 | AE, D, DC, MC, V.

Cafe Allegro. French Italian. Prints of Picasso's artwork and sculpture greet the eye as you enter this South Side restaurant. Entrees include grilled calamari, pasta del sol, and grilled seafood with red wine and peppercorn sauce. Pre-theater menu. | 51 S. 12th St. | 412/481–7788 | fax 412/481–4520 | $14–$25 | AE, DC, MC, V.

Chauncy's. American. Both business and college crowds come to this restaurant, which is also a nightclub with live entertainment, dancing, and billiards. You can get Caesar salad, Hawaiian chicken, New Orleans-style blackened sirloin steak, or lemon sole, broiled and served with butter sauce. | Commerce Ct. | 412/232–0601 | No lunch. Closed Sun. and Mon. | $11–$18 | AE, MC, V.

China Palace. Chinese. Various architectural touches help the outside resemble 19th-century Chinese buildings, while Chinese paintings and sculptures add beauty to the interior. Classic dishes are General Tso chicken, crispy walnut shrimp, and duck. | 5440 Walnut St. | 412/687–7423 | fax 412/687–5555 | No lunch Sun. | $10–$17 | AE, D, DC, MC, V.

The Church Brew Works. Contemporary. This converted Catholic Church has brewing kettles, and pews have been altered to accommodate tables for patrons. The original stained-glass windows are still in place. Buffalo and wild mushroom meat loaf, wood-fired pizzas, and pierogies are on the menu. | 3525 Liberty Ave. | 412/688–8200 | fax 412/688–8201 | www.churchbrew.com | No lunch Sun. | $10–$22 | AE, D, DC, MC, V.

Crewsers on the Water. American. You can find several sandwiches, salads, and pasta dishes along with butterflied, breaded, and lightly fried gulf shrimp here. The house specialty is tournedos oscar–twin medallions of filet mignon, topped with jumbo crab meat, fresh asparagus and béarnaise sauce. The restaurant is also known for its view of the river and live music, DJs, and dancing at night. Kids' menu. | 1501 Smallman St. | 412/281–1099 | Closed Sun. and Mon. | $8–$28 | AE, MC, V.

Kaya. Caribbean. Woodwork and tapestries hanging from the ceiling lend a Jamaican flavor to this converted warehouse, as does the reggae music. You can dine outside under a protective awning. Tropical paella, Jamaican green curry stir fry, and fish specials are on the menu. | 2000 Smallman St. | 412/261–6565 | fax 412/261–1526 | www.bigburrito.com/kaya | $10–$19 | AE, D, DC, MC, V.

1902 Landmark Tavern. Italian/American. You can feast on filets, pasta dishes, and famous New England clam chowder at this casual early 20th-century tavern. | 24 Market St. | 412/471–1902 | Closed Sun. | $14–$27 | AE, D, DC, MC, V.

Paparazzi. Italian. This glass and mirrored restaurant has live jazz and blues bands Wednesday through Sunday night. You'll have a selection of fresh fried appetizers—calamari, eggplant, ravioli, and zucchini. Low-priced sandwiches include sausage, veal, and chicken. Pizzas, calzones, and pasta dishes are also available. | 2100 East Carson St. | 412/488–0800 | No lunch | $5–$18 | AE, D, MC, V.

Pasta Piatto. Italian. A mural of St. Peter and offerings from local artisans provide an eclectic look for this local favorite, otherwise a traditional Italian restaurant. Most of the artwork can be purchased. You can enjoy pasta, chicken, and veal. Kids' menu. | 736 Bellefonte St. | 412/621–5547 | No lunch Sun. | $11–$24 | AE, MC, V.

Piccolo Mondo. Italian. The home of Rico Lorenzi has a chandeliered dining room accented in warm colors and a panoramic view of nearby Greentree's woodlands, creating a romantic country look. Soft lighting, oil paintings, and music from a baby grand add to the romance. Penne con broccoli and eggplant are house specialties. | 829 Lamar Blvd. E | 412/922–0920 | www.piccolo-mondo.com | Jacket required | Closed Sun. No lunch Sat. | $8–$25 | AE, D, DC, MC, V.

Poli. Continental. Shining brass lobsters greet you at the doorway and inside you can find a colorful interior with tapestries hanging from the ceiling. The bar area is more casual, with its grey tile floor and unique angled bar. The menu has a fresh fish platter, lobster, and crab cake. Kids' menu, early-bird suppers. | 2607 Murray Ave. | 412/521–6400 | www.polisince1921.com | Closed Mon. | $10–$25 | AE, DC, MC, V.

Shiloh Inn. Italian. This restaurant's rendition of veal parmesan adds shrimp, tomatoes, and peppers. You can also try veal Romano–dipped in egg and cheese, pan-fried, and served with lemon butter sauce, or Mediterranean—scallopini with mushrooms, green olives, diced tomato, and feta cheese. There's a variety of seafood, from swordfish steak and shrimp scampi to South African lobster tails. Reserve early for a seat at the dinner theatre show. Valet parking is available. | 123 Shiloh St. | 412/431–4000 | Reservations essential | Jacket and tie | No lunch. Closed Sun. | $11–$23 | AE, MC, V.

Soba Lounge. Pan-Asian. This restaurant has four dining levels, with granite tables on the first floor, a red velvet room on the second floor, glass sculptures on level three, and an Asian bar with low tables and couches on level four. You can try eclectic dishes like Pad

Thai, sesame-stirred rare tuna, and the pineapple hoisin-glazed pork chop. | 5847 Ellsworth Ave. | 412/362–5656 | fax 412/362–6189 | www.bigburrito.com/soba | No lunch | $10–$20 | AE, D, DC, MC, V.

Steelhead Grill. Contemporary. This restaurant's menu has appetizers such as house-smoked salmon with candied lemon and black pepper crème fraiche, and sauteed crab cake with an endive and arugula salad and sauce beurre rouge. For an entree, you can choose spit-roasted Amish chicken over truffle-scented whipped potatoes and garlic rosemary sauce, or potato-crusted Alaskan halibut over fresh tomatoes and spinach with a warm smoked bacon dressing. Also try the low-priced sandwiches, salads, and pizzas. A table by the window affords a clear view of the skyline. | 112 Washington Place | 412/918–1317 | Closed Sat. and Sun. | $9–$29 | AE, D, DC, MC, V.

Tambellini's. Continental. Once a small quaint restaurant, Tambellini's large rooms can now accommodate a large number of diners, and the current layout is elegant with chandeliers and candlelight. The house recommends its seafood and meat special. | 860 Saw Mill Run Blvd. | 412/481–1118 | fax 412/481–7565 | www.tambellini.com | Closed Sun. | $15–$30 | AE, DC, MC, V, D.

EXPENSIVE

Carmassi's Tuscany Grill. Italian. You can dine by candlelight at this elegant restaurant. The veal and crabmeat, along with the crab cake, are specialties. Pre-theater menu. | 711 Penn Ave. | 412/281–6644 | fax 412/281–6650 | www.carmassis.com | Reservations essential | No lunch Sat. | $18–$26 | AE, D, MC, V.

Casbah. Mediterranean. Mexican inlaid tiles with fish designs, a mosaic bar, and hardwood floors define a well-crafted interior, with bar stools of solid iron and handmade globe work from the Pittsburgh area. You might try the lamb tagine with pears and toasted pistachios, or the orecchiete pasta with grilled chicken. Sun. brunch. | 229 S. Highland Ave. | 412/661–5656 | fax 412/661–0616 | www.bigburrito.com/casbah | Reservations essential | $15–$28 | AE, DC, D, MC, V.

Cliffside. Continental. Dine in a restored structure that sits above Pittsburgh's skyline on Mount Washington, with glass windows providing breathtaking views of the convergence of three rivers. Veal Lafayette, medallions of beef, and chicken dragina are specialties. Live music Fri., Sat. | 1208 Grandview Ave. | 412/431–6996 | No lunch | $16–$25 | AE, D, DC, MC, V.

The Colony. Steak. The Colony's main dining room is furnished with chandeliers, two grand pianos, glass window dividers, and an open-hearth grill. The steak sauce here is so famous you can buy it on-line. You can try it with the filet mignon or New York strip steak, or forgo it for the jumbo lump crab cake. Live music Fri., Sat., jazz. | 1928 Cochran Rd. | 412/561–2060 | www.thecolonyrestaurant.com | Jacket required | No lunch | $18–$23 | AE, D, DC, MC, V.

Common Plea. Italian. All rise. The layout here pays homage to those who put criminals behind bars, with photographs of famous judges, courtroom scenes hanging on the walls, and actual courtroom benches taking the place of traditional chairs. House specials are veal San Marco and crab cake. | 308 Ross St. | 412/281–5140 | fax 412/281–6856 | www.commonplea-restaurant.com | Closed Sun. No lunch Sat. | $23 | AE, DC, MC, V.

D'Imperio's. Italian. The four dining rooms here have regional oil paintings, showing each area with its own distinct look. Entrees are filet mignon sorpresso, shrimp sorrento, and veal schilling. Live music in summer Weds., Thurs., strolling musicians. | 3412 William Penn Hwy., Monroeville | 412/823–4800 | Reservations essential | Closed Sun. No lunch Mon., Sat. | $15–$30 | AE, D, DC, MC, V.

Georgetowne Inn. Contemporary. As with most restaurants that sit atop Mount Washington, this one overlooks the city. In addition, a rustic, romantic evening is created with candles and warm color tones. You can enjoy dishes such as prime rib, swordfish, and veal and shrimp maison. | 1230 Grandview Ave. | 412/481–4424 | Reservations essential | No lunch Sun. | $15–$35 | AE, D, DC, MC, V.

Grand Concourse. Seafood. Hosts use the infamous "now boarding" call to bring you to your table in this former 19th-century railway depot. Many of its fixtures are from the depot days. Specials are fresh fish, roast rack of lamb, and pasta. Tables and chairs are scattered casually outside. Live music daily. Kids' menu, early-bird suppers. Sun. brunch. | 1 Station Sq | 412/261–1717 | fax 412/261–6041 | www.muer.com/grandcon.html | No lunch Sat. | $15–$30 | AE, D, DC, MC, V.

Laforet. French. The former Highland Park Manor is transformed into a romantic dining establishment, replete with crystal chandeliers, silk linen, and fine china. | 5701 Bryant St. | 412/665–9000 | fax 412/665–8800 | Reservations essential | Jacket required | Sun.–Tues. | $20–$29 | AE, D, DC, MC, V.

London Grille. English. Consisting of two dining areas and six dining rooms, this restaurant has a separate menu and look for each. There's a Scotch bar with a number of interesting and hard-to-come-by brands available. Prime rib, crab cake, and grilled Atlantic salmon are just a few of your choices. Open-air dining is available on the patio. Sun. brunch. | 1500 Washington Rd., Mount Lebanon | 412/563–3400 | fax 412/563–8736 | $18–$25 | AE, D, DC, MC, V.

Le Pommier. French. Don't let its outward appearance of an unassuming storefront fool you, this restaurant is full of French country charm. You can try duck, veal chop, or salmon. Eat outside at the seasonal sidewalk cafe. Parking (fee) Thurs.–Sat. | 2104 E. Carson St. | 412/431–1901 | fax 412/431–1920 | www.lepommier.com | Reservations essential | Closed Sun. | $16–$28 | AE, D, DC, MC, V.

Rico's. Italian. This country manor is high on a hilltop and its six rooms are accented by old European charm. Seafood Rico, Virginia spots, and soft-shell crab are specialties. | 1 Rico Ln | 412/931–1989 | fax 412/931–2293 | www.ricosrestaurant.com | Reservations essential | Jacket required | Closed Sun. No lunch Fri., Sat. | $10–$33 | AE, D, DC, MC, V.

Top of the Triangle. Contemporary. On the 62nd floor of the USX Tower (Pittsburgh's tallest building), the varied-level dining room here has a three-sided look at the cityscape. You can try grilled molasses-glazed fresh swordfish or Colorado lamb chops. Live music, pianist, Sat. evening. Free parking. | 600 Grant St. | 412/471–4100 | www.topoftriangle.baweb.com | No lunch Sun. | $18–$30 | AE, D, DC, MC, V.

VERY EXPENSIVE

The Carlton. Contemporary. At Carlton's you can find warmth, contemporary furnishings and fixtures, and limousine service to the theater (reservations are essential). Menu choices include prime rib, sea bass, and scallops. | 1 Mellon Bank Center | 412/391–4099 | fax 412/391–4240 | Closed Sun. No lunch Sat. | $23–$33 | AE, D, DC, MC, V.

Le Mont. Contemporary. One of several restaurants on Mount Washington, Le Mont has dark wood, candlelight and crystal accenting a unique dining area. If you visit at night, you can enjoy the city's illuminated skyline. Specialties include the roast raspberry duck and steak Diana. Live music, pianist. | 1114 Grandview Ave. | 412/431–3100 | fax 412/431–1204 | Reservations essential | No lunch | $25–$45 | AE, D, DC, MC, V.

Terrace Room. Continental. Here in the Westin William Penn, an ornate ceiling, crystal chandeliers, and elaborate floral arrangements highlight a room restored to its original 1916 appearance. You can enjoy seafood, steak, or prime rib. | 530 William Penn Pl | 412/281–7100 | fax 412/553–5252 | $20–$40 | AE, D, DC, MC, V.

Tin Angel. Continental. President Bill Clinton made this, the first restaurant established on Mount Washington, one of his stops when visiting Pittsburgh. The two-tiered rooms have floor-to-ceiling windows. The menu has ocean platter, land and sea, and black forest filet. | 1200 Grandview Ave. | 412/381–1919. 412/381–6270 | Reservations essential | Jacket required | Closed Sun. No lunch | $30–$52 | AE, DC, D, MC, V.

Lodging

INEXPENSIVE

AmeriSuites–Pittsburgh Airport. All of the rooms here are two-room suites. Besides the extra room, business suites have an oversized desk, ergonomic desk chair, and an overstuffed chair with ottoman. AmeriSuites can provide you with free van service within 5 mi of the hotel. Complimentary Continental breakfast. In-room data ports, kitchenettes, microwaves, refrigerators, cable TV, in-room VCRs (and movies). Pool. Gym. Laundry service. Business services, airport shuttle, free parking. Pets allowed. | 6011 Campbells Run Rd. | 412/494–0202 or 800/833–1516 | fax 412/494–0880 | www.amerisuites.com | 128 suites | $79–$89 | AE, D, DC, MC, V.

Best Western–Parkway Center Inn. The motel is west of Greentree, 1½ mi from downtown. Complimentary Continental breakfast. In-room data ports, some kitchenettes, cable TV. Indoor pool. Exercise equipment. Laundry facilities. Business services, airport shuttle, free parking. | 875 Greentree Rd. | 412/922–7070 | fax 412/922–4949 | www.bestwesternpa.com/pittsburgh.html | 138 rooms | $85–$110 | AE, D, DC, MC, V.

ClubHouse Inn. A representative motel of this lesser-known chain is 9 mi west of the downtown. Complimentary Continental breakfast. In-room data ports, some microwaves, some refrigerators, cable TV. Pool. Hot tub. Exercise equipment. Laundry facilities. Business services, airport shuttle. | 5311 Campbells Run Rd. | 412/788–8400 or 800/258–2466 | fax 412/788–2577 | www.clubhouseinn.com/3.pit.html | 152 rooms, 26 suites | $89–$114 rooms; $99–$119 suites | AE, D, DC, MC, V.

Clarion Hotel. Standard rooms here have wood furnishings and colorful carpeting and bedspreads, while business class rooms have an extra large desk and an ergonomic office chair. During evenings the bar has a DJ, live band, karaoke, or comedy. 17 mi northeast of downtown. Restaurant, bar (with entertainment), picnic area, room service. Some in-room data ports, some microwaves, some refrigerators, cable TV. Pool. Gym. Video games. Laundry facilities, laundry service. Business services, free parking. Pets allowed. | 300 Tarentum Bridge Rd., New Kensington | 724/335–9171 | fax 724/335–6642 | 115 rooms | $60–$70 | AE, DC, MC, V.

Four Points Barcelo Hotel–Pittsburgh Airport. The main choice here is between two double beds or one king-size bed. Otherwise, the rooms all have a large desk, chair, and lamp. Restaurant, bar, room service. In-room data ports, cable TV. Pool. Gym. Laundry service. Free parking. | One Industry Lane | 724/695–0002 or 888/625–5144 | fax 724/695–7262 | 140 rooms | $74 | AE, D, DC, MC, V.

Hampton Inn–Greentree For affordable rates 3 mi west of downtown, try this motel. Picnic area, complimentary Continental breakfast. In-room data ports, cable TV. Business services, airport shuttle, free Parking. Pets allowed. | 555 Trumbull Dr. | 412/922–0100 | fax 412/921–7631 | www.hamptoninn.com | 135 rooms | $94–$109 | AE, D, DC, MC, V.

Hampton Inn–West Mifflin. This hotel is 8 mi south of downtown and half a mile from the Century 3 Mall. In-room data ports, microwaves, refrigerators, some in-room hot tubs, cable TV. Pool. Business services, free parking. | 1550 Lebanon Church Rd. | 412/650–1000 | fax 412/650–1001 | www.hamptoninn.com | 70 rooms | $94–$115 | AE, D, DC, MC, V.

Hawthorn Suites. An all-suites hotel, it's 4 mi from downtown, off Exit 4 of I–279. You can get a spacious suite with separate living and sleeping areas nearly twice the size of a traditional hotel room. Picnic area, complimentary breakfast. Microwaves, refrigerators, cable TV. Pool. Hot tub. Business services, airport shuttle. Pets allowed (fee). | 700 Mansfield Ave. | 412/279–6300 or 800/527–1133 | fax 412/279–4993 | www.hawthorn.com | 151 suites | $99–$129 | AE, D, DC, MC, V.

Holiday Inn–Allegheny Valley. At Exit 10, Rte. 28 stands this chain hotel 9 mi north of downtown. Restaurant, bar, room service. In-room data ports, some refrigerators, cable TV. Indoor pool. Exercise equipment. Business services, airport shuttle, free parking. | 180

Gamma Dr. | 412/963–0600 | fax 412/963–7852 | www.holiday-inn.com | 283 rooms, 40 suites | $105–$150 suites | AE, D, DC, MC, V.

Holiday Inn Greentree–Central. This hotel is 3 mi west of downtown, and one mile to Parkway Center mall. Restaurant, bar (with entertainment), room service. In-room data ports, cable TV. Pool. Exercise equipment. Business services, airport shuttle, free parking. Pets allowed. | 401 Holiday Dr. | 412/922–8100 | fax 412/922–6511. www.holiday-inn.com | 200 rooms | $110–$150 | AE, D, DC, MC, V.

Holiday Inn–Monroeville. This hotel is ¼ mi from the turnpike and 12 mi east of downtown. Restaurant, bar, room service. In-room data ports, cable TV. Outdoor pool. Exercise equipment. Laundry facilities. Business services, free parking. Pets allowed. | 2750 Mosside Blvd., Monroeville | 412/372–1022 | fax 412/373–4065 | www.holiday-inn.com | 188 rooms | $79–$139 | AE, D, DC, MC, V.

Holiday Inn, North Hills. In a wooded area 6 mi from downtown, 1 mi from the Ross Park Mall's restaurants and shopping, is this hotel. Restaurant, bar (with entertainment), room service. In-room data ports, some refrigerators, cable TV. Pool. Laundry facilities. Business services, free parking. Pets allowed. | 4859 McKnight Rd. | 412/366–5200 | fax 412/366–5682 | www.holiday-inn.com | 147 rooms | $85–$139 | AE, D, DC, MC, V.

Holiday Inn–Parkway East. This hotel is 8 mi east of downtown, and 4 mi from Monroeville Mall and Expo Mart. Restaurant, bar (with entertainment), room service. Some refrigerators, cable TV. Indoor pool. Laundry facilities. Business services, free parking. Pets allowed. | 915 Brinton Rd. | 412/247–2700 | fax 412/371–9619. | www.holiday-inn.com | 180 rooms | $109–$139 | AE, D, DC, MC, V.

Holiday Inn–Pittsburgh South. Right across from South Hills Village Mall is this hotel, 8 mi south of downtown. Restaurant, bar (with entertainment), room service. In-room data ports, cable TV. Pool. Video games. Business services, airport shuttle, free parking. Pets allowed. | 164 Fort Couch Rd. | 412/833–5300 | fax 412/831–8539 | www.holiday-inn.com | 210 rooms | $89–$120 | AE, D, DC, MC, V.

The Inn on the Mexican War Streets. This stone mansion is the former home of department-store magnate Russell H. Boggs. The dining room has white walls, dark drapes, and a chandelier. Guest rooms vary—for example, you can choose Mrs. Boggs' room for a queen-size four-post bed with a white bedspread. Mr. Boggs' room has a queen-size bed with wooden head- and footboards, a loveseat, and hanging ferns. Dining room, complimentary Continental breakfast. Some kitchenettes, cable TV, in-room VCRs (and movies). Free parking. | 604 W. North Ave. | 412/231–6544 | innwarst@aol.com | 10 rooms | $79–$129 | MC, V.

MainStay Suites. In addition to bedrooms, about half of the suites here have a separate living area with a full kitchen. The other half of the suites are studio apartments with large workspaces, ergonomic desk chairs, and two-line speaker phones. Picnic area, complimentary Continental breakfast. In-room data ports, kitchenettes, cable TV. Exercise equipment. Laundry facilities, laundry service. Business services, free parking. Pets allowed. | 1000 Park Lane Drive | 412/490–7343 | fax 412/788–6097 | 100 suites | $80–$105 | AE, D, DC, MC, V.

The Priory. Built in 1888, a former home for Benedictine priests, it's now an inn that takes great pride in personal service. A fireplace dominates the parlor, and the fountain is the centerpiece of the garden courtyard. The rooms have an old European style. Complimentary Continental breakfast. Cable TV. Business services. | 614 Pressley St. | 412/231–3338 | fax 412/231–4838 | www.sgi.net/thepriory/ | 24 rooms | $116–$150 | AE, D, DC, MC, V.

Radisson Greentree. If you want to be right near the heart of the city, this hotel is 3 mi west of downtown. Restaurant, bar (with entertainment), room service. In-room data ports, some minibars, cable TV. 3 pools (1 indoor). Beauty salon, hot tub. Exercise equipment. Business services, airport shuttle, free parking. Pets allowed. | 101 Marriott Dr. | 412/922–8400 or 800/525–5902 | fax 412/922–7854 | www.radisson.com | 465 rooms | $89–$139 | AE, D, DC, MC, V.

Ramada Inn–Pittsburgh East. A hillside hotel that caters especially to business travelers, it's situated east of downtown off I–376. Restaurant, bar (with entertainment), room service. In-room data ports, cable TV. Indoor pool. Hot tub, sauna. Tennis. Business services, airport shuttle, free parking. Pets allowed. | 699 Rodi Rd. | 412/244–1600 or 800/272–6232 | fax 412/829–2334 | www.ramada.com | 152 rooms | $79–$140 | AE, D, DC, MC, V.

Red Roof Inn. Affordable rates are the earmark of this motel, 11 mi west of downtown and 5 mi from Pittsburgh International Airport. Cable TV. Business services. Pets allowed. | 6404 Steubenville Pike/Rte. 60 | 412/787–7870 | fax 412/787–8392 | www.redroof.com | 120 rooms | $53–$65 | AE, D, DC, MC, V.

MODERATE

The Appletree. A small Victorian B&B; less than two blocks from the shops and restaurants of Walnut St., it's near two colleges and two universities, 10 min from downtown. The rooms of this circa-1884 restored house are named for a different apple and given each a different "flavor." Complimentary breakfast. In-room data ports, cable TV, in-room VCRs (and movies). Business services, free parking. No smoking. | 703 S. Negley Ave. | 412/661–0631 | fax 412/661–7525 | www.appletreeb-b.com | 8 rooms | $130–$180 | AE, D, MC, V.

Doubletree. This hotel has an atrium-style lobby and a convenient downtown location across from the convention center. Restaurant, bar, room service. In-room data ports, refrigerators, cable TV. Indoor pool. Hot tub. Gym. Shops. Business services. Pets allowed. | 1000 Penn Ave. | 412/281–3700 | fax 412/227–4500 | www.doubletree.com | 616 rooms | $155–$225 | AE, D, DC, MC, V.

Inn at Oakmont. On top of a hill above the town of Oakmont lies a little golf-oriented inn. The course is across the street, downtown Pittsburgh is 15 mi away. Each room has a golf motif. Complimentary breakfast. Business services. No kids under 6. No smoking. | 300 Rte. 909, Verona | 412/828–0410 | fax 412/828–1358 | www.pittsburghbnb.com/oakmont | 8 rooms (1 with shower only) | $130–$150 | AE, D, MC, V.

Morning Glory Inn. This 1862 brick Italian Victorian townhouse is in the Southside Historical District, just over a mile from Pittsburgh's downtown. Its garden room is bright, with pink lattice and floral wallpaper, a white wicker bed and chair, and a walnut rocker. Other rooms have earth-tone, floral, or yellow-striped wallpaper. You can find clawfoot tubs in two of the rooms and a canopy bed in one. Dining room. In-room data ports, cable TV. Laundry facilities. Pets allowed. No smoking. | 2119 Sarah St. | 412/431–1707 | fax 412/431–6106 | www.morningglorybedandbreakfast.com | 5 rooms | $140–$180; 2–night minimum on selected weekends | AE, D, MC, V.

Shadyside Bed and Breakfast. This small inn 3 mi east of downtown is a few blocks from shopping and restaurants, and has a billiard room and a library. Rooms have antique and period furnishings. Complimentary Continental breakfast. Cable TV, no room phones. Spa, Library. | 5516 Maple Heights Rd. | 412/683–6501 | fax 412/683–7228 | www.ledomainebb.com | 10 rooms | $145–$225 | AE, D, MC, V.

Sheraton Station Square. This is an upscale chain hotel on the South Side riverfront. Some rooms have river views. Restaurant, bar (with entertainment). In-room data ports, cable TV. Indoor pool. Hot tub. Exercise equipment. Business services. | 7 Station Sq. | 412/261–2000 or 800/255–7488 | fax 412/261–2932 | www.sheraton.com | 292 rooms | $99–$229 | AE, D, DC, MC, V.

Victoria House Bed and Breakfast. Rooms here have plenty of floor space and large windows, and some have cushioned rocking chairs, wooden vanities, hanging light fixtures, clawfoot tubs, and elaborately carved wooden head- and footboards. You can have an evening cocktail on the veranda, overlooking the Victorian garden's brick-paved sitting area and stone benches. Dining room, complimentary Continental breakfast, room service. No TV in some rooms. Free parking. No kids under 13. No smoking. | 939 Western Avenue | 412/231–4948 | www.victoriahouse-bb.com | 5 suites | $135 | AE, D, DC, MC, V.

Wyndham Garden Hotel–University Place. This midpriced motel is 2 mi east of downtown. Restaurant, bar, complimentary breakfast. In-room data ports, refrigerators, cable TV. Wading pool. Exercise equipment. Business services, airport shuttle. | 3454 Forbes Ave. | 412/683–2040 | fax 412/683–3934 | www.wyndham.com/universityplace | 198 rooms | $109–$199 | AE, D, DC, MC, V.

EXPENSIVE

Hilton Pittsburgh & Towers. Overlooking Point State Park is a large, elegant hotel. Its grand ballroom is the largest in Pittsburgh, and has a view of three rivers and Mt. Washington. Restaurant, 2 bars (with entertainment). In-room data ports, minibars, refrigerators, cable TV. Beauty salon. Exercise equipment. Business services, airport shuttle. Pets allowed. | 600 Commonwealth Pl., Gateway Center | 412/391–4600 | fax 412/594–5161 | www.hiltonpit.com | 713 rooms | $189–$264 | AE, D, DC, MC, V.

Westin William Penn. The grande dame of Pittsburgh hotels boasts a stately lobby with crystal chandeliers and ornate moldings, and guest rooms with marble baths. The hotel is considered a landmark. Restaurant, bar (with entertainment), room service. Cable TV. Exercise equipment. Business services, airport shuttle. Pets allowed (fee). | 530 William Penn Pl. | 412/281–7100 | fax 412/553–5252 | www.westin.com | 595 rooms | $99–$3,000 | AE, D, DC, MC, V.

PORT ALLEGANY

MAP 7, E2

(Nearby town also listed: Bradford)

Originally known as Canoe Place because of the many pioneers who traveled to the area via the Susquehanna River, Port Allegany began to grow into an industrial center when natural gas was discovered in the 1800s. Today, it's best known as the producer of glass containers for the Ball Corporation and glass blocks produced at the Pittsburgh Corning Corporation.

Information: **Port Allegany Chamber of Commerce** | 42 N. Main St., Suite 3, Allegany, PA 16743 | 814/642–2526 | fax 814/642–5095 | Mon.–Fri., 8–4.

Attractions

Eldred World War II Museum. Here in Port Allegany is a museum dedicated to unsung heroes of World War II: women workers. Rosie the Riveter and other icons are on display and the museum's exhibits tell of the struggles women faced in the factories. | 201 Main St., Eldred | 814/225–2220 | fax 814/225–4407 | www.eldredwwiimuseum.org | Free | Tues., Thurs., and Sat. 10–4, Sun. 1–4, closed Mon., Wed., and Fri.

Sinnemahoning State Park. This 1,910-acre park has an abundance of wildlife and includes feeding grounds for the American bald eagle. There are 35 campsites, one rental cabin, two hiking trails, three picnic areas, and more than 1,400 acres for hunting. You can also go boating, fishing, snowmobiling, and ice fishing. | Rte. 872 | 814/647–8401 or 888/727–2757 | fax 814/647–8982 | www.dcnr.state.pa.us | sinnemahoning@dcnr.state.pa.us | Free | Daily 8 AM–dusk.

Sizerville State Park. More than 380 acres are surrounded by the Susquehannock State Forest and filled with elk. The park has 23 campsites, many picnic sites, a 105-ft pool, and Cowley Run Stream, which allows fishing. It's open to hunting and hiking and has 66 mi of snowmobile trails. | Rte. 120 | 814/486–5605 | fax 814/486–5607 | sizerville@dcnr.state.pa.us | www.dcnr.state.pa.us | Free | Daily 8 AM–dusk.

SEPT.: *The Black Forest Star Party.* Join amateur astronomers for their annual observation weekend at Cherry Springs State Park, one of the darkest sites in Pennsylvania. If you haven't entered a homemade telescope in the contest, owners of large telescopes can let you peer through their lenses. Interactive forums are held on topics such as favorite deep-sky objects and astrophotography. There's also a swap table, door prizes for adults and kids, and a pizza party. Camping available. | 716/483–0343.

Dining
Ron's Place. American. This diner is popular with the locals for its specials—spaghetti and meatballs every Tuesday, chicken and biscuits every Wednesday, and Icelandic haddock fish fry on Fridays. The restaurant makes its own gravies and roasts its beef on the premises. Breakfast also available. | 206 North Main St. | 814/642–9353 | $5–$11 | No credit cards.

Lodging
The Poet's Walk Bed and Breakfast. This 1948 white-clapboard Cape Cod has six guest rooms—one in the basement, four on the second floor, and one in the attic, which is the only room with air-conditioning and cable TV. The rooms are plainly furnished with no common design, except that three of them have queen-size beds. The neighborhood is residential and you can stroll 2½ acres of lawn with several large trees. Dining room, complimentary breakfast. No air-conditioning in some rooms, no room phones, no TV in some rooms. Pets allowed. No smoking. | 428 Arnold Ave. | 814/642–2676 | 6 rooms | $65 | MC, V.

POTTSTOWN

MAP 7, K6

(Nearby towns also listed: Limerick, Norristown, Reading)

John Potts founded this borough in 1752, just 35 mi northwest of Philadelphia. A 1989 study revealed that Pottstown, for its size, contains some of the oldest, most architecturally significant housing in the Northeast. More than 1,000 historic homes and buildings occupy its districts. Despite being close to Philadelphia, most of the borough's 22,000 residents live and work in Pottstown.

Information: **Tri-County Area Chamber of Commerce** | 135 High St., 19464 | 610/326–2900 | fax 610/970–9705 | www.tricopa.com | Mon.–Thu. 8–5, Fri. 8–4.

Attractions
Bear Stadium. Ten mi north of Pottsdown in Boyerstown, this is the home of the Boyerstown Bears, the 1982 American Legion Baseball World Series champions. The Atlantic 10 Conference college baseball playoffs are also played here. | N. Monroe St. | 610/369–2327 | Varies according to games | Apr.–Sept.

Boyertown Museum of Historic Vehicles. View southeast Pennsylvania carriages and sleighs with a section dedicated to the evolution of the automobile. Cars range from classics to current electric models. Other automobile artifacts and memorabilia are on display. | 28 Warwick St. | 610/367–2090 | fax 610/367–9712 | www.boyertownmusuem.org | $4 | Tues.–Sun. 9:30–4, closed Mon.

French Creek State Park. For many years, the timber of this 7,339-acre park was harvested repeatedly to make charcoal for the nearby Hopewell Furnace. The park is now heavily forested, and has more than 200 campsites, 10 cabins, and you can fish, swim, picnic, and hunt. | 843 Park Rd., Elverson | 610/582–9680 | www.dcnr.state.pa.us | Free | Daily 8 AM–dusk.

Hopewell Furnace National Historic Site. Hopewell's iron furnace was in use from 1771 to 1883. The iron produced here was put to many uses, including arms used by colonists during the Revolutionary War. You can enjoy a living history program that shows molding and casting demonstrations in summer. The site now has 14 restored structures, including a cold-blast furnace and the ironmaster mansion, and more than 848 wooded acres of trails. Self-guided tours using park brochures, wayside exhibits, and audio stations help you tour the site at your own pace. | 2 Mark Bird La., Elverson | 610/582–8773 | fax 610/582–2768 | www.nps.gov/hofu | $4 | Daily 9–5.

Mary Merritt Doll Museum. The preservation of old and unique dolls is the goal of this museum. Many of the dolls are clothed in their original dresses. The museum has a miniature room with antique dolls from around the world. | 843 Ben Franklin Hwy. W, Douglassville | 610/385–3809 | www.merritts.com/dollmuseum | $3 | Mon., Wed.–Sat. 10–4:30, Sun. 1–4, closed Tue.

Merritt's Museum of Childhood. Old baby carriages and postcards are some of the unique items you can find here. The museum is dedicated to items we threw away as children and pays homage to what life as a child was like. | 907 Ben Franklin Hwy. W, Douglassville | 610/385–3408 | www.merritts.com/childhoodmuseum | $3 | Mon., Wed.–Sat. 10–4:30, Sun. 1–5, closed Tue.

Pottsgrove Manor. The former home of John Potts, iron master and the founder of Pottstown, still stands today. The manor was built in 1752 and has been restored to its original appearance with antiques and period furnishings. | 100 W. King St. | 610/326–4014 | fax 610/326–9618 | www.montcopa.org | Free | Tues.–Sat. 10–4, Sun. 1–4, closed Mon.

Sunnybrook Ballroom and Entertainment Center. The "Home of Swing," Sunnybrook Ballroom was built in 1931, with folks dancing to Benny Goodman and the Dorseys; the site of Glen Miller's last American concert and Frank Sinatra's first. Today, the facility hosts dinner-dances and special events including the return of the big bands. | E. High St. | 610/326–6400 | fax 610/326–2101 | sunnybrooks4U@aol.com | $5-$18.

POTTSTOWN

INTRO
ATTRACTIONS
DINING
LODGING

ON THE CALENDAR

JULY: *July Fourth Pottstown Parade.* This is a traditional 4th of July community parade, with bands, clowns, and floats, held in downtown from mid-morning to after-dark fireworks. | 610/326–2900.

SEPT.: *Duryea Day Antique and Classic Auto Show.* This Labor Day weekend event, held in Boyertown Community Park, has antique vehicles—including cars and trucks—along with crafts, a flea market with automobile memorabilia, and Pennsylvania Dutch food. | 610/326–2900 or 610/375–4375.

Dining

Coventry Forge Inn. French. The main house was built in 1717, the guest house in 1806, and most furnishings and fixtures are early 18th century. Specials include rack of lamb, sweetbreads, and quail. | 3360 Coventryville Rd. | 610/469–6222 | Closed Mon., Sun. No lunch | $16–$27 | AE, DC, MC, V.

Ice House Deli. American. Here's traditional deli food in a former ice house. Featured items include triple-decker sandwiches, steak hoagies, and a California cheese-steak sandwich. Fries come with gravy, cheese, or jalapenos. | 1 King St. | 610/326–9999 | $3–$11 | AE, D, DC, MC, V.

Sly Fox Brewing Company. American/Continental. In the Pikeland Village Shopping Center, this is a brewpub with kettles in full view, wood fixtures, and a staircase in the middle of the room. The menu has Mediterranean yellowfin tuna, brewpub steak, and tuna Nicosia salad. | Rte. 113, Phoenixville | 610/935–4540 | fax 610/935–4541 | $9–$17 | AE, MC, V.

Lodging

Comfort Inn. This motel is about 1 mi from Pottsgrove Manor. Complimentary Continental breakfast, room service. In-room data ports, some refrigerators, cable TV. Pool. Laundry facilities. Business services. Pets allowed. | Rte. 100 and Shoemaker Rd., | 610/326–5000 |

fax 610/970–7230 | www.pottstownpacomfortinn.com | 151 rooms | $89–$119 | AE, D, DC, MC, V.

Days Inn. This two-story motel is at the end of downtown and close to highways. Complimentary Continental breakfast. Some microwaves, some refrigerators, cable TV. Pets allowed (fee). | 29 High St. | 610/970–1101, 800/329–7466 | fax 610/327–8643 | www.daysinn.com | 59 rooms | $39–$69 | AE, D, DC, MC, V.

Holiday Inn Express. This midpriced hotel caters mostly to business travelers. Complimentary Continental breakfast. In-room data ports, some refrigerators, cable TV. Pool. Business services, free parking. Pets allowed. | 1600 Industrial Hwy./U.S. 422 | 610/327–3300 | fax 610/327–9447 | www.hiexpottstownpa.com | 120 rooms | $79–$135 | AE, D, DC, MC, V.

Twin Turrets. The Twin Turrets Inn is a comfortable 19th-century mansion in the heart of a small 19th-century town. Built for Horace K. Boyer, circa 1850, the home was restored to its original Victorian splendor in 1988. The inn has period furnishings and a garden with a fountain. Complimentary breakfast. Cable TV. Business services. No kids under 12. No smoking. | 11 E. Philadelphia Ave., Boyertown | 610/367–4513 | fax 610/369–7898 | turrets@netjunction.com | www.twinturrets.com | 10 rooms (9 with shower only) | $105–$130 | AE, D, MC, V.

POTTSVILLE

MAP 7, J5

(Nearby towns also listed: Ashland, Fogelsville, Hamburg, Shartlesville)

In 1806, John Pott (different from the John Potts who founded Pottstown) purchased an anthracite-fired iron furnace and founded the city. The town grew thanks to the coal mines and is known for the Pottsville Maroons, a professional football team that won the equivalent of today's Super Bowl after beating the Chicago Cardinals at Soldier Field in Chicago. Today, Pottsville showcases its industrial roots with museums dedicated to anthracite mining and railroads.

Information: **Schuylkill Chamber of Commerce** | 91 S. Progress Ave., 17901–2987 | 570/622–1942 | fax 570/622–1638 | www.schuylkillchamber.com | Mon.–Fri. 8:30–4:30.

Attractions

Locust Lake State Park. The 1,144-acre park has a 52-acre lake, where you can go boating, fishing, and swimming. There are 282 campsites and three play areas. About 1,045 acres are open to hunting. | Exit 37, Rte. 81 | 570/467–2404, campground in summer 570/467–2772, or general state park information 888/727–2757 | fax 570/467–0234 | www.dcnr.state.pa.us | Free | Daily 8 AM–dusk.

Yuengling Brewery and Museum. This is America's oldest brewery, built in 1829. In 1976, it was placed on the National and State Historic Registers. | 5th and Mahantongo St. | 570/628–4890 | www.yuengling.com | Free | Weekdays 9–4, Sat. 10–3, closed Sun.

ON THE CALENDAR

JAN.: *Pottsville Winter Carnival.* This two-week carnival sponsored by local businesses has pageants with musical performances for elementary, middle-school, and 18-and-above young women. The carnival ends with a dance and downtown parade. | 410 Laurel Blvd. | 570/628–2702. .

Dining

Atrium Restaurant. American. Serves breakfast, lunch and dinner; crabcakes are a speciality. Lunch specials change weekly. Salad bar and Sunday buffet. | 100 S. Centre St. | 570/622–4600 | fax 570/628–5971 | $7–$22 | AE, D, MC, V.

Lodging

Pottsville Motor Inn. This two-story motel is 1½ mi north on Rte. 61. Cable TV. | 480 N. Cloudalord Blvd. | 570/622–4917 | fax 570/622–2889 | 27 rooms | $35–$65 | MC, V.

PUNXSUTAWNEY

(Nearby towns also listed: Brookville, Du Bois, Indiana)

Once a year Punxsutawney becomes a media darling when one little *marmota monax* pops its head out of a hole to determine if he can see his shadow. Punxsutawney Phil, the groundhog that has made the town famous, comes from a tradition that can be traced back to Native Americans who believed in this weather-predicting legend and passed it along to the area's newest settlers. Punxsutawney has no shortage of media attention on February 2.

Information: Punxsutawney Area Chamber of Commerce | 124 W. Mahoning St., 15767 | 814/938–7700 or 800/752–7445 | fax 814/938–4303 | pcoc@penn.com | www.punxsutawneychamber.com | Mon.–Fri. 9–5, Sat. 9–2.

Attractions

Groundhog Zoo. This is where Punxsutawney Phil lives, the famous groundhog that predicts every Groundhog Day when spring can arrive, depending on whether he sees his shadow. | 124 W. Mahoning St. | 814/938–2710 | Free | Daily.

ON THE CALENDAR

FEB.: *Groundhog Day.* This annual rite of winter attracts thousands of eager folks who come up to Gobbler's Knob each February 2 to find out whether Punxsutawney Phil can see his shadow—a sign of six more weeks of cold weather. | Wood St. | 814/938–7700.

PACKING IDEAS FOR COLD WEATHER

- ❏ Driving gloves
- ❏ Earmuffs
- ❏ Fanny pack
- ❏ Fleece neck gaiter
- ❏ Fleece parka
- ❏ Hats
- ❏ Lip balm
- ❏ Long underwear
- ❏ Scarf
- ❏ Shoes to wear indoors
- ❏ Ski gloves or mittens

- ❏ Ski hat
- ❏ Ski parka
- ❏ Snow boots
- ❏ Snow goggles
- ❏ Snow pants
- ❏ Sweaters
- ❏ Thermal socks
- ❏ Tissues, handkerchief
- ❏ Turtlenecks
- ❏ Wool or corduroy pants

*Excerpted from *Fodor's: How to Pack: Experts Share Their Secrets*
© 1997, by Fodor's Travel Publications

Dining

Pantall Hotel. Continental. The coach room serves as the hotel's restaurant and is filled with antiques, prints, paintings, and collector plates. There's also an old-fashioned Victorian bar. Known for seafood, soups, and steaks. Sun. brunch.| 135 E. Mahoning St.| 814/938–6600 | fax 814/938–8592 | www.pantallhotel.com | $7–$15 | AE, D, DC, MC, V.

Pasquale's Italian Deli. American. Specializes in a "hot" bar with meats, sides, heliuski–fried cabbage and noodles—and hot-sausage sandwiches.| State Rte. 119 | 814/938–2570 | Closed Sun. | $1–$4.50 | No credit cards.

Lodging

Stonehouse Bed and Breakfast. Built in the 1940s by the owner's grandfather, the house sits on a fieldstone foundation. Modernized in the 1990s, the rooms are furnished with Victorian antiques. Complimentary breakfast. No room phones, no TV.| 210 Center St.| 814/938–5972 | 2 | $65–$75 | MC, V.

QUAKERTOWN

MAP 7, K6

(Nearby towns also listed: Allentown, Bethlehem, Doylestown, Pottstown)

Settled by Quakers from Wales in 1715, Quakertown drew attention to itself because of its residents' disdain for a state tax to help generate funds for the war against France. Today, its German heritage is celebrated and some of the unique architecture remains. The town is very hospitable to travelers—there are several places to stay right next to the Turnpike Extension (U.S. 476), and a long strip of restaurants along Rte. 309.

Information: Bucks County Conference & Visitor's Bureau | 152 Swamp Road, Doylestown, PA 18901 | 215/345–4552 or 800/836–2825 | fax 215/345–4967 | bccvb@bccvb.org | www.buckscountycvb.org | Mon.–Fri. 8:30–4:30.

Attractions

Mennonite Heritage Center. The museum and center replicate one of the original gathering places for early Mennonite settlers. Their story is told through photographs, exhibits, and a video presentation. | 565 Yoder Rd., Harleysville | 215/256–3020 | fax 215/256–3023 | www.mhep.org | Tues.–Fri. 10–5, Sat. 10–2, Sun. 2–5.

Morgan Log House. Built in 1700, the house belonged to the grandparents of Daniel Boone. Nearly 90 percent of the log-and-stone house remains intact since it was built. Inside the house you can learn about the Welsh Quaker lifestyle and see antiques and period furnishings. Tours are given by volunteers dressed in period clothing.| 850 Weikel Rd., Kulpsville | 215/368–2480 | fax 215/368–2480 | www.morganloghouse.org | $3 | Apr.–Dec., Thu., Sat., Sun. 10–6.

Nockamixon State Park. Lake Nockamixon is the center of the park, with 5,283 acres of woodland. Equestrians have access to 20 mi of horse trails, bicyclists can follow the 2.8 mi bike trail, and hunters can explore about 3,000 acres of the park. You can also go boating, swimming, fishing, picnicking, ice skating, ice fishing, cross-country skiing, and sledding.| 1542 Mountain View Dr. | 215/529–7300, 215/538–1340, 215/538–2243, or 888/727–2757 | www.dcnr.state.pa.us | Free | Daily 8 AM–dusk.

Ralph Stover State Park. The High Rocks section of this park has an outstanding view of a horseshoe bend in Tohickon Creek and the surrounding forest. The park has 45 acres along Tohickon Creek, where you can go fishing, whitewater boating, and swimming. Other activities include hiking and picnicking. | R.R. 1, Upper Black Eddy | 610/982–5560 or 888/727–2757 | www.dcnr.state.pa.us | Free | Daily 8 AM–dusk.

OCT.: *Keystone Quilters Annual Quilt Show.* Quilts and wearable art are on display the 2nd weekend in October at the United Church of Christ. Door prizes and quilt raffle. | 215/489–0875.

Dining

Bubba's Potbelly Stove. American. The building and layout are no-frills simple, with heavy wood paneling and local mementos, but the tasty food draws people from all over. The restaurant is well-known for its steaks and seafood. | 1485 N. Rte. 309 | 215/536–8308 | fax 215/536–8390 | $8–$16 | AE, D, MC, V.

Meyers Restaurant. Continental. Traditional Dutch cooking is done in a country background, with a brightly colored interior, fresh flowers, and white linen tablecloths. Chicken pie is a specialty. All baking is done on the premises. | 501 N. Westend Blvd./Rte. 309 | 215/536–4422 | fax 215/536–0439 | $10–$12 | AE, D, MC, V.

Lodging

Best Western Motor Inn. This motel is off Rte. 309, 3 mi from the PA Turnpike Extension (U.S. 476), and 6 mi from Nockamixon State Park. Restaurant. Some kitchenettes, cable TV. Gym. Laundry service. Business services. | 1446 W. Broad St. | 215/536–2500 | fax 215/536–2508 | www.bestwestern.com | 40 rooms | $85–$105 | AE, CB, D, DC, MC, V.

Econo Lodge. This low-price hotel is off Exit 32 of the PA Turnpike Extension (U.S. 476). Picnic area, complimentary Continental breakfast. Some microwaves, some refrigerators, some in-room hot tubs, cable TV. Business services. | 1905 John Fries Hwy./Rte. 663 | 215/538–3000 | fax 2215/538–2311 | www.econolodge.com | 48 rooms | $50–$150 | AE, CB, D, DC, MC, V.

Rodeway Inn. This motel is at Exit 32 of the PA Turnpike Extension (U.S. 476). Complimentary Continental breakfast. In-room data ports, some microwaves, some in-room hot tubs, cable TV. Pets allowed. | 1920 Rte. 663 | 215/536–7600 | fax 215/536–5922 | www.rodewayinn.com | $50–$139 | AE, D, DC, MC, V.

READING

(Nearby towns also listed: Adamstown, Denver, Hamburg, Kutztown, Lancaster, Pottstown)

The explosion of outlet shopping across the country can be traced to Reading and its three outlet-shopping districts. While the rest of the country was waiting for sales at their favorite stores, residents of Reading were enjoying discounts at stores whose main goal was to get rid of merchandise that was either out of date or slightly damaged.

Information: **Berks County Chamber of Commerce** | 601 Penn St., 19601 | 610/376–6766 or 800/443–6610 | fax 610/376–4135 | www.berkscounty.com | Mon.–Fri. 8–4:30.

Attractions

Berks County Heritage Center. This is the site of the Gruber Wagon Works, the C. Howard Heister Canal Center, and other historic sites. A bike and walking tour is available around the 370-acre park. | 2201 Tulpehocken Rd. | 610/374–8839 or 610/372–8939 | fax 610/373–7049 | www.berksparkand rec.org | $5 | May–Oct., Tues.–Sat. 10–4, Sun. 12–5, closed Mon.

Conrad Weiser Homestead. A pivotal figure in the history of Pennsylvania was Conrad Weiser, and you can tour his 18th-century frontier residence. His stone home, spring house, and grave site are part of a 26-acre park. | 28 Weiser Rd. | 610/589–2934 | fax 610/589–9458 | www.berksweb.com/conrad.html | $2.50 | Wed.–Sun. 9–5, closed Mon.–Tues.

Daniel Boone Homestead. Settled in 1730 by the famous frontiersman's parents, the homestead was the site of Boone's birth in 1734 and where he lived his first 16 years. Today the site tells of the early years of Boone's life and of the settlers who came to the area. | 400 Daniel Boone Rd. | 610/582–4900 | fax 610/582–4900 | www.berksweb.com/boone.html | $4 | Tue.–Sat. 9–5, Sun. 12–5.

Historical Society of Berks County. The historical society is a popular destination for people studying genealogy. It's also home to a museum with artifacts, books, and other information about Reading and Berks County. | 940 Centre Ave. | 610/375–4375 | www.berksweb.com/histsoc | $2.50 | Tues.–Sat. 9–4, closed Sun.–Mon.

Koziar's Christmas Village. It lasts only six weeks a year, but what a show. More than 700,000 Christmas lights adorn buildings, barns, and the landscape to create a true Christmas feeling. This event started in 1948 with one man decorating a bit of his property, and has grown ever since. | 782 Christmas Village Rd., Bernville | 610/488–1110 | $6 | Mon.–Sun. 5:30–9:30.

Mid-Atlantic Air Museum. More than 30 vintage and rare airplanes, including those from World War II, highlight the exhibit. A B-25 bomber and P-61 Black Widow are in perfect running condition, as are all the other planes here. | 11 Museum Dr. | 610/372–7333 | www.maam.org | $5 | Daily 9:30–4.

Nolde Forest Environmental Education Center. Nolde Forest has more than 665 acres of woodlands; a network of trails makes the center's streams, ponds, and diverse habitats accessible. The C.H. McConnell Environmental Education Hall is the indoor site for year-round educational programs. | 2910 New Holland Rd. | 610/796–3699 or 888/PA–PARKS | www.dcnr.state.pa.us | Free | Daily 8 AM–dusk.

Outlet Shopping. Reading is considered the outlet capital of the world because the concept of outlet shopping originated in its downtown. Today three areas of the city have outlet malls, but the main hub is in a five-block radius. More than 100 stores have an array of shops and restaurants. Shuttles can take you to every store. | 801 Hill Ave. | 610/375–4085 | www.outletsonline.com/roc | Free | Weekdays 9–9, Sat. 1–7, Sun. 10–5.

Reading Phillies. The Double A affiliate of the Philadelphia Phillies has been associated with the parent club since 1967, which makes the team the fourth oldest minor league affiliate in the history of major league baseball. They are a member of the Eastern League of Pro Baseball and play at Reading Memorial Stadium. | 1900 Centre Ave. | 610/375–8469 | fax 610/373–5868 | www.readingphillies.com | $3–$7 | Apr.–Sept.

ON THE CALENDAR

JUNE: *World War II Commemorative Weekend.* This event is a kind of living history lesson with battle reenactments and appearances by World War II veterans. | Mid-Atlantic Air Museum, Rte. 183 | 610/372–7333.

Dining

Antique Airplane. American. Pictures of famous planes and aviators dress up the walls, while miniature planes and actual plane parts complete the theme. Crab cake, prime rib, and salmon are some of the specialties. Kids' menu. | 4635 Perkiomen Ave. | 610/779–2345 | fax 610/779–8348 | $8–$18 | Closed Sun. | AE, D, DC, MC, V.

Canal Street Pub/Neversink Brewing Company. Contemporary. The pub is in the old Reading Hardware building and still has its original massive wood beams running in pairs along the ceiling. A formal dining area is beyond the pub. The pub has greasy spoon-type American dishes while the main dining area has full entrees—including duck and filets. | 545 Canal St. | 610/376–4009 | $7–$15 | AE, DC, MC, V.

Moselem Springs Inn. American. The house was built in 1852 and there are many dining rooms, each with a distinctive look. Kids' menu. | 14351 Kutztown Rd. | 610/944–8213 | $11–$20 | AE, DC, MC, V.

Stokesay Castle. Contemporary. A true castle was built here in 1931 as a honeymoon cottage, with hand-carved beams, leaded-glass windows, a cathedral ceiling, and many pieces of medieval armor and weaponry. Try the chicken marsala, prime rib, grilled salmon, or even frog legs. | Hill Rd. and Spook Ln | 610/375–4588 | fax 610/375-4126 | www.stokesay-castle.com | No lunch Sun. | $15–$35 | AE, D, DC, MC, V.

Lodging

Best Western Dutch Colony Inn. This motel is 3 mi from downtown Reading. Restaurant, bar, room service. Cable TV. Pool. Laundry facilities. Business services, free parking. Pets allowed. | 4635 Perkiomen Ave. | 610/779–2345 or 800/828–2830 | fax 610/779–8348 | www.best-western.com | 71 rooms | $65–$90 | AE, D, DC, MC, V.

Comfort Inn. Three miles from the outlet malls and 8 mi from Koziar's Christmas Village is this chain hotel. Complimentary Continental breakfast. In-room data ports, some refrigerators, cable TV. Exercise equipment. Business services, airport shuttle, free parking. | 2200 Stacy Dr. (5th St. Hwy.) | 610/371–0500 | fax 610/478–9421 | www.comfortinn.com | 60 rooms | $60–$125 | AE, D, DC, MC, V.

Country Inn Motel. Independently owned, this motel 3 mi west of Reading has two-bedroom suites with kitchens. Close to outlet stores. Cable TV. | 330 E. Wyomissing Ave., Mohnton | 610/777–2579 or 800/872–8452 | fax 610/685–7981 | 8 rooms, 28 suites | rooms $39–$49, suites $49–$59 | AE, D, MC, V.

Econo Lodge Outlet Village. This chain motel has reasonable rates and is half a mile from the outlet malls. Complimentary Continental breakfast. Some microwaves, refrigerators, cable TV. Exercise equipment. Laundry facilities. Business services. Pets allowed (fee). | 635 Spring St., Wyomissing | 610/378–5105 | fax 610/373–3181 | www.econolodgewyomissing.com | 84 rooms | $54–$150 | AE, D, MC, V.

Holiday Inn. A chain hotel, it's at Exit 22 of the PA Turnpike. Restaurant, bar, room service. In-room data ports, some refrigerators, cable TV. Indoor pool. Hot tub. Exercise equipment. Business services. Pets allowed. | 230 Cherry Ln./Rte. 10, Morgantown | 610/286–3000 | fax 610/286–0520 | www.holiday-inn.com | 192 rooms | $99–$119 | AE, D, DC, MC, V.

House on the Canal Bed and Breakfast. This restored farmhouse, dating from the late 1700s, is on the banks of the Schuylkill River, with a view of Felix Dam falls. There are hardwood floors, antiques, and fresh flowers in the rooms. Complimentary breakfast. Some in-room hot tubs. Cable TV. | 4020 River Rd. | 610/921–3015 | 3 | $125–$150 | No credit cards.

Inn at Reading. This sprawling motel is 10 min away from most outlet shopping. Restaurant, bar (with entertainment), picnic area, room service. In-room data ports, cable TV. Outdoor pool. Exercise equipment. Business services, airport shuttle, free parking. Pets allowed. | 1040 Park Rd., Wyomissing | 610/372–7811 or 800/383–9713 | fax 610/372–4545 | www.inna-treading.com | 250 rooms | $89–$139 | AE, D, DC, MC, V.

Ramada Inn at the Outlets of Reading. This is a two-story chain motel. Some microwaves, some refrigerators, cable TV. Outdoor pool. Pets allowed (fee). | 2545 N. 5th St. | 610/929–4741 or 800/272–6232 | fax 610/929–5237 | 139 | $59–$79 | AE, D, DC, MC, V.

Sheraton Reading. The hotel is made up of two sections, with luxury rooms housed in a five-story tower. Restaurant, bar (with entertainment), room service. In-room data ports, cable TV. Indoor pool. Hot tub. Putting green. Exercise equipment. Business services, airport shuttle, free parking. Pets allowed (fee). | 1741 Papermill Rd. | 610/376–3811 | fax 610/375–7562 | www.sheraton.com | 255 rooms | $89–$149 | AE, D, DC, MC, V.

READING

INTRO
ATTRACTIONS
DINING
LODGING

ST. MARYS

(Nearby towns also listed: Clearfield, Du Bois, Kane)

One of Pennsylvania's first German settlements, the town was founded by the German Catholic Brotherhood and named St. Marien in honor of the Virgin Mary. Today, St. Marys pays homage to its heritage with various restaurants and an inn constructed in German architecture.

Information: **St. Marys Area Chamber of Commerce,** | 4 Shawmut Sq., 15857 | 814/781–3804 | fax 814/781–7302 | www.stmaryschamber.com.

Attractions

Elk herd. The largest natural roaming elk herd east of the Mississippi River, with almost 700 in the herd, wanders through the area. The elk are most often seen near the airport in St. Marys or in the Benezette area. Please respect any "Private Property" signs while elk-watching! The best time to see the elk is in early morning or late afternoon. The current elk range covers 227 sq mi in southwestern Cameron and southeastern Elk counties. | 814/834–3723 | fax 814/834–3725 | www.iup.edu/~ferenc/pa_elk.htmlx | Free | Daily.

ON THE CALENDAR

SEPT.: *Hometown Festival.* An annual downtown festival held the weekend after Labor Day, you see arts and crafts, hear continuous live music, storytelling, and watch juggling, and a talent show. Don't miss the firemen propelling barrels down the street with their hoses in the Battle of the Barrels. | 814/781–3804.

Dining

Bavarian Inn. German. This inn may remind you of a traditional German tavern, with a touch of local history thrown into the mix. A mural of the life of St. Mary is prominently displayed, accompanied by exposed brick walls and wooden furniture. House specials are the "Best of Wurst," spaetzels, and schnitzel. Kids' menu. | 33 S. St. Marys St. | 814/834–2161 | www.users.penn.com/~carberry/bavarianinn | Closed Sun. No lunch Sat. | $10–$19 | AE, MC, V, D.

The Towne House Inn. Continental. Built in the early 1907, the Towne House still has its original leaded and stained-glass windows and Victorian antiques, memorabilia, and a working fireplace. Pasta primavera, salmon, and steak are some of the menu options. | 138 Center St. | 814/781–1556 or 800/851–9180 | fax 814/834–4449 | www.shopstmarys.com/towne | Closed Sun. No lunch Sat. | $15–$30 | AE, D, DC, MC, V.

Lodging

Old Charm Bed and Breakfast. Home of the founder of Straub Brewery, the red brick main house and carriage house, both built in 1917, have been converted. A gift shop sells country crafts. Complimentary breakfast. Cable TV. | 444 Brussells St. | 814/834–9429 | fax 814/834–1587 | 5 rooms | $52 | AE, D, MC, V.

SCRANTON

(Nearby towns also listed: Carbondale, Hawley, Wilkes-Barre)

For nearly 60 years Scranton was known as the anthracite kingdom of Pennsylvania. That industry helped build its downtown and many mansions. When the coal industry fell on hard times, the city certainly felt it. Today it has recovered and has become a popular tourist destination because of its Victorian- and Georgian-style homes and because the Pocono Mountains are less than 30 mi away.

Information: **Scranton Chamber of Commerce** | 222 Mulberry St., 18501 | 570/342–7711 | fax 570/347–6262 | www.scrantonchamber.com.

Attractions

Archbald Pothole State Park. The 150-acre park has a 38-ft-deep glacial pot hole, a geologic feature that formed 15,000 years ago. There are hiking trails and hunting on more than 100 acres. | Rte. 6 east off I–81 | 570/945–3239 or 888/727–2757 | fax 570/945–7097 | www.dcnr.state.pa.us | Free | Daily 8 AM–dusk.

Catlin House. A former library club has become a museum in this 1912 pre-Tudor- style home. The mansion has antiques and period furnishings. | 232 Monroe Ave. | 570/344–3841 | fax 570/344–3815 | Free | Tues.–Fri. 10–5, Sat. 12–3, closed Sun.–Mon.

Everhart Museum. Founded in 1908, it originally held a collection of Dr. Everhart's ornithological items, including mounted birds, fish, and mammals. Today it has Native American relics, plants, and fossils, a stegosaurus skeleton, Japanese artwork, and folk art. | 1901 Mulberry St. | 570/346–8370 | fax 570/346–0652 | www.everhart-museum.org | $5 | Wed.–Sun. 12–4, closed Mon.–Tue.

Lackawanna Coal Mine Tour. A guided tour takes you down a 300-ft coal mine that reveals what life was like for miners while the mine was in operation. Built in early 1860, the mine closed in 1966 and was converted into a tour site with actual mining cars to take people through the mine. The walking tour takes an hour and the mine stays a constant 52 degrees. | Bald Mountain Rd. | 570/963–6463 or 800/238–7245 | www.thevisitorscenter.com | $6 | Apr.–Nov., daily 10–4:20.

Lackawanna County Stadium. The stadium is currently the home of the Scranton/Wilkes-Barre Red Barons, an affiliate of the Philadelphia Phillies. | Montage Mountain Rd. | Exit 51 off Rte. 81 | 570/969–2255 | www.redbarons.com/stadium | $4–$7 | Apr.–Nov.

Lackawanna State Park. A focal point of the 1,411-acre park is 198-acre Lackawanna Lake, where you can go swimming and fishing. There are 96 campsites, picnic facilities, more than 5 mi of hiking trails, an equestrian trail, and more than 500 acres for hunting. | Rte. 407 | 570/945–3239 or 888/727–2757 | fax 570/945–7097 | www.dcnr.state.pa.us | Free | Daily 8 AM–dusk.

Montage Ski Area. With 140 acres of snow, this resort gives you your choice of skiing or snow tubing down its 22 trails. A 1,000-ft vertical drop ensures long rides from the top of the mountain. In summer, water slides help fight the heat. | 1000 Montage Mountain Rd. | 570/969–7669 | fax 570/963–6621 | www.skimontage.com | Mar.–Dec.

Nay Aug Park. This large park adjacent to Everhart Museum has two swimming pools, a bandstand, and pavilions. Extensive walking trails can be fun, especially when you have a view of the former amusement park or nearby museum. | Arthur Ave. | 570/348–4186 | fax 570/348–0270 | Free | Daily 9–dusk.

Pennsylvania Anthracite Heritage Museum. The museum tells the story of the people who came to the region to work in mills, mines, and factories. It looks at the area's culture and lifestyles in that time period as well as the impact those industries had on the community. | Bald Mountain Rd. | 570/963–4804 | fax 570/963–4194 | $3.50 | Mon.–Sat. 9–5, Sun. noon–5.

Scranton Iron Furnaces. Four massive stone-blast furnaces formerly used by the Lackawanna Iron and Coal Company lay dormant today. The furnaces, built in 1848 and 1857, are explored in a tour that gives you a glimpse of a worker's life. These furnaces were said to be the second largest producer of iron in the United States during their prime. | 159 Cedar Ave. | 570/963–3208 or 570/963–4804 | fax 570/963–4194 | Free | Daily 9–5 (grounds); Visitor Center Memorial Day–Labor Day, daily 9–5.

Scranton/Wilkes-Barre Red Barons. The Lackawanna County multipurpose stadium was built in 1989 and it brought the return of baseball to the area after a 30-year absence. The team is the Triple A affiliate of the Philadelphia Phillies. | 235 Montage Mountain Rd. | 570/969–2255 | fax 570/963–6564 | www.redbarons.com | $4.50–$7 | Apr.–Sept.

Steamtown National Historic Site. Congress created this attraction in 1986 to tell the story of mainline railroading from 1850 to 1950. The site occupies 40 acres of the former Scranton railroad yards, and has buildings constructed in 1865. Three operating steam locomotives are on display. | 150 S. Washington Ave. | 570/340–5204 or 888/693–9391 | www.microserve.net/~magicusa/steamtown.html | $15 | Daily 9–5.

ON THE CALENDAR

SEPT.: *Montage Mountain Fall Harvest Festival.* Annual event held at the Lackawanna County Stadium has 125 juried booths of artists and craftspeople, with fine arts, flowers, and fruit. | 800/229–3526.

Dining

Cooper's Seafood House. Seafood. The variety of fish served here makes it a favorite dining spot for locals. The interior is furnished with fish nets, paddles, life rings, and fish pictures. Fish dishes include Atlantic roughy filet, stuffed flounder, and salmon filet, or you can choose other dishes such as steak. Kids' menu. | 701 N. Washington Ave. | 570/346–6883 | fax 570/346–7008 | www.coopers-seafood.com | $12–$27 | AE, D, MC, V.

Coney Island Lunch. American. In Scranton's historic downtown, locals swear by the Texas wiener, covered with firehouse chili, diced onions, and Dusseldorf mustard. Finish with a slice of Mineo's apple or coconut cream pie or some rice pudding. | 515 Lackawanna Ave. | 570/961–9004 | $1.50–$5.50 | No credit cards.

Kelly's Pub & Eatery. American/Casual. This restaurant was founded in 1990 by the Cosgrove sisters. They serve mostly pub-style food such as burgers and sandwiches. Hot wings are the house specialty – you can get them in plain, extra-mild, mild, medium, hot, or extra hot. No credit cards. | 1802 Cedar Ave. | 570/346–9758 | www.kpehotwings.com | No lunch.

Manning Farm Dairy. American. This place is known for its reputation as serving the "greatest tasting ice cream." Choose among ice-cream cones, sundaes, pies, and cakes. Dairy tours. | 210 Meadow Ave. | 570/961–1645 | $1.50–$5 | No credit cards. .

Ryah House. American. You can sit in the fireside lounge with oak tables and a lighter menu, or in the main dining room with Asian paper lanterns, exposed brick, fresh flowers and a central bamboo tree where the menu, possibly including herb-crusted roasted pork tenderloin with apple smoked bacon and provençal tomato sauce or oyster, mushroom, spinach, and salmon Napolean in phyllo dough with pesto and beurre blanc, changes seasonally. Live music Wednesday–Saturday. | 1101 Northern Blvd.; Two mi north of Scranton in Clark Summit | 570/587–1135 or 800/642–2215 | $18–$39 | AE, D, MC, V.

Vince the Pizza Prince. Pizza. This is a true family establishment. Vince Sr. ran the business from 1955 until 1995, when he passed on and his son, Vince Jr., inherited the pizza parlor. You can get hoagies, white pizza, or the "crowning pinnacle," the Prince Special pizza with everything on it. | 600 Pittston Ave. | 570/347–0675 | www.vincetheprince.com | No lunch. Closed Mon., closed Tue. except in Dec. | $4–$18.

W.T. Hackett's Brewing Co. American. This brewpub serves pasta, burgers and seafood. Beers featured are Scotch Ale, Christmas Spice Beer, and Belgian Chocolate Raspberry Beer. | 130 N. Washington Ave. | 570/961–5600 | $7–$25 | AE, D, DC, MC, V.

Lodging

Clarion Hotel Scranton. This eight-story hotel is 4 mi north of the Montage Mountain Ski Area and Lackawanna County attractions. Restaurant, complimentary breakfast. In-room data ports, cable TV. Exercise equipment. | 311 Meadow Ave. | 570/344–9811, or 800/252–7466 | fax 570/344–7799 | 135 rooms | $85–$119 | AE, D, DC, MC, V.

Comfort Suites Scranton. This is a four-story all-suites hotel on Montage Mountain, near the Lackawanna Baseball Stadium and Montage Mountain Ski Area. | 100 suites. Complimentary breakfast. In-room data ports, some microwaves, some refrigerators, cable TV. Indoor pool. Hot tub. Exercise equipment. Video games. | 44 Montage Mountain Rd. | 570/347–1551, or 800/517–4000 | fax 570/347–1511 | $83–$220 | AE, D, DC, MC, V.

Comfort Suites. The draw of this motel is that it is 1 mi from Montage Mountain ski resort. Complimentary Continental breakfast. Cable TV. Indoor pool. Hot tub. Exercise equipment. Business services, airport shuttle, free parking. | 22 Montage Mountain Rd. | 570/347–1551 | fax 570/347–1511 | www.comfortinn.com | 129 rooms | $80–$110 | AE, D, DC, MC, V.

Days Inn. This chain motel is at Exit 55A off I–81. Complimentary Continental breakfast. Refrigerators, cable TV. Business services, free parking. Pets allowed (fee). | 1226 O'Neill Hwy., Dunmore | 570/348–6101 | fax 570/348–5064 | www.daysinn.com | 88 rooms | $65–$100 | AE, D, DC, MC, V.

EconoLodge Scranton. This is a two-story hotel, 2 mi from skiing, 10 min from Steamtown and the coal mines. Complimentary Continental breakfast. In-room data ports, some in-room hot tubs. Pets allowed (fee). | 1175 Kane St. | 570/348–1000 or 800/553–2666 | fax 570/348–0683 | 64 rooms | $30–$95 | AE, D, DC, MC, V.

Holiday Inn–East. A chain hotel, it's at Exit 1 of I–380. Restaurant, bar, room service. In-room data ports, cable TV. Pool. Exercise equipment. Video games. Business services, free parking. Pets allowed (fee). | 200 Tigue St., Dunmore | 570/343–4771 | fax 570/343–5171 | www.holiday-inn.com | 139 rooms | $89–$149 | AE, D, DC, MC, V.

Inn at Nichols Village. What began as a family-owned roadside motel in the 1940s has evolved into a hotel on beautifully landscaped grounds with two restaurants and a commitment to good service. Restaurant, bar, complimentary breakfast, room service. In-room data ports, cable TV. Indoor pool. Exercise equipment. Business services, airport shuttle. | 1101 Northern Blvd., Clarks Summit | 570/587–1135 or 800/642–2215 | fax 570/586–7140 | www.nicholsvillage.com | 135 rooms | $89–$139 | AE, D, DC, MC, V.

Radisson Lackawanna Station. This upscale hotel is a 1908 structure listed on the National Register of Historic Places. Restaurant, bar. In-room data ports, some refrigerators, in-room hot tubs, cable TV. Hot tub. Exercise equipment. Business services, airport shuttle. | 700 Lackawanna Ave. | 570/342–8300 or 800/347–6888 | fax 570/342–0380 | www.radisson.com/scrantonpa | 145 rooms | $99–$189 | AE, D, DC, MC, V.

Ramada Inn. Reasonable rates are a hallmark of this chain hotel. Restaurant, bar (with entertainment), room service. Cable TV. Pool. Business services, airport shuttle, free parking. | 300 Meadow Ave. | 570/344–9811 | fax 570/344–7799 | www.ramadainn.com | 125 rooms | $89–$115 | AE, D, DC, MC, V.

SHAMOKIN DAM

MAP 7, H5

(Nearby towns also listed: Danville, Lewisburg)

A haven for nature lovers, Shamokin Dam's waterways are ideal places for boating and fishing. The town is on Route 15 next to the Susquehanna River. Canoeing and fishing are two popular pastimes and Butler University's students travel to the town for annual races on the river.

Information: **Central Susquehanna Valley Chamber of Commerce** | Rte. 11 and Rte. 15, 17876 | 570/743–4100 | fax 570/743–1221 | www.csvcc.org | Mon.–Fri. 8:30–4:30.

Attractions

Shikellamy State Park. The 131½-acre park has two overlooks on Blue Hill that are 360 ft above the confluence of the west and north branches of the Susquehanna River. Inside the park is 3,060-acre Lake Augusta, where you can go fishing and boating. There's a 1-mi paved hiking and biking path. | Bridge Ave., Rte. 147 | 570/988–5557 or 888/727–2757 | fax 570/988–5559 | www.dcnr.state.pa.us | Free | Daily 8 AM–dusk.

ON THE CALENDAR

SEPT.: *River Fest.* River Fest takes place the weekend after Labor Day in Merle Phillips Park in Sunbury on the Susquehanna River. There are canoe and kayak races, living-history exhibits, including over-night Civil War encampments, French and Indian War re-enactments, black powder cannon firing, and a choreographed Double-Dutch Jumprope Show of local junior-high students. | 570/988–1749.

Dining

Selinsgrove Brewing Company. Contemporary. Occupying the basement of a former governor's mansion, the Selinsgrove has a fireplace, books, magazines, and chessboard and backgammon games for relaxation or lively conversation. A few locals claim a benevolent ghost also resides here. You can choose among the weekly special, chili, East Indian chicken curry, or other menu options. | 119 N. Market St. | 570/374–7308 | fax 570/374–9474 | sgbrew@sunlink.net | Open Wed.–Sat. after 4PM, closed Sun.–Tues. | $5–$9 | AE, D, DC, MC, V.

Lodging

Inn at Shamokin Dam. This is a good-sized motel with affordable rates. Restaurant, bar. In-room data ports, cable TV. Pool. Business services. Pets allowed. | Rte. 11 and U.S. 15 | 570/743–1111 | fax 570/743–1190 | 131 rooms | $45–$75 | AE, D, DC, MC, V.

Inn at New Berlin. Lovely grounds bring attention to this small inn with Victorian and period furnishings. Each room is different. Restaurant, complimentary breakfast. | 321 Market St., New Berlin | 570/966–0321 | fax 570/966–9557 | www.newberlin-inn.com | 11 rooms (3 with shower only) | $83–$165 | D, MC, V.

Phillips Motel. This independently owned five-building, one-story wood-sided motel where no two rooms are alike (some have colonial furniture and quilts) has a gazebo and gardens. The suite has a four-poster bed, fireplace, and whirlpool tub. Cable TV. | Rtes. 11 & 15, and 11th Ave. | 570/743–3100 | fax 570/743–4065 | 47 rooms, 1 suite | $68–$100, suite $180–$200 | AE, D, DC, MC, V.

SHARON

MAP 7, A4

(Nearby towns also listed: Mercer, New Castle, West Middlesex)

Once known for its steel industries, Sharon today is known for having several of the "world's largest" attractions such as the "World's Largest Shoe Store," the "World's Largest Off-price Women's Clothing Store," and the "World's Largest Candy Store." One site claims the largest Christmas and Easter displays.

Information: **Shenango Valley Chamber of Commerce** | 41 Chestnut St., 16146 | 724/981–5880 | fax 724/981–5480 | www.shenangovalleychamber.com.

Attractions

Shenango River Lake. You can go boating, canoeing, or to the beach at this 300-acre lake. Campgrounds nearby allow for easy access, and walking and hiking trails wind throughout the area. | Rte. 18 W. Lake Rd. | 724/962–7746, 724/646–1124, 724/646–1115 or 877/444–

6777 | fax 724/962–7744 | www.lrp.usace.army.mil/rec/lakes/shenango.htm | Free | Daily dawn to dusk.

Winner Art Galleries. Three historic Sharon buildings comprise the Winner Art Galleries, one for sculpture and three-dimensional works, one for painting, and a third for mixed-media art. | 420 E. State St. | 724/346–3046 | Free | Daily 10–5.

ON THE CALENDAR
JULY: *Small Ships Revue.* A parade of ships, entertainment, fireworks, and food are the focus of this Shenango River-based event. | 412/981–3123.

Dining
Combine Bros. Bar and Grill. American. Three mi southeast of Sharon in Hermitage, this restaurant has pasta, sausages, pastries, and homebaked bread. | 2376 S. Hermitage Rd. | 724/983–1057 | No lunch. Closed Sunday, Monday | $6–$16 | AE, D, MC, V.

Hot Rod Café, Quaker Steak and Lube, Tully's Grille. American. These three restaurants are known locally as the "Three by the River." The Hot Rod Cafe is for folks who love the fast lane, and has a nightclub look; Quaker Steak and Lube was once a place to gas up and now is a funky place for people to fuel up; Tully's Grille has a railroad theme with prints and photographs. You can try the chicken wings, hamburger, or shrimp. Open-air dining is available on the patio. Salad bar. Live music Mon., Thurs.–Sat. Kids' menu. | 101 Chestnut St. | 724/981–7221 | fax 724/981–1504 | www.lubewings.com | Hot Rod Cafe closed Mon. No lunch | $5–$13 | AE, D, DC, MC, V.

Lodging
Tara–A Country Inn. "Gone With the Wind" is the theme here. The Southern-style inn has a library and in-room hot tubs, while the formal gardens boast 10 Remington sculptures overlooking Lake Shenango. Dining rooms. In-room data ports, some in-room hot tubs, cable TV. 2 pools (1 indoor). Hot tub. Business services. | 2844 Lake, Clark | 724/962–3535 or 800/782–2803 | fax 724/962–3250 | www.tara-inn.com | 27 rooms | $190–$450 | AE, D, MC, V.

SHARTLESVILLE

MAP 7, J6

(Nearby towns also listed: Hamburg, Reading)

At the foot of the Blue Mountains, Shartlesville is about 12 mi from Reading and is a popular stop for travelers heading toward Philadelphia on I–80. It's rich in Pennsylvania Dutch traditions and caters to travelers looking for antiques or Pennsylvania Dutch cuisine. The most popular attraction is an elaborate miniature village.

Information: **Berks County Chamber of Commerce,** | 645 Penn St., Reading 19601. | 610/376–6766 | fax 610/376–4135 | www.berkschamber.org.

Attractions
Mountain Springs Camping Resort and Arena. Home to monthly professional rodeos, demolition derbies, and horse sales, there are also hayrides, ice-cream days, and musical attractions. | 3450 Mountain Rd. | 610/488–6859 | Varies according to event | Call for hrs.

Roadside America. The largest known indoor miniature village in America, with tiny underground caverns. About 60 years ago, Laurence Gierlinger began his hobby of creating this tiny town and spent the rest of his life adding to it and perfecting it. Trains go through tunnels and over bridges, fountains bubble in a miniature zoo, a mountain trolley goes through the woodland, and aircraft swoop and dive to complete the realistic effect. | 610/488–6241 | www.roadsideamerica.com/attract/pasharoad.html | $4 | Sept.–June., weekdays 10–5, weekends 10–6.

AUG.: *Authentic Indian Powwow.* This mid-August powwow held at the Mountain Springs Camping Resort features one Native-American dance group annually that competes for $7,000 in prizes. | 610/488–6859.

Dining
Blue Mountain Family Restaurant. American. Breakfast specials include Spanish, feta and onion omelets; lunch specials are chicken pot pie; Greek dishes such as moussaka and marinated chicken or scallops over rice pilaf are available for lunch and dinner. | 24 Roadside Dr. | 610/488–0353 | $4–$10 | AE, MC, V.

Haag's Hotel Restaurant. American. Family-style food is served in a traditional hotel dining room. Homestyle classics abound such as roast chicken, pot pie, and sausage. Kids' menu. Sun. brunch. | 5661 3rd St. | 610/488–6692 | fax 610/488–6692 | $11–$14 | MC, V, D.

Lodging
Dutch Motel. This one-story motel is at the foot of the Blue Mountains, near the highway, restaurants, and 25 mi from the Reading outlets. Cable TV. Pets allowed (fee). | 1 Motel Dr. | 610/488–1479 | 14 rooms | $35–$50 | AE, D, MC, V.

SHAWNEE ON DELAWARE

MAP 7, L4

(Nearby towns also listed: Bushkill, Stroudsburg)

In the Pocono Mountains, Shawnee on the Delaware has a lot of outdoor recreation. It also was the host of the PGA Golf Championships in 1938 and was visited by many entertainers including Jackie Gleason, Bob Hope, and Fred Astaire. The town is adjacent to the 70,000-acre Delaware Water Gap National Recreation Area.

Information: **Delaware Water Gap Area Chamber of Commerce** | P.O. Box 144, Delaware Water Gap, PA 18327 | 570/420–9588 | fax 570/424–6986 | www.delawarewatergap.com.

Attractions
Shawnee Mountain Ski Area. With an elevation of 1,350 ft, you can ski, snowboard, and snow tube down the slopes. The ski area has 23 lifts, a top vertical drop of 700 ft, and its longest run is 1,500 ft. | I–80, Exit 52 | 570/421–7231 | fax 570/421–4795 | www.shawneemt.com | Dec.–Mar.

Shawnee Place Play and Water Park. Designed for children ages 2–12, the park is at the Shawnee Mountain Ski Area. There are two water slides and an activity pool with a mushroom fountain and two lemon-drop-shape fountains. Dads are free on Sundays; grandparents on Tuesdays. | Hollow Rd. | 570/421–7231 | www.shawneemt.com | $8–$14 | May–Sept., daily 11–8.

SEPT.: *Scottish and Irish Festival.* An annual Celtic festival held at the Shawnee Mountain Ski Area on the second weekend in September features traditional and contemporary Irish and Scottish bands, plus Celtic dancing and Highland games. | 570/421–7231.

Lodging
Shawnee Inn. This resort-inn has a 27-hole golf course and supervised kids' activities. Bar, dining room. Cable TV. 4 pools (1 indoor), wading pool. Driving range, golf course, miniature golf, putting green, tennis. Cross-country and downhill skiing. Video games. Kids' programs, playground. Laundry facilities. | River Rd. | 570/421–1500 or 800/742–9633 | fax 570/424–9168 | 103 rooms | $109–$149 | AE, D, DC, MC, V.

SKIPPACK

(Nearby towns also listed: Limerick, Pottstown)

The land was originally owned by William Penn, but was settled in 1702 by Pennsylvania Germans. The farm community built Skippack Pike in 1714 to haul grain to nearby Whitemarsh. Washington's troops set up camp twice in town during the Revolutionary War. Today's Skippack is best known for Skippack Village, a quaint shopping district with a 19th-century look and antiques, craft shops, art galleries, specialty shops, and fine restaurants.

Information: Perkiomen Valley Chamber of Commerce | 351 E. Main St., Collegeville, PA 19426 | 610/489–7822 | fax 610/454–1270 | www.perkvlycc.org.

Attractions

Evansburg State Park. At the Friedt Visitor Center you can learn about the German Mennonites and their lives here in the 18th and 19th centuries. The herb and sensory gardens add to the experience of history. You can fish in Skippack Creek, in season, or you can picnic, hunt, play softball, or go horseback riding on the equestrian trail. There are 6 mi of trails for hikers, and one trail for mountain bikers. This park has an uncommon feature as well: The 18-hole Skippack Golf Course is one of only two golf courses in the state park system. | 851 May Hall Rd., Collegeville | 610/409–1150 | www.dcnr.state.pa.us | Free | Daily 8AM–sunset.

Dining

La Bella Cucina. Italian. "Bella Cucina" means "beautiful kitchen," but the rest of the restaurant is attractive as well. White walls, white tablecloths, murals of Italian scenes, and black lacquer chairs exude elegance. The chefs make both Northern and Southern Italian cuisine, including cannelloni Abruzzi, pollo Marsala, and zuppa di pesce. You might want to save room for the homemade desserts. | 2665 Skippack Pk | 610/222–9193 | www.labellacucina.com | Closed Mon. | $11–$25 | AE, CB, D, DC, MC, V.

Skippack Roadhouse. Seafood. This is not what springs to mind at the word "roadhouse." Instead, this is a charming country restaurant with a white tile bar, mirrors, and fresh flowers. You can choose from seasonal items like game and fresh fish, or you can opt for traditional menu picks of beef, chicken, and lamb. Live entertainment. | 4022 Skippack Pk | 610/584–4231 | $12–$30 | AE, D, DC, V.

SOMERSET

(Nearby towns also listed: Bedford, Johnstown, Ligonier)

Two large fires weren't enough to keep this town from growing into a popular tourist destination. The city rebuilt and today has skiing, outlet shopping, and a place to rest after traveling on I–76.

Information: Somerset County Chamber of Commerce | 601 N. Center Ave., 15501 | 814/445–6431 | fax 814/443–4313 | www.somersetcntypachamber.org.

Attractions

Hidden Valley Ski Area. In winter, skiing, snowboarding, and snow tubing take over the slopes, but in summer the resort area has tennis, golf, biking, and walking. A 4-acre lake and four pools are also here. The slopes have a 1-mi run, 17 lifts, and a top vertical drop of

610 ft. | 1 Craighead Dr. | 814/443–8000 | fax 814/443–1907 | www.hiddenvalleyresort.com | Dec.–Mar.

Kooser State Park. A 250-acre wooded area with an altitude of 2,600 ft includes nine cabins and 45 campsites for overnight stays. Here you can enjoy picnicking, a 1½-mile cross-country ski trail, a swimming pool, a hiking trail, and a 4-acre lake for fishing. | 943 Glades Pike Rd. | 814/445–8673 | fax 814/445–3218 | www.dcnr.state.pa.us | Free | Daily 8 AM–dusk.

Laurel Arts. Theater, dance, classical and jazz concerts are held at various venues from October-April. There's also a summer festival and year-round arts education programs. | 214 South Harrison St. | 814/443–2433 | Varies according to event | Call for hrs and locations.

Laurel Hill State Park. It is said that George Washington's troops camped within the park's boundaries during the Whisky Rebellion of 1794. More than 3,900 acres of mountainous terrain with 264 campsites are here. Most of the land is open to hunting and fishing and the park has many hiking trails. In winter it's popular for snowmobiling, ice skating, ice boating, and fishing. | 1454 Laurel Hill Park Rd. | 814/445–7725 | fax 814/443–4439 | www.dcnr.state.pa.us | Free | Daily 8 AM–dusk.

Mt. Davis. The highest point in Pennsylvania, Mt. Davis is actually the summit portion of Negro Mountain. The mountain was named after a black resident who was slain while attempting to protect a fellow traveler. The summit portion is named after the mountain's first surveyor. It is in the Forbes State Forest and has an elevation of 3,213 ft. The view from the observation tower is said to be spectacular. | Rte. 219 | 724/238–1200 | fax 724/238–5000 | Free | Daily dawn to dusk.

Somerset Historical Center. The center tells the story of early settlers who made their way into the mountains on trading paths. It also focuses on the impact of the industrial revolution and the modernization of farm life. A frontier homestead built around 1800, a replicated barn, a general store, and a restored sugar camp are also here. | 10649 Somerset Pike | 814/445–6077 | fax 814/443–6621 | www.somersetcounty.com/historicalcenter | $3.50 | Tues.–Sun. 9–5, Sun. 12–5, closed Mon.

ON THE CALENDAR

APR.: *Maple Festival.* This spring festival celebrates the rising of the sap and has a car show, hot-air balloon rides, crafts, food, and entertainment. | Festival Park, Meyersdale | 814/634–0213 | www.pamaplefestival.com.

JULY: *Somerfest.* Somerfest is a craft festival with dancing, entertainment, food, and tours. | Philip Dressler Center for the Arts, 214 S. Harrison Ave. | 814/443–2433.

SEPT.: *Farmers' and Threshermen's Jubilee.* The farm-themed event has tractor pulls, horseshoe pitching, and a tobacco-spitting contest, plus an antique car show and flea market. | 1428 Casselman Rd. | 814/926–3142.

SEPT.: *Mountain Craft Days.* Some 150 craft demonstrations, antique exhibits, and performances are presented here. | Somerset Historical Center, 10649 Somerset Rd. | 814/445–6077.

OCT.: *Pumpkin Fest.* This annual festival of autumnal arts, crafts, and foods is held at the Confluence Community Center and features a lumberjack competition, the Pumpkin Queen Pageant, music, and dancing. | 814/395–3801.

OCT.: *Springs Folk Festival.* You can enjoy banjo and fiddle music, craft demonstrations, including candle dipping and quilt stitching, and exhibits on log hewing and apple butter boiling. | Rte. 669 | 814/662–4158 or 814/662–4298.

Dining

Country Cottage. American. You'll find down-home country looks here with local arts and crafts on display (and available for purchase). You can try comfort foods like three-piece chicken, meat loaf, and chicken salad. Kids' menu. | 2817 New Centerville Rd. | 814/926–4078 | $5–$9 | No credit cards.

Il Primo, Italian Oven. Italian. Unopened Italian wine bottles, jars of pasta, and cans of olive oil suggest the flavor of Italy, with trattoria-style wooden booths. Pasta, chicken, vegetables, and stromboli deluxe are among the specialties. | 4129 Glades Pike | 814/445–4141 | fax 814/443–6899 | $7–$16 | AE, D, DC, MC, V.

Jimmy's, An American Bistro. American. A sitting room with a fireplace and plants embellish this building, once an electrical shop, now a casually elegant dining establishment. You can try the pasta stir fry, or spaghetti and meat balls. | 373 E. Main St. | 814/444–1111 | www.jimmysbistro.com | $8–$15 | AE, D, DC, MC, V.

Oakhurst Tea Room. American/Casual. The colonial antiques, authentic period furnishings, and a fireplace provide a sense of comfort. Ham pot pie and homemade noodles are house specials. Salad bar. Kids' menu. | 2409 Glades Pk | 814/443–2897 | fax 814/445–3781 | Closed Mon. | $6–$12 | AE, D, MC, V.

Lodging

A1 Economy Inn. This motel is off Exit 10 of the PA Turnpike. Microwaves, refrigerators, cable TV, in-room VCRs (and movies). Indoor pool. Miniature golf. Exercise equipment. Video games. Playground. Laundry facilities. | 1138 N. Center Ave. | 814/445–4144 | fax 814/445–3763 | www.somersetcountry.com/a1economyinn | 19 rooms | $50–$95 | AE, D, MC, V.

Bayberry. The inn was built in 1902. Each room is distinctive. Complimentary Continental breakfast. No air-conditioning, no room phones, TV in common area. No kids under 12. | 611 N. Center Ave. | 814/445–8471 | 11 rooms (with shower only) | $55–$85 | AE, D, MC, V.

Dollar Inn. Affordable rates are the draw of this small motel. Some refrigerators, cable TV. Business services. Pets allowed (fee). | 1146 N. Center Ave. | 814/445–2977 | fax 814/443–6205 | 16 rooms | $50–$70 | AE, D, DC, MC, V.

Hidden Valley. This resort employs a social director, in case the local skiing isn't enough for you. You can choose from efficiency suites to family-size rental homes. Bars (with entertainment), dining rooms, picnic area. No air-conditioning in some rooms, cable TV. 4 pools (1 indoor). Hot tub. Driving range, 18-hole golf course, putting green, tennis. Exercise equipment, hiking, boating. Kids' programs, playground. Business services, airport shuttle, free parking. | 5 Craighead Dr., Hidden Valley | 814/443–6000 or 800/458–0175 | fax 814/443–1907 | www.hiddenvalleyresort.com/lodging_home.html | 206 rooms | $225–$350 | AE, D, DC, MC, V.

The Inn at Georgian Place. Oak paneling, ornate fireplaces, a marble foyer, and chandeliers with gold leaf nearly drip elegance. This inn is 20 min from Hidden Valley Resort, and 40 min from Fallingwater. Individual, unique rooms are in Georgian style. Restaurant, complimentary breakfast, room service. Cable TV, in-room VCRs (and movies). No kids under 5. Pets allowed. | 800 Georgian Place Dr. | 814/443–1043 | fax 814/443–6220 | www.somersetcounty.com/theinn | 11 rooms | $95–$185 | AE, D, DC, MC, V.

Knights Inn. Hidden Valley Resort is 11 mi from this motel, and Fallingwater is 40 mi away. Some kitchenettes, cable TV. Pool. Laundry facilities. Business services. Pets allowed. | 585 Ramada Rd. | 814/445–8933 or 800/843–5644 | fax 814/443–9745 | www.knightsinn.com | 112 rooms | $50–$70 | AE, D, DC, MC, V.

Quill Haven Country Inn and Bed and Breakfast. This 1918 Arts and Crafts-style inn a mile outside of town backed by farm fields and an orchard, has hardwood floors and stained-glass windows. It's near the highway, 20 mi from three ski resorts, Jennerstown Raceway, and whitewater rafting. The entire house is available for rent. Complimentary breakfast. Cable TV. Outdoor hot tub. | 1519 N. Center Ave. | 814/443–4514 | fax 814/445–1376 | www.quill-haven.com | 4 rooms | $75–$95 | AE, D, MC, V.

Ramada Inn. This motel is at Exit 10 of the PA Turnpike. Restaurant, bar (with entertainment), room service. Cable TV. Indoor pool. Hot tub, sauna. Video games. Business services,

free parking. Pets allowed. | 215 Ramada Rd. | 814/443–4646 | fax 814/445–7539 | www.ramada.com | 152 rooms | $64–$125 | AE, D, DC, MC, V.
....

Somerset Country Inn. This Victorian farmhouse is furnished with 19th-century antiques and crafts and is one-half-mile from downtown. The dining room overlooks flower gardens. One guest room is suitable for children, with two twin beds and toys. Complimentary breakfast. No room phones, no TV in some rooms. | 329 N. Center Ave. | 814/443–1005 | www.laurelhighlands.org | 5 rooms | $55–$75 | MC, V.

STATE COLLEGE

MAP 7, F5

(Nearby town also listed: Bellefonte)

"We are Penn State" is the rallying cry of this community in Centre County. Pennsylvania State University has its main campus here and its 40,000-plus student body has played a large role in its development. Established in 1855, the university has expanded to the point where it's a community-within-a-community known as University Park. The Victorian town of Bellefonte is less than 15 min away and Tusk Mountain with its skiing and biking is also not far.

Information: **Centre County Chamber of Commerce** | 200 Innovation Blvd., Suite 201, 16803 | 814/234–1829 | fax 814/234–5869 | www.cbicc.org.

Attractions

Columbus Chapel—Boal Mansion Museum. An original chapel was brought to this country from Spain in 1909. The museum exhibits heirlooms dating back to the 1400s as well as the original furnishings of the Boal family. | 300 Old Boalsburg | 814/466–6210 | www.vicon.net/~boalmus | $10 | Tues.–Sun. 10–5, closed Mon.
....

Frost Entomological Museum. The museum is dedicated to bugs, over one million of them, with over 10,000 species. There are live displays of giant cockroaches, tarantulas, scorpions, mealworms, grasshoppers, and honeybees. | Penn State Campus, Bldg. Headhouse #3, Curtain Rd. | 814/863–2865 | www.ento.psu.edu | free | Mon.–Fri. 9:30–4:30.
....

Penn's Cave. Boat travel is the path of choice through the cave's extensive tunnels. The temperature inside is a constant 52 degrees and you can see many rock formations and learn the history of the cave. | 222 Penns Cave Rd. | 814/364–1664 | www.pennscave.com | $10 | Feb.–Dec., daily 9–5.
....

Pennsylvania Military Museum. A 65-acre park surrounds the museum and has equipment, monuments, and memorials of those who fought in wars. The site has a shrine to the 28th Division that commemorates the valor and sacrifices of generations of Pennsylvania patriots. The tour is highlighted by a walk through a World War I battlefield, complete with sound and light effects. | Rte. 322, Boalsburg | 814/466–6263 | fax 814/466–6618 | www.psu.edu/dept/aerospace/museum | $3.50 | Tues.–Sat. 9–5, Sun. 12–5, closed Mon.
....

Pennsylvania State University. Founded in 1855 at the request of the Pennsylvania State Agricultural Society, in 1863 it became the state's only land-grant university. Today, it consists of 24 branch campuses and has a total enrollment of more than 80,000. Its football team, the Nittany Lions, is beloved throughout the state. | Pollock Rd. | 814/865–4700 | fax 814/863–3428 | www.psu.edu | Free | Daily.

The **College of Agricultural Sciences** was the original site of the Agriculture Experiment Station built in 1889. Known to campus residents as "Ag Hill," the hill soon became the site of a number of wooden buildings used for instruction in dairy husbandry. | Shortlidge Rd. | 814/865–2541 | www.cas.psu.edu | Free | Daily.

The main gallery of the **Earth and Mineral Sciences Museum** displays fine and rare minerals in addition to more than 22,000 rocks and fossils. It has a significant collection of glass, ceramics, and metals. It also houses the most extensive collection of paintings and sculptures pertaining to the mining industry. | 112 Steidle Building, Pollock Rd. | 814/865–6427 | www.ems.psu.edu/museum | Free | Weekdays 9–5, weekends 1–5.

Construction began in 1857 on **Old Main**; its purpose was to be the university's sole building, housing all aspects of college life. The five-story building was the college's only edifice for 20 years. By 1930, it was replaced with a new Old Main. The building's original bell and stones were used in building the updated structure. Today, it holds most of the university's offices and photographs of the university's famous dignitaries line the hallways. | Pollock Rd. | 814/865–2501 | www.psu.edu | Free | Weekdays 9–5.

Whipple Dam State Park. The 256-acre park, 12 mi south of State College, has a 22-acre lake called Whipple Lake. The lake allows fishing and boating, while the rest of the park allows swimming and picnicking. In winter, you can go ice skating, ice fishing, and snowmobiling (call for snowmobile-acceptable times). | East off PA Rte. 26, Whipple Dam State Park exit | 814/667–1800 | fax 814/667–1802 | www.dcnr.pa.us | Free | Daily 8 AM–dusk.

ON THE CALENDAR

MAY: *Memorial Day Celebration.* Over the course of the three-day weekend, the holiday is celebrated in grand style, with fireworks and entertainment, in its birthplace. | 814/231–1400.

JULY: *Central Pennsylvania Festival of the Arts.* The Penn State campus plays host to a range of performing arts and visual arts events. | 814/237–3682 | www.arts-festival.com.

AUG.: *Centre County Grange Fair.* This traditional fair has farm and livestock exhibits, rides, concessions, and entertainment. | Rte. 144 S, Centre Hall | 814/364–9674 | www.pafairs.org/centrecountyfair.

DEC.–JAN.: *First Night State College.* A New Year's Eve alcohol-free, family-oriented celebration of the arts has lighted ice sculptures, midnight fireworks, parade, dance and, theater performances, and ice skating at about 25 different sites in downtown. | 814/237–3682 | www.first-night.state-college.pa.us.

Dining

Cafe 210 West. American/Casual. A popular hangout for the college crowd, this café has a long oak bar, prints of past Penn State triumphs, and a view of Penn State University across the street. You can munch on sandwiches, steak, and nachos on the sidewalk by the main street. | 210 W. College Ave. | 814/237–3449 | fax 814/237–5405 | www.statecollege.com/mcc/cafe210 | $9–$13 | AE, D, DC, MC, V.

Duffy's Tavern. Continental. Downtown, this restaurant stands out because of its size (small) and old brick exterior. The adjoining tavern is believed to have once housed stagecoach gentry who frequently passed through. It's well known for seafood and pasta. Sun. brunch. Kids' menu. | 113 E. Main St., Boalsburg | 814/466–6241 | www.duffystavern.com | $15–$30 | AE, D, MC, V.

The Hummingbird Room. Continental. This 1847 manor house, 15 mi east of State College, has six dining rooms serving such dishes as lobster galette, saddle of rabbit in dijon sauce, or crayfish over fettucine, as well as vegetarian meals. | Rte. 45, Spring Mills | 814/422–9025 | Closed Mon.–Tues. No lunch | $18–$27. | D, MC, V.

Mario and Luigi's. Italian. This restaurant has two locations, one downtown and one along the area's busiest street. Both locations have wall hangings, simple tables and chairs, and an open kitchen. Specials are chicken, steak, and homemade pasta. Kids' menu. | 1272 N. Atherton and 112 S. Gardner | 814/237–0374 | AE, D, DC, MC, V.

Panera Bread Bakery and Café. American . Specialties include rosemary-onion focaccia with Tuscan chicken and Asiago cheese, or the Asiago cheese baguette with beef, horseradish and cheddar cheese. Pastries and muffins are homemade. | 148 Allen St. | 814/867–8883 | $5–$8 | AE, MC, V.

Spatz Cafe and Speakeasy. Cajun/Creole. Wooden floors complement this old brick building, where you can view the bustling college activity through three large picture windows. Cajun food here includes jambalaya, crab-stuffed portobello, and honey amaretto almond-crusted chicken. Kids' menu. | 142 E. College Ave. | 814/238–7010 | fax 814/237–3028 | Reservations essential | Closed Sun. | $14–$26 | AE, D, MC, V.

Tavern Restaurant. American. This colonial building has contemporary furniture and fixtures that blend well with colors that were popular during early American times. Steak, chicken, veal, and crab cake are among the menu options. | 220 E. College Ave. | 814/238–6116 | www.thetavern.com | $7–$18 | AE, D, MC, V, DC.

Lodging

The Atherton Hotel. Black cherry furniture adds a warm accent to this comfortable downtown hotel. Restaurant, bar. In-room data ports, some refrigerators, some in-room hot tubs, cable TV. Business services, airport shuttle. | 125 S. Atherton St./US 322 Business | 814/231–2100 or 800/832–0132 | fax 814/237–1130 | atherton@statecollege.com | www.atherton.state-college.com | 150 rooms, 10 suites | $95–$115, $165–$210 suites | AE, D, DC, MC, V.

Autoport. The motel is known for affordable rates. Restaurant, bar (with entertainment), dining room. In-room data ports, some kitchenettes. Pool. Laundry facilities. Business services. | 1405 S. Atherton St./U.S. 322 Business | 814/237–7666 or 800/932–7678 | fax 814/237–7456 | autoport@lazerlink | www.autoport.statecollege.com | 86 rooms | $60–$70 | AE, D, DC, MC, V.

Nittany Budget Motel. Geared for the business traveler who still wants a homey touch, this motel has workstations and modems in all rooms and an on-site beer shop and restaurant. Restaurant, complimentary Continental breakfast. In-room dataports, refrigerators, cable TV. Pets allowed (fee). | 2070 Cato Ave. | 814/238–0015 | fax 814/238–0035 | 150 rooms | $40–$63. | AE, D, DC, MC, V.

Carnegie House. You'll feel like you're in the Scottish Highlands at this small inn. Each room has a different design. Dining room, complimentary Continental breakfast. In-room data ports, minibars, some microwaves, cable TV, in-room VCRs (and movies). Business services, airport shuttle. | 100 Cricklewood Dr. | 814/234–2424 or 800/229–5033 | fax 814/231–1299 | carnhouse@aol.com | www.carnegiehouse.com | 22 rooms | $135–$185 | AE, MC, V.

Courtyard by Marriott. This three-story downtown hotel is 1.5 mi south of PSU campus. Some rooms have balconies. Restaurant. In-room data ports, some in-room hot tubs, cable TV. Indoor pool. Hot tub. Exercise equipment. Video games. Laundry facilities, laundry service. Business services, airport shuttle. | 1730 University Ave. | 814/238–1881 or 800/321–2211 | fax 814/238–3108 | www.gomarriot.com | 78 rooms | $94–$140 | AE, D, DC, MC, V.

Days Inn–Penn State. The hotel is one block from the center of Penn State campus. Restaurant, bar (with entertainment), complimentary Continental breakfast, room service. In-room data ports, cable TV. Indoor pool. Gym. Video games. Business services, airport shuttle, free parking. Pets allowed (fee). | 240 S. Pugh St. | 814/238–8454 | fax 814/234–3377 | www.daysinn.com | 184 rooms | $79–$125 | AE, D, DC, MC, V.

Hampton Inn. This chain hotel is one-half mile from the Penn State campus. Picnic area, complimentary Continental breakfast. Cable TV. Pool. Airport shuttle, free parking. | 1101 E. College Ave. | 814/231–1590 | fax 814/238–7320 | www.hampton-inn.com | 121 rooms | $75–$85 | AE, D, DC, MC, V.

Nittany Lion. A Colonial-style hotel, it's on the Penn State campus and is operated by the university. Bar, dining room. In-room data ports, cable TV. Exercise equipment. Business services, airport shuttle, free parking. | 200 W. Park Ave./US 322 Business | 814/865–8500 or 800/233–7505 | fax 814/865–8501 | jwp4@psu.edu | www.nli.psu.edu | 237 rooms | $103–113 | AE, D, DC, MC, V.

Ramada Inn. Here are standard chain accommodations, 2 mi from the Penn State campus and 1½ mi from downtown shopping. Restaurant, bar. In-room data ports, room service, cable TV. 2 pools. Exercise equipment. Video games. Laundry facilities. Business services. Pets allowed. | 1450 S. Atherton St./US 322 Business | 814/238–3001 | fax 814/237–1345 | www.ramadasc.com | 28 rooms | $85–$225 | AE, D, DC, MC, V.

Rodeway Inn. Two blocks from the Penn State campus, this is a little chain motel. Some refrigerators, cable TV. | 1040 N. Atherton St./U.S. 322 | 814/238–6783 | fax 814/238–4519 | www.rodewayinn.com | 29 rooms (3 with shower only) | $50–$70 | AE, D, DC, MC, V.

The Queen: A Victorian Bed and Breakfast. This 1890s Queen Anne-style home in a National Historic Registered residential neighborhood in Bellefonte, 13 mi northeast of State College, has one room filled with Victorian ladies' undergarments, dressing screen, and a fireplace, a two-room turret suite with hunting and fishing memorabilia and a fireplace, and an efficiency apartment. There is also a turn-of-the-century player piano. | 1 room, 2 suites. Complimentary breakfast. Some in-room TVs, TV in common room. Pets allowed. | 176 E. Lynn St., Bellefonte | 814/355–7946 | fax 814/357–8068 | www.bellefonte.com/queen | $75–$155 | AE, D, MC, V.

Starry Night Bed and Breakfast. Set on 40 acres of meadows and woodlands along the stream, Slab Cabin Run, this inn is 2 ½ mi southeast of PSU. Built in 1890, the home has sleigh beds, Turkish rugs, gas fireplaces, and antiques. Complimentary breakfast. | 1170 W. Branch Rd. | 814/234–8111 | 3 rooms | $75–$90 | MC, V.

Stevens Motel. This small motel has affordable prices. Cable TV. | 1275 N. Atherton St./US 322 Business | 814/238–2438 | fax 814/238–7548 | 18 rooms (17 with shower only) | $40–$50 | AE, D, DC, MC, V.

STRASBURG

MAP 7, J7

(Nearby towns also listed: Columbia, Ephrata, Lancaster, Lititz)

Although settled by French Huguenots, the village of Strasburg is today a community of Pennsylvania Dutch. It's best known as the railroad center of eastern Pennsylvania. Railroad buffs can easily spend a day here.

Information: **Strasburg Information Center** | Rte. 896/Historic Dr., 17579 | 717/687–7922 | www.strasburgpa.com.

Attractions

Amish Village. Tour a Lancaster County Old Order Amish farmhouse that dates back to 1840, a blacksmith shop, a one-room schoolhouse, a barn with farm animals, an operating smokehouse, Amish buggies and wagons, a waterwheel, and a watermill. | Rte. 896 | 717/687–8511 | fax 717/687–8478 | www.800padutch.com/avillage.html | $6.50 | Apr.–Sept., Daily 9–5.

Choo-Choo Barn, Traintown, USA. An elaborate train display with more than 135 animated figures and 17 continuously operating model trains, there's also a train shop with thousands of items for train displays and a store of Thomas the Tank Engine and Friends merchandise with over 500 items. | Rte. 741 | 717/687–7911 | $4 | Apr.–Dec., daily 10–5.

Mill Bridge Village. An 18th-century Colonial village provides a glimpse of Colonial life and Amish culture, and you can take guided tours of the Amish house and school, a 1738 gristmill, and a Victorian music room. There are buggy rides, a farm museum, and a movie called *Life of the Amish.* Demonstrations of quilting, broom making, and candlemaking are given. | S. Ronks Rd. Strasburg | 717/687–8181 | www.800padutch.com/mbv.html | $10 | Easter–Nov., daily 9–5.

STRASBURG

INTRO
ATTRACTIONS
DINING
LODGING

★ **The National Toy Train Museum.** The showplace of the Train Collectors Association, this museum has five huge operating layouts, with toy trains from the 1800s to present, plus nostalgia films and hundreds of locomotives and cars in display cases. | Paradise La., just north of Rte. 741 | 717/687–8976 | www.traincollectors.org/toytrain.html | $3 | May-Oct. and Christmas wk., daily 10-5; Apr. and Nov.-mid-Dec., weekends 10-5.

★ **The Railroad Museum of Pennsylvania.** Across the road from Strasburg Rail Road, this museum holds 75 pieces of train history, with 13 colossal engines built between 1888 and 1930; 12 railroad cars, among them a Pullman sleeper; sleighs; and railroad memorabilia documenting the history of Pennsylvania railroading. | Rte. 741 | 717/687–8628 | www.rrmuse-umpa.org | $6 | May-Oct., Mon.-Sat. 9-5, Sun. noon-5; Nov.-Apr., Tues.-Sat. 9-5, Sun. noon-5.

Strasburg Rail Road. The Strasburg Rail Road can take you on a scenic 45-min round-trip excursion through Amish farm country from Strasburg to Paradise on a rolling antique train chartered in 1832 to carry milk, mail, and coal. Called America's oldest short line, the Strasburg run has wooden coaches pulled by an iron steam locomotive. | Rte. 741 | 717/687–7522 | www.strasburgrailroad.com | $8.25 | Apr.-June and Sept., daily 11-4; July-Aug., 10-7; Oct.-Mar., weekends noon-3; closed 1st 2 wks in Jan. Trains depart every 30-60 min depending on season; call for schedule.

Dining

Washington House Restaurant. American. One of the restaurants at the Historic Strasburg Inn has candlelight dining in two Colonial-style rooms. The menu lists steaks, jumbo lump crab cakes, and wild game. | Rte. 896, Historic Dr. | 717/687–9211 | $15–$27 | AE, D, DC, MC, V.

Iron Horse Inn. Contemporary. This rustic pub, illuminated by candles, is in the original 1780s Hotel Strasburg. Best bets are the catch of the day, homemade breads, and, for dessert, warm apple pie. | 135 E. Main St. | 717/687–6362 | Closed Mon. Dec.-May | $25–$33 | AE, D, DC, MC, V.

Hershey Farm Restaurant. American. This is a good spot for people with big appetites: Bountiful buffets at breakfast, lunch, and dinner are available, or you can order from the a la carte menu. | 240 Hartman Bridge Rd. | 800/827–8635.

Lodging

Historic Strasburg Inn. You can enjoy the petting zoo, carriage rides, and hot air balloon rides at this sprawling 58-acre property. It's a three-level country-style brick building made of brick that dates to 1793, when the Washington House began serving travelers on the square in Strasburg. Several well-known patrons enjoyed its special hospitality, including J.P. Morgan, William Astor, and Sir Thomas Lipton. Guest registers bearing their signatures are on display in the Washington House lobby. Restaurant, bar, complimentary breakfast. Cable TV. Pool. Hot tub. Exercise equipment. Playground. Business services. Pets allowed (fee). | 1 Historic Dr.(Rte. 896) | 717/687–7691 or 800/872–0201 | fax 717/687–6098 | www.800padutch.com/strasinn.html | 101 rooms in 5 buildings | $129–$139 | AE, D, DC, MC, V.

Limestone Inn Bed and Breakfast. This 1786 Georgian home, listed on the National Register of Historic Places, has a formal living room, a library, and a sitting room and fireplace, plus a small garden with a fish pool. Bedrooms are in Colonial colors with Amish quilts and four-poster beds. Library, BP. | 33 E. Main St. | 717/687–8392 | www.members.bellat-lantic.net/~manati/ | 6 rooms (5 with private bath) | $75–$105 | BP | No credit cards.

Mill Stream Country Inn and Restaurant. This well-maintained motel overlooks a picturesque stream. Request a room in the rear to get the prettiest view. Restaurant. Pool. | Rte. 896 | 717/299–0931 | fax 717/295–9326 | 52 rooms, 3 suites | $65–$78 | AE, D, MC, V.

★ **Strasburg Village Inn.** Built around 1788, the inn is in the heart of town and has rooms appointed in the Williamsburg style. A sitting/reading room is on the second floor; an old-fashioned porch overlooks Main Street. | 1 W. Main St. | 717/687–0900 or 800/541–1055 | 6 rooms, 6 suites | $79–$99 | AE, D, MC, V.

STROUDSBURG

(Nearby towns also listed: Bushkill, Canadensis, Easton, Shawnee on Delaware, Tannersville)

Unlike the founders of many Pennsylvania towns, Stroudsburg's founder dictated that homes must be set back 30 ft from the street, thus making this borough one of a handful in the state where every house has a large front yard. What once was a fort is now a town that rests at the foothills of the Pocono Mountains and is a popular attraction for outdoor lovers.

Information: **Pocono Mountains Chamber of Commerce** | 556 Main St., 18360 | 570/421–4433 | fax 570/424–7281 | www.poconochamber.com.

Attractions

Alpine Mountain Ski Area. An elevation of 1,150 ft provides skiing and snow tubing activities. The area has 18 ski lifts, a 500-ft vertical drop, and a long run of 2,640 ft. | Rte. 447 | 570/595–2150 or 800/233–8240 | fax 570/595–2803 | www.alpinemountain.com | Dec.–Mar.

Chamberlain Canoes. Chamberlain Canoes has canoe rentals for trips down the Delaware River. Trips range from 4 to 12 mi and can last as long as 6 hours. Transportation is provided back to the launch site. | River Rd., Minisink Hills | 570/421–0180 or 800/422–6631 | www.chamberlaincanoes.com | $25 | May–Oct., daily 8–6.

Quiet Valley Living Historical Farm. Costumed "family members" guide you through 14 buildings and discuss how Penn Dutch colonials used to live. Demonstrations include cooking, farming, weaving, spinning, and tending of livestock. | 1000 Turkey Hill Rd. | 570/992–6161 | fax 570/992–9587 | www.quietvalley.org | $7 | June–Labor Day., Tues.–Sat. 10–5:30, Sun. 1–5:30, closed Mon.

Stroud Mansion. Home of the Monroe County Historical Society, it was constructed in 1795 by Jacob Stroud and is currently used as a library for genealogical study and as a museum with period fixtures, furnishings, tools, weapons, and antiques. | 900 Main St. | 570/421–7703 | Free | Tues.–Fri. 9–4, Sun. 1–4, closed Sat. and Mon.

ON THE CALENDAR
OCT.: PMCC/Shawnee Fall Foliage Festival. An annual festival held at the Shawnee Inn and Golf Resort the second weekend in October, which begins with Friday evening's "Balloon Glow"—tethered balloons fire their burners for a glowing effect. There's a mass balloon ascension, kids' entertainment, and live bands playing the polka and country western music. | 717/421–1500 or 800/742–9633 | $10.

Dining

Arlington Diner. American/Casual. The railroad diner cars of the 1950s inspired the exterior of this restaurant, and once inside you can see a traditional diner counter with stools, booths, and tables. House specialties include Arlington burgers and pot roast. Kids' menu. | 834 N. 9th St. | 570/421–2329 | $6–$12 | No credit cards.

Beaver House. Continental. You'll find a comfortable, homey air here. It's known for lobster and other seafood. Kids' menu. | 1001 N. 9th St. | 570/424–1020 | www.beaverhouse.com | No breakfast. | $6–$35 | AE, D, DC, MC, V.

Brownings in the Bury. American. Brownings has a relaxed pub scene with traditional wooden tables and chairs. You might try their steaks and chops. Kids' menu. | 700 Main St. | 570/421–2200 | fax 570/421–5561 | $7–$15 | AE, D, DC, MC, V.

The Dansbury Depot. American/Casual. As the name suggests, this is an ideal dining spot for railroad fans. There's a large collection of items from the old railway days. Steak and seafood are specialties here. Kids' menu. | 50 Crystal St. | 570/476–0500 | fax 570/476–0541 | www.dansburydepot.com | $9–$19 | AE, D, DC, MC, V.

Lee's Restaurant. Chinese, Japanese. Cultures blend by incorporating traditional Japanese and Chinese statues, murals, and paintings depicting life in Asia with this restaurant's varied menu. If you're in the mood for noodles, sushi, or other seafood, this is the place. Sushi bar. Salad bar. Sun. brunch. Kids' menu. | Rte. 611, Bartonsville | 570/421–1212 | Reservations essential | $10–$15 | AE, MC, V.

Sarah Street Grill. American. In downtown Stroudsburg, specialities include DelMonico cut steak and vegetarian dishes such as lasagna and veggie burgers. There's also a bar and lounge with entertainment. | 550 Quaker Alley | 570/424–9120 | $8–$16 | AE, MC, V.

Lodging

Best Western Pocono Inn. This motel is in downtown Stroudsburg. Restaurant, bar (with entertainment), room service. Cable TV. Indoor pool. Hot tubs. Video games. Business services. | 700 Main St. | 570/421–2200 | fax 570/421–5561 | www.bestwesternpoconoinn.com | 90 rooms | $53–$103 | AE, D, DC, MC, V.

Budget. Take Exit 51 off I–80 to reach this motel. Restaurant, bar. In-room data ports, cable TV. Video games. Business services. Pets allowed (fee). | I–80, Exit 51, E. Stroudsburg | 570/424–5451 or 800/233–8144 | fax 570/424–0389 | www.budmotel.com | 115 rooms | $55–$80 | AE, D, DC, MC, V.

Caesar's Pocono Palace. A lavish, grown-ups-only resort with many amenities, Caesar's includes unusual offerings like archery and a softball field. The hotel rooms are plush, as are the themed suites. Bar (with entertainment), dining room, complimentary breakfast, room service. Refrigerators, cable TV. 2 pools (1 indoor), lake. Hot tub. Driving range, 9-hole golf course, putting green. Exercise equipment, volleyball, water sports, boating. Ice-skating. Cross-country skiing, snowmobiling. Video games. Business services. | Rte. 209, Marshalls Creek | 570/588–6692 or 800/233–4141 | fax 570/588–0754 | www.caesarspoconoresorts.com | 189 rooms, 155 suites | $200–$350, $293–$426 suites | MAP | AE, D, DC, MC, V.

Echo Valley Cottages. This is a family resort for weekly cottage rentals, 2 mi from Delaware Water Gap National Recreation Area and Shawnee Mountain Ski Area. | 1 Lower Lakeview Dr. | 570/223–0662 | echovalley@email.com | 9 cottages | $150–$650 weekly | AE, D, MC, V.

Four Points Sheraton. A two-story downtown hotel built around an interior pool courtyard, this hotel is at Exit 48 of I–80. Restaurant, bars (with entertainment), room service. In-room data ports, cable TV. Pool. Sauna. Video games. Business services. | 1220 W. Main St. | 570/424–1930 | fax 570/424–5909 | www.fourpoints.com | 133 rooms | $139–$229 | AE, D, DC, MC, V.

Inn at Meadowbrook. A charming pondside inn with a 1842 Manor House and the 1924 Mill House, and an adjacent equestrian center, rooms here are filled with farm-style furniture. Dining room, complimentary breakfast. No room phones, TV in common area. Pool. Horse back riding. Fishing. Cross-country skiing, downhill skiing. Business services. | RD. 7, Cherry Lane Rd., East Stroudsburg | 570/629–0296 or 800/249–6861 | fax 570/629–1987 | www.meadowbrookfarmpa.com | 16 rooms | $100–$150 | AE, D, DC, MC, V.

Kovarick's. This is a one-level motel with a small pond for bass fishing or boating. Grounds have gardens and a pool. You can rent cottages by the week or month. It's 1 mi from downtown Stroudsburg, I-80 is ½ mi. Kitchenettes, no room phones. Outdoor pool. Boating, fish-

KODAK'S TIPS FOR PHOTOGRAPHING LANDSCAPES AND SCENERY

Landscape
- Tell a story
- Isolate the essence of a place
- Exploit mood, weather, and lighting

Panoramas
- Use panoramic cameras for sweeping vistas
- Don't restrict yourself to horizontal shots
- Keep the horizon level

Panorama Assemblage
- Use a wide-angle or normal lens
- Let edges of pictures overlap
- Keep exposure even
- Use a tripod

Placing the Horizon
- Use low horizon placement to accent sky or clouds
- Use high placement to emphasize distance and accent fore-ground elements
- Try eliminating the horizon

Mountain Scenery: Scale
- Include objects of known size
- Frame distant peaks with nearby objects
- Compress space with long lenses

Mountain Scenery: Lighting
- Shoot early or late; avoid midday
- Watch for dramatic color changes
- Use exposure compensation

Tropical Beaches
- Capture expansive views
- Don't let bright sand fool your meter
- Include people

Rocky Shorelines
- Vary shutter speeds to freeze or blur wave action
- Don't overlook sea life in tidal pools
- Protect your gear from sand and sea

In the Desert
- Look for shapes and textures
- Try visiting during peak bloom periods
- Don't forget safety

Canyons
- Research the natural and social history of a locale
- Focus on a theme or geologic feature
- Budget your shooting time

Rain Forests and the Tropics
- Go for mystique with close-ups and detail shots
- Battle low light with fast films and camera supports
- Protect cameras and film from moisture and humidity

Rivers and Waterfalls
- Use slow film and long shutter speeds to blur water
- When needed, use a neutral-density filter over the lens
- Shoot from water level to heighten drama

Autumn Colors
- Plan trips for peak foliage periods
- Mix wide and close views for visual variety
- Use lighting that accents colors or creates moods

Moonlit Landscapes
- Include the moon or use only its illumination
- Exaggerate the moon's relative size with long telephoto lenses
- Expose landscapes several seconds or longer

Close-Ups
- Look for interesting details
- Use macro lenses or close-up filters
- Minimize camera shake with fast films and high shutter speeds

Caves and Caverns
- Shoot with ISO 1000+ films
- Use existing light in tourist caves
- Paint with flash in wilderness caves

From *Kodak Guide to Shooting Great Travel Pictures* © 2000 by Fodor's Travel Publications

ing. | 1328 Dreher Ave. | 570/421–6842 | fax 570/421–3791 | 16 rooms, 2 cottages | $95–$125 | AE, D, MC, V.

Shannon Inn. The motel is at Exit 52 off I-80. Restaurant, bar (with entertainment), picnic area, complimentary Continental breakfast, room service. In-room data ports, some refrigerators, cable TV. Indoor pool. Laundry facilities. Business services, free parking. | US 209, East Stroudsburg | 570/424–1951 or 800/424–8052 | fax 570/424–7782 | 120 rooms | $75–$100 | AE, D, DC, MC, V.

TANNERSVILLE

MAP 7, K4

(Nearby towns also listed: Bushkill, Mt. Pocono, Canadensis, Cresco, Shawnee on Delaware, Stroudsburg)

Tannersville, in the heart of the Pocono Mountains, attracts antique enthusiasts who rummage through the many shops and boutiques in the area. The surrounding mountainside is ideal for hiking and biking in summer and skiing in winter.

Information: **Pocono Mountains Chamber of Commerce** | 556 Main St., Stroudsburg, PA 18360 | 570/421–4433 | fax 570/424–7281 | pmccpa@ptdprolog.net | www.poconochamber.com.

Attractions

Camel Beach Water Park. The eight-story 819-ft-long water slide is the largest of its kind in the world. Attractions also include miniature golf, chairlift rides, and an alpine slide in fall. | 1 Camel Back Rd. | 570/629–1661 | $22 | June–Oct., 11–sunset.

Camelback Ski Area. Camelback is the largest ski resort in the Poconos, with 33 trails. It caters to both skiers and snowboarders and has a top vertical drop of 826 ft and a long run of 1 mi. | Box 168; I-80 to Exit 45 | 570/629–1661 or 800/233–8100 | skicamelback.com | Dec.–Mar.

ON THE CALENDAR

SEPT.: *Raise the Roof Concert for Habitat for Humanity.* On the third Sunday evening of September, five choirs sing as part of a benefit for Habitat for Humanity at the St. Paul Lutheran Church in Tannersville. The single choirs join their 130 voices for four anthems to conclude the concert. | 570/629–1442 | Free.

Dining

Barley Creek Brewing Company. Contemporary. This brewpub is a 19th-century farmhouse designed like a ski lodge, with high cathedral ceilings, treated woodwork, and glass walls, where you can see brewing kettles. Dine outside on the deck or have a drink at the open-air bar with a view of the mountains. Shepherd's pie, prime rib, and homemade soups top the menu. Hear live music on weekends. Kids' menu. | Sullivan Trail and Camelback Rd. | 570/629–9399 | $10–$18 | AE, D, MC, V.

Lodging

Caesars Brookdale. A lakeside resort sprawled on 250 acres in the Pocono Mountains. Some rooms have 7 foot high Champagne glass whirlpool baths. Restaurant, bar (with entertainment), complimentary breakfast, picnic area, room service. Cable TV. 2 pools (1 indoor), lake, wading pool. Hot tub, massage, sauna. Tennis. Gym, hiking, beach, boating. Bicycles. Sleigh rides, snowmobiling, tobogganing. Video games. Kids' programs, playground. Laundry facilities. Business services. | Rte. 611, Scotrun | 570/839–8844 | fax 570/839–2414 | www.caesarspoconoresort.com | 127 rooms in 8 buildings | $250–$450 | AE, D, DC, MC, V.

Summit Resort. Called "The Poconos Honeymoon Resort," this resort is designed for new-lyweds with suites and private cottages, and four-night packages available. Two mi south of downtown and half a block from I-80. Complimentary breakfast. Cable TV. Indoor pool. Hot tub, sauna, massage. Miniature golf, 2 tennis courts. Basketball, exercise equipment, volleyball. Ice-skating. No kids. | State Hwy. 715 S | 570/629–0203 or 800/233–8250 | fax 570/629–9003 | www.summitresort.com | 140 rooms | $320–$470 | AE, D, MC, V.

TITUSVILLE

MAP 7, C3

(Nearby towns also listed: Franklin, Meadville, Oil City)

Titusville has long been known as Pennsylvania's oil town, with the distinction of being the first of three Pennsylvania cities to owe its heritage to the discovery of "black gold." In 1859, Titusville became home to the world's first commercially drilled oil well.

Information: Titusville Chamber of Commerce | 206 W. Central Ave., 16354 | 814/827–2941 | www.titusvillechamber.com.

Attractions

Drake Well Museum. Edwin L. Drake drilled the world's first oil well here in 1859. You can see a replica of Drake's engine house and an oil derrick, which offers a glimpse of how the oil industry began. Reproductions of Drake's steam engine and wood-fired boiler operate year-round. | RD #3; I-80 to Rte. 8 to Exit 3 | 814/827–2797 | $4 | May–Oct., Mon.–Sat. 9–5, Sun. 10–5; Nov.–Apr., Tues.–Sat. 9–5, Sun. 12–5, closed Mon.

Oil Creek and Titusville Railroad. Take a two-and-one-half hour train ride through "the valley that changed the world," where Colonel Drake discovered oil in 1859, in passenger cars and open gondolas, weather permitting. Trains stop at four stations along the way, providing kayakers, bicyclists, and hikers places to detrain. There are fall-foliage rides, murder-mystery dinner rides, the Haunted Train, Santa Train, and the Peter Cottontail Express. Oil City is 15 mi south of Titusville on Rte. 8. | 7 Elm St., Oil City | 814/676–1733 | www.octrr.clarion.com | $10 | Open June–Sept. Train schedules change frequently.

ON THE CALENDAR
AUG.: *Titusville Oil Festival.* This annual festival held in late August at the Ed Myer Complex in Titusville has a slow-pitch softball tournament, an oil barge race, an art festival, tug-a-war, town square carnival, gazebo concert, and nightly fireworks. | 814/827–2732.

Dining
Powderhorn Cafe. American. There are 23 variations of chicken wings, including buffalo, garlic, Cajun, and taco. There's also a Friday-night fish-fry. | 425 W. Spring St. | 814/827–2438 | $4–$7 | No credit cards.

Lodging
Cross Creek Resort. A 27-hole golf course is the focal point of this resort on 400 wooded acres. It's 4 mi south of Titusville. Restaurant, bars (with entertainment). Cable TV. Pool. Golf course. Tennis. | Rte. 8 South | 814/827–9611 or 800/461–3173 | fax 814/827–2062 | www.cross-creekresort.com | 86 rooms, 8 suites | $95–$110, $125–$140 suites | AE, D, DC, MC, V.

Knapp Farm Bed and Breakfast. Built in 1813, this B&B is still farmed as one of Pennsylvania's largest beef producers. There are 1,000 acres, with 30 mi of horseback riding trails as well as streams for trout fishing. Also popular for hunting. Three mi north of downtown, and a one-hour drive from the interstates. Complimentary breakfast. No room phones, TV in common area. Outdoor pool. Hiking. Fishing. | 43778 Thompson Run Rd. | 814/827–1092 | fax 814/827–0234 | knapping@cson.net | www.bbonline.com | 4 rooms | $65 | AE, D, DC, MC, V.

TOWANDA

MAP 7, I2

(Nearby towns also listed: Mansfield, Scranton)

Towanda, named after a Native American burial ground, was once the center of the state's lumbering industry. While many lumbering towns were damaged from fires, Towanda escaped that fate and today many of the homes and businesses built in the early 1800s remain. The town sits on the banks of the Susquehanna River. The surrounding area serves as prime hunting and fishing grounds.

Information: **Towanda Chamber of Commerce** | Box 146, 18848 | 570/268–2732 | fax 570/265–4558 | www.bradford-pa.com.

Attractions

David Wilmot's burial place. David Wilmot proposed the Wilmot Proviso that would have provided $2 million for settlement of border disputes in Mexico and also called for the prohibition of slavery in any territory acquired in the Mexico War. The Proviso failed in the Senate, but helped propel the conflict between the North and South prior to the Civil War. | Riverside Cemetery, William St. | no phone | Free | Daily dawn to dusk.

French Azilum. French refugees lived in a settlement here from 1793 until 1803. Some of the refugees, because of their loyalty to the king, had left France to escape imprisonment or death at the hands of the Revolution. Others fled to the French colony of Santo Domingo in Haiti. | R. R. 2; Rte. 6 West | 570/265–3376 | www.frenchazilum.org | $4.50 | June–Aug., Wed.–Sun. 11–4, closed Mon.–Tues.; May and Sept.–Oct., weekends 11–4, closed weekdays.

Mt. Pisgah State Park. This 1,302-acre park has the 75-acre Stephen Foster Lake for boating in summer and ice skating in winter. There are picnic facilities, a swimming pool, hiking trails, a play area, 1,100 acres for hunting, and snowmobile trails. | R.R. 3, Troy; Rte. 6 | 570/297–2734 or 888/PA–PARKS | www.dcnr.state.pa.us | Free | Daily 8 AM–dusk.

Tioga Point Museum. The manuscript of Stephen Foster's first song, "The Tioga Waltz," and other memorabilia from the noted composer, are on view here as well as a collection of rare books, Native American artifacts, and other mementos of the area's past. | 724 Main St., Athens | 570/888–7225 | Free | Tues., Thurs. 12–8, Sat. 10–1, closed Sun.–Mon., Wed., and Fri.

ON THE CALENDAR

OCT.: *Towanda Halloween Parade.* This is an annual All Hallow's Eve twilight parade in the boyhood hometown of composer Stephen Foster, replete with costume competitions, marching bands, and floats. | 570/265–2696.

Dining

P and A Chicken and Burger Pit. American. The chefs of this family-style restaurant serve freshly made meals daily. Homemade goodies include soups, sauces, burgers, chili, and real mashed potatoes. | Rte. 6 | 570/265–3169 | $5–10 | No credit cards.

Lodging

Best Western–Grand Victorian Inn. This brick, four- story hotel near Endless Slopes is 200 ft from the New York border and within 40 mi of the Corning Glass Center and Ithica State Parks. Restaurant, bar (with entertainment), room service. In-room data ports, cable TV. Indoor pool. Hot tub, sauna. Tennis. Basketball. Gym. Business services. | 255 Spring St., Sayre; Rte.

220 | 570/888–7711 or 800/627–7972 | fax 570/888–0541 | www.bestwestern.com | 100 rooms | $95–$100 | AE, D, DC, MC, V.

Towanda Motel. A small two-story motel, this is a low-cost alternative to the large resorts in the area. Some rooms have whirlpool tubs. Restaurant, bar. Cable TV. Pool. Business services. Pets allowed. | 383 York Ave./U.S. 6 | 570/265–2178 | fax 570/265–9060 | 48 rooms | $50–$70 | AE, D, MC, V.

The Williamston Inn. Independently owned, this two-story country motel is less than a mile from downtown. Restaurant, bar. Cable TV. | R.R. 6 | 570/265–8882 | 16 rooms | $59–$69 | D, MC, V.

TUNKHANNOCK

(Nearby towns also listed: Carbondale, Scranton, Wilkes-Barre)

The name Tunkhannock, loosely translated, means "small creek." Tunkhannock is 20 mi north of Scranton and is primarily a lumbering town. Fishing and hunting are two of its most popular activities.

Information: **Wyoming County Chamber of Commerce** | P.O. Box 568, 18657 | 570/836–7755 | fax 570/836–6049. | www.endlessmtns.com.

Attractions

Wyoming County Historical Society, Museum and Geneological Library. In the old Harrison Street School of Tunkahannock, the institution records "a heritage and history running as wide and deep as the Susquehanna River," with displays of Paleo-Indian sites, the colonial days, the Civil War and an archeological display. Geneological resources go back to 18th-century area newspapers and records of 90 area cemeteries. | Harrison St. and Bridge St. | 570/836–5303 | wyomingpa.freeservices.com | Free | Museum open Mon.–Fri. 10–4, Library open Wed., 10–4.

ON THE CALENDAR
AUG.:–SEPT.: *Kiwanis Wyoming County Fair.* The annual fair held on the Wyoming County Fair Grounds, on Rte. 6 West Meshoppen Rd., includes traditional agricultural displays and competitions, plus carnival rides and live entertainment. | 570/836–5502 | $7.

Dining
Fireplace. Contemporary. Rustic wood country trim with simple tables and chairs are highlighted by this restaurant's large fireplace. Specialties of the house are prime rib and stuffed sole. Kids' menu, early-bird suppers. | Rte. 6 | 570/836–9662 | $6–$20 | AE, DC, MC, V.

Shaffer's Pink Apple Restaurant. American. This former roadside cider stand is now a family restaurant that serves a full buffet daily from 11–8, with an additional weekend breakfast buffet. Specials include a pasta night and full-course meals. | 651 State Rte. 6 | 570/836–2971 | $3–$9 | AE, D, DC, MC, V.

Lodging
Shadowbrook Inn and Resort. A midsized inn with an 18-hole golf course and bowling lanes, you can relax here over breakfast in the solarium. The executive suite here has a jacuzzi. Restaurant, bar (with entertainment), complimentary Continental breakfast, room service. Some refrigerators, cable TV. Pool. Sauna. Gym, hiking. Video games. Laundry facilities. | Rte. 6 | 570/836–2151 or 800/955–0295 | fax 570/836–5655 | www.shadowbrookresort.com | 72 rooms, 1 suite | $67–$127 | AE, D, DC, MC, V.

UNIONTOWN

MAP 7, C7

(Nearby towns also listed: Connellsville, Farmington)

George Washington made Uniontown his home briefly when he built nearby Fort Necessity. Eventually the town, south of Pittsburgh, became known for its production of coal.

Information: **Uniontown Chamber of Commerce** | 11 Pittsburgh St., 15401 | 724/437–4571.

Attractions

Braddock's Grave. A single marker commemorates the final resting place of British Major General Edward Braddock. Braddock led an expedition to try and capture Fort Duquesne. | 1 Washington Pkwy., Farmington | 724/329–5512 | www.nps.gov/fone/braddock.htm | Free | Daily 9–5.

Fort Necessity National Battlefield. The park commemorates events surrounding the start of the French and Indian War. The fort got its name when a young General George Washington needed to build it out of necessity. It was the only battle where Washington surrendered.

Visitor Center. At the visitor center you can watch an orientation slide show, see exhibits, and visit the bookstore. Demonstrations, such as weapon use, are conducted daily throughout the year. Park rangers are on hand to answer questions about the fort or to relate historical tidbits.

Mt. Washington Tavern. Built around 1828 as a stagecoach stop, the tavern served travelers on the National Road, the first road built by the U.S. government that connected the settled east coast and the developing western frontier. | 1 Washington Pkwy.; Rte. 40 E | 724/329–5512 | www.nps.gov/fone/mwt.htm | $2 | Daily 9–5.

Friendship Hill National Historic Site. Albert Gallatin, an entrepreneur, politician, diplomat, financier, and scholar, lived on this estate. As secretary of the Treasury under Presidents Jefferson and Madison, Gallatin reduced the national debt and arranged financing for the Louisiana Purchase and the Lewis and Clark expedition. An audio-video presentation, exhibits, and tours of the house tell his story. | R.D. 1, Point Marion; Rte. 166 N | 724/725–9190 | www.nps.gov/frhi | Free. | Daily 9–5.

Jumonville Glen. Shots fired here were the first in the Fort Necessity Campaign. The campaign was led by General George Washington in 1754 and lasted only 15 min. | Summit Rd.; Rte. 40 E | 724/329–5512 | www.nps.gov/fone/jumglen.htm | Free | Apr.–Oct. 9–5.

Kentuck Knob. Frank Lloyd Wright designed this privately owned estate in 1953. The house overlooks the Youghiogheny River Gorge and is situated below the crest of the hill, almost appearing to be part of the mountain. | Chalk Hill, Ohiopyle Rd. | 724/329–1901 | fax 724/329–0977 | www.kentuckknob.com | $15 | Tues.–Sun. 10–4.

Laurel Caverns. With 2.8 mi of passages, this is Pennsylvania's largest cave. It is the 16th oldest developed cave in the country. Laurel Caverns has been explored since the late 1700s, with the first guided tour taken on July 1, 1964. Today, the trips last two to three hours, with most passages between 10- and 40-ft high. The cave's temperature is a constant 52 degrees. | 200 Caverns Park Rd. | 724/438–3003 or 800/515–4150 | fax 724/437–1925 | cavern@sgi.net | www.laurelcaverns.com | $9 | May–Oct., daily 9–5; Mar.–Apr. and Nov., Sat.–Sun. 10–2.

Ohiopyle State Park. This 19,052-acre park is the gateway to the Laurel Mountains. More than 14 mi of the Youghiogheny River Gorge pass through the heart of the park. Points of interest in the park include Ohiopyle Falls, Lumber Falls, Cucumber Run Ravine, scenic overlooks, and Ferncliff Peninsula—a National Natural Landmark. Enjoy whitewater rafting, picnicking, 28 mi of biking trails, more than 41 mi of hiking trails, and camping. | I-76 to Rte. 381 north | 724/329–8591 | fax 724/329–8603 | www.dcnr.state.pa.us | Free | Daily 8 AM–dusk.

SIGHTSEEING TOURS/TOUR COMPANIES

River tours. You can rent watercraft and equipment from many local companies or hire a guide to take you down the Youghiogheny River. Canoeing, tubing, and other water activities are available. Companies also rent bicycles to be used in the Ohiopyle State Park.

Laurel Highlands River Tours. The rafting tours include the Upper Youghiogheny, Cheat River, Lower Youghiogheny, and Middle Youghiogheny. Self-guided tours are offered only on the Lower and Middle Youghiogheny. You can rent canoes and other watercraft as well as bicycles here. | 4 Sherman St., Ohiopyle; I-76 to Rte. 381 | 724/329–8531 or 800/472–3846 | www.laurelhighlands.com | $17–$135 | Mar.–Oct., daily 8–8; Nov.–Feb. 9–5.

Mountain Streams and Trails Outfitters. This company has many packages for whitewater rafting, biking, hiking, kayaking, canoeing, and rock climbing. Guided tours are also available. | Rte. 381 and Lincoln, Ohiopyle; I-76 to exit 9 | 724/329–8810 or 800/723–8669 | mst@hhs.net | www.mtstreams.com | $25–$140 | Jan.–Nov., daily 9–5.

White Water Adventurers. You can rent rafts, canoes, tubes, and bicycles from this company. The adventure tours vary in difficulty and distance. | 6 Negley St., Ohiopyle, | 724/329–8850 or 800/WWA–RAFT | fax 724/329–1488 | www.wwaraft.com | $22–$59 | Season runs Mar.–Oct., daily 8–11.

West Overton Museums. This industrial village is the birthplace of H. C. Frick. You can visit a distillery, museum, and homestead. Museum exhibits show artifacts and tools, providing a glimpse of life in the 19th century. | West Overton Village, Scottsdale; Rte. 381 | 724/887–7910 | $4 | Mid-May.–mid-Oct., Tues.–Sat. 10–4, Sun. 1–5, closed Mon.; Mid-Oct.–mid-May, by appointment only.

ON THE CALENDAR

MAY: *National Road Festival.* A celebration of our nation's first federally funded highway, the wagon train, the central event of this festival, starts on both ends of Route 40, in Addison, Maryland, and Washington, Pennsylvania. You can visit yard sales and bake sales or join the crowds to re-enactments of wagon travel or other activities related to the past. place. There are community activities everywhere along Route 40, including Uniontown. | 800/916–9365 | Free | 3rd weekend in May.

Dining

Caileigh's. Eclectic. Choose from signature dishes like portabello ravioli, chicken amore with roasted red peppers, gorgonzola cheese, and tarragon, or crab cakes at this house-turned-restaurant with hardwood floors, a fireplace, and classical music. Bring your own alcohol. Kids menu. Sun. brunch. | 105 E. Fayette St. (Rte. 40) | 724/437–9436 | Closed Monday | $14–$23 | AE, D, MC, V.

Mid-Towne Cafe. American. This diner has been here for more than 30 years serving dirt-cheap breakfast specials. | 13 Morgantown Rd. | 724/439–3232 | Closed Sunday. No dinner | $1.75–$3.50 | No credit cards.

Sun Porch. American. A home away-from-home best describes the interior of this casual and cozy restaurant, which serves a family-style buffet and salad bar. Kids' menu. | U.S. 40, Hopwood; U.S. 40 west of Uniontown | 724/439–5734 | Closed Mon. No lunch Sat. | $8–$12 | D, DC, MC, V.

Lodging

Blue Mountain Motel. A mile from the center of Uniontown, this one-story motel sits at the foot of the Summit Mountain, so you are assured a green view. Each room has one queen-sized bed. | 8 rooms | Rte. 40 East | 724/439–4880 | $42 | D, MC, V.

Heritage Inn. This small one-story inn on the west edge of town is just a few hundred feet from many restaurants, both fast food and upscale. Parking is right outside room doors, and rooms have either a king-size bed or two doubles. Complimentary Continental breakfast on Sundays. In-room data ports, cable TV. Laundry service. | 222 W. Main St. | 724/425–0120 | fax 724/437–8717 | info@heritage-inn.com | www.heritage-inn.com | 19 rooms | $59–$69 | AE, D, MC, V.

Holiday Inn. This midpriced, two-story chain hotel is in downtown Uniontown. Restaurant, bar (with entertainment), room service. In-room data ports, cable TV. Indoor pool. Hot tub, sauna. Gym. Miniature golf. Tennis. Volleyball. Video games. Business services, free parking. Pets allowed. | 700 W. Main St.; U.S. 40 | 724/437–2816 or 800/258–7238 | fax 724/437–3505 | www.holiday-inn.com | 174 rooms, 4 suites | $89–$99, $150 suites | AE, D, DC, MC, V.

Inn at Watson's Choice. Built in the 1820s, this Bavarian farmhouse is on 42 acres with landscaped grounds. There are fireplaces in many guest rooms. Picnic area, complimentary breakfast. TV in common area. Laundry facilities. No kids under 12. No smoking. | 234 Balsinger Rd.; Rte. 21 W | 724/437–4999 or 800/820–5380 | www.watsonschoice.com | 7 rooms (with shower only) | $89–$145 | AE, D, MC, V.

Lodge at Chalk Hill. Each room has a private deck in this lakeside, medium-size inn. It's on 37 acres, 5 mi east of Uniontown. Picnic area, complimentary Continental breakfast. Some kitchenettes, cable TV. Business services. Pets allowed (fee). | U.S. 40 E, Chalk Hill; Rte. 40 E | 724/438–8880 or 800/833–4283 | fax 724/438–1685 | www.thelodgeatchalkhill.com | 60 rooms, 6 suites | $78–$84, $153–$179 suites | AE, D, MC, V.

WARREN

(Nearby towns also listed: Bradford, Kane)

Warren was first known as a lumbering town, then became an oil town. Its downtown is a historic district. The town is a popular destination because of its proximity to Pennsylvania's most scenic natural wonder, the Grand Canyon of Pennsylvania.

Information: **Warren County Chamber of Commerce** | 315 Second Ave., Box 942, 16365 | 814/723–3050 | fax 814/723–6024 | www.warrenpachamber.com.

Attractions

Allegheny National Forest. This forest is the only national forest in Pennsylvania, covering more than 500,000 acres with more than 600 mi of trails. The forest is popular for hiking, camping, picnicking, swimming, boating, canoeing, cross-country skiing, mountain biking, and snowmobiling.

Buckaloons Recreation Area. In the forest, the campground has 51 campsites, a hiking path that travels around the Allegheny River, and a boat launch with an access point to travel by boat to one of seven islands. | 222 Liberty St.; Rte. 6 west to Rte. 62 | 814/723–5150 or 814/726–2710 (TTY) | Free; fee for camping | Daily 8 AM to dusk.

Kinzua Dam and Allegheny Reservoir. Completed in 1965 by the U.S. Army Corps of Engineers, the flood-control dam has created the Allegheny Reservoir, which is 12,000 acres and has 91 mi of shoreline. Boating, canoeing, and camping are available. | 1205 Kinzua Rd.; Rte. 59 | 814/727–0661 | Free | Daily dawn to dusk.

Chapman State Park. This state park has 805 acres with 83 campsites, a 68-acre lake, and over 12 mi of trails. It has boating, hunting, and snowmobiling. Every year the park hosts Pennsylvania's championship dog sled races. | R.R. 2, Clarendon; Rte. 6 | 814/723–0250 | www.dcnr.state.pa.us | Free | Daily 8 AM–dusk.

Rocky Gap Nature Trails. Six miles south of Warren, you'll find a 20-mi loop of hilly, wooded trails winding through the Allegheny National Forest. Although the trails are used by bikers and hikers, and ATV riders, they are not for beginning riders. | Rte. 337 | 814/723–3050 | Open Friday before Memorial Day–Sept 24, and Dec. 20-April 1.

AUG.: *Warren County Fair.* At this annual event, held the third week in August at the Warren County Fair Grounds in Pittsfield, you can find everything you'd expect at a county fair, from animal judging and tractor pulls to a midway and live country music. | 814/723–3050 | Free | 3rd week in Aug.

Dining
Dagwood's. American. This sandwich shop serves subs and hamburgers and has beer on tap. The cartoon Dagwood appears on some of the walls, although you can also see a sports motif. | 242 Pennsylvania Ave. W | 814/723–1313 | $2–$5 | No credit cards.

Lodging
Holiday Inn. Only 2 mi from downtown, this inn is partially surrounded by the Allegheny Mountains. Rooms have double beds, and some have hot tubs. Restaurant. In-room data ports, cable TV. Indoor pool. Sauna. Health club. Pets allowed. | 210 Ludlow St. | 814/726–3000 | fax 814/726–3720 | holinwrn@penn.com | www.users.penn.com-holinwrn | 112 rooms | $80.

WASHINGTON

MAP 7, A6

(Nearby towns also listed: Monroeville, Pittsburgh)

Once the headquarters of Chief Tingoocqua of the Delaware Indian tribe, Washington today is a southern suburb of Pittsburgh. Washington and Jefferson College is here. There are over 250 acres of parkland with water access for boating and fishing.

Information: Washington Chamber of Commerce | 20 E. Beau St., 15301 | 412/225–3010 | www.washcochamber.com.

Attractions
David Bradford House. This is the former home of David Bradford, leader of the Whiskey Rebellion. The home is 18th-century architecture and most of the interior woodwork was handcrafted and brought over from England. The stairway is said to have cost a guinea a step, which was a high price in those days. | 175 S. Main St. | 724/222–3604 | www.bradfordhouse.org | $4 | May–late Dec., Wed.–Sat. 11–4, closed Sun.–Tues.

Ladbroke at the Meadows. Watch live harness racing all year or view simulcast races from all over the country. You can also eat dinner at Ladbroke's restaurant, which serves daily specials, including surf and turf or Alaskan king crab. | Box 499, Meadow Lands | 724/225–9300 | www.latm.com | Free | Tues. and Thur.–Sun. 6:30 PM, closed Mon. and Wed.

LeMoyne House. One of the stops along the underground railroad, this home belonged to Dr. Francis Julius LeMoyne, a prominent advocate of the abolition of slavery and the Abolition Party's candidate for governor in 1841, 1844, and 1847. | 49 E. Maiden St. | 724/225–6740 | fax 724/225–8495 | www.wchspa.org | $4 | Feb.–Dec., Tues.–Fri. 11–4, weekends 12–4, closed Mon.

Meadowcroft Museum of Rural Life. A living history museum that covers the past 14,000 years, Meadowcroft is one of the oldest archeological sites in the United States. It is a renovated 19th-century village with costumed volunteers who demonstrate life from that period. | 401 Meadowcroft Rd., Avella | 724/587–3412 | fax 724/587–3414 | www.cobweb/~mcroft/ | $6.50 | Memorial Day–Labor Day, Sat. 12–5, Sun. 1–5, or by appointment.

Paul R. Stewart Museum. A large collection of artifacts from prehistoric Native Americans is on display, including Greensboro–New Geneva pottery, early American glass, and a large collection of rocks and minerals. | 51 W. College St., Waynesburg; Waynesburg College campus | 724/852–3214 | www.waynesburg.edu | Free | weekdays 9 AM–noon; or by appointment.

Pennsylvania Trolley Museum. Guided tours take you through a park and visitors education center with artifacts and memorabilia. Take a train ride on the 1½-mile track. The park has over 30 working trolleys. Rides last an hour. | 1 Museum Rd. | 724/228–9256 or 877/PA–TROLLEY | www.pa-trolley.org | $6 | June–Aug., daily 11–5; Apr.–May and Sept.–Dec., weekends 11–5, closed weekdays.

Ryerson Station State Park. The 1,164-acre park features the 62-acre Ronald J. Duke Lake, where you can fish, go boating, ice skate, and ice fish. There are 50 campsites, a swimming pool, picnic facilities, a 10-mile hiking trail, 900 acres for hunting, hills for sledding, and 6 mi of snowmobile trails. | Bristoria Rd.; Rte. 21 to Bristoria Rd. | 724/428–4254 or 888/PA–PARKS | www.dcnr.state.pa.us | Free | Daily 8 AM–dusk.

ON THE CALENDAR

SEPT.: _Allegheny Rib Cook-Off._ Barbecue cooks from around the country come to this cook-off to show their talents. You can also shop for antiques and crafts, hear live music, and watch pig racing. | South Park Fairgrounds | Labor Day weekend | 412/678–1727.

Dining

Barry's on the Avenue. Eclectic. Although this place calls itself a steakhouse, you'll find rattlesnake, antelope, vennison, and buffalo on the menu in addition to porterhouse, lamb chops, and filet mignons. Dinner in the Art Deco setting is by candlelight, with jazz. Full bar. | 939 Jefferson Ave. | 724/222–6688 | $12–$40 | AE, DC, MC, V.

21st Amendment. Italian. Traditional Italian fare, including homemade pasta, lots of steak and seafood, and very little on the vegetarian side has been served here since 1973. Pictures of the owners' friends and family adorn the walls, giving it a warm "Cheers"-like sense. | 301 Oak Spring Rd. | 724/228–1353 | Closed Sun. | $13–$33 | AE, D, MC, V.

Yardley. Continental. Built in 1832, this inn was frequented by barge and boat travelers in the 1800s. The inn has retained its country charm, with antiques and large windows overlooking the Delaware River. Try the crab cakes, veal and dry scallops Napoleon, or the filet mignon. | Delaware and E. Afton Aves | 215/493–3800 | $16–$25 | AE, D, DC, MC, V.

Lodging

Econo Lodge. This motel is within walking distance of the Washington Crown Center Mall and restaurants. Picnic area, complimentary Continental breakfast. Some microwaves, cable TV. Business services, airport shuttle. | 1385 W. Chestnut St.; Intersection of I-70 and I-79 | 724/222–6500 | fax 724/222–6500 | www.econolodge.com | 62 rooms | $65–$95 | AE, D, DC, MC, V.

Hampton Inn. Although this inn is in the center of town, it's just across from I-70 and on a busy street without sidewalks, so walking around isn't recommended. Rooms have either king-size beds or two doubles. Complimentary Continental breakfast. Cable TV. Exercise equipment. Laundry service. Free parking. | 119 Murtland Ave. | 800/HAMPTON or 724/228–4100 | 111 rooms | $71 | AE, D, DC, MC, V.

Holiday Inn–Meadow Lands. Next to the Meadows Racetrack, this six-story hotel is 30 mi south of Pittsburgh. Restaurant, bars (with entertainment), room service. In-room data ports, cable TV. Pool. Hot tub. Exercise equipment. Business services, airport shuttle. Pets allowed. | 340 Race Track Rd.; Intersection of I-70 and I-79 | 724/222–6200 | fax 724/228–1977 | www.holiday-inn.com | 138 rooms | $89–$119 | AE, D, DC, MC, V.

Motel 6. This one-story motel has affordable rates and is 6 blocks from Washington Jefferson College. Cable TV. Pool. Laundry facilities. Pets allowed. | 1283 Motel 6 Dr.; I-70 to exit 7A | 724/223–8040 or 800/466–8356 | fax 724/228–6445 | www.motel6.com | 102 rooms | $45–$60 | AE, D, DC, MC, V.

Red Roof Inn. This two-story motel is 2 mi from the Pennsylvania Trolley Museum. Cable TV. Pets allowed. | 1399 W. Chestnut St. | 724/228–5750 | fax 724/228–5865 | www.redroof.com | 110 rooms | $45–$55 | AE, D, DC, MC, V.

Rush House. A mile from the center of town and 1½ mi from I-70, this late 1800s country farmhouse was built on top of Catfish Creek, and you can use a tunnel to go under the house and wade in the water. Inside, everything is Victorian, with both antiques and reproductions; outside, a patio and large wraparound porch let you get a full sweep of the rural surroundings. Complimentary breakfast. No room phones, no TV. | 810 E. Maiden St. (Rte. 40) | 724/223–1890 | jwheeler@cobweb.net | 4 rooms | $75–$110 | MC, V.

WELLSBORO

MAP 7, G2

(Nearby towns also listed: Galeton, Mansfield)

Named after founder Benjamin Wister Morris' wife, Mary Wells Morris, Wellsboro is the county seat of Tioga County. Boulevards are adorned with gaslights, sidewalks are lined with elm and maple trees, and houses with manicured lawns are set off from the streets. Nearby are vast forests and mountains, and less than an hour away is the State of New York.

Information: Wellsboro Area Chamber of Commerce | 114 Main St., Box 733, 16901 | 570/724–1926 | fax 570/724–5084 | mwwacc@epix.net | www.wellsboropa.com.

Attractions

Colton Point State Park. The 368-acre park is on the western rim of the Grand Canyon of Pennsylvania, a 1,000-ft-deep gorge. There are 25 campsites, picnic facilities, 4 mi of hiking trails, 20 mi of snowmobile trails, and areas for hunting. You can fish if you want to take the long, steep hike to Pine Creek Gorge at the bottom of the canyon. | R.R. 6; Rte. 6 in Ansonia | 570/724–3061 or 888/PA–PARKS | www.dcnr.state.pa.us | Free | Daily 8 AM–dusk.

Leonard Harrison State Park. The 585-acre park is on the eastern rim of the Grand Canyon of Pennsylvania. The park has 30 campsites and two hiking trails: Turkey Path Trail, which descends 1 mi to the bottom of Pine Creek Gorge, and Overlook Trail, with scenic overlooks of the canyon. | R.R. 6; Rte. 660 west | 570/724–3061 or 888/PA–PARKS | www.dcnr.state.pa.us | Free | Daily 8 AM–dusk.

Ski Sawmill Resort. With an elevation of 2,215 ft, the resort has skiing, snowboarding, and snowtubing. Its longest run is 3,250 ft and has a top vertical drop of 515 ft. | R.R. 1, Morris; Rte. 287 north | 570/353–7521 or 800/532–SNOW (recording) | fax 570/353–2157 | ski-sawmill.com | Dec.–Mar.

ON THE CALENDAR

JUNE: *Pennsylvania State Laurel Festival.* This eight-day festival celebrates the state flower with an 18.8-mile bike race, a family-oriented bike ride, a pet parade, arts and crafts show, and a carnival. | Packer Park, Broad St. | 570/724–1926.

DEC.: *Dickens of a Christmas.* Wellsboro's period homes and gaslit streets and boulevards create a Victorian background for this traditional Christmas celebration. | Various locations | 570/724–1926.

Dining

Pioneer Dairy Bar and Grill. American. After you gobble up your burger or cheesesteak at one of the picnic tables, then choose from soft-serve or hard ice cream or Italian Ice. The biggest seller is a Texas Hot, which is a hot dog with ground meat sauce, onions, and mustard. | 29 Tioga Rd. | 570/724–4450 | Closed Oct.-Apr. | $1.50–$7 | No credit cards.

Coach Stop Inn. American. This combination hotel and restaurant serves an array of steak and seafood entrees while you dine by candlelight and flowers. Try the seafood smorgasboard on Friday or the dinner buffet on Saturdays. Full bar. Kids menu. | Rte. 6 | 570/724–5361 | $9–$20 | AE, D, MC, V.

Laurel Cafe. Eclectic. From hummus to hamburgers, everyone in the family will find something to eat at this downtown eatery. For breakfast, try steak and eggs or a belgian waffle with real maple syrup. | 2 Tioga St. (Rte. 6) | 570/723–2233 | $6.50–$15 | AE, D, DC, MC, V.

Lodging

Canyon Motel. This frame, two-story motel, on 4 acres in the center of town, is 10 mi west of the Pennsylvania Grand Canyon. The motel has special ski packages. Some rooms have Jacuzzi baths and oversized bathrooms. Picnic area. In-room data ports, refrigerators, microwaves, cable TV, in-room VCRs (and movies). Pool. Spa. Gym. Playground. Business services. Pets allowed. | 18 East Ave. | 570/724–1681 or 800/255–2718 | fax 570/724–5202 | www.canyonmotel.com | 25 rooms, 6 suites | $55, $60–$80 suites | AE, D, DC, MC, V.

Garden Cottages Motel. Just over a mile from downtown, this motel, with efficiency units, sits on four acres of flowers and lawns and even has a small duck pond out back where you can fish. Beds are king- or queen-sized. | 12 cottages. Playground. | 66 West Ave. | 570/724–3581 | fax 570/724–2123 | genosge@yahoo.com | www.gardencottages.com | $35–$60 | AE, D, MC, V.

Kaltenbach's Bed and Breakfast. This sprawling inn on a 72-acre farm just outside of Wellsboro is ½ mile from a golf course. The inn is filled with quilts made by the owner's mother and grandmother. Some of the quilts were made in the 1920s. Picnic area, complimentary breakfast. Refrigerators, cable TV, some room phones. Playground. No smoking. | R.D. #6, Stony Fork Rd. | www.pafarmstay.com/kaltenbachs | Off Rte. 287 | 570/724–4954 or 800/722–4954 | 6 rooms, 4 suites | $80, $150 suites | D, DC, MC, V.

Penn-Wells Hotel. In the heart of downtown, this is a vintage hotel built in 1869. Guests can use the pool at the Penn-Wells Lodge down the street. Restaurant, bar (with entertainment). Cable TV. Business services. | 62 Main St. | 570/724–2111 or 800/545–2446 | fax 570/724–3703 | www.pennwells.com | 64 rooms, 11 suites | $55–$70, $75–$79 suites | AE, D, DC, MC, V.

Penn-Wells Lodge. This small hotel is downtown and down the street from its sister hotel. Cable TV. Indoor pool. Hot tub. Gym. Playground. Business services. | 4 Main St. | 570/724–3463 or 800/545–2446 | fax 570/724–2270 | www.pennwells.com | 54 rooms, 1 suite | $64–$70, $75–$79 suites | AE, D, DC, MC, V.

Sherwood Motel. This two-story downtown motel has three buildings. The newest building overlooks the swimming pool. Some rooms have Jacuzzi tubs. In-room data ports, refrigerators, microwaves, cable TV. Pool. Playground. Business services. | 2 Main St. | 570/724–3424 or 800/626–5802 | fax 570/724–5658 | www.sherwoodmotel.org | 38 rooms, 2 suites | $52–$67, $70 suites | AE, D, DC, MC, V.

Terrace Motel Choose from an efficiency unit or a fully equipped cabin for an extended stay, or a suite or a room for a shorter visit. | 15 rooms. Pets allowed. | Rr 7 | 570/724–4711 | $49–$55 | AE, D, MC, V.

WEST CHESTER

MAP 7, J7

(Nearby towns also listed: Chester, Kennett Square, King of Prussia, Philadelphia)

Brick sidewalks, hitching posts, and weathered stepping stones are still evident in downtown West Chester, which welcomed General Lafayette in 1825. A walking tour of downtown takes you by a blacksmith shop built in 1699 and various other historic buildings. The historic areas of Valley Forge, Brandywine, Paoli, and other famous sites of the American Revolution are within a short drive.

Information: West Chester Chamber of Commerce | 40 E. Gay St., 19380 | 610/696–4046.

Attractions

Brinton 1704 House. The property was settled by Quakers and has two houses, one built in 1684 and the other in 1704. The buildings are furnished to the period and include 27 original leaded-glass windows. Caretakers can answer your questions about what life was like during that time. | Oakland Rd. Dilworthtown | 610/399–4588 | $3.00 | May–Oct., weekends 11–6, closed weekdays.

Old Chester County Courthouse. A Georgian and Colonial stone structure built in 1724, this courthouse is regarded as the oldest public building in continuous use in the country. | 2 N. High St. | 610/344–6181 | Free | Weekdays 9–5 by appointment, closed weekends.

QVC Studio Tour. Get a behind-the-scenes look at the world's largest electronic retailer. See how QVC products are sourced, tested, brought to life on air, and delivered to millions of customers. There are views into the studio throughout the tour, allowing you to watch the programs in progress. | 1200 Wilson Dr. | 610/701–1000 or 800/600–9900 | fax 610/701–6300 | www.qvctours.com | $10 | Daily 10–4.

ON THE CALENDAR

DEC.: *Old-Fashioned Christmas in Historic Westchester.* Usually the first weekend in December, this festival has activities spread out around the center of town, starting Friday night with a big parade that includes dancers, jugglers, and singers. The next two days have more of the same, or you can bring the kids to sit on Santa's lap and hear the carollers sing Charlie Brown Christmas songs. | 610/696–4046.

Dining

Cafe Chicane. Continental. In a historic downtown building, this restaurant is filled with antiques and period furnishings. The adjoining dining room is a martini and cigar lounge. Steaks and seafood are specialties of the house. Live music, including jazz, is offered on Saturdays. | 15 S. High St.; Rte. 220 | 610/696–6660 | Reservations essential | Closed Sun. | $15–$25 | AE, MC, V.

Dilworthtown Inn. Continental. The inn was built in 1754 and became a licensed tavern in 1780. The restaurant is filled with antiques and several walk-in stone fireplaces. Dine by candlelight and try the Chilean sea bass or the grilled ostrich. | 1390 Old Wilmington Pike | 610/399–1390 | www.dilworthtown.com | Reservations essential | No lunch | $18–$37 | AE, D, DC, MC, V.

Duling-Kurtz House. American. This country inn has seven dining rooms with fireplaces for formal dining. Specialties include crab cakes, rack of lamb, and chateaubriand. | 146 S. Whitford Rd., Exton; Rte. 202 S to Rte. 30 W | 610/524–1830 | No lunch weekends | $17–$30 | AE, D, DC, MC, V.

Jimmy John's Pipin Hot Restaurant. American. The electric train sets on display make this local landmark a favorite dining establishment. Menu favorites are homemade soups and hot dogs. | 1507 Wilmington Pike Rd. | 610/459–3083 | Reservations not accepted | $4–$10 | No credit cards.

Magnolia Grill. Cajun. Step back into a scene from Bourbon Street at this New Orleans-style restaurant. The early 19th-century decorations show off original artwork. Taste the chicken pecan salad or the crawfish étouffée. Kids' menu. | 975 Paoli Pike; Rte. 202 and Paoli Pike | 610/696–1661 | Reservations not accepted | $9–$12 | AE, D, DC, MC, V.

Oak Grill at the Marshalton Inn. Contemporary. Enjoy a candlelight supper by the fireside in this historic country inn with period furnishings and warm colors. The restaurant is known for salmon mignon, lobster and crab imperial, filet mignon. | 1300 W. Strasburg Rd.; Rte. 202 | 610/692–4367 | Reservations essential | Closed Mon.–Tues. | $16–$35 | AE, DC, MC, V.

Lodging

Bank House Bed and Breakfast A mile from the center of town, this 250-year-old country Colonial home overlooks a 10-acre horse farm and its stenciled walls surround a mixture of country antiques and quilts made by the owner. Complimentary breakfast. No room phones, no TV. Library. No kids under 12. | 875 Hillsdale Rd. | 610/344–7388 | www.bbonlin.com/pa/bankhouse | 2 rooms (1 with private bathroom) | $75–$95 | No credit cards.

Best Western Concordville Hotel and Conference Center. This large hotel caters to business travelers and meeting planners who need fully equipped conference rooms. The hotel has a pond in front, and a lobby with marble floors and staircase. Restaurant, bar, complimentary Continental breakfast. In-room data ports, mini bars, some refrigerators, cable TV. Indoor pool. Gym. Laundry services. Business services. | Concordville; Rte. 322 and Rte. 1 | 610/358–9400 | fax 610/358–9381 | www.concordville.com | 108 rooms, 7 suites | $119, $160–$189 suites | AE, D, DC, MC, V.

Broadlawns Bed and Breakfast Six blocks north of Main Street, this 1880 Victorian home has a large wraparound porch, in addition to some private balconies off guest rooms. One room has a hot tub. The Victorian style rules here, from lace curtains to antique furniture. Full breakfast. Library. | N. Church St. | 610/692–5477 | fax 610/692–5672 | 3 rooms | $110–$150 | MC, V.

Duling-Kurtz House and Country Inn. A country inn dating back to 1830, the small inn is close to many historic sites and museums. Some rooms have four poster beds. Restaurant, complimentary Continental breakfast, room service. Cable TV. Business services. | 146 S. Whitford Rd., Exton; Rte. 202 S to Rte. 30 W | 610/524–1830 | fax 610/524–6258 | www.dulingkurtz.com | 10 rooms, 5 suites | $55–$100, $79–$120 suites | AE, D, DC, MC, V.

Holiday Inn West Chester. This hotel is downtown and 1½ mi from West Chester University. Restaurant, bar, room service. In-room data ports, cable TV. Pool. Laundry facilities. Business services, airport shuttle, free parking. | 943 S. High St.; Rte. 202 | 610/692–1900 | fax 610/436–0159 | www.holiday-inn.com | 103 rooms, 40 suites | $95–$109, $119 suites | AE, D, DC, MC, V.

WEST MIDDLESEX

MAP 7, A4

(Nearby towns also listed: Mercer, New Castle, Sharon)

West Middlesex is popular because of its closeness to I–80, Grove City, and the Pittsburgh International Airport. Travelers on I–80 visit West Middlesex to get a good night's sleep or to refuel at one of the many restaurants. The community is also close to Grove City's popular outlet shopping center.

Information: Mercer Area Chamber of Commerce | 132 S. Pitt St., 16137 | 724/662–4185 | fax 724/662–4185 | mercerchamber@pathway.net | www.pathway.net/mercerchamber.

Dining

The Tavern. American. Built in the 1850s, this tavern played a central role in the history of New Wilmington as a stopping place for weary travelers. It has authentic woodwork and antiques. Try the roasted duck, rack of lamb, or chicken marsala. | 108 N. Market St., New Wilmington; Rte. 208 | 724/946–2020 | Reservations essential | Closed Tues. | $13–$25 | AE, D, MC, V.

Lodging

Comfort Inn. Five miles from downtown West Middlesex, rooms in this isolated inn are predictable. Beds are either king- or queen-sized. | 60 rooms. Complimentary Continental breakfast. Indoor pool. Exercise equipment. | R.R. 18 and Wilson Rd. | 724/342–7200 | fax 724/342–7213 | $70 | AE, MC, V.

Holiday Inn. This midpriced, three-story brick hotel is at Exit 1N off I–80. Restaurant, bar (with entertainment), room service. In-room data ports, cable TV. Pool. Video games. Playground. Laundry facilities. Business services. Pets allowed. | 3200 S. Hermitage Rd., Hermitage | 724/981–1530 | fax 724/981–1518 | www.holiday-inn.com | 180 rooms | $80 | AE, D, DC, MC, V.

Radisson Hotel Sharon. A two-story hotel at exit 1 N on I–80, this hotel has two 2-floor suites. The building exterior is white brick trimmed in black. Restaurant, bar (with entertainment), room service. Some refrigerators, in-room hot tubs, cable TV. Indoor pool. Hot tub. Exercise equipment. Game room. Laundry facilities. Business services. Pets allowed. | Rte. 18 | 724/528–2501 | fax 724/528–2306 | www.radisson.com | 153 rooms, 5 suites | $90–$100, $150–$250 suites | AE, D, DC, MC, V.

WHITE HAVEN

(Nearby towns also listed: Hazleton, Jim Thorpe, Wilkes-Barre)

White Haven, established in 1824 on the banks of the Lehigh River, was named for Josiah White, inventor of the Bear Trap Lock System, which improved navigation on River.

Information: Greater White Haven Chamber of Commerce | Box 363, 18661 | 570/427–8182 | www.whitehaven.org.

Attractions

Hickory Run State Park. In the western foothills of the Pocono Mountains, the park has 81 campsites, swimming, picnicking, 40 mi of hiking trails, and hunting. It also has 21 mi of snowmobiling trails, 13 mi of cross-country skiing trails, ice skating, and sledding. | R.R. 1; I-80 to exit 41 | 570/443–0400 | www.dcnr.state.pa.us | Free | Daily 8 AM–dusk.

Skiing. In the Pocono Mountains, skiing is easy to find. Slopes vary from easy to difficult, and if you can't ski, there's snowtubing, snowmobiling, and ice skating to keep you busy.

Big Boulder. One of the area's oldest ski resorts with skiing, snowboarding, and snowtubing, elevation is 2,175 ft with a top vertical drop of 475 ft. There's a long run of 2,900 ft. | Lake Harmony; I–80 to exit 43 | 570/722–0100 | www.jackfrostbigboulder.com | Dec.–Mar.

Jack Frost. Why ski one mountain when you can ski two for the same price. If you buy a ticket here, you can also use it at Big Boulder down the road. Jack Frost has 20 trails, a top vertical drop of 600 ft, and a long run of 2,700 ft. It also has trails for cross-country skiing. | Lake Harmony; I-80 to exit 43 | 570/443–8425 | www.jackfrostbigboulder.com | Dec.–Mar.

White Water Challengers. Take a group of friends or your family on a guided adventuresome day trip rafting along a river, ranging from class I to V. Reservations necessary. Meal, camping, or hotel packages available. | Box 8 | 570/443–9532 | www.wc-rafting.com | $20–$149 | Mar.–Oct.

ON THE CALENDAR

AUG. OR SEPT.: *White Haven Outdoor Festival.* Regional food vendors and craftspeople show their goods on Main Street the weekend before Labor Day, from Friday to Sunday. The action also includes entertainment, mountain bike racing, a midway, and lots of stuff for kids. | 570/427–8182.

Dining

Ugly Mug. American. You can take your kids for a family dinner in the dining room, or hang out in the bar area, where you can get great deals at happy hour. The menu includes all-you-can-eat specials, with choices like chicken parmesan, barbequed spare ribs, or fried haddock. Try the tollhouse pie for dessert. Kids' menu. | 219 Main St. | 570/443–7141 | $4–$25 | AE, MC, V.

Hikory Run Plaza Restaurant. American. If you're craving breakfast at midnight, this diner offers plenty of bacon and egg combos 24 hours a day. Right off I–80, it's easy to find, and generally popular with truck drivers coming through the area. | I–80, exit 41, at Rte. 534 | 570/443–7933 | Closes Saturday at 2 PM | $3–$10 | AE, D, MC, V.

Lodging

Country Place Inn. Renovated in 2000, this inn offers basic and inexpensive rooms 2 ½ mi from the Pennsylvania Turnpike and 6 mi from downtown White Haven. Weekly discounts available. | Rte. 940 E., Box 30 | 570/443–1125 | 20 rooms | $48–$61 | AE, D, DC, MC, V.

Lehigh Tannery Bed and Breakfast. This 1850s farmhouse has three very distinct rooms, from the forest room to the Shaker and the Burgundy rooms. You can explore the several acres of land around the propery or at Hickory State Park, 4 mi away. Breakfast isn't fancy, but it's delicious and filling, usually bacon, eggs, homefries, and toast. Complimentary breakfast. No room phones, no TV. | Rte. 534 | 570/443–9239 | www.lehightannery.com | 3 rooms | $65–$95 | D, MC, V.

Mountain Laurel Resort and Spa. The large, 4-story building is split into two large wings. Established in the 1960s, the property and rooms have been upgraded. The resort is in the center of the Pocono skiing areas. Bar (with entertainment), dining room, picnic area. Cable TV. 2 pools (1 indoor). Hot tub. 4 tennis courts. Gym. Video games. Baby-sitting, kids' programs, playground. Laundry facilities. Business services. | Rte. 940 and I–80 | 570/443–8411 or 800/458–5921 | fax 570/443–5518 | www.mountainlaurelresort.com | 250 rooms | $99–$129 | AE, D, DC, MC, V.

Comfort Inn–Pocono Mountain. This motel has rooms with mountain views. Some rooms have Jacuzzi baths. Restaurant, bar. Cable TV. Pool. Video Games. Business services. | Rte. 940; I–80 to Rte. 940 | 570/443–8461 or 800/443–4049 | fax 570/443–7988 | www.comfortinn.com | 123 rooms | $119–$169 | AE, D, DC, MC, V.

Ramada Inn. A snowman-shaped indoor swimming pool and indoor miniature golf make this hotel, built in 1974, unique. Some rooms have Jacuzzi baths. Restaurant, bar, picnic area, room service. Some refrigerators, cable TV. Indoor pool. Sauna. Miniature golf. Basketball, hiking, volleyball. Video games. Laundry facilities. Business services, airport shuttle. Pets allowed (fee). | Rte. 940, Lake Harmony; I–80 to Rte. 940 | 570/443–8471 | fax 570/443–0326 | www.ramada.com | 136 rooms, 2 suites | $95–$125, $145–$200 suites | AE, D, DC, MC, V.

WILKES-BARRE

MAP 7, J4

(Nearby towns also listed: Hazleton, Scranton, White Haven)

The site of battles between Native Americans and settlers, Wilkes-Barre is named after John Wilkes and Isaac Barre. By the early 1900s, the area was the site of a coal-mine boom that transformed the rural area into a metropolis. The town has seen its share of disasters, especially after tropical storm Agnes damaged more than 2,000 businesses. Today the town is a popular destination for people traveling to the Pocono Mountains.

Information: Wilkes-Barre Chamber of Commerce | 2 Public Square, Box 5340, 18710 | 570/823–2101 | www.wilkes-barre.org.

Attractions

Frances Slocum State Park. The focal point of the 1,035-acre park is Frances Slocum Lake, which covers 165 acres for boating and fishing. There are picnic facilities, 9 mi of hiking trails, hunting on 300 acres, 100 campsites, a swimming pool, a 5-acre slope for sledding, and a 7-mi trail for snowmobiles. | 565 Mt. Olivet Rd., Wyoming; 8th St. to Mt. Olivet Rd. | 570/ 696–3525 or 888/PA–PARKS | fax 570/696–3456 | www.dcnr.state.pa.us | Free | Daily 8 AM–dusk.

ON THE CALENDAR

MAY: *Fine Arts Fiesta.* Tents are set up for this outdoor celebration of visual and performing arts on the third weekend in May at the Public Square. Students show their art for competitions, with art for sale, as well as food. | 570/822–3903.

Dining

Hottle's Restaurant American. Entrees at this sports bar and restaurant are mostly seafood, such as crabcakes, shrimp scampi, and fresh halibut. Try the peanut butter ice cream pie or homemade cheesecake for dessert. Full bar. | 243 S. Main St. | 570/825–7989 | Closed Sun. | $10–$30 | AE, D, MC, V.

Olive's Mediterrean Cafe. Eclectic. Choose from specialties such as balsamic chicken or stuffed grape leaves at this eatery with an open kitchen and stainless steel tables. Live entertainment Thursday and Saturday nights. Try a lemon possit for dessert, which is a Lebanese pudding served with fresh fruit. Full bar. | 216 N. River St. | 570/826–1101 | Closed Sunday | $10–$22 | AE, D, DC, MC, V.

Saber Room. Continental. Antiques, marble counters, fresh flowers, and crystal highlight this downtown restaurant. You can view the landscaped garden from the large picture windows. Daily specials are fish, veal, and steak dishes. | 94 Butler St. | 570/829–5743 | Reservations essential | Closed Sun. No lunch Sat. | $16–$33 | AE, DC, MC, V.

Lodging

Best Western–East Mountain Inn. A large, brick seven-story hotel, some of the rooms here have views of the Pocono foothills and the Wyoming Valley. Restaurant, bar (with entertainment). In-room data ports, some refrigerators, cable TV, in-room VCRs (and movies). Indoor pool. Hot tub. Exercise equipment. Video games. Playground. Laundry facilities. Business services. Airport shuttle, free parking. | 2400 E. End Blvd.; Exit 47A, I-81 | 570/822–1011 | fax 570/822–6072 | www.bestwestern.com | 132 rooms, 24 suites | $79–$99, $109–$129 suites | AE, D, DC, MC, V.

Best Western Genetti. This brick, seven-story hotel is in the downtown area. The front entrance is landscaped. Restaurant, bar, room service. Cable TV. Pool. Laundry facilities. Business services, free Parking. Pets allowed (fee). | 77 E. Market St.; Exit 46, I-81 | 717/823–6152 or 800/ 833–6152 | fax 717/820–8502 | www.bestwestern.com | 72 rooms, 16 suites | $79–$89, $135 suites | AE, D, DC, MC, V.

Bischwind Bed and Breakfast. Seven miles from Wilkes-Barre in Bear Creek, this 1894 English Tudor home is in the Appalachian Mountains, and there's extensive land to explore. Rooms vary greatly, but most have Victorian antiques. Ask which bed Teddy Roosevelt slept in when he was there. Breakfast is elaborate, with filet mignon, shrimp scampi, and steamed salmon. Complimentary breakfast. No room phones. | 1 Coach Rd., Bears Creek | 570/472–3820 | fax 570/472–5347 | renglish@epix.net | www.bischwind.com | 9 rooms | $150–$239 | AE, D, MC, V.

Hampton Inn–Wilkes-Barre at Cross Creek Point. The Wyoming Monument is 6 mi west of this five-story hotel. Complimentary Continental breakfast, room service. In-room data ports, cable TV. Gym. Laundry facilities. Business services, free parking. | 1063 Rte. 315; Exit 47B, I-81. | 570/825–3838 | fax 570/825–8775 | www.hamptoninn.com | 120 rooms | $60–$90 | AE, D, DC, MC, V.

Holiday Inn. In the downtown area on the business route, all rooms open to the outdoors. The motel is connected to a restaurant. Restaurant, bar, room service. In-room data ports, cable TV. Pool, wading pool. Exercise equipment. Laundry services. Business services, free parking. Pets allowed. | 880 Kidder St.; Rte. 115 and Rte. 315 | 570/824–8901 or 888/466–9272 | fax 570/824–9310 | www.holiday-inn.com | 167 rooms, 14 suites | $75–$119, $129–$139 suites | AE, D, DC, MC, V.

Ponda-Rowland. This antiques-filled bed-and-breakfast is popular with families. Built in the 1850s, this working farm is 130 acres with six ponds. Some rooms have fireplaces. Picnic area, complimentary breakfast. Some refrigerators, no room phones, TV in common area. Cross country skiing. Playground. Business services. No smoking. | R.R. 1, Dallas | 570/639–3245 or 888/855–9966 | fax 570/639–5531 | www.pondarowland.com | 6 rooms | $80–$115 | AE, D, MC, V.

Travelodge. These basic accomodations are in a commercial area, 4 mi from I-84 and a 10-min drive to Wilkes-Barre. There's plenty of lawn for the kids to play out back. Complimentary Continental breakfast. | 497 Kiedder St. | 570/829–1279 | 40 | $45–$130 | AE, D, DC, MC, V.

Woodlands Inn and Resort. Stroll the 40-acre landscaped surroundings, or enjoy the 17,000 gallon jacuzzi, the largest on the East Coast. Restaurant, bars (with entertainment), room service. In-room data ports, cable TV. 2 pools (1 indoor). Beauty salon, hot tub, sauna, massage. Basketball, tennis. Gym. Video games. Business services, airport shuttle. | 1073 Rte. 315 | 570/824–9831 or 800/762–2222 | fax 570/824–8865 | www.thewoodlandsresort.com | 160 rooms, 13 suites, private cottages with kitchens | $78–$88; $119–$195 | AE, D, DC, MC, V.

WILLIAMSPORT

MAP 7, H4

(Nearby towns also listed: Lewisburg, Lock Haven)

Millionaire's Row highlights downtown Williamsport, which for three weeks each summer explodes with youth and optimism as it hosts the Little League World Series. The west branch of the Susquehanna River cuts through the community and has excellent fishing.

Information: **Williamsport–Lycoming County Chamber of Commerce** | 100 W. Third St., 17701 | 570/326–1971 | fax 570/321–1208 | www.williamsport.org.

Attractions

Hiawatha **Riverboat.** Take a paddlewheel boat trip down the Susquehanna River. The hour cruise has live entertainment and can be chartered for private occasions. | I-80 to Rte. 22 south to Williamsport Reach Rd. | 570/326–2500 or 800/248–9287 | www.citybus.org/hiawatha | $7 | May–Oct., Tues.–Sun. 11:30 AM, 1 PM, 2:30 PM, 4 PM.

Little League Baseball Museum. What started as a three-team league in 1939 now has over 3 million participants and a museum dedicated to its growth. Pictures, memorabilia, equipment, and historical material are on display on the first floor. Downstairs you can find an interactive batting cage, a pitching machine, and a base-running track. | Rte. 15 | 570/326–3607 | www.littleleague.org | $5 | Memorial Day–Labor Day, Mon.–Sat. 9–7, Sun. 12–7; Labor Day–Memorial Day, Mon.–Sat. 9–5, Sun. 12–5.

Little Pine State Park. At one time, the Iroquois and Algonquian peoples hunted in this 2,158-acre park in the Tiadaghton State Forest. This Appalachian Mountain region also has a 94-acre lake for boating and fishing. There are 104 campsites and 1,700 acres for hunting, hiking, cross-country skiing, and snowmobiling. | I-80 to Rte. 880 to Rte. 44 N | 570/753–6000 or 888/PA–PARKS | www.dcnr.state.pa.us | Free | Daily 8 AM–dusk.

Lycoming County Historical Museum. Founded in 1907, the museum artifacts tell you the story of the people who formed Lycoming County. Native American and early settler handicrafts are on display. You can see the development of the area through old photographs. | 858 W. 4th St.; I-80 to Rte. 15 north | www.lycoming.org/lchsmuseum | 570/326–3326 | $3.50 | Tues.–Fri. 9:30–4, Sat. 11–4, Sun. 1–4. Closed Sun. Nov.–Apr.

Shempp Toy Train Collection. More than 100 engines and 300 complete trains on two working levels are on display here.

Williamsport Crosscutters. This single A affiliate of the Pittsburgh Pirates began their relationship in 1999. The team plays home games at Bowman Field, built in 1926 and the second oldest minor league park in the country. | 1700 W. 4th St. | 570/326–3389 | fax 570/326–3494 | www.crosscutters.com | $5.50 | Apr.–Sept.

Worlds End State Park. The 780-acre park has 19 rustic cabins, 70 campsites, picnic facilities, and hiking trails. Other activities permitted in the park are swimming, whitewater boating on Loyalsock Creek, fishing, hunting, snowmobiling, and cross-country skiing. | Rte. 154, Forksville | 888/PA–PARKS (reservations and information) or 570/924–3287 | www.dcnr.state.pa.us | Free (day use) | Daily 8 AM–dusk.

ON THE CALENDAR

JUNE: *Victorian Sunday.* Take tours of period homes, attend a flower show, and enjoy the live entertainment at this annual event. | W. 4th St. | 570/322–4637.

JULY: *Lycoming County Fair.* Established in 1870, this country fair shows off livestock and farm exhibits, and has rides, food, and entertainment for the whole family. | Hughesville Fairgrounds, 1 East Park St.; Exit 31B, I-80 | www.lycomingfair.com | 570/784–0487.

AUG.: *Little League World Series.* Every year, in the third week of August, Little League teams come here from all over the country to compete in the big championship. Request championship tickets in writing in December. | 570/326–1921 | Free | AE, D, DC, MC, V.

Dining

Bullfrog Brewing. Contemporary. Wooden floors, a kettle at the door and four more behind the bar tell you it's a brew pub. Ferns and other plants create a casual, cozy feeling. Known for pasta and seafood dishes. Live music Wed., weekends. Sun. brunch. | 229 W. Fourth St.; I-80 to Rte. 15 N | 570/326–4700 | $7–$15 | AE, D, MC, V.

Franco's Lounge. Italian. This is an intimate restaurant and music lounge with live jazz and blues. Photographs of visiting artists hang on the walls. Specialty dishes are pasta and grilled seafood. Live music Thurs.–Sat. | 12 W. Fourth St.; I-80 to Rte. 15 N | 570/327–1840 | Reservations not accepted | Closed Mon. and Sun. | $8–$17 | AE, MC, V.

Huckleberry's. American. A quarter mile from the center of town, you can get breakfast all day here, from strawberry-stuffed french toast to omelets or waffles. The more savory dishes include a chicken pot pie in a bread bowl or a hot pot roast dinner. Norman Rockwell paintings hang on the walls. | 445 River Ave. | 570/327–5200 | $7–$11 | AE, D, DC, MC, V.

Olive Tree. Eclectic. From falafel and baba ganoush to gyros and other Greek and Mediterranean fare, this restaurant, decorated with replicas of Greek statues, has an enormous selection, and everything is homemade. Dinner is candlelit, and you bring your own alcohol. | 169 W. 3rd St. | 570/326–4493 | $9–$20 | AE, D, MC, V.

Lodging

Econo Lodge - Williamsport. This two-story motel is 2 mi east of Lycoming College. All rooms have outside entrances. The motel is attached to a steakhouse. Restaurant, bar (with entertainment), complimentary Continental breakfast. Cable TV, in-room VCRs (and movies). Exercise equipment. Business services, free parking. Pets allowed. | 2401 E. 3rd St.; Rte. 220 | 570/326–1501 | fax 570/326–9776 | 99 rooms | $50–$60 | AE, D, DC, MC, V.

Genetti Hotel. This historical 10-story hotel in downtown was built in 1922. There are whirlpool baths in some rooms, and some rooms are poolside. Restaurant, bar (with entertainment). Some refrigerators, cable TV. Pool. Beauty salon. Exercise equipment. Laundry facilities. Business services, airport shuttle, free parking. Pets allowed. | 200 W. 4th St.; Rte. 15 to Business District exit | 570/326–6600 or 800/321–1388 | fax 570/326–5006 | www.genetti.com | 206 rooms, 42 suites | $50–$115, $86–$125 suites | AE, DC, MC, V.

Governor Shulze House. Built in 1832 by Pennsylvania's Governor Shulze, this three-story Federal Victorian 6 mi from downtown sits back from the busy road to assure you a quiet stay. Rooms are furnished with antiques, and there's a breakfast menu. Relax out on the big porch. Full breakfast. | 748 Broad St., Mountersville | 570/368–8966 | fax 570/368–8681 | govshulz@csrlink.net | www.pvisnet.com/governorshulze | 5 rooms | $55–$100 | AE, D, DC, MC, V.

Holiday Inn. The hotel is 5 mi from downtown. There are two stories and rooms have outside entrances. Suites have Jacuzzi baths. Restaurant, bar, room service. In-room data ports, cable TV. Pool. Laundry facilities. Business services, free parking. Pets allowed. | 1840 E. 3rd St./U.S. 220 | 570/326–1981 or 800/369–4572 | fax 570/323–9590 | www.holiday-inn.com | 157 rooms, 2 suites | $65–$80, $130–$139 suites | AE, D, DC, MC, V.

King's Inn Motel. One mile from Williamsport and I-80, in a very commercial district, this hotel offers more than a typical chain hotel. Choose from a moderate-size room or a VIP offering. Restaurant, bar, complimentary Continental breakfast, room service. In-room data ports. | 590 Montgomery Pike/Rte. 15 | 570/322–4707 | fax 570/322–0946 | 48 rooms | $34–$129 | AE, D, DC, MC, V.

Quality Inn. The Little League Museum is across the street from this hotel. Restaurant, bar (with entertainment), room service. Cable TV. Pool. Video games. Laundry facilities. Business services, airport shuttle, free parking. | 234 Montgomery Pike/U.S. 15 | 570/323–9801 | fax 570/322–5231 | www.qualityinn.com | 115 rooms | $65–$75 | AE, D, DC, MC, V.

Radisson Hotel Williamsport. The hotel is in the downtown center. It's a five-story building with a driveway and free parking. Restaurant, bar (with entertainmnent), room service. Some refrigerators, some in-room hot tubs, cable TV. Indoor pool. Business services, airport shuttle. Pets allowed. | 100 Pine St.; I–80/Rte. 15 | 570/327–8231 | fax 570/322–2957 | www.radisson.com | 145 rooms, 2 suites | $79–$119, $159 suites | AE, D, DC, MC, V.

Shady Lane Bed and Breakfast. Established in 1947, this cozy ranch-style building is on a mountain top with views of the Endless Mountains. Picnic area, complimentary breakfast. No room phones. TV in common area. No kids under 12. No smoking. | Allegheny Ave., Eagles Mere; Rte. 42 | 570/525–3394 or 800/524–1248 | www.shadylanebnb.com | 7 rooms | $94–$125 | No credit cards.

Super 8. Only half a mile from Williamsport, this is a typical chain motel. Rooms have doubles or a king, and you'll need a car to get anywhere because it's on a busy street. Complimentary Continental breakfast. | 2815 Old Mountoursville Rd. | 570/368–8111 | fax 570/368–8555 | www.super8.com | 43 rooms | $48–$58 | AE, D, DC, MC, V.

WILLOW GROVE

MAP 7, L6

(Nearby town also listed: Philadelphia)

A suburb of Philadelphia, Willow Grove is known for its historic downtown and for the many famous musicians, including bandleaders John Philip Sousa and Walter Damrosch, who have conducted concerts here in the summertime.

Information: Willow Grove Chamber of Commerce, | 117 Park Ave., 19090 | 215/657-2227 | fax 215/657-8564 | www.wgchamber.com.

Attractions

Bryn Athyn Cathedral. This hand-crafted cathedral was built over a period of several decades beginning in 1913. Its construction relied on the builder's vision rather than on a predetermined plan. | 1001 Cathedral Rd.; Rte. 232 | 215/947–0266 | Free | Tues.–Sun. 1–4, closed Mon.

Glencairn Museum. Exhibits include medieval objects in the Great Hall, Egyptian artwork, and artifacts from the Far East. Native American, Greek, and Roman religious items are also on display. | 1001 Cathedral Rd.; Rte. 232 | 215/938–2600 | $5 | Weekdays 9–5 by appointment, closed weekends.

Graeme Park. Built in 1722 by Sir William Keith, Provincial Governor of Pennsylvania, this house is the only surviving residence of a Colonial Pennsylvania governor. The house reflects its Scottish heritage. It has original floor boards and paneling, and is almost unchanged since its construction. | 859 County Line Rd., Horsham; I-276 to Rte. 611 | 215/343–0965 | www.state.pa.us | $3.50 | Wed.–Sat. 10–4, Sun. 12–4, closed Mon.–Tues.

Tyler State Park. The 1,711-acre park has areas for picnicking, hiking, bicycling, horseback riding, fishing, and boating. There are play areas and fields for softball, volleyball, badminton, horseshoes, and a golf course. | 101 Swamp Rd., Newtown; Rte. 232 east from Willow Grove | 215/968–2021 or 888/PA–PARKS | www.dcnr.state.pa.us | Free | Daily 8 AM–dusk.

ON THE CALENDAR

JUNE: *Willow Grove Air Show*. Watch daredevil aerial feats, listen to the U.S. Navy steel band, and see the Naval displays presented here. | Willow Grove Naval Air Station; off of Rte. 232 | 215/443–1776.

Dining

Joseph Ambler Inn. Continental. The restaurant is housed in a renovated barn and the field-house next door is for overnight guests. The buildings are on 12 acres of land with manicured lawns, and you can eat outdoors on the brick terrace and enjoy the adjacent garden. | 1005 Horsham Rd. | 215/362–7500 | www.josephamblerinn.com | No lunch | $20–$30 | AE, D, DC, MC, V.

Macaroni Grill. Italian. This eatery focuses on northern Italy, including dishes such as penne rustica, which has shrimp, grilled chicken, and prosciutto in a creamy cheese sauce with parmesan. If that sounds a little heavy, try a salad with some homemade tiramisu for dessert. Full bar and kids' menu. | 10 Park Ave. | 215/830–8844 | $8–$17 | AE, D, DC, MC, V.

Otto's Brauhaus. German. Dark wood paneling and family-style tables adorn this beerhouse. Menu specialties are sausage samplers, sauerbraten, and deviled crab. You can eat outside on a covered patio overlooking a garden and pond. Kids' menu. | 233 Easton Rd., Horsham; Rte. 611 N | 215/675–1864 | $16–$22 | AE, D, DC, MC, V.

Lodging

Courtyard by Marriott. This upscale hotel is at Exit 27 of the Pennsylvania Turnpike. Restaurant, bar. In-room data ports, cable TV. Indoor pool. Hot tub. Exercise equipment. Laundry facilities. Business services, airport shuttle. | 2350 Easton Rd.; I-276 to Rte. 611 N | 215/830–0550 | fax 215/830–0572 | www.marriott.com | 137 rooms, 12 suites | $99–$119, $169–$179 suites | AE, D, DC, MC, V.

Days Inn. One mile from Willow Grove, rooms here are spacious, with a king-size bed or two doubles. Some rooms overlook a wooded area in back. Suites have hot tubs. Complimentary breakfast. In-room data ports. Exercise equipment. Laundry service, laundry facility. Business service, airport shuttle. Pets allowed. | 245 Easton Rd. | 215/674–2500 | fax 215/674–0879 | www.thedaysinn.com/horsham06707 | 168 rooms, 3 suites | $109–$129 | AE, D, DC, MC, V.

Hampton Inn. This chain hotel is at Exit 27 of the PA Turnpike. Complimentary Continental breakfast. In-room data ports, some refrigerators, some microwaves, cable TV. Exercise equipment. Business services. Airport shuttle, free parking. | 1500 Easton Rd.; Rte. 611 N | 215/659–3535 | fax 215/659–4040 | www.hamptoninn.com | 150 rooms | $70–$85 | AE, D, DC, MC, V.

Homestead Village. Half a mile from I-611, this three-story hotel offers accomodation mostly for corporations and business people. Within walking distance of restaurants and half a mile from downtown, it can arrange guest passes to a nearby gym. In-room data ports. 1 shop. Laundry facilities. Pets allowed. | 537 Drescher Rd. | 215/956–9966 | fax 215/956–9002 | www.stayhsd.com | 116 rooms, 21 suites | $89–$109 | AE, D, DC, MC, V.

Joseph Ambler Inn. A small inn with three historic buildings, there are 12 acres of lush grounds on the property. One of the buildings dates back to 1734. Five of the guest rooms are in a separate cottage, and a stone-bank barn is the restaurant. Restaurant, complimentary break-fast. In-room data ports, cable TV. Business services. | 1005 Horsham Rd., Montgomeryville | 215/362–7500 | fax 215/361–5924 | www.josephamblerinn.com | 31 rooms, 6 suites | $100–$150, $200–$250 suites | AE, D, DC, MC, V.

WRIGHTSVILLE

MAP 7, I7

(Nearby towns also listed: Columbia, Hanover, Harrisburg, Lancaster, Middletown, York)

Wrightsville, 10 mi from York, has a history as rich as its famous neighbor. Across the river from Columbia, Wrightsville is an old industrial town where silk mills and iron foundries once prospered. Today the town cherishes its history. The narrow streets are lined with rows of carefully restored historic homes, representing a range of Federal, Colonial, and Georgian architecture.

Information: York County Convention and Visitors Bureau | 1 Market Way E, York, PA 17401 | 717/848–4000 | www.yorkpa.org.

Attractions
Samuel S. Lewis State Park. The park is 85 acres on top of an 885-ft ridge separating Kreutz Creek Valley and East Prospect Valley. It's the highest point in the area, offering a spectacular panoramic view of the Susquehanna River. You can picnic, hike the trails, fly a kite, play ball in the ballfield, and play in the playground. | Mt. Pisgah Rd.; Rte. 30 to Cool Creek Rd. to Mt. Pisgah Rd. | 717/432–5011 or 888/PA–PARKS | fax 717/432–0367 | www.dcnr.state.pa.us | Free | Daily 8 AM–dusk.

ON THE CALENDAR
OCT.: *Bridge Bust.* The first Saturday every October brings more than 300 regional ven-dors of crafts, arts, and food to this festival that takes place on the bridge between Columbia and Wrightsville. | 717/684–5249.

Dining
Accomac Inn. French. Dine in this reconstructed stone building that has a wraparound enclosed porch. Its interior has exposed brick walls and high-back cherry wood chairs. Sun. brunch. | 6330 S. River Dr. | 717/252–1521 | Reservations essential | $18–$32 | AE, MC, V.

Riverside Restaurant. American. Serving only breakfast and lunch, this eatery is in an old warehouse alongside the Susquehanna River, which you can see from the porch in sum-mer. Try the cream of crab soup or the exceptional chicken salad. A general store is attached to the restaurant. | John Wright Warehouse, Front St. | 717/252–2519 | Closed Sun. | $5–$7 | AE, D, MC, V.

Lodging

Sleep Inn. Six miles from Wrightsville, right off of Route 30 in Mountville, this suburban inn has mini golf on the premise in summer and draws business travelers as well as families. Restaurant, complimentary Continental breakfast. In-room data ports. Indoor pool. Hot tub. Exercise room. | 310 Primrose Lane, Mountville | 717/285–0444 | fax 717/285–0800 | $79–$129 | AE, D, DC, MC, V.

YORK

(Nearby towns also listed: Columbia, Hanover, Harrisburg, Lancaster, Middletown, Wrightsville)

York is the site of the first military force to resist the advancement of British Troops during the American Revolution. The town was also held for $100,000 ransom by Confederate troops on their way to Gettysburg. Much of its historic buildings and sites remain untouched.

Information: York County Chamber of Commerce | 1 Market Way E, 17401 | 717/848–4000 or 888/858–YORK | fax 717/843–6737 | www.york-chamber.com.

Attractions

Industrial and Agricultural Museum. In a former industrial building, the architecture here lends itself to the chronological, intertwining exhibits of York's argicultural and industrial history. Starting with the agrarian society of Colonial times, it covers developments all the way to World War II, when York's industries became a model for converting their production to wartime supplies. A three-story grist mill towers over you as you guide yourself through. | 217 W. Princess St. | 717/848–1587 | www.yorkheritage.org | $5 | Tues.–Sat. 10–4, Sun. 12–4.

Gates House and the Golden Plough Tavern. These museum houses represent a home and a tavern during Colonial times. The Gates house is set up as the home it once was when it was General Horatio's home. Although you won't find any beer on tap, the guided tour through the tavern shows a mix of architectural styles: The first floor is a log structure and the Medieval German-style second floor is made with bricks and timber. | 157 W. Market St. | 717/848–1587 | $5 | Tues.–Sat. 10-4, Sun. 12–4.

Weightlifting Hall of Fame. Here at the York Barbell Company headquarters, you can visit a small museum dedicated to Olympic lifting, powerlifting, and body building. An Olympic section highlights American lifters. Learn the history of strongmen to body builders. | 3300 Broad St. | 717/767–6481 or 800/358–9675 | fax 717/764–0044 | www.yorkbarbell.com | Free | Mon.–Sat. 10–4.

Bonham House. Part of the York County Heritage Trust's historic sites, this Federal house was first built in 1840, with additional rooms and another floor added throughout the 1800s. The house has all its original furnishings and fixtures. | 152 E. Market St. | 717/848–1587 | $5 | Sat. 10–4.

Central Market House. See and buy the tantalizing foods and crafts at this bazaar, the largest farmer's market in York. The Romanesque Revival structure has towering spires and has been in constant use since 1888. | 34 W. Philadelphia St.; W. Philadelphia and Beaver Sts. | 717/848–2243 | Free | Tues., Thurs., and Sat. 7 AM–dusk; closed Wed., Fri., and Sun.–Mon.

Fire Museum of York County. Two hundred years of firefighting are preserved in this building. All 72 fire companies of York County are represented, with some fire companies dating back prior to the American Revolution. You can see exhibits that detail the progress of firefighting from bucket brigades to modern equipment. | 757 W. Market St. | 717/843–0464 | Free | Apr.–Nov., Sat. 12–4, closed Sun.–Fri.

General Gates House. General Horatio Gates owned this 1751 English house, said to be the site of General LaFayette's famous toast to General George Washington. The toast was a signal to conspirators that the French would not support a plot to replace Washington with Gates. | 157 W. Market St. | 717/848–1587 | $4.50 | Weekdays 10–4, Sun. 12–4.

Gifford Pinchot State Park. A 2,338-acre park that has farm fields, wooded hillsides, and a 340-acre lake, there are 340 campsites, 10 cabins, swimming at Quaker Race Beach, boating, picnicking, fishing, and more than 1,700 acres of hunting. Trails include 4 mi for horseback riding and 18 mi for hiking. | 2200 Rosstown Rd., Lewisberry; Rte. 382 to Rte. 177 N | 717/432–5011 | fax 717/432–0367 | Free | Daily 8 AM–dusk.

Harley-Davidson Inc. You can see motorcycles assembled from start to finish here at Harley-Davidson's final assembly plant. The 90-min tour ends in the company's museum, which features a variety of models, some very rare, and all in perfect running condition. | 1425 Eden Rd. | 717/848–1177 | Free | Weekdays 9:30–1:30, closed weekends.

York County Heritage of Trust. This organization operates many of the historic sites. At the museum you can see a street of shops with prints, an apothecary, and toy stores. It also has an exhibit on the history of transportation. | 250 E. Market St. | 717/848–1587 | Donation | Mon.–Sat. 9–5, Sun. 1–4.

Ski Roundtop. With an elevation of 1,400 ft, the resort has skiing, snowboarding, and snowtubing. Its longest run is 4,100 ft and the top vertical drop is 600 ft. In summer, concerts and paintball are popular. | 925 Roundtop Rd. | www.skiroundtop.com | PA Tpk, Exit 18 | 717/432–9631 | Dec.–Mar.

York County Colonial Courthouse. The courthouse is a replica of the building where America was born. You can hear and see a narrative that shows the Continental Congress debating the Articles of the Confederation, and the original Proclamation of the United States of America. | 157 W. Market St. | 717/848–1587 | $5 | Mon.–Sat. 10–4, Sun. 1–4.

ON THE CALENDAR

SEPT.: *York Fair.* One of the largest fairs in the state, the week-long event takes place on 120 acres. Some of the attractions are livestock displays, freak shows, international foods, and high-tech carnival games. | York Fairgrounds, 330 Carlisle Rd. | 717/848–2596.

Dining

The Altland House. American. Built in 1790, you can eat surrounded by period antiques and furnishings. Guest rooms are also available. Specials of the house are rack of veal and blackened dishes. Kids' menu. Sun. brunch. | U.S. 30 (Center Sq.), Abbottstown | 717/259–9535 | fax 717/259–9956 | $7–$25 | AE, D, MC, V.

Autographs. Contemporary. Autographs of famous people deck the walls of this casual restaurant in the Yorktowne Hotel. Try the pasta, chicken, or steak dishes. There's also a salad bar, and breakfast for early risers. Kids' menu. Sun. brunch. Free parking. | 48 E. Market St. | 717/848–1111 | $14–$22 | AE, DC, MC, V.

Commonwealth Room. Contemporary. The more formal of the Yorktowne Hotel's two restaurants, its brick exterior is trimmed with terra cotta. Try medallion of Capon Bigarade and grilled trout. Free parking. | 48 E. Market St. | 717/848–1111 | Reservations essential | Jacket required | Closed Sun. No lunch | $16–$38 | AE, DC, MC, V.

North Central Railway. Contemporary. Dubbed the Liberty Limited, this is a dinner train that runs between York and New Freedom. You are entertained by a variety of shows, including murder mysteries, musicals, and comedies. Dinner specials are chicken and beef dishes. Open only on weekends. | 117 N. Front St., New Freedom | 717/235–4000 | Reservations essential | Operates on Sat. at 6 PM and Sun. at 1 PM | $40–$55 | AE, D, DC, MC, V.

Lodging

Artist's Garden Bed and Breakfast. This 1850s Victorian home, 2 mi from Route 83, has a spacious back yard with a perennial garden, overlooked by the private balconies on some rooms. Victorian furnishings, like a German carved bed, and many whimsical touches make for a lovely oasis. Ask for the large suite in April when the magnolia tree is in bloom outside your window and balcony. Complimentary breakfast. TV in common area. Library. | 440 W. Philadelphia | 717/854–7688 | Susanpeck@aol.com | 2 rooms | $75 | No credit cards.

Best Western. This hotel is a brick, three-story building with a driveway and large parking lot at the main canopied entrance. Complimentary Continental breakfast. In-room data ports, some refrigerators, cable TV. Airport shuttle, free parking. | 1415 Kenneth Rd. | 717/767–6931 | fax 717/767–6938 | www.bestwestern.com | 105 rooms | $66–$70 | AE, D, DC, MC, V.

Budget Host–Spirit of 76. Relax at the gazebo and pond on the grounds of this two-story, stucco motel. Some refrigerators, cable TV. | 1162 Haines Rd.; I-83 to exit 7 | 717/755–1068 | fax 717/757–5571 | www.budgethost.com | 40 rooms | $40–$55 | AE, D, DC, MC, V.

Comfort Inn Corporate Getaway. Two miles from the center of town, this inn caters especially to business travelers. Rooms have either a king or two queen-sized beds and range from luxurious to modest. Complimentary Continental breakfast. In room data ports, kitchenettes, some in-room hot tubs. Health club. Laundry facilies. | 2250 N. George St. | 717/699–1919 | fax 717/846–7209 | 105 rooms, 24 suites | $87–$114 | AE, D, DC, MC, V.

Four Points Sheraton. Two miles from downtown, this hotel is in York's most commercialized area, surrounded by restaurants and shopping malls. Rooms are oversized, with dark cherry woodwork. Restaurant, bar, room service. In-room data ports. Indoor pool. Hot tub. Health club. Laundry facilities, laundry service. Business services. | 1650 Toronita St. | 717/846–4940 | fax 717/854–0307 | bysher4pts@aol.com | 107 rooms, 22 suites | $89–$129 | AE, D, DC, MC, V.

Hampton Inn. This hotel is adjacent to the popular Galleria Mall. Picnic area, complimentary Continental breakfast. In-room data ports, some refrigerators, cable TV. Pool. Exercise equipment. Laundry facilities. | 1550 Mt. Zion Rd.; I-83 to Rte. 30 E | 717/840–1500 | fax 717/840–1567 | www.hampton-inn.com | 134 rooms, 10 suites | $94–$99, $125 suites | AE, D, DC, MC, V.

Quality Inn. Walk to shops and restaurants from this two-story hotel with outside entrances. Restaurant, bar, room service. In-room data ports, some refrigerators, cable TV. Pool. Business services, free parking. | 2600 E. Market St. | 717/755–1966 | fax 717/755–6936 | www.qualityinn.com | 110 rooms, 8 suites | $60–$90, $100–$110 | AE, D, DC, MC, V.

Holiday Inn–Arsenal Road. A two-story building with outside entrances, this hotel is 3 mi from downtown. Restaurant, bar, room service. In-room data ports, cable TV. Pool. Laundry facilities. Business services, airport shuttle. Pets allowed. | 334 Arsenal Rd.; I-83 to Rte. 30 | 717/845–5671 | fax 717/845–1898 | www.holiday-inn.com | 100 rooms | $79–$109 | AE, D, DC, MC, V.

Holiday Inn–East. The West Manchester Mall and the Holidome, an inside recreation center, are part of this two-story hotel, 1 mi west of downtown. Restaurant, bar, room service. Cable TV. 2 pools (1 indoor). Hot tub. Miniature golf. Exercise equipment. Playground. Business services, free parking. Pets allowed. | 2000 Loucks Rd.; Rte. 30 to Rte. 74 W | 717/846–9500 | fax 717/764–5038 | www.holiday-inn.com | 180 rooms | $84–$102 | AE, D, DC, MC, V.

Yorktowne Hotel. Built in 1925, the hotel is listed on the National Register of Historic Places. The 11-story building in downtown has Renaissance-style architecture and rooms with period furnishings. Many of the guestrooms have sitting areas. Restaurants (see Commonwealth Room), bar. In-room data ports, some kitchenettes, some in-room hot tubs, cable TV. Barbershop. Exercise equipment. Business services, airport shuttle, free parking. | 48 E. Market St.; Duke and Market Sts. | 717/848–1111 or 800/233–9324 | fax 717/854–7678 | www.yorktowne.com | 118 rooms, 27 suites | $99, $115–$225 suites | AE, D, DC, MC, V.

Virginia

Many things were born in Virginia. Of the state's many nicknames, several have a decid-edly maternal slant. Virginia is proudly called "Mother of Presidents," "Mother of Statesmen," and "Mother of States." But the moniker bandied about most often is the "Old Dominion," a reference to Virginia's status as England's first colony in the Americas.

In 1607, Virginia was vast almost beyond measure, encompassing the lion's share of the present United States and western Canada. In the ensuing centuries the domain shrunk as portions of land were deeded away or reassigned by the Crown to needy proprietors. Some parcels were lost to would-be landholders who simply muscled their way in, ignoring any prior claims of ownership.

By the mid-1800s, Virginia had been whittled down to the size and shape that it is today—a ragged triangle of land, smallish (the 36th largest) but geographically diverse. What Virginia kept for herself is prodigious natural beauty: a generous stretch of Atlantic coastline, blessed with natural harbors, beaches, and the shellfish-rich Chesapeake Bay; a rolling expanse of fertile plains; and the serene, soft-shouldered splendor of the oldest mountain range in the world.

Virginians are loyal to the past and, by extension, possess an extraordinary sense of place. It's said that you will never meet a Virginian with an inferiority complex, so high is the estimation of the state's singular heritage and the Virginian's secure place in it. The history lessons here are as tangible as they come. Throughout the state are historical landmarks that seem to stand outside the exigencies of time. The Old Dominion began as a haven for patriots, became a producer of presidents, and was the major battleground during the nation's bitter disintegration. While it's not the same commonwealth that native sons George Washington and Thomas Jefferson knew, it retains many of the qualities that endeared it to them.

CAPITAL: RICHMOND	POPULATION: 6,677,200 (1996)	AREA: 40,598 SQUARE MI
TIME ZONE: EASTERN	POSTAL ABBREVIATION: VA	WEB SITE: WWW.VIRGINIA.ORG
BORDERS: NC, TN, KY, WV, MD, D.C., ATLANTIC OCEAN		

The state has five distinct regions. The Blue Ridge Mountains cut diagonally through the western part of Virginia, a continuation of the monumental Appalachian Mountains that run from Pennsylvania to southwestern North Carolina. A series of rivers course along its western flank to form a valley. The Highlands, in the extreme southwest corner of the state, are Virginia at its rugged best—incised with gorges and dominated by the state's highest peak, Mt. Rogers. As you move east, the churned-up topography unfurls into a gently rolling terrain, called the Piedmont, Italian for "foot of the mountains." The Tidewater is the flat, sandy coastal plain between the Atlantic Ocean and the "fall line," an imaginary line running north to south that denotes the point at which the tidal rivers of eastern Virginia (the Potomac, Rappahannock, York, and James) are no longer navigable. Almost a footnote, the Eastern Shore is a finger of land on the Delmarva Peninsula on the eastern side of the Chesapeake Bay, at a happy remove from the mainland.

These are not purely geographical divides—Virginia's population is as diverse as its landscape. As you travel from the remote reaches of Chincoteague Island in the Chesapeake Bay or one of the dozing hamlets in the Shenandoah Valley to the cosmopolitan streets of Alexandria, you will witness sometimes subtle changes in everything from food to idiom. You can partake in haute cuisine or home cooking and choose between the symphony or flatfooting (an American folk dance that originated in the southern Appalachian Mountains, it's best described as percussive mountain dancing) on a Friday night. You can stroll through the farmer's market in a blink-of-an-eye town, or peruse the galleries of some of the region's premier art museums. Whatever you do, you will find that most Virginians live up to their reputation for genteel manners, that give even the capital city, Richmond, the warmth of a small town.

Virginia's single largest historical attraction is Colonial Williamsburg, which draws a million visitors each year and impresses even the most jaded of travelers. Williamsburg was the capital of Virginia from 1699 to 1780, and the restored village convincingly re-creates the sights and sounds of a country on the eve of revolution. You can easily spend several days wandering about in this time warp, watching costumed craftspeople ply their trades—arduous by our standards—and become pleasantly lost in its many landscaped gardens. A stone's throw away are Jamestown and Yorktown, other representations of this essential early epoch of American history.

In Richmond, the old mingles with the new. Vestiges of the Civil War blend with the hustle of a modern city's daily commerce. You can spend an afternoon touring museums and monuments and top it off with an evening at the opera—one of the many venues that have made Richmond one of the South's preeminent cities for the arts.

On the coast is Virginia Beach, the state's most populous city, chief beach town, and year-round playground. Those seeking a more serene communion with nature head across the Chesapeake Bay Bridge-Tunnel to Virginia's "other coastline," the quiet, largely untrafficked Eastern Shore.

Scattered throughout the state are the abodes of eight Virginia-born presidents. Some, like Thomas Jefferson's Monticello, are high-minded architectural achieve-

VA Timeline

9500 BC	AD 900		
Early Native Americans migrate across the Beringia land bridge from Siberia to Alaska, some eventually settling in the region that would become Virginia.	Virginia's aboriginal population adopts the bow and arrow as its primary hunting weapon. Early Indians begin raising crops in semi-permanent villages and making elaborate pottery and	ornaments of bone and shell. Trade routes along forest paths and rivers are extended from the Atlantic coastal areas to the north-west and south-west. Algonquian-speaking tribes	settle primarily along coastal Virginia.

ments; others are comfortable retreats that reveal the individual's private side. You can also explore the places that nurtured the minds of a constellation of statesmen and leaders, among them Robert E. Lee, Booker T. Washington, and George Marshall.

Hikers, campers, anglers, and wildlife lovers simply head west into the wilderness, to the vast reaches of the George Washington and Jefferson National Forests—or to the Shenandoah National Park, the most visited park in the U.S. park system. The Appalachian Trail, that scenic-yet-rugged pathway running from Maine to Georgia, passes through the park. Many more people hit the Blue Ridge Parkway, a 469-mi road that rides the mountain crest south through Virginia's "mountain empire" of waterfalls, forests, upland meadows, trout streams and crystalline lakes. The views are equal parts stunning and chastening, panoramas unsullied, for the most part, by power lines or billboards.

INTRODUCTION
HISTORY
REGIONS
WHEN TO VISIT
STATE'S GREATS
RULES OF THE ROAD
DRIVING TOURS

History

Native Americans had lived on the lands of Virginia for many generations before the first European incursion. The original Paleo-Indians are believed to have arrived in the area some 10,000 years ago. Around the time that Christopher Columbus was exploring the islands of the Caribbean, Indians along coastal Virginia were living in permanent villages and farming the fertile lowlands from the James River north to the Potomac River.

England's first few attempts to colonize the New World failed miserably. In 1584, British explorer Sir Walter Raleigh founded the Roanoke Island colony on behalf of Queen Elizabeth I of England, but it perished from lack of food and materials. Later, the Virginia Company of London made several equally futile attempts before three tiny vessels, the *Susan Constant,* the *Godspeed,* and the *Discovery,* sailed into the Chesapeake Bay on May 14, 1607, and founded Jamestown. The English pioneers—a motley crew of gentlemen, servants, and ne'er-do-wells—named the settlement after King James I. In honor of their Virgin Queen, Elizabeth, they called the tractless wilderness, Virginia. Far from the semitropical paradise they'd envisioned, the New World was a marshy, malaria-ridden peninsula with a debilitatingly hot and muggy climate. More than half of the colonists died before the first summer was over, and the outpost struggled for several years, weakened by famine, dire mismanagement, and devastating Indian raids.

The colony's fortunes improved dramatically in 1614. The colonist John Rolfe began exporting tobacco to Britain, and this new money maker spurred Virginia's growth. Frustration with English rule hit an all-time high after the French and Indian War (1754–1763), and the Crown's imposition of heavy taxes to pay the huge war debt. The colonists' resistance led to war against Great Britain on April 19, 1775, and the British Army invaded Virginia in 1780, striking as far inland as Charlottesville and burning Richmond, the colony's capital city, to the ground. Britain surrendered a year later on October 19, 1781. The years following the Revolution saw Virginia's sons come to prominence as leaders of the new nation. A virtual dynasty of Virginians—Thomas Jefferson, James Monroe, James Madison, and John Marshall—achieved heroic stature.

1560s			1570	1584
Siouan-speaking tribes, such as the Saponi, Occaneechi, Monacan and Manahoac, settle in the Piedmont.	Powhatan, an Indian chief, consolidates about 30 Algonquian tribes—among them the Chickahominy, Mattaponi, Pamunkey and Rappahannock—to form a Powhatan chiefdom	known as Tsenacommaco. More than 13,000 members lived in the 6,000-square-mi chiefdom.	Spain builds a Jesuit mission on the York River. Tidewater Indian tribes destroy it a year later.	Sir Walter Raleigh founds Roanoke Colony and names the new territory Virginia after Queen Elizabeth I, the "Virgin Queen." The colony soon perishes.

During the first half of the 18th century, tensions increased over the slave trade, which had been abolished in Virginia in 1778 but was still vital to the state's agricultural economy. Virginia seceded from the Union in 1861 and Richmond became the capital of the Confederate States of America. When the Civil War ended in 1865, the state was a shambles. Its currency was worthless, its slaves were gone, and thousands of its young men were dead.

The turn of the 20th century brought great changes. Virginia adopted a new constitution, and its new governor, Harry F. Byrd, reorganized the government and instituted a "pay as you go" orthodoxy. The economy diversified beyond agriculture to include textiles and tobacco manufacturing. Railroad expansion opened up the coal fields of southwest Virginia, allowing coal to be shipped directly to the port of Norfolk. Communities, most notably Roanoke, flourished along the railway routes. The two world wars spurred the expansion of the Norfolk Naval Base and Newport News shipyards and proved a tremendous boom for Hampton Roads. Today, Norfolk is one of the largest naval installations in the world.

The Native American population, so much in evidence during the colonial era, has much dwindled. Some 15,000 descendants of the five Powhatan tribes and other Indian groups currently reside in Virginia. Their names, however, are all over the map of the Tidewater region. Most of the region's principal rivers—the Appomattox, Chickahominy, Pamunkey, Rappahannock, and Potomac—testify to their influence.

Regions

1. PIEDMONT

The Piedmont region is the central plateau area of Virginia, encompassing the state's verdant midsection. The Blue Ridge Mountains are its western border, and it is bounded by the Tidewater region to the east. It extends the full length of the state, bordered on the south by North Carolina and on the north by Maryland. This region was originally settled by the colony's leading families, who acquired the best acreage and immense tobacco estates. This region also saw some of the darkest days of the Civil War; the cities of Richmond and Petersburg both were devastated. Reminders of the war dot the region, including historic battlefield parks and the preserved village of Appomattox, where the terms of surrender were signed.

The Piedmont bears the brilliant stamp of its most famous denizen, Thomas Jefferson, who likened the lush countryside to Eden. His architectural achievements can be seen throughout the region, particularly in Charlottesville. The change from urban to rural is swift in Virginia, and the Piedmont offers a satisfying taste of both. The James River, which cuts a wide swath through the region, is a magnet for outdoor activities during sweltering summers, from steamboat rides to white-water rafting, tubing, and canoeing.

1606	1607	1614	1619	1622
King James I authorizes the formation of the Virginia Company of London to settle colonists in North America.	Jamestown is established.	Colonist John Rolfe ships Virginia's first marketable tobacco to England; he also weds Pocahontas, the daughter of Indian chieftain Powhatan.	The House of Burgesses, the first representative legislative body in the New World, meets in Jamestown. The first black servants arrive from Africa.	The English-Powhatan War marks a decade of sustained warfare between English settlers and Native Americans in Virginia.

Towns listed: Alexandria, Appomattox Court House National Historical Park, Arlington, Ashland, Booker T. Washington National Monument, Brookneal, Charlottesville, Clarksville, Culpeper, Danville, Dulles International Airport Area, Emporia, Fairfax, Falls Church, Farmville, Fredericksburg, Fredericksburg and Spotsylvania National Military Park, Great Falls, Keysville, Leesburg, Lynchburg, Manassas, Manassas National Battlefield Park, Martinsville, McLean, Middleburg, Mount Vernon, Orange, Pentagon City, Petersburg, Petersburg National Battlefield, Purcellville, Radford, Reston, Richmond, Richmond National Battlefield Park, Schuyler, South Boston, South Hill, Springfield, Triangle, Tysons Corner, Warrenton, Washington, White Post, Waterford

INTRODUCTION
HISTORY
REGIONS
WHEN TO VISIT
STATE'S GREATS
RULES OF THE ROAD
DRIVING TOURS

2. NORTHERN VIRGINIA

Northern Virginia refers to a cluster of counties at the northern tip of Virginia within a rough 60-mi radius of Washington, D.C. extending as far south as Fredericksburg. These suburban counties are the most affluent, cosmopolitan part of the state—and also the most congested. Gridlock aside, northern Virginia enjoys a level of diversity lacking in other parts of the state. This area combines premier shopping and dining with a number of historical touchstones. Alexandria, chock-full of boutiques and bistros, retains an essential window into the past, with nearly 100 blocks of restored 18th- and 19th-century buildings lining its cobblestone streets. The homes of early American patriots still stand throughout the region. Steeplechase races and other equestrian sports carry on the traditions of northern Virginia's historic "Hunt Country" towns, Leesburg and Middleburg.

Towns listed: Alexandria, Arlington, Dulles International Airport Area, Fairfax, Falls Church, Fredericksburg, Fredericksburg and Spotsylvania National Military Park, Great Falls, Leesburg, Manassas, Manassas National Battlefield Park, McLean, Middleburg, Mount Vernon, Purcellville, Reston, Springfield, Triangle, Tysons Corner, Warrenton, Waterford

3. THE VALLEY

The Valley extends 150 mi, north to south, in the far western portion of Virginia. Two mountain ranges serve as its borders—the Blue Ridge on the east and the Alleghenies on the west. The northernmost part, the Shenandoah Valley, is named after the river there. The central portion, from Rockbridge County to Roanoke County, is called the Roanoke Valley. The southern end is the New River Valley, after the New River, which drains it. Native Americans referred to the Blue Ridge Mountains as "the long divide," but early European settlers called it "blue" for the soft haze hanging over it (caused by the transpiration of water from the forest below).

During the 1700s, English, German, Scotch, and Irish settlers moved into this frontier area, following the Great Wagon Road south from Pennsylvania. They formed a self-sufficient backcountry of small farms that grew wheat and other grains as their principal crops, with little dependence on the slave labor so vital to the plantation

1646	1705	1716	1754–63	1766
The Powhatan chiefdom ceases to exist. Its people live with small, independent districts or tribes, and by 1677, they live primarily on reservation lands.	The House of Burgesses produces a slave code, forcing slavery on black Virginians.	Gov. Alexander Spotswood and his Knights of the Golden Horseshoe explore the territory west of the Blue Ridge, paving the way for settlement.	The French and Indian War between Great Britain and France rages in the New World.	British Parliament repeals the Stamp Act after resistance by American colonists.

economies further east. Two of America's most scenic roadways cut through the valley. The Skyline Drive, which begins in Front Royal and ends near Waynesboro, runs the 105-mi length of Shenandoah National Park. The Blue Ridge Parkway picks up for another 364 mi, meandering through the George Washington and Jefferson National Forests. Hiking, fishing, camping, and boating make the valley a recreational mecca today.

Towns listed: Basye, Blacksburg, Blue Ridge Parkway, Clifton Forge, Covington, Front Royal, Galax, Harrisonburg, Hot Springs, Independence, Lexington, Luray, Marion, Monterey, Natural Bridge, New Market, Pearisburg, Roanoke, Salem, Skyline Drive, Staunton, Strasburg, Warm Springs, Waynesboro, Winchester, White Post, Woodstock, Wytheville

4. HIGHLANDS

The Highlands, also called the Appalachian Plateau, occupy the extreme southwest corner of Virginia, bordered by Kentucky, Tennessee, and West Virginia. These lands were the western frontier of the United States until Daniel Boone cut the Wilderness Trail through here in the mid-1700s. The state's highest peak, Mt. Rogers, rises 5,729 ft above sea level. Abingdon, the oldest town west of the Blue Ridge Mountains, is home to the longest-running professional repertory theater in the country, started during the Great Depression. Tourism is not promoted as heavily here as elsewhere in Virginia (due partly to its remoteness), but it has some of the state's most scenic, unspoiled landscape, earning it the nickname "Virginia's Switzerland." The Jefferson National Forest blankets large sections of several counties. Bristol, which straddles Virginia and Tennessee, is known as the birthplace of country music because Jimmie Rogers and the Carter Family—the nation's original country music stars—made their first recordings here.

Towns listed: Abingdon, Big Stone Gap, Breaks Interstate Park, Bristol, Wise

5. TIDEWATER

Tidewater is Virginia's coastal plain, extending east of the fall line to the Atlantic Ocean and from the Potomac River south to North Carolina. The region's four tidal rivers— the Potomac, Rappahannock, York, and James—form three peninsulas that jut into the Atlantic Ocean, respectively named the Northern Neck, the Middle Peninsula, and simply the Peninsula. The cities in this region are defined by their proximity to the Chesapeake Bay and the rivers that empty into it; both leisure and livelihoods revolve around the water.

The enormous harbor of Hampton Roads, where the James, Elizabeth, and Nansemond rivers flow together into the Chesapeake Bay, played a crucial role in the discovery and settlement of the nation. Tidewater was the first area settled by English-speaking people, and the ghostly ruins of their first lasting colony, Jamestown, can still be glimpsed.

1774
Gov. John Murray Dunmore abolishes the House of Burgesses to prevent anti-government demonstrations. The First Continental Congress meets in Philadelphia to discuss ridding the colonies of British rule.

1775
War breaks out between Great Britain and its American colonies.

1776
Congress adopts the Declaration of Independence, drafted by Thomas Jefferson. The Virginia Declaration of Rights and Virginia's first constitution, drafted by George Mason, also receive Congressional approval. Virginia forces led by Gen. Andrew Lewis bombard a British flotilla at Gwynn's Island, off the coast. Governor Dunmore (the last royal governor of Virginia) ups

INTRODUCTION
HISTORY
REGIONS
WHEN TO VISIT
STATE'S GREATS
RULES OF THE ROAD
DRIVING TOURS

Towns listed: Cape Charles, Cape Henry Memorial, Charles City, Chesapeake, Chincoteague, Colonial National Historical Park, Colonial Parkway, George Washington Birthplace National Monument, Gloucester, Great Dismal Swamp National Wildlife Refuge, Hampton, Hopewell, Irvington, Jamestown, Keysville, Lancaster, Montross, Newport News, Norfolk, Onancock, Portsmouth, Reedville, Smithfield, Suffolk, Surry, Tangier Island, Tappahannock, Virginia Beach, West Point, Williamsburg, Yorktown

6. NORTHERN NECK

This is the peninsula between the Potomac and Rappahannock rivers, a region that comprises Lancaster, Northumberland, Richmond, and Westmoreland counties. An isolated area until the mid-1800s, the Northern Neck is today characterized by small Victorian villages and plantation homes. Farming and fishing sustain the local economy.

Towns listed: George Washington Birthplace National Monument, Irvington, Lancaster, Montross, Reedville

7. EASTERN SHORE

The Eastern Shore consists of the Delmarva Peninsula and several barrier islands. The 70-mi-long peninsula is connected to the rest of Virginia via the 17½-mi Chesapeake Bay Bridge-Tunnel. Fishing villages and old railroad towns, such as Cape Charles, dominate this area, known for its unsullied beaches and quietude. The national wildlife refuge on Chincoteague and Assateague Islands is a haven for many migratory bird species, including ibises, great blue herons, peregrine falcons, and bald eagles.

Tangier Island, 3½ mi long and 1½ mi wide, is a remote fishing village with no industry and relatively little contact with the mainland.

Towns listed: Cape Charles, Chincoteague, Onancock, Tangier Island

8. HAMPTON ROADS

Hampton Roads extends southeast of Williamsburg to the Chesapeake Bay, and encompasses the cities of Newport News and Hampton. The southern rim of Hampton Roads includes Norfolk, Suffolk, Portsmouth, Virginia Beach, and Chesapeake. This region has a strong military presence—Norfolk, a major shipping port, is the headquarters of the U.S. Navy Atlantic Fleet. Virginia Beach, a resort city, is noted for its 28-mi ribbon of beach.

Towns listed: Cape Henry Memorial, Chesapeake, Hampton, Newport News, Norfolk, Portsmouth, Suffolk, Virginia Beach

When to Visit

Virginia enjoys a temperate climate year-round. Warm weather prevails from late March until early October, and sometimes even longer. Along the coast, where daytime

	1781	1788	1859	1861
anchor and flees Virginia forever.	British general Charles Cornwallis surrenders to American and French forces at Yorktown, ending the Revolutionary War.	Virginia becomes a state. (It is the 10th of the original 13 states to ratify the Constitution.)	John Brown raids Harpers Ferry in a failed attempt to arm local blacks and begin a war to free the slaves.	Virginia secedes from the Union. July 21, First Battle of Manassas (Bull Run). Union forces are defeated by Confederates in the first major battle of the war. Gen. Thomas Jackson

summer temperatures average In the 80s, the days belong to boating, surf fishing, swimming, and other water sports. Large outdoor festivals are a staple in Virginia Beach and Norfolk from Memorial Day through Labor Day. Winters in the Tidewater region are mild, with rain more likely than snow. Colonial Williamsburg's busiest tourist season is December; daytime temperatures in the 50s are perfect for a walking tour of the historic area, and evening bonfires and outdoor holiday events draw hordes of people.

In the mountainous western part of the state, temperatures are cooler by 10° to 15° year-round. Fall is a luminous season along the Shenandoah Valley and the best time to visit this region of Virginia. Indian summer often lingers, and the days are warm and clear-skied. The evenings are crisp, requiring light woolens. It's ideal weather for camping and hiking; however, be forewarned: in October, Skyline Drive and the Blue Ridge Parkway are packed with motorists out to see the fiery foliage. December to March, occasional heavy snowfall is a boon for western Virginia's four ski resorts. But if you're not headed for the slopes, it's best to delay your sight-seeing until the spring. The winter weather in this region often makes for dangerous road conditions, and parts of the Blue Ridge Parkway usually close.

Spring welcomes blossoming dogwoods and azaleas and colorful flowering bulbs. The Shenandoah Apple Blossom Festival, a major event in the Shenandoah Valley, ushers in the new season every April, while northern Virginia's "Hunt Country" begins its season of equestrian events with point-to-point races.

CLIMATE CHART
Average High/Low Temperatures (°F) and Monthly Precipitation (in inches)

	JAN.	FEB.	MAR.	APR.	MAY	JUNE
FREDERICKSBURG	47/31	50/32	58/39	67/47	75/57	83/65
	4	3.5	4	3	4	4
	JULY	AUG.	SEPT.	OCT.	NOV.	DEC.
	86/70	85/69	80/64	70/53	61/44	52/35
	5	5	4	3	3	3
	JAN.	FEB.	MAR.	APR.	MAY	JUNE
NORFOLK	46/25	49/28	60/36	78/54	85/63	87/66
	3	3	3.5	4	3.5	4.5
	JULY	AUG.	SEPT.	OCT.	NOV.	DEC.
	71/47	61/38	50/30	44/25	58/36	52/35
	3.5	3	3	2.5	3.5	3
	JAN.	FEB.	MAR.	APR.	MAY	JUNE
RICHMOND	46/26	49/28	60/36	70/45	78/54	85/63
	4	3	5	4	3	4

1862

receives his nickname "Stonewall" in this battle, which results in more than 4,600 casualties.

August 29–30, Second Battle of Manassas (Bull Run). The Union army suffers a decisive defeat. Total casualties exceed 25,000, and the stage is set for Confederate general Robert E.

Lee's invasion of Maryland.

1863

Virginia's western counties, which oppose secession, break away to form a new state, West Virginia. April, Battle at Chancellorsville. Gen. Robert E. Lee leads 60,000 troops to victory

over the much larger Union force of 134,000.

INTRODUCTION
HISTORY
REGIONS
WHEN TO VISIT
STATE'S GREATS
RULES OF THE ROAD
DRIVING TOURS

	JULY	AUG.	SEPT.	OCT.	NOV.	DEC.
	88/68	87/66	81/59	71/47	50/30	50/30
	3	3	3	3	3.5	3
	JAN.	FEB.	MAR.	APR.	MAY	JUNE
ROANOKE	44/25	47/27	58/36	67/44	76/53	83/60
	3.5	3.5	3.5	3	2	3
	JULY	AUG.	SEPT.	OCT.	NOV.	DEC.
	86/65	85/64	79/57	68/45	58/37	48/29
	4	3	3	3.5	3.5	3.5

FESTIVALS AND SEASONAL EVENTS

WINTER

Dec. **The Grand Illumination.** The highlight of the Christmas festivities in Colonial Williamsburg. After a ceremony in which all the historic area's buildings are lit with candles, the evening explodes with fireworks, musical entertainment, dancing, dramatic presentations, and caroling. | 757/253–0192 or 800/246–2099.

SPRING

Mar. **Highland County Maple Festival.** This mid-month festival in Monterey features an arts-and-crafts show, Maple Queen contest and ball, dances, and food, plus tours of local sugar camps where you can watch the process of syrup-making. | 540/468–2550.

Mar. **Virginia Festival of the Book.** Writers, editors, book agents, and bibliophiles gather at this festival in Charlottesville for readings, book signings, literary panel discussions, and other events. | 804/924–3296.

Apr. **International Azalea Festival.** This colorful event, the region's oldest festival, is packed with pomp and circumstance. Held in mid- to late April in Norfolk, the festival hosts a grand parade through downtown, the coronation of a queen and court chosen from a field of young women representing the NATO countries, an air show, a fashion show, a ball, and a weekend of live entertainment highlighted by the performance of a major recording artist. | 757/445–6647, ext. 1.

May **Shenandoah Apple Blossom Festival.** Late in the month, Winchester celebrates its area apple orchards with numerous

1864
May, Battle of Spotsylvania Court House. The clash between Union and Confederate forces results in some 30,000 casualties. Neither side can claim victory. Union general Ulysses S.

Grant presses on to Richmond.

1865
Confederate commander-in-chief Robert E. Lee surrenders his army to Union general Ulysses S. Grant at Appomattox Court House. April 2, Battle at Pamplin Park. The Union army

breaks through Petersburg's defense line. On April 3, General Lee evacuates Petersburg and Richmond. One week later, he surrenders at Appomattox Court House.

1920
Virginia women win the right to vote.

parades, live music, a circus, an arts-and-crafts show, and other events. | 540/662–3863 or 800/230–2139.

Apr.–May **Virginia Waterfront International Arts Festival.** Showcased at this two-week event in Norfolk are renowned artists from the worlds of classical, jazz, and world music, as well as dance and musical theater. | 757/664–6492.

SUMMER

June **Harborfest.** This festival in Norfolk draws upwards of 250,000 people early every June. The waterfront celebration provides nonstop live entertainment, water and air shows, sailing ships, food, and fireworks. | 757/441–2345.

June **Potomac Celtic Festival.** This event on the Oatlands Plantation in Leesburg celebrates the cultural heritage of Ireland, Scotland, Wales, Cornwall, the Isle of Man, Brittany, and Galacia with music, storytelling, dancing, workshops, and Scottish games. | 800/752–6118.

June **Cock Island Race.** The largest sailboat race on the East Coast occurs in Portsmouth where hundreds of boats gather for the competition and related festivities. | 757/393–9933.

June **Hampton Jazz Festival.** Some of the country's top blues, soul, pop, and jazz performers share the stage late in the month in Hampton. | 757/838–4203.

July **Chincoteague's Annual Pony Swim and Auction.** The wild ponies of Assateague Island are rounded up and herded across the channel to Chincoteague to be sold. Those not auctioned off swim back to Assateague. | 757/336–6161.

July–Aug. **Virginia Highlands Festival.** For two weeks in late July–early August, Abingdon celebrates the region's Appalachian culture with antiques, art, crafts demonstrations, hot air balloon rides, music, and performances. | 540/676–2282 or 800/435–3440.

Aug. **Old Fiddler's Convention and Fiddlefest.** Early in the month, this festival in Galax brings together young and old musicians who play everything from the mouth harp to the bull fiddle. The oldest and possibly largest fiddler's convention in the country, it has contests and lots of dancing. | 540/236–8541.

1925
Harry F. Byrd is elected governor, beginning a 40-year reign over Virginia politics. He revolutionizes state government through reforms and constitutional amendments.

1933
The Civilian Conservation Corps begins work on a variety of public projects and develops Virginia's first state parks system.

1935
Shenandoah National Park is established.

1954
Virginia implements the Massive Resistance movement in response to the U.S. Supreme Court's ruling that racial segregation of public schools is unconstitutional. The state legislature

withholds public funding from schools that allow black and white students in the same classroom.

INTRODUCTION
HISTORY
REGIONS
WHEN TO VISIT
STATE'S GREATS
RULES OF THE ROAD
DRIVING TOURS

Aug. **Hampton Cup Regatta.** Mid-month, the oldest and largest powerboat race in the United States is held in Hampton. Live entertainment and children's activities accompany the race. | 757/722–5343 or 800/487–8778.

Aug. **East Coast Surfing Championship.** Top-notch surfers vie for the championship off the Virginia Beach coast in mid-August. | 757/499–8822.

AUTUMN

Sept. **Neptune Festival.** This festival in Virginia Beach, held in the middle of the month, is a five-day family affair with a sand castle competition, air show, live entertainment, fresh seafood, a gala ball, and fireworks. | 757/498–0215.

Sept. **Virginia State Fair.** The event in late September in Richmond has traditional state-fair fare: agricultural exhibits, animal contests, a carnival, top-name entertainment, games, and food. | 804/228–3200 or 800/588–3247.

Oct. **Waterford Homes Tour and Crafts Exhibit.** This event early in the month near Leesburg includes the oldest juried crafts fair in Virginia, traditional music and dance, hands-on demonstrations, colonial-era and Civil War encampments, and tours of Waterford's historic homes. | 540/882–3085.

Oct. **Blue Ridge Folklife Festival.** In late October, the town of Rocky Mount near Martinsville showcases western Virginia folk culture in all its variety. Craftspeople from throughout the Blue Ridge region demonstrate folk arts, and there are horse-pulling and mule-jumping contests, sheep dog trials, and lots of mountain music and storytelling. | 540/365–4416.

Nov. **Virginia Film Festival.** This festival in Charlottesville gives fans a chance to hobnob with movie stars, filmmakers, scholars, and critics. Dozens of films are screened. | 804/982–5326 or 800/882–3378.

State's Greats

As one of the nation's original colonies, Virginia is an inexhaustible treasure trove for history buffs. From entire re-created colonial towns and Civil War battlefields to remnants of routes that early pioneers followed on their sojourns westward, the choices can be almost overwhelming. You can stroll neighborhoods that look much

1959
The General Assembly repeals Massive Resistance legislation.

1989
L. Douglas Wilder is elected governor of Virginia, becoming the nation's first elected African American governor.

1999
Virginia resident Nicole Johnson crowned Miss America.

as they did 100 or 200 years ago, step Into the homes of some of America's great former presidents, or watch archaeological excavations unravel the mysteries surrounding the country's earliest settlers.

Lovers of the outdoors will also find an overabundance of options. More than a million acres of Virginia are dedicated to national and state parks, forming an official wilderness that includes mountains, marshes, forests, and seashore. Hikers and cyclists have their pick of terrains from coastal plains and rolling countryside to steep-sided mountains. Water sports enthusiasts, fishermen, and other dabblers in the water will find plenty of opportunities to play in the rugged western fringes of the state or along the miles of coastal shoreline.

Virginia is also a great getaway destination, where a maze of two-lane country roads take you past fishing villages and rural hamlets that retain the aura of simpler times. You can browse through antiques shops, sample local cuisine, tour a winery, or hear a concert under the stars.

Beaches, Forests, and Parks

Virginia's beaches are in the far eastern portion of the state. **Virginia Beach** is a highly commercialized resort area with a boardwalk. The family-oriented beach has a long, wide stretch of sparkling sand—and crowds of people. If you seek a quieter, more private setting, try **Chincoteague Island** or **Assateague Island National Seashore** on the Eastern Shore. Their beaches are wild and undeveloped and part of the islands is designated a national wildlife refuge. So don't expect food concessions or organized water sports here.

Virginia's forests occupy the mountainous western reaches of the state and total some 1.8 million acres. The **George Washington and Jefferson National Forests** stretch from Winchester at the northern tip of the Shenandoah Valley to Big Stone Gap in the southwest corner of the state. These protected lands provide lots of opportunities for hiking, camping, fishing, swimming, picnicking, mountain biking, and hunting. A 300-mi portion of the Appalachian Trail runs through the forest.

There are nearly 30 state parks scattered throughout Virginia and a dozen more regional parks. If fishing or boating is your chief aim, head for **Smith Mountain Lake State Park** near Roanoke. The 20,000-acre lake is a popular destination for pleasure boaters and is noted for trophy sport fishing. If you're in northern Virginia, visit **Lake Anna State Park** near Fredericksburg, which has a 13,000-acre lake. The best opportunities for hiking and camping are concentrated in western Virginia. The most popular choice is **Shenandoah National Park** near Luray, which covers some 196,500 acres and features 500 mi of trails, a variety of campgrounds, and horse rentals to boot. Some of the most rugged climbing terrain can be found at the **Mt. Rogers National Recreation Area** in southwest Virginia.

If ecology is an abiding interest, visit **First Landing/Seashore State Park** in Virginia Beach, which has a protected wetlands area, or the **Great Dismal Swamp National Wildlife Refuge** near Suffolk, a 200,000-acre wilderness and one of the largest natural areas on the East Coast.

Culture, History, and the Arts

Virginia is home to two of the South's premier art museums, the **Virginia Museum of Fine Arts** in Richmond and the **Chrysler Museum of Art** in Norfolk. Both have extensive collections ranging from the ancient to the modern. The Virginia Museum of Fine Arts is noted for a collection of jeweled Fabergé eggs, while the Chrysler boasts an outstanding display of Tiffany glass.

Many of the attractions in the Hampton Roads region revolve around its maritime culture: the **Mariners' Museum** in Newport News chronicles scientific and technological developments in shipbuilding, ocean navigation, and cartography; **Nauticus,** the

INTRODUCTION
HISTORY
REGIONS
WHEN TO VISIT
STATE'S GREATS
RULES OF THE ROAD
DRIVING TOURS

National Maritime Center in downtown Norfolk has many high-tech interactive exhibits on nautical themes, from navigation to sonar submarine hunts.

Virginia's historic beginnings are explored at **Jamestown, The Original Site,** an ongoing archaeological study of the first permanent English settlement in the New World. At **Colonial Williamsburg,** a re-creation of Virginia's colonial capital, costumed interpreters provide insight into the life-styles and political preoccupations of 18th-century America.

Battlefield parks preserve the sites of pivotal events in Virginia's history. The **Yorktown Battlefield** in Yorktown was the site of the military engagement that ended America's War for Independence. A number of other historical parks commemorate Civil War battles; the largest of which is the **Fredericksburg and Spotsylvania National Military Park** in Fredericksburg with interpretive trails, historic buildings, and exhibits pertaining to four major Civil War campaigns. The historic homes of Virginia-born U.S. presidents include Thomas Jefferson's **Monticello** in Charlottesville; **Mount Vernon,** the home of George Washington, outside Alexandria; and **Montpelier,** James Madison's country estate near Orange.

The **Virginia Symphony** and **Virginia Opera** can be heard seasonally at venues throughout Virginia. The **Theatre at Lime Kiln** in Lexington hosts summertime dramatic performances and acoustic concerts in an outdoor setting. **Wolf Trap Farm Park** in Vienna, near Fairfax, is the only national park dedicated to the performing arts, and opera, jazz, folk, symphony, country, dance, and popular music can be heard there year-round.

Sports

The opportunities for outdoor recreation run the gamut in Virginia. Hikers have hundreds of miles of trails to choose from, from the best-known in **Shenandoah National Park** to the more remote in the **George Washington and Jefferson National Forests.** Cyclists can coast along the boardwalk in Virginia Beach or hurtle down mountain trails in the **Mt. Rogers National Recreation Area** in southwest Virginia. A section of the Trans-America Bicycle Trail extends 500 mi from **Breaks Interstate Park** at the western fringe of the state to Yorktown on the coast. Virginia also has some 1,000 mi of official scenic byways that are popular for biking.

Skiing, a popular winter sport in western Virginia, can be enjoyed at **Bryce Resort** near Basye, the **Homestead** in Hot Springs, and **Wintergreen,** south of Charlottesville. The rest of the year, the state offers diverse golfing opportunities, from mountain and valley courses to those that border tidal rivers and the Atlantic Ocean. Some of the best golf-course architects have designed courses in Virginia, including the Homestead's Cascades in Hot Springs, designed by William Flynn; the Golden Horseshoe Gold Course in Colonial Williamsburg, created by Robert Trent Jones; and the Stoney Creek course at Wintergreen, laid out by Rees Jones.

Whitewater rafting and canoeing is particularly good on the Shenandoah, Maury, and James rivers, while the Chesapeake Bay and its tributaries are popular for windsurfing and sailing. Mountain streams and inland lakes such as **Smith Mountain Lake, Lake Anna,** and **Buggs Island** offer terrific freshwater fishing. During the summer months, speckled trout, Spanish mackerel, bluefish, and other saltwater fish are plentiful in the **Chesapeake Bay,** while the waters off the Virginia coast are home to blue marlin, dolphin, wahoo, and yellowfin tuna.

Other Points of Interest

If roller coasters and other dizzying amusement rides appeal to you, visit **Paramount's Kings Dominion,** near Ashland, just north of Richmond, a 400-acre entertainment complex with more than 100 rides, many of them geared toward youngsters. **Water Country USA** in Williamsburg has more than 30 water rides and attractions, including a 4,500-square-ft heated pool. Another nearby theme park is **Busch Gardens**

Williamsburg, which re-creates 17th-century European countries and has more than 100 rides, shows, and exhibits.

Virginia boasts a number of underground caverns, all concentrated in the Shenandoah Valley. **Luray Caverns,** considered the largest in the East, contain thousands of colored-stone formations and a unique "stalacpipe organ." **Endless Caverns,** in New Market, so called because no end to the caverns has yet been discovered, shelters an array of giant stalactites, stalagmites, and limestone pendants.

Rules of the Road

License Requirements: To drive in Virginia you must be at least 16 years old and have a valid driver's license. Residents of Canada and most other countries may drive here as long as they have valid licenses from their home countries.

Right Turn on Red: In most places, drivers may make a right turn on a red light after coming to a full stop. The practice is prohibited in some metropolitan areas, however; watch for signs at intersections with traffic lights.

Seat Belt and Helmet Laws: Seat belts are required for drivers and front-seat passengers; restraints are required for children under the age of 4. Helmets are required for motorcyclists.

Speed Limit: The maximum speed limit on most of Virginia's interstates is 65 mph. In heavily traveled corridors, however, the speed limit is 55 mph. Check speed-limit signs carefully.

For More Information: Call the State Department of Motor Vehicles headquarters in Richmond, 804/367–0538.

The Piedmont and Tidewater Regions Driving Tour
NORTHERN VIRGINIA TO RICHMOND AND HAMPTON ROADS

Distance: 202 mi   Time: 4 to 5 days

Breaks: Spend your first night in the historic district of Fredericksburg. The area presents a range of accommodations, from budget inns to bed-and-breakfasts. Richmond, a midway point on the drive, is a good choice for your second night's stay, although their lodgings tend to be more expensive. Since Williamsburg and Hampton Roads are within a 90-mi radius of Richmond, you can make a day trip to the area keeping Richmond as your base of operations, or spend the night in Williamsburg, a tourist-heavy town with a multitude of hostelries to suit every taste.

This tour follows a southeasterly course through several distinct regions of Virginia and its most prominent, historically rich cities. From Alexandria in the Washington, D.C. metropolitan area, you travel through Piedmont to Fredericksburg and Richmond, then head through flat, coastal plains to Williamsburg and the great port city of Norfolk.

❶ Spend the morning on a walking tour of **Old Town Alexandria,** the seaport town that George Washington and Robert E. Lee called home. The neighborhood of 18th- and 19th-century homes covers about 20 blocks and can easily be seen on foot. At the **Boyhood Home of Robert E. Lee,** you can see how the future Civil War general lived and studied during his formative years. For a taste of what Alexandria's early political and social

INTRODUCTION
HISTORY
REGIONS
WHEN TO VISIT
STATE'S GREATS
RULES OF THE ROAD
DRIVING TOURS

life was like, visit **Gadsby's Tavern Museum,** a once-popular gathering place, now a venue for celebrations honoring George Washington. The venerable **Christ Church,** completed in 1773, has changed little from when George Washington and Robert E. Lee served as its vestrymen. Early medical equipment and herbal remedies common in the 18th century are on display at the **Stabler-Leadbeater Apothecary Museum,** whose customers included George and Martha Washington and James Monroe. Tour the **Carlyle House,** built by Scottish merchant John Carlyle, and discover why this 1753 dwelling was considered the most splendid of its day. Then watch art in all mediums being created at the **Torpedo Arts Factory,** a former munitions factory that now houses the studios of more than 150 professional artists and craftspeople. •

❷ In the afternoon, head south 8 mi from Old Town to **Mount Vernon,** probably the best-known country house in the nation. George Washington's farmhouse has been restored to appear as it did when the president lived here in the late 1700s. The 40 acres of grounds contain restored outbuildings, pleasure gardens, two museums, and the tombs of Washington and his wife, Martha.

Top off your day in Alexandria with an evening cruise on the Potomac River, a relaxing way to take in the monuments and landmarks of Washington, D.C. The **Potomac Riverboat Company** provides three different sightseeing excursions.

❸ About an hour south of Alexandria, 48 mi on I–95, is **Fredericksburg,** another city steeped in history. At the **Fredericksburg and Spotsylvania National Military Park** you can retrace four Civil War battles that were fought in and around the city, talk to park historians, and see exhibits depicting the bloody conflict. In Fredericksburg's historic district, tour the elaborately decorated rooms of the colonial mansion **Kenmore,** built by Fielding Lewis for his wife, Betty, the only sister of George Washington. The home of Washington's brother, Charles, has become the **Rising Sun Tavern,** where today costumed guides interpret 18th-century tavern life. The **Mary Washington House** contains the personal possessions of George Washington's mother, including a dressing glass she willed to her son. The future fifth president of the United States practiced law for a time in Fredericksburg, and the **James Monroe Museum and Memorial Library** contains many of his personal possessions and furnishings.

❹ From Fredericksburg, get back onto I–95 and continue 58 mi south to **Richmond,** the capital of Virginia. Most of Richmond's attractions lie north of the James River, which bisects the city. The **Virginia State Capitol,** designed by Thomas Jefferson in 1785, is located downtown. Among the sculptures of Virginia-born U.S. presidents here is a famous life-size statue of George Washington. The **Museum and White House of the Confederacy** was the official residence of Jefferson Davis, president of the Confederacy. This mansion has been carefully refurbished to its wartime appearance; adjacent to it is a newer building that contains a vast collection of Civil War artifacts. East of downtown, in the Church Hill Historic District, is **St. John's Episcopal Church,** where Patrick Henry delivered his memorable "Give me liberty or give me death!" speech in 1775. At the **Richmond National Battlefield Park,** a movie describes the three campaigns fought on the site, and maps outline self-guided tours of the battlefields. If art is more to your taste, visit the **Virginia Museum of Fine Arts,** one of the largest in the South. Its diverse collections range from ancient to contemporary art. Of Richmond's many house museums, probably the most unique is **Agecroft Hall,** a 15th-century English manor that was reassembled here in the 1920s. The house, surrounded by formal gardens, contains Tudor and early Stuart art and furniture. The graceful **Hollywood Cemetery** is home to the graves of James Monroe, John Tyler, Jefferson Davis, and some 18,000 Confederate soldiers. It also contains beautiful Victorian tombs and sculptures.

❺ Between Richmond and Williamsburg, along the banks of the James River, in Charles City County, one of the earliest "incorporated" settlements in America, stand four historical **plantation homes,** each architecturally significant and filled with family heirlooms. If you take the scenic (and slower) 57-mi route to Williamsburg via John Tyler Memorial Highway (Rte. 5) instead of the rather monotonous 51-mi route on I–64, you can stop off and visit one or all of these estates. Built in 1723, **Shirley** is the oldest plantation in Virginia. It has remained in the same family, the Carters, for 10 generations. Benjamin Harrison, a signer of the Declaration of Independence, and William Henry Harrison, the country's ninth president, were both born at the **Berkeley Plantation.** Virginians say that the first Thanksgiving was celebrated not in Massachusetts but here. **West-**

INTRODUCTION
HISTORY
REGIONS
WHEN TO VISIT
STATE'S GREATS
RULES OF THE ROAD
DRIVING TOURS

over was home to Col. William Byrd II, a member of the colonial legislature. At 300 ft, **Sherwood Forest** is considered the longest frame house in the country. Built in 1720, it then became the retirement home of John Tyler, the 10th U.S. president.

❻ **Colonial Williamsburg,** 51 mi east of Richmond, is a living history museum on a colossal scale. Covering 173 acres, it is a re-creation of the city that was the capital of Virginia from 1699 until 1780. After your trip back to colonial America, take a walk around the College of William and Mary, the country's second-oldest university. The college's Christopher Wren Building, which dates from 1695, is the oldest academic building in America still in use.

❼ If time permits, continue east from Williamsburg toward the enormous port of Hampton Roads. In **Newport News,** visit the **Mariners' Museum,** whose galleries contain rare maritime artifacts, miniature ships and full-size vessels, navigational instruments, and other fascinating objects of maritime history.

❽ Take the Hampton Roads Bridge-Tunnel to **Norfolk** and tour the world's largest naval installation, the **Norfolk Naval Base and Norfolk Naval Air Station,** home to about 115 ships of the Atlantic and Mediterranean fleets. If you are traveling during the warmer months, make a point to see the **Norfolk Botanical Gardens,** which blossom some of the largest collections of azaleas, camellias, rhododendrons, and roses on the East Coast. The art collection at the **Chrysler Museum** includes treasures from ancient Greece, Rome, and the Orient, decorative arts from the 12th century to the present, a major Tiffany collection, plus the work of artists such as Pablo Picasso and Andy Warhol. Round off your visit by boarding one of the boats offering harbor tours. **Carrie B. Harbor Tours** runs excursions on a replica of a double-decked 19th-century Mississippi riverboat; the trip takes you past navy ships and submarines, shipyards, and other local points of interest.

To return to Alexandria: Take the Hampton Roads Bridge-Tunnel north to Hampton and pick up I–64 west. Continue on I–64 to Richmond. At Richmond, get on I–95 north, which will take you back to Alexandria.

Western Virginia Drive
CHARLOTTESVILLE AND THE SHENANDOAH VALLEY

Distance: 135 mi; 160 mi with detour to Bath County   Time: 4 to 5 days
Breaks: Spend the first night in Charlottesville. Lexington is a good stopping place on the second night, since it's a halfway point on this tour. On the third night, you'll find numerous accommodations available in Roanoke.

This drive highlights some of the most scenic reaches of Virginia and promises terrific vistas of mountains, valleys and rolling farmlands. The tour begins in Charlottesville, the most prominent city in the Blue Ridge foothills, and heads west through national park lands to Staunton. From there, you follow the Shenandoah Valley south through Lexington, then pick up the famed Blue Ridge Parkway into Roanoke.

❶ In the foothills of the Blue Ridge Mountains, **Charlottesville** is home to two of Thomas Jefferson's greatest architectural achievements. The third president's mountaintop home, **Monticello,** contains his inventions and personal effects, which reflect quite a diverse set of interests. The grounds include various dependencies, as well as a 1,000-ft-long

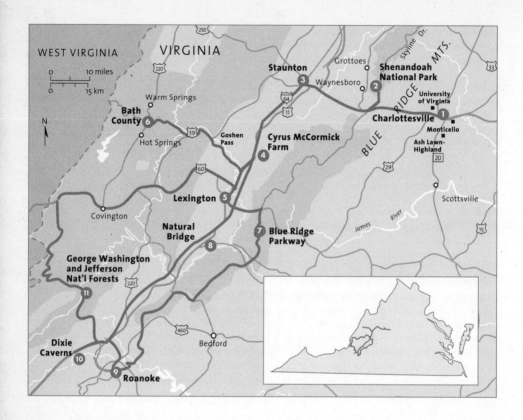

vegetable garden, vineyards, and orchards that replicate the ones Jefferson cultivated. The **University of Virginia,** founded and designed by Jefferson, features classically inspired pavilions that flank the Rotunda, a half-scale replica of Rome's Pantheon. James Monroe's estate, **Ash Lawn-Highland,** still a working plantation, displays a large collection of the fifth president's possessions.

❷ From Charlottesville, drive 28 mi west on I–64 to **Shenandoah National Park.** This breathtaking park features some of the highest and most scenic portions of the Blue Ridge Mountains. Its roughly 196,500 acres offer hiking, horseback riding, and fishing—and plenty of opportunities to see wildlife close-up. The Appalachian Trail runs the length of the park. Continue west on I–64, crossing into the Shenandoah Valley.

❸ **Staunton,** 11 mi from Shenandoah National Park, is one of the oldest cities west of the Blue Ridge. At the **Museum of American Frontier Culture,** an outdoor living history museum, learn how America's Appalachian frontier was settled. It features four authentically reassembled, 18th-century homesteads from Ireland, England, Germany, and western Virginia. The **Woodrow Wilson Birthplace and Museum** looks as it did in 1856, when the 28th U.S. president was born here.

❹ Just south of Staunton in Steeles Tavern is the **Cyrus McCormick Farm,** also known as Walnut Grove, where McCormick perfected the first mechanical grain reaper. A museum on the grounds showcases one of the original reapers.

❺ Continuing south, either on I–81 or the less-trafficked U.S. 11, proceed 55 mi to **Lexington,** a genteel, well-preserved town where two Confederate heroes had homes and were laid to rest. **Washington and Lee University,** founded in 1749, is named for two men intertwined with its past—George Washington and Robert E. Lee. Among the handsome white-columned buildings is the **Lee Memorial Chapel and Museum,** where a famous recumbent statue of Lee marks his tomb. Next door to the university are the imposing neo-Gothic buildings of the **Virginia Military Institute,** founded in 1839. The institute's **George C. Marshall Museum** preserves the memory of the VMI alumnus who served as general and secretary of state, and earned a Nobel Peace Prize. The **Stonewall Jackson House,** the only home the Civil War general ever owned, offers a glimpse of his private life. For a change of pace, visit the **Virginia Horse Center,** one of the top equine facilities in the United States. Events at this year-round arena range from miniature horse shows and pony club shows to rodeos and auctions.

❻ If you have time for a scenic detour, take Route 39 west of Lexington toward Bath County. A stretch of this roadway is known as Goshen Pass, which follows the Maury River as it winds its way through the Alleghenies. In May, the mountainside is lush with rhododendrons and other flowering plants. If you continue on to **Bath County,** a popular resort area, you can bathe in the thermal springs once used for medical treatments in the small towns, Warm Springs and Hot Springs, or check out the nearby summer and winter sports facilities.

❼ Just outside of Lexington, head south on the **Blue Ridge Parkway,** a destination unto itself. Governed by the National Park Service, this scenic roadway follows the crest of the mountains into North Carolina's Great Smoky Mountains. Free of commercial intrusions, it offers magnificent views of valley, forests, and mountain ranges.

❽ If time permits, take another detour to **Natural Bridge,** a 215-ft-high, 90-ft-long limestone arch. You can also tour caverns and a wax museum here.

❾ The Blue Ridge Parkway leads to **Roanoke,** 54 mi from Lexington, a railroad town and center for the arts in western Virginia. It's also a good jumping-off point for side trips. A restored downtown warehouse called **Center in the Square** houses a theater, a regional history museum, an art gallery, and the **Science Museum of Western Virginia and Hopkins Planetarium.** The science museum has a variety of interactive exhibits that entertain and inform youngsters on topics such as energy resources, meteorology, and oceanography. The historic **Farmer's Market** first opened in 1882 and still operates on the same site in the heart of downtown. The **Virginia Museum of Transportation** houses dozens of vintage steam, electric, and diesel locomotives, as well as antique autos, buses, and carriages. Snow leopards and other exotic animals can been seen at the **Mill Mountain Zoological Park,** home to variety of mammals, birds, and reptiles.

❿ At the **Dixie Caverns,** 7 mi from Roanoke in nearby Salem, tour guides take you up the mountain (instead of down) to see a netherworld of mineral formations.

⓫ About 10 mi west of Roanoke, the **George Washington and Jefferson National Forests** has trout streams, picnic areas, swimming, horseback riding, and miles of hiking trails. You can spend an afternoon in this wilderness or many days, thanks to dozens of developed campgrounds. The main recreation season is April through November.

To return to Charlottesville: Take I–81 north from Roanoke to Staunton. At Staunton, get on I–64 east to Charlottesville.

ABINGDON

MAP 11, C7

(Nearby town also listed: Bristol)

Near the Tennessee border, Abingdon is the oldest town west of the Blue Ridge Mountains, chartered in 1778. In 1760, Col. William Byrd cut the Great Road through what is now Abingdon onward to Tennessee. That same year, Daniel Boone camped here and gave the area its first name, "Wolf Hills," after a pack of wolves emerged from a cave and attacked his dogs. Abingdon got its present name in 1778, in honor of Martha Washington's English home. Today, the tiny town of 7,000 is a cultural crossroads in the wilderness, home to an an artist's colony and the Barter Theatre, the official state theater of Virginia and the longest-running professional repertory theater in the country. The 34-mi Virginia Creeper Trail originates just off Main Street, offering hiking, biking, and horseback riding. Tens of thousands of people visit every August for the Virginia Highlands Festival, a two-week celebration of Appalachian culture begun in 1949.

Information: Abingdon Convention and Visitors Bureau | 335 Cummings St., Abingdon, VA 24210 | 540/676–2282 or 800/435–3440 | www.abingdon.com/tourism.

Attractions

Barter Theatre. Founded in 1933 during the Great Depression, by Robert Porterfield, a local unemployed actor, this theater got its name in the obvious way: patrons who could not afford the 40¢ tickets could offer the equivalent in produce or other edibles. It now ranks as America's longest-running professional repertory theater (alumni include Gregory Peck and Hume Cronyn) and is the official state theater of Virginia. You can see a wide range of productions, from musicals and Shakespeare classics to works by contemporary playwrights such as David Mamet. | Box 867, 133 W. Main St. | 540/628–3991 or 800/368–3240 | fax 540/619–3335 | www.bartertheatre.com | Ticket prices vary with performance | Reservations suggested | Feb.–Dec.

Fields-Penn 1860 House Museum. Built by James Fields, a brick mason who was part of Abingdon's emerging middle class, this home showcases furnishings and decorative arts that evoke the lifestyle of southwest Virginians during the 19th century. The collection includes a barn loom from the 1820s. | 208 W. Main St. | 540/676–0216 or 800/435–3440 | Free | Apr.–Dec. Wed.–Sat. 1–4; Jan.–Mar. by appointment.

Mt. Rogers National Recreation Area. An outdoor recreation mecca covering some 200,000 acres, Mt. Rogers is part of both George Washington and Jefferson National Forests. At 5,729 ft, Mt. Rogers is the highest point in the state. Hiking trails and campgrounds abound. The visitor center is located on VA 16. | 3714 Hwy. 16, Marion | 540/783–5196 or 800/628–7202 | www.nps.gov | Free | Daily; visitor center Memorial Day–mid-Oct. weekdays 8–4:30, weekends 9–5; mid-Oct.–Memorial Day, weekdays 8–4:30.

Virginia Creeper Trail. This trail, a 34-mi former rail bed of the Virginia-Carolina Railroad, begins at the end of Main Street in Abingdon. You can hike or bike it, or traverse it on horseback. The trail is marked by sharp curves, steep grades, and 100 trestles and bridges. | 540/676–2282 or 800/435–3440 | www.ehc.edu/vacreeper | Free | Daily dawn–dusk.

White's Mill. A Virginia historic landmark, this water-powered gristmill, originally built in 1790, still grinds cornmeal today. Union troops destroyed the mill during the Civil War and it was rebuilt in 1866. Some of the original grinding stones, imported from France, are still on display. Tours are by appointment. | 12291 White's Mill Rd. | 540/676–0285 | Donations accepted | May–Oct. Tues.–Sun. 9 AM–dusk; Nov.–Apr. Sat.–Sun, 9 AM–dusk.

William King Regional Arts Center. Works by regional artists, rotating gallery exhibitions, folk art, and crafts are on display. There's also an outdoor sculpture garden and museum store. | 415 Academy Dr. | 540/628–5005 | fax 540/628–3922 | www.wkrac.org | Free | Tues. 10–9, Wed.– Fri. 10–5, Sat. and Sun. 1–5 | Mon.

ON THE CALENDAR
JULY–AUG.: *Virginia Highlands Festival.* A two-week celebration of Appalachian culture all over Abingdon, with live music from bluegrass to opera, as well as other performances and mountain crafts. More than 100 exhibitors display their wares, including baskets, pieced and appliquéd quilts, pewter, stained glass, jewelry, and musical instruments. | 540/676–2282 or 800/435–3440.

SEPT.: *Washington County Fair.* Livestock competitions, tractor pulls, horse shows, country music, a parade, and barnyard animals keep things lively at the Washington County Fairgrounds, the first two weeks of September. | 540/676–2282.

Dining

Dining Room. American. This classy restaurant at the Martha Washington Inn hops during local festivals. The Victorian mansion that contains the restaurant and inn used to be an all-girls school. The food specialties are the she-crab soup and the double-boned pork chops. Friday night buffet 5–9 | 150 W. Main St. | 540/628–3161 | $17–$30 | AE, D, DC, MC, V.

Starving Artist Cafe. Contemporary. An intimate café is in a white-walled gallery with monthly rotating regional artists' shows. While its patio calls to mind the Florida Keys, the café itself is minimally furnished with aluminum chairs and tables. Oysters Rockefeller, smoked Norwegian salmon, tournedos Rossini (beef fillet topped with shiitake mushrooms), specialty sandwiches at lunch are all favorites. Kids' menu. Beer and wine only. | 134 Wall St. | 540/628–8445 | Closed Sun. week of Labor Day | $17–$30 | AE, MC, V.

The Tavern. Continental. Housed in the oldest building in Abingdon, the Tavern blends an unlikely-but-inviting combination of English, German, and Japanese antiques with brick floors, stucco, and wood. The two-story building dates from 1779, and its past echoes in the surroundings. The signature dish is stuffed filet mignon. Open-air dining in the courtyard and a covered balcony. A magician performs on weekends. | 222 E. Main St. | 540/628–1118 | $13–$27 | AE, D, MC, V.

Lodging

Alpine. This one-floor, basic motel sits on the top of a small hill overlooking the mountains. The rooms have an exterior entrance to which you can pull up and park your car. Cable TV. Business services. | 882 E. Main St. | 540/628–3178 | fax 540/628–4247 | 19 rooms | $60 | AE, D, MC, V.

Camberley's Martha Washington Inn. This historic colonial landmark built in 1832 glows in the warm light of chandeliers and lanterns. The lobby entrance is marked by a large landing from which a long carpeted staircase lined with a wood banister ascends. The rooms, furnished with antique furniture, are bright with large windows and flowers. In the gardens, there is a white gazebo at the end of a brick path. Bar, dining room. Room service, cable TV. Business services. Airport shuttle. | 150 W. Main St. | 540/628–3161 or 800/555–8000 | fax 540/628–7652 | www.camberleyhotels.com | 50 rooms, 11 suites | $159–$310 | AE, D, DC, MC, V.

Comfort Inn. Easy interstate access is a plus at this standard chain hotel housed in a neutral stone building. Rooms are simply furnished. Complimentary Continental breakfast. Cable TV. Pool. Business services. | 170 Jonesboro Rd. | 540/676–2222 | fax 540/676–2222 | www.comfortinn.com | 80 rooms | $60–$82 | AE, D, DC, MC, V.

Empire. Close to downtown Abingdon, the motor lodge also has easy interstate access. The lodge's two-story buildings with blue and white-siding are on a large lot hemmed in by the surrounding mountains. Rooms are conservatively furnished in dark colors and have views of the mountains. Restaurant, complimentary Continental breakfast. Cable TV. Business services. | 887 Empire Dr. | 540/628–7131 | fax 540/628–7158 | 104 rooms | $46–51 | AE, MC, V.

ABINGDON

INTRO
ATTRACTIONS
DINING
LODGING

Silversmith Inn. Built in 1871, this three-story Italianate row house sits next door to the Barter Theater. It's also the closest lodging to the Virginia Creeper Trail. Choose from themed rooms, such as the nautically nuanced Chesapeake Room, decorated in light blues and whites with paintings by the Eastern Shore artist, Willie Crockett. Complimentary breakfast. Some in-room hot tubs, cable TV, no room phones, no smoking. No pets. No kids under 12. | 102 E Main St. | 540/676–3924 | fax 540/676–3876 | silversmith@naxs.net | www.bbhost.com/silversmithinn | 4 rooms, 1 suite | $100–$155 | AE, D, MC, V.

Summerfield Inn. This 1920s Greek Revival home in the middle of Abingdon's historic district sits only blocks from the Barter Theatre. Rooms feature walnut and oak antiques and hardwood floors accented with Oriental rugs. Most rooms have whirlpool baths. Complimentary breakfast. Some in-room hot tubs, no TV in some rooms, TV in common area, no smoking. Library. No pets. No kids under 12. | 101 W Valley Rd. | 540/628–5905 or 800/668–5905 | fax 540/628–7515 | stay@summerfieldinn.com | www.summerfieldinn.com | 7 rooms | $90–$130 | AE, MC, V.

Swiss Inn. This red brick, two-story alpine-style inn on a hilltop also offers Swiss-German dining. Carpeted rooms with mountain views are furnished in light mauve colors. Dining room, complimentary Continental breakfast. Some in-room hot tubs, cable TV. Business services. | 33361 Lee Hwy., Glade Spring | 540/429–5191 | fax 540/429–2233 | 32 rooms | $50–$55 | AE, MC, V.

White Birches Inn. This turn-of-the-century home-turned-inn surrounds you with polished antiques, stocked bookcases, and Oriental carpets atop gleaming hardwood floors. Rooms have working fireplaces and views of the surrounding gardens and lawns. Most rooms have whirlpool tubs. Complimentary breakfast. Some in-room hot tubs, cable TV, in-room VCRs (and movies), no smoking. No pets. No kids under 10. | 268 Whitesmill Rd. | 800/247–2437 | stay@whitebirchesinn.com | whitebirchesinn.com | 5 rooms | $90–$125 | MC, V.

ALEXANDRIA

MAP 11, J4

(Nearby towns also listed: Arlington, Fairfax, Falls Church, McLean, Springfield, Tysons Corner)

On the western bank of the Potomac River, just across from Washington, D.C. Alexandria was founded in 1749 by Scottish merchants eager to capitalize on the booming tobacco trade. It was named in honor of John Alexander, who bought the land of the present-day city from an English sea captain in 1699. The town emerged as one of the most important ports in colonial America, and its history is linked to significant events and individuals (George Washington among them) of the colonial and revolutionary periods.

During the Civil War, Alexandria remained under Union control, becoming a supply and hospital center. From 1863 to 1865, it was the capital of the Restored Government of Virginia, which consisted of seven Virginia counties that flew the Federal flag throughout the war. The historic district, Old Town Alexandria, is paved with cobblestones; according to tradition, the rounded stones served as ballast aboard the early sailing ships. Restored 18th- and 19th-century churches, taverns, and red brick homes line the streets; with more than 2,000 historic structures, the area is listed on the National Register of Historic Places. Among the scores of Georgian colonial and early Federal buildings are a few long, narrow structures that resemble halves of gabled houses. This unusual architectural style was born of the owners' attempts to evade taxation by reporting construction unfinished.

While Old Town retains the appearance of another century, modern-day attractions give Alexandria a vibrant, cosmopolitan air. It maintains an identity quite distinct from that of its neighbor across the Potomac. The city is dense with boutiques, antiques shops, galleries, and ethnic restaurants. At the revitalized waterfront, clipper ships dock and artisans at the Torpedo Arts Factory craft and display their wares. For architecture and history buffs, the city offers a host of house museums, and Mount Vernon George Washington's Georgian estate is only 8 mi away on the banks of the Potomac.

Information: **Alexandria Convention and Visitors Association** | 221 King St., Alexandria, VA 22314 | 703/838–4200 or 800/388–9119 | www.funside.com.

Attractions

Alexandria Black History Resource Center. The center recounts the contributions of African-Americans in Alexandria and Virginia from 1749 to the present. Next door, the Watson Reading Room, a non-circulating research library, focuses on African-American history and culture. As a port town, Alexandria was one of the largest slave exportation points in the South, with at least two slave markets. | 638 N. Alfred St. | 703/838–4356 | fax 703/706–3999 | Free | Tues.–Sat. 10–4.

The Athenaeum. Built as a bank in 1851, this edifice stands in striking contrast to the neighboring Federal-style buildings. Now the gallery of the Northern Virginia Fine Arts Association, it shows the work of local, national, and international artists. | 201 Prince St. | 703/548–0035 | fax 703/768–7471 | www.funside.com/attractions | Free | Wed.–Fri. 11–3, Sun. 1–3.

Boyhood Home of Robert E. Lee. The childhood home of the commander-in-chief of the Confederate forces during the Civil War. Lee lived here from 1812 to 1816 and from 1821 to 1825. The 1795 town house, noted for its Adamsesque woodwork, contains antique furnishings and paintings. | 607 Oronoco St. | www.funside.com/attractions | $4 | Feb.–mid-Dec. Mon.–Sat. 10–4, Sun. 1–4.

Carlyle House. Considered the grandest of Alexandria's older homes, this stone Georgian was built in 1753 by Scottish merchant, John Carlyle, and modeled after the manor houses of his homeland. Gen. Edward Braddock and five colonial governors met here to plot strategy during the French and Indian War. Take one of the tours that run every half-hour and admire the Chippendale furniture and beautiful decorative items, such as the exquisite Chinese porcelain. | 121 N. Fairfax St. | 703/549–2997 | www.carlylehouse.org | $4 | Tues.–Sat. 10–4:30, Sun. noon–4:30.

Christ Church. George Washington and Robert E. Lee belonged to this church, which was completed in 1773 and remains in nearly original condition. Made of brick and stone in a country style, the church is enlivened by an elegant Palladian window and a cut-glass chandelier brought from England at Washington's expense. Services are Sunday at 8, 9, 11:15, and 5, and Wednesdays at 7:15 and 12:05. | 118 N. Washington St. | 703/549–1450 | fax 703/686–2677 | www.funside.com/attractions | $1 (suggested) | Mon.–Sat. 9–4, Sun. 2–4:30.

Fort Ward Museum and Historic Site. During the Civil War, Fort Ward helped form a defensive ring around Washington. The museum has changing exhibitions on the Civil War as well as interpretive programs and lectures throughout the year. On Thursday evenings during the summer, free concerts are held in the 45-acre park that surrounds the restored Union fort; Scottish folk music, military bands and German dance troupes are all included on the roster. Picnicking is allowed. | 4301 W. Braddock Rd. | 703/838–4848 | fax 703/671–7350 | www.ci.alexandria.va.us/oha/fortward | Free | Tues.–Sat. 9–5, Sun. noon–5 | Mon.

Friendship Firehouse. This station built in 1855 takes its name from Alexandria's first firefighting organization, founded in 1774. Within its walls are the implements of a typical 19th-century firehouse. One of the fire engines on display was bought for the company for $140 by George Washington. | 107 S. Alfred St. | 703/838–3891 | fax 703/838–4997 | www.ci.alexandria.va.us/oha/friendship | Free | Fri.–Sat. 10–4, Sun. 1–4.

Gadsby's Tavern Museum. Dating from 1770, this Georgian tavern was the center of the city's political and social life during the late 18th century. George Washington attended the Birthnight Ball here to celebrate his birthday; the Marquis de Lafayette was entertained here during his visit in 1824. The taproom, dining room, ballroom, and bedrooms have been restored to look as they did in the 1770s. Tours of the tavern leave 15 minutes before and 15 minutes after the hour. | 134 N. Royal St. | 703/838–4242 | fax 703/838–4270 | www.ci.alexandria.va.us/oha/gadsby | $4 | Oct.–Mar. Tues.–Sat. 11–4, Sun. 1–5; Apr.–Sept. Tues.–Sat. 10–5, Sun. 1–5.

George Washington Masonic National Memorial. George Washington became a Mason in 1753 and was a high-ranking Worshipful Master at the time that he served as president. This 333-ft-tall landmark contains exhibits that explain the traditions and activities of this largely secretive order, and displays the original furnishings from Lodge No. 22, to which Washington belonged. Memorabilia include a clock that was stopped at the time of his death. A ninth-floor observation deck gives a spectacular view of Alexandria, with Washington, D.C., in the distance. | 101 Callahan Dr. | 703/683–2007 | fax 703/519–9257 | www.gwmemorial.org | Free | Daily 9–5.

A BETTER FISH TRAP?

The next time you take a boat ride on the Potomac River to view the monuments or cast a reel, take a look down into the swirling waters. You might spy what seems to be a pile of stone rubble but is actually an ancient fish trap.

The Native Americans were the first to build these ingenious devices. Large stones were stacked upon one another to make a V-shape wall 3–4 ft high, with the opened end of the "V" facing upstream. Fish were swept in by the current and eventually wound up at the narrow point, where they were forced into positions from which they could not escape. They were ensnared either by brush or by a wooden device with slats, called a weir, through which the fish would drop into a collection point below. Fish were so plentiful during colonial days that they could be scooped out with ease.

When colonial settlers moved into the region, they typically claimed the neat devices for themselves. Remarkably sturdy, the traps remained intact even after torrential floods. Some of the remains seen today are ancient traps originally built by Native Americans, then repaired and built upon over hundreds of years.

When George Washington undertook to make the Potomac River navigable in the 1780s, the stone contraptions proved a severe hindrance to boats. As head of the Potowmack Company, Washington ordered his men to tear down as many of these "fish pots" as they could find.

Washington's efforts to destroy the traps weren't thoroughly successful; over the years they were rebuilt or replaced by enterprising trappers.

In the 1930s, fish-trap proprietors and sportsfishermen were at loggerheads; the sportsfishermen viewed the traps as an unfair advantage—the traps were cheating them of good catches for themselves. As the Potomac River fell under Maryland's jurisdiction, state officials there tried to end the conflict by ordering the traps removed. When the proprietors refused to cooperate, the state blew the traps out of the water with blasting powder. They are illegal now, but the bottom layers of stone still lie tenaciously in place.

© Artville

Grist Mill Historical State Park. George Washington operated this mill on Dogue Run in 1770, grinding wheat and corn into flour and meal. It was rebuilt in the 1930s by the Civilian Conservation Corps, using materials and machinery from a similar mill of the period. A film details the history of the mill and exhibits show how it operated. Replicas of machinery also are displayed. Guided tours are available. | 5514 Mount Vernon Memorial Hwy. | 703/780–3383 or 703/550–0960 | $2 | Memorial Day–Labor Day, Mon. and Thurs.–Sun. 10–6.

Gunston Hall. This 1755 brick Georgian, 20 mi southwest of Alexandria, was the residence of George Mason, a gentleman farmer and author of the Virginia Declaration of Rights. Displayed in the home are wood carvings by one of the foremost architects of the period, William Buckland. Blossoming in the formal garden are boxwoods, some of which date to the 1760s. A nature trail leads to the Potomac River. Tours leave every 30 minutes from the porch of the visitor center. Tours begin at 10, and the last tour is at 4:30. | 10709 Gunston Rd., Lorton | 703/550–9220 or 800/811–6966 | fax 703/550–9480 | www.gunstonhall.org | $5 | Daily 9:30–5.

Lee-Fendall House. Built in 1785 by a local civic leader Philip R. Fendall (cousin of "Light Horse Harry" Lee), this clapboard house was the address of several illustrious members of the Lee family; a total of 37 members of the household lived here from 1785 to 1903. The interior reflects styles from a variety of periods and includes furniture that belonged to the family. National labor leader, John L. Lewis also resided here from 1937 to 1969. | 614 Oronoco St. | 703/548–1789 | fax 703/548–0931 | www.cais.com/webweave | $4 | Tues.–Sat. 10–4, Sun. 1–4.

Lloyd House. Lloyd House was built in 1797 in the late Georgian style, and then owned by John Lloyd, whose wife, Anne Harriotte Lee, was the cousin of Robert E. Lee. Restored in 1976, it now houses part of the Alexandria Library and a collection of rare books and archival materials relating to Alexandria and Virginia history. | 220 N. Washington St. | 703/838–4577 | fax 703/706–3912 | www.cais.com/webweave | Free | Mon.–Sat. 9–5.

The Lyceum. The Lyceum, built in 1839, has served as the Alexandria Library, a Civil War hospital, a residence, and an office building; it now houses a museum dedicated to the area's history, and a gift shop. The edifice is considered one of the city's best examples of Greek Revival architecture. Self-guided tours available. | 201 S. Washington St. | 703/838–4994 | fax 703/838–4997 | www.ci.alexandria.va.us/oha/lyceum | Free | Mon.–Sat. 10–5, Sun. 1–5.

Mount Vernon. George Washington inherited Mount Vernon and the surrounding lands 8 mi directly south of Alexandria from his half-brother, Lawrence Washington, after his death in 1752. George made major additions to the Georgian mansion (the central portion of which dates from 1740) in 1759 and 1773; among his architectural achievements is a dramatic portico with a famous view across the Potomac River. He farmed the 8,000-acre plantation before taking over command of the Continental Army. The residence contains much of the original furniture, including the bed on which Washington died, his sword, and the key to the Bastille given to him by the Marquis de Lafayette. Washington and his wife are buried in a tomb near the house. The estate's dozen outbuildings have been restored and can also be toured; there are also three gardens and a hands-on, pioneer farmer exhibit with Washington's 16-sided treading barn as its centerpiece. A museum shop is located just outside the gate. | George Washington Memorial Pkwy. Box 110, Mount Vernon | 703/780–2009 | fax 703/799–8609 | www.mountvernon.org | $9 | Mar. and Sept.–Oct. daily 9–5; Apr.–Aug. daily 8–5; Nov.–Feb. daily 9–4.

Mount Vernon Trail. You can walk, jog or bike the Mount Vernon Trail, an 18½-mi trail, which follows the banks of the Potomac River from the south end of George Washington Pkwy to Theodore Roosevelt Island, an 88-acre island with a memorial dedicated to the 26th U.S. president. The path is dotted with lookout points and parks, such as the Dyke Marsh wildlife habitat and Jones Point Park, in which stands a 19th-century lighthouse. The southern section begins at Mount Vernon, George Washington's estate; the northern end starts at the pedestrian causeway leading to Theodore Roosevelt Island. A free map indicating sights along the trail is available at the Ramsay House Visitor Center at 221 King St. (703/838–4200 or 800/388–9119). | 703/285–2601 | www.funside.com | Free | Daily dawn–dusk.

Old Presbyterian Meeting House. Scottish pioneers established the meeting house in 1774, a gathering place for patriots during the American Revolution. George Washington's funeral service was held here on December 29, 1799; the Tomb of the Unknown Soldier of the American Revolution lies in a corner of the churchyard, where many prominent Alexandrians also are interred. To visit the sanctuary, obtain a key from the church office on Royal Street. Sanctuary is on S. Fairfax St. A Presbyterian congregation still holds Sunday morning services at 8:30 and 11 here. | Sanctuary, 321 S. Fairfax St., Offices, 316 S. Royal St. | 703/549–6670 | fax 703/549–9425 | www.cais.com/webweave | Free | Sanctuary open weekdays 9–5.

Pohick Bay Regional Park. This 1,000-acre park on the Pohick Bay, 20 mi south of Alexandria, has public boat access and various boat rental options (rowboats, peddleboats, and sailboats). Hiking and horseback trails, campsites, picnic shelters, an outdoor swimming pool, an 18-hole golf course, a miniature golf course. | 6501 Pohick Bay Dr., Lorton | 703/339–6104 | fax 703/339–6813 | www.nvrpa.org | $4 per vehicle, free to northern Virginia residents | Daily dawn–dusk.

Pohick Episcopal Church. George Washington and George Mason both were long-standing vestrymen at this parish church, erected in 1774. Union troops tore out much of the interior during the Civil War to create a makeshift stable; the building was fully restored in 1917. Take the Fort Belvoir exit of I–95 to the Telegraph Road exit of the Fairfax County Parkway. | 9301 Richmond Hwy., Lorton | 703/550–9449 | fax 703/339–9884 | www.pohick.org | Free | Daily 9–4:30.

Ramsay House. Believed to be the oldest house in Alexandria, the Ramsey House was built in 1724 in Dumfries (about 25 mi south of Alexandria) and moved to its present location in 1749. It was home to the city's founder and first postmaster, a Scotsman named William Ramsay. Today, it is headquarters to the Alexandria Convention and Visitors Association, where travel counselors dispense information, brochures, and maps for self-guided walking tours. You can also obtain a free 24-hour parking permit here. | 221 King St. | 703/838–4200 or 800/388–9119 | fax 703/838–4683 | www.funside.com | Free | Daily 9–5.

Stabler-Leadbeater Apothecary Museum. Apothecary memorabilia from the 18th and 19th centuries is displayed, including old account books, medical wares, and one of the finest collections of apothecary bottles in the country (some 800 in all). The museum is housed in what is believed to be Alexandria's oldest mercantile establishment, and was once patronized by George Washington and the Lee family. | 105–107 S. Fairfax St. | 703/836–3713 | www.apothecarymuseum.org | $2.50 | Mon.–Sat. 10–4, Sun. 1–5.

Torpedo Factory Arts Center. A former munitions plant (naval torpedoes were manufactured here during both world wars), the complex was converted into studios and galleries for about 150 professional artists, and became one of Alexandria's most popular attractions. Just about every art medium is represented here, from printmaking and sculpture to jewelry, pottery, stained glass, and musical instruments. The artists' workshops are open to the public, and most of what you see is for sale at reasonable prices. Artifacts from archeological excavations around Alexandria also are on exhibit. | 105 N. Union St. | 703/838–4565 or 703/838–4399 | fax 703/838–0088 | www.torpedofactory.org | Free | Daily 10–5; archaeology program Tues.–Sat. 10–3, Sun. 1–5.

Woodlawn Plantation. Originally part of the Mount Vernon estate (8 mi south of Alexandria) Woodlawn was built for George Washington's adopted daughter, Nelly Parke Custis, who married his favorite nephew, Lawrence Lewis. Completed in 1805, the riverfront mansion and its formal gardens were designed by William Thornton, a physician and amateur architect from the West Indies who drew up the original plans for the U.S. Capitol. Succeeding residents included Quaker and Baptist settlers, a playwright, and a U.S. senator. Tours are given of the 19th-century period rooms. | 9000 Richmond Hwy., Mount Vernon

| 703/780–4000 | fax 703/780–8509 | www.nthp.org/main/site/woodlawn | $6; combination ticket for Woodlawn and Pope-Leighey House $10 | Mar.–Dec. daily 10–5 | Jan.-Feb. Frank Lloyd Wright built the **Pope-Leighey House** in 1940, which was moved on to the Woodlawn Plantation from Falls Church in 1964. An example of his "Usonian" dwellings, the building was designed to be practical, economical, and organically related to its surroundings. The building also reflects Wright's belief that people of moderate means were entitled to well-designed homes, and still contains original furnishings designed by Wright. | 9000 Richmond Hwy., Mount Vernon | 703/780–4000 | $6 | Daily 10–5.

SIGHTSEEING TOURS/TOUR COMPANIES

Ghost and Graveyard Tours Sponsored by Doorways to Old Virginia. Guides dressed in 18th-century attire lead you on a walk through Old Town, describing the histories of the many 18th- and 19th-century homes that line the cobblestone streets. The tour begins at the Ramsay House Visitor Center. Group tours are by appointment all year. | 221 King St. | 703/548–0100 | www.funside.com | $6 | Apr.–Beg. Nov. tours Fri. and Sat. 7:30 and 9, Sun. 7:30 only | Dec.-Mar.

The *Matthew Hayes* and the *Admiral Tilp.* Two boats that depart from the Alexandria City Marina directly behind the Torpedo Factory Art Center. They run three different sightseeing tours: a new 50-minute trip to Mount Vernon; a 90-minute "See Washington by Water" circuit; and the 40-minute "See Alexandria by Water" cruise. The different tours have different schedules, so if have your heart set on in particular, call ahead for times. Lots of tours leave every day of the week, and a few are held on weekend evenings. The boats have snack bars for hungary tummies, and private charters are available. | Alexandria City Marina, King St. and Union St. | 703/548–9000 | $7–$22 depending on the trip.

ON THE CALENDAR

FEB.: *George Washington Birthday Celebrations.* Festivities include a George Washington Birthday Parade through Old Town Alexandria, a 10K race and 2K fun run, and the Birthnight Banquet and Ball, a black-tie dinner followed by colonial dancing at Gadsby's Tavern. A Revolutionary War encampment and reenactment are held at Fort Ward Park | 703/838–4200 or 800/388–9119.

APR., SEPT., DEC.: *House Tours.* Privately owned Old Town homes and gardens open their doors to the public. Tickets are available at Ramsay House Visitor Center. | 703/838–4200.

JUNE: *Red Cross Waterfront Festival.* Held in Oronoco Bay Park, this weekend-long celebration of the historic seaport and the Potomac River with live music, visiting ships, fireworks, children's events, and arts and crafts draws more than 80,000 visitors each year. | 703/549–8300.

JULY: *Virginia Scottish Games.* The highlights of this festival at Episcopal High School at 3901 W. Braddock Rd. are a Retreat Parade with bagpipe bands, the Baltimore Scottish Color Guard, a ceremonial artillery salute, and a Highland dancing competition with hundreds of competitors. Scottish breed dog events and an antique automobile show round out the festivities. | 703/912–1943.

SEPT.: *Crafts Fair at Mount Vernon.* More than 75 artisans demonstrate their craft and hock handmade wares at this juried, 18th-century-style crafts festival at Mount Vernon. Colonial music, entertainment, and food also draw crowds. | 703/780–2000.

NOV.–DEC.: *Mount Vernon by Candlelight.* Learn about George Washington's Christmas traditions and take a candlelight tour of his Mount Vernon estate that includes the rarely seen third floor. On the grounds, there's a bonfire and caroling with free cookies and hot cider served. | 703/780–2000.

DEC.: *Scottish Christmas Walk.* More than 100 Scottish clans in traditional tartans play bagpipes and march through the streets of Old Town Alexandria to celebrate the city's Scottish heritage. Other activities include holiday crafts workshops, children's events, and musical performances. | 703/549–0111.

Dining

Afghan Restaurant. Afghan. The parking lot on Jefferson Davis Highway is always full, with good reason. Both Afghans and Americans agree that the kebabs are super. The interior of this restaurant is carpeted with Afghan rugs, the walls are filled with pictures, and Afghan music provides a beat you can tap your foot to. Bargain lunch buffet. | 2700 Jefferson Davis Hwy. | 703/548–0022 | Reservations essential weekends | $7–$13 | AE, D, DC, MC, V.

The Alamo. Southwestern. Gas lighting and leaded-glass windows warm the already luxurious interior of this restaurant. Two dining rooms and two bars are now housed in what was once the Corn Exchange Building, dating from 1871. There's live entertainment Thursday through Sunday, and the restaurant's house band, led by the charming Audrey Fox livens up the place until 2 AM on Fridays and Saturdays. Though there is no outdoor dining, the windows open in summer to make the place light and airy. The kitchen is known for the Texas rack of ribs, steak, and chicken. | 100 King St. | 703/739–0555 | $9–$17 | AE, DC, MC, V.

Bilbo Baggins. Eclectic. "This is the kind of place hobbits would want to visit," says one of the owners. Cozy and warm, this local gathering place is housed in two old wood-and-brick row houses with stained glass and skylights. The tortellini Chardonnay, smoked duck, Thai beef salad, gnocchi, and Mediterranean grilled lamb chops are house specialties. Fresh bread and desserts are baked in the old brick oven. Children's menu, early-bird suppers, Sunday brunch. | 208 Queen St. | 703/683–0300 | $23–$28 | AE, D, DC, MC, V.

Blue Point Grill. Seafood. This small, cozy restaurant is lit by candle at night and lightened by flowers during the summer. The raw bar with its array of lobster, jumbo shrimp, oysters, and other seafood is especially popular, while the kitchen is known for cedar-plank salmon with garlic mashed potatoes. There is open-air dining on the sidewalk and on the covered red brick patio, shaded by shrubs and cooled by circulating fans. Sunday brunch. No smoking. | 600 Franklin St. | 703/739–0404 | $20–$25 | AE, MC, V.

Calvert Grille. American. Posters hang from the walls of this neighborhood *Cheers*-style bar and restaurant. Family-style food and daily lunch and dinner specials that include meatloaf with mashed potatoes, strip steak, and crab cakes. Kids' menu. Weekend brunch. | 3106 Mount Vernon Ave. | 703/836–8425 | $10–$15 | AE, D, MC, V.

Chart House. Contemporary. Large windows look out on the Potomac River, and the U.S. Capitol can be viewed from the Capitol Room upstairs. Exotic plants create a Hawaiian-style ambience that compliments the surf and turf cuisine. Appetizers and a light café menu are served on the open-air deck. Salad bar. Kids' menu. Dock space. Free parking. | 1 Cameron St. | 703/684–5080 | Reservations essential on weekends | No lunch Mon.–Sat. | $28–$50 | AE, D, DC, MC, V.

Chez Andrée. French. Three dining rooms and a delicate cuisine echo the different faces of France: one is adorned with pottery from Normandy, one is Parisian style, and one is rustic. | 10 E. Glebe Rd. | 703/836–1404 | Reservations essential Fri.–Sat. | Closed Sun. No lunch Sat. | $14–$23 | AE, D, DC, MC, V.

Clyde's at Mark Center. Seafood. If you like decoy ducks and watersports, aim for this spot. The two bars and three dining rooms are loaded with sporty paraphenalia—kayaks and sculls hung from the ceiling in the Crew Bar (the eatery's oyster bar); gun racks and the ubiquitous ducks in the Chesapeake Room. Seafood dishes stand out—crab cakes, locally farmed oysters, and Alaskan sockeye salmon—as well as ribeye steak and other meat dishes. | 1700 N Beauregard St. | 703/820–8300 | Sun. brunch | $14–$35 | AE, D, DC, MC, V.

Copeland's of New Orleans. Cajun. This smart, casual New Orleans-style restaurant has a patio for both indoor and outdoor dining. Specialties include a seafood platter and an eggplant pirot. Live jazz at Sunday brunch. No smoking. | 4300 King St. | 703/671–7997 | $15–$30 | AE, D, DC, MC, V.

East Wind. Vietnamese. Fresh flowers and greenery add to the charm of this well-worn Vietnamese restaurant. Though the wicker furniture may be fraying, the food is quite carefully prepared and arranged, and the wait staff is helpful negotiating the menu. Specialties are marinated, charbroiled shrimp and scallops on a skewer, and the bo dun (broiled beef tenderloin marinated in wine, honey and spices, rubbed and rolled in onion, and served on bamboo skewers). Take-out available. | 809 King St. | 703/836–1515 | No lunch weekends | $16–$24 | AE, D, DC, MC, V.

Ecco Cafe. Italian/American. This cozy, comfortable restaurant has both booth and table seating, and exposed brick walls. House favorites are the chicken puttanesca and spaghetti Ecco (spaghetti with Italian sausage and peppers). Live jazz during Sunday brunch. | 220 N. Lee St. | 703/684–0321 | Reservations not accepted weekends | $10–$18 | AE, D, DC, MC, V.

Elysium. Contemporary. Housed in a re-created Federal-era manor home that is now the small Morrison House Hotel, the restaurant was designed with the help of experts from the Smithsonian. Guests are greeted by a garden area with a fountain and a replica of Rodin's sculpture *Paradise Regained*. The restaurant serves three-course, fixed-price meals. The menu of new American fare changes seasonally. Sunday brunch. No smoking. Free parking. | 116 S. Alfred St. | 703/838–8000 | Closed Mon. No lunch Tues.–Sat. No dinner Sun. | $35–$55 | AE, DC, MC, V.

Faccia Luna. Italian. Shades of Tuscany—mustards, clays, and purples—hang over this popular small-chain neighborhood restaurant, accented with tile floors and framed prints of Doisneau's black-and-white photos of Paris. Faccia Luna has been the site of at least 15 marriage proposals in the last decade. Known for wood-oven pizza, handmade pastas, salads, grinders, estate-bottled Italian wines, and 30 microbrews. Open-air dining on patio. Kids' menu. No smoking. | 823 S. Washington St. | 703/838–5998 | $9–$25 | AE, MC, V.

Fish Market. Seafood. Built of Old World bricks carried as ship's ballast to America in the 1700s, this restaurant remembers its nautical roots with a variety of fresh seafood selections, clam chowder and crispy crab cakes. A pianist performs Wednesday–Saturday. Raw bar. Kids' menu. No smoking. | 105 King St. | 703/836–5676 | $10–$28 | AE, DC, MC, V.

Gadsby's Tavern. American. Strolling minstrels provide the entertainment in this 18th-century tavern-restaurant still housed in the Georgian building in which George Washington entertained the Marquis de Lafayette. Appropriately enough, the table service is in full costume and character. Specialties include game pie, venison, rabbit, and George Washington's "Favorite Duck." During the summer, fresh crabs are served in the outdoor courtyard, which also has a bar. There are weekly and daily specials, and Friday-night beer tastings. Kids' menu. Sunday brunch. No smoking. | 138 N. Royal St. | 703/548–1288 | Reservations essential Fri.–Sat. | $18–$25 | AE, DC, MC, V.

Geranio. Italian. Housed comfortably in a historic building, this restaurant has a cozy fireplace and ceramic tile floors. The menu emphasizes modern Italian cooking and fresh ingredients. The risotto, lobster, and seabass are quite popular. | 722 King St. | 703/548–0088 | No lunch weekends | $20–$28 | AE, MC, V.

Grill Room. Contemporary. The Grill Room shares space with another restaurant, Elysium, inside the Morrison House Hotel, a grand re-creation of a Federal-era manor home. Take a seat at the mahogany bar or at one of the solid wood tables with leather chairs, and settle down for the specialty crab cakes. Live jazz piano and show tunes Thursday–Saturday. | 116 S. Alfred St. | 703/838–8000 | No lunch | $16–$25 | AE, DC, MC, V.

Hard Times Cafe. American. This onetime church is now a decidedly secular chili parlor. The relaxed, dress-down dining room adorned with Great Depression memorabilia complements the Western menu, known for the "chili mac" (chili over spaghetti). Kids' menu. Beer and wine only. | 1404 King St. | 703/683–5340 | $9–$15 | AE, MC, V.

Il Porto. Italian. A renovated 18th-century marine warehouse shelters this rustic-looking restaurant, brimming with nostalgia. Colored tablecloths brighten the warm tones of wood and brick in the country-style interior. Known for the homemade pastas, primavera and fettucine Alfredo, and extensive dessert menu. Private groups can dine in upstairs rooms with great views of King and Lee streets. Kids' menu. | 121 King St. | 703/836–8833 | $12–$17 | AE, DC, MC, V.

King Street Blues Old Town. Southern. T-shirts and shorts on the wait staff set the tone for this informal eatery, with over 100 items on the menu. Look for hearty Southern specialities like pecan-encrusted catfish and glazed pork chops. The restaurant also serves its own beer: Virginia Native Gold and Road House Red. | 112 N Saint Asaph St. | 703/836–8800 | $9–$17 | AE, D, DC, MC, V.

La Bergerie. American/French. Hearty Basque dishes get the spotlight in this china-and-crystal restaurant, in Alexandria's Olde Town. Standouts include duck confit with potatoes and wild mushrooms, and rosemary scallops served over pea risotto and drizzled with truffle oil. Remember to order your dessert souffle or apple tart at the beginning of your meal. | 218 N. Lee St. | 703/683–1007 | Reservations essential Fri.–Sat. | Closed Sun. | $16–$25 | AE, D, DC, MC, V.

Landini Brothers. Italian. Keeping with its Italian roots, Landini's is a cozy, dim, noisy restaurant. Housed in a building dating from the 1790s, the eatery retains an old-time appearance with original, exposed wooden beams, slate floors, and lots of stone and brick throughout. While the menu changes with the season's bounty, summer highlights include the soft-shell crabs and veal Tonato, while the winter's centerpiece is the venison. No smoking. | 115 King St. | 703/836–8404 | Reservations essential | No lunch Sun. | $20–$30 | AE, D, DC, MC, V.

Le Gaulois. French. As soon as you enter the door of this restaurant housed in a 120-year-old brick home filled with lace curtains, fireplaces, copper pots, and china, you will feel as if you have been transported to the French countryside. A bright flower garden brightens up the restaurant during the summer. Quiche and omelets are served all day. Open-air dining. No smoking. | 1106 King St. | 703/739–9494 | Closed Sun. | $20–$30 | AE, D, DC, MC, V.

Le Refuge. French. This "French museum," as its owner calls it, is quaintly festooned with posters of cheese, wine, and French country scenes, and the Provençal cuisine is as simple and appealing as the rest of the restaurant. Highlights of the menu are the bouillabaisse and the rack of lamb. Early-bird suppers. No smoking. | 127 N. Washington St. | 703/548–4661 | Reservations essential Fri.–Sat. | Closed Sun. | $19–$25 | AE, D, DC, MC, V.

Mango Mike's. Caribbean. Jimmy Buffett playing in the background sets the scene of this tropical restaurant, and the bright murals of the beach, tropical fruits and exotic fish make up for what Jimmy Buffet's halting baritone and sliding guitar leaves to the imagination. Ribs, fresh oysters, and fresh seafood are favorites of this so-called "cool Caribbean cafe." | 4580 Duke St. | 703/823–1166 | $14–$27 | AE, D, DC, MC, V.

Mike's Italian. Italian. Mike has served neighborhood customers for more than two decades, and the menu has stayed pretty much the same the whole time. Regulars like the piccata, the cordon bleu, and the pasta. | 8368 Richmond Hwy. | 703/780–5966 | Closed Mon. No lunch Sun. | $15–$22 | AE, DC, MC, V.

Monroe's. Italian. The walls of this invitingly spacious and airy restaurant are casually hung with local artwork. The restaurant is known for its veal dishes and seafood. Open-air dining. Kids' menu. Sunday brunch. No smoking. | 1603 Commonwealth Ave. | 703/548–5792 | No lunch | $10–$15 | AE, D, MC, V.

Mount Vernon Inn. American. The hearty American colonial-style food of this restaurant just outside of the George Washington's estate is served by waiters in character and period dress. One room has a wall of windows. When it's cold, sit by one of the three crackling fireplaces. Kids' menu. | 703/780–0011 | No supper Sun. | $12–$24 | AE, D, MC, V.

Peking Duck. Chinese. Chef "Duck Chang" has reduced the 24-hour advance notice usually needed to order Peking duck down to 6 hours. The Chang family culinary tradition spans five generations. Call ahead for the Peking duck or just show up and order the firecracker shrimp or bang bang beef, and enjoy the flavorful fireworks. Lunch buffet. | 7531 Richmond Hwy. | 703/768–2774 | $10–$12 | AE, MC, V.

Red Hot and Blue. American. Ten years ago, Republican politician and moonlighting blues musician, Lee Atwater, founded this barbecue-and-rib restaurant. The original Arlington location of what is now a chain was frequented by the political "in-crowd" in its heyday, and now houses a collection of political and blues-related photographs and posters. Blues music from the 1950s and '60s plays softly in the background of the restaurant known for authentic Memphis pit-barbecue and hickory-smoked ribs. Open-air dining on a three-tiered patio. Kids' menu. | 4150 Chain Bridge Rd. | 703/218–6989 | $6–$10 | AE, D, MC, V.

RT's. American. The cozy neighborhood restaurant, known for crab cakes and crawfish étouffée, is a hop from the popular Birchmere country, blues, and jazz club. The Jack Daniels shrimp, Acadian peppered shrimp, and she-crab soup are restaurant favorites. No smoking in dining room. | 3804 Mount Vernon Ave. | 703/684–6010 | No lunch Sun. | $14–$25 | AE, D, DC, MC, V.

Santa Fe East. Southwestern. The Southwest comes east in this brick 18th-century home. Warm yourself by either of the two brick fireplaces (one gas burning and one double-sided wood burning) or if the weather is fitting, dine outside on wrought-iron tables in a brick-paved enclosed courtyard complete with a fountain. Sunday brunch. | 110 S. Pitt St. | 703/548–6900 | $17–$24 | AE, MC, V.

Scotland Yard. Scottish. The original building, built in 1792, was a tack shop and saddlery and later became an inn. Today candlelight and stuffed deer head remind you of another simpler, quieter time. The beef wellington, shepherd's pie and venison stew baked in a puff pastry are house specialties. The restaurant has a fine array of single malt whiskeys. No smoking. | 728 King St. | 703/683–1742 | Closed Mon. No lunch | $20–$28 | AE, MC, V.

Seaport Inn. Seafood. This tourist attraction, one of Old Town's first restaurants, has fireside dining and views of the Potomac River. Shrimp and scallops in wine sauce round out the menu of seafood standards. Entertainment. Kids' menu. Sunday brunch. | 6 King St. | Reservations required Fri.–Sat. | $18–$28 | AE, D, DC, MC, V.

South Austin Grill. Tex-Mex. This funky Texas roadhouse-style restaurant is filled with copper sculptures, colorful Texas stencil paintings, and posters of Austin musicians (who can be heard in the eclectic mix of background music). Try the wood-grilled fajitas or the crab-meat quesadilla or any of the 15 different homemade salsas and sauces. Kids' menu. Weekend brunch. | 801 King St. | 703/684–8969 | $15–$25 | AE, D, DC, MC, V.

Taverna Cretekou. Greek. This long-running Greek restaurant is known for its garden patio dining and lamb- and-seafood-filled menu. Choice dishes are the chicken with apricot, papaya and mango, and lamb with sundried tomatoes. Entertainment Thursdays. Sunday brunch. | 818 King St. | 703/548–8688 | Reservations essential Fri.–Sat. | Closed Mon. | $16–$25 | AE, MC, V.

Tempo. French/Italian. Housed in a former Shell station, this restaurant has a contemporary California-style design, right down to the wait staff's patterned attire. The inventive menu emphasizes seafood, lamb and veal; specialties include the linguini with lobster and the lamb chops with fresh herbs. Limited open-air dining on patio. Sunday brunch. | 4231 Duke St. | 703/370–7900 | No lunch Sat. | $13–$18 | AE, D, DC, MC, V.

Thai Hut. Thai. This modest restaurant serves authentic, spicy cuisine that highlights the area's fresh seafood. The crispy fish in black bean sauce, the Mee Krob and the Nam Sod are always crowd pleasers. | 408 S. Van Dorn St. | 703/823–5357 | $15–$20 | AE, DC, MC, V.

Union Street Public House. American. With a bar that's as busy as a Metro station at lunch hour, Union Street Public House (originally a sea captain's home–circa 1870) is a social hub for locals as well as out-of-town notables like television reporter Katie Couric, news anchor Sam Donaldson, and G. Gordon Liddy. Known for its sandwiches, the grill, and the raw bar. Family-style service. Kids' menu. Sunday brunch. No smoking. | 121 S. Union St. | 703/548–1785 | $9–$20 | AE, DC, MC, V.

Villa d'Este. Italian. Lined with murals of the Tivoli gardens near Rome, this restaurant captures something of the air of a palazzo or Roman villa. As the music of Italian and Italian-American artists from Luciano Pavarotti to Frank Sinatra sets the scene, choose from a menu that includes such classics as linguini with lobster, clams and sea scallops in marinara sauce, and veal Ferrara with mushrooms. Kid's selections on menu. No smoking. | 818 N. St. Asaph St. | 703/549–9477 | No lunch weekends | $25–$30 | AE, MC, V.

Warehouse Bar and Grill. Seafood. Eat here enough and you could get your picture on the wall. Caricatures of regulars adorn this white-tablecloth and starched-napkin restaurant, harbored in a renovated townhouse in Alexandria's Old Town. Local seafood specialties include she-crab soup and crab cakes. | 214 King St. | 703/683–6868 | Breakfast on Sat. | $12–$22 | AE, D, DC, MC, V.

The Wharf. Seafood. Images of the Chesapeake Bay thematically link two dining rooms with otherwise drastically different personalities: downstairs is rustic, with exposed old wood; upstairs is white-tablecloth formal. Papier-mâché creations by local artist, Brian McCall, brighten both rooms. The cashew-crusted crawfish, and Chilean sea bass with black bean and sun-dried tomato are the innovative side of the menu that is as versatile as it classic. Kids' menu. Sunday brunch. | 119 King St. | 703/836–2836 | $15–$25 | AE, D, DC, MC, V.

Lodging

Alexandria Suites. Choose from studios, one-, and two-bedroom units, all with full kitchens. Though designed for corporate travelers, it's also a comfortable option for families. Take Exit 3A off I–395. Complimentary breakfast. Kitchenettes, microwaves, refrigerators, cable TV. Pool. Gym. Laundry facilities, laundry service. Business services, free parking. Pets allowed. | 420 N Van Dorn St. | 703/370–1000 or 800/368–3339 | fax 703/370–1000 | alexandriasuites@erols.com | www.alexandriasuites.com | 185 suites | $89–$173 | AE, D, DC, MC, V.

Alexandria Travelodge. A convenient choice if you're traveling in or out of Reagan National Airport, this two-story chain, renovated in 1999, is 1½ mi south of the airport. In-room data ports, some microwaves, some refrigerators, cable TV. Pets allowed. | 700 N Washington St. | 703/836–5100 | fax 703/519–7015 | 40 rooms | $55–$95 | AE, D, MC, V.

Almost Heaven Bed and Breakfast. Opened in 2000, this four-story, Colonial-style bed and breakfast is within walking distance to Old Town and the Metro. For elegance, check out the Victorian Room, accented with period furniture. Feeling sporty? Try the Paradise and Seclusion Room, with game tables for foosball, air-hockey, and pool, as well as a wet bar. Complimentary breakfast (weekends). Some microwaves, some refrigerators, cable TV, in-room VCRs. Pool. Hot tub, sauna. Bicycles free to guests. Library. Free parking. No pets. No smoking. | 6339 Brocketts Crossing | 703/921–9043 or 703/856–2355 | fax 703/783–0683 | cthorneclark@yahoo.com | 3 rooms | $79–$100 | AE, MC, V.

Best Western Mount Vernon. This four-story prefabricated, commercial chain hotel has reasonable rooms done in a green and burgundy scheme, and services and amenities common to most Best Westerns. Complimentary Continental breakfast. Some microwaves, cable TV. Exercise equipment. Business services. Free parking. | 8751 Richmond Hwy. | 703/360–1300 | fax 703/779–7713 | www.bestwestern.com/mtvernonalexandria | 84 rooms | $75–$77 | AE, D, DC, MC, V.

Best Western Old Colony Inn. The only thing "old colony" about this Best Western is its location not far from Alexandria's Old Town. The courtyard rooms are bright and have pleasant views. Complimentary Continental breakfast. In-room data ports, cable TV. Pool. Business services. Airport shuttle. Free parking. Some pets allowed (fee). | 615 1st St. | 703/739–2222 | fax 703/549–2568 | www.bestwestern.com | 151 rooms | $90–$105 | AE, D, DC, MC, V.

Bragg Towers. Choose from efficiency, one-, and two-bedroom kitchenette units in this 10-story hotel, just north of I–395 and west of the Landmark Shopping Center. Kitchenettes, microwaves, refrigerators, cable TV. No pets. | 99 S Bragg St. | 703/354–6300 | fax 703/354–6300 | 98 suites | $61–$80 | AE, D, DC, MC, V.

Comfort Inn Gunston Corner. Five miles south of Mount Vernon (Exit 163, I–95), this motor lodge is in a quiet, residential neighborhood close to Grist Mill Historical Park. Rooms face the pool and residential neighborhood. Complimentary Continental breakfast. Cable TV. Pool. Business services. Some pets allowed (fee). | 8180 Silverbrook Rd., Lorton | 703/643–3100 | fax 703/643–3175 | www.ci.gunstun.com | 129 rooms | $80–$90 | AE, D, DC, MC, V.

Comfort Inn–Mt. Vernon. This two-floor, suburban Comfort Inn is just off of Capital Beltway, that mammoth-laned expressway that zips Washington-area commuters from home to work (when they're not sitting in traffic). Rooms are predictably characterless. Complimentary Continental breakfast. In-room data ports, microwaves, cable TV. Pool. Business services. Free parking. Some pets allowed. | 7212 Richmond Hwy./U.S. 1 | 703/765–9000 | fax 703/765–2325 | www.comfortinn.com | 92 rooms | $65–$85 | AE, D, DC, MC, V.

Comfort Inn–Landmark. This modern Comfort Inn is 5 mi from Old Town Alexandria and 7 mi from Washington D.C. and is close to an International House of Pancakes. Rooms are simple and bright. Restaurant, complimentary Continental breakfast. In-room data ports, cable TV. Pool. Business services. Free parking. | 6254 Duke St. | 703/642–3422 | fax 703/642–1354 | www.comfortinn.com | 148 rooms | $80 | AE, D, DC, MC, V.

Courtyard by Marriott. This eight-floor Marriott off I–395 has spacious rooms with sitting areas and courtyard views. Restaurant, bar. Some microwaves, refrigerators, room service, cable TV. Exercise equipment. Business services. Free parking. | 2700 Eisenhower Ave. | 703/329–2323 | fax 703/329–6853 | www.courtyard.com | 176 rooms | $113–$125 | AE, D, DC, MC, V.

Doubletree Guest Suites. Five miles from Old Town, this all-suite hotel is a converted apartment complex in a residential area near the Metro and shopping at Landmark Mall. Rooms view the Potomac and courtyard. Restaurant, bar, complimentary Continental breakfast. In-room data ports, kitchenettes, microwaves, cable TV. Pool. Exercise equipment. Laundry facilities. Business services. Pets allowed (fee). | 100 S. Reynolds St. | 703/370–9600 | fax 703/370–0467 | www.doubletreehotels.com | 225 suites | $109–$119 | AE, D, DC, MC, V.

Econo Lodge Old Town. In the heart of Old Town, the budget choice is close to historical sites, shopping, and dining. The motel is housed in a multileveled stone building in a more commercial area of Old Town. Cable TV. Business services. Airport shuttle. Some pets allowed. | 700 N. Washington St. | 703/836–5100 | fax 703/519–7015 | www.choicehotels.com | 39 rooms | $65 | AE, D, DC, MC, V.

Embassy Suites Old Town Alexandria. This large chain hotel is a good choice if you want to sightsee in nearby Washington, D.C.: it's less than 100 yards from the Metro station. It's also adjacent to the George Washington Masonic National Memorial. Inside the hotel, lush greenery drapes the spacious atrium, trimming indoor fountains and the gazebo where breakfast and complimentary evening cocktails are served. Restaurant. In-room data ports, refrigerators, cable TV. Pool. Hot tub, sauna. Gym. Laundry service. Business services. No pets. | 1900 Diagonal Rd. | 703/684–5900 | fax 703/684–1403 | 268 suites | $189–$204 | AE, D, DC, MC, V.

Executive Club Suites. This all-suites, luxury complex on the north end of Old Town Alexandria has apartment-style units, furnished with rich Queen Anne reproductions and complete with cookware and dinnerware in the kitchenettes. Picnic area, complimentary Continental breakfast. In-room data ports, kitchenettes, microwaves, cable TV. Exercise equipment, gym, health club, sauna. Pool. Laundry facilities. Business services. Airport shuttle. Parking (fee). Some pets allowed. | 610 Bashford La. | 703/739–2582 or 800/535–2582 | fax 703/548–0266 | www.dcexeclub.com | 78 suites | $179–$199 | AE, D, DC, MC, V.

Hampton Inn. This typical chain accommodation, housed in a stone building bordered by shrubbery, is conveniently located close to the interstate. Complimentary Continental breakfast. In-room data ports, cable TV. Pool. Exercise equipment. Business services. Free parking. | 4800 Leesburg Pike | 703/671–4800 | fax 703/671–2442 | www.hampton-inn.com | 130 rooms | $110 | AE, D, DC, MC, V.

Hampton Inn–Olde Towne. This chain hotel in a bland stone multiple-level building is convenient to both I–95 and 395. Rooms are comfortable and bright. Restaurant, bar. In-room data ports, room service, some in-room hot tubs, cable TV. Indoor pool. Beauty salon. Exercise equipment. Business services. Airport shuttle. Free parking. Some pets allowed. | 5821 Richmond Hwy./U.S. 1 | 703/329–1400 | fax 703/329–1424 | www.hojo.com | 156 rooms | $99–$109 | AE, D, DC, MC, V.

Hilton Alexandria. Formerly the Radisson Plaza at Mark Center, this luxury hotel off of I–395 has panoramic views of the Washington monuments, a towering glass atrium, and imported Italian marble. The property is surrounded by a man-made lake and 80 acres of woods. Reagan National Airport is 10 minutes away. Restaurant, bars (with entertainment). In-room data ports, refrigerators in some rooms, cable TV. Indoor-outdoor pool. Barbershop, beauty salon, hot tub. Tennis. Exercise equipment, racquetball. Video Games. Business services. Airport shuttle. | 5000 Seminary Rd. | 703/845–1010 | fax 703/845–7662 | www.gardeninn.com/hotels/DCAAHHH | 495 rooms | $99–$179 | AE, D, DC, MC, V.

Hilton Alexandria Olde Town. Walk into the Italian-marble-adorned lobby, and you'll get the idea that this isn't your typical chain hotel. The seven-story establishment, opened in 2000, doesn't hold back on the lush appointments or the amenities. It's also conveniently located next to the King Street Metro Station, so it's a quick hop to area attractions and Reagan National Airport. Restaurant, bar, room service. In-room data ports, in-room safes, minibars, cable TV. Pool. Gym. Laundry service. Business services. No pets. | 1767 King St. | 703/837–0440 | fax 703/837–0454 | 241 rooms | $149–$329, Presidential Suite is $699 | AE, D, DC, MC, V.

Holiday Inn Eisenhower Metro. The high-rise hotel is next door to the Metro and convenient to Mount Vernon. Restaurant, bar with entertainment. In-room data ports, cable TV. Indoor pool. Exercise equipment. Game room. Laundry facilities. Business services. Airport shuttle. | 2460 Eisenhower Ave. | 703/960–3400 | fax 703/329–0953 | moli@erols.com | www.holiday-inn.com | 197 rooms | $87–$113 | AE, D, DC, MC, V.

Holiday Inn Hotel and Suites–Historic District. This modern brick Holiday Inn is in the heart of Old Town Alexandria, five blocks from the waterfront. Bar with entertainment. In-room data ports, cable TV. Indoor-outdoor pool. Hot tub. Gym. Laundry facilities. Business services. Airport shuttle. | 625 1st St. | 703/548–6300 | fax 703/548–8032 or 887/732–3318 | www.holiday-inn.com | 178 rooms | $129–$199 suites | AE, D, DC, MC, V.

Holiday Inn Select Old Town. This high-end Holiday Inn is across the street from Alexandria's town hall in the Old Town and is convenient walking distance to the Metro and the waterfront. The lobby is elegantly put-together in mahogany with chandelier lighting. Rooms are colonial-themed with a long list of amenities. Every Sunday there is a colorful market on the town square across the street. Restaurant, bars, complimentary Continental breakfast. In-room data ports, in-room safes, some in-room kitchenettes, minibars, microwaves, cable TV, some in-room VCRs. Indoor pool. Barbershop, beauty salon. Exercise equipment. Laundry facilities. Business services. Airport shuttle. Some pets allowed. | 480 King St. | 703/549–6080 or 800/368–5047 | fax 703/684–6508 | othismta@erols.com | www.hiselect.com | 227 rooms | $169–$190 | AE, D, DC, MC, V.

Homewood Suites. This comfortably modern facility is within walking distance of shopping at the Skyline Mall. Suites have large windows, neutral colored walls, and warm wood furnishings. Complimentary Continental breakfast. Kitchenettes, cable TV. Pool. Hot tub. Exercise equipment. Laundry facilities. Business services. Free parking. | 4850 Leesburg Pike | 703/671–6500 | fax 703/671–9322 | www.homewood-suites.com | 105 suites | $139 | AE, D, DC, MC, V.

Morrison House. This small hotel has rooms beautifully furnished with authentic Federal Period reproductions and marble bathrooms complete with hair dryers and terry cloth bathrobes. Tapestries and Persian rugs warm the sometimes cold marble floors, and an attentive staff makes sure your stay is as equally warm. Bar with entertainment, dining room. In-room data ports, room service, cable TV. Business services. | 116 S. Alfred St. | 703/838–8000 or 800/367–0800 | fax 703/684–6283 | www.morrissonhouse.com | 45 rooms | $150–$295 | AE, DC, MC, V.

Radisson Hotel–Old Town. Convenient to monuments and museums, the 12-floor high-rise has rooms with gorgeous views of the low-slung Washington D.C. skyline. Rooms are conservative in darker-hued colors. Restaurant, bar. In-room data ports, microwaves, cable TV. Pool. Business services. Airport shuttle. Some pets allowed. | 901 N. Fairfax St. | 703/683–6000 | fax 703/683–7597 | www.ramada.com | 253 rooms | $159–$249 | AE, D, DC, MC, V.

Red Roof Inn. This three-floor motor lodge with exterior corridors is less than a mile from the Capital Beltway, the traffic artery that encircles Washington. Rooms are simply furnished in conservative colors. In-room data ports, cable TV. Laundry facilities. Business services. Free parking. Some pets allowed. | 5975 Richmond Hwy./U.S. 1 | 703/960–5200 | fax 703/960–5209 | www.redroofinn.com | 115 rooms | $59–$79 | AE, D, DC, MC, V.

Sheraton Suites. In the heart of Old Town, the distinctive U-shaped, 10-floor building that houses this hotel is high enough that the upper rooms have decent views of the stunted Washington skyline. Rooms are bright with prominent windows. Restaurant, bar, complimentary Continental breakfast. In-room data ports, refrigerators, cable TV. Indoor pool. Hot tub. Exercise equipment. Business services. Airport shuttle. Some pets allowed. | 801 N. St. Asaph St. | 703/836–4700 | fax 703/548–4514 | www.ittsheraton.com | 247 suites | $99–$139 | AE, D, DC, MC, V.

Travelers Motel. This one-floor plain-jane motel has old-fashioned exterior entrances to all the rooms. Neutral-to-dark colors abound in this prefabricated-but-comfortable commercial accommodation. Near the Potomac River. Cable TV. Pool. Business services. | 5916 Richmond Hwy./U.S. 1 | 703/329–1310 or 800/368–7378 | fax 703/960–9211 | 30 rooms | $59–$79 | AE, D, DC, MC, V.

ARLINGTON

MAP 11, I4

(Nearby towns also listed: Alexandria, Falls Church, McLean, Springfield)

The Virginia suburb of Arlington County was carved out of Virginia and given to the federal government to help create the District of Columbia in 1791. The area was given back to Virginia (along with the rest of the land west of the Potomac River) in 1845 and was considered part of Alexandria until 1920, when it became its own county.

Named after the Custis family mansion (the home of Robert E. Lee), Arlington was an agrarian community until World War I. It then evolved into an urban center and is now dominated by large corporations, Department of Defense buildings, a bevy of upscale shopping malls, and Reagan National Airport. Connected to Washington, D.C. by four bridges, Arlington functions largely as a satellite of the capital. Its major attractions are linked to the armed forces: Arlington National Cemetery, the U.S. Marine Corps Memorial, and the Pentagon.

Information: Arlington Convention and Visitors Service | 2100 Clarendon Blvd., Suite 318, Arlington, VA 22201 | 703/358–3988 | arlcvb@us.net | www.stayarlington.com.

Attractions

Arlington National Cemetery. Some 250,000 fallen soldiers as well as many notable Americans (among them, Presidents William H. Taft and John F. Kennedy, General John Pershing and Admiral Robert E. Peary) are interred at Arlington National Cemetery, which was established as the nation's cemetery in 1864. Made up of 612 acres directly across the Potomac

River from Washington, D.C. the cemetery's rolling hills are covered with almost endless rows of simple white uniform markers. Dozens of funeral ceremonies are held here on any given day, each accompanied by a gun salute and the playing of taps. At the end of Crook Walk is the Tomb of the Unknowns, where the remains of unknown servicemen from both world wars and the Korean conflict are buried. The white marble Memorial Amphitheater honors those who have defended the nation and is the site for Memorial Day services and other ceremonies. Decorations awarded to unknown soldiers by the United States, foreign governments and other organizations are displayed in a trophy room inside. There's a 40-minute bus tour of the cemetery; tickets are available at the visitor center. | www.arlingtoncementery.org | Sept 29–March 31 Daily 8–5; April 1–Sept. 30 5–7.

Overlooking the rolling hills of white markers, between Lee and Sherman Drives, **Arlington House, the Robert E. Lee Memorial** is a Greek Revival-style mansion built between 1812 and 1817, by George Washington Parke Custis, grandson of Martha Washington, 140 years before the establishment of the national cemetery. After his death, the 1,100-acre estate went to his daughter, Mary Anna Randolph Custis. In 1831, she married Robert E. Lee, and the family lived here for the next 30 years. In 1861, Lee resigned his commission in the U.S Army to defend his native Virginia, and Union troops took over the estate, making it headquarters for the officers charged with defending Washington. The government confiscated the property in 1862 for nonpayment of taxes, and the Lees never returned. The house has been restored to its 1861 appearance and contains possessions once owned by the Custises and the Lees; the view of Washington from the front is outstanding. | 703/557–0613 | www.nps.gov | Free | Daily 9:30–4:30.

On the western end of Memorial Bridge, **U.S. Marine Corps War Memorial/Iwo Jima Statue** is based on John Rosenthal's Pulitzer Prize-winning photograph of five marines and a navy corpsman raising a flag atop Mount Suribachi on Iwo Jima on Feb. 19, 1945. Sculpted in bronze by Felix W. de Weldon, the 78-ft-high memorial is the site of Marine Corps sunset dress parades on Tuesday evenings, May through August. | Marshall Dr. | 703/228–3988 or 800/667–6267 | Free | Daily.

Next to the Iwo Jima Memorial on Marshall Drive is **Netherlands Carillon.** This bell tower was a gift from the Dutch government in appreciation of U.S. aid during World War II. | Marshall Dr. | Free | Daily.

Drug Enforcement Agency Museum. Chronologically arranged exhibits illustrate the history of drug abuse and legal efforts to curb it. The museum includes mock-facades of a 1930s drugstore, a 1970s head shop, and a 1980s crack den. | 700 Army Navy Dr. | 202/307–3463 | Free | Tues.–Fri. 10–4, by appointment only.

The Newseum. Opened in 1997, the Newseum is the first such venue dedicated exclusively to the news business. Memorabilia include Ernie Pyle's typewriter and Columbus's letter to Queen Isabella about discovering the New World. Hands-on exhibits allow you to try your hand at reporting, anchoring TV news, or delivering radio broadcasts. | 1101 Wilson Blvd. | 888/639–7386 or 703/284–3700 | fax 703/284–3770 | www.newseum.org | Free | Tues.–Sun. 10–5.

Freedom Park. Adjoining the Newseum, the one-and-a-half-acre Freedom Park features icons that symbolize the struggle for freedom, including a fallen, headless statue of Vladimir Lenin and sections of the Berlin Wall. A memorial is dedicated to some 1,000 journalists who have died in the line of duty. | 1101 Wilson Blvd. | 703/284–3725 | Free | Daily dawn–dusk.

The Pentagon. Headquarters for the U.S. Department of Defense, the Pentagon is the world's largest office building. Completed in 1943, it consists of five concentric buildings (3.7 million square ft), connected by 17½ mi of corridors, through which 23,000 military and civilian personnel pass each day. A 90-minute tour takes you down hallways lined with portraits of military leaders, scale models of air force planes and navy ships, and through the Hall of Heroes, where the names of all the Medal of Honor winners are inscribed. | 703/695–1776 | fax 703/614–1642 | www.dtic.mil/pentagontours | Free; photo ID required | Weekday tours every hour 9–3.

The Fashion Centre at Pentagon City. This mall has 150 stores, including Macy's and Nordstrom's, on three levels, a food court, and cinemas. | 1100 S. Hayes St. | 703/415–2130 | Mon.–Sat. 10–9:30, Sun. 11–6.

ON THE CALENDAR

MAY: *Memorial Day Service.* The president of the United States, or his representative, lays a wreath on the Tomb of the Unknown Soldier during this annual service. | 202/685–2851.

AUG.: *Arlington County Fair.* There are pony rides, carnival attractions, midway rides, food, exhibits, and live entertainment at the Thomas Jefferson Community Center, 3501 S. 2nd St. The local police, fire, and rescue departments give demonstrations. | 703/358–6400.

OCT.: *Marine Corps Marathon.* Starting from the Iwo Jima Monument near the Arlington Memorial Bridge, this 26-mi footrace winds its way across the Potomac and through the nation's capital, earning it the nickname of "Marathon of the Monuments." | 800/RUN–USMC | www.marinemarathon.com/index.html.

Dining

Alpine. Italian. This rustic, 5-room restaurant has had 34 years in business under the same ownership. The dining room is dimly lit by lamp centerpieces on all the tables. The solid Italian fare is highlighted by the pasta, veal, and fish. | 4770 Lee Hwy. | 703/528–7600 | Reservations essential Fri.–Sat. | $20–$25 | AE, DC, MC, V.

Bistro Bistro. Contemporary. This casual neighborhood bistro and bar is light and airy with flower centerpieces and renaissance-style art adorning the walls. At night, the place gets a bit more intimate with lots of candlelight. Friendly servers tend to know the locals, who stop by after work. Known for oyster stew, turkey chili, and veal meat loaf. Open-air dining on a smart outdoor patio under a canopy. Jazz guitarist for Sunday brunch. | 4021 S. 28th St. | 703/379–0300 | $22–$30 | AE, DC, MC, V.

Café Dalat. Vietnamese. In Arlington's Little Saigon neighborhood, this restaurant, a good budget choice for Vietnamese-food lovers, serves simple, lightly seasoned (but flavorful) grilled meat and seafood. The sweet-soy marinated pork and skewered seafood are house specialties. No smoking. Close to the Metro. | 3143 Wilson Blvd. | 703/276–0935 | $4–$9 | MC, V.

Carlyle Grand Cafe. Contemporary. The stylish restaurant offers two kinds of dining on two floors. Lively paintings spice up the interior of both dining rooms. Eat a light supper downstairs, or go upstairs for longer lunches and dinner. The daily seafood specials include soft-shell crabs in summer, and the rest of the year, the Virginia trout, baby-back ribs and smoked salmon filet are house favorites. Open-air dining on patio. Sunday brunch. No smoking. | 4000 S. 28th St. | 703/931–0777 | No lunch Sat. upstairs | $12–$30 | AE, MC, V.

Cowboy Cafe. American. Celebrating western cowboy culture, this casual family restaurant, serving cold beer and a meat and potatoes menu, is filled with cowboy artwork, cactus motifs, and western license plates. Acoustic rock-and-roll livens up the place on Thursdays, Fridays, and Saturdays. Open-air dining on screened-in sun porch. No-smoking section. | 2421 Columbia Pike | 703/243–8010 | Breakfast also available weekends | $13–$23 | AE, D, DC, MC, V.

Faccia Luna. Italian. One of a very popular small chain of restaurants in the Washington metropolitan area, this small branch is known for its wood-oven pizza, estate-bottled Italian wines and microbrews. Homemade pastas and sauces round out the largely Tuscan menu. The interior of this neighborhood restaurant is seasoned with terra-cotta, earth tones, and eggplant colors. Open-air sidewalk dining. Kids' menu. No smoking. | 2909 Wilson Blvd. | 703/276–3099 | $10–$15 | AE, MC, V.

The Grill. Contemporary. This plush restaurant has the rarified air of an old-style, English gentlemen's club. Oak wood paneling, oil paintings, sculpture, and a working fireplace define the interior, while the contemporary American cuisine is infused with the flavors of Scandinavia and France. Known for smoked gravlax, sirloin steaks, seasonal fish entrées, and a three-poached-egg appetizer with caviar and salmon. Pianist weekend evenings. Jazz trio during Sunday brunch. Kids' menu. | 1250 S. Hayes St. | 703/412–2760 | $28–$38 | AE, D, DC, MC, V.

JW's Steakhouse. American. For almost 30 years this restaurant has been on the 14th floor of the Key Bridge Marriott and its spectacular panorama of the D.C. skyline is a major draw for guests. Every table has a sparkling view of the major monuments, Georgetown, the Key Bridge, and Rosslyn. Besides the dining room there is a 50-seat oak bar decorated with dark woods and rich colors. The restaurant hosts special dinner events on major holidays (call early for information and reservations). Known for Certified-Angus beef steaks, seafood and soufflés baked to order. Guitarist plays light jazz-pop music weekends. Kids' menu. Sunday champagne brunch buffet. No smoking. | 1401 Lee Hwy. | 703/284–1407 | Business attire | No lunch Mon.–Sun. | $30–$50 | AE, D, DC, MC, V.

Kabul Caravan. Afghan. Dine outside, at one of only seven intimate tables on a front patio surrounded with wildflowers, or inside in a dining room of flickering candles and exotic Afghan decor. Either way, it's romantic. The kitchen is known for the lamb, Afghan-style pasta, and the vegetarian dishes. No smoking. | 1725 Wilson Blvd. | 703/522–8394 | No lunch weekends | $11–$18 | AE, MC, V.

La Cote D'Or Cafe. French. Provençal antiques and artwork adorn the glassed-in dining room of this restaurant. Rack of lamb and sole Mouliniere are the pick of this classic southern French menu. Early-bird suppers. Sunday brunch. No smoking. | 6876 Lee Hwy. | 703/538–3033 | No supper Sun. | $20–$32 | AE, DC, MC, D, V.

Lebanese Taverna. Lebanese. This homey restaurant with large windows is frequented by D.C. politicians and celebrities. Crowd-pleasers are the chicken shawarma, lamb kabob or sharhat ghanam. No smoking. | 5900 Washington Blvd. | 703/241–8681 | Reservations not accepted Fri.–Sun. | No lunch Sun. | $8–$16 | AE, DC, MC, V, D.

Little Viet Garden. Vietnamese. Dine in a tropical oasis in the midst of the concrete of the city. As you sit in the lounge-like interior surrounded by sheltering palm trees and plants, focus your attention from the decor to the menu that includes a tasty seafood combo special (fresh vegetables stir-fried with shrimp, scallops and squid) and the long-cooked claypot specialties in caramel sauces. Open-air cafe in the back. | 3012 Wilson Blvd. | 703/522–9686 | $15–$20 | AE, D, DC, MC, V.

Matuba. Japanese. This informal dining spot with a traditional Japanese interior (complete with Japanese paper lamps on the walls) has combo platters perfect for those who want to experiment. The chefs at the grill and adjacent sushi bar prepare sashimi and tempura in front of your eyes. | 2915 Columbia Pike | 703/521–2811 | No lunch weekends | $7–$11 | AE, MC, V.

Pasha Cafe. Middle Eastern. While the dining room is typically Middle Eastern, the menu has Egyptian dishes you won't see elsewhere. Specialties include the fetta del lahma. | 2109 N. Pollard St. | 703/528–2126 | No lunch Sun. | $15–$20 | AE, D, DC, MC, V.

Queen Bee. Vietnamese. One of the first restaurants to open in the "Little Saigon" neighborhood, Queen Bee's reputation and extensive menu is reknowned in the Washington area. The one-room dining space is quite simple and casual. Barbecue pork and the beef soup are local favorites. No smoking. | 3181 Wilson Blvd. | 703/527–3444 | $5–$10 | AE, MC, V, D.

Red Hot and Blue. American. One of a chain of eateries founded 10 years ago by Republican politician and moonlighting blues musician Lee Atwater. A soundtrack of blues music sets the scene for a menu known for its barbecue and hickory-smoked ribs. Kids' menu. | 1600 Wilson Blvd. | 703/276–7427 | $6–$10 | AE, D, MC, V.

When it Comes to Getting Cash at an ATM, Same Thing.

Whether you're in Yosemite or Yemen, using your Visa® card or ATM card with the PLUS symbol is the easiest and most convenient way to get cash. Even if your bank is in Minneapolis and you're in Miami, Visa/PLUS ATMs make getting cash so easy, you'll feel right at home. After all, Visa/PLUS ATMs are open 24 hours a day, 7 days a week, rain or shine. And if you need help finding one of Visa's 627,000 ATMs in 127 countries worldwide, visit **visa.com/pd/atm**. We'll make finding an ATM as easy as finding the Eiffel Tower, the Pyramids or even the Grand Canyon.

It's Everywhere You Want To Be®

It's time to PowerShop

PowerShopping means finding everything you want, all under one roof. For less than you expected to spend. And enjoying every minute of it.

Over 220 stores including:
Off 5th-Saks Fifth Avenue Outlet
- **Bally Outlet** • **Nordstrom Rack**
- **SYMS** • **Royal Doulton Outlet**
- **The Donna Karan Company Store**
- **JCPenney Outlet** • **Lenox** • **IKEA**
- **Fragrance Outlet** • **OshKosh B'Gosh**

...Plus 25 eateries and a 15 screen cinema!

Exit 156 off I-95
12 miles South of Washington, DC Capital Beltway

1-800-VA-Mills
www.potomacmills.com

For Metro shuttle schedules, call (703) 551-1050.
Special incentives for groups.

Red Hot and Blue–Express Location. American. This is the carry-out branch of the original restaurant known for its barbecue and hickory-smoked ribs. | 3014 Wilson Blvd. | 703/243–1510 | $6–$10 | AE, D, MC, V.

RT's Seafood Kitchen. Cajun. The colorful, upbeat dining room of this restaurant has walls hung with hand-painted pictures of hot sauces and beer bottles, and life-size papier-mâché mermaids and alligators. Known for Cajun-style seafood. Enclosed dining patio with views of an adjacent fountain. Kids' menu. | 2300 Clarendon Blvd. | 703/841–0100 | No lunch Sun. | $6–$23 | AE, D, DC, MC, V.

Tivoli. Italian. This continental-Italian restaurant directly above the Rossyln Metro station is quiet, contemporary and semiformal with paneled and mirrored walls. Napkin fans and flower vases decorate the tables. The menu invites languorous long dining and includes such classic Italian favorites as rissotto, steak with peppercorns, cognac and cream, and veal Oscar (veal tenderloin with crab meat and hollandaise). | 1700 N. Moore St. | 703/524–8900 | Reservations essential Fri.–Sat. | Closed Sun. No lunch Sat. | $18–$25 | AE, D, DC, MC, V.

Tom Sarris' Orleans House. American. Step inside the columned entrance of what seems to be a grand southern plantation home and you have actually entered the three-level Orleans House, whose interior is equal parts New Orleans and medieval European castle. Fountains, chandeliers, marble flooring, gilt-edged pictures, and suits of armor lend the dining rooms an exotic air of luxury and history. The centerpiece of the menu is the prime rib of beef. Salad bar. Kids' menu. No smoking. | 1213 Wilson Blvd. | 703/524–2929 | No lunch weekends | $13–$20 | AE, D, DC, MC, V.

Village Bistro. Continental. A healthy list of seasonal and daily specials competes with the regular menu at this popular neighborhood restaurant, housed in a fraying strip mall along Wilson Boulevard. The house specialties are the seafood served in delicate sauces that echo both western and non-western flavors. | 1723 Wilson Blvd. | 703/522–0284 | No lunch weekends | $21–$34 | AE, D, DC, MC, V.

Woo Lae Oak. Korean. This quiet Korean restaurant with branches in Los Angeles, New York and Seoul is a hit with critics and the local Korean community alike. Thirteen different types of barbecue and the chap chae (clear vermicelli noodles tossed with shredded beef and crispy vegetables) are specialties of the chef and favorites of the wait staff. | 1500 S. Joyce St. | 703/521–3706 | $13–$20 | AE, MC, V.

Lodging

Best Western Key Bridge. A half-block from the Rosslyn Metro station, this hotel, housed in a high-rise building is walking distance to Georgetown and only a short Metro ride away from Washington, D.C.'s numerous museums and cultural attractions. Restaurant. Some microwaves, cable TV. Pool. Exercise equipment. Business services. Some pets allowed. | 1850 N. Fort Myer Dr. | 703/522–0400 | fax 703/524–5275 | www.bestwestern.com | 178 rooms | $139 | AE, D, DC, MC, V.

Best Western Pentagon. This two-story lodging, made up of three buildings next to the Sheraton Four Points Hotel, is a straightforward option, with exterior corridors accessing basic rooms. In-room safes, cable TV. Pool. Gym. Laundry service. Business services, free shuttle. No pets. | 2480 S. Glebe Rd. | 703/979–4400 | fax 703/685–0051 | 205 rooms | $80–$130 | AE, D, DC, MC, V.

Comfort Inn Ballston. Three blocks from the Metro, this multilevel hotel is clothed in neutral stone colors, and has simple and sufficient rooms. Restaurant, bar, complimentary Continental breakfast. In-room data ports, room service, cable TV. Business services. Free parking. | 1211 N. Glebe Rd. | 703/247–3399 | fax 703/524–8739 | www.comfortinn.com | 126 rooms | $69–$120 | AE, D, DC, MC, V.

Courtyard by Marriott. Three blocks from the Rosslyn Metro station, this 10-floor Marriott has spacious, comfortable rooms, furnished conservatively. Restaurant, bar. Some microwaves, room service, cable TV. Indoor pool. Hot tub. Exercise equipment. Laundry facilities. Business services. Free parking. | 1533 Clarendon Blvd. | 703/528–2222 | fax 703/528–1027 | www.courtyard.com | 162 rooms, 18 suites | $139–$179 | AE, D, DC, MC, V.

Courtyard by Marriott. This fourteen-floor, high-rise hotel, in the commercial Crystal City area, is close to Reagan National Airport. Rooms have luxurious amenities and large windows. Restaurant, bar, room service. In-room data ports, in-room safes, some mini-bars, cable TV. Indoor pool. Hot tub. Exercise equipment. Laundry facilities. Business services. Airport shuttle. Free parking. | 2899 Jefferson Davis Hwy./U.S. 1 | 703/549–3434 | fax 703/549–7440 | www.courtyard.com | 268 rooms | $99–$179 | AE, D, DC, MC, V.

Crowne Plaza Washington National Airport. Less than ½ mi north of Reagan National Airport (it's actually next door), this 12-story hotel gets the nod for convenience. It's also only a block and a half south of the Crystal City Metro station. Renovated in late 1999, the hotel now has ultra-modern amenities like a complimentary computer in the lobby, plus three dining options: two dining rooms (one formal, one casual), and a deli. 3 restaurants, room service. In-room data ports, some refrigerators, cable TV. Pool. Gym. Shops. Laundry service. Business services, airport shuttle. No pets. | 1489 Jefferson Davies Hwy. | 703/416–1600 | fax 703/416–1615 | 308 rooms | $139–$289 | AE, D, DC, MC, V.

Days Inn Arlington. Located off U.S. Route 50, directly west of Fort Myer and Arlington National Cemetary, this three-story motel offers complimentary shuttle service to Rosslyn Metro Station. Restaurant, bar. Cable TV. Laundry service. No pets. | 2201 Arlington Blvd. | 703/525–0300 or 800/329–7460 | fax 703/525–5671 | 128 rooms | $81–$150 | AE, D, DC, MC, V.

Days Inn Crystal City. This large glass and white stone hotel in the commercial Crystal City area prides itself on not being "just any Days Inn." The hotel is bordered with gardens to the front and back, and rooms have large three-paned windows, bright colors, and conservative furnishings. The hotel is less than a mile from National Airport and just across the river from Georgetown in Washington D.C. Restaurant, bar. In-room data ports, room service, cable TV. Pool. Exercise equipment. Business services. Airport shuttle. Parking (fee). | 2000 Jefferson Davis Hwy./U.S. 1 | 703/920–8600 or 800/847–4775 | fax 703/920–2840 | www.daysinncrystal.com | 247 rooms | $118–$100 | AE, D, DC, MC, V.

Doubletree–Washington National Airport. The Pentagon, National Airport, and shops are all close to this gigantic hotel housed in a modern, geometrically shaped hotel. The rooms are designed in warm beige and neutral hues and have large windows. Restaurant, bar with entertainment. In-room data ports, some microwaves, cable TV. Indoor pool. Sauna. Business services. Airport shuttle. Free parking Some pets allowed. | 300 Army-Navy Dr. | 703/416–4147 | fax 703/416–4126 | www.doubletreehotels.com | 632 rooms, 265 suites | $100–$149, $200–$400 suites | AE, D, DC, MC, V.

Econo Lodge Metro. This motel, renovated in 1999, is an economical option that's close to public transportation. The lodging is three blocks from the East Falls Church Metro Station, just off I–66W at Exit 69. Complimentary Continental breakfast. Cable TV. Laundry facilities, laundry service. No pets. | 6800 Lee Hwy. | 703/538–5300 | fax 703/538–2110 | 47 rooms | $59–$169 | AE, D, DC, MC, V.

Embassy Suites–Crystal City. Two blocks from Crystal City Metro, the all-suites hotel is housed in a modern, red geometric building (the likes of which earned the neighborhood its name, Crystal City). Rooms in beiges and browns match the exterior of the building, and have large floor-to-ceiling wall mirrors and lots of lighting. Restaurant, bar, complimentary breakfast. In-room data ports, refrigerators, cable TV. Pool. Exercise equipment. Business services. Airport shuttle. | 1300 U.S. 1 | 703/979–9799 or 800/362–2779 | fax 703/920–5947 | www.embassysuites.com | 267 suites | $109–$189 | AE, D, DC, MC, V.

Executive Club Suites. In a residential area, this all-suites hotel has a columned entrance and chandeliers. The otherwise conservatively furnished suite rooms are lightened by large windows. Picnic area, complimentary Continental breakfast. Kitchenettes, microwaves, refrigerators, cable TV. Exercise equipment. Pool. Hot tub. Laundry facilities. Business services.

Airport shuttle. Free parking. Some pets allowed (fee). | 108 S. Courthouse Rd. | 703/522–2582 or 877/316–2582 | fax 703/486–2694 | www.dcexeclub.com | 74 suites | $159–$179 suites | AE, D, DC, MC, V.

Four Points Sheraton Hotel Washington DC–Pentagon. Just south of the Pentagon, off I–395 at Exit 7, this seven-story hotel was renovated in 1999. Many rooms have nice views of the city and adjacent park. Restaurant, bar, room service. In-room data ports, cable TV. Pool. Gym. Laundry service. Business services, airport shuttle. No pets. | 2480 S. Glebe Rd. | 703/682–5500 | fax 703/682–5505 | 120 rooms | $109–$209 | AE, D, DC, MC, V.

Hilton Arlington and Towers. Directly atop the Ballston Metro station, this European-style hotel has a special business and information technology area for business travellers. Rooms are light, spacious, and luxurious right down to the door handles. Restaurant, bar. In-room data ports, cable TV. Indoor pool. Hot tub. Laundry facilities. Business services. | 950 N. Stafford St. | 703/528–6000 | fax 703/812–5172 | www.hilton.com | 209 rooms, 5 suites | $99–$215 | AE, D, DC, MC, V.

Holiday Inn National Airport. Just ½ mi from the airport, this Holiday Inn has rooms dressed in dark drapery to keep out the distant roar of landing jets. Restaurant, bar. In-room data ports, cable TV. Pool. Business services. Airport shuttle. Some pets allowed. | 2650 Jefferson Davis Hwy./U.S. 1 | 703/682–7200 | fax 703/684–3217 | www.holiday-inn.com | 280 rooms | $114–$180 | AE, D, DC, MC, V.

Holiday Inn Rosslyn Westpark. Not just another link in the national chain, this high-rise hotel overlooks the Potomac River in the commercial Rosslyn area of Arlington. Rooms, brightly festooned in rose and green, have large windows, and views of D.C. and the Potomac. One block from the Rosslyn Metro Station. Restaurant, bar. In-room data ports, some refrigerators, cable TV. Indoor pool. Exercise equipment. Laundry facilities. Business services. Some pets allowed. | 1900 N. Ft. Myer Dr. | 703/807–2000 | fax 703/522–7480 | www.holiday-inn.com | 306 rooms | $120–$140 | AE, D, DC, MC, V.

Hyatt Arlington. This hotel near Key Bridge and next to the Metro is another elegant high-rise that forms the futuristic skyline just across the Potomac from D.C. With low-lighting and deep dark furniture, the rooms are enlivened by the appointment of flowers and plants. Restaurant, bars. In-room data ports, cable TV. Exercise equipment. Business services. Some pets allowed. | 1325 Wilson Blvd. | 703/525–1234 | fax 703/525–1476 | www.hyatt.com | 302 rooms | $129–$230 | AE, D, DC, MC, V.

Hyatt Regency Crystal City. Adjacent to the airport, this suburban behemoth hotel high-rise is part of a larger multi-building complex. Rooms are warm and light. Room windows are dressed with sheer linings and heavy curtains to muffle the roar of the incoming air traffic. Restaurant, bars. In-room data ports, some refrigerators, cable TV. Pool. Hot tub. Exercise equipment. Business services. Airport shuttle. Valet parking. | 2799 Jefferson Davis Hwy./U.S. 1 | 703/418–1234 | fax 703/418–1289 | wasrc1@erols.com | www.hyatt.com | 685 rooms | $89–$190 | AE, D, DC, MC, V.

Marriott Crystal City. This rounded high-rise hotel has 11 floors of rooms with full-length windows and beige and peach furnishings. On the fourteenth floor is the esteemed JW's Steakhouse (*see Dining*). Restaurant, bar. In-room data ports, cable TV. Indoor pool. Hot tub. Exercise equipment. Laundry facilities. Business services. Airport shuttle. | 1999 U.S. 1 | 703/413–5500 | fax 703/413–0192 | www.marriott.com | 345 rooms | $159–$239 | AE, D, DC, MC, V.

Marriott Crystal Gateway. The eighteen floors of this asymmetrically designed, luxury high-rise hotel have bright rooms with fresh flowers and wall art. Restaurant, bar. In-room data ports, cable TV. Indoor-outdoor pool. Hot tub. Exercise equipment. Business services. Airport shuttle. Some pets allowed. | 1700 Jefferson Davis Hwy./U.S. 1 | 703/920–3230 | fax 703/271–5212 | www.marriott.com/marriott/wasgw | 697 rooms, 17 suites | $119–$209, $199–$300 suites | AE, D, DC, MC, V.

Marriott Key Bridge. The beige stone building that contains this Marriott is surrounded by trees, and faces the Potomac, and Washington D.C. across the river. Rooms have large windows and balcony views of Georgetown and Washington D.C. Restaurant, bar with entertainment. In-room data ports, microwaves, cable TV. Indoor-outdoor pool. Barbershop, beauty salon, hot tub. Exercise equipment. Business services. | 1401 Lee Hwy. | 703/524–6400 | fax 703/524–8964 | www.marriott.com | 588 rooms | $119–$207 | AE, D, DC, MC, V.

Quality Hotel Courthouse Plaza. Two blocks from Courthouse Metro, the property has a movie theater on premises and an urban garden with flowers and flower bushes. Rooms have lots of lighting and walk-out balconies overlooking the gardens. Restaurant, bar. In-room data ports, cable TV. Pool. Exercise equipment. Laundry facilities. Business services. Some pets allowed. | 1200 N. Courthouse Rd./U.S. Route 50 | 703/524–4000 or 888/987–2555 | fax 703/522–6814 | www.qualityhotelarlington.com | 391 rooms | $90–$120 | AE, D, DC, MC, V.

Quality Inn–Iwo Jima. Walking distance of the Marine Corps War Memorial and the Rosslyn Metro, this high-rise hotel has regular, conservative rooms. Kids under 18 stay free. Restaurant, bar. In-room data ports, microwaves, room service, cable TV. Indoor pool. Exercise equipment. Laundry facilities. Business services. | 1501 Arlington Blvd. | 703/524–5000 | fax 703/522–5484 | 141 rooms | $72–$86 | AE, D, DC, MC, V.

Residence Inn by Marriott. The seventeen-floor hotel is across from the Fashion Centre shopping complex, and close to the Pentagon in a commercial area of Arlington. Rooms are bright and nondescript. Picnic area, complimentary Continental breakfast. Kitchenettes, microwaves, refrigerators, cable TV. Indoor pool. Hot tub. Exercise equipment. Laundry facilities. Business services. Airport shuttle. | 550 Army-Navy Dr. | 703/413–6630 | fax 703/418–1751 | www.marriott.com | 299 suites | $164–$240 suites | AE, D, DC, MC, V.

Ritz-Carlton, Pentagon City. This luxury hotel with a grand entrance is in a wide grey-stone building with large windows that look towards the Potomac on one side and the Fashion Center complex on the other. Rooms are clothed in elegantly luxurious fabrics and accented with thoughtful artwork. Restaurant, bar with entertainment. In-room data ports, minibars, room service, cable TV. Indoor pool. Hot tub, massage. Gym. Shops. Business services. Airport shuttle. | 1250 S. Hayes St. | 703/415–5000 | fax 703/415–5061 | www.ritzcarlton.com | 345 rooms, 41 suites | $119–$239, $299–$450 suites | AE, D, DC, MC, V.

Sheraton Crystal City. This hotel is housed in a white stone building bordered by rounded glass windows. Rooms have large windows and views of the Washington D.C. metropolitan area. A block from the Crystal City Metro station. Restaurant, bar with entertainment. In-room data ports, minibars, cable TV. Pool. Sauna. Exercise equipment. Business services. Airport shuttle. | 1800 Jefferson Davis Hwy./U.S. 1 | 703/486–1111 | fax 703/769–3970 | perrya@ix.netcom.com | www.sheraton.com | 220 rooms | $79–$149 | AE, D, DC, MC, V.

Sheraton National Hotel. A mile and a half from Reagan National Airport, this 16-story hotel has a rooftop pool and restaurant (Stars) with views of the national cemetery. 3 restaurants, room service. In-room data ports, cable TV. Pool. Sauna. Gym. Shops. Laundry service. Business services, airport shuttle. No pets. | 900 S. Orme St. | 703/521–1900 | fax 703/521–2122 | 414 rooms | $109–$219 | AE, D, DC, MC, V.

Travelodge Washington/Arlington Cherry Blossom. This three-floor, red brick motor lodge is close to two different Metro stops and the Fashion Center mall. Rooms have ceiling fans, external entrances and face the parking lots. Restaurant, complimentary Continental breakfast. Some kitchenettes, refrigerators, cable TV. Exercise equipment. Laundry facilities. Business services. Free parking. | 3030 Columbia Pike | 703/521–5570 | fax 703/271–0081 | www.travelodge.com | 76 rooms | $59–$84 | AE, D, DC, MC, V.

Virginian Suites. Atop a hill one block from the Iwo Jima Memorial, this 10-story hotel has rooms, studios, and one-bedroom suites, all with full kitchens and dishwashers. In-room data ports, kitchenettes, microwaves, refrigerators, cable TV. Gym. Laundry service. Business services. Pets allowed. | 1500 Arlington Blvd. | 703/522–9600 or 800/275–2866 | fax 703/525–4462 | www.virginiansuites.com | 262 rooms | $118–$135 | AE, D, DC, MC, V.

ASHLAND

(Nearby town also listed: Richmond)

Edwin Robinson, president of the Richmond, Fredericksburg and Potomac Railroad, created Ashland in 1848 as a health resort. Set around a mineral spring, the village, originally called Slash Cottage, became a popular destination for residents of Richmond, just 15 mi south. By 1855 it had discarded its first name in favor of Ashland, the name of native son Henry Clay's Kentucky estate. In 1866, the railroad company persuaded the Methodist Church, by means of a land donation, to move Randolph-Macon College to Ashland. Today, the village born of the railroad is essentially a college town with a historic district of Victorian homes. Paramount King's Dominion theme park is 8 mi away.

Information: Ashland/Hanover Visitor Center | 112 N. Railroad Ave., Ashland, VA 23005 | 804/752–6766 or 800/897–1479 | pritter@town.ashland.va.us | www.town.ashland.va.us.

Attractions

Paramount's Kings Dominion. This amusement park's 100-plus rides include simulated white-water rafting and 10 roller coasters. | 16000 Theme Park Way, Doswell | 804/876–5373 | www.pkd4fun.com | $25.99–$36.99, parking $10–$30 | Apr. 1– Sept. 4, Daily 10:30–10; Closing times vary.

Scotchtown. Built around 1719 in Hanover County, Scotchtown was the residence of Patrick Henry from 1771 to 1778. Dolley Payne (future wife of James Madison), whose father purchased the house around 1781, lived here as a child. | 16120 Chiswell La. | 804/227–3500 or 804/883–6917 | www.town.ashland.va.us | $6 | Apr.–Oct. Tues.–Sat. 10–4:30, Sun. 1:30–4:30.

Randolph-Macon College. Founded in 1830, this liberal arts institution is the country's oldest Methodist-affiliated college in continuous operation. The name honors statesmen John Randolph of Roanoke and Nathaniel Macon of North Carolina. Originally an all-male college, Randolph-Macon became coeducational in 1971. 45-minute campus tours, offered weekdays at 10, noon, and 2, begin at the Admissions Office (204 Patrick Street). | Box 5005, 204 Patrick St. | 804/752–7305 | fax 804/752–4707 | www.rmc.edu | Free | Daily.

SIGHTSEEING TOURS/TOUR COMPANIES

Ashland Walking Tours. An easy, self-guided amble past Ashland's Victorian shops and private homes. The free brochure, available at the Ashland Visitor Center (in the old train station) showcases the town's historical highlights. Allow about one hour to walk the circuit. | 112 N Railroad Ave. | 804/752–6766 or 800/897–1479 | Free.

ON THE CALENDAR

MAY: *Camptown Races.* This Hanover County tradition is occasion for picnics, tailgate parties, and, of course, lots of horse racing at Graymont Park on Rte. 641. | 804/752–6678.
JUNE: *Ashland Strawberry Faire.* The stars here are the strawberries, prepared every way imaginable. The fair on the Randolph-Macon College campus also hosts a pie-eating contest, hundreds of craftspeople, local entertainers, pony rides, and children's games. | 804/752–6766.
JUNE: *Hanover Tomato Festival.* Hanover County's celebrated tomatoes are served every way possible: raw, cooked, in BLTs, tomato fritters, and more. There's also live music, a tomato-eating contest, a parade, crafts, and games at the festival at Battlefield Park Elementary School, 5501 Mechanicsville Tpk. | 804/798–1712.

Dining

Ashland Coffee and Tea. Café. Catch poetry readings, live music, and comedy acts throughout the week at this lively hang-out, where local art adorns the walls. It's a good spot to grab a bagel or panini sandwich, a salad and a bowl of soup, or a quick cappuccino. | 100 N Railroad Ave. | 804/798–1702 | $4–$7 | MC, V.

Bryce Resort. American. Ski slopes and mountains grab the view through the entire back wall (it's all glass) of this lodge restaurant, remodeled in 2000. The menu includes steaks, chops, burgers, and salads. During ski season, look for wallet-friendly buffet lunches and dinners, too. | 1982 Fairway Dr. | 540/856–2121 or 800/821–1444 | Breakfast also available | $7–$19 | AE, D, MC, V.

Coleman's Basye Bistro. Contemporary. Look for fresh, organic ingredients on the menu in the cozy dining rooms of this farmhouse. The emphasis is on seafood–pan-seared scallops over pasta, for example–but you'll also find Angus steak, and free-range chicken entrées. Upstairs on weekends, listen to live music in the attic bar. | 1518 Orkney Grade | 540/856–8187 | Breakfast Fri. and Sat. | $10–$26 | AE, D, DC, MC, V.

Ironhorse. Contemporary. Riding the rails is the theme of this restaurant and bar, which is itself close to the railroad. The building, a restored turn-of-the-century department store, has a wood-paneled interior filled with train memorabilia. Visitors can even view cabinets of china used in the heyday of the iron horse. The menu changes monthly. Entertainment. | 100 S. Railroad Ave. | 804/752–6410 | Closed Sun. No dinner Mon. no lunch Sat. | $15–$25 | D, DC, MC, V.

Smokey Pig. American. The humorous touches to the interior design of this restaurant, in a turn-of-the-century building, are an eccentric blend of rusticity and the porcine. Known for barbecue, crab cakes, hush puppies, and pies. Kids' menu. | 212 S. Washington Hwy. | 804/798–4590 | Closed Mon. | $10–$20 | AE, MC, V.

Lodging

Ashland Travelodge. This well-maintained, 1960s-style motor lodge makes a good all-in-one place to stop, with a restaurant and service station. Cable TV. Pool. No pets. | 100 N. Carter Rd. | 804/798–6011 | fax 804/798–7342 | 24 rooms | $49–$55 | AE, D, DC, MC, V.

Best Western Hanover House. The hotel edged by greenery is located midway between Ashland and Richmond. The lobby of this rural hotel is large and sunlit. Huge floor-to-ceiling windows in the rooms look out on a charming patio. Restaurant. Cable TV. Pool. Laundry facilities. Business services. | 10296 Sliding Hill Rd. | 804/550–2805 | fax 804/550–3843 | www.bestwestern.com | 93 rooms | $44–$52 | AE, D, DC, MC, V.

Comfort Inn. In downtown Ashland, this relaxed hotel is close to Randolph-Macon. Rooms are brightly lit and look out on the neighborhood. Complimentary Continental breakfast. Some refrigerators, cable TV. Pool. Exercise equipment. Laundry facilities. Business services. Some pets allowed. | 101 Cottage Green Dr. | 804/752–7777 | fax 804/798–0327 | www.comfortinn.com | 126 rooms | $59–$79 | AE, D, DC, MC, V.

Henry Clay. Recreated from photographs, the exterior of the Inn is an exact replica of its predecessors. Inside, the hotel has an art and gift gallery displaying the work of local artists and artisans; a parlor that opens onto the balcony overlooking the old Ashland train station and the campus of Randolph-Macon; and a drawing room for business and social functions. Rooms have antique reproduction furnishings, and sleigh, pencil post, canopy, acorn post, and cannonball beds. Dining room, complimentary Continental breakfast. In-room data ports, no smoking, cable TV. Business services. | 114 N. Railroad Ave. | 804/798–3100 or 800/343–4565 | fax 804/752–7555 | 15 rooms, 1 suite | $90–$125, $165 suites | AE, MC, V.

Holiday Inn. The two-story chain hotel is 5 mi south of Paramount's Kings Dominion. Rooms are connected by an interior corridor and have coffee makers and lots of plaids, stripes and flowers. Restaurant, bar with entertainment. Room service, cable TV. Pool, wading pool. Exercise equipment. Laundry facilities. Business services. Free parking. | 810 England St. | 804/798–4231 or 800/923–4231 | fax 804/798–9074 | www.holiday-inn.com | 165 rooms | $45–$98 | AE, D, DC, MC, V.

Sky Chalet Mountain Top Lodge. Opened in 1937, this rustic lodge sits on 14 acres atop Supin Lick Ridge, with magnificent views of the surrounding mountains. Accommodations are spartan but comfortable, with living room fireplaces warming some suites, and decks to take in the scenery. Complimentary Continental breakfast. Some kitchenettes, no air-conditioning, no room phones, no TV. Hiking. Some pets allowed. | 280 Sky Chalet Ln. | 540/856–2147 or 877/TOP–VIEW | fax 540/856–2436 | 5 suites | $34–$79 | D, DC, MC, V.

Super 8 Motel. This two-story chain motel is just west of I–95 at Exit 92 (east of U.S. Route 1). Rooms are dependably bland, furnished with two double-beds each. Complimentary Continental breakfast. Cable TV. Pool. Business services. No pets. | 806–B England St. | 804/752–7000 | fax 804/752–7795 | 150 rooms | $45–$58 | AE, D, DC, MC, V.

BASYE

(Nearby town also listed: Woodstock)

Basye, nestled between the Blue Ridge and Allegheny mountains, was settled in the 1700s by Scotch, Irish, German and English immigrants, like much of the Shenandoah Valley. Basye is base for skiers during the winter, and golfers during warmer months, who are attracted by the nearby Bryce Resort, a popular family getaway. Just to the west of town, George Washington National Forest is also a hot spot for year-round outdoor recreation with hiking, swimming, fishing, boating and camping.

Information: Shenandoah County Travel Council | 600 N. Main St. Suite 101, Woodstock, VA 22664 | 540/459–2332 | www.co.shenandoah.va.us.

Attractions

Bryce Resort. This year-round resort on the western rim of the Shenandoah Valley has operated since 1964. It has an 18-hole golf course, tennis courts, horseback riding, miniature golf, eight ski slopes, plus two restaurants and accommodations. As if there isn't enough to do, the 45-acre Lake Laura also has swimming, boating, windsurfing, and fishing. | 1932 Fairway Dr. | 540/856–2121 | fax 540/856–8567 | www.bryceresort.com | Open year-round.

George Washington and Jefferson National Forests. (*See* Harrisonburg). Hiking trails ascending up the valley into the mountains, about 10 mi east from Basye, lead to scenic vistas. Camping, fishing, lake swimming and picnicking are all available. The visitors center is in Roanoke, far to the south at the mid-point between the two forests. | Visitor Center, 5162 Valleypointe Pkwy., Roanoke | 540/265–5100 or 888/265–0019.

ON THE CALENDAR

MEMORIAL DAY–LABOR DAY: *Shenandoah Valley Music Festival.* The summer-long outdoor music festival has symphony pops concerts, classical masterworks, folk music, and big band jazz. Arts-and-crafts shows add to the family fun, three mi southwest of Basye at the Orkney Springs Hotel, 221 Shrine Mont Circle. | 540/459–3396 or 800/459–3396.

Lodging

Best Western Shenandoah Valley. The colonial-styled two-story hotel near Bryce Resort has a large front lawn, blue and red roof and an old cannon on the front lawn. Large windows frame the bright, simple rooms. Restaurant, bar. Cable TV. Pool, wading pool. Tennis. Playground. Business services. Some pets allowed. | 250 Conicksville Rd., Mt. Jackson | 540/477–2911 | fax 540/477–2392 | www.bestwestern.com | 98 rooms | $54–$65 | AE, D, DC, MC, V.

Bryce Resort. This family-oriented resort in the Shenandoah Mountains has its own private condominiums, town houses, and chalets of all styles for rent. Restaurant, bar. Some microwaves, refrigerators, cable TV. 18-hole golf course, miniature golf, tennis court. Horseback riding. Beach, water sports, boating, fishing, bicycles. Downhill skiing. | Creekside Realty, 1932 Fairway Dr./Rte. 263 | 888/771–RENT | GeneralInfo@bryceresort.com | www.bryceresort.com | 750 chalets | $95–$250 | AE, D, MC, V.

Widow Kip's. This quaint country house, southeast around 14 mi, has a shrub-lined walkway, and is peaceful and sunny. The country-style rooms have dark wood furniture, lace canopies, flowers, lots of quilts and plaids. Picnic lunches are available. Complimentary breakfast. No smoking, TV only in common area, cable TV, no room phones. Pool. Bicycles. Some pets allowed. | 355 Orchard Dr., Mt. Jackson | 540/477–2400 or 800/478–8714 | widokips@shentel.net | www.widowkips.com | 5 rooms; 2 cottages | $70–$90, $90–$95 cottages | MC, V.

BIG STONE GAP

MAP 11, B7

(Nearby town also listed: Wise)

In the 1870s, northern businessmen came to the tiny village of Big Stone Gap and dreamed of turning it into the "Pittsburgh of the South." Near both the Powell River and a pass on Stone Mountain, it was a strategic spot where the railroads could access the coal fields. The town was founded in 1888 and coal and iron ore mining continues to be the main industry in Big Stone Gap today. Its most famous resident, novelist John Fox Jr., gave the world its first (and somewhat romanticized) story of life in the Blue Ridge Highlands of Virginia, *The Trail of the Lonesome Pine.*

Information: Big Stone Gap/Wise County Tourist Information Center | Box 236, Gilley Ave. E, Big Stone Gap, VA 24219 | 540/523–2060 | info@bigstonegap.org | www.bigstonegap.org. .

Attractions

Harry Meador Coal Museum. The history of coal mining and its influence on this region of southwest Virginia are the focus of the museum, which grew out of a collection of the personal possessions of Harry Meador, president of the Westmoreland Coal Company. Also exhibited are old medical and dental equipment. | E. 3rd St. and Shawnee Ave. | 540/523–9209 or 540/523–2060 | Free | Wed.–Sun. 9–4:30.

John Fox Jr. Museum. Built in 1888, this house was the family home of John Fox Jr., author of *The Trail of the Lonesome Pine.* The 1908 novel, a love story between a mountain girl and a mining engineer from the East, deals with the positive and negative impacts of progress on mountain culture. The play is performed each summer by a local drama troupe. Family possessions are displayed in the museum. | 117 Shawnee Ave. | 540/523–2747 or 540/523–1235 | www.bigstonegap.org/attract | $3 | June–Sept. Wed. and Sun. 2–5, Thurs.–Sat. 2–6, or by appointment.

June Tolliver House. Though June Tolliver was the fictional heroine of John Fox Jr.'s *Trail of the Lonesome Pine,* she was based on a real person. This 1890 house with period furnishings was the character's residence in the book. Today, local arts and crafts, including coal carvings and quilts, are sold there. During the summer months, Fox's novel of mountain feuding and vigilante law is dramatized in side yard of the house by local performers. | Jerome St. at Clinton Ave. | 540/523–1235 or 540/523–4707 | www.bigstonegap.org/attract | Free; performances $10 | Mid-May–mid-Dec. Tues.–Sat. 10–5, Sun. 2–6; performances June–Aug. Thurs.–Sat. at 8.

Natural Tunnel State Park. This 603-acre park in neighboring Scott County, 14 mi south of town, has a 10-story-high natural tunnel carved over thousands of centuries from a limestone ridge. The passage was used as a railway tunnel in the 1880s by the South Atlantic and Ohio Railway. Today, camping, hiking, and swimming are available. | Rte. 3, Duffield |

540/940–2674 | www.state.va.us | Memorial Day–Labor Day, weekdays $1 parking fee, weekends $2 | Daily dawn–dusk.

Southwest Virginia Museum. In this Victorian mansion built during the coal boom of 1888–93, you'll find the old mine manager's home furnishings and exhibits relating the history of the settlement of southwestern Virginia. | 10 W. 1st St. | 540/523–1322 | www.bigstone-gap.org/attract | $3 | Mon.–Thurs. 10–4, Fri. 9–4; Sat. 10–5, Sun. 1–5 | Labor Day–Dec. and Mar.–Memorial Day closed Mon.

ON THE CALENDAR

APR.: *Lonesome Pine Arts and Crafts Festival.* Local artisans display their wares; there's also live music and food at the Powell Valley Middle School, 2945 2nd Ave. E. | 540/523–6112.

JULY–AUG. *The Trail of the Lonesome Pine.* John Fox Jr.'s book about life in the Blue Ridge Highlands is the inspiration for this drama performed on an outdoor stage. | June Tolliver House | 540/523–1235 or 800/362–0149.

Dining

Victorian House–Ms. Fritzi's Tea Room. American. Inside a 1908 Victorian home, this restaurant sits next door to the Trail of the Lonesome Pine Outdoor Drama and Pine House. In July and August when the theater is open, the eatery serves dinner. The rest of the year, it opens for lunch only, offering soups, sandwiches, and homemade desserts. | 606 E. Wood Ave. | 540/523–6245 | No dinner Sept.–June, closed Sun.–Mon. | $5–$9 | AE, D, DC, MC, V.

Lodging

Comfort Inn. This three-story chain hotel has the standard offerings, but the added bonus of great views of the Appalachian Mountains. Standard rooms have queen beds; executive suites have an in-room spa, fireplace, and balcony. The hotel, located at the intersection of U.S. 58 West and U.S. 23, is 1 mi from the Trail of the Lonesome Pine Outdoor Drama and Pine House. Complimentary Continental breakfast. In-room data ports, some microwaves, some refrigerators, cable TV. Hot tub, spa. Gym. Laundry services. Business services. No pets. | 1928–B Wildcat Rd. | 540/523–5911 | fax 540/523–0726 | 61 rooms | $74.95–$144.95 | AE, D, DC, MC, V.

Country Inn Motel. The 1950s era brick motel with exterior corridors is near Jefferson National Forest, on the outskirts of town. Rooms are basic and bright with pictures adorning the walls and lamps by the bedside. Cable TV. Business services. Some pets allowed. | 627 Gilley Ave. | 540/523–0374 | fax 540/523–5043 | 42 rooms | $45–$51 | AE, D, DC, MC, V.

BLACKSBURG

MAP 11, E7

(Nearby towns also listed: Radford, Roanoke, Salem)

On a plateau between the Blue Ridge and Allegheny mountains, Blacksburg was established in 1748 as Draper's Meadow, a small farming community of German, English, Scotch, and Irish settlers. Today the town is home to the Virginia Polytechnic Institute and State University, the largest university in the state. Thanks to the university, Blacksburg has an enviable cultural calendar and abundant social life. The university's offerings range from museums, lectures, and shows by performing arts groups to NCAA Division I basketball and football. Jefferson National Forest, which forms the town's northwest border, has hiking, camping, swimming, and fishing.

Information: Blacksburg Chamber of Commerce | 1995 S. Main St. Suite 901, Blacksburg, VA 24060 | 540/552–4061 | www.blacksburg-chamber.com.

Blacksburg Regional Visitor Center | 1995 S. Main St. Suite 902, Blacksburg, VA 24060 | 540/552–4061 or 800/288–4061 | www.blacksburg-chamber.com.

Attractions

Jefferson National Forest. (*See* Harrisonburg.) Hiking, fishing, camping, and picnicking opportunities are all minutes from town. The visitor center is in neighboring Roanoke. | 5162 Valleypointe Pkwy., Roanoke | 540/265–5100.

Mountain Lake. This lake at 4,000 ft above sea level is one of only two natural freshwater lakes in Virginia and one of the highest in the East. It was formed when a rock slide dammed the north end of the valley, and has been a resort since 1857. Mountain Lake has trails throughout its 2,600 acres, boating, fishing, tennis, and horse-drawn carriage rides, and is almost 16 mi northwest of Blacksburg. | 115 Hotel Circle, Mountain Lake | 540/951–1819 or 800/346–3334 | fax 540/626–7172 | Free | May–Oct. daily dawn–dusk.

Smithfield Plantation. This 1777 frontier plantation was built by Revolutionary War hero, Col. William Preston, and was the birth site of two Virginia governors—James Patton Preston and John Floyd Jr. Costumed interpreters provide tours of the plantation, complete with period furnishings and family possessions. | 1000 Smithfield Plantation Rd. | 540/231–3947 | $4 | Apr.–Dec. Thurs.–Sun. 1–5.

Virginia Polytechnic and State University. Founded in 1872, Virginia Tech is the state's largest university with an enrollment of more than 25,000 students. Today, it is considered among the top 50 research institutions in the country. The main campus, a mix of modern and Gothic architecture, covers 2,600 acres. When classes are in session, walking tours happen weekdays at 10, 11, and 1 and Saturdays at 11 and 1, and start at the Office of Admissions (201 Burrus Hall). | U.S. 460 | 540/321–6000 | fax 540/231–3242 | www.vt.edu | Free | Daily.

ON THE CALENDAR

JUNE: *Smithfield Days.* Highlights of this festival on the Smithfield Plantation include 18th-century crafts, games, demonstrations of early pioneer work, apple-butter making, and plantation tours. | 540/552–4061.
AUG.: *Stepping Out.* This downtown festival has live music, food, and crafts. | 540/951–0454.

Dining

Anchy's. Seafood. This quiet, candlelit restaurant has a large menu, including chicken, veal, duck, and steak options, though some of the most popular dishes are the fresh seafood like Norwegian salmon filets and crab legs. If seafood isn't your thing, try the Peking steak. | 1600 N Main St. | 540/951–2828 | Closed Mon. no lunch Sat. | $8–$15 | AE, D, DC, MC, V.

Bogen's. American. This restaurant was founded and inspired by former Virginia Tech and NFL player, Bill Ellenbogen. Framed prints of the sports star hang from the walls, as does a custom stained-glass piece depicting Virginia Tech sport scenes. Upstairs on the second floor, a photo history of Blacksburg adorns the walls. The restaurant in a remodeled three-story house also has the self-proclaimed, "world's first Cyberbar" (a dubious proclamation, but fitting for a town famous as an "Electronic Village"). The bar has been featured in *Esquire* and *Reader's Digest* and is renowned for its steaks, burgers, seafood, salads, and sandwiches. | 622 N. Main St. | 540/953–2233 | $9–$15 | AE, D, MC, V.

Commonwealth Café. American. Part of the Donaldson Brown Hotel and Conference Center, this eatery serves breakfast and lunch year-round, and dinner during the school year, when it is operated by the Virginia Tech students themselves. Buffet-style lunch is popular; dinner nods include sirloin steak, chicken parmesan, fried shrimp, and sweet and sour vegetable stir fry. | 201 Otey St. | 540/231–8000 or 877/200–3360 | Breakfast also available. No dinner when school is not in session | $8–$20 | AE, D, MC, V.

Kabuki. Japanese. Built to resemble a Japanese castle, the restaurant, eight mi south of Blacksburg, greets you with a serene Japanese garden and waterfall outside the entrance. Inside, 18-ft ceilings, and embellished with antiques and a painting of a night sky, make for an elegant dining experience. Known for hibachi cooking. Sushi bar. | 120 Arbor Dr., Christiansburg | 540/381–3600 | No lunch | $11–$25 | AE, D, DC, MC, V.

PK's. American. Place your order, then go play billiards, foosball, darts, or video games while waiting for your meal at this informal eatery. There's a Philly cheese steak and a meatball sub, sandwiches, burgers, and salads, along with pastas and pizza (note the "Vegetarian Beware" topped with ham, beef, sausage, and pepperoni). | 432 N Main St. | 540/552–1577 | $5–$13 | AE, D, MC, V.

Lodging

AmeriSuites Blacksburg. One mile south of Virginia Tech University, rooms at this five-story, all-suites chain afford views of the surrounding Blue Ridge Mountains. Nosh on free popcorn every evening. Complimentary Continental breakfast. In-room data ports, kitchenettes, microwaves, refrigerators, cable TV, in-room VCRs. Pool. Laundry service. Laundry facilities. Business services. No pets. | 1020 Plantation Blvd. | 540/552–5636 | fax 540/552–5138 | 94 suites | $84–$109 | AE, D, MC, V.

Best Western Red Lion Inn. This rural Tudor-style Best Western is surrounded by trees and greenery. Rooms are warm and homey and have views of natural surroundings. Restaurant, bar, picnic area. Room service, cable TV. Pool. Tennis. Playground. Business services. Free parking. | 900 Plantation Rd./Rte. 685 | 540/552–7770 | fax 540/552–6346 | www.bestwestern.com | 104 rooms | $62 | AE, D, DC, MC, V.

Clay Corner Inn Bed and Breakfast. This hostelry, consisting of two twin houses, is next to the Virginia Tech campus and six blocks from downtown. Quaint and homey, the bed and breakfast is complete with a white mailbox and quiet garden with dogwood and magnolia trees. By the pool, there are green Asian-style umbrellas. Rooms are cozy with white spreads, pillows and large windows. Covered deck. Complimentary breakfast. Some refrigerators, cable TV. Pool. Hot tub. No kids under 12. No smoking. | 401 Clay St. | 540/953–2604 | fax 540/951–0541 | claycorner@aol.com | www.claycorner.com | 12 rooms | $85–$130 | AE, MC, V.

Comfort Inn. This bright and roomy hotel conveniently close to Interstate 81 is not far from Virginia Tech. Complimentary Continental breakfast. In-room data ports, cable TV. Pool. Exercise equipment. Business services. Some pets allowed. Free parking. | 3705 S. Main St. | 540/951–1500 | fax 540/951–1530 | www.comfortinn.com | 80 rooms | $62–$72 | AE, D, DC, MC, V.

Days Inn. This two-floor hotel with exterior corridors prides itself for its "southern hospitality." The hotel is in a commercial area, eight mi south of Blacksburg, 15 minutes from Virginia Tech. Rooms are basic, and neutral colored. Across the street is a Cracker Barrel restaurant. Complimentary Continental breakfast. In-room data ports, cable TV. Pool. Playground. Some pets allowed. | U.S. 11, Christiansburg | 540/382–0261 | fax 540/382–0365 | 122 rooms | $56–$64 | AE, D, DC, MC, V.

Donaldson Brown Hotel and Conference Center. This red brick hotel, on Virginia Tech's campus, was originally designed in 1968 as a conference and continuing-education center. Today, it serves as lodging open to all. Next door, Squire's student center has billiard and pool tables, and video games (nominal fee charged). Restaurant. In-room data ports, cable TV. Laundry service. Business services. No pets. | 201 Otey St. | 540/231–8000 or 877/200–3360 | fax 540/231–3746 | dbhcc@vt.edu | www.dbhcc.vt.edu | 128 rooms | $79–$149 | AE, D, MC, V.

Hampton Inn. This five-floor hotel housed in a white building with a green roof, eight mi south of Blacksburg, has manicured gardens and rooms of varying styles from the conservative business-oriented to the bright leisure-oriented. All rooms have ample sunlight. Shopping is nearby at the New River Valley Mall. Cable TV. Pool. Laundry facilities. Business services. | 50 Hampton Blvd., Christiansburg | 540/382–2055 or 800/426–7866 | fax 540/382–4515 | www.hampton-inn.com | 121 rooms | $63–$90 | AE, D, DC, MC, V.

L'Arche Bed and Breakfast. One block from the Virginia Tech University, this Federal-style home, built in 1908, is surrounded by a half-acre of terraced gardens, two gazebos, and fountains. Rooms are furnished with a combination of antiques and contemporary furnishings; some have canopy beds. Complimentary breakfast. Some room phones, TV in common area. No pets. No kids under 10. No smoking. | 301 Wall St. | 540/951–1808 | good@vt.edu | 5 rooms | $100 | MC, V.

Ramada Inn Limited. This hotel has a drive-thru entrance and the Ramada signature white tower. Rooms are simple with scenic view of the hotel's parking lot. 2 mi from the Virginia Tech campus. Restaurant, bar. Room service, cable TV. Pool, wading pool. Laundry facilities. Cross-country skiing. Business services. Some pets allowed. Free parking. | 3503 Holiday La. | 540/951–1330 | fax 540/951–4847 | www.ramada.com | 98 rooms | $50–$125 | AE, D, DC, MC, V.

Sheraton Four Points. Across the street from Virginia Tech campus, this hotel on a spacious property has large glass windows that flank the entrance for views of the campus. Rooms connected by interior corridors are comfortable and also have large windows. Restaurant, bar with entertainment. In-room data ports, cable TV. 2 pools (1 indoor), wading pool. Hot tub. Tennis. Playground. Business services. Free parking. | 900 Prices Fork Rd. | 540/552–7001 | fax 540/552–0827 | www.sheraton.com | 148 rooms | $89 | AE, D, DC, MC, V.

Oaks Victorian Inn. This luxurious Queen Anne Victorian inn sits atop a high hill not far from Roanoke, eight mi south of Blacksburg. Warm hospitality and memorable breakfasts are the hallmark of The Oaks. Rooms have soft, luxurious linens, down comforters, comfortable mattresses, and some in-room fireplaces. Complimentary breakfast. In-room data ports, refrigerators, cable TV. Hot tub. No kids under 14. Business services. Airport shuttle. Free parking. No smoking. | 311 E. Main St., Christiansburg | 540/381–1500 or 800/336–6257 | fax 540/382–1728 | www.innbrook.com/oaks.html | 7 rooms | $115–$150 | AE, D, MC, V.

BLUE RIDGE PARKWAY

MAP 11, G5

(Nearby towns also listed: Blacksburg, Bristol, Charlottesville, Lexington, Marion, Radford, Roanoke, Salem, Staunton, Waynesboro, Wytheville)

The 469-mi Blue Ridge Parkway is a scenic roadway that follows the crest of the Blue Ridge Mountains. A continuation of Skyline Drive, it extends south through the George Washington National Forest to the Great Smoky Mountains National Park in North Carolina. Construction of the parkway began in 1935 as a public works project of Franklin D. Roosevelt's New Deal. Since then commercial development and encroachment has been minimal and you'll see neither stop sign nor billboard, interrupting your views of mountain pastures and farms, old barns, corn and cabbage fields, and sweeping panoramas of the southern Highlands. The change in elevation is dramatic—from 649 ft to 6,053 ft.

In the spring, hillsides blaze with blooming rhododendrons, mountain laurels, and azaleas. In October, motorists flock to see the brilliant mountain foliage. The roughly 45 hiking trails are perfect side-trip digressions, and lead to stunning rock formations, waterfalls, wildflower meadows, fishing lakes, campgrounds, and picnic areas. Visitor centers, waysides, food, gas and lodging are available all along the highway. The speed limit, 45 mph, is strictly enforced, and sections of the road close during icy or snowy weather.

Information: Blue Ridge Parkway | 400 BB and T Building, 1 Pack Sq, Asheville, NC 28801 | 704/298–0398 or 800/727–5928 | www.blueridgeparkway.org. **Virginia Division of**

Tourism | 901 E. Byrd St., Richmond, VA 23219 | 804/786–4484 or 800/932–5827 | www.virginia.org.

Attractions

Chateau Morrisette Winery. Travel to the vineyards of southern France without leaving Virginia. This country winery, surrounded by the Rock Castle Gorge Wilderness area, produces a dozen different wines on signature Black Dog, Our Dog Blue, and Sweet Mountain Laurel labels. A natural amphitheater on the property is the site of the annual Black Dog Jazz Festival, usually held in September. Tours are offered and there's a restaurant on the premises. (*See Dining listing.*) | Winery Rd., Meadows of Dan | 540/593–2865 | fax 540/593–2868 | www.chateaumorrisette.com | $1 tasting fee | Mon.–Thurs. 10–5, Fri. and Sat. 10–8 Sun. 11–5.

Humpback Rock Visitor Center. This center, near the Rockfish Gap entrance to the Blue Ridge Parkway, has free maps, books for sale, picnic tables, and updates on ranger programs. A short trail leads you to a reconstructed pioneer mountain farm, with a cabin, spring house, chicken coop, and barn. | Milepost 5.8, Blue Ridge Pkwy. | 540/943–4716 | www.blueridgeparkway.org | Free | May–Oct. daily 9–5.

James River Visitor Center. At this wayside visitor center is a footbridge across the James River and a trail leading to the Kanawha Canal Lock exhibit. Before railroads became the favored mode of transport, engineers built locks to move freight along the river. The restored lock was part of a 200-mi canal system running from Richmond across the Blue Ridge to Buchanan. | Milepost 63, Blue Ridge Pkwy. | www.blueridgeparkway.org | Free | May–Oct. daily 9–5.

Mabry Mill. Probably the most visited (and most photographed) site along the Blue Ridge Parkway, Mabry Mill consists of a sawmill and a restored water-powered gristmill that produces cornmeal and buckwheat flour for sale. Keep your eye out for the regular demonstrations showcase blacksmithing and other trades. | Milepost 176.1, Blue Ridge Pkwy. | 540/952–2947 | www.swva.net/floydco | Free | May–Aug. daily 8–7; Sept.–Oct. daily 8–6.

Peaks of Otter Recreation Area. The name "Peaks of Otter" refers to two promontories, Sharp Top and Flat Top. A visitor center has exhibits on forest ecology and regional history. A walking trail takes you to the top of Sharp Top Mountain (elevation 4,004 ft), where a panoramic, 360-degree view awaits. You can see living-history demonstrations most weekends at the Johnson Farm, a homestead dating from the 1800s. A 23-acre lake is nearby. | Milepost 86, Blue Ridge Pkwy. | 540/586–4357 | www.blueridgeparkway.org | Free | Apr.–Nov. daily 9–5.

Rocky Knob Visitor Center. Housed in a converted gasoline station, this center overlooks the Rock Castle Gorge which is accessible by a 10.8-mi trail. A variety of activities, from

BLUE RIDGE
PARKWAY

INTRO
ATTRACTIONS
DINING
LODGING

WHAT TO PACK IN THE TOY TOTE FOR KIDS

- ❑ Audiotapes
- ❑ Books
- ❑ Clipboard
- ❑ Coloring/activity books
- ❑ Doll with outfits
- ❑ Hand-held games
- ❑ Magnet games
- ❑ Notepad
- ❑ One-piece toys
- ❑ Pencils, colored pencils
- ❑ Portable stereo with earphones
- ❑ Sliding puzzles
- ❑ Travel toys

*Excerpted from *Fodor's: How to Pack: Experts Share Their Secrets*
© 1997, by Fodor's Travel Publications

naturalist programs and campfire talks to guided hikes are available at the center. | Milepost 169, Blue Ridge Pkwy. | 540/745–9660 | www.blueridgeparkway.org | Free | May–Oct. daily 9–5.

ON THE CALENDAR

OCT.: *Blue Ridge Folk Life Festival.* Celebrating the mountain communities that border the parkway's twists and turns, this festival delivers a lively dose of blues, bluegrass, and gospel music, with livestock competitions and mule-jumping contests. Local crafts for sale include baskets, dolls, and pottery. The festival takes place at Ferum College, in Ferum, on the last weekend in October. | 540/365–4416.

Dining

Brugh Tavern. American. A perfect stop on Sunday drive on the Blue Ridge Parkway. This reconstructed restaurant and tavern is in an 18th-century log cabin, originally built in Botetourt County, and was moved to its present location. The filet mignon in pastry, grilled salmon, or prime rib are house specialties. | 3900 Rutrough Rd., Roanoke | 540/427–2440 | $17–$22 | AE, D, MC, V.

Chateau Morrisette Restaurant. International. The winery's three dining rooms are in an elegant stone and gabled building, which was once a private residence. Framed playbills and the vineyard's own wine labels cover the walls. Large bay windows look out at the Buffalo Mountain and the Blue Ridge Parkway. The menu changes with the seasons, and centers on fresh ingredients. Known for desserts, particularly the Chocolate Oblivion Cake. Open-air dining on patio. Kids' menu. Beer and wine only. No smoking. Milepost 171, Blue Ridge Pkwy. | Winery Rd., Meadows of Dan | 540/593–2865 | Reservations essential for dinner | No dinner Mon.–Tues. no lunch Fri.–Sun. | $20–$33 | AE, MC, V.

High Country. Contemporary. Huge windows overlook the western Piedmont of North Carolina. The menu reflects a variety of cuisines: Angus rib steak, Norwegian salmon fillet in an orange and white wine sauce and sautéed veal. Homemade pies and cakes. Live pianist performs Fridays and a jazz or blues band keeps things toe-tapping on the terrace on Saturdays. Kids' menu. Sunday brunch. | Milepost 189, Blue Ridge Pkwy., Hillsville | 540/398–2212 | Closed Mon. | $14–$23 | AE, MC, V.

Otter Creek. American. Built in the 1950s and recently remodeled, this rustic restaurant on the Blue Ridge Parkway is a short drive from the James River. There's outdoor dining on picnic tables by Otter Creek. Known for buckwheat pancakes. Kids' menu. Lunch counter and gift shop. No alcohol. No smoking. | Milepost 60.8, Blue Ridge Pkwy. | 804/299–5862 | Breakfast also available. Closed Thanksgiving–mid-Apr. | $7–$10 | MC, V.

Peaks of Otter. American. This rustic pine restaurant features a wall of ceiling-high windows with a view of Sharp Top Mountain and Abbott Lake, through which you can enjoy the glorious colors in autumn and the flowers in spring. Vaulted ceilings, exposed beams, and 35-year-old wooden tables especially built for the restaurant complete the appealing interior. Under the same roof is also a cocktail lounge and a coffee shop. There's a Friday-night seafood buffet, Sunday country brunch, and an extensive selection of Virginia wines. The baked salmon is the local favorite. Salad bar. Kids' menu. No smoking. | Milepost 86, Blue Ridge Pkwy. | 540/586–9263 | Breakfast also available | $9–$18 | MC, V.

Lodging

Doe Run Lodge. This lodge has separate condominium-style suites on the quiet mountainside. Children under 15 may stay for free. Weekly rates are available. The suites have mountain views, rustic exteriors and modern interiors that vary in style. Restaurant, bar with entertainment, picnic area. Kitchenettes, in-room VCRs and movies. Pool. Sauna. Business services. Driving range, putting green, tennis courts. | Milepost 189, Blue Ridge Pkwy., Fancy Gap | 540/398–2212 or 800/325–6189 | fax 540/398–2833 | www.doerun-lodge.com | 47 suites | $119–$299 suites | AE, MC, V.

Peaks of Otter Lodge. This mountain get-away is on a 24-acre lot by a lake, and is surrounded by coniferous trees. Rooms are simple and comfortable. Restaurant, bar. No TV in rooms, TV in common area. Business services. | Milepost 86, Blue Ridge Pkwy., Bedford | 540/586–1081 or 800/542–5927 in VA | fax 540/786–4420 | www.peaksofotter.com | 63 rooms | $80 | MC, V.

Waynesboro/Afton Mountain Holiday Inn. Atop Afton Mountain, this three-story, white-brick hotel has breath-taking views of the Rockfish Valley below. The hotel stands at the northern end of the Blue Ridge Parkway, near the junction of Skyline Drive. Restaurant, bar, room service. Cable TV. Pool. Business services. Pets allowed. | Junction of I–64 (Exit 99) and U.S. 250 | 540/942–5201 or 800/465–4329 | fax 540/943–8746 | 118 rooms | $73–$91 | AE, D, DC, MC, V.

BRISTOL

(Nearby town also listed: Big Stone Gap)

Bristol, the "Twin City," straddles the Virginia and Tennessee border. The town's main thoroughfare, State Street, divides the town between Virginia to the north and Tennessee to the south. Although it is one community, Bristol is run by two local governments. Bristol was founded in 1771 and by 1784 an important iron works center operated here. Today, the factory town produces electronics, metal goods, and textiles.

Bristol calls itself the birthplace of country music because the first nationally successful country music stars, Jimmie Rodgers and the Carter Family, made their first recordings in Bristol in 1927. That heritage is kept alive with musical performances held throughout the year at the Paramount Center for the Arts. Nestled within national forests, Bristol also has plenty of outdoor activities. You can swim, water-ski, fish, or boat at either Sugar Hollow Park on the Virginia side or Steele Creek Park and South Holston Dam in Tennessee.

I–81 passes through Bristol, linking it to Roanoke and Knoxville. West Virginia, Kentucky, and North Carolina are all within easy driving distance.

Information: **Bristol Chamber of Commerce** | 20 Volunteer Pkwy., Bristol, TN 37620 | 423/989–4850 | tourism@bristolchamber.org.

Attractions

Bristol Caverns. In this cavern, you can walk a trail that follows the banks of an underground river and leads you past many unique rock formations. | 1157 Bristol Caverns Hwy., TN | 423/878–2011 | www.svis.org/comcaves | $8 | Mar. 15–Nov. 14, daily 9–5; Nov. 15–Mar. 15, daily 10–4.

Bristol Motor Speedway. NASCAR races, including the Winston Cup Series, Busch Series, and the Craftsman Truck Series, are held here. | 151 Speedway Blvd., TN | 423/764–1161 | www.bristolmotorspeedway.com | Ticket prices vary | Ticket Office Mon.–Fri. 9–5.

ON THE CALENDAR

OCT.: *Bristol Rhythm and Roots Reunion.* Held in downtown Bristol, this event includes many live performances (bluegrass, blues, and classic country) as well as demonstrations and workshops. | 423/764–4171.

Dining

Athens Steak House. American/Greek. Enjoy a casual meal in this brick building with hardwood floors and pictures of Greece on the walls. House specialties are steak with Greek seasonings. | 105 Goodson St., VA | 540/466–8271 | Closed Sun. No lunch | $15–$20 | AE, MC, V.

Cuzz's Uptown Barbeque. American. People drive two, three, and four hours to reach Cuzz's, a renovated 1950s barn in the middle of nowhere. The hayloft is converted into a waiting lounge where there's live bluegrass, blues, and jazz on weekends. You can dine in one of two solariums and enjoy a view of the surrounding farmland and hills from the upstairs deck. The owners have recently added two log cabins for travelers who have come particularly far and need a place to stay the night. Known for thick steaks, smoked prime rib, fresh fish, Thai seafood curry, and, of course, barbecue. Semi-covered dining on deck. Live bluegrass, blues, and jazz on weekends. Kids' menu. Beer and wine only. No smoking. | Rte. 460, Pounding Mill, VA | 540/964–9014 | Closed Sun. Dec.–Feb. and 1–2 wks around July 4 | $18–$31 | AE, MC, V.

Vinyard. Italian/American. This eatery strikes a balance between upscale formality and comfortable southern hospitality. Meals, served in the dining rooms, bistro-like lounge, and gardens, are enhanced by a familiar, long-employed staff. Local favorites are the prime rib and lasagna. Open-air dining in garden. Salad bar. Holiday buffets. Entertainment New Year's and Valentine's Day. | 603 Gate City Hwy., VA | 540/466–4244 | $15–$30 | AE, D, DC, MC, V.

Lodging

Budget Host. This modest, comfortable hotel is in the heart of downtown Bristol, and borders Tennessee. Corridors and room entrances are interior, and rooms are simply furnished. Cable TV. Business services. | 1209 W. State St., VA | 540/669–5187 | fax 540/466–5848 | 24 rooms | $25–$29 | AE, D, MC, V.

Comfort Inn. This hotel in a stone building has modest, sparsely decorated rooms, and easy interstate access. Complimentary Continental breakfast. Cable TV. Pool. Business services. | 2368 Lee Hwy., VA | 540/466–3881 | fax 540/466–6544 | www.comfortinn.com | 60 rooms | $60–$85 | AE, D, DC, MC, V.

Econo Lodge Bristol. A two-story chain option that's 2½ mi south of I–381 at Exit 3. The Omelet Shoppe, open 24 hours, is next door. Some microwaves, some refrigerators, cable TV. Pets allowed. | 912 Commonwealth Ave., VA | 540/466–2112 | 48 rooms | $33–$56 | AE, D, DC, MC, V.

Holiday Inn Bristol. This 10-story hotel is just off I–81 at Exit 7, on the northeast side of town. The hotel caters to businesses, with conference facilities and meeting rooms. Restaurant, bar, room service. In-room data ports, some kitchenettes, some microwaves, cable TV. Pool. Hot tub. Gym. Laundry service. Business services. Pets allowed. | 3005 Linden Dr., VA | 540/466–4100 or 888/466–4141 | fax 540/466–4103 | 226 rooms | $74–$189 | AE, D, DC, MC, V.

La Quinta Inn Bristol. The inn in a white stone building has comfortable rooms dressed in a conservative blue and green color scheme and floral and stripe prints. Complimentary breakfast. Pool. Some pets allowed. | 1014 Old Airport Rd., VA | 540/669–9353 | fax 540/669–6974 | www.laquinta.com | 123 rooms | $52 | AE, D, DC, MC, V.

Ramada Inn. This prefabricated chain hotel is housed in a white stone building with the signature Ramada tower over the entrance. Rooms are simple rooms with modest furnishings. The hotel is in a commercial area, and several blocks away from an indoor shopping mall. Restaurant, bar. Room service, cable TV. Pool. Laundry/valet. Business services. | 2221 Euclid Ave., VA | 540/669–7171 or 888/298–2054 | fax 540/669–7171 | www.ramada.com | 123 rooms | $60 | AE, D, DC, MC, V.

Red Carpet Inn. This red brick hotel is in a valley and has a courtyard. Rooms are comfortable, and have sliding glass doors to balconies that overlook the courtyard. Cable TV. Pool. Business services. Some pets allowed. | 15589 Lee Hwy., VA | 540/669–1151 | 60 rooms | $46 | AE, D, DC, MC, V.

Super 8. A member of the budget chain, this three-floor hotel in a commercial area has simple modest rooms. Just minutes from downtown Bristol. Picnic area. Some microwaves, refrigerators, cable TV. Business services. Some pets allowed. | 2139 Lee Hwy, Exit 4000, VA | 540/466–8800 | fax 540/466–8800 | www.super8.com | 62 rooms | $37–$120 | AE, D, DC, MC, V.

BROOKNEAL

(Nearby towns also listed: Lynchburg, South Boston)

Near the confluence of the Falling and Staunton Rivers in the south-central part of the state, Brookneal was named after the Brooke and Neal families. The settlement started as a tobacco inspection depot in the 1790s and got its town charter in 1802. The present-day economy is a mix of service and manufacturing firms, and furniture, electronic equipment, pharmaceutical products, and fabric are the chief products. The town's main tourist attraction is Red Hill, a frame house where Patrick Henry lived until his death in 1799.

Information: Town of Brookneal | Box 450, 215 Main St., Brookneal, VA 24528 | 804/376–3124 | www.brookneal.com.

Attractions

Patrick Henry National Memorial (Red Hill). Red Hill was the final home of Revolutionary War patriot Patrick Henry, whose "Give me liberty or give me death" speech inspired a generation. The restored home contains numerous family furnishings. An original law office, a coachman's cabin and stable, and a formal boxwood garden also occupy the site. | 1250 Red Hill Rd. | 804/376–2044 | fax 804/376–2647 | $3 | Apr.–Oct. daily 9–5; Nov.–Mar. daily 9–4.

Staunton River. Lovely trees rise up on either side of this lazy, meandering river, edging the city's southern border. Striped bass thrive in its waters, but in recent years have been found to contain PCB toxins.

ON THE CALENDAR

DEC.: *Patrick Henry Women's Auxiliary Christmas Tea.* Christmas tea, colonial-style, is served at Patrick Henry's home, Red Hill, which is decorated for the holidays with period trimmings. Refreshments are accompanied by holiday music. | 804/376–5216.

Lodging

Comfort Suites Hotel. Conservative, quaintly well-appointed rooms are offered at the chain hotel, almost 27 mi west of Brookneal. Complimentary Continental breakfast. Some in-room hot tubs, cable TV. Business services. Some pets allowed. | 1558 Main St., Altavista | 804/369–4000 | fax 804/369–4007 | www.comfortsuites.com | 65 suites | $68–$90 | AE, D, DC, MC, V.

CAPE CHARLES

(Nearby towns also listed: Chincoteague, Hampton, Norfolk, Onancock, Virginia Beach)

Cape Charles faces the Chesapeake Bay from the western rim of the Delmarva Peninsula. Established in 1884 as a railroad town, this community on sandy point is one of the East Coast showcases of late-Victorian and turn-of-the-century buildings. It's noted for clean and quiet public beaches, a marina, and opportunities for fishing and golfing. Just south of town is Kiptopeke State Park, a popular spot for bird-watching off of U.S. 13.

Information: Cape Charles/Northampton County Chamber of Commerce | 209 Mason Ave., Cape Charles, VA 23310 | 757/331–2304 | www.ccncchamber.com. **Eastern Shore of**

Virginia Tourism Commission | Box 460, Melfa, VA 23410 | 757/787–2460 | esva-tourism@esva.net | www.esva.net.

Attractions

Kiptopeke State Park. This 375-acre park on the Chesapeake Bay in Northampton County is excellent for bird-watching—it's on the path of a major flyway for migratory birds—and its coastal dunes provide a habitat for several rare animal species. Recreational activities include hiking, camping, swimming, and fishing. Boat ramp. | 3540 Kiptopeke Dr. | 757/331–2267 | www.state.va.us | Memorial Day–Labor Day, weekdays $3 per vehicle, weekends $4; Labor Day–Memorial Day, weekdays $2 per vehicle, weekends $3 | Daily 8 AM–dusk.

ON THE CALENDAR

OCT.: *Eastern Shore Birding Festival.* This three-day festival occurs at the peak of fall migration. Hikes, bird-banding demonstrations, educational talks, canoe trips, birding field trips, and conservation activities are held. | Sunset Beach, Kiptopeke State Park | 757/331–2267 or 757/787–2460.

Dining

Eastville Manor. Contemporary. The Scalleys, who escaped the city to live the quieter life, have planted more than a dozen vegetable, herb, and edible flower gardens around their renovated 1886 Victorian farmhouse, which also has two spacious guest rooms. The grounds are spectacular in spring, when the 100-year-old boxwoods, the thousands of perennials, flowering bulbs, and shrubs bloom. Renowned chef William Scalley prepares seasonal entrées, all garnished with herbs and edible flowers from the gardens. Locals say the crab cakes are the best anywhere. Desserts include crème brûlée, strawberry shortcake, chocolate truffles. Entertainment. No smoking. Eight mi north of Cape Charles. | 6058 Willow Oak Rd., Eastville | 757/678–7378 | Closed Sun.–Mon. also Tues. Sept.–May | $12–$21 | MC, V.

Little Italy. Italian. In this Italian restaurant, 19 mi northeast of Cape Charles, family pictures hanging from the walls and low-lighting set the scene for the local favorite dishes: lasagne, eggplant parmigiana, and linguini with clam sauce. Kids' menu. | Rogers Dr., Nassawadox | 757/442–7831 | Closed Sun. and Mon. | $7–$15 | No credit cards.

Sting-Ray's Restaurant. Seafood. Don't be put off by the location (behind a service station). Offerings on the blackboard menu include surprisingly upscale fare—certified cuts of Angus beef, fried oysters, broiled crab cakes, stuffed flounder with crab imperial, and home-smoked pork barbecue. | 26507 Lankford Hwy. | 757/331–2505 | Breakfast also available | $7–$20 | D, DC, MC, V.

Lodging

Cape Charles House Bed and Breakfast. A short stroll from this Colonial-revival house, built in 1912, finds you on the edge of Chesapeake Bay. Inside, antiques harmonize with the polished maple floors and wood details. Outside, herb and flower gardens brighten the scene. Beverages and snacks are served each afternoon. Complimentary breakfast. No TV, no room phones. No pets. No smoking. | 645 Tazewell Ave. | 757/331–4920 | fax 757/331–4960 | stay@capecharleshouse.com | www.capecharleshouse.com | 5 rooms | $85–$120 | AE, D, MC, V.

Pickett's Harbor. On Chesapeake Bay, the inn offers 27 acres of private beach. The rooms, which are furnished with antiques, all face the bay. Complimentary breakfast. No TV in rooms. Beach. Fishing. Some pets allowed. | 28288 Nottingham Ridge La. | 757/331–2212 | pickharb@aol.com | 6 rooms | $110–$150 | No credit cards.

Sea Gate Bed and Breakfast. Just three houses back from the beach of the Chesapeake Bay, this 1912 Victorian home has rooms with bay-views. Hardwood floors and mahogany appointments lend a warm charm to the interior. Outside, curl up in one of the inn's beach chairs outside and enjoy an afternoon tea. Complimentary breakfast. Cable TV. Bicycles (free for guests). No pets. No kids under 7. No smoking. | 9 Tazewell Ave. | 757/331–2206 | fax 757/331–2206 | seagate@pilot.infi.net | www.bbhost.com/seagate | 4 rooms | $80–$90 | No credit cards.

Wilson-Lee House. This turn-of-the-century Colonial Revival home is appointed with a tasteful selection of Victorian antiques and art deco furnishings. Breakfast is served on a screened-in porch, with pleasant breezes off the water of the Chesapeake Bay. A stocked butler's pantry provides you with complimentary sodas. There's also a microwave and refrigerator for your use. Complimentary breakfast. No TV, no room phones. Boating, fishing, bicycles. No pets. No kids under 12. No smoking. | 403 Tazewell Ave. | 757/331–1954 | fax 757/331–8133 | info@wilson-leehouse.com | www.wilsonleehouse.com | 6 rooms | $85–$120 | AE, MC, V.

CHARLES CITY

(Nearby towns also listed: Richmond, Williamsburg)

Colonial Virginia was divided into four political units in 1619, and Charles City County is one of the oldest "incorporated" settlements in America. Its early glory days can be glimpsed along Route 5, a scenic road that follows the James River past nine plantations, the oldest dating from 1723. You can tour four of the estates (Berkeley, Evelynton, Sherwood Forest, and Shirley) on one combination ticket for $28. Benjamin Harrison, presidents William Henry Harrison and John Tyler, and the family of Robert

AN ISLAND ON THE GROW

Fisherman's Island, the southernmost barrier island off the Delmarva Peninsula which began forming in the early 1800s, is an island to keep an eye on. While all the other islands in the chain are shrinking, slowly losing sand to the constant battering of the sea, Fisherman's Island continues to increase in size.

According to local legend, the island first formed around the bones of a British vessel that had been wrecked on the shoals of the Chesapeake Bay in the 19th century. The linen cargo carried by the vessel was salvaged by local residents and gave rise to the island's original name, Linen Bar. Others, however, say the name derived from the area's sands, which are as white and smooth as linen. Either way, by 1900, the area was known as Fisherman's Island. However it earned its name, most everyone agrees that the island basically showed up one day and has been expanding ever since. Over the years, fishing parties verify that this low-lying and treeless sandbar has just kept on growing.

In 1891, Fisherman's Island became the possession of the U.S. government. For a time it was the site of a Marine hospital and quarantine station; sailing vessels would stop at the island to drop off sailors suffering from communicable diseases. At that time, the land area was reported to be 25 acres. During both world wars, U.S. armed forces used the island for harbor defense. In the 1960s, the navy gave the island—then about 52 acres—to the Chesapeake Bay Ferry District which used it to connect the Chesapeake Bay Bridge-Tunnel to the mainland.

Today the island measures roughly 1,875 acres and has become a haven for wildlife. Most of it belongs to the Eastern Shore National Wildlife Refuge, a breeding ground for marsh and water birds, shore birds, gulls, and terns.

© Artville

E. Lee rank among the county's famous residents. Ironically, there is no city in Charles City County; despite its proximity to Richmond and Williamsburg, Charles City is largely rural, with extensive timberlands and cultivated farmland.

Information: **Charles City County Tourism Board** | 501 Shirley Plantation Rd., Charles City, VA 23030 | 804/829–5121.

Attractions

Berkeley. Built in 1726, this brick Georgian was the birthplace of Benjamin Harrison, a signer of the Declaration of Independence, and of William Henry Harrison, who briefly served as president in 1841. The riverfront mansion is furnished with period antiques; the terraced boxwood gardens, too, have been restored. The Coach House Tavern restaurant has seating indoors and out. | 12602 Harrison Landing Rd. | 804/829–6018 | fax 804/829–6757 | www.jamesriverplantations.com | $8.50 | Daily 9–5.

Evelynton Plantation. This 2,500-acre working plantation, originally part of the Wover estate, was the dowry of William Byrd II's eldest daughter, Evelyn. In 1846, it was purchased by the family of Edmund Ruffin, a secessionist who fired the shot at Fort Sumter that officially began the Civil War. The house contains 18th-century English and American antiques and is surrounded by landscaped lawn and gardens. The plantation is still operated by Ruffin descendants. | 6701 John Tyler Memorial Hwy. | 804/829–5075 or 800/473–5075 | www.jamesriverplantations.com | $9 | Daily 9–5.

Sherwood Forest. This 1730 estate was the retirement home of John Tyler, 10th president of the United States; he lived here from 1845 until his death in 1862. At 301 ft, it is said to be the longest wood-frame house in the country. It has remained in the Tyler family and contains many heirloom antiques; surrounding it are a dozen acres of grounds and outbuildings, including a tobacco barn. | 14501 John Tyler Memorial Hwy. | 804/829–5377 | fax 804/829–2947 | www.jamesriverplantations.com | $9 | Daily 9–5.

Shirley. The oldest plantation in Virginia, Shirley has been occupied by a single family, the Carters, for 10 generations. Robert E. Lee's mother, Anne Hill Carter, was born here. The 1723 Georgian manor stands at the end of a drive lined by towering Lombardy poplars; inside, the hall staircase rises for three stories with no visible support. The family silver is on display, ancestral portraits are hung throughout, and rare books line the shelves. | 501 Shirley Plantation Rd. | 804/829–5121 | fax 804/829–6322 | www.jamesriverplantations.com | $9 | Daily 9–5.

Westover. This estate was built about 1730 by Col. William Byrd II, an American aristocrat who served in both the upper and lower houses of the colonial legislature at Williamsburg; he also wrote one of the first travel books about the region. While the grounds are open to the public daily, the house, a renowned example of Georgian architecture, is open only during Garden Week in late April. The grounds feature rose and other flowering gardens as well as Byrd's grave site. | 7000 Westover Rd. | 804/829–2882 | www.jamesriverplantations.com | $2 | Daily 9–5:30.

ON THE CALENDAR

JULY: *Independence Day Celebrations at James River Plantations.* Benjamin Harrison, a signer of the Declaration of Independence, is honored at a wreath-laying ceremony at Berkeley Plantation. An ice cream social and 19th-century games are held at Sherwood Forest Plantation. | 804/829–5377.

NOV.: *The First Thanksgiving Festival.* Food, music, and special events commemorate the first official celebration of Thanksgiving in the New World, which occurred at Berkeley Plantation in 1619. There are living history performances, dances, demonstrations by local Native American tribes, southern-style food, and arts and crafts. | 804/829–6018.

DEC.: *James River Plantations' Christmas in the Country.* The historic plantation homes along the James River host a variety of holiday activities, from teas and festive dinners to decorating workshops.

Dining

Coach House Tavern. Continental. This tavern on the Berkley Plantation defines rustic elegance with fresh flowers and double linens. Frenchdoors open up to a view over the gardens. Oyster stew, crabcakes, homemade breads and desserts are choice selections off the menu. Kids' menu. Sunday brunch. | 12604 Harrison Landing Rd. | 804/829–6003 | No supper Sun.–Thurs. | $25–$40 | AE, DC, MC, V.

Indian Fields Tavern. Southern. After sight-seeing at the nearby historic plantations, experience the innovative southern cuisine served in this 100-year-old farmhouse. Fresh flowers set the tables at which delicate crabcakes Harrison and Chocolate Bourbon pecan pie, as well as homemade breads and dessert are served. Open-air dining on screened-in porch. | 9220 John Tyler Memorial Hwy./Rte. 5 | 804/829–5004 | Closed Mon. Jan. | $25–$41 | AE, D, MC, V.

River's Rest Motel and Marina. American. With views of the Chickahominy River, this restaurant serves comfort fare, including barbecued chicken, teriyaki chicken, steaks, and lasagna. Entrée comes with salad and dessert. | 9100 Wilcox Neck Rd. | 804/829–2753 | Breakfast also available | $8–$12 | AE, MC, V.

Lodging

Edgewood. On five wooded acres, the inn is in a Victorian home furnished with antiques and canopy beds. Many rooms have fireplaces. Discounts on plantation tours are available. Complimentary breakfast. Cable TV, in-room VCRs. Pool. No kids under 12. | 4800 John Tyler Hwy./Rte. 5 | 804/829–2962 or 800/296–3343 | fax 804/829–2962 | www.wmbg.com/edgewood | 8 rooms (3 with shower only) | $148–$188 | AE, MC, V.

North Bend Plantation. A National Registry property, this bed and breakfast on a working plantation is one of the finest examples of Greek Revival Federal Period architecture in Charles City. Original antiques, rare books, and old dolls furnish the building that has a rich Civil War history. Rooms have canopy beds, antique armoires, fireplaces, chaise lounges, period antiques and private baths. Croquet, volleyball, horseshoes, and bicycles available. Complimentary breakfast. Pool. | 12200 Weyanoke Rd./Rte. 5 | 804/829–5176 | fax 804/829–6828 | www.jamesriverplantations.org/NorthBend.html | 4 rooms | $120–$135 | Closed Jan. | MC, V.

Piney Grove at Southall's Plantation. Antebellum splendor. This 7,000-square-ft example of Gothic architecture has stunning interiors, rich upholstery, lavish canopy beds, gold-gilded frames, lace and damask window treatments, and a double free-standing, winding staircase. The bedrooms in the main house are equipped with working fireplaces, canopy beds, and elegant bathrooms, complete with dual shower heads. Complimentary breakfast. Refrigerators, no smoking, cable TV in some rooms, no room phones. Pool. | 16920 Southall Plantation La. | 804/829–2480 | fax 804/829–6888 | 4 rooms, 1 suite | $135–$175 | No credit cards.

Red Hill Bed and Breakfast. Surrounded by pastures, farms, and cornfields, this Williamsburg-style home, built in 1989, has four rooms, each with a distinctive look. One room, for instance, is done in antiques, another in wicker and oak, another has a white iron bed. Complimentary breakfast. TV in common area. No pets. No smoking. | 7500 John Tyler Memorial Hwy. | 804/829–6213 | fax 804/829–6213 | 4 rooms | $85 | MC, V.

CHARLOTTESVILLE

MAP 11, H5

(Nearby towns also listed: Culpeper, Orange, Schuyler, Shenandoah National Park)

Thomas Jefferson's city, Charlottesville is the home of the University of Virginia, and the most prominent metropolis in the foothills of the Blue Ridge Mountains. Roughly in the center of the state, it has been an important crossroads since colonial times; Main Street follows one of the first trails from Tidewater to the West. Named in 1762 for Queen Charlotte, wife of George III, Charlottesville today is a cosmopolitan college town known for its architectural gems and lush countryside. The area's leading attraction is Monticello, Jefferson's mountaintop home. Nearby is Ash Lawn-Highland, the abode of Jefferson's friend James Monroe. The University of Virginia campus, which also bears Jefferson's architectural touch, is renowned for its beauty.

Several annual festivals have added to the city's fame, among them the Virginia Film Festival in October and the Virginia Festival of the Book, a springtime event that brings together authors, publishers, and book agents. Beyond the city limits are a constellation of wineries and Shenandoah National Park, which borders Albemarle County to the northwest and offers lots of recreational opportunities.

Information: **Charlottesville/Albemarle Convention and Visitors Bureau** | 600 College Dr., Charlottesville, VA 22902 | 804/977–1783 | caccbb@comet.net | www.charlottesvilletourism.org.

Attractions

Albemarle County Court House. Albemarle County's first frame courthouse, constructed between 1763 and 1781, was replaced in 1803 by what now serves as the north wing of the present building. The front of the building was built just before the Civil War. Thomas Jefferson visited the courthouse many times, as did his neighbors and presidential successors, James Madison and James Monroe. The only large public building in the village during the early 1800s, the courthouse was used for a range of activities, from meetings of the University of Virginia's Board of Visitors to religious services. | 501 E. Jefferson St. | 804/972–4083 | fax 804/293–0298 | www.monticello.avenue.org | Free | Weekdays 8:30–4:30.

Ash Lawn-Highland. This farmhouse retreat was James Monroe's residence from 1799 to 1826, chosen, in part, so that he could be close to his friend, Thomas Jefferson, who lived several miles away at Monticello. Part of the house was destroyed in 1840, and the main section of the building dates from the 1870s. The 550-acre property is still a working plantation, and sheep and peacocks roam the grounds. The house is crowded with the fifth U.S. president's possessions, including gifts from notable persons and souvenirs from his

© Artville

THE BLUE RIDGE FOOTHILLS

Sometimes, small is better. You won't find any great neon-hung metropolis in the foothills of the Blue Ridge Mountains, or any 24-hour sushi bars, either. Towns without a stoplight are the norm here, and the daily cadences are quiet and unhurried. But if you are keen for history and architecture, for antiques and antiquarian books, or for activities in the great outdoors, you'll find plenty to keep you busy here.

The biggest city in this region is Charlottesville. Thomas Jefferson's Monticello tops the must-see list of attractions, along with the educational institution he founded, the University of Virginia. But less famous sites are worth a visit, too. If you come during summer, stop by James Monroe's estate, Ash Lawn-Highland, and stay for an evening of opera held outdoors in the boxwood garden.

During World War II, many of Chesapeake's watermen served in the armed forces overseas and illegal dredging declined. In 1962, Congress created the bi-state Potomac River Fisheries Commission, and law and order has since reigned.

time as envoy to France; the furniture is mostly original. The outdoor Ash Lawn-Highland Summer Festival, one of the country's top-ranked summer opera companies, draws music aficionados June through August. | 1000 James Monroe Pkwy. | 804/293–9539 | fax 804/293–8000 | www.monticello.avenue.org/ashlawn | $8 | Mar.–Oct. daily 9–6; Nov.–Feb. daily 10–5.

George Rogers Clark Memorial. This memorial, unveiled in 1921 by sculptor Robert Aitken, honors the man who helped win the Northwest Territory for Virginia during the Revolution. Clark is depicted astride a horse, among scouts and Indians. | West Main St. and Jefferson Park Ave.

Historic Michie Tavern. Michie Tavern was opened by Scotsman, William Michie in 1784. The tavern was actually built 17 mi away at Earlysville and moved here piece by piece in 1927. Costumed hostesses perform historically based skits and lead tours through antiques-filled rooms. The Virginia Wine Museum is housed in the tavern's old wine cellar; the old gristmill has been converted into a gift shop. A restaurant on the premises serves a colonial-style lunch buffet. Tours are every 10 minutes. | 683 Thomas Jefferson Pkwy. | 804/977–1234 | fax 804/296–7203 | www.michietavern.com | $8 | Daily 9–5.

Lewis and Clark Monument. Charles Keck created this monument to Meriwether Lewis and William Clark in 1919. It depicts the explorers of the Louisiana Territory gazing westward, while behind them crouches Sacajawea, the Indian woman who guided them in the vast new territory. | West Main St. at Ridge St.

★ **Monticello.** Thomas Jefferson, third U.S. president and author of the Declaration of Independence, constructed this mountaintop home over a 40-year period, between 1769 and 1809. It is considered a revolutionary structure, typical of no single architectural style. The staircases are narrow and hidden because he considered them unsightly and a waste of space; contrary to plantation tradition, his outbuildings are in the rear, not on the side. Throughout the house are Jefferson's inventions, including a seven-day clock and a "polygraph," a two-pen contraption that allowed him to make a copy of his correspondence as he wrote it. Monticello's gardens have been restored according to Jefferson's specifications and include many rare varieties of fruits and vegetables. The Thomas Jefferson Center for Historic Plants, located on the grounds, includes gardens, exhibits, and a sales area. April through October, interpreters give tours of Mulberry Row, the plantation "street" where Jefferson's slaves lived and labored. He and members of his family are buried in a nearby graveyard. Rte. 53. | 804/984–9822 or 804/984–9800 for recorded info | fax 804/977–6140 | www.monticello.org | $11 | Mar.–Oct. daily 8–5; Nov.–Feb. daily 9–4:30.

The **Monticello Visitors Center** provides extensive background information on both Thomas Jefferson and the construction of Monticello. Exhibits include a wide assortment of personal memorabilia—from drafting instruments to financial ledgers—as well as artifacts recovered during recent archaeological excavations. A free film that delves into Jefferson's political career is shown every half hour. Tours leave every 15 minutes. | Rte. 20 S | 804/977–1783 | fax 804/295–2176 | www.monticello.org | Free | Mar.–Oct. daily 9–5:30; Nov.–Feb. daily 9–5.

Robert E. Lee Monument. The equestrian statue of General Lee is the work of two sculptors, H. M. Shrady and Leo Lentelli. It was dedicated in 1924. | Market St. between 1st St. and 2nd St.

Stonewall Jackson on Little Sorrel. Created by artist Charles Keck and dedicated in 1921, this statue is of a bareheaded Jackson—a unique pose—galloping forward on his favorite mount, Little Sorrel. | Jefferson St. between 4th St. and 5th St.

Shenandoah National Park. Extending 80 mi along the Blue Ridge Mountains, the park has numerous opportunities for hiking, horseback riding, fishing, and camping. Naturalists conduct daily guided hikes throughout the summer. | 540/999–3500.

Wintergreen Resort. This 11,000-acre resort in the Blue Ridge Mountains offers recreational activities year-round, though its primary draw is skiing. The facility has 17 downhill slopes, indoor and outdoor tennis courts, and 45 holes of golf, around the mountain and in the valley. Half of the property is protected as natural forest area, with hiking and bridle trails throughout. There are accommodations and restaurants on the premises. | Rte. 664, Wintergreen | 804/325–2200 or 800/325–2200 | fax 804/325–8003 | www.wintergreenresort.com | Activity fees vary | Daily.

University of Virginia. Thomas Jefferson founded this university in 1819, drafted its first curriculum, helped select its first faculty, designed the original buildings, and served as the first rector of its board of visitors. Today it ranks as the one of the nation's most distinguished institutions of higher education. The heart of the university is the "academical village," built around a rectangular, terraced green space called the Lawn. Rows of single-story rooms are accented by large pavilions, each in a different classical style. Behind are public gardens delineated by serpentine brick walls. A poll of experts at the time of the U.S. bicentennial designated this complex "the proudest achievement of American architecture in the past 200 years." | 804/924–1019 or 804/924–7969 | fax 804/924–3587 | www.virginia.edu | Free | Daily; closed during winter break in Dec.–Jan. and during spring exams the first three weeks of May; tours daily at 10, 11, 2, 3, and 4.

Anchoring the north end of the Lawn, the domed **Rotunda** is a half-scale replica of the Pantheon in Rome. It originally served as the university's library, with rooms for drawing, music, and examinations. An 1895 fire severely damaged the building; its reconstruction was undertaken by New York architect Stanford White. Tours daily at 10, 11, 2, 3, and 4. | Main St. | 804/924–7969 | Free | Daily 9–4:45.

Maps and other brochures about the university can be picked up at the **Visitors Center** located about ½ mi from campus. | 2304 Ivy Rd./U.S. 250 | 804/924–7166 | www.virginia.edu | Free | Daily.

Virginia Discovery Museum. Hands-on exhibits are meant to interest kids in science, history, and the humanities. Programs include a computer lab and make-it-and-take-it art studio. | 524 E. Main St. | 804/977–1025 | fax 804/977–9681 | www.vadm.org | $4 | Tues.–Sat. 10–5, Sun. 1–5.

Jefferson Vineyards. The winery, which offers free tours and tastings, occupies the same land that Thomas Jefferson gave in 1773 to Italian winemaker Filippo Mazzei to establish a European-style vineyard. Mazzei is said to have found the soil and climate of Virginia better than Italy's, and the modern-day operation has consistently produced award-winning wines. | 1399 Thomas Jefferson Pkwy. | 804/977–3042 | fax 804/977–5459 | www.jeffersonvineyards.com | Free | Daily 11–5.

ON THE CALENDAR

MAR.: *Virginia Festival of the Book.* More than 100 writers attend this literary celebration, which offers dozens of events for book lovers of all ages: storytelling, seminars, book fairs, readings, and book signings. | 804/924–3296.

APR.: *Commemoration of Thomas Jefferson's Birth.* A wreath-laying ceremony at Thomas Jefferson's grave at Monticello includes a speech and music by a fife-and-drum corps. | Monticello, Rte. 53 | 804/984–9822.

APR.: *Dogwood Festival.* This community event, held along McIntire Road and all around downtown, features a parade, fireworks, barbecue, carnival, and the coronation of a Miss Dogwood queen. | 804/961–9824.

APR.: *Garden Week.* The doors of more than 250 private homes and gardens throughout Charlottesville and Albemarle County open for tours for this one week only, the last in April. The Garden Club of Virginia has free guidebooks detailing the houses on the Charlottesville tour. | 804/644–7776.

MAY, OCT.: *Crozet Arts and Crafts Festival.* This nationally ranked art show on Mothers Day weekend displays the work of more than 120 craftspeople with live music and food 12 mi west of Charlottesville. | Claudius Crozet Park, Park Rd. | 804/977–0406 | $3.50.

JUNE–AUG.: *Summer Festival–Ash Lawn-Highland.* A summer-long festival of music at James Monroe's country estate, Ash Lawn-Highland, offers concerts, lectures, crafts, and family entertainment. | 804/293–9539.

OCT.: *Virginia Film Festival.* Filmmakers, critics, actors, scholars, and moviegoers gather downtown and on the University of Virginia grounds to discuss American film. The featured roster of films has a different theme every year. | 800/882–3378.

Dining

Aberdeen Barn. Steak. Owned by the same family for more than 30 years, this old-fashioned steak house has lots of regular customers that come for an intimate and semiformal dining experience. Piano Sunday–Tuesday. Music in lounge Wednesday–Saturday. Kids' menu. | 2018 Holiday Dr. | 804/296–4630 | No lunch | $16–$45 | AE, DC, MC, V.

Ashley Room. Continental. The pastel dining room of this lovely restaurant in a turn-of-the-century building has Palladian-style windows overlooking the mountains. The seasonally-changing menu is decidedly international with a combination of European and American dishes that use fresh locally grown produce. Entertainment Friday–Sunday. Sunday brunch. No smoking. | 804/979–3440 | Reservations essential | Jacket required | Breakfast available. No lunch | $58 fixed price | AE, DC, MC, V.

Bertines North Caribbean. Caribbean. The owners blend the tastes and colors of the Caribbean (their home for 10 years) in their restaurant in a 75-year-old Virginia house overlooking the forested mountains of the Shenandoah National Park almost 30 mi north of Charlottesville. One room is deep ocean blue and brightened with original Haitian artwork; another room is tan and beige and basks in the warmth of a fireplace. Reggae, steel band and French island music fill the house, shaded with enormous trees. Open-air dining on porch. Beer and wine only. No smoking. | 206 S. Main St., Madison | 540/948–3463 | Closed Tues.–Thurs. No lunch | $23–$28 | D, DC, MC, V.

C.&O. French. French country cooking meets the flavors of the American Southwest and Pacific Rim at this restaurant that merges the casual with the composed and elegant. Choose from three dining areas. Two are bistro-style, informal and cozy, with rustic barnwood paneling. The other has a dressier feel and windows that allow diners to watch the scenic C.&O. train roll by. Food ranges from simple to elegant: rustic artichoke pâté, stuffed quail, Cuban sirloin steak. Frequently requested is steak chinois, a marinated flank steak served with C.&O.'s rich mashed potatoes. Most desserts are made on the premises, and there is an extensive wine list. | 515 E. Water St. | 804/971–7044 | No lunch | $12–$24 | AE, MC, V.

Carmello's. Italian. Right across the street from University Hall, this restaurant entices alumni, students and locals alike with northern Italian cuisine. Ravioli filled with lobster or lobster bisque are menu favorites. Desserts are specially made by the chef at the Watergate Hotel in Washington, D.C. | 400 Emmet St. | 804/977–5200 | No lunch | $8–$25 | AE, D, DC, MC, V.

Duner's. Eclectic. International flavors permeate the menu, which offers such varied items as venison, samosas, carne asada, and Cajun dishes. The grilled mahi mahi, baked Rag Mountain trout, polenta, and the lasagna are all house specialties. Sunday brunch. Seven mi west of Charlottesburg. | U.S. 250 W, Ivy | 804/293–8352 | www.cvilledining.com/clients/duners/duners.html | Reservations not accepted | No lunch | $19–$26 | AE, D, MC, V.

Eastern Standard. Asian/American. Self-styled American food fused with Asian accents is the hallmark of this upper-story restaurant housed in a 100-year-old brick building opposite the Omni Hotel and an ice skating rink on the west end of Charlottesville's historic Downtown Mall. Eastern Standard is an upscale version of Escafe, downstairs. Fresh fish preparations are offered daily; there are occasional special wine and champagne dinners. House specialties are the tamarind lamb, rabbit adobo, and pork medallions with passion fruit. Open-air dining on patio. | 102 Old Preston Ave. | 804/295–8668 | www.easternstandard.com | Closed Sun.–Tues. No lunch | $16–$23 | AE, D, DC, MC, V.

Escafe. Asian/American. This trendy, café takes after its big brother, Eastern Standard, with its pleasant mix of European and Asian flavors. The facade of the building has been renovated, so that a wall of doors opens in the summer to let the outdoors in. There's also seating on a patio along the west end of the Downtown Mall, perfect for people-watching while you nibble on such delicacies as roasted vegetable lasagna or beef tenderloin with black vinegar sauce. Entertainment Sundays. | 102 Old Preston Ave. | 804/295–8668 | www.escafe.com | No lunch Mon. | $5–$16 | AE, D, DC, MC, V.

Goodfellas. Italian. With stained glass windows in both dining rooms and an inviting fireplace, this classy restaurant is warm and comfortable. The prime rib and the Goodfellas combination plate, which consists of veal marsala, lasagna, and chicken parmigiana, are local favorites. Kids' menu. | 1817 Emmet St. | 804/977–6738 | Closed Mon. No lunch | $11–$18 | AE, D, DC, MC, V.

Hardware Store. American. The extensive menu of informal American fare has been updated to include smoothies, wraps, and pannini. The vintage turn-of-the-century signs, tools, and hardware displayed on the walls retain the flavor of a bygone era. Sit at the bar by the soda fountain or at a table and savor local treats, like fried chicken, fresh fish, Virginia country ham, and hush puppies. Desserts are flown in from around the world and also baked on the premises. Open-air dining. | 316 E. Main St. | 804/977–1518 | Closed Sun. | $10–$15 | AE, DC, MC, V.

Ivy Inn. Contemporary. Regional food is served in four dining rooms warmed by fireplaces in what was once an 18th-century Victorian toll house. The tent-covered garden patio is open April to October. The menu changes daily but always includes fresh seasonal produce. Locally raised bison and loin of veal from the nearby Summerfield Farms are house specialties. | 2244 Old Ivy Rd. | 804/977–1222 | Sundays; No lunch | $17–$27 | AE, MC, V.

Maharaja. Indian. Pictures of the subcontinent and antique-like urns accent the spare dining room of this Indian restaurant. Known for tandoori chicken, lamb, seafood dishes that use the rich ginger, tamarind, cumin, cashews, almonds and yogurt that tantalize and please the palate. Open-air dining on patio. No smoking. | 20 Seminole Sq. | 804/973–1110 | No lunch Mon. | $11–$16 | AE, D, DC, MC, V.

Martha's Cafe. Vegetarian. This friendly restaurant is in a 1920s house just off the trendy Corner, close to the University of Virginia Lawn. Original artwork by the restaurant owners and by members of the community adorns the inside walls; goldfish swim in the bathtub. Dine inside, out under a cool canopy of trees on a brick patio or on the wooden front porch. Mediterranean quesadillas, eggs Chesapeake with crab cakes, spinach crab soup, black bean burgers, artichoke pasta, gourmet micro pizzas, and herb chicken linguine are all house specialties. Kids' menu. Sunday brunch. Beer and wine only. One room air-conditioned. No smoking. | 11 Elliewood Ave. | 804/971–7530 | No supper Mon.–Tues. | $6–$13 | AE, D, DC, MC, V.

Mono Loco. Cuban. This eclectic restaurant offers a menu inspired by Cuban, Caribbean, and Latin cuisines that includes paella loca, giant burritos, and margaritas. Walls are bright gold and terra-cotta, and there's an unforgettably blue and green bar. Latin kitsch—giant lizards, dragons, and carved wooden angels—add to the fun. Don't miss dessert: bananas Castro, coconut flan, lime curd with fresh fruit. Sunday brunch. | 200 W. Water St. | 804/979–0688 | No lunch weekends | $7–$15 | D, MC, V.

Northern Exposures. Contemporary. Lots of exposure at this restaurant a short walk from the University of Virginia: Dine on the roof for maximum views, or inside in the glassed-in dining room. The New York Italian specials and the broiled bistro steak sauteed in red wine, garlic and fresh mushrooms are local favorites of this restaurant that draws its inspiration from "the Big Apple." Photos of "the city" and baseball heroes fill out the interior. Sunday brunch. | 1202 W. Main St. | 804/977–6002 | No lunch Sun. | $9–$19 | AE, D, DC, MC, V.

Old Mill Room. Contemporary. The 19th-century English styling of this restaurant's dining room in the historic Boar's Head Inn belies the thoroughly modern menu. Kobe beef (Japanese marinated beef) is served with Pernod poached Maine lobster and truffle foie gras and potatoes, and so on. Jazz Tuesday–Saturday night, harpist Sundays. Kids' menu. Salad bar. Lunch buffet. Sunday brunch. | 200 Ednam Drive | 800–476–1988 or 804/972–2230 | Breakfast also available | $25 | AE, D, DC, MC, V.

Rococo's. Italian. This upscale, Italian eatery, is as its name would suggest, done in an elegant Rococo-style design. Taste the tortellini bellisima, a cheese-filled tortellini with pancetta and scallions in a cream reduction sauce, the wild mushroom pizza or any of the homemade desserts and understand why this restaurant has become a Charlottesville institution since its opening in 1988. Kids' menu. Sunday brunch. | 2001 Commonwealth Dr. | 804/971–7371 | No lunch Sat. | $15–$30 | AE, D, DC, MC, V.

Schnitzelhouse. German/Swiss. Genuine German food is served in this rustic chalet under the light of chandeliers, and candles. German pictures and cuckoo clocks add to the continental feel. The most popular dish is the Wiener schnitzel, but the menu has grown over the past 30 years to meet diverse tastes; vegetarian entrées, pasta, and smaller portions are all available. With 24 hours notice, the chef can even come up with a tasty fondue. Kids' menu. | 2208 Fontaine Ave. | 804/293–7185 | Closed Sun.–Mon. 1st wk in Jan. 1st wk in July. No lunch | $10–$26 | AE, MC, V.

Starr Hill Restaurant and Brewery. American. Award-winning brewmaster, Mark Thompson showcases seasonal drafts at this contemporary brewery in a historic, turn-of-the-century building. Try the pizza made with brewer's grains, crabcakes, or the homemade veggie burger. | 709 W. Main St. | 804/977–0017 | No lunch | $8–$17 | AE, MC, V.

Lodging

Best Western Cavalier Inn. Convenient to the University of Virginia campus, this hotel is just three blocks from Barracks Road Shopping Center. The comfortable lobby has a library with many books to choose from and a large overstuffed chair, and the rooms are just as relaxed. For two-day stays, inquire about the Getaway plan. Cable TV. Pool. Business services. Airport shuttle. Some pets allowed. Free parking. | 105 Emmet St. | 804/296–8111 | fax 804/296–3523 | www.bestwestern.com | 118 rooms | $69–$99 | AE, D, DC, MC, V.

Best Western–Mount Vernon. This large motel has six two-bedroom suites available, and large rooms. Easy access to Monticello and the University of Virginia. Cable TV. Pool, wading pool. Business services. Some pets allowed. | 1613 Emmet St. | 804/296–5501 | fax 804/977–6249 | www.bestwestern.com | 110 rooms | $56–$68 | AE, D, DC, MC, V.

Boar's Head Inn. This old English-style inn on 53 acres of grounds is actually a modern, luxury resort. In the foothills of the Blue Ridge Mountains, the symbol of the large boar's head is famous for hospitality, and the list of guest amenities and activities is long from the hot-air ballooning to the four-post beds to the Italian linens. Restaurant, bar with entertainment, dining room. In-room data ports, some refrigerators, cable TV. 2 pools. Driving range, putting green, tennis courts. Exercise equipment. Bicycles. Kids' programs. Business services. Airport shuttle. Free parking. | 22905 Ivy Rd./U.S. 250 | 804/296–2181 or 800/476–1988 | fax 804/972–6024 | www.boarsheadinn.com | 173 rooms, 11 suites | $135–185, $250–$300 suites | AE, D, DC, MC, V.

Clifton–the Country Inn. This historic 18th-century manor house has a large columned veranda and beautiful views of Monticello (4 mi away). Rooms are luxuriously individually designed with down comforters, antique beds, and fireplaces. The forty-acre grounds include a croquet court and gazebo. Tea is served at 4. Restaurant, complimentary breakfast, room service. No room phones. Pool, lake, dock. Hot tub. Tennis. Business services. No smoking. | 1296 Clifton Inn Dr. | 804/971–1800 or 888/971–1800 reservations | fax 804/971–7098 | reserve@cstone.net | www.cliftoninn.com | 14 rooms, 7 suites | $150–$265, $225–$315 suites | MC, V.

Courtyard by Marriott. This Courtyard has a large marble lobby and comfy rooms with two phones, coffee makers, irons and ironing boards. Conveniently close to shopping at Fashion Square Mall. Bar, picnic area. In-room data ports, some microwaves, some refrigerators, cable TV. Pool. Hot tub. Exercise equipment. Laundry facilities. Business services. Airport shuttle. | 638 Hillsdale Dr. | 804/973–7100 | fax 804/973–7128 | www.courtyard-marriott.com | 150 rooms | $75–$150 | AE, D, DC, MC, V.

Days Inn. This chain hotel has a landscaped courtyard, which some of the more comfortable rooms face. Conveniently close to the University of Virginia and the interstate. Restaurant, bar. In-room data ports, room service, cable TV. Outdoor pool, wading pool. Sauna. Exercise equipment. Business services. Airport shuttle. Some pets allowed. Free parking. | 1600 Emmet St. | 804/293–9111 | fax 804/977–2780 | 129 rooms | $70–$80 | AE, D, DC, MC, V.

Doubletree. Off of U.S. 29, outside of town, this luxury chain hotel is situated on 20 acres four mi from Charlottesville-Albemarle Regional Airport. Jogging trails crisscross the property, and rooms are ambiguously "just what you'd expect from a Doubletree" (in other words, plush, but a bit bland). 2 restaurants, bar with entertainment. In-room data ports, cable TV. 2 indoor-outdoor pools. Hot tub. Tennis. Exercise equipment. Business services. Airport shuttle. | 2350 Seminole Trail | 804/973–2121 | fax 804/978–7735 | www.doubletreehotels.com | 234 rooms | $99–$140 | AE, D, DC, MC, V.

1817 Historic Bed and Breakfast. A block from the University of Virginia campus, this Federal period bed and breakfast was constructed by one of Charlottesville's master artisans: James Dinsmore, who also worked on Monticello. Antiques and period reproductions, complemented by lemon and burgundy walls, grace the rooms. Complimentary Continental breakfast. Cable TV. No pets. No smoking. | 1211 W Main St. | 804/979–7353 or 800/730–7443 | the1817inn@aol.com | www.1817bandbvirginia.com | 5 rooms | $89–$259 | AE, D, DC, MC, V.

English Inn of Charlottesville. This well-apportioned, small chain hotel has an English Tudor-style exterior and lobby, complete with high ceilings and oriental rugs. Rooms are comfortably fitted with Queen Ann panache, and host a reasonable list of modern amenities, like clock radios, shower massage and automatic wake-up services. Complimentary Continental breakfast. Refrigerators (in suites), cable TV. Indoor pool. Sauna. Exercise equipment. Business services. Airport shuttle. | 2000 Morton Dr. | 804/971–9900 or 800/786–5400 | fax 804/977–8008 | www.wytestone.com | 88 rooms, 21 suites | $64–$83 | AE, D, DC, MC, V.

Foxfield Inn. Built in 1951, this house has been completely redone as a gracious inn. Personal touches include canopy beds made by hand by the proprietors. Four of the five rooms have hot tubs, fireplaces, and bay windows. The inn also boasts three acres of manicured gardens. Complimentary breakfast. Some in-room hot tubs, no room phones, TV in common area. Spa. No pets. No kids under 14. No smoking. | 2280 Garth Rd. | 804/923–8892 | fax 804/923–0963 | foxfieldin@aol.com | www.foxfield-inn.com | 5 rooms | $125–$160 | MC, V.

Hampton Inn. This one-story chain hotel off of Route 29, next to Seminole Square shopping center, has spacious rooms with warm tile flooring. The airport is 6.7 mi away. Complimentary Continental breakfast. Cable TV. Pool. Business services. Airport shuttle. | 2035 India Rd. | 804/978–7888 | fax 804/973–0436 | www.hampton-inn.com | 123 rooms | $75–$82 | AE, D, DC, MC, V.

Holiday Inn Monticello. This high-rise hotel is close to I–64 and four mi away from Monticello. Marble floors, and big comfortable furniture in the lobby are echoed in the rooms. Restaurant, bar. Room service, cable TV. Pool, wading pool. Gym. Video games. Laundry facilities. Business services. Free parking. | 1200 5th St. SW | 804/977–5100 | fax 804/293–5228 | www.holiday-inn.com | 131 rooms | $80–$130 | AE, D, DC, MC, V.

Inn at Court Square. This Federal-style home, built in 1785, gets top honors as the oldest house in Charlottesville. Opened as an inn in 2000, the building touts modern amenities and improvements, such as whirlpools in all baths, but still casts a period charm with polished antiques and fireplaces in every room. The bed and breakfast is surrounded by charming shops and restaurants; the county courthouse is across the street. Complimentary Continental breakfast. Cable TV. Hot tub. Library. No pets. No smoking. | 410 E Jefferson St. | 804/295–2800 | 4 rooms, 1 suite | $149–$259 | AE, D, DC, MC, V.

Inn at the Crossroads. Want a glimpse at how life used to be? Check out the interior walls of this four-story brick lodging, an inn since 1820: they may look like plaster, but they're an old-fashioned mixture of clay strengthened with horse hair. Nine miles south of Charlottesville, the inn's four acres are surrounded by another 8,000 acres of pasture and orchards, with views of the Blue Ridge Mountains. Some of the antique-filled rooms have fireplaces. Complimentary breakfast. No TV, no room phones. No pets. No smoking. | 5010 Plank Rd., North Garden | 804/979–6452 | www.crossroadsinn.com | 4 rooms, 1 cottage | $85–$125 | MC, V.

Inn at Monticello. Dating from the mid-1800s, this inn is nestled on a large property that encircles the beautiful Willow Lake and is dotted with dogwoods, boxwoods, and azaleas. Rooms have beautiful views of the mountains, and individually furnished with period antiques and reproductions. Some rooms have fireplaces, and four-post canopy beds. Two-night minimum stay on weekends and holidays. Complimentary breakfast. No smoking, no room phones. No kids under 12. Business services. | 1188 Scottsville Rd./Rte. 20 | 804/979–3593 | fax 804/296–1344 | www.innatmonticello.com | 5 rooms | $110–$145 | AE, D, MC, V.

Inn at Sugar Hollow Farm. Wander this inn's 70 acres of fields and forests for views of the surrounding Blue Ridge Mountains. The inn's five rooms have canopy or four-poster beds, topped with handmade quilts. Two rooms have whirlpools, four have fireplaces. Complimentary breakfast. Some in-room hot tubs, no TV, no room phones. Hiking. No pets. No kids under 12 (on weekends). No smoking. | Sugar Hollow Rd. | 804/823–7086 | fax 804/823–2002 | theinn@sugarhollow.com | www.sugarhollow.com | 5 rooms | $95–$160 | AE, D, MC, V.

★ **Keswick Hall.** East of Charlottesville, this luxury estate-hotel on 600 acres of rich green, pastoral country, in the foothills of the Blue Ridge Mountains, was built with the full regalia of Italianate architecture. Each room is decorated along a different theme, and filled with Laura Ashley designs and antiques from around the world. Restaurant, picnic area, room service, cable TV. Indoor-outdoor pool. Hot tub, massage, sauna, spa. Driving range, 18-hole golf course, putting green. Health club. Business services. Airport shuttle. | 701 Club Dr., Keswick | 804/979–3440 or 800/274–5391 | fax 804/977–4171 | www.keswick.com | 42 rooms, 6 suites | $375–$575, $575–$595 suites | AE, DC, MC, V.

Knights Inn. On Route 29, a main commercial thoroughfare, this popular one-floor motel is quite close to shops and restaurants. Rooms are relaxed and well-appointed with private entries. Some kitchenettes, cable TV. Pool. Business services. Some pets allowed. | 1300 Seminole Trail | 804/973–8133 | fax 804/973–1168 | www.knightsinnofcharlottesville.com | 115 rooms | $49–$68 | AE, D, DC, MC, V.

Omni. The sleek ultramodern architecture of this hotel cuts a rakish knife-like pose among the buildings making up the low skyline of the pedestrian Downtown Mall. In the lobby, true to form, there is a fairly flamboyant seven-story gardened atrium. Rooms are well-apportioned (the standard size being 250 square feet), and modern. Restaurant, bar. Cable TV. In–room data ports. 2 pools (1 indoor). Hot tub. Massage. Exercise equipment. Business services. Some pets allowed. | 235 W. Main St. | 804/971–5500 | fax 804/979–4456 | www.omni-hotels.com | 204 rooms | $124–$169 | AE, D, DC, MC, V.

Prospect Hill Plantation. At this family-run bed-and-breakfast a few miles east of Charlottesville, rooms are in either the 1732 manor house or its authentic 18th century outbuildings. All rooms have working fireplaces, antique furnishings, and quaint country quilts. The manor house, surrounded by 50 acres of grounds, has a large private veranda and arboretum. Breakfast is served in bed or in the dining room. Dining room, complimentary breakfast. Some refrigerators, some in-room hot tubs, no room phones. Pool. Business services. | 2887 Poindexter Rd. Trevilians | 540/967–0844 or 800/277–0844 | fax 540/967–0102 | www.prospecthill.com | 13 rooms (2 with shower only), 3 suites | $190–$275, $275–$365 suites | MAP | D, MC, V.

Ramada Inn–Monticello. This hotel, off Route 250 East at Interstate 64 (Exit 124), has comfortable rooms with a number of options, like king-size or double beds. Nearby is the Pantops shopping center. Restaurant, bar, picnic area, room service, some in-room hot tubs, cable TV. Pool. Sauna. Exercise equipment. Video games. Laundry facilities. Business services. Free parking. | 2097 Inn Dr. | 804/977–3300 | fax 804/977–3300 | www.ramada.com | 100 rooms | $89–$129 | AE, D, DC, MC, V.

★ **Silver Thatch Inn.** This bed and breakfast is housed in a charming clapboard home built in 1780, now one of the oldest buildings in central Virginia. Rooms are furnished with period antiques, canopy beds, fireplaces and floral prints. Dining room, complimentary breakfast. No room phones. Pool. No kids under 8. Business services. No smoking. | 3001 Hollymead Dr. | 804/978–4686 | fax 804/973–6156 | www.silverthatch.com | 7 rooms | $115–$165 | AE, DC, MC, V.

Sunset Mountain Bed and Breakfast. Six miles north of Charlottesville, secluded in a forest, this modern, stained-wood bed and breakfast consists of two lodges, one with a large guest room and suite, the other a 900-sq-ft cottage. Both have kitchens and fireplaces, and are furnished with antiques and four-poster beds. Picnic area, complimentary breakfast. Kitchenettes, microwaves, refrigerators, some in-room hot tubs, in-room VCRs. Pool. Hot tub. No pets. No smoking. | 3722 Foster's Branch Rd. | 804/973–7974 | fax 804/973–9608 | driff@driff.com | www.driff.com/bb, or www.sunsetmt.com | 1 room, 1 suite, 1 cottage | $95–$165 | No credit cards.

200 South Street. Built in 1856, this inn is composed of two separate buildings that were for many years a single private residence, and briefly afterwards, a girls' finishing school, and brothel. Today, old-world elegance dominates the bed and breakfast, filled with English and Belgian antiques. A wide, welcoming neoclassical veranda and solid walnut two-story banister mark the main building. Rooms have individual antique furnishings, fireplaces, canopy, four-post, and sleigh beds. One block away is the pedestrian Downtown Mall. Complimentary Continental breakfast. Some in-room hot tubs. No TV in rooms, TV in common area. Business services. No smoking. | 200 South St. | 804/979–0200 or 800/964–7008 | fax 804/979–4403 | www.southstreetinn.com | 17 rooms, 3 suites | $105–$195, $190–$200 suites | AE, MC, V.

University Econo Lodge. A popular choice for parents of students at University of Virginia, this chain motel is across the street from the school's sports arena, and fills up on weekends and when football games are played. Some microwaves, some refrigerators, cable TV. Pets allowed ($5). | 400 Emmet St. | 804/977–5591 | 60 rooms | $60–$75 | AE, D, DC, MC, V.

Wintergreen. This 11,000-acre mountaintop resort has condominium and private home housing available. Accommodations vary: some have fireplaces, but all have beautiful views. Live entertainment and movies are featured. The resort is 45 mi southwest of Charlottesville. Dining room, bar, picnic area, snack bar. Kitchenettes, cable TV. 6 pools (1 indoor), wading pool. Hot tubs, massage. 2 driving ranges, 18-hole golf courses, 27-hole golf course, 2 putting greens, tennis. Exercise equipment, boating. Bicycles. Downhill skiing. Children's programs (ages 2 1/2–17), playground. Business services. Airport shuttle (fee). | Wintergreen Dr./Rte. 664 Wintergreen | 804/325–2200 or 800/266–2444 | fax 804/325–8003 | www.wintergreenresort.com | 315 rooms | $140–$200 1–bedroom room, $205–$290 2–bedroom room | AE, MC, V.

CHESAPEAKE

MAP 11, K7

(Nearby towns also listed: Norfolk, Portsmouth, Suffolk, Virginia Beach)

At the southeastern edge of Virginia, Chesapeake is considered the boomtown of the Hampton Roads region. Once a rural, agricultural area, it is now home to a large concentration of Japanese manufacturers, big-name businesses, and service companies. The city was formed in 1963, when Norfolk County and city of South Norfolk were merged. There is still a bit of wilderness behind all the industry, however; the Great Dismal Swamp and the National Wildlife Refuge border the city on the east and west, and people boat and camp at Northwest River Park. Two branches of the Atlantic Intracoastal Waterway run south from Chesapeake, offering boaters a scenic route to Florida.

Information: **Hampton Roads Chamber of Commerce** | 400 Volvo Pkwy., Chesapeake, VA 23320 | 757/622–2312 | pnemetzg@hrccva.com | www.hrccva.com.

Attractions

National Wildlife Refuge. This 7,000-acre preserve with a visitor center is bounded by the Atlantic Ocean on one side and the bay on the other. Trails for hiking and bicycling wind through the refuge, providing glimpses of wildlife and a variety of waterfowl. | 4005 Sandpiper Rd. | 757/721–2412 | fax 757/721–6141 | www.backbay.fws.gov | $5 per vehicle | Daily dawn–dusk; visitor center weekdays 8–4, weekends 9–4.

Great Dismal Swamp National Wildlife Refuge (*See* Suffolk.) Stretching into North Carolina, this wildlife refuge has hundreds of miles of hiking and biking trails, including a wheelchair-accessible boardwalk. The Dismal Swamp Canal, which runs into North Carolina, is part of the Atlantic Intracoastal Waterway and is the oldest man-made waterway in the country. | 757/986–3705 U.S. Fish and Wildlife Service, 919/771–8333 or 888/872–8562 visitor center.

Northwest River Park. This park allows boating on both an inland lake and the Northwest River. Camping, fishing, horseback riding, and canoeing trips on Chesapeake's scenic waterways, led by park staff, are popular activities. | 1733 Indian Creek Rd. | 757/421–3145 or 757/421–7151 | fax 757/421–0134 | www.chesapeake.va.us | Free | Apr.–Dec. daily dawn–dusk.

ON THE CALENDAR

MAY: *Chesapeake Jubilee.* Celebrating the town's anniversary (it was founded in 1963), this festival finds livestock competitions, carnival rides, live music and fireworks keeping things hopping at the Chesapeake Park along the Greenbriar Parkway. | 757/482–4848.

Dining

Cara's. Contemporary. Enjoy a casual meal over views of the Chesapeake Bay wetlands. The long menu offers a wide variety of dishes. Be sure to try the fresh tuna specials or have the hot wings as an appetizer. Open-air dining on outdoor deck. Live music Thursday–Saturday. Kids' menu. | 123 N. Battlefield Blvd. | 757/548–0006 | Closed Sun.; no lunch Sat. | $11–$17 | D, MC, V.

Court House Café. American. Down the street from the court house, this restaurant plays with a legal theme, with touches like law books lining the walls. Fare includes seafood and chicken dishes, as well as prime rib. A favorite starter is she-crab soup. | 350 Battlefield Blvd. S | 757/482–7077 | $8–$19. | AE, D, MC, V.

Kyoto Japanese Steak House. Japanese. Watch steak sizzle as it is prepared table-side at this teppanyaki-style steak house. There's also a full cocktail bar and a sushi bar. Kids' menu. | 1412 Greenbriar Pkwy. | 757/420–0950 | No lunch Sun. | $10–$23 | AE, D, DC, MC, V.

Locks Pointe. Seafood. This restaurant has two dining rooms, one of which is enclosed in a glass atrium with water on three sides, and the other sports water views from all areas of the restaurant. The daily seafood specials rule the menu. Open-air dining on an open deck. Entertainment Wednesday–Sunday in summer, Friday–Saturday in winter. Kids' menu. Dock space. Sunday brunch. | 136 N. Battlefield Blvd. | 757/547–9618 | No lunch Sat. | $14–$22 | AE, MC, V.

Lone Star Steakhouse and Saloon. Steak. If you're in the mood for meat, tug on that Stetson and saunter on in to this Western-themed, family-run restaurant, where hunting trophies decorate the walls. When it comes to the food, the focus is on big steaks. The saloon, on the side of the restaurant, has TVs tuned to sporting events. | 1570 Crossways Blvd. | 757/424–6917 | $9–$20 | AE, D, DC, MC, V.

Oysterette. Seafood. The name says it all at this eatery, just east of Chesapeake Square Mall near Hodges Ferry Bridge. The menu is loaded with oysters (try the Oysters Rockefeller), clams, and other seafood selections. A tip for hungry night owls: this restaurant keeps serving well after midnight. | 3916 Portsmouth Blvd. | 757/465–2156 | $7–$12 | AE, D, DC, MC, V.

Lodging

Comfort Inn–Bowers Hill. This two-story brick motel has Spartan-but-"comfortable" rooms with exterior entrances that face the outdoor pool or the highway. Easy interstate access is a plus. Complimentary Continental breakfast. Some kitchenettes, cable TV. Pool. Business services. | 4433 S. Military Hwy. | 757/488–7900 | fax 757/488–6152 | www.comfortinn.com | 100 rooms | $79–$119 | AE, D, DC, MC, V.

Comfort Suites–Greenbriar. Homey for a chain hotel, this Comfort Suites has flowers, a chandelier or two, a variety of oriental rugs, and a working fireplace. The suites are quite comfortable. Nearby is the Greenbriar Mall. Complimentary Continental breakfast. Microwaves, refrigerators, cable TV, in-room VCRs and movies. Pool. Hot tub. Sauna, exercise equipment. Business services. | 1550 Crossways Blvd. | 757/420–1600 | fax 757/420–0099 | www.comfortsuites.com | 123 suites | $86–$110 suites | AE, D, DC, MC, V.

Courtyard by Marriott. This self-consciously business-oriented hotel ("designed by business travellers") has well-appointed rooms, some of which face a landscaped courtyard. Within 5 mi are Mitsibushi, Panasonic, Volvo Penta, and Ford Motor. Across the street is the Greenbriar Parkway Mall, and conveniently close is the Great Dismal Swamp. Restaurant. Some in-room hot tubs, cable TV. Indoor pool. Business services. | 1562 Crossways Blvd. | 757/420–1700 | fax 757/420–1939 | www.courtyardmarriott.com | 90 rooms | $96–$136 | AE, D, DC, MC, V.

Days Inn. This terra-cotta-colored and blue-trimmed hotel has rooms that echo the exterior's southwestern color scheme. Rooms are predictably Spartan. Easy access to Interstate 64. Complimentary Continental breakfast. Some microwaves, refrigerators, cable TV. Pool. Laundry facilities. Business services. | 1433 N. Battlefield Blvd. | 757/547–9262 | fax 757/547–4334 | 91 rooms | $70–$90 | AE, D, DC, MC, V.

Econo Lodge Chesapeake. This comfortably appointed, two-story chain motel, renovated in 1999, sits near I-64 off Exit 291–A. In-room data ports, some microwaves, some refrigerators, cable TV. No pets. | 2222 S Military Hwy. | 757/543–2200 | fax 757/543–0572 | 55 rooms | $42–$85 | AE, D, DC, MC, V.

Fairfield Inn by Marriott. A comfortable lounge area greets you with a large chandelier as you enter this hotel across from the exciting Greenbriar Mall. Rooms are reasonably equipped, and have work desks with lamps. Complimentary Continental breakfast. In-room data ports, cable TV. Pool. Business services. | 1560 Crossways Blvd. | 757/420–1300 | fax 757/366–0608 | www.marriott.com | 104 rooms | $78–$90 | AE, D, DC, MC, V.

Hampton Inn. This prefabricated chain hotel is just two blocks from the I-64 interchange. Rooms are furnished in luxurious shades of blue, brown and maroon, and some have couches. Complimentary Continental breakfast. In-room data ports, cable TV. Pool. Business services. | 701A Woodlake Dr. | 757/420–1550 | fax 757/424–7414 | www.hampton-inn.com | 119 rooms | $83–$90 | AE, D, DC, MC, V.

Holiday Inn. Perhaps, the pinnacle of accommodation in Chesapeake, this seven-story hotel, smack in the center of town off I-64, has a pyramidal atrium area with a large pool. Rooms vary from the standard to the executive class (which has a king-size bed and wet bar) and have security key locks. Restaurant, bar. In-room data ports, some microwaves, room service, cable TV. Pool. Hot tub. Exercise equipment. Business services. Airport shuttle. | 725 Woodlake Dr. | 757/523–1500 | fax 757/523–0683 | www.holiday-inn.com/chesapeakeva | 230 rooms | $109–$179 | AE, D, DC, MC, V.

Red Roof Inn Chesapeake. A half mile north of Greenbrier Mall, this two-story, moderately priced chain lodging stands near I–64 at Exit 289–A. Some in-room data ports, some microwaves, some refrigerators, cable TV. Pets allowed. | 724 Woodlake Dr. | 757/523–0123 | fax 757/523–4763 | 108 rooms | $41–$53 | AE, D, DC, MC, V.

Super 8 Motel Churchland. This two-story, Tudor-style chain motel sits just off I–664, Exit 8B. In-room data ports, some refrigerators, cable TV. Pets allowed. | 3216 Churchland Blvd. | 757/686–8888 | fax 757/686–8888, ext. 403 | 59 rooms | $41–$75 | AE, D, DC, MC, V.

Wellesley Inn. This modern corporate chain hotel has coffee makers in all the rooms, and love seats and pull-out sofas in some rooms. The hotel is 10 minutes from the beach, and walking distance to several malls and a supermarket. Complimentary Continental breakfast. Microwaves, refrigerators, cable TV. Pool. Laundry facilities. Business services. Pets allowed (fee). Free parking. | 721 Conference Center Dr. | 757/366–0100 | fax 757/366–0396 | 106 rooms; 16 suites | $89–$149 | AE, D, DC, MC, V.

CHINCOTEAGUE

MAP 11, L5

(Nearby towns also listed: Cape Charles, Onancock, Tangier Island)

This remote island on the Eastern Shore near the Maryland border is known for its wild ponies, descendants of horses that strayed or were abandoned in early colonial times. Every July, hordes of visitors come to witness Pony Penning Day, when ponies from Assateague Island are herded across the channel to Chincoteague to be auctioned. The event was immortalized in *Misty of Chincoteague*, a 1940s children's book, written by the island's most famous resident, Marguerite Henry.

Chincoteague is no longer the wild, secluded island of Henry's novel, but a resort community with many shops, eateries, and hotels. Seven miles long and slightly more than a mile wide, the island has largely uncrowded beaches and excellent channel fishing. Chincoteague is also the gateway to uninhabited Assateague, a wildlife preserve.

Information: Chincoteague Chamber of Commerce | Box 258, Chincoteague, VA 23336 | 757/336–6161. **Eastern Shore of Virginia Tourism Commission** | Box 460, Dept. 98, Melfa, VA 23410 | 757/787–8687 | esvatourism@esva.net | www.esv.net.

Attractions
Chincoteague National Wildlife Refuge. There are several trails for hiking and biking, including a wildlife loop and a woodland trail, in this protected area. Snow Goose Pool and Swan Cove are popular bird-watching areas. The visitor center, near the park's entrance, posts a daily schedule of events. | 8231 Beach Rd. | 757/336–6122 | fax 757/336–5273 | www.nature.nps.gov | $5 per vehicle | Daily dawn–dusk, visitor center daily 9–4.

Misty Monument. The wild pony, inspiration behind Marguerite Henry's 1947 classic, "Misty of Chincoteague," is memorialized in a bronze statue at the end of Ridge Road. | Ridge Road.

NASA's Wallops Flight Facility Visitors Center. The center features exhibits on the history of flight, early rocket launches, space travel, and the business of the Wallops Island facility, which launches suborbital rockets and balloons. | Rte. 175 | 757/824–1344 or 757/824–2298 | www.wff.nasa.gov | Free | July–Aug. daily 10–4; Sept.–June, Thurs.–Mon. 10–4.

Oyster and Maritime Museum. The Chesapeake Bay's oyster trade from the 1600s to the present is chronicled in this museum's displays of homemade tools, hand-carved decoys, shells and marine life. | 7125 Maddox Blvd. | 757/336–6117 | www.chincoteague.com/omm | $3 | Memorial Day–Labor Day, daily 10–5; Labor Day–Nov. Sat. 10–5, Sun. noon–4; Mar.–Labor Day, Sat. 10–5, Sun. noon–4.

Refuge Waterfowl Museum. This museum has mounted displays of waterfowl and other wild shore birds that make their home on the Eastern Shore. The history of decoy carving is highlighted; a resident carver sells his wares at the museum. | 7059 Maddox Blvd. | 757/336–5800 | $2 | Mar.–Nov. daily 10–5.

ON THE CALENDAR

MAR. OR APR.: *Easter Decoy and Art Festival.* Roughly 150 local and national carvers gather to show and sell their work. There are contests and an auction. | Easter weekend | Chincoteague High School, 4586 Main Street | 757/336–6161 | www.chincoteaguechamber.com/ev-easterdecoy.html.

JULY: *Pony Swim and Auction.* Wild ponies are rounded up on Assateague Island by volunteer firemen, swim across the channel to Chincoteague and are herded down Main Street to the carnival grounds for auction. Those unsold swim back to Assateague. | 757/336–6161.

COLUMBUS DAY WEEKEND: *Oyster Festival.* An all-you-can-eat feast for oyster lovers at the Maddox Campground, off Rte. 175. Tickets regularly sell out and must be purchased in advance. | 757/336–6161 | www.chincoteaguechamber.com/ev-oyst.html.

NOV.: *Waterfowl Week.* Chincoteague National Wildlife Refuge, off Route 175, has extended hours during this week; visitors can glimpse snow geese, ducks, and a variety of other migrating waterfowl. Special bird-watching programs and marsh wildlife walks are offered. | 757/336–6122.

Dining

AJ's on the Creek. Seafood. Dine inside among the candlelit tables or outside on a screened-in veranda to enjoy live music and views of Eel Creek. Though veal and hand-cut steaks are on the menu, the specialty here is seafood, with oysters, assorted shellfish in marinara sauce, and grilled tuna. | 6585 Maddox Blvd. | 757/336–5888 | $16–$41 | AE, D, DC, MC, V.

Blackboard Bistro, Ltd. Contemporary. With seating for only 18 guests, this restaurant, a converted 1901 waterman's house, is an intimate dining option. Each of three dining rooms has its own theme; the Iron Horse Room, for instance, displays a collection of model trains. Parents take note: the owners keep a few toy locomotives on hand to keep the kids busy. Menu changes nightly, but always includes seafood, such as crab cakes or sautéed flounder. | 3837 Main St. | 757/336–6187 | No lunch. Closed Wed. | $10–$17 | No credit cards.

Captain Fish's Steamin' Wharf and Deck Bar. Seafood. The big deck at this wharf restaurant makes room for the weekend crowds, which pack in for the fresh seafood and live music. Try the aptly named seafood boat: a jumble of crab meat, shrimp, and scallops, topped with melted cheese. | 3855 Main St. | 757/336–5528 | $11–$22 | MC, V.

Chincoteague Inn. Seafood. Beneath a vaulted ceiling crossed with exposed beams, captain's chairs snug up against wood tables in the spacious dining room, which overlooks Chincoteague Bay. The menu prides itself on local seafood offerings, including crab cakes, stuffed flounder, oysters, and clam strips. Take in live music on the weekends. | 6265 Marlin St. | 757/336–6110 | $10–$24 | MC, V.

Don's Seafood Restaurant. Seafood. Surrounded by Chincoteague's little shops, this restaurant has been serving its homemade crab cakes, oysters, and clams (on the half shell or steamed) since 1973. Hamburgers, steaks, ham, chicken dishes fill out the menu. | 4113 Main St. | 757/336–5715 | Breakfast also available | $7–$16 | D, DC, MC, V.

Garden and the Sea Inn. American/Continental. Romantic, candlelit dinners prepared by gourmet chef, Tom Baker, a Culinary Institute of America graduate with 35 years experience, make dining at this inn truly special. His signature dishes are shrimp, scallops, and oysters in white wine, and chicken Virginia, which is served on a bed of Smithfield ham with apple slices and brandy cream sauce. You can eat outside on the patio surrounded by lush gardens, and afterward, spend an intimate evening in one of the eight guest rooms. The Victorian front of this historic country inn, which was originally built in 1802, was added in 1896. | 4188 Nelson Rd. New Church | 757/824–0672 | Reservations essential | $28–$37 | AE, D, MC, V.

KF Chicken and Fish. American. Slip into a red vinyl booth in this relaxed, family-run restaurant, and fill up on fresh-cooked crab cakes, a shrimp basket, or a chicken sandwich. Large windows let you watch the world go by. | 6341 Maddox Blvd. | 757/336–3433 | $4–$9 | No credit cards.

Landmark Crab House. Seafood. Surrounded by the bay on three sides, this restaurant's many window tables assure you a view of the water. The menu is split between seafood entrées, like the crab imperial and sautéed crab meat in butter, and meat dishes, including New York strip steak, filet mignon, and prime rib, all using certified Angus beef. | 6172 N Main St. | 757/336–5552 | No lunch | $13–$22 | AE, D, MC, V.

Steamers Seafood. Seafood. Paintings of the famous ponies of Assateague Island by local artists mark the dining room of this casual eatery. In addition to the regular menu, there's an all-you-can-eat special. Kids' menu. | 6251 Maddox Blvd. | 757/336–5478 | Closed Nov.– Apr. No lunch | $14–$22 | D, DC, MC, V.

Lodging

Birchwood. This motel has a crabbing pier, pool with a gazebo, colorful rooms, hammocks hanging from shady pines, and picnic grounds with grills for summer barbecuing. Refrigerators, cable TV. Pool. Playground. Laundry facilities. | 3650 Main St. | 757/336–6133 | fax 757/336–6535 | www.esva.net/~birchwd | 42 rooms | $50–$89 | Closed Dec.–Mar. | AE, D, MC, V.

Cedar Gables Seaside Inn. Overlooking Little Oyster Bay and Assateague Island, the inn makes good use of its location: each room has its own deck overlooking the water, and the pool, with views of the peaceful marshlands and bay, has a see-through glass enclosure. Rooms, appointed with contemporary furnishings, all have fireplaces. Complimentary breakfast. Refrigerators, in-room hot tubs, cable TV, in-room VCRs. Pool. Hot tub. Dock. No pets, no smoking. No kids under 14. | 6095 Hopkins Ln. | 757/336–1096 or 888/491–2944 | www.cedargable.com | 4 rooms | $155–$180 | AE, D, MC, V.

Channel Bass Inn. Built in 1892, the house became an inn in the 1920s. Each room is furnished in a different period of antiques. Afternoon tea is a sumptuous affair with different desserts from around the world served in an ornate tea room. The inn is close to Assateague Wildlife Refuge. Complimentary breakfast. No kids under 6. No smoking. | 6228 Church St. | 757/336–6148 or 800/249–0818 | fax 757/336–0599 | www.channelbass-inn.com | 6 rooms | $109–$175 | Closed Jan.–mid-Mar. | AE, MC, V.

Comfort Inn. This standard chain hotel is rurally located, a mile from downtown Onley, 25 mi southwest of Chincoteague Island, 2 mi west of the Tangier Island Tour, and 4 mi north of the Historic Mitchie Tavern. The Spartan rooms are blandly furnished. Complimentary Continental breakfast. In-room data ports, refrigerators, cable TV. Pool. Exercise equipment. Business services. | 25597 Coastal Blvd., Four Corner Plaza, U.S. 13, Onley | 757/787–7787 | fax 757/787–4641 | www.comfortinn.com | 70 rooms, 10 suites | $74, $81–$88 suites | AE, D, DC, MC, V.

Driftwood Lodge. This three-floor motel has elevators for upper level room access. The comfortable rooms have views of Assateague Island, some teak-like furniture, and queen-size and king-size beds. Cable TV. Pool. Bicycles. Business services. Refrigerators. Picnic area. | 7105 Maddox Blvd. | 757/336–6557 or 800/553–6117 | fax 757/336–6558 | www.driftwood-motorlodge.com/ | 53 rooms | $89–$100 | AE, D, DC, MC, V.

Garden and the Sea. Built in 1802 as the Buxom tavern, this Victorian house, a few miles west of Chincoteague, is well-put-together with an eclectic mix of antiques and reproductions. Rooms are luxuriously appointed and you are served complimentary beverages during your stay. Tea and meals are served in an elegant dining room. The inn is 15 mi from Chincoteague. Restaurant, complimentary Continental breakfast. No room phones. Some hot tubs. Business services. | 4188 Nelson Rd., New Church | 757/824–0672 or 800/824–0672 | www.gardenandseainn.com | 8 rooms in 3 buildings | $95–$175 | AE, D, MC, V.

Inn at Poplar Corner. Built in 1996, a replica of a Victorian manor in Suffolk, VA, the inn has the look of an old home, but the comfort and amenities of a new building. The wide porch is the place to relax for breakfast each morning. Floral-patterned wallpaper, hardwood floors, and antique beds highlight each room, which also have private whirlpool tubs. Most rooms have views of Chincoteague Bay; the Main View room has its own balcony. Complimentary breakfast and afternoon tea. In-room hot tubs, no room phones, no TV. Bicycles. No pets. No kids under 10. No smoking. | 4248 Main St. | 757/336–6115 or 800/336–6787 | fax 757/336–5776 | 4 rooms | $139–$149 | Closed Dec.–early March | MC, V.

Island Manor House. This B&B has an upscale charm, with French doors and large windows to take in views of the Chincoteague Bay. The white frame house, built in 1848 as a classic "Maryland T," has been juggled and split into two separate buildings joined by a glassed-in sitting room. This rose-hued Garden Room looks across the inn's brick courtyard and fountain, and is warmed on chill evenings by a crackling fire. Inn rooms are filled with antiques, some from the 1700s. Complimentary breakfast. No room phones, no TV, no smoking, no pets. Bicycles, free to guests. No kids under 12. | 4160 Main St. | 757/336–5436 or 800/852–1505 | fax 757/336–1333 | www.islandmanor.com | imh@intercom.net | 8 rooms (6 with private bath) | $75–$130 | AE, MC, V.

Island Resort. On the Intercoastal Waterway, the inn has ocean and bay views from the lobby and balcony of every room. The former motor inn has a private boardwalk, a deep water dock, and crabbing pier. Restaurant. Room service. Picnic area. In-room data ports, refrigerators, cable TV. 2 pools (1 indoor). Hot tub. Exercise equipment. Business services. | 4391 Main St. | 757/336–3141 or 800/832–2925 | fax 757/336–1483 | 44 rooms, 16 suites | $95–$115, $105–$175 suites | AE, D, DC, MC, V.

Lighthouse Inn. This modest, two-story motel has screened-in patios and is within walking distance of downtown, and just minutes from NASA's Wallops Flight Facility Visitors Center. Picnic area. Refrigerators, microwaves, cable TV. Pool. Hot tub. | 4218 Main St. | 757/336–5091 | 17 rooms | $69–$89 | Closed Dec.–Feb. | MC, V.

Miss Molly's Inn. Right on the saltwater bay, this late-19th-century inn has period furnishings in the parlor, common area, and rooms. Marguerite Henry, the daughter of J.T. Rowely, stayed in this quaint 1886 home, while writing *Misty of Chincoteague* published in 1947. The afternoon tea in the gazebo is known for its scones. Complimentary breakfast. No smoking. No kids under 8 on weekends. Business services. | 4141 Main St. | 757/336–6686 or 800/221–5620 | www.missmollys-inn.com | 7 rooms (2 with shared bath) | $85–$130 | Closed Jan.–mid-Mar. | AE, D, MC, V.

Payton Place. On two secluded acres on the quiet, southern end of the island, this lodging sits directly on the bay, facing west to take in the sunset. This is a place to sprawl, with each 800-square-foot suite having a separate living room and bedroom and private entrance. Bring along the fishing rod to try your luck off the 350-foot-long private pier; a nearby outdoor eating area, with grill, gazebo, and tables, gives you a pleasant place to cook and enjoy your bounty. Picnic area. Microwaves, refrigerators, cable TV, no room phones, no smoking. Dock, fishing. No pets. No kids under 8. | 2569 Main St. | 757/336–3572 or 800/237–5856 | johnclang@aol.com | www.chincoteague.com/payton | 3 suites | $110–$125 | AE, MC, V.

Refuge Inn. Chincoteague ponies can be seen on the grounds of this motor inn located near the beach, off the the causeway to Assateague. Rooms vary from the standard appointments, such queen-size beds and dark varnished furniture, to the deluxe with king-size beds with mirrored and four-post bed frames. Picnic area. Refrigerators, cable TV. Indoor-outdoor pool. Hot tub. Exercise equipment. Bicycles. Laundry facilities. Business services. | 7058 Maddox Blvd. | 757/336–5511 or 800/544–8469 | fax 757/336–6134 | www.esva.net/~refugeinn/ | 72 rooms | $57–$200 | AE, D, DC, MC, V.

Sea Hawk. This prefabricated motel is near Chincoteague Channel. A wide variety of accommodations, including some efficiency apartments, are available, but all of them are Spartan and spare. Picnic area. Refrigerators, cable TV. Pool. Playground. | 6250 Maddox Blvd. | 757/336–6527 | 25 rooms; 8 apartments | $50–$85, $525–$575 (7–day minimum stay) apartments | www.esva.net/~seahawk/ | AE, D, MC, V.

Sea Shell. This old-fashioned, one-story motel is in a quiet residential area, and has a variety of accommodation and bedding options. Rooms vary with several single beds, double and queen-size beds. Picnic area. Refrigerators, cable TV. Pool. Business services. | 3720 Willow St. | 757/336–6589 | fax 757/336–0641 | 40 rooms, 5 cottages, 2 houses | $40–$74 | www.chincoteague.com/hot/sea.html | Closed Nov.–mid-Mar. | AE, D, DC, MC, V.

Sunrise Motor Inn. This modest, low-slung one-story motel is close to the wildlife refuge and the beach. Rooms are quiet and comfy. Picnic area. Some kitchenettes, refrigerators, cable TV. Pool. Playground. Business services. | 4491 Chicken City Rd. | 757/336–6671 or 800/673–5211 | fax 757/336–1226 | www.chincoteague.com/sunrise/ | 24 rooms | $40–$70 | Closed Dec.–mid-Mar. | AE, D, DC, MC, V.

Waterside Motor Inn. On the channel with a marina, this beach-house style motel has beautiful views of the water. Rooms are comfortable and have commercially standard furnishings. Picnic area. Refrigerators, cable TV. Pool. Hot tub. Tennis. Exercise equipment. Fishing. Dock. Business services. | 3761 S. Main St. | 757/336–3434 | fax 757/336–1878 | www.watersidemotorinn.com | 45 rooms | $98–$155 | AE, D, DC, MC, V.

Watson House. This inn was built in 1878 as a private home, and restored as inn in 1992. Dine outside on the veranda or inside in the dining room among the period antiques that populate both the common areas and the rooms. If the inn is full, inquire about the owner's other property in town, Inn at the Poplar Corner, another Victorian home restored in 1996. Complimentary breakfast. No smoking, no room phones. Bicycles. No kids under 9. Business services. | 4240 Main St. | 757/336–1564 or 800/336–6787 | fax 757/336–5776 | 6 rooms (5 with shower only) | $89–$110 | Closed Dec.–mid-Mar. | MC, V.

Year of the Horse Inn Bed and Breakfast. This inn, opened in 1958 as a boarding house for fishermen, sits right on the edge of the water. Rooms, with contemporary furnishings, all have their own deck for taking in spectacular sunsets across Chincoteague Bay. The inn has its own dock for boating and fishing, and picnic area with tables, chairs, and grills (charcoal supplied). Complimentary Continental breakfast, picnic area. Some kitchenettes, all rooms have refrigerators, cable TV, no room phones, no smoking. No pets. | 3583 Main St. | 757/336–3221 or 800/680–0090 | rhebert@esva.net | www.esva.net/~rhebert | 3 rooms | $80–$120 | MC, V.

CLARKSVILLE

MAP 11, H8

(Nearby town also listed: South Boston)

Clarksville, in central Virginia near the North Carolina border, got its start in the 1820s as a market town for tobacco. In the late 1940s, the U.S. Army Corps of Engineers formed Buggs Island Lake, the 50,000-acre body of water that edges Clarksville, by constructing a series of dams along the Roanoke River. The town is now an outdoor destination, with fishing, swimming, boating, and camping all readily accessible; surrounding the lake are state park and wildlife management areas, several marinas, restaurants, vacation cottages, and other lodgings.

Information: **Clarksville Chamber of Commerce** | 105 2nd St., Clarksville, VA 23927 | 804/374–2436 | clarksville@kerrlake.com | www.kerrlake.com.

Attractions

Occoneechee State Park. Named for the Native American people indigenous to the area, the 2,690-acre park is on Buggs Island Lake. The park has campsites, picnic shelters, and boat launching ramps. A visitor center has exhibits on the culture of the Occoneechee people. | 1192 Occoneechee Park Rd. 23927 | 804/374–2210 | www.state.va.us | Weekdays $1 per vehicle, weekends $2 per vehicle | Daily.

Old Clarksville. Take an amble past the homes, businesses, and churches of Clarksville, founded in 1816. Many structures are on the National Register of Historic Places. The downtown area has many antique shops and art galleries.

Prestwould. This 1795 plantation house, built by Sir Peyton Skipwith, one of colonial Virginia's few baronets, overlooks Buggs Island Lake. One-hour tours are given of the main house, which contains its original furnishings, and the outbuildings, which are the earliest surviving wood-frame slave houses in the South. | Box 872, U.S. 15, | 804/374–8672 | $8; garden tour $3 | Apr. 15–Oct. Mon.–Sat. 12:30–3:30, Sun. 1:30–3:30; or by appointment.

ON THE CALENDAR

MAY: *Native American Heritage Festival and Powwow.* A celebration of Native American culture in Occoneechee State Park, this festival has traditional dancing, drumming, food, and crafts. | 804/374–2436.

JULY: *Virginia Lake Festival.* Over 45,000 people descend on Clarksville the third weekend of July to enjoy this annual festival, centered around Main Street, in the historic district. Festivities include fireworks over the lake, arts and crafts and food booths, and live music. | 804/374–2436.

Dining

Lamplighter Restaurant. American/Casual. Don't be put off by the name of this restaurant's locale, Buggs Island Lake. You'll get bug-free views across the water through the windows of this eatery, decorated with murals harkening back to the days of the horse and buggy. Prime rib, ribeye steak, lobster tail, crab legs, and local clams and oysters highlight the menu. | 201 Virginia Ave. | 804/374–0230 | Breakfast also available | $10–$18 | AE, D, MC, V.

Lodging

Century Manor. The Victorian mansion is furnished with antiques. It's just four blocks from lake. Complimentary afternoon snacks are served, and box lunches are available. Complimentary breakfast. In-room VCRs, no room phones. | 900 Virginia Ave. | 804/374–5414 | www.bbonline.com/va/century | 4 rooms | $75–$95 | MC, V.

Kinderton Manor. On six landscaped acres, including rose gardens and a 100-yard-long alley of myrtle trees, this 1835 Greek revival plantation house has four spacious rooms, each with antiques and period wallpaper. The inn is surrounded by Kinderton Country Club's golf course. Complimentary breakfast. Cable TV. No pets, no smoking. No kids under 10. | 850 Kinderton Rd. | 804/374–8407 | fax 804/374–4439 | 4 rooms | $55–$85 | No credit cards.

Lake Motel. This horse-shoe-shaped motel is right on the lakefront. Rooms are comfortable and have lake views. Cable TV. Pool. | 101 Virginia Ave. | 804/374–8106 | fax 804/374–0108 | www.conradusa.com | 74 rooms, 3 suites | $65, $75–$85 suites | AE, MC, V.

CLIFTON FORGE

(Nearby towns also listed: Covington, Lexington, Hot Springs, Warm Springs)

Clifton Forge sits in the shadow of the Allegheny Mountains with West Virginia as its next-door neighbor. Founded in 1884, the city was named for its iron production; its rich mines produced cannons and cannonballs during the Civil War. But the area owes more of its prosperity to the Chesapeake and Ohio Railway, which established a terminal here after the war. For nearly a century, the area's economy was tied to the railroad industry; the present-day economy is a mix of manufacturing and service industries. Douthat State Park, one of the first public parks in Virginia, was completed by the Civilian Conservation Corps in 1936 and is listed on the National Register of Historic Places. The park lies between two massive ridges and is the site of many recreational activities, from swimming and boating to fishing and camping.

Information: Alleghany Highlands Chamber of Commerce, | 501 E. Ridgeway St. Suite C, Clifton Forge, VA 24422 | 540/862–4969 | ahchamber@aol.com.

Attractions

Allegheny Highlands Arts and Crafts Center. The place to find watercolors, pottery, jewelry, and quilts by local artists and crafts people. The center also displays monthly art exhibits. | 439 E Ridgeway St. | 540/862–4447 | Free | Mon.–Sat. 10–4:30.

C & O Historical Society Archives. You are welcome to peruse historical documents, photos, and drawings relating to the Chesapeake and Ohio Railway, its predecessors, and other railways that have merged with it, including the Michigan and Ohio rails. Records date from the mid-1800s. There's a gift shop. | 312 E. Ridgeway St. | 540/862–2210 | fax 540/863–9159 | www.cohs.org | Free | Mon.–Sat. 10–4.

Douthat State Park. A 50-acre lake stocked with trout, a sandy swimming beach, hiking trails, a campground, picnic areas, and mountain scenery are the main draws of this 4,493-acre park. | Rte. 1 | 540/862–8109 | www.state.va.us | Weekdays $1 per vehicle, weekends $2 per vehicle | Daily 8 AM–10 PM.

Historic Stonewall Theatre. After laying dormant for a number of years, this 1904 theater is once again turning up the stage lights. Friday and Saturday nights find the Clifton Forge Players and actors from the close Lime Kiln theater putting on musical variety shows. | 510 Main St. | 540/863–9606 | Fri. and Sat. nights.

Iron Gate Gorge. A rock formation known as "Rainbow Rock" dominates this gorge, which got its name from the iron blast furnaces put in at its northern end by the Alleghany Iron and Ore Company in the 1880s. The Jackson River has been carving out the rock for 12 million years. | U.S. 220 | 540/962–2178.

ON THE CALENDAR

OCT.: *Fall Foliage Festival.* This celebration takes place when the fall foliage in the Allegheny Mountains is at its peak. Crafts, an art show, railroad history exhibits, music, food vendors, a flea market, fair rides, and games fill the downtown Historic District. | 540/862–4463.

Dining

Cat and Owl Steak and Seafood. American. This Victorian home opened as a restaurant in 1975, aiming its sites at workers from nearby C & O Railway yards. But everyone's welcome in the dining room, appropriately decorated with railroad antiques. Specialties include charbroiled shrimp and scallops, filet mignon, and ribeye steaks. Off I-64 at Low Moor Exit. | 110 Karnes Rd. Low Moor | 540/862–5808 | No lunch. Closed Sun. | $13–$18 | AE, D, MC, V.

Lodging

Longdale Inn. This dusty-rose, gingerbread-trimmed Victorian inn is listed on the National Register of Historic Places. Built in 1873 for the Firmstone family and the Board of Directors of the Longdale Iron Works, it has been an inn since 1938 and was restored in 1989 and 1991. Rooms come in a variety of styles from Victorian to Southwestern to European, and period antiques populate the nooks and corners of the inn. Picnic area, complimentary breakfast. No air-conditioning, no smoking, no TV in rooms, no room phones, TV and VCR in common area. Playground. Business services. Some pets allowed. | 6209 Longdale Furnace Rd. | 540/862–0892 | fax 540/862–3554 | www.bbonline.com/va/longdale | 10 rooms (3 with shower only, 4 with shared bath), 2 suites | $80–$100, $130 suites | AE, D, MC, V.

COVINGTON

MAP 11, F6

(Nearby towns also listed: Clifton Forge, Warm Springs, Hot Springs)

Named for its earliest settler, Peter Covington, this town was established in 1818. It is the county seat of Alleghany County and considered the western gateway to Virginia. The town's biggest employer is Westvaco, which manufactures paper products and chemicals. The George Washington and Jefferson National Forests surround the area and attract outdoor sports enthusiasts year-round; Lake Moomaw, 19 mi north of Covington, is particularly popular.

Information: Alleghany Highlands Chamber of Commerce | 501 E. Ridgeway St. Suite C, Clifton Forge, VA 24422 | 540/862–4969 | ahchamber@aol.com.

Attractions

George Washington and Jefferson National Forests. (*See Harrisonburg.*) Boating, swimming, water-skiing, fishing, and rugged hiking are among the activities in the James River Ranger District of these national forests. | 5162 Valleypointe Pkwy., Roanoke | 540/265–5100.

Humpback Bridge State Wayside Park. The nation's only surviving curved-span covered bridge, erected in 1835, is the centerpiece of this small, 5-acre park. Made of hand-hewn timbers and locust pins instead of nails, the bridge carried traffic until 1929. It got its name because of a rise of 8 ft from the ends to the center. There's a picnic area. | Midland Trail Rd. | 540/962–2178 | www.state.va.us | Free | Daily.

Lake Moomaw. In the Bath and Alleghany counties, on the edge of the West Virginia border, this 2,530-acre lake was created when the U.S. Corps of Engineers constructed the Gaithright Dam in 1979. With 43 mi of shoreline, the lake's recreational opportunities include boating, swimming, fishing, camping, and hiking. | Rte. 687 | 540/962–2214 | www.fs.fed.us | $2 parking fee | May–Nov. daily dawn–dusk.

ON THE CALENDAR

JUNE: *International Bass Bonanza.* A competition to catch the biggest largemouth bass at Lake Moomaw off U.S. Route 220 North. | 540/962–2178.

Dining

Brass Lantern. American. Gaze out at the Allegheny Mountains from this restaurant, connected to the Best Western Mountain View (*See Lodging*). Chicken, trout, and shrimp dishes, with special prime rib dinners every Saturday. | 820 E. Madison St./Rte. 60 | 540/962–4951 | Breakfast also available | $8–$19 | AE, D, DC, MC, V.

James Burke House. American. This house, built in 1817 next to the Jackson River, serves homemade quiches, salads and other lunch fare in its cozy dining room with central fireplace. Try the chicken salad sandwich, finished off with a brownie for dessert. | 232 River-side St. | 540/965–0040 | Breakfast also available. No dinner. Closed Sun. | $5–$8 | MC, V.

Lodging

Best Western–Mountain View. The chain hostelry is close to the interstate. Rooms are painted in comfortable colors and sufficiently furnished. Restaurant, bar, complimentary breakfast, room service. In-room data ports, some refrigerators, cable TV. Pool, wading pool. Business services. Pets allowed (fee). Free parking. | 820 E. Madison St./U.S. 60 | 540/962–4951 | fax 540/965–5714 | www.bestwestern.com | 79 rooms | $74–$99 | AE, D, DC, MC, V.

Budget Inn Motel. How many chain motels let you cast a line into a quiet stretch of river looping through the backyard? This two-story lodging sits on the western edge of town, along the Jackson River and adjacent to the James Burke House Eatery. Room service. Some in-room data ports, microwaves, refrigerators, cable TV. Fishing. Laundry service. Business services. Pets allowed ($10). | 420 N Monroe Ave. | 540/962–3966 | 30 rooms | $70 | AE, D, DC, MC, V.

Comfort Inn. Two miles southeast of Covington, this Comfort Inn has beautiful mountain views from its rooms and facilities. coffee makers and irons are in every rooms. Restaurant, bar. Complimentary Continental breakfast. Some refrigerators, cable TV. Pool. Hot tub. Business services. Pets allowed (fee). | 203 Interstate Dr. | 540/962–2141 | fax 540/965–0964 | www.comfortinn.com | 98 rooms, 32 suites | $72–$74, $81 suites | AE, D, DC, MC, V.

Holiday Inn Express Covington. Opened in 1999, this four-story member of the familiar chain is a convenient, reliable option, just north of I–64 at Exit 16. In-room data ports, microwaves, refrigerators, some in-room hot tubs, cable TV. Pool. Hot tub. Laundry service. Business services. No pets. | 701 Carlyle St. | 540/962–1200 | fax 540/962–1245 | 63 rooms | $76–$125 | AE, D, DC, MC, V.

Knights Court. A comfortable small, standard hotel, with easy interstate access. Rooms are coordinated in dark muted colors. Complimentary Continental breakfast. Some kitchenettes, microwaves, refrigerators, cable TV. Some pets allowed. | 908 Valley Ridge Rd. | 540/962–7600 | fax 540/965–4926 | 72 rooms | $57–$65 | AE, D, DC, MC, V.

Milton Hall Bed and Breakfast. Built in 1874 out of solid brick, this Gothic Victorian inn has period antiques, reproduction furniture, and fireplaces to warm yourself. The building is on 44 acres and has lush gardens for wandering. Adjacent is the George Washington National forest. Complimentary breakfast. TV in rooms, common area, common area phone. Some pets allowed. No smoking. | 207 Thorny La. | 540/965–0196 | www.miltonhall.com | 6 rooms (3 with shower only), 1 suite | $100–$150 suite | MC, V.

CULPEPER

MAP 11, I4

(Nearby towns also listed: Orange, Warrenton)

Founded in 1748, Culpeper was at the forefront of the colonial rebellion against England. In 1777, the town's Minutemen marched to Williamsburg in answer to Governor Patrick Henry's call to arms. During the Civil War, several large battles were fought in Culpeper's pastures and hillsides, and the wounded were treated in the town's churches and homes. Culpeper is a center for light industry in a five-county area and maintains a strong agricultural base. The downtown district has antiques stores, crafts shops, and a handful of eateries. A major north–south artery, U.S Route 29, passes through Culpeper, making it a good stopover point on longer drives.

Information: **Culpeper County Chamber of Commerce** | 133 W. Davis St., Culpeper, VA 22701-3017 | 540/825-8628 | culpepercc@summit.net | www.co.culpeper.va.us.

Attractions

Dominion Wine Cellars. Under the direction of Williamsburg Winery Ltd., Dominion is the maker of award-winning specialty wines, such as Blackberry and Raspberry Merlot, Lord Culpeper Seyval, and Filippo Mazzei Reserve. The Dominion label was launched in 1985 by a group of 20 growers who formed the Virginia Wineries Cooperative. There's picnicking on the grounds. | 1 Winery Ave. | 540/825–8772 | www.williamsburgwineryltd.com | Free, tastings $1 | Mon.–Sat. 10–4:30, Sun. 12–4:30.

Prince Michel Winery. Jean Leducq created this award-winning winery in the foothills of the Blue Ridge Mountains, 10 mi southwest of Culpeper, in 1982. Free tastings take place in the Wine Tasting Room of a small museum dedicated to the history of winemaking. | HCR 4, Box 77, Leon | 540.547.3707 or 800.869.8242 | www.princemichel.com | Free, tastings $1 | Daily 10–5.

Museum of Culpeper History. From the footprints of Culpeper's earlier inhabitants–dinosaurs–to more recent memorabilia, you'll find a wide sweep of the town's rich history in this downtown museum. Displays include assorted artifacts and period photographs. | 803 S. Main St. | 540/829–1749 | www.culpepermuseum.com | Free | Mon.–Sat. 11–5.

ON THE CALENDAR

APR.: *Graves Mountain Spring Fling.* This weekend celebration, five or six mi west of Culpeper, has bluegrass music, cloggers, fly-fishing demonstrations, arts and crafts, hayrides, and horseback riding. | Graves Mountain Lodge, Rte. 670, Syria | 540/923–4231.
MAY: *Culpeper Day.* A festival along Davis Street with regional crafts, bluegrass and country music, and food vendors. | 540/825–7768.

Dining

Hazel River Restaurant. Contemporary. As one of the oldest buildings in downtown Culpeper (it served as a jail in the Civic War), it's not surprising to find wide plank floors and hand-hewn beams in this candlelit restaurant. The steak, duck, and chicken dishes all have a twist–grilled chicken breast, for example, is marinated in blackberry vinaigrette and served with wild mushrooms. The home-smoked salmon and organic trout are also standouts. Many of the herbs and vegetables are grown at Culpeper's Hazel River Inn. | 195 East Davis St. | 540/825–7148 | Closed Wed. | $13–$22 | AE, MC, V.

Lord Culpeper Restaurant. Contemporary. Local legend says the ghost of Culpeper's former mayor hangs out in this downtown building, built in 1933. If so, he's not going hungry, with varied choices including lemon ginger chicken, salmon with a sour cream dill sauce, and pork loin with carmelized apples and onions. Burgers, grilled fish, and steaks fill out the menu. | 401 S Main St. | 540/829–6445 | Sun. brunch | $9–$24 | AE, D, DC, MC, V.

Pancho Villa's Mexican Family Restaurant. Mexican. Murals of the legendary Mexican liberator ornament the walls of this informal restaurant. While the usual assortment of burritos, fajitas, enchiladas, and quesadillas show up on the menu, you'll also spy more innovative specialties, such as bacon-wrapped shrimp stuffed with crab meat. | 910 S. Main St. | 540/825–5268 | $7–$9 | AE, D, MC, V.

Prince Michel. French. This restaurant 10 mi southwest of Culpeper in Madison County, is nestled on the grounds of Prince Michel wineries. Two dining areas give you the opportunity to dine casually in the bistro-area with its trellised booth alcove or in a more elegant upscale room with a view of the vineyards. The soft peach and blue-green of the table linen accents the European-style place settings, and the service is as dazzling as the crystal. French master chef, Alain Lecomte is uncompromisingly committed to using local and fresh foods to create updated classic French recipes, such as filet of sole stuffed with lobster and served on a bed of spinach with lobster butter sauce or roasted duck breast with a cherry sauce served with potatoes and turnips. | HCR 4, Box 77, U.S. 29 S, Leon | 540/547–9720 or 800/800–9463 | www.princemichel.com/diningmain.htm | Jacket required | $70–$80, fixed price menu; $20–$40 entrees | AE, MC, V.

Lodging

Comfort Inn. In downtown Culpeper, this fully-carpeted hotel has coffee makers in every room, and some king-size beds and nonsmoking rooms available. Rooms are conservatively furnished. Complimentary Continental breakfast. In-room data ports, cable TV. Pool. Business services. Pets allowed (fee). | 890 Willis La. | 540/825–4900 | fax 540/825–4904 | www.comfortinn.com | 49 rooms | $60–$85 | AE, D, DC, MC, V.

Fountain Hall Bed and Breakfast. The basic structure of this bed and breakfast dates from 1859. In 1923, the building's front facade was renovated in a Colonial revival-style. Each room of the stately bed and breakfast is plush with period antiques and reproductions, and decorated in a different style: 1920s Art Deco, Victorian, and early American. Picnic area, complimentary Continental breakfast. In-room data ports, some refrigerators, some in-room hot tubs. Business services. Library. No pets. No smoking. | 609 S. East St. | 540/825–8200 or 800/298–4748 (outside VA) | fax 540/825–7716 | www.fountainhall.com | 4 rooms, 2 suites | $95–$125 | AE, D, DC, MC, V.

Graves' Mountain Lodge. This family-run resort lodge is on a peaceful, 135-year-old working farm with apple orchards and cattle, six mi west of Culpeper next to Shenandoah National Park. With many different lodgings to choose from, you can stay in anything from a motel-like room to a rustic log cabin by a running river, to a renovated one-room schoolhouse. Box lunches are available. Dining room, picnic area. Pool. Tennis. Playground, laundry facilities. Business services. Some pets allowed. | Rte. 670, Syria | 540/923–4231 | fax 540/923–4312 | www.gravesmountain.com | 48 rooms; 13 cottages | $132–$195, $110–$230 cottages | Closed Dec.–mid-Mar. | AP | D, MC, V.

Hazel River Inn. Peer out the windows of this 1880s home, a 15-minute drive northwest of Culpeper and surrounded by five acres of informal gardens and rambling hardwood forest. In the evening, take in views of the Blue Ridge Mountains while relaxing surrounded by an eclectic mix of antiques, sip a complimentary glass of local wine or beer, and listen to the logs crackle in living and dining room fireplaces. A 10% discount at the Hazel River Restaurant (in the center of town), which uses herbs and greens grown in this inn's gardens, is offered. Complimentary breakfast. No room phones, TV in common area. Pool. No pets, no smoking. | 11227 Eggsbornsville Rd. | 540/937–5854 | hazel@hazelriverinn.com | www.hazelriverinn.com | 3 rooms | $110–$130 | AE, MC, V.

Holiday Inn. The chain hotel, off U.S. Route 29 has exterior corridors connecting rooms, designed in a standard dark color scheme, and furnished with double and king-size beds. Restaurant, bar with entertainment. In-room data ports, room service, cable TV. Pool, wading pool. Laundry facilities. Business services. Free parking. | 791 James Madison Rd. | 540/825–1253 | fax 540/825–7134 | www.holiday-inn.com | 159 rooms | $69–$140 | AE, D, DC, MC, V.

Suites at Prince Michel. This winery's georgeous one-bedroom suites are luxuriously designed in French Provincial style along different themes. All suites have beautiful views, private garden patios, separate living rooms and fireplaces. Restaurant, complimentary breakfast, room service. In-room data ports, in-room hot tubs, cable TV, in-room VCRs. Business services. | HCR 4, Box 77, U.S. 29 S, Leon | 540/547–9720 or 800/800–9463 | www.princemichel.com | 4 suites | Thursday–Sunday $350–$400 | AE, MC, V.

DANVILLE

MAP 11, G8

(Nearby town also listed: South Boston)

Located on the North Carolina border, Danville takes its name from the Dan River, which bisects the city. It was initially founded in 1793 as a tobacco inspection center; the loose-leaf auction system now used throughout the southeastern United States to sell tobacco originated here in 1858. The spectacle of those market days can still be witnessed in late summer in Danville's historic warehouse district; the town remains one of the largest tobacco auction centers in the United States. The prosperity brought by tobacco is especially evident on Millionaire's Row, a line of opulent Victorian and Edwardian mansions along Main Street.

Danville is known as the "last capital of the Confederacy." President Jefferson Davis and his cabinet made their headquarters here after the evacuation of Richmond in April 1865. Sutherlin House, the mansion where Davis resided, now houses the Danville Museum of Fine Arts and History.

Information: Danville Area Chamber of Commerce | 635 Main St., Danville, VA 24541 | 804/793–5422 | dancham@gamewood.net | www.danvillechamber.com.

Attractions

Chatham. Chatham, north of Danville on U.S. 29, population 1,400, was established in 1777 during the American Revolution. The town's Main Street is lined with large Victorian homes; set on a far hill is Chatham Hall, a girls' preparatory school built in 1894 and attended by Georgia O'Keeffe. The Pittsylvania Chamber of Commerce distributes maps for self-guided walking tours of the town. | 38 N. Main St.,Chatham | 804/432–1650 | fax 804/432–1344.

Danville Museum of Fine Arts and History. The city's art museum operates out of the Sutherlin House, a building that played a key role in the waning days of the Civil War. In April 1865, after the fall of Richmond, Danville was chosen as the South's temporary capital; this 1858 Italianate mansion became Jefferson Davis's residence for several weeks and is where he signed his last proclamation as Confederate president. For this reason, Danville is known as the "last capital of the Confederacy." The museum contains original and period furnishings and exhibits on Civil War history and the arts. | 975 Main St. | 804/793–5644 | fax 804/799–6145 | Free | Tues.–Fri. 10–5, weekends 2–5.

Danville Science Center. Housed in the town's 1899 train station, this facility features a gravity well and other hands-on exhibits relating to electricity, magnetism, and light. There are also changing exhibits. | 677 Craghead St. | 804/791–5160 | fax 804/791–5168 | www.smv.org | $5 | Mon.–Sat. 9:30–5, Sun. 1–5.

Millionaire's Row. On the National Register of Historic Places, this row of houses was built in Danville's grand Victorian and Edwardian eras. Gracious mansions with gingerbread scrollwork, gables, porticos, and minarets line Main Street. Walking-tour books are available at the visitor center. | 635 Main St. | 804/793–5422 | fax 804/793–5424 | www.danvillechamber.com | Free | Visitor center Mon.–Sat. 9:30–5, Sun. 1–5.

Streetcar Diners. Virginia's only two streetcar diners are parked a block apart. Only 20 such diners are said to exist in the country. The restored Getaway Car was retired from service in Danville in 1939; the other trolley, called Streetcar Named Desire, was bought in 1937 from the Duke Power Company in North Carolina. Both are celebrated hot dog stands and listed on the Virginia Landmarks Register. | 19 S. Main St. and 1 Depot St. | 804/432–1650.

"Wreck of the Old 97" Marker. A commemorative sign marks the site of a September 27, 1903 railroad accident that inspired the folk ballad "Wreck of the Old 97." A mail express train on the Southern Railroad left the tracks on a trestle and plunged into the ravine below, killing nine people. | Riverside Dr./U.S. 58.

SIGHTSEEING TOURS/TOUR COMPANIES

Tobacco Auction Tours. At the turn of the century, Danville supported upwards of 100 tobacco companies. Though only a few major ones remain today (among them Brown and Williamson Tobacco and R. J. Reynolds Tobacco Co.), the city continues to be one of the largest tobacco auction centers in the country. Seasonal self-guided tours of the historic warehouse district let you witness the spectacle of the tobacco auction, where the loose leaves are sold in great piles. The tradition dates from 1858. Weekly schedules are provided by the Danville Chamber of Commerce. | 635 Main St. | 804/793–5422 | fax 804/793–5424 | www.danvillechamber.com | Free | July–Nov. call for times.

ON THE CALENDAR
MAY: *Festival in the Park.* Arts and crafts, food vendors, entertainment, pony rides, a petting zoo, and crafts-making are the hits at this family festival in Ballou Park. | 804/799–5200.
SEPT.: *River City Strut.* This festival at the Auctioneers Park at the Crossing has live entertainment, crafts, exhibits, contests, a 5K race, food, and various children's activities. | 804/799–5200.
DEC.: *Christmas in Chatham.* Entertainment, carriage rides, puppet shows, bowling on the green, open houses, a model train show, working craftspeople, and a strolling troubadour are all part of the festivities on Main St. in Chatham. Free ham biscuits and snacks. | 804/432–1650.

Dining

Dominic's. American. An outdoor deck by the water, a goldfish pond, and a lighted fountain set the scene at Dominic's, which opened in October, 2000. Choose from an extensive wine list (prices go from $90 to $100); entrees include steak, chicken, and seafood dishes. Try the seafood pasta served with crab, shrimp, and scallops in a chardonnay cream sauce. | 3575 Hwy. 29 N | 804/836–5700 | Closed Sun. Mon. No lunch | $10–$24 | AE, D, MC, V.

Eldon Restaurant. Continental. Enjoy dinner or Sunday brunch at this elegant restaurant, where arched doorways mark the entrance to three dining rooms with huge decorative fireplaces, large mirrors, and a handful of 19th-century antiques. The owners use produce and herbs grown on the plantation. Specialties include the fresh rack of lamb with rosemary jus lie and the chicken Sofia, an herb-grilled breast stuffed with ham and provolone cheese and served with sun-dried tomato alfredo sauce, pasta, and vegetables. Try the Maryland-style crab cakes as an appetizer, if not a main course. | 1037 Chalk Level Rd. | 804/432–0934 | No lunch. Closed Mon. Tues. No dinner Sun. | $12–$20 | MC, V.

Miyako Japanese Steak & Seafood. Japanese. Past the mural and carved woodwork in the lobby, you'll see chefs cooking hibachi style right on the tables. You can choose from chicken, red snapper, filet mignon, lobster, and scallops, or combine any of the above. Each entree is served with a shrimp appetizer, chicken soup, salad, and, for dessert, a grilled banana. | 2907 Riverside Dr. | 804/799–2599 | No lunch Mon.–Sat. | $12–$28 | AE, D, DC, MC, V.

Outback Steak House. Modern Australian. This Australian-theme chain restaurant serves salads, sandwiches, and a selection of steaks. Choose from the Outback Special (a 12-ounce sirloin), prime rib (in an 8-, 12-, or 16-ounce cut), and lobster tails; the "Bloomin' Onion," a huge onion dipped in batter and fried, makes a good starter. A favorite dessert is the "Chocolate Thunder from Down Under," a pecan brownie topped with ice cream, whipped cream, and chocolate shavings. | 111 Enterprise Dr. | 804/792–0781 | No lunch Mon.–Sat. | $9–$22 | AE, D, DC, MC, V.

Lodging

Eldon–the Inn at Chatham. Antiques are found throughout this Greek revival mansion built in 1835; the property's 13 acres are wooded and interspersed with gardens and orchards. Rooms have decorative fireplaces and some have canopy beds. Dinner is available. Complimentary breakfast. Pool. No TV. | 1037 Chalk Level Rd., Chatham, north of Danville on U.S. 29 | 804/432–0935 | www.inns.com | 3 rooms, 1 suite | $65–$80, $130 suite | MC, V.

Hampton Inn. This chain hotel opened in 1997 and is just four blocks east of Danville's historic district. Rooms include an iron with ironing board and a coffee maker. Complimentary Continental breakfast. In-room data ports, microwaves, refrigerators, some in-room hot tubs, cable TV, room phones, TV in common area. Outdoor pool. Gym. Laundry facilities, laundry service. No pets. | 2130 Riverside Dr. | 804/793–1111 or 800/426–7866 | fax 804/791–1181 | 58 | $79 | AE, D, DC, MC, V.

Holiday Inn Express. This chain hotel has a deck overlooking the river, a lobby with two sitting areas, marble countertops and cherry-wood finish throughout the rooms. Free golf nearby on weekdays, a complimentary national weekday paper, and fresh-baked cookies in the evening are among the perks. All the rooms have tables and chairs; some have a recliner or loveseat. Complimentary Continental breakfast. Some microwaves, some refrigerators, some in-room hot tubs, cable TV, room phones, TV in common area. Outdoor pool, pond. Golf privileges. Fishing. Laundry service. No pets. | 2121 Riverside Dr. U.S. 58 | 804/793–4000 | fax 804/799–5516 | www.holiday-inn.com | 98 rooms | $79–$149 | AE, D, DC, MC, V.

Howard Johnson. On a hilltop, this hotel has balconies in some rooms from which you can admire the location. The lobby area has French Provincial style furniture, and rooms have coffee makers. Restaurant, bar, room service. In-room data ports, some microwaves, cable TV. Pool. Laundry facilities. Free parking. | 100 Tower Dr. | 804/793–2000 | fax 804/792–4621 | www.hojo.com | 118 rooms, 20 suites | $74–$85, $96–$104 suites | AE, D, DC, MC, V.

Innkeeper Motor Lodge West. The motor lodge is on a major thoroughfare. Renovated in 2000, rooms are carpeted, with cherry-wood finish furniture and marble countertops in the sink areas. Complimentary Continental breakfast. Cable TV. Pool. Some in room hot tubs. Business services. Free parking. | 3020 Riverside Dr./U.S. 58 | 804/799–1202 or 800/822–9899 | fax 804/799–9672 | 118 rooms | $50–$60 | AE, D, DC, MC, V.

Innkeeper North. This A-frame hotel could very well pass for a chain hotel, as all of its rooms seem to be cut from the same mold as the corporate hotels around Danville. Rooms are conservatively furnished in bland colors. Cable TV. Pool. Complimentary Continental breakfast. Business services. | 1030 Piney Forest Rd./U.S. 29 Business | 804/836–1700 | fax 804/799–9672 | 52 rooms | $55 | AE, D, DC, MC, V.

Red Maple Inn. This 1890s house sits back from the road on a three-acre lot landscaped with dogwoods, azaleas, and redbud trees. Originally built by a doctor who used the cottage as his office, the home now has three guest rooms, one with a fireplace and private bath. The other two rooms share a bath. Complimentary breakfast. Cable TV, some room phones, no TV in some rooms, TV in common area. No pets. No smoking. | 4157 Franklin Turnpike | 804/836–6361 | 3 | $50–$60 | No credit cards.

Stratford Inn. This brown-brick hotel, built in the 1970s, has a variety of room layouts, from rooms with king-size beds and hot tubs to more standard accommodations. All rooms are comfortable and plainly furnished. Restaurant, bar, complimentary breakfast. Room service, cable TV. Pool, wading pool. Hot tub. Exercise equipment. Laundry facilities. Business services, conference center. Some pets allowed. Free parking. | 2500 Riverside Dr./U.S. 58 | 804/793–2500 or 800/326–8455 | fax 804/793–6960 | www.stratford-inn.com | 152 rooms, 5 suites | $55–$65, $85–$150 suites | AE, D, DC, MC, V.

EMPORIA

(Nearby town also listed: South Hill)

Emporia is the seat of Greensville County and has historically been the commercial hub of Southside Virginia. The town is actually the combination of two early settlements that grew up on opposite banks of the Meherrin River: the village of Hicksford, established in 1710, and Belfield, established in 1798. In 1887, they married to form Emporia.

Once strategically located on an important north–south Confederate railroad and supply line, the town has a similar advantage today of being at the crossroads of Interstate–95 and U.S. Route 58. Emporia is emerging as an industrial center, thanks to an influx of manufacturing and distribution companies such as Georgia Pacific, Beach Mold and Tool, and Perdue Farms. It is 8 mi from the North Carolina line. Since 1974, Emporia has hosted the Virginia Pork Festival, a major attraction held every June. The rural area's agricultural heritage is celebrated during the Virginia Peanut Festival, which takes place the last weekend in September.

Information: **Emporia Chamber of Commerce** | 326B S. Main St., Emporia, VA 23847 | 804/634–9441 | www.empva.com.

Attractions

Village View. This 1790s Federal-style plantation house is unusual for having remained in the same family for more than 200 years. In 1986, the last descendant of the Briggs family gave it to the town of Emporia. Many original furnishings remain in the house—even the window blinds. Throughout are finely carved fireplace mantels and moldings. The boxwood gardens have been completely restored. Call the Emporia–Greensville County Chamber of Commerce to schedule a tour. | 221 Brigg St. | 804/634–9441 or 804/634–2475 | Free | By appointment.

ON THE CALENDAR

JUNE: *Virginia Pork Festival.* Some 20 tons of pork are served 30 different ways at this festival on the Greensville Ruritan Club grounds along Rte. 640. Live music helps you digest as you pig-out. | 804/634–6611 or 800/482–7675.

SEPT.: *Virginia Peanut Festival.* Attracting more than 25,000 visitors, this annual homage to the beloved local legume along Main Street hosts carnival rides, an arts-and-crafts show, a parade, canoe races, outdoor concerts, and lots of nutty food. | 804/634–9441.

Dining

Marie's. Contemporary. This house from the early 1900s was the base for Marie's catering operation until she turned it into a restaurant in 1985. Known for its homemade breads, soups, and desserts, the restaurant also hand-cuts its own Delmonico steaks and filets. Favorite seafood dishes include the Seafood Norfolk–crab meat, scallops, and shrimp in a sour-cream mushroom sauce topped with melted cheese–and the crab cakes. Pork tenderloins, prime rib, pasta, salads, and a wine list featuring Virginia wines are also available. | 825 S. Main St. | 804/634–2213 | Closed Sun. No lunch Sat. | $8–$23 | AE,D,DC,MC,V.

Squire House. American/Casual. Built in 1903, the Squire House was converted into a restaurant with four dining rooms in 1991. Two of the rooms are decorated with Queen Anne furniture; two have fireplaces. For seafood, you can choose from talapia, jumbo scallops, shrimp, flounder, crab cakes, and salmon. Steaks, prime rib, and chicken cordon bleu are also available; homemade desserts are offered occasionally. | 632 S. Main St. | 804/634–0046 | No lunch. Closed Sun. | $8–$19 | AE,D,MC,V.

Lodging

Best Western. Built in 1992, this standard chain hotel has modern rooms with a reasonable list of amenities and exterior corridors. Complimentary Continental breakfast. In-room data ports, some refrigerators, cable TV. Pool. Exercise equipment. Business services. | 1100 W. Atlantic St. | 804/634–3200 | fax 804/634–5459 | www.bestwestern.com | 99 rooms | $55–$75 | AE, D, DC, MC, V.

Brunswick Mineral Springs. A 1,200-foot driveway with stone columns off U.S. 58 leads you to a huge oak grove and plantation house built in 1785, 20 minutes west of Emporia. The three guest suites are named in honor of people who were laid to rest in the adjacent family cemetery. Enjoy your breakfast on the glassed-in porch; dinner is served with china and crystal in the formal dining room. Dining room, complimentary breakfast, complimentary dinner. Cable TV, no TV in some rooms, TV in common area. Hiking. Library. Laundry service. Some pets allowed (fee). No children under 18. | 14910 Western Mill Rd., Lawrenceville

EMPORIA

INTRO
ATTRACTIONS
DINING
LODGING

| 804/848–4010 | fax 804/848–9110 | nanny@jnent.com | www.brunswickmineralspring.com | 3 | $105–$125 | No credit cards.

Comfort Inn. This chain hotel is 1.4 mi outside of Emporia (Exit 8, I–95). Rooms are furnished in standard corporate hostelry style. Complimentary Continental breakfast. In-room data ports, cable TV. Pool. Playground. Fishing. Business services. Some pets allowed. | 1411 Skipper's Rd. | 804/348–3282 | fax 804/348–3282 | www.comfortinn.com | 96 rooms | $49–$60 | AE, D, DC, MC, V.

Hampton Inn. The chain hotel is northwest of the Emporia, adjacent to a Shoney's Restaurant, the Sadlers Truck Plaza and a Cactus Steakhouse. Rooms painted in neutral tones are comfortably equipped with desks, and depending on the room, easy chairs and sofas. Nearby is the Interstate–95 and U.S. Route 58 interchange. Complimentary Continental breakfast. Some microwaves, refrigerators, cable TV. Pool. Some pets allowed. | 1207 W. Atlantic St. | 804/634–9200 | fax 804/348–0071 | www.hampton-inn.com | 115 rooms | $62–$70 | AE, D, DC, MC, V.

Holiday Inn. Located off I–95 at Exit 11A, this chain hotel has a playground out front for the kids; relax in the comfy lobby or have a cup of coffee in the lobby dinette area. Restaurant, bar, complimentary Continental breakfast, room service. In-room data ports, room phones. Outdoor pool. Playground. Laundry facilities, laundry services. No pets allowed. | 311 Florida Ave. | 804/634–4191 | fax 804/634–4191 ext. 720 | 144 | $68 | AE, D, DC, MC, V.

FAIRFAX

MAP 11, I4

(Nearby towns also listed: Arlington, Falls Church, Manassas, McLean, Springfield, Tysons Corner, Vienna)

In 1694, King Charles II of England gave the land that would become Fairfax County to seven English noblemen. In 1741, the land became a county named after Thomas, Sixth Lord of Fairfax. During the 18th century, the dominant industry in the area was tobacco farming, but increasingly depleted lands helped steer the county toward a more industrial base. Today, Fairfax City is a suburb of Washington, D.C., and has one of the highest per-capita incomes in the country. Its central location makes it a convenient place to stay while exploring northern Virginia's sights.

Of interest to history buffs is the Fairfax County Courthouse, built in 1800, which displays the wills of George and Martha Washington. A handful of county and regional parks offer swimming, golf, fishing, and boating. George Mason University sponsors a full calendar of concerts and performances at three venues.

Information: Fairfax County Convention and Visitors Bureau | 8300 Boone Blvd. Suite 450, Tysons Corner, VA 22182 | 703/790–3329 | www.cvb.co.fairfax.va.us. **Fairfax Visitors Center** | 10209 Main St., Fairfax, VA 22030 | 703/385–8414 | www.visitfairfax.org.

Attractions

Algonkian. This regional park, 22 mi northwest of Fairfax, has a hiking trail that runs down along the Potomac River, past riverfront vacation cottages that rent year-round. An outdoor pool, 18-hole golf course, boat launch, and visitor center also are on the grounds. | 47001 Fairway Dr., Sterling | 703/450–4655 | www.nvrpa.org | Free | Daily 6 AM–dusk.

Bull Run. In addition to the more common recreational activities—swimming, miniature golfing, camping, and picnicking—this regional park, 10 mi slightly southwest of Fairfax, has a 6-acre public shooting center where you can try sporting clays, skeet, and trap shooting. Woodlands and trails provide opportunities for hiking, including access to the 17-mi Bull Run–Occoquan Trail (no bikes allowed). | 7700 Bull Run Dr., Centreville | 703/631–0550 | www.nvrpa.org | Free | Daily dawn–dusk.

Burke Lake. The county park, four mi southwest of Fairfax, has a 218-acre lake with a fishing pier accessible to persons with disabilities. Other amenities include rowboat rental and boat tours, a miniature train, an 18-hole golf course, picnic areas, and playgrounds. Swimming is prohibited. | 7315 Ox Rd., Fairfax Station | 703/323–6601 | www.fairfax.va.us | Free.

Fairfax County Court House. This national landmark has been in continuous use ever since it was built in 1800, except for a period during the Civil War, when Union troops occupied the town and used the building as a stable. The original wills of George and Martha Washington are kept in the clerk's office in an adjacent building, the Jennings Building Judicial Center, at 4010 Chain Bridge Road. | 4000 Chain Bridge Rd. | 703/324–3151 or 703/246–2770 | fax 703/324–3926 | www.fairfax.va.us/courts | Free | Weekdays 8:30–4:30.

George Mason University. This university is home to the Center for the Arts, a glittering complex that hosts performing arts events ranging from ballet and contemporary dance to theater and opera. It has a 1,900-seat concert hall, the 500-seat Harris Theatre (which presents student drama performances), and the intimate 150-seat Black Box Theatre. Also on campus is the 9,500-seat Patriot Center, a venue for pop music acts and sporting events. | 4400 University Dr. | 703/993–1000 university switchboard, 703/993–8888 Center for the Arts, 703/993–3000 Patriot Center | fax 703/993–4622 | www.gmu.edu | Ticket prices vary.

National Firearms Museum. Exhibits examine the role firearms have played in America's history. Thousands of guns are on display; permanent collections include muzzle-loading flintlocks used in the Revolutionary War, high-tech pistols used by Olympic shooting teams, and weapons that once belonged to U.S. presidents. The museum is on the second floor of the National Rifle Association's headquarters. | 11250 Waples Mill Rd. | 703/267–1600 | fax 703/267–3913 | www.nra.org | Free | Daily 10–4.

Sully Historic Site. This Federal-period home was built in 1794 by Richard Bland Lee, northern Virginia's first representative to Congress. Restored to its original appearance and furnished with period antiques, the house includes formal and kitchen gardens and outbuildings, including a stone dairy and smokehouse. The Schoolhouse Store (now a gift shop) once served as the one-room country schoolhouse. | 3601 Sully Rd./U.S. 28, Chantilly

YOUR FIRST-AID TRAVEL KIT

- ❏ Allergy medication
- ❏ Antacid tablets
- ❏ Antibacterial soap
- ❏ Antiseptic cream
- ❏ Aspirin or acetaminophen
- ❏ Assorted adhesive bandages
- ❏ Athletic or elastic bandages for sprains
- ❏ Bug repellent
- ❏ Face cloth

- ❏ First-aid book
- ❏ Gauze pads and tape
- ❏ Needle and tweezers for splinters or removing ticks
- ❏ Petroleum jelly
- ❏ Prescription drugs
- ❏ Suntan lotion with an SPF rating of at least 15
- ❏ Thermometer

*Excerpted from *Fodor's: How to Pack: Experts Share Their Secrets*
© 1997, by Fodor's Travel Publications

| 703/437–1794 | fax 703/787–3314 | www.co.fairfax.va.us/parks | $5; grounds free | Wed.–Mon. 11–4.

ON THE CALENDAR

FEB.: *Mobil Invitational Track and Field Meet.* Men's and women's collegiate teams from around the country compete in a variety of track and field events, from relay and distance running to hurdles and pole vaulting, on the George Mason University campus at Route 123 and Braddock Road. | 703/993–3000.

JUNE: *Antique Car Show.* Model A's and other classic cars are on display on the Sully Historic Site in Chantilly. | 703/550–2450.

JUNE: *Fairfax Fair.* This fair at the Fairfax County Government Center, 12000 Government Center Pkwy. off Monument Dr., has something for everyone: national and regional entertainment, science and technology exhibits, a model train show, children's activities, a dog show, sports, and a carnival. | 703/324–3247.

SEPT.: *Sully Quilt Show and Sale.* Quilters from around the country demonstrate their skills and offer finished works for sale at the Sully Historic Site in Chantilly. | 703/550–2450.

Dining

Artie's. American. This old American-style restaurant is quite unique with its dark wood all around and classic paintings. Artie's makes its own root beers and ice cream and has a wide selection of draft beers and wines by the glass. Known for the southern flair of its cuisine, which you can taste in the ribs and Saturday night blackened 24 oz. prime rib special. Early-bird suppers Monday–Thursday. Sunday brunch. | 3260 Old Lee Hwy. | 703/273–7600 | $12–$20 | AE, MC, V.

Bailiwick Inn. Eclectic. At this restaurant flowers abound, particularly roses. You can sit outside in a secluded, brick-walled garden with the soothing sound of a fountain in the background, or inside, where the garden is visible through French doors. The chef serves five-course, fixed-price meals; the menu varies seasonally but features American fare with Mediterranean, Pacific Rim, and regional influences. Afternoon tea is served to the public Thursday and Sunday. No smoking. | 4023 Chain Bridge Rd./Rte. 123 | 703/691–2266 | Reservations essential | Closed Mon. No lunch | $55–$65 | AE, MC, V.

Blue Ocean. Japanese. Both the cuisine and the design of this restaurant are authentically Japanese. The only Western touch is a salad bar during lunch. | 9440 Main St. | 703/425–7555 | Reservations essential | Closed Mon. No lunch Sun. | $13–$23 | AE, MC, V.

Bombay Bistro. Indian. This casual but elegant restaurant has mirrorwork wall hangings and folk art from Rajastan. Regional Indian dishes include curries, tandoori, and dosas. Kids' menu. Sunday brunch. No smoking. | 3570 Chain Bridge Rd. | 703/359–5810 | $8–$12 | AE, D, DC, MC, V.

Connaught Place. Indian. This popular restaurant has consistently good Indian cuisine, served in an interior that recalls the streets of New Delhi. House favorites are chicken tikka masala and rogenjosh, a lamb dish in a creamy yogurt sauce. Sunday and Saturday Brunch. | 10425 North St. | 703/352–5959 | $8–$17 | AE, DC, MC, V.

Espositos/Pizza N' Pasta. Southern Italian. This casual restaurant has great pizzas and chicken dishes. Beer and wine only. | 9917 Lee Hwy. | 703/385–5912 | No lunch Sun. | $10–$20 | AE, DC, MC, V.

Heart-in-Hand. American. This restaurant, 9 mi southwest of Fairfax, is in a large 19th-century building with wood plank floors. There are three country-style dining rooms: the quilt room, the polo room, and the "new" room. Popular menu items are the chicken Suzanne with raspberry sauce, the homemade pecan pie, and Geva's iron-skillet chocolate pie. Sunday brunch. No smoking. | 7145 Main St., Clifton | 703/830–4111 | Closed Mon. | $15–$24 | AE, D, DC, MC, V.

Hermitage Inn. French. This intimate restaurant, 9 mi southwest of Fairfax, serves French Mediterranean cuisine in three dining levels. The first level is done in a Virginian hunting country theme, with stone fireplaces and gold, burgundy, and other rich colors. The main dining rooms on the second and third floors are done in French Victorian-period style with local artwork adorning the walls. The rack of lamb and château briand are the centerpieces of the menu. Open-air dining on a patio. Sunday brunch. | 7134 Main St., Clifton | 703/266–1623 | Closed Mon. | $30–$42 | AE, D, DC, MC, V.

Il Lupo. Italian. Healthy seafood fare and homemade desserts are the main attraction at this Northern Italian restaurant, which opened in July, 2000. The owners, two brothers, have put together a menu that includes grilled salmon and mahi mahi, chicken arraviato, and spaghetti; panini and specialty salads are available for lunch. Choose from 10 homemade authentic Italian treats for dessert, including a ricotta cheesecake. If you look around, you'll find a picture of unique Italian card decks from different regions of the country. | 4009 Chain Bridge Rd. (Rte. 123) | 703/934–1655 | No lunch Sun. | $9–$19 | AE, D, MC, V.

P. J. Skidoo's. Steak. This steak house has a separate sports bar with a long, antique bar. Open-air dining on a patio. Entertainment Tuesday and Thursday–Saturday. Kids' menu. | 9908 Lee Hwy. | 703/591–4516 | $10–$17 | AE, MC, V.

Seasons Restaurant. Continental. Brazilian shrimp, Chesapeake crab dip, and plantation chicken are among the favorite dishes at this five-room restaurant; for a lighter meal, try the chicken walnut salad. Desserts include apple strudel crisp and "Chocolate Suicide." You can take your pick of rooms: Ask to be seated in the library, or check out the patio-style room with the photolike wall murals. There's no smoking in the restaurant, but you can adjourn to the cigar lounge if you wish. Sunday brunch available. | 4069 Chain Bridge Rd. | 703/383–0949 | $10–$20 | AE, D, DC, MC, V.

Silverado. Southwestern. At the Silverado, six mi east of Fairfax, cowboys abound in photos, sculpture, and a mural by John Gable, titled "Three Horsemen." Known for fajitas, roasted chicken. Kids' menu. Early-bird suppers Monday–Thursday. | 7052 Columbia Pike, Annandale | 703/354–4560 | $12–$18 | AE, MC, V.

Lodging

Bailiwick Inn. Across from the old courthouse, this Federal-style inn was built in 1800. Rooms, named for early American heroes, are luxurious and plush with period furnishings and fireplaces. Afternoon tea served. Restaurant, complimentary breakfast. No smoking, some in-room hot tubs. | 4023 Chain Bridge Rd./Rte. 123 | 703/691–2266 or 800/366–7666 | fax 703/934–2112 | http://bailiwickinn.com/inn/ | 14 rooms | $225–$330 | AE, MC, V.

Best Western. This several-story, brown brick hotel surrounds a pool and courtyard lush with coniferous trees, and lots of shrubbery. The comfortable rooms are decorated in shades of brown. Easy access to George Mason University and historic Fairfax sites. Restaurant. In-room data ports, some microwaves, cable TV. Pool. Laundry facilities. Business services. Free parking. | 3535 Chain Bridge Rd. | 703/591–5500 | fax 703/591–7483 | www.bestwestern.com | 127 rooms | $129 | AE, D, DC, MC, V.

Comfort Inn University Center. This chain hotel has rooms with a nice variety of options, including queen-size and king-size beds, and coffee makers. Next to the hotel is a 4-acre park. Restaurant, complimentary Continental breakfast, room service. In-room data ports, some kitchenettes, some in-room hot tubs, cable TV. Indoor pool. Gym. Video games. | 11180 Main St./U.S. 50 | 703/591–5900 or 800/223–1223 | fax 703/273–7915 | www.comfortinn.com | 205 rooms | $90 | AE, D, DC, MC, V.

Courtyard by Marriott–Fair Oaks. This large three-story Marriott in the suburban wilds of Fairfax county, a mile from the large Fair Oaks mall, is surrounded by a mix of corporate offices, such as the NRA, BTG, and AT&T, and chain restaurants, like Ruby Tuesdays and the Outback Steakhouse. Rooms are well-designed with work desks, coffee makers, irons, and hair dryers. Restaurant, bar. In-room data ports, some microwaves, cable TV. Indoor pool.

Hot tub. Exercise equipment. Laundry facilities. Business services. Free parking. | 11220 Lee Jackson Hwy./U.S. 50 | 703/273–6161 | fax 703/273–3505 | www.marriott.com/courtyard/va_197.htm | 144 rooms; 12 suites | $75–$124 | AE, D, DC, MC, V.

Hampton Inn. This hotel has comfortable rooms with the standard commercial hostelry perks, like coffee makers, and connecting rooms. The fast food restaurants, Chili's and Denny's are nearby, as are George Mason University, and the Fair Oaks and Tysons Corner shopping centers. Complimentary Continental breakfast. In-room data ports, cable TV. Exercise equipment. Business services. | 10860 Lee Hwy. | 703/385–2600 | fax 703/385–2742 | www.hampton-inn.com | 86 rooms | $80–$100 | AE, D, DC, MC, V.

Holiday Inn Fair Oaks Mall. Adjacent to Fair Oaks Mall, this large hotel has an enclosed garden-like atrium. Rooms either have exterior windows or balconies that open up to the atrium, and are all well-appointed with a reasonable list of amenities. Restaurant, bar with entertainment. In-room data ports, cable TV. Indoor pool. Exercise equipment. Video games. Laundry facilities. Business services. Airport shuttle. Some pets allowed. | 11787 Lee Jackson Hwy. | 703/352–2525 | fax 703/352–4471 | www.holiday-inn.com | 312 rooms | $129–$195 | AE, D, DC, MC, V.

Homestead Village Guest Studios. This hotel caters to the business traveler on an extended visit. The burgundy-, green-, and beige-toned rooms each have a fully stocked kitchenette that's set off from the carpeted living area with a tile floor. In-room data ports, kitchenettes, microwaves, refrigerators, cable TV, some in-room VCRs, room phones. Laundry facilities, laundry service. Pets allowed (fee). | 8281 Willow Oaks Corporate Dr. | 703/204–0088 or 888/782–9473 | fax 703/204–2741 | 130 | $89–$109 | AE, D, DC, MC, V.

Hyatt Fair Lakes. This reasonably luxurious hotel has guest rooms with electronic door locks, sitting areas, individual climate controls, two phones, and desks. Dulles International Airport is just 9 mi away. Restaurant, bar with entertainment. In-room data ports, cable TV. Indoor pool. Hot tub. Sauna. Exercise equipment. Business services. Airport shuttle. | 12777 Fair Lakes Circle | 703/818–1234 | fax 703/818–3140 | www.hyatt.com | 316 rooms | $100–$299 | AE, D, DC, MC, V.

Sierra Suites Fair Oaks. A business travelers' hotel, the Sierra offers studio-style suites, each furnished with a queen-sized bed, a sofa sleeper, and a kitchenette with stove, coffee pot, toaster, and place settings. Close to shopping and business areas. Complimentary paper on weekdays. Picnic area. In-room data ports, kitchenettes, microwaves, refrigerators, cable TV, room phones, TV in common area. Outdoor pool. Exercise equipment. Laundry facilities. No pets. | 3997 Fair Ridge Dr. | 703/359–5000 or 800/474–3772 | fax 703/359–5524 | 93 | $69–$139 | AE, D, DC, MC, V.

Wellesley Inn. This white stone hotel was built in 1980. The muted tones, sofas, and chairs in the lobby create a peaceful place to relax, read, or wait for friends. Each room is equipped with a coffee maker and hair dryer. Dining room, complimentary Continental breakfast. In-room data ports, some microwaves, some refrigerators, cable TV, room phones, TV in common area. Laundry service. Some pets allowed (fee). | 10327 Lee Hwy. | 703/359–2888 or 800/444–8888 | fax 703/385–9186 | www.wellesleyinnandsuites.com | 82 | $114 | AE, D, DC, MC, V.

FALLS CHURCH

(Nearby towns also listed: Arlington, Alexandria, Fairfax, McLean, Springfield)

This community grew up around the Falls Church, founded at the intersection of two historic Virginia roadways, Leesburg Pike and Lee Highway, which was originally an Indian trail leading to the lower Potomac River falls. By 1875, it had gained township status. Now a suburb of Washington, D.C. Falls Church is near two major shopping centers, Tysons Corner Center and Galleria at Tysons II (*see Tysons Corner*).

Information: **Public Information Office, City of Falls Church** | 300 Park Ave., Falls Church, VA 22046-3395 | 703/824–6635 | fcpio@falls-church.va.us | www.ci.falls-church.va.us. **Greater Falls Church Chamber of Commerce** | Box 491, 417 W. Broad St., Falls Church, VA 22040 | 703/532–1050.

Attractions

Fountain of Faith. Composed of a dozen bronze figures, this fountain caused a scandal when it was unveiled in National Memorial Park in the 1950s because all of the figures are nude. Swedish sculptor Carl Milles spent about 15 years on the project; each statue represents someone he knew who had died. Commissioned by the cemetery's owner, Robert Marlowe, the monument was shipped from Europe in pieces. | Lee Hwy. | 703/876–1888 | Free | Daily dawn–dusk.

The Falls Church. The original Episcopal church building, erected in 1733, stood on a road leading to the falls of the Potomac River—hence its name. It served as a recruiting station during the Revolution, and as a hospital during the Civil War. The current building dates from 1769. | 115 E. Fairfax St. | 703/532–7600 | Free | Weekdays 9–4, weekends 9–1.

Untitled sculpture. Conspicuous against its background–a local car dealership–this life-size sculpture of a man slopping pigs is decorated seasonally by the artist's family. | Rte. 7 and Gordon Rd. | Free.

ON THE CALENDAR

MAY: *Memorial Day Festivities.* Held on Memorial Day every year, this Falls Church celebration includes a parade, a 3K "fun run" (some people even walk), onstage entertainment, crafts, and food booths. | 703/532–1050.

Dining

Argia's. Italian. An enormous Florentine fresco and small family photographs hang over the interior of this restaurant, named for the owner's grandmother. Pasta, like the pesto fusilli, is the house specialty, though the spinach salad with pancetta and balsamic vinaigrette is quite good. | 124 N. Washington St. | 703/534–1033 | Reservations essential weekdays lunch | $10–$20 | AE, DC, MC, V.

Bangkok Vientiane. Thai. This drab restaurant serves spicy Thai and Laotian cuisine at bargain prices. House specialties are sean nam tok (sliced grilled beef seasoned with a melange of lemon juice, mint, parsley, scallions and hot peppers), and the pad Thai (noodles with shrimp, bean curd and sprouts). Lunch buffet. | 926A W. Broad St. | 703/534–0095 | $6–$15 | AE, D, DC, MC, V.

Duangrat's. Thai. Thai artifacts are showcased behind glass at this quietly elegant restaurant. Regional Thai dishes, such as bhram (chicken in a peanut-garlic curry sauce with shallots), are served by waitresses wearing flowing Thai silk outfits. | 5878 Leesburg Pike | 703/820–5775 | Reservations essential Fri.–Sat. | $7–$21 | AE, DC, MC, V.

Haandi. Indian. Paintings of India on pastel walls adorn this restaurant serving north Indian fare. The pappadams, salmon tandoori and murg makhini (chicken in a tomato and curry cream sauce) are house specialties. No smoking. | 1222 W. Broad St./Rte. 7 | 703/533–3501 | Reservations not accepted Fri.–Sat. | $10–$16 | AE, D, DC, MC, V.

Panjshir. Afghan. Tapestries hang from the walls of this Afghan restaurant. There's lots for vegetarians on the menu, like the kadu chalow, a delectable pumpkin dish; however, the prize of the menu is the chopped lamb kebabs and the muntoo, meat-stuffed Afghan noodles smothered in yogurt, tomato sauce and mint. No smoking. | 924 W. Broad St. | 703/536–4566 | No lunch Sun. | $10–$14 | AE, DC, MC, V.

Peking Gourmet Inn. Chinese. The elegant setting features Asian screens, antiques, and artwork. Northern Chinese dishes are a specialty. The salt-baked shrimp and the string beans with pork and chili are delicious. | 6029 Leesburg Pike/Rte. 7 | 703/671–8088 | Reservations essential Fri.–Sat. | $10–$32 | AE, MC, V.

Pilin. Thai. Quiet romance is in the air of this restaurant (whose name means "blue sapphire") filled colorful paintings and softly lit by candles and dimmed lighting. The chicken satay and spicy catfish are specialties. | 116 W. Broad St./Rte. 7 | 703/241–5850 | Reservations essential Fri.–Sat. | No lunch Sun. | $8–$15 | AE, D, DC, MC, V.

Rabieng. Thai. Teakwood, Thai mirror art, and white tile tables make this restaurant cozy. Known for its country-style cooking. The signature dish is bhram, chicken with a spicy peanut sauce on napa cabbage. Also fine are the stir-fried noodles, shrimp dumplings, and chicken satay. Open-air dining on patio. No smoking. | 5892 Leesburg Pike | 703/671–4222 | $9–$17 | AE, DC, MC, V.

Secret Garden Beewon. Korean/Japanese. Shoji screens and other elements of traditional Korean design define the interiors of this restaurant, in which you can have your food prepared tableside. Try the Korean barbecue, and have them do it, or do it yourself. The kitchen is also known for its sushi and sashimi. | 6678 Arlington Blvd. | 703/533–1004 | Reservations essential Fri.–Sat. | $20–$24 | AE, D, DC, MC, V.

Lodging

Best Western. Three miles from the beltway and fifteen minutes from Washington, D.C. this chain hotel is close to a shopping center and several fast food restaurants. The rooms each have two sinks; 21 rooms have both poolside and interior entrances. Restaurant, bar, room service. In-room data ports, in-room safes, some kitchenettes, some microwaves, some refrigerators, cable TV, room phones. Outdoor pool, wading pool. Laundry services. No pets. | 6633 Arlington Blvd. | 703/532–9000 | fax 703/532–3887 | 106 | $80–$85 | AE, D, DC, MC, V.

Marriott–Fairview Park. This large marble-floored, chandelier-accented hotel has park-like grounds with a man-made lake and jogging trails. Rooms are quite comfortable with a notable list of amenities, like free newspapers, complimentary coffee, in-room iron and ironing board, hairdryer, and bathrobe. There is even a shuttle to take you to the Metro, the Washington D.C. metropolitan area public transportation system. Tyson's Corner, the largest mall on the East Coast is 4.5 mi away. Restaurant, bar, room service. In-room data ports, cable TV. Indoor-outdoor pool. Hot tub. Exercise equipment. Laundry facilities. Business services. | 3111 Fairview Park Dr. | 703/849–9400 | fax 703/849–8692 | www.marriott.com | 395 rooms | $169–$229 | AE, D, DC, MC, V.

Quality Inn Governor. This two-level motel has exterior corridors that connect the rooms. You can pull your car up the entrance of your room. Rooms are comfortable, and conservatively furnished. Three miles away is the Capital Beltway. Restaurant. Some refrigerators, cable TV. Pool. Business services. | 6650 Arlington Blvd./U.S. 50 | 703/532–8900 | fax 703/532–7121 | 121 rooms | $75–$90 | AE, D, DC, MC, V.

FARMVILLE

MAP 11, H6

(Nearby towns also listed: Keysville, Lynchburg)

The south-central, college town of Farmville, home to Hampden-Sydney College and Longwood College, was founded in 1798. Apart from the colleges, the backbone of Farmville's economy is the manufacture of furniture, shelving, and hardwoods, with retail and food distribution companies in the mix. The town has a noteworthy history. During the final days of the Civil War, Gen. Robert E. Lee made his retreat through Farmville; Confederate soldiers crossed (and then attempted to burn) High Bridge, a 100-ft-high railroad crossing above the Appomattox River. The bridge and other nearby sites, including Sailor's Creek Battlefield Historic State Park, are part of Virginia's popular Civil War Trails tour. Appomattox Court House National Historic Park is 25 mi to the west.

Information: Farmville Chamber of Commerce | Box 361, Farmville, VA 23901 | 804/392–3939 | www.chamber.farmville.net.

Attractions

Appomattox Court House National Historical Park.(*See* Lynchburg.) It was on the well-worn country lanes of this park that Robert E. Lee, Commanding General of the Army of Northern Virginia, surrendered to Ulysses S. Grant, General-in-Chief of the Union forces, on April 9, 1865. The park is 1800 acres of rolling hills speckled by the 27 original 19th-century buildings, including the surrender site, the McLean home; the village of Appomattox Court House, Virginia, the former county seat of Appomattox County; and the home and grave of Joel Sweeney, the popularizer of the five-string banjo. | 804/352–8987.

Green Front Furniture. Hand-painted floors and running fountains are found throughout this 12-building tobacco warehouse-turned-furniture store–600,000 square feet filled with home decorations and furniture. You'll find a selection of Oriental rugs, Portuguese linens, wicker and leather furniture, Chinese porcelain, Mexican mirrors, and other items from around the world. | 316–318 N. Main St. | 804/392–5943 | www.greenfront.com | Free | Weekdays 9–5, Sat. 9–5:30, closed Sun.

Saylor's Creek Battlefield Historic State Park. (See *Lynchburg*.) This 221-acre park, 22 mi northwest of Farmville, is the site of the Civil War's last major battle before the surrender at Appomattox Courthouse. On April 6, 1865—thereafter known by Confederate veterans as "Black Thursday"—the Army of Northern Virginia on its retreat from Petersburg sustained a crippling defeat, losing at least a quarter of what remained of Gen. Robert E. Lee's army. During the summer, costumed volunteers reenact the Battle of Sailor's Creek near the restored Hillsman House, which served as a field hospital for both Northern and Southern soldiers. The park also offers picnic sites and self-guided trails. | Rte. 617, c/o Twin Lakes State Park, Green Bay | 804/392–3435 | www.state.va.us | Free | Daily dawn–dusk.

ON THE CALENDAR

.**MAY: *Heart of Virginia Festival.*** A celebration of the arts, culture, and music of south-central Virginia, with fireworks, live music, puppet shows, clowns, and arts and crafts. | 804/392–3939.

Dining

Charley's Waterfront Cafe. American. Once a tobacco warehouse in the 1850s, Charley's has kept the original brick walls, which are painted with old advertisements. Try the tomato mozzarella salad (the cafe makes its own mozzarella) or the roasted red pepper and crab soup. Seafood and steak specials are available, along with ribs, Cajun chicken Alfredo, grilled tuna steak, and a portabello mushroom sandwich. | 201-B Mill St. | 804/392–1566 | fax 804/392–7538 | $7–$18 | AE, D, MC, V.

Lodging

Comfort Inn. This standard hotel is on the south side of Farmville at the intersection of U.S. 460 and Route 15. Rooms are connected by an interior corridor and have double and king-size beds. Historic sites are within driving distance of this standard hotel. Complimentary morning coffee and evening cider. Cable TV. Pool. Exercise equipment. Business services. | 2108 S. Main St. | 804/392–8163 | fax 804/392–1966 | www.comfortinn.com | 51 rooms | $53–$73 | AE, D, DC, MC, V.

Days Inn. This two-story, brown brick Days Inn is on the south side of Farmville. Rooms have interior corridors and dark conservative furnishings. Picnic area, complimentary Continental breakfast. Cable TV. Pool. Free parking. | 2011 S. Main St./U.S. 15 | 804/392–6611 | fax 804/392–9774 | 60 rooms | $50–$90 | AE, D, DC, MC, V.

Super 8. Popular with construction workers and parents of university students, this chain hotel is located five minutes from Farmville's business district. The lobby has a love seat and breakfast bar that's open until 11AM. Complimentary Continental breakfast. Some microwaves, some refrigerators, cable TV, room phones. Pets allowed. | Hwy. 15, at Hwy. 460 | 804/392–8196 | 42 | $70 | AE, D, DC, MC, V.

FREDERICKSBURG

MAP 11, I5

(Nearby town also listed: Orange)

Fredericksburg is at a strategic half-way point between Richmond and Washington, D.C. on Interstate–95, near the falls of the Rappahannock River. Founded in 1728, the city was named in honor of England's crown prince at the time. Originally serving as frontier port for nearby tobacco and wheat farmers and iron miners, the city's main sources of income are now the timber, dairy and beef cattle, bookbinding, and concrete block manufacturing industries.

George Washington grew up just across the river on Ferry Farm, and the city's relationship with the Washington family is deep. The house where Washington's mother spent her last years is open to the public, as is Kenmore, the plantation home of his sister. During the Civil War, Fredericksburg played a vital role in the Confederate defense of Richmond and became the target of many Union assaults. Four major battles were fought in and around the city, and it changed hands seven times during the war. The sites of the battles are now the 9,000-acre Fredericksburg and Spotsylvania National Military Park. Despite heavy bombardment, much of the city survived intact. Fredericksburg's 40-block National Historic District contains more than 350 original 18th- and 19th-century structures.

Historic Caroline Street, one of the city's main thoroughfares, is lined with antiques shops. Outdoor activities at nearby Lake Anna State include water-skiing and sailing.

Information: Fredericksburg Office of Economic Development and Tourism | 706 Caroline St., Fredericksburg, VA 22401 | 540/373–1776 or 800/678–4748 | www.fredericksburgva.com.

Attractions

Belmont, the Gari Melchers Estate and Memorial Gallery. The last owner of this 1790s Georgian home, 4 mi northeast of Fredericksburg, was American artist Gari Melchers, who chaired the Smithsonian Commission to establish the National Gallery of Art in Washington, D.C. Now administered by Mary Washington College, the manor house is furnished with a wide collection of antiques; Melchers's studio contains the world's largest repository of his work (he died in 1932). | 224 Washington St., Falmouth | 540/654–1843 or 540/654–1015 | fax 540/654–1785 | $4 | Mar.–Nov. Mon.–Sat. 10–5, Sun. 1–5; Dec.–Feb. Mon.–Sat. 10–4, Sun. 1–4.

Chatham Manor. This 1771 Georgian mansion, built by William Fitzhugh, looks out over the Rappahannock River on the northeast side of Fredericksburg. As the Union headquarters and hospital during the Civil War, President Abraham Lincoln conferred with his generals here, while Clara Barton and the poet Walt Whitman tended the wounded. The estate has been restored by private owners and donated to the National Park Service, which holds concerts here during the summer. | 120 Chatham La., Chatham Heights | 540/371–0802 | fax 540/371–1907 | www.nps.gov/frsp | Free | Daily 9–5.

Confederate Cemetery. The cemetery contains the remains of more than 2,000 soldiers—most of them unknown—as well as the graves of generals, Dabney Maury, Seth Barton, Carter Stevenson, Daniel Ruggles, and others. | 1100 Washington Ave. | 540/373–1776 | Daily dawn–dusk.

Ferry Farm. Visit the farm where George Washington spent his early years from 1738 to 1752—home to the famous cherry tree legend. It was here that Washington threw the silver dollar across the Rappahannock River (it was really a stone). Ferry Farm was also an important part of the Union lines during the battle of Fredericksburg. Archeological exploration has found evidence of early Native American habitation. | Ferry Farm Rd., East of Rte. 3 | 540/373–3381 ext. 28 | $2 | Mon.–Sat. 10–5, Sun. 12–5.

Fredericksburg and Spotsylvania National Military Park. Four Civil War battlefields—Fredericksburg, Chancellorsville, Wilderness, and Spotsylvania Court House—make up this 9,000-acre park. Four battles raged from December 1862 until May 1864 and cost both sides dearly in manpower and resources; the fighting resulted in the estimated loss of 65,000 Union soldiers and 40,000 Confederates. During the May 2, 1863, Battle at Chancellorsville, Stonewall Jackson was fatally wounded by his own troops. There are two park visitor centers, one in Chancellorsville and one in Fredericksburg. Since the park consists of different sites all over town and there is no single entrance, it's best to go to a visitor center to get a detailed map. All of the battlefields are within a 15-mi radius of Fredericksburg. | 540/373–6122 or 540/786–2880 | fax 540/786–1326 | www.nps.gov/frsp | Pass for all four battlefields $3, valid 1 wk | Daily dawn–dusk, visitor centers daily 9–5.

The **Chancellorsville Visitor Center** shows a 10-minute slide program on the Battle of Chancellorsville and the Civil War and offers maps for self-guiding walking and driving tours. Tape-recorded tours can be rented. Battlefield artifacts and soldiers' artwork are displayed. Historians are available to answer questions. The center is 7 mi west of I–95, and 12 mi west of Fredericksburg. | U.S. 3 W | 540/786–2880 | fax 540/786–1326 | www.nps.gov/frsp | Free | Daily 9–5.

Fredericksburg Battlefield Visitor Center screens a 10-minute slide program on the Battle of Fredericksburg and the Civil War and offers maps for self-guiding walking and driving tours. Tape-recorded tours can be rented. Historians are available to answer questions. Near the visitor center is a statue honoring a Confederate sergeant who risked his life to bring water to wounded foes. | 1013 Lafayette Blvd./U.S. 1 | 540/373–6122 | fax 540/786–1326 | www.nps.gov/frsp | Free | Daily 9–5.

While you're visiting the park, be sure not to miss the **Fredericksburg National Cemetery,** the final resting place of 15,000 Union soldiers, most of whom were never identified. | 540/373–6122 | Daily dawn–dusk.

Another important site is the **Old Salem Church,** which became a refuge for civilians fleeing the city during the Battle of Fredericksburg (December 1862) and was the site of a battle during the Chancellorsville campaign (May 1863). It later was used by both sides as shelter for the wounded. | Rte. 3 | 540/373–6122 | Daily dawn–dusk.

Fredericksburg Area Museum and Cultural Center. The museum's six permanent exhibits tell the story of the area from prehistoric times through the Revolutionary and Civil wars to the present. Displays include Native American artifacts and Confederate memorabilia. The museum is housed in the former 1816 town hall. | 907 Princess Anne St. | 540/371–3037 | fax 540/373–6569 | www.fredericksburgva.com | $4 | Mar.–Nov. Mon.–Sat. 9–5, Sun. 1–5; Dec.–Feb. Mon.–Sat. 10–4, Sun. 1–4.

George Washington Masonic Museum. In 1752, George Washington became a Master Mason in this Lodge (No. 4). The museum now contains memorabilia and relics relating to his membership, including an original Gilbert Stuart portrait of Washington. | 803 Princess Anne St. | 540/373–5885 | www.fredericksburgva.com | $2 | Mon.–Sat. 9–4, Sun. 1–4.

Hugh Mercer Apothecary Shop. Established in 1771 by Dr. Hugh Mercer, a Scotsman who served as a brigadier general of the Continental Army, the apothecary shop is now a museum that offers a close-up view of 18th- and 19th-century medicine. A costumed guide describes amputations and other operations performed before the advent of anesthetics, and exhibits include the devices used in colonial dentistry. | 1020 Caroline St. | 540/373–3362 | www.fredericksburgva.com | $4 | Mar.–Nov. daily 9–5; Dec.–Feb. daily 10–4.

James Monroe Museum and Memorial Library. The future fifth president of the United States practiced law in this one-story building from 1787 until 1789. Many of Monroe's possessions have been collected here, including a mahogany dispatch box used during the negotiation of the Louisiana Purchase. The library contains books and historical manuscripts dealing mostly with Monroe and his era. | 908 Charles St., 23401 | 540/654–1043 | fax 540/654–1106 | www.jamesmonroemuseum.mwc.edu | $4 | Mar.–Nov., daily 9–5; Dec.–Feb., daily 10–4.

Kenmore. This mid-18th-century home belonged to Col. Fielding Lewis, a patriot, plantation owner, and brother-in-law of George Washington. During the Revolutionary War, he used his fortune to operate a gun factory that supplied the American forces. The house contains ornate plasterwork on the ceilings and over the fireplaces, as well as antique furnishings that include a large standing clock belonging to Mary Washington. Admission includes tea and ginger cookies (a Washington family recipe). | 1201 Washington Ave. | 540/373–3381 | fax 540/371–3660 | www.kenmore.org | $6 | Mar.–Nov., Mon.–Sat. 10–5, Sun. noon–5; Jan.–Feb., Sat. noon–4, weekdays by reservation only.

Lake Anna State Park. This 2,058-acre park, 12 mi southwest of Fredericksburg, has 8½ mi of shoreline along the Lake Anna Reservoir, a swimming beach, fishing pier accessible to people with disabilities, boat-launch facilities (motor boats permitted), and pontoon boat rides. A visitor center traces the history of gold mining in the area and highlights the park's natural features. | 6800 Lawyers Rd. (Rte. 601), Spotsylvania | 540/854–5503 | fax 540/854–5421 | www.state.va.us | $1 | Daily 8–dusk.

Mary Washington College. Founded in 1908 as the State Normal School for Women at Fredericksburg, this state college changed its name to Mary Washington College in 1938 and began accepting male students in 1970. Its Ridderhof Martin Gallery hosts exhibitions of art from various cultures and historical periods; the DuPont Gallery in Melchers Hall features painting, sculpture, photography, ceramics, and textiles by art faculty, students, and contemporary artists. Free parking is in a lot at College Avenue and Thornton Street. | College Ave. | 540/654–1000 or 800/468–5614 | fax 540/654–1857 | www.mwc.edu | Free | Mid-Jan.–May; mid-Aug.–mid-Dec. Mon. Wed. and Fri. 10–4, weekends 1–4.

Mary Washington House. George Washington purchased this house for his mother in 1772, and she spent the last 17 years of her life here. Many of her personal effects remain, and the old English garden that she tended still has some of the boxwoods that she planted, as well as her sundial. | 1200 Charles St. | 540/373–1569 | fax 540/372–6587 | $4 | Mar.–Nov. daily 9–5; Dec.–Feb. daily 10–4.

Mary Washington Monument. A 40-ft granite obelisk, dedicated by President Grover Cleveland in 1894, marks the final resting place of George Washington's mother. It replaced a partial marble monument laid by President Andrew Jackson in 1833—one that was badly scarred by the Civil War bombardment of Fredericksburg before it could be completed. | Washington Ave. at Kenmore | 800/678–4748 visitor center | Free | Daily.

Masonic Cemetery. Established in 1784 by Masonic Lodge No. 4—to which George Washington belonged—this cemetery contains the graves of Freemasons and their relatives, including Robert Lewis, son of Fielding Lewis and Betty Washington, and secretary to his uncle, George Washington; Revolutionary War general George Weedon; plus some of Fredericksburg's leading families. It is believed to be the country's oldest Masonic cemetery. | Corner of Charles St. and George St. | 540/654–1043 | Free | Mar.–Nov. daily 9–5; Dec.–Feb. daily 10–4.

National Bank Museum. Two centuries of banking history are encapsulated in this museum, housed in one of America's oldest-operating bank buildings. Built in 1820, the Farmers' Bank has artifacts that include a scale for weighing gold dust and a counterfeit bank note from the 1800s. | 900 Princess Anne St. | 540/899–3243 | www.fredericksburgva.com | Free | Weekdays 9–1.

Old Slave Auction Block. In Fredericksburg, slaves were sold from this platform before the Civil War. The slaves were made to step up on the block, so they could be better viewed by potential buyers. | Corner of Charles St. and William St. | 800/678–4748 visitor center | Free | Daily.

Presbyterian Church. Built in 1833, this temple-like building served as a hospital for both Union and Confederate soldiers during the Civil War. It was here, in 1862, that Clara Barton, founder of the American Red Cross, nursed casualties after the Battle of Fredericksburg. | 810 Princess Anne St. | 540/373–7057 | fax 540/370–0210 | Free | Daily 9–5.

Rising Sun Tavern. In 1760, George Washington's brother, Charles, built this structure as his home. It later became the Rising Sun Tavern, a local watering hole frequented by luminaries ranging from George Washington to Patrick Henry and Thomas Jefferson. "Wenches" in period costume lead tours and act out 18th-century tavern life. | 1304 Caroline St. | 540/371–1494 | www.fredericksburgva.com | $4 | Mar.–Nov. daily 9–5; Dec.–Feb. daily 10–4.

St. George's Episcopal Church and Churchyard. A memorial window to Mary Washington and three Louis Comfort Tiffany windows adorn this church. The current structure, erected in 1849, is the third church on this site; the first was built in 1732. The churchyard contains the graves of William Paul, brother of John Paul Jones, and Martha Washington's father, John Dandridge of New Kent. | 905 Princess Anne St. | 540/373–4133 | fax 540/374–0923 | Free | Daily 9–5.

St. James House. Built in the 1760s, this is a rare example of a typical pre-Revolutionary Fredericksburg house. Called a "gentleman's cottage," it was the residence of James Mercer, Fredericksburg's first judge. The interior is furnished with period antiques. | 1300 Charles St. | 540/373–1569 | $4 | Third week of Apr. (Garden Week) and first week of Oct. daily 9–5; group tours by appointment.

Sergeant Kirkland's Museum and Historical Society. This museum presents the history of Fredericksburg and the Civil War through documents and artwork. | 912 Lafayette Blvd. | 540/899–5565 | Free | Daily 10–5.

Spotsylvania Court House. This historic Civil War site shares its name with the battle that raged here from May 8-21 in 1864. While the courthouse was reconstructed in the early 1900s, the original Doric columns remain, and you can still see the battle scars on the nearby church, now a museum for local artifacts and genealogical records. | 1013 Lafayette Blvd. | 540/373–6122 | Free | Daily 9–5.

Stonewall Jackson Shrine. This small office building is where Stonewall Jackson died on the afternoon of May 10, 1863, eight days after he was mistakenly shot by his own men during the Battle at Chancellorsville. The Confederate general had been taken to Fairfield Plantation to recover from the amputation of his left arm (necessitated by a bullet wound), but pneumonia set in and he died. The National Park Service has restored the building, and the room looks much as it did on Jackson's final day. | Rte. 606, Guinea Station | 804/633–6076 | www.nps.gov/frsp | Requires battlefield pass ($3) | Mid-June–Labor Day, daily 9–5; Apr.–mid-June and Labor Day–Oct. Fri.–Tues. 9–5; Nov.–Apr. Sat.–Mon. 9–5.

Visitor Center. The visitor center has comprehensive information about tours of the Fredericksburg, Stafford, and Spotsylvania area, including maps for self-guided tours, parking passes, and discount touring tickets ($19.75 for entry to seven sights, or $13.75 for four sights). It also offers lodging reservation services. A 14-minute film provides an overview of the area's history and its attractions. | 706 Caroline St. | 540/373–1776 or 800/678–4748 | fax 540/372–6587 | www.fredericksburgva.com | Free | Memorial Day–Labor Day, daily 9–7; Labor Day–Memorial Day, daily 9–5.

ON THE CALENDAR

APR.: *Historic Garden Week.* An opportunity to tour historic homes and gardens in Fredericksburg and the surrounding countryside of Spotsylvania County. | 540/373–1776 or 800/678–4748.

FREDERICKSBURG

INTRO
ATTRACTIONS
DINING
LODGING

APR.: *Quilt Show.* Quilts of every pattern and technique are displayed at Walker Grant Middle School. | 540/373–1776 or 800/678–4748.

MAY: *Market Square Fair.* An arts-and-crafts fair at 1200 Caroline St. it features demonstrations of 18th- and 19th-century work by artisans in period garb. | 540/373–1776 or 800/678–4748.

MAY: *Battle of the Wilderness.* Fredericksburg and Spotsylvania National Military Park, near the Chancellorsville Visitor Center on Rte. 3, hosts an annual reenactment of the Civil War battle fought there May 5–7, 1864. | 540/371–0802.

JUNE: *Fredericksburg International Scottish Games and Irish Festival.* An international competition of Highland games, Scottish and Irish food, dance, music, crafts, and folklore at Maury Field, Rte. 3. | 540/373–1776 or 800/678–4748.

DEC.: *Christmas Candlelight Tour.* A highlight of Fredericksburg's holiday season: Private homes in the historic district are bedecked with Christmas decorations and open for tours by costumed hostesses. | 540/373–1776 or 800/678–4748.

Dining

Carlos O'Kelly's Mexican Cafe. Mexican. Wood booths, old framed advertisements, and Texas artifacts decorate this casual Midwestern chain, where favorites include the fajita cheese-crisp appetizer, the fiesta sampler (including enchilada, burrito, tostada, chimichanga), and the fried ice cream. The dining room is open late on weekends and the adjacent lounge has entertainment on most nights. | 2306 Plank Rd. | 540/373–5436 | No reservations accepted | $6–$15 | AE, D, DC, MC, V.

Claiborne's. American/Casual. Originally a train depot, Claiborne's's was later transformed into a dining spot with white linen tablecloths and candle lamps. Veal, lamb chops, filet, and crab cakes are on the menu, along with a 24-ounce porterhouse steak. | 200 Lafayette Blvd. | 540/371–7080 | No lunch | $15–$30 | AE, D, MC, V.

Goolrick's Pharmacy. American. Treat yourself to a cherry, vanilla, or chocolate coke inside the 130-year-old pharmacy at what is possibly the oldest soda fountain still in existence. For lunch or an early dinner (they close at 7 PM.), take your pick of deli sandwiches, macaroni salad, potato salad, or soup. Breakfast is available, along with seven flavors of milk-shakes. | 901 Caroline St. | 540/373–9878 | Closed Sun. | $3–$6 | MC, V.

La Petite Auberge. American/French. This restaurant has high ceilings, and exposed-brick walls like the bistros of Paris. Have a drink in the lounge or dine outside on the terrace. Try any of the seafood specials or the trout setoise (trout over a bed of ratatouille with bearnaise sauce on top). Early-bird suppers Monday–Thursday | 311 William St. | 540/371–2727 | Closed Sun. | $9–$25 | AE, DC, MC, V.

Merriman's. Continental. Local artwork is displayed on the yellow walls of this restaurant. Try the crab cakes or the linguine Mykonos with shrimp, scallops, black olives, and feta cheese. Sunday brunch available. | 715 Caroline St. | No lunch Sun. | $9–$26 | AE, D, DC, MC, V.

Ristorante Renato. Italian. This restaurant offers semiformal Italian dining in a crisp, white linen dining room. Specialties are the seafood and veal menu items. | 422 William St. | 540/371–8228 | No lunch weekends | $10–$25 | AE, MC, V.

Sammy T's. Continental. Sammy T's specializes in vegetarian dishes and makes all of its sauces, dressings, soups, and desserts. Bean and grain burgers, tempeh burgers, and falafel are popular picks, or try the Camper's Special, grilled vegetables and lemon tahini sauce rolled into a grilled flour tortilla and topped with cheddar and mozzarella cheese. You can swivel and swill from the captain's stools at the bar, or settle into one of the high wooden booths. | 801 Caroline St. | 540/371–2008 | Reservations not accepted | $6–$12 | AE, D, MC, V.

Smythe's Cottage and Tavern. Southern. Lots of windows make this cozy dining room bright and airy by day; candlelight sets the tone by night. The restaurant is in what was once a blacksmith's home. Lunch and dinner menus are classic Virginia, from the seafood pie, quail, and stuffed flounder, to the Virginia peanut soup. | 303 Fauquier St. | 540/373–1645 | $10–$18 | MC, V.

Lodging

Best Western. This red-brick chain hotel opened in April, 2000. All rooms have hair dryers and coffee makers. A sports bar, restaurant, and lounge are nearby. Complimentary Continental breakfast. In-room data ports, some microwaves, some refrigerators, cable TV, room phones, TV in common area. Outdoor pool. Laundry facilities, laundry service. Some pets allowed. | 2205 William St. | 540/371–5050 or 800/937–8376 | fax 540/373–3496 | 107 | $75 | AE, D, DC, MC, V.

Best Western Central Plaza. The motor lodge is between the Spotsylvania Mall and Central Park, two mi from historic Fredericksburg, and a mile from Mary Washington College. Rooms, painted light colors, are made comfortable with floral arrangements. Complimentary Continental breakfast. Cable TV. Laundry facilities. Business services. Some pets allowed. Free parking. | 3000 Plank Rd. | 540/786–7404 | fax 540/785–7415 | www.best-western.com | 76 rooms | $40–$82 | AE, D, DC, MC, V.

Comfort Inn Southpoint. This chain facility is next to Massaponax Outlet Center. Skylights in the lobby, lots of brickwork and archways throughout the hotel, and classic bed frames set this hotel apart. Complimentary Continental breakfast. In-room data ports, cable TV. Pool. Hot tub. Exercise equipment. Business services. Free parking. | 5422 U.S. 1 | 540/898–5550 | fax 540/891–2861 | www.comfortinn.com | 125 rooms | $64–$77 | AE, D, DC, MC, V.

Days Inn–North. This two-story hotel has exterior room entrances, and is quite close to Fredericksburg's historic district. Easy interstate access is also a plus. Complimentary Continental breakfast. Cable TV. Pool. Business services. Pets allowed (fee). | 14 Simpson Rd. | 540/373–5340 | fax 540/373–5340 | 120 rooms | $30–$70 | AE, D, DC, MC, V.

Dunning Mills. Near a quiet wooded area, this all-suite motel added a new non-smoking building with ten suites in September, 2000. Every suite at Dunning Mills has a full kitchen with a sitting area. Hang out in the lobby on the comfy sofa and read a paperback from the library, or play a board game and socialize with other guests. The outdoor picnic area has barbecues. Picnic area, complimentary Continental breakfast. In-room data ports, kitchens, microwaves, refrigerators, some in-room hot tubs, cable TV, room phones, TV in common area. Outdoor pool. Library. Laundry facilities. Pets allowed (fee). | 2305C Jefferson Davis Hwy. | 540/373–1256 | fax 540/599–9041 | www.dunningmills.com | 54 | $118 | AE, D, DC, MC, V.

Econo Lodge Central. You'll find this chain hotel off I–95 at Exit 130B, near the Spotsylvania Mall. There are places to eat nearby. Complimentary Continental breakfast. Cable TV, room phones. Pets allowed. | 2802 Plank Rd. | 540/786–8379 or 800/553–2666 | fax 540/786–8811 | 96 | $50 | AE, D, MC, V.

Fredericksburg Colonial. Built in 1928, this classy lodge is in historic downtown Fredericksburg. Rooms, lined with lace and linen, are furnished with Civil War era antiques and dark varnished furniture. Complimentary Continental breakfast. Refrigerators, no smoking, cable TV. | 1707 Princess Anne St. | 540/371–5666 | fax 540/371–5884 | www.fcl1.com | 30 rooms | $65–$99 | AE, MC, V.

Hampton Inn. This two-story hotel with exterior room entrances is located at the intersection of Route 3 and I–95. Rooms are plainly furnished. Mary Washington College is nearby. Complimentary Continental breakfast. In-room data ports, cable TV. Pool. Laundry facilities. Business services. Some pets allowed. | 2310 William St. | 540/371–0330 | fax 540/371–1753 | www.hampton-inn.com | 166 rooms | $60–$90 | AE, D, DC, MC, V.

Holiday Inn. Renovated in 2000, this hotel has a large atrium. Rooms have prominent windows and are well-appointed. The hotel is in Central Park, and shopping is nearby. Restaurant, bar with entertainment, picnic area. Room service, cable TV. In-room data ports. Pool, wading pool. Exercise equipment. Business services. Airport shuttle (fee). Free parking. | 2801 Plank Rd. | 540/786–8321 | fax 540/786–3957 | www.holiday-inn.com | 195 rooms | $109–$169 | AE, D, DC, MC, V.

FREDERICKSBURG

INTRO
ATTRACTIONS
DINING
LODGING

Holiday Inn–North. This chain hotel is three mi north of Fredericksburg, near the area's Civil War battlefields. Rooms are comfortable with commercially standard furnishings. Restaurant, bar with entertainment. Room service, cable TV. Pool, wading pool. Laundry facilities. Business services. Free parking. | 564 Warrenton Rd. | 540/371–5550 | fax 540/373–3641 | www.holiday-inn.com | 150 rooms | $60–$92 | AE, D, DC, MC, V.

Kenmore Inn. Built in 1796 and redone in 1933, this colonial inn is in the downtown historic district. Rooms have high ceilings, and some have fireplaces and canopy beds. Bar, dining room, complimentary Continental breakfast. In-room data ports, no TV in rooms, cable TV in common area. Business services. | 1200 Princess Anne St. | 540/371–7622 | fax 540/371–5480 | www.kenmoreinn.com | 12 rooms | $100–$145 | AE, DC, MC, V.

Ramada Inn–South. This hotel has a large lobby with high ceilings from which the state flag hangs. Rooms either face the hotel atrium or the exterior. The hotel is easily accessible from Interstate–95. Restaurant, bar with entertainment. In-room data ports, room service, cable TV. Pool. Hot tub. Exercise equipment. Video games. Laundry facilities. Business services. Some pets allowed. Free parking. | 5324 U.S. 1 | 540/898–1102 | fax 540/898–2017 | 196 rooms | $62–$75 | AE, D, DC, MC, V.

Ramada Inn–Spotsylvania Mall. The chain facility is close to the shopping mall and 2 mi from Mary Washington College. Rooms have exterior entrances and are plainly furnished. In-room data ports, cable TV. Pool. Business services. Some pets allowed. Free parking. | 2802 Plank Rd. | 540/786–8361 | fax 540/786–8811 | www.ramada.com | 129 rooms | $60–$72 | AE, D, DC, MC, V.

Richard Johnston. This Federal-style inn was built in the mid-18th century. Each room in the antique-filled inn is individually furnished with quilts, fine linen and canopy beds. Complimentary Continental breakfast. No smoking, no room phones. No kids under 12. | 711 Caroline St. | 540/899–7606 | www.inns.com | 6 rooms, 2 suites | $95–$125 | AE, MC, V.

Roxbury Mill. Dating back to 1723, this old gristmill on the river, 13 mi south of Fredericksburg, is decorated with family antiques, including two beds from the 1850s. The house is on 3.9 wooded acres, which stretch down to the river. One of the three rooms is a 900-square-foot suite with its own kitchen and a deck overlooking the waterfall. Complimentary breakfast. One kitchenette, refrigerators, cable TV, some room phones, no TV in some rooms. Pond. Hiking. Fishing. Laundry facilities. Some pets allowed. No smoking. | 6908 Roxbury Mill Rd., Thornburg | 540/582–6611 | members.aol.com/roxburymil | 3 | $95–$150 | AE, D, MC, V.

Super 8. The rooms at this chain hotel are decorated in dark-green and maroon colors with wood furniture; there's a sitting area, a 24-hour coffee bar, and a microwave in the small lobby. Across the highway is Central Park–a complex with shops, a movie theater, a nightclub, and places to eat. Some in-room data ports, some microwaves, some refrigerators, cable TV, room phones. No pets. | 3002 Mall Ct. | 540/786–8881 | 62 | $66 | AE, D, DC, MC, V.

Super 8. This low-slung, brown-brick Super 8 has standard Spartan rooms put-together in beige and neutral tones. Complimentary Continental breakfast. In-room data ports, some kitchenettes, cable TV. Business services. | 557 Warrenton Rd. | 540/371–8900 | fax 540/372–6958 | 77 rooms | $65–$75 | AE, D, DC, MC, V.

FRONT ROYAL

MAP 11, H4

(Nearby towns also listed: Middletown, Shenandoah National Park, Woodstock)

At the northern end of the Shenandoah Valley, Front Royal is the northern gateway to Skyline Drive and the wilderness of Shenandoah National Park. This frontier village has a colorful past. In the 1700s, it was better known as "Helltown" for all the hard drinking and brawling of its residents. During the Civil War, Front Royal was a base of operations for Confederate spy, Belle Boyd. The restored downtown district preserves some of the town's 19th-century atmosphere and contains many boutiques and antiques shops.

Information: Front Royal–Warren County Chamber of Commerce | 414 E. Main St., Front Royal, VA 22630 | 540/635–3185 or 800/338–2576 | www.frontroyalchamber.com.

Attractions

Belle Boyd Cottage. This 1860s cottage was used by Confederate spy, Belle Boyd, who purportedly used her female charms to obtain military secrets from Union suitors. It contains period furnishings and memorabilia relating to the area during the Civil War. | 101 Chester St. | 540/636–1446 | $2 | Apr.–Oct. Mon. and Fri. 10–4, weekends by appointment; Nov.–Mar. by appointment.

Shenandoah National Park. (*See Shenandoah National Park.*) Front Royal is the northern gateway to Skyline Drive and the wilderness of this national park. | 540/999–3500.

Sky Meadows State Park. This 1,618-acre park on the eastern side of the Blue Ridge Mountains spreads through Fauquier and Clarke counties, 13 mi east of Front Royal. Camping, picnicking, and hiking are common activities in the park. It includes two mid-19th-century farmsteads, the Mount Bleak and Turner farms, and a circa-1830 slave log dwelling. The Mount Bleak house can be toured on weekends, April through October, at 1 and 4 PM. The park also serves as an access point to the Appalachian Trail. | 11012 Edmonds La., Delaplane | 540/592–3556 | fax 540/592–3617 | www.state.va.us | $2 parking fee | Daily 8–dusk.

Skyline Caverns. Subterranean streams, cascades, and fragile mineral formations called anthodites are featured in these caverns, discovered in 1937. Walking tours are given every 15 minutes. | U.S. 340 S | 540/635–4545 or 800/296–4545 | www.skylinecaverns.com | $12 | June 15–Labor Day, daily 9–6:30; Mar. 15–June 15 and Labor Day–Nov. 15, weekdays 9–5, weekends 9–6; Nov. 15—March 15, daily 9–4.

Warren Rifles Confederate Museum. This museum contains a variety of Civil War items—guns, soldiers' letters, and pictures—including possessions belonging to Confederate spy, Belle Boyd, and Generals Robert E. Lee and "Stonewall" Jackson. | 95 Chester St. | 540/636–6982 | $2 | Apr. 15–Oct. Mon.–Sat. 9–4, Sun. noon–4; Nov.–Apr. 15 by appointment.

ON THE CALENDAR

MAY: *Virginia Mushroom and Wine Festival.* A celebration of the shiitake mushroom, complete with food, wine tastings, live music, theatrical performances, arts and crafts, and children's rides. | 414 E. Main St. | 540/635–3185 or 800/338–2576.

AUG.: *Warren County Fair.* A traditional county fair, featuring agricultural exhibits, a Miss Warren County beauty pageant, food, crafts, and rides. | 540/635–3185 or 800/338–2576.

SEPT: *Blue Ridge Oktoberfest.* Like its German cousin, this beerfest is held at the end of September. Old Town Main Street is roped off so that you can drink beer, eat German food, and listen to live music. A commemorative mug and a beer are included in the $5 admission. | 540/635–3185, ext. 1.

OCT.: *Festival of Leaves.* The season is celebrated with music and period dancing at Belle Boyd Cottage. Folklore events, a parade, food vendors, live bands, and a beard-growing contest are also held in the surrounding vicinity. | 101 Chester St. | 540/635–3185 or 800/338–2576.

Lodging

Chester House. Built in 1905, this Georgian-style home is on a two-acre lot with elaborate terraced gardens. Marble mantels, fountains, fireplaces and statues imported from Europe mark the interior of the rooms. Picnic area, complimentary breakfast. No TV in rooms, TV in common area. No kids under 12. Business services. | 43 Chester St. | 540/635–3937 or 800/

621–0441 | fax 540/636–8695 | www.chesterhouse.com | 6 rooms, 1 suite | $95–$210 | AE, MC, V.

Quality Inn. The chain inn is close to Skyline Drive, three mi outside of Fredericksburg. Rooms were remodeled in 2000 and have heat lamps in the bathrooms. Restaurant. Cable TV. Pool. Business services. | 10 Commerce Ave. | 540/635–3161 | fax 540/635–6624 | 107 rooms | $85 | AE, D, DC, MC, V.

Relax Inn. This hotel, in the center of town near the river and Norfolk and Western train tracks, has standard comfortable rooms. Picnic area. Some microwaves, some refrigerators, cable TV. Pool. Playground. | 1801 N. Shenandoah Ave. | 540/635–4101 | fax 540/635–5765 | 20 rooms | $60–$75 | AE,D, MC, V.

GALAX

MAP 11, E8

(Nearby towns also listed: Independence, Wytheville)

The town sprang up in 1904 when a spur of the Norfolk and Western Railway opened up the neighboring timber regions, an industry which has dissipated over time. Now the town's major industries include furniture, glass and mirrors production, textiles, and clothing. The region's rich musical heritage is celebrated every August at the Old Fiddler's Convention and Fiddlefest. Galax is also the name of the white-blossomed mountain evergreen that grows profusely in the area; used in floral arrangements, galax is picked and processed here and shipped all over the country. In southwestern Virginia's Blue Ridge Mountains, Galax, the town, sits on the Carroll County and Grayson County line. The Blue Ridge Parkway is also accessible to the east off Route 97.

Information: Galax-Carroll-Grayson Chamber of Commerce | 405 N. Main St., Galax, 24333-2958 | 540/236–2184.

Attractions

Blue Ridge Parkway. A scenic ridge road traversing Virginia, this parkway provides access to camping, fishing, and self-guided hiking trails. | 828/298–0398 | www.nps.gov/blri | Free | Parts of the parkway close during winter months because of snow and ice; call for weather-related updates.

Jeff Matthews Memorial Museum. Jeff Matthews, one of Galax's first settlers, established this museum with his personal collection of Civil War items and American Indian artifacts. Two restored log cabins and a smithy remain on the grounds as well. | 606 W. Stuart Dr. | 540/236–7874 | Free, donations accepted | Wed.–Fri. 1–5, Sat. 11–4, Sun. 1–4.

Cliffview Trading Post. You can rent horses (Apr.– mid-Nov.) and bikes at this country tack store. It also stocks saddles and other horse supplies and has overnight stables, in case you have your own steed. | 442 Cliffview Rd. | 540/238–1530 | Tues.–Fri. 9:30–1:30, Sat. 9:30–5.

New River Trail State Park. This 57-mi linear park, or greenway, follows an abandoned railroad right-of-way. The trail parallels the New River for 29 mi and links to other recreational areas as far as Pulaski to the north. Its gentle slope is suitable for hiking, biking, or horseback riding. Fishing, tubing, and canoeing are popular as well. The southern terminus is on U.S. 58 in Galax. | 176 Orphanage, Dr. Foster Falls | 540/699–6778 or 800/933–PARK | www.state.va.us | $2 per car | Daily dawn to dusk.

ON THE CALENDAR
AUG.: *Old Fiddler's Convention and Fiddlefest.* One of the world's oldest, and possibly the largest, annual fiddler's convention attracts musicians from the U.S. and abroad. There are banjo, guitar, mandolin, fiddle, song, and dance competitions at Felts Park. | 540/236–8541.

OCT.: *Baywood Fall Festival.* This community-wide event includes crafts, an art show, live music, games, a horse pull, antique equipment displays, and food booths. | Baywood Elementary School | 540/236–9711.

Dining

Tlaquepaque. Mexican. A fountain welcomes you into five dining rooms, separated by arched doorways and decorated with traditional Mexican pottery and clothing; Spanish-language television and a bilingual waitstaff add to the foreign atmosphere. On the menu, you'll find fajitas, chimichangas, pescado frito, steak, shrimp, and some vegetarian options. For dessert, choose from fried ice cream, sopapillas, flan, and churros with ice cream. A mariachi band entertains twice a month. | 1003 E. Stuart Dr. | 540/236–5060 | $5–$13 | AE, DC, MC, V.

Lodging

Knights Inn. This mid-sized, one-story inn is ¼ mi west of the New River Trail State Park entrance and 10 mi from the Blue Ridge Parkway. Most rooms provide views of the Blue Ridge Mountains. Cable TV. Outdoor pool. Business services. | 312 W. Stuart Dr. | 540/236–5117 | fax 540/236–0652 | www.knightsinn.com | 48 rooms | $41–$50 | AE, DC, MC, V.

Super 8. This chain hotel is close to the New River Trails State Park, where you can go hiking, fishing, horseback riding, and canoeing. The property is 10 minutes from the Blue Ridge Parkway and 10–15 minutes from I–77. The bright, open lobby is full of plants, windows, and a seating area. Picnic area, complimentary Continental breakfast. Some in-room data ports, some kitchenettes, some microwaves, some refrigerators, cable TV, room phones, TV in common area. Laundry facilities. No pets. | 303 N. Main St. | 540/236–5127 | fax 540/236–9163 | 60 | $51 | AE, D, DC, MC, V.

GLOUCESTER

MAP 11, K6

(Nearby town also listed: Williamsburg)

Named for Henry, Duke of Gloucester, Gloucester County's history dates to the early 1600s. According to legend, it was here that the Indian princess Pocahontas saved Capt. John Smith from death at the hands of her tribe. In the Tidewater region, Gloucester County sits on a finger of land bounded by the Piankatank River on the north, Mobjack Bay and the Ware River on the east, and the York River on the south. Plantation homes from the county's tobacco-producing era still dot the rich landscape. On the banks of the York River stand the ruins of Rosewell, a circa-1725 mansion that was considered one of the finest homes built in the colonies; much of its superb brickwork survives.

The town of Gloucester maintains a restored 1766 courthouse, a debtor's prison, and other historic buildings. A research institute with public aquariums, the Virginia Institute of Marine Sciences sits at Gloucester Point.

Information: **Gloucester County Chamber of Commerce** | P.O. Box 296, Gloucester 23061 | 804/693–2425.

Attractions

Abingdon Episcopal Church. Completed in 1755, this rare cruciform colonial church midway between Gloucester Court House and Gloucester Point underwent a major restoration in 1986. Inside, you'll find a unique three-tiered pulpit and a pipe organ. The adjacent cemetery has gravestones dating back to the mid-1600s. | Rte. 17 | 804/693–2425 | Free | Sun. or by appointment.

County Courthouse. Set on the court green, Gloucester's courthouse dates from 1766 and contains plaques honoring various distinguished men and Gloucester natives, among them

Nathaniel Bacon Jr. who led the first organized rebellion against British authority in 1676, and Dr. Walter Reed, a surgeon whose research led to the eradication of yellow fever. | 6489 Main St., U.S. 17 Business | 804/693–2502 | fax 804/693–2186 | Free | Weekdays 8–4:30.

Rosewell Historic Ruins. Built about 1725 and noted for its superb brickwork, Rosewell was considered one of the most splendid and finely crafted mansions of colonial Virginia before fire gutted the mansion in 1916. The massive chimneys, elaborate doorways, window casements, and brick walls of the three-story, 33-room house remain as an indication of its previous grandeur. Tour guides are available. Picnicking is permitted on the grounds. | Old Rosewell La. | 804/693–2585 | $2 | Mon.–Sat. 10–4, Sun. 1–4, winter hours subject to change.

Virginia Institute of Marine Science, College of William and Mary. Within Watermen's Hall of the research institute you can visit the public aquariums that contain fish indigenous to Virginia and endangered sea turtles. Displays contain shells from around the world and life-size models of marine mammals. A "Touch Tank" invites you to explore hermit crabs, sea urchins, and small shoreline animals. | 1208 Greate Rd., Gloucester Point | 804/684–7000 | fax 804/684–7097 | www.vims.edu | Free | Weekdays 8–4:30.

ON THE CALENDAR

APR.: *Daffodil Festival.* Arts and crafts, a parade along Main St. music, clowns, and children's games honor this cheerful bloom of spring. | 804/693–2355.

Dining

Goodfellas. Contemporary. This large, upscale restaurant offers more than 30 pasta, seafood, and steak entrees, not including the nightly specials. Desserts are homemade. Check out the paintings and photography by local artists while waiting for your food. | 17 George Washington Memorial Hwy. | 804/693–5950 | No lunch. Closed Mon. | $10–$17 | D, DC, MC, V.

Seawell's Ordinary. Contemporary. Once a bar where several Founding Fathers socialized, the building retains its colonial-style, but the food shows French and American Southwest influences. Chicken stuffed with brie and served with raspberry sauce, oyster volcano, or fresh seafood and andouille sausage served with teriyaki cream sauce are unique favorites not likely to have been served in the 18th-century. Open-air dining on patio. Sun. brunch. | 3967 George Washington Hwy. | 804/642–3635 | Closed Mon. | $25–$35 | AE, DC, MC, V.

Lodging

Airville Plantation Bed and Breakfast. Dating from 1756, this manor house turned B&B sits on 250 acres along Chesapeake and Mobjack Bay. Listed in the National Register of Historic Homes, the main house boasts Italian black marble mantels over two fireplaces and a floating, circular, staircase. The overseers house is also available. Complimentary breakfast. Outdoor pool. Beach, dock, fishing. No kids under 12. No smoking. | 6423 T. C. Walker Rd. | 804/694–0287 | fax 804/694–0287 | airville@visi.net | www.airvilleplantation.com | 2 rooms (1 with shared bath), 1 suite (with shared bath) | $105–$150, $160 suite | No credit cards.

Comfort Inn. A quiet wooded setting, a friendly staff, and a large glass lobby create a welcoming atmosphere at this hotel, which opened in April, 2000. The rooms are done in dark green and burgundy with gold accents and dark wood. You're 1½ mi from the restored district of Gloucester and within walking distance of an antique mall. Complimentary breakfast. In-room data ports, some microwaves, some refrigerators, some in-room hot tubs, cable TV, room phones, TV in common area. Outdoor pool. Shop. Laundry service. No pets. | 6639 Forest Hill Ave. | 804/695–1900 or 800/228–5150 | fax 804/695–1901 | www.comfortinn.com | 78 | $79 | AE, D, DC, MC, V.

North River Inn. The 17th Century National Register and Virginia Landmark estate on the waterfront provides a private dock for river access. Individual rooms and complete houses contain period antiques and Franklin stoves or fireplaces. Complimentary breakfast. No smoking. Dock, fishing. Business services. | 8777 Toddsbury La. | 804/693–1616 or 877/248–0303 | fax 804/695–0303 | innkeeper@northriverinn.com | www.northriverinn.com | 7 rooms | $85–$225 | AE, MC, V.

HAMPTON

(Nearby towns also listed: Newport News, Norfolk, Portsmouth, Virginia Beach)

Now the oldest continuously existing English-speaking settlement in the United States, the English established Hampton in 1610 on a Kecoughtan Indian village. Located at the mouth of the Hampton Roads harbor, Hampton was a bustling seaport and one of colonial Virginia's principal cities. The city was partially destroyed three times: once by the British during the Revolution and again during the War of 1812, then by Confederate soldiers attempting to preempt a Union invasion during the Civil War.

The area's aviation legacy is chronicled at Air Power Park and the Virginia Air and Space Center. Hampton is also home to the country's first aviation research facility, NASA Langley Research Center. Fort Monroe preserves the local military history.

A cruise around the Chesapeake Bay provides a taste of the region's seafaring culture. Hampton is central to the state's commercial fishing industry, particularly oysters and Chesapeake Bay blue crabs. Computer technology, manufacturing, and aerospace research also are mainstays of the local economy.

Information: Hampton Visitor Center | 710 Settlers Landing Rd., Hampton, 23669 | 757/727–1102 or 800/800–2202 | www.hampton.va.us/tourism.

Attractions

Air Power Park and Aviation History Center. This 15-acre park has about 50 vintage jets, missiles, and rockets scattered throughout its grounds. An indoor museum houses model airplanes, photos, and other items relating to Hampton's aviation history. | 413 W. Mercury Blvd. at U.S. 258 | 757/727–1163 | Free | Daily 9–4:30.

American Theater. Originally built in 1908, this proscenium theater was renovated and reopened in June, 2000. Classical and jazz concerts, dance shows, and plays are performed in the 400-seat theater throughout the year. | 125 E. Mellen St. | 757/722–2787 | www.americantheater.com | $17.50–$22.50 | Call for show times.

Bluebird Gap Farm. This petting zoo has both wild and domestic animals, plus displays of farm machinery. There are picnic facilities on the grounds. | 60 Pine Chapel Rd. | 757/727–6739 | Free | Wed.–Sun. 9–5.

Buckroe Beach and Park. From Memorial Day through Labor Day a lifeguard presides over this public beach park ¾ mi long on the Chesapeake Bay. The park has several picnic shelters and an enclosed stage for special events. | E. Pembroke Ave. | 757/727–6347 | www.hampton.va.us/parks | Free | Daily 7 –dusk.

Fort Monroe. Built in stages between 1819 and 1934, this is the largest stone fort in the U.S. and the only one in active duty enclosed by a moat. Named in honor of President James Monroe, the U.S. Army installation is shaped like a seven-pointed star. Robert E. Lee and Edgar Allan Poe served here in the antebellum years, yet it remained a strategic Union stronghold in Confederate territory throughout the Civil War. After the Civil War, Confederate president Jefferson Davis was imprisoned here. | 20 Bernard Rd. | 757/727–3391 | fax 757/727–3886 | www.tradoc.monroe.army.mil | Free | Daily 10:30–4:30, closed Thanksgiving, Dec. 25, Jan. 1.

The **Casemate Museum** displays the prison cell where Jefferson Davis was confined until 1867. Exhibits of weapons, uniforms, models, drawings, and Civil War relics retell the fort's history, depict coastal artillery activities, and describe military life during the Civil War years. | 20 Bernard Rd. | 757/727–3391 | fax 757/727–3886 | www.tradoc.monroe.army.mil | Free | Daily 10:30–4:30, closed Thanksgiving, Dec. 25, Jan. 1.

Completed in 1858 by architect Richard Upjohn, the **Chapel of the Centurion** is the U.S. Army's oldest wooden structure in continuous use for religious services. Three Tiffany stained-glass windows grace this white clapboard chapel. | Free | Daily, Sunday services: Episcopal Eucharist 7:45, Protestant 9:30 and 11, Protestant Sunday School 9:30–10:30.

Hampton Carousel. A fixture at the old Buckroe Beach Amusement Park for 60 years, this 1920 carousel is an operating antique. The merry-go-round's 48 horses and two chariots, hand-carved by Russian, German and Italian immigrant artisans, will take you for a classic spin. Housed in its own pavilion, this beautiful carousel is a focal point on Hampton's downtown waterfront. | 602 Settlers Landing Rd. | 757/727–6381 or 757/727–6347 | 50¢ | Apr.–Sept. Mon.–Sat. 10–8, Sun. noon–6; Oct.–mid Dec. weekends noon–6, closed weekdays.

Hampton University. Founded in 1868 as a freed men's school, the campus holds the Emancipation Oak, a sign of freedom to Hampton's African-American population in 1863. Hampton University has a distinguished history as an institution of higher education for African-Americans, including graduate Booker T. Washington. The chateauesque main building, Virginia Hall, was designed by Richard Morris Hunt and built by students. Maps for self-guided walking tours of the campus's historic sites are available at the museum. | Queen St., at Tyler St. | 757/727–5253 | fax 757/727–5170 | www.hamptonu.edu | Free | Mon.–Sat. closed Sun.

The **Hampton University Museum** is Virginia's second oldest and is noted for an extensive collection of African art, including 2,000 pieces from 87 ethnic groups and cultures. Other holdings include Harlem Renaissance paintings, Native American artwork, and crafts and art from Oceania. A small exhibit tells the history of the institution. | Huntington Building | Free | Weekdays 8–5, Sat. noon–4, closed Sun. and holidays.

Standing at the entrance to Hampton University, the gnarled old **Emancipation Oak** tree marks the spot where Abraham Lincoln's Emancipation Proclamation was first read to Hampton slaves. The January 1, 1863 proclamation declared free all slaves residing in territory rebelling against the federal government. The tree is a National Historic Landmark. | Free | Daily.

Now a National Historic Landmark, the **Trusty House,** a pink-shingled Victorian was built by William Trusty, the first African-American councilman in the area. Shortly after the Civil War, Trusty moved to Hampton, worked at Fort Monroe, and invested in real estate; by 1870, he was a millionaire. While you can't go inside (it's privately owned), you can stroll past it; the house is now part of the Hampton University campus. | 757/988–0015. | Closed to the public.

Harborlink Ferry. The Zephyr, meaning strong wind, will take you on a 45-minute ferry ride down the Elizabeth River from downtown Hampton to downtown Norfolk. Along the way, you can see the ships at Norfolk Naval Base and Fort Monroe in the distance. Snacks and beverages, including beer and wine, are available on board. The ferry leaves from downtown Hampton, next to the Visitor Center and the Radisson Hotel. | 762 Settlers Landing Rd. | 757/722–9400 | www.harborlink.com | $4–$5 | Seasonal schedule.

Kecoughtan Indian Village Monument. This site commemorates the 17th-century Kecoughtan Native American settlement which encompassed several thousand acres on the eastern side of the mouth of the Hampton River. In 1610, English governor Thomas Gates forcibly removed the Native Americans. | 100 Emancipation Dr.

St. John's Church. Founded in 1610, this parish claims to be the oldest in continuous service in America. The 1728 church has a stained-glass window honoring Pocahontas. The communion silver on display was made in London in 1618. A taped tour is available, or you can take a guided tour by prior arrangement. The parish house has a small museum. | 100 W. Queens Way | 757/722–2567 | Free | Weekdays 9–3, Sat. 9–noon, closed Sun.

Virginia Air and Space Center and Hampton Roads History Center. The official visitor's center for the NASA Langley Research Center, this facility displays space artifacts ranging from a 3-billion-year-old space rock to the *Apollo 12* command capsule, and a dozen full-size aircraft. An IMAX theater presents films on a rotating schedule. The history center has archaeological and audiovisual exhibits focusing on the area's naval history, with partial reproductions of the U.S.S. *Monitor* and the C.S.S. *Virginia*. | 600 Settlers Landing Rd. | 757/727-0900 or 800/296-0800 | fax 757/727-0898 | www.vasc.org | $6.50, IMAX film $6 | Memorial Day–Labor Day, Mon.–Wed. 10–5, Thurs.–Sun. 10–7; Labor Day–Memorial Day, daily 10–5.

SIGHTSEEING TOURS/TOUR COMPANIES

Miss Hampton II Boat Tours. Narrated cruises take you into the Hampton Roads' harbor past Blackbeard's Point to Fort Wool for a guided walking tour. The cruise continues around the Norfolk Naval Base so you can view docked aircraft carriers, submarines, and other navy cruisers. | 764 Settlers Landing Rd. | 757/722-9102 | fax 757/722-9113 | $17 | Apr.–Oct.; call for hours.

ON THE CALENDAR

APR.–SEPT: *Summer Block Party.* Every Saturday night down on Queens Way, you can celebrate the summer with music, food, and street performers; kids can have fun with activities like face painting. The party takes place in and around restaurants, shops, and bars from 5 to 11 PM. | 757/722-6811 or 800/800-2202.

JUNE: *Hampton Jazz Festival.* This three-day musical event attracts the country's top blues, soul, pop, and jazz singers. Past performers include Ray Charles, Anita Baker, David Sanborn, and Kenny G. | Hampton Coliseum, I-64 and Mercury Blvd. | 757/838-4203.

AUG.: *Hampton Cup Regatta.* The oldest and largest powerboat races in the country, the national championship includes 10 classes of hydroplanes and competitions with speeds in excess of 140 mph. Live entertainment, concessions, and children's activities complete the event. | Mercury Blvd. Bridge | 800/800-2202.

SEPT.: *Hampton Bay Days.* The city's largest festival celebrates the Chesapeake Bay with headline musical entertainment, seafood, exhibits, an art show, children's activities, a carnival, and sporting and water events. | Downtown | 757/727-6122.

Dining

Captain George's. Seafood. A boat outside the entrance and a fountain inside the front door welcome you to this seafood restaurant, which offers an expansive buffet for $21.95. Choose from a variety of salads, Alaskan snow crab legs, manicotti, prime rib, seafood casserole, Hampton-style crab cakes, pudding, peach cobbler, and more. If you prefer to order from the menu; try the Norfolk Special–lobster, shrimp, and crab meat in a garlic butter sauce. | 2710 W. Mercury Blvd. | 757/826-1435 | No lunch. Sunday brunch. No dinner Sun. | $19–$24 | AE, MC, V.

Cheddar's. American. Locals flock to this restaurant for the ribs and the chicken tenders. Steaks, burgers, catfish, and salmon are also on the menu; the "Cookie Monster Dessert" is another favorite. The walls are decorated with old pictures of Yorktown and Virginia Beach. | 12280 Jefferson Ave. | 757/249-4000 | Reservations not accepted | $6–$12 | AE, D, DC, MC, V.

Grey Goose Tavern. Continental. Blue-crab soup, Brunswick stew, shrimp and crab salad, and croissant sandwiches are among the favorites at this cozy luncheon room. Tea-related items and Victorian tea-party prints in gilded frames decorate the room; a gift shop is adjacent. | 101-A Queens Way | 757/723-7978 | Reservations not accepted | No dinner | $3–$9 | AE, D, MC, V.

Magnolia House. French. Part antique store, part restaurant, this 1885 Victorian house serves both lunch and dinner. Lunch entrees include lobster quiche and curried seafood crepes; the dinner menu expands to include rack of lamb, porterhouse steak, and a salmon filet with saffron sauce. Sunday brunch. | 232 S. Armistead | 757/722–6881 | Closed Mon. No dinner Tues. Wed. Sun. | $17–$19 | MC, V.

Sammy and Nick's. Steak. Take a trip to the West without actually going west. This traditional steak house has longhorns on the walls, huge chandeliers, and paintings of western scenes. Kids' menu. | 2718 W. Mercury Blvd. | 757/838–9100 | Breakfast also available weekends | $15–$22 | AE, D, DC, MC, V.

Lodging

Arrow Inn. The property sits just off I-64 and U.S. 134, next to Langley Air Force Base. Basic efficiencies and kitchenettes provide you with simple comforts. Kitchenettes, refrigerators, some microwaves, cable TV. Laundry facilities. Business services. Pets allowed (fee). | 7 Semple Farm Rd. | 757/865–0300 or 800/833–2520 | fax 757/766–9367 | mb@arrowinn.com | www.arrowinn.com | 81 rooms | $40–$61 | AE, D, DC, MC, V.

Courtyard Hampton. Next to the Hampton Coliseum and just off U.S 258, this hotel caters to business travelers and families on the go. Bring your own hotdogs and hamburgers to grill poolside. Restaurant, bar, picnic area. In-room data ports, refrigerators (in suites), cable TV. Outdoor pool. Hot tub. Exercise room. Laundry facilities, laundry service. Business services, free parking. | 1917 Coliseum Dr. | 757/838–3300 | fax 757/838–6387 | www.courtyard.com | 134 rooms, 12 suites | $66–$76 | AE, D, DC, MC, V.

Days Inn. Just off I-64 at Exit 263, this chain hotel has a restaurant on the premises. You can walk to the Coliseum; a five-minute drive will take you to Buckroe Beach or the Langley Speedway. Restaurant. Some microwaves, some refrigerators, cable TV, room phones. Outdoor pool. Laundry facilities, laundry service. Pets allowed (fee). | 1918 Coliseum Dr. | 757/825–4810 or 800/325–2525 | fax 757/827–6503 | 144 rooms | $60–$85 | AE, D, DC, MC, V.

Fairfield Inn by Marriott. This 3-story inn keeps its rooms bright and spacious. Next to the Hampton Coliseum, and just off I-64, the Coliseum Mall and several restaurants are within a few blocks. Complimentary Continental breakfast. In-room data ports, cable TV. Outdoor pool. Business services. Free parking. | 1905 Coliseum Dr. | 757/827–7400 | fax 757/827–7400 | www.fairfieldinn.com | 134 rooms | $40–$65 | AE, D, DC, MC, V.

Hampton Inn. The inn is ½ mi away from the Hampton Coliseum and the Hampton Mall. Rooms have jewel tones and contemporary oak furnishings. Complimentary Continental breakfast. In-room data ports, cable TV. Business services. Some pets allowed. | 1813 W. Mercury Blvd. | 757/838–8484 | fax 757/826–0725 | www.hamptoninn.com | 132 rooms | $79–$89 | AE, D, DC, MC, V.

Holiday Inn Hampton Conference Center. Next to the Hampton Coliseum, this hotel is set on 13 landscaped acres. An executive level provides additional amenities. Almost all of the rooms have balconies – some overlook the outdoor pool, others overlook the atrium. Restaurant, bar. In-room data ports, some refrigerators, cable TV. 2 pools (1 indoor). Hot tub. Exercise room. Laundry facilities. Business services, airport shuttle, free parking. | 1815 W. Mercury Blvd. | 757/838–0200 | fax 757/838–4964 | www.holidayinn.com | 320 rooms | $99–$149 | AE, D, DC, MC, V.

Lady Neptune. Now on Buckroe Beach, this 1930 home was moved by barge from its original location in May, 1988. The veranda now overlooks Chesapeake Bay, while the back deck commands views of the marsh. One of the rooms has Louis XV furnishings; another has four-poster beds. In addition to breakfast, lunch and dinner are also available on request. Dining room, picnic area, complimentary breakfast. Some microwaves, some refrigerators, cable TV, no room phones, no TV, TV in common area. Beach, dock, fishing. No pets. No smoking. | 507 N. First St. | 757/850–6060 | smcq320907@aol.com | www.bbonline.com/va/neptune | 4 | $125–$175 | AE, D, MC, V.

Radisson. The hotel's rooms have views of historic Hampton harbor and downtown. The Virginia Air and Space Center is a block away. Honeymoon and Plaza suites have private hot tubs. Restaurant, bar, room service. In-room data ports, some refrigerators, cable TV.

Outdoor pool. Hot tub. Exercise equipment. Business services, airport shuttle. | 700 Settlers Landing Rd. | 757/727–9700 | fax 757/722–4557 | rhi_hamp@radisson.com | www.radisson.com/hamptonva | 172 rooms | $105–$125 | AE, D, DC, MC, V.

Victoria House. Enjoy the outdoors without ever leaving the house at this 1898 three-story inn, where a large two-level deck is built around the surrounding trees. There's also a screened porch, a garden, an outdoor patio area, and a sitting room furnished with antiques. The inn is in old downtown Hampton–two blocks from the water, and close to the Air and Space Museum. Popular with business travelers. Dining room, complimentary breakfast. In-room data ports, refrigerators, some in-room hot tubs, cable TV, in-room VCRs, room phones, TV in common area. No pets. No kids under . No smoking. | 4501 Victoria Blvd. | 757/722–2658 or 800/201–4642 | fax 757/723–5282 | www.bbonline.com/va/victoria | 4 | $90–$125 | AE, D, MC, V.

HARRISONBURG

MAP 11, G4

(Nearby town also listed: Shenandoah National Park)

Settled in 1739, Harrisonburg is nestled in Virginia's Shenandoah Valley. Flanked by the Shenandoah National Park to the east and George Washington and Jefferson National Forests to the west and northeast, Harrisonburg doesn't lack for outdoor recreation; fishing lakes, rugged hiking trails, and mountain wilderness abound. It is also a center of higher education, with James Madison University and Eastern Mennonite College in town and Bridgewater College 8 mi to the southwest. The region is a stronghold of Old Order Mennonites who wear a simple style of dress and drive horse-drawn buggies.

Information: Harrisonburg–Rockingham County Convention and Visitors Bureau | 10 E. Gay St., 22802 | 540/434–2319 | hrcvbdirector@rica.net | www.harrisonburg.org.

Attractions

Eastern Mennonite University and Seminary. The Mennonite Church founded this university in 1917. Private and coeducational, Eastern Mennonite has about 1,000 undergraduates and several hundred seminary and graduate students. Its 90-acre hillside campus sits on the northern end of the city, just west of I-81. Music and theater performances are held throughout the year by faculty, students, and visiting artists; call for a calendar of events. | 1200 Park Rd./Rte. 42 | 540/432–4000 | fax 540/432–4488 | www.emu.edu | Free | Daily.

On the southern end of campus, in the Suter Science Center, the **Brackbill Planetarium** provides a simulation of the heavens as seen from any point on the earth; the sun, moon, major planets, and more than 1,200 stars are projected onto a 30-ft dome, with special effects to create celestial phenomena. | 1200 Park Rd./Rte. 42 | 540/432–4400 | fax 540/432–4488 | www.emu.edu | $1, $1.50 including Museum | call for hours.

Also in the Suter Science Center, the **Hostetter Museum of Natural History** contains more than 6,000 items, from botanical specimens and crystals to stuffed African game mammals and Virginia birds. | 1200 Park Rd./Rte. 42 | 540/432–4400 | fax 540/432–4488 | www.emu.edu | $1, including Planetarium $1.50.

Fort Harrison. Also known as the Daniel Harrison House, this 1749 fortified frontier home, six mi southwest of Harrisonburg, illustrates a prosperous frontier style. Costumed interpreters discuss how the furnishings—beds with ropes as slats and hand-quilted comforters—were made. Lovely gardens surround this stone house, and an annual plant sale exhibits the gardens' abundance. | 526 N. Main St., Dayton | 540/879–2280 | Free | Mid-May–Oct. weekends 1–4.

Grand Caverns Regional Park. The underground caverns, which contain giant stalactite and stalagmite mineral formations, are the centerpiece of this park; Cathedral Hall, 280 ft long and more than 70 ft high, is one of the largest rooms of any cavern on the East Coast. South of Harrisonburg 11 mi on U.S. 340, the park also has hiking and biking trails, tennis courts, a swimming pool, miniature golf, picnic shelters, and a gift shop. | Grand Caverns Dr., Grottoes | 540/249–5705 | Caverns $13 | Apr.–Oct. daily 9–5; Mar. weekends 9–5.

George Washington and Jefferson National Forests. Encompassing some 1.8 million acres, this forest land stretches from Winchester to Big Stone Gap and covers the Blue Ridge, Massanutten, Shenandoah, and Allegheny mountain ranges; about 139,000 acres lie in Western Rockingham County. There are lakes for swimming, miles of hiking trails, and 25 campgrounds scattered throughout with the gamut of services. Trout inhabit in hundreds of streams. Horseback riding, hunting, and cross-country and downhill skiing also are available. | 5162 Valleypointe Pkwy., Roanoke | 540/265–5100 | fax 540/265–5145 | www.fs.fed.us/gwjnf | Free; parking fees are charged at some recreational areas | Daily.

James Madison University. Founded in 1908 as the State Normal and Industrial School for Women, this liberal arts university changed names three more times before becoming JMU, a well-respected institute of higher education. Today, the 472-acre campus (about eight blocks from downtown Harrisonburg) has an enrollment of more than 13,000 students. Theater, dance, and musical performances occur throughout the year. It has 27 intercollegiate sports teams, but only football, basketball, soccer, and baseball games charge admission. | 1031 S. Main St. | 540/568–3621, 540/568–3853 sports ticket office, or 540/568–7000 theater box office | fax 540/568–3634 | www.jmu.edu | Daily.

The **Warren House Life Science Museum** displays a range of stuffed mammals and live creatures, including snakes, spiders, and African millipedes. The museum also includes a walk-in dinosaur cave and seashells, butterflies, and Native American relics exhibits. | 17 Grace St. | 540/568–6378 | Free | Sept.–June, weekdays 9–3, Sat. 9–noon.

Rotating exhibits at the **Sawhill Gallery** display art with a regional and international scope. Recent shows include the work of Milton Glaser, considered the founder of graphic design. | Duke Hall | 540/568–6407 | Free | Weekdays 10:30–4:30, weekends 1:30–4:30.

Lake Shenandoah. Managed by the Virginia Department of Game and Inland Fisheries, this lake has a public boat ramp and fishing. | 804/367–1000 | www.dgif.state.va.us | Free | Daily 7 AM–dusk.

Lincoln Homestead and Cemetery. Abraham Lincoln's father, Thomas Lincoln, was born in Rockingham County at this homestead, which is now privately owned. The cemetery, which is open to the public, contains the graves of Lincoln ancestors. | Rte. 42 N, look for signs | 540/434–2319.

Natural Chimneys Regional Park. Seven free-standing limestone pillars make up the natural chimneys. An unknown natural occurrence formed the chimneys 500 million years ago. These tall pillars provide the backdrop for jousting tournaments held in June and August. Park facilities include a swimming pool, picnic area, nature and bike trails, and campsites. The park is 23 mi southwest of Harrisonburg. | Rte. 1, Mount Solon | 540/350–2510 | $3; $6 limit per car | Daily 9–dusk.

Massanutten Resort. Go golfing, hiking, snowboarding, or ski-skating on the sprawling grounds of this resort, just under 6,000 acres. The driving range becomes a snowtubing park in the winter; there's also a skateboard and rollerblade park. | Rte. 644 north of Rte. 33 | 540/289–9441 | www.massresort.com.

Shenandoah River. The Shenandoah and its two major tributaries, the North Fork and the South Fork, thread through the Shenandoah Valley, past farmland and national forest. The river flows from its headwaters in Augusta and Rockingham counties southwest of Harrisonburg, merging with the Potomac River at Harpers Ferry, West Virginia. About 225 mi of the Shenandoah are designated trout-fishing waters, and the South Fork, which flows just east of Harrisonburg, is renowned for smallmouth bass fishing. Popular summer pastimes include swimming and inner-tubing. The Virginia Department of Game and Inland Fisheries maintains many public access sites for boats and canoes. (A number of local outfitters rent canoes, kayaks, and inner tubes.) Near Harrisonburg, you can access the river in Port Republic. | 540/248–9360 Dept. of Game and Inland Fisheries | fax 540/248–9399 | www.dgif.state.va.us | Free | Daily.

Shenandoah National Park. (*See Shenandoah National Park.*) The closest entrance to access hiking, horseback-riding trails, picnic grounds, and campsites from Harrisonburg is a scenic 22 mi drive east on U.S. 33. | 540/999–3500.

Shenandoah Valley Folk Art and Heritage Center. The Center's folk art and artifacts in a variety of media reflect the culture of the Shenandoah Valley. A Civil War exhibit with an electric relief map traces Stonewall Jackson's famous 1862 Valley Campaign. The Center is six mi southwest of Harrisonburg. | 328 High St., Dayton | 540/879–2681 | $4 | Mon. and Wed.–Sat. 10–4, Sun. 1–4.

Silver Lake. The damming of Crooks Creek formed this 10-acre lake that attracts migrating waterfowl, warblers, and egrets in the spring and has a host of resident birds, including Canada geese. There is year-round trout fishing. | Rte. 701, Dayton | 540/434–2319 or 540/248–9360 | Free | Daily.

Virginia Quilt Museum. This museum focuses on the local and international quilting tradition and displays antique and contemporary quilts made throughout the mid-Atlantic region. | 301 S. Main St. | 540/433–3818 | fax 540/433–3818 | $4 | Mon. and Thurs.–Sat. 10–4, Sun. 1–4.

ON THE CALENDAR

JUNE: *Shenandoah Valley Bach Festival.* A week of professional concerts and events focuses on the works of Bach and Mendelssohn. In addition to three main concerts, there are films and chamber music recitals at Eastern Mennonite University, 1200 Park Rd. | 540/432–4367.

JUNE, AUG.: *Natural Chimneys Jousting Tournament.* Dating from 1821, this oldest continuously held sporting event in the U.S. involves competitors vying for Ring Jousting titles. A parade and crafts exhibits usually accompany the festivities, as well as live bluegrass music at Natural Chimneys Regional Park, 23 mi southwest of Harrisonburg. | 540/350–2510.

AUG.: *Rockingham County Fair.* Recognized as one of the top rural county fairs in the country, this week-long event includes agricultural and livestock exhibits, a tractor pull, a petting zoo, a circus, bull riding, a demolition derby, and live music. The fair is at Rockingham County Fairgrounds, 4808 South Valley Pike. | 540/434–0005.

SEPT.: *Big Game Trophy Show and Sportsman's Fair.* A deer, bear, and turkey trophy competition and sportsman's trade show featuring the latest in hunting equipment highlight this fair, held at the Rockingham County Fairgrounds, 4808 South Valley Pike. | 540/434–0005.

Dining

Artful Dodger. Café. This eclectic coffee shop and internet café is filled with local artwork and quirky, thrift-store furnishings in a wild mix of colors. Board games and books add to the inviting cheerfulness of the place; internet access keeps you in touch with the folks at home. Look for wrap sandwiches, salads, and vegetarian dishes. Open-air dining on sidewalk patio. | 47 W. Court Sq. | 540/432–1179 | $5–$8 | AE, D, MC, V.

Blue Stone Inn. American. Mounted animal heads peer out from the walls, seeming to join you for dinner. Known for steaks and seafood, try the mushroom caps stuffed with crab meat or the "Baked Captain's Platter" (crab cake, scallops, shrimp, oysters Casino, and fillet of flounder or mahi mahi). You can wear jeans and a T-shirt or formal evening wear at this quaint rustic inn. | 9107 North Valley Pike | 540/434–0535 | Closed Sun.–Mon. | $25–$40 | MC, V.

Calhoun's. Contemporary. Locals visit this microbrewery before or after taking in a play, live show, or movie at the Court Square Theatre, which is in the same building. In a restored

Woolworth's five-and-dime store, Calhoun's has two large dining rooms, a bar, and a large patio on top of the building with views of the square. As you enter the building, you can see the brewery through a glass window. The owners always have 4 or 5 of their 16 micro-brews on tap. The most popular are the honey blonde ale, smoked Scottish ale, and the nut brown ale. Try the stuffed mushrooms, hickory-smoked rib eye, or crab cakes. Also known for locally-raised trout, fresh fish, and quail. Entertainment Wed.–Fri. Sun. brunch. | 41A Court Sq. | 540/434–8777 | $12–$18 | MC, V.

Joshua Wilton House. Eclectic. A turreted, late-Victorian gingerbread mansion on the outskirts of the downtown area contains this quietly elegant restaurant and a bed-and-breakfast inn. Tall towers and gabled windows sparkle with candles during the winter months; terraced gardens blossom in the spring. The Shenandoah Valley Watercolor Society provides artwork for the two formal dining rooms in front, while the more casual café displays the work of a different regional artist every two months. Five-course meals with a preset menu are served in the formal dining rooms; meals are à la carte in the café. Pleasant mixes of various cuisines–French, Asian, and subcontinental flavors–tempt your palate. Try the house smoked salmon appetizer, the roasted duck, and the crème brûlée. | 412 S. Main St. | 540/434–4464 | Jacket required | Closed Sun.–Mon. first wk in Jan. No lunch Tues.–Sat. | $22–$30 (café), $45 (dining rooms) | AE, D, DC, MC, V.

Saigon Cafe. Vietnamese. Accented with Vietnamese costumes and musical instruments, an indoor fountain in one corner provides the constant, calming sound of flowing water. The restaurant has all the warmth of a family-owned establishment with a small but attentive staff. | 787 Market St. E | 540/434–5750 | $10–$17 | MC, V.

Lodging

By the Side of the Road B&B. Built in 1790, this bed and breakfast once served as a field hospital during the Civil War. Pick from five rooms, including a 5,000-square-foot suite. Rooms all have coffee makers; some bathrooms have chandeliers. Complimentary breakfast. In-room data ports, some microwaves, some refrigerators, cable TV, in-room VCRs, some room phones. | 491 Garbers Church Rd. | 540/801–0430 | fax 540/801–8148 | www.by-the-side-of-the-road-bb.com | 5 | $120–$175 | AE, MC, V.

Comfort Inn. This hotel, 1 ½ mi from James Madison University, has contemporary rooms. The lattice gazebo is a quiet place to take breakfast on summer mornings. Complimentary Continental breakfast. Cable TV. Pool. Exercise room. Business services, free parking. | 1440 E. Market St. | 540/433–6066 | fax 540/433–0793 | www.comfortinn.com | 102 rooms | $72–$119 | AE, D, DC, MC, V.

Courtyard by Marriott. Opened in September, 1999, this chain hotel is just off I–81 at Exit 247-A. The marble lobby has high open ceilings, a fireplace, sofas, and a big-screen television. The rooms are decorated with floral patterns and dark cherry wood furniture. You can walk down the hill to a small shopping center with a movie theater and some chain restaurants. Room service available Mon.–Thurs. only. Room service. In-room data ports, some microwaves, some refrigerators, some in-room hot tubs, cable TV, room phones, TV in common area. Indoor pool. Hot tub. Gym. Business services. No pets. | 1890 Evelyn Bird Ave. | 540/432–3031 | fax 540/432–3032 | 125 | $79 | AE, D, DC, MC, V.

Days Inn. Adjacent to James Madison University, this hotel is only six blocks from downtown. You can enjoy the neutral colors and a room with a king-size bed and wet bar. Easy access to I-81 provides quick entry to local sights. Complimentary Continental breakfast. Cable TV. Outdoor pool. Hot tub. Laundry Services. Business services, free parking. Pets allowed (fee). | 1131 Forest Hill Rd. | 540/433–9353 | fax 540/433–5809 | 89 rooms | $50–$75 | AE, D, DC, MC, V.

Econo Lodge. This two-story motel is 1 mi from James Madison University and I-81. The Valley View Mall is within view. Complimentary Continental breakfast. Some in-room hot tubs, cable TV. Outdoor pool. Business services. Some pets allowed. | 1703 E. Market St. | 540/433–2576 | fax 540/433–2576, ext. 240 | www.choicehotels.com | 89 rooms | $55–$85 | AE, D, DC, MC, V.

Four Points by Sheraton. The large stone fireplace in the lobby roars on cold winter days. The Valley View Mall and James Madison University are both only 1 mi away. Restaurant, bar with entertainment, room service. In-room data ports, cable TV. Indoor pool, wading pool. Hot tub. Exercise room. Business services. Free parking. Some pets allowed. | 1400 E. Market St. | 540/433–2521 | fax 540/434–0253 | www.sheraton.com | 140 rooms | $79–$109 | AE, D, DC, MC, V.

Hampton Inn. Rooms at this hill-top hotel overlook the Shenandoah mountains and the downtown district. The Valley View Mall is across the street and James Madison University is ½ mi away. Eastern Mennonite University is 2 mi north. Complimentary Continental breakfast. In-room data ports, cable TV. Pool. Business services, free parking. | 85 University Blvd. | 540/432–1111 | fax 540/432–0748 | www.hamptoninn.com | 164 rooms | $68–$62 | AE, D, DC, MC, V.

Howard Johnson. Just east of I-81, dogwoods, pine trees, and flowering annuals, beautiful in late spring, color the long front lawn. James Madison University is ¼ mi away across the interstate to the west. Restaurant. Cable TV. Outdoor pool, wading pool. Business services. Some pets allowed. | 605 Port Republic Rd. | 540/434–6771 | fax 540/434–0153 | www.hojo.com | 134 rooms | $45–$70 | AE, D, DC, MC, V.

Joshua Wilton House. One of Virginia's finest inns, this Victorian mansion sits on a corner in the historic district, four blocks from downtown and James Madison University. Rooms reflect the house's era with period antiques, some with fireplaces. Restaurant, complimentary breakfast. Business services, airport shuttle. No smoking. | 412 S. Main St. | 540/434–4464 | fax 540/432–9525 | jwhouse@rica.net | home.rica.net/jwhouse | 5 rooms | $95–$120 | AE, D, DC, MC, V.

Massanutten Resort. While most guests opt for the time-share condominiums at this four-season resort, hotel rooms are also available. Go golfing, hiking, snowboarding, or ski-skating on the sprawling grounds, just under 6,000 acres. The driving range becomes a snowtubing park in the winter; there's also a skateboard and rollerblade park. 2 restaurants, bar with weekend entertainment. Cable TV, room phones, TV in common area. 5 pools, lake, wading pool. Hot tub, outdoor hot tub, massage, sauna, steam room. Driving range, golf courses, miniature golf, putting green, tennis. Health club, hiking, racquetball, squash, volleyball. Fishing, bicycles. Downhill skiing. Shops, video games. Baby-sitting, children's programs 2–18, playground. Laundry facilities. No pets. | Rte. 644 north of Rte. 33 | 540/289–9441 | www.massresort.com | 190 | $90, call for prices on condominiums | AE, D, DC, MC, V.

Village Inn. Family owned, this countryside motel is ¼ mi south of the Rockingham County Fairgrounds. Rooms have outside entrances and decks. Restaurant, picnic area. Some in-room hot tubs, cable TV. Pool. Playground. Business services. Some pets allowed. | Rte. 11 | 540/434–7355 or 800/736–7355 | fax 540/434–7355 | 36 rooms, 1 suite | $47–$57, $60 suite | AE, D, DC, MC, V.

HOPEWELL

MAP 11, J6

(Nearby towns also listed: Charles City, Petersburg, Richmond)

Originally called Charles City Point, this town on the James River was established in 1613 by Sir Thomas Dale. Just 20 mi south of the state capital, it served as the Federal army's headquarters and supply depot during the 1864 Union campaign to capture Richmond. The City Point Unit, used by Gen. Ulysses S. Grant as his base of operations during the siege of Petersburg, is now part of Petersburg National Battlefield, southwest of Hopewell.

Hopewell was a quiet seaport town until the first World War, when E. I. du Pont established a dynamite factory on the site of Hopewell Farms, and the town became the center of an extensive munitions industry. Today, it's an industrial center producing chemicals, paper products, and synthetic textiles. Flowerdew Hundred, a working farm and museum that dates from 1619 and illustrates the city's earlier history, sits just to the east.

Information: Hopewell Visitor Center | 4100 Oaklawn Blvd. Hopewell, VA 23860 | 804/541–2461 | www.ci.hopewell.va.us.

Attractions

City Point Unit of Petersburg National Battlefield. City Point was considered the center of the Union war effort during the Civil War. At Appomattox Manor, built in 1763, Gen. Ulysses S. Grant set up headquarters in June 1864 during the siege of Petersburg. A major supply depot, this unit brought in shipments from Northern manufacturers and more than 100,000 soldiers to fight under Grant. The site is now part of Petersburg National Battlefield. The visitor center within Appomattox Manor shows a 15-minute film about the role of the City Point Unit; rangers conduct tours of the house. | 804/458–9504 | fax 804/732–0835 | www.nationalparks.org | $3, $5 limit per vehicle; house only, $1; grounds free | Park mid-June–Labor Day, daily 8:30 AM–dusk; Labor Day–mid-June, daily 8–5; visitor center daily 8:30–4:30.

Crescent Hills Driving Tour. Forty-four original mail-order homes from Sears, Roebuck and Company can be found in the Crescent Hills subdivision of Hopewell. The homes were built between 1926 and 1937 under the direction of real estate developer M.T. Broyhill. A brochure guides you through the neighborhood, pointing out different models and showing where the original owners added their own unique touches. | Visitor Center, 4100 Oaklawn Blvd. | 804/541–2461 or 800/863–8687 | Free | Visitor Center, daily 9–5.

Flowerdew Hundred. Established as a working farm in 1619, Flowerdew was the site of one of the earliest English settlements in America. Since the 1970s, archaeological digs have uncovered thousands of items, some dating from 9000 BC; many of these artifacts are now on display in the museum, housed in an 1850s school. A reconstructed and operational 18th-century wind-powered gristmill overlooks the James River. Tours are available, and picnicking is permitted on the grounds. | 1617 Flowerdew Hundred Rd. | 804/541–8897 or 804/541–8938 | $6 | Apr.–Nov. 15, Tues.–Sat. 10–4, Sun. 1–4; Nov.16–Mar. by appointment.

Merchants Hope Church. Built in 1657, this is considered one of America's oldest existing Protestant churches still in use as a house of worship. Made of red brick laid in Flemish bond, it was constructed in the meetinghouse style common throughout colonial Virginia; according to tradition, sailors built the church. Used as a horse stable, invading Union soldiers destroyed much of the church's interior during the Civil War. The flagstones that pave the center aisle—formerly ballast from English sailing ships—are all original. | 11300 Merchants Hope Rd. Rte. 641, Prince George | 804/458–6197 or 804/541–0470 | Free, donations accepted | Open daily during Historic Garden Week (third wk of Apr.); rest of the year by appointment; Episcopal service Sun. 10 AM.

ON THE CALENDAR

APR.: *Prince George County Heritage Fair.* Held at Flowerdew Hundred, an historic working farm that dates from 1619, the fair provides musical entertainment, food, crafts booths, a greased pig contest, and a carnival. | 804/541–2461 or 800/863–8687.

AUG.: *Explosion at City Point.* This living-history program at Petersburg National Battlefield City Point Unit, 1539 Hickory Hill Rd. commemorates the massive explosion that rocked the Federal supply base in 1864. | 804/732–3531.

SEPT.: *Hooray for Hopewell Festival.* Civic pride comes out in full force for this downtown festival with live entertainment, food vendors, and arts and crafts. | 804/541–2461 or 800/863–8687.

Dining

Papa Granny's. American. Papa added lemon squares to the menu at the request of his regulars, and he had to make the navy bean soup a regular item instead of a special to keep everybody happy. Leland's Chicken Salad is a major draw, but you may want to try something with Papa's special barbecue sauce. Take your time and stay as long as you like—except on Mondays and Wednesdays, when they close at 8 PM. Breakfast available. | 224 N. Main St. at Broadway | 804/541–0910 | No reservations accepted | Closed Sun. No dinner Tues. Thurs. | $4–$10 | AE, MC, V.

Lodging

Econo Lodge. Opened in July, 2000, this chain hotel is close to shopping and five minutes from downtown Hopewell. A Continental breakfast is served among greenery in the exposed-brick lobby. Complimentary Continental breakfast. In-room data ports, some kitchenettes, microwaves, refrigerators, cable TV, room phones, TV in common area. Laundry facilities. No pets. | 4046 Oak Lawn Blvd. | 804/541–4849 | fax 804/415–2016 | 50 | $69 | AE, D, DC, MC, V.

Holiday Inn Express. A ¼ mi from Fort Lee and 1½ mi the Petersburg National Battlefield City Point Unit off I-295, this hotel is easily accessible. Hunter-green colors and cherry furnishings provide traditional local appeal. Complimentary Continental breakfast. In-room data ports, some kitchenettes, refrigerators, cable TV. Outdoor pool. Hot tub. Exercise room. Laundry facilities. Business services. | 4911 Oaklawn Blvd. | 804/458–1500 | fax 804/458–9151 | holidayinnexpresshopewell.devraj@earols.com | www.basshotels.com | 115 rooms, 50 suites | $60–$95, $100–$135 suites | AE, D, DC, MC, V.

Innkeeper. This hotel is basic and accommodating within four blocks of Oaklawn Boulevard's shops and restaurants downtown and on the edge of the Cedar Level neighborhood. Complimentary Continental breakfast. In-room data ports, refrigerators, cable TV. Pool. Laundry facilities. Business services. | 3952 Courthouse Rd. | 804/458–2600 | fax 804/458–1915 | 104 rooms | $60–$88 | AE, D, DC, MC, V.

HOT SPRINGS

MAP 11, F5

(Nearby town also listed: Warm Springs)

Tucked away in the Allegheny Mountains of western Virginia, Hot Springs has been a popular resort for more than 200 years. The name comes from the famous natural mineral springs which bubble up out of the ground at 104°F and are said to have curative powers. The area has long been associated with the Homestead, a grand resort hotel that dates from 1766. The thermal springs continue as a relaxing attraction, but the area's other recreational activities draw you in as well; golf, fishing, horseback riding, and skiing are all available through the Homestead resort.

Information: Bath County Chamber of Commerce | P.O. Box 718, Hot Springs, VA 24445 | 540/839–5409 or 800/628–8092 | bathco@va.tds.net | www.bathcountyva.org.

Attractions

Homestead Ski Area. The Homestead resort opened its ski slopes in 1959 and has nine runs for downhill and night skiing, plus a snowboard park and Olympic-size ice-skating rink. You can find a ski shop and school, hourly instruction, and equipment rental at the main lodge. Special packages include accommodations, breakfast and dinner daily, lift tickets, and lessons. | U.S. 220, P.O. Box 2000 | 540/839–7721 or 800/836–5771 | fax 540/839–7744 | www.thehomestead.com | Day rates | Nov.–Mar. daily.

APR.: *Archduke Music Holiday.* The Garth Newel Music Center on U.S. 220, hosts a special holiday the weekend of April 20, with chamber music, gourmet meals, and fine wine. Some of the events are black-tie affairs. | 540/839–5018.

Dining

Chef Ed's Community Market. Contemporary. This long, narrow building doubles as a restaurant and grocery store; sit at one of the six tables, or have a seat at the high bar, where you can watch Ed cook. Favorites include the pork chops stuffed with pears, pancetta, mushrooms, and thyme; steak tournedoes of beef with roasted-garlic tomato jus; and the picata-style Allegheny mountain trout. But the real winner is the Meyer lemon gratin, a cheesecake-based dessert. Seatings at 6:30 PM and 8:30 PM, with live music on Mondays. | 3 Main St. | 540/839–3663 | No lunch. Closed Tues. Wed. | $16–$19 | MC, V.

Country Cafe. American. A dining room with blue checked tablecloths draped on each table provides down home appeal for the cafe's country cooking. Crafts and antiques line the walls. A cast iron stove sits sedately in the corner. The Friday-night specialty is steamed shrimp; Saturday is prime rib night. Known for steaks, seafood, and chicken, this restaurant serves a smattering of them all. Kids' menu. Beer and wine only. | U.S. 220 | 540/839–2111 | Breakfast also available. Closed Mon. | $15–$23 | MC, V.

Sam Snead's Tavern. American. The casual eatery contains memorabilia of local PGA golf pro Sam Snead. As you might expect, there's also a sports bar. Golf shrimp, hickory smoked spare ribs, and New York rib eye steak are staples on the menu. | Main St. | 540/839–7666 | No lunch Mon.–Wed. | $25–$30 | AE, D, DC, MC, V.

Lodging

Hillcrest Motel. Next to a small country restaurant, this one-story motel has 12 rooms. It is located three quarters of a mile south of The Homestead. Refrigerators, cable TV, room phones. Laundry service. No pets. | Rte. 220 | 540/839–5316 | fax 540/839–5320 | 12 | $46–$60 | AE, MC, V.

★ **The Homestead.** Famous since 1766 for its mineral waters, this resort is one of the country's most luxurious spas. Chippendale-reproduction furnishings and fireplaces grace the rooms in the main building. Traditional furnishings, plush patterned carpets and floral draperies accurately reflect the Georgian architecture. An orchestra performs nightly in the formal dining room. You can stroll the extensive grounds or participate in the many activities the spa supports. Extras include use of the mineral pool, skeet and trap shooting, and movies. Bar, dining room, snack bar, room service. Cable TV. 2 pools (1 indoor). Spa. Bowling, exercise equipment, hiking, horseback riding. Driving range, three 18-hole golf courses, putting greens, tennis. Ice-skating, cross-country skiing, downhill skiing, snowboarding. Game room. Kids' programs. Business services, airport shuttle. | U.S. 220 | 540/839–1766 or 800/838–1766 | fax 540/839–7556 | www.thehomestead.com | 430 rooms, 87 suites | $274–$306, $372–$810 suites | MAP | AE, D, DC, MC, V.

King's Victorian Inn. Secluded on three acres and shaded by an old maple grove, this stately 1899 Queen Anne Victorian sports turrets, bay windows, and a wrap-around porch. Inside, the regal look continues, with Oriental carpets, original and reproduction antiques, and wingback chairs. The cottages, one a converted ice house, work well for families. Complimentary breakfast. No room phones, TV in common area. No pets. No smoking. | Box 622, R.R. 1 | 540/839–3134 | www.inngetaways.net/va/kingsvic.html | 6 rooms (4 with private bath), 2 cottages | $89–$150 | No credit cards.

Roseloe. This family-owned motel is 3 mi north of Hot Springs and 2 mi south of Warm Springs. All rooms view the Allegheny mountains as this motel sits in the midst of the mountains themselves. Some rooms have patios. Kitchenettes, refrigerators, cable TV. Business services. Pets allowed (fee). | U.S. 220 | 540/839–5373 | 20 rooms | $48–$55 | AE, D, DC, MC, V.

Vine Cottage Inn. Built in 1894, this inn next to the Homestead has been a bed and breakfast since 1904. Leisure and business travelers mingle in the large living room or out on the wraparound porch. Lakes for fishing and canoeing and hiking trails are nearby. The 15 rooms, each uniquely decorated, some with shared baths, can sleep one to five people. Dining room, complimentary breakfast. No air-conditioning, cable TV, no room phones, no TV, TV in common area. Pets allowed (fee). | Rte. 220 | 540/839–2422 | 15 | $65–$90 | AE, D, DC, MC, V.

INDEPENDENCE

(Nearby towns also listed: Galax, Wytheville)

Though it has only one stoplight and a population that hovers around 1,000, Independence is the seat of Grayson County, and serves as a jumping-off point to some of the region's most magnificent natural treasures. The scenic New River, thought to be one of the oldest rivers in the world, the Jefferson National Forest, and the state's highest peak, Mount Rogers, are all found in Grayson County. Independence and its neighboring communities are a hotbed of Appalachian music.

Information: Grayson County Tourist Information Center | Box 366, 1908 Courthouse, Independence, 24348 | 540/773–3711 | grayson@ls.net | www.grayson.va.us.

Attractions

Grayson Highlands State Park. You can hike the Appalachian Trail, and get to Mount Rogers from this park. The grounds are full of Mountain Laurel, wildflowers, and inspiring views of the mountains. Along the trails you might encounter wild ponies, which are plentiful here. You can also camp, ride horses, and fish. The 4,935-acre park is about 25 mi west off Rte. 58. | 829 Grayson Highland La., Mouth of Wilson | 540/579–7092 or 800/933–7275 | www.state.va.us | Free, parking fee | Park daily; visitor center June–Aug. daily 10–6; May and Sept.–Oct. weekends 10–6.

Historic 1908 Courthouse. This fine example of Richardsonian architecture stands majestically in the center of town. The courthouse is a Virginia Historic Landmark and is on the National Registry of Historic Places. It hosts artistic and cultural events, and includes a craft shop and tourist center. | Main St. | 540/773–3711 | www.historic1908courthouse.org | Free | Mon.–Sat. 9–5.

Little Wilson Trout Farm. If you like fresh trout, stop by this fish farm. You can catch your own in the hatchery's icy spring waters or just buy what you need for a fish fry. | Rte. 58, Mouth of Wilson | 540/579–7154 | www.ls.net/~lwtrout | Free | Mar.–Sept.

New River Trail State Park. You can hike or bike this scenic trail that follows the route of the Norfolk Southern railway. The trail stretches across four counties for 57 mi, including 39 mi along the New River. Enter near the town park in Fries, off Route 94. | 800/933–7275 | www.state.va.us/~dcr/parks/newriver.htm | Free.

Oak Hill Academy. This small Baptist school, 12 mi west of Independence, is one of the area's biggest surprises: the Warriors are one of the powerhouses of high school basketball, and have produced numerous nationally ranked teams and several NBA greats. The school was founded in 1878 and is set on 250 acres. It is 14 mi west off Rte. 58. | 2635 Oak Hill Rd., Mouth of Wilson | 540/570–2619 | fax 540/579–4722 | www.oak-hill.net | Free | Daily 8–5.

ON THE CALENDAR

JUNE: *Grayson County Old–Time and Bluegrass Fiddlers' Convention.* Though in the shadow of the mammoth Galax convention, this one has been popular with local competitors since 1967. About 2,000 people attend each night, and nearly 40 bands compete for cash prizes. There are also individual competitions in areas like Clawhammer Banjo and Flatfoot Dance. The Convention is held at Elk Creek School Ball Park, Cormer's Rock Rd. 12 mi north off Rte. 21. | Fri.–Sat. last full weekend in June | 540/655–4740.

JUNE: *Wayne C. Henderson Music Festival and Guitar Competition.* Wayne Henderson may not be a household name, but he is one of the finest guitar makers in the country, and has made instruments for the likes of Doc Watson and Eric Clapton. Nationally renowned bluegrass and gospel acts perform, and individual guitarists compete for a custom-made guitar. The competition is held at Grayson Highlands Park, about 25 mi west off Rte. 58. | Third Sat. in June | 540/579–7092.

OCT.: *Mountain Foliage Festival.* The highlight of this annual festival is the wacky Grand Privy Race in which outhouses on wheels are raced around town for the honor of a chamber pot trophy. You can also browse among arts and crafts, and enjoy traditional mountain music and dancing at Courthouse Square. | 2nd Sat. in Oct. 9–3 | 540/773–3711 | www.ls.net/mtnfoliage.

Dining

Heyday's Restaurant. American. This spot recreates a 1950s diner, and is bursting with pictures of antique cars and photographs from Independence High School's 1950s yearbooks. You can't beat their burgers topped with homegrown tomatoes, or their shakes and malts. | 560 E. Main St. | 540/773–3846 | $3–$6 | No credit cards.

High Country Cafe. Southern. This is the real deal: salt-cured ham, pinto beans, and biscuits and gravy are some of the favorites. You can watch the passersby on Main Street through the picture window. | 592 E. Main St. | 540/773–2551 | Closed Sun. breakfast also available | $3–$10 | No credit cards.

Tin Star Cafe. American. Light fare like BLTs and chicken salad are served, as well as heftier dishes like spaghetti. The walls are ornamented with intertwined faux grape vines and mountain laurel, and there is a nifty collection of antique sheriff's badges. | 110 Courthouse Ave. | 540/773–2523 | Closed weekends, breakfast also available | $3–$5 | No credit cards.

Lodging

Davis-Bourne Inn. This 1864 Queen Anne Victorian has an immense wraparound porch with a lovely view of rolling hills. Rooms are furnished with a melange of antiques, including a fine walnut sleigh bed in one room. Some rooms have fireplaces. Complimentary Continental breakfast. No room phones, TV in common area. No pets. No smoking. | 119 Journey's End | 540/773–9384 | www.ls.net/~dbinn | 3 rooms | $65–$75 | No credit cards.

Duck Roost Inn. The tongue-and-groove panelling in this 1906 farmhouse has been whitewashed and hand-stencilled. One room has its own porch, with a view of horses grazing in pastures. The owner is a calligrapher and has a studio on the grounds. The inn is 12 mi west off Rte. 58. Complimentary breakfast. No room phones, TV in common area. Baby-sitting. No pets. | 777 Riverbend Rd., Mouth of Wilson | 540/773–9325 or 888/712–7551 | www.ls.net/~duckroostinn | 2 rooms | $75 | AE, D, MC, V.

Fox Hill Inn. Rooms at this 1987 inn are simple, with handsome cherry-wood furniture. The interior is rugged, and the kitchen is open. The building sits on the top of a hill, where the view of the mountains is superb. The grounds cover 70 acres. The inn is 24 mi west off Rte. 58. Complimentary breakfast. Kitchenette, no room phones, TV in common area. | 8568 Troutdale Hwy., Troutdale | 540/677–3313 or 800/874–3313 | www.bbonline.com/va/foxhill | 6 rooms | $75–$150 | D, MC, V.

IRVINGTON

(Nearby towns also listed: Irvington, Lancaster, Onancock, Tangier Island)

Irvington lies almost at the tip of Virginia's Northern Neck peninsula, near the point where the Rappahannock River empties into Chesapeake Bay. Settled in the mid-1600s, this town of less than 500 relies on farming and fishing to sustain its economy. Watermen still use the time-honored methods their fathers used to harvest fish, crab, and oysters from the bay. Apart from its fishing grounds, Irvington is noted for the Tides Inn, a golf and water-sports resort that opened in 1947. Nearby is historic Christ Church, a gem of colonial architecture built in 1735 and virtually unchanged today. Westland Beach, a small, sandy strand on the Rappahannock River, is near Windmill Point, in White Stone.

Information: **Lancaster County Chamber of Commerce** | Box 1868, Kilmarnock, 22482 | 804/435–6092 or 800/579–9102 | lancva@crosslink.net. **Northern Neck Tourism Council** | Box 1707, Warsaw, 22572 | 804/453–6303 or 800/393–6180 | www.northern-neck.org.

Attractions

Historic Christ Church. This Lancaster County church was built in 1735 as a gift of Robert "King" Carter, one of the colony's wealthiest planters. Virtually unchanged, the cruciform church has a marble baptismal font, three-decker pulpit, and the original communion silver. Carter's elaborate tomb is in the churchyard of this National Historic Landmark. | Rte. 646 | 804/438–6855 | fax 804/438–6855 | www.christchurch1735.org | Free | Apr.–Nov., Mon.–Sat. 10–4, Sun. 2–5.

The church's **Carter Reception Center,** next door, gives a slide show and displays artifacts from Christ Church and Corotoman. Guided tours are given daily.

Farmers' Market. Between May and December, an old-fashioned open-air market is held at the town commons the first Saturday morning of every month. Wander past stands heaped with everything from cheeses, seafood, and baked goods, to fresh herbs, fruit, and plants. Kids can ride horses and play games. | Town Commons | 804/438–5714 | Free | May–Dec., Sat. 8–12.

Westland Beach. This small public beach, maintained by Lancaster County, borders the Rappahannock River. | Rte. 695 | 800/393–6180 or 804/453–6303 | www.northernneck.org | Free | Daily dawn to dusk.

ON THE CALENDAR

APR.: *Kirkin' o' the Tartan.* This traditional Scottish celebration includes bagpipe playing, a marching parade, and a full Tartan-Scottish church service at the Historic Christ Church. | 804/438–6855.

JUNE: *Northern Neck Beach Music Festival.* Reservations are required for this event, an all-you-can-eat cookout dinner with seafood, live music, and dancing at the Windmill Point Resort in White Stone, a five-minute drive north of Irvington. | 804/435–1166.

Lodging

Hope and Glory Inn. This Victorian inn, built in 1890 and once an elementary school, is near Chesapeake Bay. Hollyhocks and roses bloom in the English garden; cottages have private patio gardens. All rooms are unique and furnished with antiques. Complimentary breakfast. No smoking, phones in cottages only, no TV in rooms, TV in common area. Boating. Fishing. Bicycles. Kids allowed in cottages only. Business services. Some pets allowed.

| 634 King Carter Dr. | 804/438–6053 or 800/497–8228 | fax 804/438–5362 | www.hope-andglory.com | 7 rooms, 4 cottages | $110–$195, $145–$195 cottages | AE, MC, V.

Tides Lodge Resort and Country Club. Opened in 1947, this popular golf and water-sports resort is on Chesapeake Bay. Rooms are done in tartan plaids and have a woodsy, rustic look. You can sign up for bay cruises at the front desk. Bar, dining room. Refrigerators, cable TV. Exercise room, game room, 2 pools. Driving range, putting greens, tennis courts. Marina, boating. Bicycles. Kids' programs, playground, laundry facilities. Business services. Some pets allowed (fee). | 1 St. Andrews La. | 804/438–6000 or 800/248–4337 | fax 804/438–5950 | www.thetides.com | 60 rooms | $238–$302 | Closed Dec.–late Mar. | MAP | D, MC, V.

Whispering Pines. The single-story motel is on wooded grounds. Rooms have outside entrances. Picnic area. Cable TV. Pool, wading pool. | Rte. 3, White Stone | 804/435–1101 | fax 804/436–1511 | 29 rooms | $59–$69 | AE, MC, V.

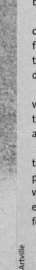

OYSTER WARS

The Chesapeake Bay hasn't always enjoyed tranquil waters. Throughout the 19th century, in fact, this region had an entrenched reputation for lawlessness. For more than a century, "oyster wars" raged on the bay and along its tributaries, particularly along the Potomac River.

It all began in the 1820s with skirmishes, sometimes armed, between bay watermen, who made their living harvesting the region's rich oyster beds, and interlopers from New England, who also wanted to make a profit from the succulent shellfish.

In 1830, out-of-staters were barred from the bay, and the battle for the almighty oyster took a different shape. Marylanders and Virginians clashed with one another over the oyster beds. Fights also broke out between law-abiding "tongers" and outlaw "dredgers." Dredging was the handiest way to retrieve oysters: Boats simply dragged a giant scoop across the river bottom. The tonging method, which entailed plucking oysters off the bottom with long hand-held tongs, was far less popular because it was arduous and time-consuming.

By the mid-1800s, some 3,000 oyster boats cruised these tidal waters. Some operated by legal means, others not; all were eager to profit from the local shellfish. Harvests reached as high as 15 million bushels a season. To prevent utter depletion, Maryland officials declared certain waters off limits to dredgers. Previously, dredging was off limits in certain areas, and now it became even more restricted.

Since dredging for oysters was a way of life for most watermen, the new law was widely ignored. Using small, fast boats, outlaw dredgers began to work under the cover of darkness. They became known collectively as the "Mosquito Fleet," and as often as not, they made a game of outrunning the patrol boats.

In 1868, Maryland stepped up enforcement by creating the Maryland State Oyster Police Force, better known as the Oyster Navy. Tensions between watermen and police hit a high point in 1884, when about 100 dredge boats entered prohibited waters and fired upon a police schooner. Four years later, another gun battle ensued between the Oyster Navy and dredgers working illegally in an area reserved for tongers. Several watermen were arrested, but most of the pirate fleet escaped.

© Artville

JAMESTOWN

(Nearby towns also listed: Charles City, Williamsburg)

Jamestown Island, separated from the mainland by a narrow isthmus, was the site of the first permanent English settlement in North America and is also known today as the Original Site. Colonists sent by the Virginia Company of London arrived on May 14, 1607, on three sailing vessels: the *Susan Constant,* the *Godspeed,* and the *Discovery*; they called the new enterprise "James Towne" after their king. The colony served as the capital of Virginia until 1699.

Now uninhabited, the island bears only tantalizing traces of that early colony. The ruin of a church tower from the 1640s, brick foundation walls, and other clues help delineate the settlement, together with artists' renderings. Jamestown Island is a historic park, full of archaeological excavations, and historians continue to uncover more evidence about the lifestyle of these early pioneers, including the discovery of the site of Jamestown's first fort. Adjacent to the park is Jamestown Settlement, a separate museum complex.

Information: National Park Service, Colonial National Historical Park | Box 210, Yorktown, 23690 | 757/898–2410 or 757/229–1733 | www.nps.gov/colo/.

Attractions

Confederate Fort. Five Confederate earthworks were constructed at Jamestown during the Civil War; at Confederate Fort, portions of two of these remain accessible to the public. | Loop Drive | 757/229–1733 | fax 757/898–6025 | www.nps.gov/colo | Free with entrance to the Original Site | Daily 9–5.

Jamestown, the Original Site. This is the site of an ongoing archaeological study of the first permanent English settlement in the New World, dating to 1607. Nothing of Jamestown remains aboveground except the Old Church Tower. Since 1934, the National Park Service has conducted archaeological explorations and has now made the outline of the town clear. Cooperative efforts by the park service and the Association for the Preservation of Virginia Antiquities (which owns 22 acres of the island, including the Old Church Tower) have exposed foundations, streets, property ditches, fences, and the James Fort site. Markers, recorded messages, and paintings around the park supplement the tour. The island is part of the Colonial National Historical Park. | Jamestown Island | 757/229–1733 | fax 757/898–6025 | www.nps.gov/colo | $5 (includes admission to all sites on the island) | Daily 9–5.

At the reconstructed **Glasshouse** on Jamestown Island, artisans demonstrate glassblowing, an unsuccessful business venture of the early colonists. The original ruins of Jamestown's 1608 glass furnace are all that remain of their efforts. | Jamestown Island | 757/229–1733 | fax 757/898–6025 | www.nps.gov/colo/ | Free with entrance to the Original Site | Daily 9–5.

In addition to maps and information about special programs and ranger-led tours, the **Jamestown Visitor Center** on Jamestown Island contains one of the most extensive collections of 17th-century artifacts in the United States. A 15-minute film provides a perspective of the island's history. Audio tapes for self-guided tours can be rented here, and books and other educational materials are sold in the gift shop. | Jamestown Island | 757/229–1733 | fax 757/898–6025 | www.nps.gov/colo/ | Free with entrance to the Original Site | Daily 9–5 (gates close at 4:30).

While no particular spot on Jamestown Island has been identified as the first landing site in 1607, a 103-ft obelisk at **First Landing Site** commemorates its founding. | 757/229–1733 | Free with entrance to the Original Site | Daily 9–5.

The **Memorial Church,** which dates to 1907, contains the foundations of two earlier, 17th-century churches—a wooden structure built in 1617 that was the first assembly place and a 1640s brick church. | Jamestown Island | 757/229–1733 | fax 757/898–6025 | www.nps.gov/colo/ | Free with entrance to the Original Site | Daily 9–5.

New Towne contains the ruins of an early country house belonging to Henry Hartwell, a founder of the College of William and Mary. Other ruins include Ambler House and a part of the old James City, which dates to the 1620s. Foundations of several statehouses also are visible. A 1-mi self-guided walking tour takes you along the old streets, where markers indicate the sites of former structures. | Jamestown Island | 757/229–1733 | fax 757/898–6025 | www.nps.gov/colo/ | Free with entrance to the Original Site | Daily 9–5.

Old Church Tower is the only structure that remains standing on Jamestown Island, marking the site of the first permanent English settlement in North America (1607). Dating from the 1640s, the tower was part of Jamestown's first brick church, which was used until about 1750 and then fell into ruin. The tower is now part of Memorial Church. | Jamestown Island | 757/229–1733 | fax 757/898–6025 | www.nps.gov/colo/ | Free with entrance to the Original Site | Daily 9–5.

Tercentenary Monument was erected in 1907 to commemorate the 300th anniversary of the Jamestown colony's founding. | Jamestown Island | 757/229–1733 | fax 757/898–6025 | www.nps.gov/colo/.

Jamestown Island Loop Drive winds through Jamestown Island's woods and marshes for 5 mi and is posted with historically informative signs and interpretive paintings that show what a building might have looked like where only ruins or foundations now stand. | Jamestown Island | 757/229–1733 | Free with entrance to the Original Site | Daily 9–5.

Dale House This building holds the laboratories and offices of the Jamestown Rediscovery Project, an ongoing archaeological investigation headed by the Association for the Preservation of Virginia Antiquities. A gallery allows you to observe the workings of an archaeological lab and see some of the items unearthed in recent digs. Archaeologists have found pieces of armor like those worn by soldiers in Europe in the late-16th and early-17th centuries, plus animal bones that indicate the early colonists survived on fish and turtles. Coins, tobacco pipes, ceramic fragments, and more are on display. | Jamestown Island | 757/229–1733 | fax 757/898–6025 | www.nps.gov/colo/ | Free with entrance to the Original Site | Daily 9–5.

Jamestown Settlement. Not to be confused with Jamestown Island, Jamestown Settlement is an adjacent living-history museum complex. Built in 1957 to celebrate the 350th anniversary of Jamestown's founding, the museum has several indoor exhibits as well as outdoor areas that provide a glimpse of life during the early 1600s. A 20-minute film and three permanent galleries—the English Gallery, the Powhatan Indian Gallery, and the Jamestown Gallery—focus on the conditions that led to the English colonization of America, the culture of its indigenous Indian tribes, and the development of Jamestown from an outpost into an economically secure entity. At the pier are full-scale reproductions of the ships in which the settlers arrived: *Godspeed, Discovery,* and *Susan Constant.* You can climb aboard the *Susan Constant,* which is manned with sailor interpreters. | Rte. 31 South, at Colonial Parkway | 757/253–4838 or 888/593–4682 | fax 757/253–5299 | www.historyisfun.org | $10.25 | Daily 9–5.

James Fort is a re-creation of the three-cornered fort that was home to the first Jamestown settlers. Within the fort at Jamestown Settlement, colonists (interpreters in costume) cook, make armor, and describe their hard life under thatched roofs and between walls of wattle and daub (stick framework covered with mud plaster). | Rte. 31 South, at Colonial Parkway | 757/253–4838 or 888/593–4682 | fax 757/253–5299 | www.historyisfun.org | Free with entrance to Jamestown Settlement | Daily 9–5.

Powhatan Indian Village. The Powhatan Indian tribe once lived between Jamestown and Richmond in Quanset huts. Today, those huts have been reconstructed as the Powhatan Indian Village, part of the Jamestown Settlement. As you walk through this living history village, you'll see people tanning furs, cooking, preserving food, and making tools. | Rte. 31 | 888/593–4682 | www.visitwilliamsburg.com | Free with admission to Jamestown Settlement | Daily 9–5.

Replica of the Three Ships. Down at the dock on the James River, you'll find full-sized replicas of the three ships that brought the first settlers to the colonies: the Susan Constant, the Discovery, and the Godspeed. You're welcome aboard the Susan Constant (unless she's out at sea, which is rare), where interpreters are on board to share stories about the 104 men and boys who landed here in 1607. Sometimes the other two ships are open to the public too. | Rte. 31 | 888/593–4682 | www.visitwilliamsburg.com | Free with admission to Jamestown Settlement | Daily 9–5.

ON THE CALENDAR
MAY: *Founders' Weekend.* An encampment, tactical demonstrations, lectures, and a concert of patriotic music commemorate the founding of the Original Site of Jamestown in 1607. | 757/898–3400.

JULY: *First Assembly Day.* This event at Jamestown, the Original Site lets you join with costumed interpreters to commemorate the nation's first legislative assembly in 1619. | 757/899–3400.

NOV.: *Foods and Feasts of Colonial Virginia.* Learning how Jamestown's colonists and Virginia's Powhatan Indians gathered, preserved, and prepared food on land and at sea is the intent of this event. | Jamestown Settlement | 757/253–4838 or 888/593–4682.

KEYSVILLE

MAP 11, H7

(Nearby towns also listed: Farmville, Lynchburg)

Keysville is in the heart of central Virginia, at the junction of several major roadways: U.S. 360, U.S. 15, and VA 40. Still, its population hovers around 600. Settled in the late 1700s, this quiet community depends on agriculture to sustain itself, with beef, corn, wheat, soybeans, and tobacco its main products.

The town's primary attraction, Twin Lakes State Park, originally began in 1950 as Prince Edward State Park for Negroes, a segregated "separate but equal" facility. In 1986, it merged with the Goodwin Lake facilities and acquired its present name. In addition to two lakes, the park has a range of overnight accommodations and a conference center.

Information: **Town of Keysville** | Box 42, Keysville, 23947 | 804/736–9551.

Attractions
Briery Church. The congregation at this Presbyterian church in the woods first formed in 1755. The original 1760 log shelter was replaced in 1824 with the current structure. Entering through the main doors, you immediately come upon the raised pulpit facing the congregation. In the 1800s, men and women sat on separate sides of the church and entered through designated doors; now you can sit wherever you want. Sunday service starts at 11:15 AM. | Rte. 15 and Hwy. 654 | 804/736–8914 (member John Lyle) | Free | Sun. 10–12 or by appointment.

Twin Lakes State Park. A multiuse trail, developed in conjunction with Prince Edward State Forest, is open to hikers, mountain bikers, and equestrians in this 270-acre park. Overnight accommodations include a full-service campground, group camping facilities, and cabins. You can swim, fish, boat, or picnic at Goodwin Lake. For family reunions or other gatherings, you can rent the Cedar Crest Conference Center on the grounds. | Rte. 2, Green Bay | 804/392–3435 or 804/767–2398 (conference center) | www.state.va.us | Free; parking $2 May–Sept., $1 Oct.–Apr. | Daily dawn to dusk.

Dining
Sheldon's. Southern. It's a homey place, right down to the wallpaper border that reads "Welcome to my country home." A buffet of fried chicken, homemade rolls, pork ribs, catfish,

assorted vegetables, and desserts is available for both lunch and dinner. The specialty of the house, however, is the baked Virginia ham, aged in the smokehouse and served with a raisin sauce. Breakfast also served. | 1450 Four Locust Hwy. | 804/736–8434 | Breakfast available | $5–$13 | AE, D, MC, V.

Lodging

The Cottage. The Cottage, sometimes called Paddy's Party Place, is a 1940s farmhouse on the 90-acre cattle farm of Paddy and Joseph Kernisky. The house has two bedrooms, two full baths, a living room, and a kitchen stocked with spices, sugar, and other necessities. You might glimpse a fox or turkey as you relax in one of the rockers on the wraparound porch that overlooks the pond, field, and woods. Weekly rate available. Pinball machine. Two-day minimum stay required. Kitchen, microwave, refrigerator, in-room VCR, room phone. Pond. Hiking, fishing. Laundry facilities. No pets. No smoking. | 3421 Briary Rd. | 804/736–2119 | paddyk@hovac.com | www.vafarmvacation.com | 1 | $75 | No credit cards.

Sheldon's. Family-owned and operated since 1940, this hotel is in a rural setting. All rooms have outside entrances and picture-postcard views of open fields, an old farmhouse, and a big red barn. Restaurant. Some microwaves, cable TV. Business services. Some pets allowed. | 1450 Four Locust Highway | 804/736–8434 | fax 804/736–9402 | 40 rooms | $40–$70 | AE, D, MC, V.

LANCASTER

(Nearby towns also listed: Irvington, Onancock, Tangier Island)

Lancaster, seat of rural Lancaster County, lies between the Potomac and Rappahannock Rivers on the Northern Neck peninsula. The area, settled in the mid-1600s, is the birthplace of George Washington's mother, Mary Ball Washington. A museum and library for genealogical research in the Lancaster Courthouse Historic District bears her name. Belle Isle State Park follows old farm roads through fields and marshes to the Rappahannock River.

Information: **Lancaster County Chamber of Commerce and Visitors Center** | Box 1868, Kilmarnock, 22482 | 800/579–9102. **Northern Neck Tourism Council** | Box 452, Reedville, 22539-0452 | 804/453–6303 or 800/393–6180 | www.virginia.org/northernneck.

Attractions

Belle Isle State Park. This 733-acre park includes 7 mi of frontage on the Rappahannock River. Many predatory birds (blue herons, osprey, hawks, and bald eagles, among others) make their home in the diverse wetlands, lowland marshes, tidal coves, and upland forests, sharing the park with wildlife such as white-tailed deer and turkey. Guided canoe trips take place during the summer. Hiking, bicycling, fishing, boating, and picnicking are available year-round. | 1632 Belle Isle Rd., Lancaster | 804/462–5030 | www.state.va.us | $1 | Daily dawn to dusk.

Lancaster County Courthouse Historic District. Several blocks long, Lancaster's Historic District includes the Lancaster County Courthouse, built in 1860. It contains complete records as far back as 1652. The Mary Ball Washington Museum and Library occupies a former tavern known as Lancaster House, dating from 1827. The county's jail and clerk's office are also open to the public. | Rte. 3 | 804/462–7280 or 804/435–6092 | Free | Daily.

Mary Ball Washington Museum and Library. Named for George Washington's mother, a Lancaster native, this museum has changing exhibits on the Northern Neck region's history and a library for genealogical research. The museum occupies Lancaster House, a former tavern dating from 1827; the genealogical library is housed in the Stewart-Blakemore building. The complex includes several other historic buildings, such as the 1797 Old Clerks

Office, which displays county artifacts, and the Old County Jail, an 1820 structure that houses the archives and historical lending library. The grounds include 18th-century herb and box-wood gardens. Guided tours are available. | Rte. 3 | 804/462–7280 | fax 804/462–6107 | www.mbwm.org | $2 | Wed.–Fri. 10–5, Sat. 10–3, Tues. by appointment.

St. Mary's Whitechapel Church. Mary Ball, mother of George Washington, attended this Episcopal parish church, which was named for the London suburb of Whitechapel. The old-est surviving part of the original church, built about 1669, is an addition built between 1739 and 1741. You'll find many old tombstones, most bearing the names of Washington's relatives on his mother's side, in the churchyard. | Rte. 622 | 804/462–5908 | Free | Week-days 9–2, tours by appointment.

ON THE CALENDAR

AUG.: *Lively Fireman's Festival.* A turkey shoot, an archery contest, hunting and fish-ing expositions, food, games, and live entertainment are all part of this two-day event. | Lively Fireman's Pavilion, Lively | 804/462–0304.

SEPT.: *Bay Seafood Festival.* With live music, exhibits, and all the steamed crabs, crab cakes, oysters, shrimp, and other seafood you can eat, it's no wonder this festival is so popular. Attendance is limited to 2,000 people. | Fleets Bay | 804/435–4171.

Dining

Northside Grill. American. When you walk in, you'll see the specials board and a room where the wine is stored. On the menu, you'll find Cajun chicken salad, Delmonico steak, and a grilled seafood platter with fried oysters. Sunday brunch. | 555 N. Main St. | 804/435–3100 | Closed Mon. No lunch or dinner Sun. | $11–$19 | MC, V.

Lodging

Dove Cottage. This secluded 1746 colonial inn sits on five acres of farmland and has two guest rooms: "Cupid's Blush," with a balcony overlooking the woods, and "Betsy's Butter-fly Garden," decorated with the work of Anne Geddes. Complimentary breakfast. Some in-room hot tubs, no room phones, no TV. Library. No pets. | 369 Browns Store Rd. | 804/580–3683 | fax 804/580–5566 | dove@rivnet.net | 2 | $85–$110 | MC, V.

LEESBURG

MAP 11, I3

(Nearby town also listed: Middleburg)

Founded in 1758, Leesburg is one of the oldest towns in northern Virginia, with numer-ous well-preserved colonial and Revolutionary-era buildings that now house offices, shops, restaurants, and residences. A staging area for the British during the French and Indian War, Leesburg subsequently served as a strategic point for troop movements during the Civil War. The 1861 Battle of Ball's Bluff took place here; the site is now a historic park.

In the 19th century, Leesburg was Loudoun County's political and legal center. As the largest town in the area, it also contained the most religious, retail, and profes-sional establishments. Leesburg continues to be the seat of government for Loudoun County, the third fastest-growing county in the nation.

Leesburg is in the heart of Virginia's "hunt country," at the foothills of the Blue Ridge Mountains. It is home to many horse farms and the site of equestrian events in the spring and fall. Nearby, two historic mansions, Oatlands and Morven Park, are open for tours. There are a number of vineyards and wineries in the area; the Loudoun Wine Trail tour includes visits to six of them.

Information: **Loudoun Tourism Council** | 108D South St. SE, Leesburg, 20175 | 703/777–2617 or 800/752–6118 | www.visitloudoun.org.

Attractions

Ball's Bluff Battlefield Regional Park. This park is the site of the 1861 Battle of Ball's Bluff, when Confederate troops pushed Union soldiers back across the Potomac River; houses on nearby King Street served as hospitals for the wounded. You can tour the Ball's Bluff National Cemetery, which contains the graves of many of the soldiers who fought and died here, or follow scenic hiking trails along the Potomac. | Ball's Bluff Rd. | 703/779–9372 or 703/352–5900 | Free | Daily dawn to dusk.

Loudoun Museum. Exhibits at this museum detail the history of the Loudoun County area, displaying art and artifacts of daily life from the time of the Native American tribes to the 20th century. | 16 W. Loudoun St. SW | 703/777–7427 | fax 703/737–3861 | www.loudoun-museum.org | $1 | Mon.–Sat. 10–5, Sun. 1–5.

Morven Park. This 1,200-acre estate is home to the Westmoreland Davis Equestrian Institute, a private riding school, and two museums—the Morven Park Carriage Museum and the Museum of Hounds and Hunting. The 1781 Greek Revival building bears a striking resemblance to the White House (it's been used as a stand-in for films) and has been home to two governors, Westmoreland Davis and Thomas Swann Jr. (a Maryland governor). The mansion is fully furnished with pieces Mrs. Davis inherited and collected on travels throughout Europe and Asia. The tour takes you through 16 rooms decorated in a variety of styles. You can also stroll the estate's gardens, which include a boxwood garden and reflecting pool. | Old Waterford Rd./Rte. 7 | 703/777–2414 | fax 703/771–9211 | www.morvenpark.com | $6 (includes admission to both museums) | Call for hours.

The **Winmill Carriage Museum** in Morven Park contains one of the largest personal collections of horse-drawn vehicles—more than 100 in all. Viola Townsend Winmill, a horsewoman, began collecting these driving carriages in the late 1920s. On display are coaches, breaks, everyday phaetons, surreys, and sleighs, plus a funeral hearse and fire engine. | Old Waterford Rd./Rte. 7 | 703/777–2414 | fax 703/771–9211 | www.morvenpark.com | Free with admission to Morven Park | Call for hours.

In Morven Park's north wing, the **Museum of Hounds and Hunting** contains art, artifacts, and literature about foxhunting, a Virginia tradition since colonial days. Paintings, hunting attire and tack, and a 1731 hunting horn are among the pieces. | Old Waterford Rd./Rte. 7 | 703/777–2414 | fax 703/771–9211 | www.morvenpark.com | Free with admission to Morven Park | Call for hours.

Oatlands. Formerly a 5,000-acre plantation, Oatlands was built in 1803 by a great-grandson of Robert "King" Carter, one of the wealthiest planters in Virginia before the Revolution. In 1903, William Corcoran Eustis bought the property and restored the Greek Revival mansion to its original beauty. Pieces from Eustis's collection of French and American art and antiques furnish the rooms, and a 4-acre formal English garden highlights the grounds. Spring through fall, Oatlands hosts public and private equestrian events and other activities, including a Celtic Festival in June. | 20850 Oatlands Plantation La. | 703/777–3174 | fax 703/777–4427 | www.oatlands.org | $8 | Apr.–Dec., Mon.–Sat. 10–4:30, Sun. 1–4:30.

Vineyard and Winery Tours. The Loudoun Tourism Council provides information on tours to a handful of award-winning operations in the Leesburg area, among them Loudoun Valley Vineyards, Tarara Vineyards and Winery, Willowcroft Farm Vineyards, Swedenburg Estate Vineyard, and Old Dominion Brewing Company (a microbrewery). Most have free tours, tastings, and picnicking on the grounds. The Loudoun Wine Trail is an itinerary that includes six area wineries. | 108D South St. SE | 703/771–2617 or 800/752–6118 | fax 703/771–4973 | www.visitloudoun.org | Free | Tourism office daily 9–5.

MAR.: *Loudoun Hunt Pony Club Horse Trials.* Riders from across the country compete in dressage, cross-country racing, and stadium jumping. | Morven Park International Equestrian Institute, Morven Park | 703/777–2890.

APR.: *Leesburg Flower and Garden Festival.* Plants, gardening equipment, and supplies are sold at this street festival, which also includes food and entertainment. | 703/777–1262.

APR.: *Homes and Gardens Tour.* The doors of more than 250 private homes and gardens throughout Virginia open for tours for one week only. The Garden Club of Virginia provides free guidebooks detailing the houses on the Leesburg tour. | Garden Club of Virginia, 12 E. Franklin St., Richmond | 804/644–7776.

MAY: *Sheep Dog Trials.* Contests involve handlers using whistles to command their border collies to herd sheep. There are crafts, music, sack races, and food, too. | Oatlands Plantation, 28050 Oatlands Plantation La. | 703/777–3174.

JUNE: *Potomac Celtic Festival.* Celebrating the cultures of Ireland, Scotland, Wales, Cornwall, the Isle of Man, Brittany, and Galacia, continuous live music plays on four stages at this festival. There are also areas for dance and storytelling, workshops, a juried crafts market, import vendors, Scottish athletics, and ethnic food. Booths manned by clans and societies help visitors trace their genealogy. | Morven Park | 703/777–2617 or 800/752–6118.

AUG.: *August Court Days.* More than 200 costumed characters interpret Leesburg's colonial history with street dramas and demonstrations. A children's fair, music, and crafts are part of the festivities. | Downtown | 703/777–2617 or 800/752–6118.

OCT.: *Morven Park Races.* Steeplechase races take place all day long at this annual event. Pony rides, children's games, crafts, and refreshments are part of the excitement. | Morven Park | 703/777–2414.

NOV.–DEC.: *Christmas at Oatlands.* Among the special holiday events at the mansion are living-history demonstrations staged on weekends. | Oatlands Plantation, 28050 Oatlands Plantation La. | 703/777–3174.

Dining

Colonial. Continental. In keeping with the name, the restaurant serves early-American food in an old-fashioned atmosphere. The property is also a bed-and-breakfast inn. Specialties include hearty homemade soups and sandwiches. Cherry and apple pies are always in season. Kids' menu. | 19 S. King St. | 703/777–5000 | $21–$25 | AE, D, DC, MC, V.

Green Tree. American. Originally a wayside inn, the Green Tree retains much of its original flavor—with just a few changes for the better. The tap room, for example, is no longer open only to men, and women don't have to take dinner alone upstairs. There's a walk-in fireplace large enough to roast a pig on a spit, and the dining room has long wooden tables, tall wicker chairs, wide-plank flooring, and tin ceilings. The dishes are prepared according to authentic 18th-century recipes, and seasonal drinks are made from original recipes researched in the National Archives. A strolling musician plays on weekends. | 15 S. King St. | 703/777–7246 | $24–$40 | AE, D, DC, MC, V.

Laurel Brigade Inn. American. Lovers of history congregate at this inn, the site of lot No. 30 in the original Leesburg plan, drawn up in 1759. The original log house served travelers between Winchester and Alexandria; it later became a tavern and then a residence. In 1945, the building was restored, and in 1949 it became a six-room bed-and-breakfast inn. It retains a quiet 18th-century aura with its authentic period furnishings, marble mantletops from France, Swiss door fixtures, and a gazebo in the garden. Baked scallops, filet mignon, and crab imperial are specialties. Outside seating is available. | 20 W. Market St. | 703/777–1010 | Breakfast also available Sun. Closed Mon. | $15–$28 | AE, D, MC, V.

Tuscarora Mill. Contemporary. Named after an Indian tribe, this bar, restaurant, and bakery is housed in an 1898 mill. The 25-ft ceilings in the main dining room let you look at the mill workings and statues of griffons, the insignia of the Mill. The wine list features 320 wines, some of which are carted around on an old grain scale. Try the roasted rack of lamb or the Alaskan halibut, both rotating house specials, or try the sesame roasted salmon. The sauteed medallions of lobster are a favorite appetizer. | 203 Harrison St. | 703/771–9300 | $12–$28 | AE, D, DC, MC, V.

Lodging

Colonial. This redbrick inn is in the heart of the downtown historic district. Early-American furniture, hardwood floors, and fireplaces give each room a special warmth. Restaurant, picnic area, complimentary breakfast. Room service, some in-room hot tubs, cable TV. Library. Airport shuttle. Some pets allowed. | 19 S. King St. | 703/777–5000 or 800/392–1332 | fax 703/777–7000 | saeidi@aol.com | 10 rooms | $78–$120 | AE, D, DC, MC, V.

Comfort Suites. Granite sinks in the bathrooms and marble floors throughout add a touch of elegance to this hotel, which opened in November, 2000. Of the 80 suites, ten have a separate living room, kitchen, and fax machine. All rooms have sofas; the desks come with ergonomic chairs. Outside, you can picnic in a gazebo equipped with grills. Picnic area, complimentary Continental breakfast. In-room data ports, in-room safes, some kitchenettes, microwaves, refrigerators, some in-room hot tubs, cable TV, some in-room VCRs, room phones, TV in common area. Indoor pool, hot tub, sauna. Gym. Laundry facilities, laundry services. Business services. No pets. No smoking. | 80 Prosperity Ave. | 866/533–7287 | www.comfortsuitesleesburg.com | 80 | $125–$149 | AE, D, DC, MC, V.

Days Inn. The location is convenient—it's near Prosperity Shopping Center, just off of Rte. 15, and less than 1 mi from Leesburg. Complimentary Continental breakfast. Cable TV. Laundry facilities. Business services. Some pets allowed (fee). | 721 E. Market St. | 703/777–6622 | fax 703/777–4119 | 81 rooms | $65 | AE, D, DC, MC, V.

Holiday Inn–Leesburg at Carradoc Hall. This hotel is on five landscaped acres, with a gazebo and duck pond. Rooms re-create the late 18th century with antique reproduction furnishings and paintings. The main building is adjacent to a 1773 colonial mansion, Carradoc Hall. Restaurant, bar with entertainment. Cable TV. Pool. Exercise equipment. Laundry facilities. Business services. Airport shuttle. | 1500 E. Market St./Rte. 7 | 703/771–9200 | fax 703/771–1575 | 126 rooms, 4 suites | $109–$129, $109–$159 suites | AE, D, DC, MC, V.

Lansdowne Conference Resort. This resort sits on rolling and wooded hills along the Potomac River in sight of Sugarloaf Mountain. Marble and brass furnishings add a touch of elegance. Restaurant, bar with entertainment, picnic area. In-room data ports, cable TV. Indoor and outdoor pools, hot tub. Driving range, putting green, tennis courts. Gym. Bicycles. Kids' programs. Business services. Airport shuttle. | 44050 Woodridge Pkwy., Lansdowne | 703/729–8400 or 800/541–4801 | fax 703/729–4111 | www.lansdowneresort.com | 305 rooms | $169–$209 | AE, D, DC, MC, V.

Little River. The rooms and cottages in this inn, built in 1820, are furnished with antiques; some have fireplaces. A path leads from the inn to the restored Aldie Mill, now a gallery where local artists show their work. Antique shops and a bakery are also within walking distance. Picnic area, complimentary breakfast. Some room phones. No kids under 10 in cottages. | 39307 John Mosby Hwy., Aldie | 703/327–6742 | www.aldie.com | 9 rooms (3 with shared bath); 3 cottages | $85–$110, $175–$195 cottages | AE, MC, V.

Milltown Farms. Like every house in Waterford, this 1765 log and stone home is on the National Historic Registry. Set on a 300-acre farm, the inn is decorated with antiques from the 1600s and a piece dating back to the Ming Dynasty. Two rooms have fireplaces; one has a private entrance. Dining rooms, complimentary breakfast. Some refrigerators. No room phones, no TV. Hiking. Some pets allowed. No smoking. | 14163 Milltown Rd., Waterford | 540/882–4470 or 888/747–3942 | www.milltownfarms.com | 5 | $100–$135 | AE, D, DC, MC, V.

Norris House. Built in 1760, this inn has a parlor, library, and dining room furnished with stately period pieces and antiques. Guest rooms have canopy, brass, or feather beds, and some rooms overlook the award-winning garden. Complimentary breakfast, picnic area.

No smoking, some room phones. No kids allowed on weekends. Business services. Airport shuttle. | 108 Loudoun St. SW | 703/777–1806 or 800/644–1806 | fax 703/771–8051 | www.norrishouse.com | 6 rooms (all with shared bath) | $90–$135 | AE, D, DC, MC, V.

Tarara Vineyard Bed & Breakfast. This contemporary stone and glass house sits on a 475-acre vineyard on a bluff above the Potomac River. Oriental rugs blanket the granite living room, where there's also a stone fireplace, a baby grand, and a wet bar. Play tennis, go hiking, wander through the apple and pear orchards, or go fishing in the lake. Choose from three bedrooms or one suite; all guests receive a complimentary bottle of wine and two etched glasses. Dining room, complimentary Continental breakfast. Some microwaves, some refrigerators, no TV. Lake. Tennis. Hiking. Fishing. No pets. No kids under 18. No smoking. | 13648 Tarara Ln. | 703/771–7100 | fax 703/771–8443 | www.tarara.com | 4 | $120–$135 | AE, D, MC, V.

LEXINGTON

(Nearby town also listed: Clifton Forge)

In the early 1730s, Scots-Irish and German colonists migrated south from Pennsylvania in search of more farmland and settled in northwest Virginia's Shenandoah Valley. It was here that they established Lexington, and in 1778 it became the seat of the newly created Rockbridge County. Wiped out by fire in 1796, it was rebuilt with the proceeds of a lottery. During the Civil War, Federal troops raided it, and many of its buildings were razed again. Today, Lexington is a college town, and tourism is a major driving force for the area's economy.

Lexington's heritage and many of its present-day attractions revolve around several great military leaders—George Washington, Confederate generals Robert E. Lee and Thomas J. "Stonewall" Jackson, and World War II hero George C. Marshall, winner of the Nobel Peace Prize. Two deeply traditional Virginia colleges, Washington and Lee University and Virginia Military Institute, sit side by side in this town.

Lexington's historic downtown can be toured on foot or by carriage ride. Northwest of town is the Goshen Pass Natural Area, a popular spot for swimming, tubing, canoeing, and picnicking. Chessie Nature Trail, a 7-mi stretch of old railbed between Lexington and Buena Vista, attracts hikers and cross-country skiers.

Information: Lexington-Rockbridge Chamber of Commerce | 100 E. Washington St., Lexington, 24450 | 540/463–5375.

Lexington Visitors Bureau | 106 E. Washington St., Lexington, 24450 | 540/463–3777 | lexington@rockbridge.net | www.lexingtonva.com.

Attractions

Blue Ridge Parkway. (*See* Blue Ridge Parkway.) | 828/259–0701.

Cave Mountain Lake Recreation Area. This park in the Jefferson section of the George Washington and Jefferson National Forests has a 7-acre lake with a beach and bathhouse, hiking trails, tent and trailer campgrounds, and picnic facilities. The campground has water hook-ups. | Cave Mountain Lake Rd. | 540/291–2189 or 540/265–6054 | fax 540/291–1759 | www.fs.fed.us/gwjnf | Parking $4 | May–Nov., daily 6 AM–11 PM.

Goshen Pass Natural Area. Between Lexington and Goshen in Rockbridge County is the 3-mi Goshen Pass area, where a dramatic gorge follows the boulder-strewn Maury River through the Allegheny Mountains. Before railroads, this was the main stagecoach route into Lexington. Rhododendron, mountain laurel, pines, maples, and dogwoods line the river and climb the steep slopes of the surrounding mountains. The scenic pass winds through a 16,000-acre wildlife management area, where a day-use park allows you to picnic or fish, swim, canoe, and inner-tube in the river. | Rte. 39 | 540/265–5100 | fax 540/265–5145 | www.fs.fed.us/gwjnf.

Lexington Carriage Company. A horse-drawn carriage takes you on a 45-minute narrated tour of Lexington. The Stonewall Jackson House, the restored historic downtown area, Washington and Lee University, and the town's residential district are some of the sights you will pass. Tours begin at the Lexington Visitor Center. | 106 E. Washington St. | 540/463–5647 | $14 | Apr.–Oct., daily 10–4:30, weather permitting.

★ **Natural Bridge.** Over millions of years, this massive limestone arch has been gradually carved out of rock by Carver Creek, which rushes 215 ft below. The Monocan Indians called this geologic formation—23 stories high and 90 ft long—the Bridge of God. Surveying the structure for Lord Halifax, George Washington carved his initials in the stone; Thomas Jefferson bought it (and more than 150 surrounding acres) from George III in 1774. During the Revolutionary War, it was used as a shot tower to manufacture ammunition. Today, this natural wonder is owned by a private corporation and is part of a tourist complex that includes caverns and a wax museum. It also supports part of U.S. 11. The Cedar Creek Nature Trail passes by the bridge. | 15 Appledore La. | 540/291–2121 or 800/533–1410 | fax 540/291–1896 | www.naturalbridgeva.com | $10 | May–Aug., daily 8–8; Sept.–Nov. and Mar.–Apr., daily 8–6; Dec.–Feb., Wed.–Sun. 8–5.

Every night at sunset there's a narrated sound-and-light show, the *Drama of Creation,* beneath the Natural Bridge. | 15 Appledore La. | 540/291–2121 or 800/533–1410 | fax 540/291–1896 | www.naturalbridgeva.com | Free with admission to Natural Bridge.

LITTLE SORREL'S LEGACY

On a summer's day in 1997, the town of Lexington witnessed one of the oddest Civil War ceremonies on record. Gen. Stonewall Jackson's beloved war horse, Little Sorrel, was buried with full military honors on the parade grounds of the Virginia Military Institute, more than a century after the steed's death.

Jackson cherished his horse (whom he also called Fancy) because of its great stamina and vigor. The horse was also fearless in the heat of battle, rarely spooked by gunfire. The general was riding Little Sorrel when he was shot by friendly fire on May 2, 1863; he died 10 days later. Afterward, Little Sorrel lived in North Carolina with Jackson's widow. In 1883, she asked VMI to stable the horse when she could no longer care for him. Little Sorrel spent his final years grazing on the institute's parade grounds, where he was known to snort and gallop about whenever the cadets fired rifles or cannons during practice. He died in March 1886 after falling and injuring his back.

For decades afterward, the bones of Little Sorrel gathered dust in a storeroom, all but forgotten. The United Daughters of the Confederacy finally stepped in, saying the time had come to inter the remains and pay tribute to one of the Confederacy's faithful servants.

The ceremony featured an honor guard, a mounted escort, an infantry escort, and a fife and drum corps of Confederate reenactors. The Fincastle Rifles, another reenactment group, fired three volleys as the box of bones was lowered into the grave. Several hundred people attended the funeral, including a Stonewall Jackson impersonator and journalists from the *Wall Street Journal* and elsewhere.

Another part of Little Sorrel remains on permanent display at VMI's museum. A taxidermist mounted his brown hide over plaster of Paris and saddled him up, as if for one more ride.

© Artville

A 45-minute tour takes you along a steep and winding pathway 34 stories down. Said to be the deepest commercial caverns on the East Coast, **Caverns of Natural Bridge** includes hanging gardens of stalactites, underground streams, and waterfalls. Tours depart every 20 minutes. | 15 Appledore La. | 540/291–2121 or 800/533–1410 | fax 540/291–1896 | www.naturalbridgeva.com | $7 | Mar.–Nov., daily 10–5.

Natural Bridge Wax Museum. George Washington and Thomas Jefferson are among the 125 life-size wax figures in this museum. Historical scenes cover the history of the Shenandoah Valley, Native American legends, and folklore. You can tour the museum's factory to see how the wax figures are made. | 15 Appledore La. | 540/291–2121 or 800/533–1410 | fax 540/291–1896 | www.naturalbridgeva.com | $5 (includes factory tour) | May–Aug., daily 9–9; Mar.–Apr. and Sept.–Nov., daily 10–6)

Natural Bridge Zoo. This 25-acre zoo next to the Natural Bridge Village and Resort is also an endangered species breeding center, raising animals such as Siberian tigers and Himalayan bears. There's a large petting zoo and an array of wildlife, from giraffes and monkeys to camels and ostriches. On weekends, you can ride an elephant for $3. Covered picnic pavilions and a gift shop are on the premises. | U.S. 11 | 540/291–2420 | fax 540/291–1891 | $7 | Apr.–Nov., weekdays 9–6, weekends 9–7.

Stonewall Jackson House. The Confederate general lived in this brick town house, built in 1801, for two years while teaching physics and military tactics to cadets at the nearby Virginia Military Institute. Furnished with period pieces and some of his belongings, it was the only house he ever owned. Guided tours are provided every half hour. There's a museum shop. | 8 E. Washington St. | 540/463–2552 | fax 540/463–4088 | www.stonewalljackson.org | $5 | Sept.–May, Mon.–Sat. 9–5, Sun. 1–5; June–Aug., Mon.–Sat. 9–6, Sun. 1–6.

Stonewall Jackson Memorial Cemetery. The grave of the Civil War general, who died May 10, 1863, from wounds received at the Battle of Chancellorsville, is marked by an Edward Valentine bronze statue that faces south. Approximately 400 other Confederate soldiers are buried here. | S. Main St. | 540/463–3777 | Daily dawn to dusk.

Virginia Horse Center. This equine complex stages a variety of horse competitions—show jumping, hunter trials, miniature and pony club shows—several days a week in an indoor arena that seats 4,000 people. The center also hosts rodeos, auctions, and Civil War encampments. | 487 Maury River Rd. | 540/463–2194 | fax 540/464–3507 | www.horsecenter.org | Most events free | Call for show times.

Virginia Military Institute. Founded in 1839, VMI is the nation's oldest state-supported military college, often called the West Point of the South. About 1,300 cadets undergo the rigors of a traditional college curriculum combined with a daily regime of military training and discipline. Stonewall Jackson and oceanographer Matthew Fontaine Maury were among its early faculty members; George C. Marshall was perhaps the most famous alumnus. By order of the U.S. Supreme Court, the male-only academy became coeducational in 1997. At Lejeune Hall, cadet guides are available for walking tours of the post. | Jefferson St. (U.S. 11) | 540/464–7000 | fax 540/464–7388 | www.vmi.edu | Daily, tours daily 10–4.

VMI's history and traditions are the focus of the **Virginia Military Institute Museum.** Look for Stonewall Jackson's stuffed and mounted horse, Little Sorrel, and the general's coat, pierced by the bullet that killed him at Chancellorsville. The university's varied collection started in 1856 with the gift of a Revolutionary War musket. | Jackson Memorial Hall | 540/464–7232 | fax 540/464–7388 | www.vmi.edu/museum | Free | Daily 9–5.

Exhibits at the **George C. Marshall Museum** trace the brilliant career of the World War II army chief-of-staff, beginning when he was aide-de-camp to John "Blackjack" Pershing in World War I and culminating with his creation of the Marshall Plan, a strategy for reviving postwar Western Europe. Marshall's Nobel Peace Prize is on display along with other medals and awards. | Box 1600, VMI Parade | 540/463–7103 ext. 231 | www.gcmarshallfdn.org | $3 | 9–5, Closed Thanksgiving, Christmas, and New Year's Day.

Washington and Lee University. Founded in 1749 as Augusta Academy, this university was later renamed Washington College in gratitude for a donation from George Washington. After Robert E. Lee served as its president following the Civil War, it received its present name. Today, with 2,000 students, the university occupies a campus of white-column, neoclassical buildings grouped around a central colonnade. | Jefferson St. (U.S. 11) | 540/463–8400 | fax 540/463–8062 | www.wlu.edu | Campus open daily; tours weekdays 10, 11, noon, 2, 3, and Sat. mornings during spring and fall; meet at Admissions Office.

Lee Memorial Chapel and Museum. Robert E. Lee supervised the construction of this Romanesque brick chapel in 1866, during his presidency at the university. After his death in 1870, Lee was entombed here and the chapel was named after him. Behind the altar is the famous recumbent statue of Lee by sculptor Edward Valentine. The Lee Museum, on the lower level, contains many relics of the Lee family, including the famous Charles Willson Peale portrait of George Washington. Lee's office, also situated on the lower level, looks much as he left it on September 28, 1870. | Jefferson St. | 540/463–8768 | fax 540/463–8062 | www.wlu.edu | Free | Apr.–Oct., Mon.–Sat. 9–5, Sun. 1–5; Nov.–Mar., Mon.–Sat. 9–4, Sun. 1–4.

ON THE CALENDAR

MAR. OR APR.: *Easter Sunrise Service.* The nondenominational Easter message is delivered beneath Natural Bridge. | Natural Bridge National Historic Landmark | Easter Sunday | 540/291–2121.

APR.: *Garden Week in Historic Lexington.* More than 250 of the state's finest homes, gardens, and landmarks are open to the public as part of "America's Largest Open House." | 540/463–3777.

MAY: *Natural Bridge National Historic Landmark Celebration.* Live entertainment, food, arts and crafts, and a Civil War encampment are attractions at this event. | Natural Bridge National Historic Landmark | 540/291–2121.

MAY–SEPT.: *Lime Kiln Arts' Theater at Lime Kiln.* The ruins of a lime kiln become the outdoor stage for original plays and musicals about Virginia's culture. Shows are Tuesday through Saturday nights during the warm-weather months. | 14 S. Randolph St. | 540/463–3074.

DEC.: *Holiday Traditions in Lexington.* Activities range from a 10K road race to a candlelight procession. A tree-lighting ceremony, caroling, and Christmas house tours are other activities. | 540/463–3777.

Dining

Frank's Pizza. Pizza. Enjoy the view of the Blue Ridge Mountains from the patio of Lexington's first pizza joint, or eat inside, a bright space with exposed brick walls. Pasta and sub sandwiches are also available. Come on a Wednesday for Frank's pizza special, a 16" pie for $4.95. Free parking available. | 511 E. Nelson St. | 540/463–7575 | $4–$7 | No credit cards.

Harb's Bistro. American. Overstuffed sandwiches, salads, burgers, soups, cookies, and brownies are served at this bistro, which offers indoor and outdoor dining. The mountain nachos with black beans are popular. Breakfast is served until they close in the mid-afternoon. | 19 W. Washington St. | 540/464–1900 | No dinner. Closed Mon. | $3–$6 | MC, V.

Il Palazzo. Italian. Scampi al palazzo in a garlic, lemon, oil, and wine sauce is the title dish at this casual restaurant, where pictures of Italian towns grace the walls. You can also order veal picatta, penne alla vodka, pizza, and seafood; try the tiramisu for dessert. | 24 N. Main St. | 540/464–5800 | $8–$20 | MC, V.

The Palms. American. Palm trees and a teal and mauve color scheme set the scene at this bright and cheerful dining spot. Steaks are hand-cut on the premises and share the menu with steamed shrimp, baby back ribs, fettucine Alfredo, burgers, and homemade soups and salads. For dessert, try the coconut cream pie. Late-night dining and a Sunday brunch are available. | 101 W. Nelson St. | 540/463–7911 | $10–$17 | AE, D, MC, V.

Redwood. American. Home-style cooking and a casual, family-friendly atmosphere are the draws here. The barbeque sandwich, overstuffed potatoes, and homemade coconut and pecan pies are favorites. Kids' menu. | 898 N. Lee Hwy. | 540/463–2168 | Breakfast also available | $7–$14 | No credit cards.

Sheridan Livery Inn. Seafood. Since opening in 1997, the patio of this former 1887 livery stable has become Lexington's favorite al fresco spot. Choose from a wide selection of appetizers, salads, soups, sandwiches, and pasta, or from heartier fare such as steaks, chops, ribs, poultry, and seafood. | 35 N. Main St. | 540/464–1887 | $8–$20 | AE, MC, V.

Southern Inn. Contemporary. Established in 1932, this Lexington landmark uses regionally grown organic produce, locally raised pheasants, and fresh seafood to create the nightly specials. Free-range chicken, shrimp, and scallops are usually on the menu, while lamb, duck, pheasant, bison, and seafood are sometimes offered. Live music on Thursday to Saturday. | 37 S. Main St. | 540/463–3612 | $6–$23 | AE,D,MC,V.

Traveller's Bar and Grill. American. Dark-burgundy brick walls and wooden tables and booths set the tone at this casual sports bar and restaurant; you can order from the bar menu until 2 AM if the restaurant's closed. Build your own burger from the bar's "burger board," which has everything from crumbled blue cheese to portabello mushrooms. The hand-cut fries with special seasoning are a good bet; filet mignon, pasta, steak tips, and sandwiches are also available. | 16 Lee Ave. | 540/462–6014 | Closed Sun. | $6–$17 | AE,D,DC,MC,V.

Whistlestop Cafe. Contemporary. Best known for its fried green tomatoes and baby back ribs, this train-themed restaurant also serves steaks, vegetarian dishes, pasta, and seafood specials. For breakfast, homemade panini rolls or sugar-fried dough "whistlepuffs" are a good choice. There's an outdoor covered patio. | 33 Soapy Pl. | 540/377–9492 | Reservations not accepted on weekends | Closed Mon. | $6–$13 | D, MC, V.

Willson-Walker House. American. The lush interior of this restaurant includes warm burgundy and gold tones, faux marble, a fireplace, and period antiques and light fixtures. The archway in the foyer was uncovered during restoration. There are two dining rooms on the lower level and a veranda for alfresco dining. There are daily specials; the local trout is a favorite, and so is the famous $5 lunch. Kids' menu. | 30 N. Main St. | 540/463–3020 | Closed Sun. and Mon. | $20–$25 | AE, D, MC, V.

Lodging

Best Western Inn at Hunt Ridge. The spacious rooms are decorated with Shaker-style furniture. Restaurant, bar. In-room data ports, microwaves (in suites), refrigerators, room service, cable TV. Indoor-outdoor pool. Laundry facilities. Business services. Some pets allowed. | 112 Willow Springs Rd. | 540/464–1500 | fax 540/464–1500 | 100 rooms, 10 suites | $74–$86, $90–$149 suites | AE, D, DC, MC, V.

Col Alto Hampton Inn. Originally the home of a Virginia governor and later willed to Washington & Lee University, this 1827 manor house set on seven acres has been converted into 10 luxury guest rooms. A redbrick hotel of similar architecture is behind Col Alto. Picnic area, complimentary Continental breakfast. Some microwaves, some refrigerators, some in-room hot tubs, cable TV, room phones. Outdoor pool. Outdoor hot tub. Gym. Laundry service. No pets. | 401 E. Nelson | 540/463–2223 or | fax 540/463–9707 | hampton1@cfw.com | www.hamptoninn.com | 86 rooms | $76, hotel; $150–$225, manor house | AE, D, DC, MC, V.

Comfort Inn. This chain hotel is near the Virginia Horse Center. Rooms on the top floor of the four-story building have views of the mountains. Complimentary Continental breakfast. Cable TV. Indoor pool. Laundry facilities. Business services. Some pets allowed. | U.S. 11 S | 540/463–7311 | fax 540/463–4590 | 80 rooms | $60–$90 | AE, D, DC, MC, V.

Days Inn Keydet-General. This mid-sized hotel is set on a hill 1 mi east of historic downtown Lexington. The rooms have mountain views. Complimentary Continental breakfast, picnic area. Some kitchenettes, some refrigerators, cable TV. Business services. Some pets allowed. | 325 W. Midland Trail | 540/463–2143 | fax 540/463–2143 | 63 rooms | $50–$75 | AE, D, DC, MC, V.

Holiday Inn Express. Restaurants and stores are within easy walking distance of this hotel, which is about three mi north of Lexington. Rooms have queen beds. Picnic area, complimentary Continental breakfast. In-room data ports, cable TV. Pool. Laundry facilities. Business services. Some pets allowed. | U.S. 11 | 540/463–7351 | fax 540/463–7351 | 72 rooms | $64–$96 | AE, D, DC, MC, V.

Howard Johnson. The motel is in a commercial district about 5 mi north of downtown Lexington. Rooms have mountain views. Restaurant. Cable TV. Pool. Laundry facilities. Business services. Some pets allowed. | U.S. 11 N | 540/463–9181 | fax 540/464–3448 | 100 rooms | $55–$75 | AE, D, DC, MC, V.

Hummingbird Inn. First built in 1780 and expanded in 1853, this Carpenter Gothic Victorian villa is at the edge of the George Washington National Forest. Most rooms have canopy beds, and three rooms have working fireplaces. Verandas overlook the gardens. Picnic area, complimentary breakfast. No smoking, some in-room hot tubs, no room phones, no TV in rooms, TV in common room. Business services. No kids under 12. Pets allowed (fee). | 30 Wood La., Goshen | 540/997–9065 or 800/397–3214 | fax 540/997–0289 | hmgbird@cfw.com | www.hummingbirdinn.com | 5 rooms | $85–$135 | AE, D, MC, V.

Inn at Union Run. This Federal-style manor house, built in 1853, is 3 mi southwest of Lexington along Union Run Creek. Venetian glass, Meissen china, and Victorian antiques fill the rooms. Some of the guest rooms have private porches. Restaurant, picnic area, complimentary breakfast. Room service, no smoking, many in-room hot tubs. No TV in rooms, TV in common room. No kids under 8. Business services. | 325 Union Run Rd. | 540/463–9715 or 800/528–6466 | fax 540/463–3526 | www.unionrun.com | 8 rooms | $90–$125 | AE, MC, V.

Lavender Hill Farm. Pet goats, sheep, dogs, and cats roam this working 20-acre farm, across the road from a river and minutes away from Lexington. The central section of the main building is a 200-year-old log cabin with simply furnished rooms and lace curtains. Lounge on the porch or head down to the stream for a little fishing. Cable TV, no room phones, no TV in some rooms, TV in common area. Fishing. No pets. No smoking indoors. | 1374 Big Spring Dr. (Rte. 631) | 540/464–5877 or 800/446–4240 | lavhill@csw.com | www.lavhill.com | 3 | $75–$110 | MC, V.

Llewellyn Lodge. Tucked away in a quiet neighborhood, this charming gray-brick colonial has been accommodating travelers since it was built in 1940. You can walk down a tree-lined street to Lexington's historic district, or relax on one of the porches. The innkeeper will be happy to put together fly fishing or hiking packages for you. Complimentary breakfast. Some refrigerators, cable TV, some in-room VCRs, no TV in some rooms, TV in common area. No pets. No kids under 10. No smoking. | 603 Main St. | 540/463–3235 or 800/882–1145 | fax 540/464–3122 | LLL@rockbridge.net | www.llodge.com | 6 | $65–$110 | AE, D, MC, V.

Maple Hall. This former plantation, dating to 1850, is on 56 acres, 6 mi north of Lexington. Some guest rooms have poster beds and gas fireplaces. All guest rooms have private baths. Dining room, complimentary Continental breakfast. Pool, tennis courts. Business services. | 3111 N. Lee Hwy. | 540/463–6693 | fax 540/463–6693 | www.innbook.com | 21 rooms (9 with shower only) | $100–$165 | D, MC, V.

McCampbell. This four-story redbrick hotel is in the heart of downtown Lexington. Rooms are filled with antiques, and most have working fireplaces. Picnic area, complimentary Continental breakfast. Refrigerators, cable TV. Pool privileges. Business services. | 11 N. Main St. | 540/463–2044 | fax 540/463–7262 | www.innbook.com | 23 rooms | $100–$145 | D, MC, V.

Natural Bridge Inn and Conference Center. This redbrick colonial-style hotel is next to the Natural Bridge tourist complex. Restaurant, bar. Cable TV. Indoor pool. Miniature golf, tennis courts. Business services. | U.S. 11 | 540/291–2121 or 800/533–1410 | fax 540/291–1551 | natbrg@aol.com | www.naturalbridgeva.com/nbva | 180 rooms in 2 buildings | $69–$89 | AE, D, DC, MC, V.

Ramada Inn. Built in 1993, this contemporary hotel has large rooms and easy access to the interstate. Restaurant, bar, room service. Cable TV. Indoor pool. Business services. Some pets allowed. | U.S. 11 N | 540/463–6400 | fax 540/464–3639 | www.ramada.com | 80 rooms | $60–$68 | AE, D, DC, MC, V.

Sheridan Livery Inn. Irish immigrant John Sheridan built this stable in 1887. It was turned into a 12-room inn in 1997 and now has a restaurant, lounge, and outdoor cafe. Three of the two-room suites have a balcony overlooking Main Street. Restaurant, bar, complimentary Continental breakfast. Refrigerators, cable TV, room phones. No pets. | 33 N. Main St. | 540/464–1887 | fax 540/464–1817 | 12 | $75–$135 | AE, MC, V.

Steeles Tavern Manor. This 1916 Georgian Manor inn on 55 acres is 6 mi west of the Blue Ridge Parkway. The rooms have sleigh beds, fireplaces, and mountain views. Complimentary breakfast, picnic area. Many in-room hot tubs, in-room VCRs and movies, no room phones. No kids under 13. Business services. Free parking. | U.S. 11 and Raphine Rd., Steeles Tavern | 540/377–6444 or 800/743–8666 | fax 540/377–5937 | hoernlel@cfw.com | www.steelestavern.com | 5 rooms | $115–$150 | AE, D, MC, V.

Stoneridge. Six miles south of Lexington off U.S. 11, this 1829 inn is beautifully decorated with reproduction furnishings and modern baths. Two of the rooms have gas-log fireplaces. Some in-room hot tubs, cable TV, TV in common area. Hiking. No pets. No kids under 12. No smoking. | Stoneridge Ln. | 540/463–4090 or 800/491–2930 | fax 540/463–6078 | 5 | $115–$160 | AE, D, MC, V.

Travelodge. This motel is 6 mi north of Lexington near an old-fashioned drive-in movie theater. Cable TV. Pool. | U.S. 11 | 540/463–9131 or 800/521–9131 | fax 540/463–7448 | 150 rooms | $55–$75 | AE, D, DC, MC, V.

Wattstull. This family-owned motel is near the Natural Bridge. Rooms have wood-beamed ceilings and outside entrances. Restaurant. TV. Pool, wading pool. Some pets allowed. | U.S. 11, Buchanan | 540/254–1551 | 26 rooms | $44–$50 | MC, V.

LURAY

MAP 11, H4

(Nearby towns also listed: New Market, Shenandoah National Park)

Nestled between the Blue Ridge and Massanutten mountains, Luray is the main gateway to the 105-mi-long Skyline Drive. German and Swiss immigrants came to the area in 1812 and established large farms, many of which are still owned by their descendants. Agriculture remains the mainstay of the local economy.

Luray is the seat of Page County, and is home to Luray Caverns, some of the most popular caverns on the East Coast. Bordered by Shenandoah National Park and George Washington National Forest, the area is a favorite for hiking, mountain biking, swimming, and camping. Several local outfitters rent canoes and kayaks for trips down the Shenandoah River.

Information: **Luray-Page Chamber of Commerce** | 46 E. Main St., Luray 22835 | 888/743–3915 | pagecoc@shentel.net | www.luraypage.com.

Attractions

Car and Carriage Museum. This transportation museum grew out of a car-collecting hobby of Luray Caverns' president H. T. N. Graves. More than 140 items are on display, including an 1892 Benz and Rudolph Valentino's 1925 Rolls-Royce. | 540/743–6551 | Admission included in caverns entrance fee | Daily 9 to 1 hr after last cavern tour (8:30 or 9 PM).

Lake Arrowhead. A man-made lake with sandy white beaches, Lake Arrowhead is surrounded by 2 mi of hiking trails threading through 34 acres. You can rent the picnic shelters for group events, play volleyball or horseshoes, or, during the summer, swim or fish for bass and perch. Follow the signs from the intersection of Main St. and Reservoir St. in the center of town. | 2½ mi SE of Luray | 540/743–6475 or 540/743–5511 | Free; $1–$2, beach | Beach closed Sept.– May.

Luray Caverns. Discovered in 1878, Luray Caverns is the state's largest caverns and home to the world's only "stalacpipe organ." This "organ" consists of stalactites that have been tuned to concert pitch and are tapped by electronically controlled rubber-tipped plungers. The cavern's chambers, 30 to 140 ft high, contain thousands of colorful mineral formations and pools that reflect them. The one-hour tour begins every 20 minutes. | U.S. 211 Bypass | 540/743–6551 | fax 540/743–6634 | www.luraycaverns.com | $14 | Mid-June–Labor Day, daily 9–7; mid-Mar.–mid-June and Labor Day–Oct., daily 9–6; Nov.–mid-Mar., weekdays 9–4, weekends 9–5.

From the grounds at Luray Caverns you can hear free musical recitals from the **Luray Singing Tower,** which contains a carillon of 47 bells—the largest weighing in at 7,640 pounds and the smallest at 12 pounds. | 540/743–6551 | Free | Mar.–May and Sept.–Oct., weekends at 2 PM; June–Aug., Tues., Thurs., and weekends at 8 PM.

Luray Reptile Center and Dinosaur Park. Besides a large reptile collection, this center has a petting zoo with deer, llamas, and other animals. More than 300 animals can been seen in 70 different exhibits. There's also a nature shop. | 1087 U.S. 211 W | 540/743–4113 | $5.50 | Daily 10–5.

Massanutten One-Room School. This 1840s clapboard building served as Page County's school before the public school system took over. It was moved from a nearby farm to its present location in 1972 and restored to its original condition. You can see some of the original desks, old writing slates, and a school bell dating from 1880. Many old photographs are also displayed. | Inn Lawn Park | 888/743–3915 or 540/743–2852 | Free | By appointment only.

Shenandoah National Park. (*See* Shenandoah National Park.) Luray is the main gateway to the 105-mi Skyline Drive, which winds through the park. | 540/999–3500 | www.nps.gov/shen/.

Yogi Bear Jellystone Park. Even if you're not camping here, you're still welcome to come and play on the 400-ft water slide or take out a paddleboat. There's a miniature golf course, too. | 2250 US 211 E. | 540/743–4002 | $15 | June–Aug., daily 12–7; Closed Sept.–May.

ON THE CALENDAR

MAY: *Mayfest.* It's a spring street festival with all the trimmings: arts and crafts, food, flower and antiques vendors, live music and entertainment, Maypole dances, clowns, and kiddie rides. Historic buildings are open for tours. | Main St., downtown | 540/743–3915.

AUG.: *Page Valley Agricultural Fair.* Animal and crop exhibits, a parade, a demolition derby, a tractor pull, and live music are the highlights of this annual fair. | Page County Fairgrounds, Collins Ave. | 540/743–3915 or 540/843–3247.

OCT.: *Page County Heritage Festival.* Clogging shows, wagon rides, apple cider, a steam- and gas-engine show, and a chili cook-off are the high points. More than 150 craftspeople display their wares. | Page County Fairgrounds, Collins Ave. | Columbus Day weekend | 540/743–3915.

Dining

Anthony's Pizza XII. Pizza. Rumored to have some of the best chicken wings in town, Anthony's serves Sicilian, Neapolitan, or white pizza topped with your choice of vegetables or meat. You can also get calzones, stromboli, pasta, and salads. Delivery and take-out available. | 1432 U.S. Hwy. 211 W. | 540/743–9300 | $6–$10 | AE, D, DC, MC, V.

Brookside. American. Peacocks are the theme at this family-style restaurant, and you'll see plenty of them roaming the grounds outside. Woods surround the property, and a babbling brook runs through it. Cabins are available, each with its own deck overlooking the water. There's a salad bar with 32 homemade items, and entrées include brizola steak, pan-fried chicken, pork barbeque, and broiled rainbow trout. You can top it off with some homemade cake or pie. Kids' menu. Beer and wine only. | 2978 U.S. 211 E. | 540/743–5698 | Breakfast also available. Closed mid-Dec.–mid-Jan. | $10–$19 | AE, D, DC, MC, V.

Dan's Steak House. Contemporary. The steaks are hand-cut on the premises at Dan's, including sirloin for two, New York strip, and prime rib. You can also order pork chops, grilled chicken, and steamed spiced shrimp. Old washtubs and feed sacks give the place an antiquey country feeling. | 8512 US Hwy. 211 W. | 540/743–6285 | Mon.–Sat. no lunch | $9–$28 | AE, D, MC, V.

Farmhouse at Jordan Hollow Inn. Contemporary. Wood floors and exposed-log walls complement white linen tablecloths and glass candles in the five dining rooms of this restored farmhouse. Although the menu changes every six weeks, some dishes (like the sherried veal tenderloin medallions, the dijon walnut-crusted lamb, and the filet mignon chargrilled with pistachios and a wild-mushroom demiglaze) remain nightly staples. Sunday champagne brunch. | 326 Hawksbill Park Rd., Stanley | 540/778–2285 or 888/418–7000 | No lunch. No dinner Sunday | $14–$25 | D, DC, MC, V.

Mimslyn Inn. American. Watercolor paintings by P. Buckley Moss, a piano, colored linen tablecloths, and fresh flowers decorate the restaurant at this three-story inn. Favorites from the menu include Delmonico steak, stuffed pork chops, and the Mimslyn chicken, a breast layered with country ham and cheddar cheese and topped with a citrus cream sauce. The desserts change so often, they're not on the menu. Sunday brunch available. | 401 W. Main St. | 540/743–5105 | $7–$18 | AE, D, MC, V.

Moment to Remember. Contemporary. Known for its specialty coffees. Order from salads, quiche, sandwiches, and wraps at the counter. The sun-dried tomato and herb and garlic wraps are two favorites. Beer and wine are available. Live entertainment on the weekends. | 55 E. Main St. | 540/743–1121 | Reservations not accepted | Closed Sun. Breakfast available | $4–$7 | AE, D, DC, MC, V.

Parkhurst at Rainbow Hill. Contemporary. Housed in what was built as a country inn, this casual spot displays paintings by local artists. Outdoor tables on the covered brick porch have views of the Blue Ridge Mountains. Specialty sandwiches—like turkey Reubens, grilled chicken breast, and artichoke and cream cheese—are favorites here. There's also an ice cream shop on the premises. | 2547 U.S. 211 W. | 540/743–6009 | $8–$15 | AE, D, DC, MC, V. .

Lodging

Best Western Intown. Rooms at this centrally located, two-story motor inn have separate outside entrances. Restaurant. Room service, cable TV. Pool. Playground. Business services. Pets allowed (fee). | 410 W. Main St./U.S. 211 Business | 540/743–6511 | fax 540/743–2917 | 40 rooms | $50–$105 | AE, D, DC, MC, V.

Cabins at Brookside. These cabins are 5 mi from Luray Caverns and Shenandoah National Park. Each cabin has its own deck overlooking a mountain brook. Stone fireplaces add to the rustic look. Some in-room hot tubs, some refrigerators, no room phones. | 2978 U.S. 211 E | 540/743–5698 or 800/299–2655 | fax 540/743–1326 | www.brooksidecabins.com | 8 cabins | $140–$185 | AE, D, DC, MC, V.

Days Inn. Three miles from the Luray Caverns and 7 mi from the entrance to Shenandoah National Park, this chain hotel offers mountain views in almost all of its rooms. Thirteen of the rooms are decorated with antiques collected by the former owner. You can picnic and play horseshoes out back. Restaurant, bar with entertainment, picnic area, room service. In-room data ports, some in-room hot tubs, cable TV, room phones, TV in common area. Outdoor pool, wading pool. Miniature golf. Hiking. Pets allowed (fee). | 138 Whispering Hill Rd. | 540/743–4521 | fax 540/743–6863 | 101 | $64–$89 | AE, D, DC, MC, V.

Jordan Hollow Farm. This restored colonial horse farm is at the base of the Blue Ridge Mountains, about 15 minutes from Luray Caverns. Horses and llamas are still boarded at the farm, and many of the rooms have an equestrian theme. The original farmhouse, built in 1780, is now the restaurant. Restaurant, bar, complimentary breakfast. No smoking, some in-room hot tubs, cable TV in some rooms. Business services. Hiking. | 326 Hawks Bill Park Rd., Stanley | 540/778–2285 | fax 540/778–1759 | www.jordanhollow.com | 21 rooms in 3 buildings | $121–$175 | D, DC, MC, V.

Little Inn at the Kite Hollow. You'll have pretty views of the surrounding area from this guest house perched on a hill. The cows may come up to the fence while you're relaxing in the outdoor hot tub. Inside you'll find a pool table, a sunroom, and a sitting room with a piano and Oriental rug. Dining room, complimentary breakfast. Refrigerators, cable TV, room phones. Outdoor hot tub. Pets allowed (fee). | 340 Taylor Dr., Stanley | 540/778–2758 | info@kitehollow-b-b.com | www.kitehollow-b-b.com | 2 | $55–$85 | No credit cards.

Luray Caverns Motels. Two separate buildings share the same management and both overlook the mountains. Rooms are done in calming greens. Restaurants are nearby. Pools. Business services. | U.S. 211 | 540/743–6551 | fax 540/743–6634 | 64 rooms | $57–$74 | Motel East closed Dec.–Feb. | AE, D, MC, V.

Mayneview Bed and Breakfast. Built in 1865, this home was once a stop on the Underground Railroad. Feather poster beds, gas-log fireplaces, and private baths make the guest rooms inviting. You can see the Blue Ridge Mountains from the veranda. Complimentary breakfast. No room phones. Hot tub. | 439 Mechanic St. W | 540/743–7921 | fax 540/743–1191 | www.mountain-lodging.com/mayneview | 5 rooms (1 with shower only) | $80–$125 | AE, D, MC, V.

Milton House. An original Sears Roebuck mail-order home built in 1915, this bed and breakfast has kept its model name. The main house welcomes you in southern colonial style with big columns and a portico. The owner has decorated with "some of this, some of that," combining Queen Anne and Victorian antiques with German memorabilia. A separate log cabin has two rooms with private fireplaces and hot tubs. No kids on weekends. Dining room, complimentary breakfast. Some kitchenettes, some microwaves, some refrigerators, some in-room hot tubs, no room phones, no TV in some rooms. No pets. No kids under 12. | 113 W. Main St., Stanley | 540/778–2495 or 800/816–3731 | fax 540/778–3451 | milhouse@shentel.net | www.miltonhouse-inn.com | 6 | $85–$160 | AE, D, MC, V.

Mimslyn Inn. This reconstructed former girls' school is in the center of downtown Luray. Rooms look out over the town and mountains. Restaurant, room service. Cable TV. Business services. Some pets allowed. | 401 W. Main St./U.S. 211 Business | 540/743–5105 or 800/296–5105 | fax 540/743–2632 | www.svta.com/mimslyn/virginia | 49 rooms (2 with shower only), 11 suites | $84–$95, $99–$139 suites | AE, D, DC, MC, V.

Piney Hill. This 1750s farmhouse is nestled in a valley with views of the Massanutten and Blue Ridge mountains. The den has a stone fireplace and a TV/VCR with a large video collection. Innkeepers Wiley Gregory and Hank Overton will cater to any special dietary needs in preparing your breakfast. Dining room, complimentary breakfast. Cable TV, no room phones, no TV in some rooms, TV in common area. No pets. No kids under 16. | 1048 Piney Hill Rd. | 540/778–5261 | pineyhill@vaix.net | www.bbonline.com/virginia/pineyhill/ | 3 rooms | $99 | D, MC, V.

Spring Farm. Built in 1795, this farm was an Underground Railroad stop during the Civil War. In a secluded setting on 10 acres, the hostelry has views of the Blue Ridge Mountains. A mixture of antiques and contemporary furniture fill the rooms. Some rooms have access to the verandas. Complimentary breakfast. No smoking, no room phones, no TV in rooms, TV in common area. No kids under 12. | 13 Wallace Ave./Rte. 656 | 540/743–4701 | fax 540/743–7851 | 5 rooms (3 with shared bath) | $75–$150 | D, DC, MC, V.

Woodruff House. This 1882 mansion has all of the trappings of romance—candelabras, roses, and lace. Afternoon dessert teas are served by candlelight. The private patio by the fountain is a pleasant place to take breakfast. The inn is 1 mi east of Luray Caverns. Complimentary breakfast. No smoking, in-room hot tubs, no room phones. No kids under 10. | 330 Mechanic St. | 540/743–1494 | fax 540/743–1722 | www.woodruffinns.com | 6 rooms (4 with shower only) | $145–$225 | MAP | D, MC, V.

LYNCHBURG

(Nearby towns also listed: Farmville, Lexington)

Established in 1786, this city of now over 65,000, takes its name from John Lynch, owner of the original town site. Tobacco was the economic stimulus of this largely Quaker community. Before the days of canal and railroad, bateaus (flat-bottomed boats) used to carry tobacco down the James River to Richmond, where it was sold. Every June, the Batteau Festival celebrates this part of the city's history.

By the mid-19th century, Lynchburg was one of the wealthiest cities in the United States. Many of the mansions built by the city's tobacco and iron magnates still stand. Some have been converted into bed-and-breakfasts; one, Point of Honor, is now a museum. During the Civil War, Lynchburg was an important Confederate supply base,

PRAISING A PUNGENT PLANT

Virginia has dozens of festivals to celebrate its bounteous harvests. Cantaloupe, strawberries, peanuts, beef, and oysters are all honored with special days of observance. Garlic, however, was for years the ignored stepchild of the state's agricultural industry. Garlic farmers were the butt of jokes, and the bulb itself didn't have a festival to its name.

In 1991, all that changed. Devotees of garlic launched a campaign for public respect, and the Virginia Garlic Festival was born. Every year since, the weekend celebration of this once-low status plant has attracted slightly larger crowds. Highlights of the festivities include a garlic-eating contest and offerings of garlic-drenched food, from garlic bread to garlic-marinated roast beef sandwiches. In the Garlic Cook-off, participants must submit original recipes that feature no fewer than three cloves of fresh garlic. (The faint-hearted—and weak-stomached—should take note: The garlic grown in Virginia is not as hot or pungent as other varieties. Local "elephant garlic" has larger cloves and a milder flavor than most garlic.)

A few fun-loving souls even dress up as giant bulbs, with sprouts shooting from their heads. And, as with any self-respecting festival, there is a royal court—in this case, a Garlic King and Queen, plus a Junior Miss Garlic. Organizers advise contestants to "come equipped with wit, inner beauty, an unusual costume, and some dubious talent."

The festival is held in early October at Rebec Vineyards in Amherst, north of Lynchburg. Several Virginia wineries participate in the event, and there's live blues and jazz. Some 50 craftspeople also make an appearance, offering a variety of goods for sale. Rebec Vineyards is located on U.S. 29 S. For more information, call 804/946–5168.

© Artville

with hospitals and an arsenal. The Pest House Medical Museum in the historic Old City Cemetery chronicles some of the medical advances made here during the war.

Often called the "city of churches" for its many houses of worship, Lynchburg is the national headquarters of Rev. Jerry Falwell, the Baptist minister who launched the Moral Majority. Falwell's Liberty University is in Lynchburg, as is Randolph-Macon Women's College, which houses the Maier Museum of Art. Sweet Briar College, another well-known women's college affiliated with the Virginia Center for the Creative Arts, is also here.

Walking tours cover some of Lynchburg's 19th- and early-20th-century residential districts; five of the seven hill neighborhoods are National Register Historic Districts. In the heart of the city is Blackwater Creek Natural Area, which is laced with walking trails. Thomas Jefferson's retreat, Poplar Forest, is minutes south of town.

Information: Greater Lynchburg Chamber of Commerce | Box 2027, 2015 Memorial Ave., Lynchburg, 24501 | 804/845–5966 | info@lynchburgchamber.org. **Lynchburg Visitor Information Center** | 216 12th St., Lynchburg, 24504 | 804/847–1811 or 800/732–5821 | realva@aol.com.

Attractions

Anne Spencer House. Built in 1903, this was the home of Harlem Renaissance poet and civil rights activist Anne Spencer (1881–1975). Visitors to her house included W. E. B. Du Bois, Martin Luther King Jr., and Thurgood Marshall. Spencer did much of her writing in a small detached cottage (called Edan Kraal) built by her husband. It overlooks the garden behind the main house. The interior has been left exactly as it was when she died, down to the glasses beside her chair. | 1313 Pierce St. | 804/846–0517 | $5, grounds free | Group tours by appointment.

Appomattox Court House National Historic Park. The quiet village of Appomattox Court House was the scene of General Robert E. Lee's surrender of the Army of Northern Virginia to Union general Ulysses S. Grant on April 9, 1865. Restored to its 1860s appearance by the National Park Service, the village is now a 1,744-acre historic park. There are 27 structures in all; you can enter most of them. Among them are the old county courthouse and the home of Wilmer McLean, where the surrender negotiations took place. During the summer, costumed interpreters cast as soldiers and villagers answer questions. | Rte. 24, Box 218, Appomattox | 804/352–8987 | fax 804/352–8330 | www.nps.gov/apco | $4 June–Aug.; $2 Sept.–May | June–Aug., daily 9–5:30; Sept.–May, daily 8:30–5.

The original courthouse in the tiny village of Appomattox Court House burned in 1892, and the county seat was moved 3 mi away to the town of Appomattox. The **Appomattox Court House Building** was reconstructed and now serves as the visitor center for Appomattox Court House National Historic Park. It has a museum and an auditorium where slide shows are given every half hour, detailing the events that led to the surrender of Lee's Army. | Box 218, Rte. 24, Appomattox | 804/352–8987 | fax 804/352–8330 | www.nps.gov/apco | Free with admission to park | June–Aug., daily 9–5:30; Sept.–May, daily 8:30–5.

Lee surrendered to Grant in the parlor of the **McLean House** on April 9, 1865. The house, now part of Appomattox Court House National Historic Park, has been reconstructed to appear as it did on that day. Apparently, officials chose the two-story brick building, owned by Wilmer McLean, for the negotiations because it was the most imposing home in the village. In 1893, M. E. Dunlap, a New York speculator, planned to move the house to Washington, so he dismantled it. His plan failed, and the materials were left to the elements and souvenir hunters. The National Park Service salvaged what was left and reconstructed the house on its original site. | Box 218, Rte. 24, Appomattox | 804/352–8987 | fax 804/352–8330 | www.nps.gov/apco | Free with admission to park | June–Aug., daily 9–5:30; Sept.–May, daily 8:30–5.

The **Stacking of Arms** site within Appomattox Court House National Historic Park marks the Stacking of Arms ceremony of April 12, 1865, when the Confederate infantry surrendered its firearms. About 22,000 Confederate soldiers relinquished their guns and other munitions to 6,000 Federal troops as part of the surrender accord. | Box 218, Rte. 24, Appomattox | 804/352–8987 | fax 804/352–8330 | www.nps.gov/apco | Free with admission to park | June–Aug., daily 9–5:30; Sept.–May, daily 8:30–5.

Other sites of historical interest in Appomattox Court House National Historic Park include the Clover Hill Tavern, County Jail, Meek's Store, and Woodson Law Office.

The local tavern at the time of the surrender, **Clover Hill Tavern,** set up a press and became a temporary printing office so it could print parole papers for Confederate soldiers. | Box 218, Rte. 24, Appomattox | 804/352–8987 | fax 804/352–8330 | www.nps.gov/apco | Free with admission to park | June–Aug., daily 9–5:30; Sept.–May, daily 8:30–5.

The **County Jail** building is a reconstruction of the jail that stood in Appomattox Court House during the 1860s; the interior's holding cells resemble those of the period. | Box 218, Rte. 24, Appomattox | 804/352–8987 | fax 804/352–8330 | www.nps.gov/apco | Free with admission to park | June–Aug., daily 9–5:30; Sept.–May, daily 8:30–5.

The partially restored **Meek's Store** was the village's general store, operated by Francis Meeks and his wife. The interior, which includes a post office, is stocked with items typical of the period. | Box 218, Rte. 24, Appomattox | 804/352–8987 | fax 804/352–8330 | www.nps.gov/apco | Free with admission to park | June–Aug., daily 9–5:30; Sept.–May, daily 8:30–5.

The one-room **Woodson Law Office** building was the law office of John W. Woodson, who died in 1864. | Box 218, Rte. 24 Appomattox | 804/352–8987 | fax 804/352–8330 | www.nps.gov/apco | Free with admission to park | June–Aug., daily 9–5:30; Sept.–May, daily 8:30–5.

Blackwater Creek Natural Area. This 300-acre nature preserve occupies a narrow stream valley in the center of Lynchburg, with steep-sided hills and forested terrain. Deer, raccoons, beavers, foxes, and other wildlife make their home here, as do a wide assortment of plants. A 4-mi paved trail runs along a series of abandoned railroad beds and is shared by walkers and bicyclists. The flat grade also makes it easily accessible for wheelchairs. | 301 Grove St. | 804/847–1640 | fax 804/528–2794 | Free | Daily dawn to dusk.

Diamond Hill Historical District. Italianate, Georgian, and Victorian mansions are set between small, charming cottages in this neighborhood four blocks southeast of the Old Court House. | Free.

Fort Early. Earthen fortifications are all that remain of Fort Early, the headquarters of Confederate general Jubal Early during the Battle of Lynchburg in 1864. During that fight, Jubal managed to blunt an effort by Union general David Hunter to disrupt important transportation and manufacturing links in the city. The grounds are open during the annual Kaleidoscope festival in September, when reenactments are held. | 3511 Memorial Ave. | 804/847–6898 | Free | By appointment.

Holliday Lake State Park. This 250-acre park, which includes a 150-acre lake, lies within the 19,705-acre Appomattox-Buckingham State Forest. Swimming, fishing, hiking, and camping are favorite activities. There are boat rentals and a bathhouse. | Box 622, R.R. 2, Appomattox | 804/248–6308 | www.state.va.us | Parking $1 ($2 summer weekends) | Daily dawn to dusk, camping Mar.–Dec.

Lynchburg Museum. Housed in Lynchburg's old courthouse, a 1855 Greek Revival building, this museum traces the area's history through exhibits that range from Monocan Indian artifacts and Quaker relics to Civil War memorabilia. The city's growth from a center for tobacco trade to a modern industrial center also is detailed. | 901 Court St. | 804/847–1459 | fax 804/528–0162 | www.lynchburgmuseum.org | $1 | 10–4, closed Thanksgiving, Dec. 24 and 25, and Jan. 1.

Lynchburg Symphony Orchestra. The Lynchburg Symphony includes both amateur and professional musicians from Lynchburg and around the nation. Students from local schools are regularly given the opportunity to audition for and perform with the group. | 621 Court St. | 804/845–6604 | www.lynchburgva.com/symphony | Varies with performance.

Monument Terrace. Life-size statues of soldiers line these 138 stone steps up to Court House Hill. You get a great view of Historic Lynchburg at the top. | Court House Hill | Free.

Old City Cemetery. Three Potter's Fields and a cemetery with over 25,000 graves, including seven Lynchburg mayors and five revolutionary soldiers are in this 1806 cemetery that is a registered National Historic Landmark. | 401 Taylor St. | Free | Daily, dawn to dusk.

Located on the grounds of the Confederate Cemetery, between 4th and Taylor Streets, the **Pest House Medical Museum** provides a look into the medical practices at the time of the Civil War and later, with displays of instruments. | 401 Taylor St. | 804/847–1465 | fax 804/856–2004 | www.gravegarden.org | Free | Daily dawn to dusk.

Point of Honor. This mansion, built on Daniel's Hill (the site of a duel) in 1815, was home to Dr. George Cabell Sr., a prominent Lynchburg physician and friend to Patrick Henry. Once part of a 900-acre estate, the house has matching polygonal bay windows and a commanding view of the James River. The restored interior is furnished with pieces from the 19th-century Federal period. The kitchen and stable building have been reconstructed. Guided tours of the house and gardens are given daily. | 112 Cabell St. | 804/847–1459 | www.pointofhonor.org | $5 | Daily 10–4, closed Thanksgiving, Dec. 24 and 25, Jan. 1.

Randolph-Macon Woman's College. This private liberal arts college, founded in 1891, was the first southern women's college to receive a charter for a Phi Beta Kappa chapter. Pearl Buck, the first American woman to win the Nobel Prize for Literature, graduated from this institution in 1914. Affiliated with the United Methodist Church, the college has an enrollment of about 700 women. | 2500 Rivermont Ave. | 804/947–8000 | fax 804/947–8138 | www.rmwc.edu | Daily.

The nationally recognized **Maier Museum of Art** at Randolph-Macon Woman's College displays work by 19th- and 20th-century American artists, such as Mary Cassatt, Georgia O'Keeffe, George Bellows, Thomas Hart Benton, and James McNeill Whistler. | 1 Quinlan St. | 804/947–8136 | Free | Late Aug.–late May, Tues.–Sun. 1–5; closed during Christmas semester break.

Riverside Park. This park contains a hull fragment from the canalboat *Marshall*, which transported Stonewall Jackson's body from Lynchburg to Lexington for burial in 1863. | 2240 Rivermont Ave. | 804/847–1640 | fax 804/528–2794 | Free | Daily dawn to dusk.

South River Meeting House. In 1791, John Lynch, the founder of Lynchurg, gave 10 acres of land to the Quaker Society of Friends for a meetinghouse; the stone structure that stands today was completed in 1798 and remained the site of Quaker worship and activity until the 1840s. South River Quakers were among the first in the South to oppose slavery, and its members were forbidden to purchase slaves. Lynch and other early leaders of the city are buried in an adjacent cemetery. Costumed guides are available on request. | 5810 Fort Ave. | 804/239–2548 | www.lynchburgchamber.org | Free | Daily 9–2, by appointment.

Thomas Jefferson's Poplar Forest. Conceived and built by Thomas Jefferson as his "occasional retreat," Poplar Forest is considered one of his most creative and original architectural designs, an octagonal house that is both simple and compact. Just as he did with Monticello, his other home 90 mi north in Charlottesville, Jefferson built Poplar Forest after his retirement from the presidency. He began work on the house in 1809, and in 1823, at the age of 80, was still supervising interior work. The 4,800-acre plantation, which came to Jefferson as part of his wife Martha Skelton's inheritance, provided him with substantial cash income from tobacco and wheat. The estate remained private property until 1984 when the private, nonprofit Poplar Forest Foundation took over; restoration is ongoing. Archaeologists continue to explore the grounds for clues about Jefferson's landscape design and plantation community, which included slaves and free workers. Every July 4, a free celebration is held here. | Box 419, Forest | 804/525–1806 | fax 804/525–7252 | www.poplarforest.org | $7 | Apr.–Nov., Daily 10–4; Dec.–Mar. by appointment.

Holliday Lake State Park. This 250-acre park, which includes a 150-acre lake, lies within the 19,705-acre Appomattox-Buckingham State Forest. Swimming, fishing, hiking, and camping are favorite activities. There are boat rentals and a bathhouse. | R.R. 2, Box 622, Appomattox | 804/248–6308 | www.state.va.us | Parking $1 ($2 summer weekends) | Daily dawn to dusk, camping Mar.–Dec.

ON THE CALENDAR

JUNE: *James River Batteau Festival.* Crews pole authentic replicas of 18th-century merchant boats down the James River from Lynchburg to Richmond, camping at various points along the route, in this eight-day event. Music, food, and exhibits add to the fun. | James Riverfront | 804/528–3950.

SEPT.: *Kaleidoscope.* A children's festival, antiques show, and a riverfront music jamboree with barbecue, bike race, crafts show, and teddy bear parade highlight this three-week-long festival. Thousands of runners also participate in a 10-mi race. | Locations vary | 804/847–1811.

OCT.: *Historic Appomattox Railroad Festival.* Festivities include a parade, antiques displays, live music, food, and children's activities. | Downtown Appomattox | 804/352–8268.

OCT.: *Virginia Garlic Festival.* Garlic-drenched food, a garlic-eating contest, a garlic cook-off, and the selection of a Garlic King and Queen and Junior Miss Garlic celebrate the pungent bulb, which is grown in these parts. Live blues and jazz and a crafts show fill out the schedule of events. | Rebec Vineyards, U.S. 29 S., Amherst | 804/946–5168.

Dining

Backyard Grill. American. Look up at the ceiling in this casual, purple-walled eatery and you can see a sparkling, aqua-blue swimming pool. House specialties include pecan-crusted salmon or penne pasta salad. | 5704 Seminole Ave. | 804/237–6208 | Reservations essential | $12–$20 | MC, V.

Big Lick Publick House. American. Vivid painted murals with everything from volcanos to pin-up girls make this a restaurant with a sense of humor. You can get traditional favorites such as sandwiches, pasta, and fajitas, or the house specialty, coconut breaded shrimp with the Big Lick's secret dipping sauce. | 4001 Murray Pl. | 804/528–3604 | $6–$12 | AE, D, MC, V.

Crown Sterling. American. In the same location for 30 years, this restaurant is known for its lightly seasoned, aged, and marbled western rib-eye steak. It also serves char-grilled tenderloin filets and lobster tails. The ice cream parfait with wine sauce is a favorite. Working fireplaces warm the rustic interior. | 6120 Fort Ave. | 804/239–7744 | Closed Sun. No lunch | $25–$30 | AE, D, DC, MC, V.

Jazz Street Grill. Contemporary. Modern, cajun cuisine is served in this sleek, contemporary restaurant. The Catfish Jazz Street, a fresh catfish fillet lightly breaded and fried, then topped with crawfish tails and seared vegetables in a white wine and Tabasco sauce is one of the house specialties. | 3225 Old Forest Rd. | 804/385–0100 | Reservations essential | $10–$20 | AE, D, DC, MC, V.

Jeanne's. Seafood/Steak. Hearty food with rich desserts describe the fare at this homey restaurant. Potatoes, bread, and salad accompany entrées, such as grilled salmon and rib-eye steak. The hot fudge cake, Boston cream pie, and strawberry shortcake are decadent treats. High ceilings create an airy feeling, and lots of windows provide views of the lake. You can also dine outside on the deck. Kids' menu. | U.S. 460 E | 804/993–2475 | No lunch Sun.–Wed. | $15–$20 | AE, D, DC, MC, V.

Landmark House. Steak. Besides its slow oven-roasted prime rib, seasoned with herbs and spices and served au jus, this steakhouse is known for its large shrimp cocktail. Each of the 15 desserts is homemade. Salad bar. Piano bar. Kids' menu. | 6113 Fort Ave. | 804/237–1884 | Closed Sun.–Mon. No lunch | $20–$33 | AE, DC, MC, V.

Lynchburg Ale House. American. There are raw, wooden plank floors and small-paned windows in this rustic pub. You can get burgers, grilled (or blackened) chicken sandwiches, and po'boys, then top it off with one of the 16 homemade brews on tap. | 2731 Wards Rd. | 804/237–2215 | $4–$8 | AE, MC, V.

Merriwether's. Contemporary. Rich, painted raspberry walls, large canvas paintings, and glossy parquet floors set the tone in this elegant restaurant. Everything on the menu is homemade, right down to the catsup. Seared spice-rubbed grouper, served on a warm cucumber-mango coulis, with sauteed spinach and grits is the house specialty. | 4925 Boonsboro Rd. | 804/384–3311 | Reservations essential | Closed Sun. | $10–$22 | AE, D, MC, V.

Milano's Italian Restaurant. Italian. This popular family-run restaurant serves up dishes with a touch of northern Italy. The dining area has both tables and booths, and the menu features favorites like tender, juicy chicken marsala and tangy chicken parmigiana. Pasta is homemade daily, so even basic dishes have a fresh flavor. | 5006 Boonsboro Rd. | 804/384–3400 | $6–$13 | AE, D, MC, V.

Sachiko's. Contemporary. The popular "early bird special," served evenings from 5 to 6, includes a bay shrimp cocktail; soup or salad; an 8 oz. rib-eye steak, grilled salmon, or grilled chicken; potato; vegetable; port-wine parfait; and coffee or tea. Or, you may want to try the salmon Wellington, baked in a puffed pastry with mozarella cheese and crab sauce. The "shocker" lives up to its name: 20 to 23 ounces of porterhouse steak. A fireplace adds to the warmth of the interior. | 126 Old Graves Mill Rd. | 804/237–5655 | Closed Sun. No lunch | $30–$35 | AE, MC, V.

T.C. Trotters. Eclectic. The variety of dining areas matches the varied menu. There are two dining rooms and a café. The masculine Claret Room has heavy benches and tables. The solarium has a big bay window with lots of light. The cigar and martini bar has a walk-in humidor, and there's a full-service bar downstairs, too. The menu includes something for every taste: American, French, Italian, and Greek dishes. Some nights there's a DJ; other nights you can hear live music. The crabcakes, made from a 100-year-old family recipe, are always popular, as are the hamburgers and hand-trimmed 10-ounce filets. In the summer, you can eat on the patio under big umbrellas. Entertainment Wed. and Fri.–Sun. Kids' menu. | 2496 Rivermont Ave. | 804/846–3545 | No dinner Mon. | $24–$30 | AE, MC, V.

Lodging

Babcock House. This inn is convenient to historical sites, including Appomattox Court House National Historic Park. A mixture of Victorian and contemporary furniture fills the rooms. The Annie Laurie room has a four-poster bed and an original claw-foot porcelain bathtub. Complimentary Continental breakfast. Cable TV. Business services. | 106 Oakleigh Ave/Rte. 131 | 804/352–7532 | www.babcockhouse.com | 5 rooms | $80–$100 | MC, V.

Best Western. This chain hotel is close to shopping areas. Complimentary Continental breakfast. In-room data ports, room service, cable TV. Pool. Business services. | 2815 Candlers Mountain Rd. | 804/237–2986 | fax 804/237–2987 | 87 rooms | $79 | AE, D, DC, MC, V.

Budget Inn. This chain motel is close to historical sites and parks, including Appomattox Court House National Historic Park. Some microwaves, refrigerators, cable TV. Pool. Business services. Some pets allowed. | 714 W. Confederate Blvd./U.S. 460 Business | 804/352–7451 | fax 804/352–2080 | 20 rooms | $45–$50 | AE, D, MC, V.

Comfort Inn. The property is close to shopping areas. Picnic area, complimentary breakfast. Some microwaves, refrigerators, cable TV. Pool. Business services. Airport shuttle. | 3125 Albert Lankford Dr./U.S. 29 | 804/847–9041 | fax 804/847–8513 | 120 rooms | $68–$80 | AE, D, DC, MC, V.

Courtyard Marriott Lynchburg. This lodging is just 4 mi from historic downtown Lynchburg and Thomas Jefferson's summer home. The River Ridge Mall is across the street. Guest rooms have modern, wood furniture and watercolor prints on the walls. In-room data ports. Cable TV. Pool. Exercise equipment. Business services, free parking. | 4640 Murray Pl. | 804/846–7900 | fax 804/846–7900 | www.marriott.com | 90 rooms | $79–$150 | AE, D, DC, MC, V.

Days Inn. Even though this chain is across from River Ridge Mall, the rooms are surprisingly quiet. Restaurant. In-room data ports, room service, cable TV. Pool. Playground. Business services. Airport shuttle. | 3320 Candlers Mountain Rd. | 804/847–8655 | fax 804/846–3297 | 131 rooms | $70–$150 | AE, D, DC, MC, V.

Dulwich Manor. This turn-of-the-century, English-style manor house, filled with antiques, is 17 mi north of Lynchburg and sits on 93 secluded, wooded acres. The largest of the guest rooms is the Scarborough, with its Victorian-mansion bed and gold inlaid sink. Some of the rooms have fireplaces. Complimentary breakfast. No room phones. Hot tub. | 550 Richmond Hwy., Amherst | 804/946–7207 | www.thedulwichmanor.com | 6 rooms (2 with shared bath) | $80–$120 | AE, MC, V.

Econo Lodge. This budget chain is close to shopping areas and the Lynchburg Stadium. Continental breakfast. Cable TV. Business services. | 2400 Stadium Rd. | 804/847–1045 | fax 804/846–0086 | 48 rooms | $50 | AE, D, DC, MC, V.

1880s Madison House Bed & Breakfast. This gabled 1880s Victorian bed-and-breakfast is in Lynchburg's Garland Hill neighborhood. Carefully selected Schumacher wallpaper, original light fixtures, and antique furnishings re-create the aura of a time past. An extensive collection of Civil War books line the library's shelves. Individual period guest rooms have private bathrooms. Plush guest bathrobes are provided. High tea is served at 4. Complimentary breakfast. Cable TV, in-room VCRs. Hot tub, exercise equipment. Airport shuttle. No kids under 18. No smoking. | 413 Madison St. | 804/528–1503 or 877/901–1503 | madison@lynchburg.net | www.bbhost.com/1880s-madison | 3 rooms, 1 suite | $89–$119 | AE, MC, V.

Federal Crest Inn. A grand staircase dominates the lobby and seven massive fireplaces add cozy warmth in colder months to this 1909 Georgian Revival with classic detailed wood and columns. There's a charming 50s-style diner adjacent to the inn where you get a view of the well-tended grounds while you eat. Some in-room VCRs. No Pets. No kids under 10. No smoking. | 1101 Federal St. | 804/845–6155 or 800/818–6155 | fax 804/845–1445 | www.federalcrest.com | 4 rooms, 1 suite | $95–$140 | AE, D, MC, V.

Hampton Inn. Bright and airy, this chain is close to the interstate. Complimentary Continental breakfast. Cable TV. Business services. | 5604 Seminole Ave. | 804/237–2704 | fax 804/239–9183 | 65 rooms | $70–$99 | AE, D, DC, MC, V.

Hilton. This five-story hotel is located across from River Ridge Mall. The rooms have reproduction antique furniture. Restaurant, bar with entertainment. Room service, cable TV. Pool. Hot tub. Exercise equipment. Business services. Airport shuttle. | 2900 Candlers Mountain Rd. | 804/237–6333 | fax 804/237–4277 | 168 rooms | $118–$150 | AE, DC, MC, V.

Holiday Inn Express. Next to River Ridge Mall, this chain has easy interstate access. Complimentary Continental breakfast. Cable TV. Pool. | 5600 Seminole Ave. | 804/237–7771 or 800/466–5337 | fax 804/239–0659 | 104 rooms | $62–$90 | AE, D, DC, MC, V.

Holiday Inn Select. Near downtown shops and the commercial area, this chain provides live piano music by the fountain in the marble-floored lobby during Sunday brunch. Some rooms have Murphy beds. Restaurant, bar. In-room data ports, refrigerators, cable TV. Pool. Exercise equipment. Business services. Airport shuttle. Some pets allowed. | 601 Main St. | 804/528–2500 | fax 804/528–4782 | basshotels.com/holiday-inn | 243 rooms | $69–$79 | AE, D, DC, MC, V.

Howard Johnson. This chain is close to shopping. Restaurant. Cable TV. Pool, wading pool. Laundry facilities. Business services. Airport shuttle. | U.S. 29 | 804/845–7041 | fax 804/845–4718 | 70 rooms | $54 | AE, D, DC, MC, V.

Mansion Inn. This 9,000-square-ft Spanish Georgian mansion is a Virginia Landmark in the Garland Hill neighborhood. There are oak and cherry floors, soaring ceilings, decorative crown moldings, and original paintings. Special touches in guest rooms include fragrant drawer liners and scented sachets. Breakfast is served on silver. Some rooms have working fireplaces. Private baths. Picnic area, complimentary breakfast. Some refrigerators, cable TV. No smoking. | 405 Madison St. | 804/528–5400 or 800/352–1199 | fax 804/

847–2545 | mansioninn@aol.com | www.lynchburgmansioninn.com | 5 rooms | $109–$144 | AE, DC, MC, V.

Ramada Inn. This large 3-story hotel has modern furniture and art prints on the walls. River Ridge Mall is 1 mi away. Restaurant, bar. In-room data ports, Cable TV. | Rte. 29, at Odd Fellows Rd., Exit 7 | 804/847–4424 | fax 804/846–4965 | www.lynchburgramada.com | 216 rooms | $47–$120 | AE, D, DC, MC, V.

The Residence. Built in 1915 and furnished in original antiques, this terracotta-tiled lodging was once home to the president of Randolph-Macon Women's College and became a bed and breakfast in 1983. There are several balconies, in-room fireplaces, and backyard fountains. You can borrow the inn's bicycles to explore the surrounding area. Some rooms have private baths. No room phones. No TVs. Hiking. Bicycles. | 2460 Rivermont Ave. | 804/845–6565 or 888/835–0387 | fax 804/845–6540 | www.the-residence.com | 3 rooms, 1 suite | $89–$140 | MC, V.

Sleepy Lamb Bed and Breakfast. This working Victorian-era farm, on 45 acres, is convenient to Appomattox Court House National Historic Park. Some rooms have decks and/or fireplaces. One of the guest rooms, the Suffolk, has a queen-size poster bed with carved pineapple ornaments. Complimentary breakfast. No TV in rooms, TV in common area. | Rte. 47, Pamplin City | 804/248–6289 | 3 rooms | $60–$65 | MC, V.

Travelodge. This 2-story motor inn is off Exit 1 on Rte. 29. Cable TV. Pool. Business services. Free parking. | 1500 Main St. | 804/845–5975 | fax 804/846–8617 | www.travellodge.com | 60 rooms | $44–$55 | AE, D, DC, MC, V.

Wingate Inn. Breathtaking views can be seen of the Blue Ridge foothills at this motel 3 mi east of the Lynchburg Regional Airport. Though slightly more expensive, the view-side rooms are well worth it. In-room data ports, Cable TV. Indoor pool, hot tub. Exercise equipment. Business services, free parking. | 3777 Candler's Mountain Rd. | 804/845–1700 or 888/498–6428 | fax 804/845–1800 | www.wingateinns.com | 131 rooms | $89–$225 | AE, D, DC, MC, V.

MANASSAS

MAP 11, I4

(Nearby towns also listed: Fairfax, Springfield, Warrenton)

Manassas, a suburb of Washington, D.C., was originally a railroad junction and then a trading center for area farms. It was founded in the 1850s and has been the seat of Prince William County since 1893. During the Civil War, the hamlet was fought over by the contending armies. It was the site of hospitals, supply depots, and fortifications used by both Union and Confederate troops, and gave its name to two Civil War battles that were fought nearby. The site of both battles is now encompassed in Manassas National Battlefield Park. Specialty shops and restaurants fill Old Town Manassas, the restored downtown area.

Information: **Prince William County/Manassas Conference and Visitors Bureau** | 14420 Bristow Rd., Manassas, 20112 | 703/792–4254 or 800/432–1792 | www.visitpwc.com.

Attractions
Freedom Museum. Memorabilia, photos, and artifacts illustrating the history of U.S. military involvement throughout the 20th century are displayed at this small museum adjacent to the Manassas Regional Airport. The museum also maintains an extensive outdoor collection of military vehicles. | 10400 Terminal Rd. | 703/393–0660 | Free | Daily, 9–6.

The Manassas Museum. Prehistoric tools, Civil War weapons and railroad memorabilia showcase the history and culture of Manassas and the northern Virginia Piedmont region.

Living history programs are held in summer. | 9101 Prince William St. | 703/368–1873 | fax 703/257–8406 | www.manassasmuseum.org | $3 | Tues.–Sun. 10–5.

Manassas (Bull Run) National Battlefield Park. This 5072-acre park was the scene of two major Civil War engagements—the First and Second Battles of Manassas—fought along the waters of Bull Run in July 1861 and August 1862. Both battles were important Confederate victories. It was on this battlefield that Gen. Thomas Jackson earned his nickname when he was observed standing "like a stone wall." Highlights of the park include several historic houses and monuments. Driving, walking, and equestrian tours are available.

Newly renovated in 1999, the **Battlefield Museum** contains permanent exhibits such as soldiers' possessions—field glasses, sashes, and the like—together with weapons and photographs. A display of uniforms highlights the 200 or so different variations. There are also changing exhibitions. | 703/361–1339 | www.nps.gov/mana | June–Aug., daily 8:30–6; Sept.–May, daily 8:30–5.

A low stone foundation, now the **Chinn House Ruins,** marks the former Chinn House, which stood in the midst of fighting during the Second Battle of Manassas as Confederate troops bore down on Union soldiers.

The small white-frame **Dogan House** building is all that remains of the wartime village of Groveton. The house also is one of only two pre–Civil War structures remaining in the park. Nearby, Groveton Confederate Cemetery contains the remains of more than 260 soldiers, only a handful of whom are identified.

The defeated Union troops crossed the **Stone Bridge** after the Second Battle of Manassas in August 1862, withdrawing to Centreville and the Washington defenses.

A former tavern on the wagon road of the Warrenton Turnpike, the red sandstone house, known as **Stone House** is one of only two intact pre–Civil War buildings within Manassas Park. During the war, it was taken over as a refuge for casualties. The house has been restored to its original appearance and is decorated with period furnishings. | 703/361–1339 | Mid-June–Labor Day, weekdays 1–4, weekends 10–4.

The **Unfinished Railroad** is a half-built railroad bed that served as a demarcation in the Second Battle of Manassas; the cut was where Stonewall Jackson's troops held the line in early fighting. His front extended about a ½ mi along this railroad, and the grade is still visible running into the woods.

The **Henry Hill Visitor Center** is the starting point for both self-guided and ranger-led tours. A 15-minute film about both battles is shown every half hour; a three-dimensional map illustrates the strategies used. You can walk or drive the battlefield; a 1-mi hike and a 12-mi auto tour, both self-guided, begin at the center. The walking tour covers highlights of the first battle, while the driving tour encompasses the main points of the second battle and areas involved in both. There's also a bookstore on the premises. | 6511 Sudley Rd. | 703/361–1339 | fax 703/361–7106 | www.nps.gov/mana | $2, $4 limit per family; valid for 3 days | June–Aug., daily 8:30–6; Sept.–May, daily 8:30–5.

Old Town Manassas. Turn-of-the-century buildings, cobblestone streets, and an old train depot can be seen in this section of downtown Manassas.

ON THE CALENDAR

MAY–AUG.: *New Dominion Shakespeare Festival.* Shakespearean dramas and comedies are performed in an outdoor amphitheater at the Cramer Center, 9008 Center St., adjacent to Manassas National Battlefield Park. | $18 | 703/365–0240.

JUNE: *Manassas Railway Festival.* The festivities along Main Street in Old Town include special train rides and railroad exhibits, hands-on children's events, a juried crafts fair, musical entertainment, and food. | 703/361–6599.

JULY, AUG.: *Reenactment of the Civil War Battle of Manassas.* This weekend event at Manassas National Battlefield Park commemorates the First Battle of Manassas, fought in 1861. Events include encampments, living history displays, hikes, concerts, and theater. | 800/432–1792.

AUG.: *Prince William County Fair.* This 10-day fair at the Prince William County Fairgrounds features agricultural exhibits, a truck and tractor pull, drag racing and other motorsports, a midway, food, and live musical entertainment. | 703/368–0173.

Dining

Carmello's and Little Portugal. Italian/Portuguese. Here you'll find cozy booths surrounded by murals of Italy and Portugal. The Portuguese dish of paelha valenciana is a combination of shellfish, calamari, chicken, sausage, and pork steamed with tomatoes and chicken broth in a saffron rice casserole. Perhaps the vitello alla reginella interests you—veal in vodka cream sauce with pancetta, asparagus, tomatoes, and mushrooms. Lots of seafood and pasta, with veal, chicken, and steaks as well. A pianist performs Saturday evenings. | 9108 Center St. | 703/368–5522 | www.carmellos.com | No lunch weekends | $11–$20 | AE, D, DC, MC, V.

Chez Marc. Continental. This small, elegant restaurant has prix-fixe specials that include such delectable dishes as tenderloin of pork with wild mushroom sauce, or lobster with saffron beurre-blanc. The light here is low and the tables have crisp linens, crystal, and fresh flowers. | 7607 Centerville Rd. | 703/369–6526 | Reservations essential | $27–$40 | Closed Sun. No lunch Mon.–Wed. | AE, D, MC, V.

Hero's. Contemporary. Seventeen draft microbrews are served, along with wine and cocktails. Menu mainstays are sandwiches, salads, and prime rib. The main floor, where live jazz is performed onstage Thursday and Saturday nights, has large windows overlooking the Old Town streets. There is an upstairs room plus open-air dining on the patio. | 9412 Main St. | 703/330–1534 | $6–$20 | AE, D, DC, MC, V.

© Artville

THE MISSING CYCLORAMA OF MANASSAS

In 1886, a massive work of art was unveiled in Washington, D.C. It was a cyclorama—a painting depicting the Second Battle of Manassas in 1862, played out on a 20,000-square-ft canvas designed to encircle the spectator. Rich in detail and painted to give the illusion of depth, it was the work of French artist Theophile Poilpot and a team of 13 other artists. Displayed in a large, circular building, the astonishingly realistic work created a sensation. It won rave reviews from many Civil War veterans and the Washington press.

By 1901, the cyclorama's novelty had worn off and it was sold. The new owner was Emmett W. McConnell, a showman and entrepreneur. He took the cyclorama on the road, making an appearance at the St. Louis World's Fair in 1904 and, three years later, at the Jamestown Tercentennial Celebration. After that, the painting disappeared.

No one is sure what happened to the cyclorama, but the National Park Service has been hunting for it since 1939. The most likely explanation for its disappearance, historians say, is that McConnell cut the cyclorama up into sections and sold the pieces. The showman owned nearly 30 cyclorama paintings that he exhibited for income, and he may have found it difficult to compete with the growing film industry.

While park service staff doubt that they will ever find the entire cyclorama intact, they believe parts of this epic painting may still be somewhere out there, collecting dust in an attic or gracing somebody's wall. As stewards of the Manassas National Battlefield Park, they are eager to learn its whereabouts and solve the mystery of the missing cyclorama once and for all.

Panino. Italian. Original local art and white linens, crystal, and china set the stage. Traditional dishes such as linguini with clam sauce share the menu with specialties like ravioli stuffed with shrimp, scallops, and lobster. More pastas are offered, plus fresh fish, veal, and chicken. Desserts and pastas are made on the premises. | 9116 Mathis Ave. | 703/335–2566 | Reservations essential Fri.–Sat. dinner | Closed Sun. No lunch Sat. | $12–$18 | AE, D, DC, MC, V.

Something Fishy. Seafood. This nautical family restaurant has a popular, all-you-can-eat seafood buffet, as well as grilled salmon steaks and Maryland-style crabcakes. | 9780 Zimbro Ave. | 703/369–3474 | $8–$15 | AE, D, DC, MC, V.

Lodging

Bennett House. This 1910 Victorian country inn is on an acre of land in the Old Town historic district, 4 ½ mi from seven Civil War battlefields. Antique reproductions and brass and wood four-poster beds are in the two guest rooms. Each room has a private bath. No room phones, no TV. | 9252 Bennett Dr. | 703/368–6121 or 800/354–7060 | fax 703/330–1106 | www.virginia-bennetthouse.com | 2 rooms | $85–$125 | AE, D, MC, V.

Best Western Battlefield Inn. A mile from Manassas National Battlefield Park and 2 mi from Nissan Pavilion Amphitheater. The grounds include a courtyard with rose garden. Restaurant, bar with entertainment, picnic area, complimentary Continental breakfast, room service. In-room data ports. Some microwaves. Cable TV. Outdoor pool. Exercise equipment. Laundry facilities. Business services. Free parking. Pets allowed (fee). | 10820 Balls Ford Rd. | 703/361–8000 | fax 703/361–8000 | www.bestwestern.com | 121 rooms | $89 | AE, D, DC, MC, V.

Best Western Manassas. This hotel is 5 mi from Manassas National Battlefield Park. Complimentary Continental breakfast. Microwaves, refrigerators, some kitchenettes. Some in-room hot tubs. Cable TV. Hot tub, sauna. Exercise equipment. Laundry facilities. Business services. Free parking. | 8640 Mathis Ave. | 703/368–7070 | fax 703/368–7292 | www.bestwestern.com | 60 rooms | $79–$99 | AE, D, DC, MC, V.

Country Inn and Suites. This lodging has contemporary furnishings like wrought-iron bedframes and dried flower arrangements. There are five restaurants within 2 mi of the hotel, and Lake Manassas is 3 mi away. In-room data ports, cable TV. Indoor pool. Hot tub. Exercise room. Business services. | 10810 Battleview Pkwy. | 703/393–9797 | fax 703/393–9898 | www.countryinns.com | 120 rooms | $85–$95 | AE, D, MC, V.

Courtyard Manassas. Each guest room has a sitting area and balcony. A breakfast-only coffee shop is on the premises and dinner delivery is available from local restaurants. The facility is 1 mi from Manassas National Battlefield and 4 mi from Nissan Pavilion Amphitheater. Restaurant, bar. In-room data ports, cable TV, in-room movies. Indoor pool, hot tub, exercise equipment. Laundry facilities. Business services. Free parking. | 10701 Battleview Pkwy. | 703/335–1300 | fax 703/335–9442 | www.courtyard.com | 149 rooms | $84–$109 | AE, D, DC, MC, V.

Days Inn Manassas. This location offers convenient I–66 access and is 1 mi from Manassas National Battlefield. Guest discounts are available at a nearby fitness center. Complimentary Continental breakfast. In-room data ports, cable TV. Microwaves, refrigerators. Outdoor pool. Laundry facilities. Business services. Free parking. | 10653 Balls Ford Rd. | 703/368–2800 | fax 703/368–0083 | www.daysinn.com | 120 rooms | $71–$81 | AE, D, DC, MC, V.

Fairfield Inn Manassas. This modern 2-story motel is just a ½ mi from Battlefield Park, and 5 mi. from Historic Old Town Manassas. Guest rooms have large work desks and contemporary furniture. In-room data ports, cable TV. Indoor pool. Hot tub. Laundry facilities, laundry service. Business services. | 6950 Nova Way | 703/393–9966 | fax 703/393–9967 | www.fairfieldinn.com | 80 rooms | $77–$98 | AE, D, MC, V.

Holiday Inn Manassas–Battlefield. This facility is at the intersection of I–66 and Route 234. Restaurant, bar, room service. In-room data ports. Microwaves, refrigerators. Cable TV. Outdoor pool, exercise equipment. Laundry facilities. Free parking. | 10800 Vandor Ln. | 703/335–0000 | fax 703/361–8440 | www.holiday-inn.com | 158 rooms | $80–$130 | AE, D, DC, MC, V.

Red Roof Inn Manassas. This branch is off I–66 1 mi from Manassas National Battlefield Park. In-room data ports. Cable TV. Business services. Pets allowed. | 10610 Automotive Dr. | 703/335–9333 | fax 703/335–9342 | www.redroof.com | 119 rooms | $84.99 | AE, D, DC, MC, V.

Super 8 Motel Manassas. This budget chain motel with exterior corridors is 6 mi from Manassas National Battlefield Park. Complimentary Continental breakfast. Cable TV. Free parking. | 8691 Phoenix Dr. | 703/369–6323 | fax 703/369–9206 | www.super8.com | 79 rooms | $49–$79 | AE, DC, MC, V.

Super 8 Motel Manassas/Washington. This motel by the intersection of I–66 and SR 234, is 1 mi from Manassas National Battlefield Park and 2 mi from Manassas Mall. Several restaurants are within ½ mi. Complimentary Continental breakfast. Some in-room hot tubs. Cable TV. Laundry service. Free parking. | 7249 New Market Ct. | 703/369–1700 | fax 703/369–4451 | www.super8.com | 150 rooms | $65.95–$69.95 | AE, DC, MC, V.

MARION

MAP 11, D7

(Nearby towns also listed: Abingdon, Independence, Wytheville)

Founded in 1835, Marion is the seat of Smyth County. The town was named after Gen. Francis Marion, known by the nickname "Swamp Fox" during the American Revolution.

Marion sits in the mountains of the Blue Ridge Highlands of southwest Virginia and offers plenty of outdoor activity. In Jefferson National Forest, which borders the town to the north and south, Hungry Mother State Park has a mountain lake for swimming and boating, cabins, and campgrounds. Built by the Civilian Conservation Corps in the 1930s, it is one of the most popular parks in the state system. Mt. Rogers National Recreational Area, south of Marion, contains Virginia's highest peak and has numerous riding and hiking trails and trout streams.

Information: **Smyth County Chamber of Commerce** | Box 924, 124 W. Main St., Marion, 24354 | 540/783–3161 | www.swanva.net.

Attractions

Hungry Mother State Park. Known for its woodlands and 108-acre mountain lake, this 2,180-acre park in Jefferson National Forest 4 mi from town has a sandy beach with a bathhouse, pleasure boats and a boat launch, a fishing pier, campgrounds, cabins, hiking and biking trails, guided horseback trail rides, and a restaurant. | 2854 Park Blvd. | 540/781–7400 | www.state.va.us | Parking $1, $2 weekends | Year-round, daily dawn–dusk.

Mt. Rogers National Recreation Area. Part of the George Washington and Jefferson National Forests, this preserve in Smyth County is 55 mi long and 10 mi wide and encompasses high plateaus, alpine meadows, and panoramic views. There are 400 mi of trails, some to the summit of Mt. Rogers—at 5,729 ft the highest point in Virginia. Campgrounds come in two varieties: rustic (pit toilets, hand-pumped water) and well-equipped (hot showers, flush toilets, interpretive programs); two campgrounds are open year-round. | 3714 Hwy. 16 | 540/783–5196 | fax 540/265–5145 | www.fs.fed.us/gwjnf | Free | Daily.

Smyth County Museum. Photographs, artifacts, and archives of the region's past are displayed at this small museum devoted to preserving the history of Appalachian Smyth County. | 203 N. Church St. | 540/783–7286 | Free | Daily, 2–5. Closed Nov.–Apr.

ON THE CALENDAR

MAY: *Whitetop Mountain Ramp Festival.* Ramps are a wild-growing, aromatic vegetable, similar to a leek. Mountain crafts, Old Time and bluegrass music, barbecue, and

a ramp-eating contest are highlights of the festival, held along U.S. 58 in Konnarock, about 25 mi south of Marion, at Mt. Rogers Fire Hall. | 540/388–3257.
JULY: *Hungry Mother Arts and Crafts Festival.* This is the longest-running state-park arts-and-crafts festival in the country. The juried art show includes the works of more than 100 artisans. | $3 per vehicle | 540/783–3161.
SEPT. *Adwolfe Summer Festival.* You can see draft-horse and tractor pulls at this festival held each fall in downtown Marion. Music and food is available for purchase. | 540/783–8855.

Dining

Courtyard Cafe. American. This casual restaurant has a large main dining area with booths and tables. The menu features tasty meat sandwiches, soups, and more substantial fare like steaks and chops. | 105 N. Park St. | 540/783–6114 | $6–$12 | AE, D, MC, V.

Marion Diner. American. This classic small-town-America diner is complete with a sandwich counter and twirly-chairs. Tried-and-true comfort foods like meatloaf with mashed potatoes, or a char-grilled burger and fries are best bets at this no-frills eatery. | Hwy. 16 | 540/783–2862 | $3–$6 | MC, V.

Lodging

Best Western Inn. The property is 5 mi from Hungry Mother State Park and close to I-81. Restaurant, bar, complimentary Continental breakfast, room service. In-room data ports, microwaves, refrigerators, cable TV. Outdoor pool. Laundry service. Free parking. Pets allowed. | 1424 N. Main St. | 540/783–3193 | fax 540/783–3193 | www.bestwestern.com | 80 rooms | $69–$73 | AE, D, DC, MC, V.

EconoLodge. Hungry Mother State Park is 5 mi away from this 2-story accomodation. Guest rooms have rollaway beds available. The motel is ½ mi off I-81 near Marion. In-room data ports, cable TV. | 1424 N. Main St. | 540/783–6031 | fax 540/782–9990 | www.econolodge.com | 40 rooms | $54–$60 | AE, D, DC, MC, V.

Fox Hill Inn. With panoramic views of the Virginia Highlands, this bed-and-breakfast sits amid 70 acres of meadows, forest, and nature trails. A 10-minute drive puts you in the Mt. Rogers National Recreation Area for hiking, horseback riding, canoeing, and biking. The kitchen and the outdoor grills are available for lunch and dinner preparation. Rooms are simple, with handsome cherry-wood furniture. Common areas include a library, living room with fireplace and satellite TV, patio, and large flower garden. Eighteen miles south of town, the inn is almost halfway between Marion and Independence. Complimentary breakfast. | 8568 Troutdale Hwy., Troutdale | 540/677–3313 or 800/874–3313 | fax 815/550–5490 | mholmes@netva.com | www.bbonline.com/va/foxhill | 6 rooms with private baths, 1 suite | $75–$85, $150 suite | D, MC, V.

Virginia House Motor Inn. This one-story motor lodge looks more like a house than a motel and is surrounded by well-trimmed lawns and lots of trees. Guest rooms have contemporary furnishings and large windows that look out onto the grounds. Cable TV. Pool. | 1419 W. Main St., 1 mi off Exit 47 on I-85 | 540/783–5112 | fax 540/783–1007 | 40 rooms | $50–$55 | AE, D, DC, MC, V.

MARTINSVILLE

MAP 11, F7

(Nearby town also listed: Danville)

Founded in 1793 near the North Carolina border, Martinsville is named for Joseph Martin, an early settler and Revolutionary War soldier. Martinsville has historically been an industrial center, home to Bassett Furniture, E. I. DuPont de Nemours, Sara Lee, and Tultex. It's now a major textiles and furniture manufacturing center. The Virginia

Museum of Natural History has its headquarters here, offering a variety of programs and changing exhibits. The Martinsville Speedway hosts major stock car races.

Nearby, Fairy Stone State Park in the Blue Ridge foothills has campgrounds and wooded hiking trails. Serious fishermen head northeast of Fairy Stone State Park to Philpott Lake, a 3,000-acre lake built by the U.S. Army Corps of Engineers.

Information: **Martinsville–Henry County Chamber of Commerce** | Box 709, 115 Broad St., Martinsville, 24114-0709 | 540/632–6401 | www.mhccoc.martinsville.com | mhc-coc@neocomm.net.

FRANKLIN COUNTY—MOONSHINE CAPITAL OF THE WORLD

Some traditions in the Blue Ridge Mountains of western Virginia die hard. Though you'll never see how-to demonstrations at local festivals, or mentions in glossy tourism brochures, "moonshining" (making homemade liquor) is woven deeply into the rich cultural fabric of this region. In fact, it's a big business. Virginia bootleggers produce an estimated $20 million worth of moonshine a year, much of it in Franklin County, which occupies the area just north of town from Philpott Lake to Smith Mountain Lake. Long known as the "Moonshine Capital of the World," this quiet, rural area also has the distinction of being home to the only moonshine-fighting police squad in the country. Drop by the county courthouse and you will see, hanging prominently on the wall, a photograph of the largest still ever seized by authorities in Franklin County.

Unlawful it may be, but the sale of untaxed liquor historically had been a way for folks in this area to make ends meet—an efficient means of making money at a time when few jobs paying a cash wage were available. In the early part of the 19th century, farming was unpredictable and factory work was hard to find. Moonshine allowed farmers to make extra money from their corn crop, which was appealing particularly if the crop was poor or late in getting to market. Today, though, modern-day bootleggers are not farmers supplementing their income but seasoned professionals motivated by big profits. Most of the "hooch" ends up in metropolitan areas such as Washington, D.C., and Philadelphia. Moonshining is now considered a lucrative business, rather than some vestige of mountain culture. Individuals who sell moonshine also are more likely to be involved in narcotics and illegal firearms, according to authorities.

To avoid detection, moonshiners have hidden their operations in almost every conceivable place. Authorities have smashed stills discovered in caves under riverbanks, in barns, chicken coops, and suburban garages. One clever bootlegger camouflaged his still by building a fake family cemetery around it, complete with headstones, flowers, and fencing. The cat-and-mouse between moonshiners and the law is the stuff of local folklore, and nearly everybody in these parts has a story to tell.

The clear, roughly 90-proof spirit carries a variety of colorful nicknames; probably the most common is "white lightning," because of its harsh, fiery effect. Other monikers include "white mule" after the moonshine's kick and "forty-rod" for the distance it makes the drinker run before passing out.

Attractions

Blue Ridge Institute. Set on the campus of Ferrum College, 27 mi northwest of Martinsville, this institute is the State Center for Blue Ridge Forklore, with a mission to preserve the heritage of the Blue Ridge region. Its archives contain thousands of photographs, videotapes, books, and other records relating to Appalachian folkways, Shenandoah Valley beliefs, folk music, and more. The archives are open by appointment. The institute's two museums highlight the region's history and culture, influenced by English, Scot, Irish, African, and German settlers. | Franklin St./Rte. 80, Ferrum | 540/365–4416 | fax 540/365–4419 | www.blueridgeinstitute.org | Mon.–Sat. 10–4.

The culture of early southwest Virginia settlements is the focus of the **Blue Ridge Farm Museum,** where an authentic German-American farmstead illustrates early 19th-century life along the Blue Ridge. The farmstead consists of a log house, outbuildings, livestock, and gardens; all the buildings were relocated from other parts of the region. Costumed interpreters work the farm, performing chores and tending the livestock and garden. | $4 | Mid-May–mid-Aug., Sat. 10–5, Sun. 1–5.

The **Museum Galleries** are the only ones in Virginia dedicated exclusively to the presentation of traditional culture. Permanent and rotating exhibits feature Virginia folklife in music, art, crafts, and customs. | Free | Mon.–Sat. 10–4.

Fairy Stone State Park. Named for the fairy stones, intricate cross-shaped crystals, often found in the area, this park, 29 mi west of Martinsville, has a 168-acre lake with a beach for swimming and fishing. Cabins, campgrounds, picnic areas, and playgrounds (one of which is in the water) are among the 4,750-acre park's other amenities. | 967 Fairy Stone Lake Dr., Stuart | 540/930-2424 | fax 540/930–1136 | www.state.va.us | Parking $1 weekdays, $2 weekends | Daily 8 AM–10 PM.

Martinsville Speedway. This track hosts the biggest NASCAR late-model stock races in the country, including the Taco Bell 300 in September and the Hanes 500 in April. | Speedway Rd., Ridgeway | 540/956–3151 | fax 540/956–2820 | www.martinsvillespeedway.com | Ticket prices vary | Races in Apr., Sept., and Oct.

Philpott Lake. The 3,000-acre lake, built by U.S. Army Corps of Engineers, has 100 mi of shoreline, a mix of beach and coves. Fishing, swimming, and boating are the primary recreational activities. The surrounding park is mostly wooded and has rental cabins and camping lodges. | 1058 Philpott Dam Rd., Bassett | 540/629–2703 | Parking $2 | Daily.

Piedmont Arts Association Museum. Three galleries house changing art exhibitions with a local and international scope. Exhibits feature works by 20th-century American artists such as Clarence Holbrook Carter and Chuck Close, ancient art and archaeological finds, and recent works by the association's member artists. There's a gallery shop and children's programs. | 215 Starling Ave. | 540/632–3221 | fax 540/638–3963 | www.piedmontarts.org | Free | Tues.–Fri. 10–5, Sat. 10–3, Sun. 1:30–4:30.

Virginia Museum of Natural History. This museum is actually a vast repository of plant and animal specimens. It has permanent exhibits of fossils, minerals, and reptiles, as well as a computer-animated triceratops. Lectures, educational activities, field trips, and other programs are offered regularly. | 1001 Douglas Ave. | 540/666–8600 | fax 540/632–6487 | www.vmnh.org | $4 | Mon–Sat. 10–5, Sun 1–5.

ON THE CALENDAR

SEPT.: *Taco Bell 300.* The Martinsville Speedway hosts the biggest NASCAR late-model stock car races in the country. The best East Coast drivers compete in this race. | 540/956–3151 | www.martinsvillespeedway.com.

OCT. *SpeedFest.* This yearly celebration coincides with Martinsville Raceway's Winston Cup race. Held in downtown Martinsville, the event features kid's activities, tasty local food, and big-name musical acts.

OCT.: *Blue Ridge Folklife Festival.* Dozens of Blue Ridge artisans demonstrate instrument making, cane carving, basket weaving, and a host of other folk arts at this celebration of western Virginia folk culture at Ferrum College. In addition, there are horse-pulling, mule-jumping, and log-skidding contests; sheep dog trials; and the Virginia State Championship Open Water and Treeing Coon Dog contest. Three performance stages feature music and storytelling. Food, bake sales, and vintage farm machinery exhibits are offered, too. | 540/365-4416.

Dining

Hong Kong. Chinese. Gold-tasseled lanterns, carved wooden chairs, and flourescent lighting provide stark contrast in this restaurant that offers such exotic dishes as lobster Cantonese or popular favorites such as lemon chicken or beef lo mein. | 58 E. Church St. | 540/632-6429 | $5-$15 | AE, MC, V.

Michael's Steak and More. American. Big-screen TVs broadcast sporting events while you eat in booths and tables at this casual, family restaurant. Prime cuts are char-grilled to perfection. Traditional chicken and seafood dishes are available, as well. The restaurant is five mi northwest of Martinsville in neighboring, Collinsville. | 2089 Virginia Ave., Collinsville | 540/647-3720 | $6-$15 | AE, MC, V.

Lodging

Best Western Martinsville Inn. Just off Business Route 220, this hotel is 2 mi from the Virginia Museum of Natural History and 5 mi from Martinsville Speedway. Restaurant, bar, room service. In-room data ports, microwaves, refrigerators, cable TV. Outdoor pool. Exercise equipment. Laundry service. Free parking. Pets allowed. | 1755 Virginia Ave. | 540/632-5611 or 800/388-3934 | fax 540/632-1168 | www.bestwestern.com | 97 rooms | $59-$65 | AE, D, DC, MC, V.

Dutch Inn. This motel, five mi northwest of Martinsville, is easy to spot—there's a giant windmill replica on the front of the building. Restaurant, bar, room service. In-room data ports, refrigerators, cable TV. Pool, hot tub, sauna. Exercise equipment. Free parking. Pets allowed. | 2360 Virginia Ave., Collinsville | 540/647-3721 or 800/800-3996 | fax 540/647-4857 | sgrodens@neocomm.net | www.dutchinn.com | 148 rooms | $75 | AE, D, DC, MC, V.

Hampton Inn Martinsville. The inn, just off Business U.S. 220 N, is three mi from Liberty Fair Mall, four mi from Virginia Museum of Natural History, and 8 mi from Martinsville Speedway. Complimentary breakfast. In-room data ports, cable TV. Some kitchenettes, some microwaves; refrigerators. Pool, hot tub. Exercise equipment. Laundry facilities, laundry service. Business services. | 50 Hampton Dr. | 540/647-4700 | fax 540/647-4119 | www.hampton-inn.com | 68 rooms | $88, $108 suites | AE, D, DC, MC, V.

Holiday Inn Express. Occupying a two-story pale-brick building with a blue tiled roof, this hotel is just off Rte. 220. Guest rooms have large windows and rollaway beds. In-room data ports, cable TV. | 1895 Virginia Ave., Collinsville | 540/666-6835 or 800/465-4329 | fax 540/666-0156 | www.basshotels.com | 70 rooms | $72-$15 | AE, D, DC, MC, V.

Super 8. This three-story stucco motel has a cozy lobby with braided rugs, overstuffed wing-back chairs, and wood-veneer cabinets in the breakfast nook. In-room data ports, cable TV. | 1044 N. Memorial Blvd./Rte. 220N–Business | 540/666-8888 | fax 540/666-8888 Ext. 122 | www.super8.com | 54 rooms | $39-$130 | AE, D, DC, MC, V.

MCLEAN

MAP 11, J4

(Nearby towns also listed: Arlington, Alexandria, Fairfax, Falls Church, Tysons Corner, Vienna)

McLean is one of the wealthiest suburbs in northern Virginia, home to ambassadors, members of Congress, and business magnates. Less than a 10-minute drive from

Washington, D.C., McLean is just off the Capitol Beltway and has major shopping areas such as Tysons Corner Center (see separate town listing). Although it has evolved into a major business center, the town has a country feel, with rolling hills and winding roads. McLean was founded in 1910 when two smaller communities, Langley and Lewinsville, were joined together. It was named after John R. McLean, publisher at that time of the *Washington Post*. About 4 mi from the center of town is Great Falls National Park, the site of a 77-ft waterfall at Mather Gorge.

Information: Fairfax County Convention and Visitors Bureau | 8300 Boone Blvd., Suite 450, Tysons Corner, 22182 | 703/790–3329 or 800/732–4732 | cvbfceda@mindspring.com | www.cvb.co.fairfax.va.us.

Attractions

Claude Moore Colonial Farm. A family in costume re-creates the activities of a tenant farm in the 1770s—planting, cultivating, and harvesting corn, wheat, and tobacco crops; and tending livestock (old breeds of cows, chickens, and hogs). Special events include seasonal harvest celebrations with flax processing and cheese-making, and 18th-century market fairs. | 6310 Georgetown Pike | 703/442–7557 | www.cvb.co.fairfax.va.us | $2, slightly higher for special events | Apr.–mid-Dec., Wed.–Sun. 10–4:30.

Colvin Run Mill Historic Site. A restored mill dating from the first decade of the 19th century still grinds corn meal and whole wheat flour. The gears and machinery are made almost entirely of wood; the milling technique was considered revolutionary in its time. The miller's house and dairy barn contain historical exhibits. You can buy a sack of flour at the general store. The mill usually operates two Sundays a month from March to November, so call ahead for opening times and information on interpretive programs. | 10017 Colvin Run Rd., Great Falls | 703/759–2771 | fax 703/759–7490 | www.cvb.co.fairfax.va.us/parks | Tour $4 | Jan.–Mar., daily 11–4; Apr.–Dec., daily 11–5.

Great Falls Park. The twin parks of Great Falls, on either side of the Potomac River, provide one of the most spectacular scenic attractions in the region. From a cliff-top path you can look down on Mather Gorge, where the Potomac River thunders 77 ft over a series of steep, jagged rocks and through a narrow gorge. This spot was a trading place for Indians and early colonists and today is a popular picnicking site for Washington-area residents. Trails take you along the edge of the falls and past remnants of a old skirting canal, constructed about 1785 by the Patowmack Canal Company, founded by George Washington. Swimming and wading are prohibited in the park, but there are fine opportunities for fishing, rock climbing, and white-water kayaking. Horseback riding also is permitted, but there are no stables in the park. | Old Dominion Dr., Great Falls | 703/285–2966 | www.nps.gov/gwmp/grfa | $4 per vehicle, $2 for pedestrians, valid for 3 days | Daily 7 AM–dusk.

Rangers at the **Visitor Center** can provide an orientation of the park. The center has a slide show on park history and changing exhibits, plus maps and books for sale. Here you can pick up maps of the Patowmack Canal Trail or the River Trail, which offers views of Mather Gorge. Staff members conduct naturalist and historical programs and walks year-round. | Apr.–Oct., daily 10–6, Nov.–Mar., daily 10–4.

Theodore Roosevelt Island and Memorial. (See Mount Vernon Trail in Alexandria.) This 88-acre island nature reserve lies in the Potomac River opposite Georgetown, separated by a narrow channel from the Virginia shore and accessible only by a pedestrian bridge. No vehicles—not even bikes—are permitted. A short trail leads to the memorial to the 26th president, a moated, granite-paved plaza with a 17-ft bronze sculpture of Roosevelt, backed by stone slabs engraved with his comments on nature, youth, manhood, and the state. Two miles of trails wind around the island, through woods and an occasional swamp, all left in their natural state. Nearly 200 varieties of wildflowers and some 50 species of trees flourish here. | George Washington Memorial Pkwy. | Free | Daily dawn–dusk.

APR.–JUNE, OCT., DEC., FEB.: *McLean Orchestra.* Monthly concerts at Langley High School, 6520 Georgetown Pike, feature classical works and performances by guest artists. | 703/893–8646.

OCT.–JUNE: *McLean Symphony.* Classical music concerts are held monthly at a variety of venues. Tickets are available at 1350 Beverly Rd., Suite 115-172, in McLean. | 703/522–7187.

Dining

Cafe Oggi. Italian. Art deco elegance is reflected in this peach and white dining room. Columns against the wall and glass-block windows frame optic-art paintings. A risotto dish is always offered—crimini and portobello mushrooms or perhaps calamari and scallops. Osso Bucco (veal shank) is another popular dish, as is the fresh liver served Venetian style, with onions and wine sauce. House-made pasta is made with a variety of fillings—artichoke, pumpkin, or veal, for instance. | 6671 Old Dominion Dr. | 703/442–7360 | Reservations essential Fri.–Sat. | No lunch weekends | $11.95–$24.95 | AE, D, DC, MC, V.

Cafe Taj. Indian. Peach walls and black tables are the backdrop for the house specialty, tandoor cooking—try the salmon. Several lamb dishes are available: consider gosht patiala (lamb with potatoes and spices) or rogan josht with its creamy yogurt sauce. Vegetarian meals are also served. Open-air dining. | 1379 Beverly Rd. | 703/827–0444 | $12.95–$18 | AE, D, DC, MC, V.

Da Domenico. Italian. This large restaurant manages a cozy atmosphere, thanks to soft colors and curtained booths. Veal is the star here, so try the peperonata (with sweet red peppers and mushrooms in spicy tomato sauce). Pastas include Ravioli alla Genovese, pasta pillows stuffed with cheese, sausage, and spinach. Several seafood, beef, and chicken dishes are served as well. Free parking at lunch. | 1992 Chain Bridge Rd., McLean | 703/790–9000 | Reservations required Fri.–Sat. | Closed Sun. No lunch Sat. | $10.95–$20.95 | AE, D, DC, MC, V.

Dante Ristorante. Italian. This 1890s Victorian house was converted to a restaurant with five dining rooms and a lounge, all with European antiques. The wraparound porch makes for pleasant outdoor dining. In addition to standards like baked ziti (with homemade mozzarella), chicken with prosciutto, and sauces with fresh tomatoes, try the quail with chestnuts and grapes, or the rabbit. | 1148 Walker Rd., Great Falls | 703/759–3131 | Reservations essential Fri.–Sat. | No lunch weekends | $15.95–$24.95 | AE, D, DC, MC, V.

J. R.'s Stockyards Inn. Steak. This clubby restaurant—white table linens, leather upholstery, mahogany walls—is across the street from Tyson's Corner Center. J. R.'s serves aged Midwestern beef cut by their private butcher. Steaks and prime rib are king here, but you will also find chicken, ribs, scallops, lobster, and lamb chops. Kid's menu. | 8130 Watson St., McLean | 703/893–3390 | www.jrsbeef.com | Reservations essential Fri.–Sat. | No lunch weekends | $15–$25 | AE, D, DC, MC, V.

Kazan. Turkish. Ornate Turkish antiques and bazaar finds add to the exotic ambience. Try the doner kebab, chopped lamb kofte, or shrimp and scallops Bosphoros. | 6813 Redmond Dr. | 703/734–1960 | Closed Sun. | $13.95–$20.95 | AE, DC, MC, V. '.

L'Auberge Chez François. French. This classic farmhouse restaurant on a winding country road emphasizes the Alsace region of France. Five-course fixed-price meals revolve around entrees such as rabbit with mushrooms and chestnuts or a medley of pheasant, duck, sausages, pork, and foie gras. Seafood and veal are also offered. A garden terrace provides a park setting for outdoor dining. No smoking. | 332 Springvale Rd., Great Falls | 703/759–3800 | www.laubergechezfrancois.com | Reservations essential | Jacket required | Closed Mon. No lunch Tues.–Sat. | $32–$39 prix–fixe | AE, DC, MC, V.

Le Petit Mistral. Continental. Bright, modern canvasses and a remarkable wrought-iron chandelier hang in the cheery, lemon-yellow dining area of this restaurant. For an appetizer, there's roasted red pepper stuffed with prosciutto, wild mushrooms, and fontina cheese. For dinner, a house specialty is mustard-crusted rack of lamb, crepes and chilled crème brûlée. | 6710 Old Dominion Rd. | 703/748–4888 | Reservations essential | $15–$30 | AE, D, DC, MC, V.

McCormick and Schmick. Seafood. A couple of the more creative dishes are Halibut stuffed with brie, and Salmon Pasta. If you like seclusion, be sure to reserve a "snug," which is a recessed booth with privacy curtains. | 8484 Westpark Dr., McLean | 703/848–8000 | Reservations essential | No lunch Sat.–Sun. | $10–$29 | AE, D, DC, MC, V.

Pulcinella. Italian. An atrium is a focal point of this restaurant with marble columns, murals of Italian landscapes, and occasional opera and cabaret. Watch the cooks shovel pizzas into the wood-fired oven from your table. Plenty of pastas, veal, and chicken, too. Try one of the grills—chicken, fish, or sausage, or shrimp with scallops. | 6852 Old Dominion Dr., McLean | 703/893–7777. | www.pulcinella.com | $7.25–$16.95 | AE, DC, MC, V.

Restaurant at the Ritz-Carlton, Tysons Corner. Eclectic. Fine art and ornate table settings impart luxurious elegance to this dining room. A harpist accompanies the Sunday champagne brunch. Dinner menu standouts include buffalo-milk mozzarella lasagna, duck with woodland mushrooms and raspberry demi-glace, and rack of lamb. Kids' menu. Sun. brunch. | 1700 Tysons Blvd., McLean | 703/506–4300 | Breakfast also available Mon.–Sat. | $21–$37 | AE, D, DC, MC, V.

Ristorante Il Borgo. Italian. Venetian glass chandeliers provide an elegant contrast to the chef's collection of horse-racing flags hanging on the walls. You won't go wrong with spaghetti malafemmena (with clams, crab, capers, and olives in spicy marinara) or linguini vittoria (lobster with garlic, brandy, dry vermouth, and sundried tomatoes). Veal is also popular. Nightly specials might include wild boar in marsala and champagne. | 1381A Beverly Rd., McLean | 703/893–1400 | www.ilborgo.net | No lunch weekends | $13–$35 | AE, D, DC, MC, V.

Serbian Crown. French/Russian/Serbian. Live gypsy music, wood beamed walls, and an extensive vodka selection compliment the Beluga caviar, smoked eel, and wild boar. Particularly recommended are the cabbage rolls and the kulibiaka—salmon for two in pastry with lobster sauce. Piano bar Tues. and Fri.–Sat, Gypsy music Wed.–Sun. | 1141 Walker Rd., Great Falls | 703/759–4150 | Reservations essential Fri.–Sun. | Closed Fri. and Sun. for lunch | $19.95–$38 | AE, DC, MC, V.

Tachibana. Japanese. Warm wood and Japanese textiles frame the sushi bar, where you can watch the chef in action. A comprehensive selection of very fresh sushi shares the menu with tempura, sashimi, and teriyaki-grilled chicken, beef, or a variety of fish. No smoking. | 6715 Lowell Ave. | 703/847–1771 | Reservations accepted Fri.–Sun. only for 5 or more | $6.50–$30 | AE, D, DC, MC, V.

Tara Thai. Thai. The dazzling, deep-blue-sea motif sports sea creatures and waves painted on the ceiling and walls. Whole-fish dishes are a popular choice—steamed rockfish with chile-garlic sauce is one option. Or try lime-marinated beef or the duck. | 226 Maple Ave. W, Vienna | 703/255–2467. | www.tarathai.com | Reservations essential Fri.–Sat. | $8–$24.95 | AE, D, DC, MC, V.

That's Amore. Italian. The big tables for the large groups this place draws make it feel like a big family gathering every night of the week. You can order single or family-size portions of traditional Italian fare. The zuppa de pesce (seafood in tomato broth over linguine), chicken abruzzi (with goat cheese, basil, and red wine), and veal asparagus are a few of the many favored dishes. | 150 Branch Rd. SE, Vienna | 703/281–7777. | www.thatsamore.com | No lunch weekends | $9.50–$20.95 | AE, D, DC, MC, V.

Wu's Garden. Chinese. Asian accents in the decor and a quiet atmosphere make this place feel serene. Try the General Tso's chicken or the shrimp imperial. | 418 Maple Ave. E, Vienna | 703/281–4410 | $8–$12 | AE, D, DC, MC, V.

Lodging

Hilton McLean Tysons Corner. This branch is 1 mi from Fairfax Square Shopping Mall, 5 mi from Tysons Corner Center. Restaurant, bar with entertainment, room service. In-room data ports, minibars, cable TV, some refrigerators. Indoor pool. Exercise equipment. Business ser-

vices. | 7920 Jones Branch Dr., McLean | 703/847–5000 | fax 703/761–5100 | mclean_hilton@
hilton.com | www.hilton.com | 458 rooms | $89–$255 | AE, D, DC, MC, V.

Holiday Inn. 1 mi from Tysons Corner Center and Galleria. Restaurant, bar with entertainment. In-room data ports, cable TV. Indoor pool. Hot tub, sauna. Exercise equipment.
Airport shuttle. Pets allowed. | 1960 Chain Bridge Rd., McLean | 703/893–2100 | fax 703/356–
8218 | www.holiday-inn.com | 316 rooms | $89–$189.95 | AE, D, DC, MC, V.

MIDDLEBURG

MAP 11, I4

(Nearby town also listed: Leesburg)

The area that is now Middleburg was surveyed by George Washington in 1763, when
it was known as Chinn's Crossroads. Strategically located midway on the Winchester-
to-Alexandria trading route (present-day U.S. 50), it was a popular stopping point for
weary travelers. The village was founded in 1787 and today, with a year-round population less than 1,000, is the capital of Virginia's "Hunt Country" and the address of
the well-to-do horsey set. Fox hunts, point-to-point and steeplechase races dominate
the calendar from April through October; polo matches are played Sundays in summer.
The town has more than 160 buildings on the National Register of Historic Places, while
Main Street is lined with a multitude of antiques shops, boutiques, and other specialty
stores. A number of nearby vineyards offer tours and tastings.

Information: Loudoun Tourism Council | 108D South St. SE, Leesburg, 20175 | 703/777–
0519 or 800/752–6118 | rogers@visitloudoun.org | www.visitloudoun.org.

Attractions

Aldie Mill. Constructed in 1809 by Charles Fenton Mercer, a noted local legislator, this brick
gristmill is believed to be the only mill in Virginia powered by twin overshot wheels. Taking water from the nearby Little River, it used the latest technological advances to grind
wheat into superfine flour for commercial export. A second, smaller country mill on the
site was used by nearby farmers for local needs. President James Monroe ground grain
here while living at nearby Oak Hill, and Confederate colonel John Singleton Mosby captured Union soldiers at the mill during the Civil War. The mill operated continuously until
1971. Restoration efforts were undertaken by the Virginia Outdoors Foundation in 2000. |
39395 John Mosby Hwy./U.S. 50, Aldie | 703/327–9777 | www.middleburgonline.com | Free
| Late-Apr.–Oct., Sun. noon–5; Nov.–late-Apr.

Meredyth Vineyards. This country winery, just south of Middleburg, produces Seyval
Blanc, Riesling, Chardonnay, and Cabernet Sauvignon wines on 56 acres. Tours are offered
daily. | Rte. 628 | 540/687–6277 | fax 540/687–3945 | Wine tasting $2 | Daily 11–5.

ON THE CALENDAR

MAY: *Delaplane Strawberry Festival.* A two-day festival at Sky Meadows State Park
offers crafts, food, a bake sale, a petting zoo, hayrides, and children's games. | 540/364–
2772 or 540/592–3556.

JUNE: *Upperville Colt and Horse Show.* The oldest horse show in the country, first held
in 1853 on the Grafton Farm in Upperville, features hundreds of horse-and-rider combi-
nations, from 8- to 10-year-olds in the pony divisions to leading Olympic and World Cup
riders and horses in hunter, jumper, and Grand Prix divisions. The highlight is the
$50,000 Budweiser/Upperville Jumper Classic. | 540/592–3858.

JUNE: *Vintage Virginia.* Virginia wines are the star at this event at Great Meadows
Field Events Center, one of the largest wine festivals on the East Coast. Area restaurants
serve food, and there are wine and food seminars, an arts-and-crafts show, and jazz,
reggae, and rock on three stages. | 800/277–2675.

Dining

Black Coffee Bistro. Contemporary. Comfort food with a contemporary twist highlights the menu at this small, family-run restaurant in a 1790s Colonial home. The dining area has light blonde wood with large windows and lots of natural light. During the summer, a house specialty is ginger-lime pork with pickled vegetables, or pan-seared breast of duck seasoned with fresh local ingredients. | 101 S. Madison St. | 540/687–3632 | Reservations essential | $8–$22 | AE, MC, V.

Red Fox Inn. Continental. George Washington once ate at this restaurant that was a former tavern built in 1728. There are two main dining rooms and a large terrace upstairs. The menu features mostly hearty, hunt-club fare like beef barbeque, filet mignon with bleu cheese walnut butter, and pork chops with fried apples. For dessert, there's rich bread pudding with Bourbon sauce. | 2 E. Washington St. | 540/478–1808 | Reservations essential | $15–$25 | AE, D, DC, MC, V.

Lodging

Goodstone Inn and Estate. Situated on 265 acres of rolling hills, this inn boasts four separate renovated homes, ivy-covered walls, shady loggias, and history going back to the mid-1800s. Guest rooms range from cozy to palatial, with rich English and French country-style furnishings, French doors, Palladian windows, massive flagstone fireplaces, and lots of privacy. You can even watch a traditional fox hunt, complete with horns and hounds, and bring your own horses to the stable. Cable TVs. Pool. Outdoor hot tub. Hiking, horseback riding. No pets. No kids under 12. No smoking. | 36205 Snake Hill Rd. | 540/687–4645 | fax 540/687–6115 | www.goodstone.com | 14 rooms | $150–$475 | AE, MC, V.

Middleburg Country Inn. The inn is in a restored former Episcopal rectory built in 1820. Rooms are individually furnished with canopied four-poster beds and period furniture; several have fireplaces. Complimentary breakfast. Cable TV, in-room VCRs, room phones, some in-room hot tubs. Hot tub. No smoking. | 209 E. Washington St. | 540/687–6082 or 800/262–6082 | fax 540/687–5603 | www.midcountryinn.com | 8 rooms, 3 suites | $165–$235, $195–$265 suites | AE, DC, MC, V.

Middleburg Inn and Guest Suites. Canopy beds and 18th-century antiques fill the spacious suites here. Sleeping quarters (with one, two, or three bedrooms) are separate from the living room and kitchen. A stone fireplace dominates the living room. Complimentary Continental breakfast. TV. | 105 W. Washington St. | 540/687–3115 or 800/432–6125 | mgs@middleburgonline.com | www.middleburg.com/mgs | 5 suites | $145–$250 | MC, V.

Red Fox Inn. The main building of this seven-building rustic lodging in downtown Middleburg was originally a tavern built in 1728. There are 24 rooms scattered throughout the seven historic buildings on the grounds. Pine floors and paneling, four-poster beds and other furnishings in 18th-century style reflect its heritage. Some rooms have fireplaces. Also on the property are an art gallery and a restaurant. Bottles of red and white wine greet you upon arrival, and the restaurant serves up excellent Continental cuisine. Restaurant, bar, complimentary Continental breakfast. Cable TV, some room phones. Business services. | 2 E. Washington St. | 540/687–6301 or 800/223–1728 | fax 540/687–6053 | www.redfox.com | 13 rooms, 11 suites | $135–$245 | AE, D, DC, MC, V.

MONTEREY

MAP 11, G5

(Nearby towns also listed: Staunton, Warm Springs)

In the foothills of the Alleghany Mountains lies the village of Monterey, the county seat of Highland County. The region is known as "Virginia's Switzerland" for its mountainous terrain. Spring is maple syrup-making season in the region. A Sugar Tour takes visitors to various "sugar camps" throughout the county to see how it's done. The season's highlight is the Highland Maple Festival, which has been called one of the top 20 attractions in the Southeast. The festival draws more than 70,000 people over a two-week period in March.

George Washington National Forest surrounds Monterey on three sides. Part of the forest is the 14,000-acre Highland Wildlife Management Area, traversed by hiking trails and dominated by the 4,200-ft-high Sounding Knob.

Information: Highland County Chamber of Commerce | Box 223, Monterey, 24465 | 540/468–2550 | highcc@cfw.com | www.highlandcounty.org. .

Attractions

Maple Museum. This museum celebrates the Highland County tradition of syrup-making. In a replica of a sugar house, you can see demonstrations of the process. Sugar-making tools and equipment used throughout the years are displayed. | U.S. 220 | 540/468–2550 | Free | Daily.

Highland Wildlife Management Area. (*see* Harrisonburg.) There are three sections to this 14,283-acre wilderness, part of George Washington and Jefferson National Forest: Jack Mountain, Bull Pasture Mountain, and Little Doe Hill. Hiking trails include a 5-mi loop up an old fire road to the 4,400-ft Sounding Knob, a viewful Highland County landmark. | Buck Hill Rd. | 540/468–2550 | fax 540/265–5145 | www.fs.fed.us/gwjnf | Free | Daily.

ON THE CALENDAR

MAR.: *Highland Maple Festival.* Here's your chance to visit sugar camps and watch how sap becomes syrup. There's also an arts-and-crafts show, a Maple Queen contest and ball, dances (including a hoedown), food, and music. | 540/468–2550.

MAY: *McDowell Battlefield Days.* This two-day event at the McDowell Battlefield showcases Civil War life through an encampment of costumed re-enactors, cooking and flintlock demos, historic lectures, and a Civil War church service. | 540/468–2550.

Lodging

Cherry Hill Bed and Breakfast. You can spend the afternoon sipping tea on the large, wrap-around porch of this Victorian home less than ⅛ mi from Rte. 250, overlooking downtown Monterey. Guest rooms and a suite have an eclectic mix of furnishings—some modern, some antique. No room phones, no TVs. | Mill Alley | 540/468–1900 | secrets@cfw.com | 2 rooms, 1 suite | $75–$95 | AE, D, MC, V.

Highland Inn. Built in 1904, this country inn is decorated with antiques to reflect the history of the building and the town. Two porches run the full length of the first and second floors, and there's a parlor. Bar, dining room, complimentary Continental breakfast. No air-conditioning; cable TV; no room phones. Business services. | 610 Main St. | 540/468–2143 or 888/466–4682 reservations | fax 540/468–3143 | highinn@cfw.com | www.highland-inn.com | 17 rooms | $55–$85 | AE, D, MC, V.

MONTROSS

MAP 11, J5

(Nearby town also listed: Tappahannock)

The small village of Montross on the Northern Neck in eastern Virginia (the region between the Potomac and Rappahannock Rivers) is known principally for Stratford Hall, the plantation house where Robert E. Lee was born in 1807. The Lee ancestral estate, whose bold architectural style sets it apart from every other colonial home, is open to the public and is still a working farm. In 1752, a Scotch merchant, William Black, built an estate here called "Mont Ross," named after the Scottish seaport from which he sailed. When the village was finally incorporated in the 1800s, it bore the name Montross. Since early on, the Potomac and Rappahannock rivers have been a source of livelihood for residents, both for fishing and as an avenue for trade and commerce. Westmoreland State Park, west of Montross, fronts the Potomac River and offers swimming, camping, fishing, and boating. George Washington Birthplace National Monument, a 550-acre park with historic buildings, is nearby.

Information: **Northern Neck Tourism Council** | 479 Main St., Warsaw, 22472 | 804/453–6303 or 800/393–6180.

Attractions

George Washington Birthplace National Monument. This 550-acre national park on the Northern Neck peninsula marks the birth site of the first president of the United States. The house in which Mary Ball Washington gave birth to George in 1732 burned on Christmas Day in 1779, but a typical 18th-century Tidewater plantation house was reconstructed here. The grounds include a kitchen, garden, family cemetery, and the Colonial Living Farm. Set on the south side of the Potomac River at Pope's Creek, the park also includes natural areas inhabited by bald eagles and whistling swans. Picnic facilities are available from April through October. | 1732 Popes Creek Rd., Oak Grove | 804/224–1732 | www.nps.gov/gewa | $2 | Daily 9–5.

The livestock and gardens at the **Colonial Living Farm** are tended by methods employed in colonial days. Historical varieties of crops are planted in an effort to re-create the milieu of George Washington's boyhood.

The **Family Burial Ground** contains the graves of 32 members of the Washington family, including Washington's father, grandfather, and great-grandfather.

Memorial House is actually a 20th-century building designed to resemble a typical Tidewater plantation dwelling during George Washington's time. Native clay was used to make the bricks, and the antiques inside were carefully selected to reflect Washington's time. Costumed interpreters lead tours.

The **Visitor Center** screens a 14-minute orientation film and provides a chronological history of the site, beginning with the purchase of the land in 1718 by Augustine Washington. On display are some of the roughly 16,000 artifacts recovered during a 1930s archaeological survey of the property; many items had been scorched by fire. | 1732 Popes Creek Rd., Oak Grove | 804/224–1732 | www.nps.gov/gewa | $2 | Daily 9–5. **Stratford Hall Plantation.** The birthplace of Robert E. Lee, this manor house three mi northeast of Montross, overlooking the Potomac River, was built in the 1730s by Lee's grandfather, Thomas Lee, president of the Council of Virginia and acting governor from 1749 to 1750. The H-shaped building, constructed with brick and timber produced on the site, is considered one of the finest examples of colonial architecture in the country. Four generations of the Lee family lived here, from the 1730s until 1822; period furnishings include some original possessions, such as Robert E. Lee's crib. Outbuildings include an 18th-century kitchen, a coach house, stables, and a school house. Farmers still cultivate 1,600 of the original acres, and their yield, a variety of cereals, is for sale. More than 2 mi of nature trails wind through the property, skirting the mill pond and the river. Lunch is served in a log cabin April through October. | Rte. 214, Stratford | 804/493–8038 | fax 804/493–0333 | www.stratford-hall.org | $7 | Daily 9–5.

Westmoreland State Park. Set on high cliffs above the Potomac River, this 1,295-acre park has a large swimming pool with a bathhouse, a boat-launching ramp, boat rentals, tent and trailer campgrounds, cabins, and a fishing pier. Hiking and biking trails pass through oak and hickory forests and meadows. A visitor center, open in summer, explores plants and wildlife indigenous to the Northern Neck region. The park also has a grocery store, restaurant, and picnic areas. | Rte. 347 | 804/493–8821 | www.state.va.us/~dcr/parks/westmore.htm | $2 | Daily dawn–dusk; visitor center May–Sept.

ON THE CALENDAR

FEB.: *President's Day Celebration.* Colonial music and dancing, plus demonstrations of weaving, blacksmithing, and ox-driving enliven the farm at the George Washington Birthplace National Monument, and hot cider and gingerbread are served. | 804/224–1732.

MAY: *Spring on the Plantation.* Costumed interpreters at the George Washington Birthplace National Monument reenact the lives of the colonial gentry, indentured servants, and slaves. Sheep shearing and ox-driving demonstrations are featured. | 804/224–1732.

JULY: *Fourth of July Celebration at Stratford Hall.* Richard Henry Lee and Francis Lightfoot Lee, both signers of the Declaration of Independence, are honored at this celebration with fireworks and music at Stratford Hall. Light refreshments are served. The hall offers a reduced admission for this event. | 804/493–8038.

Dining

John Minors Pub. Continental. Built in 1683, this pub was destroyed by fire and rebuilt in the 1790s. The original red heart-pine floorboards were salvaged and now lend an Old World rustic charm to the main dining area. For dinner, try the hickory-smoked Magret. Adjacent to the Inn at Montross. | 21 Polk St. | 804/493–0573 | Reservations essential | $10–$25 | AE, MC, V.

Lodging

Days Inn on the Potomac. This two-story motel is by the beach 4 mi from George Washington Birthplace National Monument. Complimentary Continental breakfast. Some microwaves, refrigerators; cable TV. Pool. Baby-sitting, laundry service. Business services, free parking. Pets allowed. | 30 Colonial Ave., Colonial Beach | 804/224–0404 | fax 804/224–0404 | 60 rooms | $67–$87 | AE, D, DC, MC, V.

Inn at Montross. This rustic inn adjacent to the John Minors Pub was destroyed by fire in the mid-1700s and rebuilt with the original timbers in 1790. Five guest rooms on the second floor over the pub are furnished with Colonial reproductions and tasteful watercolors. All rooms have private baths. No room phones. No TVs. | 21 Polk St. | 804/493–0573 | fax 804/493–9118 | www.theinnatmontross.com | 5 rooms | $95–$115 | AE, MC, V.

'Tween Rivers Bed & Breakfast. In this Colonial Revival home dating from the 1920s, antiques fill the upstairs sitting room, the main floor parlor, and other rooms; there's a wraparound porch outside. It is in the heart of town, 4 mi from Stratford Hall and 12 mi from George Washington's birthplace. Complimentary breakfast. No TV in rooms. No kids under 12. No smoking. | 16006 Kings Hwy. | 804/493–0692 | fax 804/493–0692 | innkeeper@tweenrivers.com | www.tweenrivers.com | 3 rooms | $95–$110 | Closed Mar. 1–15 | No credit cards.

NEW MARKET

MAP 11, H4

(Nearby town also listed: Luray)

New Market was originally known as Cross Roads because it sprang up at the intersection of two Indian buffalo trails. The first known settlers arrived from Pennsylvania in 1727 and called their village Massanutten. (It was renamed New Market in 1777.) Their livelihood was derived from farming—flax, grains, livestock, vegetables, and fruit. Until after the Revolutionary War, hemp was a major cash crop. By the mid-18th century, tanneries, lumber mills, iron smelting furnaces, and other small industries were established. The current economy is a mix of manufacturing and agriculture, especially poultry farms.

New Market is famous for a Civil War battle that took place here on May 15, 1864. Reinforcing the Confederate troops in the battle were several hundred very young cadets recruited from the nearby Virginia Military Institute (VMI). The boys were supposed to be a reserve unit, but in the confusion of battle they were placed on the front line, where 5 were killed and 15 wounded. The battlefield is now a historic park maintained by VMI. It hosts Virginia's longest-running Civil War reenactment, held in May.

A number of commercial caverns are close to New Market, including Luray, Shenandoah, and Endless Caverns.

Information: **Shenandoah Valley Travel Association** | Box 1040, New Market, 22844 | 540/740–3132 | amy@svta.org | www.shenandoah.org.

Attractions

Bedrooms of America Museum. American bedrooms from 1650 through 1930 are the focus here, with 11 rooms furnished with period accessories, bed coverings, curtains, and wall coverings. Decorating styles from William and Mary to Art Deco are represented. The museum is in a restored 18th-century building that was temporary headquarters for Gen. Jubal Early during the Civil War. | 9386 Congress St. | 540/740–3512 | $2 | Daily 9–5.

Endless Caverns. Two boys and a dog chasing a rabbit discovered these caverns in 1879. Opened to the public in 1920, they display seemingly endless configurations of stalactites, stalagmites, limestone pendants, and other formations. Visits are on guided tours, enhanced by lighting effects, especially effective in the "Snow Drift" chamber, where the rocks are white and powdery looking. The caverns are off U.S. 11. | 540/740–3993 or 800/544–2283 | fax 540/740–3717 | www.endlesscavern.com | $12 | Mid-Mar.–mid-June and Labor Day–early Nov., daily 9–5; mid-June–Labor Day, daily 9–7; mid-Nov.–mid-Mar., daily 9–4.

New Market Battlefield State Historical Park. This 260-acre battlefield park was the site of the Battle of New Market, which took place on May 15, 1864. Young cadets from the Virginia Military Institute joined the Confederate brigades to defeat Union forces here. At the Hall of Valor, the park's focal point, the courage of those 257 cadets is commemorated in a stained-glass window mosaic. The hall also contains a chronology of the Civil War and a short film that deals with Stonewall Jackson's legendary campaign in the Shenandoah Valley. An 1860 farmhouse that figured in the fighting still stands on the premises; its outbuildings have been reconstructed and equipped to show the workings of a prosperous farm of the period. Maps for self-guided walking tours are available at the visitor center. The battle is reenacted at the park each May. | 8895 Collins Dr./Rte. 305 | 540/740–3101 | www.vmi.edu/museum/nm | Hall of Valor $6, farmhouse free with Hall of Valor admission | Park daily 9–5; farmhouse mid-June–Aug., daily 9–5.

New Market Battlefield Military Museum. This museum stands in the area where the New Market battle began. The front of the building is a replica of Arlington House, Robert E. Lee's home near Washington, D.C. More than 3,000 artifacts from all American wars are displayed, beginning with the Revolution and including Desert Storm (though most deal with the Civil War). A 35-minute film covers aspects of the Civil War. | 9500 Collins Dr./Rte. 305 | 540/740–8065 | fax 540/740–3663 | $7 | Mar. 15–mid-Nov., daily 9–5.

Nickelodeon Antique Mall. Over 50 antiques dealers occupy this 8,000-sq-ft covered space, peddling everything from vintage clothing to furniture. | 9466 Congress St. | 540/740–3424 | Free | Closed Wed.

Shenandoah Caverns. Water dripping through long, narrow cracks in the limestone has created calcite formations at this famous cave; most are wet and shiny and continue to grow to this day, although at an imperceptible rate. A mile-long guided tour takes you past odd, sparkling formations with names like Grotto of the Gods and the Bacon Formation. Picnicking is allowed. | 261 Caverns Rd. | 540/477–3115 | www.shenandoah.org/caverns/ | $12.50 | Mid.-June–Aug., daily 9–6:15; Sept.–mid-Oct. and mid-Apr.–mid-June, daily 9–5:15; mid-Oct.–mid-Apr., daily 9–4:15.

MAY: *Reenactment of the Battle of New Market.* The 1864 Civil War battle is reen-acted at this living-history event at Battlefield State Historic Park. | 540/740–3212 or 540/740–3101.

OCT.: *New Market Heritage Days.* The town salutes its German, Scottish, and Irish her-itage with a parade, craft demonstrations and sales, food, and dance and musical enter-tainment. Children's activities include pony rides. | 540/740–3212. | Free.

Dining

Parkhurst Restaurant. American. The red-brick building that is home to this restaurant has been through fires and at least two incarnations as a hotel, but was re-established as a restaurant in 1978. There's a glass-enclosed porch for year-round views, and the main dining room has knotty pine trim and huge crystal chandeliers. On the dinner menu are grilled quail and chicken, sided with fresh fruit condiments, and veal Oscar, with Alaskan king crab, asparagus, and bearnaise sauce. | U.S. 211 W | 540/743–6009 | Reservations essen-tial | $20–$37 | AE, D, MC, V.

Southern Kitchen. Southern. Visitors and locals have been coming to this local restau-rant since 1955. Lloyd's Virginia Fried Chicken is the house specialty which is seasoned right down to the bone. The peanut soup is a a popular starter. | Rte. 11 S | 540/740–3514 | $5–$8 | D, MC, V.

Lodging

Budget Inn. This one-story motel with exterior corridors is 2 mi from the New Market Bat-tlefield State Historical Park and the Military Museum. Picnic area. Refrigerators, cable TV. Playground. Business services. | 2192 Old Valley Pike | 540/740–3105 or 800/296–6835 | fax 540/740–3108 | 14 rooms | $32–$55 | AE, D, DC, MC, V.

Cross Roads Inn. Little touches of the innkeepers' Austrian heritage accent the Southern and English country furnishings at this family-friendly bed and breakfast. Guest rooms have four-poster canopy beds, some fireplaces, and a blend of antique and contemporary furniture. You can relax, read, or play board games in three large common rooms. Outside there's a kids play area and a goldfish pond. Some rooms have private baths. No room phones or TVs; TV in common area only. | 9222 John Sevier Rd. | 540/740–4157 | fax 540/740–4255 | www.crossroadsinnva.com | 6 rooms | $65–$115 | MC, V.

Quality Inn Shenandoah Valley. Just off I-81 Exit 264, this two-story motel with interior corridors is 2 mi from the New Market Battlefield and 4 mi from the Shenandoah Caverns. Restaurant, room service. In-room data ports, cable TV. Outdoor pool, sauna. Miniature golf. Playground, laundry facilities, laundry service. Business services. | 162 Old Cross Rd./Rte. 211 | 540/740–3141 | fax 540/740–3250 | 101 rooms | $57–$85 | AE, D, DC, MC, V.

Red Shutter Farmhouse. Twenty acres surround this bed and breakfast at the foot of the Massanutten Mountains in the Shenandoah Valley. Built in 1790, the house is decorated in a Colonial English style, with a blend of contemporary and antique furnishings. Some rooms have private baths. No room phones, no TVs. Hiking. Library. | 1797 Farmhouse Ln | 540/740–4281 | fax 540/740–4601 | www.bbhsv.org/redshutter.com | 5 rooms | $65–$78 | MC, V.

Shenvalee. This golf resort is 2 mi from the New Market Battlefield and Endless Caverns, and 4 mi from Luray Caverns. Rooms overlook the golf course or the swimming pool. Restaurant, bar, picnic area. Refrigerators, cable TV. Outdoor pool, wading pool. Driving range, 27-hole golf course, putting green, tennis courts. Business services. | 9660 Fairway Dr. | 540/740–3181 | fax 540/740–8931 | shenvale@shentel.net | www.shenvalee.com | 42 rooms | $66–$69 | AE, DC, MC, V.

NEWPORT NEWS

(Nearby towns also listed: Hampton, Norfolk, Portsmouth, Williamsburg, Yorktown)

Newport News stretches for almost 25 mi along the James River from near Williamsburg to the mouth of Hampton Roads harbor. The city's name first appeared in the Virginia Company of London's records in 1619 as "Newportes Newes," probably in honor of Sir Christopher Newport, who captained the *Susan Constant*, one of the three ships that landed in Jamestown in 1607. Newport News was a small settlement until the late 19th century, when it became the eastern terminus of the Chesapeake and Ohio Railway. The other major catalyst to its growth was Newport News Shipbuilding and Dry Dock Company, established in 1886. Today, it is one of the largest privately owned shipyards in the world and the second-largest employer in Virginia, with about 18,000 workers. It is the only shipyard in the country capable of building nuclear aircraft carriers.

Information: Newport News Tourism Development Office | 2400 Washington Ave., Newport News, 23607 | 757/926–3561 or 888/493–7386 | mclawson@ci.newport-news.va.us | www.visit.newportnews.org. **Newport News Visitor Information Center,** | 13560 Jefferson Ave., Newport News, 23603 | 757/886–7777 | www.newport-news.org.

Attractions

Fort Eustis. On the James River at the northern tip of Newport News, Fort Eustis is home to the U.S. Army Transportation Corps. In colonial times, it was known as Mulberry Island and was the residence of John Rolfe (husband of Indian princess Pocahontas). The army bought it in 1918 in response to World War I and installed a coastal artillery replacement center for Fort Monroe and a balloon observation school. Today, army personnel are trained in rail, marine, and amphibious operations here. The fort is also the site of the U.S. Army Transportation Museum. Self-guided auto tours are available; brochures can be picked up at the public affairs office.

The only facility in the country devoted entirely to the history of military transportation, the **U.S. Army Transportation Museum** has nearly 100 vehicles, including experimental craft, on display. You can see the Flying Crane—the army's largest helicopter—plus dioramas and the world's only captive "flying saucer." | Building 300 [Besson Hall] | 757/878–1182 | Free | Tues.–Sun. 9–4:30.

Historic Hilton Village. Hilton Village was the first federal war-housing project, built between 1918–20 to provide wartime homes for workers at Newport News Shipbuilding. Today, the 500 or so English-cottage-style houses (now privately owned) are on the National Register of Historic Places as architecturally significant. The neighborhood is a mix of residences and antiques shops and other specialty stores. | 757/886–7777 or 888/493–7386 | Free | Daily.

Japanese Tea House in Virginia. This diminutive building on the Christopher Newport University campus was a gift to the people of Virginia from the Japanese firm Asahi Shimbum Newspaper and Nomura Securities. It is an exact replica of one of Japan's landmarks, the 16th-century Enan Tea House in Kyoto. Constructed of cypress, oak, and cedar and held together with doweling, tongue-and-groove fittings, and a few nails, the tea house was originally built for an exhibit at the National Gallery of Art in Washington, D.C. In 1989, it was rebuilt here. Tea ceremonies are held twice a year, in April and October. | 50 Shoe La. | 757/594–7039 | www.cnu.edu | Free | Weekdays 9–4, guided tours by appointment.

The Mariners' Museum. A world history of seagoing vessels and the people who sailed them occupies this museum in 550-acre Mariners' Museum park. Items from the RMS *Titanic* are among the exhibits. Some of the scale-model ships on view are so tiny that you must look at them through magnifying glasses; more than 50 full-size craft are also on display, including a Native American bark canoe, a gondola, a coast guard cutter, and a Chinese sampan. In one gallery, you can watch a boat being constructed; another gallery is devoted to the figureheads from the bows of sailing ships. You can also see nautical gear, a collection of scrimshaw, and photographs and paintings that recount naval history and the story of private-sector seafaring. The museum is the repository for the U.S.S. *Monitor*. Guided tours are given throughout the day. The grounds include a 5-mi walking trail, a picnic area, and a lake where you can fish. | 101 Museum Dr. | 757/596–2222 or 800/581–7245 | fax 757/591–7320 | www.mariner.org | $5 | Daily 10–5.

Mariner's Museum Research Library and Archives. The library's collection of archival material related to maritime history is the largest in North America. Because of the rarity of many of the items, the collection is noncirculating, but the library is open to the public. There are more than 75,000 volumes and 650,000 photographic images, plus maps, charts, manuscripts, and ships' logs. | 101 Museum Dr. | 757/596–2222 or 800/581–7245 | fax 757/591–7320 | www.mariner.org | Free; fee for some searches | Mon.–Sat. 10–5.

Newport News Park. This 8,000-acre municipal park offers camping, fishing, boating, nature and jogging trails, bridle paths, two 18-hole golf courses, archery, and an interpretive center. Picnic shelters and playgrounds are also on the grounds. | 13564 Jefferson Ave. | 757/888–3333 or 800/203–8322 | Free | Daily dawn–dusk.

Peninsula Fine Arts Center. This community-supported arts facility has changing exhibitions of visual arts. Tours are free, and there is a special "Hands On for Kids" program. | 101 Museum Dr. | 757/596–8175 | fax 757/596–0807 | www.pfac-va.org | Free | Mon.–Sat. 10–5, Sun. 1–5.

Virginia Living Museum. Animals indigenous to the Tidewater region live in wild or simulated wild lakefront habitats that allow you to observe their natural behavior. A trail leads to the water's edge, where otters and blue herons can be spotted, then upland past skunks, bald eagles, and bobcats. A 40-ft-tall outdoor aviary re-creates a wetlands habitat. There's also a planetarium and nature shop. | 524 J. Clyde Morris Blvd. | 757/595–1900 | fax 757/599–4897 | www.valivingmuseum.org | Museum $7, planetarium $3, combination ticket $9 | Memorial Day–Labor Day, Mon.–Wed. and Fri.–Sat. 9–6, Thurs. 9–9, Sun. 10–6; Labor Day–Memorial Day, Mon.–Wed. and Fri.–Sat. 9–5, Thurs. 9–5 and 7–9, Sun. noon–5; call for planetarium show times.

Virginia War Museum. This museum traces military history from 1775 to Desert Storm; its collection of more than 60,000 artifacts includes a 10- by 10-ft section of the Berlin Wall, a Civil War blockade-runner's uniform, weapons, wartime posters, and photographs. Exhibits on African Americans and women in the military also are featured. A Vietnam War memorial is on the Huntington Park grounds. | 9285 Warwick Blvd. | 757/247–8523 | fax 757/247–8627 | www.warmuseum.org | $2 | Mon.–Sat. 9–5, Sun. 1–5.

ON THE CALENDAR

JAN.: *Wildlife Arts Festival.* Artists from all over the East Coast come to the Deer Park Elementary School, 11541 Jefferson Ave, to exhibit paintings, sculpture, carvings, and photography, all with a wildlife theme. | 757/595–1900.

MAY–JUNE: *Children's Festival of Friends.* Kids love this event at Newport News Park with its pony rides and animal displays, crafts activities, clowns and rides, entertainment and games. | 757/926–8451.

OCT.: *Fall Festival.* About 200 artisans display their wares and demonstrate traditional crafts and trades at Newport News Park. Crafts competitions, children's activities, live entertainment, and food vendors are also included. | 757/926–8451.

Dining

Al Fresco. Italian. Distressed, handpainted walls and a mural of an Italian backyard overlooking the water set the scene here for pollo francese, calamari Fra Diavolo, vitello alla pizzaiola, and other classics. | 11710 Jefferson Ave. | 757/873–0644 | Closed Sun. | $8–$14 | AE, D, MC, V.

Das Waldcafe. German. Outside, it's a German-style building with *Fachwerk* beams on the facade. Inside, it's a friendly, homey eatery with fresh flowers on each table. Gulasch (diced beef with mushrooms), wiener schnitzel (breaded veal steak), and jager schnitzel (veal steak with mushroom sauce) are popular. | 12529 Warwick Blvd. | 757/930–1781 | Closed Mon. No lunch Sat. | $9.25–$14.95 | AE, DC, MC, V.

Herman's Harbor House. Seafood. A wonderful collection of turn-of-the-century photos of nautical subjects fills this waterfront restaurant. Check out the working sailboat models before tucking into your crab cakes, fried oysters, or soft-shell crab. Steak is also available, and there's outdoor dining on a deck overlooking the water. Kids' menu. Sun. brunch. | 663 Deep Creek Rd. | 757/930–1000 | Sat. lunch summers only | $9.95–$19.95 | AE, D, MC, V.

Lodging

Boxwood Inn. Built in 1896 in historic Lee Hall Village, this manor was a hotel for returning veterans during both World Wars. There's a large display of military uniforms, dress forms, books, and photographs that were found in the house's attic during a recent renovation. The popular Blue Willow Tea Room is on the lower floor and serves coffee, drinks, and desserts in the afternoons. No room phones, no TVs. | 10 Elmhurst St. | 757/888–8854 | 5 rooms | $75–$125 | MC, V.

Comfort Inn. This property is next to Patrick Henry Mall. Guest privileges at Bally Total Fitness Club, across the street, are available. Complimentary Continental breakfast, room service. In-room data ports, some microwaves, some refrigerators, cable TV. Pool. Laundry facilities. Business services. Airport shuttle. Free parking. Pets allowed. | 12330 Jefferson Ave. | 757/249–0200 | fax 757/249–4736 | www.comfortinn.com | 124 rooms | $94–$99 | AE, D, DC, MC, V.

Days Inn. This motel is 5 mi from Newport News Park, 6 mi from the Mariners Museum, and 8 mi from Busch Gardens in Williamsburg. Restaurant, picnic area, complimentary Continental breakfast. In-room data ports, some microwaves, some refrigerators, cable TV. Outdoor pool. Playground. Laundry services. Business services. Free parking. Pets allowed (fee). | 14747 Warwick Blvd. | 757/874–0201 | fax 757/874–0201 | 112 rooms | $65 | AE, D, DC, MC, V.

Hampton Inn and Suites. Across from Patrick Henry Mall, this hostelry is also 3 mi from the Virginia Living Museum, 4 mi from the Mariners' Museum, and 7 mi from the Virginia War Museum. Picnic area, complimentary Continental breakfast room service. In-room data ports, some kitchenettes, refrigerators, cable TV. Pool. Exercise equipment. Baby-sitting. Laundry services. Business services. Airport shuttle. | 12251 Jefferson Ave. | 757/249–0001 | fax 757/249–3911 | www.hampton-inn.com | 120 rooms, 30 suites | $84–$99, $114–$139 suites | AE, D, MC, V.

Omni Newport News Hotel. Quick access off I–64 at Exit 258A is a plus, and rooms are large, with armoires, writing desk, a sofa, and a table. Restaurant, bar with entertainment. In-room data ports, cable TV. Indoor pool. Hot tub, sauna. Exercise equipment. Laundry service. Business services. Free parking. | 1000 Omni Blvd. | 757/873–6664 | fax 757/873–1732 | www.omnihotels.com | 183 rooms, 4 suites | $129–$139, $325 suites | AE, D, DC, MC, V.

NORFOLK

MAP 11, K7

(Nearby towns also listed: Cape Charles, Chesapeake, Hampton, Newport News, Portsmouth, Virginia Beach)

South of Hampton Roads, Norfolk is linked to the peninsula by the Hampton Roads Bridge-Tunnel. The region's oldest city and the second largest in Virginia, Norfolk was established in 1680. During the Revolutionary War, the British bombarded Norfolk and the city burned to the ground; only St. Paul's Episcopal Church survived, and it remains in use today.

The city is dominated by the Norfolk Naval Base, the largest Navy installation in the world. It is also the cultural center of Hampton Roads, home base for the Virginia Symphony, Virginia Stage Company, Virginia Opera, and many other smaller arts groups. The Chrysler Museum of Art, regarded as one of country's premier art museums, is here.

The seaport's once shabby waterfront has undergone extensive redevelopment and now features Waterside Festival Marketplace, a conglomeration of shops, restaurants, and entertainment. Nauticus, the National Maritime Center, is one of the area's most popular attractions. Norfolk plays host to a variety of festivals; one of the most spectacular is June's Harborfest, which celebrates the city's maritime heritage with boat races, seafood, and entertainment by nationally known performers.

Information: **Norfolk Convention and Visitors Bureau** | 232 E. Main St., Norfolk, 23510 | 757/664–6620 or 800/368–3097 | www.norfolkcvb.com.

Attractions

Antique Alley. Starting at the intersection of Granby and 21st Street, you can pick a direction and work your way through one of the country's biggest enclaves of antique dealers catering to every budget and taste. | Corner of Granby and 21st St. | Free.

Cannonball Trail. This guide-yourself trail connects historic sites and features in downtown Norfolk, beginning at the Norfolk Visitor Information Center. Allow a minimum of 2 hours to complete the trail. | 232 E. Main St. | 757/664–6620 | Free.

The Chrysler Museum of Art. One of America's major art museums, the Chrysler has a diverse collection of more than 30,000 objects that span more than 4,000 years. You will find works by Rubens, Gainsborough, Renoir, Picasso, Monet, and Pollock, as well as art from African, Egyptian, pre-Columbian, and Asian cultures. Decorative arts include English porcelain and the Tiffany glass collection is renowned. Work by both 19th-century pioneers and contemporary artists hang in the photography gallery, and there are regularly scheduled lectures, films, and concerts. There's a restaurant. | 245 W. Olney Rd. | 757/664–6200 | fax 757/664–6201 | www.chrysler.org | $7 | Tues.–Sat. 10–5, Sun. 1–5.

Douglas MacArthur Memorial. This is the burial place of the controversial war hero General Douglas MacArthur, who designated Norfolk as the site for a monument to himself because it was his mother's birthplace. The mausoleum is in the rotunda of the old City Hall; 11 adjoining galleries house mementos of MacArthur's career, including his signature corncob pipe and Japanese instruments of surrender that concluded World War II. A 25-minute biographical film is screened continuously. | MacArthur Sq | 757/441–2965 | fax 757/441–5389 | www.whro.org | Donations accepted | Mon.–Sat. 10–5, Sun. 11–5.

Harbor Park. This ballpark is home to the Norfolk Tides, the AAA affiliate of the New York Mets. | 150 Park Ave. | 757/622–2222 | www.norfolktides.com | Varies by event.

Hermitage Foundation Museum. The largest privately owned collection of Asian art in the United States is inside this English Tudor-style house, built by the Sloanes, a textile tycoon-family at the turn of the 20th century. Ivory and jade carvings, ancient bronzes, and a 1,400-year-old marble Buddha from China are a few of the prize objects on display. There's also a decorative arts collection with Tiffany glass, Persian rugs, and furniture from the Middle East, India, Europe, and America. You can picnic on the surrounding 12 acres, which border the Lafayette River. | 7637 N. Shore Rd. | 757/423–2052 | fax 757/423–1604 | $4 | Mon.–Sat. 10–5, Sun. 1–5.

Hunter House Victorian Museum. This Victorian in Norfolk's historic Freemason neighborhood was the home of James Wilson Hunter, a merchant and banker, and it's filled with the family's Victorian furnishings. A collection of early 20th-century medical equipment also is featured. | 240 W. Freemason St. | 757/623–9814 | $3 | Apr.–Dec., Wed.–Sat. 10–3:30, Sun. 12:30–3:30, tours every ½ hr.

MacArthur Centre Mall. Nordstrom and Dillard's department stores anchor this three-level indoor mall, opened in early 1999, and there are more than 140 specialty shops. There are also 18 theaters, restaurants, a food court, and a visitor center. | City Hall Ave. | 757/622–0500 or 800/368–3097 | fax 757/627–6624 | www.shopmacarthurmall.com | Daily 10–9.

Moses Myers House. Built in 1792 by its namesake, this Federal-style redbrick structure was the home of Norfolk's first Jewish resident. A transplanted New Yorker, Myers made his fortune in Norfolk in shipping, then served as a diplomat and customs house officer. His grandson married James Madison's grandniece, his great-grandson served as mayor, and the family kept the house for five generations. The original furnishings, which include artwork by Gilbert Stuart and Thomas Sully, reflect the lifestyle and religious practices of a late-18th-century Jewish merchant family. | 401 E. Freemason St. | 757/333–6283. | www.chrysler.org | Combination ticket with Willoughby-Baylor House $5 | Wed.–Sat. 10–5, Sun. 1–5.

Nauticus, The National Maritime Center. With more than 70 maritime exhibits on three "decks" this interactive complex on Norfolk's waterfront is one of the area's busiest attractions. Exhibits cover topics ranging from ancient shipbuilding to navigation, sonar submarine hunts, and reef diving. You can also tour visiting ships docked outside at the Nauticus International Pier, watch a naval battle simulation in the AEGIS Theatre, and experience a virtual-reality submersible experience. | 1 Waterside Dr. | 757/664–1000 or 800/664–1080 | fax 757/664–1025 | www.nauticus.org | $7.50 | Memorial Day–Labor Day, daily 10–7; Labor Day–Memorial Day, Tues.–Sun. 10–5.

Housed within Nauticus, **Hampton Roads Naval Museum** contains paintings, documents, and memorabilia related to the area's naval history since the American Revolution. | 757/322–2987 | Free | Mon. 9–4, Tues.–Sun. 10–5.

Norfolk Botanical Garden. Azaleas, rhododendrons, and camellias fill this 155-acre garden. Its landscaped Japanese garden is planted with trees native to that country; a fragrance garden for the blind includes identification labels in Braille. The Tropical Pavilion houses more than 100 varieties of exotic plants. Throughout are marble statues of famous artists, carved in the late 19th century by Moses Ezekiel. From mid-March to October, boats and trams carry visitors along routes to view seasonal plants and flowers, including 4,000 varieties of roses on 3½ acres. Year-round, you can stroll 12 mi of paths. There's also a café. | 6700 Azalea Garden Rd. | 757/441–5830 | fax 757/853–8294 | www.virginiagarden.org | Garden $4, boat and tram tours $2.50 | Apr. 15–Oct. 15, daily 9–7; Oct. 15–Apr. 15, daily 9–5.

Norfolk Naval Base and Norfolk Naval Air Station. On the northern edge of the city, the naval base is home to more than 100 ships of the Atlantic Fleet. Among them is the U.S.S. *Theodore Roosevelt*, a nuclear-powered aircraft carrier with a crew of 6,300, said to be one of the largest warships in the world. You can drive into the base during daylight hours as long as you avoid the restricted areas indicated by signs. Guided 45-minute bus tours operate year-round, departing from the Tidewater Regional Transit kiosk at Waterside Festival Hall (on the waterfront) and from the Naval Base tour office (N of Gate 5 at 9079 Hampton Blvd). Designated ships are open to visitors Saturday and Sunday afternoons; on national holidays, you can see aircraft carriers. | 9079 Hampton Blvd. and I–564 | 757/444–7955 or 757/444–1577 | fax 757/445–0438 | www.pinn.net | Free; guided bus tour $5 | Daily 8–4; tour schedule varies seasonally, call ahead.

St. Paul's Episcopal Church. Constructed in 1739, St. Paul's was Norfolk's only building to survive the bombardment and conflagration of New Year's Day 1776; a cannonball fired by the British fleet remains embedded in the south wall. An earlier church was built on this site in 1641, and the churchyard contains graves dating from the 17th century. | 201 St. Paul's Blvd. | 757/627–4353 | Donations accepted | Tues.–Fri. 10–4 and by appointment.

The Waterside Festival Marketplace. This retail development overlooking the Elizabeth River is a mix of some 120 specialty shops, restaurants, a food court, kiosks, and entertainment venues. Musical performances and changing art exhibitions occupy the public spaces throughout the year. The Tidewater Regional Transit (TRT) maintains an information kiosk and is the launching point for various tours of the city, by boat or trolley. A pedestrian ferry to the Naval Shipyard Museum in Portsmouth departs from here. | 333 Waterside Dr. | 757/627–3300 | fax 757/627–3981 | Free | Memorial Day–Labor Day, Mon.–Sat. 10–10, Sun. noon–8; Labor Day–Memorial Day, Mon.–Sat. 10–9, Sun. noon–6; restaurants and entertainment centers remain open later.

Town Point Park. On the waterfront between Waterside Festival Marketplace and Nauticus, the 7-acre park is the site of many outdoor festivals and concerts, including Harborfest in spring. | 757/441–2345 performance information | Free | Daily.

Virginia Zoological Park. More than 100 species of animals live on the 55 acres here, from rhinos, reptiles, and ostriches to domesticated animals such as sheep. With the assistance of tour guides, kids are allowed to handle some of the creatures. Elephant demonstrations are scheduled regularly in summer. Adjoining the zoo is Lafayette Park, with picnic shelters and facilities for tennis, basketball, football, and softball. | 3500 Granby St. | 757/441–2706 recording or 757/441–5227 | fax 757/441–5408 | www.virginiazoo.org | $3.50 | Daily 10–5.

Willoughby-Baylor House. Built in 1794 by Capt. William Willoughby, a member of Norfolk's wealthy merchant class, this brick town house combines Federal and Georgian architectural styles. Authentic 18th-century pieces furnish the rooms; although not original to the home, the antiques follow an inventory made in 1800 by the owner. The herb-and-flower garden also is in keeping with the era. | 601 E. Freemason St. | 757/333–6283 | Combination ticket with Moses Myers House $5 | Wed.–Sat. 10–5, Sun. 1–5.

SIGHTSEEING TOURS/TOUR COMPANIES

American Rover. This three-masted topsail schooner is modeled after the Chesapeake Bay cargo schooners of the past century. Two- and three-hour narrated cruises travel through the harbor and along the Elizabeth River. | Waterside Marina | 757/627–7245 | fax 757/627–6626 | www.americanrover.com | $14–$20 | Apr.–Oct. daily; call for departure times.

Carrie B. Harbor Tours. Tour Norfolk's naval shipyards and operating base, plus historic Fort Norfolk, on a reproduction of a Mississippi-style paddle wheeler with an open-air top deck. Tours range from 1½ to 2½ hours. | Waterside Marina | 757/393–4735 | $12–$14 | Apr.–Oct. daily; call for departure times.

Spirit of Norfolk. This outfit operates dinner-dance cruises that combine sightseeing with live music and entertainment. Lunch and brunch cruises also are available. | Town Point Park, next to Waterside | 757/627–7771 | www.spiritofnorfolk.com | $20.95–$51.95 | Year-round daily; call for departure times.

ON THE CALENDAR

APR.: ***International Azalea Festival.*** One of the city's biggest events, the festival includes a parade, an air show, a concert by a major recording artist, ship visits, the coronation of Queen Azalea and her court (chosen from a field of contestants from NATO countries), a fashion show, a dinner, and a ball. | Downtown and Norfolk Botanical Garden, 6700 Azalea Garden Rd. | 757/445–6647, ext. 1.

MAY: ***Virginia Waterfront International Arts Festival.*** This eight-day festival showcases renowned artists in classical, jazz, and world music; dance; and musical theater. The Virginia International Tattoo, one of the events, includes precision drill teams, massed pipes and drums, gymnasts, folk dancers, and Dixieland jazz and swing groups. | Box office: 232 E. Main St. | 757/664–6492.

JUNE–AUG: *Bayou Boogaloo and Cajun Food Festival.* Kick back at this event with armadillo races, dancing, live Cajun and zydeco music, and lots of food: seafood gumbo, steamed crawfish, and other Cajun fare. It's in Town Point Park. | 757/441–2345.

JUNE: *Harborfest.* This major festival pays homage to Norfolk's nautical heritage with a Parade of Sail, water activities on the Elizabeth River, nautical exhibits, ship tours, and steel drum music and seafood. | 757/441–2345.

SEPT.–APR.: *Virginia Stage Company.* This professional regional theater company stages six major productions every season, in addition to smaller "second stage" shows and children's theater at the Wells Theater (110 Tazewell St.). | 757/627–1234.

SEPT.–JUNE: *Virginia Symphony.* The symphony gives more than 100 concerts a year at Chrysler Hall. In addition to a classical series, there are pops, dance, and special family concerts. Some of the concerts are held outdoors; there are occasional guest artists. | 415 St. Paul's Blvd. | 757/892–6366.

OCT.: *Virginia Children's Festival.* Kid-friendly activities at this festival, held in Town Point Park on Wayside Drive, include hands-on workshops and educational displays, costumed characters, games, arts and crafts, and local and regional children's entertainers. | 757/441–2345.

OCT.–MAY: *Virginia Opera.* This opera company typically stages five major operas, starring national and international performers, a season at Stanley L. Harrison Opera House (160 Virginia Beach Blvd.). | 757/623–1223 | www.vaopera.org.

Dining

Doumar's. American. Travel back to the 1950s at this recreated drive-in with car-hop service and seating inside. On display is the original ice cream cone–making machine used by Abe Doumar, who invented the ice cream cone in 1904. Known for sandwiches, homemade ice cream, limeade, and pork barbecue. Hand-rolled cones. | 1919 Monticello Ave. | 757/627–4163 | Breakfast also available. Closed Sun. | $1–$4 | No credit cards.

Freemason Abbey. Contemporary. Built as a church in 1873, the restaurant retains the original high ceilings, woodwork, wood tresses, and bell tower. There's also stained glass in the bar. Lobster draws the crowds; other items include prime rib and seafood. Kids' menu. Sun. brunch. | 209 W. Freemason St. | 757/622–3966 | $22–$24 | AE, D, DC, MC, V.

Kelley's. American. The patio is heated at this sports bar/pub so you can eat outdoors during the winter and catch the latest game on TV. The large cheeseburger is a favorite menu item as are hearty soups like clam chowder and broccoli-with-cheese. | 1408 Colley Ave. | 757/623–3216 | $6–$10 | AE, D, MC, V.

La Galleria. Italian. High ceilings, Italian urns, and Corinthian columns highlight this dining room. Menu favorites are Pollo di Tuscani (chicken with sun dried tomatoes, artichoke hearts, and garlic) and Cartoccio (shellfish and calamari with white wine, tomato sauce, and spaghetti, baked together in parchment). Vegetarian choices include Linguine al Mondo (linguine with fresh sliced string beans, roasted red peppers, garlic, capers, and sauced with marinara). There are also wood-fired pizzas and beef and veal dishes. Live music Mon.–Sat. | 120 College Pl. | 757/623–3939 | Closed Sun. | $10.95–$30 | AE, DC, MC, V.

Magnolia Steak. Steak. The main dining room of this turn-of-the-century storefront building is painted with magnolias. Try the house special rib-eye steak, fresh flounder or catfish, or the Santa Fe chicken. Open-air dining. | 749 W. Princess Anne Rd. | 757/625–0400 | No lunch weekends | $5.95–$20 | AE, MC, V.

The Max. American. Stop in for burgers, pizza, sandwiches, or seafood and take in the eclectic setting. Neon signs glow in electric colors, and walls are painted purple, pink, and mauve. Open-air dining on patio. Kids' menu. Sun. brunch. | 1421 Colley Ave. | 757/625–0259 | $8.99–$16.99 | D, MC, V.

Monastery. Eastern European. Dine by candlelight in this red and burgundy dining room while wait staff serve roast duck, schnitzel, and goulash. | 443 Granby St. | 757/625–8193 | Reservations essential | Closed Mon. No lunch May–Labor Day | $25–$34 | AE, D, DC, MC, V.

Ship's Cabin. Seafood. Gaze over the Chesapeake bayfront from the outside deck. Inside, the restaurant looks like a ship, with pictures of the sea, a rowboat caught in the rafters, and wooden fish hanging from the ceiling. In the winter, warm up by one of the fireplaces. Try the grilled tuna with bacon and balsamic reduction or the grilled salmon with lemon vinaigrette. Pasta, steak, and chicken are also available. Kids' menu. | 4110 E. Ocean View Ave. | 757/362-2526 | www.shipscabin.com. | No lunch | $24–$28 | AE, D, DC, MC, V.

Todd Jurich's Bistro! Continental. The seasonal menu emphasizes fresh, regional flavors—seafood from the Eastern Shore and Outer Banks and locally grown, organic produce—often with Asian influence. The signature dish is seared native yellowfin tuna with wasabi mashed potatoes. Also popular is steak with garlic mashed potatoes. Check the chalkboard for daily specials, which might include coconut tiger prawns and a variety of crab preparations. The work of local artists hangs on the earth-toned walls. | 210 W. York St. | 757/622-3210 | www.toddjurichsbistro.com. | Reservations essential | No lunch weekends | $16–$32 | AE, D, DC, MC, V.

Uncle Louie's. American. This is more a restaurant complex than restaurant; there are three dining areas ranging from casual to quietly elegant, a deli where you can stock up on cheese, meat, fish, and salads to go. If you stay, go for the Angus beef or the fresh fish, or try the scallops over spinach fettucini with red pepper cream sauce. Live music most weekends. Kids' menu. | 132 E. Little Creek Rd. | 757/480-1225 | www.unclelouies.com | Breakfast also available | $7–$20 | AE, D, DC, MC, V.

Lodging

Best Western Center Inn. Just off I-264, this hotel is within 10 mi of Norfolk attractions. Restaurant, bar, picnic area, complimentary Continental breakfast, room service. In-room data ports, some microwaves, refrigerators, cable TV. Indoor pool, outdoor pool. Hot tub, sauna. Exercise equipment. Laundry service. Business services. Airport shuttle. Free parking. | 235 N. Military Hwy. | 757/461-6600 | fax 757/466-9093 | www.bestwestern.com | 152 rooms | $59–$99 | AE, DC, MC, V.

Clarion–James Madison Hotel. Persian carpets, oak paneling and mirrors give this 1902 hotel the air of a turn-of-the-century hunt club. The lobby has soft light and elegant furnishings. Rooms are snug, with antique reproduction quilts on the beds, and a blend of traditional and contemporary furniture. Antique Alley is 1 mi from the hotel. Restaurant, bar, room service. In-room data ports, some refrigerators, cable TV. Exercise equipment. Video games, laundry facilities, laundry service. Business services. Parking (fee). Pets allowed. | 345 Granby St. | 757/622-6682 | fax 757/623-5949 | www.clarionhotel.com/hotelva332 | 124 rooms | $89–$119 | AE, D, DC, MC, V.

Comfort Inn Norfolk Naval Station. This motel is 1 mi from the Naval Station and within 8 mi of the city's points of interest. Complimentary Continental breakfast. In-room data ports, some microwaves, refrigerators, cable TV. Indoor pool. Hot tub. Laundry facilities, laundry service. Business services. | 8051 Hampton Blvd. | 757/451-0000 | fax 757/451-8394 | www.comfortinn.com | 120 rooms | $94–$99 | AE, D, DC, MC, V.

Doubletree Club. The Military Circle Mall is next door to this lodging, which is also within 8 mi of most of Norfolk's attractions. Restaurant, bar. In-room data ports, cable TV. Pool. Exercise equipment. Business services. Airport shuttle. | 880 N. Military Hwy. | 757/461-9192 | fax 757/461-8290 | www.doubletreehotels.com | 208 rooms | $119–$124 | AE, D, DC, MC, V.

Econo Lodge Oceanview. The ocean beach, complete with fishing pier, is across the street. Complimentary Continental breakfast. Some kitchenettes, refrigerators, cable TV. Exercise equipment. Laundry facilities. Business services. Pets allowed. | 9601 4th View St. | 757/480-9611 | fax 757/480-1307 | www.choicehotels.com | 71 rooms | $70–$80 | AE, D, DC, MC, V.

Hampton Inn Norfolk–Military Hwy. A mile from Military Circle Mall, Lake Wright public golf course, and free tennis courts. Complimentary Continental breakfast. In-room data ports, cable TV. Pool. Laundry service. Business services. Airport shuttle. Free parking. |

1450 N. Military Hwy. | 757/466–7474 | fax 757/466–0117 | www.hampton-inn.com | 130 rooms | $75–$94 | AE, D, DC, MC, V.

Hilton Norfolk Airport. Centrally located, the hotel has a unique architectural design. Restaurant, bars with entertainment, room service. In-room data ports, minibars, some in-room hot tubs, cable TV. | 1500 N. Military Hwy. | 757/466–8000 | fax 757/466–8802 | www.hilton.com | 250 rooms | $79–$139 | AE, D, DC, MC, V.

Holiday Sands. This beachfront hotel on Chesapeake Bay has one of the largest sun decks in the area. Complimentary Continental breakfast. In-room data ports, some kitchenettes, microwaves, refrigerators, cable TV. Outdoor pool. Exercise equipment. Laundry facilities. Business services. Airport shuttle. Free parking. | 1330 E. Ocean View Ave. | 757/583–2621 or 800/525–5156 | fax 757/587–7540 | www.holidaysands.com | 95 rooms | $65–$110 | AE, DC, MC, V.

Marriott Norfolk Waterside. The hotel is 2 blocks from Waterside Festival Marketplace and Nauticus. Some rooms have river views. Restaurant, bar, room service. In-room data ports, some refrigerators, cable TV. Indoor pool. Hot tub, sauna. Health club. Laundry facilities, laundry services. Business services. Parking (fee). Pets allowed (fee). | 235 E. Main St. | 757/627–4200 | fax 757/628–6466 | www.marriott.com | 404 rooms | $139–$179 | AE, D, DC, MC, V.

Page House Inn. This Georgian revival-style brick mansion was carefully transformed into a bed-and-breakfast with beautiful turn-of-the-20th-century antiques, china, and fine art. A sitting room/library and a rooftop patio are available for guest use, as is the stocked guest refrigerator. Rooms have four-poster beds with down comforters, some have soaking or whirlpool tubs. Suites also have fireplaces. The inn is in a residential area, next door to the Chrysler Museum. The waterside area is less than a mile away. Complimentary breakfast, room service. In-room data ports, some refrigerators, some in-room hot tubs, cable TV. Laundry service. Business services. Free parking. Pets allowed (fee). No kids under 12. No smoking. | 323 Fairfax Ave. | 757/625–5033 or 800/599–7659 | fax 757/623–9451 | innkeeper@ pagehouseinn.com | www.pagehouseinn.com | 7 rooms, 3 suites | $122–$147, $152–$200 suites, $200–$300 yacht | AE, MC, V.

Quality Inn Lake Wright Resort. This lodge is 3mi from the Botanical Gardens, 4 mi from Oceanview Beach, and 6 mi from Waterside, Nauticus, and other downtown waterfront sites. Restaurant, bar, complimentary breakfast. In-room data ports, refrigerators, cable TV. Outdoor pool. Barbershop, beauty salon. Driving range, 18-hole golf course, putting green. Laundry facilities. Business services. Airport shuttle. Free parking. Pets allowed (fee). | 6280 Northampton Blvd. | 757/461–6251 | fax 757/461–5925 | www.lakewrighthotel.com | 149 rooms, 4 suites | $89–$99, $125–$250 suites | AE, D, DC, MC, V.

Radisson Hotel Norfolk. This 12-story, modern lodging has a futuristic exterior with a circular drive. Guest rooms have lots of blonde wood and large windows. Restaurant, bar. Cable TV, in-room VCRs. Pool. Beauty salon. Gym. Pets allowed. | 700 Monticello Ave. | 757/627–5555 | fax 757/627–5921 | www.radisson.com | 339 rooms | $119–$139 | AE, D, DC, MC, V.

Rodeway Inn Little Creek. This white stucco motor inn is 5 mi east of downtown Norfolk and has a sloping, grey-shingled roof and lots of room-front parking. Cable TV. Business services. | 7969 Shore Dr. | 757/588–3600 or 800/228–8000 | fax 757/588–3700 | www.choice-hotels.com | 48 rooms | $39–$109 | AE, D, MC, V.

Sheraton Norfolk Waterside Hotel. Next to Waterside Marketplace, many rooms have a view of the working harbor on the Elizabeth River, while others have a view of the Norfolk skyline. Sleigh beds offer a romantic touch. Club-level rooms also have a private lounge with concierge services and complimentary breakfast and evening hors d'oeuvres. Restaurant, bars with entertainment, room service. In-room data ports, some refrigerators, cable TV. Outdoor pool. Dock. Business services. Airport shuttle. | 777 Waterside Dr. | 757/622–6664 | fax 757/625–8271 | www.sheraton.com | 445 rooms | $155–$165 | AE, D, DC, MC, V.

ORANGE

MAP 11, H5

(Nearby towns also listed: Charlottesville, Culpeper, Fredericksburg)

Orange County, in the rolling Piedmont region of central Virginia, is a fertile agricultural area equally rich in history. An example of Jeffersonian church architecture can be seen in the town of Orange, the county seat, which was settled in 1749. Nearby, several wineries offer tours and tastings.

Among the many estates dotting the countryside is Montpelier, the lifelong home of James Madison and his wife, Dolley. Now a house-museum with extensive grounds, Montpelier hosts popular annual events, from steeplechase races to the Fall Fiber Festival and Sheep Dog Trials, held in October.

The region also bears reminders of the Civil War. The Exchange Hotel, strategically located on the Virginia Central Railway, became a Confederate military hospital; it now houses a Civil War museum. The Wilderness Battlefield, in the Spotsylvania National Military Park at the eastern end of the county, was the scene of a May 1864 fight that left 26,000 soldiers dead and is now an historic park.

Information: Orange County Visitors Bureau | Box 133, 122 E. Main St., Orange 22960 | 540/672-1653. | www.visitocva.com.

Attractions

Barboursville Vineyards and Historic Ruins. Virginia's largest estate-bottled winery (and one of its top award winners) surrounds the ruins of a mansion Thomas Jefferson designed for his friend Gov. James Barbour. The house, built in 1814, was gutted by fire on Christmas Day in 1884, but the brick shell still offers a glimpse of Jeffersonian architecture. The 830-acre winery produces 21 wines, including Chardonnay, Barbera, and Pinot Grigio. You can picnic on the grounds and, during the first three weeks of August, catch an outdoor performance of "Shakespeare at the Ruins." | 17655 Winery Rd. | 540/832-3824 | fax 540/832-7572 | www.barboursvillewine.com | Tours free, tastings $3 | Tastings Mon.-Sat. 10-5, Sun. 11-5; tours weekends 12-4.

Exchange Hotel and Civil War Museum. During the Civil War, this Greek Revival hotel became a Confederate receiving hospital for wounded and dying soldiers, brought in by the trainload from nearby battlefields to the railroad platform in front of the hotel. An estimated 70,000 soldiers were treated here between 1862 and 1865. One gallery in the museum is a re-creation of a military surgery room; another is a hospital ward. In addition to weapons, uniforms, and personal effects of both Union and Confederate soldiers, the museum displays the often crude medical equipment used for amputations, tooth extractions, and bloodletting. | 400 S. Main St., Gordonsville | 540/832-2944 | www.gemlink.com/~exchange-hotel/home.htm | $4 | Mar. 15-May and Sept.-Dec., Tues.-Sat. 10-4; June-Aug., Tues.-Sat. 10-4, Sun. 1-4.

James Madison Museum. James Madison's Campeachy chair, an 18th-century piece made for him by his friend Thomas Jefferson, is featured in this museum, which celebrates the fourth U.S. president. Other artifacts include furnishings from his nearby home, Montpelier; presidential correspondence; and china and glassware recovered from the White House before the British torched it during the War of 1812. Another permanent exhibit details the history of Orange. | 129 Caroline St. | 540/672-1776 | fax 540/672-0231 | www.james-madisonmuseum.org | $4 | Mar.-Nov., weekdays 9-4, Sat. 10-4, Sun. 1-4; Dec.-Feb., weekdays 9-4.

Montpelier. Montpelier was home to James Madison's family for three generations, from 1723, when President Madison's grandfather was first deeded the land, to 1844, when the estate was sold. The property changed hands six times before William duPont bought it in 1900. Today, the estate includes 2,700 acres, more than 130 buildings, extensive gardens and forests, and a steeplechase course. Because the duPonts enlarged and redecorated Montpelier, the house only vaguely resembles the way it was in Madison's time; historical analysis and restoration efforts are ongoing. The visitor center has an exhibit and video detailing the life and times of James and Dolley Madison. From there, you are given headphones for an audio tour around the property, which provides descriptions of historical and natural features. The main house exhibit does not attempt to re-create Madison's home but uses the mostly empty rooms as evocative spaces to weave a story of plantation life. The landscape walking tour includes a stop at the family cemetery where Madison and his wife are buried. | 11407 Constitution Hwy. | 540/672–2728 or 540/672–0003 | fax 540/672–0411 | www.montpelier.org | $7.50 | Apr.–Nov., daily 10–4; Dec.–Mar., daily 11–3.

St. Thomas's Episcopal Church. This 1833 church is believed to be the lone surviving example of Jeffersonian church architecture. It was modeled after Charlottesville's demolished Christ Church, which Thomas Jefferson designed. During the Civil War, the building served as a hospital following four different battles; Robert E. Lee worshiped here during the winter of 1863–64. | 119 Caroline St. | 540/672–3761 | Donations accepted | Daily, tours by appointment.

ON THE CALENDAR
AUG.: *Shakespeare in the Ruins.* The Four County Players stage Shakespeare dramas outdoors in the evenings at the Barboursville Ruins about 15 mi from town; wine and picnic suppers are available. | Rte. 777, Barboursville | 540/832–5355.
OCT.: *Fall Fiber Festival and Sheep Dog Trials.* Spinning, weaving, and shearing are demonstrated at this event at Montpelier Station in Montpelier around 10 mi south of town, and vendors display fiber crafts and the fiber-producing animals—sheep, llamas, alpacas, cashmere goats, angora rabbits. The sheep dog trials are held on both days of the festival. There are children's programs, too. | Rte. 20, Montpelier | 540/672–2935 | www.fallfiberfestival.org.

Dining
Clark's Tavern. Southern. This rustic casual tavern specializes in modern versions of Southern classics. Maple-grilled breast of duck, pan-seared salmon wrapped in thin slices of country ham, or Carolina shrimp Creole are house specialties. | 14079 Plantation Way | 540/672–5982 | $10–$45 | AE, D, MC, V.

Firehouse Cafe. American. Local artwork, sculpture, and a small stage for live music on Friday nights fill this restaurant that was formerly a firehouse in downtown Orange. The menu offers basic American fare, with emphasis on meat-and-potatoes entrees and generous sides. If you want a sure bet, go with the hand-patted hamburger and fresh fries. | 137 W. Main St. | 540/672–9001 | $6–$12 | MC, V.

Tolliver House. Steak. Polished wood and captain's chairs are the order of the day in this former 1787 tavern, 9 mi south of Orange on Rte. 15. The dining area is like that of an English hunt club, and the menu includes steak and seafood dishes. The prime rib, sided with new potatoes and steamed vegetables is a popular dinner entree. | 209 N. Main St., Gordonville | 540/832–3485 | Reservations essential | $14–$23 | AE, D, MC, V.

Lodging
Hidden Inn. This bed and breakfast was built in the late 1800s by descendents of Thomas Jefferson. In addition to the main house, a carriage house, a garden cottage, and a 1940s house also serve as lodgings for guests. Rooms are furnished in period pieces or reproductions, complete with handmade quilts and wingback chairs. Dining room, complimentary breakfast. Some kitchenettes, some refrigerators, no TV in some rooms, TV in common areas, some in-room hot tubs. No smoking. | 249 Caroline St. | 540/672–3625 or 800/841–1253 | fax 540/672–5029 | www.hiddeninn.com | 10 rooms | $99–$169 | AE, MC, V.

Holladay House. This restored 1830s, Federal-style home is now a Bed and Breakfast furnished with Victorian and colonial antiques, rocking chairs in all rooms, and fireplaces in two of the guest rooms. A parlor and verandah complete the inn, which is surrounded by flower and herb gardens. Complimentary breakfast. Cable TV in some rooms, some in-room hot tubs. No pets. No smoking. | 155 W. Main St. | 540/672–4893 or 800/358–4422 | fax 540/672–3028 | www.vawinetoursbandb.com | 6 rooms, 2 suites | $95–$145, $155–$205 suites | AE, D, MC, V.

Mayhurst Inn. This Italianate Victorian mansion, built in 1859, is on 37 wooded acres. Formerly a 1700-acre plantation, it is now an antique-filled Bed and Breakfast with a parlor and a spiral staircase reaching up four floors. Most guest rooms have fireplaces, all have period furnishings. Complimentary breakfast, complimentary wine. Some in-room hot tubs, no TV in rooms. Pond. Fishing. Business services. No pets. | 12460 Mayhurst La. | 540/672–5597 or 888/672–5597 | fax 540/672–7447 | www.mayhurstinn.com | info@mayhurstinn.com | 8 rooms, 1 suite | $115–$140, $200 suite | AE, D, MC, V.

Willow Grove Inn. An encampment site during the Revolutionary War, this restored plantation house, built in 1778, sits on 37 acres. Antiques and heirloom furnishings are found throughout and a piano graces the parlor. Some guest rooms have fireplaces and/or private verandas. Prices include full breakfast and dinner; box lunches are available. Restaurant, bar, complimentary breakfast. No smoking, no TV. Some in-room hot tubs. Business services. Some pets allowed. | 14079 Plantation Way | 540/672–5982 or 800/949–1778 | fax 540/672–3674 | www.willowgroveinn.com | 5 rooms, 5 cottages | $225–$330, $275–$330 cottages | MAP | AE, D, MC, V.

ONANCOCK

MAP 11, K5

(Nearby towns also listed: Irvington, Lancaster, Tangier Island)

Onancock means "foggy place," but the town has never been obscure. Since its founding in 1680, Onancock has boasted the Eastern Shore's busiest port. And despite being tucked away on Virginia's little sliver of a peninsula, Onancock boasts plenty of charming Victorian homes, bed and breakfasts and antique shops, and a thriving arts community.

Information: **Eastern Shore of Virginia Chamber of Commerce** | P.O. Box 460, Melfa, 23410 | 757/787–2460 | www.esva.ref/~esvachamber.

Attractions

Crockett Studio and Gallery. Few artists capture the essence of life on the Eastern Shore better than Willie Crockett. You can view his fine watercolors here, as well as the sculptures of wildlife crafted by his son. There are no regular hours—the proprietor is on hand when the spirit moves him. | 39 Market St. | 757/787–2288 | www.williecrockett.com | Free | Call for hours.

Kerr Place. This 1799 brick Federal home has been painstakingly restored. Walls are painted the original Mount Vernon–era colors, and period antiques and maritime artifacts fill the rooms. | Market St. | 757/787–8012 | www.esva.com/kerrplace.htm | $3 | Tues.–Sat. 10–4.

Tangier–Onancock Cruises. It takes an hour and a half by ferry, but if you like desolate and pristine spots, Tangier Island is worth a visit. No cars are allowed, and most inhabitants descend from the original settlers who arrived in the 18th century. You can pick up traces of Elizabethan English in their dialect. The ferry departs from the Onancock Wharf. | 757/891–2240 | www.chesapeakebaysampler.com/tangierisland.htm | $20 | Memorial Day–October 15.

Dining

Armando's Restaurant. Eclectic. The best part of this inviting restaurant is the owner, Armando, who charms with his cosmopolitan ways. Veal picatta with shiitake mushrooms and marguerita shrimp sautéed in garlic are just a couple of the surprises on the menu. The room is full of photographs of jazz legends, and saxophones and other instruments hang on the walls. | 10 North St. | 757/787–8044 | Closed Mon.–Thurs., no lunch | $8–$17 | MC, V.

Danielle. Pizza. Large windows and an exposed kitchen make this dining room open and bright. You can't go wrong with a calzone or a designer pizza like the Florentine. | 13 North St. | 757/787–1081 | Closed Mon. | $4–$15 | MC, V.

Flounder's. Continental. Flounder stuffed with blue crab is just one example of this restaurant's divine menu. Ornate period wallpaper and turn-of-the century lamps complement the building's Victorian heritage. | 145 Market St. | 757/787–2233 | Closed Sun.–Mon. | $14–$18 | MC, V.

Lodging

Colonial Manor Inn Bed and Breakfast. The restored 1882 house is five blocks from the harbor. You can sit on the screened front porch or in the parlor, which has a piano. Each room has its own theme. Complimentary breakfast. Some refrigerators, cable TV, in-room VCRs, no room phones. Bicycles. No smoking. | 84 Market St., Onancock | 757/787–3521 | fax 757/787–2448 | host@Colonialmanorinn.com | www.Colonialmanorinn.com | 8 rooms (2 with shared bath), 2 suites | $65–$85, $95 suite | Closed Jan. | MC, V.

Comfort Inn Onley. The rooms here are no-nonsense but affordable in this hostelry a mile from Onancock, off Rte. 13. Complimentary Continental breakfast. Cable TV. Outdoor pool. No pets. | Four Corner Plaza | 757/787–7787 | www.comfortinn.com | 80 rooms | $58–$88 | AE, D, DC, MC, V.

76 Market Street. Floral accents brighten the rooms in this bed-and-breakfast in an 1840 home. Some have heart-of-pine floors and four-poster beds. It's four blocks from the dock. Complimentary breakfast. No room phones, TV in common area. No pets. No kids under 6. No smoking. | 76 Market St. | 757/787–7600 or 800/751–7600 | www.76marketst.com | 3 rooms | $95 | MC, V.

Spinning Wheel. This 1890s Folk Victorian home is typical of many homes on the Eastern Shore. Rooms are furnished with local antiques and an extensive antique spinning wheel collection. Comfortable quilt-covered queen-size beds, crisp cotton linens and lace complete the cool Victorian summerhouse decor of the rooms. Each guest room has an attached private bath. Complimentary breakfast. No smoking, no TV in room. No kids under 12. | 31 North St., Onancock | 757/787–7311 | fax 757/787–8555 | www.downtownonancock.com | 5 rooms | $75–$95 | Closed Nov.–mid-Apr. | DC, MC, V.

PEARISBURG

MAP 11, E6

(Nearby town also listed: Blacksburg)

Pearisburg is one of only two towns on the Maine-to-Georgia Appalachian Trail and is home to many retirees. The region around Pearisburg, in the New River valley of southwestern Virginia, is a mountainous terrain of forests, hiking trails, cliffs, cascading waterfalls, and the fish-laden New River. It was first settled in 1808 by lumbermen. The main employer now is Celanese Co., a chemical maker. Other manufacturers produce industrial equipment, stone, clay, and glass products. Much of the surrounding area, home to native trout, whitetail deer, turkey, and other wildlife, is part of the Jefferson National Forest, which provides campgrounds and other amenities.

Information: **Giles County Chamber of Commerce** | 101 S. Main St., Pearisburg, 24134 | 540/921–5000.

Attractions

Walnut Flats Campground. This remote camping area is surrounded by acres of the Jefferson National Forest, which provides ample opportunities for hunting, fishing, and hiking. The Appalachian Trail and other marked hiking and horse trails are in the vicinity, as is a wildlife pond. Dismal Creek and the Falls of Dismal are nearby; the creek is a stocked trout stream. | Rte. 201 | 540/552–4641 or 888/265–0019 | www.fs.fed.us/gwjnf | Free | Daily.

White Rocks Recreation Area. This wooded camping area in the Jefferson National Forest is considered a good site for viewing wildlife. A nature trail, the Virginia Walk, is a 1½-mi loop that starts and ends at the campground. Along one section of the trail, a wetlands area has been established by a resident beaver colony; a variety of waterfowl also make their home there. The campground has 49 sites and a trailer waste disposal station. | Rte. 613 | 540/552–4641 or 888/265–0019 | www.fs.fed.us/gwjnf | May–Sept. $4; Apr. and Oct.–Nov. $2 | Daily Apr.–Nov.

ON THE CALENDAR

OCT.: *Narrows Fall Festival.* Arts and crafts, food vendors, and a barrage of bluegrass bands are the highlights of this festival held along Main Street. | 540/921–5000.

Lodging

Mountain Lake Hotel. This remote mountaintop locale was the setting for the movie *Dirty Dancing.* The hotel was built in the 1930s from native stone. There is also a lodge, plus a number of studio, one-, two-, three-, and even four-bedroom cottages. Some rooms and cottages have fireplaces. The many activities available range from hay rides (and carriage rides and pony rides) and a daily movie screening to water sports and hiking. The resort also offers deer-hunting packages. Restaurant. Some in-room hot tubs, some microwaves, refrigerators. TV in common rooms. Pool, lake. Hot tub, massage, sauna. Tennis, health club, hiking, volleyball, beach, dock, boating, fishing, bicycles, shops, video games. Children's programs (ages 4-11), library. Laundry facilities. Business services. Airport shuttle. | 115 Hotel Circle | 540/626–7121 | fax 540/626–7172 | www.mtnlakehotel.com | 94 rooms | $165–$225, $205–$275 suites | Closed late Nov.–Apr. | MAP | AE, D, DC, MC, V.

PETERSBURG

MAP 11, I7

(Nearby towns also listed: Hopewell, Richmond)

Twenty miles south of Richmond, Petersburg stretches along the Appomattox River. It began in 1645 as Fort Henry, a frontier fort and trading center. By the early 19th century, it outshone Richmond both economically and culturally.

During the Civil War, the city experienced the longest siege of any American city—10 grueling months. Bombardment by Union forces from June 1864 to April 1865 marked the so-called "last ditch of the Confederacy." The site of the fighting is now the 2,700-acre Petersburg National Battlefield. A major railroad hub, Petersburg was a crucial link in the supply chain for Gen. Robert E. Lee's army, and its fall to the Union army prompted the evacuation of Richmond and the surrender at Appomattox.

Apart from tourism, Petersburg does a thriving business in luggage, optical lenses, and ballpoint pens. Most of the city's museums and refurbished 18th- and 19th-century buildings are in the Old Towne. Memorial Day is said to have been first celebrated here, at the old Blandford Church.

Information: **Petersburg Visitor Center** | Box 2107, 425 Cockade Alley, Petersburg, 23804 | 804/733–2400 or 800/368–3595. | www.petersburg-va.org.

Attractions

Appomattox River Park. The old Appomattox River canal system once stretched between Petersburg and Farmville—over 50 mi. This riverside park with scenic footpaths and picnic areas off River Road celebrates its canal heritage during Batteau Day in September when the canal opens for boat rides. | Ferndale Ave. | 804/733–2394 | Free | Mar.–Oct., daily dawn-dusk.

Blandford Church. This 1737 church is a Confederate shrine, surrounded by the graves of 30,000 Southern dead. The building's 15 Louis Comfort Tiffany windows are memorials donated by Confederate states. The first celebration of Memorial Day tradition is said to have taken place in this cemetery. A reception center offers exhibits of artifacts and record books. | 319 S. Crater Rd. | 804/733–2396 | fax 804/863–0837 | www.petersburg-va.org | $3 | Daily 10–5.

Centre Hill Mansion. Built in 1823 for Robert Bolling, this antebellum home was considered one of Petersburg's grandest. During the siege of Petersburg, Union general George Lucas Hartsuff established his headquarters here; Abraham Lincoln visited in April 1865, a week before his death. The house was remodeled in 1901 and is furnished with Victorian antiques. | 1 Center Hill Circle | 804/733–2401 | www.petersburg-va.org | $3 | Daily 10–5.

Farmers Bank. One of the oldest bank buildings in the nation, this 1817 structure was restored by the Association for the Preservation of Virginia Antiquities. On display are old banking record books and a machine once used to print money. Guided tours leave from the visitor center at Old Market Square. | 19 Bollingbrook St. | 804/733–2400 | www.petersburg-va.org | $3 | Apr.–Oct., Fri.–Mon. 10–5, guided tours every ½ hr.

Fort Lee. This U.S. Army base provides a number of major army supply and soldier support functions and operates the Defense Commissary Agency, the Quartermaster Center, and the Army Logistics Management College. It is home to about 4,000 military and 3,300 civilian employees and is next to Petersburg National Battlefield. | Rte. 36 | 804/734–4203 | fax 804/734–4359 | www.lee.army.mil | Tues.–Fri. 10–5; weekends 11–5.

The **Quartermaster Museum** is devoted to the history and heritage of the Quartermaster Corps. Permanent and changing exhibits feature insignia, uniforms, and equipment used by Quartermaster officers and soldiers. Highlights include Gen. Ulysses S. Grant's Civil War saddle and the Jeep used by Gen. George S. Patton during campaigns in Europe in World War II. | 1201 22nd St., Building 5218 | 804/734–4203 | fax 804/734–4359 | Free | Tues.–Fri. 10–5, weekends 11–5.

Lee Memorial Park. The principal attraction of this park is an 18-hole golf course. | Homestead Dr. | 804/733–2394 or 804/733–5667 | Free; fees for golf | Mid-Apr.–mid-Oct., daily 7 AM–dusk.

Old Towne Petersburg. The original Old Towne was wiped out in a fire in 1815, but the district was rebuilt soon after and now houses galleries, shops, restaurants, and boutiques along the Appomattox River.

Old St. Gallery. National and locally-known artists are showcased at this downtown gallery. Works on display are also for sale, and regular events are held for the openings of new shows. | 1419 W. Main St. | 804/539–0017 | Free | 10–5 Daily.

Pamplin Park. This carefully landscaped, 422-acre park crisscrosses several points of historic interest. There are picnic areas, a restaurant, and several miles of flat walking trails. You can choose from 15-, 30-, and 60-minute trails. | 6125 Boydton Plank Rd. (also called Rte. 1) | 804/861–2408 | www.pamplinpark.org | $10, $5 for kids | Daily, 9–6.

Breakthrough Trail. This trail runs along a section of the original earthworks built by the Confederate soldiers as they struggled to secure the area during the Civil War. The earthworks (some almost 12 ft high) were abandoned when Union troops broke through the line and routed the Confederates. This portion of the trail winds through 1¾ mi of woods and open fields, with interpretive waysides telling the tale of the battle. | Rte. 1, Exit 63A on I–85 | 804/861–2408 | Free with park admission | Daily 9–5.

Tudor Hall. Built in 1810, this Federal-style house has several Greek Revival-style additions and was used by General Samuel McGowan as his brigade headquarters during the Civil War. Today, half the structure has been restored to its original state as a residence, the other half looks as it did when McGowan's troops occupied the house. | 804/861–2408 | Free with park admission | Tours by appointment.

Petersburg National Battlefield. The Union Army waged a 10-month campaign here in 1864–65 to seize Petersburg, a vital railroad center that supplied Gen. Robert E. Lee's army. There are ranger-led and self-guided walking tours of the 2,700-acre park, in addition to 4-mi and 16-mi driving tours. Fortifications and entrenchments constructed by both the Union and Confederate armies can be seen throughout. Living-history programs are held June through August. You can hike the trails or follow them on bicycle or horseback. Picnicking is permitted. | Rte. 36 | 804/732–3531 | fax 804/732–0835 | www.nps.gov/pete | Memorial Day–Labor Day $5, $10 limit per vehicle; Labor Day–Memorial Day, $4, $10 limit per vehicle | Park grounds daily 8 AM–dusk, visitor center daily 8–5.

Memorials and markers are scattered throughout the park to commemorate some of the most important battles fought on the grounds. Gen. Ulysses S. Grant's army first struck the Confederate line from **Battery 5.** Later, it was the point from which he shelled Petersburg with a 17,000-pound seacoast mortar known as "The Dictator."

Battery 8 was captured by black U.S. Union troops and renamed Fort Friend for the large Friend House nearby. The fort was refaced and served as a supporting artillery position for the duration of the siege.

Battery 9 was also captured by black U.S. Union troops of Hink's Division during the first day of fighting. A short distance away is Meade Station, an important supply and hospital depot on the City Point and Army railroad line.

The Confederate attack of March 25, 1865—Gen. Robert E. Lee's last failed offensive—originated at **Colquitt's Salient**

The **Crater** is a huge depression that marks the spot where a Union mine exploded under a Confederate fort on July 30, 1864. Members of the 48th Pennsylvania Volunteers—many of them coal miners—tunneled 510 ft from the Union lines to the Confederate position known as "Elliott's Salient," where they packed a shaft containing four tons of black powder. The blast killed 278 soldiers and created a hole 170 ft long, 60 ft wide, and 30 ft deep.

The **First Maine Monument** commemorates the greatest regimental loss in a single action of the Civil War. On June 18, 1864, 632 Union soldiers from the same regiment were killed.

Several forts are commemorated at the park, including **Fort Haskell,** where Union artillery and heavy infantry fire stopped the Confederate Sward advance during the Battle of Fort Stedman.

Fort Stedman was a Union stronghold and the focus of Lee's failed attack on March 25, 1865. **Gracie's Dam** is named for Gracie's Alabama Brigade, which was stationed here during part of the siege of Petersburg. The Confederate troops built an earthen dam across Poor Creek to produce a pond that would hinder a Union attack in that portion of the lines.

Retreating Confederate forces dug in along **Harrison's Creek** when they were driven from their original line in the opening battle of June 15, 1864. In March 1865, the main Confederate advance of Lee's last offensive (Fort Stedman) was stopped along this same stream. And **Spring Garden** was the site of the Taylor family farmhouse, which became General Burnside's headquarters during the Battle of the Crater. It also served as a Union artillery position during that and subsequent battles for Petersburg. All of the original farm buildings were destroyed.

City Point Unit (*see also* Hopewell) includes City Point in Hopewell, where Gen. Ulysses S. Grant made his headquarters at Appomattox Manor for the final 10 months of the war. | Cedar La. and Pecan Ave., Hopewell | 804/458–9504.

Five Forks Unit is the site of the last major battle for the South Side Railroad on April 1, 1865. Gen. Philip H. Sheridan launched a massive Federal assault that broke the Southern lines after a nine-month stalemate. A visitor contact station is open here in summer. | 1539 Hickory Hill Rd. | 804/265–8244 | fax 804/732–0835 | www.nps.gov/pete | Apr.–June, weekends 8:30–5; July–Aug., daily 8:30–5.

In addition to maps for self-guided tours of the battlefield, the **Visitor Center** has exhibits about the Petersburg campaign, a 17-minute audiovisual map presentation, battlefield relics, and models. The 4-mi Battlefield Tour starts here; the 16-mi Siege Line Tour picks up where the Battlefield Tour ends and takes you farther afield, to the park areas south and west of Petersburg (City Point and Five Forks units). June through August, costumed interpreters reenact army life during the 10-month siege. | Mid-June–Aug., daily 8:30–5:30; Aug.–mid-June, daily 8–5.

Poplar Grove (Petersburg National Cemetery). Severe fighting occurred here in 1864 and Poplar Grove contains the graves of Union dead from the Petersburg campaign and other engagements in the area of Amelia, Dinwiddie, Prince George, and Appomattox. Bodies were collected between July 1866 and June 1869 and reinterred here; of the 6,315 grave sites, 4,110 remain unidentified. | Rte. 675 | 804/732–3531 | www.nps.gov/pete | Free | Daily 8:30 AM–dusk.

Siege Museum. This museum examines the Civil War from a purely local perspective. Exhibits concentrate on details of ordinary civilian life in embattled Petersburg during the last year of the war. A 15-minute movie narrated by Petersburg-born actor Joseph Cotten dramatizes the upheaval. | 15 W. Bank St. | 804/733–2404 | fax 804/863–0837 | www.petersburg-va.org | $3 | Daily 10–5.

St. Paul's Episcopal Church. A marker denotes the pew where Gen. Robert E. Lee worshiped during the campaign for Petersburg. Two other Confederate generals, William H. F. "Rooney" Lee—the commanding general's son—and George E. Pickett, were married in this Gothic Revival church, built in 1856. There is a memorial window of Robert E. Lee, the church bells date from 1860, and the nave remains as it looked at the time of the Civil War. | 110 N. Union St. | 804/733–3415 | fax 804/733–8705 | Free | Mon.–Thurs. 9–4 or by appointment.

Trapezium House. This unusual house, built in 1817, is named for its geometric shape: four sides, none of them parallel. The construction is said to have followed a Caribbean superstition that the owner, Charles O'Hara, learned from one of his servants—that parallel lines and right angles harbor evil spirits. The house's furnishings reflect the owner's lifestyle in the mid-19th century. Tours begin at the Siege Museum (15 W. Bank St.). | N. Market and High Sts. | 804/733–2404 | www.petersburg-va.org | $3 | Apr.–Oct., daily 10–5; tours every ½ hr.

USSSA Softball Hall of Fame Museum. This museum contains videos of great games and memorabilia of players inducted into the United States Slow-Pitch Softball Association Hall of Fame. | 3935 S. Crater Rd. | 804/733–1005 | fax 804/732–1704 | www.usssa.com | $2 | Weekdays 9–4, Sat. 10–4, Sun. noon–4.

SIGHTSEEING TOURS

Lee's Retreat. A 26-stop self-guided driving tour here follows Gen. Robert E. Lee's retreat route across part of Virginia from Petersburg to Appomattox, where he signed the terms of surrender that ended the Civil War; the 100-mi journey is often called the "Corridor of Sorrows." The route follows part of U.S. 460 and a number of country backroads, through the small towns of Sutherland, Amelia Courthouse, Jetersville, and Farmville. The starting point, the Petersburg Visitor Center, provides free maps outlining the route and sells related books and audio tapes. Interpretive signs are posted at each stop; a radio transmission also describes the journey. | 425 Cockade Alley | 804/733–2400 or 800/368–3595 | fax 804/861–0883 | www.petersburg-va.org | Free | Daily.

ON THE CALENDAR

JUNE: *Virginia State EAA Fly-In.* Hundreds of aircraft fly in from all over the eastern United States for this two-day event at the Dinwiddie County Airport. On display are antiques, classics, home-built aircraft, ultra-lights, powered parachutes, radio-controlled models, and hot-air balloons. | 804/358–4333. | www.vaeaa.org.

JULY–AUG.: *Battle of the Crater.* A night program, special tours, and living-history demonstrations at Petersburg National Battlefield commemorate the battle. | 804/732–3531.

DEC.: *Civil War Christmas.* At this old-fashioned Christmas at Pamplin Historical Park, costumed soldiers reenact a winter encampment, while storytelling, caroling, refreshments, and other activities showcase Civil War–era Christmas traditions. | 6523 Duncan Rd. | 804/861–2408. | www.pamplinpark.org.

Dining

Alexander's. Eclectic. An 1810 storefront in Old Towne Petersburg, the menu offers Italian, Greek, and American dishes. The most popular item is the stuffed chicken breast, but if you're here for lunch try the famous "grill and chill"—marinated grilled chicken breast with chilled pasta salad. Kids' menu. Beer and wine only. | 101 W. Bank St. | 804/733–7134 | Breakfast also available. Closed Sun. No dinner Mon.–Tues. | $10.99–$14.99 | No credit cards.

Lodging

Best Western. This three-story motel is just off I–95 South Exit 52 (I–95 North Exit 50D) and I–85 Exit 69. Restaurant, bar, complimentary Continental breakfast. In-room data ports, microwaves, refrigerators, cable TV, some in-room hot tubs. Outdoor pool. Video games. Laundry facilities. Business services. Free parking. Pets allowed (fee). | 405 E. Washington St. | 804/733–1776 | fax 804/861–6339 | www.bestwestern.com | 120 rooms | $57–$67 | AE, D, DC, MC, V.

Comfort Inn. This motel is ½ mi from the Softball Hall of Fame and 5 mi from the battlefields and the Quartermaster Museum. Restaurant, complimentary Continental breakfast. Some kitchenettes, microwaves, refrigerators, cable TV. Outdoor pool. Laundry facilities. Pets allowed. | 11974 S. Crater Rd. | 804/732–2900 | fax 804/732–2900 | www.comfortinn.com | 96 rooms | $74.95–$79.95 | AE, D, DC, MC, V.

Days Inn Fort Lee/South. I–95 Exit 45 and the I–295 interchange are less than ½ mi from this large two-story hostelry, set on 30 acres of green land. Victorian-style furnishings add flair to guest rooms. Restaurant, bar. In-room data ports, some kitchenettes, microwaves, refrigerators, cable TV. Pool, wading pool. Barbershop, beauty salon. Putting green. Tennis. Exercise equipment. Playground, shopping, laundry services. Business services. Pets allowed. Free parking. | 12208 S. Crater Rd. | 804/733–4400 | fax 804/861–9559 | 155 rooms | $59–$79 | AE, D, DC, MC, V.

Plaza Motel. The Andrew Johnson House is less than 1 mi from this 2-story motel that was built in the mid-60s. Guest rooms are furnished with wood-veneer pieces. Rollaway cots are available. Cable TV. | 415 N. Main St. (Rte. 100) | 540/921–2591 | 12 rooms, 2 suites | $35–$45 | AE, DC, MC, V.

Quality Inn Steven Kent. This motel is 2 mi from the Softball Hall of Fame and 4 mi from the Civil War battlefields. Restaurant, bar, picnic area. In-room data ports, some microwaves, some refrigerators, cable TV. Outdoor pool, wading pool, sauna. Miniature golf, tennis, basketball. Playground, laundry facilities. Business services. Pets allowed. | 12205 S. Crater Rd. | 804/733–0600 | fax 804/862–4549 | 136 rooms | $54–$70 | AE, D, DC, MC, V.

PORTSMOUTH

MAP 11, K7

(Nearby towns also listed: Chesapeake, Hampton, Norfolk, Smithfield, Virginia Beach)

Portsmouth, established in 1752, occupies a water-locked point of flat land near the mouth of Hampton Roads harbor, surrounded by the James and Elizabeth rivers. It is home to the Norfolk Naval Shipyard, established in 1767 and now the world's largest ship repair yard. The Olde Towne Historic District, a restored 18th-century neighborhood, is said to have the largest collection of historically important homes of any place between Alexandria and Charleston, South Carolina. Next to this district are several museums. A paddle wheeler routinely ferries passengers between Portsmouth and Waterside Festival Marketplace, across the river in Norfolk.

Information: Portsmouth Convention and Visitors Bureau | 505 Crawford St., Suite 2, Portsmouth, 23704 | 757/393–5327 or 800/767–8782 | portscvb@ci.portsmouth.va.us | www.ci.portsmouth.va.us.

Attractions

Children's Museum of Virginia. Kids can learn engineering and scientific principles by playing with bubbles and blocks at this museum, which has about 80 hands-on exhibits, from computer games to a rock-climbing wall. The museum also has a planetarium with daily shows. | 221 High St. | 757/393–8393 | fax 757/393–5228 | $5 (includes admission to Naval Shipyard Museum) | Mid-June–Labor Day, Mon.–Sat. 10–7, Sun. 1–5; Labor Day–mid-June, Tues.–Fri. 10–5, Sat. 10–7, Sun. 1–5.

Courthouse Galleries. Contemporary and ancient art rotate through these galleries, from works by regional and internationally known painters to displays of artifacts such as Henry VIII's warship *Mary Rose*. The center is in Portsmouth's 1846 courthouse. | 420 High St. | 757/393–8543 | fax 757/393–5228 | $1 | Tues.–Sat. 10–5, Sun. 1–5.

Hill House. Built by Col. John Thompson in the 1830s, this English basement house (the first floor is actually considered the basement; true below-ground basements are not possible at sea level) was inherited by his adopted son, John Thompson Hill, and remained in the Hill family until 1961. It contains all its original furnishings. | 221 North St. | 757/393–5111 | $2 | Apr.–Dec., Wed. 12:30–4:30, weekends 1–5.

Lightship Museum. This is a restored 1915 Coast Guard lightship. Historically, lightships were anchored off the coastline, with lights to warn mariners of dangerous areas and safely guide them to harbor. There are exhibits of photographs, uniforms, and equipment relating to lightship service. | London Slip, at Water St. | 757/393–8741 | fax 757/393–5228 | $1 | Tues.–Sat. 10–5, Sun. 1–5.

Monumental United Church. Monumental was the first Methodist congregation in Portsmouth. It began in 1772, when local residents heard the first Methodist sermon preached south of the Potomac River. The current structure was built in 1876 on the site of the original church, which was destroyed by fire. | 450 Dinwiddie St. | 757/397–1297 | Free | Weekdays by appointment.

Naval Shipyard Museum. Exhibits on naval history include models of 18th-century warships. You can board the retired coast guard lightship (a floating lighthouse), whose quarters below deck have been furnished authentically. A pedestrian ferry travels between the museum and the Waterside Festival Marketplace in Norfolk. | 2 High St. | 757/393–8591 | fax 757/393–5228 | $1 | Tues.–Sat. 10–5, Sun. 1–5.

Olde Towne Historic District. The handsome 18th- and 19th-century buildings here are in diverse architectural styles—Colonial, Federal, Greek Revival, Georgian, and Victorian. Imported English street lanterns stand before structures of historic or architectural significance. Bordered by Crawford, Effingham, and South Sts. and Crawford Pkwy. | 757/393–5327 or 800/767–8782.

Trinity Church. Portsmouth's first Episcopal church dates to 1762. During the Civil War, it was a Union field hospital for wounded black soldiers. A memorial window unveiled in 1868 honoring slain Confederate soldiers caused a storm of controversy; U.S. naval officers in the congregation were offended that their actions during the occupation of Portsmouth were referred to as an "invasion," and the Secretary of the Navy ordered the window's removal. Today you can see the window's two inscriptions—the old and the revised. | 500 Court St. | 757/393–0431 | Free | Weekdays by appointment.

SIGHTSEEING TOURS

Carrie B. Harbor Tours. Tour Norfolk's naval shipyards and operating base, plus Fort Norfolk, on reproduction Mississippi-style paddle wheeler with an open-air top deck. Tours range from 1½ to 2½ hours. | 757/393–4735 | $12–$14 | Apr.–Oct. daily.

Olde Towne Historic District Trolley Tours. You can view the district's many historically notable homes aboard vintage mass transit—trolleys operated by Tidewater Regional Transit. They depart from the Visitor Center. | Crawford St. | 757/393–5327 or 800/767–8782 | $3.50 | May–Sept. daily, 10:45 AM, noon, 1:15, 2:30.

ON THE CALENDAR

JUNE: *Cocks Island Race.* One of the biggest sailing events on the East Coast has more than 300 sailboats racing around obstacles on the Elizabeth River. Street dancing and musical entertainment are part of the festivities at the Olde Towne Portsmouth Waterfront. | 757/393–9933.

JUNE: *Seawall Festival.* This summer celebration downtown includes a crafts show, regional cuisine, and oldies and beach music. | 757/393–9933 or 800/296–9933.

JUNE–SEPT.: *Olde Towne Lantern Tours.* Guides in period attire lead walking tours of the city's historic district by lantern light and regale you with tales of the neighborhood's legends, folklore, and architecture. | 757/393–5327 or 800/767–8782.

Dining

The Circle. Continental. Crab cakes, prime rib, and lobster tail stand out on the menu of this local favorite restaurant. The salad bar is extensive. Pianist Mon., Wednesday–Friday. Kids' menu. Sunday brunch. | 3010 High St. | 757/397–8196 | Breakfast also available except Sun. | $7–$15 | D, DC, MC, V.

Scale O' De Whale. Seafood. Antique diving suits and bells, a classic ship engine, and scrimshaw decorate this seafarer. Try the stuffed flounder, shrimp and scallops scampi, seafood Parmesan, or New York filet mignon stuffed with crab meat, lobster, and Monterey Jack cheese. Kids' menu. Dock space. | 3515 Shipwright St. | 757/483–2772 | No lunch weekends | $10–$46 | AE, D, MC, V.

Lodging

Days Inn. This two-story chain hotel is two blocks northwest of the Historic District. Rooms have two double beds or a single king. Complimentary Continental breakfast. In-room data ports, some kitchenettes, microwaves, refrigerators. Cable TV. Business services. | 1031 London Blvd./Rte. 141 | 757/399–4414 | fax 757/399–7066 | 60 rooms | $55–$105 | AE, D, DC, MC, V.

Holiday Inn Old Town–Portsmouth. This 30-year-old, 4-story hotel is on the waterfront at the Elizabeth River. Some rooms have river views. Restaurant, bar, room service. In-room data ports. Cable TV. Pool. Exercise equipment. Dock, marina. Laundry facilities. Business services. Some pets allowed (fee). | 8 Crawford Pkwy.; Interstate 264, Exit Crawford Parkway | 757/393–2573 | fax 757/399–1248 | www.holiday-portsmouth.com | 268 rooms | $95–$115 | AE, D, DC, MC, V.

Olde Towne Bed and Breakfast. A large balcony graces the front of this cozy Federal-style house that was built around 1884. Guest rooms have fireplaces and private verandas. Furnishings are a tasteful blend of antique and contemporary pieces. The inn is ⅛ mi to the harbor, downtown museums, and antique shops. In-room hot tubs. No room phones, no TV in some rooms. No pets. No kids under 12. No smoking. | 420 Middle St. | 757/397–5462 or 800/353–0278 | www.bbonline.com/va/oldetowne | 4 rooms | $95–$120 | MC, V.

PURCELLVILLE

(Nearby towns also listed: Leesburg, Waterford, Winchester)

The town was not incorporated until 1908, but Purcellville has been around since Quakers began moving to the area in the 1760s. Purcellville, and the neighboring communities of Lincoln and Round Hill, were popular summer retreats for Washingtonians wishing to escape the muggy heat of the capital, and that history is reflected in the splendid Victorian homes along Route 7. The 45 mi Washington and Old Dominion Bike Trail wraps up at Purcellville's old train depot.

Information: Loudoun Tourism Council | 108-D South St., Leesburg, VA 20175 | 800/752–6118 | info@visitloudoudn.org | www.visitloudoun.org.

Attractions

Breaux Vineyards. You can gaze at the Blue Ridge mountains while sitting on the patio to sample a hybrid French-American wine. You can also try one of the wines in the elegant tasting room, which features stucco walls and a marble bar. The farm covers 400 acres, and the vineyards spans 43 acres. | 36888 Breaux Vineyards Ln. | 540/668–6299 | fax 540/668–6283 | www.breauxvineyards.com | Free | Nov.–Apr. 11–5, May–Oct. 11–6.

Goose Creek Meeting House. Although it's not open to the public, this Quaker meeting house is worth seeing from outside. The stone building is the oldest meeting house in Virginia. | 722 Lincoln Foundry Rd., Lincoln, .

Ketoctin Baptist Church. After many years of inactivity, services at this old church resumed in 2000. The brick structure dates from 1854, and the graveyard has some 18th-century markers. | Rte. 711 and 716, Round Hill .

Dining

Breezeway Bar and Grill. American. Caricatures of regulars hang on the walls of this pub, which is popular with locals. Shrimp and Scallop Florentine and New York Strip please this crowd. | 721 E. Main St. | 540/338–1964 | $9–$13 | AE, DC, MC, V.

Candelora's. Italian. The tile floor, exposed beams, and basement fireplace make this early 19th-century tavern seem rustic. The most popular dishes are Fusilli Petrello, prepared with sun-dried tomatoes and goat cheese, and Veal Saltimbocca. | 36855 W. Main St. | 540/338–2075 | Closed Tues. | $11–$19 | AE, MC, V.

Cate's. American. The portions of all-American dishes like meatloaf and pot roast are generous and tasty. The room is as simple as the food. | 620 W. Main St. | 540/338–7072 | Closed Sun. | $6–$12 | No credit cards.

Lodging

Buckskin Manor. The rooms in this former 18th-century tavern have log and stone walls, four-poster beds, and hardwood floors. The innkeepers run a 65-acre farm with a fine view of the Blue Ridge mountains. Complimentary breakfast. No room phones, TV in common area. No pets. No smoking. | 13452 Harpers Ferry Rd. | 540/668–6864 or 888/668–7056 | www.buckskinmanor.com | 4 rooms, 1 cottage | $125–$155 rooms, $185 cottage | MC, V.

Log House Bed and Breakfast. The common room has 22-ft ceilings, a huge stone fireplace, and views of pastures and beds of wildflowers and roses. The rooms are lean, with contemporary furnishings appropriate to a log cabin. Complimentary breakfast. Some hot tubs, no room phones, TV in common area. No pets. No smoking. | 13161 Harpers Ferry Rd. | 540/668–9003 or 800/876–9003 | www.theloghouse.com | 2 rooms | $95 | MC, V.

Springdale Country Inn. You can sleep in a bed with a red silk canopy in this 1832 Federal home. The building has served as a boarding school, a stop on the Underground Railroad, and a Civil War hospital. The inn is surrounded by six wooded acres that include a garden and a stream. Complimentary breakfast. No room phones, TV in common area. Business services. No pets. No smoking. | 18348 Lincoln Rd. | 540/338–1832 or 800/388–1832 | fax 540/338–1839 | 8 rooms | $125–$200 | MC, V.

RADFORD

MAP 11, E7

(Nearby town also listed: Blacksburg)

Radford began in 1756 as a stagecoach stop on a route that ran between the Blue Ridge and Allegheny mountains. Built along the New River, the city was incorporated in 1892 and became an important rail division point. Today, Radford University, with an enrollment of 8,000 students, provides the city with many cultural and sports events. A major attraction here is *"The Long Way Home,"* a long-running outdoor historical drama that depicts the story of Mary Draper Ingles, a pioneer mother who escaped the Shawnee Indians in 1755 and trekked 850 mi back to Radford to warn the town of an impending attack.

Information: **Radford Chamber of Commerce** | 1126 Norwood St., Radford, VA 24141 | 540/639–2202.

Attractions

Bisset Park. Set on 52 lush acres along the New River, this park just off Norwood Street has a public pool, hiking trails, fishing, and picnic areas. | 540/731–3633 | Free | Daily dawn to dusk.

Clayton Lake State Park. This 4,500-acre lake, 12 mi southwest of Radford, has a beach for swimming, boating, and fishing. The lake has white bass, catfish, and crappie. Rental boats and supplies, fuel, and refreshments are available at the marina. The Italianate Howe House, built in 1876, is the park's visitor center, with exhibits on the ecology of the lake and the surrounding area. The park also has hiking trails, picnic sites, and cabins. | 4400 State Park Rd., Dublin | 540/643–2500 | www.state.va.us | Parking $3 Memorial Day–Labor Day, $1 Labor Day–Memorial Day | Daily 6 AM–10 PM.

Radford University. Established in 1910, this university functioned as the women's division of Virginia Polytechnic Institute (in neighboring Blacksburg) until the 1960s. The university's galleries display rotating exhibits by regional and national artists; one gallery is an open-air courtyard where contemporary sculpture is displayed. | Adams St. | 540/831–5324 or 540/831–5475 | fax 540/831–5036 | www.runet.edu | Free | Daily; galleries weekdays 10–5, Sun. 1–4.

ON THE CALENDAR

APR.: *Brush Mountain Arts and Crafts Fair.* Potters, weavers, quilters, decoy carvers, and other artisans show their work at this juried art festival at the Dedmonds Center at Radford University. | 540/552–4909.

JUNE–AUG.: *"The Long Way Home."* This outdoor historical drama at the Ingles Homestead Amphitheatre tells the story of Mary Draper Ingles, who escaped from Shawnee Indians in 1755 and traveled hundreds of miles back to Radford to warn the townspeople of an impending attack. | 540/639–0679.

OCT.: *Radford Highlanders Festival.* This celebration of the area's Scots-Irish heritage on the University Campus, along Norwood Street, has Highlander games, music, dancing, crafts, storytelling, and food. | 540/831–5182.

Dining

Bus Stop Cafe and Nightclub. American. Antiques line the walls and fill out the spare corners of this small local spot, many of them related to the area's mining industry. The menu has hearty, road-house fare, like quarter-pound burgers, grilled chicken, and steaks. Desserts are made fresh, too. | 401 Front St. | 540/395–6672 | $5–$6 | No credit cards.

Sal's Italian Restaurant and Pizzeria. Italian. This casual family-friendly restaurant has large tables and roomy booths for big crowds. The dining room can get a little loud at peak times. Pasta is made daily, and the scungilli, or conch, doused in either marinara or white sauce is an excellent choice for dinner. | 709A Central Sq. | 540/963–5558 | $7–$20 | Closed Mon. | MC, V.

Lodging

Alleghany Inn. One mi from the Radford University Campus, this comfortable Victorian inn has guest rooms that have both antique and contemporary pieces, quilts on the beds, and polished hardwood floors. No room phones, no TV. | 1123 Grove Ave. | 540/731–4466 | www.beaconsystems.org/alleghanyinn | 5 rooms | $85–$115 | AE, MC, V.

Best Western Radford Inn. The 2-story chain hotel off U.S. 81 at Exit 109 has two double beds or a single king-size bed. Restaurant. Cable TV. Indoor pool, wading pool. Hot tub. Exercise equipment. Business services. Some pets allowed. | 1501 Tyler Ave. | 540/639–3000 | fax 540/639–3000, ext. 412 | www.bestwestern.com | 72 rooms | $64–$85 | AE, D, DC, MC, V.

Comfort Inn. This hillside chain hotel, 12 mi southwest of Radford, has two stories, with double beds or a single king-size. Complimentary Continental breakfast. Cable TV. Pool. Hot tub. Business services. Free parking. | Rte. 100, Dublin | 540/674–1100 | fax 540/674–2644 | www.comfortinn.com | 98 rooms | $69 | AE, D, DC, MC, V.

Dogwood Lodge. This is a quiet inn with reasonable rates, just off the highway. There are outdoor entrances, with full-size, double or single beds. Cable TV. | 7073 Lee Hwy. | 540/639–9338 | 15 rooms | $35 | D, MC, V.

Executive. This two-story hotel in the Radford University area has some in-room balconies. Refrigerators, some microwaves. Cable TV. Some pets allowed (fee). | 7498 Lee Hwy. (Rte. 11) | 540/639–1664 or 888/393–8483 reservations | fax 540/633–1737 | 26 rooms (13 with shower only) | $50–$85 | AE, D, MC, V.

Super 8. This inn is 1 mi from the Radford University campus, making it a popular stay for parents and visiting sports fans. Some in-room data ports. Cable TV. Business services. Free parking. | 1600 Tyler Ave. | 540/731–9355 or 800/800–8000 | fax 540/731–9355 ext. 400 | www.super8.com | 58 rooms | $39–$109 | AE, D, DC, MC, V.

REEDVILLE

MAP 11, K5

(Nearby towns also listed: Irvington, Lancaster, Onancock, Tangier Island)

Reedville, on eastern Virginia's Northern Neck peninula, dates from 1867. It was founded by a New England sea captain, Elijah Reed, who followed schools of menhaden fish into the Chesapeake Bay. This fishing community on Cockrell's Creek quickly prospered, and fishermen built their Victorian mansions along Main Street. A number of these houses have been converted into bed and breakfasts. Still a quiet fishing village, Reedville is a point of embarkation for pleasure cruises and fishing charters around the bay and to nearby Smith and Tangier islands.

Information: Northern Neck Tourism Council | Box 1707, Warsaw, VA 22572 | 804/453–6303 or 800/393–6180 | www.virginia.org/northernneck.

Attractions

Reedville Fishermen's Museum. You can learn about the Northern Neck's menhaden fishing and watermen's heritage at this museum, in the Walker House, a restored fisherman's home. Next store are two galleries with permanent and rotating exhibits. | 504 Main St./U.S. 360 | 804/453–6529 | $2 | May–Oct., Wed.–Mon. 10:30–4:30; Nov.–Dec. and Feb.–Apr., Fri.–Mon. 10:30–4:30 or by appointment.

SIGHTSEEING TOURS/TOUR COMPANIES

Smith Island Cruise. Boats to Smith Island leave from the Chesapeake Bay/Smith Island KOA Campground in the Smith's Point area of Reedville. The 13½-mi narrated cruise takes you across the Chesapeake Bay to Maryland's only inhabited island (population 500), with Cape Cod–style homes, rustic country stores, and the sunken remains of *Island Bell I*, one of the earliest island ferries. The ship drops anchor at Eastwell, the island's largest village, where anglers catch hard- and soft-shell crabs to send back to the mainland market. | 804/453–3430 | $18.50 | May–mid-Oct., daily departures at 10 AM (boat returns at 3:45 PM), weather permitting; reservations required.

ON THE CALENDAR

MAY: *Watermen's Heritage Day*. Along Main Street, there are demonstrations of Chesapeake Bay watermen's traditional occupations, including crab picking, crab-pot making, and net mending. The festival also has tours of crab boats, boat rides, races, seafood, and live entertainment. | 804/453–6529.

NOV.: *Oyster Roast*. This feast of oysters, raw and roasted, also presents live bluegrass music, a line-dancing show, and special museum displays at the Reedville Fishermen's Museum on U.S. 360 in the historic district. | 804/453–6529.

Dining

Crazy Crab. Seafood. With a perfect view of the Reedville Marina from the dining room or the deck outside, and a menu full of tasty seafood dishes, this eatery is popular with both locals and visitors. You can get fresh fish filleted, fried, broiled, or baked, and of course, crabcakes. The dining area has plenty of room for large parties. If you come by boat, you can dock in a boat slip at the restaurant. | 902 Main St. | 804/453–6789 | $6–$15 | AE, D, MC, V.

Lodging

Fleeton Fields. This Victorian-style inn (built in 1945) is set on 11 park-like acres on the Chesapeake Bay, outside old Reedville. The house has two stories, fireplaces, elegant grand piano, steel engravings, antiques, Oriental rugs, and rose gardens. Complimentary breakfast. No smoking. TV in rooms. Beach. Bicycles. | 2743 Fleeton Rd. | 804/453–3915 or 800/497–8215 | fax 804/453–2650 | tiptons@crosslink.net | www.fleetonfield.com | 2 suites; 2 rooms | $75–$135 suites | MC, V.

The Gables. Once the home of a sea captain, this Victorian bed-and-breakfast has the main mast of a schooner on the third floor and ballast steel in the bricks on the lower floors. Guest rooms—two in the mansion and four in the carriage house—are furnished with antiques, artifacts, and memorabilia from the Captain and the home's previous owners. All rooms have private baths. No room phones, no TVs. No pets. No kids under 13. No smoking. | 859 Main St. | 804/453–5209 | 6 rooms | $78–$120 | MC, V.

Morris House. In the heart of town, this Queen Anne Victorian (1895) was built by one of Reedville's founders. The inn is furnished with antiques, and has a wraparound porch and suites with hot tubs and fireplaces. Every room has a view of the water. Complimentary breakfast. Cable TV. Dock. Some pets allowed in cottage. | 826 Main St. | 804/453–7016 | fax 804/453–9032 | morrishs@crosslink.net | www.eaglesnest.net/morrishouse | 2 rooms, 2 suites, 1 cottage | $80–$125, $125–$150 suites, $170 cottage | MC, V.

RESTON

(Nearby towns also listed: Fairfax, Falls Church, Vienna, Tysons Corner)

This northern Virginia suburb is a planned community, developed in the 1960s by Robert E. Simon. Its town center is a local gathering place, and the pavilion here hosts music shows, an Oktoberfest, and other events. Reston is six mi east of Washington Dulles International Airport and quite close to Wolf Trap Farm Park (*see Vienna*). There are shopping outlets in neighboring Tysons Corner (*see Tysons Corner*), as well as restaurants and hotels in neighboring Herndon (3 mi to west), Centreville (15 mi southwest), and Chantilly (8 mi south).

Information: Fairfax County Convention and Visitors Bureau | 8300 Boone Blvd., Suite 450, Tysons Corner, VA 22182 | 703/790–3329 | cvbfceda@mindspring.com | www.cvb.co.fairfax.va.us.

Attractions

Algonkian. This regional park, 10 mi northwest of Reston, has a hiking trail than runs down along the Potomac River, past riverfront vacation cottages that rent year-round. An outdoor pool, 18-hole golf course, boat launch, and visitor center also are on the grounds. | 47001 Fairway Dr., Sterling | 703/450–4655 | www.nvrpa.org | Free | Daily 6 AM–dusk.

Lake Fairfax. This county park on 476 acres has an outdoor swimming pool and an 18-acre lake for fishing and boating. There are hiking trails, campgrounds, carousel and miniature train rides, and picnic areas. | 1400 Lake Fairfax Dr. | 703/471–5415 | www.fairfax.va.us | Free.

Reston Animal Park. Kids can pet domestic animals in this park, which also has its share of monkeys, zebras, llamas, and other wild beasts. | 1228 Hunter Mill Rd. | 703/759–3637 | fax 703/759–3848 | $7.95 | Mid-June–Labor Day, weekdays 10–5, weekends 10–6; mid-Mar.–mid-June and Labor Day–Oct., weekdays 10–3, weekends 10–5.

Reston Town Center. Some 50 shops and restaurants do a booming local business in this outdoor mall, with a pavilion for concerts and special events. | 11911 Freedom Dr. | 703/709–8500 | Mon.–Sat. 10–9:30, Sun. 10–6.

There's skating in the Center at the **Fountain Square Ice Rink.** | 703/709–6300 | $6; skate rental $2.50 | Nov.–Mar., Sun.–Mon. and Thurs. 11–7, Tues.–Wed. 11–9, Fri. 11–11, Sat. 10 AM–11 PM.

Washington Dulles International Airport. One of three airports serving northern Virginia and Washington, D.C., Dulles is 26 mi west of the District of Columbia and 13 mi from the Capitol Beltway on the Fairfax and Loudoun County line. Major U.S. airlines and many international carriers have service here, and their passengers are served by an abundance of hotels. | Dulles Access Rd. | 703/572–2700 | fax 703/572–5718 | www.mwaa.com | Daily.

ON THE CALENDAR

MAY: *Northern Virginia Fine Arts Festival.* Some of the country's top artists and craftspeople display their work at the nationally recognized art show that's part of this two-day festival at Reston Town Center. | 703/471–9242.

JUNE: *Summer Concerts.* Regional orchestras and singing groups perform music both popular and classical every Saturday evening in June at Reston Town Center. | 703/368–8696.

SEPT.: *Oktoberfest.* Reston Town Center's German *Biergarten*, with music and food. | 800/368–8696.

SEPT. *Reston Multicultural Festival.* This one-day celebration of national and ethnic diversity with dancing, live music, food, and crafts from six continents is held in Washington Plaza at Lake Anne.

DEC.: *Fountain Square Holiday Celebration.* Community choral groups, trolley rides, and costumed characters put in appearances for the Yuletide season at the Reston Town Center. | 703/368–8696.

Dining

Clyde's. American. Model sailboats and airplanes embellish this casual spot near the center of town. The menu includes fresh salmon and Maine lobster, along with hamburgers and a local favorite, Clyde's chili. There's open-air dining in a European style piazza, on Chippendale chairs. Early-bird suppers weekdays. Sunday brunch. | 11905 Market St. | 703/787–6601 | $10–$19 | AE, D, DC, MC, V.

Fortune. Chinese. This traditional restaurant serves dim sum, orange beef, General Tso's chicken, sautéed lobster with fresh pineapple, and other favorites in an inside dining room and a small patio outside. | 1428 N. Point Village Center | 703/318–8898 | Reservations essential Fri.–Sat. | $7–$22 | D, MC, V.

Il Cigno. Northern Italian. There's always a breeze off Lake Anne in summer—pleasant when you're dining on the terrace of this modern peach-hued dining room hung with original art. The kitchen serves veal Marsala, ravioli with fresh sea bass and herbs, and veal scallopini with wild mushrooms. | 1617 Washington Plaza | 703/471–0121 | Reservations essential Fri.–Sat. | Closed Sun. Labor Day–Memorial Day | $12–$25 | AE, DC, MC, V.

Little Place Called Siam. Thai. Contemporary Thai pictures and statues of Buddha decorate this restaurant 3 mi west of Reston, known for pad thai, Thai curry, and seafood. There's a small open-air patio in back. | 328 Elden St., Herndon | 703/742–8881 | Reservations required Fri.–Sat. | $3–$13 | AE, DC, MC, V.

Market Street Bar and Grill. Contemporary. Light floods this elegant spot as diners savor food with an Asian flavor such as sea bass in a macadamia and plantain crust with pineapple rice. There's also filet mignon and steamed codfish, and paintings by different local artists change every three months. There's a tiled dining patio in back, and live jazz Friday–Sunday. | 1800 Presidents St. | 703/709–6262 | $13–$30 | AE, D, DC, MC, V.

Palm Court. Continental. Meals are prepared tableside at this candlelit spot in the Westfield Mariott, 8 mi south from Reston; you might order lobster bisque laced with brandy, pan-roasted red snapper, or arugala salad with caramelized shallot vinaigrette. Flourless chocolate cake stars for dessert. Live piano music. Sunday brunch. No smoking. | 14750 Conference Center Dr., Chantilly | 703/818–3520 | Breakfast also available. No dinner Sun. | $26–$33 | AE, D, DC, MC, V.

Paolo's. Italian. Fresh, homemade bread sticks are a popular appetizer in this restaurant where the pizza is baked in a wood oven. The house specialty is the beggar's purse filled with wild mushrooms, spinach, and Taleggio cheese. | 11898 Market St. | 703/318–8920 | Reservations essential | $17–$30 | AE, DC, MC, V.

Russia House. Russian. White linen drapes the tables in this formal restaurant with a menu of old world beef, fish, veal, lamb, and duck dishes. It's 3 mi west of Reston. | 790 Station St., Herndon | 703/787–8880 | Reservations required Fri.–Sat. | No lunch weekends | $15–$26 | AE, D, DC, MC, V.

Tortilla Factory. Mexican. The place is California-casual, with eclectic Mexican folk art and generous portions of traditional Sonoran-style cooking. The fresh produce and meat come from local vendors, and the spices from Arizona and New Mexico. Try fajitas, tamales, and rellenos. Folk music Tues. Kids' menu. | 648 Elden St., Herndon | 703/471–1156 | $9–$17 | AE, D, DC, MC, V.

Lodging

Comfort Inn. Rooms at the three-story budget chain come with double beds or a single king-size bed. Complimentary Continental breakfast. Refrigerators, cable TV. Exercise equipment. Business services. Airport shuttle. Free parking. | 200 Elden St., Herndon

| 703/437–7555 | fax 703/437–7572 | www.comfortinn.com | 103 rooms | $89–$129 | AE, D, DC, MC, V.

Courtyard by Marriott. This hotel has spacious rooms, three stories, and some balconies. The rooms come with double beds or a single king-size bed. Picnic area. In-room data ports. Cable TV. Indoor pool, hot tub, exercise equipment. Laundry facilities. Business services. Airport shuttle. Free parking. | 3935 Centerview Dr., Chantilly | 703/709–7100 | fax 703/709–8672 | www.courtyardmarriott.com | 149 rooms | $74–$139 | AE, D, DC, MC, V.

Courtyard by Marriott. Most rooms in the 3-story hotel have balconies and double beds or a single king. Restaurant, bar. In-room data ports, cable TV. Indoor pool, hot tub, exercise equipment. Laundry facilities. Business services. Airport shuttle. Free parking. | 533 Herndon Pkwy., Herndon | 703/478–9400 | fax 703/478–3628 | www.courtyard.com/iadhc | 146 rooms | $110–$145 | AE, D, DC, MC, V.

Embassy Suites. This large, modern hotel opened in 1998 and has a soaring atrium over the lobby with a fountain and scores of plants. Guest suites have separate sitting areas with pull-out sofa beds. There's a manager's reception every evening, with snacks and beverages, and a full breakfast is included in the price of a suite. Cable TV. Pool. Hot tub. Gym. Laundry service. Business services. | 13341 Woodland Park Rd. in Herndon, 1/2 mi from Rte. 267 | 703/464–0200 | fax 703/464–6210 | www.embassysuites.com | 150 suites | $129–$249 | AE, D, DC, MC, V.

Hawthorn Suites. Guest suites have large sitting rooms and bedrooms that can easily fit an extra roll-away. In-room dataports, kitchenettes, Cable TV, Laundry facilities. | 467 Herndon Pkwy., Herndon | 703/437–5000 | fax 703/464–5800 | www.hawthorn.com | 104 suites | $89–$110 | AE, D, DC, MC, V.

Hilton. It's just 2 mi from Dulles International Airport and 6 mi from the town center. The executive level has extra amenities, including living rooms. Most rooms have double beds or a single king. Restaurant, bars with entertainment. In-room data ports. Some refrigerators. Room service. Cable TV. 2 pools (1 indoor). Barbershop. Beauty salon. Tennis courts. Exercise equipment, basketball, racquetball. Business services. Airport shuttle. Some pets allowed. | 13869 Park Center Rd., Herndon | 703/478–2900 or 800/445–8667 | fax 703/834–1996 | www.hilton.com | 301 rooms | $105–$165 | AE, D, DC, MC, V.

Holiday Inn. Most rooms in this two-story chain hotel have double beds or single king-size. Restaurant, bar with entertainment. In-room data ports. Room service. Cable TV. Indoor pool. Hot tub. Exercise equipment. Laundry facilities. Business services. Airport shuttle. Free parking. Some pets allowed. | 1000 Sully Rd., Sterling | 703/471–7411 | fax 703/834–7558 | www.holiday-inn.com | 296 rooms | $169 | AE, D, DC, MC, V.

Holiday Inn Express. This four-story budget offshoot of the chain is near the airport, and has double beds or a single king. Complimentary Continental breakfast. Some microwaves, cable TV. Exercise equipment. Business services. Airport shuttle. Free parking. Some pets allowed. | 485 Elden St., Herndon; Route 495, Exit 12 to Dulles Access | 703/478–9777 | fax 703/471–4624 | disales@bfsaulco.com | www.holiday-inn.com | 115 rooms | $139 | AE, D, DC, MC, V.

Homestead Village. This all-suites property looks more like a suburban apartment complex than a motel and is 1 mi between the Reston Parkway and the Fairfax County Parkway. In-room data ports, kitchenettes, Cable TV. Laundry facilities. | 12190 Sunset Hills Rd. | 703/707–9700 | fax 703/707–9786 | www.stayhsd.com | 149 rooms | $85–$109 | AE, D, DC, MC, V.

Hyatt. The rooms at this 13-story hotel include a sitting area, modern wood furniture, and large, bright windows with views of the airport and the city. Restaurant, bar with entertainment. In-room data ports. Microwaves, cable TV. Indoor pool, hot tub, exercise equipment. Business services. Laundry facilities. Airport shuttle. | 2300 Dulles Corner Blvd., Herndon | 703/713–1234 | fax 703/713–3410 | www.hyatt.com | 317 rooms, 4 suites | $99–$209 | AE, D, DC, MC, V.

Hyatt Regency Reston. In Reston Town Center, this 15-floor hotel is part of the Main Street complex of shops, restaurants, and movie theaters. There's a sundeck and an executive floor with additional amenities. Restaurant, bar. Some refrigerators. Room service. Cable TV. Indoor pool, gym. Business services. Airport shuttle. Free parking. | 1800 Presidents St.; Rte. 276, Exit 12 | 703/709–1234 | fax 703/709–2291 | www.hyatt.com | 517 rooms | $159–$299 | AE, D, DC, MC, V.

Marriott Suites. You can get privileges at the large health club next door to this 11-story hotel. Restaurant, bar. In-room data ports. Refrigerators. Cable TV. Indoor-outdoor pool. Hot tub. Exercise equipment. Business services. Airport shuttle. | Worldgate Center, Worldgate Dr., Herndon | 703/709–0400 | fax 703/709–0434 | www.marriott.com | 253 suites | $84–$109 | AE, D, DC, MC, V.

Marriott Washington. This three-story chain hotel is a five-minute drive from Dulles International Airport. Restaurant, bar, picnic area. In-room data ports. Cable TV. 2 pools (1 indoor). Hot tub. Exercise equipment, tennis court. Laundry facilities. Business services. Airport shuttle. | 450-20 Aviation Dr., Dulles | 703/471–9500 | fax 703/661–8714 | www.marriott.com | 368 rooms | $69–$204 | AE, D, DC, MC, V.

Residence Inn by Marriott. This chain hotel, 2 mi from the downtown shopping area, has 21 separate buildings, all two stories high. Picnic area. Complimentary Continental breakfast. In-room data ports. Kitchenettes. Microwaves. Cable TV. Pool. Hot tub. Tennis court. Playground. Laundry facilities. Business services. Free parking. Some pets allowed (fee). | 315 Elden St., Herndon | 703/435–0044 | fax 703/437–4007 | www.marriott.com | 168 rooms | $159–$209 | AE, D, DC, MC, V.

Sheraton Reston. A sleek, modern lobby with lots of recessed lighting and artful flower arrangements greets you at this large hotel. Guest rooms have modular furniture in dark wood. There is a golf course adjacent to the property. Restaurant, bar. Cable TV, in-room VCRs. Pool. Hot tub, sauna. 2 tennis courts. Business sevices. | 11810 Sunrise Valley Dr., 2 mi off Exit 12 of Rte. 267 | 703/620–9000 | fax 703/860–1594 | www.sheratonreston.com | 302 rooms, 10 suites | $119–$200 | AE, D, DC, MC, V.

Springhill Suites. Guest rooms at this all-suite hotel off the Dulles Toll Road at Exit 11 have sitting rooms, large windows, and modern furnishings. In-room dataports, kitchenettes, cable TV. Pool. Laundry facilities. | 138 Spring St. | 703/435–3100 | fax 703/435–5100 | www.springhillsuites.comherndon/reston | 136 suites | $69–$134 | AE, D, DC, MC, V.

Westfields Marriott. 15 minutes from downtown shopping, this hotel has three stories and some balconies. Picnics and box lunches can be arranged. Restaurant, bar with entertainment, picnic area. In-room data ports. Minibars. Room service. Cable TV. 2 pools (1 indoor). Hot tub, massage. Tennis court. Basketball, gym, hiking, bicycles. Business services. Airport shuttle. Free parking. Some pets allowed. | 14750 Conference Center Dr., Chantilly | 703/818–0300 | fax 703/818–3655 | www.marriott.com | 340 rooms | $119–$264 | AE, D, DC, MC, V.

RICHMOND

MAP 11, I6

(Nearby towns also listed: Ashland, Charles City, Hopewell, Petersburg)

Richmond is a city built on seven hills, straddling the Tidewater and Piedmont regions of Virginia. It was named by William Byrd II, who laid out the city at the falls of the James River in 1737; he probably named it after the English borough Richmond upon Thames. In 1780, it became the capital of Virginia, largely through the efforts of Thomas Jefferson. From secession through the Civil War, from 1861 to 1865, Richmond was capital of the Confederacy. Reminders of this historical legacy can be glimpsed around almost every city corner.

At the start of the Civil War, Richmond was the most industrialized city in the South, and it remains home base to national industries such as Reynolds Metals and tobacco manufacturers. The nerve center of Virginia's business community, it has added high technology to traditional economic bases that include shipping and banking.

Richmond has three universities and numerous professional schools, professional and amateur sports, many public parks, and a lively arts scene. Historians and amateur genealogists will find a wealth of archival information at the Virginia State Library and Archives, the Virginia Historical Society Museum of Virginia History, the Beth Ahabah Museum and Archives, and other museums in this history-minded city.

More recent significant figures from Richmond include the first elected African-American governor, L. Douglas Wilder; the first African-American tennis player to win Wimbledon, Arthur Ashe Jr.; and the first African-American woman bank president, Maggie Walker.

Information: **Metropolitan Richmond Convention and Visitors Bureau** | 550 E. Marshall St., Richmond, 23219 | 804/782–2777 or 800/370–9004 | mrcvb@richmondva.org | www.richmond.org.

NEIGHBORHOODS

After suffering years of urban decay, Richmond is on the upswing. Now a modern, sophisticated town, previously neglected neighborhoods are undergoing revitalization and rebirth.

Court End District. The heart of old Richmond, this area surrounding the State Capitol contains seven National Historic Landmarks, three museums, and 11 other buildings on the National Register of Historic Places. The Capitol, designed by Thomas Jefferson, is still the meeting place for one of the world's oldest representative legislatures. The Court End District is bounded by Broad Street, 9th Street, Franklin Street, and Governor Street; downtown Richmond's borders are Belvidere Street, Canal Street, 14th Street, and Leigh Street.

Jackson Ward. This area, west of the Capitol, became the cultural and business center of the city's black population following the Civil War. The residential neighborhood of row houses includes numerous examples of 19th-century Greek Revival and Victorian architecture. Most of the city's ornamental cast-iron porches are in Jackson Ward. Several museums are here, including the Valentine Museum, the Black History Museum and Cultural Center, and the Maggie Walker National Historic Site.

Fan District. The gaslit area west of downtown is a trendy neighborhood of restored turn-of-the-century town houses, small bistros, and specialty shops. The community is a mix of blue- and white-collar families, college students, and young professionals.

Shockoe Slip and **Shockoe Bottom.** Once a tobacco trading and warehouse district, this is now the center of Richmond's restaurants and nightlife. The Slip is east of downtown near the James River; the Bottom is downhill from the Slip.

Church Hill. Also east of downtown, this is home to St. John's Church, site of Patrick Henry's famous "Give me liberty or give me death" speech. The residential neighborhood has many 19th-century houses, and more than 70 predate the Civil War. Richmond National Battlefield Park is headquartered here.

TRANSPORTATION INFORMATION

Airports: International Airport, U.S. 64 E to Exit 197, 804/226–3000.
Train: Amtrak, 7519 Staples Mill Rd., 800/872–7245.
Bus Lines: Greyhound Lines, 2910 N. Boulevard, 800/231–2222.
Intracity Transit: Greater Richmond Transit Co. (bus service), 804/358–4782.

Attractions

ART AND ARCHITECTURE

Agecroft Hall. Built in the 15th century in Lancashire, England, Agecroft Hall was transported to its present location, overlooking the James River, in 1926. Set amid 23 acres of gardens and woodlands, this half-timbered country manor house contains an extensive collection of Tudor and early Stuart art and furniture (1485–1660) and a few priceless collector's items. The tours begin with a 10-minute slide show about the hall's original English location, and the process of shipping it to the United States. | 4305 Sulgrave Rd. | 804/353–4241 | fax 804/353–2151 | $5 | Tues.–Sat. 10–4, Sun. 12:30–5.

Jefferson Hotel. (*see* Lodging) This 1895 resurrected hostelry of the Gilded Age in downtown Richmond has a skylit rotunda above a mezzanine ringed by faux marble columns and broad staircases. A statue of Thomas Jefferson stands in the lobby. | 101 West Franklin St. | 804/788–8000 or 800/424–8014 | www.jefferson-hotel.com.

John Marshall House. Built in 1790, this was the residence of the famous chief justice of the Supreme Court. Marshall, who also served as secretary of state and ambassador to France, lived here from 1791 until his death in 1835. Fully restored, this house located in Court End combines the Federal style with neoclassical motifs; it has wood paneling and wainscoting, narrow arched passageways, and a mix of period pieces and heirlooms. | 818 E. Marshall St. | 804/648–7998 | $3, special rates for seniors and children | Apr.–Sept., Tues.–Sat. 10–5; Oct.–Dec., Tues.–Sat. 10–4:30; Jan.–Mar., by appointment.

Virginia House. An English priory built in the 16th century, this building in Windsor Farms was saved from demolition in 1925, dismantled, and brought over to the United States by Alexander and Virginia Weddell. Remade as a country estate, the mansion is furnished with treasures acquired worldwide during Mr. Weddell's career as a U.S. ambassador. | 4301 Sulgrave Rd. | 804/353–4251 | fax 804/354–8247 | www.vahistorical.org | $4 | Fri. & Sat. 10–4, Sun. 12:30–5. Mon.–Thurs. by appointment only.

Wilton. William Randolph III built this Georgian mansion in 1753 on the only James River plantation in Richmond. Wilton has the distinction of being the only Virginia home that is completely paneled, floor to ceiling, in every room. Its period furnishings include an original map of Virginia drawn by Thomas Jefferson's father. Terraced lawns overlook the river. | 215 S. Wilton Rd. | 804/282–5936 | $5 | Mar.–Jan., Tues.–Sat. 10–4:30 (last tour at 3:45).

CULTURE, EDUCATION, AND HISTORY

Beth Alabah Museum and Archives. Located in downtown Richmond, this is the area's only Jewish history museum with changing exhibits of historic documents, photographs, and religious artifacts on display. The archive, available for genealogical and historical research, contains documents, articles, and other materials relating to Richmond and the southern Jewish experience, including the records of three congregations. | 1109 W. Franklin St. | 804/353–2668 | fax 804/358–3451 | $3 (suggested) | Sun.–Thurs. 10–3 or by appointment.

Bill "Bojangles" Robinson Statue. A monument to the 20th-century dance giant. The statue stands at the site where Robinson donated a stoplight for the safety of the neighborhood children. | Intersection of Leigh and Chamberlon Aves.

Capitol Square. On a green hilltop in the heart of downtown, Capitol Square is a manicured oasis of ancient trees and rolling lawns, lined with wooden benches and surrounded by a cast-iron fence. Statues of Edgar Allan Poe, Harry Flood Byrd, and William Smith stand on display. A visitor center is in the Old Bell Tower (1824); the bell formerly served as a fire alarm and, during the Civil War, signaled Union attacks. | 804/358–5511 | fax 804/257–5571 | Free | Daily.

State Capitol. Thomas Jefferson designed the State Capitol in 1785, modeling it on a Roman temple, the Maison Carrée, in Nîmes, France. The central portion was completed in 1792; the wings were added in 1906. The Virginia General Assembly, the oldest legislative body in the Western Hemisphere, still meets here. A wealth of sculpture is contained within: busts of Virginia's eight presidents and a famous life-size statue of George Washington by Jean-Antoine Houdon, the only work for which Washington posed. In the old Hall of the House of Delegates, Robert E. Lee accepted the command of the Confederate forces in Virginia; a bronze statue marks the spot where he stood. Guided tours operate continuously throughout the day and delve into the building's history and architectural highlights. | 804/698–1788 | fax 804/257–5571 | www.legis.state.va.us/vaonline | Free | Apr.–Nov., daily 9–5; Dec.–Mar., Mon.–Sat. 9–5, Sun. 1–5.

The Executive Mansion. has been the official residence of Virginia's governors since 1813. It was designed by Alexander Parris, a Boston architect. The mansion has ornamental plaster ceilings and elegantly carved woodwork. | Capitol Sq | 804/371–2642 | fax 804/257–5571 | Free | By appointment during these hours: Mon. 2–4, Tues.–Fri. 10–noon and 2–4.

Equestrian Statue of Washington. Designed by Thomas Crawford, this bronze sculpture of George Washington was completed in 1857 by Randolph Rogers. The figures of seven notable Virginians circle the base of the monument, including Thomas Jefferson, Patrick Henry, and John Marshall. Jefferson Davis was inaugurated president of the Confederacy on this spot.

Church Hill Historic Area. Overlooking Shockoe Bottom and downtown, this hilltop neighborhood is Richmond's oldest intact residential district. For more than a century, the middle and upper classes lived here, but its fortunes gradually declined as the city expanded westward. Most of the antebellum houses are two– or three–story brick structures; they represent a range of architectural styles, including Federal, Greek Revival, Italianate, Queen Anne, and Colonial Revival. Some are beautifully restored, while others are works in progress. Some of the streets retain their gas streetlamps and brick sidewalks.

The Fan District and Monument Avenue. Named for its streets, which fan out from downtown, the Fan District extends west from Monroe Park at Belvidere Street to the Boulevard. This gaslit neighborhood is composed mostly of late-19th-century town houses in different architectural styles; it also has an abundance of sidewalk cafés and corner bistros. The campus of Virginia Commonwealth University anchors the eastern end of the Fan. The grandest of its streets is Monument Avenue, a broad, tree-lined boulevard of stately homes, the residences of some of the first families of Virginia. Laid out in 1887, the street is dotted with the statues of six famous Virginians: Robert E. Lee, J.E.B. Stuart, Stonewall Jackson, Jefferson Davis, Matthew Fontaine Maury, and, most recently, Arthur Ashe Jr. | Bounded by Grace and Main Sts. and Boulevard and Belvidere Sts.

Hollywood Cemetery. U.S. presidents John Tyler and James Monroe; Confederate president Jefferson Davis; Gens. Fitzhugh Lee, J.E.B. Stuart, and George E. Pickett; and oceanographer Matthew Fontaine Maury, "Pathfinder of the Seas," rest in this parklike hilltop cemetary at Albermarle Street. A granite pyramid built of stones quarried from the James River below marks the final resting place of 18,000 Confederate dead. Dedicated in 1849, the cemetery's monuments, ironwork, and statuary provide numerous examples of 19th-century funeral art and its symbols. | 412 S. Cherry St. | 804/648–8501 | Free | Mid-May–mid-Oct., daily 8–6; mid-Oct.–mid-May, daily 8–5.

Jackson Ward. By 1900, Jackson Ward was among the foremost African-American communities in the United States, and it remains the nation's largest historical district related principally to black enterprise and culture. Notable residents included publisher John Mitchell, Jr., banker Maggie Walker, entertainer Bill "Bojangles" Robinson, and attorney Giles B. Jackson, the first African-American admitted to practice before the Supreme Court of Virginia. | Bordered by I–95, 7th, Broad, and Belvidere Sts.

Maggie Walker National Historic Site. From 1904 to 1934, this 25-room brick building was the home of the pioneering African-American businesswoman and educator who founded Richmond's Saint Luke Penny Saving Bank and the Richmond Council of Colored Women. She was active in insurance and newspaper publishing as well. | 110 E. Leigh St. | 804/771–2017 | fax 804/771–2226 | www.nps.gov/mawa | Free | Wed.–Sun. 9–5, tours every ½ hr.

Monument Avenue. Head northwest along Franklin Avenue and it will soon change into Monument Avenue, part of old Richmond. Lined with statues and monuments, mostly Civil War heroes mounted astride their "trusty steeds," the avenue branches off into small side streets rich in Victorian architecture.

Richmond National Battlefield Park. As the capital of the Confederacy, Richmond came under attack from Union troops seven times during the Civil War. This park preserves the sites of two battles that came closest to the Union army's goal of taking over the city—Gen. George McClellan's Peninsula Campaign (1862) and Gen. Ulysses S. Grant's Overland Campaign (1864). The park's 10 units also include the sites of the Seven Days' Battle (June 26–July 1, 1862), Cold Harbor (June 1–3, 1864), and other engagements in the vicinity of Richmond, as well as fortifications used by both sides during the siege of the city. | 3215 E. Broad St. (U.S. 60 E) | 804/226–1981 | fax 804/771–8522 | www.nps.gov | Free | Parks daily dawn–dusk.

Chimborazo (Main) Visitor Center. Here you'll find maps for self-guided tours of the battlefields. You can also see shows a film that provides an overview of the 1861–1865 defense of Richmond. They also rent audio tapes for the complete park tour, which covers 80 mi. Living-history programs and reenactments are held April through October. Chimborazo Park surrounds the visitor center. The park is the site of the old Chimborazo General Hospital, an 1861 complex that treated more than 76,000 Confederates during the Civil War. | 3215 E. Broad St. (U.S. 60 E) | 804/226–1981 | www.nps.gov | Free | Daily 9–5.

Cold Harbor Visitor Center. The Cold Harbor Visitor Center, outside northeast Richmond, exhibits an electronic battle map documenting the Battle of Cold Harbor (1864). A 1-mi trail of the battlefield begins at the center. The center is east of I–295, between Routes 615 and 632. | Rte. 156 in Hanover County | 804/730–5025 | www.nps.gov | Free | Daily 9–5.

Fort Harrison Visitor Center. In the Fort Harrison unit of the national park, the center has brochures, exhibits, and a walking trail. Closed Nov.–Mar. | Battlefield Park Rd. | 804/795–2217 | www.nps.gov | Free | June–Aug., daily 9–5; weekends only Sept.–Oct. and Apr.–May, 9–5.

St. John's Episcopal Church. Virginia's second revolutionary convention met here in 1775, and it was in this church that Patrick Henry made his celebrated "Give me liberty or give me death!" speech. Richmond's oldest place of worship, its original frame building was erected in 1741. Edgar Allan Poe's mother and many famous early Virginians are buried in its cemetary. You can hear a reenactment of Henry's speech every summer on Sunday at 2 PM. | 2401 E. Broad St. | 804/648–5015 | $3 | Mon.–Sat. 10–4, Sun. 1–4; closed some weekends for private functions.

Tuckahoe Plantation. Built in 1714, and 7 mi from Central Richmond, the boyhood home of Thomas Jefferson actually consists of a set of plantation buildings overlooking the James River. | 12601 River Rd. | 804/784–5736 | By appointment.

Virginia Historical Society. With 7 million manuscripts and 125,000 books on Virginia history, the library is a key stop for researchers and genealogists. It is the only southern member of the prestigious Independent Research Libraries Association. The library also mounts regularly changing exhibits and has permanent displays, such as an 800-piece collection of Confederate weapons and equipment. | 428 N. Boulevard | 804/358–4901 | fax 804/355–2399 | www.vahistorical.org | $4 | Mon.–Sat. 10–5; Sun. galleries only, 1–5.

Virginia State Library and Archives. As the official state archival repository, the library preserves and provides access to more than 83 million manuscript items that document four centuries of Virginia history. The library also makes available to researchers more than 1½ million books, bound periodicals, microfilm reels, newspapers, and state and federal documents. Its collections include 240,000 photographs, prints, engravings, posters, and paintings. Free parking is available beneath the building. | 800 E. Broad St. (Rte. 60 E) | 804/692–3500 | fax 804/692–3556 | www.vsla.edu | Free | Mon.–Sat. 9–5.

Virginia War Memorial. The Virginia-born casualties of World War II and the Korea, Vietnam, and Persian Gulf conflicts are named and honored with this monument at the north end of the Lee Bridge. | 621 S. Belvidere St. (U.S. 1) | 804/786–2050 | Free | Daily 8 AM–10 PM.

MUSEUMS

Black History Museum and Cultural Center of Virginia. The lives and accomplishments of black Virginians, from Jamestown to the present day, are told through visual, oral, and written records. The history of the Jackson Ward, considered the first community of black professionals, is highlighted. | 00 Clay St., Richmond | 804/780–9093 | fax 804/780–9107 | www.blackhistorymuseum.org | $4 | Tues.–Sat. 10–5, Sun. 11-5.

Children's Museum of Richmond. This hands-on museum has a kids' bank, a health and safety area, a TV studio, a computer station, and an art studio among its interactive exhibits. The most popular attraction is the Cave, a 40-ft-long replica of a Virginia limestone cave where your crew can learn about earth science and rock collecting. | 2626 W. Broad St. | 804/474–7000 | fax 804/474–7099 | $5 | Mon.–Sat. 9–5, Sun 12–5.

Edgar Allan Poe Museum. The poet/author grew up in Richmond. The 1737 Old Stone House, Richmond's oldest residence, displays some of the writer's possessions, including his trunk and walking stick. The Raven Room has James Carling illustrations inspired by the writer's most famous poem. | 1914 E. Main St. | 804/648–5523 | $6 | www.poemuseum.org | Tues.–Sat. 10–5, Sun.–Mon. 11–5.

Federal Reserve Money Museum. Different forms of currency, rare bills, and gold and silver bars are among the more than 500 items on display at this museum, which chronicles the history of money. | 701 E. Byrd St. | 804/697–8108 | www.rich.frb.org | Free | Weekdays 9:30–3:30.

Meadow Farm Museum at Crump Park. Costumed interpreters demonstrate farm life in the 1860s with hearth cooking, a blacksmith forge, and barnyard animals. The farmhouse is furnished to reflect the period. The park contains nature trails, with fishing and picnicking available. An orientation center has exhibits about rural southern life. | 3400 Mountain Rd., Glenn Allen | 804/501–5520 | Free | Park daily dawn–dusk. Farmhouse and orientation center Mar.–Dec., Tues.–Sun. noon–4; mid-Jan.–Feb., weekends noon–4.

Museum of the Confederacy. This museum has one of the country's largest collections of Civil War artifacts, paintings, and documents, including the sword Robert E. Lee wore to the surrender at Appomattox. You can park free in the adjacent Medical College of Virginia visitor-patient parking deck; the museum will validate tickets. | 1201 E. Clay St. | 804/649–1861 | fax 804/649–1460 | www.moc.org | $6, museum and White House $7 | Mon.–Sat. 10–5, Sun. noon–5.

In late 1998, the **Museum of Virginia History** opened an expanded exhibition called "The Story of Virginia, an American Experience," which covers 16,000 years of history. Seven galleries chronicle the development of Virginia through the colonial period, the Civil War, and both world wars, to the present. | 804/358–4901.

Science Museum of Virginia. Aerospace and Crystal World are among more than 250 instructive exhibits here. The Universe Theater, also a planetarium, has an Omnimax theater (like IMAX, but with a curved screen) with movies and astronomy shows. The museum is housed in the city's domed 1919 train station. | 2500 W. Broad St. | 804/367–6552 or 800/659–1727 | fax 804/367–2511 | www.smv.mus.va.us | Museum $5; museum, Omnimax, and planetarium $8 | Mon.–Sat. 9:30–7, Sun. 11:30–7.

Valentine Museum. The museum documents the life and history of Richmond with changing exhibits that cover everything from architecture to relationships between the races. The museum's collection includes costumes, decorative arts, textiles, and paintings, in addition to more than 500,000 photographs of the city. The core of the holdings is from Edward Valentine, a former owner of the Wickham House mansion. The museum admission includes a tour of the restored 1812 Wickham House, a neoclassical mansion designed by architect Alexander Parris, the creater of Boston's Faneuil Hall. John Wickham was Richmond's wealthiest citizen of the time. Rare wall paintings and a free-standing staircase are on display. | 1015 E. Clay St. | 804/649-0711 | fax 804/643-3510 | www.valentinemuseum.com | $5, seniors, students, and children | Mon.–Sat. 10–5, Sun. noon–5. 30–5.

Virginia Museum of Fine Arts. Five jeweled Fabergé eggs are stellar attractions here. The encyclopedic collection ranges from ancient to contemporary art, from paintings by Goya, Renoir, and van Gogh to Art Nouveau furniture, African masks, Roman statuary, and British sporting art. Free highlight tours are given at 2:30, Tuesday through Sunday. There's a cafeteria. | 2800 Grove Ave. | 804/340-1400 | fax 804/340-1548 | www.vmfa.state.va.us | $4 (suggested) | Tues.–Wed. and Fri.–Sun. 11–5, Thurs. 11–8.

White House of the Confederacy. Preservationists have carefully recreated the interior of this mansion as it was during the Civil War, when Jefferson Davis lived here. You can tour 11 period rooms displaying many original furnishings. Constructed in 1818 of brick, the house is stuccoed to give the appearance of a stone mansion. There are occasional dinners with a Civil War theme. | 1203 E. Clay St. | 804/649-1861 | fax 804/649-1460 | www.moc.org | $7 | Mon.–Sat. 10–5, Sun. noon–5.

PARKS, NATURAL AREAS, AND OUTDOOR RECREATION

Bryan Park. This 200-acre park on Richmond's north side is treasured for its azalea gardens. Tennis courts, a fishing lake, playgrounds, and picnic shelters are available. | 804/780-5704 | fax 804/780-7680 | Free | Daily dawn–dusk.

The Crossing Golf Club. This 18-hole, par-72 course, 14 mi north of Richmond, is open to the public. | 800 Virginia Center Pkwy., Glenn Allen | 804/266-2254 | fax 804/266-2948 | www.crossinggolf.com | Mon.–Thurs. $46, Fri.–Sun. $58 | Daily 8–5.

James River Park. On 480 acres along the James River on the city's south side, this urban park has white-water canoeing and kayaking. The park is also known for good bass fishing, rock climbing, and rappelling. There are walking trails with river views. A visitor center provides maps and trail guides and interpretive tours. There are two parking lots, at 22nd Street and 42nd Street. | 804/780-5311 or 800/697-3373 | fax 804/780-5394 | Free | Daily dawn–dusk.

Lewis Ginter Botanical Garden. This 80-acre park, 7 mi north of Richmond, has specialty collections of ivy, narcissus, azaleas, rhododendrons, day lilies, and roses. Special areas are designed for various tastes, such as the Kids' garden and the Asian Valley, Wildflower Meadow, English Cottage, and Tea House gardens. The park also houses a research center and has a nature trail. | 1800 Lakeside Ave., Lakeside | 804/262-9887 | fax 804/262-9934 | www.lewisginter.org | $4 | Daily 9:30–4:30.

Maymont. This 100-acre, 19th-century country estate is now a huge park with a nature center, barn, extensive working carriage collection, and a kids' farm and petting zoo. You can tour the 1893 Maymont House, a Romanesque Revival mansion once owned by Major and Mrs. James Dooley (still furnished with original pieces), or stroll through its gardens, which include Japanese, Italian, and English designs. Carriage and tram rides are available. | 1700 Hampton St. | 804/358-7166 | fax 804/358-9994 | www.maymont.org | Donations accepted | Grounds daily 10–7; mansion, nature center, and barn Tues.–Sun. noon–5.

Pocahontas State Park. A swimming pool, boat rental, fishing, picnicking, and camping are available at this 1,783-acre park in the Pocahontas State Forest. The park includes Swift Creek and Beaver Lake, and hiking and biking trails that take you around them. The visitor center south of Richmond City has a wildlife exhibit and natural history displays. | Rte. 655 | 804/796-4255 | www.state.va.us | Parking $4 | Daily 8 AM–dusk.

William Byrd Park. This residential park near the Fan District has three lakes with paddleboat rental, fishing, a 1-mi gravel fitness course, tennis courts, ball fields, and picnic shelters. Dogwood Dell, an outdoor amphitheater, is the site of musical performances and festivals during warm-weather months. The park's landmark is the Carillon, a 240-ft Georgian bell tower and World War I memorial. | Boulevard and Idlewood Ave. | 804/646–1437 | fax 804/646–1437 | Free | Daily.

RELIGION AND SPIRITUALITY

St. Paul's Church. Built in 1845, St. Paul's is sometimes known as the Church of the Confederacy. Jefferson Davis and Robert E. Lee worshiped here during the Civil War. The church's windows are memorials to Lee. | 815 E. Grace St. | 804/643–3589 | fax 804/649–3283 | Free | Mon.–Sat. 10–4, Sun. 8–3.

SHOPPING

6th Street Marketplace. The two-level shopping center, built in 1987, caters mainly to downtown office workers on their lunch breaks and visitors attending conferences at the nearby Coliseum and Richmond Center. Specialty and chain stores sell gifts and cards, clothing, shoes, and country crafts; there's also a food court. | 550 Broad Street | 804/648–6600 | fax 804/788–0454 | Mon.–Sat. 10–6, Sun. 12:30–5:30.

Shockoe Slip. The cobblestoned district of converted 19th-century tobacco warehouses is filled with restaurants, upscale boutiques, art galleries, antiques stores, and clothiers such as Beecroft and Bull. | E. Cary St. | Daily.

Carytown. The nine-block commercial district is dense with independently owned shops, more than 250 in all. You'll find Oriental rug dealers; card and party shops; bakery and seafood stores; sidewalk cafés; wine, chocolate, and cheese stores; pet and bike shops; furniture and antiques stores; and clothing, music, and book stores. | W. Cary St. | Most stores Mon.–Sat. 10–5:30; some stores Sun.

17th Street Market. The open-air farmers' market, one of the country's oldest, is adjacent to an old railroad station in Shockoe Bottom. Flowers, meat, and fresh produce—including locally renowned Hanover tomatoes–are for sale. Restaurants, art galleries, and small antique shops operate out of restored warehouses and factory buildings at the market site. | 17th St. | Daily.

SIGHTSEEING TOURS

Historic Richmond Tours. There are daily bus tours, walking tours, and guide service. The 2½-hour tour highlights Capitol Square, Monument Avenue, and other neighborhoods. There are also theme tours that focus on Civil War battlefields, Church Hill, and Hollywood Cemetery. Pick-up is available at major hotels and the Robin Hood Road Visitors Center. Reservations required. | Tour headquarters, 707A E. Franklin St. | 804/780–0107 | $18 | Daily.

Paddle wheeler *Annabel Lee.* The narrated tours include a day-long plantation cruise 25 mi down the James River, where you can disembark and tour Berkeley and Evelynton plantations and the Westover gardens. There are also lunch, brunch, and dinner cruises, with live music, dancing, and a southern buffet. | Intermediate Terminal, 3011 Dock St. | 804/644–5700 or 800/752–7093 | fax 804/644–5760 | www.annabellee.com | $20–$46 | Mar.–Dec., daily Tues.–Sun.; plantation cruise Apr.–Oct., Tues.

Richmond Raft Co. Tours. Whitewater rafting trips cut through the city on the James River, which has Class III and IV rapids. | 4400 E. Main St. | 804/222–7238 or 800/540–7238 | Prices vary | Mar.–Nov.

SPECTATOR SPORTS

Richmond Braves Baseball. This AAA farm team to the Atlanta Braves plays at the Diamond from spring to fall. | 3001 N. Blvd. | 804/359–4444 | fax 804/359–0731 | www.rbraves.com | General admission $5, special rates for seniors and children | Apr.–Sept. Call for game times.

Richmond Coliseum. The indoor stadium hosts ice shows, basketball, wrestling, and tennis tournaments. | 601 E. Leigh St. | 804/780–4970 | fax 804/780–4606.

Richmond International Raceway. NASCAR races are held here, usually in June, September, and October. | 602 E. Laburnum Ave., State Fairgrounds at Strawberry Hill | 804/345–7223 | fax 804/321–3833 | www.rir.com | Ticket prices vary | May, Sept.

OTHER POINTS OF INTEREST

City Hall Observation Deck. From the top of City Hall you can see all of downtown, with Church Hill stretching to the east and the James River to the south. If you arrive after 5 PM or on a weekend, enter the building from its side entrance on 9th Street. | 900 E. Broad St. | 804/646–7000 | Free | Mon.–Thurs. 8–8, Fri.–Sun. 8–5.

Kanawha Canal Locks. George Washington proposed the James River–Kanawha Canal as a way of bringing ships around the falls of the James River. Dating from 1785, it was the country's first canal system. This restored lock has been incorporated into Kanawha Park. Under the park archway, a free slide show recounts the history of the canal. A scenic walk continues over a footbridge to Brown's Island, across from the ruins of the Tredegar Iron Foundry, a vital supplier of cannons throughout the Civil War. | 12th Street and Byrd Street | 804/358–5511 or 888/742–4666 | Free | Daily 9–5.

ON THE CALENDAR

APR.: *Historic Garden Week in Virginia.* At "America's largest open house" you can tour more than 250 of the state's finest homes, gardens, and landmarks. Information is

KODAK'S TIPS FOR PHOTOGRAPHING PEOPLE

Friends' Faces
· Pose subjects informally to keep the mood relaxed
· Try to work in shady areas to avoid squints
· Let kids pick their own poses

Strangers' Faces
· In crowds, work from a distance with a telephoto lens
· Try posing cooperative subjects
· Stick with gentle lighting—it's most flattering to faces

Group Portraits
· Keep the mood informal
· Use soft, diffuse lighting
· Try using a panoramic camera

People at Work
· Capture destination-specific occupations
· Use tools for props
· Avoid flash if possible

Sports
· Fill the frame with action
· Include identifying background
· Use fast shutter speeds to stop action

Silly Pictures
· Look for or create light-hearted situations
· Don't be inhibited
· Try a funny prop

Parades and Ceremonies
· Stake out a shooting spot early
· Show distinctive costumes
· Isolate crowd reactions
· Be flexible: content first, technique second

From *Kodak Guide to Shooting Great Travel Pictures* © 2000 by Fodor's Travel Publications

available at the Garden Club of Virginia (12 E. Franklin St., Richmond, 23219). | 804/644–7776.

APR.: *Strawberry Hill Races.* This steeplechase event at the Strawberry Hill Fairgrounds (600 E. Laburnum Ave.) is one of Richmond's premier social gatherings. A carriage parade and elaborate themed tailgate parties are part of the festivities. | 804/228–3200.

APR.: *Richmond Civil War Days.* Military demonstrations, period games, music, and living history presentations at Chimborazo Park in Church Hill. | 804/226–1981.

MAY: *Living History Weekend at Drewry's Bluff.* A Civil War reenactment at the Fort Harrison unit of Richmond National Battlefield Park. | 804/266–1981.

JUNE: *June Jubilee.* Music by local and regional acts, arts and crafts, food vendors, and children's games downtown. | 800/365–7272.

JUNE: *Festival of the Arts.* Several weeks of free concerts, dance performances, and dramatic productions in an outdoor amphitheater at Dogwood Dell in Byrd Park. | 804/780–5733.

JUNE: *Living History Weekend at Cold Harbor.* Artillery demonstrations and encampments take place at the Cold Harbor unit of Richmond National Battlefield Park. | 804/266–1981.

JULY: *Big Gig, Richmond's International Festival of Music.* Richmond hosts some 50 free concerts at different venues around the city; there's rock, jazz, reggae, zydeco, classical music, and more. | 804/643–2826.

AUG.: *Carytown Watermelon Festival.* Carytown, a small neighborhood west of the Boulevard in Richmond's upper Fan District, is blocked off for this community event, which has food from area restaurants, exhibits, sidewalk sales, live entertainment, and, of course, watermelon. Most of the festivities take place along Cary Street. | 804/359–4645.

SEPT.–OCT.: *Virginia State Fair.* The traditional state fair attractions are here, with agricultural exhibits, animal contests, top-name entertainers, carnival rides, and food booths, at Strawberry Hill Fairgrounds. | 804/228–3200 or 800/588–3247.

OCT.: *Richmond Children's Festival.* Music, drama, professional performances, roving entertainers, crafts, and food, at Byrd Park. | 804/355–7200.

OCT.: *Richmond Newpapers Marathon.* This is the area's biggest sporting event. Some 3,000 runners and wheelchair racers compete in a 26-mi marathon. A 13-mi half-marathon and a 5-mi race are also held. There are more activities at the finishing line downtown at 6th and Broad Sts. | 804/775–2724.

OCT.: *2nd Street Festival.* The two-day downtown (2nd St.) celebration of Jackson Ward's African-American community has jazz, ragtime, and gospel concerts; street dancing and dramatic performances; and plenty of soul food, including chitterlings, pigs' feet, and fried chicken. There are vendors selling jewelry, prints, and crafts. | 804/643–2826.

WALKING TOUR

Historic Downtown (approximately 3–4 hours)

Begin at Capitol Square, at 9th and Bank streets. Dominating this green oasis in the city's center is the **State Capitol,** designed by Thomas Jefferson. There are tours highlighting the building's history and its architectural highlights. Beyond the main entrance, note the **Equestrian Statue of Washington.** Next door to the Capitol, on the east side, is the Federal-style **Governor's Mansion,** the oldest governor's mansion in the United States still in use. Follow the path past the front of the mansion and exit the square onto Governor Street. Walk one block north to Broad Street, then west two blocks. On the corner of 8th and Broad streets is the **Virginia State Library and Archives,** where you can browse through the vast repository of books, maps, and manuscripts on Virginia history. For a different kind of perspective, cross to the other side of Broad Street and enter City Hall at the corner of 9th and Broad streets. Take an elevator to the **City Hall Observation Deck,** which has a panoramic view of downtown Richmond, with its mix of glass skyscrapers and Civil War–era buildings. Walk one block north to Marshall Street. Between 8th and 9th streets stands the **John Marshall House,** former residence of the famous U.S. Supreme Court justice. The restored home displays family furnishings and mementos. Walk one block north to Clay Street, then east about two blocks to tour the **Valentine Museum,** where Richmond's social history is traced through decorative arts, textiles, and other exhibits. Just two blocks east on Clay Street is an historical attraction of a different stripe. The **Museum of the Confederacy** showcases Confederate artifacts and memorabilia. If you have time, tour the **White House of the Confederacy,** adjacent to the museum, which has been restored to pre-wartime appearance. Head two blocks south back to Broad Street, and then walk west six blocks to **6th Street Marketplace,** an airy, indoor shopping center where you can get a refreshment at the food court and browse through specialty boutiques. Walk east two blocks to 8th Street, turn right, and go two more blocks to the intersection of Grace and 8th streets to view **St. Paul's Episcopal Church,** where Robert E. Lee and Jefferson Davis worshiped during the Civil War. To return to Capitol Square, your starting point, walk one block west on Grace Street.

Dining

INEXPENSIVE

Cafe Indochine. Eclectic. The weekday lunch-only version of Indochine down the street, this elegant café serves a fixed-price mid-day meal, including soup or salad. Order at the counter; the servers will bring the food to the table. The signature dishes are French/Vietnamese, but other Asian flavors and Mediterranean seasonings also show up. Wrap sandwiches are popular. No smoking. | 1209 E. Cary St. | 804/225–1331 | Closed weekends. No dinner | $7 | AE, DC, MC, V.

Caffe Di Pagliacci. Italian. The owner's outstanding collection of clown memorabilia is on display at this neighborhood eatery in the Fan District. Try the seafood dishes, the stuffed leg of veal, the Italian-style stuffed pork, and for dessert, the chocolate mousse. | 214 N. Lombardy St. | 804/353–3040 | Closed Sun. No lunch | $8–$19 | AE, D, MC, V.

Farouk's House of India. Indian. Saag Paneer, spinach and homemade Indian cheese over rice, is popular at this ethnic eatery. | 3033 W. Cary St. | 804/355–0378 | No lunch Mon. | 6–$18 | MC, V.

Peking Pavilion. Chinese. Asian antiques complement the traditional fare here. Sunday brunch. | 1302 E. Cary St. | 804/649–8888 | No lunch Sat. | $7–$24 | AE, MC, V.

Penny Lane Pub and Restaurant. Terry O'Neill came from Liverpool to open the Penny Lane Pub in 1978. Sample the brews and British pub grub: the cottage pie, bangers and mash, or fish and chips. | 207 N. 7th St. | 804/780–1682 | $7–$20 | AE, MC, V.

Tanglewood Ordinary. Southern. This rustic spot, 28 mi northwest of Richmond, has family-style service in a log cabin built in 1928. *Saturday Evening Post* covers dating from 1913 are on the walls, and fried chicken and Virginia country ham are on the menu. No smoking. | 2210 River Rd. W, Maidens | 804/784–7011 | Reservations essential | Closed Mon.–Tues. No lunch Wed.–Sat. | $5–$11 | No credit cards.

Winnie's. Caribbean. The bright blue and yellow bamboo chairs, palm trees, and tropical plants accent the yellow cream walls. The West Indian specialties include hot and spicy Jamaican jerk chicken, roti, curried goat, homemade lemonade, corn fritters, crab cakes, and coconut bread pudding. Kids' menu. Beer and wine only. No smoking. | 200 E. Main St. | 804/649–4974 | Closed Sun. | $7–$22 | MC, V.

Yen Ching. Chinese. An elegant room with a skylight, greenery, and an indoor fountain, serves Cantonese, Mandarin, Hunan, and Szechuan specialities. | 6601 Midlothian Tpk. | 804/276–7430 | Reservations essential | $6–$25 | AE, DC, MC, V.

MODERATE

Amici. Italian. Northern Italian fare and buffalo and wild game specials are served here. The busy first floor seats 18, the quieter second floor seats 40, and there is an open-air patio in front. | 3343 W. Cary St. | 804/353–4700 | No lunch Sun. | $14–$23 | AE, D, DC, MC, V.

Avalon. Contemporary. The menu of this restaurant in the Fan District changes seasonally, but the flavors are international. There's a full bar and an extensive list of imported and microbrew beers. There's Derk's Dallas Duck, Bangkok chicken, and filet mignon in peanut sauce. | 2619 W. Main St. | 804/353–9709 | No lunch | $13–$19 | AE, DC, D, MC, V.

Byram's Lobster House. Seafood. Along with live lobster and other seafood, steak, pasta, and lamb chops are served here. There's a full bar, where you can grab a meal if the room is crowded. Local artwork is on display. Early-bird suppers weekdays. | 3215 W. Broad St. | 804/355–9193 | $9–$16 | AE, D, DC, MC, V.

Hard Shell. Seafood. The downtown/Shockoe Slip spot has a full raw bar. Try the house pasta (mixed seafood tossed with penne), seafood quesadilla, and vegetable strudel. There's an outdoor patio courtyard and Sunday brunch. | 1411 E. Cary St. | 804/643–2333 | Closed Sun. No lunch Sat. | $12–$21 | AE, DC, D, MC, V.

Kabuto Steak House. Japanese. Chicken, steak, seafood, lobster tail, shrimp, and scallops are prepared tableside. There's a sushi bar, too. Kids' menu. | 8052 W. Broad St. | 804/747–9573 | No lunch weekends | $12–$23 | AE, D, DC, MC, V.

O'Toole's. Eclectic. The standards–steak, chicken, seafood, and pasta–are here with finger food, cold cuts, burgers, and pizza at this Irish bar. The restaurant seats 130 people at tables or booths. Kids' menu. | 4800 Forest Hill Ave. | 804/233–1781 | $9–$16 | AE, D, MC, V.

Tobacco Company. American/Continental. This is a versatile spot, with three floors in a renovated 19th-century tobacco company building. The first floor is a lounge with a bar, couches, a fireplace, and exposed brick walls. The second floor is formal; the third floor is more casual with Greenwich wicker furniture. There is also an open-air garden atrium. The menu includes prime rib, and there's a dessert buffet. Band Monday–Saturday. Sunday brunch. | 1201 E. Cary St. | 804/782–9431 | No lunch Sun. | $12–$30 | AE, D, DC, MC, V.

EXPENSIVE

Frog and the Redneck. Contemporary. This modern room has mirrored columns and murals by a local artist. Regional specialties are served: jumbo lumpmeat crabcakes, softshell crabs, local fresh fish, fresh meat and produce from local farmers, and buffalo. No smoking. | 1423 E. Cary St. | 804/648–3764 | Closed Sun. No lunch | $17–$34 | AE, D, DC, MC, V.

Half Way House. Contemporary. The restaurant serves American food in an intimate room: candlelight, low ceilings, brick walls, and a fireplace at each end of the room. The bill of fare includes filet mignon with fried shrimp and chocolate almond coconut cheesecake. | 10301 Jefferson Davis Hwy./Rte. 1 | 804/275–1760 | No lunch weekends | $24–$32 | AE, D, DC, MC, V.

Indochine. Vietnamese. The kitchen at this elegant room serves Asian spice with a French flair, with dishes like jumbo shrimp sauteed with honey and cayenne pepper, and Chilean sea bass stuffed with lump crabmeat with a saffron and cognac curry sauce. No smoking. | 2923 W. Cary St. | 804/353–5799 | Reservations essential Fri.–Sat. | Closed Sun. No lunch | $18–$28 | AE, D, DC, MC, V.

La Petite France. French. Classic cuisine is served by tuxedoed waiters. Specialties include Dover sole almondine, soft shell crabs, dessert souffles, and seasonal fruit and vegetables. The restaurant is kid-friendly and will cut or alter portions as needed. | 2108 Maywill St. | 804/353–8729 | Closed Sun.–Mon., 2 wks before Labor Day. No lunch Sat. | $19–$30 | AE, D, DC, MC, V.

Lemaire. Southern. There are eight small dining rooms serving regional Southern cooking with European classical and American contemporary influences. Their inspiration is the Jeffersonian style—marble, heavy drapes, rich colors. The nightly four-course tasting menu comes with a specially selected wine. Specialties are crab cakes, duck breast, and loin of lamb. | Main St., between Adams and Franklin Sts. | 804/788–8000 | Breakfast also available | $23–$35 | AE, D, DC, MC, V.

Mr. Patrick Henry's Inn. Continental. The chef-owned inn in a classic townhouse has a gourmet restaurant on the main floor, a pub in the English basement, and a garden patio. The fare includes fresh seafood, regional cuisine, fresh herbs and vegetables from the chef's garden, and homemade breads, desserts, and soups. The colonial-style inn has wood-burning fireplaces, porcelain and brass chandeliers, and high ceilings. There are five dining areas and four suites for overnight lodging. The deck overlooks formal gardens and the pony bridal path behind the inn. | 2300–02 E. Broad St. | 804/644–1322, 800/932–2654 | Closed Sun. No lunch weekends | $28–$40 | AE, D, DC, MC, V.

Ruth's Chris Steak House. Steak. Ruth Fertel's New Orleans-based chain opened this branch in the Bellgrade Plantation, originally built as a 1½-story farmhouse in 1732. There is open-air dining at an eight-table garden patio in the back, and an organist Tuesday–Sunday. The plantation is 14 mi southwest of Richmond. | 11500 W. Huguenot Rd., Midlothian | www.sizzlingsteak.com | 804/378–0600 | No lunch | $18–$31 | AE, D, DC, MC, V.

Sam Miller's Warehouse. Seafood/Steak. The menu includes crab cakes, crab soup, slow-roasted prime rib, hand-cut western beef, and whole live lobster. A relaxed room, with 100-year-old exposed brick walls and antique mirrors. Sunday brunch. | 1210 E. Cary St. | 804/643–1301 | $16–$29 | AE, D, DC, MC, V.

Skilligalee. Seafood. For a cross-section of the menu, order a seafood platter: shrimp scallops, oysters, fish, crab cake, and a deviled clam. There are three working fireplaces and nautical memorabilia. Kids' menu. | 5416 Glenside Dr. | 804/672–6200 | No lunch weekends | $17–$21 | AE, DC, MC, V.

Lodging

INEXPENSIVE

Amerisuites. The all-suite chain property, opened in 1997, is in Innsbrook Corporate Center, about 8 mi west of downtown, 10 mi from Richmond International Raceway, and 13 mi from the Civil War Visitors Center. Four restaurants are adjacent to the hotel. Complimentary Continental breakfast. Microwaves, cable TV, in-room VCRs. Pool. Exercise equipment. Laundry facilities. Business services. | 4100 Cox Rd., Glenn Allen | 804/747–9644 | fax 804/346–9320 | www.amerisuites.com | 126 suites | $89 suites | AE, D, DC, MC, V.

Berkeley. The 6-story hotel is in the heart of Shockoe Slip. The rooms are filled with reproduction antiques and silk and brocade fabrics, with double beds and a sitting area with couches. Restaurant, bar. In-room data ports, cable TV. Business services. Airport shuttle. | 1200 E. Cary St. | 804/780–1300 | fax 804/648–4728 | www.gateway-va.com/berkeley | 55 rooms | $110–$155 | AE, D, DC, MC, V.

Commonwealth Park Suites Hotel. This century-old, 11-story building overlooks Capitol Square, within walking distance of museums and historical sites. There are double beds or a single king. Cafe, bar. Complimentay breakfast. In-room data ports, minibars, refrigerators, room service, cable TV. Business services. | 901 Bank St. | 804/343–7300 or 888/343–7301 | fax 804/343–1025 | 9 rooms, 50 suites | $109–$115, $129–$169 suites | AE, D, DC, MC, V.

Courtyard by Marriott. The chain hotel has standard rooms with double beds. It's about 6 mi west of downtown. Restaurant. Bar. In-room data ports, some refrigerators, cable TV. Pool. Hot tub. Exercise equipment. Laundry facilities. Business services. Free parking. | 6400 W. Broad St. | 804/282–1881 | fax 804/288–2934 | www.courtyardmarriott.com | 145 rooms | $114–$149 | AE, D, DC, MC, V.

Crowne Plaza. This modern, downtown hotel has 16 stories. Upper-floor rooms have views of the James River or the city skyline. Restaurant, bar. In-room data ports, cable TV. Pool.

Hot tub. Exercise equipment. Business services. | 555 E. Canal St. | 804/788–0900 | fax 804/788–0791 | www.basshotels.com/crowneplaza | 297 rooms | $119–$159 | AE, D, DC, MC, V.

Embassy Suites. The member of the all-suites chain is in Commerce Center, about 12 mi west of downtown. There are eight stories with balconies, standard double beds, and a living room with a pull-out couch. Restaurant, bar, complimentary breakfast. In-room data ports, microwaves, refrigerators, cable TV. Pool. Hot tub. Exercise equipment. Laundry facilities. Business services. | 2925 Emerywood Pkwy. | 804/672–8585 | fax 804/672–3749 | www.embassysuites.com | 226 suites | $109–$170 suites; under 18 free | AE, D, DC, MC, V.

Emmanuel Hutzler House. In the Fan District, west of downtown, this inn has four–poster mahogany beds, flowered quilts, wallpaper, antique lamps, sofas, and dressers. Some rooms have a fireplace and sitting areas. Complimentary breakfast. No-smoking, cable TV. No kids under 12. | 2036 Monument Ave. | 804/353–6900 | fax 804/355–5053 | www.bensonhouse.com | 4 rooms | $105–$155 | AE, D, DC, MC, V.

Fairfield Inn by Marriott. The chain hotel has double beds or a single king. It's about 6 mi west of downtown. Picnic area, complimentary Continental breakfast. In-room data ports, microwaves (in suites), refrigerators, cable TV. Pool. Business services. | 7300 W. Broad St. | 804/672–8621 | fax 804/755–7155 | www.fairfieldinnbymarriott.com | 124 rooms, 1 suite | $66–$89, $129 suite | AE, D, DC, MC, V.

Hampton Inn. The 5-story building is in the Innsbrook Corporate Center, about 8 mi west of downtown. The rooms have double beds or a single king. Complimentary Continental breakfast, picnic area. In-room data ports, cable TV. Pool. Exercise equipment. Business services. | 10800 W. Broad St. | 804/747–7777 | fax 804/747–7069 | www.hampton-inn.com | 136 rooms | $89–$103 | AE, D, DC, MC, V.

Henry Clay Inn. Inspired by a small, turn-of-the-century hotel which once stood in this spot, the Henry Clay borders the railroad tracks and has views to match. Arrive directly by train, and sit in a rocking chair on the front porch to watch the other trains go by. The Inn is furnished with Georgian revival antiques and reproductions, and local art is on display. Complimentary breakfast. In-room data ports. Cable TV. Hot tubs. Gift shop. No pets. | 114 North Railroad Ave. | 804/798–3100 | fax 804/752–7555 | www.henryclayinn.com. | 16 rooms | $90–$165. | AE, MC, V.

Hilton Airport. Convenient for air travelers, the hotel is next to Richmond International Airport and 9 mi from downtown. Balconies are in the suites only. Restaurant, bar. In-room data ports, room service, cable TV. Pool. Hot tub. Exercise equipment. Business services. Airport shuttle. Free parking. | 5501 Eubank Rd., Sandston, | 804/226–6400 | fax 804/226–1269 | www.hilton.com | 160 rooms, 122 suites | $89–$109, $129–$189 suites | AE, D, DC, MC, V.

Holiday Inn–Airport. The hotel occupies two buildings—one a tower building with six floors, the other with three floors—near Richmond International Airport, 12 mi east of the city. Built in 1974. The rooms come with double beds and a table and two chairs. Restaurant, bar. In-room data ports, microwaves, room service, cable TV. Pool. Business services. Airport shuttle. Some pets allowed. | 5203 Williamsburg Rd., Sandston, | 804/222–6450 | fax 804/226–4305 | www.holiday-inn.com | 230 rooms | $99 | AE, D, DC, MC, V.

Holiday Inn Richmond Central. You're paying for location when you book a room at this two-building complex: It's smack in the center of town. Some rooms have balconies, and there is a courtyard in the back. Restaurant. Cable TV. In-room data ports. Picnic area. Outdoor pool. Exercise facility. Laundry Service. Pets allowed. | 3207 North Blvd. | 804/359–9441 or 800/465–4329 | fax 804/359–3207 | 184 rooms | $89 | AE, D, DC, MC, V.

Inn of Virginia. At the west end of Richmond, near The Shops at Willow Lawn, the Inn is just a short walk from downtown. Built in 1950, the three-floor stucco building has a lobby furnished with antique reproductions, and spare and tidy rooms. Restaurant. Lounge. In-room data ports. Cable TV. Outdoor Pool. Laundry facilities. No pets. | 5215 W. Broad St. | 804/288–4011 or 800/289–9814 | fax 804/288–2163 | www.innsofvirginia.com | 141 rooms | $44–$74 | AE, D, DC, MC, V.

Knight's Inn. This two-story building has Romanesque columns fronting a large lawn. Though 8 mi south of downtown Richmond, the hotel is nonetheless near shopping centers and restaurants. Rooms are unadorned and basic. Restaurant. Cable TV. In-room data port. Refrigerator. Microwave. Outdoor Pool. Pets ok. | 9002 Brook Rd. | 804/266-2444 | fax 804/261-5834 | www.knightsinn.com. | 63 rooms | $44–$64 | AE, V, MC, DC, D.

La Quinta. The three-story hacienda-style hotel has a bell tower and outdoor entrances to the rooms. It's convenient to shopping—about 10 mi south of downtown. It has standard rooms with double beds. Complimentary Continental breakfast. In-room data ports, cable TV. Pool. Business services. Free parking. Some pets allowed. | 6910 Midlothian Pike/U.S. 60 W | 804/745-7100 | fax 804/276-6660 | www.LaQuinta.com | 130 rooms | $60–$67 | AE, D, DC, MC, V.

Linden Row Inn. This downtown inn, built in 1833, is a four-story building with balconies. The Victorian house is filled with antique furniture. Most of the rooms have double beds. Dining room, complimentary Continental breakfast. In-room data ports, room service, cable TV. Business services. Parking is $7 per night. | 100 E. Franklin St. | 804/783-7000 or 800/348-7424 | fax 804/648-7504 | www.lindenrowinn.com | 70 rooms, 7 suites | $99–$179, $129–$200 suites | AE, D, DC, MC, V.

Lions Inn. Built in 1870, this family-run inn has been a Richmond standby for 13 years. The three-story Italianate home has gardens in the front and back, and six bedrooms with three shared baths. Rooms, which are rented by the week, have antique furniture from the late 19th century. A small cafe is fittingly named, The Secret Garden. Cable TV. No kids. No pets. | 905 W. Grace St. | 804/355-7265. | 6 rooms | $165/week | V, MC.

Marriott. Next to Richmond Centre, this chain hotel has 18 floors, some balconies, and double beds. Restaurant, bar. In-room data ports, some refrigerators, cable TV. Indoor pool. Health Club. Laundry facilities. Business services. | 500 E. Broad St. | 804/643-3400 | fax 804/788-1230 | www.marriott.com | 400 rooms | $89–$159 | AE, D, DC, MC, V.

Mr. Patrick Henry's Inn. The inn is in the Church Hill Historic District, about ½ mi east of downtown. The classic Greek-revival townhouse has a garden patio, a carriage house, and a unique pony path. The rooms and suites have fireplaces and private baths. Restaurant, complimentary breakfast. Refrigerators, room service, cable TV. | 2300–02 E. Broad St. | 804/644-1322 or 800/932-2654 | 3 suites | $95–$135 suites | AE, D, DC, MC, V.

Quality Inn. This six-story hostelry is five mi west of downtown. Complimentary Continental breakfast. In-room data ports, cable TV. Pool. Business services. | 8008 W. Broad St. | 804/346-0000 | fax 804/346-4547 | 194 rooms | $85 | AE, D, DC, MC, V.

Red Roof Inn. This two-story chain hotel has standard rooms with double beds or a single king. Some refrigerators, cable TV. Business services. Some pets allowed. | 4350 Commerce Rd. | 804/271-7240 | fax 804/271-7245 | www.redroofinn.com | 108 rooms | $50–$70 | AE, D, DC, MC, V.

West-Bocock House. Built in 1871, this bed and breakfast is in the center of downtown Richmond, walking distance to museums, restaurants, shopping centers, and Capitol Square. Each room has a private bath, French linens, and fresh flowers. Kids are fine, but let the House know in advance. Complimentary breakfast. No pets. | 1107 Grove Ave. | 804/358-6174 | brwest@erols.com | 3 rooms | $75 | No credit cards.

William Catlin House. This two-story inn was built in 1845 in the Church Hill Historic District, 1 mi east of downtown. There is one net-canopy bed, one regular canopy bed, some four-poster beds, and one room with double beds. Some balconies. Complimentary breakfast. | 2304 E. Broad St. | 804/780-3746 | 5 rooms (2 with shared bath) | $75–$98 | D, MC, V.

Wyndham Garden Hotel–Richmond Airport. This hotel has four stories, no balconies, and standard rooms with double beds. Restaurant, bar. In-room data ports, room service, cable TV. Pool. Barber shop, beauty salon, hot tub. Exercise equipment. Business services. Airport shuttle. Free parking. Some pets allowed. | 4700 S. Laburnum Ave. | 804/226–4300 | fax 804/226–6516 | www.wyndham.com | 155 rooms, 4 suites | $125–$149 | AE, D, DC, MC, V.

MODERATE

Hyatt. The five-building complex is about 5 mi west of downtown. The rooms come with double beds or a single king. Restaurant, bar (with entertainment). In-room data ports, room service, cable TV. Indoor-outdoor pool. Tennis court. Exercise equipment. Business services. Free parking. | 6624 W. Broad St. | 804/285–1234 | fax 804/288–3961 | www.hyatt.com | 384 rooms | $109–$175 | AE, D, DC, MC, V.

Omni. This 18-story hotel is in James Center in downtown Shockoe Slip, next to shops and entertainment. Restaurant, bar with entertainment. In-room data ports, minibars, cable TV. Indoor pool. Business services. | 100 S. 12th St. | 804/344–7000 | fax 804/648–6704 | www.omnihotels.com | 363 rooms, 12 suites | $105–$169, $269–$650 suites | AE, D, DC, MC, V.

Radisson Historic District Hotel. When the State's General Assembly is in session, legislators make this former Holiday Inn their home. The restaurant looks out onto Franklin Street, and the rooftop pool has a 16-story view. Restaurant. Lounge. In-room data ports. Cable TV. Outdoor pool. Exercise facility. | 301 West Franklin Street | 804/644–9871 | fax 804/344–4380 | 230 rooms | $99–$199 | AE, D, DC, MC, V.

Residence Inn by Marriott. The apartment-style motel is about 10 mi west of downtown. Many rooms have fireplaces and double beds or a single king. Picnic area, complimentary Continental breakfast. In-room data ports, kitchenettes, microwaves, cable TV. Pool. Laundry facilities. Business services. Free parking. Some pets allowed (fee). | 2121 Dickens Rd. | 804/285–8200 | fax 804/285–2530 | www.marriott.com | 80 suites | $124–$164 | AE, D, DC, MC, V.

EXPENSIVE

The Jefferson. A downtown landmark, this restored 1895 Colonial Renaissance hotel is surrounded by luxurious public areas adorned with fine art and sculpture. Restaurant, bar. In-room data ports, refrigerators, minibars, room service, cable TV. Exercise equipment. Business services. Fee for parking. | Franklin and Adams Sts. | 804/788–8000 or 800/424–8014 | fax 804/325–0334 | sales@jefferson-hotel.com | www.jefferson-hotel.com | 274 rooms, 26 suites | $219–$275, $299–$1,600 suites | AE, D, DC, MC, V.

ROANOKE

MAP 11, F6

(Nearby town also listed: Salem)

Like much of the Valley of Virginia in the southwestern part of the state, Roanoke was settled in the early 1700s by Scots-Irish and German pioneers, many of whom were escaping economic, political, and religious oppression farther north. Originally called Big Lick for its salt marshes, this community in the Blue Ridge Mountains was a crossroads for commerce. Its present-day name derives from the Indian word "Rawrenock," which were shell beads used as currency.

In 1882, the region was transformed into a railroad hub when Norfolk and Western Railroad set up its home office here. Roanoke is now the largest metropolis west of Richmond, as well as the biggest city off the Blue Ridge Parkway. As the commercial and industrial center for western Virginia, its manufactured products include railroad cars, fabricated steel, fabrics, furniture, flour, wood products, and electronic equipment. The centerpiece of its revitalized downtown is Market Square, where museums, shops, and restaurants surround the Farmers Market, the state's oldest open-air market in continuous operation. The Roanoke Symphony and Mill Mountain Theater have made the city a center for the arts in western Virginia. Within an hour's drive are many outdoor recreational areas, including Smith Mountain Lake State Park and Jefferson National Forest.

Information: Roanoke Valley Convention and Visitors Bureau | 114 Market St., Roanoke, VA 24011-1402 | 540/342–6025 or 800/635–5535 | rkecvbfox@aol.com | www.visitroanokeva.com.

Attractions

Booker T. Washington Birthplace. Born into slavery, Booker T. Washington went on to become an inspiring educator, an advisor to presidents (McKinley, Roosevelt, and Taft), and the founder of Tuskegee Institute in Alabama. This restored plantation covers 224 acres with buildings, tools, crops, and animals evocative of a childhood spent in slavery in the mid-1800s. In summer, there are interpreters in period costume. Picnic facilities are available. | 12130 Booker T. Washington Ave., Hardy | 540/721–2094 | fax 540/721–8311 | www.nps.gov | Free | Daily 9–5.

Blue Ridge Parkway. (*See also* town listing.) This scenic roadway follows the mountaintops both north and south of Roanoke, beginning in the Shannon Della National Forest and ending in the Great Smoky Mountains. Camping, hiking, fishing, bicycling, and picnicking are all available. | 540/857–2213 Vinton Ranger Station or 540/857–2458 weather–related closures | www.blueridgeparkway.org | Free | Parts of the parkway close during winter months because of snow and ice; call for weather-related updates.

Center in the Square. The cultural center has displays on history, science, and the arts. In addition to three museums, the building contains the Arts Council of the Blue Ridge, and Mill Mountain Theatre, a regional, professional theatre. | One Market Sq. | 540/342–5700 | fax 540/224–1238 | www.cits.org | Museum fees vary | Mon.–Sat. 10–5, Sun. 1–5.

Science Museum of Western Virginia. Natural history is the focus of this museum, which has many hands-on exhibits that appeal to youngsters, including live-animal programs and a Chesapeake Bay "touch tank." The Hopkins Planetarium has programs on the stars, planets, and galaxies. There's a museum shop. | One Market Sq. | 540/342–5710 | fax 540/224–1240 | Museum $5, planetarium $2.60, combined ticket $6.30 | Mon.–Sat. 10–5, Sun. 1–5; call for seasonal planetarium schedule.

History Museum and Historical Society of Western Virginia. Here's a curious collection of regional artifacts, including relics of the local Native Americans. The permanent exhibits illustrate the history of southwest Virginia from prehistoric times to the present; rotating exhibits are regularly mounted. A library and archives are open to the public by

KODAK'S TIPS FOR USING LIGHTING

Daylight
• Use the changing color of daylight to establish mood
• Use light direction to enhance subjects' properties
• Match light quality to specific subjects

Dramatic Lighting
• Anticipate dramatic lighting events
• Explore before and after storms

Sunrise, Sunset, and Afterglow
• Include a simple foreground
• Exclude the sun when setting your exposure
• After sunset, wait for the afterglow to color the sky

From Kodak Guide to Shooting Great Travel Pictures © 2000 by Fodor's Travel Publications

appointment. There's a museum shop. | One Market Sq | 540/342–5770 | fax 540/224–1256 | $2 | Tues.–Fri. 10–4, Sat. 10–5, Sun. 1–5.

Art Museum of Western Virginia. This museum's collection emphasizes regional works, particularly Appalachian folk art and area decorative arts. A gallery shows changing exhibits of traditional and contemporary art. Guided tours are available. | One Market Sq. | 540/342–5760 | fax 540/342–5798 | Free | Tues.–Sat. 10–5, Sun.–Mon. 1–5.

George Washington and Jefferson National Forests. *(See also* Harrisonburg.*)* Encompassing some 1.8 million acres, this forest land stretches from Winchester to Big Stone Gap, and covers the Blue Ridge, Massanutten, Shenandoah, and Allegheny mountain ranges. Fishing, riding, hunting, and skiing are available in these woods. The Appalachian Trail can be accessed near Rte. 311 in Salem and via U.S. 220 in Troutville. | Headquarters, 5162 Valleypointe Pkwy., Roanoke | 540/265–5100 | fax 540/265–5145 | www.fs.fed.us/gwjnf | Free; parking fees are charged at some recreational areas | Daily.

Mill Mountain Zoological Park. In this 3-acre park you'll find 45 species of exotic and native animals, including a Siberian tiger, a snow leopard, and red pandas. There's also a discovery center, Camp Wildcat, for youngsters. | Walnut Ave. | 540/343–3241 | www.mmzoo.org | $6 | Daily 10–5 (gate closes at 4:30).

Smith Mountain Lake State Park. Covering 20,600 acres, Smith Mountain Lake is Virginia's second-largest freshwater lake, with 500 mi of jagged shoreline that spans three counties, Bedford, Franklin, and Pittsylvania counties. The sprawling park rents every kind of boat—from pontoons and canoes to motorboats—and there are swimming, waterskiing, and jetskiing, a handicapped-accessible fishing pier, hiking trails, an 18-hole golf course, primitive campsites, and cabins. The lake is one of the hottest trophy fishing waters in the region, particularly for striped bass; large bass angling tournaments are regularly held here. Memorial Day through Labor Day, a public beach is open. A visitor center has nature programs and natural history exhibits. | 1235 State Park Rd., Huddleston | 540/297–6066 or 800/933–7275 | fax 540/297–1578 | www.sml-chamber.com | Free; parking $2 Memorial Day–Labor Day, $1 Labor Day–Memorial Day | Daily dawn–dusk; visitor center Mon.–Sat. 10–5, Sun. noon–5.

Virginia Museum of Transportation. This downtown museum, near Market Square, has the largest collection of diesel and steam locomotives in the country. The dozens of original train cars and engines, many built here in town, include a massive Nickel Plate locomotive. Antique autos, buses, and carriages. A library and archive are open to the public. | 303 Norfolk Ave. | 540/342–5670 | fax 540/342–6898 | www.vmt.org | $6 | Mar.–Dec., Mon.–Sat. 10–5, Sun. noon–5; Jan.–Feb., Tues.–Sat. 10–5, Sun. noon–5.

Virginia's Explore Park. This 1,100-acre park depicts life in Virginia from three distinct historical periods. Costumed interpreters represent early Native American life, the colonial frontier experience, and the life of a 19th-century settlement, complete with a schoolhouse and blacksmith's shop. The park also has 8 mi of hiking trails along the Roanoke River gorge. | Rutrough Rd. | 540/427–1800 | fax 540/427–1880 | www.explorepark.org | $6 | May–Nov., Mon.–Sat. 10–6, Sun. noon–6; Apr., Fri.–Mon. 10–6.

ON THE CALENDAR

APR.: *Vinton Dogwood Festival.* The celebration includes a parade, an antique car show, a crafts show, amusement rides, a Miss Dogwood competition, and live entertainment along Washington Avenue in neighboring, Vinton, three mi west of Roanoke. | 540/983–0613.

MAY: *Virginia State Championship Chili Cookoff.* Some 65 local and regional teams compete to represent Virginia in the annual World Chili Cookoff at the City Market on Market Square. Adjunct activities include a salsa competition, crafts, vendors, a chili-pepper-eating contest, and entertainment. | 540/342–2028 or 540/342–4716.

MAY–JUNE: *Festival in the Park.* One of the city's largest events spans 11 days: performing arts, a juried fine arts show, a parade, theater, children's activities, evening con-

ROANOKE

INTRO
ATTRACTIONS
DINING
LODGING

certs with regional and national acts, sporting events, antique shows, wine tastings, a fireworks and laser show, an illusionist, and a gala party. | 540/342–2640.

OCT.–AUG.: *Mill Mountain Theatre.* This professional theater at Center in the Square on Market Square, stages new and original works, musicals, classic dramas, and children's plays. | 540/342–5740.

Dining

Alexander's. Contemporary. The first new restaurant to locate in the old downtown area since its revival, Alexander's is housed in a three-story Victorian building dating from the 1880s. The restaurant displays artifacts from the town's past. Work by local artists hangs side-by-side with antique etchings on the walls. The kitchen specializes in fresh fish and seafood, including crab cakes and barbecued shrimp. | 105 S. Jefferson St. | 540/982–6983 | Closed Sun.–Mon. No lunch Tues., Thurs–Sat. | $13–$26 | V, MC.

Billy's Ritz. American/French. This downtown dining spot is housed in two century-old buildings in sight of the old railroads. The front dining room includes a wood-paneled, mirrored bar; the second, the building's original tin ceilings. Arched French doors lead from the third dining room to a tree-lined courtyard with open-air dining for 60. The menu includes grilled salmon with gingery greens, filet Diane, Alaskan king crab legs, crawfish pie, goat cheese salad, and chicken teriyaki. | 102 Salem Ave. SE | 540/342–3937 | No lunch | $7–$23 | AE, D, DC, MC, V.

Buck Mountain Grille. American. Housed in a former hotel along the Blue Ridge Parkway above Roanoke, the dining room is sunny and bright during the day and dimly lit at night, with a fireplace in winter. The menu includes crab cakes, steak, and vegetarian dishes. Kids' menu. | 5002 Franklin Rd. | 540/776–1830 | No lunch Mon., Sat. | $8–$20 | AE, D, DC, MC, V.

Carlos Brazilian International Cuisine. Brazilian. The intimate restaurant is in downtown Roanoke, just outside the century-old City Market. There's lots of meat here but vegetarian dishes are also available. Try *feijoada,* a traditional Brazilian dish of black beans simmered with sausage, pork, and beef, or the signature dish, *porco recheado* (pork tenderloin stuffed with spinach and feta in apple brandy sauce). | 312 Market St. SE | 540/345–7661 | Reservations essential | Closed Sun. | $9–$21 | AE, MC, V.

Charcoal Steakhouse. American. This elegant room has a dance floor and a grand piano. The menu includes prime rib, New York strip steak, and rib-eye. There's a jazz bass-and-piano duo with (occasionally) a vocalist on weekends. Kids' menu. | 5225 Williamson Rd. | 540/366–3710 | Closed Mon. No lunch Sat. | $13–$17 | AE, D, DC, MC, V.

The Homeplace. Southern. This 1907 Victorian house, northwest of Roanoke, is surrounded by farmland, down the mountain from the Appalachian Trail, and within sight of the turn-of-the-century Catawba General Store. The kitchen serves old-fashioned southern dishes including fried chicken, country ham, roast beef, pork barbecue (Thursday only), real mashed potatoes, baked apples, homemade biscuits, and peach and cherry cobblers, with family-style service. There's a gift shop. Live music every other Saturday. No alcoholic beverages. No smoking. | 4968 Catawba Valley Dr., Catawba | 540/384–7252 | Call for hrs | $9–$11 | MC, V, D.

Kabuki. Japanese. This atmospheric steakhouse displays samurai armor and masks, and Japanese antiques. Chicken and seafood dishes are served. Kids' menu. | 3503 Franklin Rd. SW | 540/981–0222 | Reservations essential Fri.–Sat. | No lunch | $14–$30 | AE, D, DC, MC, V.

The Library. Continental. The rooms are lined with bookshelves. The menu includes Dover sole and roasted rack of lamb. | 3117 Franklin Rd. | 540/985–0811 | Closed Sun.–Mon. No lunch | $13–$26 | AE, D, DC, MC, V.

Nawab Indian Cuisine. Indian. Near the glass front you can catch a glimpse of the huge neon star lit up on top of Mill Mountain at the edge of downtown. The kitchen serves chicken tikka masala, tandoori, mixed grill, lamb krahi goshat, lamb mango, and mango lassi (a nonalcoholic yogurt beverage). An extensive vegetarian menu is available as well. Buffet lunch weekdays. Sitar music Friday. | 118A Campbell Ave. | 540/345–5150 | $8–$15 | AE, D, MC, V.

Norberto's Italian Ristorante. Italian. This tiny, intimate, candlelit restaurant, owned by a Brazilian family, is in Grandin Village, just around the corner from Roanoke's Grandin Theatre. Their specialties include shrimp scampi, traditional scallopini, and salad with avocado vinaigrette. | 1908 Memorial Ave. | 540/342–1611 | No lunch | $10–$24 | AE, D, MC, V.

Pine Room Pub. American. This British pub in the century-old Hotel Roanoke is noisy at lunch hour, cozy in the evening. It consists of two rooms with knotty pine paneling, a fireplace, a billiards room, and a juke box. They have hearty soups and sandwiches, open-air dining on the patio, and live acoustic guitar on weekends. Sun. brunch. Free parking. | 110 Shenandoah Ave. | 540/985–5900 | $10–$15 | AE, D, MC, V.

Pine Tavern. Continental. The rustic seven-room lodge and restaurant are at the top of Pine Mountain, an hour's drive out of Roanoke. The walls, still covered with the original 1937 knotty pine, are hung with local photography, pottery, or paintings. Displays are changed every six weeks. The restaurant is lit with oil lamps at night. There are open-mike nights on Sundays, an occasional local dinner-theater performance, and live music twice a month on Friday nights including jazz, rock and roll, reggae, or solo violin. The menu includes seafood, vegetarian dishes, steak, pasta, and cooked-to-order chef's choice dishes. There's open-air dining on a wooden deck surrounded by huge oak trees and lovely gardens. Kids' menu. | 611 Floyd Hwy. N | 540/745–4482 | Closed Mon.–Tues. No lunch Wed.–Sun. | $12–$20 | MC, V.

Regency Room. American. The grand dining room reflects the old-fasioned elegance of the Hotel Roanoke. The kitchen serves the room's trademark peanut soup and spoonbread. There's open-air dining on the veranda, a salad bar and buffet at lunch, and early-bird suppers. A pianist or a three-piece jazz combo performs Tuesday–Saturday. Kids' menu. No smoking. Valet parking $5–$8. | 110 Shenandoah Ave. | 540/985–5900 | Reservations essential | No lunch Sun. | $25–$40 | AE, DC, D, MC, V.

Stephen's. Cajun. The theme is southern Louisiana, with dishes like "South Louisiana" (blackened fillet of Norwegian salmon with crawfish étoufée, oysters Rockefeller, and fried shrimp) and the "Gulf Shore" (fried shrimp and peanut-crusted roast pork tenderloin with barbecue sauce). | 2926 Franklin Rd. SW | 540/344–7203 | Reservations required | Closed Sun. No lunch | $11–$24 | AE, D, MC, V.

Sunnybrook Inn. American. Family-style food is served at this turn-of-the-century inn, which seats 65. The menu includes Virginia country ham, fried oysters, and peanut butter pie. There's outdoor dining in a screened-in patio with a roof, a salad bar, and daily buffets, with special buffets on weekends. Kids' menu. Beer and wine only. | 7342 Plantation Rd. NW | 540/366–4555 | Closed Mon. | $6–$18 | DC, MC, V.

Lodging

AmeriSuites Roanoke/Valley View Mall. This six-story chain hotel is near Valley View Mall and the Roanoke Regional Airport. Many restaurants are in walking distance, and the hotel is less than five mi to downtown Roanoke. Rooms are very clean, though unexceptional. Complimentary Continental breakfast. Picnic Area. Kitchenettes. Cable TV. Indoor pool. Exercise equipment. Airport Shuttle. Pets allowed. | 5040 Valley View Blvd. | 540/366–4700 or 800/833–1516 | fax 540/366–1157 | 128 rooms | $89–$139 | AE, D, DC, MC, V.

Apple Valley Motel. This one-story brick lodging is a quiet, secluded option that's still convenient to area shopping malls (less than 2 mi away), and 5 mi from downtown Roanoke. Cable TV. No pets. | 5063 Franklin Rd. | 540/989–0675 | 18 rooms | $38–$45 | AE, D, DC, MC, V.

Bernard's Landing Resort and Conference Center. Jutting out on a peninsula on Smith Mountain Lake, 45 minutes from downtown Roanoke, Bernard's is easily accessible to 500 mi of shoreline. Every room has a view of the lake. Restaurant. In-room data ports. Kitchenettes. Cable TV. In-room VCR. 2 outdoor pools. Hot tub. Exercise equipment. Racquetball. Bicycles.

| 775 Ashmeade Rd., Moneta | 540/721–8870 or 800/572–2048 | fax 540/721–8383 | 75 rooms | $95–$260 | AE, D, DC, MC, V.

Civic Center Inn. The hotel, next to the Roanoke Civic Center, has double beds or a single king. Restaurant, bar, complimentary Continental breakfast. In-room data ports, room service, cable TV. Pool, wading pool. Business services. Free parking. | 501 Orange Ave. | 540/342–8961 | fax 540/342–3813 | 150 rooms | $64–$80 | AE, D, DC, MC, V.

Claiborne House. Built in 1895, this Victorian inn has lace canopy queen-size beds. Complimentary breakfast. No smoking. Cable TV, phones in some rooms. Business services. | 185 Claiborne Ave., Rocky Mount, | 540/483–4616 | fax 540/484–1504 | 3 rooms; 2 suites | $75–$150 | MC, V.

Clarion-Airport. This four-story hotel, near the Roanoke Regional Airport, has standard rooms with double beds or a single king. Restaurant, bar, picnic area. In-room data ports, some microwaves, refrigerators, room service, cable TV. Indoor-outdoor pool. Hot tub. Tennis court. Exercise equipment. Business services. Airport shuttle. Free parking. Some pets allowed. | 2727 Ferndale Dr. | 540/362–4500 | fax 540/362–4506 | www.roanokeclarion.com | 154 rooms | $100–$110 | AE, D, DC, MC, V.

Colony House. This modern hotel has spacious rooms with double beds or a single king. Complimentary Continental breakfast. In-room hot tub, refrigerator (in suites), cable TV. Pool. Business services. Free parking. | 3560 Franklin Rd. SW; N on 81 to Exit 143 | 540/345–0411 or 800/552–7026 reservations | fax 540/345–0411 | 69 rooms | $61 | AE, D, DC, MC, V.

Days Inn–Airport/Interstate. This two-story chain hotel is close to I–81 and five mi from Roanoke Regional Airport. It has double beds in most rooms. Restaurant, bar. In-room data ports, cable TV. Pool. Business services. Airport shuttle. Free parking. | 8118 Plantation Rd. | 540/366–0341 | fax 540/366–3935 | 123 rooms | $52–$60 | AE, D, DC, MC, V.

Doubletree Hotel Roanoke and Conference Center. One block from Market Square, this six-story, restored Tudor Revival structure (1882) is set on a hillside downtown. It has elegant public areas and guest rooms with fireplaces. Restaurant, bar with entertainment. In-room data ports, some refrigerators, cable TV. Exercise equipment. Pool. Hot tub. Business services. Airport shuttle. | 110 Shenandoah Ave. | 540/985–5900 | fax 540/345–2890 | www.hotelroanoke.com | 332 rooms | $109–$149 | AE, D, DC, MC, V.

Hampton Inn–Airport. This two-story, hilltop chain hotel has outdoor entrances and spacious rooms with double beds or a single king. The regional airport is nearby. Free parking. Microwaves, refrigerators, in-room hot tubs (in suites), cable TV, in-room VCRs. Pool. Exercise equipment. Laundry facilities. Business services. Airport shuttle. | 6621 Thirlane Rd. | 540/265–2600 | fax 540/366–2091 | www.hampton-inn.com | 79 rooms | $69–$79 | AE, D, DC, MC, V.

Hampton Inn–Tanglewood. The rooms in this two-story chain hotel have a table and chairs, double beds or a single king, and outside entrances. The Tanglewood Mall is nearby. Complimentary Continental breakfast. In-room data ports, some microwaves, refrigerators, cable TV. Laundry facilities. Business services. Free parking. | 3816 Franklin Rd. SW | 540/989–4000 | fax 540/989–0250 | www.hampton-inn.com | 58 rooms | $63–$75 | AE, D, DC, MC, V.

Holiday Inn–Airport. The chain hotel, two stories with balconies, has standard rooms with double beds or a single king. Two mi to Roanoke Regional Airport. Restaurant, bar. In-room data ports, room service, cable TV. Pool, wading pool. Laundry facilities. Business services. Airport shuttle. Free parking. | 6626 Thirlane Rd. | 540/366–8861 | fax 540/366–1637 | www.holiday-inn.com | 163 rooms | $74 | AE, D, DC, MC, V.

Holiday Inn–Tanglewood. This five-story chain hotel is convenient to Tanglewood Mall. Restaurant, bar. In-room data ports, room service, cable TV. Pool. Business services. Airport shuttle. Some pets allowed (fee). Free parking. | 4468 Starkey Rd. SW | 540/774–4400 | fax 540/774–1195 | www.holiday-inn.com | 196 rooms | $67–$102 | AE, D, DC, MC, V.

Manor at Taylor's Store. The site is a trading post built in 1799, that became a post office in 1818. Rooms have four-poster beds, oriental rugs, some antiques, and fresh flowers. There's a sun room. The property covers 120 acres and includes six ponds. The Booker T. Washington National Monument is nearby. Complimentary breakfast. No smoking, no TV in rooms, TV in common area, no room phones. Exercise equipment, boating. Fishing. Library. Business services. | Rte. 122 S, Smith Mountain Lake | 540/721–3951 or 800/248–6267 | fax 540/721–5243 | www.symweb.com/taylors | 5 rooms | $90–$135 | AE, MC, V.

Patrick Henry. Three blocks from Center in the Square, this hotel has large rooms furnished with antiques. Restaurant, bar, complimentary Continental breakfast. Barbershop, beauty salon. In-room data ports, kitchenettes, refrigerators, cable TV. Business services. Airport shuttle. | 617 S. Jefferson St. | 540/345–8811 | fax 540/342–9908 | www.patrickhenry-roanoke.com | phhotel13@aol.com | 117 rooms | $89–$109 | AE, D, DC, MC, V.

Ramada Inn. Close to the Roanoke River, this chain hotel has four stories (no balconies), outdoor entrances, and standard-size rooms, most with double beds. Restaurant, bar, complimentary Continental breakfast. In-room data ports, cable TV. Pool. Laundry facilities. Business services. Some pets allowed. | 1927 Franklin Rd. SW | 540/343–0121 | fax 540/342–2048 | www.ramada.com | 126 rooms | $45–$85 | AE, D, DC, MC, V.

Rodeway Inn. This two-story stucco building is within walking distance to the Roanoke Civic Center, and to the downtown shops, restaurants, and Farmers' Market. Complimentary Continental breakfast. In-room data ports. Some microwaves. Refrigerators. Cable TV. Laundry facilities. Pets allowed. | 526 Orange Avenue NE | 540/981–9341 or 800/424–4777 | fax 540/345–8477 | VA248@apluslodging.com | www.choicehotels.com | 102 rooms | $30–$60 | AE,D, DC, MC V.

Sleep Inn. This two-story hotel, near Tanglewood Mall, has standard-size rooms with double beds. Complimentary Continental breakfast. In-room data ports, cable TV. Business services. Free parking. | 4045 Electric Rd. | 540/772–1500 | fax 540/772–1500 | 93 rooms, 10 suites | $63–$67 | AE, D, DC, MC, V.

Travelodge-North. All rooms in this chain option are at ground level, with outdoor entrances and parking in front. The rooms have double beds. The location makes for easy interstate access; it's about 10 mi north of Roanoke. Complimentary Continental breakfast. Some kitchenettes, cable TV. Pool. Playground. Business services. Some pets allowed (fee). | 2619 Lee Hwy. S, Troutville | 540/992–6700 | fax 540/992–3991 | 108 rooms | $44–$55 | AE, D, DC, MC, V.

Walnut Hill Bed and Breakfast. This turn-of-the-century home in a quiet neighborhood has a European-style interior. Each room has antiques and reproductions, and both the Blue Ridge Parkway and downtown Roanoke are only five minutes away. Complimentary Breakfast. TV in common area. | 436 Walnut Ave. SE | 540/427–3312 | fax 540/427–0273 | 4 rooms | $75–$135 | AE, MC, V.

Wyndham Hotel. This hotel is on 12 acres, with two tower buildings—one eight stories, the other seven stories—and some balconies, 2 mi from the municipal airport. It has standard-size rooms, most with double beds. Restaurant, bars. Some refrigerators, room service, cable TV. 2 pools (1 indoor). Hot tub. Tennis court. Exercise equipment. Business services. Airport shuttle. Some pets allowed (fee). | 2801 Hershberger Rd. NW | 540/563–9300 | fax 540/366–5846 | www.wyndham.com | 320 rooms | $79–$145 | AE, D, DC, MC, V.

SALEM

MAP 11, F6

(Nearby town also listed: Roanoke)

Created out of the estate of Gen. Andrew Lewis in 1806, Salem is the oldest and southernmost community in the Roanoke Valley of southwestern Virginia. The city's downtown area is lined with Victorian homes, many listed on the National Register of Historic Places. Salem grew as a town serving travelers on the Great Road westward. In the first decades of the 1800s, its local businesses included taverns, stables, blacksmith shops, grocers, and wagon and buggy repair facilities. The main industries today include the manufacture of transportation-related equipment, fiber optics, food processing, plastics and electronics. The home of Roanoke College, a private liberal arts school, Salem also has a civic center that hosts the Roanoke Valley Horse Show in June and the popular Salem Fair and Exposition in July.

Information: Roanoke County–Salem Chamber of Commerce | 9 N. College Ave., Salem, VA 24153 | 540/387–0267 | www.salem-va.com.

Attractions

Dixie Caverns. Once inside the mountain, ascend into an enormous chamber called the Cathedral Room, and into smaller cavities with names like Wedding Bell and Magic Mirror, all hung with stalactites. There's a mineral and fossil shop at the site. | 5753 W. Main St. | 540/380–2085 | fax 540/380–5655 | $7.50 | June–Sept., daily 9:30–6; Oct.–June, daily 9:30–5.

Roanoke College. Originally established in 1842 as the Virginia Institute near Staunton, this private, liberal arts college was moved to Salem five years later. The school is Virginia's only Lutheran college (and the nation's second oldest). It also was one of the few southern colleges to remain open during the Civil War. Maps for self-guided walking tours are available at the Admissions Office in Roselawn, 226 High St. | 540/375–2500 | fax 540/375–2267 | www.roanoke.edu | Daily.

Salem Museum. This regional history museum is housed in the Williams-Brown House, an 1845 structure that served as a residence, store, and post office in one. Exhibits include Native American artifacts and displays that chronicle the town's history from its early settlement days to the present. There's a gift shop. | 801 E. Main St. | 540/389–6760 | www.salem-museum.org | Donations accepted | Tues.–Fri. 10–4, Sat. noon–4.

ON THE CALENDAR

APR.: *Spring in the Valley Arts and Crafts Show.* Work by many regional artisans is displayed at the Salem Civic Center (1001 Roanoke Blvd.) at a show sponsored by the Virginia Mountain Crafts Guild. | 540/375–4044.
JUNE: *Roanoke Valley Horse Show.* One of the largest multibreed indoor horse shows in the country. There's a grand prix jumping competition with a $50,000 purse. More than 1,000 horses typically compete during the weeklong show at the Salem Civic Center (1001 Roanoke Blvd.). | 540/375–3004.
JULY: *Salem Fair and Exposition.* This two-week-long county fair at the Salem Civic Center (1001 Roanoke Blvd.) has carnival rides, games, livestock judging, food, and concerts. There's also a Roanoke Valley bake-off. | 540/375–4013.

Dining

Claudia's Blues Cafe. Cajun. The walls are covered with blues-related posters, photographs, and mementos. Blues always plays in the background at this tiny café strung with blue lights. Half the room is taken up by a crowded wooden bar, where one might often find a Roanoke College professor grading exams alongside couples on a date. Specialties include jambalaya, blackened tuna, and blackened catfish. | 300 E. Main St. | 540/387–2523 | Closed Sun.–Mon. No lunch | $12–18 | AE, D, DC, MC, V.

Mac and Bob's. American. A true neighborhood restaurant on Salem's Main Street, this eatery is close to the Roanoke College campus, antiques shops, and the weekend farmer's market. Othere are three levels, with bright sunrooms with tile floors and lots of brick, brass, and live plants. There are homemade calzones, the catch of the day, and cut-to-order steaks. Kids' menu (children eat free Sun.). | 316 E. Main St. | 540/389–5999 | $5–$15 | AE, D, DC, MC, V.

Shanghai. Chinese. The gold-and-green dining room has high ceilings, skylights, a Chinese mural, and Asian panels and vases. There's a daily buffet and Sunday brunch. Kids' menu. | 1416 Colorado St. | 540/389–4151 | No lunch Sat. | $6–$10 | AE, D, MC, V.

Lodging

Down Home Bed and Breakfast. You can eat breakfast on the 90-ft wraparound deck over-looking the property's five acres, and the Catawba Valley beyond. Inside, the 1990 wood-and-stone building is a cross between a Pennsylvania Dutch and a rugged, outdoors style. The Down Home is 10 mi north of Salem, and is surrounded by hiking trails. Complimentary Breakfast. Outdoor Pool. No pets. No kids under 12. | 5209 Catawba Valley Road | 540/384–6865 | dwnhmbb@rbnet.com | www.downhomebb.com | 2 rooms | $65 | No.

Holiday Inn. With its hilltop location, the 30-year-old, three-story hotel has views of the Blue Ridge Mountains and the city. There are standard rooms with double beds or a single king. Restaurant, complimentary Continental breakfast. In-room data ports, room service, cable TV. Pool, wading pool. Business services. Free parking. | 1671 Skyview Rd. | 540/389–7061 | fax 540/389–7060 | www.holiday-inn.com | 101 rooms | $49–$89 | AE, D, DC, MC, V.

Holiday Inn Express. This budget branch of the chain stands across from a shopping center. There are outdoor entrances to standard rooms with double beds or a single king. Complimentary Continental breakfast. In-room data ports, microwaves, refrigerators, cable TV. Exercise equipment. Business services. | 1535 E. Main St. | 540/986–1000 | fax 540/986–0355 | www.holiday-inn.com | 70 rooms | $54 | AE, D, DC, MC, V.

Inn at Burwell Place. With a wraparound porch, a front parlor, and gardens, this old home-stead is furnished in antique walnut and cherry, and has two cats—allergy sufferers beware! It is close to Salem, and easily accessible to the many hiking trails. Complimentary Breakfast. Cable TV. VCR. Some in-room hot tubs. Library. No pets. No kids under 12. | 601 West Main Street | 540/387–0250 or 800/891–0250 | burwellplace@yahoo.com. | www.burwellplace.com. | 4 rooms | $90–$130 | AE, D, DC, MC, V.

Quality Inn. This chain option has two stories with balconies, mountain views, and standard rooms with double beds. Restaurant, bar, picnic area, complimentary Continental breakfast, cable TV. Pool. Putting green. Exercise equipment. Playground, laundry facilities. Business services. Airport shuttle. Some pets allowed. | 179 Sheraton Dr. | 540/562–1912 | fax 540/562–0507 | 120 rooms | $57–$72 | AE, D, DC, MC, V.

SCHUYLER

MAP 11, H6

(Nearby towns also listed: Charlottesville, Shenandoah National Park)

Schuyler is a tiny hamlet in rural Nelson County, in the foothills of central Virginia's Blue Ridge. Apple orchards are the mainstay of the local economy. After Schuyler was founded in the 1830s, a large soapstone quarry was the backbone of the economy. For years, fans of the television series *The Waltons* have trekked to Schuyler to see the home of Earl Hamner, Jr., the show's creator. Nearby is a home of a very different sort: Oak Ridge, the estate of Thomas Fortune Ryan, another Nelson County native, who became one of the country's 10 wealthiest men.

Information: **Nelson County Division of Tourism** | 8519 Thomas Nelson Hwy., Lovingston, VA 22949 | 804/263–5239 or 800/282–8223 | fax 804/263–6823 | tournelson@aol.com | www.nelsoncountyva.org.

Attractions

Crabtree Falls Trail. This trail in the George Washington National Forest passes a series of cascades falling a distance of 1,200 ft. Winding through rugged mountainside, it has views of the highest waterfall east of the Mississippi. The trailhead is off the Blue Ridge Parkway on Route 56 E. | Rte. 56 E | 804/263–5239 or 540/265–5100 | fax 540/265–5145 | www.fs.fed.us/gwjnf | Free | Daily.

Oak Ridge Estate. The Colonial Revival mansion has formal Italian gardens, a crystal palace–style greenhouse, and more than 50 outbuildings on 5,000 acres. Built for Thomas Fortune Ryan, a Nelson County native and a leading financier at the turn of the 20th century, it is one of only two private estates in Virginia with a railroad station on a main line. There are guided tours (available by appointment) of the first floor of the mansion and sections of the grounds. The estate, still under restoration, is the site of numerous festivals throughout the year, including a Civil War reenactment held in April. | 2300 Old Ridge Rd. | 804/263–8676 | fax 804/263–4168 | www.oakridgeestate.com | $5–$10 | Open Garden Week in Apr., rest of yr by appointment.

Walton's Mountain Museum. This museum is dedicated to the popular 1970s television series, *The Waltons*. Earl Hamner, Jr., wrote the novel *The Homecoming* and the series based on it. He grew up in Schuyler and attended school in the building that now houses the museum. You'll find recreated sets, including the kitchen and Ike Godsey's store, memorabilia, and photo displays that compare Hamner's real family with his television creation. You can also watch a 30-minute documentary film of interviews with the writer and former cast members. The old Hamner homestead is nearby, but it is not open to the public. | Schuyler Community Center, Rte. 617 | 804/831–2000 | www.waltonmuseum.org | $5, special rates for seniors and children | Mar.–Nov., daily 10–4.

ON THE CALENDAR

APR.: *Civil War Reenactment at Oak Ridge Estate.* You can experience camp life and the clash of armies in Civil War battles. | 804/263–5239.
OCT.: *Apple Butter Making Festival.* Apple butter is made here at the Flippen-Seaman Packing Shed the old-fashioned way, in big kettles over an open fire. The festival also has apples, cider, other food, and live country music. | 804/277–5824.

Dining

Schuyler Family Restaurant. American. Housed in the town's first high school, next door to the Walton Family Museum, the Schuyler Family restaurant is filled with antiques and local memorabilia. The food, served inside or on the back porch, is home-style; you can try the baked chicken dinner or meatloaf, and each comes with dinner rolls, mashed potatoes, and vegetables, or you can keep it simple with hamburgers and barbecue spare ribs. | 6500 Rockfish River Rd. | 804/831–3333. | Tues.–Sat. 10–4, Fri.–Sat. 6–9, Sun. 11–4, closed Mon. | $6–$8 | No credit cards.

Lodging

High Meadows. You can lodge in Victorian- and Federal-style buildings at this working vineyard, 13 mi east of Schuyler. The surrounding 50 acres are dotted with gardens and ponds. Some rooms have fireplaces and private decks. The dining room is open Thursday through Sunday; supper baskets are available Monday through Wednesday. Dining room, complimentary breakfast. Some in-room hot tubs. Some pets allowed. No smoking. | 55 High Meadows La., Scottsville | 804/286–2218 or 800/232–1832 | fax 804/286–2124 | www.highmeadows.com | 9 rooms, 2 suites, 3 cottages | $89–$145, $119–$135 suites, $135–$195 cottages | DC, D, MC, V.

Mark Addy. A farmhouse dating from the 1840s houses this inn at the northeastern edge of the Blue Ridge Mountains, 20 mi northwest of Schuyler. Dining room, complimentary breakfast. Some in-room jacuzzis. No kids under 12. No smoking. | 56 Rodes Farm Dr., Nellysford | 804/361–1101 or 800/278–2154 | markaddy@symweb.com | www.mark-addy.com | 8 rooms, 1 suite | $149, $135 suite | MC, V.

Village Inn at Lovingston. All the rooms at this small, country-style inn 10 mi out of Schuyler are at ground level. They are clean and basic, overshadowed only by the massive wall murals by local artists. Cable TV. | 8010 Thomas Nelson Highway | 804/263–5068 | fax 804/263–5371. | 23 rooms | $38–$49 | AE, D, DC, MC, V.

SHENANDOAH NATIONAL PARK

MAP 11, H4

(Nearby towns also listed: Charlottesville, Front Royal, Harrisonburg, Luray, Middletown, Schuyler, Strasburg, Washington, Waynesboro, Woodstock)

Established in 1936, Shenandoah National Park follows the Blue Ridge Mountains for almost 80 mi from Front Royal south to Waynesboro, and its 196,466 acres encompass some of the highest peaks in northern Virginia. Its Native American name has been variously translated as "Daughter of the Stars" and "River of High Mountains." A fairly narrow band of hardwood forests, the park climbs from the Shenandoah Valley floor to more than 4,000 ft high and embraces some of the mountain range's highest peaks. To the west is the Shenandoah Valley; to the east, rolling farmland of the Piedmont region.

Shenandoah is one of the most popular parks in the national park system, with many varied species of animal and plant life, trout streams, campgrounds, gorgeous panoramas, and hundreds of miles of hiking trails, including a stretch of the Appalachian Trail; naturalists conduct daily hikes all summer. You can rent horses for wilderness rides, and there is trout fishing in nearly three dozen streams. Some 200 species of birds make their home here—from ruffed grouse to barred owl, along with white-tailed deer, woodchuck, gray fox, and black bear. Wildflowers fill the Big Meadows, the park's largest open area in April and May.

Information: **Shenandoah National Park Headquarters** | 3655 U.S. 211 E, Luray, VA 22835 | 540/999–3500 | www.shenandoah.national-park.com | www.nps.gov/shen | $10 per vehicle; $5 for motorcyclists, bicyclists, or pedestrians; permits good for 7 days | Daily.

SHENANDOAH
NATIONAL PARK

INTRO
ATTRACTIONS
DINING
LODGING

Attractions

Camping. There are developed campgrounds and backcountry camping opportunities in the park. The former are open on a first-come, first-served basis, except for Big Meadows, which requires reservations from mid-May through November. Most have coin showers, laundry facilities, a dump station, and a camp store. No RV hook-ups are available. In addition to Big Meadows (Milepost 51.3), the park's campsites are at Mathews Arm (Milepost 22.1), Lewis Mountain (Milepost 57.5), Loft Mountain (Milepost 79.5), and Dundo Group Campground (Milepost 83.7). All campgrounds have a 14-day limit and allow pets. Back-country camping requires a permit, available free of charge at the park headquarters, entrance stations, and visitor centers.

Fishing. Anglers go out year-round on some 25 streams. You must fish with a single-hooked artificial lure; the minimum size is 9 inches, with a creel limit of six fish. A Virginia fishing license, available at the park, is required for anglers 16 and older (nonresidents $6.50 for five consecutive days, $15 per year).

Hang Gliding. Hang gliders may be launched from authorized sites: two in the north and one in the central area of the park. A Hang-Gliding Special Use Permit is required. Contact the Park Communications Center in advance for an application. Permission from landowners must be obtained to land on private property below the cliff edge. To make a launch, you must have a rating of Hang 3. | Shenandoah National Park Communications Center Box 348, Rte. 4, Luray, VA | 540/999–3500.

Hiking. Some 100 mi of the Appalachian Trail runs through the park, along with some 421 mi of other footpaths of varying length and difficulty; some lead to waterfalls, canyons, old-growth forests, and rocky outcrops with sweeping views of the Piedmont and the Shenan-

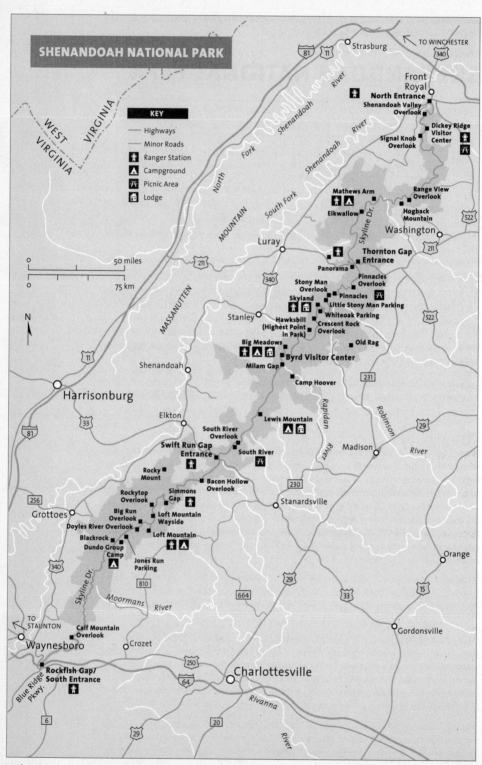

SHENANDOAH NATIONAL PARK

KEY

— Highways
— Minor Roads
👤 Ranger Station
🏕 Campground
🏕 Picnic Area
🏠 Lodge

WEST VIRGINIA

VIRGINIA

TO WINCHESTER

Strasburg

Front Royal

North Entrance
Shenandoah Valley Overlook

Signal Knob Overlook

Dickey Ridge Visitor Center

Shenandoah River

North Fork

South Fork

MOUNTAIN

Range View Overlook

Mathews Arm
Elkwallow

Hogback Mountain

Washington

Luray

Thornton Gap Entrance

Panorama

Pinnacles Overlook

Stony Man Overlook

Skyland
Pinnacles
Little Stony Man Parking

Stanley

Whiteoak Parking

Hawksbill (Highest Point in Park)

Crescent Rock Overlook

Old Rag

Big Meadows

Byrd Visitor Center

Milam Gap

Camp Hoover

Shenandoah

MASSANUTTEN

Harrisonburg

Rapidan River

Robinson River

Elkton

Lewis Mountain

Madison

River

South River Overlook

Swift Run Gap Entrance

South River

Rocky Mount

Bacon Hollow Overlook

Rockytop Overlook

Simmons Gap

Big Run Overlook

Loft Mountain Wayside

Doyles River Overlook

Loft Mountain

Stanardsville

Grottoes

Blackrock
Dundo Group Camp

Jones Run Parking

Orange

Moormans River

Gordonsville

TO STAUNTON

Calf Mountain Overlook

Crozet

Waynesboro

Rockfish Gap/ South Entrance

Blue Ridge Pkwy.

Charlottesville

Rivanna River

50 miles

75 km

N

doah Valley. Maps are available at visitor centers and entrances. Many trails are accessible from Skyline Drive. | 540/999–3581.

Interpretive programs. In summer and fall, rangers lead hikes, field seminars, evening programs around the campfire, and trips to Camp Hoover, with special offerings for kids. Schedules are posted on park bulletin boards and at visitor centers. | 540/999–3489.

Picnicking. Seven picnic areas are scattered throughout the park: Dickey Ridge (Milepost 4.6), Elkwallow (Milepost 24.1), Pinnacles (Milepost 36.7), Big Meadows (Milepost 51.3), Lewis Mountain (Milepost 57.5), South River (Milepost 62.9), and Loft Mountain (Milepost 79.5).

Guided trail rides. Wranglers lead you out of the park's Skyland Stables several times daily from May through October and on weekends in November. The route follows White Oak Canyon trail, which passes several waterfalls; you can choose a 1-hour ride or a 2½-hour ride. Book 24 hours in advance (or bring your own horse). | Skyland Lodge, Milepost 41.7, near Luray | 540/999–2210 | $21 | Apr.–Oct. daily, Nov. weekends.

★ **Skyline Drive.** This scenic highway winds 105 mi through Shenandoah National Park and connects with the Blue Ridge Parkway near Waynesboro. Seasonal activities, supervised by rangers, are outlined in the *Shenandoah Overlook*, a free newspaper you can pick up on entering the park. Skyline Drive runs the length of the park and can be entered at four points: at Front Royal, off U.S. 340; at Thornton Gap, between Luray and Sperryville, off U.S. 211; at Swift Run Gap, between Stanardsville and Elkton, off U.S. 33; and at Rockfish Gap, between Charlottesville and Waynesboro, off U.S. 250/I–64. The speed limit is 35 mph. | $10 per vehicle, $5 for pedestrians and bicyclists.

Visitor Centers. There are two in the park. The **Harry F. Byrd Visitor Center** is near the park's largest and most popular campground, Big Meadows. You'll find park maps and trail information and postings about current ranger programs. | Skyline Dr., Milepost 51 | 540/999–3293 | Free | Mar.–Oct., daily 9–5.

Near the Front Royal entrance to Skyline Drive, the **Dickey Ridge Visitor Center** also distributes maps and dispenses up-to-date information about wildlife, trail conditions, and ranger programs. | Skyline Dr., Milepost 4.6 | 540/635–3566 | Free | Mar.–Oct., daily 9–5.

White Oak Canyon and Dark Hollow Falls. There are 6 waterfalls at White Oak Canyon, 4 mi from Skyline Drive, at Milepost 51.5. At a height of 77 ft, Dark Hollow Falls is a mile from Big Meadows Lodge, next to the Harry F. Byrd Visitors Center, at Milepost 50.5. | Mileposts 50.5 and 51.5, Skyline Dr. | 540/999–3253.

Dining

Panorama Restaurant. American. This full-service restaurant serves mainly pizza, subs, and salads. Try the fried catfish or the country ham platter. After the meal, check out the many artifacts on display, and the craft store and fudge kitchen. | Skyline Drive, Mile 31.5 at U.S. Hwy. 211 | 540/999–2265. | Mid-Nov.–Apr. | Mon.–Fri. 11:30–5:30. | $4.50–$6.25 | AE, MC, D, DC, V.

Lodging

Big Meadows Lodge. The lodge and cabins date from the 1930s at Big Meadows campground in Shenandoah National Park. Restaurant, bar with entertainment. No TV in some rooms. Playground. Business services. | Skyline Dr., Milepost 51, Luray | 540/999–2221 or 800/999–4714 | fax 540/999–2011 | www.shenandoah.national-park.com/lodge | 62 rooms; 10 cabins, 20 rooms in lodge | $60–$75, $64–$75 cabins, $75–$125 lodge rooms | Closed Nov.–Apr. | AE, D, DC, MC, V.

Lewis Mountain Cabins. Right off Skyline Drive, Lewis Mountain has ten rustic, furnished cabins with private baths and outdoor grill areas. There is a camp store on site, and you have access to 500 mi of hiking trails, waterfalls, and streams. | Skyline Drive, Mile 57.5 at U.S. Hwy. 211 | 540/743–5108 or 800/999–4714 | fax 540/743–7883 | 10 cabins | $67–$94 | Nov.–Apr. | AE, MC, V.

VA

SHENANDOAH
NATIONAL PARK

INTRO
ATTRACTIONS
DINING
LODGING

Skyland Lodge. The highest point on Skyline Drive (3,680 ft) is the site of this lodge, and the views over Shenandoah Valley are wonderful. All 26 two-story buildings on the property are modern, with a balcony or patio. Box lunches are available. Restaurant, bar. Cable TV. Playground. Business services. | Skyline Dr., Milepost 41.7, Luray | 540/999–2211 or 800/999–4714 | fax 540/999–2231 | www.shenandoah.national-park.com/lodge | 177 rooms | $79–$155 | Closed Dec.–mid-Mar. | AE, D, DC, MC, V.

SMITHFIELD

MAP 11, J7

(Nearby towns also listed: Hampton, Newport News, Portsmouth, Suffolk, Surry)

Founded in 1749 on the banks of the Pagan River in southeastern Virginia, Smithfield is considered the best-preserved of the state's 18th-century seaports. The historic district has about 50 period buildings of various architectural styles, including a 1750s courthouse. St. Luke's, the oldest church in the country, is 2 mi south of town. The town is also known for the production of Smithfield hams.

Information: **Isle of Wight Tourism Bureau** | Box 37, 130 Main St., Smithfield, VA 23431 | 757/357–5182 or 800/365–9339 | smsdtour@visi.net | www.smithfield-virginia.com | Daily 9–5.

Attractions

Fort Boykin Historic Park. The original fort was built in 1623 by settlers seeking protection from Native Americans and raiding Spaniards. The site is said to have been involved in every military campaign fought on American soil since then; you can still see earthenworks from the Civil War. A gazebo overlooks the James River; there are picnic areas and a trail with markers. | 7410 Fort Boykin Tr. | 757/357–2291 or 800/365–9339 | fax 757/365–4360 | www.co.isle-of-wight.va.us | Free | Daily 8–dusk.

Isle of Wight County Museum. Housed in a former bank built in 1913, the museum highlights local history with archaeological displays, including American Indian and Civil War artifacts. There's also an exhibit on the the Smithfield ham. | 103 Main St. | 757/357–7459 | fax 757/365–9112 | Free | Tues.–Sat. 10–4, Sun. 1–5.

St. Luke's Church. Nicknamed "Old Brick," this church built in 1632 is considered the country's original Gothic church and the oldest church of English foundation in America. The interior has gables, buttresses, traceried windows, and a 17th-century silver baptismal table. Episcopal services are still held. | 14477 Benn's Church Blvd. | 757/357–3367 | fax 757/365–0543 | stlukes@visi.net | www.historicstlukes.org | Free | Feb.–Dec., Tues.–Sat. 9:30–4, Sun. 1–4.

ON THE CALENDAR

MAY: *Olden Days.* A two-day event in the historic district celebrates local history with carriage rides, a Pagan River raft race, an antique car show, arts and crafts, a children's tea party, and live entertainment. | 800/365–9339 | fax 757/365–4360 | www.smithfield-virginia.com.

AUG.: *Tastes of Smithfield–Isle of Wight.* Downtown restaurants serve their specialties, from ham and seafood to desserts. | 800/365–9339 | fax 757/365–4360 | www.smithfield-virginia.com.

OCT.: *Olde Towne Smithfield Art Show.* A juried art show in the historic district displays the works of local and regional artists. | 757/357–6276 | lmc07@erols.com.

Dining

Angelo's Seafood and Steakhouse. American. This sparsely decorated restaurant, with its bare floors, and wooden tables and chairs, opened in the 1960s, and is still a popular place for steaks, seafood, and chicken. Greek-owned, Angelo's baklava comes highly recommended. | 1884 South Church St. | 757/357-3104 | $5–$15 | AE, MC, V.

Anna's Pizza and Italian Restaurant. Italian. You can order just about every Italian dish under the sun at this large, family-style restaurant in the middle of town. Standards include manicotti, veal, chicken, and beef marsala, and shrimp, chicken and eggplants parmigiana. The linguine with clam sauce is one of the most popular items, along with the cherry cheesecake dessert. Italian music plays in the background, and the walls are lined with old Italian movie posters. | 1810 South Church St. | 757/357–4676. | Sun.–Thurs. 11–11, Fri.–Sat. 11–12 | $8–$15 | AE, D, DC, MC, V.

Battery Park Grill. American. In an old dairy barn, Battery Park has four different rooms for eating, drinking, smoking, playing pool, and general merry-making. Most of the walls are hung with old photographs, except for one, which is covered in a mural depicting a scene in a pool room. The place closes when "the owner gets tired," and though the menu is heavy on the steak side, you can also choose from pastas, salads, chicken, and seafood. | 201 Battery Park Rd. | 757/357-1747. | $5–$14 | AE, MC, V.

Lodging

Econo Lodge Benn's Church. This budget motel has some more deluxe accomodations available. Microwaves, refrigerators, cable TV. Business services. | 20080 Brewers Neck Blvd. | 757/357-9057 | fax 757/365-4108 | www.choicehotels.com | 72 rooms | $43–$70 | AE, D, DC, MC, V.

Four Square Plantation. Just west of Smithfield, the Four Square is surrounded, appropriately, by four acres of farmland. The 1807 home is filled with antiques from the original period. Complimentary breakfast. No pets. | 13357 Four Square Road | 757/365–0749 | fax 757/365–0749 | foursquareplantation@att.net | 3 rooms | $75–$85 | AE, MC, V.

Isle of Wight Inn. The inn is close to shops and the historic district. Complimentary breakfast. Some microwaves, refrigerators, cable TV. | 1607 S. Church St. | 757/357-3176 | 12 rooms | $40–$119 | AE, DC, MC, V.

Porches on the James. This two-story country-style home is 5.5 mi north of Smithfield. A wraparound porch overlooks the property's five acres and its namesake, the James River. You can arrive by car or boat, and you have access to a sandy beach on the river. Rooms have queen-size beds, overstuffed armchairs, and family antiques from the 1930s. TV and phone in common area. Hiking. Fishing. No pets. No kids under 12. | 6347 Old Stage Highway | 757/356–0602 or 866/356–0602 | 3 rooms | $85–$95 | AE, MC, V.

Smithfield Inn. This 250-year-old bed and breakfast is in the heart of town. Restaurant, bar, complimentary breakfast, cable TV. Some microwaves, refrigerators. No smoking. | 112 Main St. | 757/357–1752 | fax 757/365–4425 | www.smithfieldinn.com | 5 suites, 4 rooms | $70–$125 | AE, D, DC, MC, V.

Smithfield Station. This property is in the historic district. Restaurant, complimentary Continental breakfast. Some microwaves, refrigerators. Cable TV. | 415 S. Church St. | 757/357–7700 | fax 757/357–7700 | www.smithfieldstation.com | 20 rooms | AE, D, DC, MC, V.

SOUTH BOSTON

MAP 11, G7

(Nearby towns also listed: Clarksville, Danville)

Located in south-central Virginia, near the North Carolina border, South Boston was established in 1884 on the south side of the Dan River and called Boyd's Ferry. When floods destroyed the town around 1796, it was rebuilt on the river's north bank. South Boston historically has been a farming region and today is the second-largest tobacco market in Virginia. The manufacture of textiles, wood, furniture, electronics, and metalwork also sustains the economy. East of town, the Staunton River State Park follows the shoreline of Virginia's largest lake, Buggs Island.

Information: **Halifax County Chamber of Commerce** | Box 399, 515 Broad St., South Boston, VA 24592 | 804/572–3085 | fax 804/572–1733 | info@halifaxchamber.net | www.halifaxchamber.net | Weekdays 9–5.

Attractions

South Boston/Halifax County Museum of Fine Arts and History. Like its name suggests, this museum consists of local memorabilia and artifacts, an exhibition of the history of Virginia, a gift shop, and a revolving exhibition of local, national and international art. | 1540 Wilborn Avenue | 804/572–9200 | www.2halifax.com/museum | Free, donation suggested | Wed.-Sat. 10–4, Sun. 2–4:30.

Staunton River State Park. This 1,414-acre park on Buggs Island Lake has freshwater fishing and camping, a swimming pool, tennis courts, riverfront picnic areas, canoe rentals, boat launch, hiking trails, and a visitor center. | 1170 Staunton Trail, Scottsburg | 804/572–4623 | fax 804/572–4650 | www.state.va.us | Free; parking and pool fee | Daily dawn–dusk.

ON THE CALENDAR

MAR.: *NASCAR Winston Racing Series Race.* The NASCAR Winston Cup series takes place at the South Boston Speedway. | 804/572–4947.

MAY: *Virgilina Summerfest.* This old-fashioned festival in Virgilina, 17 mi southeast on the states' southern border, has a parade, fireworks, arts and crafts, food, and live entertainment. | 804/585–2657.

JULY: *Virginia Cantaloupe Festival.* The festival at the Halifax County Fairgrounds has live bands, barbecue, beer, and plenty of fresh cantaloupes. | 804/572–3085 | fax 804/572–1733 | info@halifaxchamber.net | www.halifaxchamber.net.

Dining

Hill's Tavern. American. Modeled after a Colonial Williamsburg Tavern, Hill's has wooden tables and booths, linen tablecloths, and fresh flowers. The walls are lined with news clippings from the area, dating back to the 1800s. Food ranges from burgers, steaks, and salads, to quesadillas and crabcakes. Try the hot fudge cake or one of an assortment of fruit pies for dessert. | 817 Wilborn Ave. | 804/572–4467 | Sun. | Mon.–Fri. 11–2, Mon–Sat. 5–10 | $9–$20 | AE, D, DC, MC, V.

Shannon's Restaurant. American. This family-owned and operated restaurant in downtown South Boston's Best Western is decked out Art Deco-style, complete with pastels, mahogany tables, and antique posters from the 1920s and 30s. Vegetarians beware: House specialties include the Steak au poivre, rib eye steak with sauteed shrimp and marinated shiitake mushrooms, and a pan-fried, peppercorn-encrusted steak on a garlic and herb cheese potato cake in brandy sauce. There is also live music every Saturday night. | 2001 Seymour Drive. | 804/575–8001 | Daily 6:30am–2am | $10–$18 | AE, D, DC, MC, V.

Torero's Authentic Mexican Cuisine. Mexican. Tucked away in the Days Inn, with a sign that's somewhat hidden from the road. Specialties of the house include fajitas and seafood platters. Mexican artwork hangs on the walls, and Central and South American music plays non-stop. | 2050 Phelpot Road, 68 West | 804/575–1491 | Daily 11–11 | $2.95–$12 | AE, D, DC, MC, V.

Lodging

Best Western Howard House Inn. This hotel is in town, right off U.S. 360 and ¼ mi from U.S. 58. Restaurant, complimentary Continental breakfast. In-room data ports, cable TV. Pool. Business services. Some pets allowed. | 2001 Seymour Dr. | 804/572–4311 | fax 804/572–2740 | www.bestwestern.com | 52 rooms | $59–$73 | AE, D, DC, MC, V.

Days Inn. The chain motel is on U.S. 58, 2 mi from town. Complimentary Continental breakfast. Some microwaves, refrigerators, cable TV. Pool. | 2050 Philpott Rd. | 804/572–4941 | fax 804/575–6750 | www.daysinn.com | 76 rooms | $50–$62 | AE, D, DC, MC, V.

Falkland Farms. There's plenty of room to roam on this cattle farm. Five rivers run along the property, and the 1911 country farmhouse, 13 mi east of South Boston, is filled with early 20th-century antiques. Complimentary breakfast. TV in common area. Hiking. | 1003 Falkland Landing | 804/575–7137 | 7 rooms | $55–$80 | No credit cards.

Holiday Inn Express. The hotel is on U.S. 58 and ½ mi from U.S. 501, 1 mi south of town. Complimentary Continental breakfast. Cable TV. Pool. | 1074 Bill Tuck Hwy. | 804/575–4000 | fax 804/575–1600 | www.holiday-inn.com | 66 rooms | $62–$68 | AE, D, DC, MC, V.

Oak Grove Plantation. On 400 acres of farm, and 10 mi out of South Boston, the Oak Grove has a parlor, sun porch, and a Victorian dining room. All the bedrooms have fireplaces and period furniture. Picnic area. Complimentary breakfast. Hiking. Horseback riding. Fishing. Bicycles. | 1245 Cluster Springs Rd. | 804/575–7137 | www.oakgroveplantation.com | 4 rooms | $55–$80 | Oct.–Apr. | No credit cards.

Super 8. This budget motel is on U.S. 58. Cable TV. Some pets allowed. | 1040 Bill Tuck Hwy. | 804/572–8868 | fax 804/572–8868 | www.super8.com | 58 rooms | $46–$50 | AE, D, DC, MC, V.

SOUTH HILL

MAP 11, H7

(Nearby town also listed: Clarksville, Emporia)

South Hill is in the rolling hills of south-central Virginia, 12 mi north of the North Carolina border, at the junction of U.S. 1, I–85, and Route 58. It was founded in 1889 and is the third-largest tobacco market in Virginia. The town is between Kerr Lake (Buggs Island) and Lake Gaston.

Information: South Hill Chamber of Commerce | 201 S. Mecklenburg Ave., South Hill, VA 23970-2619 | 804/447–4547 | fax 804/447–4461 | shchamber@meckcom.net | www.southhillchamber.com | Weekdays 8:30–4.

Attractions
Kerr Lake (Buggs Island). The lake was built on land belonging to a family named Buggs. When the dam and reservoir were created, the lake was named after the dam builder, John Kerr. Locals call the lake "Buggs Island," but there is no island in the lake. The 50,000-acre lake has 800 mi of shoreline, with fishing, swimming, a boat launch, and picnic areas. North Bend Park has a beach, fishing pier, and campsites. | Off U.S. 58 or U.S. 4 | 804/738–6143, 804/738–6101, or 804/738–6662 | fax 804/738–6541 | www.kerrlake.com | $3 per car | Daily.

ON THE CALENDAR
AUG.: *Arts and Crafts Jamboree.* Vendors sell handcrafted items at the John H. Kerr Dam. | 804/738–6143.
NOV.: *Shriner's Shrimp Festival.* Shrimp with all the trimmings are served at the Virginia Warehouse on Danville Street. | 804/447–7969.

Dining
Brian's Steak House. Steak. This is a traditional family restaurant, with local artwork on the walls. Specialties are the breakfast waffle and prime-rib sandwich. | 625 E. Atlantic St. | 804/447–3169 | fax 804/447–4127 | brian@buggs.net | $12–$20 | AE, D, MC, V.

Horseshoe Restaurant. American. The 1938 building is round, with a horseshoe-shaped dining counter, and a country motif lining the walls. Southern dishes include roasted chicken, vegetable stew, and chocolate meringue pie. | 311 West Danville Street | 804/447–7781 | Mon.–Sat. 6am–9pm, closed Sun. | $4.95–$9.95 | No credit cards.

Kahill's. American. Gourmet fare is served in this former country store, decorated with photos of celebrity diners. Popular menu choices are steaks and pasta. You can dine outdoors on the deck. Sun. brunch. | 1799 N. Mecklenburg Ave. | 804/447–6941 | fax 804/447–6941 | kahills@msinet.com | Breakfast also available | $17–$24 | AE, D, MC, V.

Lodging

Best Western. This property is in town, at the intersection of I–85 and U.S. 58. Restaurant, complimentary Continental breakfast, bar. Cable TV. Pool, wading pool. Game room, video games. Laundry facilities. Airport shuttle. Free parking. Some pets allowed (fee). | 911 E. Atlantic St. | 804/447–3123 | fax 804/447–4237 | www.bestwestern.com | 151 rooms | $65–$80 | AE, D, DC, MC, V.

Comfort Inn. This chain hotel is in town at the intersection of I–85 and U.S. 58. Complimentary Continental breakfast. Cable TV. Business services. | 918 E. Atlantic St. | 804/447–2600 | fax 804/447–2590 | www.comfortinn.com | 50 rooms | $49–$70 | AE, D, DC, MC, V.

Econo Lodge. The chain hotel is on the east edge of town, near I–85. Some microwaves, refrigerators. Business services. Some pets allowed. | 623 Atlantic St. | 804/447–7116 | fax 804/447–6985 | www.choicehotels.com | 53 rooms | $50–$70 | AE, D, DC, MC, V.

Hampton Inn South Hill. Surrounded by other hotels, the three-story Hampton is walking distance from some major shopping areas, 12 mi from Lake Gaston, and seven mi from the Bush Garden Amusement Park. Complimentary Continental breakfast. In-room data ports. Some in-room hot tubs. Cable TV. Outdoor pool. Exercise facilities. No pets. | 200 Thompson Road | 804/447–4600 or 800/426–7866 | fax 804/447–2553 | www.hampton-inn.com | 55 rooms | $72 | AE, D, DC, MC, V.

Holiday Inn Express. This two-story hotel is in the South Hill business district, walking distance from most shops and restaurants. Complimentary Continental breakfast. In-room data ports. Microwaves. Refrigerators. Some in-room hot tubs. Cable TV. Outdoor Pool. | 200 Thompson St. | 804/447–4600 | fax 804/955–2777 | www.basshotels.com | 55 rooms | $75–$85. | AE, D, DC, MC, V.

SPRINGFIELD

MAP 11, I4

(Nearby towns also listed: Alexandria, Fairfax)

This northern Virginia suburb was established in 1852. Once a farming community, Springfield is now a bedroom community for D.C. Near the junction of Interstates 95 and 395, it is minutes from the Capital Beltway (I–495). Potomac Mills, the state's biggest shopping mall (and most-visited site), is just south of Springfield. Nearby are George Washington's historic home, Mount Vernon, and the picturesque streets of Old Town Alexandria.

Information: Fairfax County Convention and Visitors Bureau | 8300 Boone Blvd., Suite 450, Vienna, VA 22182 | 703/790–3329 | fax 703/893–1269 | info@fceda.org | www.fairfaxcountyeda.org | Daily 8:30–5.

Attractions

Potomac Mills. This regional supermall has 1.7 million square ft of retail space, all on one level; more than 220 of the stores are manufacturer's outlets and discount retailers. You'll find Swedish furniture giant IKEA, plus Nordstrom Rack, Off 5th–Saks Fifth Avenue, JCPenney Outlet, TJ Maxx, and Spiegel Outlet. There are 23 eateries, including a food court. | 2700 Potomac Mills Circle, Prince William | 703/643–1203 | fax 703/643–1054 | www.potomac-mills.com | Mon.–Sat. 10–9:30, Sun. 11–7.

ON THE CALENDAR

JUNE: *Springfield Days.* This is a four-day festival held at Lake Accotink and other locations throughout the town. Highlights include a Miss Springfield pageant, carnival rides and games, food booths, and a cardboard boat race. | 703/866–3500.

Dining

Il Buon Gusto Ristorante. Italian. This northern Italian restaurant in the Backlick Center Mall has white linen tablecloths, fresh flowers, Italian art, and opera playing in the background. Try the Rollata di Pollo, a pounded chicken breast rolled in fresh herbs, and served with a brandy, cream and mushroom sauce, or the lightly-breaded veal stuffed with prosciutto and fontina. The requisite tiramisu graces the dessert menu. | 6681 Backlick Road. | 703/644–4044. | Tues.–Thur. 11:30-2:30 and 5-9, Fri. 11:30-2:30 and 5-10, Sat. 5-10, Sun. 5-9 | $9.95–$20.95 | AE, D, DC, MC, V.

Mike's American Grill. Steak. With its brick exterior and smoking green chimney, this 1940s-style eatery looks like a warehouse. The interior of the two-story building is done in cherry wood and brass. Specialties are prime rib, baby-back ribs, crab cakes, and pepper steak. | 6210 Backlick Rd. | 703/644–7100 | fax 703/866–7736 | www.gar.com | No lunch weekends | $7–$29 | AE, MC, V.

Slades. American. The menu at this mall-restaurant has few surprises, consisting mostly of steaks, burgers, and seafood. Standouts include the Island Steak, a rib eye marinated in ginger, pineapple juice, and soy sauce, grilled chicken linguine, and apple walnut cobbler. Old magazine covers and sports memorabilia are plastered on the walls. | 6705 Springfield Mall | 703/313–0479 | Mon.–Thurs. 11-10, Fri.–Sat. 11-11, Sun. 11-9. | $7–$25 | AE, D, DC, MC, V.

Springfield Family Restaurant and Pizzeria. Greek. Opened in 1990, this restaurant is the definition of "multicultural," serving Italian, American, and Greek food. Though there's practically no decor to speak of, just wooden tables and chairs, the menu is packed with everything under the sun, including pastas, pizzas, burgers, moussaka, stuffed grape leaves, and baklava. | 6416 Brandon Avenue | 703/451–4800 | Mon.–Thurs. 8–10, Fri.-Sat. 8–11, Sun. 8–9. | $5–$8 | AE, D, DC, MC, V.

Lodging

Comfort Inn. The chain hotel is next to the Springfield Mall. Complimentary Continental breakfast. In-room data ports, cable TV. Business services. Free parking. Some pets allowed. | 6560 Loisdale Ct. | 703/922–9000 | fax 703/971–6944 | www.comfortinn.com | 112 rooms | $79–$95 | AE, D, DC, MC, V.

Days Inn–Potomac Mills. This chain is 5 minutes from Potomac Mills, with easy interstate access. Complimentary Continental breakfast. In-room data ports, minibars, some refrigerators, cable TV. Pool. Exercise equipment. Laundry facilities. Business services. Free parking. No pets allowed. | 14619 Potomac Mills Rd., Woodbridge | 703/494–4433 | fax 703/385–2627 | potmillsdi@aol.com | www.daysinnpotomacmills.com | 176 rooms | $86–$113 | AE, D, DC, MC, V.

Days Inn–Springfield Mall. The moderately priced motel is just north of the Springfield Mall. Restaurant. In-room data ports, cable TV. Pool. Business services. Free parking. | 6721 Commerce St. | 703/922–6100 | fax 703/922–0708 | www.daysinn.com | 179 rooms | $75–$98 | AE, D, DC, MC, V.

Hampton Inn. The motel is next door to the Springfield Mall. Complimentary Continental breakfast. Cable TV. Pool. Free parking. Some pets allowed. | 6550 Loisdale Ct. |

703/924–9444 | fax 703/924–0324 | www.hampton-inn.com | 153 rooms | $99–$109 | AE, D, DC, MC, V.

Hilton. This hotel is next to the Springfield Mall. Restaurant, bar with entertainment. In-room data ports, some refrigerators, cable TV. Indoor pool. Business services. | 6550 Loisdale Rd. | 703/971–8900 | fax 703/971–8527 | guest@springfieldhilton.com | www.hilton.com | 246 rooms | $89–$139 | AE, D, DC, MC, V.

Holiday Inn Express. The hotel is close to the Springfield Mall and the Amtrak station. Coffeemaker, complimentary Continental breakfast. Pool. | 6401 Brandon Ave. | 703/644–5555 | fax 703/866–4557 | www.holiday-inn.com | 194 rooms | $69–$79 | AE, D, DC, MC, V.

Hunter Motel. The oldest motel in the area, the one-story, family-owned and operated Hunter is 3 mi outside Springfield. Rooms are plain and serviceable. Restaurant. Cable TV. No pets. | 8011 Backlick Road | 703/339–5400 | fax 703/339–6979 | 43 rooms | $55–$65 | MC, V.

Motel 6. This four-story brick building is less than a five-minute drive from the Springfield Mall, restaurants, Brookfield Park, and grocery stores. Rooms are standard, chain-motel style: It used to be a Ramada Inn, and not much has changed. Cable TV. In-room data ports. Laundry service. Pets allowed. | 6868 Springfield Blvd. | 703/644–5311 | fax 703/644–1077 | www.motel6.com | 190 rooms | $58–$70 | AE, D, DC, MC, V.

STAUNTON

MAP 11, G5

(Nearby town also listed: Waynesboro)

Staunton was once the seat of government in Augusta County, formed in 1738. It was briefly the capital of Virginia, when the General Assembly fled here from the British in 1781. President Woodrow Wilson was born in Staunton in 1856, and his birthplace is now a museum. The region's agrarian heritage, influenced by early Scots-Irish, German, and English settlers, is celebrated at the Museum of American Frontier Culture. The area around Staunton produces poultry, livestock, and wool. Within the city, manufacturing firms make air-conditioners, razors, candy, and clothing.

Though the town is hilly, Staunton is easily explored on foot. Unscathed by the Civil War, it contains a wealth of Victorian, Greek Revival, and Italianate architecture. Five of the town's neighborhoods are National historic districts. The Historic Staunton Foundation has detailed walking maps, available at the visitor center on Richmond Avenue.

Information: Staunton Convention and Visitors Bureau | Box 58, Dept. AAA, Staunton, VA 24402 | 540/332–3865 or 800/342–7982 | troubetzkoyss@ci.staunton.va.us | www.staunton.va.us | Weekdays 8–5.

Staunton-Augusta Visitor Center | 1250 Richmond Ave., Staunton, VA 24401 | 540/332–3972 or 800/332–5219 | fax 540/851–4005 | www.stauntonva.org | Weekdays 8–5.

Attractions

Augusta Stone Church. This Presbyterian church was built in 1749 by Scots-Irish pioneers. Constructed of native limestone, it is the oldest surviving church in the Shenandoah Valley. | 28 Old Stone Church La., Fort Defiance | 540/248–2634 | fax 540/248–5424 | Free | Mon.–Tues., Thurs. 8:30–2:30; Wed. 9–noon; Sun. service at 11.

Gypsy Hill Park. This 214-acre city park has an 18-hole public golf course, tennis courts, picnic pavilions, a pool, playgrounds, a lake, and an activity center. A 1.3-mi circular roadway is used by walkers, bicyclists, and in-line skaters. The park also has a football stadium, gymnasium, track, and a baseball field. | Churchville and Thornrose Aves | 540/332–3945 | fax 540/332–3983 | www.staunton.va.us/parks | Free | Daily 6 AM–11 PM.

Cyrus McCormick Farm. On this 634-acre farm, known as Walnut Grove, McCormick demonstrated the first mechanical grain reaper in 1831. The revolutionary invention, which harvested grain five times faster than a scythe or sickle, transformed agricultural production. You can tour the blacksmith shop, gristmill, and museum, which contains an original reaper. The farm is now a research station operated by Virginia Polytechnic Institute and State University. | Rte. 606, 128 McCormick Farm Circle | 540/377–2255 | fax 540/377–5850 | Free | Daily 8:30–5.

★ **Museum of American Frontier Culture.** This outdoor museum re-creates agrarian life in early America with American, Scots-Irish, German, and English farmsteads. Master craftsmen were brought from Ulster, Northern Ireland, to thatch the roofs on farm buildings transported from County Tyrone. Livestock has been backbred and ancient seeds germinated in order to create an environment accurate in all details. More than 70 festivals, workshops, and programs are held annually, from sheep shearing at Easter to corn husking in the fall. A visitor center has displays and a short film about the museum. | 1250 Richmond Rd. | 540/332–7850 | fax 540/332–9989 | www.frontiermuseum.org | $8, special rates for seniors and children | Dec.–mid-Mar., daily 10–4; mid-Mar.–Nov., daily 9–5.

Statler Brothers Mini-Museum. The Statlers were four country-music brothers who defied Nashville, Tennessee by cutting their records in their hometown, right here in Staunton. A converted elementary school showcases artifacts from their careers. You can buy Statler souvenirs in the gift shop. | 501 Thornrose Ave. | 540/885–7297 | Free | Tours are given Mon.–Fri. at 2 PM.

Trinity Episcopal Church. The original church on this site was built in 1763; the current early-Gothic Revival building dates to 1855 and has a number of Tiffany windows. | 114 W. Beverley St. | 540/886–9132 | fax 540/885–3096 | tecsec@rica.net | www.forministry.com/24401tec | Free | Weekdays 9–4; for a tour, stop by the rectory next door.

Woodrow Wilson Birthplace and Museum. This 150-year-old Greek Revival house has been restored to its appearance during Wilson's childhood, with some original furnishings. The 28th U.S. president was born here in 1856, son of the Rev. Joseph R. Wilson, a Presbyterian minister, and his wife, Jesse Woodrow. Some items from Wilson's political career are displayed, including his presidential limousine, a 1919 Pierce-Arrow sedan. | 24 N. Coalter St. | 540/885–0897 or 888/496–6376 | fax 540/886–9874 | www.woodrowwilson.org | $6.50, special rates for seniors, students, and children | Mar.–Nov., daily 9–5; Dec.–Feb., daily 10–4.

Walking Tours. This is the single most popular way to see Staunton. Tours run every Saturday, from June through October, beginning at President Woodrow Wilson's House and going through the Historic District. They start at 10 AM and last 1½ hours. | Free.

ON THE CALENDAR

MAY: *Art in the Park.* An outdoor art show held downtown at the Gypsy Hill Park bandstand has more than 100 local and national artists, including many wildlife painters. There's live entertainment and food. | 540/885–2028.

JULY–SEPT.: *Jazz in the Park.* Live jazz performances by regional and national artists can be heard every Thursday evening, rain or shine, at the Gypsy Hill Park bandstand. | 540/885–5854.

NOV.: *Threshing Party.* Interpreters from the Frontier Culture Museum (1250 Richmond Rd.) demonstrate how farmers in different parts of the world harvest grain. | 540/332–7850.

Dining

Buckhorn Inn. American. Built as a tavern in 1811, the inn has old mantels, cornerstones, and a spiral staircase. Buffet dinners. Popular dishes are fried chicken, peanut butter pie, and roast beef. Salad bar. Dessert bar. Kids' menu. | 2487 Hankeymountain Hwy., Churchville | 540/337–6900 | Closed Mon.–Tues. | $8–$11 | MC, V.

L'Italia. Italian. In a downtown brick building, this quiet restaurant has white tablecloths, candles, and local artwork on display. After a meal of homemade pasta, veal saltimboca, or broiled salmon, you have 15-20 desserts to choose from. | 23 East Beverly Street | 540/885-0102 | Mon. | Tues.–Sat. 11–11, Sun. 10:30-9, closed Mon. | $10–$21 | AE, D, DC, MC, V.

Mill Street Grill. American. The first restaurant as you come into Staunton on U.S. 11, the Mill Street Grill occupies the basement level of a turn-of-the-century mill. Walls are original stone and wood, and there are flour bags, stained-glass windows, and other mill relics on display. The baby back ribs are popular, as is the cajun chicken fettucine. Try the raspberry brûlée cheesecake for dessert. | 1 Mill Street | 540/886-0656 | Mon.–Sat. 4–10, Sun. 11:30–9 | $6–$20. | AE, D, DC, MC, V.

Mrs. Rowe's. American. This family-owned restaurant has been serving country food for about 50 years. Beer and wine only. | 74 Rowe's Rd. | 540/886-1833 | fax 540/885-0910 | www.mrsrowes.com | Breakfast also available | $9–$13 | D, MC, V.

Pullman Restaurant. American. Rail lovers will no doubt love the Pullman. Housed in the 1857 C & O Train Station, the restaurant arranges its tables so that you can watch the trains pull in while you eat. Though the food is generic American, there are notable local dishes, like the pecan-coated baked rainbow trout. Dessert requires a trip to the Victorian ice cream parlor next door. | 36 Middlebrook Ave. | 540/885-6612 | Mon.–Sat. 11-11, Sun. 11-9 | $10–$12 | AE, D, DC, MC, V.

Lodging

Ashton Country House Bed and Breakfast. An 1860s Greek Revival home on 25 acres of farmland, the Ashton's interior is completely furnished with antiques and reproductions. About 1½ mi from downtown Staunton, there are porches overlooking the Blue Ridge Mountains, and fireplaces in every room. Complimentary breakfast. Cable TV. VCRs. Pets allowed. | 1205 Middlebrook Ave. | 540/885-7819 or 800/296-7819 | fax 540/885-6029 | ashtonhouse@aol.com | www.bbhost.com/ashtonbnb | 6 rooms | $70–$125 | AE, D, DC, MC, V.

Belle Grae Inn. This large Victorian inn has three separate different buildings, which contain rooms with antique furniture, some fireplaces, some wet bars, and an impressive array of amenities. Dining room, complimentary breakfast. Some in-room hot-tubs, some room phones, no TV in some rooms. Business services. Airport shuttle. No kids under 12. | 515 W. Frederick St. | 540/886-5151 | fax 540/886-6641 | www.bellegrae.com | 17 rooms | $99–$199 | AE, MC, V.

Best Western. This motor lodge is 2½ mi from town and along I–81. Complimentary Continental breakfast. Cable TV. Indoor pool. Business services. Free parking. | 260 Rowe Rd. | 540/885-1112 | fax 540/885-1112 | www.bestwestern.com | 80 rooms | $72–$95 | AE, D, DC, MC, V.

Buckhorn Inn. This inn built in 1811 is in the Shenandoah Valley region of the George Washington National Forest. In 1854, Stonewall Jackson and his wife stayed at the inn, 12 mi northwest of Staunton. Restaurant, complimentary breakfast. No room phones. | 2487 Hankeymountain Hwy., Churchville | 540/337-6900 | fax 540/337-6091 | 5 rooms, 1 suite | $55–$65, $80 suite | D, MC, V.

Comfort Inn. This chain motel is 3 mi from town, along I–81. Complimentary Continental breakfast. Some refrigerators, cable TV. Pool. Business services. Some pets allowed. | 1302 Richmond Ave. | 540/886-5000 | fax 540/886-6643 | www.comfortinn.com | 98 rooms | $65–$110 | AE, D, DC, MC, V.

Econo Lodge–Hessian House. The property is 8 mi south of town, along I–81. Picnic area, complimentary Continental breakfast. Refrigerators, cable TV. Pool, wading pool. Playground. Some pets allowed (fee). | 3554 Lee Jackson Hwy. | 540/337-1231 | fax 540/337-0821 | www.choicehotels.com | 32 rooms | $45–$75 | AE, D, MC, V.

Frederick House. The bed-and-breakfast inn is composed of several different buildings. Some rooms have balconies, fireplaces, and private entrances; all rooms are cozy with period antiques. Picnic area, complimentary full breakfast. Cable TV. No smoking. | 28 N. New St.

| 540/885–4220 or 800/334–5575 | www.frederickhouse.com | 11 rooms, 12 suites | $95–$115, $115–$175 suites | AE, D, DC, MC, V.

Holiday Inn Golf and Conference Center. The hotel overlooks rolling hills, 8 mi north of town, next to I–81. Restaurant, bar with entertainment. In-room data ports, some microwaves, refrigerators (in suites), room service, cable TV. Indoor-outdoor pool. Driving range, 18-hole golf course, putting green, tennis court. Exercise equipment. Business services. Airport shuttle. Free parking. | I-81 and Rte. 275 Exit 225, Woodrow Wilson Pkwy. | 540/248–6020 | fax 540/248–2902 | higcc@cfw.com | www.holiday-inn.com | 116 rooms, 4 suites | $85–$115 | AE, D, DC, MC, V.

Iris Inn. This 1991 inn sits on a 20-acre piece of the western slope of the the Blue Ridge Mountains. But you have to travel a bit farther to get here: It's in Waynesboro, 12 mi east of Staunton. Your efforts will be rewarded with uninterrupted views of the Shenandoah Valley from the inn's wraparound porch. Inside the main building, a 28-ft stone fireplace will keep you warm in winter, and a 20-ft mural depicting local wildlife will keep you entertained, at least until you're ready to go out and see the real thing. Complimentary breakfast. In-room data ports. Hot tubs. Cable TV. No pets. No kids under 10. | 191 Chinquapin Drive | 540/943–1991 | irisinn@cfw.com | www.irisinn.com | 6 rooms | $85–$150 | MC, V.

Montclair Bed and Breakfast. This bed-and-breakfast is housed in a restored, circa 1880 brick Italianate townhouse in downtown Staunton, furnished in an entirely "Fox Hunt" interior with horses and hounds everywhere you look. The furnishings are all antiques from the original era, and each room has its own fireplace. Outside diversions include a terrace, garden, porch, and picnic area. Complimentary breakfast. Cable TV. | 320 N. New Street | 540/885–8832 or 877/885–8832 | mebang@rica.net | www.montclairbb.com | 4 rooms | $90–$170 | MC, V.

Sampson Eagon. This 1840s mansion is in Staunton's Gospel Hill district. Complimentary full breakfast. Cable TV, in-room VCRs and movies. Business services. No kids under 12. | 238 E. Beverly St. | 540/886–8200 or 800/597–9722 | www.eagoninn.com | 3 rooms, 2 suites | $98–$110 rooms, $110–$125 suites | AE, MC, V.

Shoney's Inn. This chain motel is 3 mi west of downtown, right off I–81. Restaurant, complimentary Continental breakfast. Some in-room hot tubs, cable TV. Pool. Exercise equipment. Business services. Free parking. | 42 Sangers Lane | 540/885–3117 | fax 540/885–5620 | www.shoneysinn.com | 91 rooms | $56–$69 | AE, D, DC, MC, V.

Thornrose House. This turn-of-the-century Georgian Revival inn is surrounded by landscaped gardens and across from a park with swimming, tennis, and golf. Complimentary breakfast. No room phones. No smoking. | 531 Thornrose Ave. | 540/885–7026 or 800/861–4338 reservations | fax 540/885–6458 | thornros@intelas.net | www.thornrosehouse.com | 5 rooms | $70–$90 | AE, V, MC.

Twelfth Night Inn. Built at the turn of the century, in the "Prairie" style, the inn has a wraparound veranda and a landscaped garden in the back. Each room is Shakespearean-themed, with antiques and reproductions to match. It's also right downtown, walking distance to most attractions, restaurants, and shops. Complimentary breakfast. Cable TV. Pets allowed ($10 extra). No kids under 10. | 402 Beverley Street | 540/885–1733 | fax 540/885–4213 | stay@12th-night-inn.com | www.12th-night-inn.com | 1 single, 2 suites | $75–110 | AE, D, DC, MC, V.

STRASBURG

MAP 11, H4

(Nearby towns also listed: Front Royal, Middletown, Shenandoah National Park, White Post, Woodstock)

Formerly known as Staufferstadt, Strasburg was founded by German immigrants in 1761, and rose to prominence during the 19th century by producing high-quality pottery. Strasburg's role in the 1862 Valley Campaign of the Civil War is explored at Hupp's Hill Battlefield Park. The city is known for its antiques shops; the downtown Strasburg Emporium houses roughly 110 antiques dealers under one roof. The economy today is based primarily on printing and manufacturing automotive parts.

Information: Strasburg Chamber of Commerce | Box 42, Strasburg, VA 22657 | 540/465–3187 | fax 540/465–3187 | schamber@shentel.net | www.strasburgschamber.com | Weekdays 8:30–5.

Shenandoah County Travel Council | Box 802, 125 S. Main St., Woodstock, VA 22664 | 540/459–2332 or 888/367–3934 | fax 540/459–6228 | tourism@co.shenandoah.va.us | www.co.shenandoah.va.us | Weekdays 8:30–5.

Attractions

Belle Grove. Built in 1794 with design input from Thomas Jefferson, this plantation house was owned by Major Isaac Hite Jr., James Madison's brother-in-law. Unusual features include a dressed-limestone facade and chimneys, and fan windows. The mansion served as headquarters for Union general Philip Sheridan in 1864 during the Battle of Cedar Creek. Part of the battle was fought on the farm, and a reenactment is held every October. Today, Belle Grove is a 100-acre working farm, 5 mi northeast of Strasburg, and a center for the study of traditional rural crafts. There's a museum shop. | 336 Belle Grove Rd., Middletown | 540/869–2028 | fax 540/869–9638 | bellegro@shentel.net | www.belle-grove.org | $7 | Apr.–Oct., Mon.–Sat. 10–4, Sun. 1–5.

Hupp's Hill Battlefield Park and Stonewall Jackson Museum. This museum in the Shenandoah Valley chronicles Stonewall Jackson's 1862 Valley Campaign with Civil War artifacts and reproduction weapons and uniforms. Hupp's Hill was the site of a fierce battle on October 13, 1864; remains of Confederate trenches and Federal gun positions can still be seen on the grounds. The facility also offers summer camps for kids, folkways workshops, and living-history demonstrations. | 33229 Old Valley Pike | 540/465–5884 | fax 540/465–5884 | www.nvim.com/museumamerpres | $3 | Weekdays 10–5, weekends 11–4.

Strasburg Emporium. The antiques dealers here have thousands of items for sale, including glassware, dolls, implements, furniture, and pottery. The emporium occupies a 90,000-square-ft former silk mill. | 160 N. Massanutten St. | 540/465–3711 | fax 540/465–8157 | tgse@rica.net | www.waysideofva.com | Free | Daily 10–5.

Strasburg Museum. Civil War and railroad relics, farm tools, home implements, and pottery from the mid-19th century are displayed at the museum, housed in the town's old railroad station. | Rte. 55 | 540/465–3175 | $2 | May–Oct., daily 10–4.

ON THE CALENDAR

MAY: *Mayfest.* Held at the Strasburg Town Park, this is a one-day event featuring crafts, food, local music, helicopter and hot air ballon rides, a trade show and a car show. | 540/459–2332.

MAY–OCT. AND DEC.: *Wayside Theatre.* Broadway productions, comedies, dramas, musicals, and mysteries are performed at this theatre on Main Street in Middletown. *A Christmas Carol* is staged every winter. | 540/869–1776 | www.waysidetheatre.org.

OCT.: *Battle of Cedar Creek Reenactment.* The reenactment is held in Middletown, 5 mi northeast of Strasburg, on the site of the original October 19, 1864, battle. There are artillery, infantry, and signal corps demonstrations; symposiums. | 540/869–2064.

Dining

Hotel Strasburg. Continental. The charming Victorian dining room features period antiques. The menu changes every 12 weeks, and the specialties are beef tournados and rib-eye steak. Kids' menu. Sunday brunch. | 213 S. Holliday St. | 540/465–9191 | fax 540/465–4788 | www.hotel-strasburg.com | Complimentary Continental breakfast available weekdays, full breakfast available weekends | $15–$23 | AE, D, DC, MC, V.

Old Mill Restaurant. American. Built in 1792, and transformed into a restaurant in the early 1800s, this former mill is decorated with local memorabilia. Down-home southern entrees include baked, fried, roasted, or smothered chicken. For dessert, choose from a variety of pies, cakes, and cobblers. | 886 East King Street | 540/465–5590 | Thurs–Sat. 5–8, Sun. 12–4, closed Mon.-Wed. | $8–$15 | No credit cards.

Wilkinson's Tavern. American. This restaurant is at the Wayside Inn. Kids' menu. Sunday brunch. | 7783 Main St./U.S. 11, Middletown | 540/869–1797 | fax 540/869–6038 | www.wayside-ofva.com | Reservations required Sat. | Breakfast also available. No lunch Sun. | $14–$23 | AE, D, DC, MC, V.

Lodging

Budget Inn. Three miles south of downtown Strasburg, the hotel was built in 1933. Rooms in the one-story brick building are basic and serviceable. Cable TV. Pets allowed. | 2899 Old Valley Pike | 540/465–5298 | fax 540/465–5165 | 14 rooms | $50 | AE, MC, V.

Hotel Strasburg. This restored Victorian is furnished with antiques from the Strasburg Emporium, the town's vast antique market, and nearly all are for sale. There are 21 rooms in the main hotel and four suites in each of the two adjacent houses. The hotel is 2 mi from I-81. Dining room, picnic area, complimentary Continental breakfast. In-room data ports, some in-room hot tubs, cable TV, room phones. Pets allowed. | 2133 Holliday St. | 540/465–9191 or 800/348–8327 | fax 540/465–4788 | www.hotelstrasburg.com | 29 rooms (17 with shower only) | $79–$175 | AE, D, DC, MC, V.

Wayside Inn. The restored inn, a former stagecoach stop, has been welcoming guests for 200 years. There's boating and swimming nearby. Restaurant, bar. Cable TV. Business services. | 7783 Main St./U.S. 11, Middletown | 540/869–1797 | fax 540/869–6038 | www.wayside-ofva.com | 22 rooms | $95–$145 | AE, D, DC, MC, V.

SUFFOLK

MAP 11, K7

(Nearby towns also listed: Chesapeake, Hampton, Newport News, Portsmouth, Smithfield)

Suffolk is Virginia's largest city (430 sq mi) and the self-proclaimed "Peanut Capital of the World." In 1974, Suffolk became a city when the towns of Holland and Whaleysville and the county of Suffolk were consolidated to create a new municipality. Planter's Peanuts started here in 1912 and remains one of the city's primary employers. The crop is celebrated during the Peanut Festival in October. The Great Dismal Swamp, one of the largest natural areas on the East Coast, is nearby off Route 642.

Information: Hampton Roads Chamber of Commerce | Box 327, 420 Bank St., Norfolk, VA 23501-0327 | 757/622–2312 | fax 757/622–5563 | pnemetzg@hrccva.com | www.hrc-cva.com | Weekdays 8:30–5.

Attractions

Great Dismal Swamp National Wildlife Refuge. This lush 107,000-acre wildlife area harbors bears, river otters and more than 200 species of birds. The swamp was named by Col. William Byrd in 1728; 35 years later, George Washington drained the swamp and dug a canal that is still in use today. You can hike or bike a 4½-mi road along the Washington Ditch, which ends at Lake Drummond, the largest natural lake in Virginia. There's also a 7-mi road along the Jericho Ditch that leads to the lake, and a ½-mi boardwalk. You can enter the swamp in a small boat or canoe via a 3½-mi feeder ditch on U.S. 17, about 3 mi north of the North Carolina border. The visitor center is 3 mi south of the state line, on U.S. 17 in South Mills, North Carolina. There's a picnic area and a 150-ft dock, where boaters on the

Dismal Swamp Canal can tie up for the night. | Headquarters, 3100 Desert Rd., off Rte. 32 S, Suffolk | 757/986–3705 U.S. Fish and Wildlife Service, 919/771–8333 or 888/872–8562 visitor center | fax 757/986–2353 | www.albemarle-nc.com | Free | Swamp daily dawn–dusk. Visitor center Memorial Day–Oct., daily 9–5; Nov.–Memorial Day, Tues.–Sat. 9–5.

Riddick's Folly. When this Greek Revival mansion was built by Mills Riddick in 1837, it was dubbed a "folly" because it was so big—20 rooms on four floors. During the Civil War, it became a Union headquarters for the Suffolk campaign. The house is now a museum with period furnishings and local history displays. | 510 N. Main St. | 757/934–1390 | fax 757/934–0411 | riddicksfolly@prodigy.net | www.hamptonroads.com/riddicksfolly | Free | Tues.–Fri. 10–5, Sun. 1–5.

ON THE CALENDAR

MAY: *Suffolk Spring Spectacular and Balloon Festival.* Celebrate spring with live entertainment, food, children's games, arts and crafts, and hot air balloon rides at the Suffolk Municipal Airport. | info@suffolkfest.org | www.suffolkfest.org/balloon.

OCT.: *Peanut Festival.* An annual celebration at the Suffolk Municipal Airport heralds the area's primary cash crop. Activities include a parade, the coronation of a Peanut Fest queen, live entertainment, food, and children's games. | 757/539–2111.

Dining

Bennett's Creek Marina. American. Overlooking Bennett's Creek on the outskirts of town, the menu at this coastguard-style restaurant is primarily of the surf-and-turf variety: scallops, oysters, shrimp, crabcakes, and tenderloin steaks. Sit at the bar or in the large dining room (seats 200); either inside, surrounded by mounted Marlins, or on the deck over the creek. Enjoy live acoustic music on the weekends. | 3305 Ferry Road | 757/484–8700 | Mon.–Sun. 11–9:30 | $8.95–$19.95 | AE, MC, V.

Lodging

Comfort Inn. This basic, two-story chain hotel isn't particularly close to anything: it's 35 mi from Virginia Beach, and 15 from the Chesapeake Square Mall. It is, however, one of the few lodgings available in the immediate area, and the staff will provide you with plenty of information regarding what to do in and around Suffolk. Complimentary Continental breakfast. In-room data ports. Cable TV. Outdoor pool. No pets. | 1503 Holland Rd. | 757/539–3600 | fax 757/923–3429 | 52 rooms | $60–$70 | AE, D, DC, MC, V.

Holiday Inn. The hotel is 5 mi west of town at the intersection of U.S. 58 and U.S 460 west. Restaurant. Cable TV. Pool. Business services. Some pets allowed. | 2864 Pruden Blvd. | 757/934–2311 | fax 757/539–5846 | www.holiday-inn.com | 100 rooms | $69–$109 | AE, D, DC, MC, V.

SURRY

MAP 11, J7

(Nearby town also listed: Smithfield)

On the south bank of the James River in southeastern Virginia, Surry is home to one of the country's oldest working farms, which is the centerpiece of Chippokes Plantation State Park. The park has a farm museum, tours of an antebellum mansion, swimming, hiking, and fishing.

Surry was founded in 1652, named after the English county of Surrey. The area was one of Virginia's eight original shires, designated in 1634. Forestry and agriculture support the economy—especially pork, peanuts, and pine. Virginia's Surry Nuclear Power Station, a major supplier of electricity to Virginia and North Carolina, is also important to the local economy.

Northwest of town is the Hog Island Wildlife Management Area, a 3,900-acre preserve that was named for the 17th-century practice of keeping hogs on islands, where they could forage freely but not escape.

Information: Surry County Visitors Center | Box 444, Courthouse Green, Surry, VA 23883 | 757/294–0066.

Attractions

Chippokes Plantation State Park. A working farm since the 1600s, this 1,683-acre park on the south shore of the James River has an antebellum plantation house, the Farm and Forestry Museum, and interpretive hiking trails. | 695 Chippokes Park Rd. | 757/294–3625 park or 757/294–3439 museum | fax 757/294–3299 | www.state.va.us | Mansion $3, museum $2; parking $2 weekends, $1 weekdays | Call for hours.

Hog Island Wildlife Management Area. This 2,485-acre nature preserve on the James River has ponds, paths and causeways, massive pines, and marshes. You can hike and watch for deer, ducks, geese, and other waterfowl. Fishing and hunting are permitted in season. | Rte. 650 N, Hog Island Rd. | 757/357–5224 | www.dgif.state.va.us | Free | Daily dawn–dusk.

ON THE CALENDAR

JUNE: *Chippokes Steam and Gas Engine Show.* This 2-day event is held at Chippokes Farm & Forestry Museum in the Chippoke Plantation State Park. As well as the engine exhibit, there is also a petting zoo, craft sales, food vendors and games. | 757/294–3439.
JULY: *Pork, Peanut, and Pine Festival.* The event at Chippokes Plantation State Park has barbecue pork, peanut pie, homemade foods, and hayrides. | 757/294–3625.

Dining

Surrey House Restaurant. American. The food here is about as "down-home Virginia" as it "gits." Dig in to hams (smoked down the street), crab cakes, peanut soup, apple fritters, and peanut raisin pies. | 11865 Rolfe Hwy. | 757/294–3389 | $8.99–$16.99 | AE, MC, V.

Lodging

Seward House Bed and Breakfast. The turn-of-the-century home is in town, 4 mi from the James River, where you can board the Ferry to Williamsburg. Complimentary breakfast. No smoking. | 193 Colonial Trail E | 757/294–3810 | 3 rooms (2 with shared bath), 1 suite | $65–$75, $80 suite | AE, D.

Surrey Country Inn. A small, 2-story brick hotel in the middle of town, the Surrey has a family-owned and operated restaurant in the front. Complimentary breakfast. No in-room TVs or phones. One room set aside for pets. | 11865 Rolfe Hwy. | 757/294–3389 | 11 rooms | $49–$99 | AE, MC, V.

TANGIER ISLAND

MAP 11, K5

(Nearby town also listed: Reedville)

An isolated fishing community in Chesapeake Bay, 12 mi from the mainland, Tangier Island is virtually devoid of commercialism. Cars are prohibited; you can get around by bike, motor scooter, and golf cart. Access to Tangier Island is by boat or air. Ferries leave from the town of Onancock on the Eastern Shore or Reedville on the Northern Neck. Two-and-a-half miles long and less than a mile wide, the island has no "attractions," per se, but a glimpse of its unique culture makes it an appealing day-trip. Watermen's shanties line the water, and along the village's narrow streets are white-frame houses with graves in their front yards (the tradition before cemeteries were established). The local dialect recalls the islanders' English roots, retaining many old phrases and pronunciations.

When Capt. John Smith explored the island in 1608, it was inhabited by the Pocomokes. Tangier Island was later bought from the Indians by a mainland family named West, reportedly for the price of two overcoats. During the War of 1812, the island was a base of operations for the British. Since the 19th century, Tangier's fishermen have supplied the Eastern Shore of Maryland with crabs and oysters. Fishing and swimming are permitted.

Information: Virginia Corporation Tourism | 901 E. Byrd St., Richmond, VA 23219 | 804/786–2051 or 800/932–5827 | fax 804/786–1919 | www.virginia.org | Weekdays 8–5.

Attractions

SIGHTSEEING TOURS/TOUR COMPANIES

Tangier Island Cruises. A 90-minute narrated cruise takes passengers across the Chesapeake Bay to the tiny fishing village of Tangier Island. Guided tours by locals are offered near the boat dock. The cruises depart from Onancock, about 40 mi from Cape Charles. | 757/891–2240 | fax 757/891–2586 | tocruise98@aol.com | www.chesapeakebaysampler.com/tangierisland | $20 | Memorial Day–Oct. 15., daily departures at 10 and return trip to mainland at 3.

Sandy's Place. An unlikely mix of crafts and museum pieces, Sandy's is centrally located on Main Street. Trace the history of Tangier through stories, artifacts and relics from the beach, all displayed in an 18th-century Salt Box house. | Main Street | 757/891–2234 | 50 cents | Mon.–Sat. 10–4 and 5–8.

ON THE CALENDAR

SEPT.: *Homecoming Festival*. Held in a field next to the local airport, this two-day event celebrates everything local: food, music, and crafts. | 757/891–2553.

Dining

Hilda Crockett's Chesapeake House. American. Described as "Bay cuisine," the food here runs the gamut from crab cakes, to clam fritters, to home-baked breads, all continuously passed down the long, family-style tables. The best part: It's all-you-can-eat every day. | 16243 Main St. | 757/891–2331 | Mon.–Sat. 11:30–6, Sun. 11:30–5 | $12.75 | No credit cards.

Lodging

Shirley's Bay View Inn and Bed and Breakfast. Opened in 1904, this Victorian home has a main house (with 2 rooms) and another eight cottages. Grounds are lush, and interior furnishings are comfy and cozy. There are trees outside to roam beneath, and the interior, while not furnished in keeping with any particular era, is "fixed up" to be as comfortable and inviting as your own living room. Complimentary breakfast. Cable TV. No pets. | 16408 West Ridge Road | 757/891–2396 | 10 rooms | $85 | V.

TAPPAHANNOCK

MAP 11, J5

(Nearby town also listed: Montross)

On the south bank of the Rappahannock River in eastern Virginia, Tappahannock is the seat of Essex County. It was formerly a Native American village, and its name means "town on the rise and fall of water." Founded by colonists in 1680, Tappahannock became a prosperous colonial port, though it is now supported by a mix of agricultural and industrial activity. The county is Virginia's second-largest producer of corn, grain, and barley. The principal industries here are garment, automotive parts, and sub-assembly-parts manufacturers. Forestry and fishing are also important to the local economy. Tappahannock is a gateway to the Northern Neck, with a shortcut provided by the U.S. 360 bridge. It is also the starting point for cruises to Tangier Island or down the Rappahannock.

Information: Tappahannock–Essex County Chamber of Commerce | Box 481, Tappahannock, VA 22560 | 804/443–5241 | fax 804/443–4157 | Weekdays 8:30–4:30.

SIGHTSEEING TOURS/TOUR COMPANIES

Tangier Island and Rappahannock River Cruises. An all-day trip down the Rappahannock River includes a stopover at Ingleside Plantation Vineyards in Oak Grove; another cruise goes to Tangier Island. The boats depart from Hoskins Creek. | 468 Buzzards Point Rd., Reedville | 804/453–2628 | fax 804/453–3018 | www.eaglesnest.net/tangier | $20 | May–Oct., Tues.–Sun. departures at 10, return at 4.

ON THE CALENDAR

JUN.: *Bluegrass Festival.* Regional bands play Old Time, gospel, and bluegrass music at Heritage Park in Warsaw. Food, arts and crafts, and hayrides are added attractions. | 804/333–4038.

Dining

Lowery's. American. This restaurant has a family atmosphere, gift shop, fishing well and treasure chest for children. | 528 Church La./U.S. 17 | 804/443–4314 | fax 804/443–4474 | $5–$28 | AE, D, MC, V.

Rivahside Cafe. American. Housed in a former general store dating from the early 1900s, and only one block from the Rappahannock "Rivah," the café serves a variety of food. Order a hefty burger, or choose from a wide range of soups, sandwiches, and salads (the chicken salad is most popular). Old quilts and antiques line the walls. | 221 Prince St. | 804/443–2333 | Mon.–Sat. 8–3, closed Sun. | $3–$7 | No credit cards.

Lodging

Days Inn. The moderately priced chain motel is in town, right at U.S. 360. Complimentary Continental breakfast. Cable TV. Business services. | 1414 Tappahannock Blvd. | 804/443–9200 | fax 804/443–2663 | www.days-inn.com | 60 rooms | $49–$80 | AE, D, DC, MC, V.

Linden House Bed and Breakfast Plantation. This 18th-century colonial brick home is a 10-minute drive from the center of Tappahannock. Surrounded by 203 acres of walking trails, the plantation also has an English Garden, a gazebo, and a fishing pond. The house itself has a common room with cable TV, a ballroom, and rooms furnished with both antiques and reproductions. Outside, you can relax on any one of the porches, wraparound verandas, or patios. Complimentary breakfast. Refrigerators. No kids under 10. | 11770 Tidewater Trail | 804/443–1170 or 800/443–0107 | fax 804/443–0107 | 7 rooms | $95–$135 | January. | AE, D, MC, V.

Super 8. This two-story budget motel has interior corridors and rooms furnished in dark, heavy commercial furniture. Some refrigerators, cable TV. Business services. | Box 1748, U.S. 17 and U.S. 360 | 804/443–3888 | fax 804/443–3821 | www.super8.com | 43 rooms | $49–$51 | AE, D, DC, MC, V.

TRIANGLE

MAP 11, J4

(Nearby town also listed: Manassas)

The town of Triangle in northern Virginia borders the Quantico Marine Corps Base and Prince William Forest Park. Triangle got its name from its position as a fork in the road—at the junction of the Marine Corps base, old U.S. 1, and Fuller Heights Road. The military base, built in 1918, brought economic stability to this rural farming area, which today is a small residential community.

Prince William Park protects Quantico Creek's forested watershed and has a range of outdoor activities, including hiking, fishing, camping, and ranger-led nature programs.

Information: **Prince William County/Manassas Conference and Visitors Bureau** | 14420 Bristow Rd., Manassas, VA 22192 | 703/792–4254 or 800/432–1792 | fax 703/792–4219 | www.visitpwc.com | Weekdays 8:30–5.

Attractions

Marine Corps Air-Ground Museum. This military museum displays Marine Corps air-craft, vehicles, weapons, and uniforms from both world wars and the Korean War. | Building 2014, Quantico Marine Corps Base | 703/784–2606 | fax 703/784–5856 | Free | Apr.–late Nov., Tues.–Sat. 10–5, Sun. noon–5.

Prince William Forest Park. This 18,571-acre park is the largest natural area near Washington, D.C. There are more than 35 mi of trails, campsites, and a 4-mi bike path. Stream fishing is allowed. Park naturalists offer interpretive programs on weekends. | Rte. 619 | 703/221–7181 | fax 703/221–3258 | www.nps.gov/prwi | $4 per vehicle | Daily dawn–dusk.

Weems-Botts Museum and Park. Dating from the late 1770s, the Weems-Botts has had many lives, including a bookstore, a commercial business, and a private home. Today, it's a five-room museum, with each room outfitted in the furnishings from a different era, from colonial times to the early 20th century. | 3914 Duke St. | 703/221–3346. | $3 | Tues.–Sat. 10–4, Sun. 12–4, closed Mon.

ON THE CALENDAR
JAN.: *Explore Winter Wildlife Hike.* You can take a ranger-led hike through Prince William Forest Park, the largest natural area in the Washington, D.C. metropolitan area. | 703/221–7181.
JUNE: *Historic Occoquan Spring Arts and Crafts Show.* The street festival in down-town Occoquan features the work of 150 artists and craftspeople, live entertainment and food. | 703/491–2168.

Dining

Globe and Laurel. American. A white stucco and brick Tudor building at the north end of Triangle, this restaurant serves traditional American fare, like prime rib and apple pie, in two entirely different rooms. One is of the white linen-and-candlelight variety; the other is a veritable museum of military history, with tables made of hatch covers, nautical arti-facts on the walls, and a ceiling covered with police uniform shoulder patches from around the world. | 18418 Jefferson Davis Highway | 703/221–5763 | Mon.–Fri. 11:30–1:30 and 5–9:30, Sat. 5–9:30, closed Sun. | $15–$20 | AE, MC, V.

Lodging

Quality Inn. Just off I–95, the property is close to Prince William Forest Park. Complimen-tary Continental breakfast. Some microwaves, refrigerators, cable TV, some in-room hot tubs. Pool. Game room. Video games. Laundry facilities. Business services. Some pets allowed. | 1109 Horner Rd., Woodbridge | 703/494–0300 | fax 703/494–5644 | www.quali-tyinn.com | 94 rooms | $70–$85 | AE, D, DC, MC, V.

Ramada Inn–Quantico. Despite the building's romanesque arches and columns, and the courtyard out back, rooms at this two-story stucco hotel are basic, with very little to dif-ferentiate them from any other Ramada Inn room. But the location is a plus; from here, you can walk to downtown Triangle. Restaurant. Lounge. Picnic Area. In-room data ports. Cable TV. Pool. Exercise facilities. Laundry facilities. Pets allowed. | 4316 Inn Street | 703/221–1181 or 800/2RAMADA | fax 703/221–6952 | www.ramadaquantico.com | 139 rooms | $55–$85 | AE, D, MC, V.

TYSONS CORNER

MAP 11, J4

(Nearby town also listed: Alexandria, Arlington, Fairfax, Falls Church, Reston, Vienna)

Tysons Corner is a commercial district shared by Vienna and McLean, and it's all about shopping. There are two expansive malls, a row of sophisticated shops, and enormous car dealers along Leesburg Pike. About a dozen miles from Washington D.C., Tysons Corner is a convenient spot for tourists because the hotels are countless and transportation into the city is good. Tysons Corner is an equal distance, around 16 mi, from both Ronald Reagan Washington National and Washington Dulles International Airports.

Information: Fairfax County Chamber of Commerce | 8230 Old Courthouse Road, Suite 350, Vienna, VA 22182-3853 | 703/749–0400 | www.fccc.org.

Attractions

The Galleria at Tysons Corner. Not as well-known as the main mall at Tysons Corner, the Galleria nevertheless houses department stores like Macy's, Neiman-Marcus and Sak's Fifth Avenue and lots of uppercrust shops. | 1651 International Dr., McLean | 703/847–9508 | Free | Mon.–Sat. 10–9:30, Sun. 11–7.

Leesburg Pike Shopping District. You'll find several high-end retailers directly across the street from Tyson's Shopping Center. Hermes of Paris and Tiffany and Company are just a couple of the fine shops here. | Leesburg Pike | Free | Hours vary depending on shop.

Tysons Corner Mall. There are over 250 shops at this mall, ranging from Nordstrom's and Bloomingdale's to the Disney Store. Tyson's is one of the largest and most diverse shopping malls on the East Coast. | 1961 Chain Bridge Rd., McLean | 703/893–9400 or 888/289–7667 | www.shoptysons.com | Free | Mon.–Sat. 10–9:30, Sun. 11–6.

Dining

P.F. Chang's Chinese Bistro. Chinese. Slate floors, steel bonsais, murals, and life-size statues of Chinese warriors create a sophisticated backdrop in this restaurant. You can sit in one of the high black banquettes and try the orange-peel beef, which is steak doused in a hot-and-sweet caramelized glaze, or sample Chang's fiery hot Long Life Noodles. The restaurant also has an extensive beer and wine list and makes some expert cocktails. | In Tyson's Galleria at 1716M International Dr. | 703/734–8996 | Reservations essential | $8–$18 | AE, D, DC, MC, V.

Rainforest Cafe. American. Animated, life-sized wildlife and a jungle soundtrack make this spot a big favorite of families with kids. Around lunch time it can get loud. The menu has child-friendly items like chicken fingers and burgers as well as more sophisticated disheslike Caribe Coconut Chicken and Hong Kong Stir Fry over Jasmine Rice. | In Tyson's Corner Center, 1961 Chain Bridge Rd. | 703/821–1900 | $6–$11 | AE, D, MC, V.

Lodging

Best Western Tysons Westpark. It's ½ mi from Tysons Corner Center and 2 mi from Wolf Trap Farm. Restaurant, bar. In-room data ports, microwaves, cable TV, in-room movies. Indoor pool, hot tub, sauna. Exercise equipment. Pets allowed (fee). | 8401 Westpark Dr. | 703/734–2800 | fax 703/821–8872 | www.bestwestern.com | 301 rooms, 14 suites | $89, $189 suites | AE, D, DC, MC, V.

Embassy Suites Tysons Corner. Each two-room suite has a separate living room, with TVs in both rooms. It's 1 mi from Tysons Corner Center and the Galleria. Restaurant, bar, complimentary breakfast, room service. In-room data ports, microwaves, refrigerators, mini-bars, cable TV, in-room movies. Pool, hot tub. Exercise equipment. Laundry facilities, laundry service. Business services. | 8517 Leesburg Pike, Vienna | 703/883–0707 | fax 703/883–0694 | www.embassysuites.com | 232 suites | $119–$229 | AE, D, DC, MC, V.

Hilton McLean Tysons Corner. Built in 1987 this nine-story hotel has a glass atrium with lots of marble and greenery. There's ample parking for RVs and trucks. Restaurant, bar, complimentary Continental breakfast. In-room data ports, minibars, cable TV. Indoor pool. Spa. Exercise equipment. Laundry services. Business services. Pets allowed ($50 nonrefundable deposit). | 7920 Jones Branch Dr., McLean | 703/847–5000 | fax 703/761–5100 | www.hilton.com | 449 rooms, 9 suites | $80–$235 rooms, $325–$1150 suites. Kids under 18 stay free | AE, D, DC, MC, V.

Marriott Residence Inn Tysons Corner. The utilitarian suites (some bi-level) are large enough for some families. Complimentary Continental breakfast. Outdoor pool. Hot tub. Basketball, volleyball. Laundry services. Business services. Pets allowed ($150 deposit and $5/night). | 8616 Westwood Center Dr., Vienna | 703/893–0120 | fax 703/790–8896 | www.marriott.com | 96 suites | $190–$260 | AE, D, DC, MC, V.

Ritz-Carlton, Tysons Corner. Rooms in this elegant hotel next to The Tysons Galleria and 1/4 mi from Tysons Corner Center are furnished with reproductions of classic English antiques. All have marble baths, and many have views of Washington landmarks. The club level offers a private lounge with complimentary meals and concierge. Restaurant, bar with entertainment, room service. In-room data ports, minibars, cable TV. Indoor pool. Hot tub, massage, spa, beauty salon. Exercise equipment. Baby-sitting. Laundry service. Business services. Parking (fee), free parking. | 1700 Tysons Blvd., McLean | 703/506–4300 | fax 703/506–4305 | www.ritzcarlton.com | 398 rooms, 33 suites | $340–$400, $420–$500 suites, $1400 Fairfax Suite | AE, D, DC, MC, V.

VIENNA

MAP 11, J4

(Nearby towns also listed: Alexandria, Arlington, Fairfax, Falls Church, Reston)

With a population of 15,000, Vienna is a quiet, family-oriented suburb of Washington, D.C. Church Street, one of the old town's main drags, is adjacent to the Washington and Old Dominion Trail, and features historic homes and buildings such as the Freeman House and an 1874 Presbyterian church. Vienna is also home to Wolf Trap, one of the nation's finest amphitheaters.

Information: Vienna Chamber of Commerce | 703/281–1333 | dglanz@viennacc.org | www.viennacc.org.

Attractions

The Freeman House. This home was confiscated by both Northern and Southern troops shortly after its construction in 1859, and was used as a base for officers and as a hospital. The home returned to civilian status after the war, and today contains a re-creation of a 19th-century general store, as well as a exhibits of typical household scenes from the period. | 131 Church St. | 703/938–5187 | Free | Sat. 12–4, Sun. 1–5.

Meadowlark Gardens. This 95-acre park includes two lakes, landscaped gardens with azaleas, lilies, hostas, daffodils, and other plants that provide a blooming landscape through three seasons, and it's a great place to see the cherry trees bloom. In warm weather you may glimpse a bride: the gazebos are popular for weddings. | 9750 Meadowlark Gardens Ct. | 703/255–3631 | www.nvrpa.org/meadowlark.html | Free | Daily, 10–8.

Wolftrap. International acts regularly perform at this 7,000-seat concert venue. You can dance to bluegrass out on the lawn or listen to an opera performed in the amphitheater. The Barns of Wolf Trap allow concerts to be given year-round, albeit on a smaller scale. | 1624 Trap Rd. | 703/255–1900 | www.wolftrap.org | Prices and times vary.

MAY–SEPT.: *Barns of Wolf Trap Foundation.* Children's programs, including mime, puppet, and animal shows, concerts, drama, and storytelling, take center stage at the Barns—one of the outdoor venues at Wolf Trap. The International Children's Festival takes place over several days in September and brings together performers from the United States and abroad for various children's programs—puppet shows, drama, and storytelling. | Wolf Trap Farm Park for the Performing Arts | 703/255–1900.

Dining

Aarathi Indian Cuisine. Indian. Dine amid Indian statuary on dishes from all over India, from Tandoori to curry to paneer, with many vegetarian options. Try the popular Malabar fish curry or spicy lamb vindaloo. | 409 Maple Ave. E | 703/938–0100 | $14–$24 | AE, D, DC, MC, V.

Amphora. Eclectic. Greek, Italian, and American dishes are served 24 hours a day at this local institution. Leg of lamb with rosemary and linguine with scallops are a couple of favorites. You can sit at a table, get cozy in a booth, or belly up to the counter. | 377 Maple Ave. | 703/938–7877 | $9–$23 | AE, D, MC, V.

Bistro 123. French. White table linens and wood beam ceilings are accented with fresh flowers, and a painting of Napoléon Bonaparte oversees the goings on. Start with crabmeat flan and move on to grilled swordfish in a riesling sauce, or go for the more exotic venison with huckleberry sauce. | 246 E. Maple Ave. | 703/938–4379 | Reservations essential Fri.–Sat. | Closed Sun. No lunch Sat. | $12.95–$19.95 | AE, DC, MC, V.

Bonaroti. Italian. A brick building in downtown Vienna houses this small restaurant. The comprehensive menu includes Cacciucco Livornese (seafood stew) and other fish, a dozen or more pasta dishes (lasagna, gnocchi, tortellini), plus veal, poultry, and beef. Pastas are made fresh daily. No smoking. | 428 E. Maple Ave. | 703/281–7550 | Closed Sun. No lunch Sat. | $13.95–$23.95 | AE, DC, MC, V.

Cafe Renaissance. Continental. Candlelight and fresh flowers set the French Country tone. Rack of lamb, Maine lobster, and dessert souffles are some of the scrumptious possibilities. | 163 Glyndon St. | 703/938–3311 | Reservations essential | No lunch Sat.–Sun. | $11–$27 | AE, D, DC, MC, V.

Clyde's. American. Four dining rooms, each with a different art theme, surround a central bar. Dine amid bronze sculpture or handblown glass, bird paintings, or American artifacts. Crab cakes, ribeye steak, and arugula salad are a few of the many dishes. And don't forget the famous Clyde's burgers. Kids' menu. Sunday brunch. | 8332 Leesburg Pike | 703/734–1901 | www.clydes.com | $5.25–$19.95 | AE, D, DC, MC, V.

Fedora Cafe. American. This restaurant on the outskirts of Tysons Corner is brightened by huge windows. Food offerings range from burgers to potato-crusted salmon, filet mignon, and chicken. Live jazz Wednesday–Saturday. Cigars are sold. Open-air dining on weekends. Sunday brunch. | 8521 Leesburg Pike | 703/556–0100 | No lunch. No dinner Sun. | $15–$25 | AE, D, DC, MC, V.

Hunan Lion. Chinese. This dining spot in an office building has high ceilings, large windows, and several dining rooms, some more formal and some more casual. Sample Taiwan sausages with five-spice powder, whole shrimp crusted with seasoned salt, and numerous noodle dishes. Dim sum is served on weekends. | 2070 Chain Bridge Rd. | 703/734–9828 | No lunch Sun. | $4.25–$16.95 | AE, D, DC, MC, V.

La Provence. French. Dine on one of two levels in this restaurant with large flower murals. Choose from salmon in saffron sauce, duck confit, lamb shank, and more. | 144 W. Maple Ave. | 703/242–3777 | Reservations essential Fri.–Sat. | Closed Sun. | $16.95–$24.95 | AE, D, DC, MC, V.

Le Canard. French. Impressionist art, candles, and fresh roses make for an intimate setting. The chef serves duck, the restaurant's namesake, roasted with a variety of brandies or with chestnut puree. Veal also figures heavily in the offerings. Piano bar Mon.–Sat. | 132 Branch Rd. | 703/281–0070 | www.lecanardrestaurant.com | Reservations essential Fri.–Sat. | No lunch weekends | $14.95–$24.95 | AE, D, DC, MC, V.

Marco Polo. Continental/Italian. Veal and pasta are the main offerings here. If you can't decide, try the vitello trio, a combination of veal piccata, veal marsala, and veal Marco Polo. Kids' menu. Early-bird supper Thurs. | 245 Maple Ave. W | 703/281–3922 | www.marcopolorestaurant.com. | Closed Sun. | $12–$20 | AE, DC, MC, V.

Morton's. Steak. Known in the past as a "gentleman's saloon," this steakhouse for the elite draws women, too. The dark cherry wood, white linens, LeRoy Neiman prints, and the servings all spell quality. You can have the tried-and-true Porterhouse Steak, or be daring with an order of the cajun rib eye. The lobsters are whoppers, typically weighing in at 3 to 6 pounds. All meals are a la carte. | 8075 Leesburg Pike | 703/883–0800 | Reservations essential Thurs.–Sat. | No lunch weekends | $20–$33 | AE, DC, MC, V.

Nizam's. Turkish. The owner welcomes you at the door at this restaurant filled with Turkish plates, pottery, and watercolors recalling Istanbul. It's one of a few in the United States that makes its own *doner kebob* (spit-roasted, marinated lamb). Try it or the kofte over eggplant beyendi. The bar pours Turkish beers and wines; Turkish coffee is available, too. No smoking. | 523 Maple Ave. W (Rte. 123) | 703/938–8948 | Reservations essential Fri.–Sat. | Closed Mon. No lunch weekends | $13.95–$20 | AE, D, DC, MC, V.

Panjshir. Afghan. Afghan textiles and vintage firearms adorn this eatery. Lamb, beef, and chicken kebabs are complemented by pumpkin, turnips and spinach dishes with exotic spices and sauces. | 224 W. Maple Ave. | 703/281–4183 | No lunch Sun. | $9.95–$13.25 | AE, DC, MC, V.

Phillips Seafood Grill. Seafood. The main dining room, done in rich mahogany, gets a floor show from the open, exhibition-style kitchen. Or choose one of the small, private dining alcoves. Crab cakes are the specialty, but the expansive menu includes mixed shellfish platters, hickory-grilled fish, steak, chicken, and sandwiches and salads. Patio dining is also an option. Kids' menu available. Sun. brunch. | 8330 Boone Blvd. | 703/442–0400 | www.phillipsfoods.com | Reservations required Fri.–Sat. | No lunch Sat. | $8–$30 | AE, D, DC, MC, V.

Primi Piatti. Italian. This softly lit dining room with elegantly draped windows has an open kitchen that serves a can't-miss seafood risotto with shellfish and saffron, along with veal and pastas like spaghetti with pesto and fava beans. | 8045 Leesburg Pike | 703/893–0300 | Reservations required Fri.–Sat. | Closed Sun. No lunch Sat. | $13–$29.95 | AE, DC, MC, V.

Tara Thai. Thai. The walls are hung with pictures of Thailand, and the Pad Thai and the Seafood Feast are good choices. | 226 Maple Ave. | 703/255–2467 | $8–$13 | AE, D, DC, MC, V.

Lodging

Comfort Inn Tysons Corner. The rooms here are more colorful than those in many chain hotels; the bedspreads are printed with bold floral designs. This three-story hotel has plenty of parking for trucks and RVs. Restaurant, complimentary Continental breakfast. In-room data ports, cable TV. Outdoor pool. Laundry services. Business services. | 1587 Spring Hill Rd. | 703/448–8020 | fax 703/448–0343 | www.comfortinn.com | 250 rooms | $90–$190. Kids under 18 stay free | AE, D, DC, MC, V.

Residence Inn Tysons Corner. At this hostelry 2 mi from Tysons Corner Center and Tysons Galleria, all rooms are suites and you can have dinner delivered from many local restaurants. Some rooms have fireplaces. Complimentary Continental breakfast. In-room data ports, kitchenettes, cable TV. Outdoor pool. Laundry facilities. Free parking. | 8616 Westwood Center Dr., Vienna | 703/893–0120 | fax 703/790–8896 | www.residenceinn.com | 96 suites | $189, $259 suites | AE, D, DC, MC, V.

Sheraton Premiere. This high-rise is 5 mi from Tysons Corner Center and the Galleria at Tysons II. Cherry-wood armoires and other furniture accent the guest rooms, which are done in burgundies, greens, and browns. Club Level rooms have in-room business facilities and access to an exclusive lounge. Restaurants, bar, room service. In-room data ports, some refrigerators, cable TV, in-room movies. Indoor pool, outdoor pool. Hot tub, massage, sauna. Health club, racquetball. Laundry service. Business services. Airport shuttle. Free parking. | 8661 Leesburg Pike, Vienna | 703/448–1234 or 800/572–7666 | fax 703/893–8193 | jkennedy@sptc.com | www.sptc.com | 437 rooms | $119–$229 | AE, D, DC, MC, V.

Tysons Corner Marriott. This fourteen-story hotel is ½ mi. east of Tysons Corner Center. Restaurant, bar, room service. In-room data ports, cable TV, in-room movies. Baby-sitting. Indoor pool. Hot tub, sauna. Exercise equipment. Laundry facilities. | 8028 Leesburg Pike, Vienna | 703/734–3200 | fax 703/442–9301 | www.marriott.com | 390 rooms, 2 suites | $109, $279 suite | AE, D, DC, MC, V.

Vienna Wolftrap Motel. A good bargain in this pricey region, this three-story brick motel cuts costs with minimalist rooms and no elevators. Several restaurants and a medium-size shopping center are within walking distance. Some in-room data ports, cable TV. No pets. | 430 Maple Ave. | 703/281–2330 | 116 rooms | $47–$50. Kids under 16 stay free | AE, D, DC, MC, V.

VIRGINIA BEACH

MAP 11, K7

(Nearby towns also listed: Chesapeake, Hampton, Norfolk, Portsmouth)

Virginia Beach was first settled in 1621, but thinly populated for more than a century. In the 1880s, the resort was developed along the beach, and by the turn of the century it had become very popular. In 1906, Virginia Beach became a town. The end of World War II saw the advent of suburbs and development. In 1963, it merged with Princess Anne County to form the modern city, which stretches along the Atlantic Ocean near the mouth of the Chesapeake Bay. The heart of this busy beach resort is a length of shoreline that reaches from Cape Henry south to Rudee Inlet. It consists of 6 mi of crowded public beach and a 2½-mi paved boardwalk; a bike trail runs roughly parallel to the walk. Hotels, restaurants, and shops are concentrated here, as are outfitters that rent sailing, surfing, and scuba equipment. Entertainers perform nightly, Memorial Day through Labor Day, at the 24th Street Stage. First Landing/Seashore State Park, a protected natural area, offers a less-commercial beach experience.

Information: Virginia Beach Convention and Visitors Bureau | 2100 Parks Ave., Suite 500, Virginia Beach, VA, 23451 | 757/437–4888 or 800/822–3224 | fax 757/437–4918 | www.vbfun.com | Daily 9–5.

Attractions

Adam Thoroughgood House. This 17th-century brick house is named for the original owner of the property. Thoroughgood was an indentured servant who came to Virginia in 1621 and started the first ferry service across the Elizabeth River; King Charles I rewarded him with 5,350 acres. A descendant built the English cottage-style house, a four-room dwelling with a steeply pitched roof that is considered a good example of early Virginia domestic architecture. It is furnished with period antiques and has an herb and flower garden. | 1636 Parish Rd. | 757–664–6283 | fax 757/431–3733 | $3; combination ticket with Moses Myers House and Willoughby-Baylor House in Norfolk $6 | Tues.–Sat. 10–5, Sun 1–5.

Association for Research and Enlightenment. This organization is dedicated to the late Edgar Cayce, a Virginia Beach psychic who reportedly diagnosed and prescribed treatment for medical ailments while in a trance. Cayce's former hospital is now the international headquarters for A.R.E., which shows a 30-minute film and has exhibits about the so-called father of holistic medicine. You can visit a meditation room overlooking the ocean, browse in the bookstore, or sit in on group ESP testing. Tours of Cayce's headquarters are given during the summer. | 215 67th St. | 757/428–3588 | www.are-cayce.com | Free | Mon.–Sat. 9 AM–8 PM, Sun. 11–8.

Back Bay National Wildlife Refuge. This 7,000-acre wildlife preserve is bordered by the Atlantic Ocean on one side and by the Back Bay on the other. You can hike or bike on several trails, or take a tram ride, which can be booked through the Backbay Restoration Foundation (757/498–2473). | 4005 Sandpiper Rd. | 757/721–2412 | $5 per private vehicle; on foot or bicycle $2 per person | Daily, dawn–dusk.

Cape Henry Memorial. A large granite cross marks the first landing of English settlers in Virginia, on April 26, 1607. They spent the night at Cape Henry before sailing up the James River to Jamestown Island, where they established a permanent settlement; they later returned to hammer a wooden cross in the spot where they originally landed. A pilgrimage on the fourth Sunday in April commemorates the event. | Fort Story Military Reservation | 757/898–2410 | fax 757/898–6346 | www.nps.gov/colo | Free | Dawn–Dusk.

Colonial National Historical Park. Commemorates the English Colonial Period of American History. Includes Jamestown, the first permanent English settlement in America, and Yorktown, battlefield site of the last major battle of the American Revolution. (*See* Yorktown.) | Visitors Center, Colonial Parkway, at Rte. 238, Yorktown | 757/898–3400 | fax 757/898–6346 | www.nps.gov/colo | Jamestown $5, Yorktown $4, combination $7 | Daily 9–5.

Contemporary Art Center of Virginia. The main gallery of the city's premier art museum focuses on 20th-century art. The center also offers students' exhibits, an auditorium, and regular tours. | 2200 Parks Ave. | 757/425–0000 | fax 757/425–8186 | www.cacv.org | $3.00 | Tues.–Fri. 10–5, Sat. 10–4, Sun. noon–4.

First Landing/Seashore State Park. With the Chesapeake Bay on one side and a series of creeks and lakes on the other, this 2,770-acre park is a unique natural area, with large cypress trees, rare plants, and lagoons. A boardwalk just above the water level lets you get close to flora and fauna; the park is a haven for red and gray foxes, water snakes, and other denizens of swamp and dune. More than 19 mi of hiking trails wind through the park, over dunes and through cypress swamps; there's also a bicycle trail and boat ramps. A visitor center features exhibits on the history and marsh life of the area. Campgrounds, picnic areas, and guided tours are available. | 2500 Shore Dr. | 757/412–2331 or 757/412–2300 | www.state.va.us | Apr.–Oct., $2 per vehicle weekdays, $3 weekends; Nov.–Mar., $1 per vehicle | Park daily 8–dusk, visitor center daily 9–6.

Francis Land House Historic Site and Gardens. Built about 1732 for one of the first settlers of Princess Anne County, this structure was home to four generations of the Land family. Guides in period dress lead you through the house, which has antiques and a Dutch gambrel roof. The grounds include 18th-century plantings, such as flax. | 3131 Virginia Beach Blvd. | 757/431–4000 | fax 757/431–3733 | $3.50 | Tues.–Sat. 9–5, Sun. 11–5.

Lynnhaven House. This 1725 brick house was built by the Thellaball family; the grounds feature a graveyard and period gardens. Regular cooking and crafts programs demonstrate the lifestyle of the 18th-century residents. Guided tours are optional. | 4405 Wishart Rd. (Rte. 44) | 757/460–1688 | fax 757/431–3733 | $3.50 | June–Sept., Tues.–Sun. noon–4; May and Oct., weekends noon–4.

Norwegian Lady Statue. A 9-ft bronze on Atlantic Ave. between 25th and 26th Streets commemorates the 1891 shipwreck of the Norwegian sailing vessel *Dictator*.

Ocean Breeze Water Park. The facility has a water park with slides, inner-tube course, and a wave pool; batting cages; a 36-hole miniature golf course; and a motor world, featuring mini Indy race cars and a track. | 849 General Booth Blvd. | 800/678–9453 or 757/422–4444 | www.oceanbreezewaterpark.com | Water park $16.95; golf, race track, and batting cages $2.50, with water park admission $1.25 | Call for hours.

Old Cape Henry Lighthouse. Marking the entrance to the Chesapeake Bay, this lighthouse is believed to have been the first one built in the United States. Constructed in 1792 by the federal government, it was used until 1881, when a nearby cast-iron lighthouse replaced it. The old structure is now under the command of the Fifth Coast Guard District. | Fort Story Military Reservation | 757/422–9421 | $2, special rates for seniors and children | Oct.–Mar., daily 10–4.

Old Coast Guard Station Museum. A museum in the restored 1903 lifesaving station chronicles the history of the United States Coast Guard. One gallery deals with World War II's impact on the region; other exhibits tell the story of shipwrecks along the Virginia coast. | 24th and Atlantic Ave. | 757/422–1587 | fax 757/491–8609 | www.va-beach.com/old_coast | $3 | Memorial Day–Sept., Mon.–Sat. 10–5, Sun. noon–5; Oct.–Memorial Day, Tues.–Sat. 10–5, Sun. noon–5.

Virginia Marine Science Museum. This massive facility has more than 200 exhibits representing Virginia's marine life. You can watch nesting osprey and other birds in their 10-acre marsh habitat through telescopes on an observation tower, handle horseshoe crabs, take a simulated journey to the bottom of the sea in a submarine, and study fish up close in tanks that re-create various underwater environments. There are harbor seal and river otter habitats, and a sea turtle hatchling laboratory. Seasonal boat trips include dolphin watching trips in summer and whale watching in winter. An IMAX theater shows marine and nature programs. | 717 General Booth Blvd. | 757/425–3474 | www.vmsm.com | $7.95 | Mid-June–Labor Day, daily 9–9; Labor Day–mid-June, daily 9–5.

SIGHTSEEING TOURS/TOUR COMPANIES

Blue Moon Cruise. This cruise line offers two-hour lunch and dinner sightseeing tours; you can also charter the whole boat for a private cruise around Hampton Roads. | 2109 W. Great Neck Rd. | 757/491–8090 or 757/422–2900 | $22–$41 | Daily 8–10.

ON THE CALENDAR

JAN.–DEC.: *Virginia Saltwater Fishing Tournament.* An awards program for recreational fishermen, the tournament recognizes outstanding catches in 33 species of fish. | 757/491–5160.

MAY: *Pungo Strawberry Festival.* You can sample strawberries prepared in many ways. Also featured are live music, arts and crafts, food booths, and children's activities | Memorial Day weekend | 757/721–6001.

JUNE: *Boardwalk Art Show.* Paintings, ceramics, fine arts, sculpture, and photography are displayed along a 14-block stretch of the oceanfront boardwalk. | 757/425–0000.

AUG.: *East Coast Surfing Championship.* This free event at Oceanfront between 2nd and 9th is said to be the oldest surfing contest in North America. | 757/499–8822.

SEPT.: *Neptune Festival.* A send-off to summer, this oceanfront event has live entertainment, fresh seafood, arts and crafts, and children's activities. Highlights include the Sand Castle Classic, an air show, and fireworks. King Neptune's Ball is one of the city's premier social events. | 757/498–0215.

SEPT.: *Tidewater Western Riders World Championship Rodeo.* More than 250 contestants from across the United States compete to qualify for the finals at the Princess Anne Park horse arena in Oklahoma City. There are seven rodeo events, including bull riding. | 757/721–7786.

Dining

Aldo's Ristorante. Italian. Celebrity-watch in a classy, casual place with art deco detailing. Known for seafood, veal cutlet, filet mignon. Open-air dining. Only summer patio dining. Piano Tues.–Sat. | 1860 Laskin Rd. | 757/491–1111 | fax 757/491–0597 | www.aldos.com | No lunch Sun. | $12–$30 | AE, DC, MC, V.

Blue Pete's Seafood and Steak. Seafood/Steak. Here's a spot for casual dining in a wooded, back-bay setting on a creek. A retail shop offers wine-to-go and chocolate- and rum-flavored cigars. Specialties include bouillabaisse, scallops, and fish. Early-bird suppers. Kids' menu. | 1400 N. Muddy Creek Rd. | 757/426–2005 | Tue.–Sun. 6–8:30. No lunch | $11–$40 | AE, DC, MC, V.

Coastal Grill. Seafood. This restaurant blends casual and sophisticated elements—contemporary artwork is paired with an old-fashioned sideboard. You can feel comfortable wearing jeans or dressed in a suit. Have a cocktail at the mahogany bar or on the patio. Tuna, salmon, soft-shell crab. Kids' menu. | 1427 N. Great Neck Rd. | 757/496–3348 | No lunch | $19–$21 | AE, D, MC, V.

Coyote Cafe and Cantina. Southwestern. Savor southwestern flavors in an eclectic setting. Try potato-encrusted salmon, grilled chicken fajitas, or crisped roasted duck. | 972 Laskin Rd. | 757/425–8705 | fax 757/491–3423 | Weekdays 11:30–2:30, 5–12; No lunch on Weekends | $16–$25 | MC, V.

Cuisine and Company. Continental. This small café and catering company is known for parties, weddings, bridal showers. Beer and wine only. | 3004 Pacific Ave. | 757/428–6700 | fax 757/428–0138 | cuisineandcompany@erols.com | Breakfast also available | $5–$12 | AE, D, MC, V.

Ice House. Seafood. A seashore/lighthouse theme sets the mood at this dining spot that specializes in seafood, steak, and ribs. You can dine outdoors on a deck. Kids' menu. | 604 Norfolk Ave. | 757/491–0263 | fax 757/491–4454 | Reservations not accepted | Mon.–Sun. 11–11 | $6–$15 | AE, D, DC, MC, V.

Il Giardino. Italian. This dining spot has a busy New York feeling and a brightly lit tree in the middle of the room. Popular entrees include veal chop, salmon el giardino, and chicken. Open-air dining. Entertainment nightly in season. Piano bar. Early-bird suppers. Kids' menu. | 910 Atlantic Ave. | 757/422–6464 | www.ilgiardino.com | No lunch | $11–$24 | AE, D, DC, MC, V.

Inlet. Seafood. The restaurant overlooks Lynnhaven River. Popular dishes include the seafood platter, crab cakes, and Mahi Mahi. You can dine outdoors on the deck. Raw bar. Kids' menu. Sunday brunch. | 3319 Shore Dr. | 757/481–7300 | fax 757/481–0625 | www.theinletrestaurantva.com | No lunch Mon.–Wed. | $7–$20 | AE, D, DC, MC, V.

Le Chambord. Continental. Plush couches, stucco walls, and rich neutral colors. Fireplaces warm the lounge and dining room. Cartegena, veal chop, filet mignon. Jazz pianist Fri.–Sat. | 324 N. Great Neck Rd. | 757/498–1234 | fax 757/498–0522 | Reservations essential weekends | $20–$30 | AE, D, DC, MC, V.

The Lighthouse. Seafood. Family-owned and -operated for more than 30 years, the restaurant is right on the ocean. Open-air dining. Kids' menu, early-bird suppers. Sun. brunch. | 96 Atlantic Ave. | 757/428–7974 | fax 757/422–9914 | No lunch in winter | $20–$40 | AE, D, DC, MC, V.

Lucky Star. American. This hip, chef-owned restaurant is on Virginia Beach regulars' short list. It's decorated with changing exhibits of local art, crafts, or customers' collections. Specializing in seafood, the menu changes with the season and availability of fresh ingredients. No smoking. | 1608 Pleasure House Rd. | 757/363–8410 | Reservations essential Fri.–Sat. | Closed Sun. No lunch | $16–$22 | AE, MC, V.

Lynnhaven Fish House. Seafood. This casual-to-dressy restaurant has a view of the Chesapeake Bay and the pier café has outdoor seating. Menu choices include scallops Lynnhaven, broiled Neptune Platter, stuffed jumbo broiled flounder. Candlelight dining. Kids' menu. | 2350 Starfish Rd. | 757/481–0003 | fax 757/481–3474 | www.lynnhavenfishhouse.com | Daily 11–10:30 | $22–$39 | AE, D, DC, MC, V.

Pungo Grill. American/Continental. You can dine inside, on the enclosed porch, or the garden deck. Menu specialties include crab cakes, seafood platter, and she-crab soup. Kids' menu. | 1785 Princess Anne Rd. | 757/426–6655 | Closed Mon. | $7–$22 | D, MC, V.

Rockafeller's. Seafood. The Key West–style restaurant has casual dockside dining. The verandas claim commanding views of Rudee Inlet. Try the fried flounder or lobster tails. Kids' menu, early-bird suppers. Sun. brunch. Dock space. | 308 Mediterranean Ave. | 757/422–5654 | fax 757/425–2456 | $9–$34 | MC, V, AE, D, DC.

Rudee's. Seafood. Walk in off the street or sail up to the dock for a meal of steamed shrimp, soft-shell crabs, or crab cakes. Open-air dining on deck. Raw bar. Kids' menu. | 227 Mediterranean Ave. | 757/425–1777 | fax 757/425–5107 | $10–$20 | www.rudees.com | AE, D, DC, MC, V.

Waterman's. Seafood. Every seat in the house has an ocean view, and you can dine outdoors on a wraparound porch. Classic seafood is served in a casual environment. Kids' menu. | 415 Atlantic Ave. | 757/428–3644 | $21–$35 | AE, D, DC, MC, V.

Worrell Bros. Seafood. Established in 1968 by brothers Mike and Chris Worrell, the restaurant opened the first raw bar in Virginia Beach. Try the steamed seafood sampler, shrimp scampi, or Chesapeake Bay crab cakes. Kids' menu. Raw bar. Entertainment. | 1910 Atlantic Ave. | 757/422–6382 | fax 757/425–1929 | www.worrellbros.com | $12–$35 | AE, D, DC, MC, V.

Lodging

Alamar Resort Inn. About a block and a half from the beach, this hotel's grounds are beautifully landscaped. The homey rooms are furnished with Queen Anne-style pieces. Some refrigerators. Outdoor pool. Laundry facilities. | 311 16th St. | 800/346–5681 or 757/428–7582 | fax 757/428–7587 | www.va-beach.com/alamarresort | 22 rooms | $55–$180 | AE, D, MC, V.

Barclay Cottage. This turn-of-the-century building used to be a schoolhouse. In a residential area, the house has wraparound verandas on two floors. No kids. No smoking. | 400 16th St. | 757/422–1956 | www.barclaycottage.com | 6 rooms | $85–$118 | Closed Nov.–May | AE, MC, V.

Best Western–Oceanfront. This oceanfront property faces the boardwalk and the beach. Restaurant, bar. Some refrigerators, cable TV. Pool. Hot tub. Beach. Business services. | 1101 Atlantic Ave. | 757/422–5000 | fax 757/425–2356 | www.bestwestern.com | 110 rooms | $150–$160 | AE, D, DC, MC, V.

Cavalier Hotels. The original 1927 Cavalier Hotel, a seven-story redbrick building on a hill, and a 1973 oceanfront high-rise across the street make up this resort complex in the quiet north end of town. Conventioneers and families stay here, but past guests included F. Scott and Zelda Fitzgerald. From both buildings you can see the water and access the hotel's 600-ft private beach. 3 restaurants. Indoor and outdoor pool, wading pool. Putting green, 4 tennis courts (fee for use). Exercise equipment, volleyball. Beach. Babysitting, playground. | Atlantic Ave. and 42nd St. | 757/425–8555 or 800/446–8199 | fax 757/425–0629 | www.cavalierhotel.com | 400 rooms | $140–$220 | AE, D, DC, MC, V.

Clarion-Pembroke Corporate Center. This hotel is in Virginia Beach, 12 mi from Norfolk International Airport. Restaurant, bars. In-room data ports, some microwaves, refrigerators, cable TV. Indoor pool. Hot tub. Exercise equipment. Business services. | 4453 Bonney Rd. | 757/473–1700 | fax 757/552–0477 | www.clarionhotelvabeach.com | 149 rooms | $89–$129 | AE, D, DC, MC, V.

Colonial Inn. At the quiet, family-oriented north end of the hotel strip, this inn has rooms that are renovated yearly in an oceanfront high-rise. From June through August, rooms are also available in a smaller, older building across the street. 1 restaurant. Some refrigerators. Outdoor pool. Laundry. | 2809 Atlantic Ave. | 757/428–5370 | fax 757/422–5902 | www.colinn.com | 159 rooms | $55–$110 | AE, D, DC, MC, V.

Comfort Inn. This chain hotel is one block from the beach and 7 blocks from I-264. Restaurant, complimentary Continental breakfast. In-room data ports, some microwaves, cable TV. Indoor-outdoor pool. Hot tub. Exercise equipment. Game room. Video games. Laundry facilities. Business services. Free parking. | 2800 Pacific Ave. | 757/428–2203 | fax 757/422–6043 | comfortinn@va-beach.com | www.va-beach.com/comfortinn | 135 rooms | $89–$159 | AE, D, DC, MC, V.

Comfort Inn–Oceanfront. The beachfront motel is one block from U.S. 264. Complimentary Continental breakfast. In-room data ports, kitchenettes, refrigerators, cable TV. Pool. Hot tub. Exercise equipment. Business services. | 2015 Atlantic Ave. | 757/425–8200 | fax 757/425–6521 | www.vbeach.com/hotels/comfort.html | 83 suites | $129–$259 suites | AE, D, DC, MC, V.

Courtyard by Marriott. The hotel is ¼ mi from I–264; it's about 15 mi from the beach. Bar. In-room data ports, some refrigerators, cable TV. Pool. Hot tub. Exercise equipment. Business services. Free parking. | 5700 Greenwich Rd. | 757/490–2002 | fax 757/490–0169 | www.courtyardmarriott.com | 146 rooms | $99–$169 | AE, D, DC, MC, V.

Days Inn–Oceanfront. All rooms face the ocean at this waterfront motel. Restaurant, bar. In-room data ports, some microwaves, room service, cable TV. Pool. Hot tub. Beach. Laundry facilities. Business services. Some pets allowed (fee). | 32nd St. and Atlantic Ave. | 757/428–7233 | fax 757/491–1936 | www.daysinnoceanfront.com | 121 rooms | $135–$215 | AE, D, DC, MC, V.

Econo Lodge–Oceanfront. All rooms have a private balcony and view at this beachfront motel. Restaurant. In-room data ports, cable TV. Indoor pool. Business services. | 2109 Atlantic Ave. | 757/428–2403 | fax 757/422–2530 | econo-lodge@va-beach.com | www.va-beach.com/econo-lodge | 55 rooms | $109–$199 | AE, D, DC, MC, V.

Extended Stay America. This hotel is midway between Norfolk and Virginia Beach. The walls are white, bedspreads burgundy, and furniture cherry wood. Some kitchenettes, microwaves. Laundry facilities. | 4548 Bonney Rd. | 757/473–9200, or 800/398–7829 | fax 757/473–8851 | www.extstay.com | 120 rooms | $59–$64; $299–$320 week | AE, D, DC, MC, V.

Fairfield Inn by Marriott. This chain hotel is near the interstate and about 9 mi from the beach. Complimentary Continental breakfast. In-room data ports, cable TV. Pool. Business services. | 4760 Euclid Rd. | 757/499–1935 | fax 757/499–1935 | www.fairfieldinnbymarriott.com | 134 rooms | $74–$99 | AE, D, DC, MC, V.

Flagship Motel. This early 1970s hotel is family run. Rooms are either part of the main hotel, or set up as mini-efficiencies. Their look hasn't changed since the place was built, but the rooms are clean with all the basics. Some kitchenettes, some refrigerators. Outdoor pool. Laundry. | 512 Atlantic Ave. | 757/425–6422 or 800/338–8790 | fax 757/491–6152 | www.virginiabeach.com/flagship | 55 rooms | $75–$95 | AE, D, DC, MC, V.

Founders Inn Conference Center. This hotel with Colonial-style interior is on the campus of the Christian Broadcasting Network and Regent University. Some rooms feature fireplaces. Restaurant, picnic area. In-room data ports, refrigerators, room service, cable TV. Indoor-outdoor pool. Tennis. Gym, racquetball. Bicycles. Shops. Children's programs, playground. Business services. Airport shuttle. | 5641 Indian River Rd. | 757/424–5511 or 800/926–4466 | fax 757/366–0613 | www.foundersinn.com | 238 rooms | $89–$129 | AE, D, DC, MC, V.

Hampton Inn. This chain property is 1 mi east of Norfolk, adjacent to I–264 and 2 mi from I–64. Complimentary Continental breakfast. In-room data ports, cable TV. Pool. Exercise equipment. Business services. | 5793 Greenwich Rd. | 757/490–9800 | fax 757/490–3573 | www.hampton-inn.com | 122 rooms | $82–$92 | AE, D, DC, MC, V.

Holiday Inn. This oceanfront resort hotel is 4 blocks from I–264. Restaurant, bar. In-room data ports, some kitchenettes, microwaves, refrigerators, room service, some in-room hot tubs, cable TV. Pool. Hot tub. Beach. Laundry facilities. Business services. Free parking. | 2607 Atlantic Ave. | 757/491–6900 | fax 757/491–2125 | surfside@vabeach.com | www.infi.net/~beachnet/surfside | 143 rooms, 18 suites | $159–$179, $199–$219 suites | AE, D, DC, MC, V.

Holiday Inn Executive Center. Between Norfolk and Virginia Beach, the hotel is close to I–64 and the Norfolk International Airport. Restaurant, bar. In-room data ports, some microwaves, refrigerators, room service, cable TV. 2 pools (1 indoor). Hot tub. Exercise equipment. Business services. Airport shuttle. Free parking. | 5655 Greenwich Rd. | 757/499–4400 | fax 757/473–0517 | www.holiday-inn.com | 332 rooms | $99–$119 | AE, D, DC, MC, V.

Holiday Inn–Oceanside. This oceanfront hotel is at the end of I–264; overlooks a swimming beach. Restaurant, bar. In-room data ports, refrigerators, room service, cable TV. Pool. Hot tub. Business services. | Atlantic Ave. and 21st St. | 757/491–1500 | fax 757/491–1945 | oceansid@va-beach.com | www.vabeach.com/oceansid | 150 rooms | $140–$229 | AE, D, DC, MC, V.

Holiday Inn Sunspree Resort. This oceanfront hotel with private balconies is 1 mi north of I–264. Restaurant, bar. Some kitchenettes, refrigerators, room service, cable TV. Indoor-outdoor pool. Children's programs. Business services. | 3900 Atlantic Ave. | 757/428–1711 | fax 757/425–5742 | sunspree@vabeach.com | www.vabeach.com/sunspree | 266 rooms | $142–$209 | AE, D, DC, MC, V.

Idlewhyle Motel. This motel on the beach and boardwalk usually caters to families, who can choose rooms or an efficiency apartment. The walls are covered with beige vinyl, and the furniture is serviceable. Rooms that do not face the ocean look out onto the pool in the atrium, which has a glass roof that can be opened in good weather. In winter, a free Continental breakfast is served. Some kitchenettes. Indoor pool. | 2705 Atlantic Ave. | 757/428–9341 | 23 rooms, 23 efficiencies | $35–$90 | AE, D, MC, V.

Quality Inn. All rooms face the ocean. Restaurant, bar. In-room data ports, room service, cable TV. Indoor-outdoor pool. Hot tub, sauna. Business services. Free parking. | 705 Atlantic Ave. | 757/428–8935 | fax 757/425–2769 | www.qualityinn.com/hotel/va314 | 124 rooms | $135–$175 | AE, D, DC, MC, V.

Quality Inn–Ocean Front. It's right on the beach, with shops and entertainment nearby. Restaurant, bar. In-room data ports, some kitchenettes, microwaves, refrigerators, cable TV. Pool. Hot tub. Laundry facilities. Business services. Airport shuttle. | 2207 Atlantic Ave. | 757/428–5141 | fax 757/422–8436 | 160 rooms | $130–$195 | AE, D, DC, MC, V.

Ramada Plaza Resort. Located at the residential north end of the beach, the resort has an oceanfront deck and swimming beach. Standard oceanfront rooms, but suites are not oceanfront. Restaurant, bar. In-room data ports, some microwaves, refrigerators, cable TV. Indoor-outdoor pool. Hot tub. Exercise equipment. Children's programs. Business services. | 5600 Oceanfront Ave. | 757/428–7025 | fax 757/428–2921 | www.ramada.com | 223 rooms, 24 suites | $150–$205 room's, $305–$435 suites | AE, D, DC, MC, V.

Sea Gull. The motel is on the oceanfront boardwalk. Restaurant, bar. Some kitchenettes, refrigerators, room service, cable TV. Indoor pool. Hot tub. Business services. | 2613 Atlantic Ave. | 757/425–5711 or 800/426–4855 | fax 757/425–5710 | seagullmotel@worldnet.att.net | www.seagullmotel.com | 61 rooms | $70–$110 | D, MC, V.

Virginia Beach Resort and Conference Center. This Chesapeake Bay resort has a private beach. Restaurant, bar. In-room data ports, microwaves, refrigerators, cable TV. Indoor-outdoor pool. Hot tub. Exercise equipment. Boating, jet skiing. Bicycles. Children's programs. Laundry facilities. Business services. Airport shuttle. | 2800 Shore Dr. | 757/481–9000 or 800/468–2722 (outside VA), 800/422–4747 (within VA) | fax 757/496–7429 | vb-resort@vabeach.com | www.virginiabeachresort.com | 295 suites | $104–$355 | AE, D, DC, MC, V.

WARM SPRINGS

MAP 11, F5

(Nearby town also listed: Hot Springs)

The seat of Bath County near the West Virginia border, Warm Springs is known for its natural mineral springs, popular with visitors for more than 200 years. In the late 1700s, Virginia aristocrats would arrive in the early summer and move from one spring to another; the pools at Warm Springs were the traditional starting point, followed by Hot Springs, and then Sweet Springs.

Information: **Bath County Chamber of Commerce** | Box 418, Hot Springs, VA 24445 | 540/839–5409 or 800/628–8092 | bathco@va.tds.net | www.bathcova.org | Weekdays 8–5.

Attractions

Jefferson Pools. Just as Thomas Jefferson once did, you can "take the cure" at these pools, which are filled by natural, mineral-rich thermal springs believed to have healing powers. The rustic men's and ladies' bathhouses, built in 1761 and 1836, are largely unchanged. The water temperature remains a fairly constant 96°F. The pools are operated by the Homestead resort. Swimsuits are provided. | Rte. 220 | 800/838–5346 | www.thehomestead.com | $12 per hr | Late-Mar.–Nov., daily 10–6.

ON THE CALENDAR

AUG.: *Civil War Weekend at Warwickton Mansion.* The 1864 Battle of Warm Springs is commemorated with encampments, troop formations, and weapons displays at Warwickton Mansion. The "Battle Scenario" includes music and night firing. | 540/839–3178.

Dining

Sportsman Inn Restaurant. American. This is the place to get a hamburger and fries. Bring your patience, though, because while the food is fast, many of the waitresses are slow. | 1 Route 220 | 540/839–2689 | $5–$7 | No credit cards.

Warm Springs Country Inn. German. Like a European cottage, this homey restaurant has walls of wood. The food is hearty and rich. The inn also provides lodging. | Jct. 220 and 39 | 703/839–5351 | Closed Sun.–Weds. No lunch | $10.50–$17 | MC, V.

Waterwheel. Continental. The turn-of-the-century dining room still contains the former mill's original elevator and grinding stone. The restaurant is in the Inn at Gristmill Square. Menu specialties include fresh mountain trout, roast duck, and filet mignon. Sun. brunch. | Rte. 645/Old Mill Rd. | 540/839–2231 | fax 540/83–5770 | www.gristmill.com or www.innbook./grist.html | No lunch | $19–$24 | D, MC, V.

Lodging

Anderson Cottage. A restored former tavern that was built in the 1790s, the inn has mountain views and rooms with antiques and fireplaces. Complimentary breakfast. No TV in rooms. Nearby downhill skiing. Some pets allowed in cottage. No kids under 6. | 312 Old Germantown Rd. | 540/839–2975 | www.bbonline.com/va/anderson | 2 rooms, 2 suites (1 with shared bath); 1 cottage | $60–$70; $80–$100 suites; $125 cottage | Open year-round | No credit cards.

Hidden Valley B&B. This inn on 70 acres is nestled in the valley of the George Washington Forest. On the property are farmyard animals and hiking trails. The main building is an 1848 Greek Revival mansion, which was used in the film *Sommersby.* Most rooms have 18th- and 19th-century furniture, but one has more modern pieces. Bathrooms are in the hall but private. Complimentary breakfast. No TV. | Hidden Valley Rd. | 540/839–3178 | fax 540/839–3178 | 3 rooms | $108.40 | Closed Thanksgiving and Christmas | No credit cards.

Inn at Gristmill Square. This 19th-century inn has an old gristmill and blacksmith's shop on the grounds. One- and two-bedroom units have Colonial furnishings. Restaurant, bar, picnic area, complimentary Continental breakfast. In-room data ports, refrigerators, cable TV. Pool. Sauna. Tennis. Business services. Airport shuttle. | Rte. 645/Old Mill Rd. | 540/839–2231 | fax 540/839–5770 | grist@va.tds.net | www.vainns.com/grist.htm | 17 rooms | $85–$100 | D, MC, V.

Three Hills Inn. This country inn built in 1913 by Mary Johnson, author of "To Have and To Hold," is on the National Register of Historic Places; the 40-acre property is surrounded by wide lawns and boxwood gardens atop Warm Springs Mountain. Rooms have individualized interiors, with antique furniture. Complimentary breakfast. No TV in rooms, TV in common area. Some pets allowed. Conference center. | U.S. 220 | 540/839–5381 | fax 540/839–5199 | www.3hills.com | 13 rooms | $69–$179 | D, MC, V.

Warm Springs Country Inn. You can see the mountains from the back of this farmhouse. A judge lived here in the 1800s, and there's an old jail on the property. Restaurant. Some microwaves, refrigerators. | Box 99 (Junction Rte. 220 and 39) | 540/839–5351 | www.members-xoom.com/poco.007/warmsprings.htp | 25 rooms | $55 | MC, V.

WARRENTON

(Nearby towns also listed: Culpeper, Manassas, Washington)

Warrenton is the seat of Fauquier County, in Virginia's northern Piedmont region. Once part of the hunting grounds of the Manahoac Indians, it was settled by German and English immigrants in the 1700s. During the American Revolution, many of its citizens served in the Continental Army, including Capt. John Marshall, who later became chief justice of the United States Supreme Court.

Traditional foxhunting meets and point-to-point races have made Warrenton a part of northern Virginia's so-called "Hunt Country." The state's biggest steeplechase race, the Virginia Gold Cup, is held nearby every May. Warrenton is mostly residential, with a small retail and commercial district in the town center. Historic Old Town has antiques stores, clothiers, and specialty shops. Sky Meadows State Park is north of town in Front Royal, with facilities for horseback riding, hiking, and camping. May through October, people pack picnics and head to the Flying Circus Air Show in Bealeton, 14 mi south of Warrenton.

Information: Warrenton–Fauquier County Visitors Center | 183A Keith St., Warrenton, VA 20186 | 540/347–4414 | fax 540/347–7510 | www.fauquierchamber.org | Daily 9–5.

Attractions
Old Jail Museum. The museum's two buildings, constructed in 1808 and 1823, represent the few surviving examples of early jails in Virginia. There are exhibits on local and Civil War history. | 10 Waterloo St. | 540/347–5525 | www.fauquierchamber.org | Free | Tues.-Sun. 10–4.

ON THE CALENDAR
MAY–OCT.: *Flying Circus Air Show.* These shows at the Flying Circus Airfield feature feats of daring and skill, skydiving, and formations. Open cockpit biplane rides are available. | 540/439–8661 | www.flyingcircus.com.
MAY: *Virginia Gold Cup.* The state's biggest steeplechase race is held at the Great Meadows Field Events Center in the Virginia countryside. | 540/347–2618 or 800/697–2237.
JUNE: *Warrenton Pony Show.* The oldest pony show in the country features hunters, jumpers, and side-saddle riding classes at Warrentown Horse Show Grounds on Shirley Avenue. | 540/347–9442 or 540/364–4345.

Dining
Depot Restaurant. Mediterranean. With the only garden seating in Warrenton, this restaurant appeals to young professionals and former cosmopolitans for its beautiful setting. A late-19th-century train depot has been reconstructed indoors. The "Paris" room has a fireplace and 14 french doors. The crab cakes and the large dinner salads are good. | 65 3rd St. S | 540/347–1212 | Reservations essential | Closed Mon. | $8–$20 | MC, V.

Fantastico Ristorante Italiano. Italian. This 50-year-old stone building has been expanded to become a 14-room inn with a restaurant and piano lounge. The lounge hosts live entertainment from international performers ranging from classic jazz to Cuban dance music. Known for seafood and veal. Kids' menu. | 280 Broad View Ave. | 540/349–2575 | fax 540/341–4658 | www.fantastico-inn.com | Breakfast also available. Closed Sun. No lunch Sat. | $8–$15 | AE, D, DC, MC, V.

Napoleon's. Continental. This lovely 19th-century home is now a restaurant with two seating areas and flower gardens. There's a more formal, romantic terrace upstairs where you can dine al fresco and a casual café downstairs. Known for fresh fish, Black Angus beef, veal. Kids' menu. Sun. brunch. | 67 Waterloo St. | 540/347–1200 | fax 540/347–1661 | www.napoleonsrestaurant.com | Daily 11–Late | $24–$33 | D, MC, V.

Lodging

Black Horse Inn. This antebellum estate on 20 acres is in the heart of Virginia's horse country. The original home served as a hospital during the Civil War. The rooms have antiques and fireplaces. Afternoon tea is served; box lunches are available. Complimentary breakfast. No smoking, some in-room hot tubs. Business services. | 8393 Meetze Rd. | 540/349–4020 | fax 540/349–4242 | www.blackhorseinn.com | 6 rooms, 2 suites | $125–$195; $275–$295 suites | AE, MC, V.

Cheswick Motel. With rooms rented by the week, this no-frills motel is often filled for months with regular tenants. No special facilities, but you're welcome to bring your own mini-fridge. | 394 Broadview Ave. | 540/349–1901 | fax 540/349–1109 | 33 rooms | $206 per week | AE, DC, MC, V.

Comfort Inn. The inn is ¼ mi north of town on U.S. 29 and U.S. 15. Complimentary Continental breakfast. In-room data ports, refrigerators, some in-room hot tubs; cable TV. Pool. Exercise equipment. Laundry facilities. Business services. Some pets allowed (fee). | 7379 Comfort Inn Dr. | 540/349–8900 | fax 540/347–5759 | www.comfortinn.com | 97 rooms | $59–$150 | AE, D, DC, MC, V.

Hampton Inn. This motel is in town, 1 mi from U.S. 29. Picnic area, complimentary Continental breakfast. Microwaves, cable TV, in-room VCRs and movies. Pool. Exercise equipment. Laundry facilities. Business services. | 501 Blackwell Rd. | 540/349–4200 | fax 540/349–0061 | www.hampton-inn.com | 100 rooms | $69–$75 | AE, D, DC, MC, V.

Howard Johnson Inn. You'll find no HoJo's diner here, but the motel is near the chain restaurants of the tourist section. Civil War attractions are close by. Outdoor pool. | 6 Broadview Ave. | 540/347–4141 | fax 540/347–5632 | www.howardjohnsons.com | 79 rooms | $55–$85 | AE, D, DC, MC, V.

1763 Inn. First known as Greystone House when it was built in 1763, this country inn on 50 acres was the site of considerable fighting during the Civil War. The individually decorated guest rooms have fireplaces. Restaurant, complimentary full breakfast. Some in-room hot tubs, cable TV. Pool, pond. Tennis courts. Fishing. | 10087 John Mosby Hwy./U.S. 50, Upperville | 540/592–3848 | fax 540/592–3208 | www.1763inn.com | 14 rooms, 4 cabins | $115–$195; $225 cabins | AE, D, DC, MC, V.

WASHINGTON

MAP 11, H4

(Nearby towns also listed: Shenandoah National Park, Warrenton)

Known as "Little" Washington to differentiate it from the District of Columbia, this tiny town in the rural foothills of the Blue Ridge was surveyed by George Washington in 1749. The county seat of Rappahannock County, Washington depends on farming to sustain the economy. Its chief attraction is the Inn at Little Washington, which opened in 1978. The hotel's success has carried over to the town, which now has antiques shops, galleries, custom jewelry makers, and two theaters within its roughly five blocks.

Information: Town of Washington | Box 7, Washington, VA 22747 | 540/675–3128 | fax 540/675–1742 | Mon., Wed.–Fri. 9–2.

Attractions

Shenandoah National Park. (*See* Shenandoah National Park.) The nearest entrance from Washington is at Thornton Gap. The park has 500 mi of trails, including a stretch of the Appalachian Trail (access at Beahms Gap, Milepost 28.5); naturalists conduct daily hikes throughout the summer. You can rent horses for wilderness rides, and fish for trout in some 30 mountain streams. A variety of camping options exist. Trail maps and program information are available at park headquarters (U.S. 211, 4 mi E of Thornton Gap). | 540/999–3500 | Free | Weekdays 8–4.

Farfelu Vineyard. This small farm winery in Rappahannock County produces Chardonnay, Cabernet Sauvignon, and red and white picnic wines. You can tour the winery and sample the wines, picnic on the 86-acre property and hike along the Rappahannock River. | 13058 Crest Hill Rd., Flint Hill | 540/364–2930 | Free | Mar.–Dec., daily 11–4:30; reservations suggested.

The Theatre at Washington. This venue showcases films, theater and musical performances, including a Smithsonian chamber music series, usually on weekends and for short runs. Professional theatrical troupes and college and community productions put on regular shows. | 291 Gay St. | 540/675–1253 | www.theatre-washington-va.com | Movies $5, concerts and plays $15 | Call for program schedule.

ON THE CALENDAR
JULY: *Fourth of July Celebration.* The streets of Washington are blocked off for a children's bicycle parade, live music, a crafts fair, food vendors, and fireworks. | 540/675–1253.

Dining

Bleu Rock Inn. American. The early American farmhouse has a restaurant, and five guest rooms with antiques and fireplaces. Sit on the terrace for coffee and dessert and enjoy mountain views. The chef relies on fresh, local produce, changing the menu seasonally. Menu specialties include tempura, soft-shell crab, and baked halibut. Sun. brunch. No smoking. | 12567 Lee Hwy. | 540/987–3190 | Closed Mon.–Tues. No lunch | $45–55 | AE, D, MC, V.

Four and Twenty Blackbirds. Contemporary. This restaurant focuses on seasonal specialties, with the menu changing every three weeks. Entertainment. Sunday brunch. No smoking. | 650 Zachary Taylor Hwy., U.S. 522 and Rte. 647, Flint Hill | 540/675–1111 | Closed Mon.–Tues., 1st 2 wks of Jan., and 1st 3 wks of Aug. No lunch | $30–$35 | MC, V.

Inn at Little Washington. Contemporary. Renowned chef Patrick O'Connell presents a contemporary American menu at this fabled restaurant that has garden dining. An English stage-set designer decorated the lush interior. Seven-course, fixed-price meals are served. | Middle and Main Sts. | 540/675–3800 | fax 540/675–3100 | www.relaischateaux.fr | Reservations essential | Closed Tues. except in May and Oct. No lunch | $98–$128 | MC, V.

Mrs. Coxe's Tavern. Southern. Entrees at this rambling 18th-century house include rabbit stew and country chicken cordon bleu. Lighter fare is served in the more casual Thornton's Tavern room, which also has a bar. | Main St. | 540/675–1900 | Closed Tues.–Wed. | $16–$34 | D, MC, V.

Lodging

Bleu Rock Inn. The inn on 80 acres of land with a pond and vineyards is surrounded by the Blue Ridge Mountains. There's a lounge and a terrace. Afternoon tea is served, and complimentary brandy. Restaurant, complimentary full breakfast. No room phones. Hiking. No kids. | 12567 Lee Hwy. | 540/987–3190 or 800/537–3652 | fax 540/987–3193 | www.innsand-outs.com/bleurockinn | 5 rooms | $125–$195 | Closed Mon.–Tues. | AE, D, DC, MC, V.

Foster Harris House Bed & Breakfast. This 1903 farmhouse sits on a private three-quar-ter acres in the middle of town, near small shops and restaurants. Most rooms have great views of the Blue Ridge Mountains. Complimentary breakfast. No smoking. No kids under 12. | 189 Main St. | 540/675–3757 | fax 540/675–1615 | www.fosterharris.com | 5 rooms | $95–$160 | Closed 1 wk in Feb. | D, MC, V.

Heritage House Bed & Breakfast. This B&B has two buildings: an 1837 manor house and a cottage that sleeps up to four. The rooms in the house have themes, like "Lace" or "Amish." You can walk to the Inn at Little Washington, as well as other sites and shops. Complimentary breakfast. Badminton. No smoking. | 291 Main St. | 540/675–3207 | fax 540/675–1340 | www.heritagebb.com | 5 rooms, 1 cottage | $105–$150 | MC, V.

Inn at Little Washington. The luxury inn is surrounded by the foothills of the Blue Ridge Mountains. All rooms have canopy beds, marble bathrooms, and fresh flowers. Restaurant, bar, complimentary Continental breakfast. Minibars. Room service. Business services. Air-port shuttle. | 540/675–3800 | fax 540/675–3100 | www.relaischateaux.fr | 14 rooms in 2 build-ings, 4 suites | $340–$640; $640–$865 suites | Closed Tues. except May and Oct. | MC, V.

Middleton. This country estate on the Virginia Landmark register was built in 1850 by Mid-dleton Miller, who designed and manufactured the Confederate uniform during the Civil War. Complimentary breakfast. No smoking, cable TV. Business services. No kids under 12. | 176 Main St. | 540/675–2020 or 800/816–8157 | fax 540/675–1050 | middleinn@shentel.net | www.middleton-inn.com | 4 rooms (2 with shower only), 1 cottage | $195–$360; $425 cot-tage | AE, MC, V.

Sycamore Hill House and Gardens. The contempoary stone home and property on Mene-fee Mountain are part of a National Wildlife habitat. Complimentary breakfast. No room phones. Business services. No smoking, No kids under 12. | 110 Menefee Mountain La. | 540/675–3046 | fax 540/675–3068 | www.bnb-n-va.com/sycamore | 3 rooms | $110–$175 | Closed Tues. July | MC, V.

WATERFORD

(Nearby town also listed: Leesburg, Middleburg)

Waterford, a onetime Quaker village that is now a National Historic Site, is several miles northwest of Leesburg.

Information: Loudoun Tourism Council | 108D South St. SE, Leesburg, 20175 | 703/777–2617 or 800/752–6118 | www.visitloudoun.org.

Attractions

The Mill. This 3-story mill was built in the 1830s and operated until 1939. The Mill is open to the public during the annual Waterford Homes Tour and Crafts Exhibit in October. | Main St.

Post Office. This brick Victorian building dates from 1880 and has served as a post office since 1897. Old photographs of the post office are on display. | 2nd Ave. and Main St. | 540/882–3545 | Free | Mon.–Fri. 8–1, 2–5, Sat. 8–12.

Union Cemetery. Operated by the Union of Churches, this multidenominational cematary was established in the early 19th century. Veterans from both sides of the Civil War are buried here. | Fairfax St. | 540/882–3018 | Free | Daily, dawn–dusk.

Waterford. A Quaker miller in 1733 founded the historic community of Waterford, and for many decades it has been synonymous with fine crafts; its annual October Homes Tour and Crafts Exhibit attracts as many as 30,000 visitors. Festival activities include a Revolutionary War military campus with marching fife and drum corps, and Civil War skirmishes. Many of Waterford's original buildings, constructed in the regional vernacular style, survive; the town and more than 1,400 acres around it were declared a National Historic Landmark in 1970. The Waterford Foundation provides brochures for self-guided walking tours. | 540/882–3018 (Waterford Foundation) | fax 540/882–3921 | www.waterfordva.org | Free | Foundation office weekdays 9–5.

ON THE CALENDAR

OCT.: *Waterford Homes Tour and Crafts Exhibit.* Demonstrations of traditional crafts (items are also for sale), tours of historic homes, military reenactments, art exhibits, music, dance, and food are all part of this three-day event, the oldest juried crafts fair in the state. | Waterford | 540/882–3085.

Dining

Bonnie's Country Kitchen. Southern. Fried chicken and catfish with fries are a couple of the down-home favorites here. Paintings of trains and barns give the restaurant country charm. 10 mi north of Waterford off Rte. 287. | 2 N. Berlin Pk., Lovettsville | 540/822–5285 | Closed Mon., no lunch or dinner Sun., breakfast also available Tues.–Sun. | $6–$10 | No credit cards.

La Fleur de Lis. French. Lobster and Stuffed Shenandoah Trout are a few of the delicious choices here. Pictures of the French countryside hang in the dining room. 10 mi north of Waterford off Rte. 287. | 2 S. Church St., Lovettsville, | 540/822–4700 | Closed Tues., no lunch Sat.–Sun. | $16–$36 | AE, D, MC, V.

Lodging

George's Mill Farm Bed and Breakfast. This massive stone house, dating from the 1860s, is run by descendants of the original owners. The floors are pine, and some of the antiques have been here since the place was built. The 200-acre property lies between the Shenandoah and Potomac Rivers, in the Short Hill Mountains. 10 mi north of Waterford off Rte. 287. Complimentary breakfast. No room phones, TV in common area. Pond. Fishing. Pets allowed (no fee). No smoking. | 11867 Georges Mill Rd., Lovettsville | 540/822–5224 | www.georgesmill.com | 4 rooms | $85–$115 | No credit cards.

Milltown Farms Inn. The common areas in this 1765 log-and-stone home tend toward colonial elegance, whereas the private rooms are more spare, with exposed log walls and four-poster beds. The inn sits at the end of a dirt road in the middle of 300 acres of rolling hills. Complimentary breakfast. No room phones, no TV. Pets allowed (only in one particular room). Kids allowed (with advance notice). No smoking. | 14163 Milltown Rd. | 540/882–4470 or 888/747–3942 | www.milltownfarms.com | 5 rooms | $115–$135 | AE, D, DC, MC, V.

Poor House Farm Bed and Breakfast. This 1814 brick building really was a poorhouse; today the place is much more cheerful. The rooms include four-poster beds and wicker furniture, and the front porch is a lovely place to gaze across the 13 acres of pastures. Complimentary breakfast. Some kitchenettes, cable TV. Pond. Fishing. No pets. No smoking. | 35304 Poor House Ln., Round Hill | 540/554–2511 | fax 540/554–8512 | www.poorhouse-farm.com | 3 rooms, 1 cottage | $115–$135 rooms, $155 cottage | AE, MC, V.

WAYNESBORO

MAP 11, H5

(Nearby towns also listed: Charlottesville, Shenandoah National Park, Staunton)

Named in honor of Revolutionary War hero Gen. Anthony Wayne, Waynesboro is an industrial center in the Shenandoah Valley that dates from the late 1700s. The major employers today are DuPont and Wayn-Tex Inc., which makes plastic products. The scenic Skyline Drive merges with the Blue Ridge Parkway near Waynesboro. North of Waynesboro, you can hike, fish or camp in Shenandoah National Park. The town is off I–64 near the junction with I–81.

Information: **Waynesboro–Augusta County Chamber of Commerce** | 301 W. Main St., Waynesboro, VA 22980 | 540/949–8203 or 800/471–3109 | www.augustabusiness.org | Weekdays 8–5.

Attractions

P. Buckley Moss Museum. This museum showcases the work of one of America's most recognized artists. Buckley, who moved to Waynesboro in 1964, was inspired by the "plain people"—the Amish and Mennonite communities of the Shenandoah Valley—and has made these neighbors her subject matter. Displays examine the symbolism in her paintings and drawings. Guided tours are available. Moss's studio, a converted barn about 2 mi from the museum, opens four times a year to the public. | 150 P Buckley Moss Dr. | 540/949–6473 | fax 540/943–9756 | www.p-buckley-moss.com | Free | Mon.–Sat. 10–6, Sun. 12:30–5:30.

Shenandoah National Park. (*See* Shenandoah National Park and Blue Ridge Parkway.) The southern entrance to the park is just east of Waynesboro, at Rockfish Gap. Skyline Drive winds through the park and merges with Blue Ridge Parkway near Waynesboro. Nearby park attractions along Skyline Drive include Calf Mountain Overlook (Milepost 98.9), with a 300-degree view, and Jones Run (Milepost 84.1), which offers a 3½-mi hike to the 42-ft Jones Run Falls, where moss and flowering plants grow along the cliff. | 540/999–3500 | Free | Weekdays 8–4.

Shenandoah Valley Art Center. An affiliate of the Virginia Museum of Fine Arts in Richmond, this non-profit center showcases the work of regional artists, and is a venue for music, theater performances and literary readings. There are workshops and classes for kids and adults throughout the year. | 600 W. Main St. | 540/949–7662 | fax 540/949–0300 | Free | Tues.–Sat. 10–4, Sun. 2–4.

Shenandoah Lake Recreation Area. This Augusta County recreational area has swimming, fishing, camping, hiking trails, and picnicking. | 540/261–6105 | www.southernregion.fs.fed.us | $8 per vehicle | Apr.–Nov., daily dawn–dusk.

Virginia Metalcrafters. Brass, bronze, and pewter are handcast here by the same methods used in 1890, when the works was founded. From a window in the factory showroom you can watch the craftsmen at work. Virginia Metalcrafters creates licensed products for Colonial Williamsburg, the Smithsonian Institution, Monticello, Winterthur, and the National Trust for Historic Preservation. | 1010 East Main St. | 540/949–9400 | www.vametal.com | Mon.–Sat. 9–5; Sun. 1–5; viewing Mon.–Thurs. 9–4.

ON THE CALENDAR

MAY: *Blue Ridge Soap Box Classic.* The country's largest soap box derby takes place on the streets of downtown Waynesboro. | 540/949–8203 or 800/471–3109 | russells@brsoapbox.com | www.brsoapbox.com.

OCT.: *Virginia Fall Foliage Festival.* An arts-and-crafts show with more than 200 exhibitors, a chili cook-off, a British car show, and a 10K run are highlights of the festival on Broad Street. Balloons and face painting please the kids. | 540/943–2093 or 540/949–8513.

Dining

Broad Street Inn. American, Barbecue. This restaurant is on a busy street, but cozy inside and filled with antiques. The place is family friendly, and the BBQ sauce homemade. | 1220 W. Broad St. | 540/942–1280 | Closed Mon. | $4.49–$13.96 | MC, V.

Mama Ollie's. Southern. Mama really exists, and some of her kids work in this homestyle restaurant with cloth napkins and a large buffet. | 1150 W. Broad St. | 540/949–6880 | $6.95–$12.95 | AE, D, MC, V.

South River Grill. American. The owner of this restaurant is a horse-loving Kentuckian, and the equestrian theme is prominent throughout. With two patios, a sunroom, and high ceilings, the space is full of natural light. Excellent prime rib, fresh pizzas, and calzones (they're big) are on the menu. | 23 Windigrove Lane | 540/942–5567 | $6–$19 | AE, D, MC, V.

Lodging

Belle Hearth B&B. Near the old Waynesboro part of town, this 1909 house with a gabled roof was built by a doctor who kept his office on the first floor. Most rooms have heart-pine floors, gas fireplaces, and early 20th-century furniture. Complimentary breakfast. Outdoor pool. | 320 S. Wayne Ave. | 540/943–1910 | fax 540/942–2443 | www.innguestaways.net/va/belle.html | 4 rooms, 1 suite | $80–$110 | AE, MC, V.

Comfort Inn. The property is in town about 3 mi south of I–64. Microwaves, cable TV. Pool, wading pool. Business services. Free parking. Some pets allowed. | 640 W. Broad St. | 540/942–1171 | fax 540/942–4785 | www.comfortinn.com | 75 rooms | $59–$79 | AE, D, DC, MC, V.

Days Inn. The chain hotel is 2 mi south of town, just off I–64. Picnic area. Cable TV. Pool. Business services. Free parking. Some pets allowed (fee). | 2060 Rosser Ave. | 540/943–1101 | fax 540/949–7586 | 98 rooms | $69–$85 | AE, D, DC, MC, V.

Holiday Inn Express. Near Interstate 64, this hotel in the foothills of the Blue Ridge Mountains has beautiful views. The building went up 1998, and each spacious room has a king- or queen-size bed and sofabed. Complimentary Continental breakfast. Microwave, refrigerator. Outdoor pool. Sauna. Exercise equipment. Laundry facilities. | 20 Windigrove Dr. | 540/932–7170 | fax 540/932–7150 | hie@csw.com | 80 rooms | $71–$95 | AE, D, DC, V.

Inn at Afton Mountain. The mountaintop inn has panoramic views across the valley. Restaurant, bar with entertainment. Room service. Pool. Business services. Free parking. | U.S. 250 and I–64 | 540/942–5201 or 800/860–8559 reservations | fax 540/943–8746 | www.theinnatafton.com | 118 rooms | $73–$89 | AE, D, DC, MC, V.

Iris Inn. The inn on 21 wooded acres has a great room with a 28-ft stone fireplace, and views of mountains and the Shenandoah Valley. Each room has a wildlife and nature theme. Complimentary breakfast. No smoking. | 191 Chinquapin Dr. | 540/943–1991 | fax 540/942–2093 | www.irisinn.com | 9 rooms, 2 suites | $85–$105 rooms, $140–$150 suites | MC, V.

WEST POINT

MAP 11, J6

(Nearby towns also listed: Gloucester, Irvington)

Cradled at the juncture of the Mattaponi, Pamunkey, and York Rivers, West Point is a modest community of 3,000. The Mattaponi and Pamunkey Rivers are named for Indian tribes still present in the area. West Point claims historic homes of both tobacco plantation owners and well-to-do Victorians, who prospered when the area was a center of commerce and shipping.

Information: **West Point/Tri-Rivers Chamber of Commerce** | 804/843–4620 | chamber@westpointva.com | www.westpointva.com.

Attractions

Chelsea Plantation. The original Georgian specifications have been preserved in this big 1709 brick house. Walnut panelling and family portraits of the original owners confirm the building's history. The lawn is expansive, and from the house you can walk down to the Mattaponi River. | 874 Chelsea Plantation Ln. | 804/966–2215 | www.webcentre.com/usr/chelsea | $8 | Thurs.–Sun. 10–4:30.

Pamunkey Indian Museum. Chief George Major Cook started this collection, on the grounds of the Pamunkey Reservation, in the early 20th century. The exhibits tell the history of this ancient tribe. The reservation is 15 mi north of West Point, off Route 30. | Rte. 1, Box 2011, King William | 804/843–4792 | $2.50 | Tues.–Sat. 10–4, Sun. 1–4, closed Mon.

West Point Historic District. Victorian and Gothic revival homes and businesses are concentrated here. The buildings are not open to the public. You can park at the town library at 7th Street and Main Street. | Main St. | Free | Daily.

Dining

Anna's Italian Restaurant. Italian. A good place to hang out and watch sports on the widescreen TV. Lasagna and baked ziti are typical menu items. | 3040 King William Ave. | 804/843–4035 | $2–$12 | AE, D, MC, V.

Lighthouse Restaurant. Seafood. There's no lighthouse, but lighthouse pictures and memorabilia are scattered throughout this friendly spot. Seafood over Angel Hair pasta and hefty crab cakes are the specialties. | Box 18950, Rte. 33 | 804/843–3711 | Closed Mon., breakfast also available | $7–$15 | AE, D, MC, V.

Marie's. American. Fried perch and fried chicken come with heaps of mashed potatoes and gravy. Pictures of daily life in the 1920s and 30s dot the walls. | 3690 King William Ave. | 804/843–2738 | No dinner Sat., closed Sun., breakfast also available | $2–$5 | No credit cards.

Lodging

Atherston Hall Bed and Breakfast. The main Victorian building dates from 1870, and the attached renovated slaves' quarters hark back to 1735. Oriental carpets add luxuriousness to the usual mix of antique furnishings. The B&B is 14 mi east of West Point, off Rte. 3. Complimentary breakfast. No room phones, TV in common area. No pets. No smoking. | 250 Prince George St., Urbanna | 804/758–2809 | 4 rooms | $75–$85 | No credit cards.

Comfort Inn Gloucester. The rooms in this 3-story faux mansion are generic, but serviceable. The hotel is about 15 mi south of West Point, off Route 17. Complimentary Continental breakfast. In-room data ports, cable TV. Outdoor pool. No pets. | 6639 Forest Hill Ave., Gloucester, | 804/695–1900 | fax 804/695–1901 | www.comfortinn.com | 78 rooms | $60–$100. Kids under 18 stay free | AE, D, DC, MC, V.

Dragon Run Inn. This sturdy 1913 farmhouse has a wraparound porch. Whimsical paintings and figurines depicting farm animals are scattered throughout the rooms. The inn is 13 mi north of West Point off route 17. Complimentary breakfast. No room phones, TV in common area. No pets. No smoking. | Rte. 17 and Rte. 602, Church View | 804/758–5719 | www.dragon-run-inn.com | 3 rooms | $60 | No credit cards.

Hewick Plantation. Since 1678, ten generations of Robinsons have lived in this impressive manor house on an old tobacco plantation. Today, 45 of the 66 acres are used for growing corn, wheat, and soy. The brick house, a state and national registered landmark, has eight fireplaces, a dining room and parlor decorated with 18th-century antiques, and two rooms with private baths. The house is 15 mi east of West Point, off Rte. 17. Dining room, complimentary Continental breakfast. Cable TV, some room phones. Some pets allowed. No kids under . | Intersection of Hwy. 602 and 615, Urbanna | 804/758–4214 | fax 804/758–3115 | www.hewick.com | 2 rooms | $99–$135 | AE, MC, V.

WHITE POST

MAP 11, H3

(Nearby towns also listed: Strasburg, Winchester)

White Post is named for a marker that George Washington erected to point the way to Lord Fairfax's house. This tiny community of 150 has 18th- and 19th-century buildings, and is home to White Post Restoration, a highly regarded auto restoration shop.

Information: **Berryville/Clarke County Chamber of Commerce** | 101 E. Main St., Suite 2, Berryville, VA 22611 | 540/955–4200 | info@clarkechamber.com | www.clarkechamber.com.

Attractions

Blandy Experimental Farm. Operated by the University of Virginia since 1926, this 700-acre research center has thousands of varieties of plants. Students and administrators work in former slave quarters that date from the 1830s. The farm runs many educational programs, especially for kids with topics like "Trees 'n' Me" and "Worms!" | 400 Blandy Farm Ln., Boyce | 540/837–1758 | www.virginia.edu/~blandy | Free | Daily, dawn–dusk.

Dinosaur Land. This theme park is classic American kitsch. Don't be afraid of these giant beasts, which include Tyrannosaurus Rexes battling more arcane beasts, and monsters like King Kong. Dinosaur Land has been family owned and operated since the 1960s. | Rte. 1, Box 63A | 540/869–2222 | fax 540/869–0951 | $4 | Daily 9:30–5:30, closed Jan.

Old Chapel. You can't enter the oldest Episcopalian Church west of the Blue Ridge, but you can tour its graveyard, which dates back to 1782. The church is a small, one-room stone building. A service is held once a year in the summer. | VA State Road 255 and U.S. Hwy. 340, Boyce

Dining

Battletown Inn. Southern. Smothered chicken basted in white wine and butternut squash are a couple of the taste treats here. Portraits of the original owners hang in the inn, which dates from 1809. | 102 W. Main St., Berryville | 540/955–4100 | Closed Mon., no dinner Sun. | $9–$18 | AE, D, DC, MC, V.

L'Auberge Provençale. French. Chef Alain serves such updated French classics as Prince Edward Island mussels with pesto, sun-dried tomato, fennel and vermouth and black Chilean sea bass with ratatouille broth, and herbed potato cup filled with creamy potato purée. Meals are prix fixe, service not included. | Rte. 340, White Post | 540/837–1375 or 800/638–1702 | fax 540/837–2004 | www.laubergeprovencale.com | $67 | Closed Jan. | AE, DC, MC, V.

Lone Oak Restaurant. American. Prime rib and stuffed salmon are your best bets. The room, which dates from the early 19th century, has a fireplace and wood panelling. | 12696 Lord Fairfax Hwy. | 540/837–1210 | Closed Sun.–Mon. | $6–$18 | AE, D, DC, MC, V.

Lodging

Battletown Inn. The early 1900s furniture in this inn is for sale; honeymooners have been known to buy the bed in their room. The inn dates from 1809, and you can dine on the patio. Complimentary Continental breakfast. Cable TV, no room phones. Pets allowed (no fee). No smoking. | 102 W. Main St., Berryville | 540/955–4100 | fax 540/955–0127 | www.battletown.com | 12 rooms | $95–$120 | AE, D, DC, MC, V.

L'Auberge Provençale. The inn has Victorian furnishings, fireplaces, alcove and four-post beds, and luxurious gourmet meals for guests. Restaurant, complimentary full breakfast is only meal served. Room service. No kids under 10. Airport shuttle. | Rte. 340, White Post | 540/837–1375 or 800/638–1702 | fax 540/837–2004 | www.laubergeprovencale.com | 11 rooms | $145–$250 | Closed Jan. | AE, DC, MC, V.

River House. Located 100 yards from the Shenandoah River, this landmark guest house sets itself apart with its stone fireplace, kitchen hearth and collection of antique maps. It is also known for its four-course brunch, served daily. The owners live on the premises. Complimentary four-course brunch with homemade breads. No TV in rooms; TV in common area. Business services. | 3075 John Mosby Highway, Boyce | 540/837–1476 | fax 540/837–2399 | rvrhouse@visuallink.com | www.riverhouse-virginia.com | 5 rooms (2 with shower only) | $90–$130, $115–155 on Sat. | MC, V.

WILLIAMSBURG

MAP 11, J6

(Nearby town also listed: Charles City)

On the peninsula between the York and James rivers in eastern Virginia, Williamsburg was established as Middle Plantation in 1633. After the capitol building in Jamestown burned in 1698, the capital of the colony was moved here, and Middle Plantation was renamed Williamsburg in honor of King William III. It served as Virginia's cultural and political center until 1780, when the capital was moved to Richmond to escape the invading British. Its political role diminished, Williamsburg faded in significance and fell into general decay in the 19th century.

Revival came at the hands of the local rector, W. A. R. Goodman, who convinced John D. Rockefeller Jr. to bequeath part of the family fortune to fund a restoration project. Work began in 1926, and by the 1930s restored buildings were being opened to the public. In 40 years, Rockefeller spent more than $80 million on the project. Roughly 600 post-Colonial structures were demolished, more than 80 period buildings were restored, and 40 replicas were reconstructed over excavated foundations. The historic district is approximately a mile long and ½ mi wide and surrounded by a "greenbelt" to preserve the illusion of a Colonial city. Beyond that is a modern city with numerous restaurants, lodgings, outlet shops and amusement parks. Bordering the historic district is the leafy campus of the College of William and Mary, the second-oldest university in the country.

Information: **Williamsburg Area Convention and Visitors Bureau** | Box 3585, 201 Penniman Rd., Williamsburg, VA 23187-3585 | 757/253-0192 or 800/368-6511 | www.visitwilliamsburg.com | Daily 8:30–5. **Colonial Williamburg Foundation** | Box 1776, Williamsburg, VA 23187-1776 | 757/220-7645 or 800/447-8679 | www.colonialwilliamsburg.org | Weekdays 9–5.

Attractions

America's Railroads on Parade. This attraction in the Village Shops at Kingsmill is dedicated to the model railroad and has than 4,000 square ft of multilevel, remote-controlled train layouts, with animation and scenic dioramas created by a Broadway design studio. Exhibits include limited-edition railroad art, miniature trains, and tinplate and porcelain structures. | 1915 Pocahontas Trail | 757/220-8725 | www.trainsontheline.com | $5 | Daily 10–5.

Busch Gardens Williamsburg. This 360-acre theme park has more than 35 rides as well as nine re-creations of European and French Canadian hamlets. In addition to roller coasters, the park has bumper cars and water adventures, including a "Rhine River" cruise and "Roman Rapids" for rafting. Shows and rides are included in the admission price. | One Busch Place | 757/253-3350 or 800/343-7943 | www.buschgardens.com | $35; parking $6 | Call for hours.

College of William and Mary. The second-oldest college in the United States after Harvard University, William and Mary was chartered in 1693 by the reigning king and queen of England, William III and Mary II, after whom it was named. It severed formal ties with Britain in 1776 and became state-supported in 1906. Today it has an enrollment of about 7,500 students and is regarded as a "public Ivy" for its high academic standards. Among its distinguished alumni are Thomas Jefferson, James Monroe, John Marshall, and John Tyler. | 757/221-4000 | fax 757/221-1242 | www.wm.edu.

The college's **Earl Gregg Swem Library** has more than one million volumes, three million manuscripts, and documents from many historical figures, including the papers of U.S. Chief Justice Warren Burger. | From I-64, take Exit 242A, Rte. 199 W | 757/221-3050 | www.swem.wm.edu | Free | Mon.–Thurs. 8 AM–midnight, Fri. 8–6, Sat. 9–6, Sun. 1–midnight. The first floor of the **Muscarelle Museum of Art** has changing exhibits, which range from ancient to contemporary art; the second floor showcases works from the 3,000 items in its permanent collection. Lectures and gallery talks are held regularly. | Jamestown Rd. | 757/221–2700 | fax 757/221–2711 | www.wm.edu/muscarelle | Free | Weekdays 10–4:45, weekends noon–4.

The college's original structure, the **Wren Building,** dates from 1695; its design is attributed to the celebrated London architect Sir Christopher Wren. The redbrick outer walls are original, but fire gutted the interior several times, and the present quarters are largely 20th-century reconstructions. It is the oldest academic building in use in America; there are faculty offices on the third floor and classrooms throughout. Undergraduates lead tours of the building, including the chapel where Peyton Randolph, prominent Colonist and revolutionary who served as president of the First Continental Congress, is buried. | Duke of Gloucester St. | 757/221–4000 or 757/221–1540 | Free | Tours Mon.–Sat. 9–5, Sun. noon–5 during the academic year.

Colonial Parkway. This scenic 23-mi roadway connects three historic sites—Jamestown, the site of the first permanent English settlement in North America; Williamsburg, the former Colonial capital; and Yorktown, the scene of the last major battle of the American Revolution, where America won its independence. Created in the 1930s by the Depression-era Public Works Administration, the parkway has a number of turnouts with unobstructed views of the James and York rivers; many of these are good spots for a quiet picnic. Commercial traffic is prohibited. | Colonial National Historical Park, Yorktown | 757/898–3400 | www.nps.gov | Free | Daily.

Colonial National Historic Park. Box 210, Yorktown, VA | 757/898–3400 | fax 757/898–6346 | www.nps.gov.

Colonial Williamsburg. Williamsburg was the capital of Virginia from 1699 until 1780, when it was succeeded by Richmond. Restoration of the town to its 18th-century appearance began in 1926 through the efforts of William A. R. Goodwin, rector of Bruton Parish Church, and John D. Rockefeller Jr., who financed the massive undertaking. The work of archaeologists and historians of the Colonial Williamsburg Foundation continue, and the 173-acre restored area is operated as a living-history museum. There are 88 original 18th-century buildings and another 40 that have been reconstructed on their original sites. In all, 225 period rooms have been furnished from the foundation's collection of more than 100,000 pieces of furniture, pottery, china, glass, silver, textiles, and tools. Period authenticity also governs the grounds, which include 90 acres of gardens. Costumed interpreters lead house tours and demonstrate historic trades; you can step inside nearly two dozen workshops to watch a shoemaker, gunsmith, blacksmith, musical-instrument maker, silversmith, or wig maker. The restored area can only be toured on foot; all vehicular traffic is prohibited to preserve the Colonial atmosphere. Colonial Williamsburg offers several types of admission tickets.

The Patriot's Pass, valid for one year, includes admission to all of the exhibition buildings, trade sites, homes and shops, the DeWitt Wallace Gallery, the Abby Aldrich Rockefeller Folk Art Center, an orientation walk, seasonal history walks, Carter's Grove, and Bassett Hall; there's also a discount on evening programs. The two-day Colonist's Pass includes an orientation walk and admission to all of the exhibition buildings, trade sites, homes and shops, plus the DeWitt Wallace Gallery and Abby Aldrick Rockefeller Folk Art Center. The basic one-day admission ticket includes an orientation walk, trade sites, homes, shops, and most exhibition buildings (it excludes the Governor's Palace and Wheelwright); it also includes the DeWitt Wallace Gallery and Abby Aldrich Rockefeller Folk Art Center. You can also buy a single ticket to some specific attractions. Arrangements for visitors with disabilities can be made in advance (757/220–7644 or 800/637–4677). | Jct. Rte. 5 and Rte. 31/Jamestown Rd. | 757/220–7644, 757/220–7645 or 800/447–8679 | fax 757/220–7702 | www.colonial-williamsburg.org | Patriot's Pass $34, valid for 1 yr; Colonist's Pass $30, valid for 2 days; basic admission $26; single admission to Governor's Palace or Carter's Grove $17; museums $10; annual museums pass $17; special rates for children | Daily.

Carter's Grove. Carter Burwell built this mansion on a bluff above the James River in 1755, on land purchased by his grandfather, Robert "King" Carter, one of Virginia's wealthiest landowners. Remodeled in 1919, the house retains its original wood paneling and elaborate carvings, and is furnished in Colonial Revival style. The settlement around Carter's Grove was reconstructed after extensive archaeological investigation and includes 18th-century slaves' quarters. On the grounds you can see exhibits in the Winthrop Rockefeller Archeology Museum, including displays about Wolstenholme Towne, a settlement destroyed by Indians in 1622 that is believed to have been the first planned town in British America. | 8797 Pocahontas Trail | 757/229–1000 | fax 757/220–7173 | www.colonialwilliamsburg.org | $17; admission is also included in $34 Patriot's Pass from Williamsburg | Mid-Mar.–Dec., Tues.–Sun. 9–5.

© Artville

THE SOUND OF COLONIAL WILLIAMSBURG

They are the most visible symbol of Colonial Williamsburg, their image gracing seemingly every guidebook on the area. All year long, the shrill martial music of the Colonial Williamsburg Fife and Drum Corps rings through the streets of the historic area. Sporting breeches, stockings, and brass-buckled shoes, the corps marches in tight formation, practiced and perfect.

For local teenagers, membership in this elite, 90-member group is hard-won. The level of discipline that is demanded would pose a challenge for most adults. The corps' repertoire includes more than 300 tunes, and it performs a mind-boggling 500 times a year, locally and across the country. Despite such rigors, competition to join the corps is fierce. Children volunteer as recruits at the end of 4th grade and depart upon graduation from 12th grade. Parents are permitted to put their child's name on a waiting list when he or she turns five. (At one time, applications were accepted at birth.) The waiting list, at any given time, runs to several hundred names.

Members of the corps earn points for perfect attendance, for volunteering to perform on an emergency basis, and for substituting for a colleague. Demerits are given for unsatisfactory gear, tardiness, and unexcused absences. Too many bad points and a cadet might be assigned to some of the group's less pleasant chores, like cleaning the locker-room toilets.

Founded in 1958, the Fife and Drum Corps has always prided itself on being historically accurate. The uniforms match those worn by the Virginia State Garrison Regiment when it defended eastern Virginia and the capital during the American Revolution in 1778. The corpsmen were attired in red coats with blue facings—the reverse of what soldiers wore—so that the musicians were easily distinguishable from the fighting men on the battlefield. Their role was to "beat" the tunes that guided infantrymen in assaults and retreats and to play at reveille and other ceremonies.

Of course, girls didn't march with the corps in colonial times. In the fall of 1999, however, the rules of history were bent and the previously all-male corps began accepting female members. Women are being phased in gradually and, in a few years, will be totally in the mix. The decision, which came after years of debate, has its share of critics (most of them historical purists). Supporters of the unisex corps note that Colonial Williamsburg is a 21st-century museum and therefore should be governed by 21st-century laws of fairness between the sexes—not 18th-century ones.

Colonial Williamsburg Visitor Center. Here you can purchase tickets for Colonial Williamsburg and pick up a *Visitor's Companion* guide, which lists regular events and special programs, and includes a map of the historic area. The center also shows a 35-minute introductory movie, "Williamsburg—The Story of a Patriot." Information about dining and lodging is available (there's a reservation service). Shuttle buses to the historic area run continuously throughout the day. There's also a bookstore. | 102 Information Center Dr. | 757/220–7645 or 800/246–2099 | www.colonialwilliamsburg.org | Free | Daily 9–5.

Exhibition buildings are all over Colonial Williamsburg. Anchoring the eastern end of Duke of Gloucester Street is the **Capitol,** the center of Virginia's political power from 1699 to 1781; it was here that the pre-Revolutionary House of Burgesses challenged the royally appointed council. A tour explains the development of American democracy from its English parliamentary roots. The building is a reproduction with dark-wood wainscoting, pewter chandeliers, and towering ceilings. The reconstructed **Governor's Palace,** originally built in 1720, was home to seven royal governors and Virginia's first two state governors, Patrick Henry and Thomas Jefferson. It is furnished as it was just before the Revolution, with some authentic period pieces; 800 guns and swords arrayed on the walls and ceilings of several rooms herald the power of the Crown. The **Magazine** (1715), an octagonal brick warehouse, stored arms and ammunition; it was used for this purpose by the British, then by the Continental Army, and later by the Confederates during the Civil War. Today, 18th-century firearms are on display within the arsenal. The **Courthouse** of 1770 was used by municipal and county courts until 1932; the exterior has been restored to its original appearance. Stocks, once used to punish misdemeanors, are located outside the building. **Bruton Parish Church,** built in 1715, has served continuously as a place of worship; many local eminences, including one royal governor, are interred in the graveyard. The **Public Hospital,** a reconstruction of a 1773 insane asylum, provides a look at the treatment of the mentally ill in the 18th and 19th centuries. The **DeWitt Wallace Decorative Arts Gallery** contains English and American furniture, textiles, prints, and ceramics spanning the 17th to the early 19th century. Among the 8,000 pieces in this museum's collection is a full-length portrait of George Washington by Charles Willson Peale. Nearby, the **Abby Aldrich Rockefeller Folk Art Center** showcases American folk art, from toys and weather vanes to sculptures, doll houses, and paintings. The core of the collection was acquired by John D. Rockefeller Jr.'s wife. | Colonial Williamsburg. | www.colonialwilliamsburg.org | Daily 9–5.

Historic AirTours. Learn about local history by taking a narrated flight over Colonial Williamsburg, Yorktown, Jamestown, and the Jamestown River Plantations. | 102 Mark Flight Rd. (Williamsburg Airport) | 757/253–8185 or 800/822–9247 | www.historicairtours.com | $45–$60 | Daily 8–5:30.

Water Country USA. This amusement park has more than 30 water rides and attractions, live entertainment, shops, and restaurants. The Nitro Racer is a speed slide with a 382-ft drop. The biggest attraction is a 4,500-square-ft heated pool. | Rte. 199 | 757/253–3350 or 800/343–7946 | www.themeparks.com/watercountry | $25.50, special rates for seniors and children | May 15–Labor Day, daily 10–6; June–Aug., daily 10–8.

Williamsburg Winery. You can have a tour and tasting, as well as buy wine and related items. There is a restaurant, and the winery often has festivals and special events. The Chardonnay and the Governor's White are noteworthy. | 5800 Wessex Hundred | 757/229–0999 | www.williamsburgltd.com | $6 for tour | Mon.–Sat. 11–4:30, Sun. 12:30–4:30.

York River State Park. This 2,491-acre park, 11 mi northeast in James City County is an estuarine environment, formed by the York River, Taskinas Creek, and a saltwater marsh; this unusual and delicate habitat is rich in marine and plant life. More than 20 mi of hiking, biking, and horseback-riding trails wind through the marsh, river shoreline, and upland forests. The park has fresh- and saltwater fishing, picnic pavilions, a boat launch, and bike and boat rentals. Exhibits at the visitor center highlight the history and preservation efforts of the York River and its marshes. | 5526 Riverview Rd., Croaker | 757/566–3036 | www.state.va.us | $1 per vehicle, $2 weekends Memorial Day–Labor Day | Daily 8 AM–dusk.

ON THE CALENDAR

JAN.–MAR.: *Colonial Weekends.* The Williamsburg Institute has special weekend programs that emphasize Colonial traditions and how they can be transferred to the modern-day world. Seminars and demonstrations range from period design and home decorating to needlework, woodworking, and gardening. | 757/220–7255 or 800/603–0948.

FEB.: *Antiques Forum.* The weeklong annual symposium on antiques, presented by the Williamsburg Institute, has a different theme each year. | 757/220–7255 or 800/603–0948.

FEB.: *Washington's Birthday Celebration.* Reenactments, lectures, and a military tribute are part of the festivities in the historic district on President's Day weekend; the event includes a traditional review of the troops by General George Washington. | 800/246–2099.

MAR.: *Learning Weekend.* During this event conducted by the Williamsburg Institute, you can explore the complex decisions faced by Virginians on the eve of Revolution, and experience "living history" through encounters with 18th-century character interpreters. | 800/603–0948.

MAR.: *English Country Dance Ball.* Held on the first Saturday in March at the Newport House B&B, this ball attracts more than 200 dancers who come out in full period costume. A $25 ticket includes dinner. The inn also hosts free English country dancing every Tuesday night from 8 to 10. | 757/229–1775.

MAR.–DEC.: *18th-Century Comedy.* The Company of Colonial Players presents rollicking 18th-century plays. | 757/229–1000.

MAR.–OCT.: *Military Drill.* You can observe interpreters costumed as 18th-century soldiers every afternoon as they undergo military training in the historic district. | 757/253–0192 or 800/447–8679.

APR.: *Garden Symposium.* Colonial Williamsburg's longest-running symposium series examines the style and utility of native plants. | 800/603–0948.

APR.–OCT.: *Fife and Drum Corps.* Listen to Colonial Williamsburg's Fife and Drum Corps perform daily throughout the historic district; typically, the corps parades down Duke of Gloucester Street, the main thoroughfare. | 757/253–0192 or 800/447–8679.

MAY: *Prelude to Independence.* Watch a debate by Virginia's Colonial leaders at the Second Continental Congress as they prepared to vote for independence from Great Britain, performed in the historic district. | 757/253–0192 or 800/447–8679.

SEPT.: *Publick Times.* At The Capitol, you can see a reenactment of "publick times" during the Colonial era, when planters and merchants gathered in Williamsburg for the spring and fall sessions of the General Court and House of Burgesses on | Labor Day weekend | 757/253–0192 or 800/447–8679.

OCT.: *An Occasion for the Arts.* Held every year at Merchants' Square (usually on the first of the month), this day of free events includes a juried competition of artists, as well as live Dixieland jazz and rock music. Food is plentiful, and there are things for kids to do too. | 757/220–1736.

DEC.: *Traditional Christmas Activities.* Holiday programs, tours, workshops, and concerts take place in the historic district during the Christmas season. A highlight is the Grand Illumination, when all the windows in the historic district are lit with candles; the evening event also features fireworks and 18th-century-style entertainment. | 757/253–0192 or 800/447–8679.

YEAR-ROUND: *Living History Programs.* Costumed interpreters bring Colonial traditions and concerns to light through a variety of programs in the historic district. Craftspeople such as the silversmith, wheelwright, and wigmaker demonstrate their trades each day. Regular programs feature performers practicing 18th-century entertainment; reenactments of local court sessions and trials at the Courthouse; and Continental Army encampments. | 757/253–0192 or 800/447–8679.

Dining

Aberdeen Barn. Steak. This rustic wood restaurant furnished with antiques has casual dining by candlelight. House specialties are prime rib, fresh tuna, and filet mignon. Kids' menu.

|1601 Richmond Rd.|757/229–6661|fax 757/229–4440|www.aberdeen-barn.com|Closed first 2 wks in Jan. No lunch|$14–$32|AE, D, MC, V.

Berret's. Seafood. American regional fare is served; popular dishes are the seafood feast, cuban seafood with black beans and rice, and the Virginia crab meat combination. You can dine outdoors, facing a grassy area. Raw bar. Kids' menu.|199 S. Boundary St.|757/253–1847|fax 757/220–0415|Closed Mon. Jan.–Mar.|$18–$25|AE, D, MC, V.

Bray Dining Room. Contemporary. One of several dining rooms at the Kingsville resort, this modern restaurant has picture windows overlooking the 18th green. The menu includes steaks and seafood; the house specials are the grilled tuna and the swordfish. A piano player performs in the evening, and breakfast is served daily.|1010 Kingville Rd.|757/253–3900|$19–$33|AE, D, DC, MC, V.

The Cascades. American. The restaurant overlooks a ravine with a cascading brook and serves Chesapeake Bay seafood. It is part of the Colonial Williamsburg Foundation, so the proceeds go to support the museum and educational work of Colonial Williamsburg. Kids' menu. Sunday brunch.|104 Visitors Center Dr.|757/229–1000|fax 757/220–7788|Breakfast also available|$12–$25|AE, D, DC, MC, V.

Ford's Colony Country Club. Contemporary. A formal dining room overlooking a golf course features windows on three sides, a large floral centerpiece, original artwork, fine china, and crystal stemware. The more casual grill room, which is separate from the dining room, serves lighter fare for lunch. The menu emphasizes regional American food, fresh seafood, rack of lamb. Kids' menu in the grill room.|240 Ford's Colony Dr.|757/258–4100|fax 757/258–4168|www.fordscolony.com|Reservations essential|Jacket required|Closed Sun.–Mon.|$28–$35|AE, MC, V.

Gazebo. Continental. In keeping with its name, this breakfast and lunch spot has an indoor garden theme, with lots of glass and greenery. Special breakfast menu. Kids' menu. No smoking.|409 Bypass Rd.|757/220–0883|fax 757/221–0637|Breakfast also available. No dinner|$4–$7|D, DC, MC, V, AE.

Giuseppe's. Italian. It's a casual café, with maroon walls and green tables. Kids' menu.|5601 Richmond Rd.|757/565–1977|www.giuseppes.com|Closed Sun.|$7–$18|DC, D, AE, MC, V.

Jefferson Inn. Eclectic. The servers wear Colonial attire in this English country setting. There's a full bar that serves wines from Williamsburg wineries. Kids' menu.|1453 Richmond Rd.|757/229–2296|No lunch|$19–$31|AE, DC, MC, V.

King's Arms Tavern. American. Costumed servers wait tables while Colonial balladeers entertain guests. The restaurant is part of the Colonial Williamsburg Foundation. You can dine or have a drink in the garden. The menu features regional American dishes, including peanut soup, game pie, and filet mignon. Kids' menu.|Duke of Gloucester St.|757/220–7010|www.history.org|Reservations essential|Closed mid–Jan.–Mar.; Tues. Mar., May, Sept., and Nov.–Dec.|$18–$27|AE, D, DC, MC, V.

Kitchen at Powhatan. Contemporary. Near the James River, this restaurant has candlelight dining in a Colonial atmosphere. The cuisine is American with Continental and international flavors. No smoking.|3601 Ironbound Rd.|757/220–1200|Closed Mon. Jan.–Aug. No lunch|$27–$40|AE, D, MC, V.

Kyoto. Japanese. Your personal chef prepares Japanese steak and seafood tableside. Vegetarian meals are also available, and there's a sushi bar. Popular entrees are teppanyaki filet mignon, bonsai scallops, and the Kyoto special. You can eat outdoors in a courtyard. Kids' menu. No smoking.|1621 Richmond Rd.|757/220–8888|www.kyoto.com|No lunch|$12–$25|AE, D, DC, MC, V.

Le Yaca. French. Choose from four fixed-price menus in a dining room with salmon-colored walls, flowered drapes, and hardwood floors. Southern French fare includes lamb, chicken, and beef.|1915 Pocohantas Trail/U.S. 60 E|757/220–3616|Reservations essential|Closed Sun.|$28–$50|AE, DC, MC, V.

Mr. Liu's. Chinese. Chinese art contributes to the Asian ambience. Try General Liu chicken or the Mongolian spicy beef. Kids' menu. | 1915 Pocohantas Trail/U.S. 60 E | 757/253–0990 | $18–$25 | AE, D, DC, MC, V.

Old Chickahominy House. American. This restaurant serves traditional cuisine, including chicken. Beer and wine only. No smoking. | 1211 Jamestown Rd. | 757/229–4689 | Breakfast also available. Closed 2 wks mid-Jan. | $7–$12 | MC, V.

Peking. Chinese. Traditional Chinese cuisine, including Mongolian beef, General Tso chicken, chicken with cashew nuts, and shrimp and scallops with garlic sauce. You can have the buffet or order from the menu. | 122A Waller Mill Rd. | 757/229–2288 | $8–$17 | AE, D, DC, MC, V.

Polo Club. American. On the edge of Williamsburg in James City County, this restaurant is the neighborhood place to go for a beer and burger. Enjoy your Gatlin burger with chili and cheddar cheese in a wooden booth while checking out the clutter of polo parapher-nalia around you. In addition to a variety of burgers, there are seafood specials every night, like sauteed salmon in a lemon dill sauce. Chicken, ribs, soups, and sandwiches are other regular items. | 135 Colony Sq., Williamsburg | 757/220–1122 | $8–$13 | AE, D, DC, MC, V.

Prime Rib House. Southwestern. This steak place has casual dining in elegant surround-ings. Popular menu items are steak and prime rib. Kids' menu. | 1433 Richmond Rd. | 757/229–6823 | No lunch | $20–$33 | AE, MC, V.

Regency Room. Continental. On the grounds of the Williamsburg Inn, one of the older and most elegant of the inns at Colonial Williamsburg, the Regency serves regional and French-inspired cuisine. Duck and filet mignon are among the chef's specialties. Entertainment, including ballroom dancing. Kids' menu. Sun. brunch. | 136 E. Francis St. | 757/229–2141 | Jacket required | Breakfast also available | $30–$70 | AE, D, DC, MC, V.

Season's Cafe. Continental. The restaurant has many rooms, each with a theme relating to the season of the year. The postmaster's room in the back can be reserved for groups of 10 or more. Favorite dishes are the Colonial prawn, pasta primavera, and southern cat-fish. Open-air dining. Salad bar. Sun. brunch buffet. Kids' menu. | 110 S. Henry | 757/259–0018 | $25–$33 | AE, D, DC, MC, V.

Shields Tavern. American. Williamsburg's oldest tavern serves 18th-century cuisine in eight dining rooms and the garden, while strolling balladers entertain diners. Some Colo-nial entrees include spit-roasted chicken, stuffed baked pork chops, and Atlantic seafood. Kids' menu. No smoking. Sunday brunch. | 455 Francis St. | 757/220–7677 | $22–$32.50 | AE, D, DC, MC, V.

That Seafood Place. Seafood. Regionally inspired seafood. Fresh fish, crab cakes. Open-air dining. Salad bar. Kids' menu. No smoking. | 1647 Richmond Rd. | 757/220–3011 | No lunch Fri.–Sat. Call for summer hrs | $15–$20 | AE, D, MC, V.

The Trellis. Contemporary. This 800-sq ft restaurant combine simplicity and elegance; the interior is done with yellow and green fabrics, walls of hand-blown glass, and muted golden surfaces. The garden room is a favorite dining section. | 403 Duke of Gloucester St. | 757/229–8610 | fax 757/221–0450 | www.thetrellis.com | $18–$28 | AE, DC, MC, V.

Whaling Company. Seafood. Boats decorate the rafters, along with fishing nets, a porthole, and pictures of fisherman. The menu is all about seafood, of course. Fresh tuna, salmon, hand-cut steaks. Kids' menu, early-bird suppers Sunday–Friday | 494 McLaw Circle | 757/229–0275 | No lunch | $13–$18 | AE, DC, MC, D, V.

Yorkshire Steak and Seafood House. Steak. A casual place whose owner opened the first pancake house in Williamsburg. Try one of the beef dishes, seafood shish kebab, crab cakes, or salmon. Kids' menu. No smoking. | 700 York St. | 757/229–9790 | fax 757/229–7685 | www.yorkshirewmbg.com | No lunch | $13–$19 | AE, MC, V.

Lodging

Bassett Motel. Dogwood trees and flower beds (azaleas and tulips in the spring, begonias in the fall) surround this well-run, single-story brick property on the quiet east side of Williamsburg. Rooms are variously furnished, some with tables, some with desks, in a cream color scheme. | 800 York St. (U.S. 60) | 757/229–5175 | www.williamsburghotel.com | 18 rooms | $27–$35 | Closed mid-Nov.–mid-Mar. | MC, V.

Candlewick Inn B&B. This 1946 Colonial-style farmhouse and flower garden is across the street from the College of William and Mary. The living room has a fireplace, wingback chairs, a love seat, and a sofa. The rooms have king- or queen-size canopy beds. Dining room, complimentary breakfast. Cable TV, room phones. No pets. No kids under . No smoking. | 800 Jamestown Rd., Williamsburg | 757/253–8693 or 800/418–4949 | fax 757/253–6547 | 3 | $125–$145 | MC, V.

Capitol Motel. Bird feeders and a park bench are part of the landscaping in a small strip in front of this motel's parking lot. It has family suites with kitchens and queen beds, and is only .5 mi from Colonial Williamsburg. No breakfast is served, but you can stop by in the morning for complimentary donuts and coffee. Some kitchenettes. Outdoor pool. Laundry facilities. | 924 Capitol Landing Rd. | 757/229–5215 or 800/368–8383 | www.capitol-motelhistoric.com. x | 25 rooms | $29–$79 | AE, D, DC, MC, V.

Captain John Smith Inn. At this modern hotel with an old name, the rooms are hung with floral wallpaper and beds are made with floral sheets. There is a Red Lobster restaurant across the street and an outlet mall ten minutes away. Some microwaves, refrigerators. Video games. | 2225 Richmond Rd. | 757/220–0710 | fax 757/220–1166 | 68 rooms | $29–$59. Kids under 17 free | AE, D, DC, MC, V.

Colonel Waller Motel. The suites in this two-story, family-run motel have both living rooms and bedrooms. Used primarily by families, it is within 1 mi of most historic sites. Refrigerators. Outdoor pool. | 917 Capitol Landing Rd. | 757/253–0999 | fax 757/253–0276 | www.cwmotel.com | 28 rooms | $32–$54 | AE, D, MC, V.

Colonial Capital. This three-story Colonial Revival bed-and-breakfast inn with plantation parlor and wood-burning fireplaces is furnished with antiques and Oriental rugs. Complimentary breakfast. No smoking. No kids under 8. | 501 Richmond Rd. | 757/229–0233 or 800/776–0570 | fax 757/253–7667 | ccbb@widomaker.com | www.ccbb.com | 5 rooms | $115–$145 | AE, D, MC, V.

Colonial Gardens. Three acres of flower gardens surround this brick colonial B&B built in the early 1900's, furnished inside with Federal-period antiques and comfortable new sofas. A 15 minute drive from Jamestown. Complimentary breakfast. Robe, turndown service. No kids under 14. | 1109 Jamestown Rd. | 800/886–9715 | fax 757/253–1495 | www.colonial-gardens | 4 rooms | $125–$155 | AE, D, MC, V.

Colonial Houses. Some of the 27 buildings that make up this property date from the 1800s. There are some rooms with fireplaces and/or private courtyards. You can use the recreational facilities at Williamsburg Lodge and inn. Cable TV. In-room data ports. Business services. Children's programs (ages 4–12). | 302 E. Francis St. (office) | 757/229–1000 or 800/447–8679 | fax 757/565–8444 | conferencesales@crw.org.com | 76 rooms | $100–$515 | AE, D, DC, MC, V.

Courtyard by Marriott. This chain hotel is in the Busch Corporate Center. Bar. In-room data ports, refrigerator (in suites), cable TV. Indoor-outdoor pool. Hot tub. Exercise equipment. Game room. Video games. Laundry facilities. Business services. Free parking. | 470 McLaws Circle | 757/221–0700 | fax 757/221–0741 | www.courtyardmarriott.com | 151 rooms | $99–$154 | AE, D, DC, MC, V.

Embassy Suites. This five-story, all-suites hotel (formerly known as Quality Suites) built in 1987 sits on 11 wooded acres next to a shopping center. Less than 1 mi from the restored area, it is a convenient retreat from the bustle of Colonial Williamsburg. Pale pinks, blues, and greens color the guest rooms, and there is a central atrium with fountain and greenery. 1 restaurant. Complimentary Continental breakfast. Indoor pool. Sauna. Exercise equipment. | 3006 Mooretown Rd. | 757/229–6800 | fax 757/220–3486 | www.embassysuites.com | 169 rooms | $98–$120 | AE, D, DC, MC, V.

Governor's Inn. This hotel is located three blocks from the Colonial Williamsburg historic area. Cable TV. Pool. Game room. Video games. Business services. | 506 N. Henry St. | 757/229–1000 ext. 6000 or 800/447–8679 | fax 757/220–7019 | www.colonialwilliamsburg.org | 200 rooms | $65–$100 | Closed Jan.–mid-Mar. | AE, D, DC, MC, V.

Hampton Inn. This multi-story chain hotel with interior corridors is 1 1/4 mi west of Colonial Williamsburg, 5 mi from I–64. The Williamsburg Pottery Factory and Williamsburg Winery are 3 mi away, and Busch Gardens is a 15 minute drive. Complimentary Continental breakfast. Cable TV. Indoor pool. Hot tub, sauna. Game room. Video games. Business services. | 201 Bypass Rd. | 757/220–0880 | fax 757/229–7175 | www.hampton-inn.com | 122 rooms | $89–$109 | AE, D, DC, MC, V.

Heritage Inn. This motel is 1 mi west of the historic district, and 3 mi from I–64. Cable TV. Pool. Business services. Some pets allowed. | 1324 Richmond Rd. | 757/229–6220 or 800/782–3800 | fax 757/229–2774 | www.heritageinnwmsb.com | 54 rooms | $42–$84 | AE, D, DC, MC, V.

Holiday Inn–Downtown. The chain hotel is 1/2 mi from the historic district, and 1 1/2 mi from I–64. Restaurant, bar. Microwaves, room service, cable TV. Indoor pool. Hot tub. Putting green. Exercise equipment. Game room. Video games. Laundry facilities. Business services. | 814 Capitol Landing Rd./Off Rte. 5 E | 757/229–0200 | fax 757/220–1642 | www.holiday-inn.com | 139 rooms | $80–$129 | AE, D, DC, MC, V.

Holiday Inn Express–Historic Area. This chain hotel is 4 mi from Busch Gardens. Restaurant, complimentary Continental breakfast. In-room data ports, cable TV. Pool. Business services. | 119 Bypass Rd. | 757/253–1663 | fax 757/220–9117 | www.holiday-express.com | 132 rooms | $75–$119 | AE, D, DC, MC, V.

Holiday Inn 1776. This hotel with landscaped grounds with duck ponds is just 1/2 mi from the historic district. Restaurant, bar, picnic area. Microwaves, room service, cable TV. Pool, wading pool. Tennis courts. Game room. Video games. Playground, kids' programs, laundry facilities. Business services. Free parking. | 725 Bypass Rd. | 757/220–1776 | fax 757/220–3124 | www.holiday-inn1776.com | 202 rooms | $99–$130 | AP, MAP | AE, D, DC, MC, V.

Howard Johnson–Historic Area. This chain hotel is 1 1/2 mi from the historic district and 1 mi from Busch Gardens. Cable TV. Pool, wading pool. Game room. Video games. Laundry facilities. Business services. Free parking. | 7135 Pocahontas Trail/U.S. 60 E | 757/229–6900 | fax 757/220–3211 | hojohst@erols.com | http://www.hojohst.com/ | 100 rooms | $79–$110 | AE, D, DC, MC, V.

Indian Springs B&B. The bed-and-breakfast with gardens is a 1-mi walk from the historic district. Complimentary breakfast. No smoking, cable TV, room phone in cottage only. | 330 Indian Springs | 757/220–0726 or 800/262–9165 | fax 757/220–8934 | Indianspgs@tni.net | www.indian-springs.com | 4 rooms, 1 cottage | $95–$125, $135 cottage | MC, V.

Kingsmill. This 3,000-acre resort is on the James River. Bar, dining room, picnic area. In-room data ports, microwaves (in suites), some refrigerators, room service, cable TV. 2 pools (1 indoor). Massage. Driving range, three 18-hole golf courses, putting green, tennis courts. Gym, racquetball, marina, boating. Childrens' programs. Business services. | 1010 Kingsmill Rd. | 757/253–1703 or 800/832–5665 | fax 757/253–3993 | reservationist@kingsmill.com | www.kingsmill.com | 407 rooms | $179–$637 | AE, D, DC, MC, V.

Legacy of Williamsburg. Colonial inn. Complimentary breakfast. No smoking, no TV in rooms. TV, VCR, and movies in common area. Business services. No kids under 18. | 930 Jamestown Rd. | 757/220–0524 or 800/962–4722 | fax 757/220–2211 | www.legacyofwilliamsburgbb.com | 4 rooms, 3 suites | $125–$180 | MC, V.

Liberty Rose. The inn is furnished with antiques. Garden and courtyards area, complimentary full breakfast. No smoking, in-room VCRs and movies. No kids under 12. | 1022 Jamestown Rd. | 757/253–1260 or 800/545–1825 | www.libertyrose.com | 4 rooms | $145–$205 | AE, MC, V.

Marriott. This chain hotel is in a wooded setting, 5 mi from the historic district and around the corner from Busch Gardens. Restaurant, bar. In-room data ports, room service, cable TV. Indoor-outdoor pool. Hot tub. Tennis courts. Exercise equipment. Game room. Video games. Business services. | 50 Kingsmill Rd. | 757/220–2500 | fax 757/221–0653 | www.marriott.com | 295 rooms | $99–$275 | AE, D, DC, MC, V.

Marriott's Manor Club at Ford's Colony. The chain hotel is close to outlet malls and the Berkeley Commons shopping center. Restaurant. In-room data ports, kitchenettes, microwaves, refrigerators, in-room hot tubs, cable TV, in-room VCRs and movies. 3 pools (1 indoor). Hot tubs, massage. Driving range, golf courses, putting green, tennis courts. Gym. Business services. | 101 St. Andrews Dr. | 757/258–1120 | fax 757/258–5705 | www.marriott.com | 158 suites | $147–$279 suites | AE, D, DC, MC, V.

Primrose Cottage. This Cape Cod house is set among flower gardens, including the requisite primroses. The theme continues indoors with a floral mural in the kitchen. The walls are hung with prints of scenes from the fairy tales of Hans Christian Anderson, and the furniture is a mix of wicker and pieces fashioned from iceboxes. About an 8-minute walk to Colonial Williamsburg. Complimentary breakfast. No pets. No kids. No smoking. | 706 Richmond Rd. | 757/229–6421 or 800/522–1901 | fax 757/259–0717 | www.primrose-cottage.com | 4 rooms | $90–$125 | Closed Jan. or Feb. (varies) | MC, V.

Radisson Fort Magruder Hotel and Conference Center. The property is on Rte. 60, 2 mi west of Busch Gardens and ¼ mi east of Colonial Williamsburg, on the site of a Civil War fort; dirt embankments remain. Restaurant, bar with entertainment. Minibars, room service, some in-room hot tubs, cable TV. 2 pools (1 indoor), wading pool. Hot tub. Tennis. Exercise equipment. Bicycles. Game room. Video games. Playground, laundry facilities. Business services. | 6945 Pocahontas Trail | 757/220–2250 | fax 757/221–6982 | www.radissonftmagruder.com | 303 rooms | $99–$159 | AE, D, DC, MC, V.

Quality Inn Lord Paget. This motel on 7 wooded acres is 1 mi from the historic district. Restaurant. Microwaves, cable TV. Pool, wading pool. Putting green. Laundry facilities. | 901 Capitol Landing Rd. | 757/229–4444 or 800/537–2438 | fax 757/220–9314 | 94 rooms | $79–$99 | AE, D, DC, MC, V.

Quarterpath Inn. This inn is next to a public park on the edge of the historic district. Some in-room hot tubs, cable TV. Pool. Business services. Some pets allowed. | 620 York St. | 757/220–0960 or 800/446–9222 | fax 757/220–1531 | www.hotelroom.com/virginia/wmquar | 130 rooms | $55–$69 | AE, D, MC, V.

War Hill Inn. This bed-and-breakfast inn on 35 wooded, grassy acres is 4 ½ mi from Colonial Williamsburg. There are 50 Angus cows on the property. Complimentary breakfast. No smoking, cable TV, no room phones. Playground. | 4560 Long Hill Rd. | 757/565–0248 or 800/743–0248 | fax 757/565–4550 | www.warhillinn.com | 3 rooms, 2 suites, 2 cottages | $80–$110, $120–$150 suites | MC, V.

Williamsburg Hospitality House. The hotel is close to the College of William and Mary. Restaurant, bar. In-room data ports, cable TV. Pool. Business services. | 415 Richmond Rd. | 757/229–4020 or 800/932–9192 | fax 757/220–1560 | wcorp52554@aol.com | www.williamsburghosphouse.com | 296 rooms | $89–$190 | AE, D, DC, MC, V.

Williamsburg Inn. Built in 1937 in English Regency style, this inn is a National Historic Landmark. The guest rooms are individually decorated; suites have fireplaces. Restaurant, bar with entertainment, room service. In-room data ports, some refrigerators, cable TV. 3 pools (1 indoor), wading pool. Hot tub, massage. One 9-hole and two 18-hole golf courses, putting green, tennis. Exercise equipment. Bicycles. Children's programs. Business services. Airport shuttle. | 136 E. Francis St. | 757/229–1000 or 800/447–8679 | fax 757/220–7096 | conferencesales@cwf.org | 124 rooms, 11 suites | $259–$363, $410–$750 suites | MAP | AE, D, DC, MC, V.

Williamsburg Lodge. The lodge has five different buildings, built in 1939; inside there is British regency-style furniture from the 1900s and folk art. Its just one block from the historic district. Restaurant, bar with entertainment. In-room data ports. 3 pools and wading pool. Hot tub. Golf courses, putting green, tennis courts. Exercise equipment. Bicycles. Children's programs. Business services. | 310 S. England St. | 757/229–1000 or 800/447–8976 | fax 757/220–7799 | conferencesales@cwf.org | www.histories.org | 313 rooms, 2 suites | $129–$225, $245–$450 suites | AE, D, DC, MC, V.

Williamsburg Sampler. Built in 1976 to represent an 18th-century plantation home, this bed-and-breakfast inn is ½ mi from the historic district and across from William and Mary College. Rooms have British regency furniture from the 1900s. Picnic area, complimentary full breakfast. Cable TV. Business services. No smoking. | 922 Jamestown Rd. | 757/253–0398 or 800/722–1169 | fax 757/253–2669 | wbgsampler@aol.com | www.williamsburgsampler.com | 2 rooms, 2 suites | $110, $160 suites | MC, V.

Williamsburg Woodlands. This family-oriented hotel is in a wooded section of the visitor center complex. Restaurant, picnic area. Two pools. Barbershop, beauty salon. Miniature golf, putting green, tennis courts. Children's programs, playground. Business services. Free parking. | 102 Visitor Center Dr. | 757/229–1000 or 800/447–8679 | fax 757/565–8942 | 315 rooms | $75–$150 | MAP | AE, D, DC, MC, V.

WINCHESTER

MAP 11, H3

(Nearby towns also listed: Middletown, White Post)

Located in the Shenandoah Valley of western Virginia, Winchester was settled in the 1730s by Pennsylvania Quakers, Germans, Scots, Irish, and others who stopped here while heading south on the Great Wagon Road. During the Civil War, Winchester changed hands no fewer than 70 times; five battles and many more skirmishes took place in and around the city. The private residence that Gen. Thomas J. "Stonewall" Jackson used as his headquarters has been preserved as it was during the war.

Surrounded by orchards, Winchester is the unofficial "apple capital" of Virginia. Every May, the city swells with thousands of visitors who come for the Shenandoah Apple Blossom Festival. Apples are the economic mainstay; the world's largest apple cold storage plant is located here, as is one of the biggest apple processing plants. Winchester is also known as the birthplace of country music star Patsy Cline, who grew up here and first sang on the air at a small local radio station. She is buried at the Shenandoah Memorial Park on U.S. 522, which is also known as the Patsy Cline Memorial Highway.

Information: Winchester–Frederick County Chamber of Commerce | 1360 S. Pleasant Valley Rd., Winchester, VA 22601 | 540/662–4135 or 800/662–1360 | tourism@visuallink.com | www.shentel.net/wfcedc.

Attractions

Abram's Delight. The two-story limestone structure known as Abram's Delight is Winchester's oldest structure, built in 1754 by Isaac Hollingsworth, a Quaker settler. The house features an open-hearth kitchen and is furnished with 18th- and 19th-century antiques that reflect early settlement life in the Shenandoah Valley. A restored log cabin from the same period is on the grounds. | 1340 S. Pleasant Valley Rd. | 540/662–6519 or 540/662–6550 | fax 540/662–6991 | www.winchesterhistory.org | $3.50 | Apr.–Oct., Mon.–Sat. 10–4, Sun. noon–4.

Shenandoah Memorial Park. Located in Winchester, this cemetery contains the grave of Patsy Cline, who died at age 30 on March 5, 1963. A bell tower erected in her memory stands near the gravesite. | 1270 Front Royal Pike | 800/662–1360 or 540 667–2012 | Free | Daily dawn–dusk.

Stonewall Jackson's Headquarters. This 1854 Gothic Revival house is furnished as it was when Jackson used it as his base of operations during the Valley Campaign in 1861–62; it was loaned to the Confederate general by its owner, Lt. Col. Lewis T. Moore. Among the Civil War artifacts on display are Jackson's prayerbook and camp table. | 415 N. Braddock St. | 540/667–3242 or 540/662–6550 | fax 540/662–6991 | www.winchesterhistory.org | $3.50 | Apr.–Oct., Mon.–Sat. 10–4, Sun noon–4; Nov.–Mar., Fri.–Sat. 10–4, Sun. noon–4.

The Handley Library and Archives. Winchester's regional public library occupies a 1913 Beaux Arts building. The archives on the lower level contain an extensive collection of materials on the people, places, and events of the lower Shenandoah Valley from 1732 to the present. There are census records, local and family histories, diaries, correspondence, funeral home records, genealogical research items, photographs, and oral history tapes. There are also maps in the collection, including three by Jedediah Hotchkiss, Stonewall Jackson's mapmaker. The impressive renovation of the three-story building rotunda with its stained glass dome is well worth viewing. | 100 W. Piccadilly St. | 540/662–9041 | fax 540/722–4769 | www.shentel.net/handley-library | Free | Library Oct.–Nov. and Jan.–Apr., Mon.–Wed. 10–8, Thurs.–Sat. 10–5, Sun. 1–5; closed Sun. rest of yr. Archives Tues.–Wed. 1–8, Thurs.–Sat. 10–5.

George Washington's Office Museum. Washington occupied this small log cabin while supervising construction of Fort Loudoun in 1755–56. On display are survey tools, plans for the fort's construction, and memorabilia. | W. Cork and S. Braddock Sts. | 540/662–4412 or 540/662–6550 | www.winchesterhistory.org | $3.50, special rates for children | Apr.–Oct., Mon.–Sat. 10–4, Sun. noon–4.

ON THE CALENDAR

APR.: *Historic Garden Tour.* The doors of more than 250 private homes and gardens throughout Virginia open for tours for one week only. | Info: Garden Club of Virginia, 12 E. Franklin St., Richmond, VA 23219 | 804/644–7776 or 540/662–6550.

APR.–MAY: *Shenandoah Apple Blossom Festival.* Winchester's best-known festival includes what is said to be the largest firefighters' parade in the world. More than 30 events are held over five days, including arts-and-crafts shows, live music, a 10K race, a circus, and many children's activities. Nationally-known celebrities from film, sports, and music make appearances, but none outshines the Apple Blossom Queen, crowned during the festivites. | 135 N. Cameron St., Winchester, VA 22601 | 540/662–3863 or 800/230–2139 | fax 540/662–7274 | dsaville@sabf.org | www.sabf.org.

SEPT.: *Apple Harvest Arts and Crafts Fair.* Activities include pie contests, live music, and arts-and-crafts exhibits. | Jim Barnett Park, Pleasant Valley Rd. | 540/662–3996.

OCT.: *Shenandoah Valley Hot Air Balloon and Wine Festival.* The launch of more than 25 hot air balloons is the main event at this festival. At the historic center of Long Branch in Millwood (10 mi from Winchester), you can also take a free tour of a mansion, watch powered-parachute demonstrations, browse crafts, sample a variety of foods, taste Virginia's wines, and listen to live music. There are special activities for children too. | www.southfest.com/festivals/shenandoah.html | 888/558–5567.

Dining

Ashby Inn. American. This restaurant is on the grounds of an 1829 Inn. It serves traditional American food with hints of Italy and France. A garden on the grounds supplies the kitchen. The menu changes daily, but specialties include crabcakes and sausage. Open-air dining available on the terrace.++X: seasonally?++ Sun. brunch. | 692 Federal St., Paris | 540/592–3900 | Reservations required | Closed Mon.–Tues. No lunch | $30–$40 | MC, V.

Cafe Sofia. Eastern European. This small restaurant serves top Bulgarian cuisine, including a goulash featured in *Bon Appetit* magazine. The wait staff wear traditional Bulgarian dress, and the dining room is filled with weavings, dolls, and other crafts. | 2900 Valley Ave. | 540/667–2950 | Closed Sun.–Mon. and July | $20–$23 | AE, D, DC, MC, V.

Cork Street Tavern. American. Parts of this downtown tavern date to the 1800s, and some say it is haunted by an old ghost who likes to change the silverware. The sandwiches, seafood, and barbecue are popular. | 8 Cork St. W | 540/667–3777 | Reservations not accepted | $5–$15 | AE, D, DC, MC, V.

One Block West Restaurant. American/Casual. This bistro has brick walls and columns. The menu ranges from pasta to seafood, which the chef pairs creatively—the tuna, for example, comes with wasabi mashed potatoes. | 25 S. Indian Alley | 540/662–1455 | $9–$15 | MC, D, V.

Pargo's. American/Casual. Large portions of pastas and steaks are among the varied menu items at this popular local eatery, which also has a bar. This is where high-school kids come before the prom and young professionals unwind after work. | 645 Jubal Early Dr. | 540/678–8800 | $9–$16 | AE, D, DC, MC, V.

Sweet Caroline's. American/Casual. The eclectic menu at this intimate restaurant ranges from crabcakes to kebabs. Stay late Friday or Saturday to hear some of the best blues in town. | 107 W. Boscawen St. | 540/723–8805 | $6–$15 | AE, MC, V.

Lodging

Ashby Inn. Located in the Village of Paris, pop. 59. The main Inn, now including the restaurant, was built in 1829. On the grounds are a garden that supplies the restaurant kitchen. There is also a former one-room schoolhouse with four large suites, each with a view of the Blue Ridge Foothills. Restaurant, complimentary full breakfast. No smoking, no TV in some rooms. Library. No kids under 10. Business services. | 692 Federal St., Paris | 540/592–3900 | fax 540/592–3781 | www.ashbyinn.com | 10 rooms | $130–$250 | MC, V.

Best Western Lee–Jackson Motor Inn. The hotel is located next to a regional mall, race tracks, and entertainment. Restaurant, bar, picnic area. Some refrigerators, room service, cable TV. Pool. Laundry facilities. Business services. Airport shuttle. Some pets allowed. | 711 Millwood Ave. | 540/662–4154 | fax 540/662–2618 | www.bestwestern.com | 140 rooms | $52–$56 | AE, D, DC, MC, V.

Comfort Inn Stephens City. The location is convenient to Skyline Drive. Complimentary Continental breakfast. In-room data ports, cable TV, some in-room hot tubs. Outdoor pool. Business services. | 167 Town Run La., Stephens City | 540/869–6500 | fax 540/869–2558 | www.comfortinn.com | 58 rooms | $50–$75 | AE, D, DC, MC, V.

Days Inn. This hotel is within 2 mi of the historic and business districts, and there's a city bus stop in front. Rooms are small and simple. Restaurant. Outdoor pool. Laundry facilities. Small pets allowed ($5 fee). | 2951 Valley Ave. | 800/325–2525 or 540/667–1200 | fax 540/667–7128 | www.daysinn.com | 66 rooms | $50–$69 | AE, D, DC, MC, V.

Econo Lodge–North. A member of the budget chain, this property has some rooms that are specially equipped for senior citizens, such as big-button telephones and extra bathroom safety bars. Complimentary Continental breakfast. In-room data ports, some refrigerators, cable TV. Business services. | 1593 Martinsburg Pike/Rte. 11 | 540/662–4700 | fax 540/665–1762 | www.choicehotels.com | 50 rooms | $47–$52 | AE, D, DC, MC, V.

Hampton Inn. Easy access to I–81 is an advantage here. Kids can enjoy in-room Nintendo. Complimentary Continental breakfast. In-room data ports, cable TV, hairdryers, ironing boards and coffeemakers. Outdoor pool. Business services. Free Parking. | 1655 Apple Blossom Dr. | 540/667–8011 | fax 540/667–8033 | www.hampton-inn.com | 103 rooms | $69–$77 | AE, D, DC, MC, V.

Holiday Inn. This motel is located near a regional shopping mall. Restaurant, bar serves three meals a day. Children with an adult eat free. In-room data ports, some refrigerators, room service, cable TV. Outdoor pool. Tennis court. Complimentary coupons to a Nautilus fitness center across the street. Driving distance to three area golf courses. Business services. Free parking. | 1017 Millwood Pike | 540/667–3300 | fax 540/722–2730 | www.holiday-inn.com | 175 rooms | $79–$89 | AE, D, DC, MC, V.

Howard Johnson Lodge. Set among major strip malls, this motel is 1 mi from the historic section of Winchester and close to Lord Fairfax's tomb, George Washington's headquarters and other attractions. Outdoor pool. Laundry facilities. | 2649 Valley Ave. | 540/662–2521 | fax 540/662–6683 | 70 rooms | $45–$55 | AE, D, DC, MC, V.

Inn at Vaucluse Spring. This 1785 Federal-style manor house converted to an inn is just minutes from Skyline Drive. It has 12 rooms, located in four separate buildings. The manor house has six rooms; the three rooms upstairs are decorated with oriental rugs and antique furnishings. All other rooms are more informal, including the four located in the 1850s log house and the two in one-bedroom cottages on the grounds. All rooms have fireplaces and one has a deck. Eleven of the 12 rooms have Jacuzzi tubs in the bathroom. Restaurant serves complimentary, full country breakfast daily and a Saturday night four-course gourmet meal features updated Southern classics. No smoking. Kids over 10 only. Business services. | 731 Vaucluse Spring La., Stephens City | 540/869–0200 | fax 540/869–9546 | mail@vauclusespring.com | www.vauclusespring.com | 12 rooms | $140–$215, $250–$275 suites and cottages | MC, V.

Quality Inn East. This two-story inn is across the road from Shenandoah University. The rooms are simple and exceptionally clean. The staff in general is young and enthusiastic, and knows the area well. Complimentary breakfast. Outdoor pool, wading pool. Sauna. Exercise room. Laundry facilities. | 603 Millwood Ave. | 540/667–2250 | fax 540/667–0850 | www.choice.com | 96 rooms | $69–$75 | AE, D, DC, MC, V.

Shoney's Inn. This motel has easy access to Interstate 81 and U.S. 7. Continental breakfast served at the Inn; lunch and dinner available at the adjacent Shoney's restaurant. Some microwaves, refrigerators, cable TV. Indoor pool. Sauna. Hot tub. Exercise equipment. Business services. Free parking. | 1347 Berryville Ave. | 540/665–1700 | fax 540/665–3037 | www.shoneysinn.com | 98 rooms (4 with shower only. 10 rooms feature standard tubs with whirlpool jets.) | $58–$61 | AE, D, DC, MC, V.

Travelodge. This chain hotel offers easy interstate access with its location at the intersection of Interstate 81, 50 East and E22 South. Complimentary Continental breakfast. In-room data ports, some kitchenettes, some in-room hot tubs, cable TV. Pool. Laundry facilities. Business services. Some pets allowed. | 160 Front Royal Pike | 540/665–0685 | fax 540/665–0689 | www.travelodge.com | 157 rooms | $53–$75 | AE, D, DC, MC, V.

Wingate Inn. This hotel caters to business travelers, with a full business center that has not only computer facilities but also a conference room. Rooms are larger than most. Complimentary breakfast. Indoor pool. Hot tub. Exercise equipment. Laundry facilities, laundry services. In-room data ports. Business services. | 150 Wingate Dr. | 540/678–4283 | fax 540/662–4439 | www.winchesterwingate.com | 84 rooms | $85–$100 | AE, D, DC, MC, V.

WISE

MAP 11, B7

(Nearby town also listed: Big Stone Gap)

The town of Wise occupies the Appalachian Plateau in southwestern Virginia, nestled in the Cumberland Mountains near the Kentucky border. Mining has dominated the area economy since early settlers discovered seams of high-quality coal in the late 1800s. Jefferson National Forest borders Wise to the west and south, providing ample opportunities for hiking, camping and fishing. Another good recreation area is Breaks Interstate Park, about 35 mi north of Wise.

Information: Big Stone Gap/Wise County Tourist Information Center | Box 236, Gilley Ave. E, Big Stone Gap, VA 24219 | 540/523–2060 | info@bigstonegap.org | www.coalfield.com.

Attractions

Breaks Interstate Park. Known as the "Grand Canyon of the South," the park is shared by Virginia and Kentucky. It is the site of the largest canyon east of the Mississippi River, stretching more than 5 mi and reaching a depth of more than 1,600 ft. The name "breaks" comes from the break in Pine Mountain created by the Russell Fork of the Big Sandy River, which, over centuries, has carved a gorge through the sandstone. The river is said to be one of Virginia's most scenic and also most dangerous, with white-water rapids that require expert paddlers. The 4,500-acre park also offers camping, hiking and bike trails, swimming, fishing, and paddleboat rental. A 500-mi section of the Trans-America Bicycle Trail runs from here to Yorktown. A visitor center offers natural science and historical displays. Volunteer hosts available. | Box 100, VA 80, Breaks | 540/865–4413 or 800/982–5122 | www.state.va.us | Free; parking $1 Memorial Day–Labor Day | Apr.–Dec., daily 7 AM–11 PM; Sat. before Christmas all recreation areas close until April 1. Visitor center Apr.–Dec., daily 9–5.

Jefferson National Forest. Jefferson National Forest makes up a sizable portion of Wise County and provides a range of outdoor activities.

High Knob Recreation Area, constructed in the southwest corner of the forest in the late 1930s by the Civilian Conservation Corps, includes one of the highest peaks in southwestern Virginia. The park offers a swimming and fishing lake, stocked trout streams (among them Mountain Fork), picnicking, hiking trails, camping, and bathhouses with showers. A short trail leads to an observation tower atop High Knob (elevation 4,160 ft), which has a view across five states.

North Fork of Pound Lake Recreation Area. This area is about 30 mi north of High Knob. It features fishing, boating, camping, and picnicking around a 154-acre lake. South of Wise, the 92-acre Lake Keokee provides fishing, hiking trails, picnic pavilions, and a boat launch (electric motors only). | 540/328–2931 | High Knob $3 per vehicle, $1 pedestrians; North Fork of Pound Lake $1 per vehicle; Lake Keokee free | Daily, May 1-Sept 15. Gates open dawn to 10 PM.

Lonesome Pine International Raceway. The ASA Winston Racing Series oval hosts racing events weekly in the spring, summer, and fall. | 10800 Norton-Coeburn Rd., Coeburn | 540/679–0961; racetrack phone 540/395–3338 | fax 540/395–5329 | info@lonesomepineraceway.com | www.lonesomepineraceway.com | $10 | May–Sept., Sat. evenings; call for schedule.

ON THE CALENDAR

AUG.: *Tri-State Gospel Singing Festival.* Musical groups from Virginia, Kentucky, and West Virginia perform at the Breaks Interstate Park amphitheater. | 540/865–4413.

AUG.: *Coal and Railroad Days.* The town community Appalachia celebrates its coal and railroad heritage with two days of music, crafts, food, and contests, the first weekend in August. | 540/679–0961 | www.wisecountychamber.org.

OCT.: *Wise County Fall Fling.* The season is celebrated with live entertainment, arts and crafts, music, food booths, dancing, and children's games in downtown Wise. | 540/679–0961 | rdooley@optidynamic.com | www.wisecountychamber.org.

Dining

Mosby's. American. Civil War memorabilia is to be found throughout this restaurant, which has two large banquet rooms and a central bar area. Locals recommend the cajun chicken with angel hair pasta. | 205 Ridge View Center | 508/679–0101 | $9.95–$17.95 | AE, D, DC, MC, V.

Lodging

Bedrock Inn. This Blue Ridge Mountains inn has a country setting and gardens; its interior is filled with antiques. Rooms overlook a tennis court and deck. Complimentary breakfast with homemade muffins. No TV in rooms; TV in common area. Tennis courts. Business services. Pets allowed. | U.S. 460, P.O. Box 105, Pounding Mill | 540/963–9412 | fax 540/322–3617 | bedrock@netscape.net | www.symweb.com/bedrock/index.html | 3 rooms, 2 suites | $75–$100 | AE, MC, V.

Breaks Motor Lodge. In a woodland setting, the lodge overlooks a part of Breaks Canyon; Breaks Interstate Park is nearby. All rooms have a view. A restaurant offering home cooking, picnic area. Cable TV. Pool. Hiking. Bicycles available for $4. | Box 100, Rte. 80, Breaks | 540/865–4414 | www.breakspark.com | fax 540/865–5561 | 34 rooms | $65–$122 | Closed Dec. 21–Mar. | AE, D, MC, V.

Country Hearth Inn. Built in 1999, this hotel has employees that take pride in their work. Although it is near a major shopping strip, inside it is quiet and homey, with fresh baked cookies daily and a kitchen open to guests. Complimentary Continental breakfast. Exercise equipment. Business services. Laundry facilities. | 375 Wharton Ln., Norton | 540/679–5340 | fax 540/679–5341. | www.countryhearth.com/hotels/va-norton.htm | 58 rooms | $49–$55.

WOODSTOCK

MAP 11, H4

(Nearby town also listed: Strasburg)

Woodstock, seat of Shenandoah County on the western edge of the state, possesses the oldest courthouse west of the Blue Ridge Mountains. Chartered in 1761, the valley settlement contains examples of Federal, Greek Revival, and Classical Revival architecture. The Shenandoah River provides opportunities for fishing and canoeing.

Information: Woodstock Chamber of Commerce | P.O. Box 605, Woodstock, VA 22664 | 540/459–2542.

Shenandoah County Travel Council | P.O. Box 802, Woodstock, VA 22664 | 540/459–2332 or 888/367–3934 | sctc@shentel.net | www.co.shenandoah.va.us.

Attractions

Shenandoah Caverns. This cavern is about 1-mi long and takes about one hour to tour. You can also see the owner's collection of working animated window displays, many dating from the 1950s. | 261 Caverns Road, Shenandoah Caverns, VA | 540/477–3115 | www.svta.org/caverns | $12.50 | Daily 9–6 (last tour 5:15).

Shenandoah County Court House. Built in 1795, possibly with the help of Thomas Jefferson, this is the oldest courthouse west of the Blue Ridge Mountains. During the Civil War, Union soldiers used it as stable for their horses. | 103 N. Main | 540/459–2332 or 540/459–6130 | fax 540/459–6155 | Free | Weekdays 9–5.

Shenandoah Vineyards. This is the oldest winery in the Shenandoah Valley, established in 1976. Award-winning wines include Cabernet Sauvignon, Merlot, Chardonnay, Riesling, and Chambourcin. Free tours and tastings are given hourly. The winery also has picnic tables with views of Massanutten Mountain, and a gift shop. The winery is 5.5 mi southwest of Woodstock. | 3659 S. Ox Rd., Edinburg | 540/984–8699 | fax 540/984–9463 | www.shentel.net/shenvine | Free | Mar.–Nov., daily 10–6; Dec.–Feb., daily 10–5.

Woodstock Tower. You can see for miles from the old firetower atop Massanutten Mountain that dates from the era of the Civilian Conservation Corps. The most famous view is of the seven bends of the Shenandoah River. From a precipice below, hang gliders launch out over the valley. | Woodstock Tower Rd. | 540/459–6220 | www.co.shenandoah.va.us | Free | Daily.

ON THE CALENDAR
AUG.–SEPT.: *Shenandoah County Fair.* This traditional fair, with agricultural and livestock exhibits and contests, live entertainment, food vendors, and arts-and-crafts exhibits, is held in downtown Woodstock. | 540/459–2542.

Dining
Ben Franklin. American. Service is friendly at this restaurant, which has a varied menu with everything from garden burgers to grilled salmon or chicken livers. | 476 N. Main St. | 540/459–4322 | $4.50–$6.99 | AE, MC, V.

River'd Inn. American. Part of the inn by the same name, this restaurant serves nicely presented regional dishes. Used largely by the guests of the inn, it also attracts many locals looking to have a meal with fresh linens, attentive service, and an extensive wine list. | 1972 Artz Road | 800/637–4561 | Mon.–Tues. | $40–$55 | AE, D, DC, MC, V.

Lodging
Budget Host Inn. This chain hotel is right on Main Street, US Route 11 in Woostock. Restaurant, picnic area. Cable TV. Pool. Laundry facilities. Business services. Some pets allowed. | 1290 S. Main St., Woodstock | 540/459–4086 | fax 540/459–4043 | www.budgethost.com | 43 rooms | $40–$47 | AE, D, DC, MC, V.

Comfort Inn. This hotel is near both major highways and local attractions, including Caverns Skyline Drive, Civil War battlefields, Bryce Ski Resort, and the Shenandoah Music Festival. Antique stores and collector shops are within minutes by car. Complimentary Continental breakfast. Outdoor pool. Exercise equipment. Laundry facilities. | 1011 Motel Dr. | 800/228–5150 or 540/459–7600 | fax 540/459–7601 | www.comfortinn.com | 66 rooms | $80–$109 | AE, MC, V.

Inn at Narrow Passage. A restored colonial wagon stop on the Shenandoah River, this is a unique place to stay. All rooms are furnished with Early American reproductions and antiques. Complimentary breakfast. No smoking. Business services. | 30 Chapman Landing Rd./U.S. 11 S | 540/459–8000 or 800/459–8002 | fax 540/459–8001 | www.innatnarrowpassage.com | 12 rooms (2 with shared bath) | $85–$145 | MC, V.

Ramada Inn. The chain hotel is convenient to I–81. Restaurant, bar. Some kitchenettes, some refrigerators, room service, cable TV. Pool. Business services. | 1130 Motel Dr. | 540/459–5000 | fax 540/459–8219 | www.ramada.com | 129 rooms | $62–$70 | AE, D, DC, MC, V.

River'd Inn. On a private 25 acres, this inn reaches toward high luxury, and is a bit more elegant than cozy. You cross a low bridge over the Shenandoah River to get in, and if it floods (which rarely happens), the inn is "river'd in." Restaurant. Complimentary breakfast. Some kitchenettes, some in-room hot tubs. No kids on weekends. | 1972 Artz Rd. | 800/637–4561 | innkeeper@riverdinn.com | www.riverdinn.com | 7 rooms, 1 suite | $200–$285, $325 suite | AE, D, DC, MC, V.

WYTHEVILLE

(Nearby towns also listed: Marion, Radford)

The seat of Wythe County in southwest Virginia, Wytheville was founded in 1792. It claims the only saltworks in the South. Its major manufacturers today produce masonry blocks, glass, mirrors, machine parts, and industrial plastics. Two Virginia governors were born here: Henry Carter Stuart, who served from 1914 to 1918, and Elbert Lee Trinkle, governor from 1922 to 1926. The town's historic district features pre–Civil War homes. At Shot Tower Historic State Park you can see an edifice once used for ammunition making.

Information: Wytheville-Wythe-Bland Chamber of Commerce | Box 563, 150 E. Monroe St., Wytheville, VA 24382 | 540/223–3365 | chamber@wytheville.org. **Wytheville Area Convention and Visitors Bureau,** | Box 533, Wytheville, VA 24382 | 540/223–3355 | www.wytheville.org or tkhamber.wytheville.com.

Attractions

Big Walker Lookout. This mountain-top observation tower overlooks Jefferson National Forest. A café and souvenir shop are nearby. 12 mi north of downtown Wytheville. | Big Walker Mountain Scenic Byway, US 52 North C Big Walker Mountain | 540/228–4401 | Tower: $3.50 adults, $2.50 kids | Daily April–Memorial Day, 10 –5, Memorial Day–Oct., Tues.–Sun., 10–6.

Shot Tower Historical Park. The landmark tower in this 7-acre park, built in 1807, was used by area settlers in the manufacture of munitions. Lead was carried to the top of the tower, melted, and dropped through sieves to a kettle of water on the ground 75 ft below to form rounded shots. Tours of the tower, which sits on a bluff overlooking the New River, are given on summer weekends. Twenty-five minutes north of Wythville, off I-81. | 540/699–6778 | Free; $2 parking fee | Park: Apr.–Nov., daily, dawn–dusk; Shot Tower: 10AM–6PM Memorial Day–Labor Day, tours daily.

Wytheville State Fish Hatchery. The hatchery features raceways and an aquarium room where you can watch the trout—rainbow, brook, and brown—that are being raised to stock nearby lakes and streams. | 1260 Red Hollow Road, Max Meadows, VA | 540/637–3212 | Free | Daily 8:00AM–3:30PM.

ON THE CALENDAR

JUNE: *Chautauqua Festival.* The five-day event includes live nightly entertainment, arts-and-crafts exhibits, children's activities, hot air ballooning, magic shows, drama and dance performances, and special exhibits. | Elizabeth Brown Memorial Park, 110 Monroe St., Wytheville | 540/228–6855.

AUG.: *Old Time Farm Show.* This tractor pull with live music and all kinds of children's events takes place in the High Country Arena. Call first, because there are several events a year, and the month often changes. | 540/223–3365.

Dining

Corner Cafe. Cafe. You can get a cup of coffee (the basic type) and a small bite to eat at this little cafe on the corner. | 100 West Main St. | 540/228–3749 | Hours vary | $3–$7 | No credit cards.

El Puerto. Mexican. This large dining room set inside a boxlike building is decorated with the usual ponchos and sombreros. It is popular with the local crowd, who come to unwind with the margaritas and live music. | 713 Chapman Rd. | 540/228–3159 | $10 | V, D, MC.

Fran's Foods. Delicatessen. This small, friendly deli serves huge sandwiches of Pennsylvania Dutch meats and cheeses. | 522 East Main St. | 540/228–6105 | Closed Sun.–Mon. No dinner | $2.99–$3.75 | No credit cards.

Glisan's Bar-B-Que Shack. Barbecue. Easily recognizable by its red roof, this takeout place is a Wytheville fixture, with terrific barbecue ribs. Open seasonally | 100 Grayson Rd. | 540/228–5308 | $5–$10 | No credit cards.

Log House. American. The two-story, German-style, square-cut log house built in 1776 has five dining rooms, including a gazebo offering open-air dining for 35. There is a varied menu

© Artville

THE REAL DR. PEPPER?

In the tiny crossroads of Rural Retreat, located in the Highlands region of the southwest corner of the state—about 10 mi southwest of Wytheville—stands an old pharmacy building. Here was housed the onetime business of Dr. Charles T. Pepper. If local lore is to be believed, Dr. Pepper was the creator of the popular soft drink that still bears his name.

According to the story told in these parts, some time after Pepper first mixed up "the world's most original soft drink," his teenage daughter fell in love with a soda jerk at the pharmacy. Greatly displeased, Pepper put a stop to the budding romance by packing his daughter off to school and firing the young man, whose name was Charles Alderton. The lovelorn Alderton moved to Waco, Texas, where he found gainful employment as a soda jerk at another pharmacy, Morrison's Old Corner Drug Store. There, in 1885, Alderton began serving the soda mixture originally developed by—and eventually named after—his former boss.

At least that's what Virginians will tell you. The residents of Waco (home of the one-and-only Dr. Pepper Museum) relate a very different sequence of events. For starters, Texans say, Charles Pepper was not the creator of the new drink. The credit, they say, goes to Wade Morrison, the owner of the Waco pharmacy, who helped Alderton with his soda experiments. According to this version of the story, it was actually Morrison who once worked in Rural Retreat for Charles Pepper. The Virginia pharmacist had given Morrison his first job, they say; he returned the favor by naming the new beverage after him.

A slightly different twist on the Texas tale holds that the soda's name was rooted in a romance between Morrison and the daughter of the Virginia pharmacist. In this account, Morrison names the concoction "Dr. Pepper" to curry favor with his prospective father-in-law. (Many people discredit this account, however, pointing to sources that indicate Pepper's daughter was only about eight years old when Morrison moved out of Virginia.)

Finally, a stray piece of oral history that throws a wrench in all the other theories. It maintains that the soda recipe was originally developed by a physician, whose office was across the street from Charles Pepper's pharmacy in Rural Retreat. The physician had created a great-tasting cough medicine; unfortunately, it also had a laxative effect. In this version of the story, Dr. Pepper suggested substituting wild cherry bark for the syrup of tolu, a kind of balsam tree, and using carbonated instead of sterile water. Some time later, a clerk in the pharmacy, Noel Porter, moved to Waco. From there, he wrote back to Dr. Pepper, asking permission to make and sell the fizzy cherry-bark drink.

And the rest, as they say, is history.

featuring steak, seafood and poultry specialties including chicken meringo (a mixture of tomatos, mushrooms and green olives) and chicken verde pecan. Kids' menu. Beer and wine only. | 520 E. Main St. | 540/228–4139 | Closed Sun. | $18–$25.50 | AE, D, MC, V.

Scrooge's Pub and Eatery. Contemporary. Next to the Comfort Inn, this family-oriented restaurant has a large fireplace and candles on the tables. The menu includes items like lemon-peppered sole and fettucine alfredo. The wine list is extensive, and there is also a bar. | 315 Holston Rd. | 540/228–6622 | www.wytheville.com/scrooges | $12–$15 | AE, D, MC, V.

Lodging
Wytheville Inn. This hotel was completely remodeled and updated in 2000. It still retains a friendly staff, and is 12 mi from the town's major shopping area. | 100 rooms. Complimentary breakfast. Some in-room hot tubs. Outdoor pool. | 355 Nye Rd. | 540/228–7300 | $50 | AE, D, DC, MC, V.

Index

Notes

Notes

Notes

Notes

Notes

Notes

Notes

Notes

Notes

Notes

TALK TO US

Fill out this quick survey and receive a free *Fodor's How to Pack* (while supplies last)

---

1 Which Road Guide did you purchase?
(Check all that apply.)
- ❏ AL/AR/LA/MS/TN
- ❏ AZ/CO/NM
- ❏ CA
- ❏ CT/MA/RI
- ❏ DE/DC/MD/PA/VA
- ❏ FL
- ❏ GA/NC/SC
- ❏ ID/MT/NV/UT/WY
- ❏ IL/IA/MO/WI
- ❏ IN/KY/MI/OH/WV
- ❏ KS/OK/TX
- ❏ ME/NH/VT
- ❏ MN/NE/ND/SD
- ❏ NJ/NY
- ❏ OR/WA

2 How did you learn about the Road Guides?
- ❏ TV ad
- ❏ Radio ad
- ❏ Newspaper or magazine ad
- ❏ Newspaper or magazine article
- ❏ TV or radio feature
- ❏ Bookstore display/clerk recommendation
- ❏ Recommended by family/friend
- ❏ Other:_____

3 Did you use other guides for your trip?
- ❏ AAA
- ❏ Compass American Guide
- ❏ Fodor's
- ❏ Frommer's
- ❏ Insiders' Guide
- ❏ Mobil
- ❏ Moon Handbook
- ❏ Other:_____

4 Did you use any of the following for planning?
- ❏ Tourism offices ❏ Internet ❏ Travel agent

5 Did you buy a Road Guide for (check one):
- ❏ Leisure trip
- ❏ Business trip
- ❏ Mix of business and leisure

6 Where did you buy your Road Guide?
- ❏ Bookstore
- ❏ Other store
- ❏ On-line
- ❏ Borrowed from a friend
- ❏ Borrowed from a library
- ❏ Other:_____

7 Why did you buy a Road Guide? (Check all that apply.)
- ❏ Number of cities/towns listed
- ❏ Comprehensive coverage
- ❏ Number of lodgings ❏ Driving tours
- ❏ Number of restaurants ❏ Maps
- ❏ Number of attractions ❏ Fodor's brand name
- ❏ Other:_____

8 Did you use this guide primarily:
- ❏ For pretrip planning ❏ While traveling
- ❏ For planning and while traveling

9 What was the duration of your trip?
- ❏ 2-3 days ❏ 11 or more days
- ❏ 4-6 days ❏ Taking more than 1 trip
- ❏ 7-10 days

10 Did you use the guide to select
- ❏ Hotels ❏ Restaurants

11 Did you stay primarily in a
- ❏ Hotel ❏ Hostel
- ❏ Motel ❏ Campground
- ❏ Resort ❏ Dude ranch
- ❏ Bed-and-breakfast ❏ With family or friends
- ❏ RV/camper ❏ Other:_____

12 What sights and activities did you most enjoy?
- ❏ Historical sights ❏ Shopping
- ❏ Sports ❏ Theaters
- ❏ National parks ❏ Museums
- ❏ State parks ❏ Major cities
- ❏ Attractions off the beaten path

13 How much did you spend per adult for this trip?
- ❏ Less than $500 ❏ $751-$1,000
- ❏ $501-$750 ❏ More than $1,000

14 How many traveled in your party?
___ Adults ___ Children ___ Pets

15 Did you
- ❏ Fly to destination ❏ Rent a van or RV
- ❏ Drive your own vehicle ❏ Take a train
- ❏ Rent a car ❏ Take a bus

16 How many miles did you travel round-trip?
- ❏ Less than 100 ❏ 501-750
- ❏ 101-300 ❏ 751-1,000
- ❏ 301-500 ❏ More than 1,000

17 What items did you take on your vacation?
- ❏ Traveler's checks ❏ Digital camera
- ❏ Credit card ❏ Cell phone
- ❏ Gasoline card ❏ Computer
- ❏ Phone card ❏ PDA
- ❏ Camera ❏ Other

18 Would you use Fodor's Road Guides again?
- ❏ Yes ❏ No

19 How would you like to see Road Guides changed?
- ❏ More ❏ Less Dining
- ❏ More ❏ Less Lodging
- ❏ More ❏ Less Sports
- ❏ More ❏ Less Activities
- ❏ More ❏ Less Attractions
- ❏ More ❏ Less Shopping
- ❏ More ❏ Less Driving tours
- ❏ More ❏ Less Maps
- ❏ More ❏ Less Historical information
- ❏ Other:_____

20 Tell us about yourself.

❏ Male ❏ Female

Age:
- ❏ 18-24 ❏ 35-44 ❏ 55-64
- ❏ 25-34 ❏ 45-54 ❏ Over 65

Income:
- ❏ Less than $25,000 ❏ $50,001-$75,000
- ❏ $25,001-$50,000 ❏ More than $75,000

Name:_____ E-mail: _____

Address:_____ City: _____ State: _____ Zip: _____

Fodor's Travel Publications
Attn: Road Guide Survey
280 Park Avenue
New York, NY 10017

The information herein will be treated in confidence. Names and addresses will not be released to mailing-list houses or other organizations.

Atlas

VERMONT

N
H

MASS

NEW YORK

CONN

PENNSYLVANIA

NEW
JERSEY

MARYLAND

DELAWARE

WASHINGTON, D.C.

WEST
VIRGINIA

VIRGINIA

O

NORTH
CAROLINA

SOUTH
CAROLINA

GEORGIA

FLORIDA

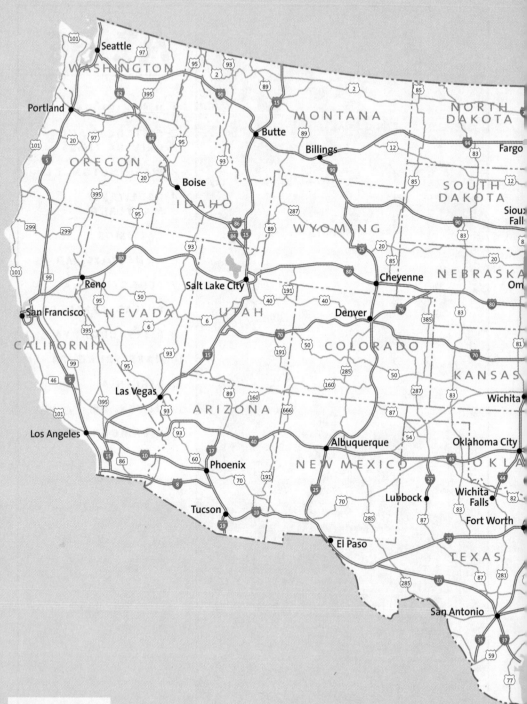

U. S. Highways

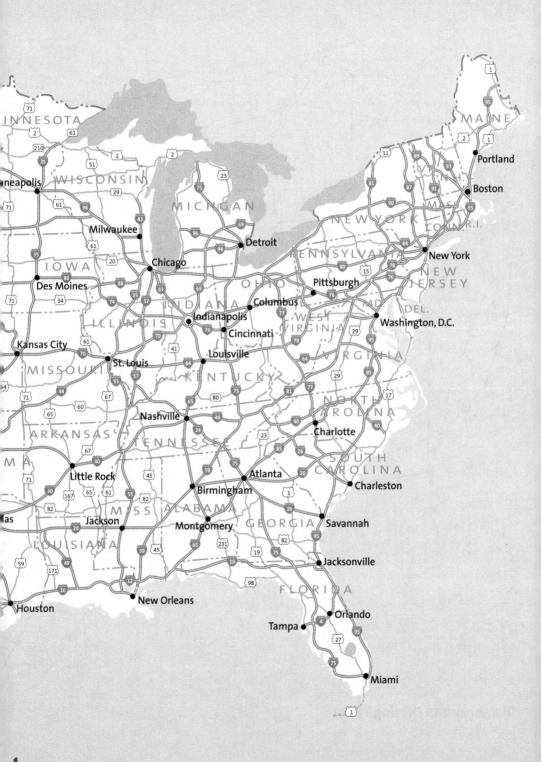

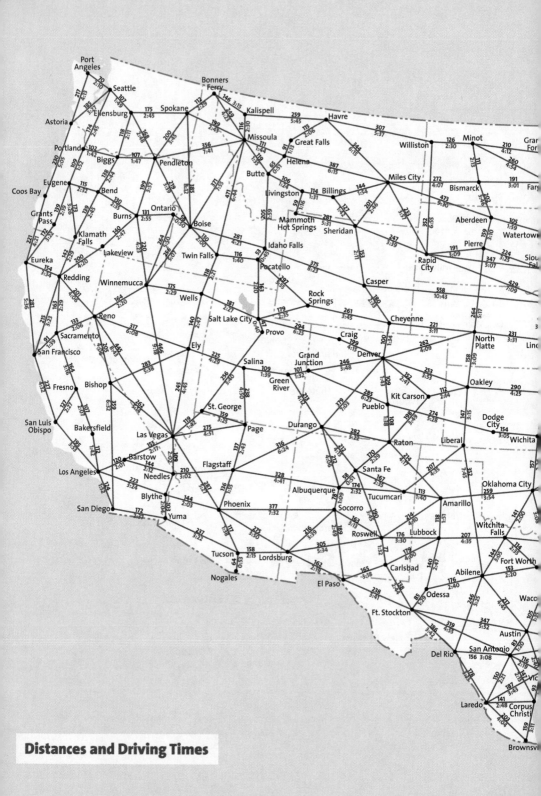

Distances and Driving Times

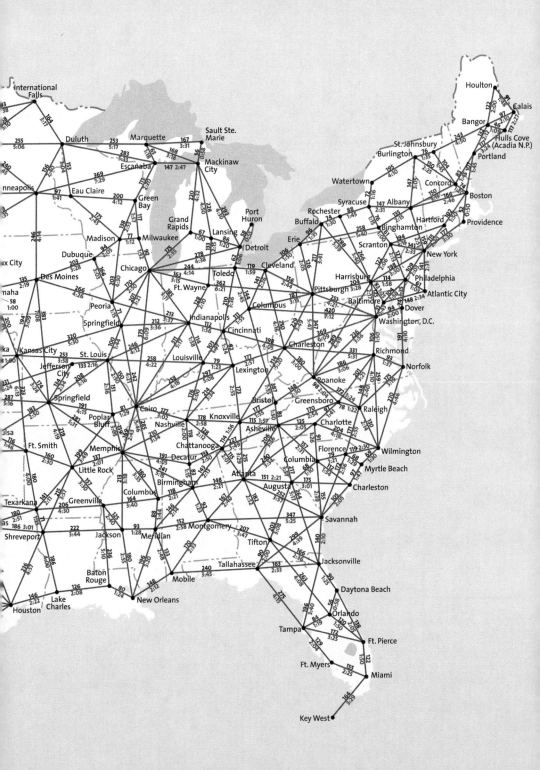

3

Washington D.C. Area

C & O Canal National Historical Park

Cabin John Reg. Park

Democracy Blvd

Rock Creek Park

Falls Rd

Persimmon

River Rd

Bradley Rd

Locks Rd

Old Georgetown Rd

Wisconsin Ave

Connecticut Ave

189

190

191

191

192

97

185

Tree Rd

Seven Locks Rd

River Rd

Wilson Ln

Bethesda

410

191

MacArthur Blvd

Goldsboro Rd

Bradley Blvd

Bradley Ln

410

185

186

CLARA BARTON PKWY

Clara Barton N.H.S.

614

191

355

Oregon Ave

Rock Creek Park

Scotts Run Nature Preserve

GEORGE WASHINGTON MEM. PKWY

Turkey Run Park

396

190

Massachusetts

Western Ave

Nebraska Ave

Connecticut Ave

Old Dominion Dr

Georgetown

Pike

123

Van Ness St

Wisconsin Ave

684

738

193

American University

Washington National Cathedral

National Zoological Park

Lewinsville Rd

Madison Blvd

123

MacArthur Canal Rd

Foxhall Rd

267

HIRST BRAULT EXPY

694

Dolley

McLean

Chain Bridge Rd

Pimmit Run

695

Glover Archbold Park

The Phillips Collection

7

123

309

693

Great Falls St

120

Georgetown University

Washington

Tysons Corner

Pimmit Hills

Leesburg Pike

Kirby

Westmoreland St

Williamsburg Blvd

Glebe Rd

650

698

695

120

309

29

George Washington University

The White House

Gallows

66

West St

694

Lee Hwy

124

50

Washing Monum

Falls Church

7

Washington Blvd

Arlington

Lincoln Memorial

110

29

237

649

338

Seven Corners

66

237

Fort Myer

Arlington National Cemetery

Jefferson Memorial

50

Graham

Arlington Blvd

Wilson Blvd

50

Arlington

Blvd

27

The Pentagon

244

1

650

Rd

Annandale Rd

613

Lake Barcroft

Pike

120

Walter Reed Dr

Glebe Rd

120

GEO WASHINGTON MEM. PKWY

Ronald Re Washing Nat'l Air

236

649

650

244

Columbia Pike

Baileys Crossroads

7

402

Mt. Vernon Ave

Jefferson Davis Hwy

400

710

Annandale

Little River Tpk

613

N. Beauregard St

395

Braddock Ln

King St

Rd

620

649

617

236

420

Alexandria

7

620

Braddock Rd

648

Edsall Rd

Duke St

Quaker Ln

7

North Springfield

401

Eisenhower Ave

236

Lake Accotink Park

Lake Accotink

HENRY G. SHIRLEY MEMORIAL HWY

Van Dorn St

95

CAPITAL BELTWAY

495

1

617

Backlick Rd

613

644

611

241

Woo Me

MARYLAND

VIRGINIA

Potomac R.

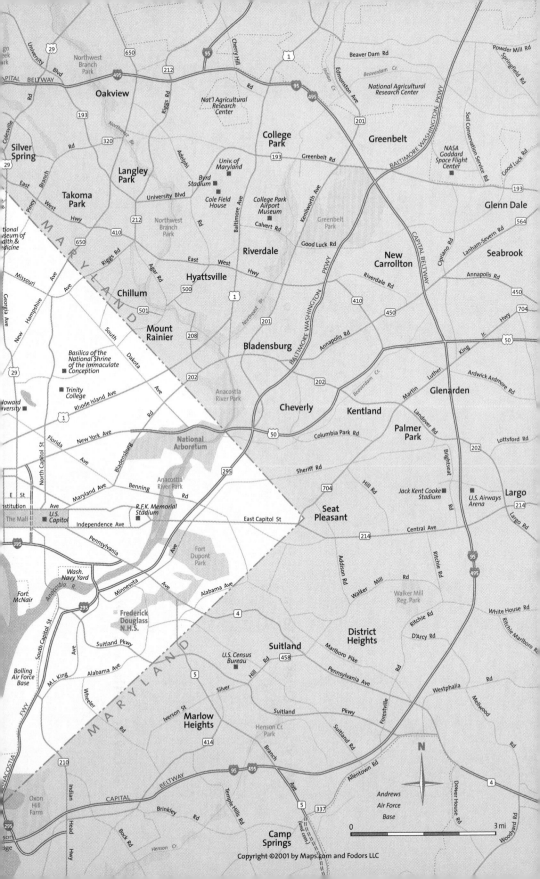

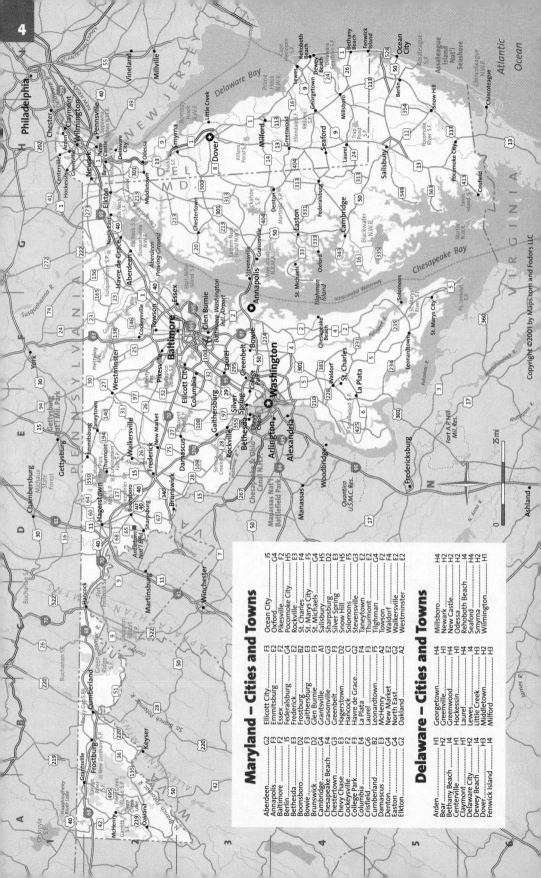

Maryland – Cities and Towns

Aberdeen	C2	
Annapolis	F3	
Baltimore	E2	
Bethesda	D2	
Boonsboro	D2	
Bowie	E2	
Brunswick	D2	
Cambridge	G4	
Chesapeake Beach	F3	
Chestertown	F2	
Chevy Chase	D2	
Cockeysville	E2	
College Park	E2	
Columbia	E2	
Crisfield	H5	
Cumberland	B2	
Damascus	D2	
Denton	G3	
Easton	F3	
Elkton	F2	

Ellicott City	E2	
Emmitsburg	D1	
Essex	E2	
Federalsburg	G4	
Frederick	D2	
Frostburg	A2	
Gaithersburg	D2	
Glen Burnie	E2	
Grantsville	A1	
Grasonville	G3	
Greenbelt	E2	
Hagerstown	D1	
Hancock	C1	
Havre de Grace	F2	
La Plata	E3	
Laurel	E2	
Leonardtown	F4	
McHenry	A2	
New Market	D2	
North East	G2	
Oakland	A2	

Ocean City	I5	
Oxford	G4	
Pikesville	F2	
Pocomoke City	H5	
Rockville	E3	
St. Charles	E3	
St. Marys City	F5	
St. Michaels	G3	
Salisbury	H4	
Silver Spring	D2	
Snow Hill	H5	
Solomons	G3	
Stevensville	F2	
Taneytown	E2	
Thurmont	D2	
Tilghman	G4	
Towson	F2	
Waldorf	F3	
Walkersville	E2	
Westminster	E2	

Delaware – Cities and Towns

Arden	H1	
Bear	H2	
Bethany Beach	I4	
Centerville	H1	
Claymont	H1	
Delaware City	H2	
Dewey Beach	I4	
Dover	H3	
Fenwick Island	I4	

Georgetown	H4	
Greenville	H2	
Greenwood	H4	
Hockessin	H1	
Laurel	H4	
Lewes	I4	
Little Creek	H3	
Middletown	H2	
Milford	H4	

Millsboro	H4	
Newark	H2	
New Castle	H2	
Odessa	H2	
Rehoboth Beach	I4	
Seaford	H4	
Smyrna	H2	
Wilmington	H1	

Copyright ©2001 by Maps.com and Fodors LLC

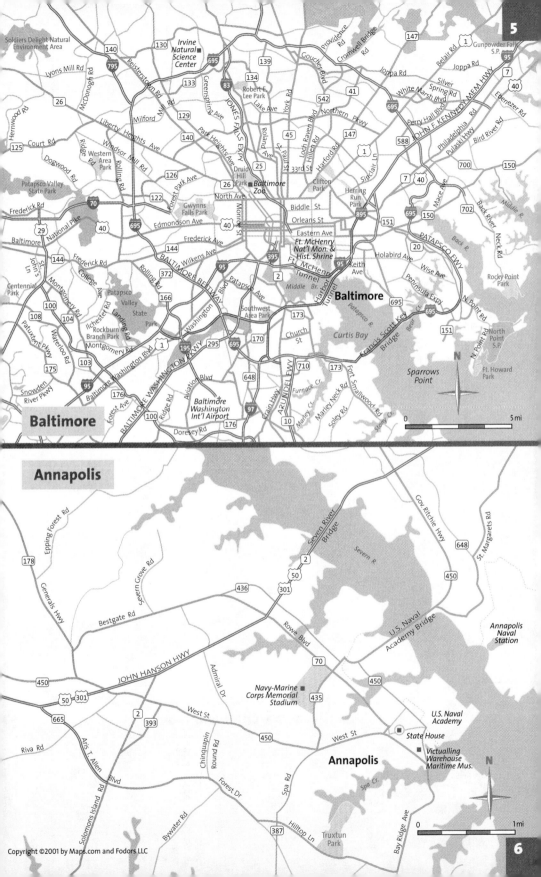

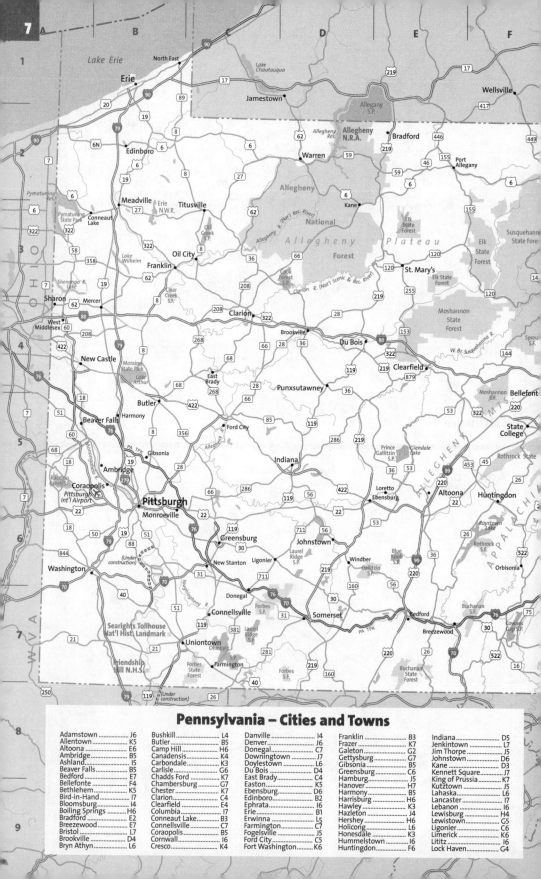

7

Pennsylvania – Cities and Towns

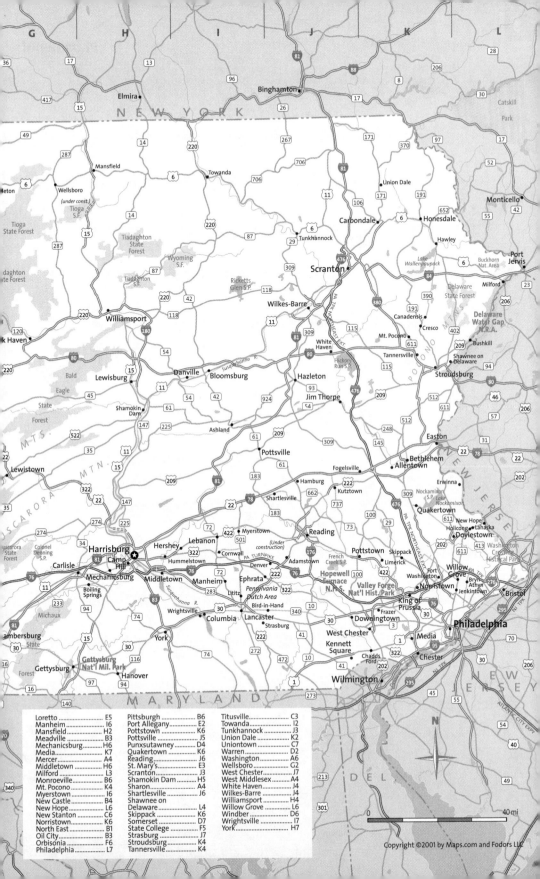

0   40 mi

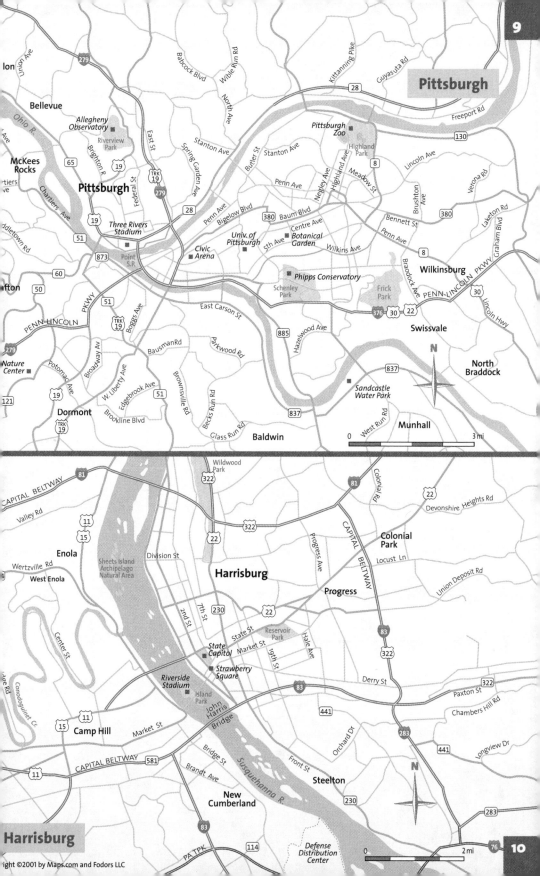

Pittsburgh

Union Ave
279
Babcock Blvd
Wible Run Rd
North Ave
Kittanning Pike
28
Guyasuta Rd
Freeport Rd

Bellevue
Allegheny
Observatory
Riverview
Park
Brighton R.
East St
Stanton Ave
Butler St
Stanton Ave
Pittsburgh
Zoo
Highland
Park
Lincoln Ave
130

McKees
Rocks
65
19
Federal St
Spring Garden Ave
Penn Ave
Negley Ave
Highland Ave
Meadow St
8
Lincoln Ave
Brushton
Ave
Verona Rd
380

Ohio R.

Pittsburgh
TRK
19
279
28
Penn Ave
Bigelow Blvd
380
Baum Blvd
Centre Ave
Bennett St
Penn Ave
8
Laveton Rd
Graham Blvd

ddletown Rd
51
Three Rivers
Stadium
873
Point
S.P.
Civic
Arena
Univ. of
Pittsburgh
5th Ave
Botanical
Garden
Wilkins Ave
Wilkinsburg
PENN-LINCOLN PKWY
30

tiers
Chartiers Ave
19

fton
50
60
Phipps Conservatory
Schenley
Park
Frick
Park
Braddock Ave
376
30
22

279
PENN-LINCOLN
PKWY
51
TRK
19
Boggs Ave
East Carson St
885
Hazelwood Ave
Swissvale
Lincoln Hwy

Nature
Center
Bausman Rd
Parkwood Rd
837
N
North
Braddock

121
Broadway Av
Potomac Ave
W. Liberty Ave
Edgebrook Ave
Brownsville Rd
51
Becks Run Rd
Sandcastle
Water Park
19

Dormont
TRK
19
Brookline Blvd
Glass Run Rd
837
West Run Rd
Munhall

Baldwin
0   3 mi

Wildwood
Park
81
322
81
Colonial Rd
22
Devonshire Heights Rd

CAPITAL BELTWAY
Valley Rd
11
15
322
Colonial
Park

Enola
Sheets Island
Archipelago
Natural Area
Division St
322
22
CAPITAL BELTWAY
Locust Ln
Progress
Union Deposit Rd

Wertzville Rd
West Enola
Harrisburg
230
22
83
322

Center St
7th St
2nd St
State St
Market St
19th St
State
Capitol
Reservoir
Park
Hale Ave
Derry St
Paxton St
322

Camp Hill
11
15
Riverside
Stadium
Island
Park
Strawberry
Square
83
441
Orchard Dr
Chambers Hill Rd

Conodoguinet Cr
Market St
John
Harris
Bridge
Front St
283
441
Longview Dr

CAPITAL BELTWAY
11
581
Bridge St
Brandt Ave
Susquehanna R.
Steelton
N
76

New
Cumberland
230
283

83
114
PA TPK
Defense
Distribution
Center
0   2 mi

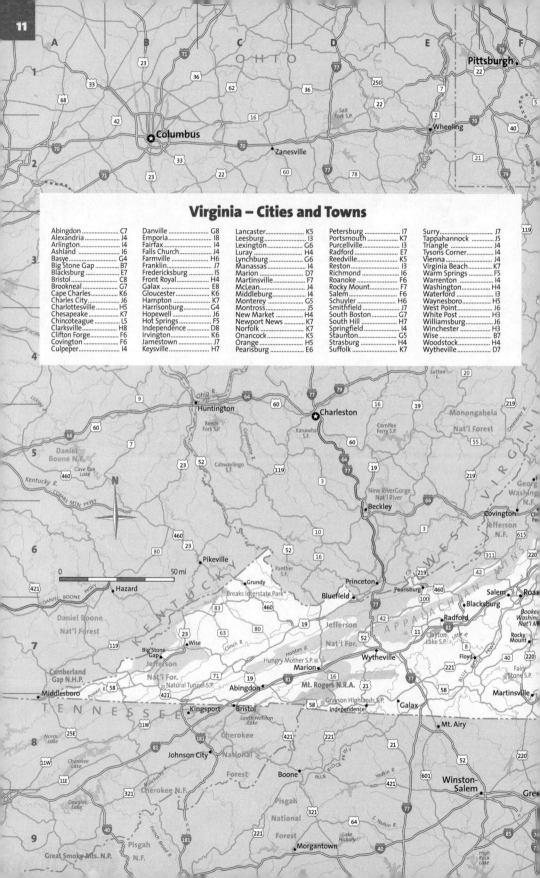

11

Virginia – Cities and Towns

Abingdon C7	Danville G8	Lancaster K5	Petersburg I7	Surry J7
Alexandria J4	Emporia I8	Leesburg I3	Portsmouth K7	Tappahannock J5
Arlington I4	Fairfax I4	Lexington G6	Purcellville I3	Triangle J4
Ashland I6	Falls Church J4	Luray H4	Radford E7	Tysons Corner I4
Basye G4	Farmville H6	Lynchburg G6	Reedville K5	Vienna J4
Big Stone Gap B7	Franklin J7	Manassas I4	Reston I3	Virginia Beach K7
Blacksburg E7	Fredericksburg I5	Marion D7	Richmond I6	Warm Springs F5
Bristol C8	Front Royal H4	Martinsville F7	Roanoke F6	Warrenton I4
Brookneal G7	Galax E8	McLean J4	Rocky Mount F7	Washington H4
Cape Charles K6	Gloucester K6	Middleburg I4	Salem F6	Waterford I3
Charles City J6	Hampton K7	Monterey G5	Schuyler H6	Waynesboro H5
Charlottesville H5	Harrisonburg G4	Montross J5	Smithfield J7	West Point J6
Chesapeake K7	Hopewell J6	New Market H4	South Boston G7	White Post H3
Chincoteague L5	Hot Springs F5	Newport News K7	South Hill H7	Williamsburg J6
Clarksville H8	Independence D8	Norfolk K7	Springfield I4	Winchester H3
Clifton Forge F6	Irvington K6	Onancock K5	Staunton G5	Wise B7
Covington F6	Jamestown J7	Orange H5	Strasburg H4	Woodstock H4
Culpeper I4	Keysville H7	Pearisburg E6	Suffolk K7	Wytheville D7

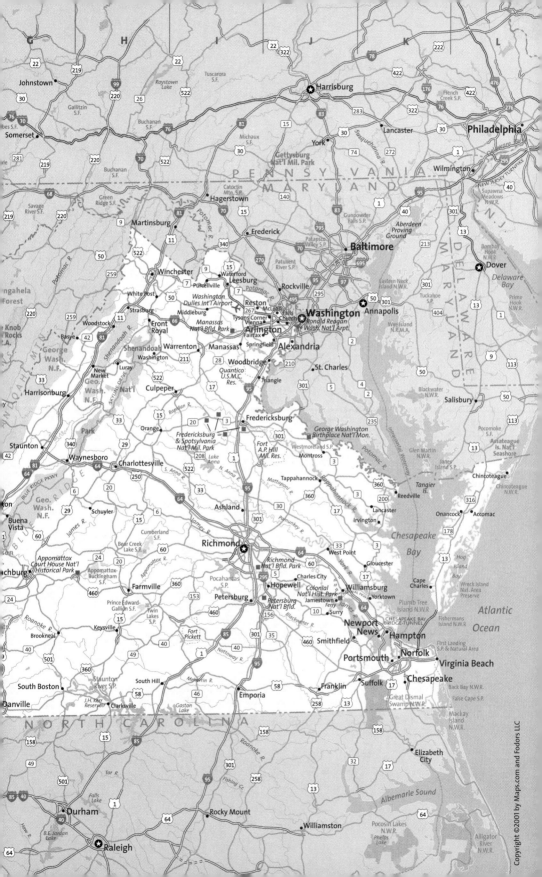

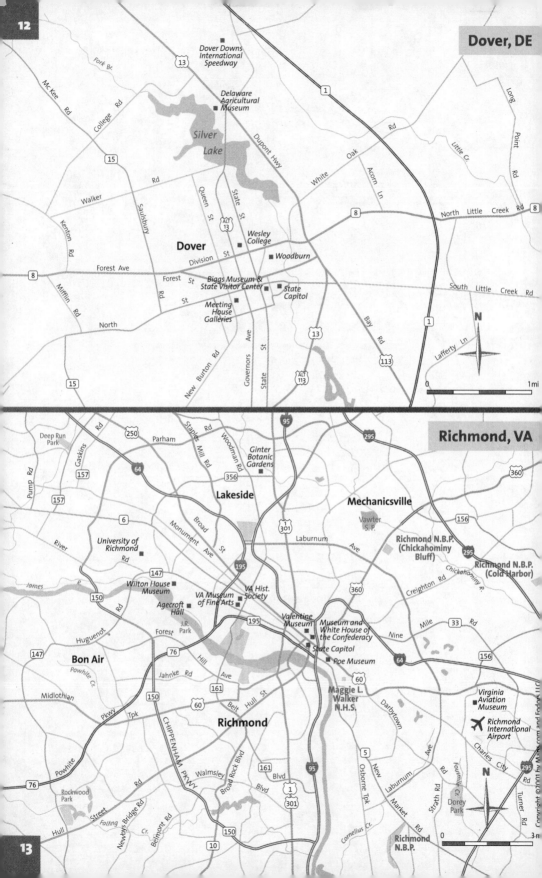

Dover Downs
International
Speedway

13

Delaware
Agricultural
Museum

Fork Br.

Mc Kee Rd

College Rd

Silver
Lake

15

Rd

Dupont Hwy

White

Oak

Rd

Acorn Ln

Little Cr.

Long

Point

Rd

Walker

Kenton Rd

Saulsbury

Queen St

State St

ALT
13

8

North Little Creek Rd

8

Dover

Wesley
College

Woodburn

Division St

Rd

South Little Creek Rd

Forest Ave

Forest St

Mifflin Rd

St

Biggs Museum &
State Visitor Center

State
Capitol

Bay Rd

1

Meeting
House
Galleries

North

New Burton Rd

Governors Ave

State St

13

113

Lafferty Ln

N

15

ALT
113

0   1mi

95

295

360

Deep Run
Park

250

Parham

Staples Mill Rd

Woodman Rd

Ginter
Botanic
Gardens

Rd

Gaskins

64

157

356

Lakeside

Mechanicsville

Vawter
S.P.

156

Pump Rd

157

6

Broad

Monument Ave

St

1
301

Laburnum

Ave

Richmond N.B.P.
(Chickahominy
Bluff)

295

360

Richmond N.B.P.
(Cold Harbor)

River

University of
Richmond
Rd

147

195

360

Creighton Rd

Chickahominy R.

James

R.

150

Wilton House
Museum

Agecroft
Hall

VA Museum
of Fine Arts

VA Hist.
Society

Valentine
Museum

Museum and
White House of
the Confederacy

Nine

Mile

33

Rd

64

156

Huguenot

147

Forest

J.R.
Park

195

State Capitol

Poe Museum

Bon Air

Powhite Cr.

76

Jahnke Rd

Ave

Hill

161

Belt

Hull St.

60

Maggie L.
Walker
N.H.S.

Darbytown

Virginia
Aviation
Museum

Midlothian

150

60

Richmond
International
Airport

Pkwy

Tpk

CHIPPENHAM PKWY

Richmond

Ave

Rd

Nine

Powhite

150

Walmsley

Broad Rock Blvd

161

Blvd

Blvd

95

5

Osborne Tpk

New

Laburnum

Ave

Fourmile Cr.

Strath Rd

Charles City

295

Rd

Turner Rd

76

Rockwood
Park

Hull

Street

Falling

Newbys Bridge Rd

Belmont Rd

Cr.

10

1
301

150

Cornelius Ct.

Market

Rd

Richmond
N.B.P.

Dorey
Park

N

0   3m